A Child's Odyssey

Child and Adolescent Development

Paul S. Kaplan
Suffolk County Community College

West Publishing Company

St. Paul   New York   Los Angeles   San Francisco

To my children:
Stacey, Amy, Jodi, and Laurie
Four of a kind
Each unique

Copyediting: Peggy Hoover
Design: The Quarasan Group, Inc.
Illustrations: Barbara Hack Barnett, Carlisle Graphics
Cover Art: A detail from Pierre Auguste Renoir, *The Meadow,* 1873, oil on canvas.
Private collection.
Cover Design: Arnold Design Group, Inc.
Composition: Carlisle Graphics

Library of Congress Cataloging-in-Publication Data

Kaplan, Paul S.
    A child's odyssey.

    Bibliography: p.
    Includes index.
    1. Child development.   I. Title.
RJ131.K36   1986   155.9   85-20341
ISBN 0-314-85253-0
1st Reprint—1986

(Acknowledgments and Photo Credits follow Subject Index)

CONTENTS IN BRIEF

CONTENTS

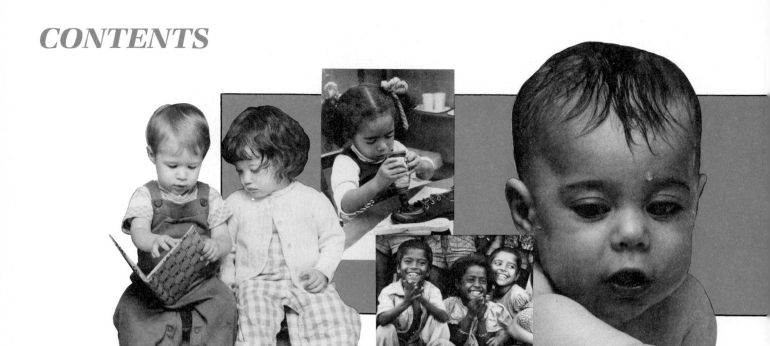

PART TWO *Infancy and Toddlerhood*   161

PART THREE *Early Childhood* 279

CHAPTER EIGHT

The Development of Language and Communication Skills 280

THE MYSTERIES OF LANGUAGE 282

CHAPTER NINE

*Physical and Cognitive Development in
Early Childhood* 312

THE DEATH OF WILL LEE 314

PART FIVE   Adolescence   529

PREFACE

The field of child and adolescent development is complicated by what seem like opposing trends. On the one hand, through scientific research, many sequences of development that hold true for children throughout the world have been discovered. On the other hand, individual differences also pervade development. Each child is unique and negotiates the challenges of childhood with his or her own style. Yet, it is a mistake to believe that these are opposites. They complement each other. We can appreciate the similarities in child development and also the individual differences.

Similar questions confront those who teach and study child development. How do we appreciate the scientific study of child development, which has yielded such impressive insights, and still marvel at the originality and beauty that is the child? How do we make generalizations about children, yet empathize with the individual child's attempts to negotiate the challenges along the way? A *Child's Odyssey* is an attempt to integrate both trends and answer these questions.

This text presents much of the modern scientific research on child and adolescent development and discusses how it answers specific questions and helps us understand the nature of development. The research on child development is enriched by its interdisciplinary nature. Research studies performed around the world by professionals representing such fields as psychology, education, health care, and nutrition add greatly to our understanding of child development. At the same time, it is important not to lose sight of each child's uniqueness and subjective experience. In this vein, I have tried to capture some of the excitement of development as well as its humor. For instance, when my daughter Jodi was four years old she looked up at my wife and me and said with pride, "I love all *my* grown-ups." My understanding of her statement was increased by my reading of Piaget, who noted that children of that age often see the world as revolving around them. At the same time, an understanding of her subjective experience and an appreciation of the originality of the child's utterance is not out of place. Throughout this text, I have tried to balance both.

This text offers many special features that I hope will be helpful to the professor and the student.

Pedagogical Features. Each chapter begins with a *True-False Motivational Quiz*. The questions are repeated next to the paragraphs in the body of the text where the answers can be found. An answer box is placed at the end of each chapter. A unique feature of this book is its *Action/Reaction* boxes. The Action/ Reaction boxes present cases that illustrate various practical situations and problems and contain questions for thought or discussion. There is no single correct answer for most of these situations, but they will cause the reader to think and spark discussion. Each chapter also contains a *Research Highlight* that explores a research study in depth. All *Key Terms* are presented in boldface and defined in the margins, a *Summary* can be found at the end of each chapter, and a *Glossary* is presented at the end of the text.

Content.   All texts in this field must cover the basic principles and research in the field, and *A Child's Odyssey* is no exception. However, it has been my experience that some of the more important topics and issues are often slighted. Among these are grandparenting, stepparenting, advertising aimed at children, bilingualism, nutrition, health, the educational experience, and cross-cultural perspectives. Such issues as day care and child abuse are often given casual treatment when they are of national concern and great interest to students. They are covered in detail here. The theoretical approaches have also been updated. For instance, the information-processing viewpoint is added to the more conventional theoretical approaches usually covered in a text. In addition, wherever possible I have substituted specific home and familial conditions that affect child development for socioeconomic status. By doing so, the specific factors that affect child development can be identified.

Organization.   This text is organized according to chronological ages and stages, with some variations, and allows for a great deal of flexibility. Two special chapters cover language development and the exceptional child. Many professors prefer to have a separate chapter on language development because the topic raises so many fascinating questions. The chapter on exceptional children offers a positive perspective on atypical development. The subject is one of major concern to child researchers and of interest to students. A chapter on genetics presents a modern perspective on how genetics affects development throughout childhood and adolescence. A full chapter is also devoted to theories. It appears as Chapter Four instead of the more traditional placement as the second chapter. A number of professors have indicated that by the time they have covered the introductory material, genetics, the prenatal period, and birth, their students no longer remember the early material on theories. The placement of theories after coverage of those topics is one way to solve this problem. However, the chapter is written so that it may easily be assigned as the second chapter.

Tables and Figures.   Careful attention has been given to tables and figures throughout the text. Many of the tables are summaries of material that will be helpful to students.

Examples and Practical Applications.   This text offers many examples and applications. The examples are an integral part of the text, and the applications indicate how the principles of child development may be used to understand and predict behavior.

Instructor's Manual with Test Bank, and Study Guide with Child Observation Exercises.   An instructor's manual with a test bank is available. A study guide with child observation exercises written by Michael Jaffe of Kean College is also part of the instructional package.

The publication of a text requires much teamwork. I wish to thank Gary Woodruff, Peter Marshall, Phyllis Mueller, Mark Jacobsen, and Jane Bacon, and so many other people at West Publishing Company, whose expertise, understanding, and encouragement is greatly appreciated. I also wish to thank those professors at the State University of New York at Stony Brook, including Dr. Everett Waters, Dr. Harriet Waters, Dr. Herbert Kaye, and Dr. Dale Hay, who helped me to better understand the mysteries of child development. Special thanks is in order for Sheryl Sassower, a genetic counselor who reviewed and made suggestions concerning the genetics chapter. In addition, I have had the good fortune to receive feedback from a number of professionals in various areas of child development who have reviewed the manuscript. I wish to express my personal gratitude to these members of the academic community:

Marilyn Bradbard
Auburn University

James Campbell
North Texas State University

Jan Deissler
Illinois Central College

Cathy Dent
University of North Carolina—
Chapel Hill

Lorraine Dieudonne
Foothill College

Jim Flanders
Florida International University

Janet Fritz
Colorado State University

Kerry Garretson
Owens Technical College

John Hamby
Clemson University

Bruce Hinrichs
Anoka Ramsey College

Albert Hollenbeck
George Mason University

Thomas Holman
University of Wisconsin—Stout

Mary Hood
Western Texas College

Ann Husmann
El Camino College

Michael Jaffe
Kean College

Elaine Justice
Old Dominion University

Jean Mercer
Stockton State College

Patricia Miller
University of Florida

Ronald Mullis
North Dakota State University

Pam Reid
University of Tennessee—Chattanooga

Ritch Savin-Williams
Cornell University

Joyce Stines
Appalachian State University

Francis Terrell
North Texas State University

Ross Thompson
University of Nebraska

Writing a text is a family affair, and I would like to thank my wife, Leslie, and my daughters Stacey, Amy, Jodi, and Laurie, without whose patience, understanding, and encouragement this text could not have been written.

PART ONE

Prospects for Personhood

CHAPTER ONE

The Study of Development

CHAPTER OUTLINE

CHILD DEVELOPMENT: A LOOK AT THE
  MYSTERY

ACTION/REACTION   Scott: On and Off the
  Timetable

DISCOVERY: RESEARCH IN CHILD
  DEVELOPMENT

RESEARCH HIGHLIGHT   **Rhyme, Reasoning,
  and Retention**

THREE PROBLEMS IN RESEARCH

ETHICAL CONSIDERATIONS

DEVELOPMENTAL PSYCHOLOGY:
  WHAT'S IN IT FOR ME?

THE PLAN OF THIS TEXT

■ *Are the Following Statements True or False?*

Try the True-False Quiz below. See if your answers correspond to the information in this chapter. Each question is repeated opposite the paragraph in which the answer can be found. The True-False Answer Box at the end of the chapter lists complete answers.

____ **1.** When asked to remember a long list of toys, young children usually use more memory strategies like rehearsal and classification than their parents do.

____ **2.** Children can learn to walk earlier if they are exposed to a special exercise program.

____ **3.** The consequences of a very poor early environment are permanent and cannot be overcome.

____ **4.** Parents who physically abuse their children are often unaware of the force they are using.

____ **5.** The very presence of a researcher may affect the behavior of a child being observed.

____ **6.** Sweetness is the most important factor in the eating habits of children under the age of four, while familiarity is more important after that age.

____ **7.** Polls taken by such popular magazines as *Psychology Today* and *Redbook* correctly mirror the opinions of their readers.

____ **8.** Expecting a child to do well increases the likelihood that the child will perform adequately on a task.

____ **9.** Most psychological experiments cause no physical or psychological harm to the people who participate in them.

____ **10.** Only children above the age of sixteen should be asked to give their permission to participate in an experiment. Below that age, the permission of parents alone should be acquired.

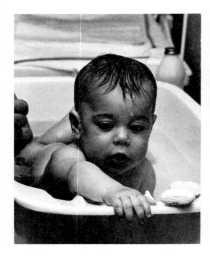

Developmental psychologists study how people change qualitatively and quantitatively over time.

Dear Tooth Fairy,
   Please leave ten dollars instead of one, since this tooth really hurt.

Scene: Moving day
Characters: Father and four-year-old son
Father: I'll pick up the heavy boxes.
Son: O.K., I'll pick up the not-so-heavy boxes.
Father: Don't say not-so-heavy, say light.
Son: O.K., I'll pick up the light boxes, you pick up the dark ones.

"What would you do if you had two apples and four people?" I asked my five-year-old daughter, Amy.
"That's easy, Daddy," she answered. "Just go out and buy two more apples."

A four-year-old, watching the rain pour off a car, asks, "Why is the car sweating?"

After coming home exhausted and worn out from work, your three-year-old tries to cheer you up by giving you her favorite stuffed animal.

After spending two hours getting dressed and made up, your three-year-old says, "Gee, mommy, you look great—just like a clown."

CHILD DEVELOPMENT: A LOOK AT THE MYSTERY

Traveling home to New York from visiting with her grandparents in California, my daughter asked, "Daddy, will you get stripes when I get older?" After a moment's reflection, I realized she meant wrinkles. She had just become aware of the aging process.

   Childhood is a time of mystery and charm. We have been led to believe that once we are adults the world of the child is permanently closed to us. In one way it is. None of us will ever again experience the first day of school or the joy on our seventh birthday when we received the toy we "always wanted." Still, our status as adults gives us an opportunity to understand that world better.

   The process of development is common to all of us, and many aspects of life unfold in a predictable way. Children sit before they walk, for example, and walk

before they run. This predictability permits the scientific study of development, of change.

But within this predictability there is individuality. The "average child" is a myth. Each child experiences different events, and each experiences the same events differently. Some children meet life's challenges enthusiastically, others are more reluctant. Some develop quickly and dramatically, others require more time. Each child is at the same time similar to others and yet unique. It is this combination of predictability and uniqueness that ensures that the scientific study of development will never dull.

Interest in child development is not new. Societies all over the world throughout history have provided training for their children. Indeed, interest in the moral development of children goes back thousands of years (Borstelmann, 1983). But the scientific study of children is recent, and from it we learn how children develop the skills and understandings they bring to adulthood. It also makes it possible for us to predict the changes and challenges that children face at different periods in their development, which in turn helps us take action that will help children negotiate such hurdles successfully.

Developmental Psychology: The Study of Change

The watchword for all development is change. **Developmental psychology** is the study of how organisms change qualitatively and quantitatively over time. Will the scientific understanding and predictions that it makes possible reduce the charms of childhood? Absolutely not. On a drive through the countryside one night, my three-year-old daughter looked at the beautiful half-moon and asked seriously, "Who cut the moon in half?" She knew what happened when her mother cut her sandwich in half, so the question made sense to her. As researchers have come to understand the reasoning of preschoolers, a new dimension has been added to our appreciation of the child. Everyone who deals with children has favorite stories. They become more meaningful when one knows how these curiosities and behaviors fit into the total pattern of children's growth and development.

developmental psychology
The study of how organisms change over time.

Research in child development attempts to answer three questions. First, how—in what stages or sequence—do children develop increasingly sophisticated skills? For example, how do children, who know nothing of mathematics as infants, acquire an understanding of addition, subtraction, multiplication, and division by the time they leave elementary school? The process is gradual and somewhat predictable.

Second, what is the nature of these changes? Researchers seek to categorize the difference between the average six-year-old's knowledge of numbers and that of the average eight-year-old.

Third, what makes these changes occur? What forces are responsible for the child's development?

The Hows of Development

To find out *how* development takes place, we must look at the way a child progressively deals with a problem or concept. For instance, how does a child develop an understanding of money? One team of researchers found that children do this in six stages (Berti and Bombi, 1981).

In the first stage, children are only vaguely aware that money has anything to do with buying or selling. In the second stage, they understand that they must pay for candy and toys, but they think all types of money are the same; to them, a quarter and a dime have the same value. In the third stage, they are aware that there is some difference in money, but they don't really understand the rules for buying and selling. In the fourth stage, they understand that different items cost different amounts, and that they may not have enough money to buy what they want, but they really don't understand why. In the fifth stage, children understand the value of various denominations and the correspondence between money and the price of the toy. In the last stage, they understand that the storekeeper should give an exact amount of change back, along with the item.

Here we see the natural development of the concept of money. The changes are predictable in terms of the order in which they will appear. What is not predictable is the exact age at which the child will exhibit a particular stage of understanding. Berti and Bombi found that of 16 four-year-olds tested, 2 were in stage one, 7 in stage two, 5 in stage three, and 2 in stage four. Each child's individuality entered into the equation. Developmental psychologists can demonstrate sequences and make some rough statements about the age distributions surrounding a behavior. For example, the average three-year-old recognized that money was necessary to buy an item, but had no idea of anything else. Most children did not achieve the sixth, or last, stage until age seven. However, we cannot say that a four-year-old is definitely in a certain stage, since children enter and leave these stages according to their own timetable.

The Nature of the Changes

Developmental psychologists must catalog the ways in which children change. For convenience, change can be divided into two categories—quantitative change and qualitative change (Appelbaum and McCall, 1983). Many changes are both qualitative and quantitative.

Quantitative Change: How Much More or Less? The average eighteen-month-old toddler uses about 10 words, while the average two-year-old uses about 29. The average two-year-old knows about 200 words. By the age of six, this has jumped to 20,000 or so (Wehrabian, 1970). The average adolescent entering high school has a vocabulary of about 80,000 words (Polermo and Molfese, 1972). Any changes that involve an increase or decrease in some characteristic are considered **quantitative.** Increases in height and weight fit into this category. In short, anything that can be expressed simply as more or less of some quantity is considered quantitative.

quantitative changes
Changes that can be considered solely in terms of increases or decreases, such as changes in height or weight.

Qualitative Change: A Change in Process or Function. The child's understanding of money is a **qualitative** change. It cannot be understood strictly in terms of more or less. At three, the child understands money differently from the way the child will understand it at six. Such changes are qualitative, that is, they involve a change in process or function. The nature of the way children understand and use money changes.

qualitative changes
Changes in function or process.

Try this experiment. Cut out sixteen pictures from various magazines. Make certain that four pictures show food, four show pieces of furniture, four show toys, and four show items of clothing. Then ask children of various ages to remember as many pictures as they can, after being given a minute or two to study them. As you would expect, the older children will remember more of the items than the younger children (Brown et al., 1983). This is essentially a quantitative change. However, if you had observed them studying the pictures, you would have noticed a fascinating qualitative change in the strategies they used to help them remember the items (Kail and Hage, 1982). Younger children do not make use of the categories, while older children do (Furth and Milgram, 1973).

In one study, Moely and colleagues (1969) isolated kindergarten, first-, third-, and fifth-grade students for two minutes to observe the strategies they would use to remember a series of pictures. A clear developmental pattern emerged. At the kindergarten level, children verbalized the names of the stimuli but did little else. By third grade, children were testing themselves, but voluntary grouping or clustering did not begin until grade five. With increasing age, children adopt new and better memory strategies. This shows a change in the quality of their functioning, not just an increase or decrease in the number of strategies used or words remembered.

1. *True or False:*
When asked to remember a long list of toys, children usually use more memory strategies like rehearsal and classification than their parents do.

Qualitative changes are particularly fascinating. A child's understanding and practice of friendship, for example, changes as the child grows (Selman, 1981). Through infancy and toddlerhood, friendship is defined by physical proximity or by a desire to play with the other child's toys. Between the ages of four and nine, children engage in one-way friendships—friendships in which they do not practice the give-and-take that characterizes later friendships. Elementary school children adopt the idea of give-and-take in friendship, but they are motivated by self-interest, not mutuality. Between the ages of nine and fifteen, children begin to share feelings as well as material things. These friendships, though, are limited by jealousy and exclusivity, qualities demonstrated by bickering and hard feelings when the children play together. The final stage, where friendship involves mutuality and trust, is seldom obtained before twelve at the earliest.

One caution must be noted here. The ages given here and throughout this text are merely reference points. They indicate only the general range during which children may be negotiating a particular stage. The sequence of stages is relatively fixed, but the ages at which children enter and leave each stage varies greatly. Again, this reflects the individuality factor noted earlier. Knowing how a child sees his or her friends, we can now predict the next progression in that child's understanding of friendship, but pinpointing the exact age at which a change to a newer conception of friendship will occur is difficult.

What Makes Changes Occur?

When we watch a baby begin to walk, we are seeing a creature impelled toward progress. Time after time, the baby will try, fall, cry, get up, and try again. In more subtle ways, the process goes on in a multitude of areas throughout one's life. The process of normal development is always forward and is propelled by maturation and learning.

maturation
A term used to describe changes that are due to the unfolding of an individual's genetic plan. These changes are relatively immune to environmental influence.

Maturation.   The unfolding of an individual's unique genetic plan is known as **maturation** (Hottinger, 1980). Maturation largely explains such things as the time a child's teeth erupt, the child's developing ability to grasp objects and to walk, and the time at which an adolescent girl first menstruates. The maturational process depends most strongly on the individual's genetic master plan. This master plan, which functions as a timetable of sorts, largely (but not entirely)

Is the child's ability to walk due to maturation, learning, or both?

determines when certain events will occur. The genetic master plan may limit progress as well. For example, before a baby can walk, he or she must have the necessary strength and balance, prerequisites that are determined largely by maturation (Stewart, 1980). The child is ready to walk only when these prerequisites are met. Nutrition is also important, and so is experience (Bower, 1977). Infants need the opportunity to practice their skills. Most of the time, these basic experiences are provided without too much difficulty or planning.

There is some evidence that environmental enrichment can optimize development. In one study, infants whose parents actively exercised the child's muscles walked two months earlier than infants who received no training (Zelazo et al., 1972). Yet the rate of maturation is not completely elastic. No one claims that such children can be trained to walk six months earlier.

There is also evidence that an overwhelmingly poor environment has a disastrous effect on the rate of maturation. Children raised under very poor conditions are often retarded in many areas of development (Rutter, 1979; Bowlby, 1969), but with extra care and attention, the negative effects of a poor environment can be overcome to some degree (Clarke and Clarke, 1976). Milder levels of deprivation do not seem to have any long-lasting effect.

The maturational process proceeds in much the same way for children of all cultures, and in all types of homes within these cultures. It is determined largely by internal signals, unlike the learning process.

2. *True or False:*
Children can learn to walk earlier if they are exposed to a special exercise program.

3. *True or False:*
The consequences of a very poor early environment are permanent and cannot be overcome.

Scott: On and Off the Timetable

ACTION/
REACTION

Scott is a playful, exuberant, happy sixteen-month-old, but his physical and mental development is slow. While most children his age are walking and starting to talk, he is just beginning to take some steps and knows very few words.

The parents are concerned. Scott's father wants him to take part in rigid exercise and cognitive stimulation programs, both of which he read about in a magazine. Now is the time to begin a program, Scott's father argues, before he falls further behind. Scott's mother doubts the wisdom of such an approach. She wants to leave well enough alone. After all, they've provided a stimulating environment for the boy, and time will take care of the rest.

A special pediatrician examined Scott and informed the parents that nothing was wrong with him as far as she could tell. As for the programs advocated by Scott's father, the pediatrician would only say not to overdo it. Scott's father argues that the programs can't do any harm, so why not try? His mother believes that forcing Scott to do things before he is ready could frustrate him and injure his relationship with his parents. The situation is complicated by the presence of a neighbor's child of about the same age who is making great progress and is well ahead of Scott.

1. If you were Scott's parent, what would you do?

Learning occurs in many forms throughout life.

learning
Relatively permanent changes in behavior due to interaction with the environment.

Learning and Experience.   Any relatively permanent changes in behavior caused by interaction with the environment are due to **learning**. These changes, by definition, cannot be the result of maturation (Rachlin, 1976). When a child recites the alphabet, imitates a brother's fear of spiders, sings along with daddy, or recognizes mommy, learning has occurred.

A child's understanding of sex roles, morality, and problem-solving are dependent on learning. Yet we cannot see learning; we can only infer it from behavioral change. The child who solves a math problem that he or she could not solve last week is said to have learned.

In contrast to maturation, learning is extremely dependent on the environment. Children learn what they see and experience. A child whose parents habitually fight, scream at their children, and encourage their children to take an aggressive stance toward other people will learn to be aggressive. A child whose parents settle disputes calmly and encourage their children to do the same is likely to learn to settle disputes in a peaceful manner. Yet the relationship is not one-to-one. Fine people sometimes emerge from traumatic environments, and a tranquil, supportive environment is no guarantee of a well-adjusted child.

Parents are not the only influence on their children. As the child's social world expands, peers, teachers, television, and a host of other environmental factors influence what the child learns. Sometimes there is conflict with what is demonstrated at home. Parents can easily control the environment of an infant or toddler, but as the child enters nursery school and elementary school, this control is reduced, and the influence other people have on the child increases. We will discuss the processes by which a child learns in Chapter Four.

The Link Between Maturation and Learning.   Learning and maturation cannot be isolated from each other. Some events, such as physical growth, are more clearly due to maturation. In other events, such as acquiring a vocabulary,

learning seems more important. Yet a complete understanding of human behavior must deal with both. Even with such maturationally determined events as walking, some interaction with the environment is necessary, and such external factors as nutrition cannot be ignored. At the same time, in order to master a skill like solving crossword puzzles, a certain degree of maturation must be attained. Reading provides a good example of the interaction between maturation and learning. Maturation plays an important role because children cannot read until they can focus on the task for a reasonable period of time and process the necessary visual information. Learning is essential because children must be able to recognize the letters and words, and pronounce the words correctly. Development is best understood as the result of the interaction of maturation and learning.

DISCOVERY: RESEARCH IN CHILD DEVELOPMENT

Discovering how and why a change occurs, and describing the nature of that change, is exciting. Researchers actively seek such information through well-defined methods of data-gathering and experimentation. These methods allow us not only to understand some of the mysteries of childhood, but also to answer many practical questions (see Research Highlight "Rhyme, Reasoning, and Retention").

One such question came to the forefront years ago when two of the best children's television shows, "Sesame Street" and "The Electric Company," were being developed (Lesser, 1976; Palmer, 1976). The question: How can we develop a high-quality, high-value show that preschoolers will want to watch? The answers were gleaned from the developers' own experiences and from numerous studies on the needs, abilities, habits, likes, and dislikes of preschoolers.

RESEARCH HIGHLIGHT   *Rhyme, Reasoning, and Retention*

Suppose you want a three-year-old to remember something. Should you use a rhyme or straight prose? Think of it. Children seem to love nursery rhymes. Common sense dictates that young children would remember rhymes better than prose.

Psychologists know that not all things that are "common sense" are necessarily true. Would the conventional wisdom that children remember rhyme better than prose stand the test of a scientific study? Donald Hayes and his colleagues designed a series of studies to answer this question.

The researchers selected two unfamiliar stories, "Old Dame Trot" and "The Little Turtle," which were written both in verse and in prose. In one study, children between three and five years of age were presented with a tape recording of either the prose form or the verse form of one of the two stories and then asked a series of questions about them. The children's liking for the stories was also measured.

The results? Children who were presented with the prose version answered 78 percent of the questions correctly, compared with only 54 percent for the children who listened to verse. The other studies extended the findings, but they did not alter the conclusion that children remember prose better than rhyme.

Although young children prefer stories told in rhyme, their retention and comprehension of such stories is inferior. Since adults often use rhymes as a memory device, there may be some age at which children will find rhymes useful again.

Why does rhyme retard understanding? Hayes and his colleagues believe that children tend to pay attention to the sound of rhymes rather than to the meaning. Children listening to prose attend to the message and retain it better. This finding runs counter to the conventional wisdom. It should be remembered that the material was presented only once, that the testing took place almost immediately, and that the children were not specifically told to listen for the meaning of the stories. If the stories had been repeated, if the testing had been performed after a longer time interval, or if the children had been specifically told to listen for content, the results might have been different. However, only further experimentation can vary these factors and present us with a clear and complete picture.

For now, these studies lead to the conclusion that if you want children to like a story, tell it in rhyme, but if you are after comprehension, then tell it in prose.

Source: D. S. Hayes, B. E. Chemelski, and M. Palmer. "Nursery Rhymes and Prose Passages: Preschoolers' Liking and Short-term Retention of Story Events, *Developmental Psychology,* 1982, *18,* 49–56.

---

replication
The scientific necessity that experimental procedures should be capable of being reproduced by others.

Research in child development offers the best of two worlds: the excitement of journeying into the unknown, and the structure of an established scientific discipline. While the excitement keeps researchers motivated, the discipline allows them to contribute to a larger body of knowledge. One of the researcher's goals is to produce a study that can be **replicated,** that is, reproduced by other researchers.

Two factors allow researchers to produce useful studies. The first is access to previous research findings. We build our knowledge brick by brick, research study by research study. The second is the body of information on research methods and data interpretation. This information eliminates the need to reinvent the wheel, for it suggests plans of action that may be useful to the researcher in designing the study.

The Importance of Research Methods

Many students ask why a knowledge of research methods is important. "It's the information that matters. Why worry about how the researcher got it?" But this attitude misses the point. The way a researcher obtains the information—the re-

The knowledge gleaned from many research studies has helped make "Sesame Street" a success.

search methods—largely determines the legitimacy of the study's conclusions. A poorly designed study will produce invalid results.

Knowing about research methods will both allow you to better understand the research presented in this text and give you a valuable technique for evaluating information. We live in an information-rich environment. Daily we read of new findings concerning parenting practices or new statistics on teenage pregnancy. Not all the studies that lead to these reports are carefully designed or unbiased. A knowledge of research methods can help you determine which information deserves your attention and which should be ignored. This is important in keeping well informed.

Laboratory vs. Field Research

Research can be performed in one of two places: the laboratory or the field. Both have advantages and drawbacks. The laboratory has the advantage of being closed and under the researcher's control. But the researcher cannot be certain that the results obtained in the laboratory will hold true for the field.

Field research is performed in the "real world" under realistic circumstances. But this world is more complex and capricious, and researchers face many frustrations and problems in controlling the environment.

Researchers have found a partial solution to these problems by simulating real-life situations in the laboratory. They do so by using an analogue, or a situation that is parallel and similar to the one being studied in the field. Some studies in child abuse, for example, have followed this pattern. Child abuse is a complicated problem with many causes (see pages 373–379). In trying to isolate these causes, psychologists have created models for how abuse develops. One such model suggests that excessive use of punishment may be involved. A parent may punish a child and receive short-term compliance. When the child resumes the troublesome behavior, the parent may use increasing amounts of punishment, and the original punishment may escalate into abuse.

To see if this could be the case, Vasta and Copitch (1981) recreated this scenario in a laboratory. They asked twenty-two undergraduates to train children to perform a memory task. These "teachers" were seated at a console separated from the children by an opaque screen. They were told that they could not see the children because their gender must be kept secret and that all teacher-student communication would be accomplished through signals that would appear on panels. In fact, there were no children, merely the illusion of children created by the researchers. Further, the researchers had programmed the student responses to decrease in accuracy. While the "students" answered 80 percent of the questions correctly at the beginning of the study, they answered only 10 percent correctly by the end of the test. And they did so no matter what the "teachers" did.

As part of the "teaching" process, the "teachers" terminated students' answers by depressing a lever. The time required for the lever to travel between the on and off positions was related to the force used and was of great interest to the researchers. The results indicated that as the number of mistakes increased, the "teachers" threw the lever with greater and greater intensity. Yet when interviewed after the experiment, the "teachers" said they were not aware that they had increased the force used to slam the lever down.

This suggests that an adult faced with a situation in which his or her best efforts to improve a child's performance or behavior are ineffective may respond with increasing force without realizing it. This possibility meshes well with clinical reports indicating that child abuse is often unpremeditated, that parents' responses to a child's misbehavior escalate rapidly to the state of abuse without them being aware of it.

This study indicates that it is possible to simulate a scenario in the laboratory that can help our understanding of a social problem such as child abuse. The next step might be to devise some method of countering this problem of escalation, to try it out in the laboratory, and finally to adapt it to the real-life concerns of the field.

4. *True or False:*
Parents who physically abuse their children are often unaware of the force they are using.

Choices in Research Design

Besides answering the question of where the research should be performed, a researcher must decide how it is to be done. Here, researchers are faced with many choices. They can simply observe the situation, or they can follow one or two children around and collect an extensive amount of data on them. They can elect to interview or survey a group of people, or even present children with a task, observe them working on it, and ask them questions about it. Or they can conduct a controlled experiment to answer the question.

Naturalistic Observation.   No matter which method is chosen, observation may enter the picture. However, there are times when a researcher will simply observe events as they occur in the native environment. In this case, the researcher does not interfere, but merely observes. This method is called **naturalistic observation.** For example, what if you wanted to find out how fathers and mothers in Mexico play with their children, and compare it to the way

naturalistic observation
A method of research in which the researcher observes people in their natural habitat.

American parents interact with their offspring? You might decide to watch such interactions as they occur at home, with the parents' permission.

This is exactly what Phyllis Bronstein (1984) did. She arranged for observers to watch and tape-record Mexican mothers and fathers interacting with their children. After entering the home, the observer sat in a corner, taking notes and recording the session. The results? Fathers were found to be more playful with their children than mothers. Mothers were more nurturant regarding their children's immediate physical needs. In addition, fathers treated sons and daughters differently. They reprimanded sons more than daughters, and they were more intellectually involved with their sons. Mothers tended to treat sons and daughters more equally. Bronstein noted that this pattern is found in many similar studies performed in the United Sates. Of course, no single study is sufficient to make any generalizations concerning Mexican or American parents, but this study adds to our knowledge of how parents interact with their children.

As valuable as naturalistic observation is, it presents us with problems. First, observers may disagree as to what they have seen. To counter this possibility, sometimes it helps to videotape the events being studied. Second, observers themselves may influence a subject. Would you act the same way if someone was watching you? The very presence of an adult sitting in a classroom or watching parents play with their children may cause subjects to act differently. For this reason, observations must be conducted with an eye to blending into the background as much as possible. Third, although naturalist observation yields interesting information, it cannot tell us anything about cause and effect. From this experiment, we can make no statement about why fathers treat sons and daughters differently. We cannot say whether some behavior in sons causes fathers to act differently, or whether some personal factor in fathers is the cause of the differential treatment.

5. True or False:
The very presence of a researcher may affect the behavior of a child being observed.

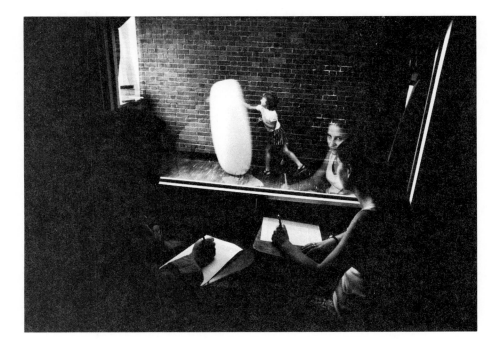

Developmental psychologists try to be as unobtrusive as possible while observing children.

case study
A method of research in which one person's progress is followed for an extended period of time.

autism
A severe mental disorder involving a lack of responsiveness to others, communication disabilities, and bizarre behavior.

Case Studies.   What if you wanted to know how a fourth-grader spends an average school day? Perhaps you could follow the child around, noting all activities for the day. A researcher following the progress of a subject over an extended period of time is conducting a **case study** (Harrison, 1979). The researcher painstakingly records the child's behavior, seeking to identify patterns. This approach sounds easy to many people, but after attempting it they often change their minds. Try it yourself. Spend an hour—or a day if you have the time—recording the behaviors of a child (with the parents' permission). You might focus on how the child responds to criticism or praise, or on the child's emotional state when interacting with others. The more activities there are to observe, the more difficult it is to record the behaviors. You will discover that there is a great deal more to observation than you first thought.

Case studies often yield interesting insights into the functioning of a particular child. In his book *The Empty Fortress*, Bruno Bettelheim spends a considerable amount of time explaining three case histories of autistic children. **Autism** is a disorder characterized by a lack of responsiveness to others, by severe problems in communication, and by strange or bizarre behavior. It develops by thirty months of age (Sarason and Sarason, 1980). Bettelheim follows Marcia, Laurie, and Joey through their stay at the Orthogenic School, where such children receive expert care. He describes in detail their early home life, the development of the condition, the behavior of the children, the trials and tribulations of working with them, and their subsequent improvement. He looks for patterns in their development and insights into their strange world. Seven-year-old Laurie's first contact with a psychologist is described in this way:

> [she] was bland; she treated him as an object. At times she grinned a little, but not in response to any obvious outer stimuli. She proceeded to build with blocks in a perfectionistic manner. Any effort on the part of the examiner to alter her arrangements upset her. With crayons she drew mostly squares, with some scribbling or "windows." If handed a half-finished square by the examiner, she finished it hastily, as if she could not tolerate open or incomplete figures. She never talked, never responded to any verbal request of any kind. She laughed in an odd manner at times, and now and then there was evidence of deep-seated agitation. When returning to the mother she seemed completely indifferent. (Bettelheim, 1967, p. 97)

Although a valuable technique, the case-study approach is of limited use. One can never be quite certain that the child being studied is similar to other children who are the same age or who have a particular condition. Therefore, it is necessary to do many case studies in order to demonstrate a common behavioral pattern, and by their very nature such observations are time-consuming and expensive. Second, the words that the observer uses can cause difficulties. Notice that the description of Laurie's behavior contains several phrases that reflect judgment on the part of the observer. Another observer might have used words with other connotations or may have described the scene differently.

survey
A method of study in which data is collected through written questionnaires or oral interviews from a number of people.

The Survey Method.   What if you wanted to collect data from a large group of people? The case-study method is too involved for this purpose. If collecting such data is your goal, consider using the **survey,** or interview, method. In a survey or interview, researchers ask a large number of people questions about their own behavior or that of their children, and the answers are tabulated and reported. Most of us are familiar with attitude surveys, such as those conducted by the Gallup organization. Their results give public officials some idea of how people are thinking and may affect public policy.

Psychologists frequently use such instruments to collect data. The results are sometimes surprising. Wikler and her colleagues (1981) researched the adjustment patterns of parents with mentally retarded children. Two incompatible theories exist in the field. The first is that parental grief is essentially a one-time event. The second recognizes the immediate grief and shock parents experience, but argues that parents continue to experience periodic crises of mourning and grieving, that their grief is not time-bound.

The researchers sought to discover which of these two theories reflected the experiences of parents and social workers familiar with the problem. Some 100 social workers were randomly selected from Dane County Department of Social Services in Madison, Wisconsin, and a list of parents was obtained from a treatment center for mentally retarded children. Questionnaires were mailed out. After a telephone follow-up, 32 completed questionnaires from parents and social workers were obtained. The majority of the respondents indicated that families experience continuing periods of sorrow. However, social workers tended to overestimate how upset parents were just after discovering their children were retarded, and they underestimated the grief the parents experienced later. The results of this study indicate that parents of such children need continued emotional support, not only counseling at the time they are told of their child's condition.

There are problems with the survey approach. For instance, in the above study it is difficult to be certain that the group of parents who received questionnaires were representative of the parents of retarded children across the nation. The researchers might be able to generalize their findings to their own community, but not any further. Second, fewer than one-third of the questionnaires were returned. Do the parents who did return the questionnaires accurately reflect the feelings and experiences of those who did not return them? In addition, can the researchers be positive that even those parents who returned the questionnaires are giving their true feelings on this emotional topic?

Finally, it is difficult to construct a fair and unbiased questionnaire. The researcher must be quite careful about how the questions sound. For example, imagine being asked a number of questions concerning how you discipline or punish your child. If the question is "How often do you spank your child?" you might answer one way, but if the question is "How often do you beat your child?" you might answer that quite differently.

The Clinical Method.   One of the most famous researchers in child development, Jean Piaget, pioneered the **clinical method.** In this method, the researcher presents the child with a verbal or physical task and both observes the child tackling the challenge and asks the child questions about it. For example, Piaget took two balls of clay, making certain that the child agreed they were equal. Next he rolled one ball of clay into a long, thin "worm" and then asked the child which had more clay. Piaget found that most children younger than seven believed the worm contained more clay because it was longer (see Pulaski, 1980).

The clinical method combines the observation and interview approaches. The researcher using this method sometimes uses different questions with different children as the need arises. In this way, the method differs from the standard

clinical method
A method of studying children which relies on both observation and individual questioning.

interview or survey method, in which the questions asked of each subject in the study are the same.

The clinical method is remarkable in its flexibility and the freedom it gives the researcher. It does have its difficulties, most important of which involve lack of standardization. Since the questions asked are not standardized, we depend on the researcher to ask the right questions and not lead the subject to give a particular answer because that's what the researcher wants to hear.

The Experimental Method.   Often the only way to answer an important research question is to conduct a controlled **experiment.** To do this, the researcher controls the situation as much as possible, manipulating one or two elements in the environment. To illustrate, let us take the problem of getting young children to eat their vegetables. Most parents have watched their children subsist on candy and french fried potatoes, while avoiding anything that contained either vitamins or minerals. In one way, it makes sense. Brussels sprouts and green beans don't compare well to potato chips and ice cream. In addition, these high-calorie, low-nutrition foods are more likely to be advertised on television and to be attractively packaged in the supermarket. Children see thousands of food messages on television each year (Peterson et al., 1984). Pronutrition commercials can now be found as well, but research shows that although children take in the nutritional information and remember the commercials, they do not seem to change their food preferences or consumption patterns (Peterson et al., 1984).

How can parents encourage their children to eat a somewhat balanced diet? Many researchers have observed the food preferences of children. In fact, Birch (1979) found that familiarity and sweetness were the most important factors in choosing food. Familiarity is most important for children under four, while sweetness becomes the primary factor for children above that age.

In another study, Birch (1980) attempted to better understand the effects other children might have on the food preferences of preschoolers. First, the food preferences of thirty-nine preschool children were assessed for nine vegetables, including carrots, celery, peas, and cauliflower. For four consecutive days a child who preferred one vegetable to another was seated with three or four children who preferred another vegetable. For example, a child who had ranked cauliflower last was seated with children who rated it number one.

After a while, the child who did not originally favor the vegetable was greatly influenced by the food preferences of the other children and began to select the nonpreferred vegetable. The child not only chose it but also actually ate it. The results were lasting. Weeks later, children continued to choose and eat their originally nonpreferred food. The food preferences of younger children were more easily modified than those of older children. In addition, older children had a greater effect on the food preferences of younger children, perhaps because the older ones were bigger and more respected. This study demonstrates that children's food preferences and their actual eating habits can be influenced by exposing the children to peers whose food preferences are different. It offers the hope that exposing a child to others who eat a greater variety of foods may encourage the child to eat a more varied diet.

The element of the situation which is manipulated by the researcher is called the **independent variable.** In this case it was the seating patterns. Children who

experimental method
A research strategy using controls which allows the researcher to answer a particular question.

6. *True or False:*
Sweetness is the most important factor in the eating habits of children under the age of four, while familiarity is more important after that age.

independent variable
The factor in a study which will be manipulated by the researcher.

did not like certain vegetables were seated with other children who did. The factors that are measured are called the **dependent variables.** In this case they were the child's choice of vegetables and the actual eating behavior. Food preferences were measured by a questionnaire, the actual consumption of the vegetable was observed. The researcher is not limited to one dependent variable, or even one independent variable. Theoretically, it is possible to measure any number of changes, but practical limitations often cause the researcher to decide on one or two of the most important factors. Experimental studies are often difficult to perform, especially in the field, since a researcher must exercise such great control over the environment. However, the effort is often worth the extra trouble since only experimental studies can demonstrate cause and effect relationships.

Correlations.   Often researchers involved in collecting and analyzing data wish to discover the relationships between two elements in the environment. For example, there is a relationship between scores on intelligence tests and school achievement. Higher intelligence scores are related to higher achievement levels in school. Researchers use the term **correlation** to describe such a relationship. A correlation may be positive or negative. A positive correlation indicates that as one factor increases, so does the other. A perfect positive correlation is written + 1.00. A negative correlation indicates that as one factor increases the other decreases. A perfect negative correlation is written − 1.00. For example, we may find a negative correlation between throwing spitballs at the teacher and grades on a child's report card: the greater number of spitballs thrown, the lower the grades.

Most correlations are far from perfect. The correlation between scores on an intelligence test and achievement in school hovers at about .60, which is high but not anywhere near perfect. Other factors besides intelligence, such as motivation and perseverance, are involved in school success. The important facts to remember about a correlation is that it tells us that a relationship exists, the direction of the relationship (whether it is positive or negative), and the magnitude of that relationship. It does not establish cause and effect.

Longitudinal and Cross-sectional Designs.   Developmental research is often concerned with measuring change over time. We may be interested in discovering how children of various ages perceive their parents, or how they approach various problems. If you were an investigator interested in the first topic, you could find groups of eight-, ten-, and twelve-year-olds, measure their perceptions of their parents, and compare them. This is an example of **cross-sectional** design (see Figure 1.1). On the other hand, you could use a group of eight-year-olds and measure how they perceive their parents today, then wait until they are ten and measure it again, then wait another two years and do it a third time. This is an example of **longitudinal** design (see Figure 1.2). Both are popular, and each has advantages and disadvantages.

Cross-sectional studies.   Cross-sectional studies are easier to perform. Groups of different-aged subjects are tested at the same time, and the results are compared. Diaz and Berndt (1982) looked into the nature of children's knowledge of their best friend and just how accurate it was. Twenty pairs of fourth- and eighth-grade friends were tested. Children were asked a series of questions that measured both their intimate knowledge and casual knowledge of the other person.

dependent variable
The factor in a study which will be measured by the researcher.

correlation
A term denoting a relationship between two variables.

cross-sectional design
A research design in which children of different ages are studied to obtain information about changes in some variable.

longitudinal design
A research design in which subjects are followed over an extended period of time to note developmental changes in some variable.

FIGURE 1.1   **Cross-sectional Studies**
In a cross-sectional study, children of different age groups are tested at the same time and
their scores on some measure compared.

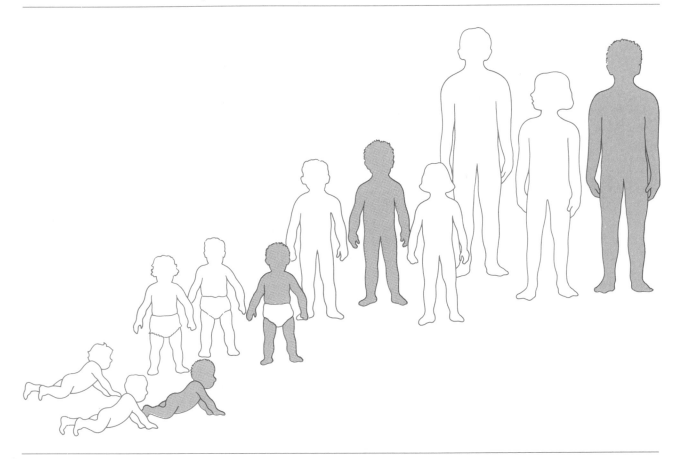

The accuracy of the knowledge was measured by comparing the pair's answers.
The researchers found that eighth-graders knew much more than fourth-graders
about their friend's personality characteristics and preferences, but there was no
difference in the knowledge of their friend's external characteristics. Older children possessed a more intimate knowledge of their friends.

Cross-sectional studies are useful, but they have their faults. It is difficult to
understand the growth and decline of any attribute over an extended period of
time, because the same people are not being followed (Nunnally, 1982). In addition, when comparing subjects who differ significantly in age, the effect of growing up in a different generation must be taken into account. This is known as the
cohort effect. Suppose you were noting the differences between fifteen-year-olds
and five-year-olds on some measure of attitude. You obtain your data and analyze it. You interpret the differences between them as age-related. But it is also
possible that the differences are caused by generational or cohort differences
(Forman and Sigel, 1979). Certain social, political, or natural events in one gen-

cohort effect
The effect of belonging to a
particular generation, of being
raised in a historical time.

FIGURE 1.2   Longitudinal Studies
In a longitudinal study, researchers test the same children over a period of time.

eration may not be repeated during the life span of the next. For example, the Great Depression of the 1930s, World War II, the rediscovery of poverty and racism in the 1960s, and the Watergate scandal in the 1970s were events that may have affected one generation and not another. The Vietnam War had a tremendous effect on teenagers growing up in the late 1960s and early 1970s, but it is only history to the younger generation today. It is difficult to screen out such cohort effects.

Longitudinal studies.   Longitudinal studies are not as easy to execute as cross-sectional studies. Subjects must be followed over some period of time and retested at stated intervals (Schaie and Hertzog, 1982). Longitudinal studies have been described as the "lifeblood" of developmental psychology (Appelbaum and McCall, 1983). They allow scientists to identify changes within subjects over age. Such questions as "Do obese children become obese adults?" and "Do aggressive children remain aggressive into adulthood?" can best be studied using longitudinal research designs.

In one longitudinal study, Eisenberg-Berg and Roth (1980) tested preschoolers between forty-six and sixty-three months of age to discover changes in how children reasoned about helping others. Subjects were interviewed twice—once at the beginning of the experiment and then eighteen months later. The researchers found an interesting developmental change. As children aged, they became more concerned with the needs of others and less with the question of whether they would get something in return for their efforts.

Longitudinal studies also have weaknesses. They are more time-consuming, and maintaining contact with subjects over the long term is difficult. Some subjects move away, others simply do not return their questionnaires at various testing periods, leaving the researcher with incomplete data. It is difficult to determine whether those who drop out differ from those who remain throughout the study.

Another problem is the effect of practice and retesting in a longitudinal study (Blanck et al., 1982). Let's say you want to measure the changes in intelligence over the years. If you use the same or a very similar test, the children might become testwise and show an improvement simply as a result of practice. On the other hand, using different measures may create problems, because one measure may not be directly comparable to another.

As in the cross-sectional approach, the cohort effect should be taken into account (see Birren et al., 1981). Longitudinal studies performed thirty years ago are interesting, but they may be confounded by specific generational problems, and such studies have to be updated.

Researchers are constantly looking for ways to improve their experiments. Some have suggested mixed models that have both longitudinal and cross-sectional components. For example, one could look at the political opinions of five-year-olds and eight-year-olds and test subjects in both groups every year for four years.

THREE PROBLEMS IN RESEARCH

As we have seen, researchers are faced with a number of choices. Should they conduct a case study, do a survey, or design an experimental study? Should a study be performed in the field or in the laboratory? Should the researcher try to follow the same subjects over a long period of time, as in a longitudinal study, or take groups of different-aged children and compare them, as in a cross-sectional study? All studies, though, share a number of problems. Three of the most common are sampling, researcher bias, and interpretational difficulties.

Sampling

Suppose you are a local school board member who is responsible for discovering how parents view elementary school's new super-improved reading program. How would you go about it? Constructing a questionnaire is a reasonable approach. Your problem is how to get the questionnaire to the people, completed, and returned to you again.

You could get a list of all the children in the school and give them the questionnaires to take home. This is a disastrous approach, if you remember anything about your old school days. Only a small number of children bring these notices home. Most of the questionnaires end up in the wastebasket or as paper planes, or lie in the middle of notebooks for weeks before accidentally being discovered.

To avoid this problem, mailing questionnaires to the parents might be advisable. But then the wait begins. Many parents will not return the questionnaires. They simply can't be bothered with them, even though filling them out would only take a minute and you have provided a stamped, addressed envelope. In addition, you cannot be certain that those parents who do respond really represent the opinion of the community at large. That is, do the 30 percent or so who spent the time and effort necessary to fill out the questionnaire differ from the others who did not? Perhaps these people are actively involved in their child's education and know all about the new reading program, while the others don't have the faintest idea that it exists. Merely sending out questionnaires may not yield the definitive results you were hoping for.

What about taking a telephone poll and reading the questions to parents? This makes some sense, but it is expensive and time-consuming. In addition, you will not be able to find everyone home, and some parents won't want to be bothered with your questions. If you call during the day, you have just eliminated many working people.

Using the telephone itself could be a problem. If every family in your neighborhood has a telephone, a concerted effort might work, but if the school serves a community that is poor, you may bias your study by leaving out those with no telephones. If you did this, you would be in fine company. In the 1930s the *Literary Digest* took a voter preference poll for President. Names and addresses were taken from the telephone directory. The survey concluded that the Republican candidate, Alfred Landon, would swamp Democrat Franklin Roosevelt. The opposite actually occurred, with Roosevelt romping to an easy victory (Freidel, 1976). What went wrong? In the 1930s, only the rich had telephones, and as a group they favored Landon. Most of the population voted for Roosevelt. The sample was not representative of the general population.

Finding a representative sample of some larger group, called a "population," is tricky. In the reading program survey situation described earlier, an attempt was made to send out the questionnaire to the entire population of the school with the hope that the portion who returned the completed forms correctly mirrored the opinions of the entire school district. In most studies it is impossible to work with an entire population, so the researcher tries to find a fraction of the population that will be representative of the larger group.

The best way to do this is to choose subjects at random from the population. In this way every member of the population would have an equal opportunity to be included in the sample. We might pick names out of a hat or have a computer do it for us.

Although this sounds reasonable, it can be a problem. What if a number of these people decide that they simply do not wish to participate in the study? Faced with this problem, researchers have resorted to advertising for volunteers. Ads for volunteers can be found on psychology department bulletin boards in most colleges and universities. But are volunteers different in some important way from nonvolunteers? This is a difficult question to answer, but it is a vital one. The more representative your sample is of the population you are studying, the more useful your research results will be.

7. *True or False:*
Polls taken by such popular magazines as *Psychology Today* and *Redbook* correctly mirror the opinions of their readers.

Many magazines, such as *Psychology Today,* conduct opinion polls. These questionnaires are answered by some of their readers and returned to the publishers or their agents, who tabulate the results and interpret their meaning. The results of such polls are tempered by two problems. First, the readership of a particular magazine is probably not representative of the population at large. The results could be misinterpreted and overgeneralized. Second, the people who send in their completed questionnaires may not have opinions similar to those of people not motivated to participate in the poll.

A few years ago, Ann Landers, the popular advice columnist, asked her readers whether they would have children all over again if they had the choice. A sizable number of those parents who responded said they would not. The results were reported in the news media across the nation, sometimes without cautioning news consumers that the sample was probably biased. It was certainly not representative of the entire nation's parents, and perhaps not even of Ann Landers' readers. Not everyone in the nation reads the column, and the characteristics of Ann Landers' readers may differ from the characteristics of those who don't care to read the column. In addition, the people who took the time to sit down and write the letter to Ann Landers in the first place were probably dissatisfied, and happy to get an opportunity to vent their anger and frustration to a willing and encouraging listener. Satisfied parents may not have been as motivated to write.

Researcher Bias

Imagine you are a science teacher who has just been informed that your students were going to take a statewide examination designed to measure their knowledge of the subject. Your students are very poor readers, but you believe they know their science. What would you do? If you do nothing, your students will fail the science test because they cannot read well.

You decide to read the questions to the students, although this is a clear violation of the rules. When the test results are returned, your students have performed much better than others in the same grade who had to read the questions themselves. A group of teachers ask you to demonstrate the manner in which you administered the test. You stand up in front of the room and read the questions out loud. However, when giving the correct answer in the multiple-choice portion, your right hand rises slightly and your voice changes somewhat. Your students may have picked up these nonverbal clues. You may have inadvertently given away some of the answers to the test.

A similar phenomenon occurs in research. When researchers seek the answer to a question, they often make a tentative guess about the results of the study called a **hypothesis.** Could a researcher's opinion bias the results? The answer is a definite yes.

In one study, Rosenthal and Fode (1963) led students to believe that the rats they were running through mazes were either dull or bright. Actually, there were no differences between the groups. The rats had been randomly assigned to students. However, students who thought that their rats were bright experienced greater success in training than those who were dealing with rats labeled "dull." In fact, students working with the "bright" rats claimed that their rats were gentler, easier to work with, and generally more cooperative. The researchers' ex-

hypothesis
An educated guess made after examining the literature in the field.

pectations that their rats were bright or dull somehow influenced their behavior, enough to bias the results of the study.

Rosenthal and Jacobson (1968) demonstrated that these expectancy effects exist in the field as well as in the laboratory. Elementary school teachers were informed that some of their students had performed extremely well on a psychological measuring instrument that could predict which students would improve dramatically over the next school year. In reality, the students so designated were chosen at random and were no different from their classmates. Even so, at the end of the year these children had spurted ahead and made impressive gains. As the researchers note, "The children from whom intellectual growth was expected were described as having a better chance of being successful in later life and as being happier, more curious and more interesting than the other children. There was also a tendency for the designated children to be seen as more appealing, better adjusted and more affectionate, and as less in need of social approval" (Rosenthal and Jacobson, 1968, p. 6). These children showed impressive intellectual gains as well. Rosenthal and Jacobson accounted for this by invoking the concept known as the **self-fulfilling prophecy,** which means that the expectation that something will happen increases the chances that it will occur. The differences between the groups were not due to any obvious teacher behavior. Such results are instead often due to more subtle, nonverbal gestures (Chaikin et al., 1974). It is unwise to generalize from one study, and indeed, other studies trying to induce similar effects have not always been successful (Brophy, 1982). Yet it is possible that researchers may influence their subjects through nonverbal behavior, and efforts must be made to eliminate this problem.

Subtle researcher bias can affect the results of any study. If the subjects are treated differently, the results may be nullified. Thus, many researchers have chosen to use **blind experimental designs,** in which the researcher is not aware of the group a subject belongs to while working with that subject. For example, suppose you were attempting to discover the effects of tutoring on children who come from poor or middle-class backgrounds. In order to counter the problem of bias, the tutor should not know the background of the child being tutored. This reduces the problem of researcher bias.

8. *True or False:*
Expecting a child to do well increases the likelihood that the child will perform adequately on a task.

self-fulfilling prophecy
The concept that a person's expectations concerning some event affect the probability of its occurrence.

blind experimental designs
An experimental design in which researchers do not know whether a subject they are working with belongs to the experimental group or the control group.

Interpretation of Data

Once a science-minded young man spent the entire night drinking scotch and soda. The next morning he awoke painfully aware of his overindulgence. He decided not to repeat his mistake, so the next night he drank bourbon and soda. The following morning his head was splitting and he couldn't feel his tongue, so he decided again not to repeat the mistakes of the past. The third evening was spent drinking gin and soda. The next morning was the worst of all, and he sat down to evaluate the disaster. He asked himself what had been common to all three evenings, and suddenly it hit him. Each night he had been drinking soda, and he solemnly promised himself he would never drink soda again (after McGraph, 1964).

Our young man made what must seem an obvious mistake. Of course, the other factor common to each evening was alcohol, but this conveniently slipped his mind. Reaching such an unfortunate conclusion is not the sole province of people who drink too much and think too little, like this young man. Researchers must be careful not to interpret the data from their studies incorrectly. Two possible sources of error have already been noted—sampling and researcher bias, but there are other sources of error.

Consider the problem of a researcher trying to investigate the effectiveness of two different types of teaching strategies. Everything is done to control the situation, but one room is quiet, while the class in the other room must contend with a great deal of street noise. The noise is not a variable included in the research design, so it could confound the results of the experiment, making interpretation difficult. Studies using infants or very young children often suffer from these difficulties. An infant may become cranky or be distracted by something in the room that no one thought would be a problem.

Another source of interpretational error involves the attention subjects may receive in an experiment. Suppose you're trying to discover whether young infants who are given a particular exercise program will be more advanced both physically and intellectually than those not given the program. You supervise the exercises with one group and leave the other group as is. You then measure the two groups and discover that your special group is more alert and advanced. You conclude that your special exercises have great benefit. But wait a moment. While your special group was receiving this training, what was the other group doing? It could be that the special attention itself, rather than your new exercise program, created the disparity between the groups. Such factors as attention, improved social relationships, and creation of an atmosphere in which the subject is made to feel special can cause differences between groups. This is often called

Hawthorne effect
The tendency for people to act differently when extra attention is paid them.

the **Hawthorne effect,** after a study performed on workers in the early twentieth century. In that study, a number of changes in the work environment boosted productivity. The factor that was important was the change in workers' attitudes and their social relationships with other workers (Maier and Verser, 1982). Subjects in a study may show a change because they are the center of attention and feel special.

How can this attentional factor be controlled? One method is to equalize the attention. For example, the parents in your group of infants who do not receive training exercises might be asked to spend time playing with their infants, thereby equalizing the amount of attention given to each child.

After reading all the things that can go wrong in an experiment, it must seem as if performing good research is very difficult. It is, but it is not impossible. No experiment is perfect, nor can one experiment be designed to answer all our questions. Many of the problems can be reduced or eliminated by carefully choosing samples, reducing researcher bias, and controlling the research environment. Yet researchers cannot always design the best possible study. They are constrained by practical factors, such as money and time, as well as ethical considerations.

ETHICAL CONSIDERATIONS

Ethical problems arise whenever research is performed. In most universities today, committees review the ethics of each research proposal involving animals or human beings (Cooke, 1982). Many professional organizations, including the

American Psychological Association (1973) and the Society for Research in Child Development (1977), have published guidelines for protecting subjects. The federal government has also published such standards (National Commission for the Protection of Human Subjects of Biomedical and Behavioral Research, 1977).

Should This Experiment Be Performed?

■ You are asked to participate in an experiment in driver education designed to discover the reactions of drivers to stressful situations. You drive past a construction site, as you were asked to, when something lunges in front of the car and you hit it. You react with horror and grief, for you believe you have just struck a human being. Later you learn it was just a dummy and that the experiment was rigged. Is this experiment ethical? (After Wood, 1974; and APA, 1973)

■ Children are continually frustrated in their attempts to reach a toy while a researcher notes their anguished responses. They show a great deal of discomfort. Should experiments that cause such adverse emotional reactions be performed?

■ A scientist wants to find out whether a particular vaccine will harm an unborn child, in order to determine whether it is safe to give pregnant women. The scientist contacts women who have decided to abort their fetuses and asks permission to inoculate them with the vaccine. After the abortion, the fetuses will be examined for abnormalities. Is such experimentation on the fetus ethical?

■ A researcher tells a young adult that the purpose of a study is to discover the effects of punishment on learning. One subject will serve as the teacher, first reading a list of word pairs and then testing another subject, who is the student. If the student does not answer correctly, the teacher throws a switch, delivering a painful shock. In reality, no one is receiving any shock at all. The researcher is really seeking to discover whether people will perform potentially damaging actions when encouraged to do so by an authority figure. The subjects have been told a lie, and the researcher is actually studying obedience, not punishment. Is it ethical to lie to a subject? (Milgram, 1963).

Most psychological experiments cause no physical or mental pain. Research studies that contain anything even remotely considered dangerous are rare. However, in the history of psychology some controversial experiments have been performed, and constant vigilance is required. For example, Watson and Raynor (1920) conditioned a nine-month-old baby to fear rats by presenting the rat and following this with a loud noise. After a number of such pairings, little Albert feared not only rats but other furry objects as well. Watson did not bother to decondition Albert to the fear, despite a month's advance notice that he would be leaving the hospital (Harris, 1979). Was it ethical to condition fear in Albert? Shouldn't Watson have attempted to decondition the young boy? The first question could be argued, but Watson definitely was responsible for deconditioning Albert.

In another experiment, Dennis (1935) sought to discover the effects of environmental deprivation on the development of motor skills. He raised twin girls in an unstimulating environment, where they were given no toys and little attention, and found that they made very slow progress. As a result, Dennis began to

9. *True or False:*
Most psychological experiments cause no physical or psychological harm to the people who participate in them.

FIGURE 1.3   **Sample Consent Form**

Any experimenter must receive the consent of the parent and the child (if the child is over seven years old) before beginning an experiment involving a child. However, even if the child is under seven years old, it is still advisable to request his or her permission.

Title of project: _____

Researcher(s) Name(s): _____
_____

The purpose of the research project that we are asking you to participate in is _____
_____
_____
_____

If you decide to participate, your part in the research project will involve (procedures, duration, which procedures are experimental) _____
_____
_____
_____

Your participation may result in the following benefits _____
_____
_____

The following risks and/or discomforts may be associated with your participation ____
_____
_____
_____
_____

Your participation in this project is completely voluntary. You do not have to participate if you do not want to. Your decision about whether to participate or not will have no effect on any other treatment or benefits which you are entitled to from the researcher or this institution. You can change your mind and withdraw from the project at any time without penalty. However, the following risks may be associated with withdrawal from the project: _____
_____
_____

Any information which we can get from this study about you, including your identity, will be held confidential. We will take the following steps to ensure confidentiality: __
_____
_____
_____

If, at any time, you have any questions about this project, please contact: _____
_____

If you have any questions about your rights as a subject, please contact: Dr. John Smith, Committee on Research Involving Human Subjects, Telephone: (100) 222-3333.

Figure 1.3 continued

If you agree to participate in this research project, please sign and print your name below. Your signature indicates that you have read the information provided above, or have had it read to you, and that you have decided to participate.

_____

Signature of Subject or Authorized Representative   *(Date)*

_____

Name of Subject

_____

Signature of Investigator   *(Date)*

Source: State University of New York at Stony Brook.

appreciate the importance of practice and stimulation on motor development. When the study was over, he gave the girls special attention and training, and they overcame their retardation. Was this experiment really ethical? What if the girls had not caught up and reached their potential?

Such experiments would probably not pass the muster of ethics committees today. Most researchers are quite concerned about the possibility of harm and seek to minimize or eliminate it. The two most common ethical problems in psychological experimentation today involve the issues of informed consent and deception.

Informed Consent

Ideally, subjects should be told specifically what is expected of them and be encouraged to decide for themselves whether they wish to participate in a study. Federal guidelines specify many important features of informed consent (Cooke, 1982). The subjects should be told the purpose of the research, the procedures involved, and the risks and benefits, and be presented with a statement noting that they are free to withdraw from the study and an invitation for the subjects to ask questions about their participation. Figure 1.3 shows a sample consent form. Some studies involve small children, who naturally cannot give their permission. In this case, the study is explained to the parents, who then consent to the child's participation. It is assumed that the parents are both capable and responsible for making decisions that are in their children's best interests. Since studies in developmental psychology are usually rather tame, such consent often centers on convenience factors, such as whether the subjects have the time to devote to the study. If the child is above seven or so, the child's consent should definitely be obtained (see Cooke, 1982). However, the researcher should try to get the permission of children even younger than seven.

Sometimes the assumption that parents always act in their children's best interests can be questioned. The parents of one severely learning disabled child refused to enroll him in a special experimental program that might have yielded

10. *True or False:*
Only children above the age of sixteen should be asked to give their permission to participate in an experiment. Below that age, the permission of parents alone should be acquired.

both valuable research information and great benefits to the child. No injury could have occurred, and the enrichment might have helped him. But the parents' suspicion and pride led them to refuse to give their consent, and the child was denied a splendid opportunity.

Deception

The most serious ethical problem confronting researchers today is deception. Some researchers argue that they cannot always inform subjects about the true objectives of their study. If they do, the subjects may alter their behavior to match the desires of the researcher. What if the researcher wants to determine whether the gender of the author of a composition would affect students' evaluations of the work. The researcher may tell the subjects that the study is concerned with the content of the story itself and not even mention the name of the author, which appears on the top of the page and clearly reflects the writer's gender. Is this deception warranted? Today, sexism and racism are not fashionable, and if psychologists are to study these areas, subtle deceptions may be necessary. Other psychologists disagree, arguing that deception is morally wrong and harmful to the profession (see Baumrind, 1985).

This difference of opinion among researchers will continue. Those researchers who use deception take on themselves extra responsibilities. After the study, subjects must be informed as to its true nature. In addition, during the study, subjects may acquire knowledge that may trouble them, and researchers must provide help for subjects trying to work through what they have learned about themselves (Holmes, 1976a; Holmes, 1976b).

DEVELOPMENTAL PSYCHOLOGY: WHAT'S IN IT FOR ME?

Whenever one approaches a new subject, it is natural to ask about its relevance. "What's in it for me?" is a common question and deserves an answer.

Personal Benefits

Most people marry and raise children. A better understanding of children leads to a greater appreciation of the problems and potential of children and will enable parents to better experience the joys of parenting. For example, an understanding of cognitive (intellectual) development may help you appreciate why your child enjoys a particular game. Very young children enjoy playing peekaboo because they are just learning that people still exist even though they can't see them. The child generates an expectation that the parent is still there, which is subsequently validated. When the child sees the expectation is correct, the child reacts with glee. This reaction means much more to a parent who understands how the child is perceiving the game.

An appreciation of where the child is in the developmental cycle can enable parents to help their child. Knowing what skills are necessary for reading would help a parent understand the best time to begin a particular activity. At the same time, warning signs can be spotted and remedial action taken. In one case, a nine-month-old had stopped babbling. The parents suspected that their child might suffer from a hearing problem, took the child for a checkup, and discovered that they were correct.

Careers in Working with Children

Teachers, mental health personnel, nurses, nutritionists, child-care workers, nursery school personnel, parent educators, playground supervisors, and many other workers need a knowledge of child development. The practical possibilities are endless. For example, teachers could avoid much frustration by understanding that the way they present questions to their students greatly affects how they answer them. Nurses may be required to communicate with children in a stressful situation, and an understanding of how to explain an operation, a separation, or even a death to a child is helpful. Nutritionists who understand the thinking processes of children are better able to develop strategies to encourage them to eat balanced diets.

Research, Teaching, and Clinical Work

Developmental psychology is a growing field. Many developmental psychologists teach in colleges and universities and perform research (APA, 1975). As you read this text, you may begin to form research questions that you may some day be in a position to answer. In addition, there has been a tremendous growth of interest in parenting courses, and developmental psychologists are often called on to design and offer such programs.

Influencing Public Policy

Research can answer practical public-policy questions. The results from scientific investigations can affect public policy toward children (Kiesler, 1979). Developmental psychologists are often called on by government agencies to create and evaluate programs aimed at improving the lot of children (Seitz, 1979). For example, child abuse is a national problem, and developmental psychologists are seeking methods of prevention and treatment. Mental health is a major national problem, and research into the causes and prevention of emotional problems is an ongoing concern (Dusek, 1974). By influencing public policy toward children on a local, state, and national level, the nation will carefully nurture its most valuable resource—its children.

THE PLAN OF THIS TEXT

This text uses a chronological approach to child and adolescent development. After the initial discussion of genetics, prenatal growth, and birth, *A Child's Odyssey* is divided into parts covering infancy and toddlerhood, early childhood, middle childhood, and adolescence. The child's physical, social and personality, and cognitive (intellectual) development are discussed in each part. Physical development involves the development of such skills as walking, running, and

holding a pencil, as well as changes in stature. Social and personality development includes how children develop their own personality and relate to others.
Cognitive development involves how children think, reason, and solve problems. These areas interact. How a child thinks affects that child's relationship
with others. Special chapters on language development and children with exceptional needs are also included.

Each chapter begins with a group of true-false questions. They are repeated
opposite the paragraph in which their answers can be found. The True-False Answer Box at the end of each chapter lists complete answers. In addition, the important terms appear in **boldface,** and a running glossary is provided in the margins. The body of the text contains a number of examples and applications that
demonstrate how research may lead to a better understanding of children's behavior as well as practical action aimed at overcoming their problems. In addition, a number of anecdotes, some humorous, are included. One hope is that
you may empathize with the child being described and put yourself into his or
her shoes, experiencing the world from the child's perspective.

Throughout the book, childhood experiences are placed into the overall
context of the life span. There is an old proverb: The child is the father of the
man. How childhood experiences affect the character and abilities of the adult
will be pointed out throughout the text.

Two other features of this book deserve mention. Each chapter contains one
or more Research Highlights, which demonstrate how research can be used to
answer some interesting question. In addition, throughout the book there are
brief case studies (called Action/Reactions) that raise practical issues. They offer
you the opportunity to apply what you are learning to realistic problems. I must
stress that there is no single correct analysis or solution to these problems. Differences of opinion are common, and you the reader, your professor, and your classmates may view the problems from different perspectives and suggest different
ways of handling them. If you think you've come up with an especially good solution, please let me know by writing to me through West Publishing Company. Finally, a summary of each chapter is provided for your review.

Just as development does not stop when adolescence ends, so it does not begin at the moment of birth. At conception our genetic blueprint is set, though
how it will be expressed later in life is not always preprogrammed. Research into
prenatal development has led to a new appreciation of this stage, and the birth
process itself has become the focus of much new interest and controversy. It is to
these experiences, which occur before infancy yet have such a lasting effect on
the child, that we turn first.

Chapter Summary

1. Developmental psychology is the study of how organisms change qualitatively and quantitatively over time.

2. There are two general categories of change. Quantitative changes involve an increase or decrease in some characteristic, such as the number of words in a child's vocabulary. Qualitative change involves some change in function or process. For example, ten-year-olds use different strategies from five-year-olds when asked to remember a list of words.

3. Most developmental psychologists are interested in how a particular behavior develops over time.

4. Changes that are relatively immune to environmental influences and are caused by the unfolding of the individual's unique genetic plan are considered maturational in nature.

5. Learning is usually defined as a relatively permanent change in behavior which can be attributed to interactions with the environment.

6. The key to understanding development is to appreciate the various ways in which maturation and learning interact.

7. The researcher has many decisions to make. It is easier to control the environment in the laboratory than in the field. However, laboratory research lacks the "real world" orientation of field research.

8. There are many types of research. In naturalistic observation, the researcher carefully observes and records what occurs in the natural environment. The case-study method involves carefully observing a subject for a substantial period of time and collecting a great deal of information about one or two people. Researchers using the survey method question a number of people, then tabulate and analyze their data. The clinical method combines careful observation and questioning. A child may be presented with a problem, and a researcher observes how the child handles it and may ask questions about the child's perception of the challenge. Researchers using the experimental method control the environment, allowing only the desired variables to vary.

9. In cross-sectional studies, children from various age-groups are tested at a particular time. In a longitudinal study, a single group of children is tested at particular intervals. Mixed research designs, which combine features of both, are also being used today.

10. Researchers face numerous problems. Three important concerns include choosing a representative sample, eliminating researcher bias, and correctly interpreting results.

11. Most psychological experiments cause no physical or psychological harm to their subjects. Today, most universities have committees that examine the ethics of each experiment. Two of the most common ethical problems involve consent and deception.

12. The study of developmental psychology yields great personal benefits, helps people deal better with their children, opens up new vocational possibilities, and suggests ways society may improve the lot of children.

■ *Answers to True or False Questions*

1. *False.* Correct statement: Young children use fewer strategies.

2. *True.* Active exercise programs may encourage early walking.

3. *False.* Correct statement: If the environment is suitably changed, even the effects of a very poor environment can be reduced.

4. *True.* Most parents are unaware that they are using too much force in disciplining their children.

5. *True.* The presence of a researcher affects the behavior of the child being observed.

6. *False.* Correct statement: Familiarity is most important for children under four, sweetness for children over four.

7. *False.* Correct statement: Readers who send in completed questionnaires may not be representative of the entire readership.

8. *True.* Expecting success is one factor leading to adequate performance.

9. *True.* Potentially dangerous psychological experiments are very few.

10. *False.* Correct statement: Consent should be acquired from any child over the age of seven as well as from the child's parents.

CHAPTER TWO

Genetic Influences on Development

CHAPTER OUTLINE

A GENETIC DILEMMA

A NEW LOOK AT GENETICS

HOW WE INHERIT: THE MECHANISMS OF
    TRANSMISSION

ACTION/REACTION   A Secret to Keep?

GENETIC INFLUENCES ON PHYSICAL
    CHARACTERISTICS

RESEARCH HIGHLIGHT   **Twin Studies**

GENETIC INFLUENCES AND DISEASE

GENETIC INFLUENCES ON DEVELOPMENT
    AND PERSONALITY

ACTION/REACTION   "Aggressive" Genes?

GENETIC COUNSELING: THE NEW
    GENETICS

HEREDITY AND ENVIRONMENT: A MODEL

■ *Are the Following Statements True or False?*

Try the True-False Quiz below. See if your answers correspond to the information in this chapter. Each question is repeated opposite the paragraph in which the answer can be found. The True-False Answer Box at the end of the chapter lists complete answers.

_____ **1.** All animal species, including human beings, have the same number of chromosomes: 46.

_____ **2.** While adult males constantly produce new sperm, females are born with all the eggs they will ever have.

_____ **3.** If a family consists of seven male children, the chances are quite small that their eighth child will be female.

_____ **4.** The emotional environment surrounding a child has an effect on the child's adult height.

_____ **5.** Dominant genetic diseases normally show themselves at birth, whereas recessive disorders show themselves later in life.

_____ **6.** At the present time, all that medical science can do for children suffering from genetic diseases is to make them more comfortable.

_____ **7.** Schizophrenia, like cystic fibrosis or Tay-Sachs disease, is directly transmitted from parent to child.

_____ **8.** Infants are born with a temperament that may remain with them throughout childhood.

_____ **9.** Left-handedness is largely determined by the environment.

_____ **10.** There is little evidence that a child's intelligence score can be raised by improving the environment.

_____ **11.** Genetic counselors have the responsibility to approve or disapprove of their clients' course of action.

_____ **12.** Evidence indicates that the great majority of people understand the information communicated to them by genetic counselors.

A GENETIC DILEMMA

Debbie and Craig were in love and planned to marry after they finished college. Craig was anxious to tie the knot, but Debbie was not. Debbie finally told Craig she would marry him, but only on the condition that they not have children. Craig could not accept this. He left the room angrily, and Debbie broke down in tears.

Debbie's unusual situation stemmed from her fear that she would have a child like her sister Elizabeth's daughter, Laura. At birth, Laura appeared to be a normal baby. She made fine progress, but as the months passed it became apparent that something was wrong. Laura was not developing normally. Elizabeth dismissed Debbie's questions about the child's development, telling her that each baby develops at a different rate.

When Laura was eleven months old, however, Elizabeth did question the pediatrician about the lack of progress. Laura could not sit up alone or crawl, and her reflexes were poor. The pediatrician examined Laura thoroughly and recommended a complete neurological examination. After examining the baby, the neurologist questioned Elizabeth and her husband, Alan, about their family history. Then the doctor informed them that Laura was suffering from a fatal illness, **Tay-Sachs disease**. They could have another child, who might be normal, the doctor said, but Alan stated that they would never try to have another child.

Infants born with Tay-Sachs disease seem normal at birth, but after about six months their progress slows. The disease involves an inborn error in metabolism. The infant's body stores an excessive amount of a material called glycolipid in the cells of the nervous system. This causes these cells to swell, rupture, and finally die. As more and more nerve cells die, the baby loses motor abilities and finally becomes retarded. The disease is incurable. At the age of two or three, the child dies.

When Debbie came home from college, she found that Laura's condition had deteriorated greatly. The child was almost blind and could not hear well. Most of the time she just lay in her crib. Elizabeth and Alan were going through an emotionally wrenching experience, watching helplessly as the child wasted away. Soon after, Laura had to be hospitalized. At this time, Debbie decided that because the disease was in her family she would never risk having a child with this disease and issued her ultimatum to Craig. Shortly after her second birthday, Laura died.

Craig made an appointment with a genetic counselor on the staff of the university medical school. After the initial consultation, Craig asked Debbie to visit the counselor with him, which she agreed to do. The counselor explained that Tay-Sachs is a disease that is encountered mostly in Jews who can trace their roots to Eastern Europe. It is caused by a defective gene that is recessive. In other words, a child will suffer from the disease only if *both* parents pass on a defective gene to their offspring. Laura's mother and father had to be carriers. They each carried one normal and one abnormal gene, and Laura had received the defective gene from both parents. The counselor suggested that Craig and Debbie take a simple blood test to determine whether they too were carriers of the defective gene.

When the results of the laboratory tests came back, they showed that while Debbie was indeed a carrier, Craig was not. They were told that no children of theirs would suffer from the disease, although there was a 50 percent chance that each of their children would be a carrier. That night Debbie and Craig had their first date in months and were married shortly after they graduated from college.

Tay-Sachs disease
A fatal genetic disease.

About a year later, Elizabeth and Alan also saw a genetic counselor. They were informed that, because they were both carriers, there was a 25 percent chance that each of their children would suffer from Tay-Sachs disease. In addition, there was a 50 percent chance that each of their offspring would be a carrier, and a 25 percent chance that each child would be perfectly normal, that is, neither show the symptoms of the disease nor carry the defective gene.

When Elizabeth protested that a 25 percent chance of having another child like Laura was too much, the counselor told her that a procedure called **amniocentesis** could determine whether the unborn child would suffer from the disease. By withdrawing some amniotic fluid at about the fourteenth week of pregnancy, the presence of the disease could be detected. If the results were positive, Elizabeth could have an abortion, but the chances were 3 out of 4 that the child would be either a carrier or genetically normal.

Elizabeth and Alan have not yet decided whether they want another child, but they now have the information needed to make a rational decision. They now have a choice—something past generations never had. (Adapted from Apgar and Beck, 1972)

In this chapter we will look at many of the great advances in genetics in recent decades. We will also consider the nature of the choices this new genetic knowledge and technology have given us. Finally, we will carefully examine the role genetic endowment plays in development.

A NEW LOOK AT GENETICS

Nature–Nurture: The Enduring Controversy

Historically, the most basic question anyone could ask involved what percentage of a particular trait could be attributed to our genetic endowment. The term

amniocentesis
A procedure in which fluid is taken from a pregnant woman's uterus and fetal cells are checked for genetic and chromosomal abnormalities.

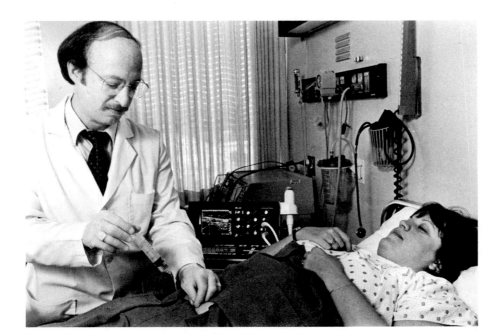

Doctors use amniocentesis to diagnose certain genetic problems. The procedure can also reveal whether the fetus is male or female.

heritability
A term used to describe how much of the variation seen in any particular trait is due to genetic endowment.

heritability refers to how much of the variation we see in people on a particular characteristic, such as intelligence, is due to genetic endowment.

Research on heritability is useful. It helps us gain an appreciation of the many aspects of our lives that are affected by our genes, and it has demonstrated that certain traits are more influenced by genetic factors than others. For example, the characteristic of height is under greater genetic influence than is skill at shooting marbles. Yet the results of such studies are often incorrectly interpreted, and when this happens the public is misled. Heritability figures are sometimes cited by the media without explanation. The percentage of any particular trait attributed to heredity depends on the specific population studied and the particular environment.

For example, what heritability figure would you place on the ability to play tennis? For most people, the ability to drive that baseline shot past an opponent will depend on the quantity and quality of practice. The heritability index is very low, near zero. However, this may not be the case for a professional tennis player. "An outstanding player must have excellent neuromuscular coordination, and people vary in the limits to which their coordination can be trained" (Sutton, 1980, p. 362). If we exposed every child in North America to an intensive program in tennis, hockey, or any other sport, some would still become more adept at the sport than others. There is some genetic influence on the necessary skills. Yet the genetic influence would be greater in the case of an expert than an occasional Saturday afternoon player.

Musical talent presents us with another illustration. A child's ability to sing passably is due mostly to practice, persistence, training, and motivation, all of which are environmental factors. However, these factors do not account for the vocal qualities of some of the great singers of our time. Almost any child might be able to learn how to sing, but not every child can become a great vocalist, no matter how much training is received. The heritability index would be different for the two groups.

Although the discussion of heritability is useful, it should not be considered the prime question in **behavior genetics**, the study of how genetic endowment affects behavior. The crucial question is not *how much* of a particular trait is influenced by our genes, but rather *how* the genetic component and environment interact to produce the behavior (Wachs, 1983; Anastasi, 1958). By focusing on the many subtle ways in which the environment interacts with our genetic endowment, we may some day be able to predict the effect a particular environment might have on a person who has a given set of genes. We could then optimize the development of that person's special talents and abilities.

behavior genetics
The study of how genetic endowment influences behavior.

Our Human Inheritance and Uniqueness

In order to understand behavior genetics, we must be aware that experience can be evaluated on two levels. First, each child's experiences are unique and individualistic. No two children experience life in exactly the same manner. Second, there are general rules of development that help us understand why a child acts in certain ways at a particular stage of life. When we look at how our genetic endowment can affect our life, we must investigate both levels. Each of us is biologically unique. The size and functioning of our organs, the volume of hormones produced, even our susceptibility to disease, show marked differences from individual to individual. Indeed, research has tended to stress these differences.

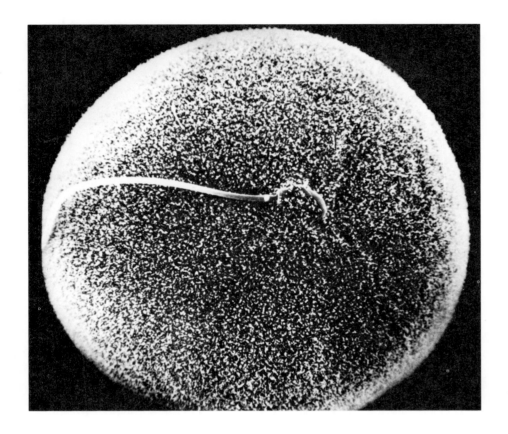

Our genetic endowment is set at the time of conception.

On the other hand, all people have much in common. As human beings, we possess a common biological heritage that is often taken for granted. Every normal child has two eyes, two ears, one stomach, two legs, and a brain. Human beings have much in common. In addition, despite some variations in timing, we develop in a similar fashion. Children sit before they walk, and walk before they run. These maturational sequences are under genetic control (Scarr and McCartney, 1983). We develop spoken language without much formal instruction. Children learn language in a remarkably similar fashion whether they are raised in New York City, on a farm in Iowa, or in the Amazon jungle.

HOW WE INHERIT: THE MECHANISMS OF TRANSMISSION

At the moment of conception, when the male's sperm penetrates the female's egg cell, our genetic endowment is set. Genetic individuality is assured by nature itself.

Genes and Chromosomes

The basic unit of heredity is the **gene**, which is composed of deoxyribonucleic acid (DNA). Genes are carried on rod-shaped structures of various sizes called **chromosomes** (Pai, 1974). Each animal species has its own number of chromosomes. The normal human being has a complement of 46 chromosomes, or 23

1. *True or False:*
All animal species including human beings, have the same number of chromosomes, 46.

gene
The basic unit of heredity.

chromosomes
Rod-shaped structures that carry the genes.

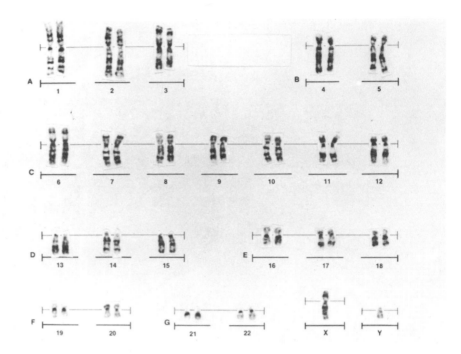

Genes are carried on chromosomes. Each normal human being has 23 pairs of chromosomes.

gametes
The scientific term for the sex cells.

meiosis
The process by which sex cells divide to form two cells, each containing 23 chromosomes.

crossing over
The process occurring during meiosis in which genetic material on one chromosome is exchanged with material from the other.

monozygotic or identical twins
Twins that develop from one fertilized egg and have an identical genetic structure.

2. *True or False:*
While adult males constantly produce new sperm, females are born with all the eggs they will ever have.

pairs. The same 46 chromosomes are found in every cell of the body except the **gametes**, or sex cells. In a process called **meiosis**, the sex cells divide to form two cells containing 23 chromosomes. This allows human beings to maintain the same complement of 46 chromosomes from generation to generation. However, these cells do not have to split right down the middle. Their splitting is more random. Which chromosome ends up in which of the split cells is a matter of chance. There are over 8 million different possibilities in this process alone.

But this is not the end of the story. During the process of meiosis, some of the genetic material on one chromosome may be exchanged with the material from another. This exchange, called **crossing over**, further complicates the situation (Pai, 1974). When crossing over is taken into consideration, the chances that any two individuals are genetically identical are practically zero. Although human beings share a common species inheritance, each person is also genetically unique. The only exception is identical, or **monozygotic**, twins who share the same genetic composition. The similarity of such identical twins in personality as well as appearance is sometimes quite astonishing (see Research Highlight "Twin Studies").

The randomness of conception is quite impressive. The average man's semen contains between 50 million and 125 million sperm for each cubic centimeter of ejaculate (Rosen and Rosen, 1981). Only one sperm is necessary for conception.

While sperm are continually being produced in the testicles of the male, females are born with their full complement of egg cells. The average female infant comes into this world carrying approximately 2 million eggs. About 25,000 are usable when the young girl reaches puberty, though throughout her reproductive life she will probably use only about 350 (Smith and Neisworth, 1975).

FIGURE 2.1 **Determination of Sex**

The child's mother can contribute only an X while the child's father can contribute an X or a Y. Statistically, 50 percent of the conceptions will produce males and 50 percent will produce females (see below). However, conditions in the vagina, among other factors, influence whether the X or Y carrying sperm will reach and penetrate the egg.

Father

	X	Y
X	XX	XY
X	XX	XY

Mother

The Sex Chromosomes

Twenty-two of the 23 pairs of chromosomes look identical. However, the twenty-third pair is different. These chromosomes, called the **sex chromosomes**, are responsible for determining the gender of the offspring. There are two types: the X chromosome and the Y chromosome. The genetic composition of a male is XY, while females have two X chromosomes. When meiosis occurs, a male contributes an X chromosome and a Y chromosome, while the female contributes two X chromosomes. If during conception the sperm carring the X chromosome penetrates the egg's membrane, the offspring will be female. If the sperm carrying the Y chromosome penetrates, the child will be male. Figure 2.1 shows the chances are fifty-fifty that the offspring will be a male.

The chances are the same for each conception. Even if you have seven boys, the chances are fifty-fifty that you will have a girl next. Many people fail to understand this basic point, and it is true for all inherited characteristics as well. Some people incorrectly believe that if their first child has a particular genetic problem, the chances of having a normal child are increased or decreased. Reproduction does not work that way. Every conception starts from square one again, and the same odds exist for every pregnancy.

sex chromosomes
The twenty-third pair of chromosomes, which determines the gender of the organism.

3. *True or False:*
If a family consists of seven male children, the chances are quite small that their eighth child will be female.

Transmitting Dominant and Recessive Traits

How do parents transmit traits to their offspring? How did Laura contract Tay-Sachs disease even though neither of her parents had it and no one in the family suffered from the disorder? Tay-Sachs is caused by a defective pair of genes and it

If this couple chooses to have another child, what are the odds that it will be another boy?

manifests itself only when both parents transmit the defective gene to their child. The genetic counselor stated the chances that Laura's mother would bear another child with the disorder, either a carrier or a genetically normal child. These possibilities are easily calculated, because the transmission of the Tay-Sachs gene is simple and direct (see Figure 2.2).

Traits that follow this simple pattern are known as **Mendelian traits**, after the person who discovered and described this method of inheritance. In the last half of the nineteenth century, Gregor Mendel, an Austrian monk with an excellent mathematical background, cross-polinated tall plants with short plants. The result was many more tall plants. Tallness is a dominant trait while shortness is recessive. The trait that is expressed when only one gene is present is considered **dominant**, while the trait that is masked is called **recessive**. Recessive traits become visible only when two recessive genes are present.

A number of genetic diseases (including Tay-Sachs), as well as some physical characteristics in human beings, follow this pattern. For instance, dark hair is dominant over blond hair, freckles over no freckles, and dimples over no dimples. These characteristics are all due to one gene pair. If the offspring inherits two genes for freckles, then the child will show freckles (see Figure 2.3(a), frame 1). At the same time, if the child inherits two genes for no freckles, the youngster will not have freckles (see Figure 2.3(a), frame 4). But what if a father passes on to his daughter a gene for freckles, but the gene from the mother is for no freckles?

FIGURE 2.2   **Transmission of Tay Sachs Disease**

When Neither Carries the Gene

Neither parent carries the gene. It is impossible for any offspring to suffer from the disorder (see below).

Father

	Normal gene	Normal gene
Normal gene	Normal gene Normal gene	Normal gene Normal gene
Normal gene	Normal gene Normal gene	Normal gene Normal gene

Mother (labeled on left side)

When One Parent Carries the Gene

When either the mother or the father (as in this case) carries the gene, there is a 50 percent chance that any offspring will be a carrier. Since the Tay Sachs disorder is recessive, none of their children will actually have the disorder (see below).

Father

	Normal gene	Tay Sachs gene
Normal gene	Normal gene Normal gene	Normal gene Tay Sachs gene
Normal gene	Normal gene Normal gene	Normal gene Tay Sachs gene

Mother (labeled on left side)

When Both Parents Carry the Gene

When both the mother and the father carry the gene for Tay Sachs Disease, the chances are 25 percent that an offspring will have the disease (Tay Sachs–Tay Sachs), 50 percent that the child will be a carrier (Tay Sachs–Normal) and 25 percent that the child will not have the disorder nor be a carrier (see next page).

Figure 2.2 continued

Father

	Normal gene	Tay Sachs gene
Normal gene	Normal gene Normal gene	Normal gene Tay Sachs gene
Tay Sachs gene	Tay Sachs gene Normal gene	Tay Sachs gene Tay Sachs gene

Mother (label appears between the two mother-rows on the left)

Since freckles is a dominant trait and no freckles is recessive, Susan will show freckles (see Figure 2.3(a), frame 2).

But what would happen if Susan, who has one gene for freckles and one gene for no freckles, married Harry, who has no genes for freckles. To understand this possibility, we must now introduce two new terms, *genotype* and *phenotype*. The **genotype** of a person refers to the specific composition of that person's genes. It is a description of the "kinds of genes possessed, regardless of whether they are expressed" (Sutton, 1980, p. 11). Susan's genotype includes one gene for freckles and one for no freckles. The **phenotype** refers to the "observable characteristics of an individual" (Sutton, 1980, p. 11). In our case, Susan's phenotype shows freckles. We should expect to see freckles on Susan's face, because her genotype has one gene for the trait and freckles are dominant.

When Susan and Harry get married, what are the chances that any of their children will have freckles? Since Harry does not have freckles, we can assume that both his genes for the trait are no-freckle genes. (Remember, if he had even one gene for freckles, he would show the trait because it is dominant.) Susan has one gene for freckles and one for no freckles. While Harry can contribute only a gene for no freckles, Susan can contribute either a gene for freckles or a gene for no freckles. As you can see in Figure 2.3(b), there is a 50 percent chance that each of their children will have freckles. Remember that this fifty-fifty chance holds for each child. If Susan's first two children did not show freckles, the same odds hold for her next child. Each conception is new, but the odds always remain the same.

Transmitting Defective Genes: Cystic Fibrosis

A more serious example of genetic transmission is **cystic fibrosis**, the most common severe children's genetic disease in the United States. Cystic fibrosis is caused by a single pair of defective genes. It is estimated that the disease occurs in one out of every 1,200 births. About one person in 20 or 30 is a carrier (Reed, 1975).

genotype
The genetic configuration of the individual.

phenotype
The observable characteristics of the organism.

cystic fibrosis
A severe genetic disease marked by digestive and respiratory problems.

FIGURE 2.3   **Transmission of Freckles**

(a) When Both Parents Have One Gene for Freckles

When both parents carry one gene for freckles, there is a 25 percent chance that a child will have two genes for freckles and thus have freckles. There is a 50 percent chance that a child will carry one gene for freckles and, since this is a dominant trait, have freckles. There is only a 25 percent chance that a child will not have a gene for freckles and so will not have freckles (see below).

Father

	Freckles	No Freckles
Freckles	1 Freckles Freckles	3 Freckles No Freckles
No Freckles	2 No Freckles Freckles	4 No Freckles No Freckles

Mother

(a)

(b) When One Parent Has One Gene for Freckles

When one parent has one gene for freckles, there is a 50 percent chance that the child will have freckles (see below).

Father

	No Freckles	No Freckles
Freckles	Freckles No Freckles	Freckles No Freckles
No Freckles	No Freckles No Freckles	No Freckles No Freckles

Mother

(b)

Cystic fibrosis is a genetic disorder that involves serious respiratory and digestive difficulties.

Cystic fibrosis is a disorder of the glands that produce mucus, saliva, and sweat (Apgar and Beck, 1974). It affects many organs, including the lungs, liver, and pancreas (Fishman, 1979). A number of serious symptoms can be present, including digestive and respiratory problems. The person with cystic fibrosis has a low resistance to respiratory diseases and a tendency to dehydrate as a result of an excessive amount of salt in the sweat.

New antibiotics have increased the life span of children with this disorder. Between 70 and 80 percent survive to at least age twenty if the disease is discovered early and excellent medical treatment is received (Apgar and Beck, 1972). Treatment must be continuous and hospitalization during periods of crisis can be expected. At this point there is no cure. Even with excellent care, the disease often worsens. The entire family experiences a great deal of stress. Cystic fibrosis is responsible for more deaths than any other genetic disease in the United States today (Berdine and Blackhurst, 1985).

Since the disease is caused by two recessive genes, the only way a child can be afflicted with it is for both parents to have the defective gene. Neither the mother nor the father need show any symptoms of the disorder, because both also have a dominant gene, which is normal. Suppose that two carriers of the disorder marry. What are the odds that each of their children would suffer from the disorder? Before looking at Figure 2.4 for the answer, try working it out yourself.

FIGURE 2.4   **What If Two Carriers of Cystic Fibrosis Marry?**

If both parents contribute their normal gene as in frame 1, the child will be normal genotypically (his genes are normal) and phenotypically (the offspring will not show the disorder). If one parent contributes a Cystic Fibrosis gene and the other a normal gene as in frames 2 and 3, the child will be phenotypically normal (will not show the disorder) but genotypically abnormal (the Cystic Fibrosis gene is present). This child is a carrier. The disorder will not be shown, however, since it is recessive and requires two such genes. If the child receives a Cystic Fibrosis gene from both parents as in frame 4, the offspring will be both genotypically and phenotypically abnormal. That is, the Cystic Fibrosis gene is present in the genetic composition of the offspring and he or she will show the disorder (see below).

Father

		Normal gene	Cystic Fibrosis gene
Mother	Normal gene	1 Normal gene Normal gene	3 Normal gene Cystic Fibrosis gene
	Cystic Fibrosis gene	2 Cystic Fibrosis gene Normal gene	4 Cystic Fibrosis gene Cystic Fibrosis gene

In this case, both parents can contribute either a normal gene or a cystic fibrosis gene. If both contribute a normal gene, the child will be normal. This child will be normal in both phenotype and genotype. In other words, the child would not have cystic fibrosis, nor would the composition of the child's genes necessarily allow it to be passed on to the next generation. There is a 25 percent chance that this may occur.

If one parent contributes a normal gene and one contributes a defective gene, the offspring will not show any trace of the disease. Since normal functioning is dominant, it masks the defective gene. However, the composition of the child's genes includes an abnormal gene that can be passed on to the next generation. In this case, the phenotype is normal but the genotype is abnormal. There is a 50 percent chance that this would occur.

Finally, what if both mother and father contributed their defective gene? Then the child would be both genotypically and phenotypically abnormal. The child would have cystic fibrosis and could pass the gene on to the next generation. There is a 25 percent chance of this occurring.

Polygenic Inheritance

If the relationship between genetics and behavior was always so simple, predicting traits would be easy. But genetic transmission is not always so direct. Mendel's success was due partially to luck. He chose very simple characteristics that

---

A Secret to Keep?

*ACTION/
REACTION*

Kathy and Tom met in their second year of college and became engaged two years later. They agree on most things and are sensitive to each other's feelings. A few nights ago, they watched a television special on cystic fibrosis. The sufferings of a child afflicted with the disorder were depicted graphically, as were the parents' problems in dealing with the child's illness and their own emotions.

Tom stated categorically that he couldn't take that and that "no life was better than that existence." Kathy felt a pang. Her sister had died from the disease five years before she and Tom had met. Kathy had told Tom that her sister had died of pneumonia.

Kathy doesn't know whether she should tell Tom. She knows something about the disease, and since it doesn't run in Tom's family, their children can't be afflicted with it. Why tell Tom something that could upset their marriage plans, when it couldn't have any effect on their children? On the other hand, Kathy recognizes that not being completely honest with Tom is a poor way to start a marriage.

1. If you were Kathy, would you tell Tom? Why or why not?
2. If you were Kathy's parents, would you insist that your child tell Tom?
3. If you were Tom, would you want to know? How would you react to the news?
4. Do people have a moral obligation to inform anyone about their genetic background?

were determined by a single gene pair. Comparatively few human traits are transmitted in this manner. In addition, most of the characteristics discussed so far are caused exclusively by a person's genotype. The effects of the environment on the expression of one's genetic endowment have scarcely been mentioned. In the real world, the relationship between genotype and phenotype is more complicated (Scarr and Kidd, 1983). Simple models of prediction soon break down as we consider characteristics determined by many gene pairs and that are affected by the environment.

polygenic or multigenic traits
Characteristics that are influenced by more than one pair of genes.

When a characteristic is influenced by more than one pair of genes, the mechanism of inheritance is **polygenic** or **multigenic**. The term **multifactorial** describes a trait that is both polygenic and influenced by the environment. However, the terms polygenic, and multigenic, and multifactorial are often used interchangeably. Skin color is a polygenic trait. A number of gene pairs are responsible for this trait (Mange and Mange, 1980), but the environment also influences the phenotype. If you have light skin and spend time in the sun, you tan. Your genotype has not changed, but your outward appearance, or phenotype, has.

multifactorial traits
Traits that are influenced both by genes and by the environment.

Another example is height. Although attainment of adult stature is greatly affected by an individual's genes, the environment also plays a part. Nutrition and health are two prime environmental factors. Japanese teenagers are taller than their parents because their health and nutrition have improved (Curtis, 1975). Even the emotional environment affects growth, since it influences the secretion of growth hormones. Cases of stunted growth occurred in some orphanages where children's psychological needs for love, tenderness, and contact were not addressed even if the children were adequately fed (Gardner, 1972). The environment makes a contribution even in the determination of a trait that is largely influenced by genetic factors.

4. *True or False:*
The emotional environment surrounding a child has an effect on the child's adult height.

Incomplete Dominance

Other mechanisms of inheritance may explain some of the great variation we see in the world around us. For example, if a man has straight hair and his wife has curly locks, would their children have straight or curly hair? Curly hair is dominant over straight hair. It is tempting to construct a chart with only curly and straight as the alternatives. However, this is not correct. Although curly hair is dominant, it is incompletely so over straight hair. If you have two genes for curly hair or two genes for straight hair, you would have curly or straight hair. But if you received one gene for curly hair and one for straight hair, your phenotype might well be *wavy* hair (Pai, 1974).

Sex-linked Traits

If you look at a picture of human chromosomes, the pairs appear identical except for one: the twenty-third pair, which are the sex chromosomes. A female has two X chromosomes, while a male has an X and a Y. The X is three times as large as the Y. It contains many more genes than the Y, and many of the genes found on the X chromosome do not exist at all on the Y. This has profound consequences for males.

Consider what might happen if a female had one defective recessive gene and one dominant normal gene on the twenty-third chromosome. Let us also assume that these genes are found only on the X, not on the Y. The female would not show the effects of the recessive gene because she possesses a gene for normal functioning to counter it. But what would happen if she had children? She could pass on both her normal gene and the abnormal gene, but unlike our previous cases the child's gender becomes crucial.

Look at Figure 2.5. Notice that if the female contributes an abnormal X chromosome and her husband contributes a normal X, the child will be a female who will show no signs of the disease but who will be a carrier like her mother. If the female contributes her normal X and her husband contributes his X (which is also normal). the offspring will be female and will neither show any signs of the disease nor pass it on to the next generation.

But what if the child is male? If the mother contributes her normal X and her husband contributes his Y, the offspring will be a male who will neither show any signs of the disorder nor be able to pass it on. Because the X is normal, there is no need to be concerned. However, if the mother transmits the defective X and the father a Y, the resulting male offspring will show signs of the disorder and may pass it on to the next generation. The defective gene on the X has no corresponding normal gene on the Y to counter it, so the defective gene on the X is in a posi-

---

FIGURE 2.5   **Sex-linked Inheritance**

In sex-linked traits, females may carry the defective gene but do not develop the disorder. Males who have inherited a defective gene develop the disorder because they have no corresponding normal gene on the Y chromosome to counter the defective gene found on the X chromosome. In frame 1, the offspring is female but although she carries the defective gene she will not develop the disorder because she has a normal gene to counteract the defective gene. In frame 2, the offspring is again female but has not inherited the defective gene and, of course, will not develop the disorder. In frame 3, the offspring is a male who will develop the disorder. Notice that he has inherited a defective gene from his mother and has no normal gene on the Y to counteract it. In frame 4, the offspring is again male. This offspring has received a normal gene on the X chromosome and cannot develop the condition.

	X^n	Y^0
X^d	1 $X^d X^n$	3 $X^d Y^0$
X^n	2 $X^n X^n$	4 $X^n Y^0$

Mother

n = normal
d = gene for a disorder, for example, hemophilia or color blindness

sex-linked traits
Traits that are inherited
through genes found on the
sex chromosomes.

tion to manifest itself. **Sex-linked traits** involve female carriers, but it is the male who inherits the trait.

A considerable amount of interest in sex-linked traits exists today. Among the proven sex-linked traits are hemophilia and color blindness. Most of the scientifically documented sex-linked traits are both recessive and pathological (Lips and Colwill, 1978). Both hemophilia and color blindness are determined by defective, recessive genes found on the X chromosome. Because a female has two X chromosomes, her chances of being a hemophiliac are negligible. She is also much less likely to be color blind.

hemophilia
A sex-linked inherited blood
disease.

Hemophilia is a severe blood disease involving a deficiency in the blood's ability to clot. When the affected individual is injured, a major crisis may ensue. Even a simple wound may cause a considerable loss of blood. Today, some progress has been made in controlling the disorder through the administration of cryoprecipitate, better known as the clotting factor. The treatment is continuous and extremely expensive.

Could some of the differences between males and females be genetically determined? Perhaps the fact that women normally outlive men can be explained by genetic endowment (Kermis, 1984). Psychologists differ sharply on such questions. Except for some genetic diseases and physical traits, the interaction of genes with the environment is crucial to understanding the end product. Still, the possibility of explaining some sex differences using the mechanism of sex-linked genetic transmission is tempting.

How does genetic endowment affect development? We now turn to three areas of genetic influence: physical characteristics, genetic diseases, and rate of development and personality.

GENETIC INFLUENCES ON PHYSICAL CHARACTERISTICS

The most striking genetic influence involves physical appearance. Hair and skin color, the shape of the nose, body build, and a thousand other physical characteristics are directly influenced by genes. But if we are genetically unique, why do we still look like some other family members? To answer this question, try the following exercise. The next time you're in class, ask yourself how you recognized the person coming in the door as John, Ted or Frank? You probably used their body build and facial features as recognition aids. In this regard, some physical features are more important than others. These features are only a very few of the physical characteristics of the individual, but for identification purposes they are crucial.

Another reason for familial similarity involves limitations in our gene pools. Consider the number of different nose shapes and eye colors that any individual might inherit. The variety is impressive. However, there may be only a small number of nose shapes or eye colors in a person's gene pool. When we say that two siblings (who are not identical twins) look alike, we are judging them on the basis of a very small number of physical traits whose variety is limited by their gene pool. We ignore their unique genetic endowment, which may be responsible for physical features that are not as useful for recognition purposes.

RESEARCH HIGHLIGHT   *Twin Studies*

The "Jim" twins were a fascinating pair. Separated at four weeks of age, they finally met thirty-nine years later. Their similarities were incredible. Besides their appearance, both had taken law-enforcement training and served as deputy sheriffs. Both men owned Chevrolets and vacationed in Florida. Both married and divorced women named Linda and remarried women named Betty. Even their dogs shared the same name—Toy.

Twin studies have always fascinated the public. Every time a twin pair is reunited after a number of years apart, the media cover every aspect of their reunion. Not far behind the newspeople are the psychologists, waiting for their turn to evaluate the twins.

Identical twins raised apart give psychologists a unique opportunity to evaluate the effect of different environments on various areas of development. Since these monozygotic twins share the same genotypes, any differences must be due to the effects of the environments in which they were raised. Despite being raised in very different environments, some of these twins show remarkable similarities in personality, habits, and developmental patterns that are very difficult to explain.

Perhaps the most famous case involves two identical twins, Oskar Stohr and Jack Yufe, who were separated shortly after birth and did not meet for forty-seven years. Oskar was taken to Germany by his mother and became a Nazi. His brother, Jack, was raised by his father as a Jew in the Caribbean and spent some time working on a communal farm in Israel. The similarities were obvious from the moment they met. Both sported wire-rimmed glasses and mustaches and they shared a number of food preferences. But some of the similarities seem to defy explanation. They both flush the toilet before using it and

read magazines from the back to the front. A psychologist, Thomas Bouchard, who tested these twins found remarkable similarities in their temperaments as well.

Can these unusual similarities be explained as mere coincidences? This is a matter of dispute. As more twin pairs who have been raised apart are found and tested, unusual similarities become more difficult to dismiss as statistical accidents. Perhaps genetic endowment plays a larger role in the development of personality and behavior than we thought.

But not all twins reared apart manifest such similarities. While twins reared apart who show striking similarities are inherently interesting, those who do not are often lost in the shuffle. Some twin pairs are quite different, but only the twins who share interesting similar habits and personality traits become newsworthy and gain national media exposure.

In addition, twins separated at birth may actually have more in common than those who have been raised together (Farber, 1981; Holden, 1980). Twins raised together often must assert their individuality from the other. Some twins show a pattern where one is more dominant or outgoing than the other. When they are raised apart, this may not be necessary.

At the present time, there is no accepted explanation for these similarities. Only one thing is certain. The general public will continue to be fascinated by twins reared apart and reunited, and psychologists will continue to try to unravel the complicated questions that surround both their similarities and their differences.

Sources: S. Farber, "Telltale Behavior of Twins", *Psychology Today*, January 1981, 58–62, 79–80; C. Holden, "Twins Reunited: More Than the Faces Are Familiar", *Science*, November 1980, *197*, 555–559.

GENETIC INFLUENCES AND DISEASE

We have already discussed a few genetic diseases: Tay-Sachs disease, cystic fibrosis, and hemophilia. There are many more. According to the March of Dimes Birth Defects Foundation (1980), there are 1,117 confirmed or suspected recessive disorders and 1,489 confirmed or suspected dominant genetic disorders cataloged. There are also 205 sex-linked genetic disorders that are transmitted through the X chromosome. More will probably be added to the list. Many of

These identical twins, who were separated as infants and reunited many years later, shared some unusual similarities.

the diseases are fairly rare and show a great variability in the severity of their symptoms. The major genetic and chromosomal disorders can be found in Table 2.1.

Why do genetic diseases continue to exist? First, not all genetic diseases are life-threatening. Second, the onset of some of these diseases, such as Huntington's Chorea is late in life (Roberts, 1970). In both cases, people have children, thereby passing on the genetic disorder.

Huntington's Chorea

Huntington's Chorea is a rare, dominant genetic disease that affects the central nervous system. The onset is typically in early middle age, after the prime child-bearing years. The average age of onset is thirty-five, but variation occurs. The individual suffers from progressive mental deterioration and pronounced involuntary muscle movements. The well-known folksinger Woody Guthrie died from this disease.

The symptoms of Huntington's Chorea were described many years before the disease was truly understood. Some families can trace their problem back to a village in Great Britain (Roberts, 1970). Families with symptoms of the disease arrived as early as 1630 in Massachusetts, and the symptoms were so bizarre that a number of sufferers were burned as witches.

The first true understanding of the disease came with the studies by George Huntington. He was taking a ride through the woods of Long Island when he and his father came across two women grimacing and twisting. As they stared at these women in amazement, George then and there decided to make the study of the disorder his life's work. Fifty years later, in 1872, he published his work on the subject.

If an individual possesses the dominant gene and marries someone who is genotypically normal, there is a 50 percent chance of transmitting the disease

Huntington's Chorea
A dominant genetic disorder affecting the central nervous system.

5. *True or False:*
Dominant genetic diseases normally show themselves at birth whereas recessive disorders show themselves later in life.

gene to offspring (see Figure 2.6). At the present time, there is no completely reliable method of predicting which children in an affected family will inherit the disorder. People can never know for certain whether their offspring will inherit the gene for the disease. They must decide whether to have children based only on possibilities and odds. For example, what if someone's father died from the disease and there is no record of the malady in the mother's family? That person would then have a 50 percent chance of possessing the gene. On the more hopeful side, the person would also have a 50 percent chance of being completely free of the disorder. Would this knowledge affect your decisions concerning marriage and childbearing? The ability to detect the presence of the gene would give affected individuals the information necessary to plan their lives and make decisions based on what is, rather than on what might happen. At present, carrier detection for Huntington's Chorea is still experimental, but it will hopefully be available for general use in the near future.

Phenylketonuria: A Success Story

Studying genetic disorders can be depressing, especially if you consider Huntington's Chorea or Tay-Sachs disease. However, research has made tremendous strides in treating a number of genetic diseases. Perhaps the greatest success story involves the strange case of **phenylketonuria**, mercifully known as PKU for short.

    PKU is a rare disorder occurring in approximately one in 10,000 births (Rainer, 1972). It involves the inability to digest a particular protein called phenylalanine. If left untreated, brain damage results. Not too many years ago, doc-

phenylketonuria (PKU)
A recessive genetic disorder marked by the inability to digest a particular protein and leading to mental retardation.

FIGURE 2.6 **Genetic Transmission of Huntington's Chorea**

If one parent possesses the gene for Huntington's Chorea, a dominant trait, there is a 50 percent chance that the offspring will inherit the condition which in the case of this particular disorder, shows itself in middle adulthood.

	Father	
	Normal gene	Huntington's Chorea gene
Normal gene	Normal gene Normal gene	Normal gene Huntington's Chorea gene
Mother		
Normal gene	Normal gene Normal gene	Normal gene Huntington's Chorea gene

TABLE 2.1   Major Genetic and Chromosomal Disorders

Disorder	Description/ Identification	Incidence	Cause
Cleft Palate and Cleft Lip	Two sides of upper lip or palate fail to close	One in 700 births or about 5,000 per year	Multifactorial; multiple causes including genetic, prenatal insults, malnutrition, and drugs
Club Foot	Ankle and foot deformities; foot twisted in and down	One in 400 births or about 9,000 cases per year; twice as frequent in boys	Multifactorial
Congenital Heart Defects	Heart defects of varying degrees of severity	20,000 cases per year or one in 175 births	Multifactorial; often cause is unknown
Cystic Fibrosis	Enzyme deficiency causes mucus obstructions and problems in controlling production of mucus, saliva and sweat; often diagnosed through analysis of perspiration which contains high salt content	One in 1,000 births	Two abnormal recessive genes
Diabetes	Pancreatic problem involving insufficiency in insulin production	Diabetes among adults is relatively common with estimates of up to five million Americans with the disease; one child in 2,500 suffers from juvenile diabetes	Thought to be partially genetic (recessive transmission), but environmental variables are important
Down's Syndrome	Distinctive physical appearance allows for early identification	One in 600 births; one in 50 among births to older parents	Chromosomal abnormality; extra chromosome #21
Hemophilia	Lack of blood clotting	One in 10,000 births	Sex linked disorder
Huntington's Chorea	Deterioration of central nervous system and body during middle age	Extremely rare	Dominant gene
Hydroencephalus	Excess fluid buildup in brain	One in 500 births	Multifactorial
Kleinfelter's Syndrome	Abnormal sexual development, sterility, absence of secondary sex characteristics: about half are mentally retarded: Identification in adolescence	One in every 600 male births	Chromosomal abnormality: XXY configuration on 23rd chromosome
Muscular Dystrophy	Progressive muscular deterioration; there are many diseases which fall under this title; the most common form, called Duchenne, begins in childhood	About 200,000 Americans have some form of the disease	Duchenne is X linked (only boys are affected); other forms follow other patterns
Phenylketonuria (PKU)	Inability to process phenylalanine prevents brain development; blood test can identify disorder two days after birth	One in 10,000 births; more often found among North Europeans	Two abnormal recessive genes

Problems	Treatment	Prenatal Detection	Carrier Detection
Speech and cosmetic problems	Surgery	No	No
Walking difficulties	Casts and/or surgery	No	Possible
Depends upon severity of disorder; can be fatal	Surgery	Sometimes through ultrasound	No
Respiratory and digestive problems; most die in adolescence or early adulthood	Advances in medical care have raised hopes for a more normal life span	No	No
Depending upon severity, diabetes may lead to serious medical problems, blindness, and death	Administration of insulin, dietary restrictions	No	No
Moderate to severe retardation and physical problems especially involving circulatory and respiratory systems	Good medical care and surgery to correct structural heart problems; special education and help for parents to enable them to care for child at home	Yes	Possible in only 5 percent of cases.*
Potential life threatening crises whenever injured	Blood transfusions and administration of "clotting factor"	Yes (but not by amniocentesis)†	Yes
Disorder is fatal		Experimental at present time	Experimental at present time
Brain damage; can be fatal	Surgery	Sometimes	No
Mental retardation, emotional problems	Administration of testosterone	Yes	No
Weakening and wasting away of muscles leads to physical incapabilities and death	Physical therapy and surgery	No	For some forms but not others
If left untreated condition leads to mental retardation, restlessness, and irritability	Low phenylalanine diet; no cow's milk	No	Yes (but test is not 100 percent reliable)

*About five percent of Down's Syndrome incidence is due to an unbalanced translocation (chromosomal rearrangement). Such cases are independent of maternal age. If one of the parents is known to "carry" this chromosome rearrangement (translocation) in a balanced fashion, then all pregnancies should be monitored by prenatal diagnosis. Carriers of chromosomal translocations are identified by performing a chromosomal analysis of their blood.

†Fetal blood must be sampled by a process called fetoscopy. This has a risk of miscarriage of 3 to 5 percent as compared to the ½ of 1 percent risk associated with amniocentesis.

TABLE 2.1—Continued

Disorder	Description/ Identification	Incidence	Cause
Pyloric Stenosis	Digestive difficulties caused by an overgrowth of muscle in the lower stomach; identification early in infancy since infants cannot keep food down and do not gain weight	One in every 200 boys and one in every 1000 girls	Multifactorial
Rh Disease	Blood disorder	7000 babies per year	If mother is Rh negative and baby is Rh positive some of mother's antibodies may kill baby's red blood cells
Sickle Cell Anemia	Blood disorder causes damage to vital organs; diagnosed through blood test	One in every 400–600 Blacks; one in every 1000–1500 Hispanics	Two abnormal recessive genes
Spina Bifida	Spine fails to close; noticeable at birth	One in 1,000 births	Multifactorial
Tay Sachs Disease	Enzyme deficiency causes buildup of fat in nerve cells; leads to retardation, blindness, and convulsions; identification through exaggerated startle response and psychomotor retardation in infancy	One in every 25 American Jews is a carrier	Abnormal recessive gene
Thalasemia (Cooley's Anemia)	Severe anemia and listlessness; identified through blood test	3 to 10 percent of Greeks and Italians are carriers; about 1,000 cases per year	Abnormal recessive gene
Turner's Syndrome	Short stature, delayed sexual development, infantile genitalia, swelling of feet, hands, and neck, heart abnormalities	One in every 2,000–3,000 live births	Chromosomal problems: Forty-five chromosomes, single X on 23rd chromosome

6. *True or False:*
At the present time, all that medical science can do for children suffering from genetic diseases is to make them more comfortable.

tors were perplexed by the disorder. Seemingly normal babies rapidly became retarded and developed behavioral disroders. Some 90 percent of these children had to be institutionalized. The normal treatment for children who are not thriving is more nourishment, but in the case of PKU, that is exactly what triggers the problem.

The disease was first recognized in the 1930s, and a urine test for the disorder was developed. About fifteen years later, doctors began treating the disorder with a special diet, low in phenylalanine. Phenylalanine is found in all protein-rich foods, including fish, meats, poultry, eggs, milk, and bread products, so the diet is very restrictive (Schild, 1979). Special preparations are required to meet the child's protein needs. This preventive treatment is very successful (Carter, 1970). Today a blood test to determine whether a newborn baby has PKU is given, usually on the day the baby is scheduled to be discharged from the hospital.

Problems	Treatment	Prenatal Detection	Carrier Detection
Can be fatal if not corrected	Surgery	No	No
Blood problems, multiple medical difficulties; can be fatal	Transfusions; prevention possible if mother receives shot of Rh immune globulin after birth, miscarriage, or after prenatal diagnosis	Yes	Yes
Problems vary depending upon severity of disorder; can be fatal	Medical care to reduce pain and severity of disorder	Yes	Yes
May lead to paralysis and problems in bladder and bowel control	Surgery, physical therapy, and training in personal hygiene	Yes	No
Disease is fatal in all cases; death occurs usually between the ages of three to five years	None available	Yes	Yes
Severe anemia causes many physical problems	Blood transfusions and bone marrow transplants	Yes	Yes
Child has normal intelligence although perceptual deficits are common; physical stature and sexual problems may lead to social problems	Hormone therapy, counseling	Yes	No

Sources: L. F. Annis, 1978; V. Apgar and J. Beck, 1973; D. Bergsma, 1979; R. M. Goodman and R. J. Gorlin, 1983; N. J. Karagan, 1979; A. P. Mange and E. J. Mange, 1980; March of Dimes, FACTS, 1984; S. Sassower, 1985; D. W. Smith, 1982; R. Thompson and A. P. Thompson, 1980.

Three important points about PKU should be kept in mind. First, it is an example of a genetic disease that can be successfully treated. Second, the ravages of the disease do not occur unless it is triggered by the environment. If every individual in a particular culture were to receive a diet low in the offending protein, the disease would never show itself. PKU illustrates how important the environment can be in the emergence and treatment of genetic disorders.

Third, the difficulty of keeping children on the regimen should be noted. Imagine having to keep a child on an extremely strict diet for years. During middle childhood the diet can usually be relaxed or even abandoned safely, although women who have PKU should consult a doctor about their diet before and during any pregnancy. Now imagine you are a child who cannot eat this or that, while all your friends can. Some parents have had difficulty keeping their children on such a diet (Reed, 1975). Prescribing a diet is a great deal easier than following one.

Sickle Cell Anemia: What To Do with Our Knowledge

sickle cell anemia
An inherited defect in the structure of red blood cells.

Sickle cell anemia is an inherited defect in the structure of red blood cells. The sufferer, especially during periods of physical exertion or low oxygen, experiences considerable pain. Although most victims live normal lives, severe cases may suffer heart and kidney problems (Fogel, 1984). Periods of crisis requiring hospitalization are not unusual. Resistance to disease is decreased, and the health of the child is usually poor.

Approximately one in ten American blacks is a carrier, and whether one is a carrier can be determined by a simple blood test. We can calculate that, on the average, one marriage out of every 100 between American blacks has the potential for producing a child who will suffer from sickle cell anemia. At present, antibiotics and improved medical treatment can help alleviate the symptoms, but some who suffer from severe cases of the disease die in childhood (Roberts, 1970). With improved treatment, many of these children will live more normal lives.

Because the detection process is relatively simple and the gene is rather common, some authorities have suggested that mandatory mass genetic screening be instituted. This would make people more aware of their genetic standing so they could make marriage and childbearing decisions accordingly. On the surface, this might appear to be reasonable. After all, it would still be an individual decision.

While no one has any objection to voluntary screening for carrier status, mass involuntary screening raises several important ethical questions (see Shaw, 1976). Some people point out that such screening would be aimed principally at a minority group and see something sinister in this. It should be noted that Latin populations are also at risk for the disorder, although the rates for Latins are lower than that for blacks in the United States. Aside from the racial issue, how ethical is it to force someone to take a test? Do people have the right not to know whether they are carrying a "genetic defect"?

One way to sidestep the issue is to recommend the test but not require it. Such a program might not be as effective as one that is mandatory, but it would avoid some difficult ethical issues. On the other hand, recommendations from the government can easily turn into quasi-requirements. Insurance companies and potential employers may learn that an individual is a carrier and increase premiums or refuse that person employment.

But no one argues against education, and this may be the key. All populations at risk for genetic diseases should be educated about them. In this way, each individual can decide whether he or she wants to submit to a carrier detection test.

Chromosomal Abnormalities

Some inherited diseases are due to chromosomal abnormalities rather than genetic defects. Three of the most important are Down's Syndrome, Klinefelter's Syndrome, and Turner's Syndrome.

Children suffering from Down's Syndrome have a distinctive physical appearance and are mentally retarded.

Down's Syndrome.   "Some of you know what it's like to look forward to the birth of your child with eagerness and anticipation, a child with whom to share your world and your life, and then be told after the birth that your hopes and expectations have just been shattered by some chromosomal accident. It is a grief process, because there is real grief over the loss of the child you expected and grief over the devastation of your dreams and hopes" (Martz, 1964, pp. 34–35, quoted in Kirk and Gallagher, 1979).

These are the thoughts of a parent who has been told that his child has **Down's Syndrome**, or **mongolism**, as it used to be called, the most common chromosomal disorder. Down's Syndrome occurs approximately once in every 600 births and is caused by the appearance of an extra chromosome on the twenty-first pair. The child has 47 chromosomes instead of the normal 46. The frequency of the disorder increases with the age of the mother. The risk for women under thirty is one in more than 1,000, while women over thirty have a one in 750 chance of having a child who suffers from Down's Syndrome. The risk for women over forty increases to one in 70 births (Blackhurst and Berdine, 1981) and to one in 50 for mothers over forty-five (Rainer, 1972). The disorder is also linked to the father. Problems in cell division in the sperm are estimated to be the cause of the difficulty about 20 to 25 percent of the time, and there is evidence that the disorder is more common when the father is under twenty or over fifty-five years of age (Arehart-Treichel, 1979).

Most children who suffer from Down's Syndrome are identified either at birth or shortly after by their physical appearance (Hirsch, 1979). Unusual phys-

Down's Syndrome (mongolism)
A disorder caused by the presence of an extra chromosome, leading to a distinct physical appearance and mental retardation.

ical features include folded eyes (which gave the disorder its original name), short digits, flat face, protruding tongue, and harsh voice (Sue et al., 1981). Retardation is the rule, with most children scoring somewhere between 30 and 50 on intelligence tests (Crandall and Tarjan, 1976), although the degree of retardation can vary.

Children with Down's Syndrome have a reputation for being lovable, cheerful, and easy to work with, although this is not always so (Bridges and Cicchetti, 1982). While years ago most children with this disorder were institutionalized immediately after birth, this is not the case today. Many of these children are now raised at home, which is usually beneficial to the child. Many are still institutionalized, however. Milunsky and his colleagues found that in Massachusetts one-third of Down's Syndrome children are institutionalized at birth, another one-third by the age of ten, and the rest by age thirty (in Reed, 1975). These children require extensive help for their entire lives.

Not too long ago the life expectancy for Down's Syndrome children was ten years or less. Congenital heart problems are common (Crandall and Tarjan, 1976), and resistance to disease is low. However, medical advances have substantially increased the life span of these children. If they survive the first few years, their death rates are about the same as the general population until age forty (HEW, 1973). After the age of forty, people with Down's Syndrome appear to be more susceptible to diseases that are related to old age.

Sex-linked Chromosomal Disorders.   Down's Syndrome is not the only chromosomal abnormality. Two of the more common chromosomal disorders are caused by problems that occur on the sex chromosomes. In Klinefelter's Syndrome, the male receives at least one more X chromosome than he should, thus creating an XXY genotype. This is found in approximately one in 600 male births. Children afflicted with this disorder have small sex organs and are sterile, and many, though not all, are mentally retarded.

Turner's Syndrome is caused by a lack of an X chromosome. The genotype is expressed as XO. These females are sterile, short, and do not mature normally. They often require estrogen treatments to attain adult stature. Though they often have specific learning problems, they are not usually mentally retarded (Kalat, 1980). Turner's Syndrome appears in about one out of every 2,000 female births (Sutton, 1980).

Predispositions to Disorders: Schizophrenia

Not all disorders with a genetic base are transmitted directly. Sometimes a predisposition to a disorder, rather than the disease itself, is passed from parents to children. This is the case with the serious emotional disorder known as schizophrenia.

schizophrenia
A severe mental disorder marked by hallucinations, delusions, and emotional disturbances.

Schizophrenia is a severe mental disorder characterized by hallucinations, delusions, emotional disturbances, apathy, and withdrawal. About 2 million people in the United States suffer from the disorder (Martin, 1977). About 25 percent of the first-time admissions to mental hospitals are diagnosed as schizophrenic, and about 50 percent of the residents of mental hospitals at any one time suffer from the disorder. It is a major international health problem.

A number of twin studies have suggested that a genetic base for schizophrenia exists. If an identical twin is schizophrenic, his or her twin is fifty times as likely to become schizophrenic than any other individual in the general population (Altrocchi, 1980). But identical twins also share a common environment as well as a common genotype. To control for environmental differences, a number of studies have compared identical, or monozygotic, twins (who develop from one sperm and one egg cell), to fraternal, or dizygotic, twins (who develop from two different sperm and egg cells). Dizygotic, or fraternal, twins are no more genetically similar than any pair of siblings. If there is a substantial genetic component, we would expect that if an identical twin became schizophrenic, the other would have an excellent chance of also suffering from the disorder. We would expect that with fraternal twins in which one becomes schizophrenic, the other twin would have a greater chance than the average person on the street of also suffering from the condition, since these twins have about half their genes in common. However, their risk would not be as great as identical twins, who share all their genes in common.

These hypotheses are confirmed by the research in the field. The risk for identical twins in which one becomes schizophrenic is three to six times as great as for fraternal twins in which one shows signs of the disorder (Rosenthal, 1970). The degree of similarity between twins is called the **concordance rate**. It approaches 50 percent for identical twins and 9 percent for fraternal twins, when one of the twins has schizophrenia (Gottesman and Shields, 1972).

Other studies have been performed on twins separated at birth and raised in different homes. If an identical twin became schizophrenic, it would be interesting to see whether the twin sibling, raised under different circumstances, would also suffer from the disorder. Studies of twenty-eight pairs of such twins show the same 50 percent concordance rate as is commonly found in identical twins raised together (Gottesman, 1978). In another study, Heston (1966) studied 47 children born to schizophrenic mothers who were adopted by nonschizophrenic parents shortly after birth. He compared these children with a control group of children whose mothers were not schizophrenic but were also adopted early. Five out of the 47 children born to mothers suffering from the disorder become schizophrenic, while none in the control group did.

There is little doubt that a significant genetic component underlies the disorder (Scarr and Kidd, 1983; Weisfeld, 1982). The evidence also indicates a strong environmental component. What appears to be transmitted is not the disease itself, but rather a tendency, or predisposition, to acquire the disorder. In other words, all environmental factors being equal, an individual with a family history of schizophrenia is at a greater risk for the disease than someone with no family history of schizophrenia. Just what in the environment may trigger the disorder is not definitely known at the present time.

concordance rate
The degree of similarity between twins on any particular trait.

7. *True or False:*
Schizophrenia, like cystic fibrosis or Tay-Sachs disease is directly transmitted from parent to child.

GENETIC INFLUENCES ON DEVELOPMENT AND PERSONALITY

The importance of one's genetic endowment goes beyond the specific physical disorders caused by genetic and chromosomal abnormalities. One's temperament, behavioral traits, hand preference, and intelligence are also affected by one's genes.

TABLE 2.2   **Measuring Children's Temperament**
Alexander Thomas, Stella Chess, and Herbert Birch found the majority of children could be classified as "easy," "slow to warm up," or "difficult" according to how they rate in key categories on a nine-point personality index (color). The categories offer only a general guide and 35 percent of the children in the study displayed a mixture of traits, being "easy" in some ways and "difficult" in others.

Type of Child	Activity Level *The proportion of active periods to inactive ones.*	Rhythmicity *Regularity of hunger, excretion, sleep and wakefulness.*	Distractibility *The degree to which extraneous stimuli alter behavior.*	Approach Withdrawal *The response to a new object or person.*
"Easy"	Varies	Very regular	Varies	Positive approach
"Slow to Warm Up"	Low to moderate	Varies	Varies	Initial withdrawal
"Difficult"	Varies	Irregular	Varies	Withdrawal

Temperament

At a recent social gathering, two couples (let's call them the Allens and the Johnsons), were discussing their youngsters. Both had given birth at about the same time, and they all came from similar ethnic, social, and economic backgrounds.

The Allens described their child as happy, eager, regular, and flexible. As Mr. and Mrs. Johnson gripped themselves, the Allens went on to say how easy it was to travel with their child. The child seemed to adapt easily to new situations, and everyone remarked on how well behaved the baby was.

The Johnsons tried to change the subject, but it was too late. Mr. and Mrs. Allen asked the listeners about their own child. After all, common courtesy called for them to exchange roles and listen while the Johnsons bragged.

"Well, our child is a bit different," Mr. Johnson began tentatively, wishing he had not accepted the invitation to the gathering in the first place. "A lot different," Mrs. Johnson continued. "He is very intense and stubborn. He cries a great deal and doesn't accept any changes in routine. He's hard to satisfy and doesn't seem to fit any pattern as far as eating and sleeping is concerned."

Parents who have children like the Johnson's baby are sometimes reluctant to talk about them. At other times, they are desperate to find someone who will not only listen but also help them deal with these children. It isn't unusual for someone to blame a child's difficulties on some parental action. Indeed, at times the parents may be the problem. According to a considerable body of evidence, however, the Johnsons might be better off accepting their child as is and stop blaming themselves. The infant was born with a certain temperament.

According to Thomas, and his colleagues (1970, p. 2), each child is born with a **temperament**, an "individual style of responding to the environment." Three general types of temperament have been identified and validated by scientific research.

"Easy" children are born that way. Like the child described by our first couple, the "easy" baby is generally happy, flexible, and regular. These children get

8. *True or False:*

Infants are born with a temperament that may remain with them throughout childhood.

temperament
A group of characteristics reflecting an individual's way of responding to the environment and thought to be genetic.

Adaptability	Attention Span and Persistence	Intensity of Reaction	Threshold of Responsiveness	Quality of Mood
The ease with which a child adapts to changes in his environment.	The amount of time devoted to an activity, and the effect of distraction on the activity.	The energy of response, regardless of its quality or direction.	The intensity of stimulation required to evoke a discernible response.	The amount of friendly, pleasant, joyful behavior as contrasted with unpleasant, unfriendly behavior.
Very adaptable	High or low	Low or mild	High or low	Positive
Slowly adaptable	High or low	Mild	High or low	Slightly negative
Slowly adaptable	High or low	Intense	High or low	Negative

Source: A. Thomas, et al., 1970.

along well with almost everyone and present few problems to parents or, later, teachers.

"Difficult" children, on the other hand, are intense, demanding, inflexible, and cry a great deal.

The third category, "slow to warm up" children, do not respond well to changes in their environment, but their reactions are not intense. They exhibit a low activity level and have a tendency to withdraw from new stimuli.

Approximately 40 percent of the sample in the study by Thomas et al. (1970), could be characterized as "easy," about 10 percent as "difficult," and another 15 percent as "slow to warm up." The remaining 35 percent could not be put in any of these categories because they showed a mixture of behaviors.

What kinds of behaviors comprise a temperament? Nine behavior patterns were used in the study (see Table 2.2). They include (1) the level and extent of motor activity, (2) the degree of regularity of such functions as eating and sleeping, (3) the distractibility of the child, (4) the response of the child to new objects or people, (5) the adaptability of the child to changes in the environment, (6) the child's persistence, (7) the intensity of the child's responses, (8) sensitivity to stimuli, and (9) the child's general disposition.

Thomas and his colleagues urge parents to work with their child's temperament rather than try to change it. For example, if a child is slow to warm up, parents and teachers should allow the child to warm up to the environment at the child's own pace. Gentle encouragement is best. If the child is "difficult," they advise parents to be very consistent and objective in their handling of the child. Teachers should realize that "difficult" children do poorly in nonstructured, permissive situations and may be easily frustrated by tasks they cannot handle immediately. Firmness and patience are required. "Easy" children may also face problems related to temperament, sometimes being unable to resolve conflict between their own desires and the demands of others.

TABLE 2.3 Temperament over Time

Temperament is revealed very early in life and tends to remain constant in quality. As children mature, their temperament manifests itself through different behaviors. However, their temperamental quality remains the same. The color indicates the temperamental characteristics that are crucial to classifying a child as "easy," "slow to warm up," and "difficult."

Temperamental Quality	Rating	2 Months	6 Months
Activity Level	High	Moves often in sleep. Wriggles when diaper is changed.	Tries to stand in tub and splashes. Bounces in crib. Crawls after dog.
	Low	Does not move when being dressed or during sleep.	Passive in bath. Plays quietly in crib and falls asleep.
Rhythmicity	Regular	Has been on four-hour feeding schedule since birth. Regular bowel movement.	Is asleep at 6:30 every night. Awakes at 7:00 A.M. Food intake is constant.
	Irregular	Awakes at a different time each morning. Size of feedings varies.	Length of nap varies; so does food intake.
Distractibility	Distractible	Will stop crying for food if rocked. Stops fussing if given pacifier when diaper is being changed.	Stops crying when mother sings. Will remain still while clothing is changed if given a toy.
	Not Distractible	Will not stop crying when diaper is changed. Fusses after eating, even if rocked.	Stops crying only after dressing is finished. Cries until given bottle.
Approach/Withdrawal	Positive	Smiles and licks washcloth. Has always liked bottle.	Likes new foods. Enjoyed first bath in a large tub. Smiles and gurgles.
	Negative	Rejected cereal the first time. Cries when strangers appear.	Smiles and babbles at strangers. Plays with new toys immediately.
Adaptability	Adaptive	Was passive during first bath; now enjoys bathing. Smiles at nurse.	Used to dislike new foods; now accepts them well.
	Not Adaptive	Still startled by sudden, sharp noise. Resists diapering.	Does not cooperate with dressing. Fusses and cries when left with sitter.
Attention Span and Persistence	Long	If soiled, continues to cry until changed. Repeatedly rejects water if he wants milk.	Watches toy mobile over crib intently. "Coos" frequently.
	Short	Cries when awakened but stops almost immediately. Objects only mildly if cereal precedes bottle.	Sucks pacifier for only a few minutes and spits it out.

1 Year	2 Years	5 Years	10 Years
Walks rapidly. Eats eagerly. Climbs into everything.	Climbs furniture. Explores. Gets in and out of bed while being put to sleep.	Leaves table often during meals. Always runs.	Plays ball and engages in other sports. Cannot sit still long enough to do homework.
Finishes bottle slowly. Goes to sleep easily. Allows nail-cutting without fussing.	Enjoys quiet play with puzzles. Can listen to records for hours.	Takes a long time to dress. Sits quietly on long automobile rides.	Likes chess and reading. Eats very slowly.
Naps after lunch each day. Always drinks bottle before bed.	Eats a big lunch each day. Always has a snack before bedtime.	Falls asleep when put to bed. Bowel movement regular.	Eats only at mealtimes. Sleeps the same amount of time each night.
Will not fall asleep for an hour or more. Moves bowels at a different time each day.	Nap time changes from day to day. Toilet training is difficult because bowel movement is unpredictable.	Food intake varies; so does time of bowel movement.	Food intake varies. Falls asleep at a different time each night.
Cries when face is washed unless it is made into a game.	Will stop tantrum if another activity is suggested.	Can be coaxed out of forbidden activity by being led into something else.	Needs absolute silence for homework. Has a hard time choosing a shirt in a store because they all appeal to him.
Cries when toy is taken away and rejects substitute.	Screams if refused some desired object. Ignores mother's calling.	Seems not to hear if involved in favorite activity. Cries for a long time when hurt.	Can read a book while television set is at high volume. Does chores on schedule.
Approaches strangers readily. Sleeps well in new surroundings.	Slept well the first time he stayed overnight at grandparents' house.	Entered school building unhesitatingly. Tries new foods.	Went to camp happily. Loved to ski the first time.
Stiffened when placed on sled. Will not sleep in strange beds.	Avoids strange children in the playground. Whimpers first time at beach. Will not go into water.	Hid behind mother when entering school.	Severely homesick at camp during first days. Does not like new activities.
Was afraid of toy animals at first; now plays with them happily.	Obeys quickly. Stayed contentedly with grandparents for a week.	Hesitated to go to nursery school at first; now goes eagerly. Slept well on camping trip.	Likes camp, although homesick during first days. Learns enthusiastically.
Continues to reject new foods each time they are offered.	Cries and screams each time hair is cut. Disobeys persistently.	Has to be hand led into classroom each day. Bounces on bed in spite of spankings.	Does not adjust well to new school or new teacher; comes home late for dinner even when punished.
Plays by self in playpen for more than an hour. Listens to singing for long periods.	Works on a puzzle until it is completed. Watches when shown how to do something.	Practiced riding a two-wheeled bicycle for hours until he mastered it. Spent over an hour reading a book.	Reads for two hours before sleeping. Does homework carefully.
Loses interest in a toy after a few minutes. Gives up easily if she falls while attempting to walk.	Gives up easily if a toy is hard to use. Asks for help immediately if undressing becomes difficult.	Still cannot tie his shoes because he gives up when he is not successful. Fidgets when parents read to him.	Gets up frequently from homework for a snack. Never finishes a book.

TABLE 2.3—Continued

Temperamental Quality	Rating	2 Months	6 Months
Intensity of Reaction	Intense	Cries when diapers are wet. Rejects food vigorously when satisfied.	Cries loudly at the sound of thunder. Makes sucking movements when vitamins are administered.
	Mild	Does not cry when diapers are wet. Whimpers instead of crying when hungry.	Does not kick often in tub. Does not smile. Screams and kicks when temperature is taken.
Threshold of Responsiveness	Low	Stops sucking on bottle when approached.	Refuses fruit he likes when vitamins are added. Hides head from bright light.
	High	Is not startled by loud noises. Takes bottle and breast equally well.	Eats everything. Does not object to diapers being wet or soiled.
Quality of Mood	Positive	Smacks lips when first tasting new food. Smiles at parents.	Plays and splashes in bath. Smiles at everyone.
	Negative	Fusses after nursing. Cried when carriage is rocked.	Cries when taken from tub. Cries when given food she does not like.

The genetic basis for temperament is now well established (Goldsmith and Gottesman, 1981), and temperament can be readily measured (Wilson and Matheny, 1983). It is also relatively stable in infancy (Matheny et al., 1985) and childhood (Thomas et al., 1970). As Table 2.3 shows, although the temperamental quality remains constant, these qualities manifest themselves differently as children mature.

Other genetically based behavior patterns have been identified. Infants differ in the degree to which they require cuddling (Schaffer and Emerson, 1964). All infants need the rich sensory stimulation that results from being held, but some children do not seek the contact as much as others do. Research has identified two primary groups: cuddlers and noncuddlers. Noncuddlers are not eager to be held and often struggle when physically confined. They twist, turn, and sometimes cry. Cuddlers, on the other hand, enjoy the close physical contact and seek it out. These differences are inborn preferences.

Imagine a parent who yearns for a child to cuddle but finds that the child twists and turns every time he or she is held. The parent may react with apathy

1 Year	2 Years	5 Years	10 Years
Laughs hard when father plays roughly. Screamed and kicked when temperature was taken.	Yells if he feels excitement or delight. Cries loudly if a toy is taken away.	Rushes to greet father. Gets hiccups from laughing hard.	Tears up an entire page of homework if one mistake is made. Slams door of room when teased by younger brother.
Does not fuss much when clothing is pulled on over head.	When another child hit her, she looked surprised, did not hit back.	Drops eyes and remains silent when given a firm parental "No." Does not laugh much.	When a mistake is made in a model airplane, corrects it quietly. Does not comment when reprimanded.
Spits out food he does not like. Giggles when tickled.	Runs to door when father comes home. Must always be tucked tightly into bed.	Always notices when mother puts new dress on for first time. Refuses milk if it is not ice-cold.	Rejects fatty foods. Adjusts shower until water is at exactly the right temperature.
Eats food he likes even if mixed with disliked food. Can be left easily with strangers.	Can be left with anyone. Falls to sleep easily on either back or stomach.	Does not hear loud, sudden noises when reading. Does not object to injections.	Never complains when sick. Eats all foods.
Likes bottle; reaches for it and smiles. Laughs loudly when playing peekaboo.	Plays with sister; laughs and giggles. Smiles when he succeeds in putting shoes on.	Laughs loudly while watching television cartoons. Smiles at everyone.	Enjoys new accomplishments. Laughs when reading a funny passage aloud.
Cries when given injections. Cries when left alone.	Cries and squirms when given haircut. Cries when mother leaves.	Objects to putting boots on. Cries when frustrated.	Cries when he cannot solve a homework problem. Very "weepy" if he does not get enough sleep.

Source: A. Thomas, et al., 1970.

or even hostility. On the other hand, what if a child is a cuddler and seeks physical contact constantly. There may be difficulties if the parents are not emotionally able to handle this.

Temperament can affect the relationship between parents and their children. A child is lucky if the inborn temperament meshes with the parents' abilities and styles. The "difficult" child thrives in a structured, understanding environment, but not in an inconsistent, intolerant home. The "slow to warm up" child does best if the parents understand the child's need for time to adjust to new situations. If they do not, the parents may only intensify the child's natural tendency toward withdrawal.

Behavioral Traits

If your parents are friendly and affectionate, will you be the same? Is extroversion (being outgoing) or introversion (being directed inward) an inherited predisposition? There is evidence that a genetic component underlies this personality dimension (Vandenberg, 1967). Such traits as sociability, emotionality, and activity level also have underlying genetic components (Daniels and Plomin, 1985; Goldsmith, 1983; Gottesman, 1966), as do authoritarianism and rigidity (Rose and Ditto, 1983). The tremendous influence of the environment on personality is obvious, but a genetic basis for various personality traits may exist.

Just how would genes affect behavior? Gottesman (1966, p. 199) notes, "There are no genes for behavior. The genes exert their influence on behavior through their effects at a more molecular level of organization. Enzymes, hormones, and neurons mediate the path between the genes and those psycho-social aspects of behavior termed personality." In other words, genes influence the individual's physiology, which in turn affects behavior.

Handedness

9. *True or False:*

Left handedness is largely determined by the environment.

Over 90 percent of the general public shows a preference for the right hand. Such preferences are genetically based (Hicks and Kinsbourne, 1976). Usually, children show little preference for either hand until about four months of age, and a few do not develop a preference well into early childhood. However, the majority show a right-hand preference at a young age.

It is a right-handed world. Look around a classroom and note how many desks are left-handed. Probably very few. Demonstrations in class are usually performed by a right-handed teacher for right-handed students and this makes imitation difficult for left-handed students.

If both parents are left-handed, there is better than a 40 percent chance that each of the children will follow suit (Cratty, 1970). If one parent is left-handed,

---

**ACTION/
REACTION**

"Aggressive" Genes?

"You're just like your father!" Jane yelled at Steven. "Go on, hit me! Show what kind of a man you are!"

All the neighbors know Jane and Steven—they are constantly fighting. The entire neighborhood can hear them, and their arguments often erupt into violence, with Steven hitting Jane.

When interviewed, Jane noted that Steven's father had also behaved violently toward his wife, so "it must be in his genes." "His father had a terrible temper, just like Steve does." Steven agrees. He states that, although he loves Jane, he can't seem to control his temper, just as his father couldn't.

Steven had been a very aggressive child and was subject to temper tantrums. When a psychologist suggested that he could change, Steven looked astonished, shook his head, and said, "Once it's in your genes, you can't get rid of it." Both Jane and Steven also told the psychologist that their son was showing the same behavior pattern. They offered this as further proof of their genetics argument.

1. If you were the psychologist, how would you deal with Steven and Jane's attitude?
2. If you were Jane, what would you do?

the chances drop to 17 percent, and if both parents are right-handed the chances are only 2 percent that any of their children will be left-handed.

There are environmental considerations as well. Some parents strongly encourage their children to be right-handed by placing implements in the right hand or handing them toys in a way that forces the child to use the right arm. In some parts of the world, left-handedness is socially unacceptable, and children are forced to be right-handed.

Many people believe that left-handed children have more difficulty learning particular skills, but any difficulty they have is due to the environment's right-handed bias rather than any inborn deficiency. Generally, children who develop their handedness early do better than those who develop it later or not at all (Williams and Stith, 1980). It does not make any difference whether that preference is right or left, just so long as there is some preference.

Rate of Development

It is no secret that children develop at their own rate. The maturation rate reflects their unique genetic master plan. Such activities as standing, crawling, walking, and talking are largely, but not exclusively, dependent on the child's genetic endowment (Mischel, 1976).

Statistics show that the "average" child walks or talks at a particular age, but wide variations exist within the range of normal development. When children fall far behind these norms, as Laura in our opening vignette did, the problem should be investigated.

It is important to recognize that within the broad "normal" range some children develop faster than others. Serious consequences may follow from pushing a child to do something before that child is ready. The concept of **readiness** implies that there is a point in development when a child has the skills necessary to master a particular task. When parents and teachers do not understand this, problems can result. For instance, if a child who does not understand the concept of "number" is forced by parents to try to add two numbers, that child is destined to fail. The child becomes frustrated, since an understanding of numbers is essential to success in learning how to add. Bitter and unnecessary failures, and repetition of such experiences, may lead to a lack of self-confidence. The same argument may hold for any physical or mental challenge.

readiness
The point in development at which a child has the necessary skills to master a new challenge.

Intelligence

In the history of psychology no issue has been more bitterly debated than the influence of genetics on intelligence (Loehlin et al., 1975). Two questions are usually asked: How much of the variable we call "intelligence" can be attributed to hereditary factors? and How modifiable is intelligence?

The first question involves discovering the heritability of intelligence. The existence of a genetic component in intelligence is well accepted, but someone who offers a numerical figure is likely to be criticized. Some authorities claim that it is impossible to estimate true heritability figures for human traits because we cannot control the environment (Feldman and Lewontin, 1975). After all, people with similar levels of intelligence tend to establish similar environments.

Highly intelligent people create more stimulating environments than less intelligent people. Despite these difficulties, the effort continues.

The closer two people are related, the more likely they are to have similar intelligence levels. The correlation between identical twins reared together is + .87, for identical twins reared apart it is + .75, for siblings reared together, it is + .55, and for parents and their children generally it is + .50. Correlations for intelligence scores between first cousins is approximately + .26 and for unrelated children reared together + .23 (Erlenmeyer-Kimling and Jarvik, 1963). A more recent review of the literature concludes that the figures are a bit lower (Bouchard and McGue, 1981).

None of these correlations is perfect, although some are high. Genetic influence on intelligence is indicated, but the genetic explanation falls far short of explaining all the differences in intelligence between people. An understanding of the environmental factor is needed to accomplish that.

Such correlations may be interpreted in another way. The closer the relationship between two people, the greater the chance that they were raised in similar environments. The results of these studies can be interpreted as demonstrating the importance of the environment as well.

The data from adoption studies generally indicate that the intelligence levels of adopted children are more closely related to their biological parents than their adoptive parents (Horn, 1983; Jencks, 1972). Jencks argues that genetic factors are responsible for about half the variation in intelligence we see among people. Others have offered higher and lower figures. Jensen (1969) argues that it approaches 80 percent, while Kamin (1974), who thoroughly criticizes the studies purporting to demonstrate the heritability of intelligence, places the figures at a much lower level. While older studies have ascribed as much as 80 percent of intelligence to genetic factors, newer studies yield values closer to 50 percent (Plomin and DeFries, 1980). This would ascribe approximately half to genetic factors and the other half to the environment.

Any heritability figure should be interpreted cautiously. Problems in defining what we really mean by intelligence, and difficulties in research design, combine to provide ammunition for both sides (Walker and Emory, 1985; Horn 1985). Even the same set of data can be interpreted differently, especially if one researcher concentrates on one area of the study while another person favors data from a different portion (McCall, 1981). In addition, most psychologists today accept the fact that an important environmental element underlies intelligence, since none of the correlations in the data noted previously is perfect (Willerman, 1979). No matter which estimate of heritability one uses, both environmental and genetic factors are involved in intelligence (Scarr and Kidd, 1983).

Modifying Intelligence.   The second question, that of modifiability, is more important. A number of studies testify to the modifiability of intelligence, but one by Skeels (1966) stands out. In the 1930s, Skeels was working in a bleak orphanage, where the children received little attention and were subjected to a rigid schedule. They had no toys, and the environment was depressing. Skeels took a special interest in two girls who rocked back and forth and spent most of their time in bed. These two girls were later transferred to a mental institution, where they came under the influence of an older, retarded woman who showered them with attention. Their behavior changed, and they became much more responsive.

Skeels decided to find out more about this phenomenon. A number of children were removed from the sterile setting of the orphanage and allowed to live with older retardates in a better environment. Their intelligence scores improved an average of 29 points, and one child's intelligence score actually rose by more than 50 points. The group that stayed in the depressing environment of the orphanage were found to have even lower intelligence scores than when the study had begun.

The conclusion that a change in environment accounts for the improvement in intelligence has been accepted by most psychologists today, although the methodology has been severely criticized (Longstreth, 1981). Some creative programs have successfully increased the intelligence scores of particular groups. For example, Israel has had considerable success in narrowing, and sometimes even eliminating, the differences in intelligence that were present among many of the diverse groups who settled there. Through an intensive program of enrichment, these differences tended to disappear (Smilansky, cited in Reed, 1975).

The genetic influence on intelligence does not limit its malleability (Scarr-Salapatek, 1975). Rather the genetic factor affects the elasticity of intelligence. Few would argue that any enrichment program could turn a child of below-average intelligence into a genius, but a radical change for the better in the environment would probably have a significant effect on the child's intelligence score. A number of programs have attempted to lift the intelligence scores of young children through a variety of educational programs aimed both at children and at their parents. Many have been successful in the short term. Much more will be said about these programs in Chapter Nine.

Genes, Intelligence, and Race.   In 1969, the heredity-environment question took a different turn. Arthur Jensen (1969), in a long detailed study suggested that the differences in intelligence scores between racial groups was due primarily to genetic rather than environmental factors. Three major points were advanced by Jensen: (1) intelligence tests can measure general ability, (2) individual differences in intelligence can be attributed mostly to genetic considerations, (3) educational programs have been ineffective in increasing intelligence test scores (see Loehlin et al., 1975). Each of these points can be argued.

Considerable controversy exists concerning the validity of intelligence tests, because the background and motivation of the child taking the test is so important. Jensen's second point, that most of the differences in intelligence can be attributed to genetic considerations, is not accepted by many experts in the field. Although most agree that genetic factors influence intelligence, the significance of this contribution is debatable. Jensen's third point, concerning the ineffectiveness of programs that attempt to increase intelligence scores, depends on how soon the intelligence test is administered after the enrichment program has ended and the extent to which a permanent change in the environment is made.

If these had been Jensen's only theses, they would have attracted some attention, but it was his suggestion that differences between Caucasians and blacks in intelligence test scores were due to genetic differences between the races that caused a great outcry. Jensen did not deny the importance of environmental factors, but he did relegate them to a distinctly second-place position.

Children's environment affects their development. Studies indicate that if the environment of children like these was improved, many aspects of their development, including their intelligence, would be enhanced.

10. *True or False:*
There is little evidence that a child's intelligence scores can be raised by improving the environment.

You can imagine the uproar this caused. When such statements come from rank amateurs, they can easily be dismissed, but when a respected social scientist argues that there are racial differences in intelligence, the arguments cannot be ignored. In the early 1970s this issue was probably the hottest issue in psychology, and it sparked quite a bit of research. Based on the results of much of that research, most psychologists have now rejected Jensen's conclusions.

Few deny that significant differences exist between blacks and Caucasians on intelligence scores, but this does not indicate anything about what causes the differences. Many minorities in the United States, including blacks, suffer from a steady diet of unequal opportunity, poverty, poor housing, and poor health care. These are significant environmental factors that have a great effect on intelligence scores.

Jensen's assertion that the heritability of intelligence was as high as 80 percent was denouced at once. Many researchers accept much lower figures, ranging from about 30 percent to 50 percent (Gardner, 1983). Even those who argue for a substantial heritability figure do not relate it to an individual's ethnicity or race. In addition, these heritability factors often are computed within Caucasian populations, and their usefulness in comparing intelligence scores between races is dubious at best.

Jensen's argument that programs designed to improve the intelligence scores of children with below-average scores have failed may be based on a faulty assumption. We now have evidence that these programs can increase children's scores, although not all the effects are long-lasting (Lazar and Darlington, 1982). The lack of permanence may be the result of failure to improve the environment to which these children return after the programs have ended. Even if some programs have not lived up to the long-term expectations of their designers, it does not mean that better-planned and better-executed programs must fail.

For example, perhaps you have tried to teach a child how to tie shoelaces. Despite your best efforts, the child just can't do it correctly. However, just as you and the child are both losing patience, you switch tactics and try a different approach which succeeds. If you had concluded that the child could not learn, you would have been mistaken. While some remedial programs may not have been as successful as many people had hoped, many of these programs were organized quickly and mistakes were made. It does not mean that a well-considered, well-organized, and efficiently run program cannot succeed. There is a major difference between cannot and did not.

It is impossible to describe the heritability of any characteristic, including intelligence, without first specifying the child's environment. This point was demonstrated well by Whitten and Kagan (1969). Most people would agree that there is a significant genetic influence on height. Children from rural areas of South America are often much shorter than children who come from urban areas, but these differences are due not to genetic differences but to disease and improper diet. The farther you travel from the major cities, the worse the medical care becomes. Over the past twenty years, however, extension of medical services into these rural areas, and dietary improvement, have altered the situation somewhat. The differences in height between rural and urban children are much less than in the past.

If the heights of all the children in your suburban elementary school were tabulated, you might reasonably attribute most of the differences to heredity (if we could state that nutrition, health care, and other environmental factors were about equal). Only when environments are similar can we begin to suggest that differences in a particular trait may be substantiallly due to genetic considerations.

The same argument could be made for intelligence. Only when we equalize environmental factors—health care, nutrition, opportunity, housing, and so many others—can we give heritability figures which make sense. If not, such comparisons are misleading.

The importance of the environment is demonstrated in an interesting study involving the adoption of ninety-nine black children by Caucasion families in Minneapolis, Minnesota. All these children had been adopted by more affluent families. Scarr-Salapatek and Weinberg (1976) found that these children's intelligence scores were much higher than would have been expected had they not been adopted. The earlier they were adopted, the more likely they were to benefit from the superior environment. This in no way makes any statement about interracial adoptions, but it does indicate the powerful effect that environment has on intelligence.

GENETIC COUNSELING: THE NEW GENETICS

In our opening vignette, Laura's parents and her aunt Debbie, both sought genetic counseling. Genetic counseling changed her aunt's life by giving her the knowledge she needed to carry out her wish to marry and have a family. It offered Laura's parents hope that their other children could be normal.

Genetic counseling is a marvelous tool. Its basic functions include (1) diagnosing and describing particular disorders, (2) calculating the probabilities that a disorder will be transmitted to offspring, (3) helping people reach a decision based on genetic information as well as on moral, ethical, religious, economic, and cultural concerns, and (4) describing the treatments and resources available to those seeking such information (Sperber, 1976). On the surface it seems to present few problems. However, appearances are deceiving. In reality, genetic counseling is fraught with complicated ethical problems whose solutions are quite difficult.

For example, will those seeking the information understand it? Sibinga and Friedman (1971) reported that only a small percentage of their sample adequately understood the facts that had been communicated to them about phenylketonuria (PKU). It was their emotional reactions to what they had been told, not their intelligence level, that interfered with their understanding of the facts. There are also problems involved in communicating information about particular defects to parents who are emotionally involved (Walzer et al., 1975). People often use defenses to deny or reject such information (Sperber, 1976). The realization that something is "wrong" with their genes, that they might carry a "defect," can be alarming and startling and can change someone's life. Consider the fact that Debbie's discovery that her niece would die from a genetic disorder caused Debbie to cancel her plans to get married and have children. Genetic

11. *True or False:*
Genetic counselors have the responsibility to approve or disapprove of their clients' course of action.

12. *True or False:*
Evidence indicates that the great majority of people understand the information communicated to them by genetic counselors.

counselors must be sure that their clients understand what they are being told. It is also the duty of the counselor to help clients deal with their emotional reactions to the information (Walzer et al., 1976).

Most people seeking genetic counseling are faced with some kind of decision. A family with one child who has suffered from a genetic difficulty may have to decide whether to have other children. Some may have to decide whether they should even begin a family. Still others may be forced to decide whether to terminate a pregnancy, based on laboratory tests showing that the unborn child has some serious genetic defect. Can genetic counselors help people make their decisions without allowing their own biases to influence their clients? Marc Lappé and Julie Brady (1976) have effectively stated the case. Anyone in the position of counselor has a great deal of standing, and therefore power. A counselor must be careful to explain the information in terms that will not affect the decision itself. Yet because helping people deal with their feelings is one of a counselor's tasks, counselors can be placed in a difficult position. People often ask them what they should do. Genetic counselors can influence these decisions inadvertently by the way they provide the information.

Genetic counseling is just one example of how the advances in genetics have affected modern life. If genetic counseling is used correctly, it can ease people's minds, allowing them to make important decisions in an informed manner. People can leave genetic counseling knowing that they are armed with knowledge, that will allow them to make difficult decisions more rationally.

HEREDITY AND ENVIRONMENT: A MODEL

Genetic factors are important to any understanding of development. Heredity influences just about every important area of development. Yet the nature of those influences is greatly misunderstood. With the exception of a few major genetic diseases, one cannot understand these genetic influences without also specifying the nature of the environment in which they are operating. Heredity and environment interact and complement each other. It is impossible to speak of one in the absence of the other.

A number of models have been advanced to explain the nature of the interaction between heredity and environment. Some note the sensitivity of individuals to various environments at different ages. For example, McCall (1981) argues that, during infancy, mental development is essentially under genetic control and develops normally in many environments. A self-righting tendency exists, and even when deflected from the normal path by illness or a poor environment, the child usually returns to it. After infancy, however, the individual becomes much more sensitive to environmental factors, and individual differences become more stable. During childhood there are a number of genetically induced paths an individual may take, and it is the environment that determines which path the child follows. We are now making some tentative attempts to understand how environment and genetics interact, and these explanations will become very complicated as time goes on.

Some people yearn for the "good old days," when general statements about what was inherited and what wasn't could be made. Things were certainly easier then, even if they were almost always incorrect. The more modern view of the nature-nurture controversy is certainly more complicated and precludes making grandiose statements about heredity causing one thing and the environment causing another. However, it also gives us the opportunity to marvel once again at the complicated process by which a tiny, one-cell fertilized egg develops into a living, lovable infant, and how that infant fulfills its great human promise.

Chapter Summary

1. The basic units of heredity are genes, which are carried on chromosomes. Human beings have 23 pairs of chromosomes. In the sex cells, however, the chromosome pair splits, so that each sex cell contains 23 chromosomes. This split is random, assuring genetic individuality. The 23 chromosomes found in both the egg and the sperm cells combine during fertilization to maintain the same 46 chromosomes found in normal human beings.

2. The first 22 pairs of chromosomes appear to be alike, but the twenty-third pair, the sex chromosomes, is different. A female has two X chromosomes, while male has an X and a Y. The male determines the sex of the offspring, since he can contribute an X or a Y, while the female contributes only an X.

3. A trait that is expressed even if only one gene for it is present is called dominant. The trait that requires two genes to express itself is called recessive.

4. The term *genotype* describes the genetic composition of the individual, while the term *phenotype* refers to the person's observable characteristics. An individual's phenotype and genotype may be different.

5. When a particular characteristic is influenced by many genes, we consider the mechanism of transmission to be polygenic, multigenic, or multifactorial. The word *multifactorial* is sometimes used to denote characteristics influenced by a number of genes as well as the environment.

6. Since the X chromosome is three times larger than the Y, a number of genes found on the X are not present on the Y. When there is some defect on the X, a male may not be able to counter its effects, since males possess only one X and the gene may not be found at all on the Y. Traits inherited in this manner are called sex-linked traits. Females normally do not show them, because they have two X chromosomes and only one normal gene is necessary to mask the effects of the defective gene. Hemophilia and color blindness are transmitted in this way to males.

7. Our genetic endowment affects our physical characteristics. Since people react to us on the basis of some of these, they can become socially important even if they are biologically trivial.

8. A number of genetic diseases have been discovered, including cystic fibrosis, Tay-Sachs, phenylketonuria, Huntington's Chorea and sickle cell anemia.

9. If an extra chromosome somehow attaches itself to the twenty-first pair, the infant is born with Down's Syndrome, sometimes called mongolism. These infants are usually retarded and have a number of distinctive physical attributes.

10. There is a significant genetic component in schizophrenia. However, what is transmitted is not the disease itself, but rather a tendency or a predisposition to suffer from the disease given a particular environment.

11. Our genetic endowment influences our personality, probably by affecting our biological functioning. Human beings are born with a temperament, an individual way of responding to the environment. In addition, a number of our personality traits, such as introversion and extroversion, sociability, and activity level, appear to have a genetic basis.

12. Genetic factors are also important in determining handedness and a child's rate of development.

13. There appears to be a genetic basis for intelligence, although there is much dispute over the heritability figure. However, no matter what figure is used, an individual's environment greatly affects how these genes will be expressed. Educational programs can raise the intelligence scores of children.

14. Genetic counseling offers couples an opportunity to find out more about their genetic background and the probabilities that they might have a child with a particular disorder.

15. Heredity and environment interact in many subtle ways. We cannot speak of one in the absence of the other. We must consider both if we are to fully understand how people fulfill their human potential.

■ Answers to True or False Questions

1. *False.* Correct statement: Each species has its own number of chromosomes.

2. *True.* Females are born with their full complement of eggs, while males continually produce sperm.

3. *False.* Correct statement: The odds stay the same for each conception.

4. *True.* Constant stress can retard growth.

5. *False.* Correct statement: Huntington's Chorea is a dominant disease that manifests itself later in life.

6. *False.* Correct statement: This is an overly pessimistic view, as the success in treating phenylketonuria demonstrates.

7. *False.* Correct statement: What is transmitted is apparently a predisposition to the disorder, not the disorder itself.

8. *True.* Temperament is rather stable throughout childhood.

9. *False.* Correct statement: Although there is some environmental input, handedness is largely determined by genetic considerations.

10. *False.* Correct statement: Some efforts to increase intelligence scores have been successful. Questions surround the permanence of the change.

11. *False.* Correct statement: Genetic counselors offer information that allows their clients to make an informed decision.

12. *False.* Correct statement: Because clients are so emotionally involved, they may not understand the information.

CHAPTER THREE

Prenatal Development and Birth

■ *Are the Following Statements True or False?*

Try the True-False Quiz below. See if your answers correspond to the information in this chapter. Each question is repeated opposite the paragraph in which the answer can be found. The True-False Answer Box at the end of the chapter lists complete answers.

_____ **1.** The frequency of identical twins is uniform across various cultural and racial groups.

_____ **2.** The first organ to function is the heart.

_____ **3.** The fetus may suck a thumb in the womb.

_____ **4.** The average male infant born in the United States weighs more than the average female infant.

_____ **5.** Boys are more neurologically mature at birth.

_____ **6.** Smoking during pregnancy has been linked to increased weight gain in infants.

_____ **7.** Alcohol consumption during pregnancy leads to an Rh problem.

_____ **8.** Some 70 percent of all birth defects are caused by prenatal insults rather than genetic disorders.

_____ **9.** The number of women bearing children after age thirty-five has decreased in the past decade.

_____ **10.** Severe malnutrition during pregnancy leads to a condition in which the infant has fewer brain cells.

_____ **11.** Maternal stress does not affect the fetus because the systems of the mother and the fetus are separate.

_____ **12.** Cesarean births have decreased in the past twenty years, as doctors have come to appreciate the medical risks to the mother and child.

_____ **13.** The Lamaze method of birth emphasizes the importance of leaving the mother alone to meditate on her experience.

_____ **14.** Premature infants today are no more at risk for developmental problems than normal infants.

_____ **15.** Providing the premature infant with extra stimulation leads to hyperactivity.

Fraternal twins develop when two sperm fertilize two eggs. Fraternal twins are no more similar than any other pair of siblings.

zygote
A fertilized egg, or ovum.

dizygotic or fraternal twins
Twins who develop from two fertilized eggs and are no more genetically similar than any other sibling pair.

1. *True or False:*
The frequency of identical twins is uniform across various cultural and racial groups.

monozygotic or identical twins
Twins who develop from one fertilized egg and have an identical genetic structure.

THE DEVELOPING ORGANISM

Margaret and Tim are thrilled at the thought of becoming parents, but their friends and relatives offer all kinds of advice about what Margaret should and shouldn't do during pregnancy, and the newspapers are filled with articles about things that could go wrong during pregnancy and birth. With each report, the concerns of the expectant parents grow. They've also read about new ways to manage birth, and they don't know which is best. Everyone has a different opinion. Like all expectant parents, they want a happy, healthy baby, but they're afraid something will go wrong. How realistic are their fears?

It is easy to be overwhelmed by the number of environmental, physical, and viral agents that can cause difficulties during pregnancy. Although the threats are real enough, the overwhelming majority of infants will develop normally and emerge from the birth canal ready for life. The birthing choices available today offer an opportunity for parents to become more involved in this important experience. But although these alternative birth methods are often highly touted in the media, research concerning their true value is difficult to find.

This chapter deals with the development of the organism in the womb and the most important odyssey the infant will ever take—birth. Myths and half-truths abound in these areas, and they deserve special attention.

PRENATAL DEVELOPMENT

The Beginning

During ovulation, one egg is allowed to pass into the fallopian tube, where it is exposed to any sperm that are present. Although many sperm may surround the egg cell, only one will penetrate its outer wall. At this moment of conception, the mother's egg cell is fertilized by the father's sperm. When this occurs, there is a rearrangement and an exchange of genetic material, and the genetic endowment of the new being is set for life. This fertilized egg, or **zygote**, continues to travel down the tube into the uterus, or womb.

In some cases, two eggs may pass into the fallopian tubes and be fertilized by two different sperm. The result is **dizygotic**, or **fraternal**, twins, two separately developing organisms that are no more genetically similar than any pair of siblings. The frequency of fraternal twins differs widely among racial groups. They occur more often among African groups than among Caucasians, and more often among Caucasians than among Orientals (Bulmer, 1970).

The frequency of **monozygotic**, or **identical**, twins is uniform across racial groups and cultures at about 4 pairs in 1,000 pregnancies. Identical twins develop from a single egg and a single sperm. A cell division takes place very early in development, and these twins have the identical genetic makeup. Those rare cases in which the division into two separate zygotes is incomplete result in twins joined together, or Siamese twins.

From the moment of conception, the developing organism is affected by its genotype and its environment. During the nine months in the womb, its weight will increase 1 billion times over (Annis, 1978), and an infant will emerge with all biological systems ready for life outside the womb (see Table 3.1).

The Germinal Stage

It takes anywhere between a week to ten days or so for the fertilized egg to embed itself in the lining of the uterus. During this period, called the **germinal stage**, the fertilized egg divides again and again and begins the process of specialization that results in the formation of its organs. On the second day, about 30 hours after fertilization, the cell divides into two new cells (Singer and Hilgard, 1978). At 60 hours, the two cells divide to become four cells (Curtis, 1975). This division continues until, at the end of the first week, over 100 cells are present.

On the fifth day after conception, the cells rearrange to form a cavity. The hollow ball of cells is now called a **blastocyst** (Balinsky, 1970). The majority of cells are found in the outer layer, called a trophoblast, while the smaller number are found in the inner layer, called the inner cell mass. The outer layer will become structures that enable the embryo to survive, including the yolk sac, the allantois, the amnion, and the chorion. The yolk sac produces blood cells until the developing organism can do so on its own, at which point it disappears. The allantois forms the umbilical cord and the blood vessels in the placenta. The amnion eventually envelops the organism, holding the amniotic fluid, which protects the organism. The chorion becomes the lining of the placenta. The inner cell mass becomes the embryo.

The survival of the fertilized egg depends on its ability to burrow into the lining of the mother's uterus and obtain nourishment from her system. This process

germinal stage
The earliest stage of prenatal development, lasting from conception to about two weeks.

blastocyst
The stage of development in which the organism consists of layers of cells around a central cavity forming a hollow sphere.

Identical twins develop from a single fertilized egg. The genetic endowment of such twins is exactly the same.

TABLE 3.1 Prenatal Development and Behavior
Prenatal development is orderly and predictable.

Time Elapsed	Embryonic or Fetal Characteristics	Time Elapsed (in weeks)	Behavior
4 weeks 1 month	¼–½ inch long Head is one-third of embryo Brain has lobes, and rudimentary nervous system appears as hollow tube Heart begins to beat Blood vessels form and blood flows through them Simple kidneys, liver, and digestive tract appear Rudiments of eyes, ears, and nose appear Small tail		
8 weeks 2 months	2 inches long $1/30$ of an ounce in weight Human face with eyes, ears, nose, lips, tongue Arms have pawlike hands Almost all internal organs begin to develop Brain coordinates functioning of other organs Heart beats steadily and blood circulates Complete cartilage skeleton, beginning to be replaced by bone Tail beginning to be absorbed Now called a fetus Sex organs begin to differentiate	8 9 10½ 11 11½	Stroking mouth region produces flexion of upper torso and neck and extension of arms at the shoulder. Some spontaneous movements. More of the whole body responds when mouth is stroked. Stroking palms of hands leads to partial closing of the fingers. Other parts of face and arms become sensitive. Sensitive area spreads to upper chest.
12 weeks 3 months	3 inches long 1 ounce in weight Begins to be active Number of nerve-muscle connections almost triples Sucking reflex begins to appear Can swallow and may even breathe Eyelids fused shut (will stay shut until the 6th month), but eyes are sensitive to light Internal organs begin to function	12½ 14 15	Specific reflexes appear: lip closure, swallowing, Babinski, squinting. Entire body is sensitive, with more specific reflexes such as rooting, grasping, finger closing. Can maintain closure of the fingers (grasp) with muscle tightening, muscle strengthening.
16 weeks 4 months	6–7 inches long 4 ounces in weight Body now growing faster than head	16 to 18 19	Defined periods of activity and rest begin. Chest contractions begin, but are not sustained. Grasping with hand appears.

Time Elapsed	Embryonic or Fetal Characteristics	Time Elapsed (in weeks)	Behavior
	Skin on hands and feet forms individual patterns		
	Eyebrows and head hair begin to show		
	Fine, downylike hair (lanugo) covers body		
	Movements may now be felt		
20 weeks 5 months	10–12 inches long		
	8–16 ounces in weight		
	Skeleton hardens		
	Nails form on fingers and toes		
	Skin covered with cheesy wax		
	Heartbeat now loud enough to be heard with stethoscope		
	Muscles are stronger		
	Definite strong kicking and turning		
	Can be startled by noises		
24 weeks 6 months	12–14 inches long	25	Respiration is sustained for up to twenty-four hours. Eyelids open spontaneously, eye movements occur, and Moro reflex appears.
	1½ pounds in weight		
	Can open and close eyelids		
	Grows eyelashes	27 to birth	Few new responses appear, except for sucking at twenty-nine weeks. Rhythmic brain waves appear. After this age it becomes less easy to elicit reflexes in the fetus up until the time of birth.
	Much more active, exercising muscles		
	May suck thumb		
	May be able to breathe if born prematurely		
28 weeks 7 months	15 inches long		
	2½ pounds in weight		
	Begins to develop fatty tissue		
	Internal organs (especially respiratory and digestive) still developing		
	Has fair chance of survival if born now		
32 weeks 8 months	16½ inches long		
	4 pounds in weight		
	fatty layer complete		
38 weeks 9 months	Birth		
	19–20 inches long		
	6–8 pounds in weight (average)		
	95 percent of full-term babies born alive in the United States will survive		

Source: Adapted from Cox, 1984 and Fogel, 1984.

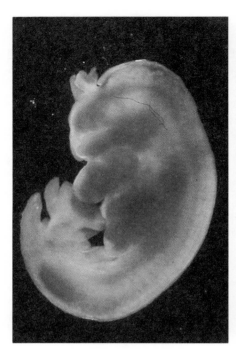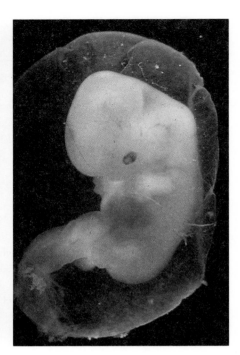

(Left) Human embryo between the fourth and fifth week; (right) human embryo at six to seven weeks.

is called *implantation*. It does this by secreting digestive enzymes that allow the blastocyst to embed itself in the maternal tissues. It now develops the ability to feed off its host. It also prevents menstruation by releasing a hormone that maintains the conditions necessary for support.

At about seven or eight days, the inner cell mass has differentiated into two distinct layers: the ectoderm and the endoderm. The ectoderm will develop into the organism's external coverings, including the skin, hair, sense organs, and nervous system. The endoderm becomes the digestive system, the respiratory system, and the glands. At about the sixteenth day, another layer, the mesoderm, appears between the ectoderm and endoderm and develops into the muscles, connective tissues, and the circulatory and excretory systems.

As development continues, the amnion swells and covers the developing organism. The trophoblast develops projections, or villi, which penetrate the uterine wall, allowing the developing organism to get nutrients more efficiently.. The villi on one side organize into the placenta, which is connected to the developing organism by the umbilical cord. The placenta delivers nutrients, removes wastes, and helps combat infection. The germ cell at the end of the first two weeks of life measures about 1/175 inch long (Annis, 1978).

The Embryonic Stage

embryonic stage
The stage of prenatal development beginning at about two weeks and ending at about eight weeks, when bone cells begin to replace cartilage.

The **embryonic stage** begins at two weeks and ends at about eight weeks after conception. At two weeks, the tiny mass has just begun to depend on its mother for everything. It is hardly recognizable as a human being. Six weeks later, 95 percent of the body parts will be present (Annis, 1978). During the embryonic period, changes occur at a breathtaking pace. Each system's development follows a par-

 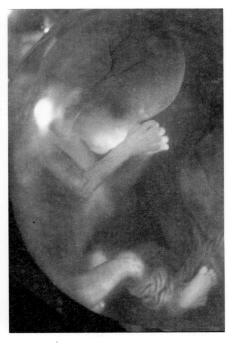

(Left) Human fetus showing close-up of hands at eight weeks; (right) human fetus at approximately ten weeks.

ticular sequence. At day 31, the shoulders, arms, and the hands develop; on day 33, the fingers develop; and on day 34 through day 36, the thumb is completed. The organs form and begin to function in a primitive manner. The first organ to function is the heart, which circulates the blood to the placenta and throughout the developing body. The circulatory system of the embryo is completely separated from the mother's, and no exchange of blood occurs. All exchanges of nutrients and oxygen occur by diffusion. By the end of the first month, the ears, nose, and mouth begin to form, and arms and legs make their appearance as buds. Fingers and toes become defined. Internal organs are now rapidly developing. During this time of extremely rapid growth, the organism is most vulnerable to environmental insult. The embryo is capable of some primitive behavioral reactions. Reflex action occurs as early as the middle of the seventh week and the beginning of the eighth. If the mouth is stimulated, the embryo flexes its neck to the other side (Richmond and Herzog, 1979).

2. *True or False:*
The first organ to function is the heart.

The Fetal Stage

During the last seven months of development, the **fetal stage**, the fetus grows and develops at a tremendous rate. At the beginning of the third month, the average fetus is 1¼ inches long and weighs less than one-third of an ounce. By the end of third month it is 3 inches long and weighs 1 ounce. Hormonal action during this third month causes the genitals to become defined. If the male hormone, testosterone, is secreted into the fetal system, it causes the development of male genitalia. In the absence of the male hormone, the fetus will develop female organs. During this third month, the major organs are completed and bones begin to appear and muscles develop. The fetus now moves, kicks its legs, swallows the amniotic fluid and digests it, and removes waste products through urination.

fetal stage
The stage of prenatal development, beginning at about eight weeks until birth.

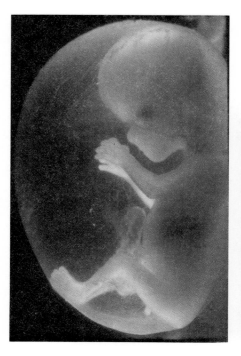 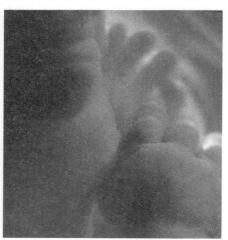

(Left) Human fetus between 14 and 16 weeks; (right) human fetus between fifth and sixth month with thumb in mouth.

3. *True or False:*

The fetus may suck a thumb in the womb.

During the fourth month, the fetus continues to grow at a fantastic pace. By the end of this month it is 6 inches long and weighs 6 ounces. As it grows, it develops internally. By the fifth month, the fetus sleeps and wakes at regular intervals, and some reflexes, such as hiccupping and swallowing, have developed (Fitzgerald et al., 1982). The fetus cries and may suck a thumb. At this point, the fetal movements are likely to be felt by the mother, though some mothers experience movement earlier. This is known as *quickening*. During the sixth month, the fetus attains a weight of about 2 pounds and a length of 14 inches. The facial features are clearly in evidence, and the fetus can make a fist.

During the last three prenatal months, the fetus gains a layer of fat that will help keep the infant warm after birth. By the end of the twenty-eighth week, the fetus measures about 17 inches and weighs about 3 pounds. Traditionally, seven months is considered the age of *viability*, since the fetus has a reasonable chance of survival if born at this time. However, this is misleading, for there is considerable individual variation in weight, health, and developmental readiness. Some seven-month-old fetuses are more ready for an independent existence than others. The availability of excellent *perinatal* (after birth) medical care is also an important factor in the survivability of the infant. Many technological innovations are improving the survival chances of these tiny infants.

During the last two prenatal months, the fetus gains about half a pound a week. Its heretofore red, wrinkled appearance disappears somewhat as it puts on weight. The development of the lungs is especially important during these last months. By the end of its normal period of prenatal development, approximately 266 days, the average American male infant weighs approximately 7½ pounds and measures approximately 20 inches. The average female weighs slightly less,

4. *True or False:*

The average male infant born in the United States weighs more than the average female infant.

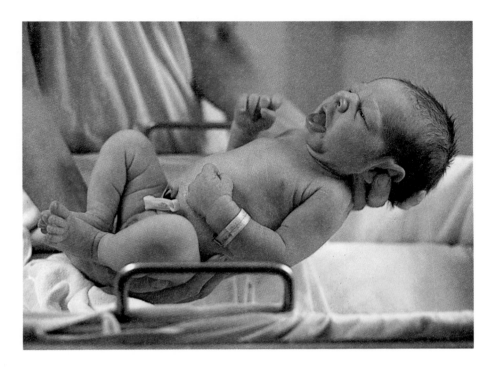

The newborn infant.

about 7 pounds, but appearances can be deceiving. In reality, the average female is more ready for life. She is about four weeks more mature, as measured by skeletal age (Annis, 1978) and is more neurologically advanced.

The entire process of fetal development proceeds without any need for conscious maternal intervention. It is directed by genetic forces that we are only just beginning to understand. However, the fetus is also affected by the environment.

5. *True or False:*
Boys are more neurologically mature at birth.

Developmental Myths

People used to think that everything a woman did could have an effect on the unborn infant. Unusual occurrences in a pregnant woman's daily life were thought to influence the personality and physical well-being of the child. For instance, if a rabbit crossed her path, some believed the child would be born with a *hare*lip (Annis, 1978). Or if she ate or squashed strawberries, it was said to lead to a strawberry-shaped birthmark.

This belief in total environmental control came to be replaced by the idea that nothing the mother did really mattered. The placenta was viewed as a barrier that did not allow any dangerous elements into the infant's environment and rendered various poisons harmless. In fact, the term *placental barrier* can still be seen in some publications.

Today we know that neither viewpoint is correct. The placenta is far from being a total barrier. It allows a number of substances to pass into the system of the fetus. On the other hand, although we no longer believe the superstitions concerning strawberries and rabbits, we know that the environment greatly affects the health of the fetus.

THREATS TO THE DEVELOPING ORGANISM

A variety of drugs and other agents have been linked to birth defects (Stechler and Halton, 1982) (see Table 3.2). The consequences of these agents differ widely. Some cause death, some cause severe or mild disabilities. Others affect the weight of the infant or may injure the brain in subtle ways that may not be discovered until well into childhood (Wilson, 1973). The effects of these agents may depend on such factors as the type of agent, the dosage, and the time at which the fetus is exposed, as well as on the genetic characteristics of the fetus.

Drugs—Legal and Illegal

On the surface, determining whether a particular drug is dangerous to the fetus appears to be a simple matter. Follow the pregnancies of drug-takers and compare the rate of birth defects in their children with that of the children of non-drug-takers. However, this strategy does not work well. Many people take a variety of drugs, not just one, and trying to fix responsibility on any one agent is difficult (McGlothlin et al., 1970). In addition, some pregnant women who take drugs are also undernourished and have not had adequate prenatal care. Finally, the effects of some drugs may be very subtle or may not show up for years.

It is difficult to state with certainty that a particular drug causes this or that defect, but we do have substantial evidence that particular drugs lead to specific problems. Two famous cases that show the dangers even some prescription drugs may pose involve thalidomide and diethylstilbestrol (DES).

thalidomide
A drug taken to combat nausea during pregnancy and responsible for birth defects.

phocomelia
A condition in which the infant is born without arms or legs or with underdeveloped extremities.

Thalidomide. The drug **thalidomide** was widely used in Europe in the 1960s. It was marketed by a West German firm as treatment for morning sickness—the nausea sometimes experienced by pregnant women especially in the early months of pregnancy. A vast increase occurred in the number of infants born either without limbs or with extremities that were grossly underdeveloped, a condition called **phocomelia**. Between 1949 and 1959, fifteen cases pf phocomelia were identified in West Germany, but in 1960 hundreds of cases appeared, and by 1961 there were thousands (Annis, 1978). Still, it was difficult to discover the link between the drug and these birth defects.

When their child was born with grossly underdeveloped limbs, Karl and Linde Schulte-Hillen were told that the infant suffered from a genetic deformity. But the couple did not accept this diagnosis. The parents' assertions were dismissed by many doctors before Karl was able to interest a pediatrician named Lenz in the child's condition. After much detective work, they isolated the connection to thalidomide.

This was only the beginning. The public had to be made aware of the problem, the authorities had to be convinced that the drug should be taken off the market, and special help had to be secured for the affected children. The drug companies did not appreciate these efforts, nor were they convinced that their product had caused the problem. As the evidence mounted, however, the campaign was successful, finally ending in a settlement that helped compensate the victims of the drug (Levy, 1968). In parts of Germany there are now entire classrooms set aside for these children, which enables them to obtain the best possible education (Annis, 1978).

TABLE 3.2 **Common Teratogens**
Research into the effects that drugs, chemicals, and other elements of our environment may have on the unborn child is an ongoing process. It is certain, though, that the lists such as the ones below will grow longer.

Factors Known To Cause Birth Defects in Humans	Factors Suspected of Causing Birth Defects in Humans	Factors Not Yet Proven, but Potentially Dangerous
Drugs and Chemicals		
Tranquilizers and hypnotics		
Thalidomine	LSD	
Barbiturates	Marijuana	
Anesthetics		
Narcotics (Heroin)		
Alcohol		
Stimulants		
Amphetamines	Caffeine	
Nicotine		
Analgesics		
Antibiotics		Aspirin
Streptomycin, tetracycline		
Hormones		
Other Drugs		
		Antihistamines
		Diuretics
		Antiallergens
		Antacids
Chemicals and Radiation		
Mercury	Asbestos	Pollutants
	Lead	Cleaning Fluids
	Agent Orange	Paints
	Pesticides	Cosmetics
	X-Rays	Deodorants
Nuclear Radiation		Additives and preservatives
		Microwaves
Foods		
Excessive amounts of vitamins (esp. A)		Dietary supplements
Poor nutrition		
Disease		
Rubella ⎫		
Influenza ⎬ Viral		
Smallpox ⎪		
Chicken Pox ⎭		
Polio	Some vaccines	
Syphillis		
Toxoplasmosis		
Diabetes		
Hypertension		
Obesity		
Toxemia		
Maternal factors		
High stress		
RH incompatibility		
Age		
Multiple pregnancy		
Low SES		
Poor prenatal care		

Source: A. Fogel, 1984.

The thalidomide tragedy, which affected some 10,000 infants (Annis, 1978), demonstrates two things. First, taking any drug when not absolutely necessary should be discouraged. Thalidomide was considered safe by many European doctors, but many families learned to their sorrow that it wasn't. Second, the thalidomide story shows how much a dedicated individual can accomplish.

Relatively few American women took the drug. American families were spared the heartache of thalidomide-induced phocomelia because of one courageous doctor's refusal, in the face of great pressure from the drug industry, to certify the drug for distribution in the United States. Dr. Frances Kelsey of the U.S. Food and Drug Administration was unimpressed with the research on the drug and pressed for more studies. Her refusal to back down was rewarded when the work of Schulte-Hillen and Lenz became public.

When a thalidomide baby was born, the disability was apparent. It matched the popular stereotype of a birth defect as visible and detected early in life. New parents breathe a sigh of relief at the sight of a healthy, functioning child. It rarely occurs to anyone that something that occurred during the prenatal period may haunt a person years later.

diethylstilbestrol (DES)
A drug taken during pregnancy to prevent miscarriage and responsible for some cases of cancer in female offspring during late adolescence or early adulthood.

Diethylstilbestrol (DES).   Appearances can be deceiving, as the case of children whose mothers took the synthetic estrogen called **diethylstilbestrol** (known as DES) shows. From the 1940s through 1971, DES was widely administered to pregnant women (N.Y.S. Department of Health, 1979). It was thought that the drug would reduce the incidence of miscarriage, and it was prescribed for women who had a history of diabetes. Although some studies doubted the effectiveness of DES, doctors continued to prescribe it. About 1 million women took the drug (Planned Parenthood, 1979). At first, there seemed to be little cause for concern. The children born to these women were healthy as infants, but in 1971 Dr. Arthur Herbst discovered a link between prenatal administration of DES and eight cases of a kind of cervical cancer usually found only in women over fifty. Some 300 to 400 cases of such cancer in daughters of women who took the drug have been confirmed (Avery, 1981). This makes a DES daughter's chance of having the cancerous condition about 1 or 2 in every 1,000 (Orenberg, 1981). However, many DES daughters suffer from genital tract abnormalities. All women whose mothers took the drug should be watched carefully by their doctors. DES sons are also affected by the drug. They sometimes suffer from genital-tract abnormalities and benign cysts that require attention from a urologist (N.Y.S. Department of Health, 1979; Planned Parenthood, 1977). Recent evidence also indicates that mothers who took DES run an additional risk of developing breast cancer twenty years after they take the drug (Herbst, 1984).

How does a person find out whether one is a DES child? The easiest way is to ask your mother whether she took anything besides vitamins during her pregnancy or had a history of bleeding or miscarriage. Her medical records may also be checked for such information. If you are a DES child, your state may have a confidential registry that will inform you of the newest research in the field.

The DES story demonstrates that the effects of drugs taken during the prenatal stage may not show up for some time. The best advice seems to be to approach all drugs with caution during pregnancy.

Medications.   A number of medications have been linked to birth defects in the fetus, but the research findings on others are contradictory. Tetracycline, a commonly prescribed antibiotic, has been linked to permanent discoloration of the teeth and defective bone growth (March of Dimes, 1983a). The contraceptive pill, if taken right before or during pregnancy, can cause such birth defects as congenital heart disease and other structural abnormalities (U.S. Department of Health and Human Services, 1981). That is why many doctors recommend that a woman who wants to become pregnant stop taking the pill some months before she plans to get pregnant. Scientists are also concerned about the possible effects that such commonly described prescription drugs as Valium and Librium may have on the unborn child. A large study called the Collaborative Perinatal Project concluded that these "minor tranquilizers" have been linked to the incidence of cleft palate, a birth defect affecting the formation of the roof of the mouth (Zimmerman, 1976). However, the evidence is mixed, and another study did not find this pattern (Rosenberg et al., 1983). With such contradictory research, it is difficult to sort out which drugs are safe and which are not.

People often make blanket statements that no drugs should be taken during pregnancy. Although that is a reasonable dictum, there are times when doctor and patient are forced to decide in favor of administering a potentially dangerous medication to combat a severe condition. For example, certain antibiotics, hormones, anticoagulants, steriods, and antihistamines have been linked to birth defects in animals and human beings. But when there is no other alternative available to treat a particular condition, a **risk-benefit analysis** must be performed, weighing the risk to the mother and fetus against the possible benefit to the mother and the baby if the condition is left untreated.

Most drugs taken during pregnancy are not prescribed by doctors. They are available either legally, as in the case of nicotine and alcohol, or illegally, as with narcotics.

Smoking.   One of the more common drugs taken by pregnant women is nicotine from smoking cigarettes (Dalby, 1978). It is estimated that more than 40 percent of American women who are pregnant smoke (March of Dimes, 1985). Nicotine causes a rise in heart rate, blood pressure, and respiration and constricts the flow of blood. The amount of oxygen the fetus receives is reduced (Martin, 1976). Although the effects of nicotine are dose-related, smokers are twice as likely as nonsmokers to have low-birth-weight babies (Simpson, 1957). The infants of smokers weigh an average of 200 grams (about .5 pounds) less than infants of nonsmokers (HEW, 1979). Smoking has been related to prematurity (Leavitt, 1974) and to increased numbers of fetal deaths (McIntosh, 1984). Other research suggests that the decrease in oxygen may lead to brain abnormalities and cleft palate (Stechler and Halton, 1982).

Injurious long-term effects from maternal smoking have also been noted. A major study found that at seven years of age children of smokers had lower reading abilities and demonstrated more problems with social adjustment than children of nonsmokers (Davies et al., 1972). Another study found a positive correlation between smoking during pregnancy and hyperactivity, low achievement, and minimal neurological dysfunction (Landesman-Dwyer and Emanuel, 1979). Maternal smoking during pregnancy has also been linked to poor attention span during the preschool years (Streissguth et al., 1984). One hopeful sign comes from a study that found that mothers who were light smokers or who had stopped smoking prior to their fourth month of pregnancy reduced their risk of having low-birth-weight infants (Butler et al., 1972). A major U.S. government

Studies show that smoking during pregnancy presents a danger to the unborn child.

risk-benefit analysis
A detailed analysis of the risks versus the benefits of a particular choice.

6. *True or False:*
Smoking during pregnancy has been linked to increased weight gain in infants.

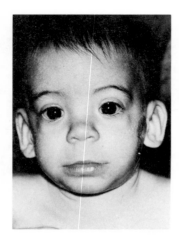

Mothers who drink heavily run the risk of bearing a child with fetal alcohol syndrome. The child pictured above suffers from this syndrome.

fetal alcohol syndrome
A number of characteristics, including retardation, facial abnormalities, growth defects, and poor coordination, caused by maternal alcohol consumption.

report noted that mothers who smoke increase their chances of spontaneous abortions and miscarriages, fetal death, and birth problems. It concludes that "maternal smoking may adversely affect the child's long-term growth, intellectual development, and behavioral characteristics" (U.S. Department of Health and Human Services, 1981, p. 238). The research on the long-term effects of smoking is not unanimous, and one major study failed to find significant differences between children of smokers and children of nonsmokers physically, intellectually, emotionally, or in the realm of personal and social functioning at age ten (Lefkowitz, 1981). However, the overwhelming majority of the research demonstrates not only a clear danger to the developing fetus but also the possibility that the child will be adversely affected as he or she matures.

Often, nicotine is only one of a number of common substances a pregnant woman takes. We are just beginning to appreciate the effects that combinations of chemicals may have on the fetus. For example, the combination of smoking and moderate-to-heavy drinking reduces the infant's alertness. These offspring cough and sneeze more, and they perform poorly on simple learning tasks (Landesman-Dwyer and Emanuel, 1979).

Alcohol.   The children of alcoholic mothers show a distinct physical appearance and pattern of development. They are shorter and lighter than other children, and their growth and development is slow. They show a number of cranial and facial abnormalities, heart defects, poor motor development and coordination and tend to be retarded (Furey, 1982; Streissguth, 1977). Their mortality rate is also higher than average (Jones et al., 1974). These characteristics describe the **fetal alcohol syndrome.**

Damage caused by alcohol appears to be permanent. Even when children of alcoholic mothers are raised in an improved environment, they continue to lag behind, both in physical growth and intellectual development (Hanson et al., 1976).

Since most women are not alcoholics, people generally consider the negative consequences of drinking something that happens to other people. However, even moderate drinking may affect the unborn child (Streissguth, 1977). The fetus is sensitive to alcohol, especially in the last trimester, when brain growth is great (Stechler and Halton, 1982). In a sample of seventy-four moderate drinkers who drank about 2 ounces of 100-proof alcohol each day before and during their pregnancies, Hanson (1977, cited in Annis, 1978) found that about 12 percent of their offspring showed one or more of the characteristics described as fetal alcohol syndrome. The effects of alcohol on the fetus seem to be dose-related, with lower doses resulting in some but not all of the characteristics of the syndrome (Clarren et al., 1978). A woman consuming about 2 ounces of 100-proof whiskey or one to two cans of beer a day has about a 10 percent chance of visibly damaging her baby. Consuming a six-pack or 10 ounces of whiskey a day leads to a 50 percent chance of damaging an unborn child (*Science News*, March 26, 1977). These figures refer only to the gross abnormalities noted above, not to damage that may not reveal itself in years to come. Although very small amounts of alcohol may not produce birth defects or developmental disabilities, as little as one drink a day increases the risk of miscarriage during the middle months of pregnancy (Kline et al., 1980; Harlap and Shiono, 1980). A study of 31,604 pregnant women found that consuming even one drink a day could lead to decreased fetal growth (Mills et al., 1984). As no minimal safe level of alcohol has so far been found, the best advice may be to severely curtail—even better, abstain from—drinking during pregnancy.

Narcotics. Babies of heroin addicts are born addicted to heroin and must go through withdrawal (Brazelton, 1970). They often show disturbances in activity level, attention span, and sleep patterns (Householder et al., 1982). Because these infants are frequently premature and very small, this is sometimes a life-or-death situation. We don't know whether it is the drug itself—or the poverty and poor diet that often accompany addiction—that leads to this life-threatening situation. Either way, these women and their offspring require extra help. Comprehensive programs that offer medical help, counseling, and parental education are often successful in improving the lot of these infants (Suffet et al., 1981).

Marijuana and LSD. Some research shows that marijuana use leads to fetal abnormalities and lack of fetal growth in animals (Annis, 1978). Evidence with human beings is still controversial, and scientists still do not understand the full effects marijuana, angel dust, hashish, or other psychoactive drugs have on the fetus (March of Dimes, 1983b). Studies of LSD are difficult to perform, since most users also take other drugs. However, some anecdotal evidence shows a relationship between LSD and congenital malformations (Apgar and Beck, 1974). Fetal abnormalities have been found when LSD is given to pregnant mice (Alexander et al., 1967). Some evidence points to alterations in white blood cells, but studies are inconclusive (Fitzgerald et al., 1982). In addition, higher rates of spontaneous abortion and miscarriage are found among LSD users (Annis, 1978).

Caffeine and Aspirin. The status of many commonly taken drugs is still controversial. Caffeine, which is found in coffee and tea, is one example. There is some evidence that high doses of caffeine increase the frequency of birth defects in animals (March of Dimes, 1983b). Most recent evidence has failed to reliably link moderate caffeine intake to birth defects (University of California, 1985).

Aspirin has been shown to cause damage to the unborn in animal studies (Stechler and Halton, 1982). In human beings, however, the main finding is that aspirin, if taken excessively in the later months of pregnancy, may adversely affect blood-clotting in both mother and baby (March of Dimes, 1983b).

Pollution and Radiation

Pollution and radiation can also affect the unborn child adversely and are therefore causes for concern. For example, mercury has been linked to severe malformations (Stechler and Halton, 1982). In Japan a number of mothers who had eaten fish laden with mercury gave birth to extremely handicapped children who suffered from cerebral palsy and physical defects (Miller, 1974). And PCB, a contaminant sometimes found in water and fish, can cause immature motor responses as well as other behavioral abnormalities (Jacobson et al., 1984). Other chemicals may cause fetal abnormalities as well, but for many, not enough research exists to label them dangerous to the unborn infant (U.S. Department of Health and Human Services, 1981).

Radiation too has been linked to fetal deaths, as well as to a number of structural defects in infants. Studies after the atomic bombings of Hiroshima and Nagasaki during World War II found that exposure to radiation increased the rates of spontaneous abortions, miscarriages and mutations among pregnant women (Annis, 1978). Even lower doses may not be safe. Because radiation accumulates in the body, repeated X rays may be dangerous. There is no safe level of radiation. Although there are times when an X ray is medically required, pregnant women should avoid radiation as much as possible.

Disease and Pregnancy

Our society has been spared the terrible epidemics of the past. We are not concerned about smallpox, diphtheria, and polio. It is often thought that the more serious a disease is to the mother, the greater the chance it will harm the baby. Although this may generally be true, there are many exceptions.

rubella (German measles)
A disease responsible for many
cases of birth defects.

Rubella.   Commonly called German Measles, **rubella** is a very mild disorder. Normally, the sufferer has a rash, feels a bit under the weather for a day or two, and perhaps runs a low-grade fever. Complications are rare. Yet the effects of the rubella virus on a developing embryo can be serious. In the epidemic of 1964–1965, about 50,000 babies were affected. Many died, while many others suffered injuries of varying degrees (Rugh and Shettles, 1971). Figures on the percentages of fetal deaths vary from 14 percent to 39 percent (Stevenson, 1973). Among the damage caused by rubella are congenital cataracts and other eye disorders, ear damage, congenital heart disease, and central nervous system damage (Monif, 19069). The effects of the disease on the unborn fetus is greater in the first three months of pregnancy—the first trimester—than later on (Rhodes, 1961), although there is evidence that rubella may also be dangerous in the second trimester, resulting in hearing loss and retarded development (Stevenson, 1973). With the advent of a vaccine that prevents rubella, epidemics should become a thing of the past. Unfortunately, not every child is being protected, and isolated cases of rubella-induced defects may still occur.

Venereal Disease.   Venereal diseases, such as syphilis, gonorrhea, and herpes, pose significant dangers to the unborn child (Mascola et al., 1984; Knox, 1984). A large number of unborn children are exposed to these diseases, which are usually transmitted during sexual intercourse.

Syphilis in the expectant mother can cause a number of defects in the infant, including bone and facial deformities, nerve deafness, and fetal death. A number of these children will develop syphilis as well. If the mother-to-be receives treatment before the sixteenth week of pregnancy, the fetus may not be infected (Cave, 1973). After that time, however, certain tissues that protect the infant break down. By the eighteenth week of pregnancy, there is an 80 percent chance that the fetus will be infected if the mother has not been treated (Thompson and Grusec, 1970), but prompt treatment, even after this time, will often prevent damage.

Many women who have gonorrhea may be totally unaware of it, because they may not show any outward symptoms. Fetuses exposed to gonorrhea are often premature and blind. The standard practice of placing a solution of silver nitrate in infants' eyes at birth is to protect against blindness in case the mother has gonorrhea. Antibiotics treat gonorrhea successfully. Before the discovery of such medication, however, about 25 percent of all the children admitted to special schools for the blind could trace their blindness to gonorrhea (Grossman and Drutz, 1974).

Women who have herpes may transmit it to the baby during the birth process. It is estimated that up to half the infants of infected mothers acquire the disease and that only about half survive. In order to prevent the spread of the disease, doctors often check for lesions in the birth canal and may recommend a Cesarean section.

The Mother's Medical Condition. While noting some of the diseases that may affect the fetus, one should not forget the medical condition of the mother. For example, about 6 to 8 percent of all pregnant women suffer from hypertension. Maternal hypertension is related to poor fetal growth, increased perinatal death, and many neurological and developmental problems. Diabetes is also related to many birth defects (U.S. Department of Health and Human Services, 1981). These disorders are dangerous to the mother as well. In both these cases, as with so many other maternal medical conditions, competent medical advice and prompt treatment may improve the chances of delivering a healthy child and safeguarding the mother's health.

The Rh Factor

Mrs. Kay was pregnant with her fifth child. On the surface, everything looked fine. The Kays were blessed with good health, a happy marriage, and financial security. Yet they suffered through nine months of agony that few people today will have to experience. The doctors told Mrs. Kay she had little chance of delivering a healthy child. In addition, her chances of miscarriage and spontaneous abortion were greater than average. The Kays have an Rh problem. The **Rh factor** consists of a particular red-blood-cell antigen found in most human beings. Approximately 85 percent of all Caucasians, 93 percent of Blacks, and nearly 100 percent of all Asian people, Native Americans, and Eskimos have the factor, that is, they are Rh positive (Stevenson, 1973).

In about 13 percent of Caucasian unions, the woman is Rh negative and the man is Rh positive. In such a situation, the baby may be Rh positive and a problem may arise: The mother's body reacts to the Rh positive antigen in the fetus as it would to an invading germ or virus. Since the blood of the fetus does not mix with that of the mother during the pregnancy, she is not likely to manufacture antibodies that might injure the fetus. Few fetal blood cells cross the placenta. During the birth, however, especially if it is long and difficult, some cells do cross the placenta, and the mother will manufacture the antibodies. Since the first child of these parents is not likely to be exposed to many of these antibodies, the infant's chances of survival are good. But once these antibodies are manufactured, they tend to remain in the mother's body. She also becomes more sensitive to this factor in later pregnancies. During the *next* pregnancy, the fetus will be exposed to the mother's antibodies, which will cross the placenta and destroy the red blood cells of the fetus (Apgar and Beck, 1974). In each successive pregnancy, the risk to the fetus becomes greater and greater, until the chances that a child will be born healthy is quite low.

7. *True or False:*
Alcohol consumption during pregnancy leads to an Rh problem.

Rh factor
An antibody often, but not always, found in human beings.

RESEARCH HIGHLIGHT   *New Technology, New Questions*

If Missy had been born thirty years ago, no decision would have been necessary. Missy was born with spina bifida, a defect that occurs in about one out of every 500 births. *Spina bifida* is a malformation in which there is a "lack of closure of the bony spinal canal" (Wyne and O'Connor, 1979, p. 535). In Missy's case, a number of physical defects were also present.

Until the early 1960s, around 80 percent of these children died, but today modern surgical techniques have lowered that figure to about 25 percent. Those that do survive suffer from symptoms of the disorder for their whole life, including physical disabilities of varying severity, and face numerous operations.

Missy's disorder was serious. The doctors informed her parents that surgery would be necessary to save her life. They carefully described the treatment, costs, and future outlook. Without surgery Missy would probably die from meningitis or would suffer additional handicaps. If the surgery was successful, Missy would never be free from braces and crutches, would need physical therapy for the rest of her life, and would have a 90 percent chance of developing water on the brain. Missy's parents decided against surgery.

After being discharged from the hospital, Missy's parents continued to visit her daily to feed and hold her. They became attached to her, and two weeks later, when Missy began to show signs of meningitis, they changed their minds and requested that surgery be performed. The surgery was successful, and Missy was soon released from the hospital. At four months, Missy developed water on the brain and required a shunt to drain the fluid. At six months, she was making progress, and her parents seemed to have adjusted well to caring for her special needs.

Have the doctors and her parents acted properly in this case?

Years ago there were no choices. Nature simply took its course. Today extraordinary efforts are made to save children, often resulting in an alive but severely disabled child, who may be constantly in pain. With our new choices come a variety of issues. We can often sustain life—but what of the quality of that life, and the cost?

The most direct solution is to argue that we have a moral responsibility to sustain life at any cost. Using this argument, no medical procedure should be called optional or extraordinary. Even if medical procedures will entail a massive amount of professional attention and cost (sometimes measured in thousands of work hours and hundreds of thousands of dollars), and result in a severely mentally and physically disabled infant, the doctor and parents are duty-bound to perform these services.

The second view differentiates between normal treatment and extraordinary treatment, noting that society has the responsibility to provide the former but not the latter. For instance, society is obligated to provide food and normal medical care but not extensive, experimental surgery, which would prolong patients' lives but not improve the quality of their existence. This view implies that people should have some say in deciding whether they should receive such life prolonging experimental treatment. Some dying and severely burned adults have, at times, been given input into such a life–death decision. However, when dealing with pediatric cases, this is impossible, and other people must make the decision for the child.

Other considerations are important as well. Should the knowledge that Missy will need a number of operations and continuous professional care be taken into account in choosing how to treat her? If the first step is taken, we may be morally committed to continuous treatment. Perhaps a decision to treat the child should be based on some reasonable hope of success, but success is a difficult term to define.

Finally, can we say that the benefits Missy receives from her treatment are proportional to the investment of time, energy, resources, personnel, and all the rest? Is the special cost of providing all these services appropriate in view of our society's full range of needs for medical care? Will Missy be a contributing member to society, or is that less important than society's obligation to care for members who may not contribute as much economically? We don't have a morally reasoned approach for answering these questions at the present time.

Missy's case is not unique, and a number of variations can be found. For instance, there have been cases reported in the media of infants fed and cared for but not given the extra care needed to allow them a better chance at life. Is it the doctor's responsibility to provide all care, regardless of the consequences, to prolong a life? What of the handicapped infant's right to survive? How do we determine the meaning of the term *extraordinary care,* and what should be done if the doctor wants to treat the patient but the parents refuse? Should such experimental procedures as fetal surgery (Henig, 1982) be considered a right of parents and the newborn?

> These are just a few of the questions raised by the new technology. As one voice argues for doing everything possible no matter what, another reminds us that our resources are limited and must be allocated. The new technology brings with it a host of questions that never had to be asked before, yet alone answered.
>
> *Sources:* W. T. Reich and H. Smith, *On the Birth of a Severely Handicapped Infant* (New York: Institute of Society, Ethics, and the Life Sciences, 1982); R. M. Henig, "Saving Babies Before Birth," *New York Times Magazine,* February 28, 1982, pp. 18–22 +; M. D. Wyne and P. D. O'Connor, *Exceptional Children: A Developmental Approach* (Lexington, Mass.: D. C. Heath, 1979).

Since 1968, a preventive vaccine for Rh problems has been available. Within seventy-two hours after each birth, miscarriage, or abortion, a shot of the vaccine RhoGAM is administered to block the production of these antibodies. Before this vaccine was available, about 10,000 babies died every year, and 20,000 more were born with severe birth defects from Rh disease (Apgar and Beck, 1974). The Kays had their first child before the discovery of RhoGAM and therefore could not take advantage of the vaccine. But they were fortunate. Although the baby had a number of problems, the child is healthy and happy today. (See Research Highlight "New Technology, New Questions" on page 96).

Why Can't We Prevent Birth Defects?

The public is constantly exposed to information about drugs, radiation, and diseases that can harm the fetus. Yet pregnant women continue to take drugs and expose their infants to danger. The figures are astounding and depressing. In a study in Scotland, 82 percent of the pregnant women used a prescribed medication (Martin, 1976). Some 65 percent were "self-medicated." A study in the United States showed that 54 percent of the pregnant Caucasians and 42 percent of pregnant black women smoked. The average number of drugs taken during pregnancy was 10.3. About 15 percent were taking drugs to suppress appetite. About half the pregnant American women drink regularly (Martin, 1976).

In Chapter Two, we looked at some of the major genetic diseases. The chance of bearing a child with a genetic deformity is slight, compared with the possibility that a fetus will be injured in the prenatal period. Genetic factors account for only 20 percent of infant defects; chromosomal abnormalities add another 10 percent to the picture. The remaining 70 percent of infant defects are caused by drugs, pollution, disease, and other environmental insults that occur during the prenatal stage (Martin, 1976). As we learn more about which environmental substances are harmful to the fetus, many of the tragedies become preventable.

If we know so much about **teratogens** (agents that cause fetal defects), why have we failed to prevent birth defects? The main reason is ignorance. Some women do not have an adequate understanding of the dangers in the environment.

The poor and the young are most at risk. The poor have a higher infant mortality rate and a greater number of prenatally caused infant problems (Birch and Gussow, 1970). They are often undernourished or malnourished, undereducated, and exposed to a number of teratogens. Inadequate prenatal care is a great problem. Many young women do not see a doctor regularly. One study found that 30 percent of pregnant teens under seventeen, 22 percent of the seventeen- to nineteen-year-olds, and 18 percent of the older group (twenty- to thirty-year-olds) failed to see a doctor for prenatal care until the third trimester of their pregnancies. About 4 percent of the teens received no prenatal care at all (Hutchins et al., 1979).

8. *True or False:*
Some 70 percent of all birth defects are caused by prenatal insults rather than genetic disorders.

teratogens
Any agent that causes birth defects.

Teenage births have increased greatly. The younger the mother, the more likely it is that she will suffer complications and her infant will show some abnormality (Birch and Gussow, 1970). It is difficult to get the information across to pregnant teens and motivate them to change their health habits.

Another reason for the failure to stem the tide of prenatal insults arises from a biological fact of life. During the first three months of pregnancy, the developing fetus is most sensitive to environmental insult. The systems of the fetus are developing rapidly. As a rule, the system that is developing most rapidly at the time of insult is the one that will be affected by the drug or virus. A **critical period** for the growth and development of specific body systems exists. During this time, the system is most vulnerable to damage. For instance, if a mother contracts rubella (German Measles) in the first four weeks of pregnancy, the chance of the baby's being born with one or more defects is about 50 percent. This drops to about 17 percent in the third month and is much lower after the third month (Rhodes, 1961). There are similar critical periods for some drugs, including thalidomide (Lenz, 1966). But in the earliest months of pregnancy, a woman may not know she is pregnant and may expose her unborn infant to some environmental insult. By the time some women are aware they are pregnant, the critical period may have passed and the damage may already have been done.

In addition, people often choose not to believe facts that run counter to their own day-to-day experiences. Whenever I discuss the dangers inherent in even moderate drinking or smoking, some of my students refuse to believe it. After all, some of their friends were smokers, and their babies turned out healthy. Most drugs or environmental pollutants do not act as radically as thalidomide. They act in tandem with other environmental insults to produce their effects. Thus, the causal linkage is more difficult to discover, and many simply refuse to believe it. Perhaps the best way to see the effects of smoking, some types of pollution, and mild malnutrition on the fetus is to say that these increase the chances that a problem may develop.

Finally, people have difficulty relating events that occur during pregnancy to its outcome. The time lag involved makes the connection difficult.

NEW TRENDS: FOUR IMPORTANT ISSUES

As scientists learn more about the prenatal period, new issues are raised and old issues are perceived differently. Four such issues are especially current: (1) the relationship between the age of the mother and the health of the fetus, (2) maternal nutrition during pregnancy, (3) emotional stress during pregnancy, and (4) the father's responsibilities during pregnancy.

The Age of the Mother

"It wasn't easy to wait," Barbara told me while holding her two-month-old infant. "Everyone was having babies, all my married friends were pregnant, but we decided to wait."

Barbara was thirty-three when her first child was born, and she is part of a growing movement, especially among professionals, to wait before starting a family. The years between twenty and thirty are the safest for childbearing. As a woman ages, the incidence of high blood pressure and delivery complications in-

---

Margin notes:

critical period
The period during which a particular event has its greatest impact.

9. *True or False:*
The number of women bearing children after age thirty-five has decreased in the past decade.

creases (Stevenson, 1973). Later parenting may also present social problems. It may be difficult for parents in their late fifties or sixties to guide adolescents. And the older parent is at a greater risk for personal injury, incapacitating illness, and death. Still, an increasing number of people choose to start their families in their thirties.

Between 1973 and 1978, the number of babies born to mothers age thirty to thirty-four increased 70 percent. An increase of 22 percent occurred for mothers in the thirty-five to thirty-nine age-group (Goldstein, 1980). Although the number of births, 11 in 1,000 for women over thirty, is certainly not large, the trend is unmistakable. These couples normally postpone having children for economic and career reasons. While the physical risks are greater, the availability of modern diagnostic procedures such as amniocentesis and better prenatal care reduces the risk somewhat. For instance, the incidence of Down's Syndrome increases with age, but it can be diagnosed by amniocentesis. If there is no evidence of chronic disease, the outlook for the intelligent mother entering into the world of parenting in her thirties is quite good (Goldstein, 1980).

A dramatic increase in the birth rate for women at the other extreme is more troublesome. Between 1969 and 1979, the childbearing rate decreased for most age-groups. However, the rate for the fifteen- to seventeen-year-old group increased by 21.7 percent (Hutchins et al., 1979). In 1982, some 523,531 infants were born to women below twenty years of age (National Center for Health Statistics, 1984). The age breakdown looks like this:

Many people are beginning their families later in life.

- 18–19 years   332,596
- 15–17 years   181,162
- under 15 years   9,773

More than 1 million adolescents become pregnant every year, and about 60 percent go on to have their babies (Fosburgh, 1977). Women between the ages of twelve and nineteen now account for 21 percent of all births in the United States. Although half are unmarried, 94 percent of these women elect to keep their babies. The formidable social, economic, and familial problems of these young parents will be discussed in detail in Chapter Fourteen.

The pregnant teenager belongs to the highest-risk group both for birth complications and for fetal abnormalities (Fogel, 1984). Adolescent mothers suffer the greatest number of prenatal and postnatal problems. This high rate of complications may be explained by the relationship between adolescent pregnancy and such factors as low socioeconomic status, poor education, and poor health care (Stevenson, 1973).

Hutchins and colleagues (1979) evaluated the outcome of teenage pregnancies at Temple University Hospital between July 1, 1970, and December 31, 1975. During that time, there were more than 4,000 deliveries involving women under twenty years of age. This Philadelphia hospital is located in a depressed socioeconomic area of the city, and more than 40 percent of the deliveries in the hospital were to teenagers. Some 35 percent of these teenage mothers were having second pregnancies. This contradicts the popular notion that having a baby will "teach them a lesson." Teenage mothers are likely to have repeat pregnancies.

Out of fear, ignorance, or the desire to deny the pregnancy, many teens do not seek prenatal care until the last minute. This leads to an increased rate of premature births and fetal deaths. In Hutchins' study, 30 percent of those under seventeen and 22 percent of the seventeen- to nineteen-year-olds did not seek prenatal care until the third trimester. About 4 percent never received any prenatal help. The rate of low-birth-weight babies, as well as the fetal and neonatal mortality rates, was higher than the rate of their twenty- to thirty-four-year-old counterparts.

The combination of youth, poverty, lack of knowledge, poor nutritional habits, poor health care, and lack of motivation to act on warnings is difficult to combat. Teenage pregnancy is part of a larger social and economic problem that must be approached educationally and medically. This may be nowhere more clear than in the case of maternal nutrition.

Maternal Nutrition

Here are a few of the misconceptions about nutrition during pregnancy:

- Eat whatever you want—you're eating for two.
- The baby has first call on all nutrients.
- The more vitamins you take, the better.
- If you are overweight, you should try not to gain any weight during pregnancy.
- There's no reason you can't go on a diet during a normal pregnancy.
- Every baby costs the mother another tooth.
- The brain is the last part of the baby's body to be hurt if the mother is malnourished.

10. *True or False:*
Severe malnutrition during pregnancy leads to a condition in which the infant has fewer brain cells.

Each one of these statements is false, yet many believe them. In the past two decades, there has been renewed interest in maternal nutrition during pregnancy. The finding that chronic malnutrition during the prenatal stage leads to an irreversible condition in which the infant has fewer brain cells—as much as 20 percent fewer than the normal baby (Winick, 1976)—did much to spur the interest. Malnutrition is related to fetal deformities and impaired physical and intellectual development. Mental retardation, low birth weight, cerebral palsy, and increased susceptibility to disease have been traced to malnourishment during pregnancy (Annis, 1978). Infants who were malnourished during the prenatal stage also show abnormal behavioral patterns, such as withdrawal and irritability (Birch, 1971). The significant correlation between nutritional status and prematurity is especially troublesome because extremely underweight infants are at risk for a variety of developmental problems (Ricciuti, 1980).

Although nutrition during pregnancy is crucial to the health of the child, the mother's nutritional history before pregnancy is important too. She may have suffered from nutritional problems that affect her own physical development and health, reducing her ability to bear a healthy child. All these factors—past and present nutritional status, prematurity, and infant mortality—are related to poverty and lack of education. Henry Ricciuti, a noted specialist in this area, states:

> The risk of low birth weight or prematurity is substantially increased in mothers who are relatively young (under 19 years) or old (above 35 years), whose nutritional and growth histories are relatively poor, who have had poor health care, nutrition and weight gain during pregnancy, and who have had a large number of closely spaced pregnancies. Since these risk conditions tend to be more prevalent in poor populations, it is not surprising that in all regions of the world the general incidence of low birth weight is substantially higher in the lowest socio-economic groups (as high as 40 percent of live births in some instances) than in economically and educationally more favored groups (8 percent). (Ricciuti, 1980, p. 4)

The effects of severe malnutrition on the fetus are well established. But what is the effect of lesser degrees of malnutrition on the fetus? Severe malnutrition is rare in the United States, but many American mothers suffer from some form of malnutrition involving vitamin and mineral deficiencies or even protein deficiencies. Such inadequate diets are often found in young pregnant females (Eichorn, 1979).

Specific nutritional inadequacies in the expectant mother do cause certain fetal problems. Lack of iodine leads to physical deformities and mental retardation. Deficiencies in vitamin B_6 are related to convulsions and neurological damage (Dakshinamurti and Stephens, 1969). A vitamin D deficiency leads to skeletal malformations (Rector, 1935). Vitamin A deficiencies are linked to spontaneous abortion and miscarriage, and visual problems. Inadequate supplies of vitamin C cause skeletal deformities (Annis, 1978). Inadequate folic acid intake is related to anemia (Stevenson, 1973). We do not know how much deficiency is required to cause a particular problem. A small deficiency may cause subclinical problems that may reduce the infant's ability in some area, such as in fighting off infection. In addition, nutritional deficiencies may combine with other factors, such as drugs or disease, to produce a fetal abnormality.

This does not mean that pregnant females should go on eating binges (Whitney and Hamilton, 1984). Today, doctors often recommend a weight gain of about 24 pounds, but the recommended weight gain over pregnancy has changed markedly over the years and may do so again. Too much gain is a problem for both mother and infant. The best advice is to eat healthful, nutritious foods and to ask a doctor's opinion on these issues.

Stress During Pregnancy

From the beginning of her pregnancy, Amelia was responsible for the care of her aging parents. Then in her third month her father suffered a stroke that left him partially paralyzed. Her mother died from a massive coronary soon after. Amelia's husband and two young children tried to ease the emotional pain, but her husband's new job required a great deal of traveling, and the children were too young to be of much help. Then the five-year-old fell and broke an arm during Amelia's sixth month of pregnancy.

Amelia was both anxious and depressed for most of her pregnancy. Will Amelia's stressful experiences have any effect on the physical or emotional well-being of her baby? So many factors confound the situation that this is a difficult question to answer. For instance, the depressed and anxious Amelia probably did not eat or sleep well. In addition, the stress may continue after the baby's birth, making it difficult to separate prenatal factors from postnatal factors when deciding what caused a problem.

Some studies have related continuous stress to the birth of infants who are irritable, squirming, and generally more difficult to care for (Stechler and Halton, 1982: Sontag, 1944, 1941). These babies do not feed as well, and they cry more than infants whose mothers have not been under constant stress (Copans, 1974). The mechanism by which stress leads to these problems is not entirely understood. Stress increases the production of hormones, particularly adrenalin, that may cause such reactions. There is also a relationship between anxiety and physical problems in pregnancy. The more stress a woman is under, the greater the chances of complications during pregnancy and delivery (Gorsuch and Key, 1974).

11. *True or False:*
Maternal stress does not affect the fetus because the systems of the mother and the fetus are separate.

The Father's Role

After noting the many maternal behaviors that affect the fetus, students often complain that the child's father seems to get away with everything during the prenatal stage. To some extent this is true, since a father's drinking, drug-taking, and stressful experiences do not directly affect the fetus. If we look a bit deeper, however, his behavior and experiences also affect the pregnancy and the subsequent health of the fetus.

Paternal drug-taking prior to pregnancy may affect the father's genes and in turn directly affect the child. Aside from this, the father's behavior influences the expectant mother's actions. If women heed the warnings about drinking, smoking, and drug-taking, they will increase their chances of giving birth to a healthy child, but if the father is indulging, the mother will find it more difficult to refrain from such behavior. In addition, the mother's need for emotional support places a responsibility on the father's shoulders. He can reduce the stress and anxiety experienced by the mother. A father's willingness to understand the expectant mother's special needs for support and assistance can help her through this unique time in their lives.

THE EXPERIENCE OF PREGNANCY

Pregnancy is a family experience. Both the mother-to-be and the father-to-be are affected by the pregnancy. Although it can be a difficult time for both, personal growth from meeting new challenges can be the result.

The Mother's Experience

"I felt wonderfully alive throughout my pregnancy. When I felt life at about five months, I couldn't believe it was real."

"I was frightened when I began to suspect I was pregnant. For the first time in my life I felt truly vulnerable. As the months went on, the feeling of uneasiness decreased somewhat, but I still did not feel like myself."

"Throughout the entire pregnancy I felt that the dark cloud of gloom was following me around. I had mood swings and would cry so easily, then feel embarrassed."

"I had the normal morning sickness, but that stopped after the third month. I couldn't wait to give birth. It was the most exciting time of my life. It would have been so wonderful if my husband had felt the same way."

Every woman experiences an emotional reaction to her pregnancy. For some, pregnancy is a time of anxiety, for others it is a time of joy. For some women, the annoying negative side effects of pregnancy—including breast tenderness, morning nausea, mood swings, frequent urges to urinate, and sometimes hemorrhoids—are quite troublesome. For others, they do not exist, or are not severe if they do. Some women seem to grow emotionally from the experience, others do not.

The pregnancy experience is a very personal one. Not only will each woman experience her pregnancy differently, but her second pregnancy may not be anything like her first. Such factors as the woman's perception of the physical changes occurring in her body, her capacity to handle the stresses of pregnancy, the family situation (including her relationship with the father of the child), and the psychological meaning the pregnancy has for her all affect how she will react to pregnancy (Williams, 1977).

The physical changes begin immediately after conception. Breasts become tender and enlarged, and the menstrual cycle ceases. The frequency of urination, which will become more obvious during the last trimester, increases. Still, each of these symptoms could be from other causes. For instance, emotional strain or certain medications can lead to a missed period, and frequency of urination might indicate a urinary infection. Confirmation of pregnancy involves a laboratory test in which the woman's urine is tested for the presence of the hormone HCG or human chorionic gonadotropin.

During the last five or six months of pregnancy, the woman's body shape changes dramatically. She may react negatively to this change, feeling insecure about her partner's love, and she may feel vulnerable because of added weight and lack of vigor. On the other hand, she may be proud of her state, and the joy of feeling the baby move at about the fifth month may overwhelm any negative feelings. Mood swings in the pregnant woman may be due to chemical changes in the body, and the need for assurance may be greater than normal.

Does pregnancy cause emotional upheaval in a couple's life? The evidence is contradictory. Some claim that it is a time of emotional instability (Coleman, 1969), others claim that the experience is too individualistic to allow for generalizations (Hooke and Marks, 1963). Leifer (1977) followed nineteen middle-class pregnant women at each trimester of pregnancy, on the third day after birth, and at the two-month and seven-month marks after birth. She utilized extensive interview procedures and psychological tests. The women in her study experienced a good deal of "emotional upheaval." Some of them grew and matured from the experience, others did not. The second group had considerable difficulty coping with their new status and responsibilities. A woman's attitude and adaptation to her pregnancy as early as the third month was predictive of good mothering behavior after birth. Leifer concluded: "Reactions during pregnancy are usually indicative of future mothering behavior and as such may be important diagnostic aids in identifying those women for whom the mother-child interaction is likely to be difficult" (p. 92).

Leifer sees the developmental tasks of pregnancy as acceptance of the fetus and the formation of an emotional attachment. The movements of the baby, called quickening, seemed to evoke powerful maternal feelings. Some of the behaviors associated with pregnancy, such as introversion, increased need for assurance from the baby's father, and reduced interpersonal relations are indications that the mother's attention is focusing on her new role and on developing an emotional attachment to the fetus. Finally, Leifer notes that anxiety during pregnancy is normal. Some women expressed anxiety about the fetus, others seemed preoccupied with their own status. Mothers who were anxious about the health and well-being of their unborn babies were reflecting their emotional attachment to the fetus. Those who were concerned only about their own well-being were very minimally attached to their babies.

Leifer's study leads to two conclusions. First, the pregnant woman's attitude toward and adaptation to the pregnancy can predict future problems. Second, bonding to the infant begins before birth. While each woman may experience pregnancy differently, she must successfully cope with the trials and tribulations of her new state.

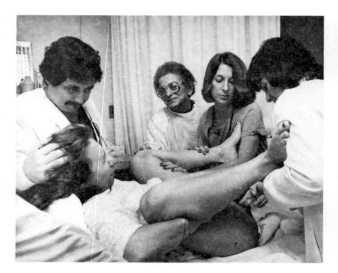 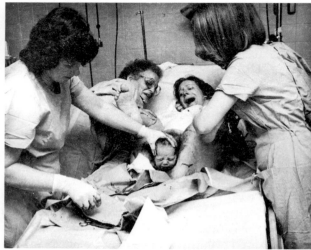

In the delivery of a child, after the cervix is fully dilated the mother is encouraged to push. Normally, the baby's head emerges first, followed by the body. Moments after the birth, the mother has the opportunity to hold her child. Notice that in this case, the woman's husband and mother, as well as a midwife, are attending and that the birth is taking place in a homelike atmosphere.

The Father's Experience

And what of the father? So much has been written about the growing relationship between mother and infant that it seems the infant's father has been neglected. Pregnancy may bring on extra stresses in the father's life as well (Golanty and Harris, 1982). These stresses may cause an expectant father to reach the breaking point, and some evidence points to increasing physical abuse by the father on the mother during pregnancy (Gelles, 1975). Pregnancy may exaggerate already serious marital problems.

The expectant father may experience conflicting feelings: joy at becoming a father and anxiety about the new burdens that being a parent brings. At the same time, he must assure the mother of his love and try to understand her own anxiety and her feelings of vulnerability. Finally, his relationship to the mother undergoes some change, and their lifestyle may be affected both by the pregnancy and later by the new baby.

BIRTH

The process of birth has been shrouded in secrecy. Unlike other societies, young people in the United States have little experience with birth. A century ago, most women gave birth at home, but today the overwhelming majority of births take place in hospitals. It is only recently that films of actual births have been shown on television. A child is likely to develop an attitude of fear rather early from overhearing horror stories about birth complications. Some television programs show labor and birth in the worst light. The dynamics of birth are rarely taught in high school, and young parents may be ignorant of the basic facts surrounding the event.

The Three Stages of the Birth Process

The birth process is divided into three stages (Curtis, 1975). During the first, or **dilation**, stage the uterus contracts and the cervix flattens and dilates in order to

dilation
The first stage in labor, in which the uterus contracts and the cervix flattens and dilates to allow the fetus to pass.

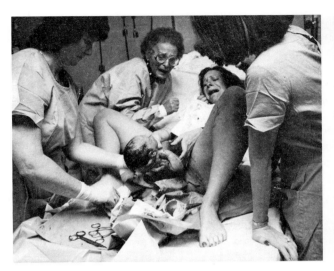
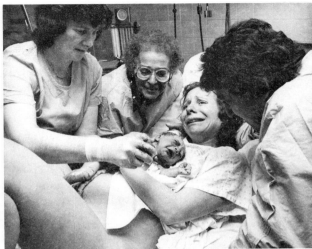

allow the fetus to pass through. The general term **labor** describes this process. This stage can last from about two to sixteen hours, or even longer. It tends to be longer with the first child. When the contractions start, they usually come at approximately 15- to 20-minute intervals and are generally mild. As they continue, they become stronger and more regular. Near the end of this first stage, a change in the nature of the contractions occurs. The contractions become more difficult, last longer, and are more frequent. This period, lasting about an hour, is called **transition** and is the most difficult time of labor for many women (Tucker and Bing, 1975). By the end of this stage, the cervix is open about 10 centimeters, and contractions are occurring every minute or so.

The second stage of birth involves the actual delivery of the baby. This **expulsion** stage is quite variable and can last anywhere from 2 to 60 minutes. The baby's head appears, an event referred to as **crowning** (Rugh and Shettles, 1971). The rest of the body soon follows.

The third stage of the birth process involves the **delivery of the placenta** or afterbirth. During this stage, mild contractions continue for some time. They help reduce the blood flow to the uterus and reduce the uterus to normal size.

Cesarean Birth

If it has been determined that there may be a problem in the birth process, the doctor may advise that the baby be removed surgically through the wall of the abdomen and uterus. This is major surgery that typically involves a longer hospital stay (often five days, as opposed to three or fewer for a vaginal delivery). **Cesarean sections**, as this type of birth is called, have become much more common in the past decades, increasing 300 percent (Gleicher, 1984). Before 1965, Cesarean sections were performed in about 2 to 5 percent of all births. Today the rate approaches 12 to 15 percent, and more in some areas.

A number of explanations for the dramatic increase in Cesarean sections have been advanced. The safety of the operation has improved markedly both for the mother and for the fetus. The fetal mortality rate from Cesareans is less than one-third of that reported in the 1950s (Bottoms et al., 1980). The use of a

labor
A term used to describe the general process of expelling the fetus from the mother's uterus.

transition
A period late in labor in which the contractions become more difficult.

expulsion
The second stage of birth, involving the actual delivery of the fetus.

crowning
The point in labor at which the baby's head appears.

delivery of the placenta
The third and last expulsion stage of birth in which the placenta is delivered.

Cesarean section
The birth procedure by which the fetus is surgically delivered through the abdominal wall and uterus.

12. *True or False:*
Cesarean births have decreased in the past twenty years, as doctors have come to appreciate the medical risks to the mother and child.

fetal monitor
A machine that monitors the condition of the mother and the fetus.

Cesarean section can improve the chances that a fetus in distress will be born healthy and normal. The increase in malpractice suits may also play a part. Today obstetricians have a number of technological aids for diagnosing problems. Most women are monitored from the moment they enter the labor room by machines called **fetal monitors**, which reflect the condition of the fetus (Paul, 1971). For example, babies sometimes have the umbilical cord wrapped around their necks. During labor, the cord is compressed, which can reduce the blood supply to the fetus. Doctors can use the fetal monitor to check the baby's heart rate during and after a contraction and diagnose the problem. From that point, the doctor must use his or her knowledge and experience to determine whether a Cesarean is necessary. Doctors faced with evidence of such a problem may decide to practice a conservative, defensive type of medicine rather than risk a difficult vaginal delivery.

The Effects of Obstetrical Medication

In the United States, obstetrical medication is almost routinely administered to women in labor. Beginning in the 1960s researchers began doubting the wisdom of medicating mother and incidentally the fetus during the delivery (Brackbill, 1982, 1979).

About 95 percent of all deliveries in the United States utilize drugs for control of discomfort during labor. Medicated infants are more sluggish than and not as alert as nonmedicated infants. However, according to a leading critic in this area, Yvonne Brackbill, obstetrical medications cause longer-term problems. These drugs affect development of the child's gross motor abilities, limiting the rate of progress in the areas of sitting, standing, and walking. They retard the development of language and cognitive skills, and these deficits are especially obvious when the tasks are challenging. Brackbill also claims that these drugs make the baby more difficult to comfort when crying. Medicated infants have also been found to eat less and gain less weight than nonmedicated infants.

Brackbill argues that the newborn is less able to deal with these drugs than the adult. The brain of the newborn is still not completely formed and is especially vulnerable. In addition, the liver and kidneys, which are responsible for eliminating drugs from the system, are also immature and not capable of doing this job efficiently. Brackbill (1979) concludes:

1. Drugs administered to mothers during labor have negative effects on the behavior of their babies. No study, she adds, has ever found that drugs are an advantage to the infant.

2. The effects of the drugs on a child appear to be related to dosage.

3. The effects of the drugs on a child's behavior are long-lasting.

4. Medication affects certain areas of a child's behavioral functioning more than others.

5. More research is needed to determine the factors that affect individual susceptibility to the influence of obstetrical drugs. The evidence on such factors as race, socioeconomic status, gender, and other individual factors is still weak and requires further investigation.

While the sluggishness of medicated babies is real and directly related to drug intake, the question of longer-term deficits is controversial. Some studies find few differences in infant behavior due to medication (Stechler and Halton, 1982; Murray et al., 1981), while others argue that there are behavioral differences (Lester et al., 1982).

Obstetrical medication may affect the infant-mother relationship, thereby partially explaining the longer-term effects. Attempts of a mother to stimulate an infant who is less alert and more lethargic may be quite frustrating for both and contribute to problems in the relationship which may continue even after the full effects of the medication have worn off.

The effects of such medication depend on the type of drug, the time of administration (Moya and Thorndike, 1962), the dosage, and a number of individual factors not well understood. Some studies that found no effect of drugs on infants' later behavior used samples that were given light doses of medication (Stechler and Halton, 1982). Perhaps the standard practice should be to limit the dosage and number of drugs used to that required by the individual patient. This is not to say that medication is unnecessary or should be avoided in every case. It may be needed, but it should be tailored specifically to the patient's needs, keeping the developmental welfare of the infant in mind.

A NEW LOOK AT BIRTH: ALTERNATIVE METHODS

Alternative methods of birth are gaining in popularity. These procedures emphasize the importance of the experience for both parents. In the past, parents were robbed of the experience. The mother was medicated, sometimes to the point of oblivion, and she was frequently separated from her infant for quite some time after the birth. Fathers were forced to wait outside and could have no part in the process. Even visitation hours for the family were restricted. But a minor revolution in these procedures has recently occurred. Medical and hospital procedures are gradually changing (see Research Highlight "The Advantages of Rooming-in" on page 109).

The Lamaze method of birth, which was part of the personal experience related below, and the Leboyer method, are but two of a number of alternative methods of birth that parents are choosing.

A Personal Experience

I had attended the six **Lamaze** (prepared childbirth) sessions, but I didn't think I would be too affected emotionally by the birth of the baby. After all, I had seen films of births, so it wouldn't be as new to me as it would to someone who didn't have a background in the field.

Every week my wife and I attended the Lamaze class sessions with a group of ten or eleven other couples. During the sessions, the nurse answered all questions and taught the women methods of relaxation. We were introduced to the process of birth through a film and were taught a number of exercises that could reduce the discomfort of labor. As coaches, the father-to-be was to be responsible for reminding the woman of the techniques, supporting her, and recognizing changes in her condition during labor. The nurse stated repeatedly that women who successfully complete the program usually require less, and sometimes no, medication during labor, but that if it was needed, a woman should ask for it.

Lamaze method
A method of prepared childbirth that requires the active participation of both parents.

The success or failure of the Lamaze system does not hinge on whether the expectant mother could eliminate the need for medication during childbirth. The nurse emphasized preparing both parents to experience a great moment in their lives and to participate actively in the birth. The atmosphere was relaxed.

Upon arriving at the hospital, my wife was examined and admitted. Instead of saying good-bye to her and waiting in a room for hours, I was welcomed into the labor room. As the contractions became stronger, I helped her find a comfortable position and reminded her of the breathing exercises. When she was 7 centimeters dilated, the contractions became stronger and more difficult to deal with. Nurses checked her progress more frequently, and after some long contractions the baby's head began to show.

In the delivery room, the doctor told my wife when to push and when to stop. I stood at her head and watched everything, and a mirror was set up for her to watch too. After a short time, the baby emerged and began to cry. There she was, covered with liquid and still attached to her mother through the long, thick, braided umbilical cord. "You have a round little baby girl," the doctor said, showing us the baby, cutting the cord, and delivering the placenta.

The feelings were difficult to describe. They were both joy and relief, a high that will remain with both of us forever.

The Lamaze Method

13. *True or False:*
The Lamaze method of birth emphasizes the importance of leaving the mother alone to meditate on her experience.

The most popular alternative birthing method was developed by Fernand Lamaze. Lamaze advocated not only the father's presence but also his active participation in the birth process (Lamaze, 1970). Women are taught specific techniques for managing the discomfort, which reduces the need for painkillers. Relaxation techniques, breathing methods for the various stages of labor, and a

In this prepared-childbirth class, both mothers and fathers are getting ready for the experience of the birth of their child, as well as learning how to reduce the discomfort and pain of labor.

RESEARCH HIGHLIGHT   *The Advantages of Rooming-in*

The entire field of childbirth is in the throes of change. Some of the changes are due to technological improvements. *Sonograms*, which use sound waves to produce a picture of the fetus, have largely replaced X rays. The condition of the fetus is closely tracked by fetal monitors.

Change is also apparent in the social and psychological realm. Hospital procedures that once were rigid are being relaxed. It used to be that fathers were not permitted to visit their newborn infants, but now they are encouraged to hold and feed them. Siblings, once forbidden to come near the newborn, are now welcome too. The care of infants in the nursery was formerly left strictly to hospital personnel, but mothers are now encouraged to care for them as much as possible.

Do such changes make any real difference? Is it beneficial to encourage family participation from the beginning? These were two of the questions investigated in a Swedish study.

"Rooming-in" is an increasingly popular alternative that involves placing the newborn in a bassinet at the side of the mother's bed. The mother is encouraged to care for her own infant as much as possible. This is not the standard procedure, for in many hospitals the infant is separated from the mother and kept in a nursery for most of the day.

In the Swedish study (Greenberg et al., 1973), one hundred mothers and their firstborns were randomly assigned to either a rooming-in unit or a conventional unit. The rooming-in group cared for their infants eight hours a day, while the conventional group handled their babies for 20-minute intervals during feeding. The same nurses cared for both the rooming-in and the conventional groups. All infants were fed on a regular schedule.

A questionnaire was administered to women in both groups. The results show that rooming-in does make a difference. The rooming-in mothers judged themselves more competent than the mothers of infants assigned to the conventional group. Fewer rooming-in mothers felt they would need help at home with the care of the child. It is interesting to note that rooming-in mothers were satisfied with the time they had spent with their infants, whereas the mothers in the other group wanted more contact. Mothers in the rooming-in group also appeared to have developed maternal feelings faster than mothers in the conventional group.

There were no differences on a number of variables including how great a responsibility the mothers considered their infant, their anxiety about the caring for the baby, and attitudes toward child-rearing, toilet-training, crying, or feeding.

The researchers concluded that mothers in the rooming-in situation gained self-confidence and competence. Rooming-in mothers felt they could better understand their child's cry, although conventional group mothers thought they could learn to know their child faster. Perhaps, the researchers argue, the conventional group mothers did not know what to expect. In a related experiment, the authors found that mothers in a conventional group were not able to ask relevant questions because they did not know much about their infant's behavior. A certain amount of knowledge is required to ask questions, and the lack of contact led to a lack of familiarity with the infant's behavior.

This study demonstrates that early contact gained through a rooming-in procedure leads to increased levels of self-confidence and competence. The experience of rooming-in familiarizes the mother with the peculiarities of her infant's behavior, allowing her the opportunity to gain enough knowledge to ask intelligent questions. The feeling of confidence and competence is important, especially when the mother leaves the hospital and must shoulder a greater share of the burden of child care. More research is needed to evaluate the effects of other arrangements, but it appears that these new programs may be beneficial to the entire family.

Sources: M. Greenberg, I. Rosenberg, and J. Lind, "First Mothers Rooming-in with Their Newborns: Its Impact upon the Mother," *American Journal of Orthopsychiatry,* 1973, *43,* 783–788.

---

number of other procedures help reduce the discomfort. Finally, the importance of experiencing the birth and of sharing an emotional experience is emphasized.

Lamaze procedures accomplish their goals. They reduce the amount of medication required, and women giving birth using Lamaze techniques report less discomfort and a more positive attitude toward the process (Cogan, 1980). The importance of the father's experience is also substantiated by research. Peterson and colleagues (1979) examined the attitudes of forty-six middle-class Canadian couples planning various delivery methods, from the sixth month of pregnancy to six months following the birth. The father's participation was found to be significantly related to the father's attachment to the infant. The researchers conclude:

> Medical tradition has often posited that the father's attachment is determined prior to the delivery and that the actual birth process has little effect upon the fathers' involvement. This study demonstrates that the father's experience of birth and his behavior towards his spouse and his baby during delivery are more important than the prenatal attitude in determining the father's involvement. Evidence such as this supports a model of behavior based on animal studies which claim that the birth experience acts as a powerful catalyst for nurturing behavior from any observer (p. 337).

The researchers advocate better prenatal education for the father and structuring the birth and home environment to encourage active participation by the father.

The Leboyer Method

Leboyer method
A method of childbirth emphasizing the importance of the birth experience for the child and encouraging such things as dim lights, low voices, delay in cutting the umbilical cord, a bath, and a massage.

The Lamaze method focuses on the needs and experiences of the parents. Another method, formulated by Frederick **Leboyer**, emphasizes the importance of the birth experience for the infant. Leboyer's book *Birth Without Violence* (1975) is not written with the scientific-minded public in mind. It is anything but subtle, and it is not filled with facts, figures, and research studies. Rather, it is an empathic, impassioned plea for treating the infant gently and effecting a smooth transition from life within the womb to life outside.

Leboyer argues that the cries and shrieks of the newborn are not inevitable. They result from a kind of torture, the traumatic removal from a warm, dark,

---

ACTION/
REACTION

Under Pressure

When Lisa discovered she was pregnant, everything seemed perfect. Her husband, Simon, was happy, and both sets of grandparents were thrilled. After reading some articles about childbirth, Lisa mentioned to Simon that she wanted to use the Lamaze method of childbirth to deliver the baby, but Simon was not happy about that. Neither was her mother, who shook her head and said, "After you feel the first labor pain and get to the hospital, have them put you out." Simon's mother was just as direct. "They've been delivering babies in the hospital the regular way for generations with no problems. Why try something new?"

Since Simon doesn't want to be in the labor or delivery room, Lisa asked her best friend, Betty, to be her coach, but Simon saw this as an attack on his manhood, and everyone is pressuring Lisa to change her mind. She is terribly upset and can't sleep.

1. If you were Lisa what would you do? What would you say to Simon and the two mothers?
2. If you were Lisa's friend, how would you advise her?
3. If you were Lisa's doctor, and saw how much pressure she was getting from others, would you step in and make suggestions?

quiet, supporting environment to a cold, bright, noisy one filled with need. He argues that the baby feels everything and truly experiences the birth process, and that what is easiest for the doctor may not be best for the baby. Among other things, Leboyer advocates using dimmed lights and whispering in the delivery room, placing the infant on the mother's abdomen after birth, waiting minutes before cutting the umbilical cord, providing a bath in which the father plays a leading role, and having both parents massage the infant. He also notes the importance of preparation for childbirth.

Leboyer's theories have not been met with overwhelming medical support. Some disagree with specific procedures, such as dimming the lights, but the main difficulty involves the lack of scientific evidence presented by Leboyer and his supporters to demonstrate the practical value of such procedures. His supporters tend to stress the experiential value of the method and construct their cases on the theory that the first moments of life are more important both for parents and for child than was first thought (Berezin, 1980).

Leboyer uses his clinical experiences and theoretical clarity as arguments in favor of his procedures. One study found that babies born by the Leboyer method were physically and behaviorally more advanced than would have been expected (Trotter 1975), but this study has been criticized because it lacked adequate controls.

One excellent study was performed at the McMaster University Medical Centre in Hamilton, Ontario. Women interested in the program were first matched for social class and number of prior pregnancies, then randomly assigned to either a Leboyer group or a non-Leboyer group. Only women who were considered "low risk" were allowed to participate in the experiment. All Leboyer procedures were carefully followed with this group. For the control group, standard medical practices were used. The lighting was not dimmed, the cord was cut within 60 seconds of delivery, and no bath was given. But in both groups, mothers and fathers actively participated in the birth process, and gentle handling, a norm at this hospital, was given to all infants.

The results showed no significant advantages for the Leboyer method. The researchers stated: "The infants born by the Leboyer method were neither more responsive nor less irritable than the control infants during the neonatal period, nor were there any differences in infant temperament or development at eight months of age" (Nelson et al., 1980, p. 659). Mothers' perception of the two deliveries did not differ either. The only reported difference was that "mothers in the Leboyer group were more likely to attribute differences in the behavior of the infants to the delivery experience" (p. 659). The researchers also reported that fears that there would be a greater danger to both infants and mothers were also not supported by the study.

While many hypotheses are offered to account for the lack of significant advantages to this method, the most striking one involves the nature of the control group. In this hospital, even without the use of Leboyer's methods, the delivery and postnatal care was gentle. Hospital procedures encouraged both parental participation and early parent-child interaction. It may well be that the group being compared with the Leboyer sample makes all the difference. Comparing Leboyer babies to a highly medicated, roughly treated, parental-separated sample may be unfair, for hospital procedures are changing in the direction of greater family participation and gentler birth.

On the other hand, the fact that the danger for low-risk mothers and infants appears to be minimal would allow for a greater amount of choice for parents in determining which method of birth to use under normal circumstances.

COMPLICATIONS OF BIRTH

Most pregnancies and deliveries are normal, but sometimes problems do occur. Problems such as anoxia and prematurity may have serious consequences later in childhood.

Anoxia

anoxia
A condition in which the infant does not receive a sufficient supply of oxygen.

Anoxia, a deficiency in the oxygen supply getting to the baby, is the most common cause of brain damage. Such damage may be inflicted either during the birth process or for some time during the prenatal period, when the placenta is detached or infected. Anoxia may lead to a number of birth defects, including cognitive and behavioral problems (Wenar, 1982). Except for the more extreme cases, however, making predictions about the future development of anoxic children is difficult. Some anoxic children compare well with peers who did not suffer any anoxia. Anoxia increases the risk for developmental disability in both cognitive and behavioral areas, but many anoxic children develop normally and show little difference from their peers when they enter school (Wenar, 1982). The quality of care may be most important in staving off possible problems (Sameroff and Chandler, 1975). The better the care, the less likely mildly and moderately anoxic children are to develop these disabilities.

Prematurity: Born at Risk

"She has a head too large by half for her body. With little to flesh them out, her features are skull-tight and wizened. Her arms and legs are no thicker than her mother's fingers. Her ears have no cartilage. Her shoulders and back are covered with lanugo, the fine body hair of the immature fetus, and in her body creases there are smeared traces of the waxy secretion called vernix. Her posture is floppy, and her skin, through which her veins are clearly visible, is as thin and shiny as Saran Wrap" (Fadiman, 1981, p. 47).

This is the way Anne Fadiman described Frances, a 2 pound 10 ounce infant born after a gestation period of only 28 weeks, as opposed to the normal 40. The experience of seeing an infant of this size stays with you. Fifteen or twenty years ago, the outlook for this child was almost hopeless. However, many of these infants will survive today because of improvements in medical care.

prematurity
Any infant weighing less than 5 1/2 pounds or born less than 37 weeks after conception.

small-for-date babies
Infants born below the weight expected for their gestational age.

What Is Prematurity?   **Prematurity** can be defined in terms of birth weight or the length of the gestation period. Currently, a baby weighing less than 2,500 grams (about 5½ pounds) or one who has been born less than 37 weeks after conception is considered premature. Generally, low-birth-weight infants are categorized into two groups. In the first group are infants born below the weight we would expect for their gestational age. Some of these babies are born at their normal term, others are born earlier. These infants are called **small-for-date** babies.

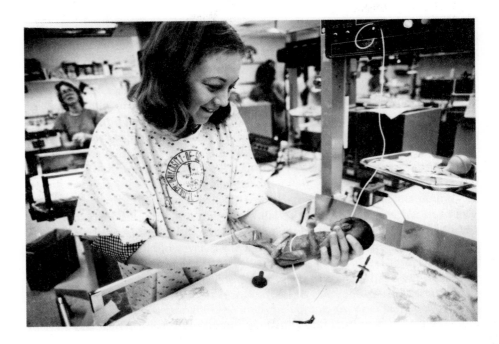

Many premature infants spend their early infancy in the hospital attached to life-sustaining machinery. Today, scientists are concerned with the psychological development as well as the physical development of premature infants.

The other group involves what are called **pre-term** infants, those whose birth weights are appropriate for their gestational age but who are born at 37 or fewer weeks after conception (Kopp and Parmelee, 1979).

pre-term infants
Any infant born before 37 weeks of gestation.

Some authorities use a measure of biological functioning to determine whether an infant is premature (Caputo and Mandell, 1970), others include head circumference and body length in their equation (Fitzgerald et al., 1982). These differences in defining prematurity present problems in evaluating research, because comparisons among different samples chosen using different criteria is difficult. Most of the studies that will be cited here define prematurity in terms of both weight and gestational age (Goldberg, 1978).

The Consequences of Prematurity.   Premature infants are "at risk" for a number of physical and intellectual deficits during childhood (Lawson et al., 1984). Children who are premature are more likely to show intellectual problems and learning difficulties than children who are not premature, and they are more likely later to be in classes for the retarded (Caputo and Mandell, 1970). Such children are also at risk for developing a number of social difficulties, being especially prone to hyperactivity. Many show neurological problems (Drillien, 1964). In addition, premature infants are more likely to die during the first month of life, accounting for about half of all the deaths that occur during this time (Fitzgerald et al., 1982) (see Figure 3.1).

14. *True or False:*
Premature infants today are no more at risk for developmental problems than normal infants.

Although both sexes suffer from being born prematurely, males are more likely to experience learning difficulties and other school-related problems (Davies and Stewart, 1975). And children who were premature are also more likely to be abused by their parents. Although premature infants comprise only about 7 to 10 percent of the total live births in the United States, somewhere between 23 percent and 31 percent of all abused children are premature (Kennell et al., 1979).

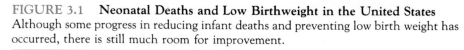

FIGURE 3.1   Neonatal Deaths and Low Birthweight in the United States
Although some progress in reducing infant deaths and preventing low birth weight has occurred, there is still much room for improvement.

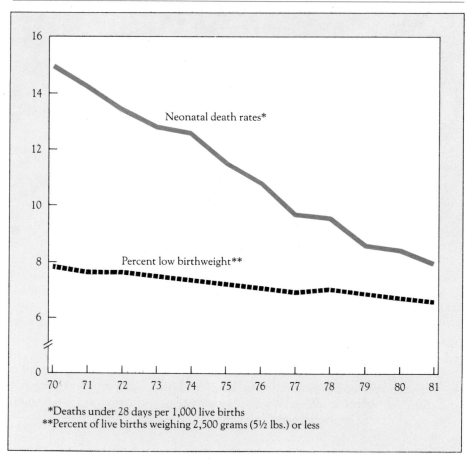

Source: National Center for Health Statistics and state health departments.

The situation is complicated by the fact that not every premature infant suffers these setbacks. Some premature babies grow up to be superior children and to function well as adults. A variety of outcomes are possible, depending on the size and gestational age of the infant and on subsequent care and upbringing. The lower the birth weight and the shorter the gestation period, the more potentially serious are the consequences (deHirsch et al., 1966; Drillien, 1964).

Why are premature infants as a group subject to such risk? First, fetuses that are diseased or have some genetic abnormality are likely to be born early. Second, the premature infant is also likely to be born into a disadvantaged environment (Scarr-Salapatek and Williams, 1973). While prematurity is found in every socioeconomic group, it is far more common in women living in poverty (Birch, 1968).

The Causes of Prematurity. Sometimes the cause of the prematurity is obvious. For instance, the human uterus is designed to carry one fetus at a time. Twins don't always share the food supply equally, and one twin may weigh much less than the twin sibling (Ross Laboratories, 1977). At other times, an illness or disease may bring on labor too early. But often the cause is unknown. A number of factors have been implicated, including the mother's health and nutrition prior to pregnancy, the mother's age, height, and weight, her weight gain during pregnancy, smoking, use of drugs, uterine problems, and lack of prenatal care (Kopp and Parmelee, 1979). These factors correlate with social class. For instance, the poor are less likely to eat a nutritious diet during pregnancy and are much less likely to avail themselves of prenatal care. Their health prior to the pregnancy is also likely to be worse, and the crowded environment is not ideal because the woman is probably exposed to more diseases. It is no wonder that these children are at a double risk. They are more vulnerable at birth and more likely to be exposed to a poor environment afterward.

Helping the Premature Infant Develop. As late as the 1940s and the very early 1950s, premature infants were placed in oxygen-rich environments at cold temperatures and fed a weak formula. The oxygen-rich environment was thought to be necessary to aid breathing, and the light formulas were a reaction to the in-

ACTION/
REACTION

What If Something Happens?

Often the actual reason a child is born prematurely remains a mystery. So it was with Sandy and Bob's baby. Cynthia, born after six and a half months, was given only a small chance of surviving. After a few days in the hospital, Sandy went home. She returned to the hospital each day to feed Cynthia and spend time with her, but Bob refused to see the baby at all. He told Sandy that if the baby died it would be worse for him if he had become attached to her. Sandy felt the same way, but she told Bob it was their responsibility to care for Cynthia. What if she too refused to see the baby? Bob said he would understand, and that if she didn't want to see Cynthia until chances improved, he could respect that. Sandy was very angry at her husband's attitude and behavior.

Now Cynthia is home and apparently will be all right. Bob now shows her a great deal of love, but Sandy is distant with Bob because she is still angry with her husband. "He gave me no help when the baby was in the hospital," she complains. Her estimation of Bob has been reduced. Bob says that he understands Sandy's feelings but that continuing her cool behavior is pointless.

1. If you were Sandy, how would you have dealt with Bob's behavior at the hospital?
2. If you were Sandy, how would you deal with Bob at home?
3. If you were Bob, and felt the same way he did, how would you have dealt with the infant?
4. If you were the pediatrician, would you have intervened?

retrolental fibroplasia
A disorder involving blindness caused by an oversupply of oxygen most often administered to premature infants.

fant's tendency to throw up and develop pneumonia. However, too rich an oxygen supply led to **retrolental fibroplasia**, a disorder that causes blindness. Lack of proper nourishment led to developmental problems, and the lower temperatures probably caused the infant to expend all resources trying to maintain body heat, thus preventing the infant from gaining weight (Kopp and Parmelee, 1979).

In the 1980s the medical situation is different. Improved knowledge of nutrition coupled with effective tube-feeding techniques help the premature infant to thrive. Monitoring of vital signs with sophisticated machinery is now the norm, and general medical care has improved greatly.

While the survival outlook is brighter, however, more effort must be made to improve the child's environment, in order to minimize the developmental problems that are often seen in this population.

Reducing the separation from parents caused by the child's enforced confinement in the hospital is one possibility. After all, the child may remain there for weeks, maybe months, and have little or no contact with the parents. The bond between parent and child is quite important, as we shall see in Chapter Seven, and this limited-contact situation is certainly not conducive to the growth of such a bond (Klaus and Kennell, 1976). To remedy this situation, most hospitals encourage parents to spend time with their premature infants. In addition, since parents may feel anxious or upset by these children, some hospitals provide group discussion sessions for parents to talk about their feelings. Finally, parents require information about the child's special needs.

On a different level, the effects of the deadening, nonstimulating aspects of hospital care must be reduced. A number of studies have shown that extra rocking and tactile stimulation are highly effective in improving the neurological, motor, and psychological development of premature infants. Premature babies given five minutes of stroking by nurses in the hospital (tactile stimulation) were healthier and gained more weight than a similar group not given such stimulation (Solkoff et al., 1969).

15. *True or False:*
Providing the premature infant with extra stimulation leads to hyperactivity.

Parents can be taught to do the same thing. Ruth Rice (1977) trained parents of fifteen premature infants to give each infant a program of tactile stimulation for fifteen minutes four times a day for a month. Another group of premature infants received no such treatment. At four months, each infant was examined by a pediatrician, a psychologist, and a pediatric nurse. None of these professionals had any idea whether the baby had received any tactile stimulation. The results were remarkable. The stimulated infants were superior in mental development, weight gain, and neurological development. Increased tactile, visual, and kinesthetic (movement) stimulation plays a crucial role in helping premature infants develop more normally.

LOOKING FORWARD

The study of prenatal development and birth is both hopeful and most frustrating. We know so much about preventing birth defects, yet every day we observe pregnant women drinking, smoking, eating improperly, and not availing themselves of proper prenatal care. Despite our knowledge of how to minimize the deficits that seem too often to follow the premature infant through life, relatively few hospitals have excellent postnatal wards where the child's total needs are taken into account. And while teenagers are giving birth at alarming rates, little effort is expended to teach these young parents about the special needs of their infants (Counseling and Personnel Services Clearinghouse, 1982). We have some of the answers to our problems, but improving programs to serve the needs of families during this important time of their lives is expensive. We pay for these failures in the years to come, since problems that develop at this stage often lead to psychological, social, and medical problems later in life that force their attention on us. Professionals who decry our efforts in the area of prenatal and perinatal education and medical attention are supported by figures showing that a number of other developed countries have lower infant mortality rates than the United States (see Table 3.3).

But what does all this mean to Margaret and Tim, the expectant couple introduced at the beginning of the chapter? Increasing knowledge allows them to make important decisions during pregnancy about what to avoid. Although there are no guarantees that their baby will be born healthy, they now have the information necessary to improve their chances of having a healthy infant. They are also more aware of alternative methods of birth and the choices available to them.

The average full-term infant weighs about 7½ pounds and is 20 inches long. Boys tend to be slightly longer and heavier than girls. Infants come into the world more ready for life than was first thought, and we shall turn to the newborn's capabilities and needs in Chapter Five. But before we deal with questions of how the infant develops physically, emotionally, socially, and intellectually, we must take a detour. Human development takes on a new significance when we become aware of the various approaches to viewing development that are available today. It is to these approaches that we turn next.

TABLE 3.3

Comparison of Infant Death Rates per 1,000 Live Births in Selected Developed Countries

As this table shows, a number of other developed countries have lower infant mortality rates than the United States.

Country	Rate
Sweden	7.0
Japan	7.1
Netherlands	8.2
Denmark	8.4*
Switzerland	9.1*
Canada	9.6
France	9.6
Austrailia	10.0
Spain	10.3
Federal Republic of Germany	11.6
New Zealand	11.7
United States	11.7
United Kingdom	12.0*
German Democratic Republic	12.3
Austria	12.6

*1980 Rate

Source: United Nations Statistical Office, 1981.

Chapter Summary

1. Fertilization occurs when a sperm cell penetrates an egg cell. Monozygotic, or identical, twins develop from a single fertilized egg. Fraternal, or dizygotic, twins form when two egg cells are fertilized by two sperm cells.

2. The germinal stage lasts from conception until about two weeks. During this stage, the fertilized egg travels down the fallopian tube and embeds itself in the womb. The embryonic stage lasts from two to eight weeks. During this time, the heart starts to beat and 95 percent of the body systems are present. During the fetal stage, from two months until birth, the developing organism continues to develop internally and put on weight.

3. A number of environmental factors may adversely affect development, including drug-taking, pollution, radiation, and various diseases.

4. Thalidomide was once prescribed to relieve the symptoms of morning sickness. It produced many deformities. Diethylstilbestrol (DES) was prescribed for women who had histories of miscarriages. Although the infants were born healthy, some female offspring developed cancer of the cervix and showed structural abnormalities.

5. Smoking has been linked to low-birth-weight babies and possibly to learning disabilities, prematurity, and cleft palate. The children of alcoholics suffer from fetal alcohol

syndrome, a condition of retardation and physical defects. Even moderate drinking may cause some fetal abnormality. The combination of smoking and drinking is especially dangerous.

6. The babies of heroin addicts are born addicted and must go through life-threatening withdrawal.

7. Various diseases, such as rubella, gonorrhea, and herpes, cause fetal abnormalities.

8. The Rh factor is a particular red-blood-cell antigen. When the mother is Rh negative and the father is Rh positive, the offspring may be Rh positive and problems may arise. Antigens from the mother may pass through the placenta and kill red blood cells in the fetus. Today, women with such problems receive a shot of RhoGAM, which blocks the creation of the antibodies.

9. Many women use some kind of drug during their pregnancy. Most birth defects are caused by prenatal insults rather than genetic diseases. Many women expose their unborn children to danger because they do not understand the danger, do not believe the warnings, do not realize they are pregnant at the time, or have difficulty motivating themselves to stop a potentially dangerous activity.

10. A critical period is the time at which an event has its greatest impact. Some teratogens are more dangerous at some times than others.

11. More women over thirty are having children. Although the risk is greater for both mother and baby, good prenatal care can reduce the risk somewhat. The birthrate for adolescents has increased. Many pregnant teens do not get proper prenatal care, are exposed to many teratogens, and may suffer from malnutrition. The risk factor is very high for this group.

12. Serious malnutrition can lead to fewer fetal brain cells. Specific vitamin and mineral deficiencies may lead to fetal deformities. The effects of mild and moderate malnutrition are controversial but malnutrition may serve to weaken the fetus.

13. Maternal stress has been linked to babies who are irritable as well as to obstetrical problems.

14. During the first stage of birth, the uterus contracts and the cervix dilates. The infant is delivered in the second stage and the placenta during the third.

15. Cesarean births have increased greatly during the past fifteen years, due to improvements in safety, new technological aids allowing doctors to know sooner if something is wrong, and the tendency for doctors to practice defensive medicine.

16. Babies who are medicated are sluggish and not very alert. The long-term effects of obstetrical medication are controversial at the present time.

17. The Lamaze method of prepared childbirth emphasizes the importance of both parents' participation in the birth process. Relaxation is used to reduce discomfort, and usually less medication is required.

18. The Leboyer method emphasizes the importance of the infant's experience. It involves delivering the child with dimmed lights and whispers, placing the infant on the mother's abdomen, waiting minutes before cutting the umbilical cord, and bathing and massaging the infant.

19. A premature infant is one who weighs less than 5½ pounds or who has spent less than 37 weeks in the womb. Infants born below the weight expected for their gestational age are small-for-date babies. Preterm infants are those whose birth weights are appropriate for their gestational age but who are born at or before 37 weeks. The cause of most cases of prematurity is unknown. Prematurity is related to infant mortality and intellectual, neurological, and developmental disabilities.

20. The premature infant has special needs, and parents must learn to cope with these greater demands. Studies show that extra stimulation reduces the possibility that the infant will develop a disability.

■ *Answers to True or False Questions*

1. *True.* The rate is constant across cultures, at about 4 pairs of twins per 1,000 pregnancies.

2. *True.* The heart is the first organ to function during the prenatal period.

3. *True.* The fetus is capable of a number of behaviors, including sucking a thumb.

4. *True.* On the average, male newborns weigh more than females.

5. *False.* Girls are more neurologically advanced at birth than boys.

6. *False.* Correct statement: Smoking is linked to lower-birth-weight infants.

7. *False.* Correct statement: An Rh disorder is not caused by alcohol consumption.

8. *True.* An infant is more likely to suffer a prenatal insult than to be the victim of a genetic disorder.

9. *False.* Correct statement: The number of women bearing children in this age-group has increased.

10. *True.* Severe malnutrition may lead to an abnormally low number of brain cells.

11. *False.* Correct statement: Maternal stress is linked to irritable infant and obstetrical problems.

12. *False.* Correct statement: The number of Cesarean sections has increased markedly.

13. *False.* Correct statement: The Lamaze method encourages the father to participate actively in the birth of the child.

14. *False.* Correct statement: Despite improvements in medical care, the premature baby is still at a greater risk for developmental problems than the normal infant.

15. *False.* Correct statement: Providing the premature infant with carefully planned extra stimulation increases the chances that the infant will develop normally.

CHAPTER FOUR

Perspectives on Development

■ *Are the Following Statements True or False?*

Try the True-False Quiz below. See if your answers correspond to the information in this chapter. Each question is repeated opposite the paragraph in which the answer can be found. The True-False Answer Box at the end of the chapter lists complete answers.

___ **1.** Theories are neither right or wrong, just useful.

___ **2.** Good theories can describe, but cannot predict future events.

___ **3.** The stage of cognitive development a child is negotiating is accurately determined by considering the child's chronological age.

___ **4.** Through careful observation, the sequence of stages leading from sitting to walking to running can be discovered.

___ **5.** Freud emphasized the importance of the parent-child interaction to a child's later behavior.

___ **6.** It is difficult to perform experimental studies in order to validate Freud's theories.

___ **7.** It is dangerous for a small and vulnerable toddler to develop a sense of autonomy.

___ **8.** Child development specialists are impressed by the similarity between children's thinking and adults' thinking.

___ **9.** All psychologists agree that children develop in stages.

___ **10.** In an attempt to understand how we solve problems, psychologists often equate the human mind with the computer.

___ **11.** Psychologists who use learning theory to explain children's behavior emphasize the importance of thinking and consciousness.

THE CASE OF JOHN BAKER

John Baker's problems came to the attention of the school psychologist after students apprehended for extorting money from their classmates identified him as the brains behind the scam. School officials were not surprised, for John had been a problem for quite a while.

Now that he is in sixth grade, John's tendency to disturb the class and his lack of academic progress have become more serious. They can no longer be attributed to immaturity. Quiet when the teacher is looking, John misbehaves when the teacher's attention is elsewhere. He always appears to be angry. Smaller than his peers, he rarely participates in fights, but often instigates them. He also taunts the girls in the class, and once he threw a tremendous tantrum when asked to sit beside Nancy, a classmate. Nonetheless, he has not been involved in any serious misdeed—until now.

John performed poorly on readiness tests before starting school, and his reading has been well below average since first grade. Though his teacher believes he is bright, John's progress in other subjects has also been marginal. He lags behind his classmates in reading, writing, and math. He lacks confidence in his work, and occasionally throws it away before the teacher can correct it.

During a conference with the school psychologist, his mother noted that John had walked and talked late but was "never any trouble" at home. John's father, a plastics salesman, admitted disappointment in his son, noting he may have expected too much from him too soon. He tries to motivate John to achieve, but often loses his temper.

John is the youngest of three children. His mother's face lit up as she described her older son as a "genius." His sister, an average student, excels in athletics.

John's parents have caught him lying a number of times. He always takes the easy way out, and his father's efforts at instilling morals have had little effect. Once a cashier gave the boy an extra five dollars in change. When his father asked him to return it, John shrugged, saying it was the cashier's bad luck and that he needed the money to buy a record album. When questioned about his relationship with his parents, John told the psychologist he loved his mother but felt nothing toward his father. He vehemently denied any anger, although he clenched his fists when speaking of his father.

John's parents and teachers have a number of questions. How did John's problems develop? How can they help him? What will the future bring?

THEORETICAL PERSPECTIVES ON CHILD DEVELOPMENT

Why Bother with Theory?

Many students react to the word *theory* with a groan. A student once told me, "We want the facts, not a bunch of theorizing." It's unfortunate that theory has such a bad reputation, for it is the most useful aspect of psychology. Without a theoretical perspective, data cannot be interpreted. Theory gives facts their meaning (Arndt, 1974).

Imagine that you have access to a computerized data base of research findings in child development. You ask for data on intellectual (cognitive) development. The computer spews out thousands of pages of data from study after study.

How do you know which studies are germane to your questions? How do you pull the information together to make it intelligible? To give cohesiveness to this voluminous data, you adopt a theory (Thomas, 1979).

A theory can help us relate one fact to another. Asked to determine who has behaved worse—Larry, who broke four dishes while helping to clear off the table, or Howard, who broke two dishes while trying to sneak an extra cookie—most five-year-olds respond, "Larry." Because young children do not take intent into consideration when judging an action, they see Larry's actions as worse because he broke more dishes (Piaget, 1932). Children who are eight or nine years old begin to factor intent into the equation and say Howard's actions were worse. To understand this developmental progression fully, you need a theory that relates the phenomenon at one age to behavior at another age.

Theory can be of practical help as well. Imagine a mother at the end of her patience. Her five-year-old twins are complaining because one claims that the other's glass contains more soda than her cup. The mother has demonstrated that the cup and the glass contain the same amount of liquid, but the twins continue to fight. Later, they argue over which piece of clay is bigger—the one shaped like a ball or the one flattened to look like a worm—even though she has shown them that both have the same amount of clay. The mother wants to know if this constant bickering will ever end. (See page 410 for a discussion of this problem.) By relating earlier behavior to later actions and one behavior to another, theory can help explain why the twins continue to fight.

Theory is also useful in formulating the right questions. Proponents of the various theoretical perspectives ask different questions about the same behavior. A behaviorist, for example, would be interested in discovering the rewards and punishments in John Baker's environment. A social-learning theorist might look for the models in John's life. A psychoanalytic theorist, a follower of Sigmund Freud, might look at the unconscious forces that impel behavior and find them in John's early relationship with his parents. Maturationally oriented psychologists might try to understand how John's growth and rate of development have affected his actions. Each theorist seeks to understand why John acts the way he does, but each approaches the problem differently.

Good Theory—Bad Theory

How can we tell a good theory from a bad one? Although authorities differ on the number and importance of specific criteria for a good theory, some of the most important are usefulness, testability, predictability, and inclusiveness.

Usefulness. Theories are not right or wrong; they are only useful. The best theory is the one that is most useful in understanding and making predictions about the phenomenon in which you are interested. No single theory explains every aspect of child development. Some theories explain some areas better than others, and some theories are aimed at particular areas of interest.

For instance, Lawrence Kohlberg has spent many years investigating the reasoning behind moral decisions. He presents subjects with moral dilemmas—complex situations that involve conflicting values and goals—and asks them for their opinions. Kohlberg has constructed an elaborate sequence of stages that describe the development of moral reasoning (see page 469). The more specific a theory,

1. *True or False:*
Theories are neither right or wrong, just useful.

the more limited its application. Thus, while Kohlberg's theory may be useful in looking at the moral decisions an individual makes, it would not be useful in understanding unconscious psychological motives.

The usefulness of a theory is partly determined by the developmental phenomenon we are investigating. When a new theory becomes more useful in understanding and predicting phenomena, it should replace an older one. This does occur, but only rarely, because a new theory is seldom more useful in every way. It is more common that both remain.

Testability.   Ideally, a theory is testable. Researchers should be able to perform experiments that test its hypotheses. This seems simple enough, but this requirement can create quite a problem. Certain theories are less easily tested than others. The psychoanalytic or Freudian theory, for example, is difficult to test experimentally (Sarnoff, 1971).

2. *True or False:*
Good theories can describe, but cannot predict future events.

Predictability.   Good theories can be used both to understand present events and to predict future behavior. Think for a moment about the twins' complaining over who got the most soda. One of the mother's first questions was, "When would they ever stop?" A good theory would predict the point in the twins' development when they would be able to understand that the cup and the glass could hold the same amount of soda.

Inclusiveness.   A theory should be as inclusive as possible. No single theory explains all the concerns of development, but, a theory formulated to help us understand cognitive or social development should answer as many related questions as possible.

Other Criteria.   A number of other criteria may be used. For instance, a good theory is economical, that is, it introduces as few new terms and concepts as possible and is clear and concise. Finally, good theories tend to spark a great deal of valuable research and give people in the field a new slant on a particular issue.

Theoretical Approaches

The theoretical approaches to explaining child behavior and development differ in a number of ways. Some emphasize maturation, others stress the importance of learning. Some see development as occurring in stages, others view development as more continuous. Stage theories are popular in developmental psychology, and most share certain similarities.

3. *True or False:*
The stage of cognitive development a child is negotiating is accurately determined by considering the child's chronological age.

Stage theories present development in terms of age-related periods in which children are faced with particular problems and have specific abilities. Each child progresses through the same stages and cannot skip a stage, but children may enter or leave a particular stage at different times, so it is incorrect to simply equate ages and stages. The ages that will be given throughout the text are nothing more than averages and guides and should not be thought of as absolutes.

In this chapter a number of theories will be discussed and their strengths and weaknesses noted. We will also look at how each perspective can contribute to our understanding of John Baker's behavior, as described at the beginning of this chapter.

GESELL'S MATURATIONAL PERSPECTIVE

If you carefully filmed the progress of children from the moment they were born, you would find that each child progresses through the same sequence of stages. Children sit before they walk and walk before they run. Children negotiate these and other developmental steps at their own individual rates. But we can predict what will happen next. Human beings seem to be genetically programmed to develop according to a particular pattern.

Gesell's Growth Gradients

Arnold Gesell and his colleagues were so impressed with this sequential format that they based an entire theory of development on it. Gesell emphasized the importance of the maturational process in determining growth and development. He understood that the environment could affect behavior, but he believed that most normal environments merely allowed genetically programmed behavior to proceed in an orderly fashion (Gesell, 1954; Gesell and Ilg, 1949).

Francis Ilg and Louise Bates Ames, who worked with Gesell and took over the directorship of the Gesell Institute after his death, wrote: "Our observations of child behavior have led us to believe that almost any kind of behavior you can think of (eating, sleeping, talking, moving about, getting on with other people, even thinking about religion or understanding such complicated things as time and space) develops by means of remarkably patterned and largely predictable stages" (Ilg and Ames, 1955, p. 3).

In one study, Gesell presented infants with a paper and crayon and studied what they did with these items at various ages. He noted: "At 36 weeks the initial response may be to the paper. The infant fingers it, picks it up, grabs it grossly, or slaps it. Rarely is the activity confined to the paper. Characteristically he picks up the crayon and puts it immediately into his mouth. He may mouth without further manipulation. Any marking of the paper which may occur is apparently adventitious" (Gesell et al., 1934, p. 213). Gesell also observed the infants' behavior at 40 weeks, 44 weeks, and so on, and carefully described the results. Such observation makes it possible to understand the sequence through which a child develops the ability to work with paper and crayon.

By combining observations of many activities, we can get a picture of the "average" child at a particular age. For example, Gesell's colleagues described two-and-a-half-year-olds as "rigid and inflexible." This is a stage where children want exactly what they want when they want it. A two-and-a-half-year-old cannot adapt, give in, wait awhile. Everything must be done just so. For any domestic routine, there is a rigid sequence of events that the child wants to follow in exactly the same manner (Ilg and Ames, 1955).

Some ages are easier than others. Periods of equilibrium are followed by periods of disequilibrium. This leads to the prescription that parents gnashing their teeth at the frustrating behavior of a two-and-a-half-year-old be patient. Their child is only going through a stage.

Gesell's theory can help us understand some of John Baker's problems. John had been slow to develop, and his father tried to push him to perform. Because John wasn't ready for many of the skills his parents wanted to teach him, he failed at them. This produced a pattern of failure at home that carried over to

It is a mistake to equate age with stage. These two children are about the same age, yet one may be developmentally ahead of the other.

4. *True or False:*
Through careful observation, the sequence of stages leading from sitting to walking to running can be discovered.

school. In fact, John's lack of readiness to attend school may have led to his in-ability to read. Perhaps things would have been different if his parents had un-derstood and appreciated his individual rate of maturation.

Application and Value

Gesell's focus on maturation as a fundamental element in explaining behavior has considerable value. His appreciation of the unfolding of the genetic blue-print, of individual rates of maturation, and of the concept of readiness have achieved some acceptance. His excellent use of observations and original use of photography are valuable methodological advances. Finally, psychologists have accepted some of his principles of growth, which will be discussed in Chapter Five.

Criticisms and Cautions

Some of Gesell's ideas have not been accepted. Gesell did much of his work dur-ing a time when researchers were only just beginning to appreciate the impor-tance and subtleties of the environment. As a result, he attributed only a small influence to the environment, and nothing at all to formal training. His extreme maturationalist view has been rejected by many, as has its consequence—waiting for a child to leave the stage. This wait may lead to a lack of action where some is required. John, for example, clearly requires intervention, and has for some time.

Gesell's work also has some methodological and sampling problems. Since he believed that all human beings develop according to their maturational ten-dencies, Gesell felt that it made little difference which youngsters were studied. As a result, he has been criticized for focusing mostly on middle-class children in New England.

FREUD'S PSYCHOANALYTIC THEORY

Gesell was a physician as well as a psychologist. His theory has a genetic, biologi-cal slant. Another physician whose theories have affected the course of develop-mental psychology is Sigmund Freud, the founder of psychoanalysis.

Levels of Consciousness

Have you ever been unaware of the reasons behind your actions? Have you ever taken an instant dislike to someone without any apparent reason? Have you ever made a slip of the tongue, an error in which an embarrassing word or phrase slipped out in place of the more conventionally acceptable one? If your answer to any of these questions is yes, you may have experienced the unconscious in action.

Sigmund Freud (1933, 1923, 1900) posited three levels of awareness. The **conscious** involves one's immediate awareness and comprises only a small por-tion of the total mind. The **preconscious** comprises memories that can easily be-come conscious. For example, you may remember the correct answers to the questions on the exam only after the test is over (Kline, 1972). Finally, some

conscious
Freudian term for thoughts or memories of which a person is immediately aware.

preconscious
Freudian term for thoughts or memories that although not immediately conscious can easily become so.

memories are stored in the **unconscious**—the portion of the mind that is beyond normal awareness. Motives may arise from here. The unconscious shows itself in many ways, for instance, through dreams and slips of the tongue.

Freud's insistence that we may not be aware of our true motives and wishes, probably because their gratification is forbidden by society, was criticized by many when Freud suggested it (Eidelberg, 1968). If a child who is angry at mother kicks a younger sibling, a situation referred to as **displacement**, the child may refuse to admit to feelings of hostility toward his mother. The child is not lying, but is probably unaware of those feelings.

The Constructs of the Mind

Freud explained the workings of the mind using three constructs (Freud, 1940, 1923)—the id, the ego, and the superego. The **id** is the source of all wishes and desires. It is unconscious and exists at birth. The id wants what it wants when it wants it and cannot tolerate delay. It functions through the **primary process**, which entails instant gratification for every wish and desire. The infant is, in this sense, complete id.

Within the first year, the **ego** comes into being. Some needs, such as hunger, can be satisfied only by interacting with the real world. The ego, which is partly conscious, operates through the **secondary** or **reality process**. It is responsible for dealing with reality and satisfying the needs and desires of the id in a socially appropriate manner. Whereas the id knows only its subjective reality (I want), the ego must also understand the world outside the mind and the self (Hall and Lindzey, 1957). As the child grows and matures, the ego becomes stronger, being able to delay gratification and balance the desires of the id with the restraints of the third construct, the superego.

The **superego** is analogous to one's conscience. It contains a set of principles gathered from interacting with others in society and serves as an internal gyroscope. The superego compares your behavior to your **ego ideal**, that is, what you think you should be like. The superego is perfectionistic, seeking to inhibit the id's antisocial desires and causing an individual to experience guilt when transgressing, or even considering a misdeed. The ego must mediate between the strictures of the superego and the desires of the id. Tension may arise from the pull of the id, the nature of society's prohibitions, and the weight of superego restraint. Life is a compromise, and proper adjustment is a matter of maintaining a delicate balance.

People whose ids are in control and who have not developed a sufficiently strong ego may not be able to delay gratification or restrain their activities. We see this in young children who have little or no ability to wait for attention or food. An individual who has failed to adequately develop a superego may not act in an ethical manner. John Baker does not appear to have a solid superego or a strong ego. He is unable to delay gratification.

Defense Mechanisms

The ego has a difficult job. Sometimes it is overwhelmed, and the tension that results is experienced as anxiety. If the anxiety becomes too great, the ego may defend itself by using a large number of protective maneuvers called defense mecha-

unconscious
Freudian term for memories that lie beyond normal awareness.

displacement
The process by which an emotion is transferred from one object or person to another more acceptable substitute.

id
The portion of the mind in Freudian theory which serves as the depository for wishes and desires.

primary process
The process by which the id seeks to gratify its desires.

ego
The part of the mind in Freudian theory which mediates between the real world and the desires of the id.

secondary or reality process
The process by which the ego satisfies the organism's needs in a socially appropriate manner.

superego
The part of the mind in Freudian theory which includes a set of principles, violation of which leads to feelings of guilt.

ego ideal
The individual's positive and desirable standards of conduct.

defense mechanism
An automatic and unconscious process that reduces or eliminates feelings of anxiety or emotional conflict.

repression
A defense mechanism in which memories are barred from consciousness.

nisms. A **defense mechanism** is an automatic and unconscious process that serves to relieve or reduce feelings of anxiety or emotional conflict (Laughlin, 1970). One of the most prominent defense mechanisms is repression (Brenner, 1955). In **repression**, some memory is "barred" from consciousness and no longer directly bothers us. Laughlin (1970) describes the case of a five-year-old girl who was asked to look after her two-year-old sister. She became bored with the assignment and went to play with some friends. The two-year-old walked across the road, down to a bay, and drowned. The five-year-old experienced tremendous feelings of guilt, but after a while she no longer talked about or even seemed to remember the tragedy, a state of mind encouraged by her family. She had repressed the entire event. There are many other defense mechanisms, which are described in Table 4.1.

The Psychosexual Stages

One of the most challenging Freudian concepts is that of infantile and childhood sexuality, the idea that infants and children experience sexual feelings (Noam et al., 1982). However, Freud did not believe that young children experienced *adult* sexual feelings. His idea of sexuality resembles what we might consider sensuality and pleasure. Freud saw life as the unfolding of the sexual instinct. This sexual instinct is called **eros**, and the energy emanating from it is known as the **libido**. The libido attaches itself to different portions of the body as the child grows and matures. This is the basis for Freud's **psychosexual stages**. Freud stressed the importance of early experience in the formation of behavior and focused attention on parent-child interactions.

eros
In Freudian theory, the positive, constructive sex instinct.

libido
In Freudian theory, the energy emanating from the sex instinct.

psychosexual stages
Stages in Freud's developmental theory.

oral stage
The first psychosexual stage, in which sexuality is centered on the oral cavity.

The Oral Stage.   At birth, the infant's oral cavity (the mouth) is well developed. Infants gain pleasure through sucking and then later biting, which are both oral activities. During the **oral stage**, the child's needs for oral experiences take precedence over all others. But this time, children's oral activities are restricted by parents when they bite someone or spit, and they encounter authority in the form of their parents' demands (DiCaprio, 1983). If a child is either frustrated or overly stimulated, the child may become fixated, that is, a part of the child remains in a previous stage of psychosexual development, and development is partially arrested (Eidelberg, 1968). But this does not mean that a child does not progress to the next step. Rather, the child's *personality* shows some characteristic of this fixation. According to Freud, fixation at this stage, if it involves sucking, may lead to gullibility, accepting anything that is presented (Hall and Lindzey, 1957), being dependent and inactive, and believing that others will provide the comforts of life for him (Kline, 1972). Freud also noted an increase in such oral activities as eating and drinking in orally fixated individuals. Fixation at the biting stage may result in a sarcastic or "biting" personality that is always in conflict with others.

Freud, then, views various childhood experiences as predetermining a number of personality traits. According to him, it is not genetics or even maturation that causes the development of these traits, but rather problems in the early interaction between the child and, at least in the oral stage, the child's mother. Nowhere is this so noticeable as in the next stage, the anal stage.

5. *True or False:*
Freud emphasized the importance of the parent-child interaction to a child's later behavior.

TABLE 4.1 Defense Mechanisms

Defense mechanisms are used to reduce or eliminate unpleasant feelings such as anxiety or emotional conflict. This table shows some of the more prominent mechanisms.

Defense Mechanism	Description	Example
Rationalization	Making up plausible, but inaccurate, excuses to explain some behavior.	A student who is getting poor grades in school explains it away by telling you, "It's what you learn, not your grades, that are important" or, "Schools teach nothing useful anyway"
Denial	A person refuses to believe something has occurred.	A child refuses to believe that his dog has died.
Compensation	Making up for a real or imaginary deficiency by placing effort into a similar area (direct compensation) or into a different area (indirect compensation).	An unathletic child who feels physically inferior may buy body-building equipment and work out until he is a first-class weight lifter (direct compensation), or place his efforts into schoolwork to become the best student he can (indirect compensation).
Reaction Formation	An individual experiences feelings that are unacceptable so he or she acts in the exact opposite manner.	A junior high school girl who likes a boy may act very rude or even hit him to prove to her friends that she doesn't really like him.
Projection	Feelings that are unacceptable to oneself are transferred to someone else.	A child who feels angry at his mother for not driving him to the ball game asks her, "Why are you angry at me?" instead of telling her that he is angry at her.
Regression	Returning to a time in life which was more comfortable.	A three-year-old boy who is talking and toilet-trained begins to talk baby talk and wet his pants after his baby brother is brought home from the hospital.
Repression	Memories are barred from consciousness so that they no longer bother a person.	A child who accidently struck another with his bat during a baseball game cannot remember the incident.
Displacement	The transfer of feelings from one person or object to another.	A child is angry at his father but yells at his brother.
Rechannelization (Sublimation)	Unacceptable impulses are rechanneled into socially appropriate pursuits.	An aggressive child learns to express himself through sports or music.

Freud argued that early interaction between child and parent was very important in determining the course of development.

anal stage
The second psychosexual stage, in which sexuality is centered on the anal cavity.

The Anal Stage.   At about eighteen months of age, the muscles responsible for elimination mature to the extent where some control is possible. The libido becomes attached to the anal cavity from that age to about three, and this coincides with attempts to toilet train the child.

The **anal stage** can be divided into the anal expulsion and the anal retentive substages. In the first substage, the child gains pleasure from expelling the body's waste products. In the second, gratification is obtained from withholding them. If the parents create a situation in which a power struggle rages over bowel and bladder control, an anal retentive character may arise. In that case, the child will gain satisfaction from holding back feces and be likely to have such character traits as miserliness, obstinacy, and incredible orderliness and neatness. If, on the other hand, the child relents and gives feces, especially at inappropriate times, the anal expulsive traits such as cruelty and messiness result. Again, according to Freud's theory, childhood experiences predetermine later personality traits.

phallic stage
The third psychosexual stage, in which sexuality is centered on the genital areas.

The Phallic Stage.   At about the age of four, the libido becomes attached to the genital organs: the penis in males and the clitoris in females. There is no difference in the development of males or females in the oral or anal stages (Deutsch, 1945), but beginning in this **phallic stage**, the experiences of boys and girls differ greatly.

According to Freud, the young male experiences sexual feelings toward his mother and desires to possess her sexually. His father is a rival for the mother's affections, and he desires to rid himself of the father. Freud called this the **Oedipal complex**. The child's sexual attachment to his mother is defined by exclusivity and jealousy (Mullahy, 1948). At the same time, the child realizes that he is at a great disadvantage in competing with the father because of the differences in size and fears that his father will discover his desires and castrate him. He experiences **castration anxiety**. The young boy resolves this dilemma of wanting mother but fearing father's retribution by identifying with father and repressing—burying—these feelings toward his mother deeply in his unconscious.

In the case of the female, the situation is more complicated, and Freud admitted there was an insufficient amount of knowledge on this subject (Mullahy, 1948). Nevertheless, he did posit a type of Oedipal situation (often called the **Electra complex**) for young girls. The young girl is first attached to her mother, but she turns her affection and attention to her father when she realizes that she does not have a penis. She blames her mother for this situation and desires to take her mother's place in her father's affection. This gives rise to "penis envy" and a desire to possess the male organ. Since castration is no threat to her, the resolution of the Electra complex is not as important or severe as in males. Instead of simply repressing her feelings toward her mother, a girl identifies with her mother and continues to build on the relationship she established before the phallic stage (Chodorow, 1981).

Problems in the phallic stage lead to a variety of disturbances in personality. For example, when the resolution of the Oedipal conflict is not positive, a boy will resent his father and generalize this resentment to authority figures later in life (Nye, 1975). A number of sexual problems also date from difficulties in the phallic stage.

The Latency Stage.   The phallic stage ends with the resolution of the Oedipal situation. The child then enters the **latency stage**. From about six up to puberty, the child's sexuality lies dormant. Since a boy has identified with his father, he tends to imitate him at every turn. Some of the antismoking campaigns use this fact in an attempt to encourage fathers to stop smoking. Boys have also repressed their feelings toward their mothers, but since they are so young, this repression generalizes to all females. Thus, eight-year-old boys are likely to stay apart from eight-year-old girls. The sexes appear to segregate, and boys play with boys and girls with girls. This can be seen in John Baker's case, as he refused to have anything to do with the girls in his class and often teased them.

Realizing that the resolution of the Electra complex is less abrupt in females, we would expect much less of this behavior with girls. Girls do show this aversion to boys, but usually on a much less intense level. In addition, whereas boys of this age often do not like physical contact with their mothers, girls are not likely to show this type of conduct as often.

The Genital Stage.   The emergence of puberty, with its hormonal changes and sexual arousal, throws the child out of the latency stage into the **genital stage**. The young adolescent boy turns his attention to a girlfriend, while the young adolescent female seeks a boyfriend. This is the beginning of mature adult sexuality.

Oedipal complex
The conflict during the phallic stage in which a boy experiences sexual feelings toward his mother and wishes to do away with his father.

castration anxiety
A male's fear of castration, usually used to indicate a boy's anxiety during the phallic stage.

Electra complex
In Freudian theory, the female equivalent to the Oedipal complex, in which the female experiences sexual feelings toward her father and wishes to do away with her mother.

latency stage
The psychosexual phase in which sexuality is dormant.

genital stage
The final psychosexual stage, occurring during adolescence, in which adult heterosexual behavior develops.

Application and Value

Child development specialists differ greatly on the value of psychoanalytic theory to the understanding of children's behavior, but certain aspects of Freud's theory offer useful insights. Freud's emphasis on the importance of the early interaction between parent and child has been largely accepted by psychologists. He felt that injuries during the early stages left indelible marks on children, but today we have a more flexible view that allows for subsequent experience to ease the negative effects of poor early experiences. In addition, Freud's theory presented the development of the child in a stage setting that has become very popular. Some of Freud's ideas concerning the unconscious have been of great interest as well, and his description of defense mechanisms has allowed psychologists to obtain new understandings of what were in the past incomprehensible behaviors. Freud's idea that sexuality begins early in life is also challenging. Even though many of his disciples disagreed with the emphasis he placed on sexuality, we owe Freud gratitude for raising the issue of childhood sexuality at a time when such ideas were unacceptable. Finally, Freud's theory has served as a focal point for criticism and as a basis for the development of other theories.

A psychoanalytic theorist would see John Baker's problems as reflecting his disturbed relationships with his parents. John's denial of his feelings toward his father appears to be an example of repression.

Criticisms and Cautions

6. *True or False:*
It is difficult to perform experimental studies in order to validate Freud's theories.

Psychoanalytic theory was formulated on the basis of Freud's clinical experiences (Cairns, 1983). His patients were troubled, and psychoanalytic theory may have more to say about abnormal development than normal development. It may be a mistake to base our ideas concerning normal development and child-rearing on clinical experiences with emotionally troubled people. In addition, Freud's formulations are difficult to test empirically. Some of his concepts, such as instinct and psychic energy, are vaguely or even poorly defined, and none is defined in a manner that would make testing easy (Baldwin, 1967). Finally, Freud's emphasis on sexuality may have grown out of the society in which he lived. Sexuality was frowned on in Vienna at that time, and the idea that sexuality is sinful and unhealthy may have been the cause of many of the problems Freud treated. His ideas may not be as universal as he thought.

ERIKSON'S PSYCHOSOCIAL THEORY

epigenetic principle
The preset developmental plan in Erikson's theory consisting of two elements: that personality develops according to maturationally determined steps and that each society is structured to encourage challenges that arise during these times.

Although accepting some of his concepts, a number of Freud's followers, have rejected others. Freud's emphasis on sexuality has troubled many, as has his lack of consideration for the effect cultural differences may have on the child's development. Of all Freud's followers, Erik Erikson has had the greatest influence on the study of child development. Erikson (1968, 1963) argued that human beings develop according to a preset plan called the **epigenetic principle**. This principle consists of two main elements. First, personality develops according to predetermined steps that are maturationally set. Second, society is structured so as to invite and encourage the challenges that arise at these particular times.

The Psychosocial Stages

According to Erikson, each individual proceeds through eight stages of development from cradle to grave (Table 4.2). Each stage presents the individual with a crisis. If a particular crisis is handled well, a positive outcome ensues. If it is not handled well, the resulting outcome is negative. Few people emerge from a particular stage with an entirely positive or negative outcome. In fact, Erikson argues that a healthy balance must be struck between the two poles. However, the outcome should tend toward the positive side of the scale. Although people can reexperience these crises during a life change, by and large the crises take place at particular times in life. The resolution of one stage lays the foundation for negotiating the challenges of the next stage.

TABLE 4.2   Erikson's Eight Stages of Psychosocial Development
According to Erik Erikson, we negotiate new challenges at each stage of life.

	Psychosocial Stage	*Task or Crisis*	*Social Conditions*	*Psychosocial Outcome*
Stage 1 (birth to 1 year)	Oral-sensory (infancy)	Can I trust the world?	Support, provision of basic needs, continuity	Trust
			Lack of support, deprivation, inconsistency	Distrust
Stage 2 (2 to 3 years)	Muscular-anal (toddler)	Can I control my own behavior?	Judicious permissiveness, support	Autonomy
			Overprotection, lack of support, lack of confidence	Doubt
Stage 3 (4 to 5 years)	Locomotor-genital (early childhood)	Can I become independent of my parents and explore my limits?	Encouragement, opportunity	Initiative
			Lack of opportunity, negative feelings	Guilt
Stage 4 (6 to 11 years)	Latency (middle childhood)	Can I master the skills necessary to survive and adapt?	Adequate training, sufficient education, good models	Industry
			Poor training, lack of direction and support	Inferiority
Stage 5 (12 to 18 years)	Puberty and adolescence	Who am I? What are my beliefs, feelings, and attitudes?	Internal stability and continuity, well-defined sex models, and positive feedback	Identity
			Confusion of purpose, unclear feedback, ill-defined expectations	Role confusion
Stage 6 (young adulthood)	Young adulthood	Can I give fully of myself to another?	Warmth, understanding, trust	Intimacy
			Loneliness, ostracism	Isolation
Stage 7 (adulthood)	Adulthood	What can I offer succeeding generations?	Purposefulness, productivity	Generativity
			Lack of enrichment, regression	Stagnation
Stage 8 (maturity)	Maturity	Have I found contentment and satisfaction through my life's work and play?	Sense of closure, unity, direction	Ego-integrity
			Lack of completeness, dissatisfaction	Despair

Source: Adapted from Erik Erikson, *Childhood and society,* New York: Norton, 1950.

Erik Erikson noted the importance of a child's gaining a sense of trust early in life. A warm, supporting environment enables the child to develop a sense of trust, which is the positive outcome of the first psychosocial stage.

trust vs. mistrust
Erikson's first psychosocial stage, in which the positive outcome is a sense of trust while the negative outcome is a sense of suspicion.

7. *True or False:*
It is dangerous for a small and vulnerable toddler to develop a sense of autonomy.

autonomy vs. shame or doubt
The second psychosocial stage, in which the positive outcome is a sense of independence, and the negative outcome is a sense of doubt about being a separate individual.

initiative vs. guilt
The third psychosocial stage, in which the positive outcome is a positive view of one's own desires and actions, the negative outcome a sense of guilt over one's actions.

Trust vs. Mistrust: Stage 1.   The positive outcome of the stage of infancy is a sense of **trust**. If children are cared for in a warm, caring manner, they are apt to trust the environment and develop a feeling that they live among friends. If the parents are anxious, angry, or incapable of meeting a child's needs, the child may develop a sense of **mistrust**. Trust is the cornerstone of the child's attitude toward life.

Autonomy vs. Shame or Doubt: Stage 2.   Two- and three-year-olds are no longer completely dependent on adults. Toddlers practice their new physical skills and develop a positive sense of **autonomy**. They learn that they are someone on their own. If children of this age are either not allowed to do the things they can do, or are pushed into doing something for which they are not ready, they may develop a sense of **shame or doubt** about their own abilities and fail to develop self-confidence. Parents do not help children acquire a sense of autonomy by allowing them to do everything for themselves. Rather, encouraging children to do what they *can* do is the key to their developing a sense of autonomy.

Initiative vs. Guilt: Stage 3.   By the time children reach about four years of age, they can begin to formulate a plan of action and carry it through. The positive outcome of this stage is a sense of **initiative**, a sense that one's desires and actions are basically sound. If parents encourage children of this age to form their own ideas, the children will develop a sense of initiative. If a child is punished for expressing his or her own desires and plans, the child develops a sense of **guilt**, which leads to fear and a lack of assertiveness.

Industry vs. Inferiority: Stage 4.   During the middle years of childhood, children must learn the academic skills of reading, writing, and math, as well as a variety of social skills. At this point, children are required to learn the skills society considers necessary for their future. If a child succeeds in aquiring these new skills and the accomplishments are valued by others, the child develops a sense of **industry** and has a positive view of the achievements. But children who are constantly compared with others and come up a distinct second may develop a sense of **inferiority**. If a child's cultural, religious, or racial group is considered inferior, a sense of personal inferiority may also develop.

John Baker is experiencing this psychosocial crisis in school. His work is not up to par, and he throws away his assignments rather than handing them in. John expects to fail, and he is developing a sense of inferiority regarding his work. His parents continue to compare him with his more gifted or talented siblings, and again he suffers in the comparison.

Identity vs. Role Confusion: Stage 5.   During adolescence, children must decide on their vocational and personal future and develop a sense of who they are and where they belong. The adolescent who develops a solid sense of **identity** formulates a satisfying plan and gains a sense of security. Adolescents who do not develop this sense of identity may develop **role confusion**, a sense of aimlessness and being adrift without an anchor or plan.

Intimacy vs. Isolation: Stage 6.   In young adulthood, the psychosocial crisis involves attainment of **intimacy**. Intimacy requires a sense of identity, because identities are shared in marriage. Although marriage is not the only vehicle for achieving intimacy, most people in this age-group do marry. An individual who is fearful or opts not to enter into very close interpersonal relationships may develop a sense of **isolation**, of being alienated from society, essentially lonely and alone.

Generativity vs. Stagnation: Stage 7.   By middle age, most people have set routines, and they can easily become **stagnated**, absorbed only with their own needs and comforts. This negative outcome may be avoided by giving oneself to the community and to the younger generation. Helping other people is a means of remaining productive and achieving the positive outcome of **generativity**.

Integrity vs. Despair: Stage 8.   The last psychosocial stage, that of old age, revolves around integrity and despair. Older people must cope with the death of others, increasing illness, and their own approaching end. Yet if they can look back with pride at a life of accomplishment, they can develop a positive sense of ego **integrity**. If, on the other hand, all they see is missed opportunities, they may become depressed and bitter, developing a sense of **despair**.

Socialization, Culture, and History

Erikson broadened Freud's conception of growth and development by stressing the importance of socialization, culture, and history. The resolution of each crisis depends on a person's interaction with their culture. The search for identity is different for an American than for a South Sea Islander. In our society, industry, the positive outcome of middle childhood, is somewhat dependent on formal school achievement. This is not true in other cultures. Erikson also noted the importance of the historical period in which people live (Erikson, 1975). Each gen-

industry vs. inferiority
The fourth psychosocial stage, in which the positive outcome is a sense of confidence concerning one's accomplishments, while the negative outcome is a sense of inadequacy concerning one's achievements.

identity vs. role confusion
The fifth psychosocial stage, in which the positive outcome is a sense of knowing who one is, while the negative outcome is a sense of purposelessness.

intimacy vs. isolation
The sixth psychosocial stage, occurring during young adulthood, in which the positive outcome is a development of deep interpersonal relationships, while the negative outcome is a flight from close relationships.

generativity vs. stagnation
The seventh psychosocial stage, occurring during middle adulthood, in which the positive outcome is a sense of giving to others, while the negative outcome is a self-absorption and stagnation.

integrity vs. despair
The eighth and last psychosocial stage, occurring during old age, in which the positive outcome is a sense of satisfaction with one's life while the negative outcome is a sense of bitterness concerning lost opportunities.

eration is raised under different social, political, and technological circumstances. Erikson has applied his theories to many great historical personalities, including Martin Luther and Gandhi (Erikson, 1969, 1958).

Application and Value

Erikson's theory, which is clear and easy to understand, serves as an excellent introduction to the general concerns of people at different ages. His emphasis on the importance of culture, socialization, and the historical moment extends our view of the factors that influence children. Erikson sees psychosocial development as continuing throughout life rather than stopping at adolescence. Finally, Erikson's conception of identity has become a cornerstone for understanding adolescence.

Criticisms and Cautions

Criticisms of Erikson's theory follow the criticisms of Freud's theory. Erikson's theory is difficult to test experimentally. Some support for Erikson's concept of identity exists (Hjelle and Ziegler, 1975), but little research has been done on the other stages. In addition, Erikson's theory is rather general and global, and some authorities doubt the existence of all of his stages (Thomas, 1979). Despite these criticisms, Erikson's theory offers a convenient way of viewing development throughout the life span.

PIAGET'S THEORY OF COGNITIVE DEVELOPMENT

■ Fill two glasses equally with water and ask a five-year-old to confirm that each glass has the same amount of water. Then pour the water from one of the glasses into a wider, more squat container, perhaps a cup. Now ask the child which container has the greater amount of liquid in it. The child will probably tell you that the glass contains more.

■ Sit a six-year-old at a small table with some object in the middle. Sit at the other end of the table and ask the child to draw it from your point of view—the way it appears to you. You may find that the child is incapable of doing this correctly.

■ Draw a picture of a group of flowers,—perhaps three tulips and two lilies. Ask the young child whether there are more flowers than tulips or more tulips than flowers. The child may say that there are more tulips than flowers.

Children are not little adults. They think and deal with problems differently. Jean Piaget devoted a great deal of his adult life to studying the ways in which children think and develop their notions of time, space, mathematics, and reality. Much of his work is sweeping and monumental in scope, and at this point it is the most complete theory of **cognitive development** available today.

Basic Concepts in Piaget's Theory

For most people, knowledge is a set of facts or concepts that an individual has been taught. This rather static view of knowledge allows only for adding more

8. *True or False:*
Child development specialists are impressed by the similarity between children's thinking and adults' thinking.

cognitive development
A general term denoting intellectual development.

Jean Piaget conducted research by presenting children of varying ages with problems to solve, noting how they approached them and the nature of their mistakes.

facts to our storehouse. To Piaget, knowledge is equated with action. As Thomas (1979, p. 292) notes, "To know something means to act on that thing, with the action being either physical, mental or both." An infant's knowledge of a toy hammer consists of the physical manipulation of that object. As the infant grows, the child uses the hammer in qualitatively different ways and talks about its use to others.

Factors in Development.   According to Piaget, development involves the continuous alteration and reorganization of the ways in which we deal with the environment (Piaget, 1970). Development is defined by four principal factors: maturation, experience, social transmission, and the process of equilibration. We have already discussed *maturation*, the gradual unfolding of our genetic plan for

equilibration
In Piagetian theory, the process by which children seek a balance between what they know and what they are experiencing.

life. *Experience* involves the active interaction of the child with the environment. *Social transmission* refers to the information and customs that are transmitted from parents and other people in the environment to the child. We can consider this the educational function in the broad sense. Finally, the process of **equilibration** defines development. Children seek a balance between what they know and what they are experiencing. When they are faced with information that calls for a new and different analysis or activity, children enter a state of disequilibrium. When this occurs, they change their way of dealing with the event or experience, and a new, more stable stage of equilibrium is established. In this way, children progress from a very limited ability to deal with new experiences to a more mature, sophisticated level of cognitive functioning.

Sequence of Development.   Piaget's theory emphasizes the importance of the interaction between the child and the environment. Children are no simple, passive receivers of stimulation. They deal actively with the world. Their active experiences impel them to new heights in cognitive functioning and action. Formal learning is only one of the factors involved in development, and Piaget deemphasizes it.

Piaget's research was aimed at discovering how a child's interactions with the environment change over the years. Piaget was interested in the development of children's conceptions of such things as numbers, space, time, movement, and speed. He discovered a sequence of development that ranged from inability to understand the concept at all to a complete and accurate understanding of the concept.

For instance, Piaget investigated the development of a child's understanding of a one-to-one correspondence between glasses and bottles (Piaget, 1952). This understanding is important in learning mathematics. Piaget placed six small toy bottles and a set of glasses on a tray. He arranged the bottles and glasses in different ways, asking children of different ages whether there were more glasses than bottles and other such questions. During the first stage, there is no understanding of exact correspondence. When confronted with four bottles placed very close to each other and six glasses spread out far apart so that their row is longer, the child believes that rearranging the glasses to make the same length as the bottles will produce equivalence. Thus, any understanding of one-to-one correspondence is global and tentative. The child makes a global comparison based on spatial evaluation of the length of rows rather than on a true mathematical comparison. Stage two is a transitional stage. Here the child can understand the one-to-one correspondence easily if the bottles and glasses are placed opposite one another. However, the stage two child still confuses the physical length of the rows with the one-to-one correspondence. The child can understand the correspondence only when the glasses and bottles are visually equal in spacing. When they are not, the child loses the ability to make such a correspondence. Stage two children, even if they verbally tell you there are six glasses and six bottles, still depend in the final analysis on their visual processing of the situation. In this transitional stage, children can perform the correspondence task, but they are easily tripped up by changes in the situation. In stage three the child can now understand and accept the one-to-one correspondence even if the spacing of the items is changed.

Throughout Piaget's works there are numerous examples of such developmental sequences. As the child matures and is allowed to interact with the environment, the child progresses from a less mature stage to one that is more mature. The changes in the child's ability to perform a one-to-one correspondence are qualitative.

Schemes.   Watch a three-year-old try to pick up a block. The child easily uses thumb and fingers, examines the block, and places it on top of another block. The blocks are combined in a primitive way to form a building. It is easy to forget the tortuous steps that led to this behavior. Hand the block to an infant, and the infant places it in the mouth. Infants explore the environment in their own way by sucking on it. Sucking is an example of what Piaget calls a **scheme**.

The concept of scheme is difficult to define (Flavell, 1977) but relatively easy to understand. When the infant places a block in the mouth and sucks on it, the sucking scheme is being used. A scheme is a "property of an action that can be generalized to other contents" (Phillips, 1975). The infant places many things in the mouth using this scheme. Other infant schemes include looking, listening, grasping, hitting, and pushing (Flavell, 1977). Schemes are tools for learning about the world. They become more sophisticated as a child matures and new schemes are developed. For example, an infant presented with a block may first use the sucking scheme, but later the child may look at the block and bang it against the side of the crib. Gradually the child learns to coordinate the schemes, finally being able to pick the block up, examine it, and place it on top of another (a building scheme).

Adaptation.   Every being must adapt to its environment in order to survive (Phillips, 1975). Adaptation can be understood in terms of adjustment. As the forces in the environment change, so must the individual's ability to deal with them. Adaptation involves two processes that complement each other—assimilation and accommodation.

Assimilation refers to the "taking-in process, whether of sensation, nourishment, or experience. It is the process by which one incorporates things, people, ideas, customs and tastes into one's own activity" (Pulaski, 1980, p. 9). In other words, when we assimilate something, we alter the form of information to adapt it to our already existing actions or structures (Brainerd, 1978). For example, if a child sees an odd-shaped piece of paper and uses it as a paper airplane, the child has assimilated the paper into the child's structure and knowledge of an airplane. You could say that the child has incorporated it into his or her already existing idea of an airplane. A child may bang a rattle against the side of the crib, but when given another toy, perhaps a plastic block, the child will assimilate it by banging it against the crib as well.

Accommodation involves "modifying existing schemes to satisfy the requirements of a new experience" (Salkind, 1981, p. 191). When we accommodate, we create new schemes or modify old ones (Brainerd, 1978). For example, a child may be very good at using a one-handed pickup scheme, that is, lifting an item with one hand, but when faced with a heavier item, the child has to accommodate, that is, use a two-handed pickup scheme.

Assimilation and accommodation work together. Suppose you are riding in a car with a young child and she points to a large Cadillac automobile and says "Car." "That's right," you remark as you continue driving. She then spots an old, rusty Volkswagen beetle and says "Car." You are suitably impressed. After all, even though the Cadillac and Volkswagen are noticeably different, the child un-

scheme
A method of dealing with the environment which can be generalized to many situations.

assimilation
The process by which information is altered to fit into one's already existent structure.

accommodation
The process by which one's existing structures are altered to fit new information.

TABLE 4.3   **Highlights of Piaget's Stages of Development**
According to Jean Piaget, children progress through four stages in their cognitive development—sensorimotor, preoperational, concrete operational, and formal operational (column one). The indented material under the sensorimotor stage represents the six substages of the first stage of cognitive development. The second column indicates the type of behavior commonly found in children negotiating a particular stage, while the third column notes activities that can optimize the child's cognitive development. Remember, the ages are simply guidelines, and are not absolute.

Stage	*Child's Activity*	*Adult's Activity*
Sensorimotor (birth to 2 years)		
Reflex activity (birth to 1 month)	Refines innate responses	Respond to and stimulate the child's senses (sight, sound, taste, touch, and smell)
Primary circular reaction (1 to 4 months)	Repeats and refines actions which once occurred by chance	Stimulate the senses through objects the child can interact with—rattles, bells, or mobiles
Secondary circular reactions (4 to 10 months)	Manipulates objects Repeats actions by choice Develops object permanence	Provide toys to handle with various shapes, textures, and colors Partially hide a toy while child watches
Coordination of secondary schemata (10 to 12 months)	Combines previous activities for new results Imitation begins	Provide toys: familiar dolls, balls, or boxes Encourage imitation
Tertiary circular reactions (12 to 18 months)	Experiments with objects to discover new uses Locates an object with eyes and tracks it	Provide experience with water, sand, textures Include toys which can be manipulated to turn, nest, roll, open, or close

derstood that they were both cars—an example of assimilation. As you drive on, the child points to a large truck and says "Car." You correct her, saying, "No, that is a truck." After a while the child points out a few more examples of trucks. She has accommodated. Now she has separated her conception of car from that of truck. The child then sees a van. She may put it in either category, or even ask you what it is. In this way, using assimilation and accommodation, the child begins to understand her world.

A nonverbal example of how assimilation and accommodation work together can be seen in an infant investigating a rattle. The child may try to assimilate the rattle by using the old sucking scheme, but he or she must also accommodate the mouth to the size of the rattle. Pulaski (1980) notes that when an infant begins to understand that there are objects that can go in the mouth and are suckable but not swallowable, the child begins to divide objects into the edible and nonedible. With experience and a timely "no" from a parent, this scheme will be further defined so that the child will not place anything in the mouth that is not food.

Stage	*Child's Activity*	*Adult's Activity*
Invention through mental combination (18 to 24 months)	Practices deferred imitation Applies old skills in new situations	Provide opportunities to apply old skills to new experiences Provide peer contact and interaction
Preoperational (2 to 7 years)	Language appears Imaginative player, deferred imitation, egocentrism prevalent Can complete simple operations, but cannot explain why	Provide dolls, cars, blocks, crayons, paste, paper, scissors, books, musical instruments, etc. Communicate at child's level or above Provide experience with liquid, mass, and length informally Encourage decision making (red shirt or yellow, apple or orange, bath before dinner or after)
Concrete operational (7 to 11 years)	Applies simple logic to arrive at conclusions Reasons deductively Performs simple operations with physical objects Conserves	Provide opportunity to pursue areas of interest Use questions to understand child's reasoning processes but do not question too much
Formal operational (11 to 15 years)	Reasons abstractly Solves problems through inductive reasoning Employs logical thought	Propose hypothetical problems for the child to solve Discuss ethical questions Encourage personal decision making and problem solving

Source: J. Thibault and J. McKee, 1982.

The Stages of Cognitive Development

Piaget argued that children's cognitive development can be viewed as occurring in a sequence of four stages (see Table 4.3). Each of these stages represents a qualitative advance in a child's ability to solve problems and understand the world. The most common example is that of **conservation**. Earlier it was suggested that you present a five-year-old with equally filled glasses and pour the contents of one of them into a squat cup. The average five-year-old who is in an earlier stage of cognitive development will say that the taller glass contains more liquid. The child fails to understand that water is conserved even if it is transferred to another container. The average nine-year-old in a more advanced stage has no trouble with this problem.

The Sensorimotor Stage.   Between birth and about two years of age, infants progress through the **sensorimotor stage**. They investigate their world using the senses (sight, hearing, etc.) and motor activity. They develop **object permanence**—the understanding that objects and people do not disappear merely

conservation
The knowledge that quantities remain the same, despite changes in their appearance.

sensorimotor stage
The first stage in Piaget's theory of cognitive development, in which the child discovers the world using the senses and motor activity.

object permanence
The knowledge that objects exist even if they are outside one's field of vision.

because they are out of sight. For instance, when a parent leaves the room an infant is likely to cry. Young infants may believe that the parent has disappeared. Reappearance of the mother or father brings joy and relief. Object permanence is also seen in the child's ability to search for some object (Flavell, 1977). The child's abilities in this stage are limited by an inability to use language or symbols—things that stand for other things. Children must experience everything directly through their senses and through feedback from motor activities.

The Preoperational Stage.   From about age two through age seven, children negotiate the lengthy **preoperational stage**. Now the child can use one thing to represent another, for instance, a piece of wood may symbolize a boat. The child's emerging use of symbolism shows itself in expanding language abilities. Language allows children to go beyond direct experience, opening up a new and expanded world. There are a number of limitations in this stage, though. Children cannot understand conservation problems, and they believe that inanimate objects are alive. This animism is responsible for some of the charm children of this age have. Stuffed animals may have a life of their own, and when one is so old that the stuffing has come out, a youngster may insist on a funeral and burial. The preoperational child is also **egocentric**, believing that each person sees the situation just the way the child does. If a parent is tired or not feeling well, little Kevin may bring him a favorite toy. He doesn't understand that daddy or mommy would rather have some peace and quiet and the evening newspaper.

The Concrete Operational Stage.   From age seven to about twelve, children progress through the stage of **concrete operations**. In this stage, many of the preoperational deficiencies are slowly overcome, and children develop the ability to conserve. They gradually become less egocentric. The child in the stage of concrete operations has difficulty with abstract terms, such as *freedom* or *liberty*. Things are understood concretely and literally. A saying like "You can lead a horse to water, but you can't make him drink" is often met with a questionable frown, and political cartoons mean nothing. In short, children in this stage understand the world on a concrete, tangible level.

The Formal Operational Stage.   During adolescence, children enter the stage of **formal operations**. They now develop the ability to test hypotheses in a mature, scientific manner and can understand and communicate their positions on complex ethical issues that demand an ability to use abstractions.

Application and Value

Piaget's basic ideas are very influential in American preschools. His explorations into the way children develop their concepts of time, space, and math, for example, show that children see the world differently from the way adults do. Parents and teachers must understand children's thought processes in order to serve the needs of youngsters better.

Piaget deemphasized formal learning in his theories, stressing maturation and experience as the foremost factors in cognitive development. This translates into some practical conclusions. For example, Piaget advocates elaborating on concepts that children already know rather than accelerating their progress. If a child seems to understand addition, the next step is to use the skill in as many

---

preoperational stage
The second stage in Piaget's theory of cognitive development, during which children cannot understand logical concepts such as conservation.

egocentric
A term used to describe a preschooler's tendency to believe everyone is experiencing the environment the same way that the child is.

concrete operations
The third stage in Piaget's theory of cognitive development, in which the child develops the ability to conserve and becomes less egocentric.

formal operations
The fourth and last stage in Piaget's theory of cognitive development, in which the adolescent develops the ability to deal with abstractions and engage in scientific logic.

Dealing with the Stubborn Child

Lee is an active, engaging two-and-a-half-year-old. He has a mind of his own and a good vocabulary to go along with it. Both his mother, Sharon, and his father, Will, are keenly aware of the importance of providing a stimulating atmosphere for Lee. Both play with him a great deal, but lately Will has been saying that the child is ready for bigger and better things. Will is trying to teach him such concepts as "in" and "out" and "up" and "down," as well as some of the letter sounds. Some number concepts are included in the lessons, as is the concept of grouping things into categories (squares and triangles, for example).

According to Will, however, Lee is "stubborn." He refuses to work even for a short period of time with his parents. He seems to give the wrong answers on purpose. Will believes that Lee knows the right answers but for some reason just won't try. Sharon has read a few books on child development and thinks that things would be better if Lee is left alone to play as he wishes. She tells Will, "Piaget says to leave the child alone."

1. If Will asked your opinion of his teaching strategies and approaches, how would you respond?
2. If you were a psychologist, how would you respond to Sharon's ideas about cognitive development?

ways as possible. Too many people are interested in accelerating cognitive development, asking the question "How fast?" rather than the Piagetian question of "How well?"

Piaget was not very interested in formal teaching strategies, but some educators have applied Piagetian concepts to schools (Furth and Wachs, 1975). For example, Yelon and Weinstein (1977) note six implications of Piaget's theories for teachers. These include using Piagetian tasks to determine the intellectual level of students, teaching students with their cognitive level in mind, remembering that children's thought processes are different from those of adults, being careful to sequence instruction carefully, testing children to find the results of teaching, and encouraging social interaction to facilitate learning. Of these implications, two require some explanation.

First, Piaget stresses the importance of understanding sequences. If teachers understand the sequence of development for a particular concept, such as one-to-one correspondence, they can elaborate on what the child knows, allowing the child to practice and preparing the youngster to move to the next level. Second, Piaget's methods of testing children were unique. He presented children with tasks at various stages of development and noted the mistakes they made. Their approach to the problem demonstrated their cognitive level.

Piaget's emphasis on the active, searching mind of the child has fascinated many. His theory implies that children should be encouraged to discover and to experience, that they are not mere passive receivers of stimulation. They both initiate action and react to stimuli in the environment. They are both shaped by and actively shape their own environment.

Piaget's theories can tell us something about the view of the world that John Baker has. John's development was slow, and his parents did not take his individual rate of progress into consideration. If John's teachers had understood where he was, they might have elaborated on what he could do instead of forcing him to progress at a rate that exceeded his ability. The pressure John's father placed on him was counterproductive, for John did not have the abilities needed to function at the high level his father insisted on. This caused John to fail and to develop feelings of insecurity and frustration. If some of Piaget's ideas had been used in forming an educational program to meet John's needs, he may not have experienced the frustration and failure that plagued his school career.

Criticisms and Cautions

Critics of Piaget's theory argue that Piaget underestimated the influence of learning on intellectual development. In addition, there is evidence both for and against the idea that children progress through a series of stages in cognitive development (Flavell, 1982). Some Piagetian concepts, especially egocentrism, have also come under fire. For example, Falvell (1975) showed children in the preoperational stage a number of proposed gifts for their fathers and asked these children to choose the appropriate one. Most of the children chose appropriate gifts, demonstrating that they are able to take the point of view of others when they have had experience in these areas. The nature of the task and the past learning experiences of the child may be more important than Piaget realized.

Piaget's method of research, the presentation of problems to children followed by observation and questioning, is a source of criticism. This subjective approach is marked by interpretation rather than formal statistical data. His experiments are not well controlled (Baldwin, 1967). Piaget has in effect blazed a trail using his particular method, leaving the research validating his concepts to others. In a series of conversations with Jean-Claude Bringuier (1980), Piaget answered his methodological critics:

> *Bringuier:* But surely, some questions have to be included in order to produce statistics. (*Piaget wrinkles his nose.*) Just to have a coherent body of information.
>
> *Piaget:* Exactly. Once the work of clearing away, of groundbreaking, has been done, which consists of discovering new things and finding things that hadn't been anticipated, you can begin to standardize—at least if you like that sort of thing—and to produce accurate statistics. But I find it more interesting to do the work of groundbreaking.
>
> *Bringuier:* And you're not afraid the individual cases will be too individual?.
>
> *Piaget:* Why, no. What's so remarkable is that the answers show an unbelievable convergence. While you were preparing this interview, I was classifying the new documents that just came. Twenty-five kids I don't know, and they all say the same thing! At the same age!
>
> *Bringuier:* Because they're from the same social class and the same city?
>
> *Piaget:* I don't think so.
>
> *Bringuier:* Because they're at the same level of evolution?
>
> *Piaget:* Yes.

(Bringuier, 1980, p. 25)

Piaget saw himself as a scientist performing groundbreaking experiments. The extent to which his formulations have been validated by subsequent statistically based research can be debated. While much research supports Piaget's theory, some does not.

The theories formulated by Freud, Erikson, and Piaget are all *stage theories*. Although developmental specialists are partial to stage theories, other approaches can be useful as well. Three such theories will be discussed. The first, information-processing, looks deeply into the cognitive roots of our abilities. Two other non-stage theories—the behavioral approach and social-learning theory—emphasize the importance of learning.

9. *True or False:*
All psychologists agree that children develop in stages.

THE INFORMATION-PROCESSING APPROACH

If a speaker announced, "How you ask your question partly determines the answer you receive from another person," you wouldn't see this as a startling breakthrough. After all, ask a question to a child in one way, and you may receive a blank stare in return. Perhaps your question was not phrased in a way the child could understand. Were the words too difficult? Did the child understand what you were referring to? Could it be the child's memory that is at fault?

I can remember trying to discover who was pilfering cookies from the cookie jar a few years ago. A full box of cookies would be poured into the jar, and less than a day later the jar would be completely empty. Since each child was only allowed two cookies a day, and there were only three children, the numbers didn't add up. We asked each daughter separately whether she had taken the cookies and received the suitable wounded look and innocent response. After a number of days in which again the cookie goblin struck, I had an idea. I asked my three-year-old whether she had taken extra cookies, and got the same negative response. Then I took two different cookies out of the jar and asked her to point to the type she had been taking from the jar and eating that day. With glee she pointed to the chocolate chip cookie. Since the children had not had their two cookies yet, at least we knew what had happened on that day. (At that point my wife shook her head and noted, "All that psychological education has just impressively succeeded in trapping a three-year-old into a confession.")

Although this was not one of the prouder moments in my career, it does indicate the importance of the way you ask questions and how a child's developmental stage may affect your own strategies as a parent. I don't think this strategy would have worked with my older children.

Information-processing emphasizes the way children take in information, process it, and then act on the information. Such factors as attention, perception, memory, the mediating process by which an individual does something to the information, and a response system are important. For instance, my three-year-old's attention was focused on the cookie in both questions. Somehow her program for denying the act was used in the first instance but not in the second. When asked to point out the type of cookie she had taken, the question tripped a different program, which we might call the recognition program.

Researchers advancing the information-processing viewpoint look at ways we take in information, process and store it, and finally retrieve it. They are interested in precisely how people represent information in their memory. One finding suggests that we remember the meaning of a sentence rather than the exact words we hear or read.

You can demonstrate this by trying the simple exercise you will find below. First, read each sentence in Part A to yourself, then count to five before answering the question that goes with the sentence. After you have answered the question go on to the next sentence and repeat this procedure until you have read all the sentences in Part A.

Part A

Sentence	*Question*
The girl broke the window on the porch.	Broke what?
The tree in the front yard shaded the man who was smoking his pipe.	Where?
The hill was steep.	What was?
The cat, running from the barking dog, jumped on the table.	From what?
The tree was tall.	Was what?
The old car climbed the hill.	What did?
The cat running from the dog jumped on the table.	Where?
The girl who lives next door broke the window on the porch.	Lives where?
The car pulled the trailer.	Did what?
The scared cat was running from the barking dog.	What was?
The girl lives next door.	Who does?
The tree shaded the man who was smoking his pipe.	What did?
The scared cat jumped on the table.	What did?
The girl who lives next door broke the large window.	Broke what?
The man was smoking his pipe.	Who was?
The old car climbed the steep hill.	The what?
The large window was on the porch.	Where?
The tall tree was in the front yard.	What was?
The car pulling the trailer climbed the steep hill.	Did what?
The cat jumped on the table.	Where?
The tall tree in the front yard shaded the man.	Did what?
The car pulling the trailer climbed the hill.	Which car?
The dog was barking.	Was what?
The window was large.	What was?

STOP. COVER THE SENTENCES FROM PART A. Now read the sentences in Part B. After each sentence, indicate whether the sentence is new or old. A sentence is new if it is not a repetition of any of the sentences that appeared in Part A. It is old if it is identical to one that you have just read in Part A.

Part B

The car climbed the hill.	old _____ new _____
The girl who lives next door broke the window.	old _____ new _____
The old man who was smoking his pipe climbed the steep hill.	old _____ new _____
The tree was in the front yard.	old _____ new _____
The scared cat, running from the barking dog, jumped on the table.	old _____ new _____
The window was on the porch.	old _____ new _____
The barking dog jumped on the old car in the front yard.	old _____ new _____
The tree in the front yard shaded the man.	old _____ new _____
The cat was running from the dog.	old _____ new _____
The old car pulled the trailer.	old _____ new _____
The tall tree in the front yard shaded the old car.	old _____ new _____
The tall tree shaded the man who was smoking his pipe.	old _____ new _____
The scared cat was running from the dog.	old _____ new _____
The old car, pulling the trailer, climbed the hill.	old _____ new _____
The girl who lives next door broke the large window on the porch.	old _____ new _____

The tall tree shaded the man.   old _____ new _____
The cat was running from the barking dog.   old _____ new _____
The car was old.   old _____ new _____
The girl broke the large window.   old _____ new _____
The scared cat ran from the barking dog that jumped on the table.   old _____ new _____
The scared cat, running from the dog, jumped on the table.   old _____ new _____
The old car pulling the trailer climbed the steep hill.   old _____ new _____
The girl broke the large window on the porch.   old _____ new _____
The scared cat which broke the window on the porch climbed the tree.   old _____ new _____
The tree shaded the man.   old _____ new _____
The car climbed the steep hill.   old _____ new _____
The girl broke the window.   old _____ new _____
The man who lives next door broke the large window on the porch.   old _____ new _____
The tall tree in the front yard shaded the man who was smoking his pipe.   old _____ new _____
The cat was scared.   old _____ new _____

That seemed easy didn't it? Count the number of sentences that you labeled as old. How many did you count? Actually, none of the sentences in part B are identical to those that appeared in Part A. However, their meanings are very close. People often make mistakes in this exercise because they automatically encode the *meaning* of these sentences rather than the words themselves. Even a minute or so after reading the sentences in Part A it is difficult to accurately determine which sentences you have read before.

The information-processing viewpoint seeks to discover just how information is taken in, processed, remembered, and finally acted upon. Although the perspective is still young, it shows great promise for improving our understanding of just how human beings understand and cope with the world around them.

Source: From Jenkins, 1974. Copyright 1974 by the American Psychological Association. Reprinted by permission.

The Computer Analogy

Information-processing specialists often use the computer as an analogy to the workings of the human mind, but this does not mean that they see human beings as computers or robots. The computer analogy helps us understand how children solve problems and use information. What we type into the computer, called the "input," is roughly analogous to information we gather from the environment through our senses. Some operations are performed on the information according to the program, and the information is encoded and stored in some way that is retrievable. Some processes must occur in our minds which enable us to attend to a particular stimulus, organize it, and remember it so it may be used in the future. The information that is retrieved and used if the proper command is given could be considered "output." In the human being, the output could be some motor activity, such as moving the right arm to catch a baseball, or be verbal, as when you come up with the answer to a math problem. Finally, an individual receives feedback—information noting whether the answer or movement was effective. Just as the title of a computer program gives some clue as to what the general results of the program will be, human beings may have an upper executive plan, which coordinates the activities described above and guides purposeful behavior. Information-processing theorists are interested in following the information through the system in order to learn how it is encoded, processed, and retrieved (Hagan et al. 1975; Trabasso, 1975). Thus, they look at cognition on a very detailed level, investigating the processes of perception, attention, representation, memory, and finally retrieval.

10. *True or False:*
In an attempt to understand how we solve problems, psychologists often equate the human mind with the computer.

Application and Value

The information-processing approach allows us to delve more deeply into the same kinds of phenomena that interested Piaget. The Piagetian and information-processing viewpoints can complement each other, giving parents and teachers new ways to analyze a child's cognitive growth. The information-processing viewpoint shows great promise as a diagnostic aid in dealing with problem-solving concerns. It also opens up new and exciting possibilities in working with children who have hearing, visual, or other sensory handicaps, as well as with the mentally retarded. Much research is now under way in an attempt to determine how these children take in information and process it. This may give us some idea of their strengths and weaknesses, allowing us to design better curricula for them.

For instance, the visually impaired tend to experience a room as a number of discrete elements and have difficulty putting these elements together to form a general impression. As sighted individuals, we get a general impression of the room as we walk into it. If you were blind, however, you would have to rely on the senses of hearing and touch for such information. Neither sense provides the individual with a general impression or information that would relate one element to the other. The blind person first gains a distinct, item-by-item view of the world and then puts it all together. Such findings have led to attempts to provide blind children with help in building general views from the specific sensory information available to them.

The information-processing view can help psychologists, teachers, and parents understand the process by which knowledge is obtained and used. In the case of John Baker, an analysis of what he can and cannot do may allow his teacher to formulate a plan that will be effective and will efficiently teach John the skills he lacks. In this way, his deficiencies may be reduced and he might be able to catch up with his classmates.

Criticisms and Cautions

The information-processing perspective is so new that it is difficult to analyze it critically at this point. It is hardly a unified field. A number of models have been advanced to account for the numerous subprocesses such as encoding, memory, and retrieval involved in processing information. No one yet knows how far the computer analogy can be taken. More importantly, we also do not know whether the mind will yield to the step-by-step analysis of subprocesses vital to the success of the information-processing approach. Although the viewpoint is interesting, much work remains before we can truly judge its value for understanding how children develop and process information.

THE BEHAVIORAL APPROACH

"Give me a dozen healthy infants, well-formed, and my own specified world to bring them up in and I'll guarantee to take any one at random and train him to become any type of specialist I might select—doctor, lawyer, merchant, chief, and yes, even begger-man and thief, regardless of his talents, penchants, abilities, vocations and the race of his ancestors" (Watson, 1930). This passage was taken from the writings of John Watson, a psychologist who changed the history of psychology. Watson argued that psychologists should study only behavior that is observable. He ruled out studying mental processes like thinking directly. For instance, Watson would study John Baker's *actions*, including taunting the girls in class and throwing temper tantrums. These are overt behaviors that can be easily observed.

As you can infer from the passage quoted, behaviorists argue that the environment determines behavior and that if the environment is altered adequately, behavior change will follow. How does this occur? Behaviorists such as Watson and, later, B. F. Skinner explain behavior in terms of the processes of learning, including classical and operant conditioning. For example, they would argue that John Baker had learned to behave (or in this case misbehave) and that now he must learn a new set of behaviors.

Classical Conditioning

Classical conditioning involves the pairing of a neutral stimulus with a stimulus that elicits a particular response until the stimulus that was originally neutral elicits the response (Reese and Lipsett, 1970). For instance, a hungry baby is usually pacified by being fed. After a while, the sound of mother's footsteps is sufficient to quiet and soothe the hungry child. The child knows what is coming next, since the sound of the mother's footsteps always precedes the feeding. The child has associated the mother's approach with food.

If the consequences are severe, sometimes only one or two pairings are necessary for conditioning to occur. For instance, suppose Kenny is lying down when the sky becomes dark and he hears a great thunderclap. Lightning strikes the house, and a small fire results. A commotion follows, during which Kenny's mother puts out the fire. No serious damage or injury occurred, but now each time the sky darkens or he hears thunder, Kenny runs to the middle of the house or joins his mother and father in bed, crawling under the covers for protection. The darkening of the sky and the thunderclap had never caused this type of behavior before, but when they were paired with the lightning causing a fire and a great commotion, the child was frightened. This was sufficient to set up a fear response every time the sky darkened.

Kenny may also show fear of any number of very loud noises or darkening environments. This is called **stimulus generalization**. With experience, Kenny may learn to differentiate between loud noises that signify a storm and those that do not. When this occurs, Kenny has learned to **discriminate** between the noises. He will then run to the center of the house only in response to a storm, and not to the sound of a plate being accidentally dropped and broken. Will Kenny's fear ever end, or will he grow up being afraid of storms? Perhaps after many experiences in which the storm does not result in any catastrophe his fear will be **extinguished**, that is, he will no longer respond in a fearful manner.

Classical conditioning has a number of interesting uses, such as in treatment for **enuresis**, or bed-wetting. The child sleeps on a special pad that is connnected to a buzzer. If the child urinates, it completes a circuit, and the buzzer wakes the child up. After a while, the child becomes conditioned to wake up when the bladder is full (Mowrer, 1938). This treatment is effective, with a cure rate of about 85 percent (Sacks and DeLeon, 1973; DeLeon and Mandel, 1966).

11. *True or False:*
Psychologists who use learning theory to explain children's behavior emphasize the importance of thinking and consciousness.

classical conditioning
A learning process by which a neutral stimulus is paired with a stimulus that elicits a response until the originally neutral stimulus now elicits that response.

stimulus generalization
The tendency for a person to react to similar stimuli in the same manner as he or she reacts to the conditioned stimulus.

stimulus discrimination
The process by which a person learns to differentiate among stimuli.

extinction
The weakening and disappearance of a learned response.

enuresis
The scientific term for bed-wetting.

Operant Conditioning

operant conditioning
The learning process in which behavior is governed by its consequences.

reinforcement
An event that increases the likelihood that the behavior that preceded it will reoccur.

In **operant conditioning**, the child's behavior is followed by some event that increases or decreases the frequency of the behavior that preceded it. If the event increases the likelihood that the behavior will recur, the action is said to be **reinforced**. If it decreases the chances of its occurring, it is said to be punished. In operant conditioning, then, behavior is governed by its consequences. Suppose a two-year-old brings you the newspaper. You respond with a smile, a hug, or a thank you. You may then find that this toddler brings you not only the newspaper but also your keys, wallet, handkerchief, and anything else the child can find on the table. The youngster has been reinforced for being helpful.

Reinforcement is a potent force in shaping behavior, but the same reinforcement is not effective in every situation or with every individual. An offer of two more lamb chops to someone who has just finished Sunday dinner is not an effective reinforcement. And if someone hates lamb chops, it won't be effective either.

Parents are the most important givers of reinforcement during the child's early years. As children grow and their social world expands, reinforcements delivered by peers, teachers, and siblings also become important. In fact, parents and siblings may reinforce children for different behaviors. My three-year-old daughter stuck out her tongue and made a funny face at the dinner table. My wife and I ignored it, but her older sisters thought it very funny and reinforced the behavior by giving her plenty of attention. She naturally continued to make faces. In fact, she showed stimulus generalization by beginning to make faces in front of her grandparents and aunts when they visited, but she soon learned stimulus discrimination because she received no attention from these people for her behavior. Behaviors extinguish when they are not reinforced, and we finally had to tell her sisters to ignore her behavior and not reinforce it with attention. It took some time before she finally stopped.

As my daughter discovered, the setting conditions are very important. We learn that if we behave in a certain way in some circumstances we will be rewarded, while that same behavior under other conditions will not be. My daughter learned to make funny faces only in front of her sisters. Generalization and discrimination are important concepts and explain many behaviors. If Pat is reinforced for being aggressive by getting what he wants, he will show this behavior in many contexts. He begins by taking toys away from a younger brother and generalizes this behavior to peers in school. However, he soon learns when this will work and when it will be counterproductive. In other words, he must learn to discriminate. Using profanity with friends may be acceptable, but it is inappropriate in front of grandma. Being aggressive and hostile may be successful in getting his way in early childhood with some peers, but it is ineffective in late adolescence when trying to talk his way out of a speeding ticket.

The behavioral perspective emphasizes the past history of the organism, the setting conditions, and the reinforcements available. No mention is made of what occurs within the mind, of thought processes, or of memory.

Behavior Modification

behavior modification
The use of learning theory to alter behavior.

The use of learning theory to change human behavior, known as **behavior modification**, has proved useful at home and in school. Teachers and parents can be taught how to use reinforcement to improve the functioning of the children under their care. Some of the more prominant operant techniques are summarized in Table 4.4.

Behavior modification can also be used by children. In one study, Gray and his colleagues (1974) trained students who had acquired poor reputations to reinforce their teachers and thus change their teachers' attitudes and behaviors. For the first two weeks, students were told to simply keep records of their interactions with their teachers. These students could easily recognize the negative interactions, but they had difficulty labeling an interaction as positive. The students were trained to smile at their teachers, to show interest in the lectures, and to praise their instructors at the appropriate time. They even learned how to deal with criticism. The results were interesting. The number of positive interactions between students and teachers increased, while the number of negative interactions decreased.

Every day we see the results of reinforcement. If someone gives a child a present and the child is excited and thankful it is reinforcing to the giver. Children are more likely to get more gifts this way than if they accept a gift silently and do not say thank you.

The behavioral approach is useful in both understanding and changing John Baker's behavior. John's parents and teachers must both be taught to reinforce John at the appropriate times, and John must learn how to reinforce his parents and teachers to encourage them to act more positively toward him.

*ACTION/
REACTION*

The Temper Tantrum

Almost every parent has to handle a child's temper tantrum at one time or another. But what do you do when it's an everyday occurrence?

Carrie is four years old and a bright, playful child, but when she doesn't get her own way she screams and throws things. She becomes unconsolable. Carrie engages in this behavior with both her parents, but most often with her mother. The mother's response is to give in, try to reason with her or turn her attention to something else. Carrie's father usually gives in to her before the tantrum begins. When he doesn't, her father spanks her. The girl then runs to her mother and screams even more. Since the mother doesn't believe in spanking, she tries to quiet Carrie by playing with her. She has told her husband that the girl will become afraid of her father when she gets older.

Carrie's mother is at the end of her rope. She can't take the screaming. Her father wants her to ignore it or "spank the kid," which the mother does not believe to be the best policy. She also doesn't know why the tantrums began or why they are getting worse—only that she has to do something.

1. If you were Carrie's parents, how would you handle her tantrums?
2. If you were her mother, how would you deal with your husband's behavior toward the child?

TABLE 4.4   **Summary Chart of Operant Techniques**
The techniques explained in this chart are often highly effective in altering behavior.

Positive Reinforcement

Presentation of a positive reinforcer contingent upon the occurrence of a specified response. A positive reinforcer is defined empirically as anything that increases probability, strength, or frequency of the response. E.g., praising a child for mowing the lawn.

Negative Reinforcement

Cessation of an aversive stimulus contingent upon a specified response to increase the probability, strength, or frequency of the response. E.g., allowing a child who has been "grounded" to begin seeing friends again contingent upon a polite apology for the offense being punished.

Punishment

Presentation of an aversive stimulus contingent upon a specified response to reduce the frequency of the response. As in the case of a positive reinforcer, a punisher is defined empirically by its effects on the response. E.g., scolding a child who has taken a toy from a younger brother or sister.

Extinction

Nonreinforcement of a response to reduce its frequency. E.g., completely ignoring a child whenever the youngster speaks in a "whining voice." Should normally be combined with positive reinforcement for some alternative desired behavior (such as speaking in a normal voice).

Token Reinforcement

Presentation of a symbolic positive reinforcer contingent upon a desired response. The token is later exchanged for a backup reinforcer such as money, food, or privileges. E.g., allowing a youngster to paste a star on a daily chart each day the youngster remembers to empty the trash; at the end of a week or month, etc., the youngster exchanges the filled chart for a trip to the zoo.

Response Cost

A fine imposed contingent upon a specified response. Used in conjunction with a token economy. E.g., in addition to earning stars for a specified behavior, the youngster may lose a star on his/her chart every time he/she fights with a sibling.

Time-out from Positive Reinforcement

The child is removed from *all* positive reinforcers contingent upon a specified response. E.g., a child is told to sit on a chair away from the rest of the family whenever he/she uses foul language.

Differential Reinforcement of Other Behavior (DRO)

A specified response is reduced in frequency by consistent, positive reinforcement of alternative responses incompatible with the undesired response. E.g., shouting and speaking quietly are incompatible, and a parent reinforces the child whenever a quiet voice is used in speaking.

Behavior Shaping

A novel response is developed by careful, immediate reinforcement of successive approximations to the novel response beginning with some behavior already in the child's repertoire. E.g., a youngster may be taught to make a bed by first reinforcing straightening of sheets, then straightening of sheets and blankets, then correct placement of pillows, etc.

Modeling

Imitation of a desired behavior first emitted by a model is reinforced. E.g., Mary, age 5, observes Johnny, age 10, washing dishes. Mary asks if she may help wash dishes and is praised by her parents for helping.

Contingency Contracting

An explicit, mutual contract is developed in which each party agrees to perform (or refrain from performing) specified behaviors in order to obtain desired positive reinforcement from the other party. E.g., mother and Johnny agree that regular bathing is important, and if Johnny bathes regularly for one week, mother will help him complete a club project.

Source: B. Suran and J. Rizzo, 1983.

Reciprocal Interaction

Children both affect and are affected by the people around them. Spend some time observing the interactions between a parent and an infant. Perhaps the parent fondles the baby, who responds with a smile. The parent then says something to the baby, who then reacts with a vocalization. The baby's vocalization brings a string of verbal praise from the parent. For years, psychologists have looked at the caregiver-child relationship in terms of what the mother or father did to the child. The effect of the child on the parents was rarely considered. Today, however, child development specialists look at how each affects the other.

In the above example, the actions of both parties served as both responses and stimuli, which prompted new actions. The baby's smile stimulated the parent to speak to the child, and this stimulated the baby to vocalize. The interaction proceeded rapidly, with both parties affecting the behavior of the other. We can best understand behavior by looking at the **reciprocal interactions** between the parties. The system is bi-directional, with information flowing from one party to the other and back again (Bell, 1979, 1968). Reciprocal interaction can be useful in understanding the social interchanges of the disabled. Traditionally, physically disabled people are viewed negatively by society. Yet this is only half the story. How people project themselves to others is equally important. If they are pleasant, talk freely with others, and help others feel at ease, it sets in motion positive social interactions, but if they reject other people, they are also likely to reject or avoid that person, thus increasing his or her isolation. Social interactions cannot be viewed simply in terms of what society does to a person, in this case someone who is physically disabled, but rather as a series of interactions in which the person plays at least some part. As you read further in this book you will note a number of these interactions.

reciprocal interactions
The process by which an organism constantly affects and is affected by the environment.

Application and Value

The behavioral view is valuable in pinpointing the importance of the environment. Even those who criticize behaviorism usually acknowledge that the environment has a tremendous effect on behavior (Rogers, 1980; May, 1969). The question is whether it has total control or whether internal, cognitive factors such as thinking and information processing abilities must also be taken into account to understand the organism better. Another contribution of behaviorism is its emphasis on experimental methodology. Although it may seem stifling at times, experimental methodology does produce high-quality work. Finally, the idea that children are not only just affected by their environment but also can themselves change it forces us to look at how children affect people near them.

Criticisms and Cautions

The most common criticism of the behavioral view of human development is that it is too mechanical. This approach makes human beings seem too predictable, and the avoidance of such concepts as consciousness, thinking, and subjective experience is a problem. It is doubtful that all human development can be understood on the basis of the principles of learning.

SOCIAL-LEARNING THEORY

Learning Through Observation

Children learn by observing and imitating others. Imitation is so common that we may not fully appreciate its importance. Youngsters use words they hear and often imitate the gestures they see. One little girl of two pointed as if lecturing and called out with a straight face, "You better do that"—an exact imitation of the way her mother would do it. **Social-learning theory** investigates the process of imitation and observation learning.

Sometimes a child's imitation can be embarrassing to parents. One of my friends has a large family spread out over eighteen years. The three-year-old adored his eighteen-year-old brother, who was a senior in high school. Each morning the eighteen-year-old would wake up bleary-eyed and late and walk around the room getting dressed with his eyes only half open. He could never seem to find a pair of socks that matched, and when opening his drawer he would curse. A couple of days later, his mother was opening the drawer to put away his brother's socks. Immediately, the three-year-old ran over and put himself in her way. "Mommy," he said, "You forgot to say &%#!@!"

Imitation can be seen in many behaviors. For instance, children imitate the drug-taking habits of their parents (Dusek-Girdano and Girdano, 1980), and aggressiveness in children is influenced by the models they observe (Bandura, Ross, and Ross, 1961). Eating and dressing are also influenced by observation, as are fears. For instance, if children see others being afraid of the dark, they may follow suit. One mother was very afraid of spiders but did not want her children to have the same fear. She made a conscious effort to pick up a spider and smile, believing that by modeling this type of behavior her children would be less likely to develop a fear of spiders. This may be beyond the sensitivities of many people who experience a fear, but it has been used in therapeutic situations. In one study, a group of children who were afraid of dogs were exposed to a film showing other children playing with dogs freely and happily. This exposure reduced their fear (Bandura, Grusec, and Melove, 1967).

Imitation normally has a component of reinforcement at the end. People notice what happens to others. If someone is reinforced for a behavior, a child may follow suit. If someone is punished, a child may learn from that person's experience. Perhaps this is why younger children often profit from the experiences of older siblings. They may watch and observe, finally noting how their brothers and sisters succeeded and failed in their attempts to get what they wanted from their parents.

Rarely are behaviors imitated exactly. You may watch Jimmy Connors or Chris Evert Lloyd play tennis and try to imitate their play, yet you will be limited by your physical ability. We adapt what we see in a creative way that mirrors our own understanding of the situation and our abilities. Behavior, then, is a compromise between what we see and understand and what we are able or willing to do.

The Process of Imitation

The process of imitation can be explained using a four-step process (Bandura, 1977, 1969). First the individual must pay attention to the model, then encode the message and remember it. After that, the person reproduces the behavior, and

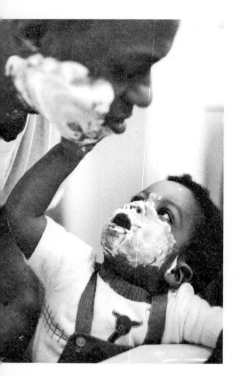

Children imitate what they see around them early in life.

social-learning theory
A theory of learning emphasizing the importance of imitation and observation learning.

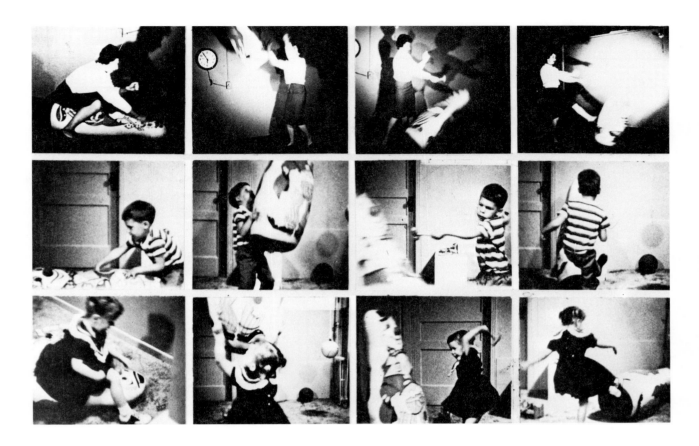

finally, some reinforcement must be available. Reinforcement provides children with information about what may happen in the future if they perform a particular action. It may also motivate them. They remember the consequences of the act and later can use this information to attain their own ends. Children do not have to experience the reinforcement personally. They can learn by watching others.

But who will the child imitate? Children imitate people whom they consider competent and whom they respect. For example, children learn to be cooperative and generous partly by observing others. If children see their parents, whom they respect, giving to charity, the youngsters are likely to follow suit. Children also imitate people who are successful. For example, suppose one day a child witnesses his father avoiding responsibility for failure by blaming it on his mother. Because the child respects the father and sees him as a powerful figure, he remembers the father's behavior. At a later time, when the situation is appropriate, the child reproduces that behavior. His mother interrupts his homework when she calls him for dinner, and he makes an error. He tells his mother that she caused the mistake. Notice that the response may have been learned weeks before, but the action wasn't imitated until the situation was appropriate.

Boys and girls who had watched an adult modeling violence were more likely to show violent behavior in that same situation than children who had not witnessed the model's violent behavior.

Application and Value

Social-learning theory reminds us of the importance of imitation and observation learning in determining behavior. It is useful in understanding the genesis of

TABLE 4.5   **Summary of Developmental Theories**

Theory	Basic Premises	Value and Strengths	Criticisms and Weaknesses
Gesell's Maturational Perspective	1. Development is guided by the unfolding of the individual's unique genetic plan. 2. Developmental sequences in growth and development are discoverable through observation.	1. Increases our appreciation of the importance of the individual's rate of maturation. 2. The verbal pictures provided of children at different ages are useful to parents and professionals alike. 3. The study of maturational sequences such as how children use crayon and paper allows us to predict future development. 4. Excellent use of observations and photography.	1. Underestimates importance of environment. 2. Extreme maturationist view may lead to a wait-and-see prescription which may be counterproductive in some cases. Little room for intervention. 3. Some problems in samples used in studies.
Freud's Psychoanalytic Theory	1. Behavior is motivated by unconscious thoughts, memories, and feelings. 2. Life is the unfolding of the sex instinct. 3. The child's early experience is crucial to his later personality. The manner in which the mother satisfies the child's basic needs is important to later mental health. 4. Children develop through a sequence of stages called psychosexual stages. 5. People protect themselves from anxiety and other negative emotions through unconscious and automatic reactions called defense mechanisms.	1. Encourages child developmental specialists to look beyond the obvious visible behavior and seek insights into the unconscious. 2. Emphasizes the importance of the child's early experience and relationships which in turn focuses our attention on the caregiver-infant relationship. The idea that later problems may be due to disturbed early relationships is challenging. 3. The concept of stages in Freudian theory has become a popular way of viewing the development of children. 4. Emphasis on sexuality, while debatable, still alerts us to the existence of sexuality at all ages. 5. Serves as a focal point for other theorists.	1. Since theory is based upon clinical experiences with troubled people it may have more to say about unhealthy than healthy development. 2. Hypotheses are very difficult to test. 3. Failure to appreciate the importance of culture.

TABLE 4.5—Continued

Theory	Basic Premises	Value and Strengths	Criticisms and Weaknesses
Erik Erikson's Psychosocial Theory	1. Explains development in terms of the epigenetic principle. Personality develops according to predetermined steps which are maturationally set. Society is structured to encourage the challenges which arise at these times in a person's life. 2. Describes development in terms of eight stages from cradle to grave. Each has positive and negative outcomes. 3. Emphasizes the importance of culture and the historical period in which the individual is living.	1. Sees development as continuing over the life span. 2. Importance of culture and historical period adds to our appreciation of factors that affect children's development. 3. Provides a good general overview of crises that occur at each stage of a child's life. Some of these crises such as identity versus role confusion have become important in understanding specific periods in a child's life.	1. Difficult to test experimentally. 2. Theory is rather general.
Piaget's Theory of Cognitive Psychology	1. Children do not think or solve problems in the same manner as adults. 2. Emphasizes the importance of the child's active interaction with the environment. 3. Sees maturation and experience as more important than formal learning in the child's cognitive development. 4. Views cognitive development as occurring in four stages. Each stage shows a qualitative leap forward in the child's ability to solve problems and reason logically. 5. Most complete description of cognitive development from infancy through childhood available.	1. Emphasizes the importance of active experience in child's development. Leads to a view of young children as little scientists sifting through information and actively coping with the world. 2. Descriptions of the way in which children think and approach problems very helpful in understanding their behavior. 3. Many of the sequences for understanding specific concepts are very challenging.	1. May underestimate the influence of learning on cognitive development and the nature of task on the child's performance. 2. Piaget's style of research has been criticized. He presented children with a problem and sought to discover how they reasoned and tried to solve the problem. His experiments were not controlled.

TABLE 4.5—Continued

Theory	Basic Premises	Value and Strengths	Criticisms and Weaknesses
Information Processing	1. Emphasizes the importance of the manner in which children take in information, process it, and then act upon it. 2. Such processes as attention, perception memory, and processing strategies are studied.	1. Yields a detailed look at the processes involved in taking in and processing information. 2. May serve as a diagnostic aid in discovering where children have difficulties in solving problems.	1. It is not a unified field. A number of models have been advanced. 2. It still awaits adequate testing.
Radical Behavioral Approach	1. Human behavior may be explained by the processes of learning including classical and operant conditioning. 2. The behavioral approach has been successful in modifying the behavior of children in many situations. 3. The behavioral approach does not deny consciousness and mental processes like thinking, but rather deals with behavior and development in a different manner. 4. Development is seen as continuous with no stages posited to explain progress.	1. Learning theories are clear, precise, and laboratory tested. 2. The emphasis on the environment is important.	1. Some consider it too mechanical. Its avoidance of mental processes such as consciousness and thinking may yield only a partial picture of behavior. 2. Sees little qualitative difference between humans and animals.
Social Learning Theory	1. Human behavior is partially explained through the process of imitation and observation learning. 2. The process of imitation may be explained using a four step process involving attention, encoding and memory, behavioral reproduction, and, finally, reinforcement.	1. Is useful in understanding certain behaviors such as altruism and aggression. 2. Encourages us to look at the models in the child's environment.	1. Lacks a developmental framework. The process of imitation is viewed as the same no matter who is observing. 2. Does not explain age related changes.

many behaviors—from giving to chairty to being aggressive (Bandura and Walters, 1963), from choosing clothing to understanding speech patterns. In the case of John B., we might look at the models in John's environment. He does not respect his father, and the people he does respect may not be very concerned with the rights of others. Few warm, accepting, competent models exist for John to imitate.

Criticisms and Cautions

Social-learning theory is not without limitations. In the realm of child development, it completely lacks a developmental framework (Cairns, 1979). The process of imitation is described in terms that give little consideration to maturation or to the differences between the imitative behavior of a toddler and that of an adolescent (Thomas, 1979). So, although social-learning theory explains some behaviors very well, it has difficulty with age-related developmental changes.

HOW TO USE THEORIES

Each theory in this chapter has its own way of looking at development (see Table 4.5). The decision to use a particular theory leads a researcher to ask specific questions. For instance, if you used a behavioral approach you might concentrate on what reinforcements were present in John Baker's environment and look at what behaviors he had learned throughout childhood. If you used a Freudian perspective you might ask questions about John's unconscious motivations. If you used an information-processing approach you would consider how John is interpreting his environment and deciding what his alternatives are. Each theory adds something to our understanding of development.

Many child development specialists are aware that there are many ways to look at a particular behavior. This is a strength, not a weakness, for each approach has something different to offer. Some child development specialists are **eclectic**, that is, they adopt the most useful aspects of various theories rather than working from only one perspective. Such eclecticism is healthy if it allows us to appreciate the many ways a particular behavior can be studied (Rychlak, 1985).

Throughout this book we will be describing behavior from a number of different perspectives. Each may look at the subject from a different point of view, but each has as its purpose a better understanding of the developing child.

eclectic
Picking and choosing elements from many different theories rather than depending solely on one theory to explain human behavior or development.

Chapter Summary

1. Theories give facts their meaning and help us interpret data. Theories allow us to relate one fact to another and predict behavior.

2. A good theory is determined by its usefulness, testability, and ability to predict behavior.

3. Arnold Gesell stressed the importance of understanding the sequential format of development, which is largely determined by maturation. Each child negotiates the same steps, though not at the same rate. Gesell's theory is noteworthy because of its excellent descriptions of children's behavior and its use of maturation to explain development. It has been criticized because it underestimates the importance of the environment and offers no practical basis for intervention.

4. Psychoanalytic theory emphasizes the importance of the early parent-child relationship. Freud argued that children progress through five psychosexual stages that involve the unfolding of the sexual instinct. Some of his concepts, such as unconscious motivation and defense mechanisms, are also of interest. Freud's concepts of stage development, infantile and child sexuality, unconscious motivation, and defense mechanisms are noteworthy. Psychoanalytic theory has been criticized because it is difficult to test, considers sexuality the prime motivation, and emphasizes deviancy.

5. Erik Erikson argued that people proceed through eight stages from the cradle to grave. Each stage presents people with different tasks. If a task is successfully negotiated, there is a positive outcome, if not, there is a negative outcome. Erikson's theory is noteworthy because it provides a good framework for viewing development, emphasizes the importance of culture and history, and sees life as continuing throughout the life span. It has been criticized because it is overly broad and general and difficult to explore experimentally.

6. Jean Piaget investigated the cognitive, or intellectual, development of the child. He noted that children do not think like adults and described four stages through which children pass between birth and adolescence. Piaget's theory is noteworthy because of his discovery of the sequences of development leading to an adult understanding of math, time, space, and a number of other concepts. Piaget also views the child as actively involved with the environment and stresses the importance of discovery. The theory has been criticized because it underestimates the importance of formal learning.

7. Information-processing theory focuses on the way people take in information, process it, and finally act on it. Such factors as attention, perception, memory, and response systems are investigated. It is a noteworthy approach because it yields specific information on how a child solves a particular problem. However, it is not as well developed as other theoretical approaches, and only additional experimentation will determine how useful it will be.

8. Learning theorists or behaviorists do not emphasize the concept of stages but stress the importance of classical conditioning, operant conditioning, and social-learning theory (imitation) to the understanding of child development. It is a noteworthy approach because learning is one cause of change. Learning theory also presents us with useful techniques to modify behavior. It has been criticized for being too mechanical, and not adequately taking consciousness and thought processes into consideration.

9. The continuous interaction between the child and others in the environment is known as reciprocal interaction. Child development specialists are now looking at how the child affects his or her parents, not just how the parents affect the child.

10. Developmental psychology lacks a unified theory that covers every aspect of development. A researcher will choose the theory that seems most useful in understanding the developmental phenomena of interest. Many researchers are eclectic, that is, they take portions from various theories, depending on the problem they wish to study.

■ Answers to True or False Questions

1. *True.* The value of a theory depends on its usefulness.

2. *False.* Correct statement: A good theory not only describes development but can predict it.

3. *False.* Correct statement: Children enter and leave a particular stage at different times. Ages noted by most theorists are averages and are meant only as rough guides.

4. *True.* Through painstaking, regular observations, many developmental sequences have been discovered.

5. *True.* Freud emphasized the importance of early parent-child interactions.

6. *True.* Psychoanalytic theory is difficult to validate empirically.

7. *False.* Correct statement: Developing a sense of automony is an important outcome of the toddler stage.

8. *False.* Correct statement: The differences between the thought processes of children and adults have been more impressive.

9. *False.* Correct statement: A number of theories attempt to explain children's behavior without resorting to stages.

10. *False.* Correct statement: Scientists using the information-processing approach do not equate human minds with computers. They merely use the computer as an analogy for how processing may occur.

11. *False.* Correct statement: Behaviorists argue that they can explain behavior without studying cognitive processes or exploring consciousness.

PART TWO

Infancy and Toddlerhood

CHAPTER FIVE

Physical Development in Infancy and Toddlerhood

■ *Are the Following Statements True or False?*

Try the True-False Quiz below. See if your answers correspond to the information in this chapter. Each question is repeated opposite the paragraph in which the answer can be found. The True-False Answer Box at the end of the chapter lists complete answers.

____ **1.** The newborn infant resembles the pictures on babyfood jars.

____ **2.** The newborn infant is poorly equipped to enter the world.

____ **3.** The newborn infant is very nearsighted at birth.

____ **4.** Infants are born deaf but develop their sense of hearing quickly.

____ **5.** Newborns are relatively insensitive to pain.

____ **6.** Infants dream less than school-age children.

____ **7.** Most of the infant's reflexes become stronger with time.

____ **8.** There is a relationship between brain weight and intelligence.

____ **9.** An infant can be adequately fed using prepared formula instead of breast milk.

____ **10.** The injurious effects of malnutrition can be reduced by a good environment.

____ **11.** African infants develop faster than European infants.

____ **12.** The infant's cry of pain is qualitatively different from other types of cries.

____ **13.** The sound of a heartbeat has a special property that quiets a baby.

____ **14.** The first smile is an innate behavior.

____ **15.** Blind infants smile at about the same time as sighted infants.

____ **16.** Females are more mature at birth and continue to develop at a faster rate.

____ **17.** Parents see male infants as sturdier than female infants.

____ **18.** Parents treat boys and girls similarly during infancy.

THE APPEARANCE OF THE NEWBORN

The Newborn at a Glance

1. *True or False:*
The newborn infant resembles the pictures on babyfood jars.

neonate
The scientific term for a newborn infant.

lanugo
The fine hair that covers a newborn infant.

vernix caseosa
A thick liquid that protects the skin of the fetus.

fontanels
The soft spots on the top of a baby's head.

The newborn infant does not resemble the pictures we see on babyfood jars, in soap advertisements, or in the movies. The **neonate**, or newborn, is covered with fine hair called **lanugo**, which is discarded within a few days. The baby's sensitive skin is protected in the womb by a thick secretion called **vernix caseosa**, which dries and disappears. The head is elongated and about one-fourth of the baby's total length. The thin skin appears pale and contains blotches caused by the trip through the birth canal. The head and nose may be out of shape, because their soft, pliable nature allows an extra bit of "give" during birth. They will soon return to normal, but it will be about a year and a half before the bones of the skull will cover the soft spots, or **fontanels**. The legs are tucked in under the baby in a fetal position and will remain that way for quite a while. The infant wheezes and sneezes and appears anything but ready for an independent existence.

The Importance of Being Small and Cute

The protruding forehead and large eyes of the neonate seem to draw out a protective feeling in most of us. In fact, the infant's appearance has survival value (Morris, 1977). Some ethologists, scientists who study organisms in their native habitat, argue that the appearance of young organisms can elicit strong protective emotions from adults. In one study, twenty-five undergraduates were shown line drawings of human heads that varied in head shape, as does the human organism, from birth through childhood. Subjects' responses could be predicted from the babyishness of the head shape. Even though all the drawings showed attractive facial features, undergraduates reliably chose the illustrations of the infant heads as the cutest (Alley, 1981). The same may hold true for the infant's big eyes and protruding forehead. Indeed, the total appearance of a newborn elicits strong positive and protective reactions that encourage caregiving behavior.

The newborn cannot survive without care. The infant appears to be ill-prepared for entrance into the world. But appearances can be deceiving. Science has recently begun to draw a new and different picture of the capabilities of the newborn. We now know that infants are born well prepared for survival. The neonate is better adapted to the environment and more capable than most people think.

2. *True or False:*
The newborn infant is poorly equipped to enter the world.

HOW THE INFANT EXPERIENCES THE WORLD

Vision

Adults rely on the sense of vision for much of their information about the world. So do infants. At birth the visual apparatus of an infant is immature but functional (Cohen et al., 1979). What can an infant see?

visual acuity
The ability to see clearly at various distances.

Acuity and Accommodation. You have probably had your **visual acuity**—your ability to see objects clearly at various distances—examined using a

Snellen chart. You stand 20 feet away and are asked to read letters that get progressively smaller until you have difficulty identifying them. Researchers cannot use an eye chart with infants, but an infant's eye movements can be watched to determine whether the baby senses a difference between a figure and its background—in one case, stripes. Dayton and his colleagues (1964) varied the width of the stripes until the neonates showed no eye movements. These researchers argue that neonates have an acuity of 20/150, that is, they can see at 20 feet what normal adults see at 150 feet. Other estimates are a little worse, approaching between 20/200 and 20/300 (Dobson and Teller, 1978). The newborn infant is very nearsighted. The infant also has difficulty focusing. The best focal distance for the newborn is about 19 centimeters, or 7 1/2 inches (Haynes et al., 1965). Infants cannot focus well on distant or approaching objects (Wickelgren, 1967).

3. *True or False:*
The newborn infant is very nearsighted at birth.

As poor as their visual acuity is, though, it serves them well. When a newborn is held by the mother, the baby's face is usually a bit less than 6 inches away, so the baby is able to see her during feeding. Visual abilities improve quickly. Within six months the infant's visual acuity approaches that of an adult (Cohen et al., 1979), and by about two months the ability to focus approaches adult status (Aslin and Dumais, 1980).

Form and Preference.   If you were shown two pictures—one of a beautiful mountain scene and the other of a green square on a white background—chances are you would look longer at the first scene. Your interest could be measured by the amount of time you spent looking at it. This is the same approach used in investigating visual preferences in the newborn.

Consider the fact that you have quite a bit of visual experience and a green square isn't very exciting. Yet what of a newborn, who has had no visual experiences? Would newborn infants focus on anything in particular or just allow their eyes to wander aimlessly?

Newborns do have visual preferences. They prefer curved lines to straight lines (Fantz and Miranda, 1975), a patterned surface over a plain one (see Figure 5.1) (Fantz, 1963), and high-contrast edges and angles (Cohen et al., 1979). The infant's scanning is not random. It is directed by rules (Haith, 1980) that cause the baby to concentrate on the outline of a figure rather than explore its details (Milewski, 1976). By eight weeks or so, infants develop more adult patterns of scanning and will investigate the interior as well as the contours of a figure (Maurer and Salapatek, 1976).

A preference for faces?   How can visual patterns and preferences help the newborn survive? The newborn depends on others for the basic necessities of life, so a visual preference for human faces would be adaptive. In fact, the discovery by Fantz (1961) that this was true greatly excited the scientific world. Fantz showed infants two pictures—one off to the infant's right, the other to the left—and measured the time the infant's eyes spent fixated on either one. Fantz found that infants preferred patterns to nonpatterned surfaces and that a picture of a face attracted the most attention. Perhaps the infant comes into this world preprogrammed to recognize faces. Fantz's argument that infants have a natural preference for faces may be premature. His conclusions have been reinterpreted in terms of the complexity of stimuli, and other researchers have not replicated his work (Cohen et al., 1979). At the present time, there is no final answer to this question. Perhaps both sides are correct, but looking at the issue at different lev-

FIGURE 5.1   Infant Visual Preferences
The importance of pattern rather than color or brightness was illustrated by the response of infants to a face, a piece of printed matter, a bull's-eye, and plain red, white, and yellow disks. Even the youngest infants preferred patterns. Solid color bars show the results for infants from two to three months old; tinted color bars, for infants more than three months old.

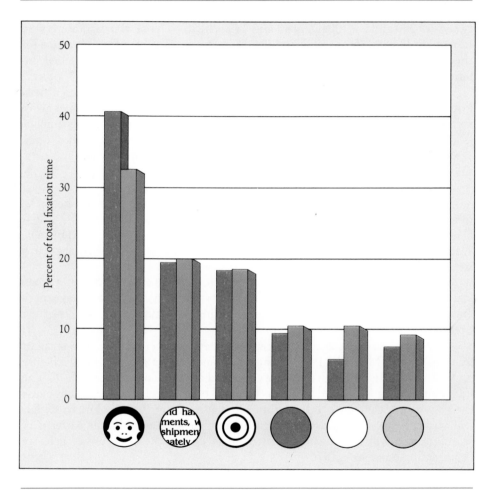

Source: R. Fantz, 1961.

els. On a more detailed level, the infant has a preference for complex stimuli, while on a behavioral level this translates into an interest in faces, which are common complex stimuli in the infant's environment.

Color Vision.   Color vision has been found in infants as young as three months (Banks and Salapatek, 1983; Bornstein, 1976). At present, it is impossible to say whether neonates see color the same way older people do. Until some methodological breakthrough occurs, this will continue to be merely an assumption. However, infants as young as four months do show the same color preferences as adults, gazing more at blue and red than at yellow (Banks and Salapatek, 1983; Bornstein, 1975).

Spatial and Depth Perception.   Do babies live in a two- or three-dimensional world? Bower and his colleagues (1970) found that infants will move their heads back and place their hands in front of them when viewing a ball coming toward their face. An impressive 70 percent of the infant's hand extensions were in the direction of the ball, and infants made contact with the ball 40 percent of the time (Bower, 1977). When the infants could not contact the ball, they seemed surprised and upset. If this is true, it shows astonishing spatial peception at a very young age. Ball and Tronick (1971) projected a shadow of a ball that was shown as becoming larger and larger, giving the babies the impression that the ball was heading for them. Two-week-old infants drew back and interposed their hands between face and object.

A number of other researchers have attempted to replicate these studies. Some have noted various aspects of reaching but do not believe they are a coordinated defensive attempt to avoid the oncoming stimulus (DiFranco et al., 1978). Infants ages seven days to fifteen days were placed on a pillow in which their heads were slightly elevated. A ball was suspended from a rod and moved to one of three positions, which were 7 to 8 centimeters from their eyes, and their movements were photographed (Ruff and Halton, 1978). Only 36 percent of the reaches were near contact, and only 7 percent resulted in contact. This is far below Bower's finding. Most of the arm-reaching could not be interpreted as directed at the target.

In another study, Hofsten (1982) used a moving object to test eye-hand coordination and spatial perception in five- to nine-day-old infants. As the ball moved back and forth, the infant's movements were videotaped. Hofsten found evidence that eye-hand coordination does occur in the newborn. The infant has the ability to direct both eyes and hands toward an external stimulus. Obviously catching and grasping are not well developed in the infant, and at best these behaviors can only be interpreted as the very early beginnings of the ability.

In order to test an infant's depth perception, an ingenious experiment was designed by Gibson and Walk (1960). A stand was constructed above the floor, and an infant was placed on the stand, which contained two glass surfaces. The first was a checkerboard pattern, the other half was a clear sheet of glass. Underneath this clear sheet was another checkerboard pattern, giving the impression of a cliff. This experiment, using what is called the **visual cliff**, showed that children six months or older would not crawl from the "safe" side over the cliff even if their mothers beckoned (see Figure 5.2).

visual cliff
A device used to measure depth perception in infants.

But what of younger children? Because of their inability to crawl, testing very young infants on this apparatus is difficult. However, Joseph Campos and his colleagues (1970) placed infants as young as two months on the deep side of the cliff. The heart rate of these infants decelerated, indicating interest not fear. Although young children develop depth perception very early, it is only at six months or later that they develop a fear of the cliff. This contrasts with animals such as dogs, goats, and cats, which show a much earlier avoidance of the cliff.

These experiments show that an early primitive form of depth and spatial perception exists in very young infants. They can locate objects in the visual field and show some minimal eye-hand coordination. The meaning of an infant's re-

FIGURE 5.2 The Visual Cliff

Six-month-old infants refused to crawl over this visual cliff demonstrating depth perception.

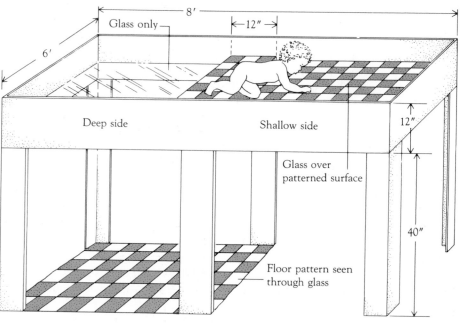

Source: Gibson and Walk, 1960.

sponses to visual stimuli, though, is a matter of controversy. Some authorities, like Bower, tend to interpret them as indicating an early, purposeful series of actions, while others disagree sharply. Perhaps the movements Bower observed represent infants visually tracking and orienting themselves to the approaching object that rises on the visual plane. Despite these differences of opinion, it appears that the beginnings of spatial and depth perception are visible in the young infant. Later perceptual capabilities may have their basis in these earliest abilities.

Visual Tracking.   Infants can track slowly moving objects. Haith (1966) presented one- to four-day-old neonates with a stationary light and a moving light that traced the outline of a rectangle. The infants reduced their sucking behavior more when presented with the moving light than when they were shown the stationary light. Kremenitzer and her colleagues (1979) found that infants one to three days old looked in the direction of a moving target, although the skill was not well developed.

Taken together, studies of the neonate's visual capabilities show that newborns can indeed see and process information, on a very limited basis. They can see forms (Bond, 1972) and track objects, although their visual acuity and ability to focus are poor. Finally, they scan the field according to rules that may be innate, indicating that part of visual processing is indeed inborn.

The perceptual abilities of the infant develop rapidly. During the first weeks, the visual process is directed by prewired programs, but these quickly give way to more adult patterns of scanning, and the infant's visual abilities approach that of adults (Cohen, 1979). As Cohen notes, this is quite a change from about twenty years ago, when researchers were arguing over whether the infant could see.

Hearing

A researcher stood in a delivery room with a clicker and on the birth of a child sounded the instrument in either the right ear or the left ear of the newborn. Amazingly, this neonate only seconds old turned eyes toward the right or left, depending on where the sound was coming from (Wertheimer, 1961). In another experiment, neonates as young as three days old turned their heads in the direction of a continuous sound (Muir and Field, 1979).

The newborn can hear. In fact, the neonate's auditory capability is better developed than the visual abilities. Studies have shown that newborns react to pitch, loudness, and even rhythm (Eisenberg, 1970). Deafness can be tested by allowing the infant to suck and then presenting the baby with a loud noise. A hearing infant will interrupt the sucking, a deaf infant will not (Semb and Lipsitt, 1968).

The neonate's visual abilities have survival value, and the same can be said for the newborn's auditory abilities. Human neonates respond to most sounds within the human voice range (Webster et al., 1972) and are more responsive to sounds within the normal human voice range than outside it (Kearsley, 1973). They are also more sensitive to higher-pitched sounds (Aslin et al., 1983) and can discriminate one sound from another. DeCasper and Fifer (1980) reported that by three days neonates could discriminate between their mother's voice and that of a stranger as measured by differential sucking on a nipple. Infants are also tuned in to language from birth (Aslin et al., 1983). As young as one month old, they can tell the difference between the sound of a *p* and a *b* (Eimas et al., 1971). Infants are also partial to music (Walk, 1982). Rhythmic sounds tend to soothe a baby (Salk, 1960).

4. *True or False:*
Infants are born deaf but develop their sense of hearing quickly.

Smell

The newborn can also use the sense of smell. Neonates move away from an unpleasant-smelling solution (Lipsitt et al., 1963). Infants as young as seven days old turn differentially to their mother's breast pad even if offered another woman's breast pad (MacFarlane, 1975), but this ability was not present in two-day-old neonates. Such discrimination on the basis of smell is impressive.

Taste

Infants can taste. They can tell the difference between plain water and a sugar solution (Desor et al., 1973). They tend to reject plain water, but if sugar is added, they accept it. Newborns one to three days old prefer sucrose to glucose (Engen, Lipsitt, and Peck, 1973). They can even tell the difference between sour and bitter substances (Jensen, 1932). They prefer sugar to salt (Pratt, 1954). Some researchers note that the newborn is more sensitive to taste stimuli in early infancy than at any other time (Reese and Lipsitt, 1973). While that is difficult to prove, we can conclude that the sense of taste is functional in the neonate and well developed during infancy and toddlerhood.

Pressure and Pain

5. *True or False:*
Newborns are relatively insensitive to pain.

Neonates are responsive to tactile stimulation, especially around the mouth, but relatively insensitive to pain at birth. This reduces the infant's discomfort during the birth process. Within a few days, a dramatic increase in this sense occurs (Lipsitt and Levy, 1959), and this contributes to the baby's ability to respond to painful stimuli that might be injurious. The sense of pain reaches a plateau in later infancy and then stays rather stable throughout childhood (Birren et al., 1981).

The neonate, then, is born with a number of sensory abilities that develop rapidly throughout infancy and toddlerhood. The infant actively seeks out variation and new stimuli during attempts to experience and understand the world. This process is facilitated by changes in the sleeping-waking cycle. As infants mature, they spend more time awake and alert, which allows for even more exploration of the environment.

THE SLEEPING-WAKING CYCLE

rapid eye movements (REM)
The movements of the eyes during sleep that are related to dreaming.

Neonates spend about sixteen or seventeen hours a day sleeping (Parmelee et al., 1964). The nature of these periods shows some interesting differences between neonates and older children and adults. For example, when both children and adults are awakened from sleep in which they show **rapid eye movements (REM)**, they report vivid dreams. The normal adult spends about 20 percent of sleep time in REM. Normally, the adult begins in non-REM sleep and after about 50 to 70 minutes switches to REM. About 50 percent of infants' sleep, an astounding one-third of their day, is spent in REM (Roffwarg et al., 1966). Premature infants show even more REM. An infant born between 35 and 38 weeks following conception spends about 58 percent of sleep time in REM. That percentage jumps to 67 percent in infants 33–35 weeks, and 80 percent for infants born after a gestation period of 30 weeks. In addition, infants typically begin their sleep patterns in REM. By the age of three months, however, the amount of REM sleep is reduced to about 40 percent, and they are no longer beginning their nights in that state (Minard et al., 1968).

6. *True or False:*
Infants dream less than school-age children.

The functions of sleep and REM are probably quite complex in the newborn (Brierly, 1976). Perhaps newborns use the extra REM to provide a self-stimulatory experience, because they sleep so much of the day. The fact that REM sleep decreases as waking time increases provides some evidence in that direction (Roffwarg et al., 1966). Other psychologists argue that the REM sleep fosters brain organization and development, which is particularly rapid at this stage of development (Berg, 1979).

Just about every parent is familiar with the pattern of the newborn infant's day. The newborn shows no differentiation between night and day, equally distributing sleep time. By about four weeks of age, though, infants sleep longer at night, and by sixteen weeks they have sustained periods of sleep at night and longer periods of wakefulness during the day (Parmelee et al., 1964; Parmelee and Stern, 1972). Brain maturation contributes greatly to this change in the sleeping-waking cycle (Berg, 1979).

It is relatively easy to describe waking and sleeping in adults. Not so with infants. While waking and sleeping appear in the newborn, a number of transitional states are present which fit into neither. As the infant grows, these decrease and the infant's state can more easily be measured and classified. Peter Wolff (1966) argues that infants show seven states:

1. *Regular Sleep.* During this state the infant lies quiet, subdued, with his eyes closed and unmoving. The child looks pale and his breathing is regular.

2. *Irregular Sleep.* In this state he does not appear as still. He shows sudden jerks, startles and a number of facial expressions including smiling, sneering, and frowning. The eyes, though closed, sometimes show bursts of movement and breathing is irregular.

3. *Periodic Sleep.* This is an intermediate stage between regular and irregular sleep. The infant shows some periods of rapid breathing, and jerky movements followed by periods of perfect calm.

4. *Drowsiness.* In this state he shows bursts of "writhing" activity. The eyes open and close and have a dull appearance. Respiration is variable but regular.

5. *Alert Inactivity.* The infant is now relaxed and has a bright shining appearance, but is inactive. He searches the environment and their breathing is irregular.

6. *Waking Activity.* The infant in this state shows a number of spurts in activity involving the entire body. Respiration is irregular. The intensity and duration of these movements vary with the individual.

7. *Crying.* In this familiar state the infant cries and this is often accompanied by a significant motor activity. The face may turn red.

It is estimated that 67 percent of the time infants are in sleep, 7 percent in drowsy, 10 percent in alert inactivity, 11 percent in waking activity and 5 percent in crying (Berg, Adkison, and Strock, 1973).

The concept of infant state is important because the response of an infant to a stimulus is a function of the state in which he is tested (Parmelee and Sigman, 1983; Lenard and Prechtl). Some reflexes are stronger and more reliable in one state than the other. The infant's sensory thresholds are also mediated by the baby's state. In the alert inactive stage, infants may turn away from strong auditory stimuli toward more gentle voices (see Parmelee and Sigman, 1983). Before comparing studies, the infant's state must be taken into consideration. The concept of state has practical implications for parents as well (Brazelton 1980). During the transition states, the infant can go either way. If the stimuli awaiting the infant are pleasant the infant is drawn out into an alert stage and is more responsive.

THE INFANT'S ABILITY TO LEARN

If newborns are to survive, they must learn about their new world. Even neonates can learn through the three processes described in Chapter Four—classical conditioning, operant conditioning, and imitation.

Classical Conditioning

Researchers report some success using classical conditioning with infants (Blass et al., 1984; Sameroff and Cavanaugh, 1979). For example, Lipsitt and Kaye (1964) succeeded in classically conditioning the sucking reflex by sounding a tone that acts as the conditioned stimulus and following it by inserting a nipple in the mouth of the infant. Other researchers using a variety of other reflexes have also reported some success (Connolly and Stratton, 1969; Kaye, 1965). Little (1970) delivered a tone and a puff of air that caused ten- to forty-day-old infants to blink. After a number of pairings, the infants blinked to the tone alone.

Despite these successes, there have been a number of significant failures. After reviewing the literature in the area, Fitzgerald and Brackbill (1976) found that only about half the studies reported in the past thirty years or so were successful in classically conditioning the newborn. The interpretation of many studies is complicated by methodological problems (Sameroff, 1971). Perhaps infants experience difficulty associating the conditioned and unconditioned stimuli (the tone and the air puff in Little's example) because of lack of experience. While acknowledging that the research results are mixed, we can conclude that classical conditioning has been established in the neonate (Sameroff and Cavanaugh, 1979).

Operant Conditioning

No such problem exists with operant conditioning. In one study, Siqueland (1968) successfully trained newborns to turn their heads for a chance to suck on a nipple. Most operant-conditioning experiments have involved either head-turning or sucking responses (Sameroff and Cavanaugh, 1979). The creativity of researchers working with young infants is shown by the Butterfield and Siperstein (1972) study concerning the musical preferences of young infants. In this study, infants were allowed to suck on a nipple and were rewarded by being allowed to hear music. The longer they sucked, the more music they heard. Two-day-old infants sucked longer and longer to hear the music, but would not do so if sucking led to the music's being turned off.

One experiment shows how much easier it is to demonstrate operant conditioning than classical conditioning. Siqueland and Lipsitt (1966) used the fact that touching an infant's cheek leads to the head turning about one-quarter of the time. The researchers sounded a tone, then touched the infant's cheek. The infant's head-turning was then reinforced by administration of a sweet solution. Operant conditioning could be said to occur if the infants significantly increased their head-turning in order to get the sweet solution, while classical conditioning would be established if they turned their head in response to the tone. The infants learned to turn their heads in response to the touch on the cheek, but not to the tone alone. The researchers had demonstrated operant conditioning but not classical conditioning.

Imitation

Can neonates imitate? Meltzoff and Moore (1977) claim that twelve- to twenty-one-day-old infants imitate facial and manual gestures. Infants opened their mouths and stuck out their tongues when the same behaviors were modeled by an adult. Infants only 60 minutes old show imitative responses. In another study, newborn infants ages .7–71 hours imitated an adult's facial gestures of opening the mouth and sticking out the tongue (Meltzoff and Moore, 1983). While some researchers doubt such early imitation in infants (Hayes and Watson, 1981), these findings tentatively demonstrate that it may indeed exist, even at this early age.

Habituation

Imagine looking at the same picture hanging over your desk day after day. Eventually you wouldn't even notice it. But what if someone changed the picture

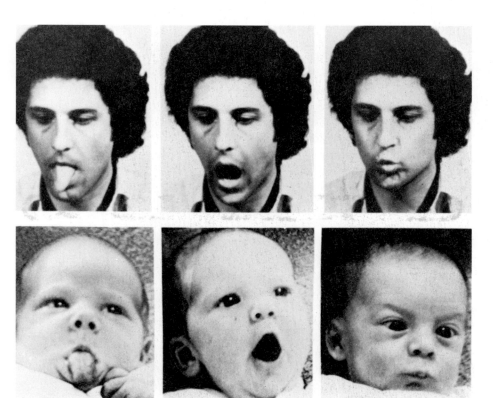

Infants show imitation at very early ages. In the top row, Andrew Meltzoff makes facial gestures at an infant. In the bottom row, you can see the infant's responses.

habituation
The process by which organisms spend less and less time attending to familiar stimuli.

while you were out of the room? Would you notice the change? The process by which you spend less and less time attending to a familiar stimulus is known as **habituation** (Brierly, 1976). In order to respond to the new picture, you must notice that it is different.

Psychologists have used the process of habituation to test a number of infant perceptual abilities (Kisilevsky and Muir, 1984). An infant is presented with one stimulus, and the baby's behavior is observed closely. At first the infant shows some interest, but after a time the baby pays less attention to it, finally perhaps ignoring the stimulus altogether. Now you present the infant with another stimulus and observe the behavior. If an increase in attention occurs, the infant has noticed the difference between the pair of stimuli.

This habituation design has been used on infants as early as the first few days afer birth. One-and-a-half- to three-day-old infants habituate to a checkerboard pattern placed on the side of the crib (Friedman and Carpenter, 1971). The three-day-old infants habituated faster to the visual stimuli than younger infants did.

Learning and Development

Infants' ability to profit from their experience improves with age. Older infants are easier to condition, and their ability to imitate is impressive. As infants develop, their brains become more capable of processing a greater amount of information at a faster rate. Infants' memory and cognitive abilities allow them to make better judgments about elements in the environment (Parton, 1976). Their improved learning ability is the result of experience with the environment and the infants' developing neurological systems.

Psychologists today have a new respect for the sensory and perceptual abilities of the neonate. The infant comes into this world well prepared to take in and process information as well as to learn. Special patience is needed to work with neonates, because their responses are mediated by their state, and they move in and out of these states so quickly. A researcher may turn around and have a sleeping baby on hand instead of an infant who just a few seconds before was awake and ready to participate in the study. Since the infant's abilities are so limited compared with those of the older child, special experimental designs are needed to unlock the secrets of their functioning. Even so, the creative work of researchers around the world has demonstrated that human neonates possess impressive perceptual abilities that develop rapidly.

REFLEXES IN THE NEWBORN

reflex
A relatively simple automatic reaction to a particular stimulus.

Infants also enter the world preprogrammed with a number of specific responses to the environment in the form of reflexes that enable them to deal efficiently with stimuli in their environment (see Table 5.1). A **reflex** is a simple automatic reaction to a particular stimulus (Kalat, 1980). If you are tapped just below the kneecap, there is an automatic response in which your leg kicks up. Infants are born with quite a number of these automatic responses. While the functions of some are obvious, we can only guess at the purposes of others.

TABLE 5.1   **Some Neonatal Reflexes**

Reflex	Eliciting Stimulus	Response	Developmental Duration
Babinski	Gentle stroke along sole of foot from heel to toe	Toes fan out, big toe flexes	Disappears by end of 1st year
Babkin	Pressure applied to both palms while baby is lying on its back	Eyes close and mouth opens; head returns to center position	Disappears in 3–4 months
Blink	Flash of light, or puff of air delivered to eyes	Both eyelids close	Permanent
Diving reflex	Sudden splash of cold water in the face	Heart rate decelerates, blood shunted to brain and heart	Becomes progressively weaker with age
Knee jerk	Tap on patellar tendon	Knee kicks	Permanent
Moro reflex	Sudden loss of support	Arms extended, then brought toward each other; lower extremities are extended	Disappears in about 6 months
Palmar grasp	Rod or finger pressed against infant's palm	The object is grasped	Disappears in 3–4 months
Rage reflex	Place both hands on side of alert infant's head and restrain movement; block mouth with cheesecloth or covering for 10 seconds	Crying and struggling	Disappears in 2–4 months
Rooting reflex	Object lightly brushes infant's cheek	Baby turns toward object and attempts to suck	Disappears in 3–4 months
Sucking reflex	Finger or nipple inserted 2 inches into mouth	Rhythmic sucking	Disappears in 3–4 months
Walking reflex	Baby is held upright and soles of feet are placed on hard surface; baby is tipped slightly forward	Infant steps forward as if walking	Disappears in 3–4 months

Source: J. P. Dworetsky, 1984.

Oral Reflexes

Reflexes connected with feeding are well established in the newborn. Place something in an infant's mouth and the baby will **suck** vigorously. The infant also shows the **rooting reflex**. If you stroke the neonate's cheek, the baby turns toward that side to find the breast. The swallowing reflex is also well developed in the newborn.

Digestive Reflexes

Almost every parent is well aware that the infant also has a number of **digestive reflexes**, including hiccuping, burping, and regurgitation, to name a few. They allow the child to regulate the intake of food and eliminate gases. Infants are especially likely to demonstrate these when their parents are in a hurry. When parents are getting ready for an evening out, the infant's schedule is likely to be disrupted. The parent feeding the infant is apt to be in a rush, thereby increasing the chances that the infant will exhibit these reflexes.

sucking reflex
A reflex found in young infants, in which they automatically suck when something is placed in their mouths.

rooting reflex
The reflex in young infants in which a stroke on a cheek causes them to turn in the direction of the stimulus.

digestive reflexes
A group of reflexes such as hiccuping and burping.

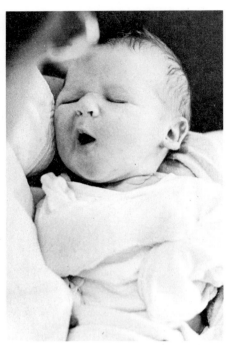

(Left) The sucking reflex is perhaps the most familiar reflex in young infants. (Right) If an infant's cheek is stroked, he turns his head in that direction.

grasping reflex
A reflex in which a stroke on the palm causes the infant to make a fist.

Babinski reflex
The reflex in which stroking the soles of the feet results in the toes fanning out.

The Grasping Reflex

If you slide your finger along the palm of a neonate, the infant's fist will close. This **grasping reflex** is strongest at birth, weaker by two months, and usually disappears by about three months (Illingworth, 1974). In the evolutional perspective, the grasping reflex might have some survival value. Most primates must hold on to their mothers for protection, and this reflex would facilitate that attachment. The reflex may have once had the same purpose for human infants. Persistence of this response well past the three- to four-month period may indicate brain damage.

The Babinski Reflex

If someone tickled you on the sole of your foot, what would happen to your toes? In adults, the toes curl in, but when the infant's sole is stroked, the toes fan out. This reflex, known as the **Babinski reflex**, normally disappears by the end of the first year.

Stepping and Swimming Reflexes

Among the most interesting reflexes are those that involve behaviors similar to later walking and swimming. If infants are held upright and pitched a bit forward, and the soles of their feet make contact with some hard surface, they will show stepping motions (Cratty, 1979). The stepping reflex cannot be elicited every time (Rushworth, 1971). Some research demonstrates that systematic exercise of the stepping reflex encourages the early development of walking (Zelazo et

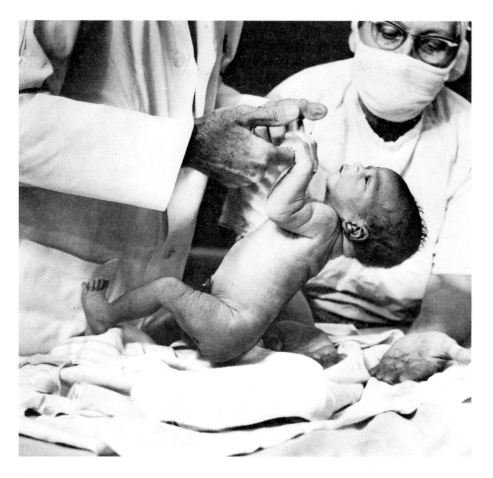

The grasping reflex is quite strong in newborns.

In the Babinski reflex, the toes fan out when the sole of the infant's foot is stroked.

The young infant shows swimming motions when placed in water.

al., 1972), but this conclusion is still controversial. The stepping reflex normally ends by the fourth month or so.

You may have seen reports on television of very young infants being "taught" to swim. Basically the "instructors" are capitalizing on the swimming reflex. If infants are placed in water with their stomachs down, they make swimming movements. These babies do not swallow water and can hold their breaths. However, *extreme caution* must be taken, because these infants cannot hold their heads above the level of the water and may easily drown. It is best to get both a physician's opinion concerning this activity and an expert's participation because there is such an obvious danger in this practice. The swimming reflex normally disappears by about the fourth month or so.

The Moro Reflex

Moro reflex
A reflex elicited by a sudden loud noise or momentary change in position, causing the back to arch, an extension of the arms and legs, and finally their contraction into a hugging position.

Of all the reflexes, perhaps the strangest is the **Moro reflex**. This reflex may be elicited in a number of ways. A sudden loud noise or a momentary change in position may cause infants to extend their arms and legs while arching the back, then contract them into a hugging position. The infant also cries. This reflex may even be set off by the baby. "When he startles, it upsets him even more, and he prolongs the vicious cycle by crying, startling, crying from the startle and so on" (Brazelton, 1981, p. 116). What survival value might this reflex have? Brazelton (1981) describes a film of a mother chimpanzee feeding while her baby plays at her side. She hears danger and "claps" the chimp on its back. The baby chimp exhibits the Moro reflex, ending the baby's hugging himself to the mother's chest, and they leave the scene of danger. It is quite an efficient system.

7. *True or False:*
Most of the infant's reflexes become stronger with time.

Only 20 percent of normal infants in one study showed the Moro reflex at five months of age (Rushworth, 1971), and its presence past six months or so is a sign that some neurological dysfunction may be present. Many other reflexes exist in the newborn. Most of these decrease and terminate with time, being replaced by behaviors that are voluntary.

ASSESSING THE NEWBORN

Every normal infant comes into this world with impressive sensory abilities and inborn behavioral responses. But infants show individual differences in their appearance, their sensory abilities, and the behavioral responses that can be measured at birth. Spend a little time watching neonates in a hospital nursery. You will notice that they are not all alike. Some are very still, others are fussy. Some are more alert than others. They also differ in their appearance and physical functioning. If we could determine which infants are more likely to suffer physical problems or even die, individual treatment programs suited to their special needs could be designed. A number of newborn-assessment scales are available. The Apgar Scale and the Brazelton Neonatal Behavioral Assessment Scale are two of the more popular scales used in hospitals today.

The Apgar Scoring System

The simplest approach to rating neonates, the **Apgar Scoring System**, was developed by Virginia Apgar (1953) and measures five physical characteristics—heart rate, respiration, reflex response, muscle tone, and color (see Table 5.2). The neonate is given a score of 0, 1, or 2 for each item according to specific criteria. For instance, if the newborn has a heart rate of 100 to 140 beats a minute, the infant receives a score of 2; for 100 beats a minute or below, a score of 1 is noted; and if there is no discernible heart beat a 0 is given. This rating is often done more than once. The first time is generally about a minute after birth, the second is usually either three, five, or ten minutes later (Self and Horowitz, 1979). Most neonates score between 7 and 10 on the scale (Williamsen, 1979). The lower the Apgar score, the greater the chance of behavioral problems or infant death (Apgar et al., 1958; Apgar, 1953). Babies who die from sudden infant death syndrome tend to have low Apgar scores as well (see Research Highlight on page 181). Some studies suggest that differences between infants who have received

Apgar Scoring System
A relatively simple system giving a gross measure of infant survivability.

TABLE 5.2   **The Apgar Rating System**
The Apgar Rating System is a relatively simple scale used to rate newborns. Each child is rated on the five behaviors indicated below. If the total score is greater than 7, no immediate threat to survival exists. If the score is lower than 4, the infant is presently in critical condition. Any score lower than 7 is cause for great concern.

	Score		
Area	*0*	*1*	*2*
Heart rate	Absent	Slow (< 100)	Rapid (> 100)
Respiration	Absent	Irregular	Good, infant crying
Muscle tone	Flaccid	Weak	Strong, well flexed
Color	Blue, pale	Body pink, extremities blue	All pink
Reflex irritability:			
Nasal tickle	No response	Grimace	Cough, sneeze
Heel prick	No response	Mild response	Foot withdrawal, cry

Source: V. Apgar, 1953.

scores of 7, 8, and 9 and those with a perfect 10 exist. Infants with a perfect Apgar score show more mature patterns of attention to stimuli than infants with good but not perfect scores (Lewis et al., 1967). Infants who receive a score of less than 7 need additional watching and care. The Apgar score can alert those responsible for the infant's care that a possible problem exists.

The Brazelton Neonatal Behavioral Assessment Scale

Brazelton Scale
A rather involved system for evaluating the infant's reflexes and sensory and behavioral abilities.

The **Brazelton Neonatal Behavioral Assessment Scale** is a more complex system. It provides information concerning reflexes and infant behaviors (see Table 5.3) (Jacobson et al., 1984). Among the behavioral items are measures of decreased responsiveness to visual stimuli, reactions to a bell and a pinprick, and the quality and duration of the infant's alertness and motor activity (Lester and Brazelton, 1982; Brazelton, 1973). The scale is a diagnostic tool, but it is also used to research cross-cultural differences between infants. For example, Freedman and Freedman (1969) found major differences between a group of Chinese-American and European-American infants. The Chinese-American infants

---

TABLE 5.3   The Brazelton Behavioral Assessment Scale

The Brazelton Scale is used for both diagnostic and research purposes. The examiner rates the child on each of these behaviors while the infant is in particular state. For example, the child's response to an auditory stimulus (e.g., the examiner's voice), is noted only when the infant is in the quiet alert state. The examiner is interested in discovering what the infant *can* do, not what he or she does.

1. Response decrement to repeated visual stimuli
2. Response decrement to rattle
3. Response decrement to bell
4. Response decrement to pinprick
5. Orienting response to inanimate visual stimuli
6. Orienting response to inanimate auditory stimuli
7. Orienting response to animate visual stimuli—examiner's face
8. Orienting response to animate auditory stimuli—examiner's voice
9. Orienting responses to animate visual and auditory stimuli
10. Quality and duration of alert periods
11. General muscle tone—in resting and in response to being handled, passive and active
12. Motor activity
13. Traction responses as he is pulled to sit
14. Cuddliness—responses to being cuddled by examiner
15. Defensive movements—reactions to a cloth over his face
16. Consolability with intervention by examiner
17. Peak of excitement and his capacity to control himself
18. Rapidity of buildup to crying state
19. Irritability during the examination
20. General assessment of kind and degree of activity
21. Tremulousness
22. Amount of startling
23. Lability of skin color—measuring autonomic lability
24. Lability of states during entire examination
25. Self-quieting activity—attempts to console self and control state
26. Hand-to-mouth activity

Source: B. M. Lester and T. B. Brazelton, 1982.

RESEARCH HIGHLIGHT   *Sudden Infant Death Syndrome*

A seemingly healthy baby goes to sleep. In the morning the baby is found dead. There is no sign of a struggle, no sign of any fight for life. An autopsy fails to discover any life-threatening condition. The cause of death is listed as *Sudden Infant Death Syndrome* (SIDS), commonly called crib death.

Perhaps as many as 10,000 infants in the United States die from this mysterious killer every year (De-Frain et al., 1982). Victims are most likely to be between two and four months of age. Some 90 percent are younger than six months, 97 percent are younger than one year. SIDS is more common among the poor, but no family, regardless of income and social status, is immune. The child's mother is more likely to be a smoker, to have received less medical care, and to be either young or have had many children with short intervals between pregnancies (Guntheroth, 1982). However, many mothers of SIDS victims do not fit this pattern.

The cause of Sudden Infant Death Syndrome remains elusive. SIDS is indicated only where no other cause of death can be found. It is strange that a healthy infant would die in the night with no apparent cause. However, research has found that these infants may not be as healthy as they first seem. Between 40 and 50 percent of SIDS victims suffer from some respiratory infection right before their death. Some have a history of stress both before and after birth. The Apgar scores of these infants are significantly lower than those of babies who did not suffer SIDS (Guntheroth, 1982). These babies, then, appear to be members of an "at risk" population, although they are essentially normal.

Because many victims of SIDS suffer from mild respiratory infections, research interest has centered on finding a relationship between SIDS and respiration. Many infants stop breathing for brief periods during sleep. These pauses are called apneic pauses. Perhaps the SIDS victim does not recover from these periods. But why? The SIDS victim may be weaker and possibly does not develop the ability to react to threats to survival. One theorist, Lewis Lipsitt (1978), argues this position. In the first month or so, the infant's defensive reactions to respiratory distress are reflexive. However, a learned reaction soon takes its place. Perhaps the victim of SIDS fails to learn to defend against such dangers because of some subtle neurological problem. Other suggested causes of Sudden Infant Death Syndrome include botulism (poisoning due to a toxin transmitted by bacteria), heatstroke, and hormone imbalances (Fogel, 1984). Perhaps no single cause will explain every case of SIDS; a number of different agents are implicated in the disorder.

At times we can predict which infants will be at risk for the disorder, but again, not all SIDS victims fit any specific pattern. Among those who are most at risk are infants who have suffered an oxygen deficiency, have a high apnea rate, or have almost died once from the disorder (near misses). These infants may be monitored in their own home using an apnea monitor. This device rings an alarm if the infant stops breathing for a specific period of time, allowing parents to respond to the problem. But use of a monitor does not guarantee the infant's survival, and the monitor may cause parents much distress. Parents may feel they cannot go out or use a noisy appliance because they will not be able to hear the monitor ring (Guntheroth, 1982).

Sudden Infant Death Syndrome is a family tragedy. Parents suffer self-doubt, guilt, and pain. There is a high rate of marital problems and divorce following the experience. When a child is born very prematurely or suffers some lingering disease, parents have time to prepare for the possibility of an impending death, but SIDS does not afford parents that opportunity. The shock is great, the questions are many, and the answers are few.

Parents of SIDS victims can be helped to cope with their grief. Social support is available from groups of parents who have suffered similar tragedies, where parents of SIDS victims discuss their feelings and help one another. Professionals may also aid the family by offering parents the facts as we know them today. Sometimes just the knowledge that an autopsy shows no cause of death alleviates some of the guilt.

Sudden Infant Death Syndrome is a mystery. Today, there is hope that with research we may learn more about its causes and eventually be able to prevent this silent killer from striking.

evoked potentials
A technique of measuring the brain's response to particular stimuli.

were calmer, showed fewer defensive behaviors, habituated to a light more quickly, and were easier to soothe than European-American infants.

The search for new ways to assess specific capabilities in infants goes on. One of the most important new techniques involves the use of visual **evoked potentials**. Electrodes are attached to the scalp of the infant, who is then shown a pattern, such as a checkerboard. As the color of the checks is changed, the waves from the part of the brain that is involved, the occipital cortex, produce a pattern that can then be measured against that produced by other infants. In this way, amblyopia, a disorder in which the person suffers dim and indistinct vision even though the eye is structurally normal, can be discovered (Patrusky, 1980). A number of other new techniques being evolved should lead to early diagnosis and treatment of sensory difficulties. This is especially important, because a critical period in which the brain learns to process information may exist. Lifelong disability may result if these dysfunctions are not discovered in early infancy.

BRAIN DEVELOPMENT

8. *True or False:*
There is a relationship between brain weight and intelligence.

At birth, the infant's brain weighs between 325 and 350 grams, while an adult male's brain weighs about 1,400 grams and a female's weighs 1,200 grams. (There is no relationship between brain weight and intelligence, although an adult brain of less than 1,000 grams is usually indicative of intellectual retardation.) The newborn's brain weighs about 25 percent of a mature adult's. It develops rapidly. By six months it weighs 50 percent of the adult brain's weight, and at two years of age it weighs three-quarters of what an adult's brain may weigh (Brierly, 1976). Brain growth allows the infant to develop new skills and capabilities.

Brain Development and Behavior

Most areas of the brain are not well developed at birth. The brain stem and spinal cord are most advanced (Hutt and Hutt, 1973), because they are involved in critical psychological functions and behavioral responses. Most areas of the upper region of the brain, the cortex, are relatively undeveloped. The sensory and motor areas are functional, but at a primitive level. The neurons that carry instructions from the cortex to the motor nerves lack the insulating cover called a *myelin sheath*, which is necessary for efficiently conducting impulses (Brierly, 1976). The process of myelinization is faster for the sensory tract than for the motor cortex. This has survival value, because the infant requires the information from the senses in order to safely negotiate the environment.

Between three and six months a very important change occurs. The upper portion of the brain, the cortex, develops. This switch from control by the lower, more automatic section of the brain to control by the upper, more voluntary centers affects behavior. For instance, most neonatal reflexes disappear within the first half-year of life. The upper centers of the brain are inhibiting these reflexes (Kalat, 1981).

The development of the brain is swift, and between three and six months a major changeover occurs. A number of factors can inhibit the development of the brain at this point, leaving the infant with a possible lifelong disability.

The Brain and Experience

The brain does not develop in a vacuum. Rosenzweig and his colleagues (1972), for instance, showed that the brains of rats who are raised in an enriched or impoverished environment differ. Experience makes an imprint on the brain, and lack of basic experience may hinder the brain's development. Wiesel and Hubel (1965) sewed one eye of a kitten closed for the first four to six weeks of life. After cutting the sutures and allowing the kitten the full use of its eyes, the cells that would normally process visual information for that eye were unable to do so. There is a critical period of four to six weeks in which the cortical cells develop an ability to process information from the eye. After that period, suturing the eye had little or no effect on the kitten.

For ethical reasons, experiments like this cannot be performed on human beings, but some evidence suggests that there may also be such a critical period in the development of human sensory abilities. People who are cross-eyed have difficulty focusing both eyes and sometimes undergo operations to reverse the condition. If the operation is performed early in life, up to three years, the condition is corrected and something like normal vision is restored. However, this is not true for adults who have the operation; they still show poor focusing even after the operation (Banks et al., 1975).

INFANT NUTRITION

Breast-feeding and Bottle-feeding

One of the first choices parents must make is whether to breast-feed or bottle-feed the baby. Infants' nutritional needs are different than those of adults (see Figure 5.3) and nutritional decisions throughout infancy and childhood are important to the future health of the child. Although bottle-feeding is very popular in the United States, there has recently been a resurgence of breast-feeding. In underdeveloped nations, a trend away from breast-feeding can be seen, which is unfortunate because without the medical and social checks available in the United States these infants may not be getting the proper nutrition. Some infant deaths from misuse of prepared infant formulas have been reported. In addition, many parents in underdeveloped countries cannot afford the formula. Some laborers in Africa spend as much as one-third to one-half of their income to buy prepared formula, which means their families must often go without other necessities of life (Wade, 1974). In an attempt to encourage breast-feeding, some countries now severely restrict the importation and use of infant formulas.

Are there benefits to breast-feeding? The answer is a definite yes. Mother's milk is the natural food for human infants and meets all the requirements for infants, with the possible exception of vitamin D (Woodruff, 1978). Vitamin D deficiency is rarely seen in breast-fed infants, though, since that vitamin is synthesized with the help of a normal amount of exposure to sunlight.

Mother's milk contains a number of helpful substances not found in prepared formulas. Some antibodies protect the infant against intestinal disorders, and immunities are passed on in breast milk. Mother's milk also contains chemicals that promote the absorption of iron. In addition, breast-feeding produces

FIGURE 5.3 **Comparison of the Nutrient Needs of a Three-month-old with Those of an Adult Male per Unit of Body Weight**
The infant's nutritional needs are vastly different from those of his parents. In the graph the adult's needs are set at 100 percent.

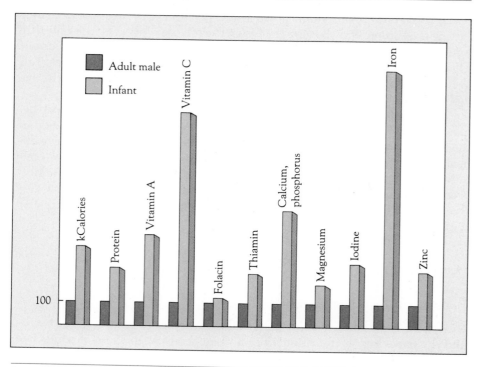

Source: Hamilton, et al., 1985.

fewer fat infants, and the incidence of allergies is less than in infants raised on artificial formulas. Breast-feeding also promotes better tooth and jaw alignment (Hamilton, et al., 1985). There are significant psychological benefits to the infant who is breast-feeding. The close contact between mother and child encourages the growth and development of the mother-infant bond and satisfies the infant's need for warmth and physical contact. Environmental pollutants, such as insecticides, are sometimes found in breast milk, but to date there is no evidence that these chemicals lead to any illnesses in the infant (Rogan et al., 1980).

Breast-feeding is nutritionally sound. But what of bottle-feeding with prepared formulas? Some advocates of breast-feeding make outlandish, unsubstantiated claims about the benefits of breast milk, and this may make mothers who wish to bottle-feed feel guilty, but there is no evidence of long-term differences between breast-fed and bottle-fed babies (Schmidt, 1979). However, whereas the infant's natural nutritional and psychological needs are normally satisfied naturally during breast-feeding, bottle-feeding may require more thought and concern. The caregiver must be certain to hold the baby close to give the child the physical contact that is so important to infants.

Today, many infant formulas meet the nutritional standards set by the Committee on Nutrition of the American Academy of Pediatrics. Most formulas are based on fortified cow's milk, but the incidence of allergies to cow's milk is estimated to be less than 1 percent of infants (Woodruff, 1978). In conclusion, although breast-feeding may be preferable, there is no reason that a loving, caring parent should feel guilty about bottle-feeding an infant.

Infant Malnutrition

It is difficult to look at the pictures of starving children in underdeveloped countries and not feel depressed. Perhaps these children would be better off if the pictures aroused anger in us. Since anger is an energizing emotion, that might lead to positive action. Laboratory studies of inadequately fed animals indicate that malnutrition leads to deficits in the size and number of brain cells (Dobbing, 1975), and autopsies of severely malnourished infants show they have between 15 and 20 percent fewer brain cells than average healthy infants (Winick, Russo, and Waterloo, 1970; Winick and Russo, 1969).

Infants who are severely undernourished may develop **marasmus**, a condition that involves severe weight problems. These children are literally all skin and bones. The heart is weakened, and resistance to disease is low. Between the ages of one and three, a common form of malnutrition in the Third World involves a protein deficiency. This is called **kwashiokor**, which comes from the Ghanaian word meaning "the evil spirit that infects the first child when the second child is born" (Hamilton and Whitney, 1982). This occurs in the newly weaned child when the child is subjected to a diet that is very deficient in protein. In this disorder, the child becomes apathetic and inactive, which is prob-

9. *True or False:*
An infant can be adequately fed using prepared formula instead of breast milk.

marasmus
A condition of severe underweight, heart irregularities, and weakened resistance caused by malnutrition.

kwashiokor
A nutritional problem often found in toddlers and preschoolers who are newly weaned and then subjected to a protein-deficient environment.

ACTION/ REACTION

Doing What Comes Naturally

Penny believes in breast-feeding. She believes it is the natural way to feed an infant and better for both the child and mother. She has told her younger sister, who is pregnant, that there is no other alternative and that mothers who bottle-feed are just plain lazy or ignorant. Penny thinks that the benefits of breast-feeding should be taught in high school, and she approves of the trend away from bottle-feeding. She has convinced several of her friends to breast-feed as well.

Last week, Penny and a friend went to a restaurant for lunch. Penny took her baby with her and asked for the last booth. While waiting for her lunch, she began to breast-feed the child. The owner of the restaurant asked her to leave, but Penny refused. She told the owner, "No one has to watch, and what I'm doing is normal and natural. If I had bottle-fed the child, no one would care."

1. If you were the owner of the restaurant, what would you have done?
2. If you were Penny's friend, what would you have advised her to do?

ably the body's defense against the malnutrition. Fluid fills the abdomen and legs, and the child is quite weak. Often normal childhood diseases become life-threatening. Most of the time, protein and calorie deficiencies are found together (Hamilton and Whitney, 1982). In the Third World, this combination, called **protein-calorie deficiency**, is the most common nutritional problem, contributing to the death of literally millions of children each year.

Although such severe cases of malnutrition are rare in Western, developed countries, they do sometimes occur in the poorest areas of those nations. However, a number of other deficiencies exist in developed countries. The most common is iron deficiency anemia. In addition, deficiencies in vitamin A, vitamin C, and riboflavin (a B vitamin) are not unusual (Eichorn, 1979). The effects of severe vitamin deficiencies are physically obvious, but the consequences of mild to moderate deficiencies are controversial.

The Long-term Consequences of Malnutrition

Malnourished children suffer severe growth problems, and malnutrition may permanently affect their intellectual and emotional development (Eichenwald and Fry, 1969). Recently, researchers have become more cautious in the interpretation of data (Ricciuti, 1980a), for we now know that the relationship between malnutrition and intellectual development is much more complex than first thought.

Malnutrition is found mostly among the poor. It is difficult to evaluate the "independent" effects of malnutrition on the child (Ricciuti, 1980b). A malnourished child is probably experiencing poor housing, poor sanitation, little or no medical care, increased exposure to disease, poor feeding and child-care practices, and severely limited educational and vocational opportunities (Ricciuti, 1980b). Much of the earlier evidence linking malnutrition to intellectual and emotional deficits may have confused the injurious effects of nutrition with those of poverty.

The evidence now indicates that the effects of malnutrition are mediated by a person's environment. Korean children suffering from various degrees of malnutrition and adopted before the age of two by middle-class families developed normal intelligence and did well in school (Winick, Meyer, and Harris, 1975). Richardson (1976) discovered that Jamaican children suffering from early severe malnutrition, whose families scored fairly high on social background measures, had intelligence scores only slightly lower than average. Malnourished children whose families scored low on social background factors scored far below children whose families scored higher. Malnutrition may have a greater impact on children who come from poor environments. The injurious effects of malnutrition may be moderated by improvements in the home environment.

Malnutrition is likely to lead to permanent physical and intellectual damage if it is prolonged, if it occurs early in life, and if it is left untreated (Ricciuti, 1980a; Ricciuti, 1980b). Fieldwork in Guatemala among children who suffer mild to moderate malnutrition demonstrates that dietary supplements can somewhat improve intellectual functioning (Townsend et al., 1982). Some programs that include nutritional education and improved health care have been more successful. The improvement depends some on the age at which the program is begun (McKay et al., 1978). Merely providing nutritional supplements in cases of mild

---

protein-calorie deficiency
The most common nutritional deficiency in the world, in which neither the number of calories nor the protein consumed is sufficient.

10. *True or False:*
The injurious effects of malnutrition can be reduced by a good environment.

to moderate malnutrition may not be sufficient. If these children are to develop normally, their entire environment must be substantially improved as well.

Obesity

They call it "baby fat," but according to a recent theory, it may not dissolve with the years. A child's initial birth weight is not related to later obesity, but over-feeding in the first year or two of life could lead to a lifelong battle with obesity.

Fat cells are manufactured by the body in the first year or two of life and in adolescence (Garn et al., 1975). If an infant is overfed, there will be more fat cells. In fact Hirsch and Knittle (1970) found that obese people had as much as 100 per-cent more fat cells than normal individuals. Their fat cells contained only about 20 percent more fat than the normal-weight individual. These fat cells stay with a person throughout life. The amount of fat stored in these cells decreases when that person goes on a diet, but the abnormally high number of fat cells remain. Infants who are overfed may be programmed for weight problems throughout life. A radical restructuring of infant feeding is not warranted by these findings, but parents should beware of shoving a bottle at the baby every time the child cries, and they should try to keep toddlers away from junk food.

GROWTH AND MOTOR DEVELOPMENT

As we have seen, the neonate is born with many impressive perceptual and learning abilities, which develop rapidly. Parents are always surprised and pleased when their infant masters some skill or performs some new action for the first time. Nowhere is this rapid development any clearer than in the areas of growth and motor development.

Growth and weight gain during infancy and toddlerhood are shown in Table 5.4 and Table 5.5. Heights and weights that fall between the 25th and 75th percentile are usually considered normal. Those that fall outside these figures should be investigated by a doctor but may not indicate any problems.

Gather together pictures of yourself or a sibling from birth to three years of age. The changes in physical appearance tell a story all their own. If your parents kept a record of your growth and weight gain, you will notice a decrease in the *rate* of growth and weight gain over that period of time. In Chapter Three, the tremendous increase in both length and weight during the prenatal period was noted. Sometimes the unborn child's weight doubles within a month. Obviously, that rate must slow down. The slowing-down process is evident in the first three years of life. Within six months the infant has grown more than 5 inches, and in the next three months 3 more inches will be added to the baby's length. In the entire second year the child grows approximately 4 inches (Lowrey, 1978).

A self-correcting process also takes place. If a baby's father is tall but the mother is short, the child's growth may be limited in the womb, but the child may catch up during the first six months and return to a normal growth rate (Tanner, 1970). Each child has a preordained path to travel in physical develop-ment (Waddington, 1957). Illnesses, stress, and nutritional inadequacy may de-flect the path for a time, but a self-righting tendency called **canalization** takes place. The child's natural growth trajectory may be permanently deflected from

canalization
The self-righting process in which the child shows a catch-up in growth despite a moderate amount of stress or illness.

TABLE 5.4   **Growth During Infancy and Toddlerhood**
All data is presented in centimeters. To convert to inches multiply by .39.

Sex and Age	*Percentile*						
	5th	*10th*	*25th*	*50th*	*75th*	*90th*	*95th*
Male	*Recumbent length in centimeters*						
Birth	46.4	47.5	49.0	50.5	51.8	53.5	54.4
1 month	50.4	51.3	53.0	54.6	56.2	57.7	58.6
3 months	56.7	57.7	59.4	61.1	63.0	64.5	65.4
6 months	63.4	64.4	66.1	67.8	69.7	71.3	72.3
9 months	68.0	69.1	70.6	72.3	74.0	75.9	77.1
12 months	71.7	72.8	74.3	76.1	77.7	79.8	81.2
18 months	77.5	78.7	80.5	82.4	84.3	86.6	88.1
24 months	82.3	83.5	85.6	87.6	89.9	92.2	93.8
30 months	87.0	88.2	90.1	92.3	94.6	97.0	98.7
36 months	91.2	92.4	94.2	96.5	98.9	101.4	103.1
Female							
Birth	45.4	46.5	48.2	49.9	51.0	52.0	52.9
1 month	49.2	50.2	51.9	53.5	54.9	56.1	56.9
3 months	55.4	56.2	57.8	59.5	61.2	62.7	63.4
6 months	61.8	62.6	64.2	65.9	67.8	69.4	70.2
9 months	66.1	67.0	68.7	70.4	72.4	74.0	75.0
12 months	69.8	70.8	72.4	74.3	76.3	78.0	79.1
18 months	76.0	77.2	78.8	80.9	83.0	85.0	86.1
24 months	81.3	82.5	84.2	86.5	88.7	90.8	92.0
30 months	86.0	87.0	88.9	91.3	93.7	95.6	96.9
36 months	90.0	91.0	93.1	95.6	98.1	100.0	101.5

Source: P. V. V. Hamill, et al. 1977.

its course only if environmental deficiencies continue for a long period of time or are very severe.

Factors Affecting Growth

Genetic considerations are most important in determining growth, but environmental elements are important too. One environmental element is nutrition. Severe malnutrition that occurs early in life and remains untreated may lead to a permanently small stature (Eichenwald and Fry, 1969). Nutrition works both ways. Improvement in nutrition over the past 100 years in the United States have added significantly to the average height of the population. Improved nutrition in Japan over the past thirty years has produced significant increases in the average height of Japan's younger generations (Curtis, 1975). Disease is another factor that can affect the inborn trajectory. Finally, stress has been implicated in lack of growth.

Gardner (1972) investigated the growth patterns of children in orphanages where poor treatment and great stress were present. These children were retarded in growth. Such growth retardation due to lack of affection and excessive stress is known as **deprivation dwarfism.**

deprivation dwarfism
Growth retardation due to emotional factors such as stress.

TABLE 5.5   **Weight Gain During Infancy and Toddlerhood**
All data is given in kilograms. To convert to pounds multiply by 2.2.

Sex and Age	Percentile						
	5th	10th	25th	50th	75th	90th	95th
Male	*Weight in kilograms*						
Birth	2.54	2.78	3.00	3.27	3.64	3.82	4.15
1 month	3.16	3.43	3.82	4.29	4.75	5.14	5.38
3 months	4.43	4.78	5.32	5.98	6.56	7.14	7.37
6 months	6.20	6.61	7.20	7.85	8.49	9.10	9.46
9 months	7.52	7.95	8.56	9.18	9.88	10.49	10.93
12 months	8.43	8.84	9.49	10.15	10.91	11.54	11.99
18 months	9.59	9.92	10.67	11.47	12.31	13.05	13.44
24 months	10.54	10.85	11.65	12.59	13.44	14.29	14.70
30 months	11.44	11.80	12.63	13.67	14.51	15.47	15.97
36 months	12.26	12.69	13.58	14.69	15.59	16.66	17.28
Female							
Birth	2.36	2.58	2.93	3.23	3.52	3.64	3.81
1 month	2.97	3.22	3.59	3.98	4.36	4.65	4.92
3 months	4.18	4.47	4.88	5.40	5.90	6.39	6.74
6 months	5.79	6.12	6.60	7.21	7.83	8.38	8.73
9 months	7.00	7.34	7.89	8.56	9.24	9.83	10.17
12 months	7.84	8.19	8.81	9.53	10.23	10.87	11.24
18 months	8.92	9.30	10.04	10.82	11.55	12.30	12.76
24 months	9.87	10.26	11.10	11.90	12.74	13.57	14.08
30 months	10.78	11.21	12.11	12.93	13.93	14.81	15.35
36 months	11.60	12.07	12.99	13.93	15.03	15.97	16.54

Source: P. V. V. Hamill, et al. 1977.

Principles of Growth and Development.   Infants do not develop in a hap-hazard manner. Their development follows consistent patterns (Shirley, 1931) and is governed by principles that are now well understood. For instance, the head and brain of the infant are better developed at birth than the feet or hands. The **cephalocaudal principle** explains that development begins at the head and proceeds downward ("cephalocaudal" means from head to tail). Control of the arms develops ahead of control of the feet.

A second rule of development notes that organs nearest to the middle of the organism develop before those farthest away. The **proximodistal principle** explains why the internal organs develop faster than the extremities. It also correctly predicts that control of the arms occurs before control of the hands, which pre-dates finger control (Whitehurst and Vasta, 1977).

Muscular development follows a path from control of **mass to specific** muscles. First, the individual develops control over the larger muscles responsible for major movements. Then, slowly, control is extended to the fine muscles. This is why younger children use broad, sweeping strokes of the forearm or hand when coloring with a crayon. It is only later that the child gains the dexterity to use finger muscles in a coordinated manner.

Development is also directional. It moves from a state of largely involuntary, incomplete control toward one of voluntary control, from undifferentiation to-

cephalocaudal principle
The growth principle stating that growth proceeds from the head downward to the trunk and feet.

proximodistal principle
The growth principle stating that development occurs from the inside out, that the internal organs develop faster than the extremities.

mass to specific
The developmental principle stating that the larger muscles develop before the fine muscles.

ward subtle differentiation. Under normal circumstances, the movement is forward, with new abilities arising from older ones.

Motor Development

Development occurs within a predictable sequence. Nothing demonstrates this as well as the development of such motor skills as crawling, walking, and finally running.

The first step a child takes is a milestone for the child and a joyous occasion for the parents. A new world of exploration is now open to the child. Many parents may not be fully aware of the series of accomplishments that lead up to walking. Today we can predict what advancements in motor control will occur next, but not necessarily when they will happen. Mary Shirley (1933) made exhaustive observations of a group of children beginning on the day of their birth. These infants all progressed through the same sequence, leading up to walking. Shirley was interested only in when the baby would first perform any of the acts on her chart (see Figure 5.4), such as sitting with support or standing with help, not how well they performed it. Each of these abilities is perfected with practice.

A word about the ages included in Shirley's chart is in order. Although the sequence of motor development is standard, the ages noted are merely guidelines. Radical departures should be brought to the attention of a pediatrician, but there are no "average" babies. Each infant will negotiate each stage at his or her own rate. Some will stay longer at one stage than others. The age at which a child develops these abilities is a function of that child's maturation rate as long as the child is well fed and healthy and has an opportunity to practice these skills.

While Shirley's sequence is well accepted, other researchers have placed different age norms on these accomplishments. These differences are due to a number of factors, including the criteria used to assess success at a task or the timing of the observations. Perhaps you have met parents who tell you how early their children sat up or scooted over to the sofa on their own. Precocious motor development does occur, but it is not related to higher intelligence scores on its own (Illingworth, 1974). However, early emergence of motor abilities allows the child more freedom to explore the environment, to do things on his or her own, and to learn. Studies of the gifted show that they walk about a month earlier than average (Kirk and Gallagher, 1979), which is certainly not a significant advantage. Greatly retarded motor development should always be investigated, but even some children who demonstrate delayed development may have normal intelligence.

The Question of Cultural Differences.   Although individual differences in the rate of motor development are well accepted, the question of cultural differences is more difficult to resolve. Almost thirty years ago, Geber and Dean (1957) noted that African infants were more advanced motorically at birth than European infants. A number of other cross-cultural studies followed. Some research supported these findings (Keefer et al., 1978), while other research cast doubt on the conclusions (Warren and Parkin, 1974). Just how African and European infants differ at birth is still a controversial question. However, most researchers agree that African infants reach motor milestones like sitting and walking before

European or American infants (see Super, 1981). How can we explain these differences?

The most obvious explanation involves a difference in the rate of maturation, which is largely influenced by genetics. While this may be partially true, another explanation is possible. In many African societies, infants are reinforced for their motor behavior, even at very early ages. Parents play games with them using these emerging motor skills. In some tribes, mothers begin walking-training very early, and African children are placed in a sitting position and supported much more often than American babies. Differences in child-rearing procedures may partly explain the motor advancement. African infants are precocious on motor skills on which they receive the most practice (Super, 1981).

This raises two questions. First, what is the effect of lack of practice on the development of motor skills? Second, can motor skills be accelerated through a special training program?

The Effects of Practice and Stimulation.   No one doubts that some opportunity to practice motor skills is necessary for development of those skills, but there are many roads to mastering them. Dennis and Dennis (1940) found that Hopi Indian children who were reared in a restrictive environment through the use of the cradleboard still walked at about at the same age as infants not reared on the cradleboard. These children received excellent stimulation and were allowed off the cradleboard more often as they matured.

Flexibility in developing motor skills was shown in another study. Dennis and Najarian (1957) investigated the development of children growing up in an orphanage in Lebanon. These children showed retarded development in their first year, but by the time they reached four to six years of age, they were normal. The greater opportunities these children experienced after age one was sufficient to counter their poor early environments. Although Dennis admitted that severe malnutrition results in motor retardation, he does not believe that this caused the retardation. Instead, Dennis argued that it was due to environmental restriction and that this deficit could be remedied. If corrected, the effects of a deprived environment could be reduced and children can motorically catch up. If nothing improves, these children would not develop normal motor abilities. Finally, Dennis argued that Shirley's mean ages at which children achieve motor milestones are met only under favorable environmental conditions (Dennis, 1960). In other words, maturation alone is not sufficient to explain motor development. The environment must be stimulating and provide opportunities for practice as well.

In most homes, children receive at least minimal stimulation and some opportunity to explore the environment. The question, then, is not one of overcoming stimulus deprivation. Instead, parents are interested in the possibility of hastening motor development. To that purpose, a number of programs aimed at improving motor development have been advanced, and some research has shown them to be effective. In one experiment, Zelazo and his colleagues (1972) found that a specific program of practice capitalizing on the stepping reflex enabled children to walk at an earlier age than expected. This is still a controversial question, however, and evidence for both sides exists (Ridenour, 1978). Parents should be wary of stimulation programs that promise large gains in motor and cognitive development. Our efforts would better be spent on optimizing the envi-

11. *True or False:*
African infants develop faster than European infants.

FIGURE 5.4   The Sequence of Motor Development Leading to Walking

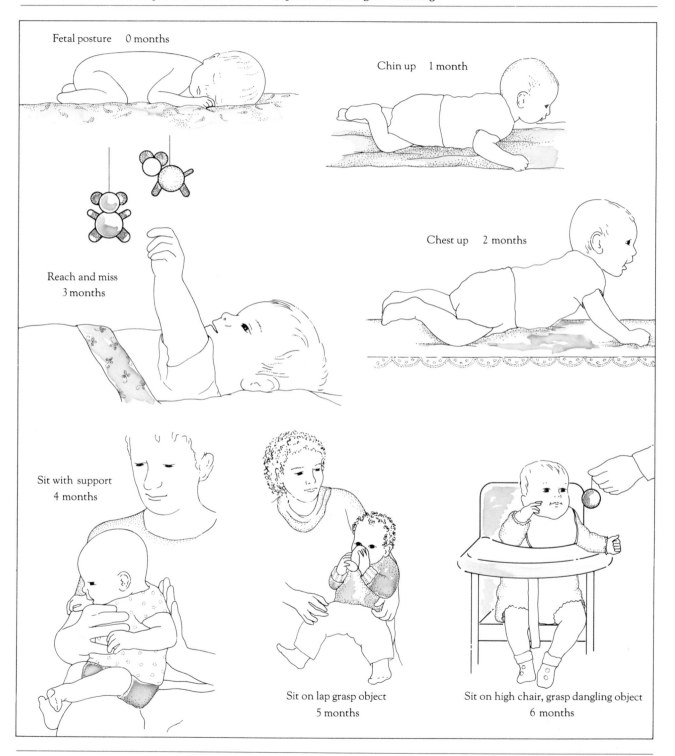

Fetal posture   0 months

Chin up   1 month

Chest up   2 months

Reach and miss
3 months

Sit with support
4 months

Sit on lap grasp object
5 months

Sit on high chair, grasp dangling object
6 months

Figure 5.4 continued

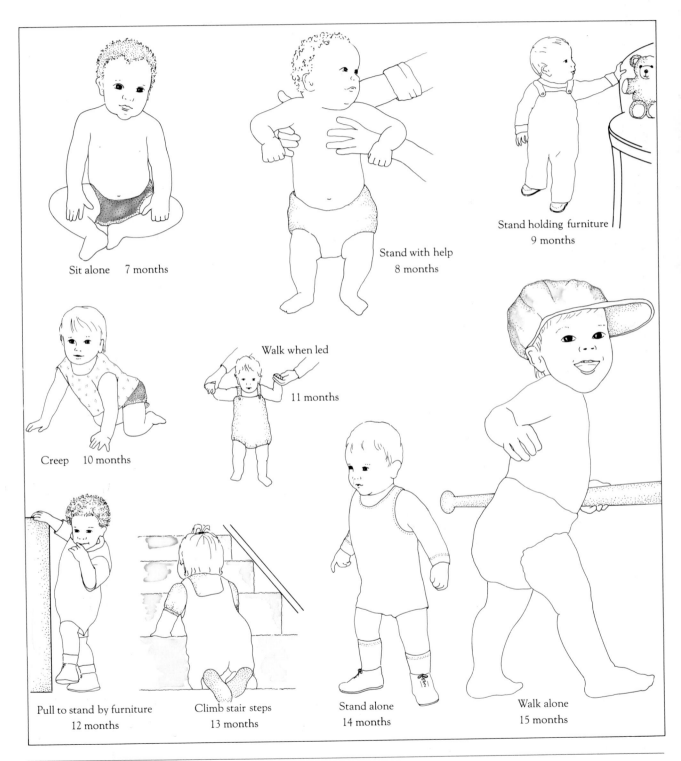

Sit alone   7 months

Stand with help
8 months

Stand holding furniture
9 months

Creep   10 months

Walk when led
11 months

Pull to stand by furniture
12 months

Climb stair steps
13 months

Stand alone
14 months

Walk alone
15 months

Source: M. M. Shirley, 1933.

Toddlers are active explorers and show a great deal of curiosity.

ronment, allowing each child to take advantage of opportunities to explore and learn when that child is ready.

Focus on the Toddler

Physical and motor development follow a predictable course. Using this knowledge, a verbal picture of the infant and toddler (the child between eighteen months and about three years old) can be constructed. Gesell and his colleagues (1940, pp. 34–35) describe the motor abilities of the two-year-old in the following way:

> Two is decidely motor-minded. His most numerous and characteristic satisfactions are muscular. He greatly enjoys gross motor activity. In this respect he is like eighteen (months), but he has made important advances in postural control. Two is more flexible at the knees and ankles, has a better balance and consequently can run, while Eighteen propels himself with a wobbly, stiff, flat gait. Two no longer needs personal assistance in walking up and down stairs, but he has to shift into "marking time" at each tread. He can jump down from the first tread without help, one foot leading the other as he leaps. He can walk up to a ball and kick it on command. (Eighteen simply walks up to the ball.) He can hasten steps without losing equilibrium, but he cannot yet dart about, making short turns and sudden stops.

Gesell's descriptions offer us a verbal picture of the child in action at various ages and give parents an idea of what to expect. These descriptions are valuable for parents and physicians. For instance, most pediatricians do not make exhaustive observations of their young patients during their monthly examinations. They rely instead on parental reports of what the average child is doing at this or that age. For instance, a doctor might ask the parents of a six-month-old whether the child is putting toes in the mouth in order to ascertain developmental progress in the most general terms. The doctor can then roughly gauge the child's developmental rate and be alerted to problems in the areas of growth and development.

Toddlers in Action.   At about eighteen months the child enters the toddler stage. The youngster has been walking for a few months but is still unsteady. A new world is open to toddlers. They go until they drop, often becoming very cranky but refusing to take a nap. They prefer the wide open spaces and dislike confinement. Sometimes toddlers will just drop and sleep wherever they have been playing.

There is an exciting quality to their newfound capabilities, and they go from one activity to another with breathtaking speed. No one can mess up a room like a two-year-old. Their energy seems unbounded. Yet they can easily get themselves in trouble. They seem to miss the edges of tables by inches—accidents are common at this age. The toddler is often thrilled by the underside of sinks and cabinets, mainly because these items are at eye level. Toddlers often become interested in things that parents miss on a casual inspection of an area. This is why it is important that the caregiver carefully evaluate the child's environment. It is a good idea to get down on your knees to look at the room as a toddler might. One parent who did this found nails sticking out of a piece of paneling, which could have caused injury to a child.

Toilet-training.   An important event in toddlerhood is the beginning of toilet-training. One of the most common questions is how early to start? In one study, McGraw (1940) started to train one twin from each of two pairs as early as two months of age, while their siblings were allowed to wait. The early training did not help. The later-trained children trained much more quickly and were soon up to the others. Training started later is faster (Sears et al., 1957). It is best to train a child when the child is ready.

Some parents place a great deal of importance on early training. The expectation that a one- or two-year-old is going to be completely dry day and night not only is unreasonable but also may be harmful, for it leads to criticism from parents when the child has an accident. Toilet-training is a complicated affair (Wesley and Sullivan, 1980). The child must learn to pay attention to the signals that the bladder is full, then learn to hold it in until a bathroom is available. This is a complete change from the diaper stage.

Besides the obvious maturational need to control the muscles, there are individual and environmental factors involved in training. Some children do not like being soiled. Others may be aware that friends are not wearing diapers and may train easily and quickly. Still others may require more time and have many accidents.

Once a child is maturationally ready, toilet-training should not take long, according to Azrin and Foxx (1977) authors of a book on the subject. They do not recommend training a child much younger than two years old, and they advocate using reinforcement and imitation. The toddler is carefully taught the mechanics of going to the bathroom, including how to lower and raise his or her pants, being positively reinforced each step of the way. Then a doll that wets is used to illustrate the elimination process. The child sees the doll placed on a potty and wet. The child is then reinforced for doing the same. Sometimes a candy is used to prompt the child to eliminate. Using this learning technique, the child who is ready can be trained quickly.

The toddler is an active, engaging being who is rapidly gaining the ability to control internal and external aspects of the environment. Control over bladder and bowel movements give the child a sense of accomplishment and more freedom from the caregiver. At the same time, developing motor abilities allow toddlers more range to explore their environment.

COMMUNICATION IN THE YOUNG CHILD

The toddler can communicate verbally. Eighteen-month-olds are using the word *no* constantly and understand commands even though they may be unable or unwilling to carry them out. By age two a child may know anywhere between 300 and 1,000 words and is beginning to put two and three words together (Elkind, 1978). Verbal communication is not the first attempt at social communication though. The infant communicates using both the cry and the smile.

Infant Crying

A crying infant is totally distressed. At times the lips quiver, and the baby seems to be inconsolable. Then a parent comes, speaks a few soft words, lifts the child from the crib to the shoulder, pats the back, and the world is whole again. The cry seems to effect other infants as well as adults (see Research Highlight "Are Infants Sensitive to the Crying of Other Infants" on page 198).

The cry of an infant has survival value. It informs not only others of the baby's condition but also encourages the parents to care for the infant. Many young parents are concerned that the child will be spoiled if they pick the baby up, or that they won't understand what the infant is communicating through the cry. Research indicates that they need not worry. There are qualitative differences between the cries (Wolff, 1965), and parents are often able to understand the meaning of these cries from environmental cues (Murray, 1979).

Types of Cries.   The infant emits a number of different cries. Besides the birth cry there is a hunger cry, a pain cry, and a "mad" cry. Each of these can be measured, and each elicits a different response from the infant's caregiver. The first cries are probably more reflexive than communicative, although they may soothe the mother by letting her know that the child is alive and all right. Wolff (1965, 1969) isolated the three types of early cries—the hunger cry, the mad cry, and the pain cry. The *hunger cry* is heard when the infant is hungry, but it is also heard if there is any environmental disturbance. The cry is rhythmical and follows this pattern:

- CRY
- SILENCE
- WHISTLE SOUND WHILE TAKING IN AIR
- SILENCE
- CRY

Parenting style is more important than the form of crying in eliciting parental reactions. Parents do not respond to the hunger cry in any fixed way. Some always give the bottle or breast when they hear the cry, others check diapers first. Experienced parents do not come as quickly when they hear this cry as do inexperienced parents.

The *mad cry* follows the same general pattern as the hungry cry, except that it is more forceful as more air is pushed past the vocal cords. Most parents have no difficulty noting the differences between these cries. Parental response to the mad cry was less varied than the response to the hunger cry. Parents did go immediately to the crib to check, but they were not overly concerned—they were a bit amused at this early show of "rage."

The *pain cry* is different. The first cry is much longer, as is the first rest period. It lasts as long as seven seconds, during which time the infant lies still, holding his or her breath. This is followed by the gasping intake of air and cries of shorter and varying durations. The pain cry is easily recognized. The loud pain cry begins suddenly, and no moaning occurs before it. The first cry is quite long, and a long period of breath-holding occurs. Both parents and nurses recognize the pain cry and rush to attend to the infant. Concern shows both on their faces and in the way they approach their caregiving responsibilities.

Control of Crying.   If you've ever cared for an infant, you've probably faced the age-old problem of how to comfort a crying child. A number of strate-

12. *True or False:*
The infant's cry of pain is qualitatively different from other types of cries.

Just Let Her Cry?

Karen and Burt have two children, Eileen (age four years) and Brenda (age four months). The only word that describes Eileen, according to her parents, is "spoiled." She whines and expects everything, and Karen and Burt don't want the same thing to happen with Brenda.

Burt believes the problem stems from their early child-rearing practices, when they always picked Eileen up when she cried. This reinforced her for crying. Karen is not sure about that, but she admits that Eileen is now a bit of a problem.

When Brenda cries, the parents face a decision. They think they know when she is in pain or has wet diapers, and they always attend to those needs. But when the child is "just crying for attention," what should they do? Should they wait or pick her up? They both find letting the child cry a difficult course of action, but believe it will be best for all concerned.

Karen's parents don't agree. They see nothing wrong with Eileen and believe it is more important to pick Brenda up and comfort her than to "train her."

1. If Karen asked you how to handle the situation, what advice would you give her?

2. If you were Karen's parents, would you have offered advice even if though you were not asked for it?

gies have been tried, and their success depends on the age and state of the infant. A softly crying child is more likely to be easily mollified than an infant crying loudly and completely embroiled in discomfort.

It is a popular misconception that the sound of a heartbeat has some special property that quiets a baby. To study the effects of sounds on cry suppression, two-day-old infants were exposed to the sounds of a metronome, non-English lullabies, a tape recording of a human heart, or simply a no-sound condition (Brackbill et al., 1966). Each of these regular rhythmic sounds reduced crying, but heartbeats had no greater success than any of the other sounds. Although continuous, low-level stimulation will often quiet a baby, the most effective way—as most parents know—is to pick up and and hold the baby (Korner and Thoman, 1972). But won't this spoil the child?

Not so, say Bell and Ainsworth (1972), who followed twenty-six infant-mother pairs to examine maternal responsiveness to infant crying. Parents tried to reduce crying by giving the babies toys or pacifiers, feeding them, or rocking them. Close physical contact was most often used. Infants whose mothers responded promptly cried less frequently in the later months of infancy than those infants whose mothers did not respond as quickly. Picking the baby up did not lead to any more crying later in infancy. Infants who were picked up were more secure and required less contact later in the first year. This strategy fosters mother-infant communication and strengthens the relationships.

13. *True or False:*
The sound of a heartbeat has a special property that quiets a baby.

On the surface, Bell and Ainsworth's study seems to cast doubt on the behavioral or learning theory approach to infant crying. After all, infant crying, like any other behavior, should be affected by the rewards and punishments available in the environment. Etzel and Gewirtz (1967) found that crying could be reduced if it was ignored, especially if smiling behavior was reinforced at the same time.

Five years after the appearance of this study, Gewirtz and Boyd (1977) wrote a rejoinder to Bell and Ainsworth's study. They pointed out what they saw as technical flaws in the work and noted that Bell and Ainsworth had failed to note the differences between responses to various cries. For instance, behaviorists never advocated ignoring pain cries. Rather, they are interested in reducing crying for attention. In addition, Bell and Ainsworth's conclusions can be explained using a behaviorist perspective. For example, children may have cried less at one year because their mothers responded to precry vocalizations rather than the cry. These vocalizations were reinforced by their mothers' behavior. In their reply, Ainsworth and Bell (1977) defended both their methodology and their conclusions.

Whether a child can be spoiled by being picked up remains a controversial question. We know that crying can be shaped through attention or lack of attention, but it is doubtful whether responding to an early infant's cry spoils the child. One factor should be taken into consideration, though. When parents re-

---

RESEARCH HIGHLIGHT   **Are Infants Sensitive to the Crying of Other Infants?**

When we hear someone crying, it usually has some emotional effect on us. This is true for children as well. In a series of experiments, Simner (1971) exposed newborns to tape-recorded cries of other neonates. These infants responded by beginning to cry. They were more sensitive to the cries of a five-day-old neonate than to either a cry engineered through a computer or the cry of a five-and-a-half-month-old infant. Could such empathy be innate?

Grace Martin and Russell Clark (1982) presented forty infants whose average age was a bit over 18 hours with tape recordings of their own cry or that of another neonate. These recordings were presented when the infants were either crying or calm. The infants demonstrated a remarkable degree of empathy. Infants who were originally calm tended to cry when they heard the sounds of another neonate crying. Crying infants tended to continue to cry when exposed to the cries of other infants, but stopped when they heard recordings of their own cry. Calm infants, hearing their own cries, did not begin to cry.

In a second study, newborns were presented with tapes of a crying chimpanzee, an eleven-month-old child, or another newborn. Newborns exposed to the cry of another newborn tended to cry, but not those who heard the cry of an eleven-month-old or the chimpanzee.

Martin and Clark conclude that neonates as young as 18 hours can distinguish among their own cries, that of another infant or an older child, and that of a chimpanzee and respond differentially. More research is needed to discover just how they can make these discriminations.

Scientists are only beginning to appreciate the astounding abilities of newborn infants. The neonate was once viewed as an inactive, incapable organism with few, if any, sensory abilities. But science is now constructing a new view of the neonate. The newborn is an alert, active organism with a functional if immature sensory system and an interesting behavioral repertoire.

Sources: G. B. Martin and R. D. Clark, "Distress Crying in Neonates: Species and Peer Specificity," *Developmental Psychology,* 1982, *18,* 3–9; M. Simner, "Newborn's Response to the Cry of Another Infant," *Developmental Psychology,* 1971, *5,* 136–150.

spond to the needs of their child a bond forms between them which contributes to the development of a sense of trust and security in infants.

Infant Smiling

Every infant in every culture smiles. In fact, the development of smiling is parallel in every society. Smiling is infrequent in the first month or two, then it increases dramatically until four months or so, after which it declines (Super, 1981; Gewirtz, 1965). Blind infants smile in response to social stimuli at about the same time as sighted children, even though they could not have seen any smiles (Freedman, 1965). After four or five months, the frequency of smiling becomes dependent on one's culture and family environment.

14. *True or False:*
The first smile is an innate behavior.

15. *True or False:*
Blind infants smile at about the same time as sighted infants.

The smile begins as an inborn response, but it soon develops from that undifferentiated response to internal stimuli to a response that is attached to social stimuli and reinforcement. If infants are rewarded for smiling by being picked up, talked to, and handled, the frequency of their smiling increases (Brackbill, 1958). The smile contributes to the establishment and maintenance of the infant-caregiver relationship (Eveloff, 1971). Most parents take great pleasure in interpreting their child's smile as a positive response to their own activity. Their actions are thus reinforced by the child.

The child's physical growth and motor and perceptual development affect the reactions of people around. The more alert and responsive the child, the more reinforcing the child is likely to be to the caregiver. One last physical factor is crucial to the way others react to the baby—the infant's gender.

SEX DIFFERENCES

■ "It's a boy!" the doctor announced. "A boy," repeated George Ellsworth with a look of wonder on his face. He began to think of all the things he wanted for his son and the things they would do together—like play ball and work on model airplanes. "How strong he looks," he said to a friend as they looked at the infant through the nursery window.

■ "It's a girl!" the doctor announced. "A girl," repeated George Ellsworth with a look of wonder on his face. He began to think of all the things she would do, like play with dolls. "How cute and delicate she looks," he said to a friend as they looked at the infant through the nursery window.

The first announcement made to parents is the baby's sex. In fact, the first question people ask when told a new baby has arrived concerns gender (Intons-Peterson and Reddel, 1984). How important is gender to the way infants are treated? Do any inborn physical differences exist at birth?

Sex Differences at Birth

The question of what sex differences are present at birth is difficult to answer. There are contradictions throughout the literature. When differences are demonstrated, they tend to be moderate and unstable (Moss, 1974). Many experimental findings of sex differences have not held up under further investigation (Birns, 1976). Overlap is also common. For instance, if newborn females are more sensitive to certain stimuli, as when a blanket is removed (Bell and Costello, 1964), this does not mean that *every* female infant will be more sensitive than every male infant. Individual differences must also be taken into account. Still, some differences do appear in the first few days after birth.

16. *True or False:*
Females are more mature at birth and continue to develop at a faster rate.

One of the most consistent differences is that females are more mature at birth and continue to develop at a faster rater. Girls are four weeks more advanced in skeletal development at birth (Tanner, 1970), and they reach motor milestones faster than males. The average female child sits up, walks, toilet trains, and talks earlier than the average male child (Kalat, 1980). Another difference is that the average female infant performs more rhythmic behaviors, such as sucking and smiling, than the average male infant (Feldman et al., 1980; Korner 1973; Moss, 1967). Still another is that males exceed females in large musculature movements, such as kicking. They also show greater muscular strength and can lift their heads higher at birth (Korner, 1974).

Other reports of sex differences are not adequately replicated by research. For instance, Wolff (1969) noted that two-week-old females are more sensitive to physical contact, and some research shows females to be more sensitive to taste (Nisbett and Gurwitz, 1970). Most of the research attempting to show that one sex or the other is superior in perceptual development has failed to find positive results. The similarities are far more impressive than the differences.

How Parents View Sons and Daughters

These early differences may affect parental behavior, magnifying the effects of the differences. The more developmentally superior females may be more responsive. Being capable of doing things at an early age may be more reinforcing to the parents. Advanced development could then lead to more attention and different types of interaction with the caregivers.

17. *True or False:*
Parents see male infants as sturdier than female infants.

Differences in parental response to male and female infants can readily be found. The trick is to interpret and place them in perspective. For example, even when male and female infants are the same size, weight, and physical condition, parents see daughters as weaker and more sickly and see males as sturdier and more athletic (Provenzano and Luria, 1974). Parents show more concern for the health of daughters than sons (Pedersen and Robson, 1969), even though the male infants are more likely to become seriously ill.

Some indirect evidence indicates that this labeling process continues throughout infancy and toddlerhood. College students were shown videotapes of nine-month-old infants demonstrating negative responses to a loud buzzer (Condry and Condry, 1976). When subjects were told that the infants were male, they described the emotion as anger, but if the infants were described as female, the emotion was labeled fear. In another study, Meyer and Sobieszek (1972) showed videotapes of seventeen-month-old children, describing them as either males or females to male subjects. When the child was labeled male, the men described the child in such stereotyped terms as "independent," "aggressive," and "active." They interpreted those same actions as delicate, passive, and dependent when they were told the toddler was a female. From birth on, we perceive and interpret the behaviors of males and females differently. Men are more likely than women to see sex-stereotyped behavior. But does this differential perception lead to differential treatment?

Do Parents Treat Sons and Daughters Differently?

The first treatment difference begins in the hospital nursery, where pink signs for girls and blue signs for boys are pasted onto the tiny bassinets in which newborns are placed. In some hospitals, other differences can be found. In one, the female's hair is combed into a curl, while a male's locks are combed straight. These small differences are plentiful, but do they have any effect on later behavior? In their mammoth review of the literature on sex differences, Maccoby and Jacklin (1974) were more impressed with the similarities in treatment than with the differences. Although their conclusions have been criticized by some (Block, 1976), we should be wary of claims that a particular difference in treatment leads to some recognizable difference later in life. Most studies are not constructed to allow the jump from early infant treatment to later behavioral differences.

Some studies do find differences in parental treatment, but again, interpretation is difficult. At birth, mothers appear to talk and smile more to girls than to boys (Thoman et al., 1972). The qualitative nature of their speech differs as well. They use longer sentences and more repetition than do mothers of boys (Cherry and Lewis, 1976). Male infants receive more physical contact than females, but this changes by three months, when girls receive more contact (Moss, 1967). In later infancy, mothers talk to and play more with daughters than sons. By thirteen months, daughters touch their mothers more than sons (Goldberg and Lewis, 1969).

The opposite pattern is found in fathers' interactions with their infants. In early infancy, fathers spoke more to daughters than to sons (Rubelsky and Hanks, 1971). This changed at about three months, with fathers verbalizing more to male infants than to female infants. However, the evidence indicates that fathers do not interact much with their infants at this stage. Since most infants spend so much more of their time with their mothers, the verbal interchange between mother and child is perhaps more important in promoting language development than that between father and infant.

As boys and girls develop, other differences in treatment become more noticeable. Smith and Lloyd (1978) noted how a mother's behavior is affected by her perception of gender. Seven toys were placed on a table within reach of a subject, who was asked to play with an infant between five and ten months old. Some of these toys were considered stereotyped "male," such as the squeaky hammer and stuffed rabbit wearing trousers and the bow tie. Some were stereotyped "feminine," such as a doll and a squeaky bambi. A squeaky pig, a plush ball, and an hourglass-shaped rattle were considered neutral. The baby's mother presented the infant to the subjects by name. Each baby was dressed in clothing that made the gender seem obvious. Actually, these babies were properly identified to the subject as to gender only sometimes—at other times they were cross-dressed and misrepresented. The subjects presented the doll and hammer to the baby only when they appeared to be gender appropriate, and they reinforced babies perceived as males more often for efforts to crawl, walk, or use their large muscles. Thus, males are reinforced in their attempts to develop their gross motor actions, which involve large-scale physical play (Smith and Lloyd, 1978).

18. *True or False:*
Parents treat infant boys and girls similarly during infancy.

 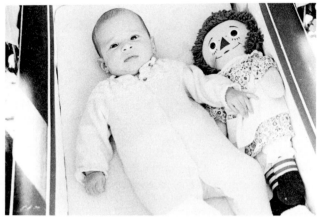

Differences in parental treatment of sons and daughters begin very early in life.

These differential patterns of reinforcement are also seen with samples of two-year-olds. Fagot (1978) observed parent-child interactions in 24 families, rating 46 child behaviors and 19 parental reactions to them. Boys were allowed to play alone, and parents were more likely to join in play with boys than with girls. Girls receive more praise and more criticism than boys. Both parents were more likely to stop the play activities of boys. Parents gave more positive feedback to boys when they played with blocks, and more negative reaction when they played with dolls. Parents reacted more negatively when girls manipulated objects than when this was done by boys. Girls also received more positive responses when they played with dolls than did boys. Again consistent with other research, fathers seemed more concerned with sex-appropriate behavior, giving more negative feedback to boys playing with dolls and other soft toys. Parents criticized girls more often when they attempted to participate in large motor activities like running, jumping, and climbing. More positive responses were given for their daughters' requests for help.

But parents did not want to restrict their children's playmates to a single sex, nor would they avoid buying a sex-inappropriate toy if the child wanted it. They showed a willingness to allow the child to follow his or her own pattern of interests as the child grew older, no matter whether they were stereotyped sex-appropriate or not. Some 80 percent planned to encourage a sexual equality attitude in their children as they grew.

Interpreting Early Differences

In summary, studies show that the sex of the child does affect parental treatment. Females receive more verbal feedback and are given more praise for helping and playing with dolls, as well as more negative feedback for using gross motor skills. On the other hand, males receive positive encouragement to develop their gross motor skills and are not encouraged to play in a stereotyped sex-inappropriate manner.

While gender is a biological fact of life, people's reactions often exaggerate its importance. Three main conclusions stand out quite clearly from the research in sex differences in early life.

First, the initial differences between the sexes are quite limited at birth (Bee, 1978), confined mostly to the greater number of mouth movements and the faster maturation of females. These may have meaning, because the female infant is more likely to reinforce her parents for social behaviors than the young male.

Second, the treatment of males and females tends to be more similar than different, although the differences may in the end turn out to be important. Parents give both sons and daughters affection and do not generally tolerate aggression from either. However, there is evidence that different patterns of behavior, even in the early years, are reinforced differentially. Males receive greater reinforcement for engaging in physical play, while girls are positively reinforced for asking for help from others and for helping others. Both are reinforced for playing with sex-appropriate toys. Their rooms are even furnished differently. Rheingold and Cook (1975) found that boys' bedrooms not only had more toys but were also gender-related. Animal furnishings and athletic equipment were more commonly found in boy's rooms, while the rooms of girls contained more dolls and flowers. The environment itself is shaped at an early age to encourage sex-stereotyped behavior.

Third, although parents often do not vocalize their sex-stereotyped opinions, they may show them in some of their behaviors toward their children. Fathers are stricter in reinforcing these stereotyed sex-apppropriate behaviors, especially in their sons, than are mothers. This conclusion is supported by research as well as everyday experience, as a story related by Shirley Weitz (1977) indicates. Weitz was gift-shopping for a pregnant friend. She rejected the thought of buying something pink, which would be inappropriate if the baby were male, and looked for something blue, which could be worn by both males and females, or a neutral yellow. She was considering an outfit that had a few ruffles but wasn't frilly or feminine when the saleswoman said, "I wouldn't buy that if I were you. If the baby's a boy, the *father* won't want him to wear that" (Weitz, 1977, p. 66). She realized the saleswoman was correct and made another choice. The saleswoman knew it would be the father, not the mother, who would object. Parents are frequently unaware of how they may affect the development of their children and may need consciousness-raising if they are to follow their stated aim of allowing children to develop their own abilities.

In this chapter, we examined the perceptual, motor, and physical development of the child from birth through toddlerhood. The pattern of increased abilities and skills is impressive. The child makes even more impressive gains in ability to relate to the world, process information, and communicate. It is to the infant and toddler's developing cognitive abilities that we turn next.

Chapter Summary

1. The neonate is born with characteristics and abilities that make survival possible. Newborns can see, hear, smell, and taste. Although relatively insensitive to pain at birth, this sense increases dramatically in the next few days.

2. Neonates spend 16–17 hours a day sleeping and spend a great deal more time than adults in dream sleep. The infant's state is related to behavior.

3. Classical and operant conditioning has been demonstrated in the infant. Infants can also imitate.

4. The neonate is born with a number of reflexes, such as the sucking, rooting (turning the head toward a source of stimulation when a cheek is stroked), grasping, stepping, and swimming reflexes. The functions of other reflexes, such as the Babinski reflex (fanning of the toes when soles of the feet are stroked) and the Moro reflex (extending arms and legs while arching the back, then contracting them in a hugging manner) are not known.

5. The Apgar Scoring System and Brazelton scales are ways of assessing the survivability and abilities of the infant.

6. The brain grows rapidly in the months following birth, and such factors as nutrition and experience are important in optimizing such growth.

7. There are nutritional and health advantages to breast-feeding, but there is no evidence of long-term differences between children who were breast-fed and those who were bottle-fed. Malnutrition is a major problem in the Third World and leads to many developmental problems, including a smaller number of brain cells. The effects of lesser degrees of malnutrition is more controversial. The effects of malnutrition are mediated by the environment.

8. Genetic considerations and nutrition both affect development. Acute illnesses and stress may deflect children from a normal growth projectory, but a self-righting process enables them to return to normal when the stress is past. Development occurs in a consistent pattern from the head downward (cephalocaudal) and from the inside out (proximodistal), and muscular development progresses from mass to specific.

9. Motor development also follows a specific pattern. The rate may be affected by culture, genetic endowment, and the environment.

10. During toddlerhood, the child begins toilet-training. Children who are trained later take less time to train. The toddler's physical abilities often outweigh the child's judgment, making home safety a first priority.

11. A number of cries have been identified, including the hunger, pain, and mad cries. The first smile is reflexive, but with social reinforcement it becomes attached to specific situations.

12. Sex differences in infancy are moderate and unstable. Girls are more mature at birth and develop at a faster rate than males. Females show more oral and facial movements. Males show more large musculature movements such as kicking and greater muscular strength.

13. Parents treat their infant sons and daughters differently. Activities requiring gross motor control are more likely to be reinforced in male infants. In toddlerhood, girls are given more praise and criticism than boys. Fathers are more rigid in sex-stereotyping behavior than mothers.

■ *Answers to True or False Questions*

1. *False.* Correct statement: The newborn doesn't look like the pictures in advertisements.

2. *False.* Correct statement: The newborn is well equipped to survive, with aid, in the world.

3. *True.* The newborn is nearsighted at birth, but by six months visual acuity approaches that of a normal adult.

4. *False.* Correct statement: Newborns can hear at birth.

5. *True.* Newborns are relatively insensitive to pain, but sensitivity to pain develops quickly.

6. *False.* Correct statement: Infants dream a great deal more than school-age children.

7. *False.* Correct statement: Many infant reflexes become weaker and finally terminate.

8. *False.* Correct statement: Except for very small brains, there is no relationship between brain weight and intelligence.

9. *True.* Many infant formulas meet nutritional standards for infants.

10. *True.* We now know that a good environment can reduce the injurious effects of malnutrition.

11. *True.* African infants attain milestones of motor development more quickly than European infants do.

12. *True.* The pain cry is qualitatively different and recognizable.

13. *False.* Correct statement: Any regular rhythmic sound will reduce crying.

14. *True.* The first smile is innate.

15. *True.* Even though blind infants could not have seen a smile, they still begin to smile at about the same time as sighted infants.

16. *True.* The average female infant is more mature at birth and develops at a faster rate than the average male infant.

17. *True.* Parents see their infant sons as sturdier and their infant daughters as weaker and more sickly.

18. *False.* Correct statement: Although there are many similarities in how parents treat their sons and daughters, there are some important differences.

CHAPTER SIX

Cognitive Development in Infancy and Toddlerhood

■ *Are the Following Statements True or False?*

Try the True-False Quiz below. See if your answers correspond to the information in this chapter. Each question is repeated opposite the paragraph in which the answer can be found. The True-False Answer Box at the end of the chapter lists complete answers.

___ **1.** A baby banging a toy against the side of a crib is showing "intelligent" behavior.

___ **2.** The two-month-old infant believes that mother has disappeared when she leaves the room.

___ **3.** Three-month-old infants can recognize their mother's face.

___ **4.** Psychologists can accurately predict later intelligence from scales measuring infant intelligence.

___ **5.** Programs that teach parents how to interact with their children have largely failed to improve the intellectual functioning of these children.

___ **6.** Parents of competent infants spend many hours of time teaching them concepts.

___ **7.** Interactions with infants and toddlers of less than one minute have no effect on their cognitive development.

___ **8.** Overstimulation is as great a problem as lack of stimulation.

___ **9.** Child development specialists equate fast development with superior development.

___ **10.** If children do not receive the optimal stimulation by the age of two, they will underachieve throughout the childhood and adolescent years.

■ A six-year-old reads the word *tiny* from a comic book.

■ A four-year-old tells his mother that the television show she is watching is "totally awesome."

■ A three-year-old puts a simple puzzle together.

■ A two-year-old tells her father that she wants a polar bear for a pet.

■ An eight-month-old bangs a rattle against the side of the crib again and again.

intelligence
In the Piagetian view, any behavior that allows the individual to adapt to the environment.

1. *True or False:*
A baby banging a toy against the side of a crib is showing "intelligent" behavior.

If you were asked which of the above events shows **intelligence,** you would probably say the first four. After all, three of these show verbal abilities, while putting together a puzzle demonstrates problem-solving skills. Few people would consider the baby's repeatedly banging the toy against the crib intelligent behavior. But isn't it? If intelligence is considered adaptive behavior, then this eight-month-old is learning about causality—that banging the rattle will lead to a predictable noise.

THE WONDER OF COGNITIVE DEVELOPMENT

During the first two years of life, children develop a basic understanding of the world around them. They learn to recognize objects and people, to search for objects that are not in their field of vision, to understand cause and effect, and to appreciate the concept of space. The average adult takes this knowledge for granted, but a child's understanding of these concepts takes many months to develop.

How does this development occur? An infant does not go to bed one night without understanding cause and effect and wake up the next morning comprehending this basic concept. The understanding is developed gradually over many months. This chapter will investigate the process by which this transformation occurs. In addition, many recent books advocate a particular program of infant exercises and stimulation. Some claim that if parents follow the author's advice, they will increase their child's intelligence. Is the acquisition of such seemingly simple concepts as cause and effect related to later intelligence? And if so, what should parents do to maximize a child's intellectual potential? These very practical issues will be examined later in the chapter.

PIAGET'S THEORY OF SENSORIMOTOR DEVELOPMENT

sensorimotor stage
Piaget's first cognitive stage, during which the infant learns about the world using sensory and motor abilities.

representation
The ability to create a mental picture of what is transpiring in the environment.

The manner in which infants develop an understanding of their world was described in detail by Jean Piaget. The infant is negotiating the first stage of cognitive development, the **sensorimotor stage.** This stage lasts from birth to the appearance of language and consists of six substages (Piaget, 1962). It is called "sensorimotor" because infants learn about their environment through their senses (hearing, vision, touching) and motor activity (reaching, grasping, kicking) (Piaget, 1967). How else does anyone know the world?

Much of our knowledge of the environment is symbolic. It is based on words and language and requires an ability to **represent,** or create a mental picture of, what is going on around us. For instance, when your friend tells you not to sit on

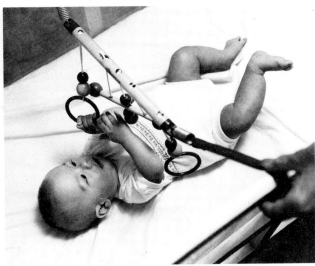

the chair that has spilled coffee on it, you don't have to see the coffee or get your pants soggy. You understand the idea behind the statement and can create a mental picture of what has happened. All this is far beyond the abilities of the infant.

In the sensorimotor stage, infants learn about their world through their senses and motor activity.

Trends and Premises in Infant Cognitive Development

Two important trends underlie Piaget's view of cognitive development in infancy. First, there is a trend from dependence solely on the objective content of the environment toward internal representation. At first the infant must experience everything. Later children can create mental images of the world and understand and use language. Second, the infant develops an appreciation that he or she is separate from other objects in the world and that the existence of those objects does not depend on the infant's perception of them (Brainerd, 1978).

Piaget's theory is based on two important premises. First, children are active participants in their own development. Second, development takes place in stages, and each stage acts as a foundation for a succeeding stage (Petersen, 1982). No stage or substage can be skipped, and each must be negotiated in turn.

Interpreting Ages and Stages

As with any stage theory, the standard caution should be kept in mind. Piaget considered the substages of the sensorimotor stage to be invariant, that is, infants go through substage one, then proceed to substage two, then to substage three, and so forth. They never revert to a previous substage, nor do they skip a substage. However, the age at which children negotiate these substages varies from child to child. The ages used here are meant as guideposts and not as absolutes. Children proceed through these substages at their own rate, and the time at which they enter and leave each substage varies.

The Substages of Sensorimotor Development

It is easy to overlook the basic cognitive advances in infancy. The ideas that objects exist even if they are out of sight, or that by tugging at a string with a toy on the end the toy will come toward you must be learned. Piaget describes the development of such elementary concepts in terms of six substages.

Reflexes (0–1 Month).   In substage one, the infant is basically an organism reacting to changes in stimuli. The behavior of infants is rigid and reflexive. They are almost entirely dependent on these inborn patterns of behavior. Yet infants do learn and can be conditioned. During the first month, reflexes are often modified in an infant's everyday experience. For instance, an infant may suck harder if a bottle containing milk, instead of a toy, is placed in the mouth (Ault, 1977).

Primary Circular Reactions (1–4 Months).   The most prominent feature of substage two is the emergence of actions that are repeated again and again. These are called **primary circular reactions.** They are primary because they are focused on the infant's body rather than on any outside object (Phillips, 1975). They are circular because they are repeated. The infant tries to recreate some interesting happening. For example, the infant may have had a thumb drop into his or her mouth by accident. This is pleasurable, so after the thumb falls out, the infant attempts to find the mouth again (Ault, 1977).

primary circular reactions
Actions that are repeated over and over again by infants.

Secondary Circular Reactions (4–8 Months).   An important change occurs in substage three. **Secondary circular reactions** are observed. Infants now focus their interest not on their bodies but on the consequences of some action on the external environment. That is why they are secondary reactions rather than primary. The infant does something that is intended to create some environmental reaction. For instance, an infant shakes a rattle and is surprised to find that it produces a sound. The child may pause, then shake it again, hear the sound, and continue the activity (Flavell, 1985). Piaget (1952) observed that his daughter Lucienne shook her bassinet by moving her legs rapidly, which made the cloth dolls swing from the hood. She looked at them and smiled and continued the movements.

secondary circular reactions
Repetitive actions that are intended to create some environmental reaction.

Coordination of Secondary Reactions (8–12 Months).   In substage four, the child coordinates two or more strategies to reach a goal. This shows intention. Means and ends are now separated. The child begins to show perseverance in spite of being blocked. For instance, if you place your hand in front of a toy, the child will brush it away. The change can also be seen in terms of play activities. Children will enjoy stacking items again and again, or banging a pot with a spoon over and over (Willemsen, 1979). This activity, so charming at the beginning, may become annoying after a while.

Tertiary Circular Reactions (12–18 Months).   We now begin to see **tertiary circular reactions,** stage five. Although actions are still repeated and thus circular, they are no longer carbon copies of each other. Children now seek out novelty (Ault, 1977). They are now little scientists, experimenting with the world in order to learn its characteristics and mysteries and seeking out novelty. The

tertiary circular reactions
Repetitive actions with some variations each time.

substage five child picks up objects from the crib and throws them out, listening and watching intently to learn what they sound like and how they look on the floor (Willemsen, 1979). When you put them back in the crib, the child may do it again.

Ault (1977) describes the difference between the child's employing secondary circular reactions and tertiary circular reactions. Suppose the child is placed in a playpen with lots of toys. The infant in the secondary circular reaction stage drops a block from a particular height again and again. He does not vary the action. The child in the stage of tertiary circular reactions may drop different items out of the playpen and vary the distances from the ground.

Invention of New Means Through Mental Combination (18–24 Months). Substage six marks the beginning of representation (Flavell, 1977). The child can now think of an object independent of its physical existence. The character of play and imitation changes. Children are now capable of **deferred imitation,** that is, they can observe some act and later imitate it. Before going to bed, an eighteen-month-old may make pedaling motions with the feet, just as the child saw older siblings do while riding bicycles hours before. Children also show some pretend play in this substage (Belsky and Most, 1981). Until now, spoons were something to suck on, eat with, or bang. Now a spoon may stand for another, unrelated object, such as a person or a piece of corn on the cob.

deferred imitation
The ability to observe an act and imitate it at a later time.

Object Permanence

How a child acquires the concept of an object, as Piaget describes it, is just as impressive as the child's cognitive development from the reflexive stage to mental representation.

Suppose you put your coffee cup on a table and leave it there while you go to the refrigerator for a snack. You return to find the cup gone. You remember where you had put it and reason that someone must have moved it. You search for the cup and finally find it. This sounds simple, but such a plan of action re-

In early infancy, babies do not show object permanence, the understanding that objects exist even though they are out of sight.

quires quite a bit of knowledge. First, you understood that even while you weren't watching it, your coffee cup still existed. In other words, the cup exists whether or not you are attending to it. Second, you remembered where you had put it. Third, you developed some search pattern. We take for granted that objects and people are permanent, that is, they exist outside our perception of them. Most students are surprised to discover that infants must torturously develop this understanding over a number of months.

Some of Piaget's findings in the area of **object permanence** are especially challenging. For instance, if you have a nine-month-old infant available for study, try this experiment. Show a toy to the infant and then put it behind a cover. The infant easily retrieves the toy. Now, put the toy behind a different cover while the child is watching. The infant will still go to the first cover to recover the toy! This finding has been observed in many studies (Petersen, 1982).

How Infants Develop Object Permanence.   Researchers study the development of object permanence by hiding objects in a variety of ways and observing children's search patterns. Infants develop their ability to understand object permanence in a series of stages identifed by Piaget (1954). In stage one (0–2 months), infants look at whatever is in their visual field but will not search when the item or individual disappears. For instance, the infant looks at mother but doesn't search for her when she leaves the room (Ault, 1977). Instead, the infant looks at something else.

During stage two (2–4 months), the infant looking at some item will continue to look in the direction of the item after it disappears. However, Piaget does not see this as true object permanence because the search is basically passive (Piaget, 1954).

During stage three (4–8 months), we begin to see some active search for items. Now if an object is partially covered by a handkerchief, the infant tries to lift the cloth to discover the rest of the object (Diamond, 1982). Children who drop something from a high chair look to the ground for it. It is as if they can now anticipate the movement of an item. The child at this stage does not show complete object permanence, however, for the search for the hidden object consists only of a continuation of eye movement, some expectation that something in motion may continue its trajectory. The child will not search for an object if it is completely hidden from view.

In stage four (8–12 months), the child will now search for an item that is completely covered by a handkerchief. However, if the child is allowed to find the item in one place, and the item is then hidden elsewhere while the child watches, the child will search in the first location. The child has simply identified the object with a particular location (Diamond, 1982).

In stage five (12–18 months), children can follow the object through the displacements. They no longer search for an item under the first pillow if it has been moved to a second one while they are watching. Piaget (1954, p. 265) describes it this way:

> Observation 53: Jacqueline watches me hide my watch under cushion A on her left, then under cushion B on her right; in the latter case she immediately searches in the right place. If I bury the object deep she searches for a long time, then gives up, but does not return to A.

The stage five child's understanding of object permanence is far from perfect, however. Piaget designed a simple test to demonstrate the child's limitations. His

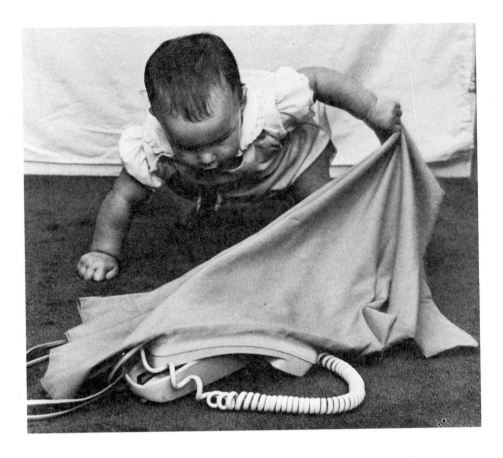

Later in infancy, children develop object permanence. This child isn't fooled by the presence of the blanket that conceals the telephone.

daughter had been playing with a potato and placing it in a box that had no cover. Piaget (1954, p. 266) notes:

> I then take the potato and put it in the box while Jacqueline watches. Then I place the box under the rug and turn it upside down thus leaving the object hidden by the rug without letting the child see my maneuver, and I bring out the empty box. I say to Jacqueline, who has not stopped looking at the rug and who has realized that I was doing something under it: "Give papa the potato." She searches for the object in the box, looks at me, again looks at the box minutely, looks at the rug, etc. but it does not occur to her to raise the rug in order to find the potato underneath.

Notice that in this stage the movement from one hiding place to the other must be performed under the child's gaze. The child's search for a hidden object is still based on visual information. No logical inferences are formed.

During the last stage (18–24 months), children becomes free from the concrete information brought in through their senses. They can now construct a mental representation of the world and locate objects after a series of invisible displacements. They can imagine where an item might be (Diamond, 1982).

Object Permanence and Infant Behavior. Piaget's description of the infant's cognitive development explains some common infant behaviors. For instance, children in substage five of the sensorimotor period who are dropping toys out of their playpens despite pleas to stop are not doing this out of any malicious intent, they are practicing tertiary circular reactions. And take the exam-

The game of peekaboo allows the child to test his assumptions concerning object permanence.

ple of the old game of peekaboo, in which you cover your face with your hands, then take them away. As a child gains more knowledge of object permanence, the child will pull down your hands, exposing your face. The child is validating the expectation that you are still there. Or perhaps a four-month-old begins to cry hysterically after playing alone for a while. You notice that the baby has dropped a toy out of sight. Since children younger than six months do not search for hidden objects, you may find that merely picking it up and placing it in the baby's field of vision is enough to stop the crying.

Piaget's Theory Under Scrutiny

Piaget's description of infant and toddler cognitive development which is summarized in Table 6.1, is accepted by many psychologists. Because his findings are partly based on his observations of his own children, it is fair to ask whether the theory has stood up well to rigorous scientific study. A great deal of research has been performed in an attempt to test Piaget's contentions in this area empirically.

Before such research could be performed, reliable scales to test an infant's cognitive abilities at a particular point in time were needed. After years of research, Uzgiris and Hunt (1975) developed a scale for measuring such Piagetian tasks as object permanence and causality. For example, the observer presents the infant with a certain task, such as following a slowly moving object through a 180-degree arc, and notes the infant's reaction. This scale is used to investigate Piaget's contention that children proceed through a series of stages in their development of object permanence.

The most popular approach to this problem has been to present tasks that a child in one stage should be able to do, but not a child in a preceding stage, and note whether the progression holds. Brainerd (1978, p. 75) puts it this way: "If X is an earlier stage than Y, then children should always pass the X test before they pass the Y test and they should never pass the Y test before the X test."

These experiments have generally supported Piaget's views (Kramer et al., 1975; Uzgiris, 1973). In fact, Piaget's theory is quite popular with psychologists all over the world (Nyiti, 1982), and studies of cognitive development in infancy using Piaget's concepts have been done in many countries from the Ivory Coast, Zambia, and Botswana in Africa to the Indian subcontinent (Super, 1981). The results from studies around the world show that Piaget's descriptions hold under a variety of environmental conditions, although the development of object permanence and causality is delayed in some cultures and more advanced in others.

While these differences are interesting, the similarities are more impressive. After reviewing the research in this area, Dasen and Heron (1981, p. 305) state:

> Differences in the chronological age at which the substages of sensori-motor intelligence are attained do occur. However, in emphasizing these cultural differences, we may overlook the amazing commonality reported by all these studies: in fact, the qualitative characteristics of sensori-motor development are identical in all infants studied so far, despite vast differences in their cultural environments.

Problems with Piaget's Views.   Although Piaget's views have been largely supported by research, some problems remain. First, the way that Piaget presented the tasks to the infants may have affected their reactions. Second, a fundamental error in logic may have crept into these studies. Just because infants do not successfully complete a particular task does not mean they can't do it. Perhaps the child has the ability to perform some task but either is not motivated to do so or cannot perform the motor activity required. Third, though the concept of substages does serve to focus our attention on particular aspects of a task, why choose six substages? Why not twelve or fifteen (Gratch, 1979)?

The Competency-Performance Argument. These arguments are too logical to dismiss without further consideration. The most intriguing argument may be the contention that children may be capable of doing something but for some reason cannot or do not. Have you ever "known" something but were unable to put it into words? Perhaps you failed an essay test but felt that you knew the information. You just could not perform the required action of putting your knowledge on paper. Perhaps you didn't have the vocabulary or the time. Maybe the pressure was too great. Perhaps the questions were phrased in such a way that the correct response in your memory wasn't tripped.

There is another, even simpler explanation. Let's say you are asked to write a paragraph about the administration of Warren Harding but sprained your wrist. You can't write, and trying to do so with your other hand is folly. You might fail the test because you could not write the information down on the paper. In this situation, you would speak to the teacher, but that option is not available for an infant. It is clearly possible for someone to know something, that is, be competent, yet not be able to perform a certain activity.

Whenever an infant cannot perform a particular task, Piaget interprets it in terms of competency: the child does not have the cognitive sophistication necessary. But some psychologists are not so sure about that. If we change the physical composition of the task, maybe the results would be different. Psychologists working with infants must sometimes use novel and unusual approaches to discover what infants know about their world. (See Research Highlight "Can Infants Tell the Difference Between Two and Three?" on page 218.)

Characteristics of the Task and the Infant. Some evidence suggests that infants are more capable than Piaget believed. Individual and situational factors influence the performance of the infant. For example, when testing for object permanence, the infant's motivation is important. Lingle and Lingle (1981) used the Uzgiris-Hunt scale to test infants between the ages of eight months and thirteen months on object permanence. Three different objects were used. One was a familiar object that the child had played with for a week, the second was an attached object that had been used to comfort the child, such as a bottle or rattle, while the third was an unfamiliar object. Since each task on the Uzgiris-Hunt scale is administered twice, two different examiners administered the object-permanence test. The older infants performed better on the object-permanence test than the younger infants, which would be expected for Piaget's theory. However, the infants tested for the attached object by one of the examiners performed better than infants tested in the other conditions.

Why did the examiner make such a difference? After ruling out examiner expectations for success, the researchers suggest that motivation might account for this unusual finding. If one of the examiners increased the infants' feelings of ten-

TABLE 6.1   **A Multidimensional View of Development During the Sensorimotor Period**

As this table indicates, the advances in cognition during the sensorimotor period are quite impressive.

Stage	Developmental Unit	Intention and Means-end Relations	Meaning	Object Permanence
1	Exercising the Ready-made Sensorimotor Schemes (0–1 mo.)			
2	Primary Circular Reactions (1–4 mo.)		Different responses to different objects	
3	Secondary Circular Reactions (4–8 mo.)	Acts upon objects	"Motor meaning"	Brief single-modality search for absent object
4	Coordination of Secondary Schemes (8–12 mo.)	Attacks barrier to reach goal	Symbolic meaning	Prolonged, multi-modality search
5	Tertiary Circular Reactions (12–18 mo.)	"Experiments in order to see"; discovery of new means through "groping accommodation"	Elaboration through action and feedback	Follows sequential displacements if object in sight
6	Invention of New Means Through Mental Combinations (18–24 mo.)	Invention of new means through reciprocal assimilation of schemes	Further elaboration; symbols increasingly covert	Follows sequential displacement with object hidden; symbolic representation of object, mostly internal

sion or uneasiness, we would expect that the infants tested by this examiner would be more likely to seek out the object that in the past had been comforting. In addition, we might expect that the infants tested by the higher-stress examiner would not perform as well on unattached objects as the infants tested by the lower-stress examiner. This exact pattern was found. When examining object permanence studies, such factors as familiarity with the object and motivation must be taken into account.

Space	Time	Causality	Imitation	Play
			Pseudo-imitation begins	Apparent functional autonomy of some acts
All modalities focus on single object	Brief search for absent object	Acts; then waits for effect to occur	Pseudo-imitation quicker, more precise. True imitation of acts already in repertoire and visible on own body	More acts done for their own sake
Turns bottle to reach nipple	Prolonged search for absent object	Attacks barrier to reach goal; waits for adults to serve him	True imitation of novel acts not visible on own body	Means often become ends; ritualization begins
Follows sequential displacements if object in sight	Follows sequential displacements if object in sight	Discovers new means; solicits help from adults	True imitation quicker, more precise	Quicker conversion of means to end; elaboration of ritualization
Solves detour problem; symbolic representation of spatial relationships, mostly internal	Both anticipation and memory	Infers causes from observing effects; predicts effects from observing causes	Imitates 1. complex, 2. non-human, 3. absent models	Treats inadequate stimuli as if adequate to . imitate an enactment—i.e., symbolic ritualization or "pretending"

Source: J. L. Phillips, 1975.

The testing procedures may also lead investigators to make the logical error that performance always reflects competency. Even the type of cover used when hiding an object seems to make a difference. Rader and his colleagues (1979) studied object permanence in infants whose median age was 160 days. They hid plastic keys in a well and covered the keys with either a 12-by-12-inch washcloth or a 7-by-7-inch piece of manila paper covered with blue felt. Infants differed in their success with the task. Some succeeded in uncovering the keys when the paper

---

RESEARCH HIGHLIGHT   *Can Infants Tell the Difference Between Two and Three?*

Infants cannot count, but that does not mean they have no concept of quantity, according to researchers Mark Strauss and Lynne Curtis. Since the verbal abilities of infants are so limited, special procedures must be used to test their ability to tell the difference between two and three, or three and four.

Strauss and Curtis tested 96 infants (48 males and 48 females) between the ages of ten and twelve months in one of two conditions. In the heterogeneous condition, half the infants were presented with a series of slides in which only the number of items remained constant, while the type of item varied (dogs, houses). In the homogeneous condition, both the type of item (chicks) and the number remained the same, while the size and position of the stimuli varied.

To compensate for the problem of communicating with preverbal infants, a habituation design was used. The subjects first looked at a blinking light. As soon as the infants attended to it, the light was terminated and a stimulus slide was projected. The infant was allowed one unlimited look at the stimulus. When the infant stopped looking, the blinking light returned. The experiment consisted of habituation and test trials. During the habituation trials, infants were shown a series of slides on which the number of items were kept constant. The exact slide shown depended on whether the infant was being tested in the homogeneous or heterogeneous condition.

Habituation was defined in terms of the amount of time each infant spent looking at the slides. If the fixation time on three consecutive trials was less than 50 percent of the average of the first three fixations, the infants were considered habituated and ready for the next step. After habituation occurred, the infants were presented with four test trials with two slides containing the same number of items as the habituation series, alternated with two slides containing either one less or one more item. If the infant had been habituated to slides containing three items, the test trials would contain slides of three items alternating with slides containing two or four items. Would infants notice the difference in numerosity?

The results clearly showed that infants did perceive the difference between two and three items, but were unable to do so for four and five items. A sex difference appeared in the three versus four condition. Females discriminated between the items in the homogeneous condition, while males were able to make the distinction in the heterogeneous condition. The researchers suggest that male and female infants were differentially attracted to the stimuli. On trials using the three-four array, males looked longer in the heterogenous condition, while females spent more time gazing at the slides in the homogeneous condition.

The results of this study lead to the conclusion that the infant has primitive abilities in quantity. Infants can perceive differences if the amounts are not very great. This is not to say that infants have a cognitive awareness of numbers or can count. However, the origin of number concepts may be found in infancy. Again, we see that infants have abilities far beyond what was thought even a generation ago. With more research, perhaps we will come to an even greater appreciation of the impressive abilities a seemingly helpless infant has and how these abilities develop into the more advanced skills we see in later life.

Source: M. S. Strauss and L. E. Curtis, "Infant Perception of Numerosity," *Child Development*, 1981, 52, 1146–1152.

---

cover was used, but not when the cloth cover was hiding their toys. The awkwardness of the covers used in an object-permanence test may affect its outcome. The infant's physical abilities may be an important confounding factor in tests of object permanence.

The very nature of the three-dimensional task may affect the infant's search pattern. Young infants have difficulty when an object is placed inside another object. When a rattle is placed in a box, infants are confused, because they see the rattle not as being hidden but as having been replaced by the box (Bower, 1979). Bower and Wishart (1972) found that infants who could not find an object that was hidden under a cup could grasp an object dangling in front of them when the lights were turned out in the room. Infants can successfully retrieve objects from behind a two-dimensional barrier, such as a screen, before they can do so from a three-dimensional barrier, such as a box. In addition, their performance on object-permanence tests depends on the spatial characteristics of the barrier. The response demand of the search, such as whether a researcher demands successful retrieval or mere looking, is also a factor (Dunst et al., 1982).

Bower (1971) argues that object permanence develops much sooner than Piaget believed. Infants do not show it because most studies force children to engage in an active search, which involves eye-hand coordination and motor skills. Another possible confounding variable is memory. Infants of about eight or nine months were presented with the standard task of watching a researcher hide an object in Place A, then move it to Place B. The babies were forced to wait different amounts of time before being allowed to search for the item. If the infants were allowed to search immediately, they did not make the mistake of searching in Place A first, but if the babies were held back from searching for anywhere between 3 to 15 seconds, some of them made the common error of searching in Place A (Gratch et al., 1974). Memory, then, is a factor as well.

Putting It All Together

We have two sets of findings. First, much evidence substantiates Piaget's contention that infants progress through a series of substages during the sensorimotor stage. Second, there is evidence that such factors as how the task is structured and the infant's memory, motivation, and physical skills affect performance on sensorimotor tasks. These findings do not disprove Piaget's theory, but rather extend it.

Piaget's description of infant cognitive growth is an excellent starting point. His descriptions of how a child progresses in infancy are well accepted. His descriptions have focused our attention on this area and encouraged us to form more detailed questions (Gratch, 1979). At the same time, however, the evidence showing that other factors may affect performance should make us wary of making generalizations concerning what an infant or toddler can or cannot do. The specific type of task presented to the infant, the object being hidden, and the nature of the barrier must always be noted. Infants follow Piaget's progression if tested in the standard Piagetian way. However, infants are very sensitive to the demands of the task. An analysis of what skills are necessary for success may yield information concerning why a child fails at a task. When a child must retrieve a hidden object, eye-hand coordination skills, motor skills, three-dimensional perception, and memory abilities are required. Piaget did not detail these skills. That task remained for others. Children who fail a particular task may lack any one (or more) of these skills or abilities.

MEMORY

Recent research has added a new dimension to our knowledge of infant cognition by considering the specific skills needed to successfully perform the tasks that Piaget described so well. One of the most notable skills, which has been the focus of much recent interest, is memory. The idea that infants remember things is easy to demonstrate experimentally but difficult to comprehend. We rarely re-

recognition
A way of testing memory in which the subject is required to choose the correct answer from a group of choices.

recall
A way of testing memory in which the subject must produce the correct response given very limited cues.

3. *True or False:*
Three-month-old infants can recognize their mother's face.

trieve memories from infancy or toddlerhood, yet memory is basic to the learning process.

Research on early memory focuses on recognition and recall. **Recognition** involves the ability to choose the correct response from a group of answers and is similar to the multiple-choice questions on a test. **Recall** involves producing the correct response on the basis of very limited cues and is similar to the task you face when taking an essay test.

To illustrate the difference, suppose you were presented with a list of one hundred famous people and asked to underline those who were Presidents of the United States. You would probably do well on this type of recognition examination. On the other hand, what if you were asked to list all the Presidents you can remember? This test of recall is much more difficult. As a rule, our ability to recognize is far better than our ability to recall information (Wingfield and Byrnes, 1981).

The Development of Recognition

Testing recognition in infancy is not a difficult task. Very young infants habituate to stimuli. If shown a stimulus, such as a face, the infant will pay attention to it, but if we continually show that face to the infant, the amount of time the baby spends attending to it becomes less and less. Testing recognition involves familiarizing infants of various ages with a stimulus. The infants pay less and less attention to it. Now we present them with another stimulus. If they pay more attention to it, they have noticed the difference, thus showing recognition memory.

Using this method, three-month-old infants were presented with pictures of their mother. They were later able to tell the difference between their mother's face and that of a stranger (Barrera and Maurer, 1981). Some researchers are impressed not only with infants' ability to recognize but also with their retentive abilities. Infants as young as two months were able to recognize a visual pattern and retain it for 24 hours (Martin, 1975). Fagan (1973) found that five- to six-month-old infants familiarized with a face for only two minutes were able to recognize it after a delay of two weeks. And this recognition memory is relatively impervious to interference.

Suppose that after attending a lecture in history on the important figures in British history you then attend a literature class in which American historical figures are discussed. You may confuse one with the other. One experience has interfered with your memory of the other. Infant memory is surprisingly robust. After performing a series of experiments, Fagan (1977) concluded that loss in recognition is the exception rather than the rule. Recognition does improve with age. Older infants show superior retention on tests of recognition (Rose, 1981).

The recognition memory of infants is impressive, but what are the stimulus characteristics that they recognize and retain? Infants do not retain everything equally well. For example, three- to four-month-old infants were trained to produce movement in a blue or green mobile. These infants remembered the color of the mobile, but this was more quickly forgotten than the fact that it would move if kicked (Fagan, 1984). Strauss and Cohen (1978) familiarized five-month-old infants with a three-dimensional styrofoam figure. The figure varied as to shape, color, size, and orientation, and the infants' recognition was measured at various time intervals from 10 minutes through 24 hours. These infants showed recognition on every dimension when tested immediately, but they recognized only color and form after 10 minutes and only form after 24 hours. Form is probably the most important element in recognition for infants at this age. Perhaps other experiments will discover a developmental progression in what infants recognize and retain.

The Development of Recall

Studies of recall are not as plentiful as research on recognition. Recognition is a relatively simple type of memory, recall is something else. Piaget (1968) argues that children do not show true recall before one-and-a-half to two years of age. The two-year-old certainly shows recall (Goldberg et al., 1974), but whether recall has been shown in children much under two years is a subject of debate (Labarba, 1981).

Some experiments demonstrate a memory process similar to recall in eight-month-old infants. Brody (1981) first trained infants to touch a lighted face. When they did so, they were reinforced by the pleasant sounds of a music box, the sequential illumination of eleven lights around the panel, and a view of puppets rotating on a turntable for three seconds. After the infants had learned to touch the light for the reward, they were presented with a delay. After the face was lighted, the light was turned off and a screen covered the face for 250 milliseconds. Then the screen was lifted and the infants were reinforced for touching the face that had been illuminated before the lowering of the screen. After the infants had learned this response, the researcher varied the amount of time in which the screen covered the face by three, six, and nine seconds. Brody found that eight- and twelve-month-old infants could remember the location of the stimulus during the 250 millisecond delay but that only the twelve-month-old infants could tolerate the longer delays.

An increase in recall occurs between eight and twelve months. This period is one of rapid change in the infants' cognitive abilities. Neurological changes that improve memory occur (Kagan, 1979a, 1979b). The infant develops an ability to retrieve older information spontaneously and apply it to current circumstances.

This has behavioral implications. For instance, stranger anxiety is rare before seven months, but it increases rapidly between this time and the end of the first year. Separation anxiety occurs when an infant shows anxiety at being left by the parent or caregiver. It emerges at about eight or nine months, rises to a peak at thirteen to fifteen months, then declines until at the age of three it is rare. Kagan argues that these events are partly explained by the growth of the infant's memory abilities, which include the ability to retrieve past memories and anticipate future behavior based on past experiences. Suppose the father of a ten-month-old leaves the room. The child remembers his former presence and compares it with the current scene in which he is not there. If the child cannot resolve the difference, distress may occur. In addition, the ten-month-old may cry when mother walks toward the exit without leaving. Kagan believes that this child can now generate hypotheses about what might happen in the future and anticipates the mother's exit.

COGNITIVE DEVELOPMENT IN THE FIRST YEAR: A SUMMARY

Infants are hardly passive beings just waiting for the world to teach them something (Restak, 1982). They are quite active and develop their abilities quickly. During the first year, the infant becomes a goal-directed being and develops some idea of causality. By one year, the child can search for completely covered objects and has developed some measure of object permanence. The child's memory is also developing, as is the ability to anticipate particular outcomes—as Kagan's analysis of stranger anxiety shows. At about one year, the child utters his or her first word(s). This is the culmination of a year of verbal and nonverbal communication with caregivers. The one-year-old knows the difference between a stranger and a loved one, and may be walking or about to walk. Children of this age explore their world, often getting into trouble. Recent research shows that they can begin to form concepts as well.

COGNITIVE DEVELOPMENT IN THE SECOND YEAR: A SUMMARY

Cognitive development during the second year is impressive. The ability to walk allows children of this age to explore the environment more fully, and their vocabulary grows. They master the finer points of object permanence and, in the last six months of their second year, can no longer be confused by difficult hiding procedures. White (1975) notes that the one-year-old will take off a handkerchief that covers a toy but will be frustrated if it is covered by three such handkerchiefs. The two-year-old thinks nothing of demolishing all three barriers. Their ability to form concepts increases as well. By the end of the second year, the child has developed representational thought, that is, can now think without acting (Ault, 1977). Children at this point are no longer sensorimotor in the truest sense of the term, relying solely on the information they have obtained through the senses and motor activity. They can now construct a mental image of the world. They can also defer imitation, seeing an event at one time and later imitating it. At the end of the second year of life, the child enters a new stage of cognitive development known as the *preoperational stage*, which will be discussed in Chapter Nine.

PREDICTING INTELLIGENCE IN LATER CHILDHOOD

Psychologists are always interested in predicting some future behavior on the basis of past or present behaviors or circumstances. For instance, what if we knew what behaviors or capabilities in early infancy are forerunners of intellectual achievement during the school years (ages six through twelve)? We could then isolate these important abilities that predict later achievement, and perhaps help children develop them.

   This may sound simple, but it isn't. Before this can be done, a number of interesting questions must be answered. For instance, do general measures of infant capabilities predict later cognitive development? Is there a relationship between early care, the home environment, and later achievement? What do infant intelligence tests really measure?

What Do Infant Intelligence Tests Measure?

Infant tests of mental abilities do not measure the same intellectual abilities as the intelligence tests you may remember taking in school (Horner, 1980). Those tests mostly measured verbal abilities, although some may have included such tasks as assembling puzzle parts or telling the examiner what part of a picture is missing. Since young children do not have the verbal abilities necessary to succeed on such tasks, some measure of motor and perceptual abilities must be used instead. These are generally not the skills that are required for success on verbally oriented items given on intelligence tests and school achievement tests. The relationship, if any, between these motor skills and later academic abilities is difficult to grasp.

Predictions from Tests: The Bayley Scales

The most popular way of measuring the intellectual abilities of the infant and toddler was devised by Nancy Bayley and her colleagues (Bayley, 1969; Bayley and Oden, 1955). The **Bayley Scales of Infant Development** can be used to assess the abilities of infants from two months through two and a half years. The Mental Scale measures such functions as perception, memory, learning, problem-solving, and vocalization (Anastasi, 1976). The Motor Scale measures such motor abilities as sitting, standing, stair-climbing, hand skills, and coordination. The Infant Behavior Record is designed to assess such qualities as attention span, persistence, and emotional and social behavior (Anastasi, 1976). The observer is asked to rate the infant on responsiveness, cooperativeness, fearfulness, and activity level. The Bayley Scales yield a valid description of the child's intellectual development at the time (Bayley, 1970), but do they predict later intellectual development? Can we administer the scales to a child of six months and make any statement concerning that child's intelligence as a second-grader at age seven? Do they have any predictive validity?

Attempts to predict later intelligence on the basis of infant measures have been disappointing. Most studies have failed to find much predictive validity for normal infants between their scores on the Bayley Scales and their later cognitive abilities (McCall, 1979; McCall et al., 1977; McCall, Hogarty, and Hurlburt, 1972). Even the infant behavioral record does not seem to have much predictive validity. Although the behavioral report of the Bayley Scale is useful for describing the child's functioning at the point in time it is administered, it does not predict later functioning (McGowan et al., 1981).

Why don't these scales predict later behavior in normal children? Perhaps the abilities measured by these scales are too unstable to possess predictive abilities. Perhaps we are simply measuring the wrong abilities, and other infant capabilities may be predictive of later behavior.

The Bayley Scales are more useful in predicting the intelligence of infants who are neurologically impaired or have some other defect (Rubin and Balow, 1979; McCall, Hogarty, and Hurlburt, 1972). These scales may also predict later problems in language development. In addition, the scales are helpful in detecting infants who are at risk for developmental delay (Siegel, 1981).

Bayley Scales of Infant Development
A test of intelligence administered to infants between two months and two and a half years of age.

4. *True or False:*
Psychologists can accurately predict later intelligence from scales measuring infant intelligence.

We now have a problem. Infant scales such as the Bayley Scales may be able to assess the present functioning of the infant, but they have predictive power only when applied to atypical populations. The normal infant's behavior prior to one year is not predictive of intellectual functioning later in life. Only after eighteen months does the child's score on infant intelligence tests have any predictive abilities, and then only when added to some measure of socioeconomic status (McCall, 1979). Lately, some researchers have tried to isolate particular infant behaviors that may predict later development. One behavior that has shown some promise in this regard is the speed of habituation during infancy, which is related to measurements on Piagetian tasks such as object permanence during early toddlerhood (Miller et al., 1977) and speaking vocabularies at twelve months (Ruddy and Bornstein, 1982). However, only future research will demonstrate whether this or other behaviors will predict academic achievement in later childhood.

Predictions from Socioeconomic Status

If scores on infant tests do not predict later intellectual abilities, what of some scale measuring the child's early environment? There is evidence that socioeconomic status affects the development of the child (Kagan and Lapidus, 1978). The socioeconomic status of the child in the first twelve to eighteen months is a good predictor of later intellectual development (McCall et al., 1972). Bee and her colleagues (1982) found that the mother's educational level was related to the child's later intelligence, especially if it was below the high school level. The relationship was not significant if the mother's educational level was at or above the high school level.

Socioeconomic status is usually analyzed in terms of income, parental educational level, and occupational ratings (Rubin and Balow, 1979). Low-socioeconomic-status homes differ greatly from middle- and higher-socioeconomic-class homes, especially in the area of verbal behavior (Tulkin and Kagan, 1972). Lower-socioeconomic-class mothers talk much less to their infants. Perhaps because of lack of education or the stresses of poverty, they may not provide the verbal stimulation or the environment necessary for their children to develop adequate cognitive skills.

Yet there is something unsatisfactory about the entire concept of socioeconomic status. It is far too broad and too general a consideration, and it ignores the wide variations that exist in intelligence within socioeconomic levels. It would be better to focus on the differences among families (Ramey et al., 1979). General statements noting that the low-socioeconomic-status parent does this or that ignore these differences and stigmatize an entire group of people. Finally, socioeconomic status is not an easy variable to change. Poverty, lack of education, and a low-status job cannot be altered overnight by a child development specialist. Because these factors are so important, professionals may have a societal responsibility to help improve the lot of the poor. However, a more specific approach stressing behaviors and specific environmental variables rather than social class may be more helpful in uncovering clues to intellectual development. These behavioral or environmental factors may be more susceptible to change. For instance, if we find that children of parents who are responsive and who speak to them are intellectually advanced in middle childhood, we can help parents develop these skills and change their pattern of parent-child interactions. If we find that the absence of books in the house makes a difference, we can not only provide the books but also teach parents how to use them. We have recently made a start in this direction. We discovered specific types of parent-child interactions and discrete elements of the physical environment surrounding the child which facilitate cognitive growth.

Predictions from the Home Environment

One instrument frequently used to measure various aspects of the home environment is called the **Home Observation for Measurement of the Environment,** called **HOME** for short. This scale provides a measure of the quality and quantity of the emotional and cognitive elements in the home setting (Elardo et al., 1977). The inventory measures six factors, including the mother's emotional and verbal responsivity, the avoidance of restriction and punishment, the organization of the environment, provision of appropriate play materials, maternal involvement with the child, and opportunities for variety in the daily routine (see Figure 6.1). Information is collected through interviews and observation.

HOME Scale
A scale that provides a measure of the quality and quantity of the emotional and cognitive elements in the home.

FIGURE 6.1   The HOME Inventories: Assessing a Child's Home Environment

The importance of a child's home environment is a favorite theme of developmental psychologists. Dr. Bettye M. Caldwell has formulated a tool which attempts to assess this crucial element in the child's development. An observer spends about an hour in the family's home watching the normal daily routine and occasionally asking a question. The observer checks off items on the inventory.

This instrument, called the HOME Inventory, exists in two forms. The first is meant to assess the home environments of children from birth to three and consists of forty-five items, the second is used to assess the environments of preschoolers (three- to six-year-olds) and contains eighty items. Although the full inventories are too long to present here, the main categories are noted below. Studies have shown that there is a significant relationship between scores on the HOME Inventory at six months and scores on an intelligence test at three years. The HOME Inventory may be used to focus on problems within the child's home which may be correctable.

Home Observation for Measurement of the Environment (Birth to Three Years)

Categories

1. Emotional and verbal responsivity of mother
2. Avoidance of restriction and punishment
3. Organization of physical and temporal environment
4. Provision of appropriate play materials
5. Maternal involvement with child
6. Opportunities for variety in daily stimulation

Home Observation for Measurement of the Environment (Three to Six Years)

1. Provision of stimulation through equipment, toys, and experiences
2. Stimulation of mature behavior
3. Provision of a stimulating physical and language environment
4. Avoidance of restriction and punishment
5. Pride, affection, and thoughtfulness
6. Masculine stimulation (involves time spent with father and the availability of toys such as jump ropes, swings, and balls which encourage large-muscle development)
7. Independence from parental control

Using the HOME instrument, Bradley and Caldwell discovered a "substantial relationship between home-environment in the first year of life and IQ at age three" (1980, p. 1145). The HOME score is an effective predictor of IQ and language. Certain elements of the HOME scale are better predictors than others, depending on the sex of the child. Bee and her colleagues (1982, p. 1146) note: "Boys' IQ appears associated with a highly organized environment, one where a variety of appropriate play materials are available and one where encouragement of development is provided. For girls, the level of maternal responsivity, the level of punishment, and the amount of variety in stimulation also appear to be strongly related to IQ."

Evaluations of specific elements of the home are more efficient in predicting future intellectual growth than either infant tests or parental education (Elardo et al., 1975). For example, the intensity and variety of stimuli is related to intellectual development (Wachs, 1971). Carew and his colleagues (1975) found that positive experiences in verbal and symbolic learning such as labeling objects; perceptual, spatial, and fine-motor experiences such as matching; color discriminations; and problem-solving activities were related to IQ scores at three years.

At this point, some tentative conclusions can be drawn. Such factors as the responsivity of the caregiver, parental involvement with the child, the variety of stimulation available, the organization of the environment, the caregiver's restrictiveness, and the play materials available at an early age predict later cognitive development. One point should be kept in mind, though. A healthy environment in infancy is usually carried over throughout childhood. An unhealthy environment in infancy rarely improves greatly in childhood. Some of the relationship between the environment during infancy and later intellectual ability is a reflection of the cumulative effects of the environment throughout childhood and does not solely demonstrate the importance of the earliest environment.

APPLYING WHAT WE KNOW ABOUT COGNITIVE DEVELOPMENT

These lessons are easily translated into general prescriptions for child-rearing, but caution is necessary. Some parenting books make impossible promises. They imply that if you follow their regimen your child will become a superior student in school and be ready for an Ivy League college and eternal bliss after adolescence. But there are no magic formulas for producing a genius, and cognitive development is only one aspect of childhood growth and development. In addition, parents may become too involved in technique, ignoring the importance of spontaneity, joy, and play.

The cognitive development of their infant boy became an obsession for one professional couple. They smothered him with stimulation and pressured him to master certain skills. If a child requires stimulation, they reasoned, the more the better. But too much noise and confusion can be harmful to the very activity they want to promote (Wachs, 1976), and there is no reason to believe that higher levels of stimulation are better than moderate levels.

The genetic component in intelligence should be kept in mind too (Lunde and Lunde, 1980; Scarr and Weinberg, 1978). Even the best environment and care will not produce an Einstein in every case. In addition, environmental varia-

How Do You Tell a Mother?

Nancy is a social worker with a problem. She has been working with unwed mothers to improve their parenting skills. She is aware of their problems and has been generally effective and helpful. One case particularly disturbs Nancy.

Lana is nineteen years old. She survives independently on state assistance and a few dollars earned from working part time. Nancy has visited Lana's home. The home is physically acceptable and her toddler, Melissa, is well cared for—that is, the child is fed and clothed, and the apartment is warm and safe. But Lana does not seem to know how to deal with Melissa's intellectual needs. She rarely plays with Melissa, and the child spends most of her time in the crib or playpen in front of the television.

Nancy has tried to tell Lana about the child's needs for stimulation, but to no effect. Lana argues that she doesn't need anyone's help and that Nancy is butting in where she doesn't belong. Neither Lana's parents or Melissa's father show any interest in Lana or the child.

1. Should Nancy continue to try to work with Lana? If so, what approach should she use?
2. Taking the situation from Lana's viewpoint, why won't she take Nancy's advice?
3. Nancy has reported the problem to her supervisor. Should her supervisor take action?

bles and genetic factors interact in a highly complex manner. Each child matures according to his or her own genetic blueprint, and particular strategies and environments must be tailored to the child's individual rate of maturation. A child who is developing more quickly may be able to handle a more advanced problem or toy. Children can also influence their own environments. Brighter children may create a better environment for themselves because they are more responsive and reinforcing to their caregivers (Bradley et al., 1979). Children who are developing more slowly require playthings that are closer to their ability level.

Other factors also enter the picture, for example, the socioeconomic status of the family, the number of children, the nutritional status of the family, and the child's general health. One or more of these factors may limit the parents' ability to create the optimal environment for a child.

Still, some lessons can be learned from studies of cognitive development. We can teach parents how to interact with their infants in ways that help the children develop their intellectual abilities.

Infant Learning Programs

It seems almost criminal to have information that may improve a child's chances for success in later life and not share it with those who need it most. Parents who read books on the subject and are most interested in creating optimal home environments are often those who need the information least. Children will be more advanced cognitively (or less retarded) if we provide them with experiences that will stimulate all their senses, label the environment for them, provide exploratory experiences, and the like. This information ought to be communicated to parents, and they should be taught how to help their own children. Indeed, such programs have been developed and show considerable success rates.

Reaching Out to Parents.   Working with parents is the most efficient approach to improving a child's environment, but ensuring parental involvement in a program is often difficult. If you have ever attended a conference on some aspect of parenting, you probably noticed that the parents who need it most seem to be absent. How can we encourage people to attend these programs and consider professional suggestions? Evidence collected over almost three decades shows that children of parents who participate in such programs operate at a more advanced cognitive level than children of parents who have not done so (Beller, 1979). When parents are helped to improve the environment of their home, it helps all the children in the home and may carry over to new arrivals. Community support is also enlisted when these strategies work. Finally, friends and relatives who come into contact with these participants obtain at least a smattering of knowledge and may themselves consent to participate at a later time.

Teaching Parents to Parent.   In the mid-1960s, I. J. Gordon instituted a program in which people in the community were trained to function as educators. They received an intensive five-week program on the principles of child development, interviewing skills, recording procedures, and specific exercises and games that were to be played with infants and taught to parents. Gordon based these games on Piaget's theory, so they involved basically manipulative and exploratory activities and encouraged verbal interaction between parents and their children. A bit later, games that relate to object permanence were used, such as attaching an object to a string and hiding it out of sight, which requires the infant to pull the string to bring it into view. Parents were visited once a week by the paraprofessional, who demonstrated the activity.

The results? Children who had been involved in the project for two to three years were superior to a control group on measures of both intellectual and academic performances. In the third grade, these infants were superior in reading, math concepts, and math problem-solving (Beller, 1979).

Other home-based programs exist. The most interesting is a verbal interaction program under the directorship of Levenstein (Golden and Birns, 1975; Madden, 1976). This program is beautiful in its simplicity. Beginning in the second year of life, 200 lower-income families participating in the study received a visit from a demonstrator who showed parents how to read to their children and use certain toys. These materials were provided by the program. However, a large part of the instruction emphasized verbal interaction between parent and child. For instance, parents were encouraged to label things according to form and color, to elicit responses from children through questions, and to give a considerable amount of positive reinforcement to their child. These children showed dramatic increases in intelligence, and the longer they were involved, the better the results (Beller, 1979). Their reading skills in elementary school were superior as well.

These programs really have two purposes (Cataldo, 1982). One is to help children develop their cognitive skills and abilities through play activities, stimu-

5. *True or False:*
Programs that teach parents how to interact with their children have largely failed to improve the intellectual functioning of these children.

lation, and an environment filled with appropriate materials. The second purpose is to help infants develop their interpersonal relationships, their individuality, and their selves.

If these programs are largely successful, why are they not expanded? Money is one limiting factor, as they are costly. In addition, many people believe that the family has the sole responsibility to care for children, that society should take little interest or part in child-rearing. Infant programs, day care, and early childhood education are considered extras. In addition, people still hold fast to the idea that parenting is a simple skill, something that is "instinctual." However, not all parents know how to develop their children's potential. One common question parents ask is, "Just what can you do with a baby or a toddler?" Today, when we know what can be done to improve a child's development, it is unfortunate that such programs are not more widespread.

The Role of Father.   Another area that requires a look is the role of the father in cognitive development. Most of the programs involve teaching mothers to do this and that. The assumption is that since the mother is the primary caregiver in most cases, and has the greatest number of interactions with the infant, it is most effective to deal with her. This assumption is reasonable, but more thought ought to be given to educating fathers to take part in the early development of their children. Fathers can make a significant impact on their children's cognitive development, but they often do not feel comfortable dealing with very young children. With experience and some training, fathers too can learn to help their children develop their cognitive abilities.

How Parents Can Encourage Cognitive Development

Parents do make a difference in the development of their children. Burton White (1971) studied the differences between mothers of competent infants and mothers of infants who are less competent and found three major differences. The mothers of competent children were designers, that is, they constructed an environment in which children were surrounded with interesting objects to see and explore. They were able to understand what meaning an activity or experience might have for a child and build on it. Second, parents of competent children interacted frequently with their children in interplays of 20- to 30-second duration. The children were not smothered with attention, but these parents were constantly available and ready to help their children experience events. They often labeled the environment for them and helped share their child's excitement. Third, the parents of these children were not overly permissive or overly punishing. They had firm limits, but they were not unduly concerned about such minor problems as mess and bother.

The research on cognitive development can be translated into a number of parental activities that encourage the cognitive growth of children. Some of these are as follows.

Provide Opportunities for Exploration.   Children are active learners and require the stimulation of all their senses. Such environmental stimulants as a mobile above the crib and a few safe, brightly colored toys are important. A bit later, try to provide experiences for the infant which involve materials of different colors, textures, and shapes.

6. *True or False:*

Parents of competent infants spend many hours of time teaching them concepts.

The intellectual level of the home and the nature of the parent-child interaction may affect later cognitive abilities.

7. *True or False:*
Interactions with infants and toddlers of less than one minute have no effect on their cognitive development.

Label the Environment.   It is important to label the environment. When the child appears to be communicating in a prelinguistic mode, it is beneficial to say, "So you want a cookie" while holding the cookie up and emphasizing the word.

Encourage Verbalizations.   As children grow, the number of verbalizations they utter will increase. The child begins to use words usually in the second year of life. Encourage communication even in the prelinguistic stage. When children become older and begin using words, encourage them to expand on their vocabulary. Children require a willing audience and encouragement in order to develop their linguistic skills.

Read to the Child.   This can start early, and you can tailor the technique you use to the age and ability of your child. For instance, young children can point to various objects in a book, such as a ball. Later your questions can expand to questions of color, shape, and so on.

Ensure Brief Interactions Between Parents and Child.   Those 20- to 30-second encounters can be valuable. Some people believe that spending every minute of their time with their children is desirable. This is not the case. As children mature, their attention span will increase, and interactions can become more involved and longer. However, sharing even a brief experience with a child is beneficial.

Tailor Activities to the Child's Developmental Level.   Most child specialists writing books about parental activities that may optimize children's cognitive growth note that these activities should be low-key and fun. A problem arises when parents believe that they are conducting an academic activity and place pressure on their children to achieve this early (Zinsser, 1981). Parental disappointment, anxieties, and expectations can be communicated to young children quite early and may hinder the very development that parents seek to improve. Infants and toddlers have limited attention spans and may go from activity to activity quickly. Equally important is understanding that enriched environments do not always lead to accelerated or enhanced cognitive or perceptual development. Enhanced environments help when there is a match between the encounter and the child's abilities (Hunt, 1961).

CONTROVERSIAL QUESTIONS

Optimizing cognitive development is a controversial theme that raises a number of questions and issues. These include the issues of overstimulation, maturational and environmental influences on development, and the question of elaboration versus acceleration, better known as the "American question."

Is Overstimulation a Danger?

8. *True or False:*
Overstimulation is as great a problem as lack of stimulation.

Walking into the Parker home is an experience. Thirteen-month-old Kathie Parker has just about every educational toy the local toy store sells. Pictures are everywhere. So many toys lie in the crib that there is little room for the child.

Parents often make the mistake of believing that if a little is good then a lot is better. This is not the case. Before about six weeks, babies simply turn away from too much stimulation, and it is not a great problem (White, 1975). Overstimulation does not produce the desired results (Wachs et al., 1971). In an overstimulated environment, children may block out stimuli of normal intensity and begin to respond only when stimuli become more and more intense (Wesley and Sullivan, 1980). The difficult question is just how to define overstimulation. What is a normal noise level in one home is deafening for those raised in another. At present, overstimulation remains a vague term.

But overstimulation does not seem to be as great a problem as lack of stimulation. Considerably more is known about the tragic effects of understimulation and stimulus deprivation, which lead to retardation (Spitz, 1945; Goldfarb, 1943).

Infants crave and require a moderate level of stimulation, and such stimulation should match their abilities. However, there is no evidence that the greater the intensity of the stimulation the more beneficial the effects.

Cognitive Development: Heredity and Environment

Just how modifiable is the child? The subtle interaction between environment and genetics is a topic to which we return again and again. The extent to which a superior environment can improve cognitive functioning is a matter of controversy at this point. If cognitive development, especially in infancy, is mostly a question of maturation and experience, then merely presenting the child with a reasonable environment would be sufficient. But if cognitive development is more a question of learning, then environmental factors become more important.

Cognitive development is affected by maturation. Each child conforms to his or her own timetable. On the other hand, in order for this timetable to un-

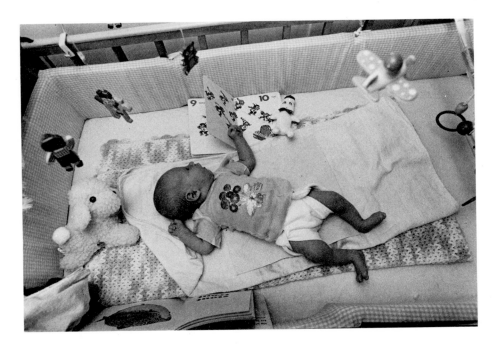

How much is too much? More stimulation does not always produce better results.

How Much Is Too Much?

In the past decade the importance of cognitive stimulation in infancy has been increasingly noted by authorities in the field. One night, Lauren and Peter, who are expecting their first child very soon, were invited to Lester and Judy's home for the evening. Lester and Judy have a baby boy, William, and naturally the conversation turned to child behavior and child-rearing.

Lester and Judy believe that early intelligence predicts later academic success. "Children need a head start from their parents," they argue. They are determined to work with William as he matures and to help him to maximize his cognitive abilities. They both give William plenty of attention, have three mobiles over the crib, and have written the name of each item in the house on strips of paper, which are pasted on each piece of furniture. They surround the child with plenty of pictures and are very involved in two exercise and cognitive growth programs. They tell their friends that to do anything less is to reduce William's chances of becoming a top student.

Lauren and Peter were impressed by the way their friends had structured the baby's environment but they wonder if the environment is too structured, too stimulating, and too confusing for the infant. They must decide just what course to chart for their own new baby.

1. If you were Lauren or Peter, what course would you choose?

fold, children must have opportunities to interact with their environment, which includes both animate and inanimate elements. Yet the extent to which this timetable may be affected by direct instruction from parents in the form of games and exercises is still unknown. The evidence indicates that when these activities match the child's developmental rate, they provide the opportunities necessary for children to grow (Endler et al., 1976). The interaction between maturation and environment is complicated, and only further research can clarify the role of each. This raises an issue that is the crux of the entire parenting dilemma: to what extent can this timetable be accelerated, and should we even attempt to accelerate it?

The Question of Acceleration: The "American Question"

American educators and parents are often interested in the question of how fast or how early a child can accomplish some academic task. We are impressed with the child who is reading at the age of three or solving algebraic equations at eight. Reflecting this fascination with speed, researchers have raised the question of whether infants can be accelerated through the various periods of sensorimotor experience. The entire idea really runs counter to Piaget's ideas.

Piaget was reluctant to make any recommendations to teachers or parents concerning how to maximize a child's potential, let alone how to accelerate the child (Vernon, 1976). Remember that Piaget's theory emphasizes the importance of maturation and giving children an opportunity to interact with their environment. It deemphasizes formal instruction. Parents may help their children by designing an environment that is appropriate for the children at their particular point in development and elaborating on that environment, giving children plenty of opportunity to discover things on their own. For instance, when presenting children with objects of different textures, it is beneficial to have a variety of such objects in the environment and to allow the children to explore them at their own rate. This does not mean that the parents remain passive. Indeed, parents should be available, answer questions, interact with the child, and so on, but the emphasis is on discovery, not formal teaching and programming.

Perhaps we should put the question a different way. The purpose of improving interaction with parents and designing a stimulating and appropriate atmosphere for infants is to provide the optimal atmosphere for children to develop their cognitive potential. Particular experiences at certain stages are beneficial, but the goal should not be to see how fast a child can get through Piaget's stages. Instead, the goal should be to provide experiences that will help that child develop according to his or her own rate and abilities. Such an environment is child-centered, providing the infant with the opportunities to interact and learn.

There are times when parents and professionals must be more active in designing a program of stimulation. Rose (1980) found significant differences in the recognition memories of full-term and preterm infants, but when preterm infants had received extra stimulation during the early weeks of life, their performance on memory tasks was similar to that of full-term infants. Infants who are not at risk might benefit from a more active program as well, but the power to accelerate development is not unbounded. If cognitive development can be accelerated, an upper limit to this acceleration probably exists. And there are risks. Parents may place pressures on their infants to perform and hold unreasonable expectations that may interfere with the child's normal development.

The value of trying to accelerate infants through the sensorimotor period is doubtful, especially since correlations between sensorimotor intelligence and later cognitive achievement are so low. Lewis and McGurk (1972) administered the Bayley Scales and a scale of object permanence at three, six, nine, twelve, eighteen, and twenty-four months to twenty infants. At two years these children were also given the Peabody Picture Vocabulary Tests, a test of intellectual level. Scores on the Bayley at three months did not predict the scores at six months. In addition, the Bayley did not predict the child's score on the test of object permanence. Finally, neither test predicted the child's performance on the Peabody. This indicates that the idea of acceleration should be deemphasized. The best course is to design stimulating environments for children and to teach parents how to interact with their infants so that they may gain the appropriate skills. Rushing a child through this stage accomplishes little. Because development is faster does not necessarily make it any better.

9. *True or False:* Child development specialists equate fast development with superior development.

CONCLUSIONS

Although the idea of accelerating children like a slingshot through the substages of Piaget's stages is undesirable, teaching parents how to care for and provide stimulation for their children is of great value. Piaget notes how important it is for children to have a variety of experiences and to be able to explore their environment. Yet many parents do not provide these opportunities and have little idea of how to play with their children. Parent education and training programs should be encouraged.

The evidence is clear that such activities as providing a stimulating atmosphere, labeling the environment, interacting in a positive manner with children, and encouraging them to investigate and explore are helpful in promoting cognitive development. Parents can and should be active in these areas, but they must also beware of overdoing it, of pressuring their infants, of believing that somehow faster is always better, of thinking in terms of how fast rather than how well, or becoming schoolteachers rather than parents. Elkind (1973) notes that parents are sometimes made to feel guilty if they do not cover the entire room with mobiles or purchase the newest educational toys. Although mobiles certainly give children something interesting to look at and have value, a homemade mobile made from clothespins is just as good as a fancy one bought from a store. As Elkind (1973, p. 40) notes, "Toys for infants should be chosen on the basis of their safety and their immediate entertainment value, rather than in terms of their long range educational benefit."

Finally, there is no magic age at which it is "all over." Cognitive development in infancy is important, but it is possible to improve the lot of a child who has not experienced an optimal early environment—if a significant change occurs in the environment later (Clarke and Clarke, 1977). Although we should not underestimate the importance of such development in infancy, neither should we overestimate it.

We have now seen how the child develops from a newborn infant with few cognitive skills to a two-year-old who has an impressive repertoire of cognitive abilities. Yet the rush of interest in cognitive psychology should not blind us to importance of the child's personality and social development. After all, we want our children not only to be intellectually advanced but also to develop their personality and their social abilities. It is to these qualities that we turn next.

10. *True or False:*

If children do not receive the optimal stimulation by the age of two, they will underachieve throughout the childhood and adolescent years.

Chapter Summary

1. According to Jean Piaget, infants are negotiating the sensorimotor stage, during which they use their senses and motor skills to learn about the world. They do not have the ability to create mental images or use language or symbols to represent anything.

2. The development of object permanence, the understanding that an object or person exists even if it is out of sight, is an important achievement in infancy.

3. One should not equate competency (knowledge and ability) with performance. Performance depends on motivation, the type of task presented to the infant, and other environmental factors.

4. Infants have the ability to recognize faces very early. Infants between eight and twelve months have some recall abilities.

5. Scores on infant intelligence tests do not predict later intellectual ability very well.

6. There is a relationship between later cognitive development and the responsiveness of the caregiver, parental involvement with the child, the variety of stimulation the child receives, the organization of the environment, and the play materials available.

7. The best way to optimize the child's intellectual ability is to improve the home environment. Programs aimed at improving the home environment and parent-child interaction have been successful.

8. Allowing children to explore their own world, labeling the environment, encouraging communication, reading to the child, brief interactions in which parents share some experience with the child, and tailoring activi-

ties to the child's development level promote cognitive growth.

9. Moderate levels of stimulation are best for the child. The question of how flexible infant cognitive development is has not yet been fully answered.

10. The so-called "American question" asks whether we can accelerate cognitive growth. Such acceleration was discouraged by Piaget, who believed that by designing an appropriate environment and giving children an opportunity to discover the mysteries of life children can develop their cognitive abilities.

■ *Answers to True or False Questions*

1. *True.* If intelligence is defined in terms of adaptive behavior, the baby is showing this quality by trying to understand physical laws.

2. *True.* At this age it is literally "out of sight, out of mind."

3. *True.* Research shows that three-month-old infants can recognize their mother's face.

4. *False.* Correct statement: For normal infants, scores on infant intelligence tests do not predict later intelligence.

5. *False.* Correct statement: Most programs that have concentrated on teaching parents to be more effective have succeeded.

6. *False.* Correct statement: Parents of competent infants do not smother their children with attention.

7. *False.* Correct statement: Interacting briefly with children to share experiences with them is one way to encourage cognitive development.

8. *False.* Correct statement: Lack of stimulation is a more serious problem than overstimulation.

9. *False.* Correct statement: Faster development does not necessarily translate into superior development.

10. *False.* Correct statement: An excellent later environment can reduce the injurious effects of a poor early environment.

CHAPTER SEVEN

Social and Personality Development in Infancy and Toddlerhood

■ *Are the Following Statements True or False?*

Try the True-False Quiz below. See if your answers correspond to the information in this chapter. Each question is repeated opposite the paragraph in which the answer can be found. The True-False Answer Box at the end of the chapter lists complete answers.

____ **1.** A child's first emotions are reflexive.

____ **2.** Fear of strangers is considered an abnormal response in infants and toddlers and indicates insecurity.

____ **3.** Infants show more fear of strange adults than of strange children.

____ **4.** Poor mothering in early infancy results in permanent retardation even if the child's environment is later improved.

____ **5.** The quality of a child's attachment to the mother can change over time.

____ **6.** Older mothers have a more positive attitude toward motherhood than younger mothers do.

____ **7.** Firstborn children receive more attention than later-born children.

____ **8.** Early and extended contact immediately after birth is necessary if infants are to develop a healthy attachment to their mothers.

____ **9.** Infants become attached to their fathers as well as to their mothers.

____ **10.** Most children in need of day care attend licensed day-care centers.

____ **11.** Children in day care form attachments to their caregivers at the expense of attachment to the mother.

____ **12.** The father is generally more active in child care when the mother is employed.

____ **13.** Maternal employment has no effect on the child's social or cognitive development.

____ **14.** Toddlers interact more if many small toys, rather than a few larger toys, are available.

SETTING THE STAGE

The Dilemma of Lisa and Tim Walters

Like so many American families, Lisa and Tim Walters needed every penny to keep their heads above water. With two children (Beth, age two, and Jon, eight months), a modest home, and two cars, they were just breaking even each month. They had decided that Lisa would stay home and be a full-time home-maker until the youngest child entered elementary school. Then she would re-turn to work. Both agreed that this was the best strategy. It combined their belief that the early relationship between mother and child was important, and the re-ality of needing a dual income as the children grew.

But Tim was laid off from his job. Unable to afford a long layoff, he took a lower-paying position and returned to school for retraining. Trapped by car pay-ments and a hefty mortgage, Lisa and Tim fell into debt. They finally decided that Lisa should go back to work.

Lisa and Tim are concerned. The two-year-old will have to enter a day-care program, while the baby will either be in day-care too or be taken daily to Lisa's mother. The parents have a host of questions. How will the experiences affect the children? How will these constant but temporary separations affect their rela-tionship with their youngsters? How will Lisa's working affect the family? Is day care harmful to children?

Before making their decision, Lisa and Tim had talked with friends and heard conflicting opinions. Some claimed that day care was actually better for children, and that the early relationship between child and mother was not as critical as people once thought. Their advice was "Don't worry, it really can't hurt." Others warned of the dire consequences of such a lifestyle. "Haven't you ever heard of maternal deprivation? Nothing can replace the mother." Accord-ing to this school of thought, the day-care experience interferes with the mother-child relationship, and separation will lead to emotional problems in the chil-dren. In addition, the baby will be confused, not knowing which caregiver is the mother. Which school of thought is correct?

The Changing Patterns of Child Care

Many American families face the same questions. Approximately 11 million chil-dren attend nursery schools, day-care centers, or group baby-sitting arrange-ments (*New York Times*, June 27, 1984). Over the past thirty years, the number of women in the labor force and the proportion of working mothers has increased dramatically (see Table 7.1 and Figure 7.1). Some 18 percent of mothers with preschoolers worked in 1948, 20 percent in 1960, 29 percent in 1970, and 49.9 percent in 1982 (Gerson et al., 1984; U.S. Dept. of Labor, 1983). In 1981, there were nearly 6 million working women with children under six (American Coun-cil of Life Insurance, 1982). Many people equate the working mother with the single parent, and indeed over half of all single parents work. However, more than 51 percent of all parents in two-parent families also work (American Coun-cil of Life Insurance, 1981).

So, the Walters' dilemma is not unusual, and the questions they ask are vital. This chapter will investigate the social, emotional, and personality development of infants and toddlers and provide some answers. But first, one qualification must be made.

TABLE 7.1   **Women in the Labor Force with Young Children (numbers in thousands)**

Today, many women are entering the labor force when their children are small.

Presence and Age Group of Children	Civilian Noninstitutional Population	Civilian Labor Force	Civilian Labor Force Participation Rate
Total women, 16 years and over	92,485	49,210	53.2
No own children under 18 years*	60,200	29,666	49.3
With own children under 18 years	32,285	19,544	60.5
Children 6 to 17 years	16,884	11,514	68.2
Children 6 to 13 years	11,447	7,781	68.0
Children under 6 years	15,401	8,030	52.1
Children under 3 years	9,248	4,407	47.7

*Children are defined as "own" children of the family. Included are never-married daughters, sons, stepchildren, and adopted children. Excluded are other related children, such as grandchildren, nieces, nephews, and cousins, and unrelated children.

Source: Bureau of Labor Statistics, 1984.

Mothers and Caregivers

For years, researchers used the term **mothering** to describe the caregiving that young children most often receive from their mothers, but the primary caregiver need not be the biological mother. Thousands of children are adopted in the United States every year, and some youngsters are being raised by single men. Even though the term caregiver may be better, the act of caring for a child is still called "mothering." Therefore, mothering refers to the early care children receive from the caregiver, no matter who it is.

mothering
A general term used to describe the caregiving activities of *all* interested parties, not just the mother.

EMOTIONAL DEVELOPMENT

How Emotions Develop

One of the Walters' concerns involves the emotional development of their children. Emotional development in infancy follows a distinct pattern. Early emotions reflected in the infant's cry and the smile are reflexive. As the child develops they become attached to specific environmental stimuli. Mother's voice may trigger a smile, and later in infancy seeing the trappings of the doctors-office may lead to crying. Specific emotions develop out of these first patterns (Bridges, 1933). Emotions such as fear, anxiety, joy, and pleasure become more specific and more differentiated. These are now triggered by environmental stimuli, as infants begin to differentiate themselves from the rest of the environment (Yarrow, 1979). Both experience and central nervous system development are implicated in the child's expanding repertoire of emotions.

Infants cannot tell us how they feel. We must depend on their facial expressions and heart rate as measures of emotional expression. Although we do not know at what age infants first become aware of their emotional states, Sroufe (1979a) suggests that emotional development occurs in the stages outlined in Table 7.2.

1. *True or False:*
A child's first emotions are reflexive.

FIGURE 7.1   Percentage of Women in the Labor Force

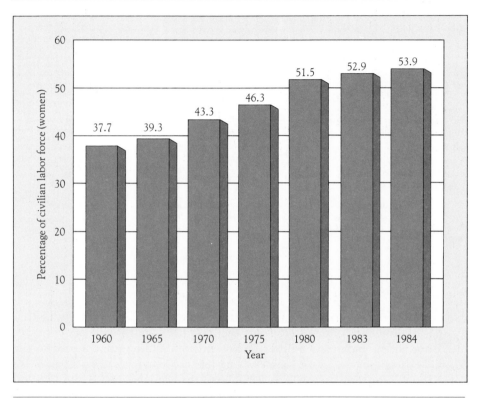

Source: Bureau of Labor Statistics, 1984.

We are able to draw a number of conclusions about emotional development. First, there is a relationship between cognitive and emotional growth. As Sroufe (1979a, p. 491) notes, "Only with recognition is there pleasure and disappointment; only with the development of causality, object permanence, intentionality, and meaning are there joy, anger, and fear; only with self-awareness is there shame." As children's cognitive skills develop, children can make finer distinctions in the environment. Second, children's emotional repertoires become more varied and differentiated as children develop. Some emotions develop before others, as shown in the table. Finally, a child's emotional development may affect the caregiver. When parents label emotions in the first few months, they rely on the context to appreciate what the child is experiencing. Although context remains important, children's emotions become more recognizable as children develop. Later, parents learn to elicit positive emotions in their infants, such as smiling, which in turn reinforce the parents' own behavior.

Fear and Anxiety

Two situations commonly produce fear or anxiety in infants and cause parents concern: fear of strangers and separation anxiety. Both Beth and Jon Walters

TABLE 7.2   The Development of Some Basic Human Emotions*
Emotions develop in a sequential pattern becoming more complex as the child ages.

Month	Pleasure-Joy	Wariness-Fear	Rage-Anger
0	Endogenous smile	Startle/pain	Distress due to: covering the face, physical restraint, extreme discomfort
1	Turning toward	Obligatory attention	
2			
3	Pleasure		Rage (disappointment)
4	Delight Active laughter	Wariness	
5			
6			
7	Joy		Anger
8			
9		Fear (stranger aversion)	
10			
11			
12	Elation	Anxiety Immediate fear	Angry mood, petulance
18	Positive valuation of self-affection	Shame	Defiance
24			Intentional hurting
36	Pride, love		Guilt

*The age specified is neither the first appearance of the affect in question nor its peak occurrence; it is the age when the literature suggests that the reaction is common.
Source: S. L. Sroufe, 1979.

show some fear of strangers, and their parents want to know if this is normal. In addition, Beth and Jon don't like being left with a baby-sitter, and the parents wonder how the children will react to being left in a day-care environment.

Fear of Strangers.   Sometime in the second half of the first year, parents are often surprised by the reaction of their infants to kindly strangers. In the past the baby showed curiosity, but now the baby shows fear. Until about four months of age, infants even smile at strangers, but after that they smile less and less (Bronson, 1968). Most children go through a stage in which their reaction to strangers, and even relatives they do not see regularly, is one of anxiety. This stage usually comes between seven and ten months and may last through a good portion of the second year (Lewis and Rosenblum, 1974; Morgan and Ricciuti, 1969). About 15 percent of infants show some fear of strangers at six months, but the majority show it at ten months (Schaffer and Emerson, 1964).

Fear of strangers is a well-established fact, but recent studies question whether it is inevitable that children exhibit a negative reaction to strangers. Rheingold and Eckerman (1973) allowed an adult female to interact with infants

2. *True or False:*
Fear of strangers is considered an abnormal response in infants and toddlers and indicates insecurity.

fear of strangers
A common phenomenon beginning in the second half of the first year, consisting of a fear response to new people.

Sometime in the second half of the child's first year, most infants develop a fear of strangers.

and their mothers for ten minutes before making any attempt to pick up the babies. The mothers acted in a friendly manner toward the stranger. The infants were neither fearful nor upset, and showed positive responses to the stranger. Infant responses to strangers depend on the stranger and the context. An infant may indeed show fear, but the child may also show interest and a positive emotional reaction (Horner, 1980).

Research findings that infants do not always show this fear of strangers may be explained by the two different methods used to measure the phenomenon. First, one can have a stranger enter the room and approach the infant. In these cases, stranger anxiety is often displayed by the baby. The second method is to allow the infant free rein while the stranger remains quiet and stationary. In this situation, infants do not show fear and may even approach the stranger, although they rarely make contact. When infants are allowed to investigate the situation on their own, they do not always show the stranger anxiety so often associated with this stage.

3. *True or False:*
Infants show more fear of strange adults than of strange children.

The nature of the particular stranger is another variable. Lewis and Brooks-Gunn (1972) used the first method to test stranger anxiety in a group of infants ranging from seven months through nineteen months. As part of the experiment, an infant was seated in an infant seat facing a door 15 feet away, with the mother seated alongside. A stranger knocked on the door and the mother said, "Come in." The stranger entered the room and walked toward the infant, smiling, and finally touched the infant's hand. Negative emotions were displayed when the child was approached by adult male and female strangers, but positive affect was observed with the child stranger. Why did the four-year-old receive a warm welcome? Infants may show positive responses to other children because they use themselves as referents.

Size is one factor in stranger anxiety, but there are other factors. In another experiment, Skarin (1977) varied the familiarity of the setting, the presence of the mother, the sex of the stranger, and the distance separating the infant and the stranger. The infants were tested at home with the mother present, at home with the mother absent, in the lab with the mother present, and in the lab with the mother absent. The infant was approached by both a male stranger and a female stranger in each of the four conditions. Again the first method was used, and the stranger approached infants age five to seven months and ten to twelve months. The findings are very detailed and cannot all be covered here, but we can say that Skarin found that the context, the sex of the stranger, the distance from the infant, and the presence or absence of the mother made a difference, especially in the older group. Generally, the older infants showed more fear of strangers than the younger subjects. And children were much more likely to show negative reactions in the lab than in the home. In addition, the older groups showed more negative reactions when the mother was not present, while the increase was not significant for the younger group. Male strangers caused more anxiety than did female strangers.

Stranger anxiety, then, is mediated by a number of factors, and Lisa and Tim Walters can be assured that a fear of strangers is normal at their children's ages. Research has shown that stranger anxiety can be reduced if the meeting takes place in a familiar setting, in the presence of the mother (or perhaps the father), and if the child is allowed time to warm up to the stranger. Unfamiliar Aunt Gertie would do better to get acquainted again with mother and dad before trying to interact with eight-month-old Jon.

Separation Anxiety.   Parents are familiar with **separation anxiety.** As they are about to go out for the evening, the younger children begin to cry and protest loudly. The memory of that scene may haunt the parents throughout the evening.

Separation anxiety begins at about eight or nine months and peaks at between twelve and sixteen months (Metcalf, 1979). It may continue throughout the second year but is not as intense, if found at all, in the third year. Some separations are predictable, as in the case of the mother who every weekday morning takes her child to the day-care center. The child can anticipate predictable separations and knows that mother will return. The environment is familiar, and hopefully the child is well acquainted with the substitute caregivers. After a while, children become used to an environment, such as a day-care center, and do not show much if any separation anxiety when mother leaves (Maccoby, 1980). Unpredictable separations, such as when a child must enter the hospital, are different. The child is now presented with an unfamiliar environment, strange people who wear frightening uniforms, and a novel situation.

How a child reacts to any separation depends on the child's age, how familiar the situation is, and previous experiences. In addition, the manner in which the mother leaves the child's presence is important (Dunn, 1977). If children have familiar toys or a companion (such as a sibling), or are left with a substitute caregiver for whom they have an attachment, separation anxiety will be reduced. Kagan (1976) found that children who had a history of day care and home care still reacted with separation anxiety when tested in the laboratory. However, children familiar with day care did not show protest in the day-care center (Maccoby, 1980). When children are left in their own homes with a grandmother, the separation anxiety is reduced (Bowlby, 1969). Even the possibility that the mother

separation anxiety
Fear of being separated from caregivers, peaking at between twelve and sixteen months.

protest
The initial reaction to separation in which the infant cries and refuses to be cared for by substitutes.

despair
The second stage in prolonged separation from the primary caregivers, in which the child becomes apathetic.

detachment
The last stage in prolonged separation from the primary caregivers, in which the child cannot place trust in anyone else and becomes detached from other people.

might leave may be enough to provide some problems, especially in the unpredictable situation. For example, when mother begins to pack for a trip, the child may start to cry and cling to her. The child is anticipating the loss. Any increase in the risk of a separation may trigger some anxiety (Bowlby, 1982).

The psychological impact of separation depends partly on the length of the separation. Robertson and Bowlby (1952) argue that the child's reaction to *prolonged* separation goes through three stages—protest, despair, and detachment. In the **protest** stage, children cry and do not allow anyone else to care for them (Schaffer, 1977). In the next stage, **despair,** the children become apathetic and may gaze at the ceiling from the crib for hours at a time. Then the final stage, **detachment,** is reached. Now a child "comes to terms with the situation but at a cost of his emotional tie with his mother and his ability to put his trust into any relationship" (Schaffer, 1977, pp. 96–97). If the separation is temporary, upon reunion the child may react to the parents with a detached attitude. A bit later the youngster may become clingy and refuse to be left alone.

What are the long-term effects of *prolonged* separation? The early work of Bowlby showed that these breaks could lead to emotional disturbances, but we now know that experience is cumulative and that an excellent later environment can mitigate the effects of a poor early environment. A study of children raised in institutions for the first few years and then adopted found no evidence of extensive emotional disturbance. They also developed good relationships with their adoptive parents (Tizard, in Schaffer, 1977). In addition, many of the problems Bowlby attributed to separation may have been due to problems that existed before the breaks (Rutter, 1979). Finally, the separations were frequently long and severe, not the type of predictable temporary separations so common when children are involved in a day-care situation.

How, then, might we handle separations in order to make them easier for the child? Let's say that mother or baby must go to the hospital for a relatively short stay. It is best for the other child or children to be left in their own home (or one with which they are very familiar) with their own toys and with someone who has cared for them in the past. Keeping to the regular routine as much as possible is also recommended. Is it best to spend a great deal of time preparing the child, or merely to inform the youngster of what is going to happen? Because of the many variables involved in separation anxiety, generalizations are risky. In one study, Adams and Passman (1981) varied the amount of information toddlers received about an immediate but brief separation. Children were introduced to a playroom, and one of two scripts was read to them. In one script, the mother told the child that she was leaving but would be right back and to play with the toys. She also read six very short nursery rhymes to the child. In the second script, she read only two nursery rhymes but spent the rest of the time telling her child in different words about the separation. Only the time spent giving the information differed. The brief preparation (script one) was superior in allaying the children's fears. Toddlers given brief preparation played more with toys and stayed in the playroom longer than children given the extended treatment. The extended treatment may have differed from the customary procedure and increased the distress. At least for brief separations, brief preparations are probably best. The researchers also quote evidence that the more time a parent spends playing with the child just prior to departure, the greater the distress. This does not mean that the child should be ignored, but sitting down to play with a child and then getting up abruptly and leaving is likely to cause problems. When children must go to the hospital, it is best to allow a parent to stay with them. Allowing liberal sibling and parental visitation also allays a child's fears to some extent.

Lisa and Tim Walters can now understand the difference between predictable and nonpredictable temporary separations. To reduce their children's anxiety, they should acquaint them with their new environments and make an attempt to maintain a routine so that the separations will be predictable. Allowing the children to take a familiar toy with them at the beginning may be necessary, and allowing them time to get used to their new environment is important. Finally, individual differences abound in separation anxiety. Some children react better than others and, Lisa and Tim will have to be alert to these individual patterns.

ATTACHMENT

When children show a fear of strangers or anticipate a separation, they often stay close to or seek contact with the caregiver. Children develop a relationship with the mother as the primary caregiver and cling to her for safety. Lisa and Tim Walters are aware of the importance psychologists place on the early mother-infant bond and are concerned that the day-care experience will somehow affect this relationship.

The Nature of Attachment

Study of the caregiver-infant relationship usually centers on the concept of **attachment.** According to Mary Ainsworth (1974, p. 135), "An attachment is an affectional tie that one person forms to another specific person, binding them together in space and enduring over time." Attachment is specific, but an infant may be attached to more than one person. It implies an emotional bond that is a positive force in an individual's life. Infants become attached to the primary caregiver, in most instances the mother. How this occurs and the functions of this attachment are still a matter of controversy.

Today, the most persuasive theory of attachment emphasizes its biological roots. Attachment is necessary for the survival and normal development of the infant (Ainsworth, 1974; Bowlby, 1973). Attachment takes time to form, and it develops along with the child's cognitive abilities. The infant is not born with a natural affinity to the mother. This affinity is learned (Waters and Deane, 1982). So, although attachment has biological roots, learning and cognition also play a part.

attachment
An emotional tie binding people together over space and time.

Attachment Behavior

Infants begin to recognize the difference between strangers and familiar people in the first four months. Only at about six months do proximity-maintaining behaviors, such as seeking out the caregiver when afraid, occur. Such behaviors as crying when the mother leaves the room, or following the mother around, begin at about six months (Ainsworth, 1967; Schaffer and Emerson, 1964).

The concept of attachment differs from "attachment behavior." **Attachment behavior** involves actions that result in a child's obtaining proximity to

attachment behavior
Actions that result in a child's gaining proximity to caregivers.

another person who is viewed as better able to cope with the world (Bowlby, 1982). In other words, under certain circumstances, such as stress or anxiety, children are motivated to seek out the individual to whom they are attached. Such behaviors are not shown all the time, only when a child's world is threatened in some manner. Infants from about nine months on develop an ability to anticipate what is going to occur and may cry when the mother turns to walk out of the room. When children approach the third year, these attachment behaviors change somewhat, and they can now accept temporary separations from the mother. They may feel secure enough to be left with a warm substitute figure without creating so much fuss. Even here, though, acceptance of separation is conditional (Bowlby, 1982). The child must be familiar with the sitter, not be anxious or unhealthy at the time, and be secure enough to be able to resume contact with the primary caregiver in a short period of time.

Although shown less frequently and less urgently after the third birthday, attachment behavior is not completely absent. During years four, five, and six, and even though early middle childhood, children may seek out their parents when they have been frightened or have had a difficult day. If, as Bowlby believes, this attachment is necessary for the emotional growth and development of the infant, we would expect children who have not been able to develop such attachments to suffer greatly.

MATERNAL DEPRIVATION

Many theorists argue that the early interactions between mother (the primary caregiver) and child are crucial to a child's later development. Freud (1935) believed that difficulties in this early relationship were the foundation for emotional disturbance. Children who do not receive adequate care become anxious and are unable to relate to others.

The Results of Poor Mothering

It is not ethical to deprive a child of mothering and then observe the results, but in cases of parental death or national upheavals, such as war, we have been able to study children who have never had the opportunity to form attachments.

Many early studies found that the consequences of a breakdown in the early mother-child relationship were serious (Rutter, 1979). Spitz (1965, 1945) compared children who were raised in an orphanage, where they received impersonal care from the staff, and another group raised by their mothers in what amounted to a prison nursery. The children raised in the prison nursery thrived, while those raised in the orphanage without much attention suffered greatly. Emotional disturbances, failure to gain weight, and retardation were common. The orphanage-raised children also suffered many more physical illnesses. Spitz coined the term **hospitalism** to describe these symptoms.

Some studies of maternal deprivation have been performed on animals. The results offer more evidence about the tragic effects of maternal deprivation (Harlow, 1971, 1959; Harlow and Suomi, 1971). Harlow raised rhesus monkeys with either a terrycloth monkey or a wire monkey. When frightened, the infant monkeys clung to the terrycloth mothers even if the wire mother had done the feeding. They were greatly comforted by the softness of these dolls. But even though

hospitalism
A condition in children found in substandard institutions, marked by emotional disturbances, failure to gain weight, and retardation.

Harlow's experiments show the importance of contact comfort. When frightened, this infant monkey clung to its terrycloth substitute even if it was fed by the wire substitute mother.

the monkeys raised on the terrycloth mother were more normal than those raised on the wire mother, abnormalities were still present. These monkeys could not play normally, showed rocking movements, bit themselves, were withdrawn, and could not function sexually.

Perhaps human infants also have this need for **contact comfort.** In other studies, Harlow demonstrated that the injurious consequences of a lack of mothering need not be permanent (Harlow and Harlow, 1962). If placed with companions before six months of age, the effects of a motherless environment were not as severe and were gradually reversed, but if the situation was not reversed early, these problems remained.

Researchers have reported similar problems in human infants. Dennis (1973) followed children raised in an orphanage in Lebanon. They received little attention, and their life was one of uninterrupted boredom. When tested after the first year, they were extremely retarded, but after being adopted they recovered quickly. Those adopted prior to the age of two recovered well. At about six years of age, those who were not adopted were transferred to other institutions—one for males, the other for females. The institution serving the females was just as bad as the one from which they had come. When tested during middle childhood, the girls were quite retarded. The institution for males, however, was run differently and provided a more stimulating environment, filled with toys, educational equipment, and films. The boys had an average IQ of 80, far above the intelligence scores for the girls. Dennis' observations lead to two conclusions. First, these children had suffered from **stimulus deprivation,** that is, their environments were so unstimulating that it prevented them from developing normally.

contact comfort
The need for physical touching and fondling.

4. *True or False:*
Poor mothering in early infancy results in permanent retardation even if the child's environment is later improved.

stimulus deprivation
The absence of adequate environmental stimulation.

Second, the consequences of these unfavorable environments, although quite serious, could be remedied to some degree by placing them in a better, more stimulating environment. The earlier this occurred, the better.

The Effects of Institutionalization

The work of Spitz, Bowlby, and Dennis led to great changes in institutional practices. Children's needs for attention, fondling, warmth, and care are now more fully appreciated. Ways to meet their need for a stimulating environment comprised of human beings as well as things to see, hear, and handle have been incorporated into many institutional environments. Caregivers now provide extra stimulation for premature infants, who spend so much of their time isolated from the outside world. We have learned at least some of our lessons. Institutionalization, then, need not lead to retardation (Saltz, 1973; Wolins, 1970). It is not the institutionalization itself, but rather the quality of the care provided, that determines the outcome. This is further demonstrated by studies showing that some symptoms of maternal deprivation are found in children who are raised in intact homes (Fischoff et al. 1971).

THE CAREGIVER-CHILD RELATIONSHIP

Trust vs. Mistrust

According to Erik Erikson (1963), our basic attitude toward people develops from the early relationship with our caregiver. If our early needs are met in a warm environment, we develop a sense of **trust,** a feeling that we live among friends and that we can trust others. If, on the other hand, our needs are met with rejection or hostility, we develop a sense of **mistrust,** perceiving the world as a hostile, nonaccepting place and developing an inability to relate warmly to others. Children's relationships and early experiences form the basis for how the children will see the world later in life.

But what is it about the nature of this early relationship that affects children so greatly? Can we focus on the elements of the relationship that may contribute to the development of a healthy personality? It is only in the past two decades that developmental psychologists have been successful in this area.

Attachment Behaviors

Classification of Attachment Behaviors.   Attachment behaviors can be measured using a standardized procedure called the **strange situation** (Ainsworth and Whittig, 1969). The "strange situation" consists of eight standardized episodes in which children are brought to an unfamiliar room where a series of brief separations and reunions with their mothers are observed (Waters and Deane, 1982). Infants are classified as **secure** if they greet their mothers positively, actively attempt to reestablish proximity during the reunions, and show few if any negative behaviors toward them. Secure infants explore the room just prior to the separation episodes and use their mothers as a base of operations to explore the environment when the mother is present (Sroufe, 1979a; Ainsworth, 1979).

trust
The positive outcome of Erikson's first psychosocial stage, a feeling that one lives among friends.

mistrust
The negative outcome of Erikson's first psychosocial stage, an attitude of suspiciousness.

strange situation
An experimental procedure used to measure attachment behaviors.

secure attachment
A type of attachment behavior in which the infant in the "strange situation" uses the mother as a secure base of operations.

Secure infants explore the environment more than insecurely attached infants. Behavioral differences are found even three years later. Here, a child heads for parts unknown.

Two other classifications can be grouped under the heading **anxious attachment.** Infants who are classified as being **anxious/avoidant** ignore their mother's entrance into the room in the reunion episodes and may actively avoid reestablishing contact. Infants classified as **anxious/ambivalent** show an angry resistance toward the mother upon reunion (Joffe and Vaughn, 1982). These babies show a great deal of anxiety upon entering the room even before the session begins and are quite distressed by the separation. In the reunion they are ambivalent, seeking close contact and yet resisting it (Ainsworth, 1979).

Stability of Attachment Patterns.   Some disagreement as to the stability of these patterns is found among researchers (see Waters, 1983; Thompson et al., 1983). Waters (1978) found that 48 out of 50 infants who had been classified at one year of age and subsequently reclassified six months later could be placed in the same category. However, Thompson and colleagues (1982) found that only 53 percent of their sample of middle-class infants showed a stable pattern. A study using infants from a low-socioeconomic-class sample found that about 60 percent were stable (Vaughn et al., 1979). More important, though, these researchers discovered a relationship between stress and the quality of mother-infant attachments. Mothers of anxiously attached infants had greater stresses than mothers of securely attached children. In addition, where the classification changed from secure to anxiously attached, the mothers had suffered more stressful events than mothers whose children were classified both times as secure.

anxious attachment
A general classification of insecure attachment shown in the "strange situation," consisting of either avoidant behavior or ambivalent attachment behavior.

anxious/avoidant
A type of attachment behavior shown in the "strange situation," in which the child avoids reestablishing contact with mother as she reenters the room after a brief separation.

anxious/ambivalent
A type of attachment behavior shown during the "strange situation," in which the child both seeks close contact and yet resists it during the mother's reentrance after a brief separation.

5. *True or False:*
The quality of a child's attachment to the mother can change over time.

Changes in Attachment Patterns.   Attachment patterns, then, can change. It is best to view attachment as a relationship rather than a trait (Waters, 1983). A child may show an anxiously attached pattern with one parent and a secure pattern with another (Main and Weston, 1981). In addition, changes in the relationship between mother and child can be improved through the intervention of a grandparent. Egeland and Sroufe (1981) looked at the attachments of children who had been neglected or abused. As expected, a much smaller number of these children could be classified as securely attached than was the case with well-cared-for children at twelve months. Patterns of attachment remained constant for those in the securely attached group between the ages of twelve months and eighteen months. However, over 50 percent of the maltreated infants changed classification. The difference between infants who had changed attachment patterns and those who did not were the presence of supportive family members and a more structured lifestyle. Although attachment patterns are generally rather stable over time, movement can occur if there are major changes in the family situation.

Relationship of Attachment to Later Behavior and Personality.   There is a relationship between the quality of an infant's attachment to the caregiver and later behavior and personality characteristics. Infants who were classified as securely attached at eighteen months were more enthusiastic, more persistent, and less easily frustrated than the infants from the other two groups at two years of age (Matas et al., 1978). Securely attached infants are more socially and cognitively competent as toddlers (Waters, 1978). The ability of securely attached infants to explore their environment carries over into early childhood (Arend et al., 1979). Infants who were securely attached at twelve months explored their environment more and scored higher on tasks of spatial ability during the preschool years than did anxiously attached children (Hazen and Durrett, 1982). They were also more likely to accept suggestions from mother (Matas, et al., 1978), were cooperative, and complied more readily with their mother's instructions (Londerville and Main, 1981).

Secure infants also differ in their play. Donald Pastor (1981) paired securely attached infants with either anxiously avoidant, anxiously ambivalent, or other securely attached infants in a play situation. Securely attached infants were more sociable both toward their mothers and toward their peers. The anxiously avoidant toddlers participated in the play session but were more negative in their orientation toward mother and peers. The anxiously ambivalent group were quite negative toward mother and ignored all peers. This showed that attachment classifications are related to competence in interpersonal situations (Waters et al., 1979).

The Effect of the Parent-Child Relationship on Attachment

Securely attached infants are superior to anxiously attached children on many measures of behavior and development, a superiority that continues at least through early childhood. But what is it in the early parent-child relationship that may lead to these differences?

The home environments of securely attached and anxiously attached infants differ. Mothers of securely attached infants pick them up and hug them more often than do parents of anxiously attached infants. Most of the research has focused on the parents of anxious/avoidant children, because their mothers appear to be more rejecting than mothers of securely attached and ambivalently attached infants (Ainsworth, Bell, and Slayton, 1971). Whereas parents of anxious/avoidant infants disdain physical contact with their infants (Ainsworth, Bleher, Waters, and Wall, 1978), they do show affectionate behavior. They tend to kiss their infants, but do not encourage physical contact (Tracy and Ainsworth, 1981). These children avoid contact in the "strange situation." Not all modes of showing affection are equal (Tracy and Ainsworth, 1981). When infants are upset, they require physical contact. Perhaps avoidant children desire the contact but realize that they will not receive it from their mothers. The avoidance may be a defensive reaction to past disappointments in this area.

Factors Determining the Patterns of Parent-Child Interaction

A child's relationship with the primary caregiver is important. Some caregivers are more competent than others and we have some idea of what characteristics comprise competent caregiving (see Table 7.3). If we could predict the nature of the parent-child relationship and target parents who are at risk for poor parent-child relationships, we could then prevent some problems from occurring. The situation is complicated, however, because a number of factors affect such interactions.

Characteristics of the Parent.   The parent's age, the parent's attitudes about caregiving, the parent's background, and the parent's sensitivity to the needs of an infant are some factors that affect parent-child interaction.

Age.   Age, especially of the mother seems to be one factor. Although some people believe that a younger person has the vitality necessary to care for a child better, this does not seem to be the case. Older mothers have a more positive attitude toward parenthood and are more responsive to the needs of their children. They also report spending less time away from their children than younger mothers (Ragozin et al., 1982). Perhaps older mothers are more secure and more likely to have realistic expectations of parenthood.

Attitudes about parenting.   The ability of an individual to visualize oneself as a parent seems to be an important aspect of parenting (Heinicke et al., 1983). Some people find that the responsibility of parenting conflicts with their life goals. Related to attitudes are expectations. Some parents do not understand the type of care that infants require. Their expectations can be quite unrealistic. The parent who thinks a newborn is going to sleep through the night at one week of age is going to be disappointed. The parent who believes that the baby will always be quiet during a favorite television program is in for a surprise. As the child grows into an ambitious explorer, these expectations may become even more unrealistic and cause tension between parent and child. The parent who thinks a child won't touch the walls with dirty hands is likely to be angry very often. I can remember entering a hardware store where a woman was obviously having a bad time with a cranky toddler. After numerous unsuccessful attempts to deal with the child she shouted, "Why can't you stop acting like such a child?" This was a combination of frustration and weariness talking, but the basic idea is

6. *True or False:*
Older mothers have a more positive attitude toward motherhood than younger mothers do.

TABLE 7.3   Characteristics of Competent Infant Caregivers

On the left side of this table, the desirable characteristics of caregivers are shown, on the right side, the behaviors which reflect these characteristics. Research shows the caregiver's ability to provide for the infant's physical, social, cognitive, and psychological needs is an important factor in the infant's development.

Desired Caregiver Characteristics	*Cues to Desirable Caregiver Characteristics*
I. Personality Factors	
A. Child-centered	1. Attentive and loving to infants 2. Meets infants' needs before own
B. Self-confident	1. Relaxed and anxiety free 2. Skilled in physical care of infants 3. Individualistic caregiving style
C. Flexible	1. Uses different styles of caregiving to meet individual needs of infants 2. Spontaneous and open behavior 3. Permits increasing freedom of infant with development
D. Sensitive	1. Understands infants' cues readily 2. Shows empathy for infants 3. Acts purposefully in interactions with infants
II. Attitudes and Values	
A. Displays positive outlook on life	1. Expresses positive affect 2. No evidence of anger, unhappiness, or depression
B. Enjoys infants	1. Affectionate to infants 2. Shows obvious pleasure in involvement with infants
C. Values infants more than possessions or immaculate appearance	1. Dresses practically and appropriately 2. Places items not for infants' use out of reach 3. Reacts to infant destruction or messiness with equanimity 4. Takes risks with property in order to enhance infant development
III. Behavior	
A. Interacts appropriately with infants	1. Frequent interactions with infants 2. Balances interaction with leaving infants alone 3. Optimum amounts of touching, holding, smiling, and looking 4. Responds consistently and without delay to infants, is always accessible 5. Speaks in positive tone of voice 6. Shows clearly that infants are loved and accepted
B. Facilitates development	1. Does not punish infants 2. Plays with infants 3. Provides stimulation with toys and objects 4. Permits freedom to explore, including floor freedom 5. Cooperates with infant-initiated activities and explorations 6. Provides activities which stimulate achievement or goal orientation 7. Acts purposefully in an educational role to teach and facilitate learning and development

Source: A. L. Jacobson, 1978.

instructive. Many parents, especially if they have had little or no contact with very young children, may not understand babyish or childish behavior.

Age is a factor in such expectations. Many young parents have unrealistic expectations for their infants, imagining them to be toys or dolls (Wise and Grossman, 1980). Reality may come as a shock, and this may affect the relationship with their children. Parents who have positive expectations about parenting adapt well to their new roles, while those who are overly anxious do not (Maccoby and Martin, 1983).

Background.   The background of the parent can be important too. Children who were abused or maltreated grow up to use similar (but not necessarily identical) strategies with their own children (Martin, 1975). People generally believe that what they have experienced is the normal way of interacting with others. If children are raised with kindness and love, they will find it easier to give such attention to their own children.

Sensitivity.   Most authorities on caregiving emphasize the importance of a parent's being sensitive to the cues and needs of an infant (Schaffer, 1977). Parents who form warm and loving relationships with their infants are sensitive to the baby's signs and interpret the baby's behavior. This sensitivity to signals from the child is an everyday phenomenon. Many parents can tell when their children will be ill from the way they look a day or two before the onset of an illness.

At times, this sensitivity is difficult to explain. One day my wife was sitting on the carpet next to a couch talking to her friend when my eleven-month-old daughter, Amy, decided to do an Evel Knievel dive off the couch. Amy stood up slowly on the couch and flung herself off it. My wife caught her in midair, turned her rightside up, and Amy continued on her way. The visitor was astounded. She had been looking straight at the child, and it had never occurred to her that the child would jump. My wife had correctly read a cue. My daughter did this only when my wife or I was there and ready to act. Could Amy also have been accurately reading our own signals?

Characteristics of the Child.   In the past, it was popular to look only at the parents' contribution to the parent-child relationship, but we now realize that certain characteristics of the child can also help or hinder that relationship, for instance, the baby's capabilities, appearance, birth order, temperament, and sex.

Capableness.   The responsive, capable infant is more likely to elicit favorable responses than an infant who is unresponsive (Brazelton et al., 1974). If a parent attempts to interact with a child in a way that is beyond the child's capabilities, the parent may feel rejected, and then become anxious and interact less with the child.

Appearance.   The appearance of the child often elicits nurturant feelings, but an infant who is deformed may elicit different behaviors. Parents may not know how to handle their own feelings. They are taught that they should love their children, and their feelings may not be equal to that ideal. Children who have some physical handicap are also more likely to be abused (Friedrich and Boriskin, 1976). The appearance of children affects the way they are treated.

Birth order.   Firstborn children normally receive the most attention from parents, for everything the child does is new and exciting. Recent research has

7. *True or False:*
Firstborn children receive more attention than later-born children.

shown that adults have different expectations for the oldest and youngest child in the family. The oldest child is expected to be more outgoing, dominant, obedient, and responsible, as well as secure and self-confident. The youngest is expected to be likeable, sociable, and not as obedient or as secure (Baskett, 1985). It is possible that these expectations affect how they are treated.

Temperament.   Temperament is also a factor. Parents behave very differently with children of various temperaments (Dunn and Kendrick, 1981). In Chapter Two, three types of temperament—easy, slow to warm up, and difficult—were presented. "Easy" children usually have no problem entering a relationship because they are not demanding. The slow-to-warm-up child also causes few problems. But demanding difficult children elicit different reactions from caregivers. Parents who consider their children difficult were less responsive to their children than parents who did not consider their infants difficult (Donovan et al., 1978).

Gender.   Are girls really more delicate than boys? Parents think so (Rubin et al., 1974), even though the scientific evidence shows the opposite. Parents are more concerned with the health of their daughters than of their sons (Pedersen and Robson, 1969), although females are actually more robust. The parents' perception, though, is more important. If parents want to see something, they will see it, and this behavior will affect their reactions to their infants.

Socioeconomic Status.   Socioeconomic status, which is a difficult variable to analyze because it is so large and general, may also be a factor in the development of the parent-child relationship. For example, parents from lower socioeconomic groups believe that they have less control over their child's development (Tulkin and Kagan, 1972). Middle-class parents respond more frequently to their infants' behavior (Tulkin, 1970). But it is incorrect to assume that just because individuals are members of a certain social class their relationship will be any less warm or loving. When talking of differences in social class, one should always be cautious.

Bi-directionality.   Parent-child interactions are actually a chain of quick actions and reactions. An action on the part of the child prompts an action on the part of the parent, which may then elicit another action on the part of the child, and so on and on. The beginning and the end are difficult to define. Infants are small but powerful. "Their power lies in the baby's ability to compel action by its eye-to-eye gaze, smiling, crying, appearing helpless, or thrashing" (Bell, 1979, p. 824). The child's behavior elicits behavior from the parents. For example, many abusing parents report that their children were annoying, showed persistent crying, and were generally "abrasive." These behaviors elicited abusive behavior from their parents.

The Synchrony Between Parent and Child.   Any understanding of the parent-child relationship must look at the second-by-second interactions between the two. This is often summarized under the heading **synchrony**—referring to the basic rhythms that underlie the interaction between parent and child (Schaffer, 1977). Watch a mother feeding her baby some mushy cereal, and the meaning of *synchrony* becomes obvious. The infant's head turns, the baby looks here and there, spits out a little, blows a bubble, and kicks both feet. At just the

synchrony
The coordination between infant and caregiver in which each can respond to the subtle verbal and nonverbal cues of the other.

right second, as the baby looks up at the mother, she has the spoon ready. The timing is amazing. The infant was an active participant too, looking at mother at just the right moment, knowing what was coming. The timing was based on an accurate reading of cues for both.

People who do not have regular contact with a particular infant often find it difficult to do things with the child. For instance, they may not be able to read the child's signals and may find themselves shoveling cereal into a closed mouth.

Mother and child must cooperate, and each must adapt to the other's behaviors (Osofsky and Connors, 1979). The development of the warm relationship hinges on the development of this synchrony, this understanding of what will happen next. The beginning of this mutual understanding, as well as the basic attachment sequence discussed earlier, starts at birth.

HOW IMPORTANT IS EARLY MOTHER-CHILD CONTACT?

Yet in many cases mothers do not have contact with their infants for some time after birth. Is early contact vital to the development of a healthy mother-child relationship? For many species, separation immediately after birth results in rejection. If a goat is separated right after delivery from her kid, she will reject it when reunited, but if the separation occurs ten minutes after delivery, no rejection occurs (Klaus and Kennell, 1976). In other species, a critical period for attachment has also appeared. Lorenz (1937) found that geese will follow and attach themselves to the first object they see. When the goslings opened their eyes and saw Lorenz, he became the object of attachment. They followed him everywhere. The geese were only capable of forming such a relationship in the first day and a half. This unlearned, rather rigid, irreversible behavior pattern is called **imprinting.** Could there be such a sensitive period in attachment for human beings? Could the first minutes, hours, or even days after birth be critical for the formation of a bond between mother and child?

When these goslings hatched, the first thing they saw was Konrad Lorenz. These goslings have imprinted on Lorenz and now will follow him everywhere.

imprinting
An irreversible, rigid behavior pattern of attachment.

Klaus and Kennell stirred up controversy by arguing that such a sensitive period in human beings existed (Klaus et al., 1979). The normal procedure in many hospitals was routine separation after birth, with the mother going to the recovery room and the infant to the nursery. Even days later, contact was often limited. Klaus and Kennell suggested that this lack of early contact was responsible for some later problems in the parent-child relationship.

Such a radical viewpoint was certain to stimulate research. Some research did show that mothers who maintained early contact with their infants demonstrated more maternal behaviors. For example, mothers who were given more contact with their infants were compared with a control group of mothers who were not. At one month, mothers in the early-contact group showed more soothing behaviors and more eye-to-eye contact and fondling during feeding, and were more "reluctant" to leave their children with someone else, than mothers in the control group. Differences were still present after a year, with the early-contact group reporting more preoccupation with their babies and showing more soothing behavior while infants were undergoing physical examinations (Kennell et al., 1974).

But are the differences due to the early contact (directly after birth) or the extended contact (providing more contact during the time the new mother is hospitalized)?

Grossman and her colleagues (1981) studied the effects of both early and extended contact on tactual contact with newborns among fifty-four middle-class German mothers. One group had neither early nor extended contact, while another group had early contact. A third group had extended contact, and a fourth had early and extended contact. It is customary in Germany to stay in the hospital for eight to ten days, as opposed to the three or so traditional in the United States. Maternal-infant interactions were videotaped during feeding. For the first five days, mothers given early contact (but not extended contact) caressed their infants more. By the end of their hospital stay, even this effect had disappeared. The early-contact differences involved such behaviors as soft stroking, tender patting, and kissing and were related to whether the pregnancy was desired. In other words, early contact only *seemed* to have an effect on mothers who had planned their infants. The fact that the differences ended after such a brief time indicates that attachment is based on the cumulative effects of mother-child interactions rather than on a single brief encounter (Sroufe and Waters, 1977).

Some studies have not found any differences between mothers allowed early contact and those not allowed early contact (Svejda et al., 1980). Even when separations were rather long, as in the case of premature babies, no significant differences in security of attachment were found between infants separated from their parents at birth and those who were not separated (Rode et al., 1981). Early contact is not absolutely necessary for healthy mother-to-infant attachment to occur (Svejda et al., 1980), and the claims of Klaus and Kennell appear to be "exaggerated" (Belsky, 1982, p. 33).

Although Klaus and Kennell have overstated their main argument, their work has promoted a needed revolution in the way we look at childbirth and aftercare. Today, women giving birth are less likely to be treated as if they were ill. Babies are not as isolated, and fathers and siblings are often encouraged to visit them. In addition, although early contact is not essential, it is probably desirable. More research is needed to determine just which mothers are more likely to benefit from early contact.

THE FATHER-CHILD RELATIONSHIP

Up to this point, it must have seemed as if children only had one parent—the mother. Where is the father? We know a great deal about the mother-child bond, but what about the father-child relationship? Is it important? Interest in the father's influence is quite recent (Hodapp and Mueller, 1982), and some of the latest research findings in this area are surprising.

Where Is Father?

When my daughter Stacey was about ten months old, I noticed a curious thing. When she was hungry, she crawled right past me and communicated with her mother, but right after eating she would crawl to me, pull on my knee to come to a stand, and make unmistakable motions that she was ready to play. If she was frightened, she would normally go to her mother, but if my wife was either unavailable or too far away, she sought my comfort. I found this to be the case with many of my friends whose children were raised in similar circumstances.

Many fathers appear to be taking a more active interest in their youngsters, and psychologists are now appreciating the importance of the father-child relationship.

8. *True or False:*
Early and extended contact immediately after birth is necessary if infants are to develop a healthy attachment to their mothers.

Child specialists are taking a long look at the father-child relationship. So are fathers, who are more interested and involved in their role than they were generations ago. This "paternal consciousness" (Lamb, 1979) may be a response to changes in society. The number of single male parents is increasing, and movies such as *Kramer vs. Kramer* have dealt with the problems and possibilities of father involvement. However, most of the Hollywood treatment of this issue has involved older children, not infants and toddlers. The mother-infant relationship has a sanctity about it that has established a psychological roadblock of sorts around questions concerning the father-infant relationship. In addition, fathers are not as involved in infancy and toddlerhood as they are later on. Most females have had more experience handling and caring for infants and toddlers than males have. This lack of experience, combined with the cultural prescriptions favoring mothers, causes fathers to be wary of interacting with their young children. This may be changing somewhat, as fathers are becoming more involved, but it is wrong to become overenthusiastic and to begin speaking in terms of the egalitarian family where fathers and mothers are equally involved (Chibucos and Kail, 1981).

How Involved Is Father?

Mothers greatly exceed fathers in the amount of time spent with their children. Full-time female homemakers greatly exceed the number of full-time male homemakers. Even when the mother works outside the home, she is much more likely than the father to take time off to care for the children.

In some countries this is changing. The Swedish government allows parents to take up to nine months paid leave from their jobs (Lamb et al., 1983), which may be divided any way they wish. About 60 percent of Swedish fathers take some time off, and about 15 percent take a month or more (Parke, 1981). In the United States, the mother is much more likely to be the one to interrupt her career, and even when she is working she is usually the person primarily responsible for making child-care arrangements.

Even taking cultural factors into consideration, though, American fathers spend little time with their infants. Pedersen and Robson (1969) found that although fathers were available about 26 hours a week when the baby was awake, their interactions with nine-month-old infants averaged about 8 hours per week. A wide range of individual differences were present. Some fathers reported spending forty-five minutes with their infants, while others spent the entire 26 hours with them. Fathers are certainly not as involved as mothers. Even when fathers are home, mothers interact more. However, since the quality of the time spent with a child is more important than the quantity, a look at the type of interactions between father and infant may be interesting.

How Do Fathers Interact with Infants?

Mothers and fathers generally do not interact with their infants for the same reasons, nor do they share the caregiving duties equally. Fathers are much more likely to play with their infants than to care for them (Parke, 1981). In a series of studies among middle-class Boston families, Kotelchuck (1972) found that 64 percent of the mothers were totally responsible for the child care and only 7.6 percent of the

Studies show that mothers and fathers interact differently with their young children.

fathers shared infant-caregiving responsibilities equally with the mother. Only 25 percent had *any* regular daily caregiving responsibilities, and, as Kotelchuck (1976, p. 338) notes, "Even more remarkably, 43 percent of all the fathers reported they never changed diapers at all!" The routine day-to-day child care falls squarely on the mother's shoulders.

The nature of the interactions also differ. Both parents play with their children, but differently. Fathers play more physically with their infants than mothers do (Hodapp and Mueller, 1982). These differences remain fairly constant throughout infancy. Fathers are more likely to engage in physical-social games than mothers (Clarke-Stewart, 1978). Fathers also engage in more unconventional, unpredictable play (Lamb, 1977).

These differences in interaction explain why children seek out each parent for different reasons (Biller, 1982). This is not a function of gender, but the type of interaction that mothers and fathers engage in. The preference is based on the past experience of the child. This interactional difference is culturally determined. Swedish fathers and mothers do not play differently with their infants (Lamb et al., 1983), but American fathers interact with their infants differently from mothers and spend much less time with their children. Do infants form an attachment to their fathers even though their interaction with them is limited?

Do Infants Become Attached to Their Fathers?

9. *True or False:*
Infants become attached to their fathers as well as to their mothers.

Infants do form an attachment to their fathers. In fact, they become attached to many people, not just the mother. The quality of this attachment depends on the history of the interactions the child has had with a person. Many people think of love as a type of pie in which a child can give only a certain amount, that if love is portioned out to too many people, the amount available for mother is less. But this is not true. "Love even in babies has no limits" (Schaffer 1977, p. 104).

Many studies have demonstrated that infants do become attached to their fathers (Parke, 1979; Lamb, 1976). This attachment occurs in much the same manner as with mothers. Infants who are attached to their fathers spend more time looking at them and react emotionally when their fathers enter or leave the room. In addition, "well-fathered" infants are more curious and more likely to explore the environment, more secure, and more advanced in motor development (Biller, 1982). When mother, father, and a stranger are present, the child will stay closer to the mother than to the father, and closer to the father than to the stranger (Cohen and Campos, 1974). In the "strange situation," children protest the departures of both mothers and fathers, and their play decreases (Kotelchuck, 1972). Summarizing the course of preference, Lamb and his colleagues (1983, p. 451) note: "In stress-free contexts, both at home and in the laboratory, infants under thirteen months of age show no preference for either parent. During the second year of life, boys show preferences for fathers whereas girls continue to show no preferences." Infants choose mother over father when they are hungry, wet, or under stress, but in a stress-free environment they show no preference and may even seek out fathers when they want to play. Fathers and mothers mean different things to children, based on the salience of their roles (Parke, 1981). The attachment to both can be quite strong.

Fathers as Caregivers

But how is Father as a caregiver? Equating competence and performance in parenting is a mistake. Fathers may not show as many caregiving behaviors as mothers, but they may be capable of them. Low involvement does not mean low competence (Parke and Sawin, 1976). Experience is important. One man who had to help care for the baby when his wife went back to work stated, "There is nothing I can't do for that baby. After his first three months, when Nan returned to work [after a three-month unpaid maternity leave], he got so used to my feeding him he complained when I left. Now Nan and I split everything: bathing, feeding, changing—it doesn't matter" (Kammerman, 1980, p. 49).

Given the opportunity and enough encouragement, fathers can do a fine job with their children and show many nurturant behaviors. Fathers are just as likely as mothers to hold newborn infants, to rock them, and to talk to them in the hospital (Parke and Sawin, 1976). Fathers are very interested in their children, and they act in a nurturant manner even though they do engage in fewer caregiving chores (Parke, 1979). Fathers can accurately recognize the meaning of infant cries and are responsive to the infant's signals, sounds, and mouth movements (Parke, 1981).

The Cultural Context of Fathering

If fathers are capable of such behaviors, why aren't they more involved in the daily child-care activities when they are available? The answer is found in our American culture and its gender expectations, which begin very early in childhood. In our culture, little girls often run to a toddler and say "How cute," while little boys try to look as bored as possible. Raising children is considered woman's work. Throwing a baseball to a son or daughter is another story. In this area, fathers are supremely confident. Many fathers do not have the confidence, the experience, the encouragement, or the social supports necessary to take a more active role in the day-to-day care of their children.

Parenthood training might provide the knowledge and experience necessary to encourage fathers to take a more active interest in their child's development. (See Research Highlight "The Effects of Parenthood Training" on page 260.)

RESEARCH HIGHLIGHT   *The Effects of Parenthood Training*

In the past, whenever child development specialists wanted to improve the parent-child relationship they concentrated on modifying the mother's behavior. But this focus ignores both the father-child relationship and the influence of the child's behavior on both parents.

Jane Dickie and Sharon Gerber looked into the possibility of training mothers and fathers to be more competent as well as into how such training might affect infant behavior. Parental competency involves such factors as anticipating infant needs, reading infant cues, and providing experiences that are conditional or contingent on the infant's behavior. Such contingent behavior is important. For example, the baby may vocalize, and the parent then responds with a smile. The smile is said to be contingent on the baby's vocalization. The baby reads the smile and smiles back in response. The baby's smile is said to be contingent on the mother's smile. Infant competency involves such factors as providing readable predictable cues and reacting contingently to parental and environmental stimulation.

Thirty-eight parents (nineteen mothers and nineteen fathers) and their normal infants aged four to twelve months participated in this study. Families were matched for neighborhood residence and randomly assigned to the experimental or control group. The experimental group received a sixteen-hour course over eight weeks involving lectures, discussions, and demonstrations emphasizing child development, individual infant variation, knowledge of the infant's temperament and cues, provision of contingent experiences, and an awareness of the infant's effect on the parent and the parent's effect on the infant. Discussions focused on identifying parent needs and on problem-solving. The control group received no such training, but training was offered to them at the end of the experiment.

Observers were sent to the homes of control and experimental subjects and rated many aspects of the parent-infant interaction for a two-hour period. A twenty-minute videotape was made of the infant in free play and his or her interaction with each parent. Various factors were rated, such as a parent's attempt to elicit infant behavior and an infant's attempts to elicit parent behavior. Each parent also completed an eighty-item questionnaire that measured the subject's sense of competence and view of his or her spouse's competence.

The researchers' hypothesis that training would increase the overall competence of mothers and fathers was supported by the data from the home observations and videotapes. Trained parents anticipated infant needs, responded more appropriately to cues, and provided more frequent verbal and nonverbal contingent responses. In addition, infants in the experimental group were more responsive and predictable.

Two unexpected results were found. Parents in the experimental group did not report feeling more competent, although they did view their spouses as becoming more competent. If all measures favored the training groups, why didn't they feel more competent? The researchers believe that training increases both social competence and the awareness of specific weaknesses, and that thus the overall sense of competence may remain the same.

The unexpected finding that training induced fathers to take a more active role and mothers a less active role during videotaping demonstrates the importance of examining both fathers and mothers in their interactions with their children after training. Perhaps the videotaping procedure, which required the presence of both parents, emphasized the mothers' role as encouraging the father to interact more with the child. Studies have shown that when fathers are present mothers interact significantly less, and this tendency is increased when fathers are expected to be involved.

The results of this study demonstrate that parenting courses do succeed in improving parent-child interactions. Such courses would be best concentrating on both mothers and fathers. However, the study also shows that the social competence of infants is improved as well. When parenting training is given, it changes the entire fabric of the parent-child relationship.

More research on such training programs is needed to discover which areas of training are most effective. With our newfound knowledge, however, we must also move in the direction of establishing such voluntary programs nationwide to encourage greater competence on everyone's part.

Source: J. R. Dickie and S. C. Gerber, "Training in Social Competence: The Effect on Mothers, Fathers, and Infants," *Child Development,* 1980, *51,* 1248–1251.

Such courses might start at the high school level (Parke, 1979), and both males and females might benefit. In one study, fathers who were given the opportunity to learn and practice caregiving skills in the hospital were more involved in the care of their infants and in household tasks at three months (Parke, 1979). The infant's attachment to the mother is not the result of any biological rule of nature. Children attach themselves to many people, depending on the nature of the interactions. The quantity of the interactions is not as important as their quality. When one asks just what the role of the father is in the family, the answer given by Schaffer (1977, p. 104) is "just what he and his wife choose it to be."

At the beginning of this chapter, the problems of the Walters family were presented. They had been told by some friends that attachment was overstated, while other friends told them that it was of great importance. There is some truth to both views. On one side, attachment is very important, and the nature of that attachment is related to later behavior. On the other side, infants form close attachments to other people besides mother, and the quality of the interaction with the parents is more important than the quantity. If Lisa Walters does go to work, what will be the effects of substitute care on their children's development?

THE ISSUE OF DAY CARE

Day care has been around for a long time, but it wasn't always called day care. Many mothers left their children with relatives and friends a few times a week for hours at a time. They called it baby-sitting. Still others who worked often left their children with grandmothers and aunts. Again, it was rarely called day care.

Forms of Day Care

Most people think of day care today in terms of large urban care centers, but most day care does not take place in such centers. About half the working mothers of the 8 million preschoolers in 1982 arrange their schedules so that either their husband or a relative cares for them (Clarke-Stewart, 1982). About 47 percent of the preschoolers were cared for in their homes either by a relative (29 percent) or by a nonrelative (18 percent). For 37 percent of the children, child-care was provided in someone else's home, evenly divided between a relative and a nonrelative (Low and Spindler in Etaugh, 1980). This is often called family day care. A bit less than 8 percent were cared for in group care centers, 7 percent by the mother while she worked, and less than 1 percent cared for themselves. The overwhelming majority of infants under one year of age whose mothers work were cared for by relatives or the parents themselves (Klein, 1985). Thus, many forms of day care exist and the day-care center is the answer for the minority. Among those who do attend a day-care center, only 17 percent attend a center that is licensed (Zigler and Muenchow, 1983).

In summary, children are found in a wide variety of day-care arrangements, and those attending facilities outside the home are not likely to find themselves in licensed day-care establishments. The quality of day-care facilities varies, and each state has its own regulations. This variability makes research in the field difficult.

10. *True or False:*
Most children in need of day care attend licensed day-care centers.

About 60 percent of women with children aged three to five work. By 1990, it is estimated that more than half the mothers of all children under six will be employed. Relatives will care for some of these children; many will be cared for in day-care centers (New York Times, July 12, 1985).

Research on Day Care

Most people have some opinion about day care—whether it helps, hinders, or has no effect on a child's development. Those who claim day care is injurious often base their opinions on personal experience or the early research on maternal deprivation. Those who argue that day care doesn't hurt sometimes also claim that it can even help some children. Both sides have their weaknesses.

Factoring out personal experience is difficult. How can we ignore the day-care reared brat next door who is always getting into trouble? How can we discount our parents' teaching that "women ought to raise their own children." One woman in my class noted that her grandchildren, whom she considered spoiled and ill-mannered, were in day care and their behavior was enough "evidence" of day care's effect on children for her. Predicting the effect day care may have on a particular child is difficult. Research gives us information on general populations and suggests factors that might be important in determining how the experience of day care might affect a child, but from there, individuals must evaluate the possibilities for themselves.

The relevance of the research on maternal deprivation to the day-care situation is doubtful. Most studies were performed in institutions among abandoned, abused, or neglected children, so the studies cannot serve as a basis for an argument against day care (Norman, 1978).

The major error made by supporters of day care has to do with their reluctance to appreciate the cautions contained in most studies. Almost all day-care studies have been conducted in very high quality day-care centers (Clarke-Stewart, 1982; Etaugh, 1980; Belsky and Steinberg, 1979). To generalize from these studies to children attending poorer day care centers is impossible. Excellent day-care centers can be very expensive, and beyond the reach of most people (Zigler and Muenchow, 1983), but these centers are the subject of research because they are often connected with universities, are run by professionals confident of their standing, and have nothing to hide.

Other problems with research abound. Some studies use measures of intelligence for comparing home-reared and day-care-reared children, but the use of intelligence tests with young children is questionable. In addition, studies of day-care children versus home-care children sometimes assume that any difference represents a distinction between home care and day care, but this is not always true. Parents who send their children to day care may differ in some unknown way from those who do not (Clarke-Stewart, 1982). Suppose you investigate the difference between home-raised children and children who attend a day-care center in a particular community. If the community suffers a high divorce rate, you may find that more children of divorced parents attend the day-care center than children from intact homes. Differences between day-care and home-care children might reflect differences in the home situations of the children, not the fact that some attend a day-care center. Divorce is an obvious factor that can be taken into consideration, but other, more subtle differences may be at work here. When evaluating the research on the effects of day care, it is important to keep these problems in mind.

Children may form attachments to grandparents and child-care workers.

Day Care and Attachment

Lisa Walters is concerned that the day-care professional will become a mother substitute and will affect Lisa's relationship with her children. Although some studies have occasionally shown differences between home-reared and day-care children on measures of attachment in the "strange situation" (Blehar, 1974), these have been exceptions rather than the rule. After reviewing a number of studies in this area, Belsky and Steinberg (1978) concluded that the vast amount of literature has failed to show any differences between home-reared and day-care children on measures of attachment.

Lisa's children will form an attachment to their substitute caregivers. Children show less distress when left with a familiar caregiver than when left with a stranger, and they show some distress when separated from the caregiver (Ricciuti, 1974). Anderson and her colleagues (1981) found that the extent of this attachment depended on the quality of the day-care worker's interaction with the

11. *True or False:*
Children in day care form attachments to their caregivers at the expense of attachment to the mother.

child. Children showed attachment behaviors to high-interaction competent caregivers and low levels of attachment to low-interaction caregivers. In the presence of a high-interaction caregiver, the child feels secure enough to explore the environment. Again, the quality, not the quantity, of interaction is most important for the development of positive interpersonal realtionships. Finally, the strength of the attachment to mother is no less in the day-care-raised child compared with the home-raised youngster (Caldwell, 1973).

Day Care and Intellectual Development

We might assume that if a child went from a stimulating environment to a good day-care center, little gain or loss should occur. But if a child came from a nonstimulating environment to a stimulating environment, some gain should result. If a child came from a stimulating environment to a poor day-care center, negative effects should be seen. Indeed, the research supports these notions (Belsky and Steinberg, 1979).

Day care has no injurious effects on the cognitive development of low-risk children (Belsky and Steinberg, 1978). For disadvantaged children, an enriched day-care program may encourage cognitive development. In some studies, disadvantaged children reared at home showed a decline over the first three years or so in intelligence scores, while those enrolled in day care did not.

Day Care and Social Development

The evidence on the effects of the day-care experience on social development is mixed. Studies show that generally the overall social emotional adjustment of day-care children is good and compares well with that of home-raised children (Watkins and Bradbard, 1984; Etaugh, 1980). Some differences have been noted. Children who experience day care are more outgoing and cooperative, but also more aggressive and boisterous (Clarke-Stewart, 1982). Children enrolled in day care incline toward more aggressiveness, impulsivity, and egocentrism (Belsky and Steinberg, 1978). They also interact more with their peers. But these results may be due to cultural factors rather than to day care, for studies in other countries do not find these differences. The philosophy of the day-care group may also contribute to these findings. If social skills are stressed, the children will become more socially motivated. In summary, some differences do exist in the social-emotional area, but no evidence indicates that day care causes serious emotional or social problems.

The Quality of Day Care

Much depends on the quality of the day-care center. All the effects described above are mediated by the characteristics of the day-care center and the home. But how can we evaluate a day-care center? The Day-Care Center Checklist shown in Figure 7.2 may be of some help. In addition, some studies single out certain factors as exceptionally important.

One study found that "groups composed of smaller numbers of children and caregivers are consistently associated with quality day care for preschool children" (Smith and Spence, 1980, p. 720). Small centers are better than big ones.

FIGURE 7.2   A Day-Care Checklist

It's not easy to choose a day-care facility. The following checklist can be used as a basis for comparing day-care centers.

Yes	No	*Space and Equipment*
____	____	1. There is adequate space to play.
____	____	2. Sufficient storage for materials is available.
____	____	3. The furniture is child-sized and in good condition.
____	____	4. The temperature is comfortable (68 to 70 degrees).
____	____	5. The lighting is adequate.
____	____	6. Materials are available in sufficient numbers so children don't have to wait long to use them.
____	____	7. There is enough space outside or inside (a playground or a gym) for children to run or engage in other physical activities.
____	____	8. There is adequate space for resting.
____	____	9. The eating area is clean and bright.
____	____	10. Bathroom facilities are designed for small children.
____	____	11. Bathroom facilities are convenient.
____	____	12. Electrical outlets are covered when not in use.
____	____	13. First aid supplies are available.
____	____	14. All equipment is in good repair (no broken toys or sharp edges).
____	____	15. Material is available such as pots or cages for growing things or taking care of animals.
____	____	16. Books are visible.
____	____	17. Puzzles are available.
____	____	18. Adequate space is available for dramatic play (raised platforms, rows of wooden crates, etc).
____	____	19. Emergency procedures are clear and environment allows for safe exit in case of emergency.
____	____	20. Smoke detectors and fire extinguishers are evident.

The Program

Yes	No	
____	____	1. There is an organized daily program.
____	____	2. There is variety within the program.
____	____	3. Students are encouraged to talk with each other.
____	____	4. Children participate in projects.
____	____	5. Activities are planned to encourage children to learn by using their senses.
____	____	6. Self-expressive activities such as painting and various forms of art are programmed.
____	____	7. Children are generally busy, not just sitting around.
____	____	8. Children show evidence of learning through discovery and asking questions of the staff.
____	____	9. Small group activities are encouraged.
____	____	10. Reading and storytelling are part of the program.
____	____	11. Activities that develop the large muscles are evident.
____	____	12. Activities that develop fine muscle control are evident.
____	____	13. Boys and girls are encouraged to participate in all activities.

Teacher-Child/Teacher-Parent Relationships

Yes	No	
____	____	1. Sufficient staff is available so each child may receive individual attention at some point in the day.

Figure 7.2 continued

____ ____	**2.**	A warm relationship with the children is evident.
____ ____	**3.**	Staff circulates among all children: does not spend an inordinate amount of time with only one child.
____ ____	**4.**	Staff offers suggestions in a positive manner.
____ ____	**5.**	Staff trusts and respects children.
____ ____	**6.**	Staff encourages children to do things.
____ ____	**7.**	Staff does not use threat or punishment.
____ ____	**8.**	Staff does not smoke around the children.
____ ____	**9.**	Children understand their responsibilities.
____ ____	**10.**	Staff has sufficient training in the field.
____ ____	**11.**	Children seem happy.
____ ____	**12.**	Children seem to get along with each other.
____ ____	**13.**	Staff appears vigilant, knows what is going on at all times.
____ ____	**14.**	Staff and administrator encourage parents to visit and become involved.
____ ____	**15.**	Adequate communication with parents such as written notices of special events or changes in program.
____ ____	**16.**	Adequate check on who can take child home (dismissal procedures).
____ ____	**17.**	Staff/teacher conferences are held regularly.

Staff/Child Ratio

Minimum staff-child ratio for day-care centers:

Age	Maximum group size	Staff/child ratio
birth to 2 years	6 children	1 adult: 3 children
2 to 3 years	12 children	1 adult: 4 children
3 to 6 years	16 children	1 adult: 8 children

Source: Adapted from Stines, 1983 and Clarke-Stewart, 1982.

In addition, the caregiver-to-child ratio is important. If attention and face-to-face interactions are vital to development in early childhood, the better the ratio of caregivers to children, the better the chances that day care will be a positive experience. If the caregiver-to-infant ratio is too great, the children cry more and become withdrawn or apathetic (Ruopp et al., 1979).

Another relevant factor is the professionalism of the workers. Day-care workers are more child-oriented if they are better educated and trained. The stability of the staff is another factor. If caregivers are changed too often, infants show insecure attachments and anxiety (Farber and Egeland, 1982). Although children's ability to form attachments is flexible, this plasticity is not unending.

Another factor to be considered is the nature of the program. Although day care should not be thought of in terms of school, such activities as reading to children and playing social games can contribute to social and intellectual growth. Other factors, such as safety, ventilation, security, cleanliness, convenience, and cost, should also be taken into consideration.

In summary, day care is neither a panacea nor a hell. Some day-care facilities are excellent, others are horrible. The nature of the interactions between the day-care workers and the child will in part determine the quality of the experience. Research to date shows that children given high-quality day care do not suffer, and in some cases may even benefit from the experience.

THE WORKING MOTHER

Most parents send their children to day-care centers because they work. About half the mothers of preschool children are employed outside the home. Even among mothers who live with their husbands and have children under three years of age, one out of three is employed (Hoffman, 1979). What effect does a mother's working have on the development of a child? Here are three scenarios:

1. Lisa Walters comes home after a tough day at work. After making dinner, she talks and plays with the children. The telephone is always off the hook between 7:00 and 8:00 so that they will not be disturbed. Tim Walters does not come home until 9:30 at night.

2. Lisa Walters comes home exhausted from work. She is so tired and angry at her boss that she puts dinner on the table and lies down. After dinner she parks the children in front of the television until it is time for bed, while she talks to her friends on the telephone.

3. Lisa Walters comes home tired from work. She puts dinner on the table and ignores the misbehavior of the children. She feels guilty for working and is always bringing home treats. She can't say no to her children. They have complete freedom and go to sleep any time they choose.

No matter what children's day care experience, home environment does affect their development. To simplify matters, I allowed Tim Walters to come home too late to really help out. This is not far from the truth. Even in families where both parents work, the mother does the bulk of the child-care and homemaking chores.

Right at the start, you may say that asking what effects a mother's working has is a sexist question. What about the father? This is a reasonable criticism, but since mothers usually act as the primary caregivers, the question is proper. In addition, working itself may be too broad a variable to be useful. The child's experiences in the day-care arrangement, the amount of time the parents are away, and what happens when they come home are crucial mediating concerns (Allnut, 1979). All these factors should be kept in mind when looking at the question of how a mother's employment affects her children's development.

Mother-Child Interaction: Working vs. Nonworking Mothers

There are differences of opinion as to whether working mothers interact differently with their children. Some studies show that employed and nonemployed mothers interact very similarly with their children (Hock, 1980), that child-rearing practices do not vary according to whether the mother is employed or not (Yarrow, 1962). But other studies came up with different findings. One found that nonworking mothers give more positive attention, including affectionate touching, and vocalize more to their infants than mothers who work (Cohen, 1978). In another study, parent-child interactions in a traditional southwestern community were examined. Although daughters received the same amount of attention whether the mother was employed or not, sons received less.

The attitude of the parents toward the mother's working was found to be important. More problems arose in families where negative attitudes toward maternal employment existed. For example, if parents believed that it was harmful to the children to have the mother work, or that the children required full-time mothering, more rejection and criticism was directed toward the children. Whether the mother is employed outside the home or a full-time homemaker, how she feels about her role is as important as what that role is. After reviewing some of the research in this area, Rutter (1981, p. 17) concludes:

> Clearly, what remaining at home or having a job does for the mother's mental state is likely to make a big difference to the children. It may well be more important to have a satisfied, happy mother than to have a mother at home all day. Whether maternal employment is or is not beneficial is likely to depend on whether or not mother wants to work. Presumably, too, it matters whether the job proves to be a satisfying one and not so tiring as to lead to role strain or conflict.

Recently, the stereotype of the unhappy homemaker has become common. Depression and boredom were supposedly related to full-time homemaker status. The happy, satisfied working woman was held in high esteem. There may well be some advantages for self-esteem for women who work (Rutter, 1981). However, the personal benefits are much more likely to be found in mothers who are working because they want to than for those who are working because of financial necessity (Alvarez, 1985). The stereotype of the unhappy homemaker is only partly true. Most studies simply compare working mothers with nonworking mothers and report the differences so popular in the magazines. However, if you split homemakers into those who want to work and those who don't, a different picture becomes apparent (Fiddell and Prather in Tavris, 1976). The stereotype is accurate only for the woman who finds herself trapped and wants out. The homemaker who is satisfied is just as happy as the working woman.

Father's Role When Mother Works

Although the way employed and nonemployed mothers interact with their children is not very different, the amount of attention paid to the children by the working mother is usually less. Now that the mother cannot spend as much time with the children, does the father step into the void and interact more with his children?

12. *True or False:*
The father is generally more active in child care when the mother is employed.

Generally, the father does take on more of the child-rearing responsibilities when the mother goes to work (Rutter, 1981), and the qualitative differences between mother-child interactions and father-child interactions decline somewhat (Stuckey et al., 1982). Fathers tend to supervise more on weekends, to participate more in child care, and to do more of the household chores. The age of the children is a factor. Males become more involved as their children get older. The father's attitude is another variable. If he is against his wife's working, he may not lift a finger to help. But despite father's help, mother remains the focal point of the home. Fifty-fifty splits are unusual. Mother makes the child-care arrangements and continues to be the primary caregiver.

Effects of Maternal Employment on Children

Does the mother's working affect a child's development? Before answering this question, a few cautions are necessary. Even if a mother is home, it does not necessarily mean that she is paying much attention to the children. A home-based mother does not mean a full-time mother (Hoffman, 1979). In addition, while we uncritically accept the belief that full-time mothering is best, this may not be the

Where Is Daddy?

As is true with all infants, Elaine and Sean's baby requires a great deal of attention. Even though Elaine works part-time, Sean doesn't lift a finger to help. At night he nudges Elaine when he hears Eddie crying. He rarely helps out around the house, and he spends very little time with the infant. Sean does help when Elaine specifically requests it, but his technique with the baby is so poor that she tries not to ask him to do much.

What irks Elaine more is Sean's seeming lack of interest in the infant. Sean doesn't seem to know what to do with a baby. Sean agrees, but shrugs his shoulders and says, "When Eddie can play ball or a board game, you'll see how much time I spend with him."

Still, Elaine is not happy with the situation, and she has suggested that they see a child psychologist who might help Sean with the problem. Sean shot back, "What problem?" but he agreed to go.

1. If you were Elaine, how would you have handled the situation?
2. If you were the psychologist, how could you help?

case. Although boys who received full-time mothering during the preschool period are more intellectually advanced, they are also more fearful, more conforming, and more inhibited as adolescents (Moore, 1975). The full-time mother may be overinvolved. In addition, the effect of employment is mediated by such factors as the type of day care provided, the attitude of the parents, and their behavior when they return home from work.

But some differences between children of working and nonworking mothers have surfaced. These depend on the child's gender and social class. Maternal employment does not have a negative effect on girls and may actually be a positive influence on their development. Daughters of working mothers tend to be higher achievers, and the mother may serve as an achieving role model (Hoffman, 1979). Sons of working mothers do not have the traditional sex stereotypes that children of nonworking mothers frequently have.

Social class is another variable. Males from low socioeconomic backgrounds may view the need for their mothers to work as a reflection of their father's failure to earn a living. This would lead to a strain in the father-son relationship. Generally, though maternal employment does not adversely affect the cognitive development of lower-income males. However, studies of middle-class youngsters sometimes show some differences in cognitive development. A study of middle-class toddlers showed that children of nonemployed mothers were more cognitively advanced than those of employed mothers. These differences are most likely to be found in males. Some studies of middle-class males show that they do not do as well on intelligence tests as children raised by their nonworking mothers (Hoffman, 1979). Although the majority of studies have not shown this superiority in cognitive development, it has cropped up enough to indicate that there is room for additional research in this area. Why this may occur is open to question. Perhaps the care received by some middle-class children in day care does not match that provided by a nonemployed mother. Perhaps some working mothers are not as involved with their children when they get home.

Of all the areas of concern, none is more controversial than the effects of the mother's working on both the supervision of children and their socioemotional development. Children of working mothers take on more responsibilities, and supervision becomes difficult. The periods right before or after school are stressful. The mother may have to leave for work at 8:00 A.M. when the school does not accept children before 8:30. Getting children to and from after-school activities is a problem as well. Despite these supervision problems, no relationship exists between maternal employment itself and juvenile delinquency or personality disorders (Hoffman, 1979, 1974).

Differences in social behavior between children of working and nonworking mothers do appear, but they are minor. Schachter (1981) found that preschool children of employed mothers are more peer-oriented and self-sufficient. Children of nonemployed mothers seek out more help and protection and show more jealousy. No differences in emotional adjustment were found.

13. *True or False:*

Maternal employment has no effect on the child's social or cognitive development.

In summary, the differences in social behavior are neither great nor negative. The effects of maternal employment can be either negative or positive, depending on many factors. It does not lead to massive personal or emotional problems, although there is room for some concern about the cognitive development of middle-class males. This possible problem may be reduced by providing better substitute care and encouraging parents to become more involved in their children's cognitive development.

Some employed mothers do attempt to compensate for working. In the beginning of this section, three different approaches to working women dealing with their children were noted. One mother was guilt-ridden, another was overwhelmed, but the first mother built healthy interactions with her children into the evening schedule. She compensated for the lack of time with quality interaction.

RELATIONSHIPS WITH GRANDPARENTS, SIBLINGS, AND PEERS

So far we have looked at the nature of children's social relationships to their mothers, fathers, and day-care workers. But, many children also form early relationships with grandparents and siblings.

Grandparents and Their Grandchildren

Grandparents often develop special relationships with their grandchildren. In some states, grandparents may go to court for visitation rights in case of a divorce between a child's mother and father (Moss, 1985). Grandparents often help in the early child-care as well.

For some children, grandparents are the nice, easygoing, loving individuals who give them cookies. Grandparents often ignore minor problems and are more indulgent. The type of grandparent-child relationship depends on the quality of their interactions. The nature of these interactions depends on the style of grandparenting undertaken by the child's grandparents.

formal-style grandparents
Grandparents who, although interested, are uninvolved in the raising of their grandchildren.

Neugarten and Weinstein (1964) interviewed seventy pairs of middle-class grandparents and isolated five grandparenting styles. The **formal style** involves

Some grandparents develop close relationships with their grandchildren.

grandparents who are not really involved in the upbringing of the child other than a baby-sitting chore here and there but who are interested in the grandchildren. **Fun-seeking** grandparents are playtoys for their grandchildren. They are indulgent and enjoy taking part in activities with them. The **surrogate parent,** which is much more common for grandmothers than for grandfathers, is especially important. This grandparent takes on a parenting role, often so that the child's mother can work. The style known as the **reservoir of family wisdom** involves an older style of grandparenting in which the grandparent, more often the grandfather, is the titular head and the authority figure for the entire extended family. His position is supreme. Finally, the **distant figure style** involves a noninvolved grandparent who may have very little contact with grandchildren except for a birthday party.

Each style of grandparenting has a direct or indirect impact on the child. Grandparents may have an indirect impact on a child by providing a safety valve for new parents who need help adjusting to their role and who benefit from advice (Spock, 1974). Grandparents have a direct impact through their relationship with their grandchildren. Although most of the grandparents in the study by Neugarten and Weinstein (1964) were happy with their role as grandparents, about one-third were uncomfortable with it. Some felt uncomfortable about becoming grandparents, others felt some tension over differences with their children on matters relating to child-rearing.

As children get older, their relationship with grandparents changes. At four or five years of age, grandchildren are apt to value their grandparents for what they get from them. It is later in middle childhood that the grandparents' posi-

fun-seeking grandparents
Grandparents who play with their grandchildren and enjoy many activities with them.

surrogate-parent grandparents
Grandparents who take on the parental role often so the mother can work.

reservoir-of-family-wisdom grandparents
An older style of grandparenting in which the grandparents or, more commonly, the grandfather serves as head of the family.

distant-figure-style grandparents
Grandparents who are basically uninvolved with their grandchildren and have little contact with them.

**ACTION/
REACTION**

Can Anyone Else Care for My Child?

Because Rita and Todd had not been away without their baby for more than a year, they decided to take a trip and made arrangements to go on a week-long cruise. Everything seemed set, with Todd's parents ready to baby-sit.

One night before they were to leave, when Todd's parents were baby-sitting, Rita noticed a few things that disturbed her. The baby didn't seem to want to eat when Todd's mother tried to feed her. And her mother-in-law didn't seem to have the right approach. Rita told Todd about her doubts, but he dismissed them. When Rita brought up the subject with her mother-in-law, the older woman became indignant and noted that she had been the one who raised Todd. Things have cooled between Rita and her mother-in-law, and Todd's mother is going through with the baby-sitting only because the tickets have already been purchased.

1. If you were Rita, what would you do?
2. If you were Todd and witnessed this rift between your wife and your mother, what would you do?
3. If you were the mother-in-law, what would you have said to Rita? What would you do now?

tive qualities and personal wisdom are appreciated (Kahana and Kahana, 1971). If grandparents spend a considerable amount of time in active interaction with their grandchildren, an attachment will probably grow and develop. Grandparents may indeed play a part in the development of their grandchildren.

Sibling Relationships

From our earliest days, we have significant relationships with our siblings. Sibling relationships are variable and can produce help and protection or anger and despair. And the presence of other children may affect how much attention a child receives.

Most parents provide siblings for their child. Older siblings may even provide some small measure of caring for an infant by feeding, playing with, or in some way comforting the baby (Bank and Kahn, 1982). This can be a mixed blessing, however. The younger child may expect and desire a protective, warm relationship and receive anger and hostility instead, thus forming a lasting pattern of poor sibling interactions. On the other hand, older siblings may have a sense of pride in their position as the oldest.

Infants can become attached to their siblings. Infants who had a brother or a sister present with them in the nursery were much less distressed when separated from parents (Dunn, 1977). The siblings were only two or three years old themselves, so the comfort did not result from being mothered. In one fascinating case, Meyerhoff (1971) shows how a separation from older siblings might affect a toddler. A nineteen-month-old girl was placed in her aunt's home along with her five-year-old brother and three-year-old sister. Her mother had been suddenly

Older siblings may provide emotional support for younger ones.

hospitalized. At first, the little girl's adjustment was fine, but after a week she had to be moved to the home of another relative without her two siblings.

> Within the next week, the child had become stuporous, had lost her power of speech, refused food, was withdrawn and agitated, and resisted the affections of anyone, including mother and father when she was reunited with them. She looked as if she were dying, and would sit listlessly, sometimes calling out her siblings' names. Only after her brother and sister were returned to her, did she seem emotionally responsive, begin to look alive, regain her speech and usual demeanor, and once more become physically active. (Bank and Kahn 1982, p. 29)

This sibling bond does not compare with the child's primary attachments. Because of sibling immaturity, the bond is often inconsistent and anxiety-provoking. However, infants do form attachments to older children, imitate them from early infancy, and follow them around. These interactions may influence their social and emotional development.

Peer Interactions

As infants develop into toddlers, their relationship with peers becomes a factor in their development. Few parents structure peer interactions into the daily schedules of infants, but infants react to the presence of other children, and by the end of their first year they are interacting with them. The parent-infant relationship may set the stage for infants to develop peer relationships even at this early age. They provide children with an "orientation to the social world" which generalizes to infant-peer interactions (Easterbrooks and Lamb, 1979, p. 386).

Social behavior progresses with age and experience (Mueller and Vandell, 1979). Visual recognition of peers begins at about 2 months. If placed near each other at 3 or 4 months, infants will touch. At 6 months or so, infants begin to direct their attention to other infants and to smile in response to the coos of their peers. By 7 or 8 months, they follow a peer. Between 9 and 12 months, we begin to see exchanges involving social play. Children begin to play social games with balls or peekaboo. By 13 or 14 months, they imitate their peers.

After the first year, the peer interactions take on a more recognizable quality. The number of interactions increase, and some negative ones, such as tugging with another child for a desired toy, are seen. Although even one-year-olds share (Hay, 1979; Rheingold et al., 1976), cooperative and sharing behaviors increase greatly during the second year. In this second year, children will turn less toward their mothers and more toward both toys and peers if placed in a novel play setting (Eckerman et al., 1975). As toddlers age, the sophistication of their social games increases (Ross, 1982). The amount of social interaction will depend on a number of factors. Children interact more with familiar peers, and when only one other toddler is present, rather than a group. Large toys or no toys encourage interactions, and more interaction takes place in familiar settings (Mueller and Vandell, 1979). In conclusion, infants and toddlers do interact with each other from early ages. They come to prefer peers in certain situations, perhaps because their behavior is more novel than that of parents, and their actions are more easily imitated (Eckerman et al., 1975).

To return to our scenario at the beginning of the chapter, Lisa and Tim Walters now have some of the answers concerning their fears that day care and maternal employment might be harmful to their children. They must be certain that the day care provided is of excellent quality. Tim's attitude toward Lisa's working bears scrutiny, as does his ability and willingness to help with the child-care and homemaking chores. Finally, both parents must realize that their responsibilities do not end when they come home from work. They must build active involvement with their children into their schedules. If they choose to leave their children either at a day-care center or with the grandmother, the children will develop some attachment to others, but it will not be at the parents' expense.

MANY ROADS TO TRAVEL

We now have a tentative picture of how a child forms relationships and becomes a social being. The caregiver-child attachment is important. Securely attached children are superior to anxious/avoidant and anxious/ambivalently attached children on a variety of measures. The child forges bonds and close relationships with many people, including mother, father, grandparents, day-care workers, siblings, and peers. The quality of the interactions is more important than the quantity.

In the last three chapters the astounding progress that infants make cognitively, socially, emotionally, and physically has been discussed. Their communicational development that forms a bridge to the next stage will be covered in the next chapter. These advances are summarized in Table 7.4. Much has been said about meeting the needs of the child, and warm, responsive, understanding adults are required if children are to develop socially and emotionally in a healthy manner. Yet if research has taught us anything, it is that there is no single

14. *True or False:*
Toddlers interact more if many small toys rather than a few larger toys, are available.

way that these needs may be met. As Chess and Thomas (1981, p. 221) note, "Just as the child's nutritional requirements can be met successfully with a wide range of individual variation, so can his psychological requirements." Many roads can be traveled to arrive at the same destination. Some roads are more difficult than others. Evidence indicates that parents can provide for the needs of their children in many ways, taking into account the personality of the child, the children's own needs and requirements, and the family's circumstances.

Chapter Summary

1. The infant's earliest emotions are reflexive. As the child develops, emotions become more differentiated and attached to social stimuli.

2. A child's fear of strangers begins sometime in the second half of the first year and lasts through most of the second year. The child will show less fear of strangers if the stranger is small or female, or if the child is allowed to get used to the stranger.

3. Beginning at about eight months of age, and peaking somewhere between twelve and sixteen months, children show separation anxiety. Long-term separations from the caregiver may lead to protest, despair, and finally a detachment that can end in death.

4. Infants must attach themselves to a caregiver if they are to develop normally. Children who have not had the opportunity to do so often suffer retardation. The tragic consequences of maternal deprivation may be reduced if the child receives excellent care later on.

5. Erik Erikson argues that the psychosocial crisis during infancy is trust versus mistrust. If the child's needs are met, the child develops a sense of trust. If not, a sense of mistrust may develop.

6. Attachment behaviors can be measured using a standardized procedure of brief separations and reunions known as the "strange situation." Three classifications of attachment behavior have surfaced: secure attachment, anxious/avoidant attachment, and anxious/ambivalent attachment. Children classified as securely attached are superior to the other classifications on a variety of measures.

7. Many factors affect the parent-child relationship, including the age of the parent, attitudes and expectations concerning the new role as parent, the parents' background, and sensitivity to the infant's needs. The infant's abilities, appearance, birth order, temperament, and gender also af-

fect the relationship. While the parent affects the child, the child also affects the parent.

8. Although early and extended contact between mother and infant is desirable, it is not absolutely necessary to the establishment of a healthy mother-child relationship.

9. Infants form attachments to their fathers as well as to their mothers. Mothers and fathers interact differently with their infants—mothers often performing more of the daily caregiving chores, and fathers playing with them more physically. Infants often seek out their fathers when they want to play and their mothers when in distress. The involvement of fathers with their infants varies from culture to culture and family to family.

10. The day-care experience may be a positive, neutral, or negative one, depending on the quality of the day care, the attitudes of the parents, and the parent-child interactions after work. Studies show that, in general, day care does not injure the child, and in some instances may actually promote development.

11. Maternal employment does not have a negative effect on daughters, and working mothers may serve as an achieving role model. There is some evidence that middle-income males whose mothers are employed are not as cognitively advanced as sons of nonemployed mothers. This may be remedied by providing extra attention after work. The differences in social behavior between children of working and nonworking mothers are minor.

12. Children may become attached to their grandparents and siblings. Grandparents differ in their style of grandparenting.

13. Interaction with peers begins very early in infancy. Peer interaction increases as the child matures.

TABLE 7.4 **Summary of Cognitive and Social Development in Young Children**
This chart shows some types of infant behavior along with various examples of each. The ages listed are rough guides. Normal children are highly varied and variable and no child fits all the patterns presented here.

Behavior	Birth to 6 Months	6 to 9 Months	9 to 18 Months	18 to 24 Months	24 to 36 Months
Thinking	Baby discriminates mother from others, is more responsive to her Baby acts curious, explores through looking, grasping, mouthing Recognizes adults, his bottle, discriminates between strangers and familiar persons Shows he's learning by anticipating situations, responding to unfamiliarity, and reacting to disappearance of things Uses materials in play such as crumpling and waving paper Looks a long time at objects he's inspecting	Baby shows persistence in doing things Becomes aware of missing objects Makes connections between objects—pulls string to secure ring on the other end, uncovers a hidden toy Increases his ability to zero in on sights or sounds he's interested in Baby's attention span is prolonged Baby shifts his attention appropriately, resists distraction	Baby unwraps an object, takes lids from boxes Recognizes shapes in a puzzle board Names familiar objects Baby becomes increasingly curious about surroundings, sets off on his own to explore further than ever before Becomes more purposeful and persistent in accomplishing a task	Child says the names of familiar objects in pictures Explores cabinets and drawers Begins to play pretend games	Child can name many objects Begins to grasp the meaning of numbers Child's memory span is longer Child's ability to reason, solve problems, make comparisons develops Child grasps the concepts of color, form and space Begins to respect and obey rules Shows strong interest in investigating the functions and details of household objects
Language	Baby coos expressively, vocalizes spontaneously Baby vocalizes over a sustained period of time to someone who is imitating his sounds Baby babbles in word-sounds of two syllables	Baby babbles to people Says "da-da" or equivalent Notices familiar words and turns toward person or thing the speaker is referring to Shows he understands some commonly used words	Baby jabbers expressively Imitates words Says two words together	Child uses two-word sentences Has vocabulary of 20 to 50 words Begins to use "me", "I", and "you" Follows verbal instructions Listens to simple stories	Child uses language as a way of communicating his thoughts, representing his ideas, and developing social relationships Child enjoys using language, gains satisfaction from expressing himself and being understood Understands and uses abstract words such as "up", "down", "now", "later"
Body Expression and Control	Baby develops own rhythm in feeding, eliminating, sleeping and being awake—a rhythm which can be approximately predicted Baby quiets himself through rocking, sucking, or touching Adjusts his posture in anticipation of being fed or held (in crib, on lap, at shoulder) Head balances Baby turns to see or hear better Baby pulls self to sitting position, sits alone momentarily Eye and hand coordinate in reaching. Baby reaches persistently, touches, manipulates	Baby sits alone with good coordination Manipulates objects with interest, understands the use of objects—rings a bell on purpose Practices motor skills, crawls, stands up by holding on to furniture Uses fingers in pincer-type grasp of small objects Increases his fine-motor coordination of eye, hand, and mouth	Baby stands alone, sits-down, walks with help Is gradually gaining control of bodily functioning Throws ball Becomes more aware of his body, identifies body parts Stands on one foot with help Walks up and down stairs with help Needs adult as a stable base for operations during his growing mobility and curiosity	Hand coordination is increasingly steady—child can build tower of many blocks Climbs into adult chair Runs with good coordination Climbs stairs, using rail Uses body actively in mastering and exploring surroundings—an active age	Child can jump and hop on one foot Child walks up and downstairs alternates his feet at each stair Begins to notice the differences between safe and unsafe activities Expands his large muscle interests and activities Tries hard to dress and undress himself

Social Play and Responsiveness	Retains objects in hands, manipulates objects, transfers from hand to hand Baby engages in social exchange and self-expression through facial action, gestures, and play Baby imitates movements Gazes at faces and reaches toward them, reacts to disappearance of a face, tracks face movements Responds to sounds Smiles to be friendly Mouth opens in imitation of adult Baby likes to be tickled, jostled, frolicked with Makes social contact with others by smiling or vocalizing Quiets when someone approaches, smiles A mutual exchange goes on between adult and child through smiling, play, voice, bodily involvement	Baby cooperates in games Takes the initiative in establishing social exchanges with adults Understands and adapts to social signals Shows ability to learn by demonstration	Baby plays pat-a-cake, peek-a-boo Responds to verbal request Imitates actions Stops his own actions on command from an adult Uses gestures and words to make his wants known Focuses on mother as the only person he'll permit to meet needs	Child scribbles with crayon in imitation of adults' strokes on paper Likes parents' possessions and play that mimics parents' behavior and activities Follows simple directions Controls others, orders them around Tests, fights, resists adults when they oppose or force him to do something Child is able to differentiate more and more between people	Child tests his limits in situations involving other people Says "no" but submits anyway Shows trust and love Enjoys wider range of relationships and experiences, enjoys meeting many people other than parents Likes to try out adult activities, especially around the house, runs errands, does small household chores
Self-Awareness	Baby smiles at his own reflection in the mirror Looks at and plays with his hands and toes Feels things about himself through such actions as banging	Baby listens and notices his own name Makes a playful response to his own image in mirror Begins to assert himself	Baby becomes aware of his ability to say "no" and of the consequences of this Shows shoes or other clothing Asserts himself by "getting into everything", "getting into mischief" Wants to decide for himself	Child recognizes body parts on a doll Identifies parts of own body Child takes a more self-sufficient attitude, challenges parents' desires, wants to "do it myself" Child's sense of self-importance is intense—protests, wants to make own choices	Child becomes aware of himself as a separate person, can contrast himself with another Expresses preferences strongly Expresses confidence in own activities Expresses pride in achievement Values his own property
Emotions	Baby shows excitement through waving arms, kicking, moving whole body, face lighting up Shows pleasure as he anticipates something, such as his bottle Cries in different ways to say he's cold, wet, hungry, etc. Makes noises to voice pleasure, displeasure, satisfactions Baby laughs	Baby expresses some fear toward strangers in new situations Pushes away something he does not want Shows pleasure when someone responds to his self-assertion Shows pleasure in getting someone to react to him	Baby shows preference for one toy over another Expresses many emotions and recognizes feelings in other people Gives affection—returns a kiss or hug Expresses fear of strangers Shows anxiety at separation from mother, gradually masters this	Child desires to be independent, feed self, put on articles of own clothing Shows intense positive or negative reactions Likes to please others, is affectionate Shows some aggressive tendencies—slaps, bites, hits—which must be dealt with Shows greater desire to engage in problem-solving and more persistence in doing so Develops triumphant delight and pride in his own actions Becomes frustrated easily	Child strives for mastery over objects Child can tolerate more frustration, more willing to accept a substitute for what he can't have Shows strong desire for independence in his actions Gradually channels his aggressive tendencies into more constructive activities Uses language to express his wishes and his feelings toward others Shows a developing sense of humor at surprises, unusual actions, etc.

Source: Day Care: Serving Infants. D.H.E.W. Pub. #78-31056, 1978.

■ *Answers to True or False Questions*

1. *True.* The infant's first emotional reactions are reflexive.

2. *False.* Correct statement: A fear of strangers is common in older infants and toddlers.

3. *True.* Infants show much less anxiety when confronted by a small child than an adult.

4. *False.* Correct statement: Studies show that the effects of a poor early environment may be at least partly reduced by a significant improvement in the child's later environment.

5. *True.* Although they are usually stable, attachment patterns can change.

6. *True.* Older mothers have a more positive attitude toward parenthood than younger parents do.

7. *True.* Firstborn children receive more attention than their later-born siblings.

8. *False.* Correct statement: Although such contact may be desirable, it is not absolutely necessary for the development of a healthy mother-child relationship.

9. *True.* Infants become attached to their fathers as well as to their mothers.

10. *False.* Correct statement: Only a very small percentage of the children in day-care situations are cared for in licensed group day-care centers.

11. *False.* Correct statement: Although children will form an attachment to substitute caregivers, it will not be at the expense of their relationship with their mothers.

12. *True.* Although mothers continue to perform most of the child-care and homemaking duties, fathers generally pitch in more when the mother is employed outside the home.

13. *False.* Correct statement: The effects of maternal employment may be positive or negative, depending on a number of factors.

14. *False.* Correct statement: Toddlers tend to interact more with their peers if there are a few larger toys present.

PART THREE

Early Childhood

CHAPTER EIGHT

The Development of Language and Communication Skills

CHAPTER OUTLINE

THE MYSTERIES OF LANGUAGE

THE NATURE OF LANGUAGE AND
    COMMUNICATION

THE DEVELOPMENT OF LANGUAGE

HOW WORDS ARE USED

HOW WE LEARN LANGUAGE

CURRENT ISSUES IN LANGUAGE AND
    COMMUNICATION

ACTION/REACTION   A Heavy Choice

RESEARCH HIGHLIGHT   ***Day Care and Language
    Development***

A WONDER REDISCOVERED

■ *Are the Following Statements True or False?*

*Try the True-False Quiz below. See if your answers correspond to the information in this chapter. Each
question is repeated opposite the paragraph in which the answer can be found. The True-False Answer Box
at the end of the chapter lists complete answers.*

___ **1.** Infants as young as one month can under-
stand the spoken word.

___ **2.** Scientists have been unable to determine the
meaning of an infant's babbling.

___ **3.** When infants babble, they utter every sound
the human vocal apparatus is capable of producing.

___ **4.** The syntax of a six-year-old approaches that
of an adult.

___ **5.** Children produce many more words than
they can understand.

___ **6.** The learning processes of reinforcement and
imitation can explain the acquisition of a child's vocabulary.

___ **7.** Parents use well-formed sentences when
speaking to their toddlers.

___ **8.** On the average, American girls acquire lan-
guage faster than American boys.

___ **9.** Black English is a dialect of Standard English.

___ **10.** Middle-class children use more complex sen-
tences and fewer commands than children of working-
class parents.

___ **11.** Before the age of about two, cognitive
growth does not depend on the child's linguistic progress.

THE MYSTERIES OF LANGUAGE

Most of you have taken a foreign language in high school or college. There you sat, sweating over a text, trying to learn a different grammar and vocabulary. The task is time-consuming and frustrating. Has it ever occurred to you that infants who come into this world with no prior knowledge of any language learn their own language on the basis of very little formal teaching within a few years? Somehow infants master the basics of their native tongue perfectly, including the difficult sounds and pronunciations that wreak such havoc on students desperately trying to master a second language. How does the child accomplish this feat?

A related mystery involves children's ability to generate sentences they have never heard before. Spend an hour or so listening to preschoolers converse. The creativity involved in generating a new thought will amaze you. While riding through the Mojave Desert from Los Angeles to Las Vegas, my daughter of a little over two years of age was quiet. The night was very dark, and the trip was monotonous. Suddenly, as we approached Las Vegas, she looked at the city and exclaimed "Oo, I see lots of lights." She may have heard each of these words separately before, but not in that exact sequence. She had generated an original thought using words that were easily understood by those around her. The simplicity of her communication should not interfere with our wonder over how a young child creatively uses language.

But why single out language development for special treatment? A number of considerations led to the decision to devote a special chapter to this area of study. First, the acquisition of language is perhaps the greatest intellectual feat a person will ever perform. Children are born without knowing language, and within five years or so they are communicating almost as well as the adults around them. Second, language defines humanity. No other species seems to show the depth and complexity that human beings show in language formation and use. Third, the seemingly simple issue of how children acquire language is really quite complex and requires the kind of full explanation possible only when an entire chapter is devoted to discussing the many facets of language development. Finally, the issues involved in language, such as bilingualism, the importance of the environment, and language and subculture, to name just a few, transcend all ages and stages, making chapter coverage desirable.

The acquisition of language is one of the most difficult accomplishments to explain. Before trying to unravel some of its mysteries, let us define some terms and survey the normal course of language development in children.

THE NATURE OF LANGUAGE AND COMMUNICATION

communication
The process of sharing information.

language
The use of symbols to represent meaning.

Language and communication are not the same. Language is only one part of communication. **Communication** is the process of sharing information (Shatz, 1983). It entails a sender, a receiver, and a message. **Language** involves "strings of symbols that represent meaning in some perceptible medium" (Shatz, 1983, p. 844). It involves arbitrary symbols with agreed-on meanings. While communication is a process, language is the means of conveying meaning to someone else. The medium is usually speech, but it doesn't have to be.

For instance, consider the plight of a two-and-a-half-year-old who wants a cookie but can't reach the jar. The child wants to send a message to mommy, who is reading a magazine. He can communicate with her in a number of ways. He can verbally interrupt her by saying, "Mommy, gimme cookie," but there are other avenues of communication open. He can cry, make nonlanguage sounds to gain her attention, or physically lead her to the cookie jar and point.

As the receiver of the communication, the mother must interpret it—not always an easy task. Children mispronounce words or express their thoughts in individualistic ways. Parents and children often have special words or phrases that stand for particular things. If a child said, "My stomach hurts," it would normally indicate that the child was experiencing gastric distress. However, one of my daughters would use that phrase to indicate that she was either hungry or very full. We understood the phrase, and it carried a specific meaning for us, but when the child visited her grandmother, this phrase was interpreted differently, leading to a nap and no more cookies (much to my daughter's distress).

Once the mother has interpreted the message, she must communicate an answer. The roles are now reversed: the mother becomes the sender, the child becomes the receiver. Let's say that mother nods her approval. As long as the child understands that this means yes, it is as effective as verbal communication.

There are three important points here. First, communication may be verbal or nonverbal. Although we are mostly interested in verbal communication, the

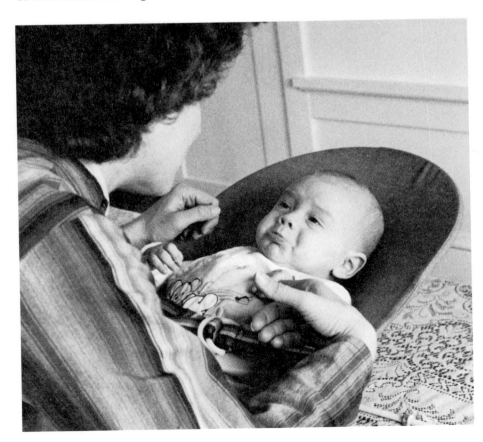

Children communicate with their parents using a variety of gestures and facial expressions.

importance of gestures and facial expressions should not be forgotten. Second, communication involves a sender, a receiver, and some message. Third, a discussion involves rapidly exchanging the roles of sender and receiver.

THE DEVELOPMENT OF LANGUAGE

Few events bring parents as much joy as their child's first word. It is easy to forget that much has taken place before the child says "Dada" or "Car." Under normal circumstances, every human child proceeds through similar steps in reaching linguistic competence (see Table 8.1). If possible, tape-record your own child's linguistic development from the baby's earliest sounds through the first primitive sentences. The developmental sequence leading to a mature use of language is impressive.

Prelanguage Communication

1. *True or False:*
Infants as young as one month can understand the spoken word.

Communication between infants and their caregivers does not require language. Smiles, cries, gestures, and eye contact all form a basis for later communication (see pages 195–199). The nonlanguage interaction between parent and infant approximates a conversation. Although very young infants cannot understand words, they do respond to their caregiver's language (Fernald and Simon, 1984), and some linguistic abilites are present almost from birth (Molfese et al., 1982). One-day-old infants respond to speech sounds by moving their bodies in rhythm to them (Condon and Sander, 1974). One-month-old infants are able to discriminate between certain vowels, such as "i-u" from "i-a" and "pa" from "pi" (Trehub, 1973).

proto-conversations
The infant's responses to verbal and nonverbal cues which resemble turn-taking, as in a conversation.

The infant's ability to respond to language and other nonverbal cues leads to a kind of turn-taking called **proto-conversations** (Bateson, 1975). A parent speaks, and the baby responds by smiling or later cooing. The parent then says something else, and the pattern continues. The interactions are spontaneous. Let's say mother is feeding the baby. When the infant spits the nipple out, the mother says, "No, I don't want any more. I want to burp." These interactions are the beginning of a conversation mode as the infant learns the basis for later communication.

These conversations are not as random as they seem. When speaking to infants younger than six months, mothers use a rising pitch when their infants are not paying attention and the mothers want eye contact (Stern et al., 1982). In addition, yes-no questions are spoken with rising pitch, whereas questions having to do with what and where and various commands are accompanied by a falling pitch.

cooing
The verbal production of single-syllable sounds, like "oo."

The infant is also the master of another ability, **cooing**. Cooing involves production of single-syllable sounds, such as "oo." Vowel sounds are often led by a consonant, resulting in a sound like "moo." Infants enjoy listening to themselves vocalize, but these early noncrying vocalizations are not meant to be formal communication.

TABLE 8.1 Patterns of Normal Speech Development

The development of speech and language is orderly and sequential. However, keep in mind that the ages specified here are guidelines and only indicate averages.

Child's Chronological Age	Child's Normal Speech Development	Child's Chronological Age	Child's Normal Speech Development
6 months	Repeats self-produced sounds; imitates sounds; vocalizes to other people; uses about 12 different speech sounds (known as phonemes).		words in length; 7 percent of the sentences are compound or complex and averages 203 words per hour; rate of speech is faster; relates experiences and tells about activities in sequential order; can say a nursery rhyme; asks permission (such as Can I? or Will I?).
12 months	Commonly uses up to 3 words besides mama and dada; may vocalize such words as bye-bye, hi baby, kitty, and puppy; and uses up to 18 different phonemes.	48 months	Commonly uses up to 1500 words in sentences averaging 5 to 5½ words in length; averages 400 words per hour; counts to 3, repeats 4 digits, names 3 objects and repeats 9-word sentences from memory; names the primary colors, some coins, and relates fanciful tales, enjoys rhyming nonsense words and using exaggerations; demands reasons why and how; questioning is at a peak, up to 500 a day; passes judgment on own activities; can recite a poem from memory or sing a song and uses such words as even, almost, now, something, like, and but.
18 months	Commonly uses up to 20 words and 21 different phonemes; jargon words or phrases are present and often automatically repeats words or phrases said by others (echolalia); uses names of objects that are familiar, one-word sentences such as go or eat, and uses gestures; uses words such as no, mine, good, bad, hot, cold, nice, here, where, more, and expressions such as oh-oh, what's that, and all gone; the use of words at this age may be quite inconsistent.		
24 months	Commonly uses up to 270 words and 25 different phonemes; jargon and echolalia are infrequent; averages 75 words per hour during free play; speaks in words, phrases, and 2- to 3-word sentences; average 2 words per response; first pronouns appear such as I, me, mine, it, who, and that; adjectives and adverbs begin to appear; names common objects and pictures; enjoys Mother Goose; refers to self by name such as Bobby go bye-bye, uses phrases such as I want, go bye-bye, want cookie, up daddy, nice doll, ball all gone, and where kitty.	54 months	Commonly uses up to 1800 words in sentences averaging 5½ to 6 words but now averages only 230 words per hour and is satisfied with less verbalization; does little commanding or demanding; about 1 in 10 sentences is compound or complex and only 8 percent of the sentences are incomplete; can define 10 common words and count to 20; asks questions for information and learns to control and manipulate persons and situations with language.
30 months	Commonly uses up to 425 words and 27 different phonemes; jargon and echolalia no longer exist; averages 140 spoken words per hour; says words that name or identify items such as chair, can, box, key, and door; repeats 2 digits from memory; average sentence length is about 2½ words; uses more adjectives and adverbs; demands repetition from others (such as do it again); almost always announces intentions before acting; begins to ask questions of adults.	60 months	Commonly uses up to 2200 words in sentences averaging 6 words; can define ball, hat, stove, policeman, wind, and can count five objects and repeat 4 or 5 digits; definitions are in terms of use—can single out a word and ask its meaning; makes serious inquiries (such as what is this for, how does this work, etc.); uses all types of sentences, clauses, and parts of speech; reads by way of pictures and prints simple words.
36 months	Commonly uses up to 900 words in simple sentences averaging 3 to 4 words per sentence; averages 15,000 words per day and 170 words per hour; uses words such as when, time, today, not today and can repeat three digits, name one color, say name, give simple account of experiences, and tell stories that are understandable; begins to use plurals and some prepositions; uses commands such as you make it, I want, and you do it; verbalizes toilet needs.	66 months	Commonly uses up to 2300 words in sentences that average 6½ words in length; grammatical errors continue to decrease as sentences and vocabulary become more sophisticated.
42 months	Commonly uses up to 1200 words in mostly complete sentences that average between 4 and 5	72 months	Commonly uses up to 2500 words in sentences averaging 7 words in length; relates fanciful tales, recites numbers up to 30; asks the meaning of words; repeats five digits from memory; can complete analogies such as: A table is made of wood, a window of _____. A bird flies, a fish _____.

Source: Adapted and abridged from Weiss and Lillywhite, 1976.

Babbling

2. *True or False:*
Scientists have been unable to
determine the meaning of an
infant's babbling.

3. *True or False:*
When infants babble, they
utter every sound the human
vocal apparatus is capable of
producing.

"Cada cada bil." The next step in language development is **babbling**. Babbling involves both vowel and consonant sounds strung together and often repeated. Babbling may begin as early as three months and gradually increases until about nine to twelve months of age. Then it decreases as the child begins to use words (deVilliers and deVilliers, 1978). Most infants are babbling by the age of six months (Dale, 1976). Is the babbling infant trying to communicate something?

If infants use babbling as a form of language, then we must admit we haven't been able to understand it. Although some parents swear that their child's babbling has some particular meaning, this does not appear to be the case. Scientists have not figured out what meaning any particular babble may have.

A number of myths have surrounded babbling. One very popular myth is that when children babble they vocalize every possible speech sound the human vocal apparatus is capable of producing. This is not the case. Although the variety and range of speech sounds produced is impressive, it does not approximate all the sounds that humans can produce (deVilliers and deVilliers, 1978).

Another myth is that social stimulation is necessary for babbling to begin. No one really knows why infants begin to babble, but we do know that they do so both when they are alone and when they are in the presence of other people. Perhaps babbling has some self-stimulatory function or is part of a drive to master an emerging ability. Whether it be sitting, standing, or vocalizing, infants have a drive to practice and gain control of their emerging abilities. Further evidence that social stimulation is not necessary for infants to begin babbling comes from work with children raised by deaf parents. These children begin to babble as well (Lenneberg et al., 1965). Even though infants do not need social stimulation to begin to babble, babbling can be increased through social reinforcement (Dodd, 1972). Although babbling begins as a relatively uncoordinated activity, social stimulation does affect the amount of babbling children produce.

A third myth is that children who babble a great deal will talk more. The relationship between babbling and talking is unclear at the present time. A gender difference is found here. The rate of babbling is more indicative of later speech for females than it is for males (Minton, 1979). No one definitely knows why this is so.

The First Word

What was your first word, and when did you utter it? Deciding when a child has really uttered the first word is more difficult than it seems. Parents often read into their children's babbling. One parent swore her three-month-old child asked for bread and butter.

What exactly constitutes a child's first word? Specialists in language development use two criteria (deVilliers and deVilliers, 1978). The word must approximate some adult word, and it must be used consistently in similar situations. If the baby says "ca" whenever he sees a car, it meets both criteria, but if the infant says it only once, it may be pure coincidence. Trying to convince a proud parent of this is useless.

Children usually utter their first word anytime between ten and fifteen months, but there is considerable individual variation. Children's first words are not usually those they hear most often. Nelson (1973) studied the early word acquisition of a number of children and divided the children into two categories. **Expressive children** used words that were involved primarily in social interactions, such as "bye-bye" and "stop it." The early language of **referential children** involved the naming of objects, such as "dog" and "penny." These differing styles followed the linguistic style used by the children's caregivers. The parents of referential children named objects very frequently, while those of expressive children directed their children's activities and emphasized social interactions. The early language of both groups differed. Referential children used many more different words. Expressive children begin to use language in a social context, referential children use it in cognitive context, such as labeling items when looking at a book (Nelson, 1981).

Words are used at first in isolation and are gradually generalized to similar situations. Babbling continues during this one-word stage. For years, psychologists have argued about the meaning of these one-word utterances. Francis (1975) asks what a child really means when uttering the single word *jam*. Does it mean that some jam is on the table or that the child wants jam on a piece of bread? Psychologists call this one-word utterance a **holophrase**, meaning a single word that stands for a complete thought. For instance, a child says "Up" and means "Pick me up," or the child says "Wet" and wants to be changed. Parents must go beyond the word and use the context in order to interpret the child's ideas. The child saying "Wet" may be labeling the condition and not want to be changed at all. This interpretation casts some doubt on whether the child is really using one-word expressions to indicate entire thoughts. If the child wanders over to the refrigerator and says "Jam," mother may say, "So you want some bread and jam." When parents interpret their children's one-word utterances so loosely, establishing what a child really means becomes difficult.

Words to Sentences

The beginning of grammar occurs when a child uses two-word sentences. "Mommy up," "Give pencil," and "Timmy dirty" are all common multiple-word utterances. There is less doubt as to the meaning. The two-word stage appears to be universal (Brown, 1973), but it is difficult to explain. The finding that children use one word as a pivot and another as an open word excited many psychologists for a time (Braine, 1963). *Pivot words* are action-oriented words, such as "look," "see," or "go," which are often found along with a variety of nouns called *open words*. For example, the word "look" may be a pivot word, and the young child may place open words, such as "mommy," "daddy," or "sister," in front of it. The child's expressive vocabulary contains few pivot words and many open words. Using a small number of words, the child can express many thoughts. When the child says "Mommy up" or "Daddy up," it shows a type of primitive grammar. Notice that the child is not simply imitating the adults, for parents do not use this type of construction.

Not all the evidence supports the use of pivot and open grammar, and not all two-word utterances show this construction (deVilliers and deVilliers, 1978). Pivot and open grammar is too simple an approach to children's language acquisition. In addition, although more specific than one-word verbalizations, pivot and open grammar does not completely define the meaning of a child's utterances either. For example, "Look Daddy" may mean "Look at me, Daddy" or "Look at Daddy."

expressive children
Children who use words involved in social interactions, such as "stop" and "bye."

referential children
Children whose early language is used to name objects, such as "dog" or "bed."

holophrase
The use of one word to stand for an entire thought.

Telegraphic Speech

The child's early speech, whether it is constructed of two- or three-word sentences, leaves out small words like "a" or "to" or "from" and concentrates on the more important words. This is called **telegraphic speech**, because it is similar to the language found in telegrams where the sender includes only the words absolutely necessary for communication. For example, "Mommy go store" may mean "Mommy is going to the store" or may be thought of as a command: "Mommy, go to the store!" Parents still must interpret the child's meaning according to the context of the remark, but the thoughts are communicated more precisely at this stage. If the child has just discovered that there are no more cornflakes in the house, the mother may interpret "Mommy go store" as a command. If Mother has just taken her coat off the hanger and begun to put it on, the child's comment may simply indicate that Mother intends to go to the store.

Whatever this utterance means, the child has used only those words which are intended for the meaning. These important words are commonly stressed by other speakers in the environment, which makes them easier to imitate and learn (Brown, 1973).

The use of telegraphic speech by children at about eighteen months to two and a half years is easy to recognize. At times, these children may use words like "the" or "a" in their speech. If the child learns that a particular object in the environment is called "the bank" or "a statue," the youngster may use those small words. The article has become part of the noun itself.

Approaching Mastery

By about three and a half years of age, children begin to use sentences of approximately four or five words, and by five years their syntax is quite good. The three-year-old has a vocabulary of about 900 words and begins to use plural nouns and the past tense. By four, conjunctions are being used and the sentence structure is more complex. By the age of five or six, the syntax has improved and approaches that of an adult (Smith and Neisworth, 1975), although tense errors and other grammatical irregularies still occur in speech until eight to ten years of age.

HOW WORDS ARE USED

Overextensions and Underextensions

"Look! Daddy!" the child says when noticing the picture of a man on the wanted poster in the post office, to the embarrassment of mother. As they learn language, children make certain kinds of mistakes. For instance, a young child looking at a magazine might label every picture of a man "Daddy" and every four-legged animal a "dog." Such a child does know the identity of his or her father and is probably aware of the difference between a cat and a dog.

The type of error in which children apply a term in a broader manner than is correct, called **overextension**, is probably more a problem in production than a problem in comprehension (Whitehurst, 1982). That is, children understand the differences, but they have difficulty producing the correct labels. This was demonstrated well in a study by Nelson and her colleagues (1978), who found that a

telegraphic speech
The child's use of sentences in which only the basic words necessary to communicate meaning are used and helping words such as "a" or "to" are left out.

4. *True or False:*
The syntax of a six-year-old approaches that of an adult.

overextension
A type of error in which children apply a term in a wider manner than is correct.

child who would call all sorts of vehicles, such as an airplane, a truck, or even a helicopter, a car could pick out the correct object when asked to do so. In another study, a child who overextended the word apple to include a number of different foods was able to choose an apple from a group of foods when asked to do so (Thomas and Chapman, 1975).

Children also **underextend** (Anglin, 1977), that is, they use a term to cover a smaller universe than it should. Young children often use the term *animal* to define only mammals and may deny that people, insects, or birds are animals as well (deVilliers and deVilliers, 1978).

Why do children overextend and underextend? Perhaps children learn nouns in terms of their features (Clark, 1978), for example, dogs have four legs and fur. If this were so, the child would call all four-legged animals with fur "dogs." Categorization problems may also arise from the speech that is directed at children by adults (Anglin, 1977). When a child is young, parents are apt to use such terms as "car" and "dog" rather than "Chevrolet" and "German shepherd." This is functional, because children need to recognize the difference between a car and a truck, but not between a Chevy and a Dodge, but it restricts the child's experience with labels and explains these phenomena. Overextension and underextension may also simply reflect the child's prevailing mental abilities and difficulty in categorizing items.

underextension
A type of error in which children apply a term in a narrower manner than is correct.

"I drinked the waters!" Once children begin to master the rules of grammar, they often overgeneralize them.

Overextension of Rules

"I drinked the waters!"

Once children begin to acquire some of the basic rules of English they over-use or, as psychologists say, **overgeneralize** them. For example, to pluralize a noun, we ordinarily add an "s" to its end, as in "dogs" or "pencils." However, exceptions abound, and the plural of "man" is not "mans" but "men" (Francis, 1975). When creating a past tense, we normally add the suffix "-ed" as in "walked" or "talked." Again, exceptions are plentiful; the past tense of "go" is not "goed" but "went," and the past tense of "see" is not "seed" but "saw." Children will often overuse these rules and use words like "seed" or "goed." They may have used the word correctly in the past, but now that they know the rule they apply it to every case, producing such grammatically incorrect forms. With experience, children correct themselves, and most gradually learn the exceptions with little or no formal training.

Comprehension and Production

So far we have looked at the **production** of language, but there is another important area—**comprehension**. Psychologists have tended to focus more on production than comprehension because it is easier to study production. A child produces a word, and parents become aware of the child's linguistic growth. The child's advancement is easy to detect. Studying comprehension is more difficult. A child may understand an order but be physically unable to carry it out. In addition, only action-oriented comprehension, as when a parent shouts "Sally, give me the crayon before you write all over the walls," can be measured. Even in this example, the child may give the parent the crayon but not understand some parts of her parent's command. Mother's menacing tone (intonation) or manual gestures (standing with her hand outstretched) may be enough for Sally to figure out that she had better hand the offending instrument over to her mother immediately.

As noted, infants can differentiate between sounds very early. By about three months, children react to the tonal quality of someone's voice (Wolff, 1963). The baby shows pleasure and contentment when exposed to a pleasant, soothing voice. Later, children can understand words they cannot produce (Bloom, 1974). A fourteen-month-old child could point out his own shoe and his mother's shoe when asked to do so, even though he was unable to speak a word (Huttenlocher, 1974).

At every age, children understand more words than they can produce. As children grow into adulthood, they use a greater variety of words in their writing than in their speech. We recognize many more words in print and in someone else's speech than we ourselves use, and this imbalance remains throughout life.

HOW WE LEARN LANGUAGE

The simplest questions are often the most difficult to answer. This is especially true in the area of language learning. For years, psychologists have been struggling over the question of how a child develops from a being that understands and produces no language to one that can use language with great ease. This all

---

overgeneralization
A type of error in which children overuse the basic rules of the language. Once they learn to use plural nouns, they may say "mans" instead of "men."

language production
The ability to verbalize language.

comprehension
The understanding of language.

5. *True or False:*
Children produce many more words than they can understand.

occurs within the space of about five or six years, at which point the child's understanding of the rules of grammar approximates what it will be in adulthood. Older children and adults do learn some new words, and they may even improve their grammar if exposed to a course on the subject, but these improvements cannot match the dramatic linguistic growth during the first five years of life.

Reinforcement and Imitation

At first glance, it appears that children learn language through imitation. This is true of vocabulary. Words are symbols that stand for things or ideas. The vocabulary of each language differs. The Spanish word for chair is "silla," and in Hebrew it is "keesay." The only way children can learn vocabulary is through imitation. Children learn the word "cookie" when they have need for the word. They master words in an attempt to communicate with others. When they finally say "chair" they have imitated what they have already heard in their environment.

The vocabulary growth of children that is shown in Figure 8.1 is impressive. Between one and a half and six and a half, the child learns about ten new words each week, yielding a rate of one and a half new words per day (Smith, 1926 in Whitehurst and Vasta, 1977).

The effects of imitation on word acquisition is evident. A parent who labels common everyday items is more likely to have a child who has a superior early vocabulary (Nelson, 1973). Children may also pick up unusual words that have shock value. My two-year-old daughter learned the words "horrible," "ridiculous," and "disgusting" very early. She would try some new food, make a face, and say "Disgusting" with all the intonation the word requires. She generalized the use of this word, and after receiving a big kiss from one of her great-aunts wiped her face and said "Disgusting." The power of the environment is shown by the way children learn words from older siblings and peers, often using them at the wrong time.

It is a mistake, however, to think that, because the child learns vocabulary through these processes, all language development can be explained by imitation and reinforcement. There is more to it. Children must acquire rules for changing tense, creating word order, and the like in order to use language correctly. These organizational rules are referred to as **syntax.** Consider the sentences "Johnny hit Mary" and "Mary hit Johnny." The word order makes quite a difference. Some of the rules we master are quite complicated. Try describing the rule by which you would use the phrase "a thing" or "the thing." Most of us use the rule perfectly, but we would be hard-pressed to formulate it. Can children learn the syntax of a language through the processes of reinforcement and imitation, or is language too complicated to be explained by these processes?

According to Skinner (1957), operant conditioning, including the processes of reinforcement, generalization, and discrimination (see pages 150–153) are responsible for language development. Children learn language the same way they learn everything else. They are reinforced for labeling the environment and for asking for things. Through the process of generalization and discrimination, children come to reduce their errors and use the appropriate forms. Of course, imitation also enters the picture, as the child imitates parental speech. Skinner looks at the acquisition of grammar as a matter of generalizing and making infer-

6. *True or False:*
The learning processes of reinforcement and imitation can explain the acquisition of a child's vocabulary.

syntax
The way words are put together to form sentences in a particular language.

FIGURE 8.1   **Children's Average Vocabulary Size**
Children's average vocabulary size increases rapidly between the ages of one and a half and six and a half. The number of children tested in each sample age group is indicated above the appropriate bar in the graph. Data is based on work done by Madorah E. Smith of the University of Hawaii.

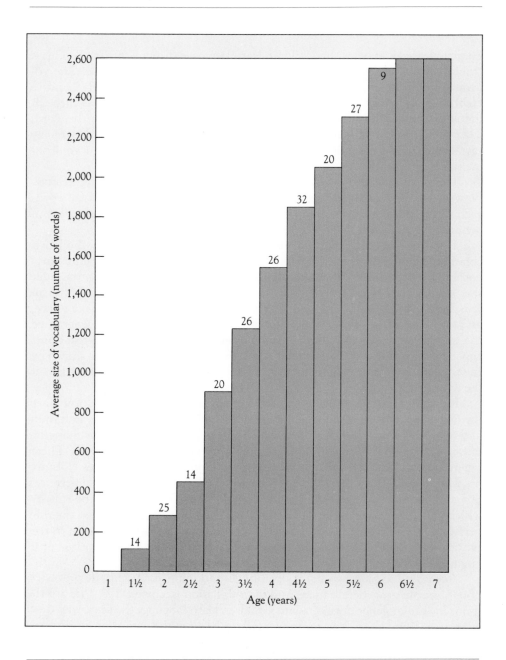

Source: Moskowitz, 1978.

ences. For example, a child may learn the meaning for the phrase "my teddy bear" and then infer that it is also "my cookie," "my television," "my" everything.

Although learning must be involved in language acquisition, the theory does not seem sufficient to totally explain how a child acquires language. Learning theory easily explains acquisition of vocabulary, but how does a child learn to create an original sentence with all the wonder and mystery involved? It is difficult to explain the simple but brilliant creativity and originality of a child's sentences. All children create original sentences they have not heard before. In addition, how can a child of limited cognitive abilities master the complicated rules of grammar that even adults cannot explain—and do all this without formal training (Bloom, 1975)? Finally, if only the processes of learning are involved, why do children make the same mistakes as they develop their language abilities, and why do they produce such childish speech patterns as telegraphic speech, which they do not hear around them? These problems, among others, have led some authorities to argue that some innate biological mechanism must be responsible for language acquisition.

Is Language Acquisition Innate?

Noam Chomsky (1972, 1965, 1959), the leading advocate for the biological or **nativist explanation**, argued that human beings are preprogrammed to learn language. Children require only exposure to the language prevailing in their own culture. Human beings are born with an innate, biological ability to learn language called a **language-acquisition device**. Children can acquire the grammar of the particular culture's language because their brain is innately patterned to understand the structure of languages. Children can understand the basic rules of language and form hypotheses about them, which they then test out.

Chomsky's position excited many psychologists and **psycholinguists**, scientists who study the nature of languages. It explained the interesting similarities that we find in language development around the world. Children proceed through the same steps when learning language in all cultures (Slobin, 1972) and

nativist explanation
An explanation of language development based on biological or innate factors.

language-acquisition device
An assumed biological device used in the acquisition of language.

psycholinguistics
The psychological study of the nature of language, language acquisition, and its use.

Studies show that children in all cultures proceed through the same stages in their mastery of language.

make the same mistakes. These similarities could be explained if the acquisition of language rests on some shared neurological foundation. Language acquisition becomes a maturational activity coinciding with brain development. Some authorities claim that there is a critical period in developing language between birth and adolescence (Lenneberg, 1967). If not developed during that time, the individual's language would be permanently disordered. In addition, Chomsky noted that languages from all around the world shared certain similarities, thus establishing a fit between the structure of the mind and human language in general.

The distinction between Skinner's and Chomsky's theoretical approaches was nicely demonstrated by Grover Whitehurst (1982). He asks that we imagine moving to Washington, D.C., and trying to find our way around the new city under one of two conditions:

> Suppose I knew nothing about the layout of streets. Gradually through many forays, mistakes, instructions from others, I would get my bearings. If I lived in the city long enough, I might even get to a point at which I had a kind of cognitive map. But this cognitive model of Washington's structure would be induced from my experience. In the second case I imagine going to Washington with a street map in my possession and constantly in use. I would check all my experiences against the map, filling in details with time. I would not have to discover, for example, that streets are laid out like spokes and wheels, that being given by the street map. I would have to discover the physical appearance of the various streets, that not being evident from the map. If I imagine that the map is given innately in the second case instead of by Exxon, I have a grasp of the essentially philosophical difference between Chomsky and Skinner (1982, p. 369).

Nature vs. Nurture—Again

The Chomsky-Skinner debate is a variation of the nature-nurture debate. Current evidence indicates that both nature and nurture are involved in the acquisition of language. Even those who believe in the nativist position admit that the environment is important. As Aitchison (1978, p. 89) states, "Both sides are right: Nature triggers off the behaviour, and lays down the framework, but careful nurture is needed for it to reach its full potential."

It is equally difficult to take a completely environmental perspective. Human beings are born with an impressive vocal apparatus, allowing them to develop speech (Aitchison, 1978), and all societies seem to use this ability in some way (Bowerman, 1981). Most of us speak very quickly and do not appreciate the intricate steps it takes to produce various sounds and intonations. To illustrate this, try to speak a sentence and become aware of how your tongue, lips, throat, and breathing apparatus all contribute to a clear, concise speech pattern.

In addition, a number of factors already noted imply some biological root for language acquisition. Human infants are able to make impressive phonetic distinctions and are attentive to speech quite early in life. Some strategies for processing language may in fact be innate (Slobin, 1973; McNeill, 1970). Finally, particular informational processes, such as memory and attention, may develop according to maturational rules that we are only just beginning to appreciate. Some biological or innate factors are at work in language acquisition, but a complete biological position does not match the facts.

The weaknesses in the nativist position are evident. For example, the existence of a language-acquisition device has not yet been proven. In addition, even if we agree that a neurological basis for language exists, it does not explain the processes involved in language learning. Finally, although the similarities between how children learn language around the world are impressive, recent evidence shows that there are some differences that reflect the nature of the language being learned. In one study, children were tested on their order of acquiring four types of statements: true affirmatives such as "You are a child," false affirmatives like "You are a baby," false negatives like "You aren't a child," and true negatives like "You aren't a baby." Three- and four-year-old Japanese-speaking and English-speaking children were asked whether such statements were right or wrong. The English-speaking children found verifying true negatives most difficult, whereas the Japanese-speaking children had the greatest problem with false negatives. The difference in acquisition pattern is due to linguistic differences between English and Japanese (Okiyama, 1984). So, although some biological foundation for learning language is probable, the nativist position does not fully explain language acquisition either.

The strictly learning theory and nativist positions thus fail as complete explanations for language acquisition. One expert, George Miller, put it well: "We had two theories of language learning—one of them, empiricist associationism (learning theory), is impossible; the other, nativism, is miraculous. The void between the impossible and miraculous remained to be filled" (in Bruner, 1978, p. 33). Two other approaches to language acquisition, emphasizing the importance of cognitive and social factors, are now popular and have begun to fill this void.

Cognitive Theory and Language Development

Language learning involves such cognitive processes as attention, information-processing, and retention. The development of these skills affects a child's language abilities. For example, how could children create sentences if they did not have the cognitive ability to remember words? In addition, children must understand something about an object or an idea before using words in a meaningful manner. Linguistic growth necessarily parallels cognitive growth. Children may learn language by first understanding the meaning of words spoken in their environment and then coming to appreciate the relationship between what the words mean and the language used (MacNamara, 1972). The child first uses simple words for things, then proceeds to define classes in terms of their more abstract qualities, such as color. Language learning follows cognitive advancements. Simple expressions become more exact as a child's cognitive development proceeds. Children may understand some concept and desire to communicate it, yet not have the proper word in their vocabulary. In fact, if children cannot express a thought using a word that they know, they will invent one (Nelson, 1974). Modern cognitive approaches to linguistic development are searching for identifiable sequences in which the relationships between cognitive advancement and linguistic expression are related. Although this approach is interesting, only further experimentation will determine how fruitful the search will be.

At the present time, no single perspective explains the mysteries of language acquisition well. Children learn more than just mere words and phrases. They learn meaning and master complex rules of language. Children do not acquire language in a vacuum. They are affected by the linguistic environment that surrounds them. But just what kind of linguistic environment is the average child exposed to?

Children are exposed to language from birth.

7. *True or False:*
Parents use well-formed sentences when speaking to their toddlers.

motherese
The use of simple, repetitive sentences with young children.

Social Interaction and Language Development

Consider the situation in which infants find themselves. They can hear and discriminate certain sounds, but everyone is talking in a quick, complex, difficult-to-understand manner, and there is little repetition. At first glance, the linguistic environment appears to be confusing, and its level much too high for infants. Yet children learn to communicate through language in a relatively short time. It was just such a scenario that appealed to the psychologists who argued in favor of an innate language mechanism. After all, children acquire language on the basis of very fragmented and cognitively advanced input. It all seemed impossible.

However, this particular argument in favor of the innate mechanism has been laid to rest. Communication aimed at children is neither fragmented nor confusing. Infants receive verbal stimulation from the first days of their lives. This verbal input is well structured and tuned to their level. It begins in the hospital nursery. Certainly new mothers and fathers speak to their newborn infants from birth, but both male and female hospital workers not only use soothing sounds and baby talk but actually speak to newborns as if they expect them to understand speech (Rheingold and Adams, 1980). At times, they engage in a dialogue, as the child's movements encourage the adult to say something. Sometimes the staff ask and answer their own questions as they think the baby would. These infants are treated as individuals from birth, called by their names. In all, this earliest verbal communication is anything but impersonal and random. Infants elicit a great deal of stimulation and from the first are exposed to a linguistic environment.

The old idea that early verbal interchanges are confusing and too difficult for infants is in error. When people talk to infants, they modify their speech. Parents talk to their older infants in shorter sentences, but these sentences are very well formed (Bowerman, 1981; Newport et al., 1977). The language that parents use to talk to toddlers is simple and repetitious (Snow, 1977). It contains many questions and commands, few past tenses, few hesitations, is highly pitched, and is spoken with an exaggerated intonation (Garnica, 1977). In short, parents' speech to their linguistically limited children is restrictive and involved with common nouns and comments on what their children are doing (Molfese et al., 1982). The use of simplistic, redundant sentences is normally referred to as **motherese**. All adults, and many older children, tailor their language use to the age and comprehension ability of younger children. The way parents talk to their children, then, is anything but random. They use motherese, with its emphasis on the present tense and simplified, well-formed sentences, in order to communicate with their youngsters. So young children are likely to be exposed to speech on their own level.

The child's reaction to parental speech determines the speaker's choice of words (Bohannon and Marquis, 1977). If a two-year-old shows a lack of comprehension, an adult immediately reduces the number of words in the next sentence. Children are not merely passive receivers of information. Their show of comprehension or noncomprehension serves to control their linguistic environment.

Verbal exchanges between adults and young children do not constitute formal language lessons. The idea that parents somehow sit down and teach their children how to talk is not supported by the facts. For example, parents do not correct their children for their grammatical errors or reward them for using correct grammar. They are more interested in the correctness of their children's utterances (Brown et al., 1969). If little Sharon says, "Me girl," her mother is likely to say, "That's right, you are a girl." On the other hand, if Sharon says, "I am a boy," her mother is likely to straighten her out immediately. Some readers may be skeptical about this. They can remember having some of their grammatical constructions—perhaps the use of *ain't*—corrected by their parents. However, these corrections are few and far between. Most parents do not correct their children's grammar, and pay more attention to the correctness of what their children say.

Language acquisition involves learning a social skill that is useful in the interpersonal context. Language is purely functional. The purpose of speech and language is to communicate thoughts, ideas, and wishes to others. Psychologists have become more interested in the nature of this give-and-take on the part of parents and their children. Children begin actively communicating with their parents, even before learning language, through gestures and vocalizations (Bruner, 1978a, 1978b). These prelinguistic modes are replaced by standard linguistic modes. Indeed, the child is an active and willing partner. The interactions between mother and child are very much structured in the form of a dialogue and show a progression from the simple to the complex. Even though parents may not be aware of their role as teachers, they do teach their children their native tongue. The infant begins to communicate and mother responds. The interaction between the two is intense and functional.

Language is used to direct the actions of others. The child learns that communication involves signaling meaning, sharing experiences, and taking turns. These are prerequisites to learning language. One expert in this area, Jerome Bruner (1978), sees language development in terms of problem-solving. Children must solve the problem of how to communicate their wishes and thoughts to others. They learn language through this interaction with others and by actively using language. Grammar and vocabulary are acquired because they are useful to children in accomplishing their aim of getting what they want and what they are thinking across to others. Notice that in this conception of language development parents tune their linguistic input to the ability level of the child. This theory is sometimes called the **fine-tuning theory**. It explains the finding that children encounter language in a very structured and progressively more difficult and complex manner. Language is learned as an extension of nonlinguistic communication.

Bruner also believes that cognitive development precedes linguistic development. Children know what they want to communicate, and language becomes the necessary vehicle for doing so when they are mature enough to produce it. This view sees language acquisition as arising from need, being based on carefully fine-tuned interactions between mother and child and as an outgrowth of solving the problems of communicating with another individual. When studying a child's linguistic progress, the transactions between mother and child should be investigated. Bruner (1978, p. 38) notes that language learning is not a "solo flight in search of rules, but a transaction involving an active language learner and an equally active language teacher."

CURRENT ISSUES IN LANGUAGE AND COMMUNICATION

So far, we have looked both at the general sequence of development and at some theoretical viewpoints that explain how children develop language. The general process by which language unfolds is universal, although individual differences

Even young children reduce the length of their sentences when faced with a younger sibling who does not understand.

fine-tuning theory
A theory noting that parents tune their language to a child's linguistic ability.

do exist in the paths a child may follow in getting there (Nelson, 1981). Although the theoretical attempts to answer the simple question of how children learn language seem confusing, we might surmise that innate factors, cognitive growth, the processes of learning and social interaction are involved in some complicated manner. With this basic knowledge in hand, let's look at some of the fascinating issues in the area of language development.

Sex Differences in Language Acquisition

8. *True or False:*
On the average, American girls acquire language faster than American boys.

Do girls learn language faster than boys? The evidence on this question is mixed. Many early studies found that girls acquire language more quickly than boys (McCarthy, 1954). Smith (1926) found that two- and three-year-old girls had larger vocabularies than boys of the same age, although the differences were negligible by the age of four. Some later studies confirmed this, while the results of other studies did not. This led Maccoby and Jacklin (1974), who reviewed the literature in this area, to conclude that the only consistent female advantage is found in the area of verbal fluency. Females are more fluent in language than males. However, some additional, recent evidence again supports the earliest evidence that girls speak earlier and use longer utterances than boys (Schachter et al., 1978). We may conclude, then, that although not all studies are in agreement, the evidence does generally favor females in this area.

This advantage would not be surprising, because girls are physically more advanced at birth and mature more quickly. If language acquisition partially involves the maturation of some complex neurological structures, we would expect girls as a group to develop language faster than boys. Perhaps the greater responsiveness of females encourages verbal communication from those around them. Some studies suggest that mothers talk more to daughters than sons (Goldberg and Lewis, 1969).

This early superiority may also be a function of culture. One study investigating sex differences in early vocal responsiveness discovered that Greek infant males raised at home were superior to infant females also raised at home on a measure of verbal responsiveness (Roe et al., 1985). In addition, Greek mothers spoke differently to their infant sons and daughters, showing more affection in their voices to sons than to daughters. Perhaps we should keep in mind that many of the studies showing female superiority in early language development were performed in the United States, and consider the possibility that cultural forces are operating. The researchers who performed the study in Greece cite evidence that "male children in Greece are much more welcomed, valued and interacted with than female children" (Roe et al., 1985, p. 372). This pattern is more pronounced than in the United States. Thus, when speaking of sex differences in language, we must be careful to note the culture.

Does the linguistic superiority of American girls compared with American boys last? Until about the age of three, girls seem to be superior, but boys do catch up. In middle childhood no differences are found except among very poor groups, in which girls remain superior to boys (Bee, 1978). In adolescence, females again begin to show greater verbal abilities than males (Maccoby and Jacklin, 1974). Of course, individual differences are plentiful, and it is easy to find a male who is superior in language acquisition.

Black vs. Standard English: Difference or Deficit?

"By the time I get there, he will have gone."
"Time I git dere, he be done gone."

If you were asked which of these sentences would be best received by an English professor, you would certainly choose the first. While the first sentence illustrates Standard English, the second is Black English. **Black English** is a dialect spoken throughout the United States by lower-income blacks and understood by almost all black people (Raspberry, 1970). It contains a consistent, logical, and coherent grammar (Labov, 1970).

At one time it was thought that Black English was simply mispronounced, poorly spoken Standard English, and it was accorded no respect. In fact, since children from ghetto areas have many language difficulties, it was thought that such problems were caused in part by their initial exposure to and learning of this dialect. This led to what has been called the **deficit hypothesis**. Basically, this dialect was considered to be a deficit, something wrong, not merely different. It was something that a child should give up somewhere along the educational ladder.

Beginning in the late 1960s, however, social scientists began to reconsider this position. After all, if black English is understood in the child's environment and has a consistent set of rules, why treat it differently from Spanish or French? In some ways, it is even more precise than Standard English. When a teacher asks a black child why his father couldn't make a meeting the night before, the child might answer, "He sick." However, when asked why the father has not attended any of the meetings during the year, the child says, "He be sick" (Raspberry, 1970). Inclusion of the word "be" shows an ongoing chronic status. In Standard English, the answers to both questions might simply be that the father was ill.

Black English is closer to Standard English than French or Spanish, but the black child who has mastered Black English might best be considered bilingual for educational purposes. Standard English could be taught as a second language. This extreme position is not accepted by most authorities, who argue instead that Black English is a valid dialect. Black children suffer not from linguistic deficits but from **linguistic differences**, and differences are not necessarily deficits (Hardman et al., 1981).

If teachers consider Black English to be inferior to Standard English, they may reject these children's ideas, essentially turning them off and reducing communication between teacher and child. Students may also develop feelings of inferiority. Teachers must understand that Black English is a dialect and accept the child's ideas without reacting negatively to the dialect. When a teacher misunderstands Black English, it may also lead to frustrating situations for both teacher and pupil. Dale (1972) notes that black children read the words "I saw it" as "I see it," since both *see* and *saw* are pronounced "see" in this dialect. Correcting this error is difficult, because black children do not understand that this is an error.

Whether it is called a deficit or a difference, lower-income children from ghetto areas have difficulty with Standard English. Caratz (1969) asked third-graders and fifth-graders in Washington, D.C., to repeat thirty sentences. Half the students were white, the other half were black. Fifteen of the sentences were given in Black English, while fifteen were in Standard English. The white children learned the sentences given in Standard English better than the black chil-

Black English
A dialect spoken throughout the United States by lower-income blacks but understood by the overwhelming majority of blacks.

linguistic deficit hypothesis
The belief that a dialect such as Black English is a hindrance to learning.

linguistic difference hypothesis
The belief that a dialect such as Black English is different from Standard English but not a deficit.

9. *True or False:*
Black English is a dialect of Standard English.

dren did. The black children learned the sentences given in Black English better than the white children. This might show merely that children learn verbal material that is more meaningful to them. However, Caratz found that black children translated the Standard English sentences into Black English, and that white children translated the Black English sentences into Standard English. From an information-processing point of view, the problem of black children who are taught to read from kindergarten using Standard English involves the extra time-consuming and inefficient process of not only recognizing the words but also translating them into their own dialect. It has been suggested that black children begin learning to read using books written in Black English, but this is a highly controversial and radical proposal.

Perhaps both the deficit hypothesis and the difference hypothesis miss the mark in one regard. Children must be able to deal with their environment, and therefore Black English has its uses. However, although Black English may be accepted as a dialect, children must learn Standard English if they are to succeed in school and in the world of work. Sandra and Francis Terrell sent six black college women for job interviews. Those that spoke Black English were given shorter interviews and fewer offers. The offers that were made were for lower-paying positions. These researchers suggest that children who are encouraged to speak Black English in order to keep their heritage risk being handicapped in the job market (Raloff, 1982b).

Most people who wish to accept Black English as a dialect agree wholeheartedly that black children must learn to speak and write Standard English. Perhaps there has been too much focus on the deficit and difference hypotheses and not enough on *how* one teaches children a different dialect that they will not hear around their homes or neighborhoods very much. Some suggest using techniques that have been developed to teach children a foreign language. The most modern way of learning a foreign language is total immersion—living, breathing, and thinking that language for weeks at a time until one is thoroughly familiar with it. This is not a practical strategy in this case. Becker and colleagues (1971) developed a very directed and highly structured program designed to upgrade the skills of culturally disadvantaged children. This very behaviorally oriented program involved the use of immediate reinforcement, fast-paced instruction, and breaking complex tasks into simpler learning tasks. One of the areas of concern was the learning of Standard English, and some success has been claimed for the program. However, it has been criticized as too structured, and it is not clear whether the results are long-lasting. More research is needed on ways of teaching Standard English to children who speak other dialects.

The Bilingual Puzzle

What of the thousands of children in the United States who come from homes in which a foreign language, commonly Spanish, is the primary language at home (see Table 8.2)? These children, who often come from impoverished backgrounds, face many of the same problems blacks do, although their language itself is accepted as a true language. English is the second language for these children, and their success in the United States depends partly on learning Standard English.

Imagine you are a teacher of second-grade children. About half your students are primarily Spanish-speaking and find it easier to speak and understand

TABLE 8.2 **Languages Other Than English Spoken at Home**
Many people are surprised by the number of children who come from homes in which a language other than English is spoken. As this table indicates, many of these children have difficulty with English.

Current Language Spoken	Total (1,000)	Difficulty with English (percent)
Total persons	47,494	—
Speaking a language other than English	4,568	14.0
Spanish	2,952	15.4
Italian	147	5.4
French	223	6.8
German	192	6.2
Polish	41	5.7
Chinese	114	20.9
Greek	66	5.2
Philippine languages	63	8.9
Portuguese	68	10.3
Japanese	34	18.7
Korean	60	17.0
Vietnamese	64	36.0
All other	544	12.3

Source: U.S. Bureau of the Census, 1980.

their native tongue than English. You notice that when taking math, social studies, and science tests your non-Spanish-speaking students do better, yet you know that your Spanish-speaking students are just as intelligent and curious. Since all the teachers in the school are faced with the same situation, you bring it up for discussion at a faculty meeting.

Some teachers propose that a bilingual program be introduced into the school, that subjects such as math and social studies be taught to Spanish-speaking students in Spanish until the children gain sufficient ability in English to function effectively in that language. At the same time, these children would receive instruction in Standard English. There is some evidence that these programs help students improve scholastically (U.S. Commission on Civil Rights, 1975) and that without these programs bilingual children have difficulty gaining acceptance into a non-Spanish-speaking culture (Genosce et al., 1976). Other teachers disagree sharply. They note that in the past every other non-English-speaking group in the United States had the same language problem and that teaching children in their native language will only delay their acquisition of English. They also note that there is a shortage of bilingual teachers and that these programs do not ensure that children will learn English.

The debate is still going on. Congress has passed legislation encouraging bilingual education, and the courts have mandated it when appropriate, so bilingual education is a fact of life in the United States. However, the psychological issues surrounding bilingualism are still with us, and the debate over the consequences of bilingualism continues.

The term **bilingual** itself is not as easy to define as one would think. The older definitions involve almost equal acquisition of two languages from birth, but this is no longer the case with many bilingual children. For example, the pri-

bilingual
A term describing people who can function in more than one language.

mary language in many Hispanic homes is Spanish, not English. The child hears much more Spanish than English. Spanish is spoken by family and friends, while English is largely the language of the school and government bureaucracy. Modern definitions of bilingualism do not stress the equality of both languages. Rather, bilingual individuals are people who function in society using two languages (Segalowitz, 1981).

At first glance, knowing more than one language seems like a great advantage. However, research in the 1950s indicated that bilingual children did poorly in school and suffered retarded language development in both languages (Segalowitz, 1981). These studies have been criticized for their poor methodology and the questionable testing devices used.

Recently, though, an about-face on the issue of bilingualism has occurred. In one review of the literature, McLaughlin (1977) exposed a number of myths concerning bilingualism. One of the theoretical underpinnings of the bilingual deficits viewpoint was that a critical period exists during which language could be learned. McLaughlin (1978, 1977) noted that there is not much evidence for this position and that older children seem to learn a new language quite well. There are some exceptions to this rule. The appropriate accents are much harder to attain after childhood. In addition, some sounds are very difficult to acquire when learning a second language, such as the English sound for "w," which does not exist in many languges.

McLaughlin also found that a child learning a second language uses the same processes as a child learning a first language. In addition, the evidence for linguistic interference is slight if the child learns both languages simultaneously and is given a balanced input. This is not the case in many homes, where the input of languages is unequal in quality and quantity. In such cases, interference does occur.

This interference may involve pronunciation or syntax. For example, in Spanish there is no sound for "th," "z," "zh" as in "pleasure," or "sh" as in "shop," according to Wiig (1982). There is no differentiation between "b" and "v," and the "r" and "l" are pronounced differently in Spanish. This leads to problems in spelling, reading, and writing. There are examples of syntactical problems as well. In Spanish, comparatives and superlatives are formed by using forms of "more" and "most," whereas in English we use suffixes. Thus, Wiig notes that, in Spanish, sentences like "Elephants are more big than cows" are common. The word order is also different. The extent to which this interference is a major factor in learning a second language is a matter of controversy at the present time (deVilliers and deVilliers, 1978).

Finally, McLaughlin found no clear evidence that bilingualism leads to intellectual or cognitive problems in school. Indeed, some evidence leads to the opposite conclusion: that bilingual children are higher in verbal and nonverbal intelligence scores and show more cognitive flexibility (Segalowitz, 1981).

What conclusions can we make, then, concerning the bilingual child? First, there is nothing inherently inferior about bilingualism, and some evidence indicates that bilingual children have certain advantages over their monolingual peers. Second, poverty and bilingualism are often confused. Many minority groups in the United States that speak a language other than English suffer from the degradations of poverty, with all that entails, including poor self-concept, disillusionment, discrimination, poor opportunity, and so forth. It may be that the clash of cultures, rather than bilingualism, actually causes many of the problems experienced by teachers in the public schools. Finally, a number of people point to the success many immigrant groups have had in learning their a language and discount the need for bilingual programs. This is unfortunate, because times have changed. Although discrimination has always existed, the need for advanced education and training has not. Fifty years ago an advanced education was not required and the importance of academic advancement could be minimized. Today, our technological world has changed all this, and education is a prerequisite to vocational success.

If bilingual programs in the schools are to work, however, they must ensure that *all* children learn English in a way that allows them to function reasonably well in the outside world. If children leave school knowing math, science, and social studies but functioning poorly in such language-related areas as reading, writing, and speaking, their prospects for educational advancement and jobs will be poor. Continous evaluation of such programs is necessary to be certain that these children are learning and using English.

As noted, most children are not truly bilingual in the pure sense of the word. That is, they do not receive the same quality and a quantity of linguistic input from both languages. Thus, children may receive more exposure to one language than to another. The child's home and cultural environment is a key concern. But just what can parents do to improve their children's language skills?

The Home Environment: Does It Make a Difference?

The Linguistic Environment.   Children learn language through an active process that involves exposure to a particular linguistic environment. The exact

---

A Heavy Choice

José is a bright Hispanic seventh-grader who came to the United States a year and a half ago. He is trying to learn English, but it isn't easy, because Spanish is spoken both at home and in the neighborhood.

José and his parents face a decision. The school has a new, experimental bilingual program in which he may enroll. Since José is doing fairly well in school, despite his lack of ability in English, he does not have to enter the program, but his parents can request it. In this program, all subjects other than English will be taught in Spanish, allowing José to keep up with his studies in other areas. At this point, his deficiency in English is hampering his progress in math, science, and social studies.

José's father believes that the only way to learn English is to live it. He does not want José to enter the program because he is afraid his son will come out of it with a poor knowledge of English. His mother argues that knowing perfect English won't help if José is far behind in his studies. Teachers in the school are split over the program. José is not sure which path is best either, but he must decide in the next few weeks whether to request entrance into the program.

1. If you were José, would you voluntarily enter the program?

manner in which language is learned is unknown. Although imitation and operant conditioning play some part, we know that the child actively contributes to
this process. From the earliest age, children interact with people in their environment and learn that they can influence people and events.

The development of language is anything but random. The input children
receive is also definite and patterned, as demonstrated by motherese (Molfese et
al., 1982) and the fine-tuning of the parent-infant interaction (Bruner, 1978b).
The repetitive, simplified speech found in motherese aids the child's comprehension. These interactions affect the manner in which children produce speech. In
one study, children who asked more questions had mothers who did the same
(Lord, in Holmes and Morrison, 1979), but this is not to imply that we are re-
turning to the old imitation theory of language acquisition. Rather, it demonstrates that the linguistic atmosphere surrounding the child is important to the
child's language acquisition. Children raised in a linguistically rich environment
are superior in their later use of language.

A number of studies have found that language usage among middle-class
and working-class people differ. Middle-class youngsters use more expansive language and do better in language activities in school. Children of working-class
parents use simpler sentences and more commands (Olim et al., 1967). The linguistic environment of middle-class children, and their interactions with their
parents are more expansive (Hess and Shipman, 1967; 1965). However, we must
remember that language is functional and that these children are not deficient in
their own native environment. What is somewhat lacking are the specific language abilities required in school. When we look at how well a child knows his or
her own dialect, there is no deficiency in rate and amount of linguistic knowledge (Menyuk, 1977).

10. *True or False:*
Middle-class children use more
complex sentences and fewer
commands than children of
working-class parents.

How Parents Can Help.   But because schooling is so important, how can
parents encourage maximum progress in language development? Most of the suggestions offered for improving linguistic competence are based on the premise
that children learn language both by listening and by participating. Parents
should not take an artificial attitude toward language development, for the natural flow of parent-child interactions is sufficient for the child to learn the appropriate language. Parents can do more harm than good by trying to force a child
to say something the youngster isn't ready to say, or by providing the child with a
language environment that is too complex and inappropriate. Nevertheless, parents can help their children in the development of their language.

Give the child an opportunity to talk.   Acquisition of language is an active process. Children need an opportunity to talk and to communicate their thoughts
(Cazden, 1981). This should be done with a minimum of criticism and impa-
tience.

Expand on the child's statements.   Middle-class parents often expand on their
children's statements. For example, if the child says, "Throw ball," a parent
might say, "Throw the ball to Daddy." Such expansions have a positive effect in
broadening the child's language usage in some areas (Hovell et al., 1978).

Label things in the environment.   Children benefit from listening to speech
which labels the environment. When a baby points at the bottle, it is worthwhile
to say, "You want your bottle."

RESEARCH HIGHLIGHT   *Day Care and Language Development*

What happens to the language development of children when they attend a day-care center for long periods of time? That depends on the day-care center, according to Kathleen McCartney (1984), who investigated the language development of 146 preschoolers attending nine day-care centers in Bermuda. Because language skills are so important for later success in school, the effect of the day-care experience on the development of these skills is an issue worth addressing.

Previous research demonstrated that the amount and nature of the verbal interchanges between parents and their children are major factors in determining language skill. McCartney hypothesized that the amount and nature of the verbal interchanges between children and caregivers at the day-care center would also predict language skill.

Many aspects of the day-care environment, and the children's intellectual and language development as well as their homes and backgrounds, were carefully measured. Verbal interactions with caregivers and peers were divided into four dimensions. *Control statements* involved commands like "Stop talking." *Expressive comments* involved the expression of feelings and attitudes such as "I like your shirt." *Representational statements* were defined as the giving and receiving of information, as in the statement "The toys are over there," and *social comments* were aimed at establishing and maintaining social relationships, as in the statement "Let's play with this."

McCartney found that the overall quality of the day-care center was a positive predictor of children's language development, as was the amount of verbal interaction between caregiver and child. The type of caregiver-child interchange was important as well. The proportion of control utterances was a negative predictor of language development. That is, children who received many commands were hampered in their development of important language skills. It is interesting to note that control and representational statements were inversely related to each other. The more control statements (as in commands) given by the caregivers, the fewer the representational statements (giving and receiving information) communicated to them. On the other hand, the proportion of representational statements was positively related to language skills. Children benefit when they are given and asked for information.

Another important predictor of linguistic abilities was a child's willingness to initiate a conversation with a caregiver. This was related to the atmosphere created by the caregiver. Children's language skills are optimized when children are encouraged to initiate conversations.

Some specific aspects of the day-care center were particularly important in determining the child's language abilities. Children did better in more-structured centers with low noise levels and little time for free play. This does not mean that children should be regimented, nor should we conclude that any one educational theory is superior. It does demonstrate that children benefit when caregivers structure the children's activities to some extent and create an organized environment.

But how about peer exchanges? After all, children do talk to each other in day-care centers. McCartney found that the greater the number of peer conversations, the lower the language scores of the children. Perhaps peer conversations of lesser quality replaced important caregiver talk.

This study demonstrates that a number of factors predict children's language abilities, including the amount and type of caregiver utterances, children's willingness to initiate interactions with the caregivers, and the overall quality of the day-care center, as well as some specific aspects of the center's organization. Good things seem to occur together. It is likely that all these factors exist in the best centers, that is, that superior day-care centers are well organized with structured activities, create an atmosphere in which children talk more with their caregivers, and contain personnel who are more concerned with giving and receiving information than with giving commands.

Studies like this one emphasize the importance of the environment in determining language skills. No matter which theory of language acquisition one subscribes to, the child's linguistic environment is a major predictor of language skill. The challenge is to create a linguistic environment that will help children develop language skills to the fullest. It is clear from this study that day-care centers have a role to play in this area.

Source: K. McCartney "Effect of Quality of Day Care Environment on Children's Language Development," *Developmental Psychology,* 1984, *20,* 244–260.

Allowing the child to participate in the story may aid the child's language development.

Read to the child.   Reading to a child is beneficial, but there are many ways to do this. When the child is old enough to give some response, try to ask questions that are age-appropriate and allow the child to participate in the story. When reading a story, you may ask the youngster to point to the cow or the dog. In time, when children can talk some, they can label things themselves and answer such questions as what color it is. Even later, the story may lead to a discussion about farm life and the like.

Modeling.   Children tend to copy the expressions of their parents, so reasonably good linguistic models are important. Finishing sentences, answering questions in an expanded way, using adjectives, and so on, contribute to a rich linguistic environment.

Encourage verbal interaction.   Rather than forcing a child to speak and verbalize, using praise and engaging the child in meaningful verbal interactions are worthwhile (Hess and Shipman, 1967).

Language, Thought, and Cognition: The Chicken and the Egg Revisited

Have you ever tried to communicate a feeling or an experience to someone else and been unable to put it into words? You stand there frustrated, knowing what you want to say and unable to find the words to express it. Perhaps you may remember having more difficulty putting ideas into words when you were younger. Young children often know something but simply can't express themselves. In one now-famous experiment, Piaget (1976) asked preschool children to crawl and then explain what they had done. It was not until five or six years of age that children could explain what they had done, albeit in a simple manner, even though the younger children complied with the researcher's request to crawl.

Cognitive development involves a great deal more than reading, writing, and speaking. It involves thought and action as well. The relationship between thought, language, and cognition has long fascinated scientists, and there is no consensus yet on exactly how they are related. Piaget argued that language is independent of thought and action, especially in younger children. The study of crawling demonstrates, among other things, that language is not necessary for action and that children know things but may not have the linguistic ability to express them. Numerous studies support his ideas that language follows cognitive growth. Sinclair-de-Zwart (1973) found that even if young children were taught the meanings of such relationship words as "more" or "less," they did not show any ability to use these concepts when tested. In other words, teaching the meaning of these words in a linguistic context had no effect on the child's cognitive growth and performance. Flavell (1977) notes that two- to four-year-olds can group objects on the basis of physical relationships yet not be able to name these categories or relationships. Thus, according to these psychologists, language follows cognitive growth, and cognitive growth is independent of language.

Most agree that, until about the age of two, cognition does not depend on language. The impressive cognitive growth of children between birth and age two takes place with either no language or very limited language usage. However, some argue that after age two, language, thought, and cognitive growth become intertwined. This point of view is best demonstrated by the Russian scientists Vygotsky (1962) and Luria (1959). At around the age of two, children begin to use words in thinking. Words gradually begin to control actions. The progression of this control is uniform. At first, language shows little control over behavior, but the verbal expressions of other people may control a child's behavior. Then children may control behavior, but only if their language is overt, that is, verbalized. Finally, this process is internalized, and nonexternalized thought controls behavior. While the great Soviet scientist A. R. Luria (1959) found such a progression, American researchers have had difficulty replicating his work (Miller et al., 1970), perhaps because of problems in translation, the lack of detailed description in Luria's publication, or the experimental methodology used to test out Vygotsky's and Luria's ideas (Frauenglass and Diaz, 1985).

However, Tinsley and Waters (1982) have succeeded in demonstrating this progression. Two-year-old children were asked to hit a peg into a pegboard once with a hammer. The children were divided into a number of groups. One group received no verbal accompaniment, the other groups were asked to say either the word "one" or the word "toy" when hitting the peg. The last group was asked to say "one" and then hit the peg. The results showed that children in the groups that said either "toy" or "one" successfully completed the task, while the group who received no verbal accompaniment did not. In other words, these overt verbalizations enabled the child to control motor behavior. Whether the child said "toy" or "one" did not matter. The verbalization itself, not the content, was critical. The success of such verbalizations depended on age factors and the difficulty of the task. As the age of the subjects increased, the need to use overt verbaliza-

11. *True or False:*

Before the age of about two, cognitive growth does not depend on the child's linguistic progress.

tions decreased. In addition, when the task was more difficult even older children benefited by using these verbalizations. Such verbalization procedures may be helpful to some older children and adults in controlling and managing situations.

For example, Meichenbaum and Goodman (1971) changed the behavior of impulsive children by teaching them to use self-instructional statements. Fifteen children between the ages of seven and nine were divided into three groups. The first group, called the "cognitive-training group," received training in which they were told to verbalize some statements concerning the task they were asked to carry out. The second group met with the researchers but received no training in self-statements. The third group did not even meet with the researchers. The results showed that the cognitive-training group did indeed profit from the experience, and that the verbal statements decreased their impulsiveness. The accuracy of their work on the motor task improved as well. The researchers concluded that teaching children to talk to themselves may be an effective strategy for improving their performance.

The relationship between thought, language, and cognitive development is a complicated one, and any conclusions at the present time appear to be premature. The available evidence indicates that, at the earliest ages, cognition does not depend on language. As children develop, however, cognition, thought, and language become intertwined, and children begin to use language to control their behavior. At first the language comes from others, then the child verbalizes out loud, and finally the child takes thought in the form of language to promote and control action. The ability of such internal verbalizations to control behavior is complicated, depending on such personality factors as impulsiveness, the age of the child, and the difficulty of the task. Our ability to control our own actions using thought develops slowly and in a developmental fashion. The exact relationship between cognition, thought, and behavior remains, however, a subject of much debate.

A WONDER REDISCOVERED

Language development is an area of developmental psychology that is filled with controversy. We have looked at many of the issues surrounding language acquisition, especially the question of how language is acquired. The certainty with which so many psychologists embraced Skinner's and Chomsky's work has long passed. Neither the radical innate posture of Chomsky nor the behavioral-learning ideas of Skinner seems sufficient to explain the development of language in children, although they both explain some aspects of language learning. The more modern approach takes both the laws of learning and the biological basis for language learning into consideration, but it also looks at the nature of the interactions between the developing child and the child's parents. This stance views language development as a carefully orchestrated progression of interchanges between an active learner and active teachers, who may not be aware of the role they are playing in the child's language development.

As we begin to tear down the curtain of mystery that surrounds language development, we can appreciate the wonder of it all. The simple sentence of a child is not just an imitation of what the child has heard, nor is it something prewired in. It is the creative expression of an inherently human ability. Looking at it from this standpoint, learning our native tongue is perhaps the greatest intellectual feat that anyone of us ever performs.

Chapter Summary

1. Communication is the process of sharing information. It may be verbal or nonverbal. Language is a set of agreed-on, arbitrary symbols used in communication.

2. Infants communicate with the people around them by smiling, crying, and gesturing. They are sensitive to speech sounds from the moment they are born.

3. Babbling, which involves verbalization of vowel and consonant sounds, begins as early as three months. Children utter their first word anytime between ten and fifteen months of age. Some psychologists argue that children use one word, called a holophrase, to stand for an entire thought. The child's early sentences are called "telegraphic," because they contain only those words absolutely necessary for communicating meaning to other people.

4. The length of children's sentences gradually increases, and conjunctions begin to be used. By the age of five or six, a child's syntax approaches that of an adult.

5. Young children make predictable errors. They "overextend," using words in a wider manner than is proper. They also "underextend," using words in a more restrictive sense than is appropriate. Children also overgeneralize rules. When children begin to learn the rules of a language, they use them indiscriminantly and have difficulty with exceptions.

6. Behaviorists, such as B. F. Skinner, use the processes of reinforcement and imitation to explain language acquisition. Noam Chomsky argues that a human being is prewired to learn language and merely requires exposure to a language in order to master it. This nativist position sees language acquisition as having a biological basis and stresses the importance of maturation.

7. Cognitive psychologists argue that such factors as attention and memory are involved in language acquisition. In addition, a child must know something about an object in order to use a word correctly.

8. Adult speech to young children is well constructed and consists of short, simple sentences with many repetitions. Social interaction is important in language acquisition, because children learn language through interaction with caregivers, who fine-tune their language to the developmental level of the child.

9. Black English is a dialect spoken by lower-income blacks and understood by most black people in the United States. It has a consistent, logical, and coherent grammar. Many authorities believe that it should be accepted as a valid dialect and that teachers should not reject the ideas of students who use this dialect. However, children who use Black English often have difficulty with Standard English, which is necessary for success in the academic and vocational world.

10. Early studies seemed to show that bilingualism was a deficit to learning. However, newer studies stress the bilingual child's advantages. It is important that every child learn Standard English.

11. The linguistic environment that surrounds a child is important in the acquisition of language. Middle-class parents tend to use expansive language, while working-class parents tend to use more restricted speech patterns. Parents can help to optimize their children's linguistic progress.

12. The relationship between thought, language, cognitive growth, and behavior is a complex one. Up until about the age of two, language and thought and action appear to be separate. According to Piaget, language follows cognitive growth. After age two, however, the Russian scientists Vygotsky and Luria argue that language, thought, and cognitive growth are intertwined.

■ *Answers to True or False Questions*

1. *False.* Correct statement: Although young infants can differentiate between sounds, they cannot understand language.

2. *True.* We have been unable to discern the meaning of an infant's babble.

3. *False.* Correct statement: Although the range of sounds babbled by infants is impressive, it does not approach every sound humans are capable of producing.

4. *True.* The syntax of a six-year-old is similar to that of adults.

5. *False.* Correct statement: Both children and adults understand many more words than they use in their own speech.

6. *True.* Learning theory explains the child's acquisition of vocabulary very well, but it is less successful in explaining how children create original sentences.

7. *True.* Although the sentences are shorter, they are well formed.

8. *True.* Generally, American girls learn language faster.

9. *True.* Today, Black English is generally accepted as a dialect of Standard English.

10. *True.* Children from middle-class families use a more expansive language than children from working-class families.

11. *True.* Before the age of two, cognition appears to be unrelated to language.

CHAPTER NINE

Physical and Cognitive Development in Early Childhood

CHAPTER OUTLINE

THE DEATH OF WILL LEE
PHYSICAL DEVELOPMENT
COGNITIVE DEVELOPMENT

ACTION/REACTION   Why Did Tabitha Die?

THE ENVIRONMENT AND COGNITIVE
  DEVELOPMENT

ACTION/REACTION   The Nursery School Gambit

PROJECT HEAD START

RESEARCH HIGHLIGHT   ***How Effective Is Early
  Childhood Education?***

TESTING THE PRESCHOOL CHILD
QUESTIONS FOR THE FUTURE

■ *Are the Following Statements True or False?*

Try the True-False Quiz below. See if your answers correspond to the information in this chapter. Each question is repeated opposite the paragraph in which the answer can be found. The True-False Answer Box at the end of the chapter lists complete answers.

____ **1.** During early childhood, the rate of growth increases.

____ **2.** Children grow in spurts during early childhood.

____ **3.** The leading cause of death among preschoolers is accidents.

____ **4.** During the preschool years, the child begins to reason in a manner that is very similar to that of the average adult.

____ **5.** Surprisingly, preschool children often use effective memory strategies, like rehearsal, on their own.

____ **6.** Preschoolers average about two hours of television-watching each day.

____ **7.** There is evidence that television advertising aimed at children is very effective.

____ **8.** Preschool children cannot tell the difference between commercials and the programs they accompany.

____ **9.** Children who watch "Sesame Street" alone gain more than if they watch it with parents.

____ **10.** Nursery school activities do not vary much from one school to another.

____ **11.** Generally speaking, children from lower-income groups who attend nursery school are more cognitively advanced than their peers who do not attend such programs.

____ **12.** Reading-readiness tests can be used to predict how well a child will learn to read in first grade.

THE DEATH OF WILL LEE

When Will Lee, who played Mr. Hooper the shopkeeper on the children's television show "Sesame Street," died in December 1982, the program's writers were in a quandary. How should they explain his absence to the millions of preschoolers who watch the program every day? It wouldn't be honest to tell viewers that he had moved to Florida, so the writers decided to deal with the difficult concept of death (*New York Times*, August 31, 1983).

But they did not do this with explanations of the causes of death or the process of aging. Instead, the resident five-year-old on the show, Big Bird, was forthrightly informed that Mr. Hooper had died. Like most preschoolers, Big Bird didn't understand the irreversibility of death, and asked when his friend Mr. Hooper was coming back. Later, as the reality sunk in, Big Bird's attention centered on his own loss. "Who will make me birdseed milkshakes and tell me stories?" he asked. Told that his friend David would do that, Big Bird remained unhappy, knowing it would never be the same. He drew a picture of Mr. Hooper and hung it over his nest. But Big Bird's mood brightened as a new baby was presented on the show, demonstrating the continuity of life.

Explaining birth, death, and illness to preschoolers is difficult and frustrating. Some parents either avoid their children's questions or do not answer them honestly, strategies that lead to misunderstanding and misconceptions. Infants and toddlers are too young to understand much of what is going on around

When Will Lee, who played the shopkeeper on "Sesame Street," died, the writers had to decide how to explain his death to the many young children who watched the program daily.

them, but during the preschool years, children become more and more aware of changes in their environment and struggle to understand what is going on. They yearn to know and to understand, but their understanding is limited and their reasoning is incomplete.

The physical development of preschoolers parallels their cognitive growth and contributes to this desire to uncover the mysteries of the environment. The physical and cognitive domains are linked. Expanding motor abilities allow preschoolers to attend to what is going on around them instead of having to concentrate just on how they walk and hold things, for example. They can now easily take part in many physical activities, satisfying some of their curiosity about the world and learning from their experiences. Their physical skills lead to more independence. They now interact more frequently with other children, learning from their social interactions. Eating is no longer a great physical challenge, either, for they can handle eating implements with some skill. They can eat by themselves and are affected by the nutritional information around them, especially on television. Finally, many children now attend a preschool in which the development of their physical and sensory abilities is used as a tool to encourage social and cognitive abilities. Preschool programs are becoming more popular, although there is controversy about them.

In this chapter we will look first at the physical changes that occur during the preschool years, then explore how preschoolers think. We will also consider the tremendous growth of preschools in the United States and the effect such schools can have on a child's physical, cognitive, and social development. Finally, we will look at the problems and possibilities of testing preschoolers.

PHYSICAL DEVELOPMENT

Growth and Development

The rate of growth slows during the early childhood years. About twice as much growth occurs between the first and third years as between the third and fifth years (Cratty, 1970). However, growth is still readily apparent during this period. The average three-year-old girl stands about 37 inches (94.1 cm) tall and weighs about 29 pounds (13.11 kg). By the age of six, she stands just over 45 inches (114.6 cm) tall and weighs almost 40 pounds (17.8 kg). Boys are a bit taller and heavier throughout this stage, and remain so until about the age of eleven. The average three-year-old boy stands just over 37 inches (94.91 cm) tall and weighs about 32 pounds (14.62 kg). By the age of six, he stands almost 46 inches (116.1 cm) tall and weighs 45.5 pounds (20.69 kg) (Hamill, 1977). The preschool child grows approximately 3 inches a year.

These figures can be misleading however, because variation from the statistical average is to be expected. In addition, simply comparing a child's height or weight to an average does not tell a doctor or a parent whether the child has a growth problem. If the average six-year-old boy weighs 45.5 pounds, what would you say about one weighing 42.5 pounds? Should this alert us to some possible growth problem? In order to take such natural variations into account, scientists usually speak of a *range* of heights and weights which is usual for a child of a certain age in a particular culture. The heights and weights of many children are

1. *True or False:*
During early childhood, the rate of growth increases.

measured and then divided into percentiles, the 50th percentile being the average (see Table 9.1 and Table 9.2). Then the height and weight below which 25 percent and above which 75 percent of all boys or girls of a certain age fall is found, and this becomes the range that is considered normal. For example, the average five-year-old girl weighs about 38.8 pounds (17.66 kg), but any weight between about 35.8 pounds (16.29 kg) and 42.6 pounds (19.39 kg) is considered normal (Hamill, 1977). Even if a child's height or weight is above the 75th percentile (larger than 75 percent of his age-mates) or below the 25th percentile (smaller than 25 percent of his age-mates), it may not indicate a problem. Perhaps the parents are very short or very tall. However, it may alert us to a *possible* problem, and many physicians will look into the situation.

Myths and half-truths abound in the area of children's growth. For example, many people believe that children grow in fits and starts, that is, they grow, then fill out, then grow again. But if measurements are taken carefully, the rate of growth is actually fairly regular (Tanner, 1978). Another often-repeated statement is that doubling a two-year-old's height is a good approximation of the child's adult height. Although this has some merit, it is a much better predictor for boys than for girls.

During the preschool period, body proportions change. At two, the head is about one-fourth the total body size, while by five and a half it is one-sixth the body size (Cratty, 1970). The preschooler gradually loses that babylike appearance. The amount of fat decreases during this period, with the added weight resulting from the growth and development of muscle tissue. Generally, boys have

2. *True or False:*

Children grow in spurts during early childhood.

TABLE 9.1   **Growth in Early Childhood**

The slowing rate of growth during early childhood is shown in this table. The data is given in centimeters. To convert to inches, multiply by .39.

Sex and Age	Percentile						
	5th	10th	25th	50th	75th	90th	95th
Male			*Stature in centimeters*				
3.0 years	89.0	90.3	92.6	94.9	97.5	100.1	102.0
3.5 years	92.5	93.9	96.4	99.1	101.7	104.3	106.1
4.0 years	95.8	97.3	100.0	102.9	105.7	108.2	109.9
4.5 years	98.9	100.6	103.4	106.6	109.4	111.9	113.5
5.0 years	102.0	103.7	106.5	109.9	112.8	115.4	117.0
5.5 years	104.9	106.7	109.6	113.1	116.1	118.7	120.3
6.0 years	107.7	109.6	112.5	116.1	119.2	121.9	123.5
Female							
3.0 years	88.3	89.3	91.4	94.1	96.6	99.0	100.6
3.5 years	91.7	93.0	95.2	97.9	100.5	102.8	104.5
4.0 years	95.0	96.4	98.8	101.6	104.3	106.6	108.3
4.5 years	98.1	99.7	102.2	105.0	107.9	110.2	112.0
5.0 years	101.1	102.7	105.4	108.4	111.4	113.8	115.6
5.5 years	103.9	105.6	108.4	111.6	114.8	117.4	119.2
6.0 years	106.6	108.4	111.3	114.6	118.1	120.8	122.7

Source: P. V. V. Hamill, et al., 1977.

TABLE 9.2   **Weight Gain in Early Childhood**
The data is given in kilograms. To convert to pounds, multiply by 2.2.

	Percentile						
Sex and Age	*5th*	*10th*	*25th*	*50th*	*75th*	*90th*	*95th*
Male	*Weight in kilograms*						
3.0 years	12.05	12.58	13.52	14.62	15.78	16.95	17.77
3.5 years	12.84	13.41	14.46	15.68	16.90	18.15	18.98
4.0 years	13.64	14.24	15.39	16.69	17.99	19.32	20.27
4.5 years	14.45	15.10	16.30	17.69	19.06	20.50	21.63
5.0 years	15.27	15.96	17.22	18.67	20.14	21.70	23.09
5.5 years	16.09	16.83	18.14	19.67	21.25	22.96	24.66
6.0 years	16.93	17.72	19.07	20.69	22.40	24.31	26.34
Female							
3.0 years	11.61	12.26	13.11	14.10	15.50	16.54	17.22
3.5 years	12.37	13.08	14.00	15.07	16.59	17.77	18.59
4.0 years	13.11	13.84	14.80	15.96	17.56	18.93	19.91
4.5 years	13.83	14.56	15.55	16.81	18.48	20.06	21.24
5.0 years	14.55	15.26	16.29	17.66	19.39	21.23	22.62
5.5 years	15.29	15.97	17.05	18.56	20.36	22.48	24.11
6.0 years	16.05	16.72	17.86	19.52	21.44	23.89	25.75

Source: P. V. V. Hamill, et al., 1977.

more muscle tissue, while girls have a bit more fat, but many individual differences can be found. At the beginning of this preschool period, children generally have their full set of baby teeth, and by the end of the period they begin to shed them. Preschoolers look forward to visits from the "tooth fairy," which bring glee, and money (the tooth fairy now brings as much as a dollar per tooth in some families).

Motor Abilities

By the beginning of the early childhood period, children have mastered the basics of walking and no longer have to pay much attention to standing steadily on two feet. Now they attempt to master the physical environment. They are as likely to run as to walk, their movements are smoother, and they turn corners better. The four-year-old can stand on one foot for 2 seconds and can negotiate a 6-centimeter walking board with a bit of stepping off (Heinicke, 1979). Large muscles are still much better developed than fine muscles, but by four the child can hold a pencil in something that resembles an adult's style and can fold a paper in a diagonal manner (Heinicke, 1979).

Children at this stage master many motor skills, including running, jumping, hopping, skipping, and climbing. The motor development of children in the preschool period is summarized in Table 9.3. Children younger than about eighteen months do not usually have the power or balance to leave the ground with both feet in the air, making running and jumping difficult. By the age of three, however, 42 percent can jump, and by four and a half years, 72 percent can (Cratty, 1970). By about three and a half, most children can hop from one to

TABLE 9.3   **Development of Locomotor Skills**

This table describes the development of locomotor skills in early childhood. Keep in mind that some children will develop these skills earlier than other children.

Locomotor Skill	Three-year-old	Four-year-old	Five-year-old
Running	Run with lack of control in stops and starts Overall pattern more fluid than 2-year-old Run with flat foot action Inability to turn quickly	Run with control over starts, stops, and turns Speed is increasing Longer stride than 3-year-old Non-support period lengthening Can run 35 yards in 20–29 seconds	Run well established and used in play activities Control of run in distance, speed, and direction improving Speed is increasing Stride width increasing Non-support period lengthening
Galloping	Most children cannot gallop Early attempts are some variation of the run pattern	43 percent of children are attempting to learn to gallop During this year most children learn to gallop Early gallop pattern somewhat of a run and leap step	78 percent can gallop Can gallop with a right lead foot Can gallop with a left lead foot Can start and stop at will
Hopping	Can hop 10 times consecutively on both feet Can hop 1 to 3 times on one foot Great difficulty experienced with hop pattern Attempts characterized by gross overall movements and a lot of arm movement	33 percent are proficient at hopping Can hop 7 to 9 hops on one foot Hop pattern somewhat stiff and not fluid	79 percent become proficient during this year Can hop 10 or more hops on one foot Hop characterized by more spring-like action in ankles, knees, and hips Can hop equally well on either leg
Climbing	Ascends stairs using mark time foot pattern During this year, ascending stairs is achieved with alternate foot pattern Descending stairs mostly with mark time foot pattern Climbing onto and off of low items continues to improve with higher heights being conquered	Ascends stairs using alternate foot pattern Descends stairs with alternate foot pattern Can climb a large ladder with alternate foot pattern Can descend large ladder slowly with alternate foot pattern	Climbing skill increasing 70 percent can climb a rope ladder with bottom free 37 percent can climb a pole 32 percent can climb a rope with bottom free 14 percent can climb an overhead ladder with 15 degree incline Climbing included more challenging objects such as trees, jungle gyms, large beams, etc.
Balance	Balance beam walking pattern characterized by mark time sequences Can traverse 25 foot walking path that is one inch wide in 31.5 seconds with 18 step-offs Can walk 3 inch wide beam forward 7.4 feet, backward; 3.9 feet 44 percent can touch knee down and regain standing position on 3 inch wide beam	Balance beam walking pattern characterized by alternate shuffle step Can traverse 25 foot walking path that is one inch wide in 27.7 seconds with 6 stepoffs Can walk 3 inch wide beam forward 8.8 feet, backward 5.8 feet 68 percent can touch knee down and regain standing position on 3 foot wide beam	Balance beam walking characterized by alternate step pattern Can traverse 25 foot walking path that is one inch wide in 24.1 seconds with three stepoffs Can walk 3 inch wide beam forward 11 feet, backward 8.1 feet 84 percent can touch knee down and regain standing position on 3 foot wide beam

Locomotor Skill	Three-year-old	Four-year-old	Five-year-old
Skipping	Skip is characterized by a shuffle step	14 percent can skip	72 percent are proficient
	Can skip on one foot and walk on the other	One footed skip still prevalent	Can skip with alternate foot pattern
	Actual true skip pattern seldom performed	Overall movement stiff and undifferentiated	Overall movements more smooth and fluid
		Excessive arm action frequently occurring	More efficient use of arms
		Skip mostly flatfooted	Skip mostly on balls of feet
Jumping	42 percent are proficient	72 percent are proficient	81 percent are skillful
	Jumping pattern lacks differentiation	Jumping pattern characterized by more preliminary crouch	Overall jumping pattern more smooth and rhythmical
	Lands without knee bend to absorb force	Can do standing broad jump 8–10 inches	Use of arm thrust at take-off evident
	Minimal crouch for take-off	Can do running broad jump 23–33 inches	More proficient landing
	Arms used ineffectively	90 percent can hurdle jump 5 inches	Can do standing broad jump 15–18 inches
	Can jump down from 28 inch height	51 percent can hurdle jump 9½ inches	Can do running broad jump 28–35 inches, vertical
	Can hurdle jump 3½ inches (68 percent)		Can jump and reach 2½ inches
			90 percent can hurdle jump 8 inches
			68 percent can hurdle jump 21½ inches

Source: C. B. Corbin, 1980.

three steps, but they cannot do it with much precision or control. By about five, most can hop for 10 seconds or so. Girls are better than boys in this. Skipping is more difficult and is generally not well developed until about five years of age or so (Corbin, 1980). Catching a ball is a skill that also develops in early childhood. At about three and a half, the child waits with arms held straight out and elbows fixed. By about four, the hands are at least open to receive the ball, although the elbows are still fixed. By about five, the arms and elbows are held to the sides of the body, allowing them to give when the ball arrives. The development of such motor skills allows children to explore and physically master the world around them.

Fine Motor Control

The three-year-old riding a tricycle is the picture many people have when they think of a preschooler. Indeed, the development of gross motor skills, such as running, hopping, and climbing, is readily visible. But the advances in fine motor control are also impressive, although fine motor control lags behind gross muscle development and control. The more subtle development of fine motor control shows itself in the way a child controls a crayon or pencil.

Children's Art.   Children have a natural affinity for drawing and painting, and their artistic ability can be viewed within a developmental framework as shown in Table 9.4. Give a one-year-old a crayon and a piece of paper, and the scribbling will begin, but the sweeping motion of the arm and the manner in which the crayon is held testify to the immaturity of the child. The scribblings may not remain confined to the paper. There is a kinesthetic enjoyment in scribbling. This lack of voluntary control belongs to the early scribbling stage—the

---

TABLE 9.4   Emergence of Scribbling, Printing, and Drawing
The child's ability to write and draw develops in the sequence shown below. The sequence is relatively fixed but the ages at which each ability is first shown varies. Children should be encouraged to draw but it is wise to appreciate just where they are developmentally.

Year	Selected Behaviors
1	
	Scribbling emerges, repetitive in radial or circular patterns
2	Multiple and single line crossings
	Variety of scribbling patterns, various positions on a page
3	Simple cross may be drawn, using two lines
	Encloses space; a variety of patterns emerge
	Figures placed in simple combinations using two figures
	Aggregates, more than two figures combined
4	"Suns" drawn with extra lines, sometimes forming faces
	Human figures emerge, crudely drawn
	Crude buildings and houses appear
	Human figures contain more detail; trunks usually absent; "stick" arms, legs, and fingers
	Boats and cars crudely drawn
	Circles and squares may be drawn
5	Animals drawn, trees appear in drawings
	Refined buildings and houses
	Better drawings of means of transportation—cars, airplanes, boats, etc.
6	
	Triangles drawn reasonably well
7	
	Diamonds drawn
8	
9	
	Three-dimensional geometrical figures drawn
10	
11	
	Linear perspective seen in drawings
12	

Source: B. Cratty, 1979.

first stage of artistic development (Allen and Herley, 1975; Kellogg, 1970). Later, eye-hand coordination and small muscle control will improve, so that the children can better control a writing instrument. Both maturation and practice are responsible for this improvement in control and coordination. During this advanced scribbling stage, the child can stay within the confines of the paper, and more voluntary control is in evidence.

At about age three, such basic forms as circles, crosses, and ovals appear over and over again in drawings. The transition between drawing these basic forms and the pictorialism of later childhood art is exhibited in drawings of mandalas, suns, and radials at about age four or five. A mandala is a circle or a square divided by one or more lines inside it (Allen and Herley, 1975). Suns are not necessarily round, but may be square or rectangular. After this stage, shapes are combined to form human beings.

Drawing is a valuable childhood activity. It helps develop children's fine motor and eye-hand coordination skills, and it gives children an opportunity to display their creativity. Yet adults often judge children's art by adult standards. Whitener and Kersey (1980) tell about a five-year-old boy who after seeing a baby hippo at the zoo became fascinated with the animal. At home, the child began to draw purple hippos with pink noses and ears. A knowledgeable first-grade neighbor told him that hippos weren't purple, and he received similar feedback from other children and well-meaning adults. He stopped drawing hippos, and later began to draw the standard scene consisting of a house in the middle of the paper near the bottom with a tree on one side, a few flowers on the other side and a blue sky.

Whitener and Kersey saw many such drawings in their travels from school to school, and wondered why children draw so many of these standard scenes. Their answer: because of the approval the children receive from adults for such drawings. Children learn to conform to their parents' view of the world and keep their creativity within the bounds of adult acceptance. Certainly children must learn the difference between reality and fantasy, but this need not mean having to draw absolute realism. Rain can be green or pink or purple without injuring a child's sense of reality.

Parents can help children in this area by providing materials that allow them freedom to express their creativity. Children require the room, the appropriate clothing (especially for painting), and a variety of materials so they can experiment with color and texture. Parents are wise to avoid interpreting children's art, but this can be difficult. What do you do when a preschooler asks you what you think a drawing is depicting? Perhaps the best response is to deflect the question so that the child tells you. Most of the time, children are so excited about what they have drawn that this strategy works. One interesting technique is to write a title at the top of the drawing when the child explains it to you. This shows the child that words may be used to describe a work of art.

The nature of children's drawings will depend on the child's physical and cognitive development as well as on any experiences with artistic materials. Children enjoy these experiences, but if they get negative feedback or are restricted in their expression, they may begin to draw the ever-present house with two trees flanking it, and the value of the activities will be diminished.

When people think of preschoolers, they often have a mental picture of three-year-olds riding tricycles.

Children's drawings indicate their state of development (drawing by Laurie Kaplan, age 5).

Growing Independence and the Need for Supervision

One of the pleasant characteristics of the preschool stage is the children's ability to do things on their own. They can dress themselves with some degree of care, eat by themselves, and play by themselves for significant periods of time. Their advances in both gross and fine motor control open new opportunities for private play. Preschoolers no longer need to be watched every second, and active, independent preschoolers are engaging beings. They can think of things they want to do and carry them out. Yet their motor skills and desire for independence are greater than their mental ability to understand what is good for them. This can lead to problems in the areas of safety and nutrition.

3. *True or False:*
The leading cause of death among preschoolers is accidents.

Safety.   Accidents are the leading cause of death during the preschool years, accounting for more than one-third of all deaths among children (Talbot and Guthrie, 1976). The danger from disease has decreased steadily over the past fifty years, but the same cannot be said of accidents. The most common causes of accidental death are motor vehicle accidents, drowning, fires, and poisoning.

Preschoolers frequently run into the street and are struck by cars. Many accidental deaths also result from crashes in which children are passengers in a motor vehicle. The use of secure restraints can prevent many of these tragedies. Some parents believe that holding babies or preschoolers is sufficient to protect the children from injury during a short stop or an accident, but it is not. One of the themes of parenting in the preschool period is the formation of good safety habits. Buckling up for safety is more than a slogan; it must be an inflexible rule. Since preschoolers observe others in the car, the driver and other passengers must do the same.

The second leading cause of death among preschool children (third among school-age children) is fires and burns, which occur most often in the home.

Some deaths and many injuries are caused by scalding. One three-year-old sitting on her mother's lap turned over a pot of boiling water on herself and was seriously burned. Most deaths from burns, though, result from fires. Stories of children playing with matches and setting fire to the apartment when left alone or in the company of an incompetent sibling or sitter are common. Not all such tragedies, can be prevented, but leaving a preschooler in the company of a seven-year-old sibling is asking for problems.

Drowning is the next largest cause of accidental deaths and is second among school-age children. Children can drown in very shallow water. Many preschoolers wander into unfenced pools. Again, supervision is the key.

Poisoning is another prominent cause of accidental death. Children often ingest medicines and household chemicals. One answer is childproof medicine bottles, but parents do not always reseal containers properly. Household cleaners should be placed completely out of the reach of preschoolers. In a number of homes, these cleaners are kept in cabinets below the sink, sometimes with special latches. Unfortunately, preschoolers show great ingenuity in opening these latches, and the result can be ingestion of a poisonous substance. A poison control center's telephone number should be available at all times just in case of such an accident. Even better, though, is prevention.

Not all accidents can be prevented, because they occur so suddenly. As children grow and parents relinquish control over their every action, adults are limited in what they can do. However, many accidents are preventable. Using proper restraints in automobiles, placing plastic stoppers in electrical sockets, and locking dangerous chemicals in overhead cabinets can do much to reduce injuries and fatalities among preschoolers.

Preschoolers are more independent and do much by themselves.

Nutrition.   Infants eat, or don't eat, what you give them. However, preschoolers know what foods are in the house and can tell you what they want. They may want a particular cereal and cry until they get it, refusing anything else. They are old enough to take certain foods, especially snacks, by themselves.

It is not surprising that the diet of many preschoolers is filled with high-calorie, low-nutrition foods—especially snacks. A desire for sugar is probably innate, and no one would argue that asparagus and cauliflower can beat a bar of chocolate and two cookies in a taste contest. However, preschoolers receive much of their nutritional information from watching television. Spend a Saturday morning watching children's television, and you'll find that the commercials are often more colorful and impressive than the programs themselves. The cartoon characters selling sugar-coated cereals are appealing to the preschoolers who watch these commercials and then demand these foods. Most commercials glorify processed and sweet foods, encouraging poor eating habits. One study found that 22 percent of the calories ingested by preschoolers came from snacks (Beyer and Morris, 1974). Many parents also use sweets as rewards, which is another mistake. Learning to eat right is an important skill learned in childhood. An apple or a carrot can be a snack; it doesn't always have to be cookies or candy.

Children's appetites are variable. At about twelve months their appetites usually decrease, probably in accordance with the decrease in the rate of growth (Hamilton and Whitney, 1982). It is not unusual for preschoolers to have periods in which they eat very little. Breakfast is often their best and most important meal, for they are usually hungry in the morning, and more likely to be cooperative. Unfortunately, many families place little emphasis on breakfast; thus, a plan to improve children's diets should begin with providing youngsters with a nutritious breakfast.

The advances in motor control and coordination in early childhood enable preschoolers to master the physical environment and learn about their world. They actively encounter the physical world and, as we shall see, try to comprehend the phenomena they see around them. In Piagetian theory, children actively learn through their physical and social interactions. It is natural that their expanding physical abilities would allow them to experiment with all sorts of activities and bring them into contact with many novel social situations. Their physical development therefore has an impact on their cognitive development. As we turn to the cognitive domain, we should remain aware of how the preschoolers' expanding physical abilities make experimentation and interaction possible, thus encouraging cognitive growth.

COGNITIVE DEVELOPMENT

Understanding Death, Illness, and Birth

Preschoolers are too old to be oblivious to what is going on in the world but too young to understand life as adults do. Nothing shows this as well as their problems with understanding death, illness, and birth. Even when children are given the facts, they don't understand them in an adult manner.

Death is not real to preschoolers. They are unable to understand the finality of the situation (Koocher, 1973). To the preschooler, death is transitory and reversible. Parents may be annoyed when a child asks when grandpa is coming back after having been told that he has died. Children, when they finally ac-

---

ACTION/
REACTION

Why Did Tabitha Die?

Tabitha was Jeffrey's favorite friend. Every day he would spend hours petting and playing with his pet cat. When the cat began to sit for hours on the windowsill and do nothing, Jeffrey's mother became concerned and took the animal to the veterinarian. After an operation, the cat died. Jeffrey was told the cat was very sick, but he expected the cat to come home.

Jeffrey's mother is concerned. When she told Jeffrey the cat had died, he cried, but an hour later he was asking when the cat was coming home. Jeffrey's father believes that simply getting another cat would help. The mother is having difficulty answering Jeffrey's questions: Why did Tabitha die? Am I going to die to when I get sick? Did Tabitha do something wrong? Where is Tabitha now?

1. If you were Jeffrey's parents, how would you explain Tabitha's death to him?

knowledge that grandpa is not going to visit them any more, may ask who is going to bring them candy. This may infuriate the grieving parent, who would like grandpa remembered for other reasons. Yet children often think instrumentally at this age, and no disrespect is meant. Preschoolers also believe that the causes of death involve misbehavior like "eating a dirty bug" (Koocher, 1973). They may parrot adult explanations, but they really don't understand the concept of death.

This combination of awareness that something has happened and the inability to understand adult explanations shows itself in preschoolers' understanding of illness as well. Kister and Patterson (1980) examined preschooler, kindergarten, second- and fourth-grade children's views about contagion and the causes of illness. A cold was used as an example of a contagious disease, a toothache for a noncontagious disease, and a scraped knee for an accident. Children were asked: "If a boy your age went to school one day, and the girl sitting next to him had [the ailment], would he have to be careful so he wouldn't catch [the ailment] from her?" (Kister and Patterson, 1980, p. 840). Almost all the children understood that some ailments were contagious, but the younger children overextended the concept to include both noncontagious illness and accidents. Ten of fifteen preschoolers believed that scraped knees, toothaches, or headaches were contagious, while only one of fifteen fourth-graders overextended the concept. The younger children also believed in the concept of immanent justice for both illness and accident. In other words, people get sick or injured because they have done something wrong. When children were told that a boy misbehaved and later caught a cold, many preschoolers believed that one caused the other. Children were more likely to use the immanent-justice argument to understand illness than misfortune. Many preschoolers believe that someone had to do something wrong to die, or that the child may have caused the death by being unpleasant or disobedient.

The third area, the creation of life, is another source of confusion to the preschooler. Many preschoolers believe that babies are bought. Bernstein and Cowan (1975) asked children where babies came from. These children had seen their mothers pregnant with younger siblings and had had their questions answered factually by their parents. Preschoolers could not understand the biological explanations involving sperm, egg, and prenatal development. They thought in terms of their own experiences, such as buying something new in a store. When faced with development within the womb, many believed that the mother swallowed something that grew, or that after buying the bones and other organs from a store she assembled them in her tummy. Preschoolers take bits and pieces from what they are told, combine them with their own experiences, and come out with explanations that cause us to ask ourselves, "Where did they get that from?"

Preoperational Thought

The studies describing how preschoolers understand birth, death, and illness demonstrate the qualitative differences between preschool and adult thought patterns. According to Piaget, the child from about the ages of two to seven progresses through the **preoperational stage**. It is a stage marked by many advances but, at the same time, many limitations.

Seriation involves the ability to place things in size order. Some studies show that if we reduce the difficulty of some tasks, such as seriation, preschoolers can perform them.

preoperational stage
Piaget's second stage of cognitive development, marked by the appearance of language and symbolic function and the child's inability to understand logical concepts, such as conservation.

Symbolic Function

The preoperational stage begins when the child is able to use one thing to represent or **symbolize** another (Mandler, 1983). One major illustration of this ability is the acquisition of language. Words represent particular concepts and objects. The ability to use symbolism also manifests itself in nonlinguistic areas. Children may use a spoon to represent a hammer, or a toy person to represent the mail carrier. Parents who are attentive to children's play may gain valuable insights into a child's view of the world. Another manifestation of the ability to use symbolism is known as **deferred imitation.** The child can see something occur, store the information, and perform that action at a later date. To do this, the child must preserve a symbolic representation of the behavior during the intervening time. For example, hours after a child sees a brother or sister doing exercises, the child may be found doing a version of the same exercises.

How Preschoolers Reason

To understand preschoolers, one must realize that they reason differently from adults. Adults reason either inductively or deductively. **Inductive reasoning** proceeds from the specific to the general. For instance, after examining a number of cases, we may say that children who do not do their homework do not receive good grades. Adults also use **deductive reasoning,** beginning with a general rule and proceeding to specifics. They may form a rule concerning homework and grades, and then apply it to specific cases.

Transductive Reasoning and Causality.   Preschool children, though, reason from particular to particular, in a **transductive** manner. The simplest example of such reasoning is that if A causes B then, according to the preschooler, B causes A. For example, Piaget found that his daughter believed that since his shave required hot water the appearance of hot water meant that daddy would shave (Phillips, 1975). The child's understanding of *causality* is based on how close one event is to another. As Pulaski notes, "The road makes the bicycle go; by creating a shadow one can cause the night to come. The thunder makes it rain, and honking the horn makes the car go" (1980, p. 49).

Seriation and Classification.   Parents are often surprised when preschoolers show a different logic or have difficulty with a particular problem that seems so simple to adults. For instance, ask preschoolers to put a series of sticks in order from biggest to smallest, an operation called **seriation** (see Figure 9.1). They simply can't seem to do it. Nor can they **classify** items, at least at the beginning of the preoperational stage (see Figure 9.2). When young children are given a number of plastic shapes, including squares, triangles, and rings of different colors, and asked to put things that are alike into a pile, most children younger than five do not organize their choices on any particular logical basis. They may put a red triangle and a blue triangle together, but then throw in a red square. No central organizing principle is evident. Some young children do not understand the task at all (Ault, 1977). Late in the preoperational stage some progress in classification is made. They can sort items on the basis of one overriding principle, most often form, but they fail to see that multiple classifications are possible.

Margin glossary and question

symbol
Anything that can represent something else, such as words symbolizing an object.

deferred imitation
Imitation of an action viewed earlier at a later time.

4. *True or False:*
During the preschool years, the child begins to reason in a manner that is very similar to that of the average adult.

inductive reasoning
Reasoning that proceeds from specific cases to the formation of a general rule.

deductive reasoning
Reasoning that begins with a general rule and then is applied to specific cases.

transductive reasoning
Preoperational reasoning in which young children reason from particular to particular.

seriation
The process of placing objects in size order.

classification
The process of placing objects in different classes.

FIGURE 9.1   **Seriation**
Young children have difficulty placing things in size order.

Preschool children also have difficulty understanding subordinate and superordinate classes (see Figure 9.3). For example, a child may be shown seven green beads and three white beads, all made of wood, and asked whether there are more green beads or more wooden beads. The child will usually say more green beads. Show children a picture of a bouquet containing five roses and three tulips and ask them whether there are more roses or more flowers. They will often say more roses. Preschoolers cannot make comparisons across levels and usually get the problem wrong.

Transitive Inferences.   Preschoolers also cannot seem to understand **transitive inferences.** If Ed is taller than Sue, and Sue is taller than Tim, then Ed is taller than Tim is an example of such an inference (see Figure 9.4). The preoperational child views comparisons as absolute (Piaget and Inhelder, 1974) and does not understand that an object can be larger than one thing and at the same time smaller than another.

transitive inferences
Statements of comparison, such as "If X is taller than Y, and Y is taller than Z, then X is taller than Z."

FIGURE 9.2   **Classification**

Young children have difficulty with tasks that require the ability to classify items into various groupings.

Conservation Problems.   Nowhere are the preschooler's difficulties so obvious than in the child's inability to solve conservation problems (see Figure 9.5). **Conservation** involves the ability to comprehend that quantities remain the same regardless of changes in their appearance. You can test this out yourself in a number of ways:

Take two equal lumps of clay and roll each one into a ball. Then, in the child's view, roll one ball into a worm and ask the child which clay form has more clay. The preschooler fails to understand that they are still equal, and believes that one has more clay.

conservation

The concept that quantities remain the same despite changes in their appearance.

FIGURE 9.3 **Subordinate and Superordinate Classes**
Are there more green beads or wooden beads? Young children answer more green beads because they have difficulty making comparisons across levels.

"Green beads."

"Are there more green beads or wooden beads?"

FIGURE 9.4 **Transitive Inferences**
If Ed is taller than Sue and Sue is taller than Tim, then Ed is taller than Tim. Young children have difficulty understanding such inferences.

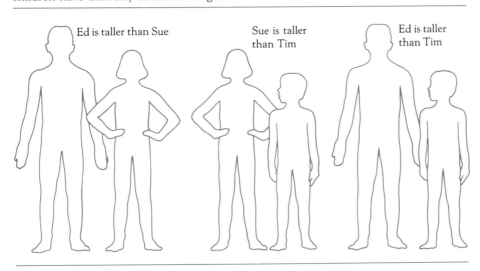

Ed is taller than Sue

Sue is taller than Tim

Ed is taller than Tim

FIGURE 9.5   **Conservation**
When presented with the problems in the figure below, preschoolers give answers (indicated in the right column) that differ from those of older children. Preschool children have difficulty with conservation problems.

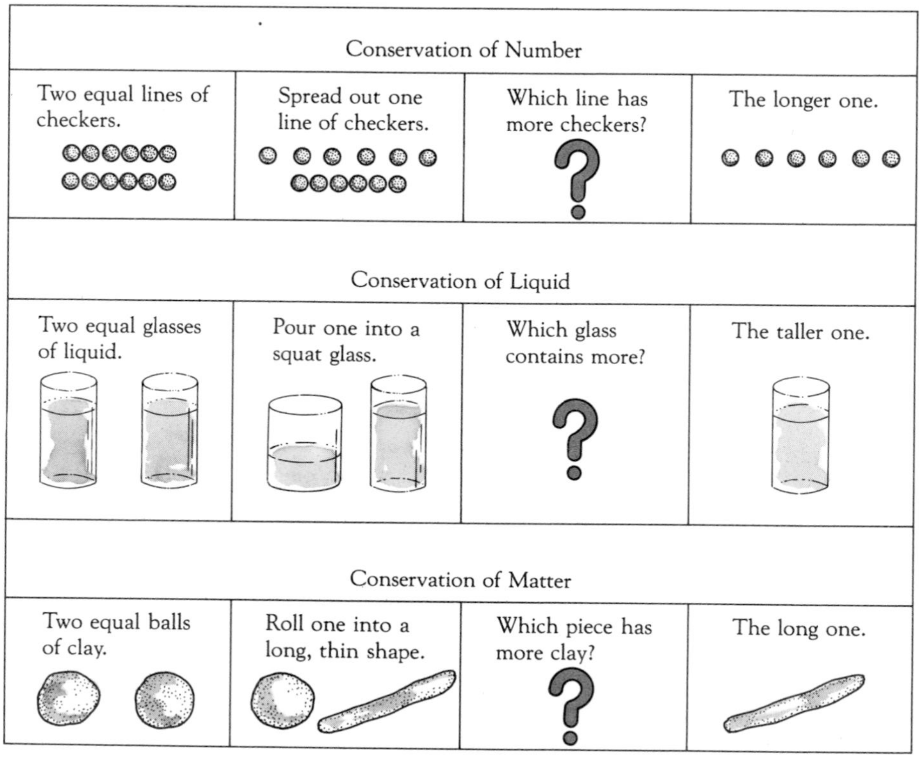

Conservation of Number			
Two equal lines of checkers.	Spread out one line of checkers.	Which line has more checkers?	The longer one.

Conservation of Liquid			
Two equal glasses of liquid.	Pour one into a squat glass.	Which glass contains more?	The taller one.

Conservation of Matter			
Two equal balls of clay.	Roll one into a long, thin shape.	Which piece has more clay?	The long one.

Present a preschooler with two identical half-filled beakers of water. The child will tell you they are equal. Now, transfer one to a squat cup and ask the child which has more. The answer will usually be that the taller beaker contains more liquid.

Show a preschooler displays of seven pennies in which the coins are either grouped in close together or spread out. The four-year-old is certain that the spread-out display has more pennies than the one that is packed closer together.

All these exemplify the preschooler's failure to understand and successfully perform conservation tasks. The fact that preschoolers cannot correctly judge that pouring a liquid from a tall beaker to a squat beaker does not change the amount of the water has fascinated psychologists for years.

But why can't preschoolers solve these simple tasks? The answer lies in certain characteristics of preschoolers' thinking.

Characteristics of Preschoolers' Thinking

centering
The tendency to attend to only one dimension at a time.

Centering.   A preschool child can concentrate on only one dimension at a time (Piaget and Inhelder, 1969). This is known as **centering.** For instance, try to

Preschoolers do not show the ability to conserve.

explain to a preschooler that a cup and a glass hold the same amount of liquid. Because the containers are shaped differently, preschoolers believe that one is larger than the other. They visually think that the taller glass contains more liquid than the fatter cup. Preschoolers can attend to only one measure at the same time, and appearances confuse them. In the same way, they have no difficulty telling you that two balls of clay are the same. If one is rolled into the shape of a worm, however, they compare the clay shapes on the dimension of length and cannot take both the length and the width into account.

Irreversibility. Preschoolers cannot **reverse** operations. If a clay ball is rolled into a worm in front of them, they cannot mentally rearrange the clay back to its original form.

Show a child three balls of the same size, each of which is a different color. Place the balls in a cylinder in a certain order (e.g., blue, green, yellow). The preschooler has no difficulty understanding that they will come out the bottom in the same order, but if you rotate the cylinder 180 degrees, the child will continue to predict the original order and is surprised that the balls leave the canister in the opposite order (Piaget, 1967).

This inability to reverse an operation affects preschoolers' answers to what seem like simple questions. When a preschooler was asked whether he had a sis-

reversibility
Beginning at the end of an operation and working one's way back to the start.

ter, he answered yes and gave her name. When asked whether his sister had a brother, he replied no.

Transformations.   When preschoolers notice that change has occurred, they can point to the beginning and the end, but do not realize the sequence involved in the change. For example, when young subjects were asked to draw the successive movements of a bar falling from a vertical position to an upright position, the children did not draw, nor did they later understand, that it went through a series of intermediate positions between the first and last position (Phillips, 1975). In the same way, children faced with a conservation task judge equality on the basis of the beginning and end states. They cannot take intervening states into consideration.

egocentrism
A thought process described by Piaget in which young children believe everyone is experiencing the environment in the same way they are. Children who are egocentric have difficulty understanding someone else's point of view.

Egocentrism.   Underlying all the child's reasoning processes is a basic **egocentrism.** The use of this term is unfortunate, because it connotes selfishness. Piaget argued that children see everything from their own viewpoint and are incapable to taking someone else's view into account. Young children believe that everything has a purpose that is understandable in their own terms and relevant to their own needs. For instance, a boy once asked Piaget why there were two mountains above Geneva. The answer the boy wanted was that one was for adults to climb while the other little one was for children (Pulaski, 1980). Preschoolers see the entire world as revolving around them. The sun and moon exist to give them light; mothers and fathers exist to give them warmth and to take care of them.

This egocentrism is seen in childrens' interpretations of their physical world and their social world. Children who know their left hand from their right may not be able to correctly identify the left and right hands of a person standing opposite. Nursery school teachers are aware of this, and when facing preschoolers they raise the left hand when requesting that the children raise their right (Davis, 1983). Piaget showed a model of three mountains to young children and asked them to consider how the display might look to a doll sitting in different positions around the model (see Figure 9.6). Preschool children could not do this accurately. They reason that everyone sees the world as they do.

Egocentrism is found in many social behaviors as well. Piaget (1965) studied the way children played marbles. Children between the ages of two and six understood the rules in a totally different manner, but were still able to play together. Neither watched the other; they all simply played the game their own way, each trying to win from his or her own point of view. I can remember coming home on a particularly hard day. It was 98 degrees and the humidity was horrendous. The car had broken down, and a number of other smaller catastrophies had occurred. Seeing me tired and upset, my four-year-old came over and asked if I wanted her to read a story to me. Since stories make her feel better, she supposed they would do the same for me.

animism
The preschooler's belief that everything, animate or inanimate, is conscious or alive.

Animism and Artificialism.   One of the charming aspects of early childhood is the child's belief that everything is capable of being conscious and alive, which is called **animism** (see Figure 9.7). A paper turtle can be alive; a hammer has a life of its own. This results in unusual behavior. If you step on the turtle, you've just killed something, not just smashed a small toy. A preschooler may

FIGURE 9.6   **Egocentrism**
In Piaget's three-mountains experiment, preschool children had difficulty visualizing the doll's perspective of the three-mountain display.

bump into a desk, smack it, and say "Bad desk." A book that falls from a shelf didn't want to be with the other books. A balloon that has soared to the ceiling didn't want to be held. Animism is most characteristic of the early part of this stage, but it becomes less evident as children reach the age of four or five (Bullock, 1985).

The child's reasoning also reflects **artificialism,** the belief that natural phenomena are caused by human beings (Pulaski, 1980). This is a natural outgrowth of what children see around them. Everything is viewed as intentional and organized for human use, so children explain the world in terms of human causation (Piaget, 1927). Thus, the lake near Geneva was created not by natural forces but by a group of men digging (Pulaski, 1980).

artificialism
The belief that natural phenomena are caused by human beings, common among preschoolers.

FIGURE 9.7   **Animism**
Young children often ascribe characteristics of living things to inanimate objects.

Training Preschoolers to Think

The characteristics of preschool thought, as demonstrated in Figure 9.8, greatly limit the child's ability to solve problems. For example, the problems with conservation limit children's understanding of the world and seriously restrict progress in math. The ability to perform conservation tasks successfully develops gradually during middle childhood, but one might ask whether it could be taught to children earlier. Can children be trained to succeed on such tasks as those requiring conservation or reversibility?

There are two questions here. First, is it possible to train children to perform these tasks? Second, if it is, why would we want to? Some psychologists have tried to train children in these skills as a way of testing, expanding, and modifying Piaget's theories, which stress social experience and maturation and deemphasize formal learning in the development of these abilities. This type of research may help us appreciate the relative importance of these factors, but if the idea behind training children in these skills is simply to move them through the stages faster, the value of such studies is questionable. In developmental terms, *faster does not imply better.* There is now a disturbing tendency to rush children through childhood as if it was a bother, something of little value (Elkind, 1981; LeShan, 1974). The practical benefits of teaching Piagetian skills to children who would not normally be ready for them are elusive, and the advantages of rushing children through the stages are nonexistent.

It used to be popular to conclude that children could not be trained in such Piagetian skills as classification and conservation. Early studies reinforced the Piagetian notion that it was impossible to teach children skills they were not ready to master (Piaget, 1970). However, just the opposite conclusion has recently been reached by some psychologists (Gelman and Baillargeon, 1983). In the older studies, logical operations were simply demonstrated to young children. They were shown how to weigh the balls of clay, that changing the shape did not change the weight, and that adding and then subtracting did not result in any net change. These studies did not succeed, and it was concluded that children were simply not ready for these learning experiences (Ault, 1977). However, researchers then began to use a different strategy. Piagetian tasks were broken down into their component parts. Children were taught subskills that were relevant to the final skill. For example, Kingsley and Hall (1967) taught five- and six-year-olds what the terms *longer* and *shorter* meant, how to measure with a ruler, that the ruler was more reliable than visual cues, that the length was changed only when quantity was added or subtracted from the ends, and that moving an object did not change its length. These children later showed the ability to conserve length. Gelman (1969) trained children to conserve by teaching them to respond to the relevant cues and to ignore the apparent visual ones. Other skills, such as classification, have also been taught to young children (Judd and Mervis, 1979).

Many authorities now admit that children can be trained to conserve or classify, but interpretation of such studies is complicated by methodological problems (Brainerd, 1978). In addition, there are questions about the stability of the results and whether these skills transfer to other problems (McGhee, et al., 1982). For instance, once trained to succeed in one classification task, can the child then perform well in another similar but not identical task? These questions remain unanswered, but we can conclude that it is possible to influence the acquisition of such skills through instruction. Formal learning may be more important than Piaget realized.

Recent Challenges to Piaget's Views

Preschool children have made great strides since infancy and toddlerhood. They can use language more efficiently and show deferred imitation. However, it is their limitations that are often emphasized. The child is described as lacking communication skills, number concepts, order concepts, memory skills, and having problems in causal relationships, as well as being egocentric, perception-bound, and unable to understand states and transformations (Gelman and Baillargeon, 1983; Gelman, 1979). Preschoolers are described more by what they cannot do (Flavell, 1977) and their charm is due to their ignorance.

However, many of Piaget's ideas concerning the limitations of preschool thought have recently been challenged. These challenges are not just based on

FIGURE 9.8   Examples of Preoperational Thought
During the preoperational stage, a child's thought tends to be characterized by irreversibility, transductive reasoning, and the inability to decenter.

Irreversibility

A four-year-old subject is asked:
"Do you have a brother?" He says, "Yes."
"What's his name?" "Jim."
"Does Jim have a brother?" "No."

From Phillips (1969)

Transductive Reasoning

At two years, 14 days, Jacqueline wanted a doll dress that was upstairs. She said "Dress," and when her mother refused to get it, "Daddy get dress." As I also refused, she wanted to go herself "To mommy's room." After several repetitions of this she was told that it was too cold there. There was a long silence, and then: "Not too cold." I asked, "Where?" "In the room." "Why isn't it too cold?" "Get dress."

From Piaget (1951)

Egocentrism

After interviewing children on how they play the game of marbles, Piaget concludes: ". . . how little children from the same class at school, living in the same house, and accustomed to playing with each other, are able to understand each other at this age. Not only do they tell us of totally different rules . . . but when they play together they do not watch each other and do not unify their respective rules even for the duration of the game. The fact of the matter is that neither is trying to get the better of the other: each is merely having a game on his own, trying to hit the marbles in the square, i.e., trying to 'win' from his point of view. [In other situations, such as sitting around the sandbox] one can observe in children between 2 and 6 a characteristic type of pseudo-conversation or 'collective monologue' during which children speak only for themselves . . . and each is concerned only with himself."

From Piaget (1965)

Centering

When the child is asked to put a set of sticks which vary in length in order, the following arrangement is constructed:

Apparently, the child "centers" on only one aspect of the problem (e.g., the tops of the sticks) and cannot simultaneously consider other aspects (e.g., the bottoms of the sticks).

Concreteness, irreversibility, centering, and states

A four-year-old is asked: "Have you got a friend?"
"Yes, Odette."
"Well look, we're giving you, Clairette, a glass of orangeade (A1, ¾ full), and we're giving Odette a glass of lemonade (A2, also ¾ full). Has one of you more to drink than the other?"
"The same."

Figure 9.8 continued

"This is what Clairette does: she pours her drink into two other glasses (B1 and B2, which are thus half filled). Has Clairette the same amount as Odette?"

"Odette has more."

"Why?"

"Because we've put less in." (She points to the levels in B1 and B2 without taking into account the fact that there were two glasses.)

(Odette's drink was then poured into B3 and B4.) "It's the same."

"And now?" (Pouring Clairette's drink from B1 and B2 into L, a long thin tube, which is then almost full.)

"I've got more."

"Why?"

"We've poured it into that glass (L) and here (B3 and B4) we haven't."

"But were they the same before?"

"Yes."

"And now?"

"I've got more."

"But where does the extra come from?"

"From in there." (B1)

From Piaget (1952)

---

the age at which these abilities appear. Psychologists are beginning to realize that preschoolers may not be as limited as first thought. Perhaps they can classify, are not so egocentric, and can perform transitive inferences—if the situation is structured correctly. These new findings will have a great impact on preschool education.

The observations Piaget made of preschoolers using his standard testing procedures are well founded, and no one seriously doubts their reliability (Gelman and Baillargeon, 1983). If you test a preschooler in the same way Piaget did, you will get the same results. However, the assumption that because preschoolers fail these tests they cannot seriate, classify, or decenter is questionable. Perhaps if we tested the children differently, they might succeed. Indeed, this is exactly what researchers have found.

Preschoolers can arrange things in size order, classify items, and understand inferences if we design the task in a manner that is ideal for the preschooler's interests and abilities. First, we have to strip away anything that might distract the preschooler, leaving only the most essential elements of the task. Second, the task situation must be familiar (Brown et al., 1983). Preschoolers are easily sidetracked and do poorly in situations that are strange to them. Their abilities are also easily taxed, so that memory and lack of comprehension can affect performance (Trabasso, 1975).

At times, simple modifications in Piaget's method change the results of the experiment. For example, Inhelder and Piaget (1964) argue that children can seriate if they can place the items in correct order, put additional items into the series, and correct any errors that have been made. So far this is reasonable. But Piaget used a total of ten sticks in his observations—and concluded that true seriation did not occur at this stage. Koslowski (1980) used a similar approach, but instead of ten sticks she used four. Using the same criteria, she found that three-quarters of the three- and four-year-olds tested could put the sticks in size order, about four-fifths could insert two new sticks into the order, and all the children could correct the incorrect insertions. The ability to seriate is present in these children, but ten sticks is simply too many for the preschooler to deal with at one time.

Piaget's concept of egocentrism has also been the focus of much criticism (Ford, 1979). Under specific circumstances, preschoolers are not egocentric, that is, they can understand the viewpoint of others. Flavell and his colleagues (1981) found that preschoolers understood that objects with different sides, like a house, look different from various perspectives but that objects with identical sides, like a ball, look the same. In another experiment, one- to three-year-old children were given a hollow cube with a picture pasted to the bottom of the inside. The children were asked to show the picture to an observer sitting across from them. Almost all the children who were two years or older turned the cube away from them and towards the observer. Thus, they demonstrated some understanding of the other person's perspective (Lempers et al., 1977).

As far as transitive inferences are concerned, Trabasso (1975) found that children had difficulty with transitive inferences because they are unable to remember and understand the problem (Trabasso, 1977, 1975). When preschoolers were trained so as to improve their memories for this type of inference, they did much better (Trabasso, 1975; Bryant and Trabasso, 1971). Some of this research is controversial, however. For example, Breslow (1981) argues that Trabasso's procedures enabled children to solve transitive problems in an noninferential manner. Some recent research has also shown that children can reason deductively under highly structured circumstances (Hawkins et al., 1984).

Harmonizing the Views

Putting this new information into perspective is difficult. It is only fair to ask for a conclusion concerning the preschooler's mental abilities—can preschoolers draw inferences, decenter, or understand causality in a more-or-less mature manner? At first glance, the research seems contradictory, but it really is not. Under certain circumstances, preschoolers can do things that Piaget did not think possible.

The key phrase here is "under certain circumstances." Preschool skills are fragile and delicate, and children's abilities in these areas are just developing. Preschoolers can classify, seriate, and are not as egocentric if they have experience in a particular skill, if the task is clear, if it does not tax their memory, and if they can understand the verbal instructions. On the other hand, if the situation is complicated or requires more memory and verbal skills than they have, preschoolers fail at these tasks.

This newfound information is valuable. People working with preschoolers must design an environment in which tasks are simplified and memory requirements are minimized. They must be certain that preschoolers understand what is required of them if they are to bring out these newly developing skills. If this is done, preschoolers can do some very surprising things. Situational and task factors, then, are of paramount importance. This is also shown in the preschool child's ability to use memory to solve problems.

Memory Skills

If children are to defer imitation, use symbols effectively, and eventually understand other people's perspectives, they must be able to use their memories effectively. Preschoolers' memory skills are far superior to those of toddlers. Between two and four years, their already good recognition skills improve (Perlmutter and Myers, 1979). Their ability to use language allows them to store memories using words. On the other hand, if you compare preschoolers with children in the middle years of childhood, their deficiencies seem overwhelming.

The Conventional View of Preschool Memory.   The memory abilities of preschoolers are limited by their inability to spontaneously use memory strategies that many of us take for granted. For instance, suppose you were shown a group of pictures and asked to remember them. You might first group them into categories (foods, buildings, people), then rehearse them. Preschoolers do not use these strategies on their own (Kail and Hagen, 1982). In order to remember successfully, you had to understand the task, have some idea of its difficulty, and then devise an appropriate strategy. You had some idea of what was involved in the memory task. This knowledge of memory processes is called **metamemory.**

If you had been presented with only two items to remember, you probably would have used only a bit of rehearsal. When preschoolers were asked to remember a string of digits, they did not spontaneously use any rehearsal—the simplest strategy, but if they were instructed in the use of rehearsal, their ability to remember the list improved greatly (Flavell and Wellman, 1977). Children can be taught to use rehearsal. However, at a later time, children will not use this strategy spontaneously when confronted with the same task with no instructions on rehearsal (Keeney et al., 1967). In other words, young children apparently can use this strategy, but do not unless they are told to do so.

Children's lack of understanding concerning the demands of the task was demonstrated in another study. Appel and his colleagues (1972) presented pictures to four-, seven-, and eleven-year-old children using two different instructions: "Look at the pictures" or "Remember the pictures." If *you* were told to remember the pictures, you would repeat them to yourself or write them down. If you were told to look at them, you wouldn't do anything special. However, you understand the problem, whereas preschool children do not. They don't seem to know that the problem requires some voluntary, purposeful cognitive activity. Indeed, the four-year-olds did not act any differently when presented with either instruction, but the older children did. Perhaps preschoolers show such poor use of memory strategies because they do not understand what is involved in memory tasks (Flavell and Wellman, 1977).

The memory of the preschooler has traditionally been viewed as rather passive, nonstrategic, and nonplanful (Brown et al., 1983). However, if we look more deeply we can see the beginnings of strategy use, and at times children will surprise you with their memories. Again, the characteristics of the task and the test conditions are most important.

A More Recent Look at Memory Skills.   Many studies have used artificial situations that require remembering new information for its own sake (Paris and Lindauer, 1982). When the information and situation are more familiar, and the

metamemory
The knowledge of memory processes that one has.

5. *True or False:*
Surprisingly, preschool children often use effective memory strategies, like rehearsal, on their own.

goals of remembering are clear, preschoolers show the beginnings of memory strategies, and their ability to recall improves markedly. For instance, Istomina (1975) asked children three to seven years of age to remember a list of five words under two different conditions. In one condition, children played a game of grocery store and had to recall the items so they could buy them. In the second condition, children were simply told to remember the items. Children recalled significantly more in condition one than in condition two. When children were tested on the task of remembering a list, young children did quite well when the words were comprised of familiar categories, such as names of their teachers and television shows (Lindberg, 1980).

Even the idea that preschoolers are nonstrategic needs rethinking. Preschoolers do use some strategies to remember such as pointing and looking (Kail and Hagen, 1982). They are competent when asked to use these motor and sensory strategies, but their ability to use verbal strategies, such as rehearsal, is greatly limited.

Memory Reconsidered.   This more recent look at the memory skills of the young child matches the newer appreciation of what preschoolers can and cannot do in other cognitive areas. If we watch the children in their normal day-to-day life, amid familiar situations and tasks whose goals are clear, we find they can remember more and do begin to use strategies. The abilities of preschoolers, though, are fragile. Young children are easily confounded, and artificial tasks are likely to show their limitations. Taken as a group, the studies in cognition and memory should make us wary about making generalizations about what abilities children do or do not have. Even though they may not show these abilities when tested in a certain way, it does not necessarily mean that they don't have them. Rather, it is important to note in what situations children can and cannot successfully perform particular tasks.

THE ENVIRONMENT AND COGNITIVE DEVELOPMENT

Jason lives in a home filled with books. His mother reads to him daily, and he watches "Sesame Street" at least once a day. He attends nursery school, where he plays with other children, takes short trips around the neighborhood, and learns about colors and shapes. Jason's parents encourage him to describe what he sees around him.

Craig's parents put him in front of a television set right after breakfast to watch cartoons for hours. They never read to him. Craig mostly plays by himself, and his parents speak to him only to demand something. They never have much time for Craig, and he is often cared for by his older brother, who would rather be doing anything else.

When Jason and Craig reach elementary school, the differences between them are obvious. Craig is not ready for the experience and is having difficulties, while Jason is progressing nicely. Will Craig catch up? For most such children, the answer is unfortunately no. In fact, just the opposite occurs: they often fall even more behind.

The fact that most preschoolers who are developmentally behind do not catch up does not indicate that the game is all over by age five. Early experience is important, but later experience may compensate for poor earlier experiences.

However, if the environment is not improved, the child will not catch up. Only if a concerted and time-consuming effort is made on the part of his teachers will Craig close the gap between himself and Jason. It would have been easier to prevent this problem, to structure the environment so that Craig was as ready as Jason for elementary school. Before we can do this, we must understand what features of the preschooler's environment encourage cognitive growth and school readiness. To begin this investigation, we will look at the main influences on the child: the home, television, and nursery school.

The Home

The atmosphere at home is important. Children who are more cognitively advanced come from homes in which language is used in an expansive manner. The children are encouraged to express themselves, to label the environment, and to describe their world (Chazan and Cox, 1976). Parents who give information, explain events, and encourage curiosity and exploration develop their children's minds so that when they enter elementary school they are ready for new challenges (Katz, 1980). In a study of sixteen five-year-old readers and nonreaders, Briggs and Elkind (1973) found that early readers came from homes in which the parents' occupation and educational level were high and parents read to their children.

Even when not directly involved in a parent-child interaction, the children observe those around them. An environment filled with books is unstimulating unless the books are read. If preschoolers see their parents and older siblings enjoying reading, they are more likely to develop a positive attitude toward the activity.

Two Views of Parents as Teachers.   Since parental influences are so important, a natural question is: What approach should parents adopt if they want to optimize a preschooler's cognitive development? There are two different models here.

The first views parents as environmental engineers who at the appropriate times provide materials and opportunities that help their children explore and learn about the world. The parents construct an environment rich in opportunities, allowing the children to discover the world at their own pace and stimulating them to think. Although Piaget never listed recommendations on child-rearing (Vernon, 1976), this type of strategy is in line with his thinking. The child learns through discovery, and readiness is taken into consideration. Formal instruction is deemphasized. The day-to-day experiences of the child are educational. A simple walk around the neighborhood becomes a learning experience. There are traffic signs, people working, and a hundred different things to discuss.

The other approach emphasizes the importance of formal instruction. Parents are encouraged to teach their preschooler skills. There is less emphasis on self-discovery and more on planned activities that impart knowledge to the child.

The Pitfalls of Both Views.   Both extreme positions are dangerous. The parent who merely produces an environment suitable for a child but does not actively interact with the youngster is not maximizing the child's experiences. On the other side, too formal or unnatural a structure may cause a child to resent the parents and reject the instruction. It becomes a "grim business" (Zinsser, 1981). There is no joy, merely pressure. In addition, not all preschool children can be early readers. Many preschoolers do not have the physical abilities, such as the ability to focus on printed words, necessary for success in reading (Moore and Moore, 1973). In such cases, children may feel that they cannot live up to their parents' expectations, and tension could develop, which would interfere with normal development.

Television

The entire home environment affects the preschooler. In the last two generations, this environment has included the television, which has become a member of the family (Singer and Singer, 1976). Some 98 percent of all American households have television sets, and 52 percent have more than one, the extra set for the children (Parke and Slaby, 1983). Young children view between three and four hours of television every day (Hayes et al., 1981) and some figures are even higher (Singer, 1983). Many parents use the television set as an electronic baby-sitter. If children spend that much time in one activity, it stands to reason that its effects may be substantial (Rubinstein, 1983).

But exactly what do children learn from what they see and hear on television, and how do they process this information? For example, do children understand the differences between commercials and regular programs? Do they comprehend the purpose behind advertising?

6. *True or False:*
Preschoolers average about two hours of television-watching each day.

Young children view between three and four hours of television each day.

Advertising Aimed at Children.   The average child is exposed to about 20,000 commercials a year. About 5,000 of these are for some type of food (Stoneman and Brody, 1981). By the time a child is twenty years old, he or she has watched 1 million commercials (*U.S. News and World Report*, 1981). Commercials are as carefully produced as the programs they accompany. Children's advertising has three goals: to increase a child's desire for a particular product, to influence the child to ask parents to purchase the item, and to change consumption patterns, that is, encourage a person to use more of the product (Atkin, 1981).

Advertising is effective in achieving each of these goals. Children do remember what they see on television and ask their parents to purchase the items. Lyle and Hoffman (1972) found that 75 percent of the mothers of preschoolers interviewed noted that their children sang commercial jingles by age three, and 91 percent reported that their children asked for the toys they saw advertised on television. In another study, 90 percent of the children exposed to a particular cereal commercial wanted to eat that brand, compared with about 67 percent of a control group (Atkin and Gibson, 1978, in Atkin, 1980). Most advertising aimed at children involves toys, cereals, candy, and fast-food restaurants (Barcus, 1980). As children get older, more personal products take center stage (Liebert et al., 1973).

And children do attempt to influence the purchasing patterns of their parents. Galst and White (1976) followed children ages three through eleven who were exposed to commercials in a lab setting on a trip to the supermarket. On the average, children tried to influence the purchases of particular foods fifteen times. Children who paid more attention to the advertisements made more requests. The extent to which these attempts are successful will vary from parent to parent. Young children make more efforts to influence parental purchases, but older children are more successful. Mothers report yielding more often to older children than to younger children (Ward and Wackman, 1972, cited in Liebert et al., 1973).

Children exposed to a particular commercial are more likely to increase their use of the product as well (Atkin, 1980). As children watch the programs, they are reminded of the product, and this alters their consumption patterns.

Television advertising aimed at children is controversial. It is too easy to condemn advertising in general. Advertising is a useful process by which people are introduced to a product. However, adults have the ability to recognize and interpret the commercials for what they are—attempts to persuade one to buy. Until recently, it was thought that young children could not even make the distinction between commercials and the television program they were watching, but we now know that children as young as three years old can tell the difference between commercials and regular programs though the ability increases with age (Levin et al., 1982). This does not mean that children understand the intent and motives behind commercials. Such understanding is not expressed until ages seven or eight (Levin et al., 1982). By the sixth grade (age eleven or so), children are downright cynical about commercials (Rubinstein, 1978).

The effectiveness of commercials is increased by the skillful manner in which they are produced. Advertisers know how to capture and maintain the attention of children. About 80 percent of the cereal ads use animation in conjunction with nonanimated scenes (Barcus, 1980). Advertisers frequently use unusual

7. *True or False:*
There is evidence that television advertising aimed at children is very effective.

8. *True or False:*
Preschool children cannot tell the difference between commercials and the programs they accompany.

Preschool children watch many commercials on television that encourage them to eat sugar-coated cereals.

sound and visual effects, violent activity, magic, and fantasy to attract attention. Few rational arguments are presented. Cereal ads usually concentrate on taste and texture and give little information about the ingredients except to say that the product is "fortified with essential vitamins" (Barcus, 1980).

The combination of efficient and effective psychological techniques of persuasion and an audience incapable of understanding the motives behind these commercials may cause us to consider whether television commercials aimed at young children should be permitted at all. What do children learn from commercials? Most ads for cereals, snacks, and gum serve to downgrade the importance of good nutrition and good health habits. When was the last time you saw a children's commercial for candy end with a suggestion that children eat a balanced diet and brush after meals? And toy advertising often deceives children, using photographic techniques to make a doll look larger than it actually is. If there is some statement such as "assembly required," it is presented so fast that children do not understand it.

Cleaning up children's advertising would seem to be a simple matter, but there are political and economic forces at work (Adler, 1980). In addition, censorship and freedom-of-speech issues are often raised (Heinz, 1983), and these should not be taken lightly. Finally, many of the recommendations to improve children's advertising are based on what seems appropriate rather than on solid evidence (Rossiter, 1980). Even so, children do not have the cognitive sophistication to understand the motives behind the commercials and to resist the messages that are presented so well. Children do need some additional protection.

Advertisements are found only on commercial stations. Prior to the late 1960s, children's programs had little focus. Although some were produced by concerned individuals, they were not based on the needs and abilities of young children, as determined by psychological research. That all changed when public television began showing their blockbuster children's programs "Sesame Street" and "Mister Rogers' Neighborhood." Children's television will never be the same.

Sesame Street.   Big Bird. Grover. Bert and Ernie. Oscar the Grouch. Most preschoolers know these characters quite well. Since 1969 the face of television has irreversibly changed as bold new experiments in television programming demonstrated that children's programs can be both entertaining and educationally valuable. Today, "Sesame Street" is broadcast in fifty countries (Rubinstein, 1978) and watched by millions of preschool children every day.

"Sesame Street" is directed toward teaching inner-city youngsters basic numerical, language, and problem-solving skills (Lesser, 1976). It emphasizes cognitive concerns, although over the years prosocial behavior, tolerance for others, and attitudinal issues have been covered. The producers of "Sesame Street" knew it had to compete with commercial television to be successful (O'Bryan, 1980), that it had to be entertaining as well as educational. The show was fitted to the needs and level of its intended audience. The pace is varied and quick, the now-famous Muppets are present, and animation, splashy color, repetition, and music are used. "Sesame Street" is fun to watch, and children do watch it.

"Sesame Street" is the most evaluated television program in the history of that medium. Children who watch it regularly learn its central concepts and have an advantage over those who do not watch. These advantages seem to hold regardless of the socioeconomic level, sex, or ethnicity of the viewer (Ball and Bogatz, 1972, 1970, Bogatz and Ball, 1971). Children gain more from the program if they watch with a parent, who can interpret the material and act as a guide (Peters, 1977). Children also imitate the cooperation they see if they are placed in a situation like the one on television, but no generalized effects have been found (Watkins et al., 1980).

The show is not without critics. The very fast, perhaps frenetic, pace does not leave room or time for rehearsal (Tower et al., 1979). "Sesame Street" also shows negative behaviors (Coates et al., 1976), such as violence and trickery. Finally, some claim that the effects of the show are not as pronounced as some of the research leads us to believe (Cook et al., 1975).

Mister Rogers' Neighborhood.   A show with a completely different format is "Mister Rogers' Neighborhood." This is a slower-paced, adult-led show that emphasizes interpersonal skills, imagination, and understanding one's emotions (Tower et al., 1979; Singer and Singer, 1976). Research on "Mister Rogers' Neighborhood" shows that it is successful in promoting prosocial behaviors, although the effect is not lasting (Friedrich and Stein, 1973). In one study, for nine weeks preschool children were exposed to daily viewing of either "Mister Rogers' Neighborhood," aggressive cartoons, or neutral programs. Children who saw "Mister Rogers" improved in task persistence and prosocial behavior, such as cooperation. Watching "Mister Rogers" also led to an increase in fantasy play and imagination (Tower et al., 1979; Singer and Singer, 1976). This increase is noteworthy, since fantasy and pretend play are considered important aspects of a child's development (Rubin et al., 1983). Children who show more imaginative play have better social skills, show greater concentration and more positive af-

9. True or False:
Children who watch "Sesame Street" alone gain more than if they watch it with parents.

Mr. Rogers.

fect, are less impulsive, and show more internal control (Tower et al., 1979). The success of "Mister Rogers' Neighborhood" demonstrates that a deliberately slow-paced, repetitive show can be successful in aiding both cognitive and effective development (Singer and Singer, 1983).

"Mister Rogers' Neighborhood" has also been criticized. Its slow pace sometimes makes young children restless (Singer and Singer, 1976), and some parents may have difficulty getting their children to watch the program. But there is a trade-off in pacing. In one study, kindergarten and first-grade children attended more to high-paced programs but showed greater recall for the material in low-paced shows (Wright et al., 1984).

Television has a great potential for helping preschoolers develop cognitively and socially. Commercial television has learned something from the success of these shows, and its offerings have improved. However, television has a long way to go to reach its potential in this area.

Nursery School

Thus far, we have looked at the home environment and television as features of a child's environment that encourage cognitive development. However, more children are now attending nursery school, and an increasing number of school systems have opted for all-day kindergartens. Preschool education is popular with educators. In one survey, three-quarters of the educators questioned believed that school should begin at age three for the average child (Shane and Nelson, 1971).

The Trend Toward Early Childhood Education.   The growth in nursery school attendance is impressive. In 1968, some 33 percent of all the three- to five-year-olds were attending preschool. By 1970, that percentage had increased to 37.5 percent, and by 1983 it stood at 52.5 percent. The percentage of children attending a preschool increases with age. Most five-year-olds attend kindergarten. Still, the number of three- and four-year-olds attending preschools has increased significantly in the past two decades (U.S. Bureau of the Census, 1985). The need for many women to work and the growth of one parent families account for part of the increase (Busch-Rossnagel and Vance, 1982). In other cases, parents worry that unless their children get a preschool education they will enter elementary school at a disadvantage.

Many authorities no longer differentiate between nursery schools and day-care programs. Today, day-care programs, community preschools, and experimental early education programs are all included under the heading of early childhood education (Clarke-Stewart and Fein, 1983). One additional term should be introduced here. **Compensatory education** involves an attempt to compensate for some difference between one group and another. Many preschool programs, such as Head Start, try to help children from economically disadvantaged families develop the attitudes and skills necessary for later success in school.

The Variety of Approaches.   What should the goals of a preschool be? Suppose you would like to send your three-year-old to nursery school. There are two schools in your neighborhood. One focuses on developing cognitive skills,

compensatory education
The use of educational strategies in an attempt to reduce or eliminate some perceived difference between groups.

the other emphasizes social skills and developing healthy attitudes toward learning. Which school would you choose?

Nursery schools vary greatly. One may emphasize social and personal growth—getting along with others and gaining a feeling of mastery over the environment. Another may stress the importance of training the senses and developing motor abilities. Still others may emphasize cognitive growth in one of two ways. A cognitively oriented school may follow a Piagetian format—by structuring the program to encourage children to discover the world around them and to learn from their own experiences. A second cognitive approach emphasizes the teaching of academic skills and uses a behavioral viewpoint involving repetition and reinforcement. Many preschools claim to have goals in all these areas, so putting one school in a particular category can be difficult. Even so, nursery schools can sometimes be classified according to their goals and programs.

The Traditional Nursery School.   The traditional nursery school emphasizes social and emotional development and may not follow any specific educational theory (McClinton and Meier, 1978). The program varies considerably from school to school, but it is often characterized by a great deal of freedom, choice, and flexibility. Activities may include story time, listening to music, moving to music, all types of artistic endeavors, trips in the neighborhood, perhaps to the fire department or a donut shop, growing plants, and observing the environment, along with free play. Children are encouraged to cooperate and share. Some Piagetian influence may be in evidence, as teachers often create situations in which children can learn through self-discovery. When used in education, the term *traditional* unfortunately connotes something old-fashioned and out-of-date. This is not the case here. There is nothing wrong with the goals or practices used in the traditional preschool (Smart and Smart, 1978).

The Montessori School.   Montessori schools, which use the approach developed by Maria Montessori at the beginning of the twentieth century, have gained popularity all over the world. They stress the importance of educating the senses (Cole, 1950), because Montessori believed there is a close relationship between the senses and the intellect. Training the senses lays the groundwork for reading and writing. As Deasey (1978, p. 82) notes, "Passing fingers across the letters with his eyes shut, listening to the names of the letters, and tracing them with his index finger and then a pencil, the Montessori pupil linked the sound of the alphabet with touch, sight and muscluar co-ordination. He had to learn how to write before writing." Every activity in the Montessori school has an educational purpose (Montessori, 1977). For instance, when children color, they do so to improve their ability to hold a writing implement, not to create something beautiful (Cole, 1950).

Many Montessori activities are self-correcting, so that children can proceed at their own rate and no pressure is placed on them. There is no punishment for not finishing an exercise, nor is there much use of reinforcement. In the Montessori classroom, each item has its proper place, and children are expected to keep the room clean and pick up after themselves. The teacher must be specially trained in the Montessori method.

Montessori's system is not without its critics. Play is considered unimportant, and this is troubling to those who consider play to be important part of a

10. *True or False:*
Nursery school activities do not vary much from one school to another.

Preschool programs differ widely in their goals and contents.

child's development (Rubin et al., 1983). Understanding one's emotions is also not a primary goal. Social interaction is present, but it is not really stressed either. Children do not act out plays, nor does the teacher tell stories. There is little use of imagination. These activities are not forbidden, but they are not encouraged. Montessori's methods have been in and out of favor with many educators around the world since their inception. Today, with the emphasis on cognitive growth, they are again in fashion.

The Piagetian Preschool.   If you walked into a traditional preschool, you would see evidences of Piaget's influence. Some ideas from one philosophy or practice are often accepted by others. Montessori's idea of using child-sized furniture is now the norm in preschools. Piaget's ideas of learning through doing are also accepted. In contrast to the Montessori method, Piagetian-based preschools stress play as a learning activity. During play, children are exposed to the viewpoints of others, which challenge their egocentric view of the world. Developing curiosity, independence, and self-confidence, learning to cooperate, and gaining physical control of the environment are definite goals. In the Piagetian preschool, children are not given formal instruction. Instead, teachers act as guides, helping children discover things through active participation. The children are exposed to a wide range of materials that help them gain experience in classification and seriation.

The Englemann-Bereiter Approach.   Nowhere is the goal of academic growth addressed as much as in the program developed by Englemann and Bereiter known as DISTAR. In this program, children are taught the concepts that are considered necessary by the educational staff. The teacher has an objective and presents the material in a standardized fashion to small groups of children for about 20 minutes or so with periods of rest, music, or other activities alternating with instructional periods. The exchanges are rapid, and the teacher reinforces the children for the correct answers. This is a teaching approach, and it is based on the idea that children can be taught the desired concepts if the material is presented clearly and appropriately. For example, children may be taught the concept of equality—that both sides of an equation must be equal. The teacher may present the concept in an appropriate way, ask the children questions, and give much positive reinforcement for the correct responses. Englemann and Bereiter argue that disadvantaged children require additional help in cognitive areas, especially language. Their program is an attempt to provide such cognitive training.

Do Nursery Schools Achieve Their Goals?

Generally speaking, nursery schools accomplish their purposes. Research indicates that children who attend nursery schools are generally more advanced than their nonattending peers. This is especially true for children in the lower-income groups (Minuchin and Shapiro, 1983). Children who attend preschool programs are more socially competent, outgoing, self-assured, curious, independent, and persistent on a task than those who do not attend. In elementary school, they are better adjusted and more task-oriented, goal-directed, persistent, cooperative, and friendly (Clarke-Stewart and Fein, 1983). In a review of 56 studies of children attending nursery school, only 3 showed no difference between those attending and those not attending (Sjolund, 1971). Some 53 showed advantages for those attending preschools. Of 36 studies on the cognitive development of children attending and not attending nursery school, 21 found higher

11. *True or False:*
Generally speaking, children from lower-income groups who attend nursery school are more cognitively advanced than their peers who do not attend such programs.

ACTION/
REACTION

The Nursery School Gambit

Anna and Al decided to send their three-year-old daughter, Lindsay, to nursery school, choosing one that was close to home with an excellent reputation. They believed that Lindsay was very bright, and they wanted the teacher to introduce her to letter sounds and concepts that would lead to early reading and writing.

After three months in the school, they saw no visible improvement and went to see the teacher, Ms. Baxter. The teacher explained that the purpose of nursery school was not to teach children to read but to help them develop social skills and a feeling that learning is enjoyable. In the school's program, children learn to cooperate with one another and learn about the world in which they live. They are even "studying" dinosaurs. Ms. Baxter also noted that forcing children to read at an early age is undesirable, that they will learn when they are ready.

But Anna and Al are not satisfied. They believe that Lindsay is ready for more than she is getting. They wonder whether they should switch to another nursery school.

1. If you were Lindsay's parents, what would you do?
2. If you were Lindsay's teacher, would you have explained the school's philosophy any differently?

intellectual performance for children who attended nursery school (Sjolund, 1971).

Comparing Nursery School Approaches

Studies comparing the various preschools have been difficult to evaluate. Most measured intellectual and cognitive growth, and their findings are equivocal (Minuchin and Shapiro, 1983). Miller and Dyer (1975) conducted a careful study comparing the effects of the (1) Engelmann-Bereiter approach, (2) the Montessori approach, (3) a program called Darcee, which emphasized parental involvement, development of good work habits, positive attitudes towards learning, and cognitive growth, and (4) an enrichment program that was similar to a traditional nursery school program. Four-year-olds from impoverished backgrounds were assigned at random to fourteen classes: two Montessori, four traditional, four DISTAR (Englemann-Bereiter), and four DARCEE. The children were carefully tested and compared not only with each other but also with a group of children who did not attend any preschool. The children were followed through the preschool program and into kindergarten, first grade, and second grade.

Regardless of which preschool the children attended, all showed gains in both cognitive and noncognitive skills and were superior to those who did not attend preschool. However, in comparing the approaches with one another, Miller and Dyer found that each approach was successful in reaching its own goals. The DARCEE group was most successful in motivation and attitude change, the DISTAR group was most successful in teaching cognitive skills, the enriched traditional program increased curiosity in the children, and the Montessori children scored high on inventiveness and curiosity. Continued observation of the children through the first and second grades indicated that the gains in intelligence did not last, while the noncognitive gains remained. These children were more curious and less aggressive than those who had not attended preschools. The intelligence gains that appear at the end of preschool programs may not last, whereas changes in attitudes and increases in curiosity and task perseverance are more stable.

A follow-up of these students in the sixth, seventh, and eighth grades was also conducted (Miller and Bizzell, 1983). Intelligence scores did not differ much among the groups attending different types of preschools, but differences in reading and math skills were found to be related to the type of preschool program and to the sex of the child. Males from the Montessori and the traditional programs were significantly better in reading than those from the Englemann-Bereiter and DARCEE projects. The Montessori males scored the highest, averaging seven points higher than their nearest rival—the traditional group of boys. In math as well, the Montessori males were more advanced. This was not evident until eighth grade, when they were significantly better than the Englemann-Bereiter males, the closest group. Females from the Englemann-Bereiter and DARCEE programs were superior to those from the other two programs in reading, but no differences in math were found. The researchers note that the superiority of the Montessori children in achievement, which began to show itself at the end of second grade, was still present at the end of the sixth grade, and this superiority was primarily shown by the males. A later follow-up of these children in ninth and tenth grade again demonstrated the superiority of males from the Montessori program and females attending the DARCEE program (Miller and Bizzell, 1984).

It is difficult to draw any firm conclusions from this one series of studies. Certainly the Montessori method as measured on academic variables appears to be of great benefit, especially to males, but if other variables were used, there might be different results. All approaches can claim some school-related gains. Studies show that preschool graduates are less likely to be retained in grade or found in remedial classes (Lazar et al., 1982). In order to firmly establish one method as greatly superior to any others, more research using a number of variables is needed.

PROJECT HEAD START

The finding that children, especially from poor backgrounds, are likely to benefit from the preschool experience is important (Lazar et al., 1982). If children from poverty backgrounds enter school behind their middle-class counterparts, these children are likely to fall further behind as they progress through school. Perhaps if these children could attend a preschool that would help compensate for their different experiences, this cycle could be stopped and they would have a reasonable chance for academic success. This was partially the thinking behind one of the greatest educational and social experiments of the past fifty years: Project Head Start (Cooke, 1979).

Since its inception in 1964, millions of American children have taken part in the great experiment called **Project Head Start** (Zigler and Valentine, 1979), and the program still continues today (see Figure 9.9). Head Start was developed at a time when we were ready to conquer poverty (Zigler and Anderson, 1979) and when the dominant view in psychology emphasized the plasticity of cognitive development. The hope was that a program instituted early enough could give children in poverty situations a head start in school and reduce or eliminate the class differences in educational achievement that were so noticeable (Zigler and Berman, 1983).

Project Head Start
A massive federal compensatory education project aimed at reducing or eliminating the differences in educational achievement between poor and middle-class youngsters.

The Head Start Program

Head Start is far from being a unified program. Although each Head Start center is governed by guidelines, the programs are not standardized. Different Head Start centers emphasize different areas of concern. Two children may attend Head Start centers, and yet their experiences could be, and probably are, very different. While it is true that Head Start was initiated to try to break the cycle of poor school achievement, it had other noncognitive goals (Richmond et al., 1979). Head Start encouraged programs that would help children "learn to work and play independently; become able to accept help and directions from adults; learn competence and worth; sharpen and widen language skills; be curious; grow in ability to channel inner, destructive impulses" (Head Start Rainbow Book No. 4, 1965, cited in Miller, 1979). There were also health goals (Richmond et al., 1979). Besides the diversity intentionally built in to allow for innovation, a number of experimental model programs were run (Miller, 1979). Cognitive growth was not viewed as divorced from social and emotional development, and an attempt was made to educate the whole child.

FIGURE 9.9 **Head Start Program Enrollment, 1965–1982**
The Head Start Program involves hundreds of thousands of children in preschool activities.

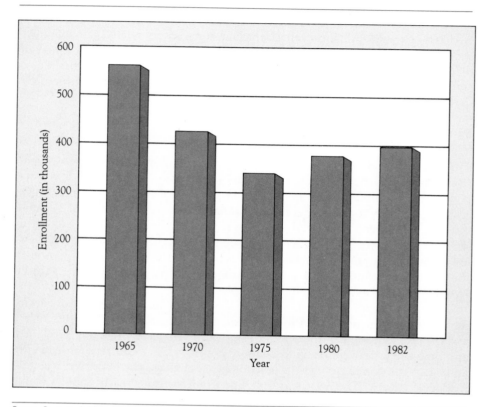

Source: Statistical Abstract of the United States, 1985.

Evaluations of Head Start

Hopes were high for Project Head Start, but soon controversy, disappointment, and disillusionment set in. The first evaluations were impressive. Studies showed sizable gains in cognitive abilities and self-esteem (Zigler and Berman, 1983), but it was soon found that the intelligence gains noted did not continue as the child progressed through second and third grade (Weinberg, 1979; Westinghouse Study, 1969). This was often called the fade-out phenomenon (Weinberg, 1979). In other words, the cognitive gains were temporary, and by the second grade or so, Head Start children did not differ from their classmates in intelligence. This led to a period of intense skepticism on the part of critics, and defensiveness on the part of the program's supporters.

The determination of the program's advocates to see the program through its hard times was rewarded, for more recent research demonstrates the beneficial effects of the Head Start experience. They are obvious—once you know where to look. The later studies looked at other measures besides intelligence and reported that students who attended a Head Start program were significantly less likely to be retained in grade or to be found in special education classes. The results of studies concerning the reading and math achievement of children who attended a Head Start program are mixed, with some showing Head Start children achieving more in math and reading (Lazar and Darlington, 1982; Darlington et al., 1980; Palmer and Andersen, 1979).

Other advantages have been found, especially for Head Start programs in which parental participation is encouraged and high (Mann et al., 1978). Involvement in the program is often the first community involvement for many parents. In one Wisconsin community, not only did a majority of the parents become involved in the program, but 44 percent continued to serve in other community organizations for years after (Zigler and Berman, 1983). Parental involvement helps parents deal with younger siblings as well. Gray and Klaus (1970) found that the younger siblings of children who had attended the program had significantly higher intelligence scores, perhaps because the improved parental interactions carried over to other children. On the whole, Head Start has been successful.

The Future of Compensatory Education

What of the future of Head Start and other compensatory education programs? Experience tells us that we should not rely on the IQ as a valid measurement of

---

RESEARCH HIGHLIGHT *How Effective Is Early Childhood Education?*

The positive short-term effects of preschool programs are now well established, but what about their long-term effects? Do they have any lasting positive effects, or do their benefits fade out during elementary school? A group of investigators collaborated on a research effort specifically designed to measure the long-term effects of such programs. These researchers conducted studies of preschool programs in the 1960s and performed follow-ups when their subjects, most of whom were from lower-income backgrounds, were between nine and nineteen years old. The data was combined and analyzed by Irving Lazar and Richard Darlington.

The results indicated that preschool programs do have important long-term effects in all four outcome areas studied: school competence, abilities, attitudes, and selected family outcomes. Children attending these programs were less likely to be left back or placed in special-education classes. Early education also improved children's performance on intelligence tests and achievement tests. The improvements in intelligence were not permanent, but program graduates performed better academically than those who did not attend preschool programs. They also manifested a more positive attitude toward academic achievement and school. Finally, mothers of children

who attended were more satisfied with their children's school performance and had consistently higher occupational expectations for them.

The researchers did not find these programs more effective for any one group. For instance, there was no evidence that boys were more affected than girls, or that children from one-parent families gained more than children from intact families.

We now have evidence from these well-designed studies that early childhood education programs do have important long-term positive effects. Consider, for example, the reduction in the number of children left back or placed in remedial classes. Educationally, it is surely better for children to progress through a regular educational program whenever possible. Economically, retaining a child in grade or placing the child in a special remedial class is expensive. In short, the effects of preschool programs do last. Such programs are a relatively small investment that can yield large dividends later on.

Source: I. Lazar et al., "Lasting Effects of Early Education: A Report from the Consortium for Longitudinal Studies," *Monographs of the Society for Research in Child Development,* Serial Number 195, 1982, 47, Nos. 2–3.

the outcome, that we need to look at the broader picture. It also shows that we must continue to perform longitudinal long-term studies of early childhood intervention programs (Weinberg, 1979). We also must tailor programs to the individual differences in children's cognitive styles and learning patterns and understand the nature of the child's motivation. Since parental involvement is so important, we should strive to increase it (Sprigle and Schaefer, 1985), as well as to help parents improve their parenting skills through participation in parent education programs. Finally, the history of Head Start is one of great ups and downs that can be blamed on premature and overly dramatic interpretations of research findings. The earliest highs and subsequent lows indicate that educators must be extremely cautious in noting successes and prematurely criticizing failures. It is also important to take an in-depth look at testing procedures with young children and be aware of the difficulties in this area.

TESTING THE PRESCHOOL CHILD

The Difficulties of Testing Preschoolers

Imagine you are a school psychologist who has been asked to test an active four- or five-year-old girl. While you are trying to administer the test, her attention is elsewhere. She soon gets bored with the testing process, and becomes frustrated if she doesn't know something. At times you are not certain she understands your questions. What do you do?

Psychologists are sometimes faced with this situation when testing preschool children, many of whom are not noted for their cooperativeness or attention span. The testing situation must be viewed from two points of view. The psychologist is trying to find out something of interest about the child, from the child's perspective, the whole process is unimportant. Children often show little or no interest in their own performance (Sattler, 1974). This is especially disturbing because tests are predicated on the idea that people will try to do as well as they can on a test.

Many suggestions have been made for improving the test performance of preschoolers, including ridding the room of such distractions as toys, making the room cheery, adjusting the speed of administering the test to the individual child, watching for signs of fatigue or boredom, being friendly, and praising the child (Goodenough, 1949, in Sattler, 1974). These are excellent suggestions, but they do not eliminate the difficulty.

Intelligence Testing

A number of intelligence tests can be used with preschoolers. One of the best known is the Wechsler Preschool and Primary Scale of Intelligence (WPPSI). This test contains a number of subtests, which yield a performance score, a verbal score, and a composite intelligence score. Examples of verbal subtests are vocabulary, arithmetic, similarities, and comprehension. Subtests such as block design (making shapes from blocks) and picture completion (telling the examiner what is wrong in a picture) are typical of the performance subtests.

Problems and Pitfalls

The problems involved in using preschool intelligence tests rest not only on the difficulties of testing all preschoolers but also on the reasons for testing them, the possibilities for abuse, and the confounding influence of motivation on the child. It is well to question why a preschooler's intelligence must be measured. In the case of Head Start, the intelligence test was basically a research tool to evaluate the program. The test administrators did not contemplate taking any action concerning any individual child on the basis of the test performance.

However, the use of intelligence tests to categorize children at an early age can lead to problems. It is possible to justify intelligence testing if it is believed that there is a problem that requires remediation, but the very existence of a handicap may make testing impractical. Before any test is administered, some idea of why the test is being given and how the results will be used should be forthcoming. In addition, the problem of abuse has been especially bothersome in this area. A child could be labeled for life by someone who does not understand intelligence testing well and misinterprets the results.

The last problem is probably the most difficult to overcome. In early childhood, the relationship between motivation and cognition is great. In fact, motivation and cognition form a generalized competence factor (Scarr, 1981). Since motivational and emotional factors influence the results, we must be cautious in interpreting intelligence scores.

Reading-Readiness Tests

Reading-readiness tests are commonly given in kindergarten or early first grade. One of the major tasks of elementary school is to teach children to read. Basically these tests tell whether a child has the necessary skills to learn to read (Brown, 1983). Such skills as identifying consonants, sound-letter understanding, matching, listening skills, auditory and visual discrimination, perceptual motor coordination, and the like are commonly tested. These tests allow teachers to evaluate the child's skill level. If a problem is discovered, a decision as to the best course of remedial action can be made.

Reading readiness and intelligence are related (Jensen, 1980; Anastasi, 1976). However, at the end of the first year, reading-readiness tests are better predictors of achievement than intelligence tests. This is not surprising, since they are designed to assess the specific areas necessary to succeed in learning to read (Anastasi, 1976).

reading-readiness tests
Tests that measure a child's attainment of the skills necessary for success in reading.

12. *True or False:*
Reading-readiness tests can be used to predict how well a child will learn to read in first grade.

QUESTIONS FOR THE FUTURE

As we have seen, cognitive development during the preschool period is impressive. Piaget described the preschooler's abilities and limitations, while new research shows just how sensitive young children are to the type of task and environment surrounding the challenge. Psychologists have gained a genuine respect for the preschool child's abilities.

We now also have a better understanding of how important it is for children to be ready for the formal school experience. As more children experience some type of preschool education, two questions constantly appear. First, how is progress to be measured—on a single factor, such as intelligence or reading achievement, or on a broader measure, which may include personal growth and other factors along with cognitive measures? Second, should academic demands be made on these young children (Maeroff, 1983)? Should nursery schools specialize in helping children gain social skills and develop a positive attitude toward school, or should they try to impart information and skills in some semi-formal manner? There is no single answer to these questions, and only further research can give us information on the possibilities and problems involved in adopting a particular course of action.

In the midst of our tremendous interest in preschool education and cognitive development, we should not forget that children are more than just cognitive beings. Their social and personal development must also be recognized and appreciated. It is to the preschooler's development in these areas that we turn to next.

Chapter Summary

1. During the preschool years, the rate of growth declines.

2. Preschoolers develop a number of motor skills, including jumping, running, and hopping. The development of the large muscles precedes that of the fine muscles.

3. The leading cause of death among preschoolers is accidents, some of which can be prevented.

4. According to Piagetian theory, children between about two and seven are in the preoperational stage. These children can now use symbols and have the capacity to view an action, remember it, and repeat it later.

5. Children in the preoperational stage also tend to be egocentric (see everything from their own point of view), believe that everything is capable of being conscious and alive, and reason transductively (from specific event to specific event).

6. Preschoolers have difficulty placing things in size order (seriation) and at least at the beginning of this stage have problems sorting items into different classes (classification).

7. Preschoolers cannot solve conservation problems (challenges that involve the understanding that quantities remain the same even if their appearance changes). Their tendency to center on one dimension and their inability to reverse operations and to understand transformations are responsible for their problems in this area.

8. New evidence shows that many of these abilities are present if preschoolers are tested on tasks that are meaningful to them, simple, and clearly defined. However, these abilities are fragile, and preschoolers will not show these skills all the time.

9. Preschoolers do not spontaneously use verbal strategies, such as rehearsal, as memory aids, but they do show such strategies as looking and pointing. Children do better in familiar situations and with tasks that are meaningful.

10. Parents who label the environment, encourage their children's curiosity, and read to them tend to maximize their children's cognitive development.

11. Advertising aimed at children is very effective. Children often ask for the products they see on television.

12. "Sesame Street" and "Mister Roger's Neighborhood" are two successful television shows combining entertainment with education.

13. More and more preschoolers are attending early childhood education programs. These programs differ in philosophy and methods of teaching. The evidence generally shows that children who attend preschools gain from the experience. Each type of preschool is successful in developing areas of competence that it views as most important.

14. Project Head Start is an attempt to provide experiences to help close the gap between children from lower socioeconomic backgrounds and their peers from middle-class backgrounds. While the immediate gains in intelligence are not sustained throughout elementary school, children who attend these programs are less likely to be left back or to be found in special education classes. Some studies show that they do better in math and reading as well.

15. Testing the preschool child is difficult because preschoolers become bored and easily distracted during testing procedures. Although some measures of intelligence do exist, they should be administered and interpreted with care.

16. Measures of reading readiness often help teachers diagnose specific problems that might hinder a child's ability to learn to read.

■ *Answers to True or False Questions*

1. *False.* Correct statement: The rate of growth decreases markedly during early childhood.

2. *False.* Correct statement: If measurements are taken often and carefully, a rather constant rate of growth within a particular period is found.

3. *True.* Accidents are the number-one cause of death during early childhood.

4. *False.* Correct statement: Even though new research shows that preschoolers can do more than we originally thought, their logic does not approach that of the average adult.

5. *False.* Correct statement: Preschoolers may use rehearsal if they are directed to do so on a particular task, but do not use it on their own.

6. *False.* Correct statement: The conservative figure for television-watching by preschoolers is three to four hours a day.

7. *True.* Children who view commercials aimed specifically at them often ask their parents for the item.

8. *False.* Correct statement: New evidence shows that preschoolers can tell the difference between the commercials and the programs, but do not understand the motives behind the advertising.

9. *False.* Correct statement: Children who watch "Sesame Street" with a parent learn more from the show than if they watch it by themselves.

10. *False.* Correct statement: Although many nursery schools have incorporated methods from a variety of specific programs, there are significant differences between nursery schools based on the Piagetian, Montessori, and Englemann-Bereiter approaches.

11. *True.* Children who attend nursery schools gain from such programs.

12. *True.* Correct statement: Reading-readiness tests can be helpful in predicting who will have difficulty learning to read.

CHAPTER TEN

Social and Personality Development in Early Childhood

■ *Are the Following Statements True or False?*

Try the True-False Quiz below. See if your answers correspond to the information in this chapter. Each question is repeated opposite the paragraph in which the answer can be found. The True-False Answer Box at the end of the chapter lists complete answers.

___ **1.** Boys show significantly more rough-and-tumble play than girls.

___ **2.** Parents should never interfere in sibling arguments.

___ **3.** Children of parents who allow the child maximum freedom with few if any restrictions are usually self-reliant and show excellent self-control.

___ **4.** In the long run, the more severe the punishment, the more likely the child is to refrain from misbehaving.

___ **5.** The incidence of sexual abuse is overreported to the police.

___ **6.** Parents who abuse their children have a distinct personality profile.

___ **7.** A child's personality may predispose the child to abuse.

___ **8.** Research has not yet established any consistent differences in personality or behavior between the sexes.

___ **9.** Girls generally receive more punishment than boys, while boys receive more praise.

___ **10.** Fathers are more likely than mothers to treat their sons and daughters equally.

"After I cook dinner, I'm going to read the newspaper and play with my children," four-year-old Matthew announced while playing in nursery school. The teacher was astonished and decided to explore this unusual statement with Matthew's mother during a regular parent-teacher conference. "Well, it's simple," Matthew's mother explained. "When my husband comes home from work, he always asks me what's for dinner. I usually reply, Anything *you* cook. You see, my husband is an excellent cook. He cooks, and I clean up." As far as Matthew is concerned, cooking is part of a male's role.

Parents are often fascinated by their preschooler's play. One mother watched her two preschool children pretend to argue. After a minute or so, one child sat down to read an imaginary newspaper, while the other just looked annoyed. Finally, the child who was reading turned to the other and said, "Darn it, I don't know what you *suspect* of me." That evening she told her husband about the little scene. "Is that how they see us?" he asked, a bit embarrassed. "Isn't that the way it happens?" the mother retorted, with less of a smile.

In their play, children often imitate what they see around them, but the result is not always accurate. Children interpret what they see and hear, often making mistakes, such as when the child used the word *suspect* instead of *expect*.

Carper (1978) describes a dialogue between two four-year-olds in a nursery school setting. The little boy told a female peer, "You stay home with the mommies and the babies. I'm going fishing." When the little girl protested that she wanted to come too, she was quieted by a promise to take her to a Chinese restaurant when he got home. The teacher reported this confrontation to the boy's mother, who told her that the only time her husband went fishing the whole family came along.

Carper reminds us that children's's play does not always accurately reflect home surroundings. Play can be very imaginative. In fact, the ability to use imagination is a major difference between toddlers and preschoolers. There are other differences too. Children between the ages of three and six have gained many skills. While the toddler still stumbles a bit, five-year-olds confidently show off their motor abilities. Their powers of comprehension and speech are far superior to what they were in the toddler stage. Five-year-olds understand more of what is going on around them and can play with, not just alongside, other children.

Erik Erikson (1968) notes that at this age the child's social world has opened up, and it challenges the youngster to master new skills. The ability to walk, run, and talk allows the child to interact with peers. Preschool children can plan, and they enjoy being on the move and taking the initiative (Erikson, 1963). Erikson considers **initiative** the positive outcome of this preschool stage, while the negative outcome is **guilt**. If parents appreciate the importance of encouraging their preschooler's self-guided initiatives and curiosity, the child will leave the stage with a sense of initiative. If a child's curiosity and activities become bothersome to parents, and they react with verbal scorn and restrictions, the child is likely to become timid and fearful.

In this chapter we will look at the preschooler's growing social relationships. Specifically, such areas as play, parental and sibling relationships, child abuse, and sex roles will be explored. The preschooler's social world expands greatly. It is in early childhood that children become aware that they will be males or females forever. It is during the preschool period that children show a noticeable

initiative
The positive outcome of the psychosocial crisis of the early childhood period, involving development of a respect for one's own wishes and desires.

guilt
The negative outcome of the psychosocial crisis of the early childhood period, resulting in a sense that the child's acts and desires are bad.

increase in social interactions with other children. It is in early childhood that many children will, for the first time, be away from home under the watchful eyes of a nursery school teacher and be forced by circumstances to get along with others. These patterns make this period one of tremendous change and growth.

THE MYSTERIES OF PLAY

What Is Play?

Play is such an obvious part of childhood that one would think that our knowledge of the subject would be massive, but we actually know very little about play (Weisler and McCall, 1976). One reason is that play itself has defied definition.

Stop to think about it. Just what is play? Do adults play too? Is a child painstakingly assembling a model of the starship *Enterprise* with a determined look playing? No single definition of play is accepted today, but this does not mean that we cannot study it, for play has some unique characteristics (Vandenberg, 1978).

Play is an activity that is performed for sheer enjoyment with no ulterior motive. The focus of play is on the child rather than on what the child is holding, bouncing, or coloring. Play activities are performed for their own sake (Vandenberg, 1978); there is no payoff in candy, attention, or money. Finally, play is enjoyable.

Exploration is not identical to play. Exploration occurs prior to play. Exploratory behavior is dominated by the object or situation and entails an element of uncertainty (Weisler and McCall, 1976). Play, unlike exploration, is more likely to occur when children feel safe and secure (Switzky et al., 1974). A child entering a new environment may look around, then proceed to explore it. Or the child may not be happy about being in a novel environment and may show signs of stress. While play engenders a positive mood, exploration does not always do so.

Why Do Children Play?

Two young boys were asked why they continued to throw a rubber ball to each other for hours at a time. The boys answered, "We like it." When asked what they liked about the activity, the children just shrugged their shoulders. To the casual observer, the activity seems to have little value or purpose.

Isolating the functions of play is difficult. For some activity to be considered play, it must be voluntary, enjoyable, and essentially purposeless. The fact that the activity is enjoyable masks the fact that play is essential to a child's development. Since we often think that only work is valuable, we overlook all the possible values of play.

For instance, the children playing ball are exercising their muscles and improving their eye-hand coordination. Play often involves muscular activity, which is vital for optimal physical development. Play also helps develop a child's mental abilities. Preschoolers often use their imagination during play. They may imagine themselves flying, or take on the role of some fictional character. Through such play, they develop their problem-solving abilities and their mental abilities. Children often exchange roles during play, pretending that they are

Child's play! Play serves many functions in childhood.

play
An activity dominated by the child and performed with a positive feeling.

doctors, nurses, fathers, and mothers. This encourages them to begin to understand the roles of others. This sort of play becomes more sophisticated during middle childhood.

The social functions of play are more obvious. Children who play with others soon learn the need for cooperation and sharing. They learn that they may not always win, that compromises are sometimes necessary. Their interactions with other children teach them the social skills necessary to live in society.

Play is also a vehicle for learning skills that will be useful later in life. In primates, play serves the purpose of allowing the organism to learn particular skills without fearing the unpleasant consequences of failure (Bruner, 1972). Skills can be mastered in a nonthreatening environment and then used to solve problems later in life. Bruner theorizes that an ape's ability to use tools comes from early play experiences. Perhaps when children play with building blocks they learn something about mechanics, spatial relationships, and tool use that may be helpful at a later date.

A child's skills improve with practice. At first, the child may explore the toy and finally put two blocks together. As the months pass, the child becomes better at building, and this increased sophistication can be seen in the sturdiness of a construction. Children can now pile many blocks on top of each other, supporting them with other blocks. Children's movements take on a refined look. When the blocks are first introduced, a child's attempts are jerky and show no appreciation of space or form, but with practice a smoother style manifests itself, and the child builds many different structures. Every finished structure really contains a number of substructures, each of which took time to learn. These substructures are finally combined, giving the project a relatively polished look. Through play, children learn how to combine these subroutines and use their minds in a creative manner to solve problems.

In addition, children at this age can control situations while playing that are impossible in real life. Through play, young children create a world in which they can increase their control and dominate situations. They use play to cope with a sense of powerlessness.

Play is also an outlet for pent-up frustration and anger. Children can express some of their anger in a safe and secure environment. This is essentially the Freudian or psychoanalytic viewpoint. Children act out their problems and thereby reduce their anxieties (Erikson, 1959). One four-year-old played house with small doll-like figures. At home, this little girl had to share the attention of her parents with her baby sister, who naturally required much care. In her play, Daddy would come home and instead of kissing her and going to see the baby, he would way, "I want to play only with you, not that silly baby. I don't care about her." In her play, she was expressing her true feelings. Observing a child's play often allows professionals to gain deeper insights into a child's problems (Axline, 1969).

Children are also able to experiment with new roles, and they often reverse them from one of submission to dominance. This role reversal is a salient feature of play (Sutton-Smith and Roberts, 1981). The five-year-old acting the part of a doctor has experienced being a patient quite often. In play, children try out other roles. They can actually control the behavior of the people in these roles in a way that is impossible in the real world. Once children realize that they will not be ridiculed or made to suffer the consequences of a mistake, they will try out new ways of behaving and relating to other people. Thus, play becomes a vehicle for exploring new ways of acting, in a safe and secure environment.

The Development of Play

Try this experiment. Visit a playground and watch the children play. Try to estimate their ages, and then note *how* they are playing. You will probably notice a definite progression (Rubin et al., 1983).

A baby is probably uninvolved with the other children. Anything that occurs may be of interest to the infant for only a few seconds. Such unoccupied behavior is the first stage of play, since these children may stroke their bodies, play with their hands, or hug a stuffed animal. Later in the first year, children play with simple toys, banging them against something or dropping them. They are basically exploring the properties of the toy and are uninvolved with any other children around them. They may play simple peek-a-boo games with a parent, but the other individual is essentially a toy, and no mutuality is evidenced.

Solitary or independent play can be seen in young children and remains important in the second and third year of life. However, the transition to a more social type of play can be seen in what Parten (1932) has called **onlooker play**. During this stage, children watch others with considerable interest and frequently ask questions about what they are doing. Yet they are not able to join in, and thus remain on the outside. This leads to a type of play in which children may seek out the company of others but still not interact with them.

During the second year, children are often brought together with their peers. These two-year-olds engage in **parallel play**. They play in the presence of other children, but not with them. They do not really interact or cooperate with one another. We get the feeling that if one child left, the other could go on without any problem. The quality of the sand castles built by either child does not depend on the participation of the other. Parallel play is found throughout the preschool period, but it decreases with age. It is the primary play behavior in two-year-olds and in some three-year-olds (Smith, 1978).

Active interaction with others emerges during early childhood. Preschoolers actively **associate** with other children and may share, cooperate, have verbal arguments, and play together, but few of these periods are sustained. There is a flightiness to the play and their interactions with others. Much of the play of preschoolers involves physical practice of skills that have been, or are being, mastered. Their play is active and physically exhausting.

Beginning in the later part of the preschool period and continuing into middle childhood, children actively **cooperate** with each other. This involves a more-or-less unified group playing a particular game, often in which one or two children lead. Children are able to take specific parts in a game, and they have a more mature understanding of what their role is in the group. If you watch a group of five-, six- or seven-year-olds at the park, you may see this type of behavior. Some children act as leaders and allot roles to the others. Sometimes rebellions break out in the ranks, but their need for one another is obvious.

Between the late toddler stage and the late preschool stage, the importance of the peer group changes. The toddler may have an occasional interaction, almost accidental at times, with another child, but the late preschooler is actively involved in cooperating and sharing. Many of this child's activities show a need for other children the same age. The amount of social and dramatic play also increases.

Dramatic play involves taking the roles of others. This requires imitation and the ability to place oneself in the position of another. As we discussed in Chapter Nine, this ability is very primitive in preschoolers, but it develops as children find themselves in different social situations. Preschoolers are essentially

---

solitary play
Independent play in which the child shows no interest in the activities of others.

onlooker play
A classification of play in which the child watches others play and shows some interest, but is unable to join in.

parallel play
A type of play common in two-year-olds in which they play in the presence of other children but not with them.

associative play
A type of play seen in preschoolers who are actively involved with one another but cannot sustain these interactions.

cooperative play
A type of play seen in the later part of the preschool period and continuing into middle childhood, marked by group play, playing specific roles, and active cooperation for sustained periods of time.

dramatic play
A type of play in which children take on the roles of others.

egocentric, but you can see some attempts at role-taking in their dramatic play. Usually this play takes a standard form. Garvey (1977) observed a number of preschool children at play. Each child was paired with another and allowed to play undisturbed in a room that contained a number of play materials. Children as young as two and three years of age engaged in some dramatic play, often involving mother and infants. Most of the dramatic play centered on common home situations and everyday challenges. However, some involved participation in fantasy, including protecting others from monsters and putting themselves in fairy tales as characters. This dramatic play was spontaneous and flexible. The sophistication of such play increased with age.

Sex Differences in Play

As you watch the children play, see if you notice any sex differences. Many studies indicate that boys and girls play in characteristic fashions. Simply stated, boys play much more roughly than girls. This difference is also seen in animal studies performed on chimpanzees. When chimps were allowed contact only with their peers, characteristic play patterns could be seen. The males were more aggressive. Since they were separated from their parents at birth, they could not have learned these patterns from them, and some biological factor, perhaps hormones, must be responsible (Harlow and Harlow, 1966).

Humans also show these sex differences in play. Males are both more aggressive and show more rough-and-tumble play. This difference appears in cultures around the world, whether essentially tribal or technologically advanced (Whiting and Whiting, 1975). We are not talking about mere variations in activity level, for preschool girls are almost as active as preschool boys. However, girls seldom act aggressively toward one another or engage in rough-and-tumble play.

Sex differences in play are well documented. DiPietro (1981) brought same-sex groups of four-and-a-half-year-old children three at a time into a mobile home from which the furnishings had been removed. A few toys were present, including a beach ball, a small trampoline, and a Bobo doll. DiPietro noted that the girls organized themselves and made rules. The girls argued, but they did not resort to physical means of persuasion. The boys, however, played in a rougher fashion, often wrestling. They did not seem angry, nor did they attempt to injure one another. They simply played differently.

It is difficult to perform the kind of controlled studies necessary to understand the causes of sex differences. As we will see later in the chapter, this is a field of great interest and controversy at the present time. Although Harlow's experiments with chimps are interesting and suggestive, they are not conclusive. Such research may suggest models and hypotheses, but we must be careful when we try to generalize from animal research to human beings. Any cross-species generalizations are dangerous. Research on cats may not generalize to dogs or horses, let alone to human beings. We may question whether the same cognitive processes involved in thinking, planning, and interpreting, which are so obvious in human beings, should be automatically ascribed to other species. Although animal research is interesting, generalizations should be made with care.

While some may argue that males are biologically predisposed to aggressive patterns, other explanations are possible. For example, various societies may expect males to act more aggressively, so males may then simply be complying with

1. *True or False:*
Boys show significantly more rough-and-tumble play than girls.

society's expectations. The possible presence of some biological predisposition does not negate the importance of learning.

THE RISE OF THE PEER GROUP

In their play, preschoolers are more socially oriented than toddlers and prefer to play with familiar peers (Rubin et al., 1983). As the child's interpersonal world expands in early childhood, peers gain influence.

With increasing age, children spend more time with their peers and less with their parents. While the peer group does not have the power it will have during middle childhood and adolescence, it still influences the preschooler. The growth of early childhood programs has exposed many more children to the social demands of other children very early. While toddlers show some ability to participate in social activities, it is in early childhood that these activities become closer to what we might call friendship. A considerable degree of sharing and cooperation begins to manifest itself, and the play of the child becomes more social, more dramatic, and more sophisticated. As preschoolers mature, the number of children they play with at one time also increases. Preschoolers are no longer merely limited to one-on-one situations. Groups of three and four children are not uncommon.

Most of the preschooler's interactions with others are positive (Hartup, 1970). Fewer arguments occur than one might think. Children are accepted on the basis of how friendly and outgoing they are. Preschoolers are not very sympathetic to others, probably because of their egocentric mentality. However, cooperation as well as competition increase with age.

The peer experience sometimes modifies parental authority, but the preschooler's family remains the primary influence on the child's activities. Parents and siblings are still the most significant persons in the interpersonal environment of the child.

SIBLINGS

"My children fight like cats and dogs," a mother of two active boys told me one night. She had come for counseling because she could no longer take the noise, the bickering, the constant fighting. She and her husband had just broken up some "vicious" verbal exchanges, and peace seemed unobtainable.

Can you remember the arguments you had with your siblings? Can you remember the times you depended on them for advice and assistance? The very presence of siblings affects a child's development. Unlike friends, siblings do not leave your home at night. You can limit your contact with them, but you cannot totally avoid them. They compete for parental attention, and their joys and pains affect everyone in the household.

Sibling Support

Discussions of siblings usually revolve around sibling rivalry, but psychologists have noted that siblings encourage prosocial actions and fill definite psychologi-

A Case of Jealousy

What does it mean to treat children equally? The Smiths must answer that question. They have two sons: Jerry, age six, and Henry, age four. Henry needs more attention. He has suffered from continuous health problems, some of which are moderately serious, and tends to be depressed because he can't always play with friends. Henry must be kept still, which sometimes means giving in to his whims and spending a great deal of time with him. Although Jerry knows his brother has not been well, he is jealous of the attention Henry gets and tries to put him down as much as possible. He taunts his brother, and his favorite statement to his parents is "You're not fair."

The Smiths believe that children ought to have responsibilities, and Jerry is required to set the table and run some errands. The Smiths are worried because Henry's problems may continue through middle childhood. He may not be able to do his household chores because he will need extra time to study. They want to be fair, but are not sure they can be. They try to give Jerry more attention, but find that whatever they give is not enough. Jerry continues to complain. They have tried to buy Jerry new toys and to reason with him, but to no avail. He still taunts his brother and complains.

1. If you were Jerry's parents, what would you do to alleviate the problem?

cal needs. Not only do siblings play together and experience each other's joys and pains first hand, but they often help one another (Brody et al., 1985). They can sometimes provide the support and affection that may not be forthcoming from the parents (Dunn and Kendrick, 1982). In one study, preschool children acted as substitute attachment figures for their younger siblings in the presence of a stranger (Stewart, 1983).

Siblings have the advantage of being in the same generation, which gives them a special social status, especially during adolescence. Siblings affect each other, and any complete understanding of personality development must take this sibling experience into account.

Sibling Arguments

Siblings bring both joy and pain to one another, and sibling conflict is inevitable. However, arguments disturb the harmony of the house. Should parents intervene in sibling arguments? Let's say a parent stops the older child from picking on the younger. The older child is apt to complain, "You always take his side." If a parent lets it go, the younger one may complain that the parent really doesn't care.

Not all sibling arguments should be lumped together. Acus (1982) classifies sibling quarrels into three different categories. *Nuisance quarrels* start when children are bored or in a bad mood. These are noisy and begin over nothing at all. They end quickly, usually cause no damage, and are forgotten as fast as they start. Parents can't follow them, and trying to get to the bottom of one of these quarrels is next to impossible.

A second type, called *verbal debate quarrels*, can be constructive. These involve rational disagreements that, although loud and strident at times, can serve as training in debating and assertiveness techniques. Each sibling forcefully gives an opinion, although most siblings will not be budged from their opening positions. If the two siblings begin viciously attacking each other, however, it can easily turn into the third kind—the *destructive quarrel.*

The destructive quarrel can cause physical or emotional damage to at least one of the participants. If the quarrel is physical, the smaller child is likely to be hurt. If it is verbal, it often entails picking on the weakest point in a child's armor.

Parents frequently intervene in quarrels between young children, especially when one child is very young. The intervention is determined partly by the child's sex. In one study of preschoolers with infant siblings, mothers responded more consistently to aggression by a male toddler than aggression by a female toddler. Perhaps mothers have an idea of what level of aggression to accept in their sons but not in their daughters (Kendrick and Dunn, 1983).

As children mature, parents intervene less, and many parents do not know when and if they should step in. Two considerations should guide parents in this decision. First, if a child will suffer any physical damage, a parent must intervene. One parent was proud that she never intervened in sibling arguments no matter how serious they became. "They have to work out their own problems," she noted. But she changed her tune after the older brother "accidentally" pushed his sister down a flight of steps, breaking her leg. Anyone could see that this was coming. Unable to keep up verbally with his sister, the boy resorted to physical means of persuasion. Children must be taught how to use other means besides physical violence to settle disputes.

The second consideration is more subtle. When siblings argue, they often resort to verbal abuse and name-calling. This may become serious if one child picks on some physical or intellectual deficit of the other. For instance, one child who suffered from a learning disability was constantly subjected to abuse focused on that problem. The child was sensitive about his lagging progress, and his older brother knew he could always be upset by referring to this problem. The parents took a sound approach. Realizing that this was injuring the child emotionally, they told the offending older brother in absolute terms that he could not resort to such tactics. They used the analogy of a prize fight. There are rules, and one of them is no hitting below the belt. He was free to call his brother names, but he had to steer clear of the problem area.

Some may argue that a child with a learning disability must learn to cope with this kind of taunting. Parents have little control over such statements in the outside world, but in the home they do. Children will receive enough hurt from peers; they need not be confronted with it at home.

Competition or rivalry between children can be intense. It is probably impossible to eliminate sibling jealousy and rivalry, but it can be reduced. Some parents encourage rivalry without knowing it. For instance, they may compare their children. By doing this, they are setting up a contest and increasing sibling rivalry.

Parents can also become more sensitive to statements and actions of their children which may demonstrate rivalry and reduce it by playing up each child's

What should parents do when siblings argue—leave them alone or intervene?

2. *True or False:*
Parents should never interfere in sibling arguments.

strengths. Encouraging competition between children is undesirable (Smart and Smart, 1978). In one case, a parent promised to give the child with the best report card a moped. Two of the children actively joined in the competition, sometimes disturbing the other on purpose, and doing nothing to help each other. The third sibling did not feel able to compete and simply gave up. This child's marks were quite low. The contest caused sibling rivalry to increase greatly.

Family Size and Intelligence

Siblings play a part in children's social and personality development. Could the number and spacing of children in the family have some effect on their cognitive development and intelligence level? Some researchers believe so (Zajonc, 1976). Looking into possible reasons for the decline of scores on the Scholastic Aptitude Test (SAT), Zajonc noted that one factor might be the increased number of children per family between the end of the Second World War and the early 1960s. There are more later-born children in school, and a decline in intelligence scores occurs as we progress from the first born to the second born, and so on. Some claim that there is a relationship between the number of children in the family and intelligence scores (Zajonc and Markus, 1975). Firstborn children have the best intellectual environment because they are the focus of the parents' attention. They share it with no one. When the second child arrives, each will now get 50 percent of the attention. With three, the attention and subsequent stimulation is reduced to one-third, and so on. Remember also that the presence of a younger sibling means that the parents must interact with this sibling on a lower level, reducing the amount of stimulation available on an older child's level. Zajonc argues, then, that the prevailing intellectual level of the family decreases with each newborn child.

Just how much of the decline in SAT scores can be attributed to the number and spacing of children is questionable. Zajonc and Bargh (1980) argue that family factors explain only a small portion of the decline, about 10 percent. If this is so, they may be one factor in the decline, but certainly not the most important one.

Some researchers have challenged Zajonc's research on theoretical and methodological grounds (Rodgers, 1984; Galbraith, 1982a, 1982b). Others claim that since lower-income families are more likely to have more children, Zajonc's conclusions may be confounded by social-class effects (Brackbill and Nichols, 1982). The question of how family size and spacing affect children's development is the basis for an ongoing debate (see Berbaum and Moreland, 1985; McCall, 1985; Berbaum, 1985). At this point, we can only conclude that while the number and spacing of children within a family may have some effect on intellectual development, the evidence remains mixed.

PARENTS AND PRESCHOOLERS

Peers and siblings are indeed strong influences on the preschool child in early childhood, but the parents still have the greatest influence on a child's social and personality development. However, the preschooler's relationship with his or her parents is very different from what it was in toddlerhood.

New Competencies

Preschoolers are more verbal and have a greater attention span and a better memory than toddlers. They can engage in simple craft work and participate in storytelling. As preschoolers achieve more independence, their relationship with their parents changes. Parents are now faced with a number of decisions. First, with maturity comes a decrease in dependency and an expanding social world. Second, parents are faced with the questions of discipline and punishment.

Early evidence indicated that family size affected achievement, with children from smaller families achieving more than children from larger families. Newer evidence has cast doubt on this point.

Dependency and Increased Independence

Preschoolers engage in less holding on and less tugging and pulling. The child still requires physical contact but does not seek it as often. Nor does the preschooler demand all mother's attention. Dependent behaviors that are tolerated in a toddler may now be annoying. Parents expect preschoolers to do more on their own and to attain some measure of independence. Children who do not do this may find their behavior rejected by their parents. The constantly clinging four-year-old may draw criticism from parents, who may have to carry a younger child as well. The more the child wants to be close, the more some parents may reject this behavior. These parents push the child away, not wanting to reinforce dependence. But this strategy has the opposite effect and is based on the mistaken notion that dependency in preschoolers is related to dependency in adulthood. It is not. In addition, if children are frustrated in their attempts to obtain nurturance and warmth, their dependent behavior increases, as they try to satisfy their needs. On the other hand, children who receive consistent nurturance feel safe and protected. They venture forth, knowing they have a secure base.

The Effects of Parenting Style

Parents differ in the way they control their children's behavior. Some exercise a great deal of direct control, others believe that having fewer rules is better.

The effects of differing parenting styles were investigated by Baumrind (1980, 1978, 1971, 1967), who isolated three different parenting styles.

authoritarian parenting style
A style of parenting in which parents rigidly control their children's behavior by establishing rules and value obedience while discouraging questioning.

permissive parenting style
A style of parenting marked by open communication and a lack of parental demand for good behavior.

authoritative parenting style
A style of parenting in which parents establish limits but allow open communication and some freedom for children to make their own decisions in certain areas.

3. *True or False:*
Children of parents who allow the child maximum freedom with few if any restrictions are usually self-reliant and show excellent self-control.

Authoritarian parents try to contol their children's conduct by establishing rules and regulations. Obedience is greatly valued, and the threat of force is used to correct behavior. A parent's decisions cannot be questioned. The authoritarian parent's word is law.

Permissive parents make few demands on their children. They are nonpunishing, open to communication, and do not attempt to shape the children's behavior. The children regulate their own activities. When necessary, permissive parents use reason rather than power to control their children.

Authoritative parents encourage verbal give-and-take and explain the reasons behind a family policy. Both autonomy and discipline are valued. Limits are set, but the child's individuality is taken into consideration. The parents are warm, and do not see themselves as infallible (Baumrind, 1971).

As a group, the children of authoritative parents are the most self-reliant, self-controlled, explorative, and contented. The children of permissive parents are least self-reliant, explorative, and self-controlled. The children of authoritarian parents are the most discontented, withdrawn, and distrustful.

Authoritative parents combine firm control, encouragement of individuality, and open communication, producing children who are independent and competent. They are also warmer and more nurturant than authoritarian parents. Some permissive parents are warm, while others show a coolness and detachment toward their children.

Parental control does not interfere with independence as long as children are given an opportunity to develop their own abilities and make their own decisions, within limits. Yet the total parental control that authoritarian parents use leads to children who are less competent, less contented, and suspicious. Warmth and discipline are the keys to producing independent, competent children.

Discipline and Punishment

discipline
An attempt to control others in order to hold undesirable impulses in check and encourage self-control.

punishment
The process by which some physical or emotional pain is inflicted in order to reduce the probability that misbehavior will reoccur.

For many families, punishment is synonymous with discipline, but there are important differences. **Discipline** involves the control of others for the purpose of holding undesirable impulses or habits in check and encouraging self-control. It may include reasoning and positive reinforcement for the correct behavior; Discipline also occurs before the infringement. **Punishment** is a process by which an undesirable behavior is followed by a negative consequence. It is administered after the damage is done and is always negative. Its purpose is to decrease or completely eliminate a behavior in a particular circumstance. Most behaviors are correct in one instance but not in another. Whereas hitting another child to get a toy is unacceptable, defending oneself when being hit by another child is acceptable. Punishment may teach a child what not to do but does not provide any instruction in what the child should do under the circumstances.

Discipline Style

power-assertive discipline
A type of discipline relying on the use of power, such as physical punishment or forceful commands.

love-oriented discipline
A type of discipline relying on the use of reasoning or love.

Parents' attempts to control their children's behavior can be placed under two headings. **Power-assertive discipline** involves physical punishment, yelling, shouting, and forceful commands, while **love-oriented discipline** includes praise, affection, reasoning, showing disappointment, and withdrawal of love

It isn't always easy to know how to discipline a child.

(Maccoby and Martin, 1983). Authoritarian parents use power-assertive discipline, authoritative parents use both power-assertive and love-oriented discipline. Permissive parents use very little discipline, but when discipline is necessary, they use reasoning, a love-oriented approach.

These discipline styles interact with the emotional tone of the parent-child relationship. When restrictiveness occurs within a context of warmth and acceptance, it can lead to obedience, nonaggressiveness, and other positive outcomes. When it occurs in the presence of hostility, it leads to withdrawal and anxiety (Becker, 1964). When investigating techniques of discipline, both the type of approach (power-assertive or love-oriented) and the emotional tone of the relationship (warm or hostile) must be considered.

Discipline and Verbal Abilities

Preschoolers can get into more trouble than infants or toddlers, because their physical abilities are greater, but their ability to use language gives parents more options in dealing with misbehavior. As children mature, they respond to a more rational approach. In a study of one-and-a-half, two-and-a-half, and three-and-a-half-year-olds, toddlers responded better to simple commands than to suggestions or questions, whereas preschoolers responded more to suggestions (McLaughlin, 1983). Parents who realize that their preschooler's verbal abilities give them more options are likely to change their discipline strategy and use more complicated verbal techniques instead of mere commands.

Method	Percentage
Yelling at or scolding children	52
Spanking children	50
Making children stay in their rooms	38
Not allowing children to play	32
Not letting children watch television	25
Making children go to bed	23
Threatening children	15
Giving children extra chores	12
Taking away an allowance	9

Source: Adapted from General Mills, 1977.

4. *True or False:*
In the long run, the more severe the punishment, the more likely the child is to refrain from misbehaving.

Each of the three parenting styles uses discipline in a different way, resulting in different outcomes. Authoritarian parents rely on punishment, which gets them obedience in the short term and rebellion in the long term. Permissive parents rarely use any type of discipline, and this sometimes results in a child without direction. Authoritative parents use both approaches, depending on the situation, but they encourage independence by allowing children freedom within limits. Perhaps authoritative parents notice the change in a child's verbal and physical abilities and tailor the discipline to the emerging abilities of the child.

Punishment: Uses and Abuses

Psychologists recognize that there is often a need for punishment under certain circumstances, but they are concerned about the type of punishment used and the way it is administered. Punishment can be administered in two ways (Karen 1974). First, a positive reinforcer may be removed. A parent may remove a toy or turn off the television set to punish a misbehaving child. The second procedure involves following the undesirable action with a negative action. A child who whines may be yelled at or spanked. The results of one survey of parental punishment methods are found in Table 10.1.

While punishment can be effective in decreasing the frequency of an undesirable behavior, it is often administered incorrectly and fails in its purpose. It is overused by some parents, who rarely if ever compliment their children but are always ready with a criticism, and even the strap. In order to be effective, punishment should be moderate, swift, sure, and combined with rewards for the correct behavior (Altrocchi, 1980). Unfortunately, parents often delay punishment, are inconsistent, use overly severe punishments, and constantly threaten their children, practices that are ineffective over the longer term.

The Effects of Harsh Punishment.   Some parents are proud that they are severe disciplinarians and do not spare the rod. They claim success and have difficulty understanding parents who don't use as much punishment. To the casual observer, the harshly disciplined child may seem well behaved, but a deeper look reveals a different picture.

Harsh punishment is effective in temporarily decreasing the undesirable behavior, but over the long term it is less successful and even damaging (Martin, 1975). Children may correct their behavior temporarily, especially in the presence of the feared parent, but their frustration and anger builds up and eventually explodes. These children may be sullen and suspicious of authority. According to Martin (1975), many children who are problems in school are harshly disciplined at home. Thus, the stereotype that the problem child in school is rarely disciplined at home may not be accurate.

Effective Punishment.   Punishment has a place in child-rearing, but using punishment correctly is more difficult than most parents realize. The effects of a poorly administered punishment may linger for some time. In addition, parents often forget to include reinforcement for good behavior along with punishment for inconsiderate actions. A punishment is likely to be more effective if children know that they have the ability to meet their parents' standards of conduct and that the parent will notice when they do, and praise them for it.

The aim of punishment is to decrease or eliminate a behavior, so if a parental action, no matter how severe, fails to do so, it has been a failure. Here are some general guidelines for effective punishment.

1. Be as consistent as possible about which behaviors are acceptable and which are not.
2. Although a warning is certainly in order at times, continually threatening a child without carrying through a *reasonable* disciplinary action decreases the adult's standing with the child.
3. Never threaten to give a child a punishment that either cannot be carried out ethically or that you would not be willing to administer.
4. Especially when dealing with younger children, punishment should be as immediate as possible. However, if you know yourself to be emotional, be careful not to administer punishments that are too severe for the misbehavior. You may regret the overreaction later.
5. Moderate punishments are normally better than severe ones. After you have dropped your "atom bomb" on the child, you have nowhere to go from there. In addition, if the punishment is too severe for the "crime," the child tends to reflect on the punishment rather than on what was done to deserve it.
6. Do not use the "Wait until father (or mother) comes home" approach.
7. Give your child a chance to answer any accusations.
8. Punishment is most effective when it is combined with reinforcement for the correct response. Using positive reinforcement together with a disciplinary action increases the effectiveness of both.
9. Overreliance on punishment decreases communication, as children become afraid to confide in adults. Be certain to keep the lines of communication open.
10. Use the minimum amount of punishment that will successfully accomplish your goal.

CHILD ABUSE

Sometimes punishment goes beyond the point of reason and leads to abuse. Most people would like to think of child abuse in terms of mental illness, but although parents who abuse their children suffer from a number of psychological problems (Lystad, 1975), only about 10 percent can be confidently classified as mentally ill (Kempe and Kempe, 1978).

For two reasons, however, the general public clings to the belief that there is a connection between mental illness and child abuse. First, the media report only spectacular examples of child abuse. When a woman puts a child on a hot gas burner to free the youngster from the devil, or when a man punishes his children for misbehavior by tying them to the bed and systematically torturing them, we all react with disgust. Since these are the cases that make headlines, it is easy to label these people mentally ill and go about our business. Second, if we can label these people as ill, we can separate them from ourselves. The idea that child-abusing parents have any similarity to us at all is usually denied. Somehow, these abusers must be totally different, not even approaching human.

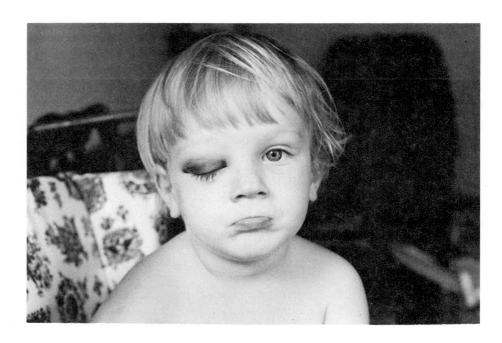

Child abuse is a major problem in all Western nations.

In the vast majority of cases, however, this is not true. Child-abusing parents cannot be picked out of a group by looking at them, nor is it easy to identify them before the abuse takes place.

What Is Child Abuse?

child abuse
A general term used to denote an injury intentionally perpetrated on a child.

Child abuse is said to occur when parents intentionally injure their children. Sometimes it is not easy to label an instance as abuse. For example, what of cases in which the injury was unintentional? What if a child sustains an injury due to parental carelessness but with no intent to injure the child? In one study, 38 percent of the professionals believed this to be abuse, 34 percent did not, and 28 percent could not make up their minds (Gil, in Starr, 1979). Even though there are some differences of opinion on the boundaries of abuse, most people do agree on the more serious cases. No one doubts that a child who has been beaten or burned or has a broken arm or extensive head injuries caused by his parents has been abused.

Sexual Abuse

One type of individual abuse, sexual abuse, has recently been the subject of much discussion in the media. Beginning in the mid-1970s and continuing in the 1980s, the public has been swamped with well-publicized cases of sexual abuse (Finkelhor, 1984). Sexual abuse is fraught with a host of definitional and legal problems, as well as an even greater stigma than other types of child abuse (Fontana, 1984). It is often a hidden type of abuse that goes unreported. When it is brought to the attention of the authorities, building a case may be difficult, because the damaging acts are often performed in private with only the child's word to substantiate the charge. The accused adult may question the credibility of a very young victim, charging that the child has been encouraged to make the accusation or is doing it for attention.

Sexual abuse may involve forcible rape, statutory rape, sodomy, incest, and "indecent liberties," such as genital exhibition and physical advances (Sarafino, 1979). The incidence of sexual abuse is acknowledged to be grossly underreported, and it is the least reported type of child abuse (Schultz and Jones, 1983); about 23,000 cases were reported in 1982 (Finkelhor, 1984). Abusers are mostly men, and girls constitute the majority of victims (Canavan, 1981). Sexual abuse may occur between victims who are related, such as father and daughter, or between strangers and children. The consequences of sexual abuse may be physical, such as venereal disease and pregnancy, and emotional. Emotional consequences vary widely, but include withdrawal, suicidal tendencies, sleep disturbances, aggression, sexual problems, anger, guilt, and the inability to trust others (Adams-Tucker, 1982).

Parents often ask what they can do to prevent sexual abuse. Knowing where children are, what they are doing, and who they are with are obvious precautions, but parents cannot foresee every circumstance. For instance, one six-year-old boy was abused by an older boy when he went to the bathroom of a supermarket while his mother waited in the checkout line (De Vine, 1980). Parents should remind their children not to accept money or favors from strangers, and not to accept a ride or go anywhere with someone they do not know. If they think they are in danger, they should be told that making a scene by running away and screaming for help is acceptable. Since the sexual abuser may be someone they know and trust, children should be told that they do not have to agree to demands for physical closeness even from relatives. Finally, children should be encouraged to report any instances of people touching them in intimate places or asking them to do the same (Queens Bench Foundation, 1977). The increase in publicity surrounding sexual abuse has led to a frank public discussion of the problem. This offers some hope that we can reduce its incidence through prevention and its consequences through early discovery and treatment.

Emotional Child Abuse

Does child abuse have to be physical? What of the parent who constantly screams at and berates her children? Imagine a four-year-old who has just spilled some juice hearing a parent shout, "You're a stupid, rotten kid. If I had any sense, I'd give you away!"

Attempts to define **emotional abuse** have been largely unsuccessful. Certain parental actions lead to a loss of self-esteem in the child and interfere with emotional development, but defining these actions and describing what remedial actions should be taken are difficult tasks. In the absence of such guidelines, the courts have thus far taken a hands-off attitude toward everything but the most extreme forms of emotional abuse. Perhaps, in the future, the more obvious cases of emotional abuse will be identified and some help for parents will be forthcoming. At this point, however, emotional abuse is a concept in search of a solid definition and some guidelines for action.

How Much Child Abuse Goes On?

Estimating the number of children abused each year is difficult. The law tends to cover only the most severe cases. Most never get to the attention of the authori-

5. *True or False:*
The incidence of sexual abuse is overreported to the police.

emotional abuse
Psychological damage perpetrated on a child over an extended period of time by a parent.

ties, because abuse may be hidden or accepted. The public is also often unwilling to become involved in such cases. Many believe that parents have the right to punish their own children and are wary of interfering. Only when the abuse is most extreme is action taken. This often depends on the age of the child.

For example, suppose you are in the supermarket and you see a mother spank an infant hard for crying. Most people would intervene, either directly or by calling the police. We can think of no reason to treat an infant in this way. However, imagine that you witnessed a parent spanking a five-year-old hard for picking up a box of cookies. In such cases, people are less likely to intervene, for we do not have that same protective feeling toward children. If the parent went too far and began smacking the child in the face with a can, however, we might do something. Notice that our standards have changed. The same behavior with an infant is not tolerated, but it is with a young child.

Estimates vary as to how many children are abused each year. About 2,000 children in the United States are abused to death every year (Turbak, 1979). The number of reported cases of abuse has steadily risen, probably the result of increased public consciousness of abuse, better reporting procedures, and improvements in the law. The number of child abuse reports in 1984 is estimated to be over one million (New York Times, Feb. 17, 1985). Of course, not all reports are substantiated. Gelles (1978) found that about 3.5 percent of all parents he surveyed admitted to having acted aggressively toward their children in a way that could have caused injury at least once. If Gelles' results are generalized to the entire population, about 1.5 million children are treated in a way that could cause them significant physical harm.

Child abuse is a world problem. In West Germany, more than 1,000 children are abused to death each year. The figure stands at about 700 in England and about 100 in Canada (Turbak, 1979).

Causes of Child Abuse

In order to understand the causes of child abuse the characteristics of the parent and child involved, and the situation, must be taken into account.

The Abusive Parent.   What kind of parent abuses a child? Is there a recognizable personality pattern that indicates the potential for abuse? If we could discover the differences between parents who abuse and those who do not, we might be able to intervene before abuse takes place.

Abusing parents are impulsive, have unmet dependency needs, have a poor self-concept and sense of identity, are defensive, and project their problems onto their children (Green et al., 1974). They are immature, socially isolated, believe in the value of physical punishment, are afraid of spoiling their children, and have difficulty empathizing with their offspring (Martin, 1978). They also tend to be young, but this factor may be confounded by socioeconomic status (Kinard and Klerman, 1980). Although child abuse can be found in every age-group and economic level, it is concentrated among young parents. Young parenthood, though, is related to poverty, poor health care, poor housing, poor family background, and other social factors, so it may not be age itself, but the socioeconomic situation and impoverished background, that contributes to the abuse.

These characteristics are general ones. Many parents who are impulsive and isolated do not abuse their children, and this fact has led many professionals to deny that there is any definite "abusive" personality (Green et al., 1974). Although abusive parents differ in some of their reactions to family situations (Frodi and Lamb, 1980), it is difficult to predict abuse simply from a personality profile of a parent.

Many (but not all) parents who were abused or neglected as children abuse their own children. In a study of 46 families with 73 abused children, Galdston (1975) found that two factors kept appearing in abusive parents. One was sexual frustration within the marriage, the other was the lack of a healthy relationship with their own parents. Abusive parents who experienced neglect or abuse in childhood do not think what they are doing is wrong. They know no other way to relate to their children. Violent individuals were often the victims of physical brutality or rejection in their own childhoods. Thus, abusive parents create hostile, disturbed, unhappy children who grow up and perpetuate the cycle.

The Abused Child.   Certain characteristics of a child may predispose that child to being a victim of abuse. This statement causes some people to feel uneasy. Any suggestion that the child contributes to the problem is usually met with hostility. The reaction is understandable. It is easier to see a child as a helpless victim of a vicious adult than to look at characteristics of a child that may bring out the worst in a parent. No one is excusing such behavior or blaming an innocent victim. However, a child's personality or physical and intellectual characteristics may combine with an inadequate parent to cause problems (Parke and Collmer, 1975).

For instance, children who are premature, who have physical handicaps, or who are mentally retarded are abused more often than children who do not suffer from these conditions (Friedrich and Boriskin, 1976). In addition, children who have difficult temperaments, that is, whose emotional reactions are intense and demanding, are also prone to being abused (Parke and Collmer, 1975). The common characteristic in all these groups is the need for special care. The child whose needs are greater is at risk for abuse.

Abusing parents often hold unreasonable expectations for their children and distorted perceptions of what their children can do (Martin, 1978). Children with physical, emotional, or mental handicaps cannot meet their parents' expectations and are more likely to be abused.

Again, prediction is difficult. Looking at the characteristics of the child makes sense only when you also consider the characteristics of the caregiver (Belsky, 1980). Consider the premature baby, who requires a great deal of care. The demand may be more than an impulsive, unrealistic parent may be able to take, and the parent may resort to violence to quiet the child. As the child grows, the pattern is reinforced, as physical violence keeps the child in line, until it is well established and continues throughout childhood. In order to understand parent-child relationships we must look at how the child affects the parent's behavior as well as how the parent affects the child. The child whose needs are greater, who engenders anger in a parent, or who is difficult to care for is more likely to set in motion abusive parental responses that may become the standard parent-child interaction.

Characteristics of the Situation.   Certain situations encourage abuse. One of the most common involves unemployment and economic tension. Steinberg and colleagues (1981) found that there is a direct relationship between unem-

6. *True or False:*
Parents who abuse their children have a distinct personality profile.

7. *True or False:*
A child's personality may predispose the child to abuse.

displacement
Transferring feelings from one
person or object to another.

ployment and other undesirable economic trends within a community and child abuse. Simply stated, neglect and abuse increase when economic tensions increase. Unemployment and underemployment cause stress. The child may become the object of a parent's anger and frustration. Parents may displace their negative feelings onto the child. **Displacement** involves transferring feelings from one person or object onto another.

Any situation that raises tension and stress may promote abuse. Social isolation and marital discord raise tensions and encourage an abusive reaction. We can see how important it is to take all three elements into consideration. Some parents are better able to handle stress than others, and this, combined with a demanding child and an impulsive nature, may lead to abuse.

Acceptance of Violence.   We live in a society that largely condones violence with respect to children. In fact, laws covering physical abuse are relatively new. In the nineenth century the Society for the Prevention of Cruelty to Animals went to court, arguing that, because children were human beings and human beings were animals, children should be protected at least as much as dogs or cats (Lystad, 1975). Shortly after this, some tentative steps toward protection were taken. Physical punishment is largly accepted in the United States, even though other methods for discipline are available.

Preventing Child Abuse

Attempts to deal with child abuse have centered on two general approaches. Primary programs identify the families that are most likely to become abusive and then try to prevent the abuse. Secondary programs try to rehabilitate families where abuse has already taken place.

Primary programs of prevention involve enrolling parents in educational programs, having professionals visit the homes of potential abusers, and offering courses on child development in high school. In such courses, teenagers are taught child-care techniques, given information concerning children's nutritional and emotional needs, and told where parents can turn for help. The results of such programs are encouraging (Starr, 1979).

Many approaches have been used to treat child abusers. Social work, individual and family therapy, self-help groups like Parents Anonymous, which provides emotional support, and group treatment can all claim some success. The figures for improvement range widely from about 40 percent to 80 percent (Starr, 1979). Generally, about half the parents involved in abusive situations can be helped to at least stop physically abusing their children.

The victims of abuse also need help. Abused children show many disturbed behavior patterns, from hypersensitivity to pain to aggressiveness, from withdrawal to fearfulness. Many improve even when there is only a mild to moderate improvement in the home situation (Jones, 1979). Early identification is one factor in successful treatment. Some of the symptoms of abuse and neglect are summarized in Table 10.2. These should be considered warning signs and indicate a need for further investigation.

The problem of child abuse is a serious one in many societies. The first steps in improving the situation are admitting that the problem exists and identifying its causes. Today we know that early intervention and a comprehensive treatment program can improve the family situation so that the children will have a chance at a decent and productive life and the cycle of child abuse can be broken.

CHILDHOOD FEARS

It would be incorrect to conclude that such problems as fearfulness and withdrawal were largely the result of child abuse. Many children raised in happy, secure environments still develop fears. In fact, almost every child develops some sort of fear during the course of childhood (Poznansky, 1973). The fears of noise, unexpected changes in the environment, or abandonment are common. Preschoolers often continue to fear separation from parents. Children's increasing awareness of their environment and knowledge of their inability to control events leads to many fears, such as fears of dogs, death, and doctors (Verville, 1967). The preschooler's vivid imagination also contributes to fears of darkness, strange creatures, monsters, and goblins. Children at this age magnify and distort events, thinking of the terrible things that could happen (Ross Laboratories, 1979).

At times, a particular experience can make a child quite fearful. A sudden move from a dog or commotion in the street during the night may be the basis for a fear. In addition, some television programs may frighten preschool children, who may insist that the light be kept on in their room to guard against some imaginary creature. Children usually outgrow their fears.

Parents should not ridicule children for their fears or shame them before others (Ilg and Ames, 1955). It may also be harmful to force the children to face their

Every child must deal with fears.

TABLE 10.2   **Symptoms of Abuse and Neglect**
These symptoms should be interpreted as warning signs. They signal the need for additional investigation or attention. They do not automatically indicate abuse or neglect.

Symptoms of Abuse	*Symptoms of Neglect*
Evidence of repeated injury	Clothing inappropriate for weather
New injuries before previous ones have healed	Torn, tattered, unwashed clothing
Frequent complaints of abdominal pain	Poor skin hygiene
Evidence of bruises	Rejection by other children because of body odor
Bruises of different ages	Need for glasses, dental work, hearing aid, or other health services
Welts	Lack of proper nourishment
Wounds, cuts, or punctures	Consistent tiredness or sleepiness in class
Scalding liquid burns with well-defined parameters	Consistent, very early school arrival
Caustic burns	Frequent absenteeism or chronic tardiness
Frostbite	Tendency to hang around school after dismissal
Cigarette burns	

Source: W. H. Berdine and A. E. Blackhurst, 1985.

fears. Children's fears should be respected, and parents are wise to make time for a period of withdrawal before helping children adjust to the stimulus. If a child is afraid of dogs, allow him or her to stay close to you and away from the canine for a while.

Children also notice how adults react to particular stimuli, such as insects, dogs, and the dark. If a parent stands on a chair and screams at the sight of a spider, the child learns to fear spiders too. Children tend to show many of the same fears their parents have (Bandura and Menlove, 1968). Exposing children to models who cope with the feared stimulus can be effective in reducing fear reactions in children. Bandura and colleagues (1967) exposed forty-eight preschool children with a fear of dogs to a model situation in which a four-year-old child approached a dog in a nonfrightened manner. Some of the children were exposed only to the dog, while a control group simply participated in a play period. The children who had witnessed the preschooler approach the dog without fear showed considerably less tendency to avoid the dogs. Thus, a peer model, patience, and understanding appear to help children overcome fears.

During the course of this chapter, we have described a number of influences on the preschooler, including peers, parents, and siblings. There are, of course, many others. A child's expanding world may include nursery school, books, and the television set. The greater the number of influences on the child, the more difficult it is to focus on the exact cause of a behavioral pattern. Nowhere is this more obvious than in the case of the child's acquisition of his or her sex role.

SEX-ROLE ACQUISITION

The research on sex-role acquisition is voluminous, and a number of terms are now used in this area. The terms *sex differences, gender identity, gender or sex roles, sex typing,* and *gender stereotypes* are often thrown around. Each has a different meaning.

Sex Differences

sex differences
The differences between males and females that have been established through scientific investigation.

8. *True or False:*
Research has not yet established any consistent differences in personality or behavior between the sexes.

The term **sex differences** describes differences between the sexes that have been established by scientific research. For example, the average female matures more rapidly than the average male. Maccoby and Jacklin (1974) reviewed over 1,600 studies concerning sex differences and concluded that only four differences appeared consistently. Most studies indicate (1) that males are generally more aggressive than females, (2) that girls have greater verbal ability, (3) that boys excel in visual spatial ability, and (4) that boys excel in mathematical ability. A number of supposed differences were not supported by scientific studies. The hypotheses that girls were more suggestible, had lower self-esteem, had lower motivation, were more social, were better at rote learning, were less analytical, were more affected by heredity, and learned better using their auditory sense than boys were dismissed as not supported by the research. A number of other hypotheses were still in question. These include the questions of male dominance, female compliance, female nurturance, male activity level, female passivity, and male competitiveness.

The work of Maccoby and Jacklin, as valuable as it is, is hardly the last word on the subject. A number of criticisms have arisen. For example, Block (1976) noted a number of technical objections to the way the review of the literature had been performed. She objected to the way studies that researched sex differences were placed together even though they measured the differences in different ways. Others had reviewed much of the same literature and come to different conclusions. Bardwick (1971) argued that the research demonstrates that females do show more dependency than males. Eagly (1978) suggests that women are more suggestible and more fearful than men. Minton and Scheider (1980) suggest that while males and females do not differ in general ability, they do differ in specific abilities: "Females generally surpass males in verbal fluency, reading comprehension, finger dexterity, and clerical skills, whereas males are superior on mathematical reasoning, visual spatial ability, and speed and coordination of large bodily movements" (p. 319). These authors also argue that "females are better at rote memory especially of verbal and social material" (p. 319).

Vital Considerations

The study of sex differences has become frenetic. Some consider any positive finding on sex differences sexist, others seem unable to wait to demonstrate one gender's superiority over the other in some area.

 Three considerations should be kept in mind whenever anyone announces a positive finding on sex differences. First, even though a difference between the genders on some characteristic, such as verbal ability, is found, that tells us nothing about its cause. Is the fact that males are generally more aggressive than females due to some environmental factor, such as reinforcement, or to some genetic or hormonal factor? Even the finding that some genetic or hormonal element may underlie the behavior does not mean the behavior itself cannot be modified. Genetic contribution does not imply immutability. Rather, the individual's genotype may influence the range of possible behaviors, but it remains the environment that determines the behavior itself.

 Second, most sex differences should not be seen as absolute. The overlap between the sexes is tremendous. The average difference between the sexes on any particular trait is normally very small, even if it does exist. The differences between individuals within the same gender are far greater than the average differences between males and females. Thus, although males seem to be better at math, you will find excellent female math students and males who receive terrible math grades. Stating that males are better in one trait, or females are superior in another trait, should not blind us to the overlap that exists in these skills or characteristics. The sexes are more similar than they are different.

 This leads directly to the third consideration. Just how much of any particular trait can you predict on the basis of an individual's sex alone? As Plomin and Foch (1981, p. 383) ask, "How much do we know about an individual's verbal ability if all we know is the individual's sex?" These researchers note that sex differences provide only about 1 percent of the variation on verbal ability, and only about 4 percent of the differences in mathematical ability. Hyde (1984) suggests that only about 5 percent of difference in aggression between males and females is due to gender. Although these differences do exist, they explain very little about the variation between individuals on any of these traits.

Gender Identity, Gender Stability, and Gender Consistency

gender identity
One's awareness of being a male or a female.

gender stability
Children's knowledge that they were of a particular gender when younger and will remain so throughout life.

gender consistency
Children's knowledge that they will remain a boy or a girl regardless of how they act, dress, or groom.

The term **gender identity** refers to one's awareness of being a male or a female. Evidence indicates that at about age two children are aware of the labels "boy" and "girl" (Schaffer, 1981), but they do not use them correctly all the time.

Children develop their understanding of gender in a developmental progression described in a study by Slaby and Frey (1975). First, children establish a **gender identity.** That is, they know whether they are boys or girls. After establishing gender identity, children learn that their gender is **stable.** In other words, children know that they were boys or girls when they were younger and will become men and women when they grow up. Finally, children develop **gender consistency**, the understanding that boys remain boys whether or not they have long hair or play female-oriented games.

This progression has been found in many other studies (Eaton and Von Bargen, 1981) and in many different cultures (Munroe et al., 1984). Gender identity is more easily understood by children than gender consistency, with gender stability lying somewhere between. The mean (average) age of attaining these understandings differs widely. For example, although the average age for attaining gender consistency was 55 months in Slaby and Frey's study, some attained it as early as 41 months, while others did not understand the concept until 67 months of age.

This developmental progression explains some of the unusual behavior we find in young children. If children have not gained an understanding of gender stability or consistency, they may believe that if daddy grows his hair long he will become a female like mommy. A little girl might believe that if her brother wore a dress, he would become a girl like her.

One important aspect of gender consistency involves its ability to direct attention toward appropriate models. Children attend more to same-sex models only when they have acquired gender consistency (Ruble et al., 1981; Slaby and Frey, 1975). Older siblings of their gender, parents of the same sex, and television commercials that show peers of the same sex are more likely to influence behavior after children have learned gender consistency. Once children know that gender is permanent and does not change with the situation, they seek out important information from the environment on what is appropriate for their particular sex and what is to be avoided. In seeking to provide preschool children with effective models, it may be important first to understand just where they are in their development of gender consistency. It is no wonder that toy manufacturers are so careful about how they market their toys and who is seen on television playing with them.

Sex Typing and Sex Roles

sex typing
The process by which people acquire, value, and behave in a manner appropriate to one sex more than the other.

In the beginning of this chapter, four-year-old Matthew casually mentioned that he expected to cook for his family when he got older. Matthew was raised in a family in which both mother and father prepared the meals. To Matthew, cooking could be a male or a female activity. However, many children and adults would consider it a female chore. **Sex typing** is the process by which an individual acquires, values, and behaves in a manner appropriate to one sex more than the other sex (Mischel, 1976). Women cook, take care of the children, ask for help, are rescued from trying circumstances (by men), and play with dolls. Men work full-time jobs, don't ask for help, are action-oriented, and are strong. Sex-typed behavior can be seen in many areas of development. Boys play with trucks, girls play with dolls. Such behavior patterns as methods of aggression, behavior while dissecting a frog, and emotional expressiveness are examples of sex-typed behavior. Girls are taught that crying is acceptable when they are sad, males are taught to hold it in. Boys avoid showing concern for babies, females pay more attention to infants. Studies in laboratory settings show that males of all ages, from preschoolers to young adults, spend less time speaking to and playing with babies than females do (Blakemore, 1981).

When we add up all the behavior patterns and psychological characteristics that seem appropriate for each sex, we are describing the concept of **sex roles**. Sex roles are diffuse and permeate other roles (Maccoby, 1978). Not only are they involved in one's choice of occupation (truck drivers are men, nurses are women), but they also relate to a number of social expectations. For example, consider the social conventions that exist between males and females in the areas of dating and family life. The male picks up the female at her house for the date and drives the car. The male is the breadwinner of the family. Some of these conceptions are changing, but many are still with us today.

Just how children acquire the behaviors that are considered "appropriate" for their gender is a matter of great interest and controversy. We will now look at some theories that seek to explain how children learn their sex roles.

sex roles
Behaviors expected of people in a given society on the basis of whether they are male or female.

The Biological Approach

Freud once stated that biology was destiny, in other words, that the physiological differences between males and females explained the behavioral differences. Few people would go that far today. No single biological explanation successfully explains why males may act one way and females another. Instead, a number of biological factors that may be taken into account when studying sex roles are suggested.

Hormones.   Males produce more testosterone, while females produce more estrogen. In laboratory studies, the hormone testosterone is linked to aggressive behavior (Rogers, 1976; Josselyn, 1973). However, variations in human behavior cannot be explained merely by citing hormonal differences. Learning is also important. Money and Erhardt (1972) studied children who were born with ambiguous genitals. Some were surgically altered very early in childhood, and these children made successful adjustments to their gender if the surgery took place before the age of two. Those who became female did, however, show a tomboyish nature, including more rough-and-tumble play. This tendency might be caused by the greater concentrations of testosterone in their systems. Perhaps males are more inclined to be aggressive than females. Despite the inclination, both males and females can be taught to settle disagreements by nonaggressive means.

Differences in Maturation.   The average female is born more ready for life than the average male. Females are more advanced in central nervous system development and bone formation. Some sex differences may be caused by the inter-action of rates of maturation and the environment surrounding the child. For example, while gross muscle development in males is superior, females develop fine muscle control more quickly (McGuinness, 1977, 1976). Since children are apt to do both what is easiest and what yields the most positive reinforcement, males may turn their attention to activities in which gross muscle ability and re-action time are vital. Females, on the other hand, having better fine motor con-trol, are apt to concentrate on tasks involving such control.

This is a most challenging view. It has always been assumed that a simple learning explanation was sufficient to understand why, for instance, males play baseball and females sew. McGuinness argues that society is merely reinforcing a difference in abilities that is already present. Boys find baseball easier, succeed at it, and then are reinforced for their efforts. Girls find activities that require fine motor control easier, succeed at them, and are reinforced. McGuinness also ar-gues that schools discriminate against boys. The average boy is just not as ready for school as the average girl. This explains why boys have so many more reading problems than girls. Females also have a greater attention span, and their eyes are better developed, by the time they enter school. Female superiority in lan-guage development and reading does not excuse males from learning to read. It shows that the average male may find language skills more difficult and may re-quire more instruction.

The specifics of McGuinness' arguments are less important than the general points. Biology itself is not the cause of these behavioral differences. Rather, par-ticular tasks become easier to master and are reinforced by society. The differ-ences are viewed in terms of the developing individual's interactions with society. In addition, any sex differences that might result must be understood, and edu-cational programs should be created to compensate for them.

Genetic Differences.   We have already discussed the possibility that genetic differences may affect behavior. The male Y chromosome contains many fewer genes than the female X chromosome, and some characteristics, such as color blindness, are sex-linked. There is evidence that this may also be true of spatial ability, although some modern studies have cast some doubt on this (Vanden-berg and Kuse, 1979).

The assignment of unequal roles on the basis of some biological argument cannot be condoned and is not justified by the evidence (Archer, 1976). In the case of sex roles and behavior, biology is not destiny. At this point in time, the biological contribution to our understanding of how a child acquires a sex role is a large question mark. While some differences between males and females, such as hormonal levels and rate of maturation, appear to be consistent, how they af-fect behavior is still a matter of conjecture. Perhaps the only conclusion possible at present is that while we cannot ignore the possible biological differences, they do not by themselves explain the acquisition of sex-role behaviors.

Behavior Theories

The most obvious reason that males and females act differently is that they learn different behaviors. These learning experiences can be divided roughly into two compartments. First, boys and girls are treated differently and reinforced for different actions. Second, we might look at the models that surround the child, because children learn by observing others.

Different Treatment for Sons and Daughters. Are boys and girls reinforced for different behaviors? Do parents treat boys and girls differently? Parents do expect different behaviors from their sons and daughters, expecting sons to be stronger and tougher (Oakley, 1972). Parents provide their sons with different toys and decorate their rooms in a "sex-appropriate" manner (Rheingold and Cook, 1975).

Differences in treatment are not difficult to find. Parents encourage sons to be more independent, competitive, and achieving (Block, 1979). They encourage daughters to be more passive and to seek protection (Chafetz, 1972). Girls are viewed as more fragile, and parents play with sons more roughly than they do with daughters (Bee, 1978). Parents also supervise daughters more, allowing sons more freedom (Block, 1979). Males are punished more, and parents are more likely to be physical with sons than with daughters. Girls tend to receive more praise than boys, but also more criticism (Fagot, 1974).

Fathers are more likely than mothers to treat sons and daughters differently (Bee, 1978). A father is more likely to criticize his son when he sees him playing with dolls, than he is to criticize a daughter who is observed beating up a Bobo doll. Mothers are more likely to treat sons and daughters equally.

Boys are more strictly sex-typed than girls. Even though preschool boys and girls both prefer sex-stereotyped toys, boys avoid cross-sexed toys more often than girls do (Williams et al., 1975). Indeed, preschool boys chose sex-typed toys and cling to their choices even if told that the toys not chosen were appropriate for both boys and girls (Frasher et al., 1980). It is also easier to get girls to switch toy preference than boys.

These differences, though, do not tell the entire story. Some authorities are more impressed by the similarities in the way males and females are treated by their parents than the differences (Maccoby and Jacklin, 1974). The evidence does not indicate that a simple, straightforward reinforcement approach can answer the question of sex typing. For example, Maccoby and Jacklin (1974) did not find that boys were necessarily reinforced for aggressiveness more than girls.

The question is not whether boys and girls are treated differently, but whether these differences are enough to explain later sex-typed behavior patterns. Although some differences in treatment do exist, it is difficult to see how these could be the sole determinants of later personality and behavioral differences between the sexes. They are, then, only one part of the puzzle. Another part may be found in an understanding of the role models that surround a child.

Role Models and Imitation. Let us return to the case of the little boy who thought nothing of daddy's cooking dinner. Where did he get the idea that it was manly to cook dinner for the family? Probably not through direct reinforcement, for little boys hardly get a chance to cook spaghetti dinners for their families. He simply observed his father doing so, and sees cooking as an activity that is performed by both sexes.

The use of modeling and imitation to explain the acquisition of sex role is appealing. Indeed, the strength of the imitative response is especially noticeable in

It is easier to get girls to play with male-stereotyped toys than to get boys to play with female-stereotyped toys.

9. *True or False:*
Girls generally receive more punishment than boys, while boys receive more praise.

10. *True or False:*
Fathers are more likely than mothers to treat their sons and daughters equally.

This child may believe that cooking is both a male and a female activity.

young children, who may act like their mothers or fathers or imitate older brothers or sisters, to the delight or despair of the parents. Since parents are the most important people in the life of preschoolers, the children may model themselves after them (Mischel, 1970). For example, daughters of working mothers have less-traditional role concepts and have higher aspirations than girls whose mothers do not work (Hoffman, 1974). They benefit from observing that their mother as well as their father is valued in the labor market and performing useful functions outside the home.

Unfortunately, attempts to explain the acquisition of sex roles as a simple matter of observation learning or modeling have not succeeded. Until the age of six or so, children do not appear to model themselves after the parent of the same sex (Maccoby and Jacklin, 1974). The characteristics of both parents may be more important than their gender. Hetherington (1967) found that dominance and warmth were the most important factors in determining the extent to which children will copy their parents' sex-typed behaviors. Dominance appears to be more important in male socialization, while warmth is a primary factor with females. Paternal dominance for boys and maternal warmth for girls are critical elements in determining effective identification.

Hetherington's study suggests that different parental characteristics affect masculinity and femininity and the acquisition of sex roles. Children copy the behaviors of the most dominant parent, but this need not be the parent of the same sex. In addition, Hetherington suggests that because males are granted more independence, outside influences may be more important for identifying with the masculine role, while home and family influences would be more crucial for the female, since she is kept closer to home.

Peers, Teachers, and Heroes.   It is a mistake to assume, then, that boys simply identify with their fathers and that daughters identify with their mothers. The situation is much more complex. Children are also exposed to models in the outside world, for instance, peers, teachers, and the characters in children's books. The most popular boy or girl in the class may be an important role model for a child.

Children are also affected by what they see on television. Perhaps Mrs. Ingram, the star of a family situation comedy, is shown as needing protection, depending on the handyman for everything, and always concerned about wax buildup on her floors and the shine on her nose. Mr. Ingram, on the other hand, tackles the business world each day, conquers his problems on his own, and is involved in all kinds of physical and mental activities. The message is clear and consistent. Television, the most powerful of the mass media, presents different pictures of males and females. Females on television are more likely to be seen in family-oriented parts, with a strong hint of sexual overtones, and play light roles. They are most often unemployed. Males are more likely to play serious roles and to initiate aggression. Females are usually seen by viewers as attractive, happy, warm, sociable, fair, and peaceful, while males are rational, smarter, more powerful, stable, and tolerant (McGhee, 1975). Television presents sexual stereotypes, and there is a relationship between the amount of time spent watching television and the acquisition of stereotyped and traditional sex roles (Freuh and McGhee, 1975).

Children are also exposed to teachers, who serve as role models too. Although teachers reinforce boys and girls equally, they reinforce behaviors that are traditionally considered feminine in nature (Etaugh et al., 1975). Perhaps female teachers are more tolerant of the kinds of behavior patterns shown by girls and reinforce these behavior patterns irrespective of the gender of the child. Preschool teachers may also not be aware of sexist practices in nursery schools (Simmons, 1976). Perhaps the teacher asks boys for help during certain situations, like putting something together, but charges the girls with cleaning up or decorating.

It would be simple if we could trace sex differences to differential treatment in schools. Some research indicates that in some areas boys and girls are treated equally. For instance, although boys are more aggressive, they are not reinforced for it in nursery school, and adults do not tolerate aggression, whether it is committed by boys or by girls (Smith and Green, 1975). Easy answers to the acquisition of sex-linked behavior patterns are untenable.

Textbooks may also contribute to the perpetuation of traditional sex roles. An interesting exercise is to go to the library and analyze the sex roles shown in children's books. A number of the books are blatant, not only in their narrative but also in their pictures. In one series of books on vocational possibilities, males were introduced to models who were engineers, scientists, and businesspeople, while females were shown as clerks, typists, and occasionally teachers. Even in math books this bias showed itself. When verbal problems that involved action sequences were given, such as Tom mixing chemicals from his chemistry set or fixing his bicycle, the person was most often male. When something was being done to someone, it was most often female. Frasher and Walker (1972) analyzed a number of readers used in elementary school and found a great deal of sex-role stereotyping in the texts. Males were most often the protagonists in stories, and few working women were noted. Mothers are most often shown as homemakers, but well out of proportion to the numbers performing that function full-time in real life. These texts also stereotyped children's activities, showing boys to be more active and girls playing many more quiet games. Publishers are now aware of these problems and are making progress in this area.

Are children really aware of the sex roles of the characters in stories? The evidence indicates that they are. Jennings (1975) found that children did remember the sex roles of children in stories, especially if these roles ran counter to their expectations. Jennings reversed some stories, allowing a girl to be a mail carrier and a boy to be a ballet dancer. The children remembered this switch and preferred the traditional sex roles in their stories. Children resist changes. Schools may help broaden children's ideas of appropriate sex roles, but they do not function in a vacuum. The child comes to school with some knowledge of sex roles.

In order to understand the acquisition of sex roles using a learning perspective, the child's entire environment, including family, friends, school, books, and television-viewing habits, must be taken into account. Just looking at parental treatment is not likely to be fruitful.

Psychoanalytic Theory

No theory is more controversial than Freud's ideas about the development of sex-typed behavior. According to Freud, the development of sex roles arises from events that occur during the **phallic stage**. Until early childhood, both boys and girls have similar psychosexual experiences. However, in the phallic stage, the **Oedipal** situation occurs. The little boy experiences sexual feelings toward his

phallic stage
Freud's third psychosexual stage, occurring during early childhood, in which the sexual energy is located in the genital area.

Oedipus complex
The conflict in Freudian theory in which the boy experiences sexual feelings toward his mother and wishes to rid himself of his father.

mother and wishes to rid himself of competition from his father. He also fears the father and is afraid that the father will find out about his wishes and castrate him. The little boy represses his feelings toward his mother and identifies with the father. In this way he becomes like his father and takes on the appropriate sex role.

The process with females is a bit convoluted. It is sometimes called the **Electra complex.** The little girl is also originally sexually attached to the mother, but slowly turns her attention to her father when she realizes she does not have a penis (Mullahy, 1948). Blaming her mother for her lack of a penis, she competes with her mother for the father's attention. She does not have to resolve this situation fully, since she doesn't have to worry about castration. She may never fully accept her "appropriate" sex role. Because of this, Freud felt that women were heir to more personality difficulties than men (Freud, 1933; Schaffer 1981).

One of the most important ideas underlying the psychoanalytic concept of sex roles is **identification.** Children identify with the parent of the same sex and acquire the appropriate sex role. Perhaps the most controversial portion of this theory involves Freud's argument that the girl's discovery that she lacks the male organ is a turning point in her life, which is now dominated by the desire to attain one through her father and later through her husband by having a baby. Freud sees every imaginable character trait of females beginning with this "penis envy," including inferiority, physical modesty, envy, and psychosexual difficulties. In the end, however, Freud's ideas in this realm have been largely rejected by developmental psychologists, for supporting evidence is lacking (Sears et al., 1965). The clinical problems Freud noted can be interpreted in terms of the social roles thrust on women by society (Horney, 1967, 1939). In addition, even though the Oedipal situation has been found in a number of societies (Kline, 1972), it is certainly not universal (Mead, 1974).

Sex-role Theories Reconsidered

No single theory can adequately explain how a child acquires a sex role, but each can add greatly to our knowledge. Behavior theory makes us aware of how important the differential treatment of boys and girls by parents and teachers can be. Social-learning theory stresses the importance of imitation and the models that surround the child. While few scientists today believe that biological explanations by themselves are sufficient to explain sex roles, maturational, hormonal and genetic differences add pieces to the puzzle. Finally, despite the problems inherent in the Freudian approach, the importance of identification and the part that both sexes may play in the socialization of the child are important to remember.

The Limitations of Traditional Stereotypes

Does it really matter whether you have a narrow or a broad definition of what is appropriate for your sex? The answer is a definite yes. Let's say that little Joey feels like crying, but refuses to do so because he thinks it is not manly. He decides that it's best not to express his emotions. Emotional expression remains inconsistent with his definition of gender role. Later in life, Joey may have difficulty expressing his feelings. His definition of being male limits his flexibility. Little Katie, who believes that girls don't get dirty or take leadership positions, has also limited her future activities unnecessarily.

Electra complex
The female equivalent to the Oedipus complex in which the female experiences sexual feelings toward her father and wishes to do away with her mother.

identification
The process by which children take on the characteristics of another person, often a parent.

*ACTION/
REACTION*

But He's a Boy!

The day Greg Martin came home from the hospital, his father bought a football and put it in his crib. He dreamed of his son being an "All-American." As Greg grew, Mr. Martin continued to give him tennis rackets, baseball gloves, basketballs, and the like. But last week four-year-old Greg asked for a Cabbage Patch doll, and his father hit the ceiling. "My son is not going to be a sissy and play with dolls. No way." Greg's mother sees nothing wrong with his playing with dolls. In fact, she secretly bought him one a few months ago, but allows Greg to play with it only when his father is not home, so he won't find out.

Greg's nursery school teacher told Mr. Martin that there was nothing wrong with a boy playing with dolls and that he was old-fashioned to think that way. Mr. Martin refused to believe that it wouldn't hurt the child, and took offense at the teacher's comments.

1. If you were Greg's mother, how would you handle the situation?
2. How would you rate the teacher's handling of the problem?

Children are greatly affected by the sex-role stereotypes they learn from their environment. **Sex-role stereotypes** are constellations of characteristics that people believe characterize men more or less than women (Best, 1977). For example, men are often seen as competitive, rational, aggressive, unemotional, objective, dominant, and assertive, whereas females are considered to be tactful, gentle, talkative, warm, and expressive (Broverman et al., 1972). Whether these characteristics actually represent sex differences is unimportant. The fact that people believe they do is enough to alter their expectations in social situations and to force children into narrow behavioral patterns.

Sex-role stereotypes appear early. Children as young as two or three years old have already learned some of them. For example, Kuhn and her colleagues (1978) found that both boys and girls believe that girls are more likely to talk, never hit, ask for help, clean, become nurses, cry, and cook. Boys are considered more likely to become bosses. Boys believe that they are more likely to become doctors and misbehave. Girls think they are more likely to look nice, kiss, and take care of babies, whereas boys are more likely to fight. Children have no stereotyped ideas for such activities as playing ball, being kind, being neat, or saying "I love you." Perhaps some sex-role stereotypes are declining. Some of these stereotypes may mirror what children see in real life. What can we expect if children see nothing but male doctors, men as authority figures, and their mothers cooking?

Sexual stereotypes are slow to change, but some evidence indicates that they are indeed changing. With so many women being added to the labor force, and the success some women have had in becoming executives and professionals, there are more role models for women than ever before. In addition, the women's movement has sensitized us to the limitations of the traditional sex-role stereotypes.

sex-role stereotypes
Groups of characteristics that people believe characterize one gender more than the other.

Androgyny: The Best of Both Worlds

Think of the stereotyped sex-role characteristics of males and females. List them if you can. Perhaps your list looks like the one in Table 10.3 on pages 390–

391. Broverman and his colleagues (1972) found that some of the more positive characteristics were stereotyped as feminine, while many more were considered masculine. For example, tactful, gentle, religious, expressive, and enjoying art and literature are positive. Broverman calls this the warmth-expressiveness cluster. On the other hand, on the competency cluster, such male characteristics

---

TABLE 10.3   A Listing of Sex-Trait Stereotypes

This table lists the prevailing sex-trait stereotypes indicated by the responses of 74 college men and 80 college women to a sex-role questionnaire. These qualities can be grouped into two clusters: a competency cluster, in which masculine traits are more desirable, and a warmth-expressiveness cluster, in which feminine traits are more desirable. As you can see, the desirable masculine competency qualities far outnumber the desirable feminine qualities found within the warmth-expressiveness cluster.

Competency Cluster: Masculine Pole Is More Desirable

Feminine	*Masculine*
Not at all aggressive	Very aggressive
Not at all independent	Very independent
Very emotional	Not at all emotional
Does not hide emotions at all	Almost always hides emotions
Very subjective	Very objective
Very easily influenced	Not at all easily influenced
Very submissive	Very dominant
Dislikes math and science very much	Likes math and science very much
Very excitable in a minor crisis	Not at all excitable in a minor crisis
Very passive	Very active
Not at all competitive	Very competitive
Very illogical	Very logical
Very home oriented	Very worldly
Not at all skilled in business	Very skilled in business
Very sneaky	Very direct
Does not know the way of the world	Knows the way of the world
Feelings easily hurt	Feelings not easily hurt
Not at all adventurous	Very adventurous
Has difficulty making decisions	Can make decisions easily
Cries very easily	Never cries
Almost never acts as a leader	Almost always acts as a leader
Not at all self-confident	Very self-confident
Very uncomfortable about being aggressive	Not at all uncomfortable about being aggressive
Not at all ambitious	Very ambitious
Unable to separate feelings from ideas	Easily able to separate feelings from ideas
Very dependent	Not at all dependent
Very conceited about appearance	Never conceited about appearance
Thinks women are always superior to men	Thinks men are always superior to women
Does not talk freely about sex with men	Talks freely about sex with men

Warmth-Expressiveness Cluster: Feminine Pole Is More Desirable

Feminine	Masculine
Doesn't use harsh language at all	Uses very harsh language
Very talkative	Not at all talkative
Very tactful	Very blunt
Very gentle	Very rough
Very aware of feelings of others	Not at all aware of feelings of others
Very religious	Not at all religious
Very interested in own appearance	Not at all interested in own appearance
Very neat in habits	Very sloppy in habits
Very quiet	Very loud
Very strong need for security	Very little need for security
Enjoys art and literature	Does not enjoy art and literature at all
Easily expresses tender feelings	Does not express tender feelings at all easily

Source: Broverman et al., 1972.

as activity, logical, worldly, direct, and competitive were considered more desirable.

Actually, whether these characteristics are really positive or negative depends on the situation. For instance, emotionality and subjectivity may be adaptive in some situations but not in others. The individual who has the best of both worlds is in the most flexible position to react, being capable of both showing emotions and not showing them, being subjective or objective. Furthermore, some of the characteristics that are not considered positive can easily be replaced by positive phrases. For instance, substitute "cooperative" for "not-at-all competitive," and the phrase has a different meaning. There are times when competition is undesirable and cooperation is better. There are times when an individual is better off being a follower than a leader, and vice versa.

Bem (1975, 1974) claims that people are better off if they have the flexibility to combine the best characteristics of males and females. Such people are called **androgynous**. Both extremely high masculinity and femininity is associated with very poor adjustment. These people are limited by the narrowness of their conception of sex role. Androgynous college students have higher self-esteem (Spence et al., 1975). Fathers who score high in androgyny tend to spend more time with their children (see Research Highlight "Just How Involved Is Daddy?" on page 392). The more flexible androgynous individuals also have a wider number of behavioral choices and are capable of adapting to new situations more easily.

An androgynous individual is no less a man or a woman. It is very important for a child to develop a strong gender identity (Lamb, 1979), but people benefit by widening their ideas of what behaviors go along with a gender label. When a woman feels secure enough to act assertively, and a man is secure enough to show emotion without being afraid that it is unmasculine, both have gained.

Socializing children into androgynous roles is not easy. My daughters have often been examined by female pediatricians, yet one surprised me by stating that boys can be doctors while girls are nurses. She certainly didn't get that limitation from us, or from her medical experiences. However, her peers and the me-

androgyny
The state of possessing the best characteristics of masculinity and femininity.

It's no secret that mothers do most of the child-rearing duties in the average family. Fathers do not bathe, dress, or feed their children very much. Mother predominates, even in such activities as playing, reading stories, and helping children with their schoolwork. This is especially disheartening, since studies show that paternal involvement in child-rearing is related to a child's academic competence as well as to a number of other desirable outcomes. Just what keeps fathers from being more involved with their children? Could it be that fathers view diapering, feeding, and comforting as feminine activities and not appropriate for a male?

This was the question Graeme Russell sought to answer. Russell reasoned that fathers who score high on the androgyny scale would be more likely to perform such child-rearing tasks as diapering and feeding and would interact more frequently with their children than men who score low on the androgyny dimension. Androgynous individuals combine the best stereotyped male and female traits and show more role flexibility than nonandrogynous people. Because the role of mother is so well stereotyped, whether or not a woman is androgynous probably would not matter as much.

To test this hypothesis, Russell interviewed forty-three couples living in the Sydney, Australia, area. He asked questions relating to the amount of time each parent spent at home or at work, the amount of time father and mother spent in child-rearing activities, and the kinds of activities that parents and children participated in together. Each parent was also given the Bem Sex Role Inventory, which measures androgyny.

Some of Russell's results are found in Table A. Notice that the father diapered the child only 19 percent of the time and fed the child only 14 percent of the time. One reason often advanced for this dismal record is the lack of time. If father works all day and comes home late at night, he simply doesn't have the time to interact with his children. But this explanation does not fit the facts. Although all the fathers in Russell's sample had full-time positions, almost half the women were also employed either full- or part-time. In addition, duties that are performed mostly at night, such as helping children with schoolwork, playing with them, attending to their needs before bed, and reading them stories, are also heavily weighted toward mother, even though most of the fathers were home and available. These percentages are very close to those found in studies performed in the United States (see Table B).

Russell also found a relationship between father-child interaction and androgyny. The degree to which fathers interacted with their children was related to their scores on the androgyny scale, while mother's interactions were not. Androgynous fathers interacted more with their children and performed more of the child-care responsibilities than nonandrogynous fathers. Perhaps androgynous fathers are more nurturant because they do not label child-care activities as strictly mother's work.

Russell also found that fathers low in androgyny married to women high on the characteristic participated more in child care than low-androgyny fathers married to low-androgynous women. High-androgynous mothers may insist that their husbands participate, whether or not they think the duties are appropriate. Situational factors, such as employment status or physical health, may also be at work here.

To summarize, fathers do not perform many child-care duties, but androgynous fathers are more involved with their children than nonandrogynous fathers. Since paternal involvement is so important in child development, a redefinition of the father's role in child-care is necessary. Fathers must be convinced that helping to care for the children is not an exclusively female task.

Source: Graeme Russell, "The Father's Role and Its Relation to Masculinity, Femininity, and Androgyny," *Child Development,* 1978, *49,* 1174–1181.

TABLE A   **Mean Parent-Child Interaction for Mothers and Fathers Expressed in Hours/Week (H) and Percentage of the Total Mother- and Father-Child Interaction (%)**

	Feed	*Dress*	*Change Diapers*	*Bath*	*Attend at Night*	*Read Stories*	*Help School*	*Play*
Mothers:								
H	10.5	3.39	1.43	1.52	.38	1.37	.29	13.73
%	86	86	81	74	72	70	62	61
Fathers:								
H	1.76	.5	.34	.52	.15	.59	.17	8.88
%	14	14	19	26	28	30	37	39

TABLE B **Australian Data Compared to U.S. Data**	*Mother*		*Father*	
	Australia	*United States*	*Australia*	*United States*
Time present	9.0	10.0	3.2	5.4
Feeding	1.5	1.5	.25	.26
Cleaning	.91	1.1	.19	.3
Play	1.96	2.0	1.3	1.25

Note: Figures are in hours/day.

dia often stereotype these roles, and she picked them up. Trying to broaden children's conceptions of sex roles is sometimes an uphill battle, but it is worth the effort.

READY FOR NEW CHALLENGES

Early childhood is a time of great change. The preschooler's social world is expanding rapidly. Parents, peers, nursery school teachers, and siblings all have an effect on the child. Preschoolers are active, curious, and playful. If parents and teachers encourage their healthful activities, they gain the sense of initiative that Erikson believes is so important. If parents set limits in a loving atmosphere and allow preschoolers some freedom to choose, the children become competent and independent and develop a positive view of themselves.

This is demonstrated well by the story of the little girl who was happily playing in the grass early one spring morning. After a neighbor watched her for a while, she asked the youngster where her parents were. "They're sleeping," came the response. "And how about your brothers?" "Oh," said the little girl, "they're also in the house." "Aren't you lonely?" asked her neighbor. "Lonely," repeated the child, "no, I'm not lonely, *I like me*." This child is ready for the challenges of middle childhood and school, which come next.

Chapter Summary

1. Play helps develop a child's mental, physical, and social abilities. It serves as an outlet for the child's frustrations and allows the child to experiment with new roles. The complexity of play increases with age. Boys play in a rougher fashion than girls.

2. Siblings may offer support and help as well as serving as sources of discord. Parents should intervene if sibling arguments become physically or psychologically damaging.

3. Baumrind identified three types of parenting styles. Authoritarian parents seek to control their child's every action, leading to children who are suspicious and withdrawn. Permissive parents rarely use discipline and allow almost total freedom. These children do not show much self-control or self-reliance. Authoritative parents give their children freedom within limits. These children are competent and self-controlled.

4. Discipline involves training in self-control; punishment involves inflicting pain for violating a rule. Punishment is most effective when it is moderate, swift, certain, and combined with positive reinforcement for the correct behavior.

5. Child abuse is a major problem. In order to understand abuse, the characteristics of the parents, child, and situation must be taken into consideration. Many abusing parents can be helped to stop abusing their children.

6. Research has generally found that males are more aggressive than females, that girls have greater verbal abilities, and that boys excel in visual spatial tasks and ability in math. Sex differences tells us nothing about the cause of the difference and account for very little of the behavioral differences between individuals. In addition, a great deal of overlap exists between the sexes.

7. Sex roles involve the behavioral patterns and psychological characteristics appropriate for each sex. Biological factors, including hormonal, genetic, and maturational differences, have been advanced to explain these differences, but a completely biological explanation is untenable. Children learn their sex roles through operant conditioning and the imitation of the role models in their environment. Freud saw sex roles in terms of the resolution of the Oedipal situation in the phallic stage, when children identify with the parent of the same sex.

8. People who have the best of both stereotyped male and female characteristics are said to be androgynous and are more flexible in their behavior.

■ Answers to True or False Questions

1. *True.* Boys play much more roughly than girls.

2. *False.* Correct statement: The type of quarrel and its possible damaging results determine whether parents should intervene in a sibling dispute.

3. *False.* Correct statement: The children of permissive parents do not show much self-reliance or self-control.

4. *False.* Correct statement: Harsh punishment may lead to temporary improvement in behavior, but over the long term it is not as effective as moderate punishment.

5. *False.* Correct statement: The incidence of sexual abuse is grossly underreported.

6. *False.* Correct statement: Abusive parents do not have a distinct personality pattern that would definitely allow them to be identified before abusing their children.

7. *True.* Any child who requires special care due to some exceptionality is more likely to be abused.

8. *False.* Correct statement: Some consistent sex differences have been found.

9. *False.* Correct statement: Boys are punished more, and girls generally receive more praise.

10. *False.* Correct statement: The opposite is true. Mothers are more likely to treat their sons and daughters equally than fathers.

PART FOUR

Middle Childhood

CHAPTER ELEVEN

Physical and Cognitive Development in Middle Childhood

CHAPTER OUTLINE

THE PHOTO EXERCISE

PHYSICAL DEVELOPMENT IN MIDDLE
   CHILDHOOD

ACTION/REACTION   The Battle at the Dinner Table

THE STAGE OF CONCRETE OPERATIONS

MEMORY

THE BASIC SKILLS: THE THREE Rs

ACTION/REACTION   Read, Please Read

ACTION/REACTION   Education or Indoctrination?

FACTORS AFFECTING ACADEMIC
   ACHIEVEMENT

RESEARCH HIGHLIGHT   *Teacher Evaluations:*
   Gender Bias in Action?

TESTING THE SCHOOL-AGE CHILD

NEW FRONTIERS

EDUCATIONAL REFORM

■ *Are the Following Statements True or False?*

Try the True-False Quiz below. See if your answers correspond to the information in this chapter. Each question is repeated opposite the paragraph in which the answer can be found. The True-False Answer Box at the end of the chapter lists complete answers.

___ **1.** During the elementary school years, the child's growth rate increases.

___ **2.** On the average, girls weigh more than boys at age ten.

___ **3.** Physical education in elementary school leads to a decrease in academic performance.

___ **4.** Children underestimate their ability to recall items on a list.

___ **5.** When elementary school children claim they understand something, a parent or teacher can be reasonably certain that they do.

___ **6.** Reading achievement has declined among elementary school children in the past ten years.

___ **7.** In general, the more time spent watching television, the lower a child's academic achievement and reading ability.

___ **8.** American children are superior to Japanese children in mathematics.

___ **9.** A child's understanding of numbers is reflected in the ability to count from one to ten.

___ **10.** People are more likely to claim that their high schools are excellent than that their elementary schools are.

___ **11.** By the end of elementary school, girls are doing better in reading, while boys excel in math.

___ **12.** Intelligence is highly related to school achievement.

___ **13.** Tests of intelligence can also be used to measure creativity.

THE PHOTO EXERCISE

Collect a group of your childhood photographs. Then guess what age you were when they were taken. Baby pictures are easy. The infant's distinctive look is a giveaway. The changes between ages one and two, two and three, and perhaps three and four are so distinctive that you probably have little difficulty guessing your age. But look at your school photographs. It is difficult to tell whether you were seven or eight, nine or ten. You may make the decision by looking at other cues, such as your hairstyle or clothing. As children develop during the school years, physical changes occur at a slower rate. Children appear to be marking time, filling in.

PHYSICAL DEVELOPMENT IN MIDDLE CHILDHOOD

Middle childhood is indeed a time of horizontal growth. The gradual changes in height, weight, and appearance can lead us to conclude that little of interest is going on. As we shall see, this is a mistake. Though the changes may be less spectacular than those that occur in earlier years, they are no less important.

Growth

1. *True or False:*
During the elementary school years, the child's growth rate increases.

The rate of growth continues to decline during middle childhood until about age ten, eleven, or twelve (Williams and Stith, 1980). Girls are a bit shorter than boys, until adolescence, but because girls experience their adolescent growth spurt about two years earlier than boys, girls are actually taller for a couple of years (see Table 11.1). By fourteen or so, boys regain their height advantage (Tanner, 1978).

The average six-year-old boy stands about 45 inches (116.1 cm). By age eight he has achieved a stature of about 50 inches (127 cm), and by age ten he is about 54 inches tall (137.4 cm). The average female at six years stands about 45.1 inches (114.6 cm). By eight she has grown to almost 50 inches (126.4 cm), and by the age of ten she stands 54.4 inches tall (138.3 cm). But averages can be deceiving. Normal height and weight are best viewed in terms of a range of values—between the 25th and 75th percentiles. Thus, the normal height of an eight-year-old female may be anywhere between 48.1 inches (122.2 cm) and 51.4 inches (130.6 cm). If her height does not fall within these marks, it still does not automatically indicate a problem. Her parents may be unusually tall or short. However, large deviations should be investigated.

Growth Problems.   People often pay lip service to the fact that children mature at their own pace. One child may lose baby teeth at an earlier age or grow faster during childhood than another child. Still, this mental acceptance of individuality often does not coincide with our feelings. Parents are concerned if a child's development is slower than they expected, although it may still be within the normal range.

We are genetically programmed to reach an optimal height in adulthood. No amount of stretching, health food, exercise, or hormone treatments will make a fairly healthy five-foot-seven-inch male into a six-foot-eight-inch basketball star.

TABLE 11.1 Growth in Middle Childhood

Stature is noted in centimeters. To convert to inches multiply by .39.

Sex and Age	Percentile						
	5th	10th	25th	50th	75th	90th	95th
Male	Stature in centimeters						
6.0 years	107.7	109.6	112.5	116.1	119.2	121.9	123.5
6.5 years	110.4	112.3	115.3	119.0	122.2	124.9	126.6
7.0 years	113.0	115.0	118.0	121.7	125.0	127.9	129.7
7.5 years	115.6	117.6	120.6	124.4	127.8	130.8	132.7
8.0 years	118.1	120.2	123.2	127.0	130.5	133.6	135.7
8.5 years	120.5	122.7	125.7	129.6	133.2	136.5	138.8
9.0 years	122.9	125.2	128.2	132.2	136.0	139.4	141.8
9.5 years	125.3	127.6	130.8	134.8	138.8	142.4	144.9
10.0 years	127.7	130.1	133.4	137.5	141.6	145.5	148.1
10.5 years	130.1	132.6	136.0	140.3	144.6	148.7	151.5
11.0 years	132.6	135.1	138.7	143.3	147.8	152.1	154.9
11.5 years	135.0	137.7	141.5	146.4	151.1	155.6	158.5
12.0 years	137.6	140.3	144.4	149.7	154.6	159.4	162.3
Female							
6.0 years	106.6	108.4	111.3	114.6	118.1	120.8	122.7
6.5 years	109.2	111.0	114.1	117.6	121.3	124.2	126.1
7.0 years	111.8	113.6	116.8	120.6	124.4	127.6	129.5
7.5 years	114.4	116.2	119.5	123.5	127.5	130.9	132.9
8.0 years	116.9	118.7	122.2	126.4	130.6	134.2	136.2
8.5 years	119.5	121.3	124.9	129.3	133.6	137.4	139.6
9.0 years	122.1	123.9	127.7	132.2	136.7	140.7	142.9
9.5 years	124.8	126.6	130.6	135.2	139.8	143.9	146.2
10.0 years	127.5	129.5	133.6	138.3	142.9	147.2	149.5
10.5 years	130.4	132.5	136.7	141.5	146.1	150.4	152.8
11.0 years	133.5	135.6	140.0	144.8	149.3	153.7	156.2
11.5 years	136.6	139.0	143.5	148.2	152.6	156.9	159.5
12.0 years	139.8	142.3	147.0	151.5	155.8	160.0	162.7

Source: P. V. V. Hamill, et al., 1977.

Although nutrition, health, and medical care are important in reaching optimal height, each person will do that in his or her own way. But we use chronological age as the marker, and therein lies the problem.

Imagine that you have three well-nourished, healthy ten-year-old boys standing next to each other. By coincidence, all were born on the same day in the same year. Would they be the same height? Probably not, you might answer, because their genetic endowment differs. This is true, but there is another possibility. What if I tell you that Boy 1 is only 8.5 years old in biological or maturational terms, Boy 2 is exactly 10, and Boy 3 is 11.5 years old. Boy 3 is far older than Boy 1 biologically, even though their **chronological ages** as measured in birthdays are the same (Krogman, 1980). This concept of **maturational age** can help us better understand the timing and rate of children's growth. Perhaps we should think of growth from the prenatal period to adulthood as a race that some of us run faster and some run slower. At any point in the twenty years, some of us may be ahead, some just on schedule, and some behind. Those that are ahead are maturationally more advanced than those that are behind (Krogman, 1980).

chronological age
The person's age according to birthdays.

maturational age
The child's level of maturation relative to his or her peers.

If we think in terms of maturational age, we are forced to consider development as an individual process. In addition, maturational age is a better measure of what can be expected of a child than chronological age (Krogman, 1980). Consider a six-year-old who is maturationally behind yet who may be the same height as another child who is "right on schedule." The child "on schedule" will be more advanced and more ready for school. In fact, there is a relationship between body maturation and achievement in first grade (Williams and Stith, 1980).

If maturational age is more important than chronological age, why isn't it used more often? Consider how each is determined. Calculating chronological age is easy. All it entails is a bit of arithmetic, but measuring maturational age is more involved. It involves an examination of X rays, and this is done only when there is a definite reason for it.

For example, a young boy may be lagging behind his peers and have a history of chronic illness, and his doctors and parents may be concerned about his lack of growth. If the doctor believes that a problem may exist, an X ray of the child's wrist might be ordered. The wrist is used for many reasons. First, the amount of radiation that is required is minimal, so X rays can be repeated at regular intervals. The dosage is about 4 millirads, about the same amount a child would get spending a week in the mountains (Tanner, 1978). Second, excellent atlases of bone development in the wrist allow us to determine just how advanced a child is on the way to maturity. We may find that the subject is well behind biologically

The maturational age of a child is easily discovered through an X ray examination of the child's wrist.

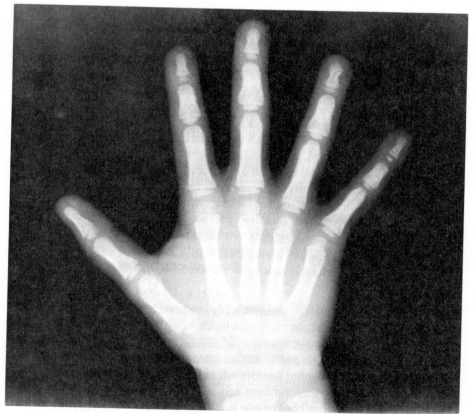

and has a long way to go to reach adult height. In other words, the boy will grow a great deal more. On the other hand, the X ray may show that his skeletal age is very mature and that he is approaching his adult height.

Doctors are most likely to be challenged by cases of extremely short children whose parents are of normal height. Why are some children very short? A number of reasons, including illness, metabolic problems, and emotional difficulties, have been advanced. Various metabolic disorders that involve the thyroid or pituitary glands affect height, as do some inherited defects. Children who lack emotional security may not grow as much as those who have a secure home life. However, the chief worldwide reason for short stature is malnutrition, especially in underdeveloped nations. Malnutrition, stunted growth, and retarded development are well correlated (Krogman, 1980). This is less likely to be the case in Western nations, where most of the difference in height during middle childhood is due to variations in genetic endowment.

What can be done if a child is extremely short for his or her age? If the condition is due solely to an endocrine problem, administration of growth hormone may help. It speeds up growth, but will not change the genetically programmed end point. Such treatments may have psychological benefits for the child.

Weight

Although boys are heavier at birth, both sexes are of about equal weight at eight and a half years of age (see Table 11.2). Girls then become heavier at about nine or ten, and this remains true until about fourteen and a half years, when boys equal and surpass girls (Tanner, 1978). The average male at six years of age weights 45.5 pounds (20.69 kg), by eight and a half years 58.7 pounds (26.66 kg), and by age ten 69 pounds (31.44 kg). The average six-year-old girl weighs almost 43 pounds (19.52 kg), by eight and a half she weights 58.5 pounds (26.58 kg), and by ten, 71.6 pounds (32.55 kg). Again, we should be wary of averages and speak in terms of percentiles. For example, a ten-year-old girl may weigh anywhere between 63 pounds (28.71 kg) and 82.6 pounds (37.53 kg) and still be considered "normal." Substantial deviations from these marks should be investigated. Many deviations may reflect differences in physique or developmental age, but some may indicate physical problems. Substantial deviations in weight may contribute to psychological problems, as in the case of the overweight or obese child.

Childhood Obesity.   Obesity is more difficult to define than one would think. Some people consider obesity simply 20 percent over chart weight, but this is not an adequate definition. Some very muscular athletes may weigh more than this but are not obese. Today some scientists measure body fat by investigating the layers of fat, usually around the tricep areas, and an abritrary measure of obesity is set (Krogman, 1980; Corbin, 1980). More than 20 percent of school-aged children are obese (Hamilton and Whitney, 1982). These children are more likely to be shunned (Richardson et al., 1961), to have fewer friends (Staffieri, 1967), and to have a poor body image (Mendelson and White, 1985).

Parents often fall victim to the "baby fat" theory, thinking that a fat child is a healthy child. Other parents argue that children who are obese will grow out of it. Both points of view are wrong. Obese children are not especially healthy, and juvenile obesity is related to adult obesity (Corbin, 1980a; Williams and Stith, 1980). The longer a child is obese, the more difficult it is to modify the condition.

2. *True or False:*
On the average, girls weigh more than boys at age ten.

TABLE 11.2   **Weight Gain in Middle Childhood**
All data is given in kilograms. To convert to pounds multiply by 2.2.

Sex and Age	Percentile						
	5th	10th	25th	50th	75th	90th	95th
Male	*Weight in kilograms*						
6.0 years	16.93	17.72	19.07	20.69	22.40	24.31	26.34
6.5 years	17.78	18.62	20.02	21.74	23.62	25.76	28.16
7.0 years	18.64	19.53	21.00	22.85	24.94	27.36	30.12
7.5 years	19.52	20.45	22.02	24.03	26.36	29.11	32.73
8.0 years	20.40	21.39	23.09	25.30	27.91	31.06	34.51
8.5 years	21.31	22.34	24.21	26.66	29.61	33.22	36.96
9.0 years	22.25	23.33	25.40	28.13	31.46	35.57	39.58
9.5 years	23.25	24.38	26.68	29.73	33.46	38.11	42.35
10.0 years	24.33	25.52	28.07	31.44	35.61	40.80	45.27
10.5 years	25.51	26.78	29.59	33.30	37.92	43.63	48.31
11.0 years	26.80	28.17	31.25	35.30	40.38	46.57	51.47
11.5 years	28.24	29.72	33.08	37.46	43.00	49.61	54.73
12.0 years	29.85	31.46	35.09	39.78	45.77	52.73	58.09
Female							
6.0 years	16.05	16.72	17.86	19.52	21.44	23.89	25.75
6.5 years	16.85	17.51	18.76	20.61	22.68	25.50	27.59
7.0 years	17.71	18.39	19.78	21.84	24.16	27.39	29.68
7.5 years	18.62	19.37	20.95	23.26	25.90	29.57	32.07
8.0 years	19.62	20.45	22.26	24.84	27.88	32.04	34.71
8.5 years	20.68	21.64	23.70	26.58	30.08	34.73	37.58
9.0 years	21.82	22.92	25.27	28.46	32.44	37.60	40.64
9.5 years	23.05	24.29	26.94	30.45	34.94	40.61	43.85
10.0 years	24.36	25.76	28.71	32.55	37.53	43.70	47.17
10.5 years	25.75	27.32	30.57	34.72	40.17	46.84	50.57
11.0 years	27.24	28.97	32.49	36.95	42.84	49.96	54.00
11.5 years	28.83	30.71	34.48	39.23	45.48	53.03	57.42
12.0 years	30.52	32.53	36.52	41.53	48.07	55.99	60.81

Source: P. V. V. Hamill, et al., 1977.

Obesity is a complicated disorder that may be caused by a number of factors. Genetic endowment can play a part. Studies performed on the Pima Indian tribe in Arizona, where alarming rates of obesity and diabetes are found, have led some authorities to that conclusion. Perhaps being able to store fat more efficiently was beneficial when food supplies were very low, but this same efficiency becomes counterproductive if food is plentiful and obesity is the result (Brody, 1980a).

Obesity seems to run in families. A child has only a 7 percent chance of becoming obese if neither parent is overweight, a 40 percent chance if one parent is overweight, and an 80 percent chance if both are overweight (Winick, 1975). But this does not prove that obesity is inherited, because children learn how and what to eat during childhood. Perhaps they are reinforced for eating everything and taking second helpings. Perhaps they witness their parents overeating or consider the evening gluttony the highlight of their day. Some children learn to eat the wrong foods and consume thousands of empty calories from junk food each day. Lack of exercise may also be an important consideration. Obese children are less active than their nonobese peers, although they may not always be aware of it (Bullen et al., 1964).

Scientists have identified two different types of obesity. **Hyperplastic obesity** involves the formation of too many fat cells, whereas **hypertrophic obesity** involves the swelling of fat cells with fat no matter what the number (Gelfand et al., 1982). Obese people may have twice as many fat cells as nonobese people (Hirsch, 1970). Hyperplastic obesity may be the result of overfeeding during the early years of childhood (Hirsch and Knittle, 1970; Knittle and Hirsch, 1968). A person suffering from this type of obesity may find long-term weight loss especially difficult because fat may be liberated from cells but the cells stay with us. This theory is still controversial, and the exact manner in which fat cells are developed is still not known (Tanner, 1978). However, it remains one of the more challenging theories in this area.

Childhood obesity is difficult to correct (Becker and Drash, 1979), and very heavy dieting may injure children as they develop. Three approaches to childhood obesity include watching caloric intake, providing psychological support, and increasing the amount of exercise the child gets (Williams and Stith, 1980). Of course, any dietary plan should be executed under a doctor's care.

Besides height and weight gains, a number of other physical changes occur during middle childhood. The forehead becomes flatter, the arms and legs more slender, the nose grows larger, the shoulders squarer, the abdomem flatter, and the waistline more pronounced (Williams and Stith, 1980). These changes occur gradually. The more noticeable changes are the shedding of the baby teeth and the eruption of the permanent teeth.

hyperplastic obesity
Obesity caused by the formation of an excessive number of fat cells.

hypertrophic obesity
Obesity caused by the swelling of fat cells with fat.

ACTION/ REACTION

The Battle at the Dinner Table

Hope is a bright, cheerful, resourceful nine-year-old. She is also obese. Both her parents are concerned about the problem, because it seems to be getting worse. When Hope was an overweight preschooler, her mother believed she would grow out of it, but she didn't. Her father has recently put Hope on a strict diet, but she cheats at every opportunity.

Hope's mother asked her whether she wants to lose weight, and her answer was "I guess so." Still, her weight goes up, and Hope's parents are becoming less patient. They watch what Hope eats, but they can't control her eating away from home or even from sneaking snacks at home. They made an appointment for Hope to talk to a friendly neighbor Marge, hoping the child would open up to someone. Hope confided in Marge that she wanted to lose weight but just couldn't. Hope burst into tears. She dislikes her father for harping on her problem.

1. If you were Hope's parents, how would you deal with the situation?

deciduous teeth
The scientific term for "baby teeth."

The Tooth Fairy Cometh

The shedding of **deciduous teeth** is perhaps the most obvious physical occurrence during early middle childhood. When a child loses a baby tooth, the tradition is that the Tooth Fairy leaves a coin or a dollar bill in place of the tooth under the child's pillow. Losing their teeth is a sign for children that they are growing up. But the gaps left in the mouth can cause temporary cosmetic problems as well as some difficulty in pronunciation.

Human beings have a complement of twenty baby teeth and thirty-two permanent teeth (see Figure 11.1(a) and (b)). The first permanent tooth is usually the "six year molar," which does not replace any baby tooth (Smart and Smart, 1978). This tooth may actually erupt at any time between four and a half and eight years of age (Krogman, 1980). It is not easily recognizable and may be decayed and lost if not properly maintained. Most parents do not put much effort into dental care for their young children thinking they have "only baby teeth" anyway, but this is unfortunate, because premature loss can lead to dental problems, including difficulties with the bite (Williams and Stith, 1980). As a rule, girls lose their baby teeth before boys.

Motor Skill Development

The pattern of gradual growth and development that we saw with height, weight, and changes in proportion is also shown in the areas of motor and skill development.

The loss of baby teeth is one of the hallmarks of middle childhood.

FIGURE 11.1   **Average Ages for (a) The Eruption and Shedding of Baby Teeth and (b) The Eruption of Permanent Teeth**
Both the eruption and shedding of baby teeth and the replacement of baby teeth by permanent teeth are maturational changes.

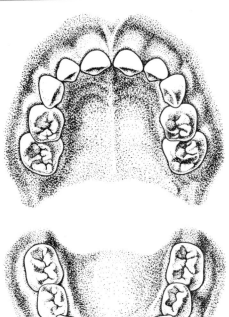

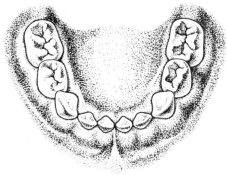

(a)

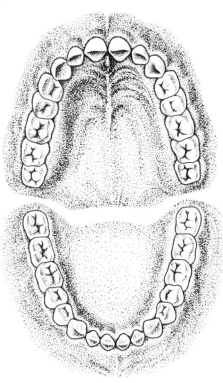

(b)

Upper teeth	Eruption date	Shedding date
Central incisor	8–12 months	6–7 years
Lateral incisor	9–13 months	7–8 years
Canine (cuspid)	16–22 months	10–12 years
First molar	13–19 months	9–11 years
Second molar	25–33 months	10–12 years

Lower teeth	Eruption date	Shedding date
Second molar	23–31 months	10–12 years
First molar	14–18 months	9–11 years
Canine (cuspid)	17–23 months	9–12 years
Lateral incisor	10–16 months	7–8 years
Central incisor	6–10 months	6–7 years

Upper teeth	Eruption date
Central incisor	7–8 years
Lateral incisor	8–9 years
Canine (cuspid)	11–12 years
First premolar (first bicuspid)	10–11 years
Second premolar (second bicuspid)	10–12 years
First molar	6–7 years
Second molar	12–13 years
Third molar	17–21 years

Lower teeth	Eruption date
Third molar	17–21 years
Second molar	11–13 years
First molar	6–7 years
Second premolar (second bicuspid)	11–12 years
First premolar (first bicuspid)	10–12 years
Canine (cuspid)	9–10 years
Lateral incisor	7–8 years
Central incisor	6–7 years

Source: American Dental Association.

Take a few minutes to watch elementary school children during recess. Then visit a nursery school and compare the differences between the children's activities at each school. Differences are definitely there but difficult to describe. The elementary school children run, hop, jump, and throw more easily than the nursery school children. As you watch the elementary school children playing ball or tag, notice how easily they run and balance. By the time children enter elementary school, they have developed many motor skills. They can run, climb, gallop, and hop. Skipping is just being mastered, as are throwing, catching, and kicking, while balancing is reasonably good. During the next six years, skills are refined and modified (DeOreo and Keogh, 1980).

During middle childhood, running speed and the ability to jump for distance increases (DeOreo and Keogh, 1980). The ability to throw both for accuracy and for distance also improves (Cratty, 1970), as does balance. These improvements are due both to maturation and to practice.

Are boys better than girls at these skills? Boys are superior in running speed and throwing, while girls excel in tasks that require agility, rhythm, and hopping (Cratty, 1970). Boys are also stronger than girls during this period, but girls show more muscular flexibility. Although balance is good in both sexes, girls between the ages of seven and nine tend to be superior (Cratty, 1970). Boys can jump higher and longer, girls tend to hop better. Girls also learn to skip sooner (DeOreo and Keogh, 1980).

These differences may seem more important than they really are. The overlap between the sexes is great (Lockhart, 1980), and training and motivation are important factors. Frequently, boys are more motivated to perform on tests of physical ability and are more likely to practice certain skills, such as throwing, which involve the large muscles. In addition, the differences between the average boy and girl on many of these tasks are not very great. If girls are encouraged to develop their skills, they can improve them immensely.

As boys and girls get older, however, differences in their physical abilities become more noticeable. Differences in performance before the age of about eleven or twelve are small (Corbin, 1980), but during adolescence males continue to improve, while females level off or may even decrease in physical ability (Espenschade, 1960). The decreased performance may be due to lack of motivation, fear of physical injury to female internal organs, or fear of appearing too masculine (Corbin, 1980B). It may also be due to society's expectations. For example, males are expected to participate in rugged sports that require strength. Females are more likely to be encouraged to engage in physical activity involving agility. Females may not be taught the same physical skills as males. Society's different expectations for the physical abilities and training of males and females are somewhat reduced today from what they were even twenty years ago, but they are still present. This is unfortunate, because the benefits of physical fitness are great for both sexes.

Physical Fitness and Health

Children who are physically fit are healthier and more resistant to fatigue and stress (Krogman, 1980). Physical fitness may prevent adult heart trouble and increase stamina (Brody, 1980A). Physical activity is also needed to support normal growth and development. For example, exercise increases bone width and mineralization (Bailey, 1975). It also has social benefits, since group sports are often important social activities and being excluded may interfere with social development (Williams and Stith, 1980). Exercise is also a form of entertainment.

Exercise can effect learning. Consider the normal school day. The child is expected to stay in his seat, is allowed to walk around only when necessary and leads an inactive life. This is not in keeping with the image of the child as an active being who needs and desires physical activity. Providing regular physical activity improves learning. French doctors and educators were concerned about the heavy intellectual load in French schools that was almost unrelieved by any physical education or recreation. Beginning in 1951 the town of Vanves, a suburb of Paris, inaugurated a new program in which the gross amount of time spent in academic activities was reduced, the time being replaced by physical education, art, music, and other activities. Children did their schoolwork in the mornings. Parents were concerned that their children would fall behind academically or would catch more colds, but just the opposite occurred. Children's academic performance actually improved, and they were more resistant to stress. They also appeared happier, were in better health, and showed a more positive attitude toward their work. By 1969 this pattern had spread throughout the rest of France (Bailey, 1975).

3. *True or False:* Physical education in elementary school leads to a decrease in academic performance.

The benefits of physical education are many, but what type of physical education is necessary? In the United States, too much of it falls under the heading of competitive sports (Krogman, 1980). Winning may be the most important thing in professional sports, but it may be counterproductive for children in the elementary school years, where the "losers" may be turned off to physical activities. In addition, certain contact activities so common in football may lead to physical injuries. Even in baseball, a child who pitches should be watched for elbow and arm problems. Roller-skating and bicycling are physical activities that are less competitive but still enjoyable. Too much time may also be spent on the few who are the best—who train the easiest—and not enough time on those who need it the most. Physical education has a great many potential benefits for all children, and a physical education program must address each of these criticisms.

Readiness for School

Think of all the physical, mental, and behavioral skills necessary for academic success. Children must be able to sit in one place, listen to an adult, and attend to lessons (Blank and Klig, 1982). They must be intellectually mature enough to understand what is going on, emotionally emancipated from their parents, so that they can form relationships with others, and have some measure of self-control (Kohen-Raz, 1977).

In almost every culture, children begin to attend school sometime between the ages of five and seven (Blank and Klig, 1982). Traditionally, we use the child's chronological age to indicate school readiness, but only a very weak case can be made for this practice. Many children are simply not ready to master schoolwork (Ilg and Ames, 1972).

Reading is the most important skill a child learns in first grade, and parents are anxious that their children learn to read as soon as possible. Yet many children are not ready to read in kindergarten or first grade (Perkins, 1975). A mental age of about six and a half is often considered necessary for acquiring the skill (Durkin, 1970), but this presents a problem, because some children may not be mentally, physically, or emotionally mature enough to tackle the challenge. Parents can help in some ways (see Figure 11.2). If children cannot recognize shapes, they cannot begin to learn their letters (Blank and Klig, 1982). Parents may intro-

---

FIGURE 11.2   "What's a Parent To Do?" A Guide to Helping Your Child Succeed
Parents can help their children succeed in elementary school.

Read to your child and with your child. Your presence communicates assurance of love and support; your shared interest in reading shows its importance, value, and pleasure.

Maintain close, supportive interest in what your child is doing in school. "Sure, you may be worn out, but take the time to go over those papers the kids bring home" is an example cited by elementary-school principal Dick Lucas.

Know your child's teacher. Effective schooling is a partnership, not a contest. Get to school whenever possible. Let the teacher know you are interested. Compare notes with the teacher.

Pay heed to periodic health screening, signs of excess pressure, or frequent absence.

Put some bounds on television watching. This remarkable invention contributes greatly to many aspects of your child's learning. But it is also addictive and is no substitute for a good book.

Broaden your child's first-hand experience. Within a mile of any home in America is a gold mine of activity and experience involving natural environments, people, and things. The concepts of math and language and the richness of nature and the arts are there to be explored together, whether you live next to a woodlot or a parking lot. The richer the direct experience, the more sense is made of the words in schoolbooks.

Accept differing rates of progress. Don't compare children. "It may sound too blunt," said one first-grade teacher, "but tell parents to lay off. Don't push for early achievement."

Communicate a sense of your backing to your child's school and teacher. Support the process of schooling with gifts to your child of books and materials that encourage learning. Show that reading has a purpose and is gratifying.

Become politically active for your children. Attend school-board meetings and demand comparative facts on class size in primary grades and high school. Most systems heavily favor the secondary schools, allowing only 10 to 15 students in advanced science classes, for example, while permitting enrollments of 28 to 30 in the crucial kindergarten-to-third-grade years. When the football crowd asks for another assistant coach, it's probably in your child's best interests to take all of the first-grade parents to the school-board meeting and demand a reading teacher instead. Organize the parents of young children and get elected to the school board.

Become informed about promising educational practices. School systems are recognizing the wide variations in readiness among young children by organizing kindergarten-through-second-grade continuous-progress programs, or "primary blocks," that reduce failure by varying rates of progress. Other schools have interage groups, with two-year age spans. In England, many schools have "family groupings" where the class stays together with the same teacher for more than one year.

Source: Roberts, 1980.

duce their children to shapes, read to them, provide a home where reading is considered an enjoyable activity, and generally instill in their children a positive attitude toward learning, but even with this excellent background some children, especially boys, will not be ready for reading instruction (Ilg and Ames, 1972).

The lack of readiness may be due to a deficiency in many areas. Children may not have the necessary physical attributes, such as the ability to focus on the material to be read (Moore and Moore, 1976), or they may lack a left-right sequence. They may be too immature behaviorally to sit in a chair, listen to the teacher, and follow directions. They may also lack the cognitive ability to understand the work.

Many schools now give *reading-readiness tests* to determine whether a child is ready to learn to read. Reading-readiness tests measure a number of skills and abilities, including associating pictured objects with the spoken word for that object, visual discrimination, sentence comprehension, the ability to count and write numbers, word recognition, and auditory discrimination (Heilman, 1967).

Once a child's weaknesses are discovered, a decision is made about how to remedy the deficiency. Sometimes a program of instruction is required, at other times maturaiton must be allowed to take its course. If children are taught reading before they have the requisite skills, only frustration can result. Since children develop at their own rate, some children will be ready to read before others—a point anxious parents should keep in mind.

THE STAGE OF CONCRETE OPERATIONS

The school experience during the middle years of childhood is so important that these years are often called the school years. As children enter first grade, at about the age of six or so, the long preoperational stage is drawing to a close, and children are entering the stage of concrete operations.

The shift from the preoperational stage to the **concrete operational stage** is gradual. A child does not go to sleep one night in the preoperational stage and wake up the next morning in the concrete stage. The child does not go to sleep egocentric, unable to fully understand classification and conservation, and wake up with fully developed abilities in these areas. These skills develop gradually over the years.

To understand this stage, we must first look at its name. The stage is called "concrete" because the children still deal with concrete objects, rather than with abstractions, when they consider change (Forman and Kuschner, 1977; Mayer, 1977). They must either see or be able to imagine objects. If children in this stage are presented with a purely verbal problem that involves hypotheses, they cannot solve it, but if you explain it in real, concrete terms, they have no difficulty with the challenge (Wadsworth, 1971). The second part of the name, "operations," has two meanings. First, it has to do with being able to develop internalized reversible strategies for dealing with problems (Phillips, 1975). Second, it may refer to the nature of the logical structures that underlie performance. For example, Piaget calls the preschool years *preoperational* because preschoolers cannot reason logically. He considers cognitive functioning in the school years in terms of *concrete operations* because school-age children can perform operations on concrete items. Finally, during the *formal operations state*, as we shall see in

concrete operational stage Piaget's third stage of cognitive development, lasting roughly from seven through eleven years of age, in which children develop the ability to perform logical operations, such as conservation.

Chapter Fifteen, adolescents can deal with hypothetical information and use scientific logic.

The Decline of Egocentrism

Children in the concrete stage of operations become less egocentric. They understand that other people see the world differently. They now know that others can get different results from the same data, and they seek to validate their own view of the world (Wadsworth, 1971). This is accomplished through social interaction, during which they can share their thoughts and verify their view of the world (Piaget, 1928). In addition, they can now take the perspective of the other person and can imagine what others are thinking of them in a relatively simple way (Harter, 1983). They are capable of being more sensitive to the feelings of others and imagining how others would feel in various situations. Language becomes less egocentric. Preschoolers often use such pronouns as *he* or *she* without offering adequate information to the listener concerning the person to whom they are referring. They figure that since they know who they are talking about, so do you (Pulaski, 1980). As the child matures, this tendency is greatly reduced.

Reversibility, the Ability to Decenter, and Transformations

During middle childhood, the limitations of preoperational thought begin to fade slowly. Children develop the ability to reverse operations, to realize that if you roll a clay ball into a long worm you can reverse your operation and recreate the ball of clay. They develop the ability to decenter, to take into consideration more than one dimension. Children now realize that the increase in the length of the clay worm compensates for the decrease in its width. They also begin to understand transformations—to understand that as objects change position or shape they progress through a series of intermediate points. Piaget did not find these abilities in the preschooler (see pages 330–332).

Conservation

The crowning achievement of the concrete operational stage is the ability to conserve. The simplest example is the famous beaker experiment described in Chapter Nine, in which a researcher takes two identical beakers that are long and thin and pours equal amounts of liquid in each. Then, in front of the child, the contents of one tall beaker are poured into a squat beaker. The preschool child cannot take both height and width into consideration, cannot reverse the operation of pouring, and attends to the end state rather than transformations, making conservation impossible (Piaget and Inhelder, 1969). But school-age children find such problems relatively easy. They may even show surprise when younger children don't get them right. But conservation is not a single entity. Conservation of number, substance, weight, and volume occur at different ages but in a specific order.

Conservation of Number.   Show children displays of seven pennies in which the coins are either grouped in very close density or spread out. The four-year-old is certain that the spread-out display has more coins than the other one.

The six- or seven-year-old develops a sense of conservation of number and knows that the spacing does not matter.

Conservation of Substance.   The clay ball example described on page 328 demonstrates conservation of substance. The child now knows that no clay was lost in transforming the ball to a worm and back again. At about age seven or eight, children discover conservation of substance (Piaget and Inhelder, 1969).

Conservation of Weight.   The seven-year-old may understand that no clay was lost during the transformation, but this child probably will not understand that they both still weigh the same. Conservation of weight comes later, at about nine or ten (Piaget and Inhelder, 1969).

Conservation of Volume.   The last conservation problem to be solved correctly is conservation of volume. Make two balls of clay and put them in two identical beakers containing equal amounts of water. The child should understand that the clay balls are equally large and equally weighted. Then put the clay balls in the containers and show that they displace the same volume of liquid because they cause the level of the water to rise the same amount. Now change the shape of one of the balls and ask whether it would still make the water rise to the previous height (Diamond, 1982). Typically, conservation of volume appears at about the age of eleven or twelve (Piaget and Inhelder, 1969).

Seriation and Classification

School-age children also further develop the ability to seriate and to classify. They can easily arrange a series of sticks in terms of length, and later weight and finally volume (Wadsworth, 1971). Their ability to classify also greatly improves. In fact, the school-age children are known for their propensity to collect things (Kegan, 1982). They will collect anything, and thereby practice their skills of classification. They begin to realize that an item can be classified in many ways and belongs to a great many classes at a particular time.

Logic and Thinking

The school-age child's thought processes are certainly a great improvement over those of the preschooler. The preschooler's logic often defies analysis for the parent who is unfamiliar with Piaget's theories. Irreversibility, egocentrism, and the rest are very different from what we encounter in adult life. The more logical, less egocentric ways of the elementary school child are more recognizable. The children go beyond what the situation looks like and infer reality from it. In the conservation situation, they are not taken in by the fact that the amount of liquid in one beaker looks greater. They can now decenter and take many more elements of the problem into consideration. This helps them not only in the physical world but also, as we shall see in Chapter Twelve, in judging events. In addition, school-age children develop a quantitative attitude toward tasks and problems. They now understand that problems have precise, quantifiable solutions that can be obtained by logical reasoning and measurement operations. For example, take six matches and place them end-to-end but in a jagged fashion. Then take five matches and lay them in a perfectly straight line. The display of five matches appears longer than the six because it is laid out straight while the other is crooked. Now tell preschoolers and school-aged children that these match lines are two roads and ask them who makes the longest trip—the person who drives a car the entire length of the first (crooked) road or the driver who drives the entire length of the second (straight) road? The preschooler is fooled by the appearance of the roads and says the second. The school-aged child answers the first. The older child is not fooled by how the roads look and recognizes that the total lengths can be divided into subparts and measured (see Flavell, 1977).

Not all children develop these skills at the same age. Cultural and individual differences must be taken into account. Although the sequence of acquisition may be similar across cultures, the ages at which children develop particular Piagetian skills differ.

Cultural and Individual Differences

Piaget was well aware that children in other cultures show variability in the age at which they develop concrete opeational skills (see Bringuier, 1980). Children in the rural areas of Iran showed a two-, three-, even four-year delay in passing through the same stages, compared with their urbanized peers. The environment becomes more important as a child becomes older. Many studies show that children with no schooling who have little contact with Westerners and who live in poor rural environments do poorer on Piagetian tasks than urbanized, youngsters who attend school (Laboratory of Comparative Human Cognition, 1983). Such factors as schooling, urbanization, and the relevance of a particular skill for a particular society affect the onset of concrete operational abilities (Dasen and Heron, 1981).

Limitations of Concrete Operational Thought

While impressive, the cognitive abilities of the school-age child show a number of limitations. For instance, ask seven-year-olds to interpret a proverb like "You can lead a horse to water, but you can't make him drink." You will be very surprised with the answers. They may say something about not being able to force an animal to drink or show a puzzled expression, or they may attempt a literal interpretation of the saying. They do not understand the more general, abstract meaning of the saying. Political cartoons also require the ability to think in the abstract, and children do not understand them very well.

Children also have difficulty with hypothetical situations. Ask a child, "If all dogs were pink and I had a dog, would it be pink too?" Children often rebel at such statements (Ault, 1977). They insist that dogs are not pink and that's that. Children in the concrete stage of operations have great difficulty accepting hypothetical situations.

Applying Piaget to Education

Piaget's ideas about the cognitive abilities of school-age children have been applied to education. Teachers can provide practice in such skills as classification and seriation. Piagetian teaching encourages the use of social interaction in the learning process. Children who work in groups may learn social skills and alter their egocentric way of looking at the world. In addition, Piaget believes in learning through activity and emphasizes the importance of direct experience (Biehler and Snowman, 1982). Finally, teachers often do not realize that children do not understand abstract or hypothetical explanations at this age. It may be necessary to explain the concept of democracy in more concrete terms that children can understand, perhaps through elections in class, than to define it in abstract dictionary terms.

MEMORY

School-age children have made impressive gains in cognitive skills, which allows them to meet the challenges of elementary school. Success in elementary school requires a good memory. Think back to all the tests you took in your early school years. You had to memorize poems, lyrics to songs, lists of presidents, state capitals, and the twenty-eight exports of whatever country. Such rote learning does not and should not imply understanding on the part of the student. As an experiment, I asked children in elementary school to write out the Pledge of Allegiance. Each of them had recited it every day and had it memorized perfectly. Yet I sometimes found it written incorrectly, for example, as "I pledge allegiance to the flag of the United States of America and to the Republic for *Richard stands* one nation *invisible* under God with liberty and justice for all." You may also note this tendency in children memorizing prayers for the first time.

Recall, Recognition, and Memory Strategies

Children are sometimes expected to make conceptual sense out of the material, not just to memorize it sentence by sentence. A teacher may use a multiple-

An agile memory is necessary for success in elementary school, whether it be in science, math, social studies . . . or music.

choice test, which measures *recognition*—choosing the correct answer from a group of alternatives—or an essay examination, which measures *recall* to test knowledge (see pages 220–221).

No matter how it is measured, memory improves as children negotiate middle childhood. Short-term memory improves with age from five to ten years. The typical five-year-old can recall four or five numbers after a single presentation, whereas a ten-year-old can recall six or seven (Williams and Stith, 1980). Retention is also superior in both recall and recognition. Qualitatively, children and adults recall stories in the same manner. That is, they remember the general form of the story and the main events. Yet there are many differences. Older children are more likely to integrate sentences and ideas. Let's say that a child hears "The batter hit the ball. It sailed into left field." An older child will simply integrate them and tell you, "The batter hit the ball into left field," but a younger child does not (Kail and Hagen, 1982, p. 357). In addition, older children make inferences as part of their performance. When a person describes a familiar action like baking, eleven- and twelve-year-olds infer that the action occurred in an oven, even if that was not stated. Six- and seven-year-olds do this much less often. Recognition memory is generally good at all ages, and always superior to recall, but it also shows improvement with age. Dirks and Niesser (1977) found an improvement in performance with age when they showed first-, third-, and sixth-grade children and adults very complex scenes and then tested them on recognition when elements of the scene were omitted or rearranged.

Just why this improvement occurs is a matter of dispute (Wingfield and Byrnes, 1981). Some maintain that memory capacity improves with age. Others argue that changes in the child's ability to attend to the material and use memory strategies such as rehearsal and classification can explain the improvement (Dempster and Rohwer, 1983). Still others believe that both factors are important (Sternberg and Powell, 1983).

Indeed, children in middle childhood begin to use verbal memory strategies. Flavell and colleagues (1966) showed pictures to five-, seven-, and ten-year-olds. The researchers pointed to certain pictures that were to be remembered and measured the rehearsal strategies used by the children. Only 10 percent of the five-year-olds showed any rehearsal, while 60 percent of the seven-year-olds did once, but only 25 percent used the strategy regularly. Some 85 percent of the ten-year-olds verbalized, and 65 percent did so with consistency. As one might expect, recall improved with age. Preschoolers can be trained to use verbal strategies, and these do improve their performance, but when faced with similar problems, preschoolers do not use them spontaneously. Perhaps they do not understand the memory process well enough to know they should. Children in the school years begin to use the strategies more consistently.

In another experiment, Kreutzer and colleagues (1975) asked children in kindergarten and first, third, and fifth grade how they could be sure to remember an invitation to a birthday party. They were also asked to list different methods of remembering. As you might expect, the older children thought of many more strategies than the younger children. The older children considered writing a note and leaving it where they would find it. Younger children had difficulty devising useful strategies.

The developmental progression in the use of strategies is quite clear. Preschoolers may occasionally name an item to be remembered, point, or show greater attention to it, but they do not use any verbal strategy. Children in the middle years of childhood rehearse, use repetition, and later demonstrate planning and flexibility in their use of strategies (Brown et al., 1983).

Metamemory. If you were faced with a memory task, you would analyze the task and choose a particular strategy. You understand the process of memorization and are aware of your memory capacity. People's knowledge of the memory process is known as **metamemory**, and their awareness of their own thought processes is called **metacognition**. Children's knowledge of these processes increases with age.

A pioneer in this research, John Flavell, suggests that metamemory should be understood in terms of two major categories. The first is sensitivity, the second involves three types of variables or factors that interact to determine how well an individual performs on various memory problems (Flavell, 1977). These include knowledge of one's own memory characteristics, knowledge about the task presented, and knowledge of which strategies are more effective in which situations (Wingfield and Byrnes, 1981).

Sensitivity. If you ask children to remember where they put their shoes, they first must understand what the word *remember* means. The term *remember* is one of the earlier mental verbs used. It can be found as early as two and a half years of age (Wellman and Johnson, 1979). There is evidence that children as young as four understand the difference between *remember* and *forget*, but their understanding is not complete. Young children understand these verbs only in terms of overt behavior (remembering where they hid a shoe). Whether young children really understand what it means to "remember" something such as a group of pictures, is open to question and seems to depend partly on the nature of the task (Flavell, 1977). By the time children enter middle childhood, they have an idea of what remembering and forgetting mean and show some sensitivity to various types of instructions.

Variable One: Knowledge of One's Own Memory Abilities. Are you better at remembering faces or names? If your boss orally gave you fifteen things to do, would you understand that you can't remember them and inform the boss of that fact? Most of us are aware of the circumstances under which our memory tends to fail us, but young children are not.

Flavell and colleagues (1970) showed ten pictures to children of various ages and asked them to estimate the number they could remember. Most preschoolers and children attending kindergarten thought they could remember all ten pictures, while very few older children thought this. In reality, none could possibly remember them all. Young children overpredict their ability to recall items (Yussen and Levy, 1975).

In another study, Markman (1973) found that second- and fourth-graders were better than kindergarteners and first-graders in understanding whether they knew items after studying them. Many younger children studied the items and said they knew them when in fact they did not. This was less likely to occur with older children.

Taken together, the evidence is strong that as children mature they become more aware of the limitations and the capacity of their memories and are less likely to overpredict their memory capacity.

metamemory
People's knowledge of their own memory processes.

metacognition
People's awareness of their own cognitive processes.

4. *True or False:*
Children underestimate their ability to recall items on a list.

Just because a child says he understands the work doesn't mean that he actually does.

5. *True or False:*
When elementary school children claim they understand something, a parent or teacher can be reasonably certain that they do.

Variable Two: Task Variables.   Almost all college students understand that recognition as tested on multiple-choice tests is generally easier than recall as tested on essay tests. If faced with a test on textbook material, one is likely to try to pick out the important facts, the definitions and concepts. This ability is not well developed in young children, who often experience difficulty separating the important material from the not-so-important material (Brown and Smiley, 1977).

As children mature, their ability to understand the difficulties produced by a particular task increases. Moynahan (1973) found that third-graders and fifth-graders were more likely than first-graders to understand that categorizing items (foods, types of furniture, etc.) made it easier to remember than memorizing a list of unrelated items. In another study, Rogoff and colleagues (1974) told six-, eight-, and ten-year-olds that they would be tested on their recognition of forty pictures after a few minutes, a day, or a week. Only the older children studied longer when told they would have to remember the material for a longer period of time.

Variable Three: Knowledge of Strategies.   Would you study differently for a multiple-choice test or an essay test? Some studies suggest that when faced with different requirements eleven-year-olds, but not five-year-olds, adopt different strategies (Horowitz and Horowitz, 1975). As children mature, they gain not only an ability to use more strategies but also the knowledge of which strategies might be more useful under certain conditions.

Implications of Metamemory

We can conclude that with increasing age children become more aware of their own capacities, can better understand a task, and can match their strategies to the problem (Masters, 1981). The study of metamemory has some interesting applications for parents and teachers. For example, if you were teaching children a particular skill and asked whether they had any questions, they might shake their heads, and you might conclude that they understand it. But teachers found that this is not so, and metamemory research confirms this. Children may not be aware that they do not understand instructions or some concept. They may really believe they do. Markman (1977) tested children of various ages by giving them instructions for a game that had a number of obvious omissions. Young children were not aware of them, and failed to seek any clarification of the rules.

Academic progress may be related to children's ability to comprehend their own level of understanding. John Holt, in his influential book *How Children Fail* (1964), noted that part of being a good student is understanding one's level of comprehension. Good students may be those who often say they do not understand, because they are aware of their level of knowledge. Poor students may not really know whether or not they understand the material. Holt (1964, p. 29) notes, "The problem is not to get students to ask us what they don't know; the problem is to make them aware of the difference between what they know and what they don't."

Can children be taught to monitor their understanding and memory strategies? Some evidence indicates that they can (Masteus, 1981). We may be able to train children to better monitor whether they are truly understanding the material. This is important, because children who are superior on measures of metacognition are better readers (Stewart and Tei, 1983). Good readers can use a variety of strategies for understanding passages, such as rereading, forming an image in their mind, and changing speed. Asking questions is another skill that appears to separate good and poor readers. Again, some of these skills can be taught (Brown et al., 1979). Children might become better readers if they are helped to develop better metacognitive skills.

This may be an important advance. The years between the ages of six and twelve are dominated by the school experience both socially and cognitively. Children are faced with a variety of challenges in school, including development of the basic skills of reading, writing, and arithmetic. Not only are these skills necessary for later academic and vocational success, but they affect how a child sees himself or herself. Erik Erikson sees the psychosocial crisis of this stage in terms of **industry vs. inferiority**. Children who do not measure up to other children in these skills may feel inferior, while children who do well develop a positive sense of achievement. Recently, as we have begun to look critically at our educational system, interest in how children acquire these basic skills has increased.

THE BASIC SKILLS: THE THREE Rs

Reading

Consider the incredibly complicated process involved in reading. First, the eye must take in a certain amount of information in one brief action lasting between 150 and 300 milliseconds. Then it moves to another position. The information must be recognized as letters and words by comparing them with visual information available in memory storage. Then the entire process of comprehension whereby words and phrases take on meaning must take place (Dodd and White, 1980). Reading is a sophisticated cognitive skill that involves perception, attention, memory, and evaluative thinking (Paris and Lindauer, 1982).

Reading is fundamental to school achievement, and learning to read at the appropriate time is crucial to academic success. Failure to learn to read by the end of the first grade is associated with later academic failure. The level of reading achievement by the end of the sixth grade can predict academic achievement in high school (Bloom, 1976). This does not mean that a poor reader in the second grade cannot be helped, but without special help, children who are behind tend to stay behind.

Since reading is such an important skill, student achievement in this area is constantly monitored. Recent evidence indicates that the reading achievement of children in grades one to three is rising. An analysis of reading tests given in 1970 and 1980 shows that the reading scores of nine-year-olds increased about 4 percent, while the scores of thirteen-year-olds were up less than 1 percent. The reading achievement of seventeen-year-olds decreased about 0.7 precent, mostly due to a problem in inferential comprehension (showing understanding of a passage that goes beyond the literal meaning of the paragraph) (Micklos, 1982).

The Great Debate.   Reading specialists have debated the strengths and weaknesses of the phonics and whole-word methods of reading instruction for

During middle childhood, children negotiate the psychosocial crisis of industry versus inferiority. Doing well in school is one factor in developing a sense of industry.

industry vs. inferiority
The psychosocial crisis that takes place during the middle years of childhood.

industry
The positive outcome of the psychosocial crisis in the middle years of childhood, involving a feeling of self-confidence and pride concerning one's achievements.

inferiority
The negative outcome of the psychosocial crisis in the middle years of childhood, involving the child's belief that his or her work and achievements are below par.

6. *True or False:*
Reading achievement has declined among elementary school children in the past ten years.

Today we have a new appreciation for the complicated process of reading.

many years. The advocates of the whole-word method note that students can read words and sentences almost immediately. Phonics will come later naturally.

The advocates of the phonics approach point out that beginning readers require training in word-attack skills and that the whole-word method is inefficient because it does not teach skills that can be transferred from one word to another. At least in the early years, decoding skills are vital because it is difficult for students to attend to meaning if they must concentrate so much on word recognition (Curtis, 1980).

This debate has been going on for about 350 years (Carter, 1981). In the last decade or so, the phonics, or word-attack, approach has become more popular (Cooperman, 1978). The evidence available showing a superiority in either system weighs in favor of the phonics approach, at least at the present time (Williams, 1979; Cooperman, 1978; Chall, 1977).

Besides the changeover to phonics, a new emphasis has been placed on viewing reading as an active process that goes beyond a literal interpretation of the text material (Athey, 1983; Chall, 1977). In addition, educators now appreciate that many factors affect the reading process (Samuels, 1983). Reading skill is affected by such external factors as the size, style, and legibility of the print, the format and organization of the material, the style and readability of the text, and the difficulty level of the text. Internal factors, such as one's knowledge base and the reader's purpose for reading, also affect the ability to understand a passage. These factors interact. The content of the passage is an external factor, but it interacts with the depth of the reader's knowledge about the topic. With some topics, students may indeed show poor comprehension, but for other topics may demonstrate a reasonably good understanding of the text's message.

Finally, we now recognize that different skills are required to understand different types of written material. Each reading activity is not identical with every other. Consider the difference between reading for fun, reading a text for detail, and reading the newspaper for general information. Each may require a different strategy. Poor readers generally do not adjust the strategy to the task. They don't know when to skim and when to read over a paragraph (Forrest and Waller, 1979). Modern reading instruction, then, is more likely to use a phonics approach, to emphasize word-attack skills, to stress inferential as well as literal comprehension, and to show an awareness of the need to develop different skills for different reading materials.

Early Reading. Because reading is such an important skill, parents sometimes try to force their children to learn to read, but this approach does not work. In fact, nonaccelerated children catch up with accelerated readers later on (Wall, 1975). The child's general cognitive level and concrete operational abilities, such as classification, are related to reading achievement (Arlin, 1981; Harrison, 1981). Besides the cognitive factors involved, attitudinal and environmental concerns are important (Bettelheim and Zelan, 1982, Purves, 1977). Parents can do much to encourage a positive attitude toward reading in their children, so that when the children are ready they will want to read. Children whose parents read to them, ask them questions that go beyond the text, and see reading as a valued activity are motivated to master the skill.

Why don't children read more? People often blame television. Some evidence does indicate that there is a negative relationship between television-watching and reading and academic achievement (Johnson et al., 1982). Television, the argument goes, has replaced reading as a leisure-time activity. Indeed, when fifth-graders were asked to rate leisure-time activities, reading was rated seventh out of nine categories, with television ranked first (Greaney, 1980). Yet it would be a mistake to blame poor reading skills on television-watching. The cog-

7. *True or False:*
In general, the more time spent watching television, the lower a child's academic achievement and reading ability.

ACTION/
REACTION

Read, Please Read

Alex Wilson doesn't read. Perhaps that is an overstatement. His reading skills are about a year behind those of the average ten-year-old. He is barely passing his courses in school. The problem is that Alex refuses to read at home, either out loud or to himself.

His parents admit that they don't set much of an example. After a hard day's work in which both Mr. and Mrs. Wilson sit in an office and do paperwork, neither feels much like reading at home. Still, they have been told by the child's teacher that Alex needs to do extra reading at home. When Alex comes home from school, he turns on the television set and it stays on. His parents feel like hypocrites turning the television off, since they themselves watch so much of it.

When asked why he doesn't read more, Alex simply says he doesn't like to read. His parents don't understand this, since they have bought many interesting books for him to read.

1. If you were Alex's parents what would you do?
2. Can Alex's teacher do anything to help?

nitive abilities of the child, the values of the home, and the child's attitude toward reading are also important factors that enter the equation. Some excellent readers watch quite a bit of television (Neuman, 1982). Thus, television may be one factor that inhibits reading, but it cannot shoulder the entire blame, which must be shared with the home and the school.

This section can be concluded on a hopeful note. Recent tests indicate that the reading abilities of elementary school children have improved modestly and may continue to do so in the future. In addition, psychologists and reading specialists now understand the entire reading process better, and this may lead to new instructional approaches that will help every child develop this most important of all basic skills.

Writing

Consider the following teacher's method of developing writing skills in a class. The teacher informs the class the day before that they will be asked to write something. The next day the teacher writes the topic on the board and reminds the students about the importance of such things as complete sentences and good grammar. Paper is distributed, and thirty minutes later the teacher suggests that the students finish and check their papers for errors. Students then recopy the material and are told that they must submit their compositions the next day. The teacher marks the papers carefully at home, correcting all the errors. After handing them back, several students who have done the assignment well are asked to read them out loud to the class (Daigon, 1982).

The ability to write is certainly an important skill and essential for academic achievement. Test results for writing achievement are similar to those for reading. Basic writing skills have shown some improvement in the lower grades but writing in junior and senior high schools remains a serious problem (Wheeler, 1979).

As in the case of reading, educators are taking a new look at writing. How would you rate the teacher in the above example? According to Daigon (1982), the teacher is well-meaning, but the instructional technique runs counter to what we now know is important in teaching writing skills. First, the assignment came out of the blue. Writing should come from experience, from something that is going on in the classroom. If a class of second-graders sets up a small community store, they might be asked to write to the candy company requesting stock. In addition, just as in the case of reading, various types of writing have different purposes. Writing can emphasize a number of aspects of thinking, including persuading, defending, comparing, and contrasting (Slater, 1982). Writing a story differs from writing a letter to a company complaining about a poorly manufactured toy, and this differs from writing to try to change someone's opinion.

Second, the teacher's reminders about proper form are poorly timed and probably a waste of time. The first task in any assignment is not form and grammar but the formation of a plan to tackle the assignment. The teacher would be more helpful if she discussed the subject and the objectives of the assignment and helped students generate ideas.

Third, the teacher's suggestion after thirty minutes that they check for errors and make a final draft is also ill-timed. The teacher would be better to encourage students to jot down their ideas freely, uninterrupted by attention to mechanical or grammatical blunders. Maintaining the creative flow of ideas is more important at this stage. Daigon (1982) admits that punctuation, capitalization, and grammar are crucial, but these elements are best attended to later.

In addition, the teacher assumed that after thirty minutes the children could merely check their papers. No time was left for revision. Most writers consider revision the real task of writing. Revision entails a reorganization and extensive reevaluation of the product, not mere proofreading. Students probably need more help in this area than in the others. One of the last processes in this area is proofreading, where the technical mistakes are corrected.

Asking the top students to read their own masterpieces is also a mistake. This only emphasizes the other students' inadequacies. A better idea is to allow students to draft, revise, and draft again, until a good product emerges, and publish them in some form. Letters may be sent, or stories may be placed in booklet form and given to other classes or displayed somewhere.

Daigon also believes that evaluation is critical and should be a learning experience. Commenting on a composition's strengths and weaknesses, providing time for student conferences, and allowing students to show their best work are among the suggestions. For some, Daigon's ideas may seem like heresy, but he is not advocating slipshod and ungrammatical writing. He is suggesting that the old methods have failed and cites research showing that successful writers have a purpose, draft and redraft, and only at the end seem to make the technical corrections that are so important.

Arithmetic

Most adults have become so familiar with basic arithmetic skills that they take them for granted. Counting the number of apples in a basket, checking the amount of change one should receive, figuring out how to divide a cake into pieces so that everyone receives a fair share, and calculating which items cost more or less are activities we perform without consciously evaluating them. It is difficult to overemphasize the importance of mathematics in our lives.

The concept of *quantity* is probably universal (Posner, 1982), but schools are charged with the responsibility of teaching the operations of addition, subtraction, multiplication, and division. Studies show that American students spend less time on math and do more poorly than children in many other societies. In one study, first-grade and fifth-grade students in Japan, Taiwan, and the United States were tested. Students in Japan and Taiwan were superior to elementary school students in the United States on basic mathematical skills (Stigler et al., 1982). The differences can be explained by the time devoted to these skills as well as by the practice demanded of these students. Math achievement may also be related to teachers' attitudes toward the subject (Schofield, 1982).

The early years of math learning involve computation. The picture most people have of learning math is a child sitting at a desk memorizing a multiplication table. Indeed, math does involve learning by rote, but many experts have criticized this aspect of math instruction, emphasizing that thinking and the child's approach to problems are more important than merely obtaining the correct answer (Kamii, 1982). The older method stressed memorization of formulas rather than understanding. The newer method emphasizes the importance of beginning with concrete objects in order for students to gain an idea of how math

8. *True or False:*
American children are superior to Japanese children in mathematics.

Research shows that Japanese students are well ahead of American students in math.

can be used and developing a better understanding of mathematical processes. When these are learned, the children can gradually decrease their dependence on concrete objects (Marjoribanks and Walberg, 1975).

This was brought home to me watching my daughters learn various mathematical operations. When I went to school, using pennies or objects to count or add was considered wrong and doing so was punished, but I was astounded to see my children routinely use pennies and other objects to learn the basics of mathematical operations. Later, as the theory predicts, they gave up these aids.

The new look in math, emphasizing thinking, exploring, and understanding and deemphasizing rote learning, is a direct result of Piaget's work on how children develop number concepts. Before discussing Piaget's work, a caution is required. As in all of Piaget's work, subjects are presented with tasks and the manner in which they attack them is noted. However, failure to perform on some mathematical task does not necessarily mean that the child does not know the basic concepts (Resnick, 1981). Perhaps the size of the numbers (Gelman and Gallistel, 1978) or the memory requirements of the task (Brainerd, 1983) are the problems. Mathematical skills are fragile and depend on the situation. The importance of the nature of the task to performance should be kept in mind.

Piaget on the Development of Mathematical Concepts

The development of mathematical concepts depends on the child's knowledge of reversibility, classification, conservation, and seriation. For example, you know that $3 + 5 = 8$, but you also know that this is reversible: $8 - 5 = 3$. Your understanding of the reversibility of addition allows for better mathematical reasoning. Understanding seriation is important in comprehending the concept of first, second, third, etc. called ordinal numbers. There is relationship between performance on such Piagetian tasks as classification and seriation, and mathematical achievement (Vaidya and Chansky, 1980).

Education or Indoctrination?

The first cosmonaut was a citizen of the Soviet Union, Communist Yuri Gagarin. He made a flight around the earth in 108 minutes. How many hours and how many minutes did the first flight around the earth last?

In our country the world's first atomic icebreaker, *Lenin,* was built. What is the length and width of this icebreaker if it is known that $\frac{1}{8}$ of its length consists of 16 meters 75 centimeters, and $\frac{1}{5}$ of its width is equal to 5 meters 52 centimeters?

A brigade of oil workers must drill 6 kilometers 650 meters per year. In the first half year it drilled 4 kilometers 900 meters, and in the second 1 kilometer 50 meters less. Did the brigade fulfill its annual plan? If it overfulfilled it, by how much?

A *sovkhoz* [state farm] pledged itself to give the state 3,350 tons of cotton. But it gave 4,200 tons, then added another $\frac{1}{10}$ of this quantity. By how many tons did the *sovkhoz* overfulfill its obligation?*

These aren't the sort of problems you are likely to find in American textbooks. However, in the Soviet Union, every subject is used to indocrinate their young, even math.

Imagine an American math book in which the problems were phrased in similar terms. What if a problem asked how long it took the first nuclear powered submarine, the *Nautilus,* to travel around the world, or how many minutes it takes the most efficient General Motors plant to produce a car? What if a problem were even more blatant and, for example, compared crop production on an efficient private farm to that on an inefficient state farm?

How would you feel if your child came home with a math text that not only covered the subject but did so with a political slant? Note that the problems presented are rather difficult. How many American third or fourth graders do you think could solve them?

Piaget argues that children learn mathematical concepts through a process of discovery (Piaget, 1965; Piaget and Szeminska, 1941). Trying to teach children these concepts is an exercise in frustration if they are not ready for them. This does not mean that parents should do nothing. Indeed, practice in grouping, using numbers in everyday life (you want two cookies), and other simple skills emphasizing quantity are appropriate, because children's understanding comes from their direct experience. You can easily get children to count at very early ages by rote, but true understanding of math involves much more. Young children may see two pens and say "two," but Piaget feels that this is intuitive and corresponds only to the perceptive figure. The idea of an indefinite series of numbers is not present during early childhood. In fact, Piaget believes that an understanding of numbers and the operations of addition and subtraction, multiplica-

9. *True or False:*
A child's understanding of numbers is reflected in the ability to count from one to ten.

*From D. K. Shipler, *Russia: Broken Idols, Solemn Dreams.* Times Books, A Division of Random House, 1983.

tion and division, are normally developed after age seven (Piaget, 1967). In order to understand these concepts, the ability to seriate and to classify must be developed. A child must understand both the idea of cardinality (1, 2, 3, 4) and that of ordinality (first, second, third, fourth).

One of the first skills needed in math is number conservation. Piaget presented his subjects with a bunch of flowers and several vases and asked the children to arrange the flowers, one flower for each vase, as many vases as flowers. Early preschoolers could not understand the one-to-one correspondence between them. Later they could do this, but were fooled if the researcher set the vases in a line and the flowers in a cluster. Children could not decenter, reverse the process, and showed the limitations of preschool thinking. Children in the concrete operational period are positive of their performance and not fooled when the researcher arranges the set into clusters. They have mastered conservation of number.

The concepts of cardinality and ordinality develop gradually from experiences with such correspondence (Pulaski, 1980). Classification is one skill necessary for understanding cardinality. The child must understand the concept of "five," treating the objects as equal with respect to the class. Seriation is necessary for ordinality, since the child must recognize that objects must be placed in order. Numbering, then, is a combination of these two skills and involves an understanding of both ordinality and cardinality (Phillips, 1975). The concepts of ordinality and cardinality proceed together side by side; one does not precede the other (Pulaksi, 1980).

One of Piaget's most famous experiments in this area involves presenting a child with ten dolls, each graduated in length, and ten sticks, each graduated in length. The child is told that the dolls are going for a walk and asked to arrange the dolls and sticks so that each doll can easily find its own stick. If the child can do this, seriation has been mastered. The researcher then disarranges the sticks so that they no longer visually correspond to each other, then picks up a doll and asks the child to choose the proper stick. The child must understand ordination in order to match the fifth longest stick with the fifth longest doll (Piaget and Szeminksa, 1941). As you might expect, the youngest children could not seriate. Later in the preoperational stage, some children can seriate, if given the time, and even match the sticks to the dolls, if both are arranged in the same order. If the two series are reversed, though, they fail again. Children in the concrete operational period can perform this task, showing that they understand the true nature of numbering.

How does Piaget's work translate into teaching strategy? Piaget did not develop a theory of education, but his theory of cognitive development leads to an approach to education based on the importance of active learning experiences, readiness, individuality, and the role of the teacher as classroom manager rather than as pure lecturer (Wadsworth, 1981). Piaget stresses the importance of such skills as seriation, conservation, and classification in learning math. Obviously, some children will be ready for math earlier than others. The child who cannot reverse may be able to tell you that 3 plus 4 equals 7, but not 7 minus 4 equals 3. The teacher who is dealing with children who do not understand these concepts should provide them with materials to manipulate in order to provoke the desired thinking (Copeland, 1971). It is also important to begin with the concrete and proceed to the abstract (Juraschek, 1983). When teaching volume, children can determine the volume of a regular solid by immersion and compare their results with those found by measuring and using the formula. Students can determine the area of an irregular pentagon by using a ruler and the formula for the area of triangle.

The new look in math does not deny the importance of learning the basic skills, including practice in the multiplication table. Indeed, practice in the basic skills is critical. However, it also takes into consideration the cognitive level of the child, introduces math on a concrete level, and emphasizes thinking and discovery. In addition, there has been a major emphasis on how a child reasons when faced with problems (Kamii, 1982), rather than simply on obtaining the right answer. For instance, Groen and Parkman (1972) investigated how young children do simple addition, such as 3 + 4. They found that children took the largest number and increased it the number of times of the smaller value. We are becoming more interested in how children think and solve problems and hope that this will teach us something we can use in developing math skills in children.

New vs. Old Emphases

The obvious conclusion from this overview of advances in reading, writing, and math is that more emphasis is being placed on the process of learning a particular skill and placing learning within a meaningful context. We now better understand children's cognitive abilities and the importance of exploration and discovery. These changes do not negate the value of the very popular back-to-basics movement, however. The Gallup poll indicates that parents are very much in favor of emphasizing the basic skills, but this does not mean going back to strategies that did not work and throwing away what we have learned in the past twenty years. Rather, educators should use the knowledge we have gained through painstaking research to improve their teaching skills and the achievement level of their students.

Reading, writing, and mathematical achievement do not develop in a vacuum. The general achievement of any student in an elementary school depends on a number of factors, including the nature of the school experience, the child's home, and the student's personal characteristics. It is popular to blame any one of these for pupil failure, but educational achievement is affected by each of these variables.

FACTORS AFFECTING ACADEMIC ACHIEVEMENT

The School Experience

Each school has its own atmosphere, its own "feeling." Some are orderly, others have a carnival atmosphere. Interest in education has increased in the last few years, due mostly to government reports highlighting problems in education. Recent evidence indicates that achievement in the basic skills is improving, and the elementary school has escaped some of the blasts of criticism. Secondary schools bear the brunt of this criticism (Donaldson, 1978). In fact, surveys show that people are much more likely to rate their elementary schools as excellent than their high schools (Elam, 1983) (see Figure 11.3). The back-to-basics movement adopted by many elementary schools and favored by most parents (Brodzinsky, 1977, Gallup, 1983) is one reason. The realization that schools can and do make a difference is another.

10. *True or False:*
People are more likely to claim that their high schools are excellent than that their elementary schools are.

FIGURE 11.3 How People Evaluate Their Schools

People tend to evaluate their local schools as superior to the national average. Note also that, despite the many problems our schools face, most people rate them favorably.

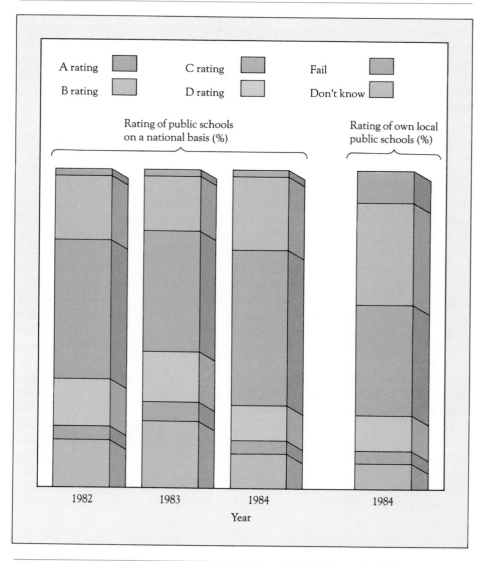

Source: Phi Delta Kappan, 1983–1984.

Some schools are doing their job much better than others. Although just what characterizes an effective school is controversial, such factors as a safe and orderly environment, an understanding of the goals of the school, administrative leadership, a climate of high expectations, allocation of time to instruction in the basic skills, and frequent monitoring of student progress have been suggested (Lezotte, 1982; Cohen, 1982). A good relationship between the home and the school is also important. Especially in the early grades, and in schools where students require remedial work, smaller classes are an advantage (Rutter, 1983).

One difficulty in labeling one school as effective and another as poor is the variation in achievement among children in different classrooms within the same school. Children in one class may be doing very well, while students in the class next door may not be. Many researchers have attempted to discover what attributes form the personality or abilities of superior teachers, but no one pattern dominates. Some have emphasized the importance of flexibility, the ability to personalize teaching, the ability to empathize with students, the willingness to try out new approaches, skill in asking questions, knowledge of subject areas, being appreciative of positive student behavior, and using an informal, easygoing style (Hamachek, 1969). Other studies find that effective teachers are task-oriented, businesslike, responsible, enthusiastic, imaginative, and well organized (Centra and Potter, 1980). One aspect of teaching that is well related to effective learning is the amount of time spent in direct instruction (Davis, 1983; Brophy, 1982; Rutter, 1980).

In summary, research indicates that certain schools and teachers are more successful than others. A number of instructional approaches are successful, but most involve spending time and effort on direct instruction in the basics. In addition, monitoring student progress and providing remedial work when necessary are important.

The Self-fulfilling Prophecy

One aspect of teacher behavior has led to more research than any other: the relationship between teacher expectation and student achievement. Research results indicate that teachers' expectations have an important effect on students' academic achievement. Sometimes these expectations are verbalized. The teacher returns work that is unacceptable and compliments students when their work has met standards. Teachers may also communicate their expectations to students on a less-than-conscious level and may not be aware of what they are telling their students (Chaiken et al., 1974; Rosenthal and Jacobson, 1968).

In the late 1960s, Rosenthal and Jacobson (1968) published the findings of their provocative study. Children were first given a test called the Harvard Test of Inflected Abilities, which was supposedly designed to indicate which students would show unusual academic gains during the next year. The test really showed no such thing, but Rosenthal and Jacobson chose some students at random and informed their teachers that they had scored high on this test. Although there was no reason to believe these children would do better than any other children, they actually showed excellent gains in academic performance and were highly rated by their teachers in adjustment. These effects were significant for the first two grades.

The publication of this study caused much controversy. Some believed that teacher expectations explained the lower success rates of students from lower socioeconomic groups in school. These students did not achieve, it was reasoned, because their teachers did not expect them to. This is called the **self-fulfilling prophecy**—the phenomenon that the expectation that something will happen increases the likelihood that it will: if you believe that your students cannot do it, they won't.

The study also met with severe criticism. Some believed that the conclusions were overdramatized and inaccurate. Others thought the study suffered from design and methodological problems (Elashaff and Snow, 1971). Attempts to repli-

self-fulfilling prophecy
A phenomenon in which the belief that something will occur increases the probability that the event will take place.

cate these results have yielded mixed results (Brophy, 1982; Cooper, 1979). The question of teacher expectations and student achievement is certainly not as simple a matter as earlier studies had indicated.

No one doubts that expectations can and do have self-fulfilling prophecy effects, yet their importance in the classroom, their strength, and their generalizability are doubtful (Brophy, 1982). Many authorities now believe that these expectations exert only a very weak effect on student achievement (West and Anderson, 1976), constituting about 5 to 10 percent of the difference in raw scores on achievement tests (Brophy, 1983).

Just looking at the school ignores the fact that some students come to school better prepared than others. Students differ on many characteristics. Some are more intelligent, while the basic personality problems of some interfere with achievement. The characteristics of the child and the home environment are important indicators of future achievement. In this regard we will now look at some of the most important factors that affect school performance.

Socioeconomic Status

The fact that children from poor socioeconomic backgrounds do not do as well in school as children from middle-class families is well established (Anderson and Faust, 1973; Coleman, 1966). Why is this so? Children from poor families live in crowded conditions, with poorer health care, are not exposed to middle-class experiences, such as trips and books, have lower career aspirations, and may not know how to succeed in school (Biehler, 1982; Mandell and Fiscus, 1981). Children from lower socioeconomic backgrounds come to school less advanced cognitively. This leads to failure, and a vicious cycle ensues. Failure leads to lack of interest and motivation, which leads to more failure. The children's expectations for success are lower as well, although they increase with age (Fulkerson et al., 1983).

Some of these generalizations are now being challenged. In a review of the literature, White (1982) found that correlations between socioeconomic status and academic achievement were indeed positive but ranged anywhere from a low of .1 to a high of around .8. (Remember, a correlation of 1.00 is perfect). Although socioeconomic status is correlated with achievement, it can explain on the average only 5 percent of the final results in academic achievement. The traditional indicators of socioeconomic status are occupational level, education, and income, but many studies add to these such factors as the size of the family, educational aspirations, ethnicity, the presence of reading material in the home, and mobility. These measures of home atmosphere correlate more highly with academic achievement than with any single or combined group of the traditional indicators of socioeconomic status.

White's findings lead to two important conclusions, First, although socioeconomic status and achievement are related, the strength of the relationship should not be generalized to the individual student. As White notes, "When the student is the unit of analysis, SES [socioeconomic status] and academic achievement are only weakly correlated." (1982, p. 474). Second, we should concentrate on what home factors affect academic achievement. Many poor families promote academic achievement in their children. For example, parents read to their children, help them with homework, take them to the library, and expand on their language. If we know that these home variables are more predictive of academic achievement, they should be the units of analysis. In addition, these factors can be changed more readily than socioeconomic status. These behaviors are also absent in some middle-class homes. By concentrating on home environments rather than on socioeconomic status, we will turn our attention away from any particular group and toward particular parent-child relationships, home variables, and child-rearing strategies. Socioeconomic status may mask the truly important home variables that do predict academic achievement.

Gender

Do girls or boys do better in elementary school? Even though no sex differences exist in intelligence, girls perform better than boys on measures of reading, spelling, and verbal abilities, while boys, at least in the later elementary school years, do better in math and problems involving spatial analysis (Busch-Rossnagel and Vance, 1982; Burstein et al., 1980). A great deal of overlap occurs, with some girls performing better than boys in math, and some boys reading better than girls. In addition, many of these gender differences, such as those found in verbal ability, are relatively small (Hyde, 1981), and the differences in math achievement normally show themselves only in the later years of elementary school (Dembo, 1981) or at the onset of puberty (Paulsen and Johnson, 1983).

11. *True or False:*
By the end of elementary school, girls are doing better in reading, while boys excel in math.

Why should these differences exist? Perhaps girls are more ready for school and this physiological readiness gives them a push toward academic achievement (McGuinness, 1979). Perhaps the atmosphere of school is considered feminine, with its great percentage of female teachers and its emphasis on obedience and sitting still. Boys and girls experience school in very different ways, and both male and female teachers value the stereotyped feminine traits of obedience and passivity rather than aggressiveness and independence (Etaugh and Hughes, 1975). At least in the early grades, boys may find school achievement more difficult and not in keeping with their view of the masculine role model.

Attitudes, Work Habits, and Motivation

Every teacher has stories about students who, though lacking certain academic skills, worked so hard that they did well in class. On the other hand, most people also know of students who, despite having a good grasp of the basic skills, fail tests because they don't care or don't study. A child's attitudes toward school, the teacher, and the subject itself influence academic achievement. One reason put forward for male superiority in math in the later grades is that males expect to do better. These higher expectations are found as early as the first grade, even though boys' grades and abilities are not superior to those of girls (Entwisle and Baker, 1983). Attitudes toward math are particularly important, because they are related to mathematical performance in both sexes (Paulsen and Johnson, 1983). Differences in performance are not inevitable, especially when females have positive attitudes toward math (Paulsen and Johnson, 1983).

Work habits also affect academic achievement, and this is an area of great concern today. Students are frustrated when they study for a test but do not do well because they either do not know how to study or studied the wrong material. Efficient and effective work habits contribute to achievement. Finally, motiva-

| RESEARCH HIGHLIGHT | *Teacher Evaluations: Gender Bias in Action?* |

Are elementary school teachers partial to girls? A number of studies have indicated that teachers interact differently with male students and female students. Teachers are more likely to reject boys, and usually rate girls' academic ability and performance higher. Boys receive lower grades, even if they have the same ability, and boys receive more criticism than girls.

A plausible explanation is that teachers perceive girls more positively than boys and have higher expectations for them and that this affects the children's achievement. However, another explanation is possible. Perhaps teachers are correctly perceiving real differences between boys and girls in elementary school. For example, teachers may be reacting to real differences in reading ability rather than to gender. In that case, teachers' perceptions would actually reflect the true situation and not indicate any bias on their part.

Richard Prawat and Robert Jarvis addressed the question of just how important gender is in a teacher's perceptions, compared with real differences in reading and intelligence. Female elementary school teachers in an urban midwestern district were asked to rate students on an inventory that measured many variables, including need achievement, aggression, anxiety, academic problems, and extroversion. Standardized reading and intelligence tests were administered to the students.

The results may surprise you. Intelligence was found to be the most important factor affecting teachers' ratings. Academic ability was also significant. Gender, however, was a relatively unimportant factor. The researchers also found that teachers underestimated actual sex differences in achievement at the primary level and slightly overestimated such differences later in elementary school. Prawat and Jarvis conclude that teachers are less influenced by the sex of the student than by the student's intelligence and level of academic achievement. Even when gender is a factor in teachers' perceptions, it is still less important than IQ scores in explaining student evaluations. Only on the variable of aggression is gender a predominant variable.

This study does not demonstrate that the child's gender is inconsequential. It does demonstrates that the child's intelligence and achievement level are more important in determining teachers' perceptions. It also points out the importance of looking at alternative explanations for various phenomena. It would have been easy to explain teachers' differential evaluations on the basis of gender bias and reach the wrong conclusion in this case. Perhaps the moral is to investigate before accusing.

Source: R. S. Prawat and G. Jarvis, "Gender Difference as a Factor in Teachers' Perceptions of Students," *Journal of Educational Psychology,* 1980, *72,* 743–749.

tion is important (Nicholls, 1979). Motivation may affect attention in class or influence the amount of study time devoted to a particular subject, directly influencing academic achievement.

Personalities

Certain behaviors, especially aggressiveness and the inability to attend to instruction, may affect academic achievement. Both may cause problems between teacher and child and affect the amount of time spent on academic work. A personality clash between some students and teachers may also affect academic achievement (Ruhland et al., 1978). One personality variable that is of special interest is locus of control. Children who have an **internal locus of control** believe that they are in control of what happens to them. These students are likely to try harder than children who have an **external locus of control** and believe that their destiny lies in the hands of others or of fate (Maehr, 1974; Clifford and Cleary, 1972). In addition, children respond differently to academic problems. When faced with difficulties, some adopt a mastery-oriented strategy, intensify-

internal locus of control
The belief that one is in control of one's own destiny.

external locus of control
The belief that one's destiny is determined by others or by fate.

ing their efforts and concentration, while others show a helpless orientation, in which they decrease their effort and concentration. Licht and Dweck (1984) found that children who had a helpless orientation were especially hindered when encountering problems in subjects, like math, in which major new skills are taught.

Cognitive Style

Consider the case of two children, Glenn and Sal. Glenn is quick to answer but makes many mistakes. He is always the first to hand in his paper. Sal thinks things through and takes his time before answering. Which child do you think will do better in school?

Psychologists have been interested in **cognitive styles**, the stable ways children process information regardless of whether the source of information is internal or external (Witkin, 1977), for about thirty years. Two dimensions of cognitive style have become popular with researchers—impulsivity-reflectivity and field dependence–field independence.

Impulsive-Reflective Styles. Consider the case of Glenn and Sal. Glenn is **impulsive**. He does everything fast, and consequently makes many mistakes. Sal is **reflective**. He takes his time and reflects on his work. Children who have a reflective cognitive style generally make fewer errors on a variety of different tests, including those involving recognition memory, inductive reasoning, and visual discrimination (Borkowski et al., 1983). Impulsive children make more errors in reading (Kagan, 1965) and are more likely to fail in the early grades (Messer, 1970). Reflective children also use different problem-solving skills. They gather more information and more thoroughly analyze the problem and their answers. Reflective children also have higher metamemory scores, that is, they are more aware of how they solve problems (Borkowski et al., 1983). Reflective children can adapt to a faster pace if necessary, whereas impulsive children are locked into a less adaptive style (Kogan, 1983; Bush and Dweck, 1975). Although reflectivity seems better than impulsivity, extremes of either cause problems. Most people fall somewhere in between.

The cognitive style of the teacher also enters the picture. Consider the impulsive teacher who presents material very rapidly and expects rapid-fire answers. The reflective child, though more adaptable, is still likely to experience some difficulty.

Although these styles are rather stable, they can be altered. For example, children with impulsive styles can be taught to be more reflective (Kogan, 1983). One way is to teach them to utter certain self-statements in which children monitor their own progress and remind themselves to "go slow" (Meichenbaum and Goodman, 1971).

Field Dependent–Field Independent Styles. Another dimension of cognitive style involves what psychologists call field independence–field dependence, sometimes known as analytical vs. global style. People with a **field independent style** are likely to use internal, independent factors as their guides in processing information. **Field dependent** people are more likely to use information gleaned from the outside world (Witkin, 1977). One way to test this dimen-

cognitive style
The stable ways that children process information, whether the source is internal or external.

impulsive cognitive style
A cognitive style marked by a cursory examination of a problem and answering questions very quickly.

reflective cognitive style
A cognitive style marked by a thorough exploration of a problem, a consideration of various alternatives, and, finally giving an answer to the question or performing the task.

field independent style
The use of internal, independent factors as guides in processing information.

field dependent style
The use of information absorbed from the environment as the principal guide in processing information.

sion is to discover the extent to which an individual can overcome distracting background elements. A person is presented with a figure that is embedded in a complex geometric pattern. People who are field independent or analytical perform better on this test than people who are more global and field dependent. Field independent children would be less influenced by context and other people, relying more on their own judgment than field dependent people. Field dependent people are more likely to look to others in social situations to define their own attitudes, are more socially sensitive than field independent people (Witkin and Moore, 1974), and are less attentive to detail. This is especially true in situations where the available information is unclear or vague. Field dependent people are more likely to describe themselves as interested in people and to be socially outgoing than field independent people (Withkin, 1977).

Social reinforcement has a greater effect on field dependent people than on field independent people (Dembo, 1981). In the learning area, field independent people perform better in mathematics (Vaidya and Chansky, 1980). Field independent children are also likely to do better on unstructured tasks, because they can impose their own structure on the learning situation (Davis and Frank, 1979). Field dependent children require more detail and clarity in order to do well. They may also form concepts differently. Field independent children prefer a more active discovery approach than field dependent children (Witkin, 1977).

Teachers are also affected by their standing on this dimension. Field dependent teachers are more socially oriented, preferring class discussion, while field independent teachers favor either lecture or discovery techniques. A mismatch here can also cause difficulty, and children and teachers who are matched on this dimension like each other better than those who are mismatched (Witkin, 1977). In addition, mismatched students do not seem to learn as much (Packer and Bain, 1978).

Neither type of information processing is superior to the other, they are merely different (Kogan, 1983). Although it may be impractical to match teacher and student on cognitive style, it is a factor in academic achievement that should be taken into consideration.

Intelligence

Of all the factors that contribute to academic achievement, none is more controversial than **intelligence**. What does it mean to say that someone is intelligent? How important is intelligence to overall school achievement, and should the term even be used?

There is a high correlation between school achievement and intelligence, about .7 (Zigler and Berman, 1983), that is, children who score high on intelligence tests are more likely to do better in school (Gardner, 1983). Many factors, including motivation, cultural background, and the nature of the test setting, affect how a child performs on an intelligence test. In fact, some psychologists believe that such factors as motivation and adjustment must be assessed if we are to measure the intellectual competence of children (Scarr, 1981). Intelligence itself may be defined in a number of ways, and various intelligence tests may tap different skills. Intelligence has been defined as the ability to profit from one's experiences, a cluster of abilities such as reasoning, the ability to do well in school, and

intelligence
A measure of one's rate of development relative to the rate of development of one's peers. The ability to profit from experience. A cluster of abilities, such as reasoning and memory.

12. *True or False:*
Intelligence is highly related to school achievement.

even what an intelligence test measures. Intelligence has also been considered a measure of one's rate of development relative to the rate of development of one's peers (Blank, 1982). No matter how one defines intelligence, the use of intelligence tests in schools is controversial. And testing has a special meaning in middle childhood because scores on intelligence and achievement tests are likely to affect school placement.

TESTING THE SCHOOL-AGE CHILD

Intelligence tests can be divided into individual tests and group tests. An individual test is administered by a professional on a one-to-one basis and may take anywhere from 45 minutes to an hour and a half. Group intelligence tests are pencil and paper tests that are distributed to a class like any other test, collected as a group, and usually scored by a computer. Both tests have recently been strongly criticized.

Individual Intelligence Tests

In the early 1900s, Alfred Binet was asked to create a test that would identify students who could not benefit from traditional education. Binet used a series of tests that measured a sample of children's abilities at different age levels. At each level, some children performed better than others. Binet simply compared children's performance on these tests to that of others in the age-group. If the average child had less knowledge than another child of the same age level, that child was less intelligent; if the child knew more, the child's intelligence was higher. Binet used the term **mental age** to describe the age at which the child was functioning. Later, another psychologist, William Stern, proposed the term **intelligence quotient** or IQ, in which the mental age of a child is divided by the child's *chronological age* (age since birth) and then multiplied by 100 to remove the decimal. The problem with the IQ is that it assumes a straight-line (linear) relationship between age and intelligence. This is not the case, especially after age sixteen. Today a more statistically sophisticated way of calculating the intelligence score, called a deviation IQ, is used. The original Binet test has gone through a number of revisions, and today it is called the Stanford-Binet Intelligence Test.

Beginning in the 1930s, David Wechsler began to develop another set of individualized intelligence tests. The Wechsler Intelligence Scale for Children (revised edition) contains a number of subtests that can be divided into two categories: verbal and performance. Two of the verbal subtests have to do with comprehension and vocabulary. Two of the performance subtests are block design (copying a pattern with blocks) and picture completion. A composite, or total, intelligence score may also be obtained.

These tests differ in a number of ways. The Wechsler tests are arranged by subject, while the Binet tests are given by age levels. The Binet is more heavily verbal (Brown, 1983). The subtests of the Weschler test provide additional information about the student's strengths and weaknesses, which may give it some advantage over the Stanford-Binet in some circumstances. The correlation between the two tests varies, but for the full scale it is .73. Thus, the tests do not tap identical skills.

mental age
The age at which an individual is functioning.

intelligence quotient
A method of measuring intelligence by dividing the mental age by the chronological age and multiplying by 100.

Individual intelligence tests are expensive to give and are used mostly as diagnostic aids. They are often administered to children who are thought to be mentally retarded, learning disabled, or intellectually gifted. Since these tests are normally used for diagnostic and placement purposes, it was natural that the challenge to them would come from children placed in special classes on the basis of scores on these tests.

In 1971, a group of parents of black children who were placed in classes for the retarded sued in federal court, claiming that the children's placements were discriminatory because they were based on intelligence tests that were culturally biased. Eight years later, the court issued its opinion that IQ tests were the primary criterion for such placement and that the tests were culturally biased. This famous case, *Larry P. v. Riles*, is well known. However, about nine months later, in another case, *PASE v. Hannon*, after hearing similar testimony and looking over the test one question at a time, a judge decided that these intelligence tests, when used with other criteria for determining educational placement, were not discriminatory (Bersoff, 1981a; 1981b). At the present time, psychologists in favor of and against the use of these tests have dug in for a long fight. The question of bias is an important one because it affects the **validity** of the test—whether the test is really measuring what it is designed to measure.

After reviewing the research on test bias, one psychologist, Nancy Cole, reached three conclusions (Cole, 1981). First, most tests do not show large-scale, consistent bias against minority groups. Second, even such a lack of bias does not make the test socially beneficial, and improvements are possible. Even the appearance of bias, as when many more minority group students are placed in educable retarded classes, in undesirable. Problems with how the tests are used rather than the technical fairness of the tests may be at the center of the controversy (Reschly, 1981). Third, there is still much to learn about the subtle aspects of the testing situation.

Group Intelligence Tests

Since group intelligence tests are administered in a group setting, the possibility for abuse is greater. For instance, young children may not understand the directions and may be afraid to ask questions. Because no psychologist is watching them, children may go astray or give unusual answers and still be marked wrong. The interpretation and use of such tests in placement has also come under fire (Kaplan, 1977). They are often used to categorize children. For instance, one of my acquaintances was shocked when her child's fifth-grade teacher told her that her son was doing fine, considering he had an IQ of "only" 105. Under such circumstances the self-fulfilling prophecy may operate, to the detriment of the individual child. These tests are not even the best predictor of school achievement available. Antonak and his colleagues (1982) found that the best predictor of school achievement at grade four was not a group intelligence test but rather early school achievement and concluded that there is no longer any reason for schools to give these tests.

The tremendous fight over intelligence testing in the schools is not over. The concept of intelligence itself carries with it excess baggage, such as the public's belief that it reflects the child's innate capacity and potential. In addition, measuring intellectual competence requires more than merely an intelligence test, it also

validity
The extent to which a test measures what it is designed to measure.

involves measures of motivation and adjustment. There is no reason to give children group intelligence tests in the schools at all, but in some instances individual intelligence tests may be required. In such cases, multiple safeguards are needed to ensure that the tests are being used properly and that bias does not enter into test construction, interpretation of the results, or the use of the tests.

NEW FRONTIERS

In this chapter we have looked at many age-old educational concerns. New discoveries in these areas will affect how children are taught in the future. However, two relatively new areas are of educational importance and are increasingly found in the news. First, with the emphasis on the basics, how do we foster creativity? Second, where does the computer fit into education?

Creativity and Education

When you think of **creativity** in education, do art and music come to mind? This is natural, and even teachers have that same concept of creativity (Dirkes, 1978). But creativity means more than that. One of the goals of education is to produce people who can think independently and creatively. Yet the definition of creativity is difficult to agree on (Barron and Harrington, 1981), and various tests of creativity, administered under different conditions, lead to different results (Hattie, 1980). The most common conception of creativity today views it as a type of thinking. Guilford (1967) differentiated between two kinds of thinking—convergent and divergent. **Convergent thinking** involves arriving at an answer when given a particular set of facts and is the type of thinking measured by intelligence tests. **Divergent thinking** involves the ability to see new relationships between things that are still appropriate to the situation. It is measured in many ways, but the most common is ideational fluency—the ability to come up with a large quantity of ideas (Kogan, 1983; Milgram et al., 1978). This correlates highly with other indices, such as originality and flexibility, but is easier to work with. There is a positive relationship between intelligence and creativity, but there are many exceptions. The assumption that an intelligence test can identify creative students is a fallacy (Goetzels and Jackson, 1962).

Children curb their creative tendencies when they realize that creativity will not be appreciated. At first, educators thought that open classrooms, which were less teacher-centered, would allow children to develop their creativity, but more recent research shows that this is not true (Kogan, 1983). We now know that, whether the child is in a traditional classroom or an open classroom, it is the atmosphere and acceptance of creative ideas that make the difference. Programs that involve incentives, models, and stress activities that offer children creative experiences can be successful in enhancing the level of divergent thinking (Kogan, 1983).

Computers

The personal computer is becoming commonplace in elementary and secondary schools (Steele, 1983). The use of computers in education is a booming en-

creativity
The ability to approach problems in novel, original ways.

convergent thinking
A type of thinking in which people solve problems by integrating information in a logical manner.

divergent thinking
A type of thinking in which people see new and different relationships between elements of a problem which are still relevant to the situation.

13. *True or False:*
Tests of intelligence can also be used to measure creativity.

A knowledge of computers may be indispensable to a child's future. Hundreds of thousands of computers are now in use in elementary and secondary schools.

terprise, but some have asked what will be left after the boom is over (Walker, 1983).

Educational uses for the computer can be divided into two major categories. The first is computer-aided instruction, the second is learning about the computer itself, sometimes called computer literacy.

The use of computer-like devices for learning is not new. Similar models of instruction, called programmed instruction, were advocated years ago. In programmed instruction, students are presented with various tasks. When they answer a question correctly, they progress to the next task. When they answer incorrectly, they are taken through small steps to learn the material (Skinner, 1968). This allows for individualized instruction and efficient practice. The advent of microcomputers has sparked new interest in this process. Computers may be used to help children learn to read and to improve their academic skills (Marsh, 1983). Computers can be used as aids in practice and drill, or as a way to present students with step-by-step instruction.

Even though computers are here to stay in the elementary school classroom, they offer no miracle to improve student achievement (Bernstein, 1983). They also do not replace teachers, and some worry about the depersonalization of instruction (Parsons, 1983). The computer can be an instruction aid, but more study is needed to discover the best ways to use the tool.

Computers have crept into every area of our lives, and a person who does not understand their use may be at a disadvantage in the job market. The term **computer literacy**, which has recently become part of our vocabulary, refers to the "knowledge and skills the average citizen needs to know (or do) about computers" (Anderson, 1982, p. 19). This involves some knowledge of how computers can be used and the consequences of computerization. Introducing the computer to children early is one way to foster computer literacy, because children learn to be more comfortable with computers. Thus, the use of a computer for

computer literacy
The knowledge and computer skills an individual needs to function in a technological society.

such educational experiences as a math drill may also have the benefit of improving computer literacy, even in the early grades (Steele et al., 1983).

But computers can be expensive, teachers need to be trained in the best way to use them, and maintenance can become a problem. In addition, there is a computer gap between rich and poor school districts. The richer districts have more computers and are forging ahead in computer-aided instruction and computer literacy. If computer literacy is important, poorer children will again be left behind.

EDUCATIONAL REFORM

The middle years of childhood are dominated by children's school experiences. School-aged children are expected to learn to read, write, and do mathematics proficiently. When children succeed in school, they develop a positive sense of achievement about their work that Erik Erikson calls industry. As we have seen, the nature of childrens' school experience depends upon many factors. Recently, calls for educational reform appear in the media almost every day. Two approaches are emphasized. One calls for stricter standards for both teachers and students, the other believes that educational salvation will come from exploring new and better approaches to teaching and learning (Hechinger, 1983). The first is politically much easier to sell to the public and is the less expensive course. Who is against the firing of incompetent teachers, requiring solid achievement from students, and assigning more homework? On the other hand, this simplistic solution will only take us so far. We now know much more about what types of instruction do and do not work. If our educational system is to improve, we must learn to use what we know to foster competence in the basic skills so that every child develops his or her academic potential.

Calls for educational reform have appeared frequently in recent years.

Chapter Summary

1. During middle childhood, the rate of growth slows. Children's motor skills improve and are refined with maturation and experience. Physical changes during this stage are gradual.

2. In almost every society, children begin their education or training at about age six. Still, some children may not be ready to learn to read or to successfully perform their school tasks due to physical, cognitive, or behavioral immaturity.

3. According to Piaget, the school-age child is negotiating the stage of concrete operations. Egocentrism declines, and improvements occur in the ability to solve problems that entail reversibility, the ability to decenter, transformations, seriation, and classification. The crowning achievement is the development of the ability to conserve. The child develops the ability to conserve number, substance, weight, and finally volume.

4. Piaget may have underestimated the importance of learning and formal instruction in the acquisition of concrete operational skills. Still, cross-cultural studies have generally supported most of Piaget's ideas about the order in which various skills are acquired.

5. Children in the stage of concrete operations are limited by their inability to understand abstractions and hypothetical problems.

6. During middle childhood, children's memory abilities increase. In addition, they begin to use verbal memory strategies, such as rehearsal and classification, spontaneously.

7. The term *metamemory* describes an individual's knowledge of the memory process, while *metacognition* refers to an individual's awareness of his or her own thought processes. Metamemory and metacognitive abilities increase during the school years.

8. As children proceed through elementary school, they are expected to learn how to read, write, and success-fully solve mathematical problems. Recent studies show that the reading achievement of elementary school students has increased slightly in the past decade, while that of high school students has not. We know more about the processes of reading and writing, which may lead to new methods of teaching.

9. According to Piaget, true knowledge of math concepts involves an understanding of number conservation, cardinality (1, 2, 3, 4), and ordinality (first, second, third, fourth). Such Piagetian skills as seriation, conservation, and classification are also involved in developing math concepts.

10. A child's academic achievement is affected by the nature of the school and teachers, the pupil's socioeconomic status, the home environment, gender, attitudes, work habits, motivation, personality factors, cognitive style, and intelligence. The teacher's expectations for a child also affect academic achievement.

11. Intelligence is related to school achievements but other factors, such as motivation and adjustment, are important. Individual or group intelligence tests are used in schools. Both have been criticized for a variety of reasons, and their value is still being debated.

12. Creativity involves divergent thinking and is measured by the number of different solutions to a problem a child may offer (ideational fluency). Teachers may encourage or discourage creativity in their classrooms.

13. Computer usage in schools is booming. The computer may be used as an instructional tool either to introduce some concept using a step-by-step approach or as a way of helping children practice some skill. In addition, children are being educated to understand the uses of computers.

■ *Answers to True or False Questions*

1. *False.* Correct statement: During these years, the child's growth rate actually decreases.

2. *True.* Generally, ten-year-old girls both weigh more and are slightly taller than ten-year-old boys.

3. *False.* Correct statement: The opposite is true. Physical education tends to improve academic performance in elementary school.

4. *False.* Correct statement: Children actually overestimate their ability to recall items.

5. *False.* Correct statement: The research on metamemory clearly shows that many children do not understand their own level of comprehension.

6. *False.* Correct statement: Reading achievement among elementary school students has shown a modest improvement over the past decade.

7. *True.* The amount of time a child spends watching television is negatively related to the child's academic achievement.

8. *False.* Correct statement: Japanese children tend to score higher on tests of mathematical knowledge.

9. *False.* Correct statement: Children often learn to count through imitation. Counting itself does not necessarily demonstrate an understanding of numbers.

10. *False.* Correct statement: Just the opposite is true. People are more likely to be favorably disposed toward their elementary schools than their high schools.

11. *True.* In general, girls do better in reading, and boys (at least in the later elementary school grades) perform better in math.

12. *True.* Intelligence is positively related to school achievement, but other factors, such as motivation and adjustment, can also influence learning.

13. *False.* Correct statement: Although scores on intelligence tests are positively related to creativity, such tests fail to identify many students who are creative.

CHAPTER TWELVE

Social and Personality Development in Middle Childhood

■ *Are the Following Statements True or False?*

*Try the True-False Quiz below. See if your answers correspond to the information in this chapter. Each
question is repeated opposite the paragraph in which the answer can be found. The True-False Answer Box
at the end of the chapter lists complete answers.*

____ **1.** Friendly contacts between boys and girls increase during middle childhood.

____ **2.** Parents show less physical affection for their children during the elementary school years.

____ **3.** Children raised in permissive environments tend to be responsible and independent.

____ **4.** After a divorce, the custodial parent tends to become stricter and the other parent more permissive.

____ **5.** Generally speaking, boys are more adversely affected by divorce than girls.

____ **6.** As children progress through middle childhood, their conceptions of sex stereotypes become more rigid.

____ **7.** Girls have stricter ideas about sex roles than boys do.

____ **8.** Girls receive more attention from elementary school teachers than boys do.

____ **9.** As children progress through the elementary school years, they are more likely to judge right and wrong on the basis of the consequences of an action rather than intent.

____ **10.** As children mature, they tend to share with other children more often.

____ **11.** Children who are happy generally give more than those who are sad.

____ **12.** Aggression is one of the most common types of interactions between children.

____ **13.** As a rule, the frequency of aggressive acts declines throughout the elementary school years.

____ **14.** There is a scientifically recognized relationship between watching violence on television and aggressive behavior.

____ **15.** Aggressive children are likely to choose to watch violent television programs.

PETER PAN REVISITED

> *Hook:* T'is some fiend fighting me! Pan, who and what art thou?
> *Peter:* I'm joy, I'm a little bird that has broken out of the egg.
>
> (Barrie, 1956, p. 84)

The essence of middle childhood is found in J. M. Barrie's great play *Peter Pan*. Peter is joyful, adventurous, peer-oriented, and playful.

The chief conflict of middle childhood is also echoed in this brilliant play:

> *Peter:* Would you send me to school?
> *Mrs. Darling:* Yes.
> *Peter:* And then to an office?
> *Mrs. Darling:* I suppose so.
> *Peter:* Soon I should be a man?
> *Mrs. Darling:* Very soon.
> *Peter:* I don't want to go to school and learn solemn things. No one is going to catch me, lady, and make me a man. I want always to be a little boy and to have fun.
>
> (Barrie, 1956, p. 92)

Children in middle childhood are caught between the desire to grow up and enjoy the privileges of adulthood and the desire to remain children, with all the

The essence of middle childhood, the conflicting desires to remain a child and yet grow up, are found in the play Peter Pan.

liberties and freedom from responsibility that state entails (Elkind, 1978). During this period, children's social world expands rapidly. They begin to attend school, and the number and importance of friendships increase. Their relationship with their parents undergoes a subtle but definite shift toward greater independence. Children receive feedback from many more sources and must develop a sense of their own abilities, strengths, and weaknesses. They are also considered more responsible for their own actions and develop a sense of right and wrong. The fact that these changes take place slowly over a number of years should not blind us to the fact that they are real and important.

CONCEPTIONS OF MIDDLE CHILDHOOD

Industry, Inferiority, and Measuring Up

Erik Erikson (1963) stresses the importance of developing a positive view of one's own work. School-age children become project-oriented and are faced with many academic challenges. If they succeed, they gain a sense of **industry**, the sense that their work and efforts are valued. If not, they develop a sense of **inferiority**, a belief that they are incompetent and do not measure up to their peers. During this stage, children take comparisons seriously. If parents compare their

industry
The positive outcome of the psychosocial crisis in the middle years of childhood, involving a feeling of self-confidence and pride concerning one's achievements.

inferiority
The negative outcome of the psychosocial crisis in the middle years of childhood, involving the child's belief that his or her work and achievements are below par.

Damaging Comparisons?

*ACTION/
REACTION*

"There's nothing we can do," Lester Chase told the counselor. "David is a superior student, a better athlete, and quicker than his brother Gary. If anything could change that, I would try, but that's just the way things are."

Mrs. Chase was less blasé about it. "I'm aware of the problem between the two boys. I try not to compare them, but they compare themselves. They're only two years apart, so comparisons are always going to occur."

The problem is not uncommon. David and Gary do get along, but Gary has stopped trying in school. He refuses to try out for any teams or to do anything but the minimum amount of schoolwork. The Chases have a policy of rewarding good grades, but so far Gary hasn't earned any reward. The Chases don't want Gary to feel bad, so they have resorted to taking David out for his ice cream reward secretly. But Gary knows what is going on.

Gary's father told the counselor that he won't stop rewarding the superior student. He made this statement even though the counselor did not suggest that he stop. When Gary saw the counselor, he spoke enviously but lovingly about his brother. He wished he was as smart, as athletic, and as musical, but admitted he wasn't.

1. If you were Gary's parents, what would you do?
2. If you were David, what would you do?
3. If you were the counselor, what would you suggest?

work unfavorably with that of their siblings, they may stop trying. One of the more difficult parenting tasks is valuing the competencies of each child in the family, especially when one child may be superior to the others in a number of areas. Even if parents avoid direct comparisons, implicit comparisons are still present.

These comparisons can cause a special problem for minority group children. Children are aware of their racial and religious identifications before middle childhood, but now they become aware of their group's standing compared with that of the majority. These children often learn that their group is not as valued (Spurlock and Lawrence, 1979) and develop a sense of inferiority.

The Misunderstood Latency Phase

latency stage
The psychosexual phase, occurring during middle childhood, in which sexuality is hidden.

In Freudian theory, the child has now negotiated the Oedipal situation and enters the **latency stage**. This phase is often misunderstood. A boy resolves his Oedipal problem by identifying with his father ("me and you, dad") and repressing his feelings toward his mother, and indeed all females. Girls experience less pressure to completely resolve their conflicts in this stage, and many do not fully do so. Sexuality in this phase is hidden or latent, and a segregation of children by gender appears. Boys play with boys, and girls play with girls.

1. *True or False:*
Friendly contacts between boys and girls increase during middle childhood.

During middle childhood, the sexes tend to segregate—boys playing with other boys, and girls playing with other girls.

Why does this segregation occur? A Freudian might explain that these children have repressed their feelings toward the opposite sex in order to resolve their Oedipal conflicts and that contact may reawaken these disturbing emotions. In addition, because girls are developmentally ahead of boys, this grouping allows each sex to explore issues in sexual curiosity and fantasies at its own rate in a more comfortable and less stimulating manner (Solnit et al., 1979). Sexuality, however, is not absent in this stage, as has often been asserted, but rather hidden from view.

THE SELF-CONCEPT AND SELF-ESTEEM

How the Self-concept Affects Behavior

School-age children are faced with many social and emotional tasks. They are beginning to emancipate themselves emotionally from their parents and to move into the broader social world (Powell, 1979). They receive more feedback from others and actively evaluate their own experiences, further developing a picture of themselves which we call the **self-concept**. They also put a value on various aspects of the self which psychologists call **self-esteem** (Kaplan and Stein, 1984).

A child's self-concept colors how the child interprets situations as well as his or her behavior and attitudes (see Figure 12.1) (Burns, 1979). Consider nine-year-olds presented with a difficult division problem. Those who believe themselves to be poor math students react with displeasure and show less perseverance, but those who have a positive view of themselves as good mathematicians approach the problem with the attitude that they *can* solve it. And children with a positive view of their physical self will join in and play baseball with the other children, but those who do not think they are good enough in this area will refuse to join the group, to avoid embarrassment. A vicious circle may ensue, for children who do not practice their motor skils will not develop them to their fullest. They fall further and further behind their peers, until they do not measure up to them. This causes them again to refuse to play, leading to a further lack of development.

Various aspects of the self affect each other. Children with a poor physical sense of self who refuse to play ball may place themselves at a social disadvantage, because such games form a part of the social scene at this age. They interact with fewer children, and therefore find it more difficult to develop social skills.

The self-concept also affects how information is processed. If children believe they are "bad," they will believe such feedback from other people. In this way, the self-concept can cause a self-fulfilling prophecy to develop. Believing that someone will say something negative causes children to anticipate poor evaluations and even to interpret neutral feedback as negative.

Early Development of the Self-concept

Children are not born with a self-concept; it develops as they mature. We can trace its inception to infancy, when children differentiate themselves from the outside world. In early childhood the self-concept is based on external factors, like physical characteristics (Burns, 1979), possessions (Damon and Hart, 1982), and activities, such as "I play basketball." In middle childhood, especially after eight years of age, a shift from physical to psychological conceptions of the self takes place (Damon and Hart, 1982). Personality characteristics now take center stage, as children separate the external world from their feelings (Damon and Hart, 1982). Children compare themselves with others, and this is reflected in such self-concept statements as "I am taller than Steven." Social conceptions of belonging, such as being a member of a family, are also common. Children between seven and fourteen years old often make statements referring to personal attributes, interests and hobbies, beliefs, attitudes, values, and relations with the opposite sex. A decrease in statements concerning possessions and appearance

self-concept
The picture people have of themselves.

self-esteem
The value people put on various aspects of their self.

FIGURE 12.1   **First Graders Reveal Aspects of Their Self-Concepts in Their Self-Portraits**
These drawings and statements give hints to how these children perceive themselves.

I am James Robert
I like to ride my bike.
I like to read books.
I like spaghetti, chili dogs,
   my puppy and my fort.
I like Marie, Jack, Harry,
   and Mommy.
I like to play baseball.
I can do exercises, ride
   my bike, tie my shoes,
   dress myself, brush my
   teeth, pick up my
   things, shower and
   shampoo.
I am special because there
   is nobody else like me.
I love Snoopy, Mommy,
   Sister, Daddy and Jesus.

I am Feisal.
I cannot ride a bike but I want
   to learn.
I came from India with my family.
I like to play with Layon and
   Daron.
I like baseball, football, and
   basketball.
I want to have a walkie-talkie.
I like to watch cartoons on T.V.
I can do cartwheels.
I can make a fort.
I can change my clothes and
   tie my shoes.
I can do almost everything.
I am special because no one is
   like me.

I am Michael.
I am a little boy.
I have a cat and two dogs.
I have a mamma, grandmamma,
   a twin brother, and a sister.
I like spaghetti and big wheels.
I like a nice home, ice-cream,
   and cookies.
I can leap, sleep, eat, run, walk
   and play football.
I am special because I am a boy;
I see; I can ride a big bicycle.

I am April.
I am six years old.
I help take out the trash and set
   the table.
I put up my clothes sometimes.
I like pretty clothes, dogs, food,
   coloring books, and things to
   ride.
I can play ball, tie my shoes, read,
   and button my clothes.
I am special because I am me and
   my Mother's baby girl.

I am Robert.
I am a little boy.
I have brown eyes and
   brown hair.
I have good manners.
I like to swim.
I like to watch speed racers
   on T.V.
I like to play with other children.
I can do most of the things I like to do,
I can jump rope, swim and ride my bike.
I am special because I am the oldest boy
   in my family.
I am special because I like all kinds of people.

I am Becky.
I am six.
I can ride my bicycle.
I am going to get a guinea pig for my
   birthday.
I like to change my room around by
   myself.
I like spaghetti best of anything to eat.
I can do tricks on the trapeze.
I can make mobiles by myself.
I am special because I am me and
   my mom thinks I can print better
   than she can.

Source: J. W. Williams and M. Stith, 1980.

occurs (Livesly and Bromley, 1973). The self-concept develops from an external frame of reference to a more internal frame of reference.

How the Self-concept Develops

The self-concept evolves from a combination of the feedback a child receives from others and the child's evaluation of his or her own subjective experiences. The child gets feedback from many people, including peers, parents, and teachers. If a parent continually tells a daughter that she has no mechanical ability, she may believe it. She then refuses to try anything mechanical, and whatever abilities she did have are not developed. A vicious circle is completed, as she actually does become mechanically incompetent. However, children are not just passive recipients of feedback. They also evaluate their own experiences. They experience themselves as being good, bad, aggressive, calm, and honest and compare their experience against a standard set by the society, parents, peers, and finally themselves. Even in the absence of direct feedback, they evaluate these experiences. If a child's experience is not in keeping with that youngster's sense of self, the child may reject her subjective experience. For instance, children may believe that they are honest and have difficulty coming to grips with the fact that they copied from a friend during an exam. Their experience of dishonesty does not match their conception of themselves as honest.

During middle childhood a number of factors add to the complexity of the development of a self-concept and self-esteem. First, children are receiving feedback from many more sources. They encounter more children and adults, not all of whom will like them. Some of this feedback is likely to be negative, or at least conflicting. The child who has been the center of attention at home may find that is not the case in school (Williams and Stith, 1980). Second, children's newly developing cognitive skills affect the development of their self-concept. Children in the concrete operational stage can reason more logically, allowing them to verify the attributes of their self. Children are especially good at developing a self-theory from inductive (specific) experiences. For example, they may come to the conclusion that they are smart because they are good at reading and math (Harter, 1983). They test their self-concepts by making comparisons with others, and because they are no longer as egocentric, they develop the ability to imagine what others are thinking of them. This allows them to anticipate evaluations, correct their behavior, evaluate the action, and react to it emotionally with pride or disappointment.

The self-concept and self-esteem of a child, then, clearly affect the child's understanding of, and attitudes toward, every event and interaction that arises in the course of a day. In order to understand the nature of these events and interactions better, we shall look at the most important areas of the child's experience in middle childhood—the family, peers, and school.

THE FAMILY

Family Relationships

The family is the most powerful influence on a child's development and mental health (Bower, 1979). On paper, the family may seem relatively simple—a mother, a father, child one, child two. But appearances are deceiving. A myriad of variables influence the nature and quality of family interactions, including stress, economic problems, the physical environment, and illness. In addition, the family is not a static institution. Parents may change over time, and relationships in the family are reciprocal—the child affects the parents just as the parents affect the child (Hartup, 1979). Studying family interactions is more complicated than it may seem, but despite these difficulties, psychologists have learned much about the nature of family interactions during middle childhood.

The relationship between parent and child changes in middle childhood. Parents show less physical affection for their children, are not as protective, and generally spend less time with them (Maccoby, 1980). Children are quite verbal, and parents reason with them more. Children also perceive their parents differently (Williams and Stith, 1980). During the early years of middle childhood, children strive to please their parents and teachers. They derive great pleasure from reaching the goals these adults set for them and from acting in a way that meets their standards. Later in this stage, the child's peers become more important, and fitting in and being accepted in the group take center stage. Children begin to identify less with adults and more with peers. They may become more argumentative, discourteous, and rebellious and complain of what they perceive as unfairness. Parents are now seen as human beings who can be, and often are, arbitrary and wrong. Parents are no longer seen as infallible. Children question more, and parents may get a bit tired of explaining the reasons for certain rules. But this does not mean that children need their parents any less. Children require a haven from the struggles of the outside world. Children have strengths and weaknesses, experience trials and tribulations, successes and failures. They need a place where they can be appreciated and accepted for what they are. Children who are accepted are more cooperative, friendly, honest, straightforward, emotionally stable, deliberate, enthusiastic, and cheerful. Children who perceive themselves as rejected are more restless, get into more trouble, show a resentment toward authority, and are more quarrelsome (Williams and Stith, 1980). Rejection in childhood is also related to bouts with depression, both in middle childhood and in young adulthood (Lefkowitz and Tesiny, 1984).

Child-rearing Strategies in Middle Childhood

The type of child-rearing strategy used by parents is also important. Baumrind (1971, 1967) identified three child-rearing strategies (see pages 369–373).

The authoritarian strategy involves the use of demands, power, placing strict limits on children's behavior, and no discussion of rules. Parents control their children, value obedience and respect, and leave no room for verbal give-and-take. Children raised this way are likely to be resentful and socially withdrawn and show little independence. Boys show high rates of anger and defiance.

Permissive parents make few demands on their children and are willing to discuss issues. They let their children regulate their own behavior and adopt a very tolerant attitude toward aggressiveness. Few rules are formulated, and parents make little use of punishment. Children of permissive parents lack self-control, self-reliance, social responsibility, and independence.

Authoritative parents expect mature behavior, enforce firm rules, encourage independence and communication between parents and children, and recognize the rights of both parents and children. Children of authoritative parents are

2. *True or False:*
Parents show less physical affection for their children during the elementary school years.

3. *True or False:*
Children raised in permissive environments tend to be responsible and independent.

more competent, independent, and socially responsible. A factor that complicates any analysis of child-rearing strategies is nurturance. Parental warmth is related to positive outcomes while coldness and hostility are related to negative outcomes.

Baumrind (1979) based her original study on observations of children in nursery school. She continued her studies, looking at the behavior of these children when they were eight or nine years old. The problems of authoritarian-raised children continued at those ages, especially for boys. Boys showed less interest in achievement and withdrew from social contact. Children who were raised permissively lacked self-confidence and were not achievement-oriented. The authoritative-raised children were again superior. The combination of firm rule enforcement, demands for more mature behavior, better communication, and warmth led to a desirable outcome.

This combination leads to greater self-esteem as well. In a now classic study, Coopersmith (1967) found that fifth- and sixth-grade boys who possessed high self-esteem had parents who set and enforced high standards for competence, did not often use coercion, practiced a more democratic style of decision-making in which children could question parental judgments, and used punishments that the children deemed fair and just. There was a warm relationship between these children and their parents. The child-rearing style in which parents used power and were not open to rational argument was associated with low self-esteem in boys. In another study, Loeb and his colleagues (1980) found that high self-esteem was associated with parents who offered suggestions but left the child some freedom of choice, rather than with a directive style, in which parents told the child what to do. These researchers suggest that children raised in the authoritarian style believe they are not trusted to work independently and do not see themselves as competent.

Despite the difficulties of conducting research in this field, we can conclude that neither the unbridled use of power nor the permissive style benefits most children. Simply demanding total, unquestioning obedience, or nothing at all, does not lead to independence or social maturity. Children of authoritarian parents lack social competence with peers, do not take the initiative, lack spontaneity, and have external rather than internal moral orientations to right and wrong. Boys raised in this environment also fail to develop their intellectual abilities to the fullest. Children from permissive families are impulsive, aggressive, and lack independence and responsibility. Children of authoritative parents are independent, take the initiative in the cognitive and social areas of life, are responsible, control their aggressive urges, have self-confidence, and are high in self-esteem (Maccoby and Martin, 1983).

Taken as a whole, the research on parenting in middle childhood yields no surprises. Children benefit when their parents show warmth and acceptance, set appropriate rules and enforce them, show some flexibility in that they listen to their children and are responsive to them, and give their children some room for personal choice, responsibility, and freedom.

The Changing Family

These prescriptions seem viable in every family context, but the family of the 1980s is a far cry from what families were even thirty years ago. As society changes, so does the family. Today the structure of the family is more variable.

Many children are raised in one-parent families. Others have experienced a variety of family configurations. Consider the case of an eight-year-old boy who, until age four, lived in a more-or-less traditional family with two parents: father worked, mother stayed home. Later, his mother also worked full-time and the boy spent a portion of the day in alternative child care. Then his parents were divorced and he lived with the mother. His mother then remarried, and the stepfather had custody of his own child—a six-year-old. Now both the boy's mother and his stepfather work, and he sees his biological father on weekends. How do these new conditions affect the child?

The traditional family of a mother who is a homemaker, a father who works, two children, and a dog is less common today. Many women with young children work full-time or part-time. The number of single-parent families increased more than 75 percent in the 1970s (Skolnick and Skolnick, 1983). By 1990, one-third of the nation's children will live in homes in which their parents have been divorced (Kurdek, 1981). Many divorced parents will remarry, but their children will spend an average of six years in a family headed by a single parent (Hetherington, 1979). Some 90 percent of these families are headed by mothers, and 10 percent are headed by fathers. This represents a 300 percent increase in the number of father-headed single households over the past decade (Hetherington, 1979).

The divorce rate in the United States has been rising since the middle of the nineteenth century. Figure 12.2 shows the divorce rate in the United States from 1960–1981. There is usually a bulge in the number of divorces following wars. The end of World War II saw a tremendous increase in the number of divorces. However, the divorce rate during the years from 1950 to 1962 was quite low. From 1962 on, the rate has increased sharply (Cherlin, 1981). If the current rate persists, about half of all new marriages will end in divorce (Skolnick and Skolnick, 1983). About 65 percent of all divorces and annulments involve children

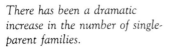
There has been a dramatic increase in the number of single-parent families.

FIGURE 12.2 **Divorce in the United States**
The number of divorces in the United States has risen steadily over the past 25 years.

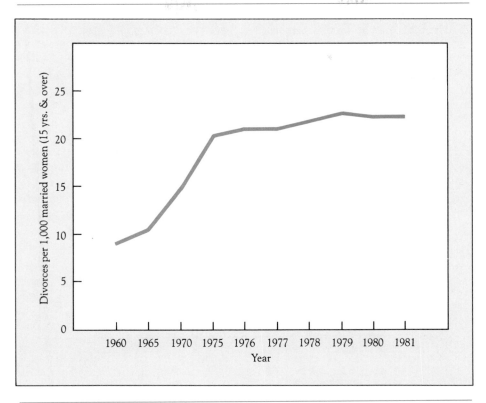

Source: Statistical Abstract of the United States, 1985.

under the age of eighteen, and since 1972 over 1 million children a year have been involved in such divorces (see Figure 12.3) (Wallerstein and Kelly, 1979).

The reasons for this increase are many and varied, including the lessening of sanctions for divorce, the growing realization that it may be better for a child to grow up in a happy one-parent family than in an unhappy two-parent family, and a liberalization of the divorce laws. Whatever the reasons, the one-parent family is on the increase. Some 45 percent of all children born in 1977 will grow up for a period of time in a one-parent family (Emery, 1982). With figures like this, the problems of these children are of great concern to psychologists.

The Experience of Divorce

Divorce is not only an event, it is an experience that affects the entire family forever. Five and ten years after a divorce, it remains the central event in childhood years and casts a "long shadow" over those years (Wallerstein, 1983, p. 233).

Divorce itself brings many changes. Not only is the child's world torn asunder, but the entire lifestyle may be disrupted. Due to financial problems, the fam-

FIGURE 12.3 **Estimated Number of Children Involved in Divorce (in thousands)**

At one time, the presence of children may have caused parents who were thinking of divorce to reconsider. Today, this does not appear to be the case as the number of children involved in divorce each year has topped the one million mark.

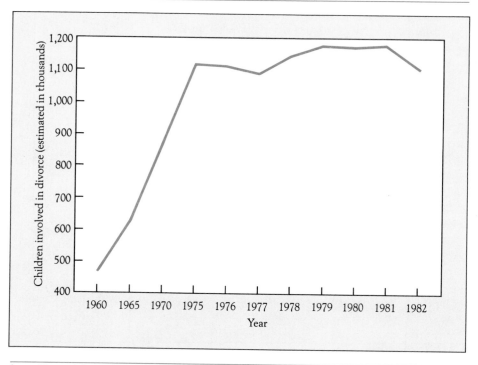

Source: National Center for Health Statistics, 1985.

ily may be forced to move to a new neighborhood, and the daily routine will be altered. Most children do not see these changes in a positive light even years after the divorce.

Immediate Reactions to Divorce. Almost all children find divorce a painful experience. The early symptoms may differ, but they include anger, depression, and guilt (Hetherington, 1979). Children often show such behavioral changes as regression, sleep disturbances, and fear (Wallerstein, 1983). Parent-child relationships may also change. The custodial parent, usually the mother, becomes stricter and more controlling, while the other parent becomes permissive and understanding, though less accessible. Both parents make fewer demands for children to mature, become less consistent in their discipline, and have more difficulty communicating with the children (Hetherington et al., 1978).

How quickly a child recovers from the initial shock depends on whether there is a stable environment after the divorce and on the social supports available to the child (Kurdek, 1981). Often those supports are not present. Parents are confused and most rearrange their own lives. Grandparents, aunts, and un-

4. *True or False:*
After a divorce, the custodial parent tends to become stricter and the other parent more permissive.

cles are often judgmental, and their relationships with both parents and children may change. Peer relationships may suffer, as some children feel guilty about what is happening. Family friends may be forced to take sides and maintain contact with only one parent. The main social supports are weakened at a time when increased support is required.

Long-term Effects of Divorce.　　Many of these initial reactions either become less severe or disappear by the end of the first year (Hetherington, 1979), but the long-term effects of divorce on children can be severe. In one study of children whose parents divorced during their middle childhood years, the functioning of half had improved, while about one-quarter of the subjects had become significantly worse (Kelly and Wallerstein, 1976). Children from one-parent families do not differ in academic ability or intelligence, but they are absent from school more often, are more disruptive, have lower grades, and are viewed by teachers as less motivated (Minuchin and Shapiro, 1983). Perhaps the home environment is less stimulating (MacKinnon et al., 1982). Perhaps the turmoil in the home makes studying difficult and personal problems become more important than schoolwork. Parent-child relationships may also worsen. Children in divorced families often perceive their relationships with their parents, most often their father, more negatively than children from intact families (Fine et al., 1983).

The long-term effects of divorce on children, then, can be severe, but these long-term effects are dependent on a number of variables. For instance, authorities agree that if parents continue to quarrel whenever they meet after the divorce, children will suffer (Wallerstein, 1983). On the other hand, the child benefits if both parents remain concerned and active in the child's life. It is difficult to predict just what the involvement of the noncustodial parent will be. Wallerstein and Kelly (1980) followed sixty children whose parents had divorced, and they could not predict the visitation frequency from the predivorce father-child relationship. However, adjustment problems will be less severe if financial problems and parental conflict are minimized and if social supports exist (Kurdek, 1981).

The quality of the parent-child relationship also contributes to the reduction in long-term problems. Children do better when parents form and maintain a warm relationship with their children (Hess and Camara, 1979). The child's general adjustment before the divorce is still another factor (Fine et al., 1983). Unfortunately, the parents' difficulties involving finances, loneliness, fear, anxiety about the future, and loss of social supports reduce their ability to give the children what they need in order to soften the blow.

Divorce and the Age of the Child.　　At what age does divorce have its greatest impact on children? Studies indicate that older children generally cope better than younger children (Kurdek, 1981). Preschoolers are the most vulnerable, although most do recover from the initial shock after a year or so (Wallerstein and Kelly, 1979). Continued deterioration after one year is linked to continuing family disorder. Why are younger children more vulnerable? The preschooler does not understand what is going on, and parents don't explain much to preschoolers. Many parents are oblivious to the behavioral deterioration in their young children (Wallerstein and Kelly, 1979). In addition, preschoolers negotiating the Oedipal situation may experience guilt when the father leaves the home. Not everyone agrees with the special vulnerability of the pre-

That Seven-Letter Word *Divorce*

The fighting was unbearable. The only practical solution was divorce, as far as Stanley and Christina were concerned. However, their feelings were not matched by their children's. Emil, age eleven, and Rose, age nine, both blamed their mother for "throwing their father out." In truth, Christina did ask Stanley to leave after a particularly bad argument, and they both agreed to seek a divorce.

During the legal proceedings, relationships between the parents worsened. Stanley would complain that Christina's lawyer was trying to get all his money. Christina became angry, believing that Stanley was turning the children against her.

Now that the divorce is finalized, things haven't changed much. Whenever Christina and Stanley talk to each other, they argue. The children still blame Christina and want to live with their father. Christina has had to be stricter with them, but finds it difficult. She hopes that some day they will appreciate her efforts to be certain they do their homework and act respectfully, but she doubts it. She must work to supplement her income and comes home tired and depressed.

Recently Christina was called to school because Emil had been caught lying about his homework and forging his mother's signature to notes. Stanley blames it on Christina and her "active" social life. Christina quips back that if Stanley would give her more financial support and stopped undercutting her authority, things would be better.

1. If you were Christina or Stanley, what would you do?

schooler, arguing simply that the younger the child the greater the effects (Kalter and Rembar, 1981).

Children faced with the divorce crisis at various ages must negotiate different problems (Wallerstein and Kelly, 1979). For instance, younger children experience fears of abandonment and a lack of warmth. School-age children experience loyalty problems, including feelings that they have to choose between their parents. Older children have a difficult time coping with anger. Even if younger children are more vulnerable to stress-related problems, their predivorce adjustment, their relationship with their parents, and the family's economic problems may increase or decrease the difficulties they experience (Kalter and Rembar, 1981).

5. *True or False:*
Generally speaking, boys are more adversely affected by divorce than girls.

Does Divorce Affect Boys and Girls Differently?   One almost unanimous research finding is that the long-term effects of divorce are greater for boys than for girls (Kurdek, 1981; Hetherington et al., 1979). Boys are much more likely to suffer psychological, social, and academic problems. We can only guess at the reasons for this. In most families, the mother gains custody, and the absence of the male authority figure may have an especially injurious effect on boys (Huston, 1983). In addition, a change may occur in the father-son relationship. Father-daughter relationships are more stable than father-son relationships following divorce (Wallerstein and Kelly, 1980).

Although the long-term effects of divorce on girls are not as great, psychologists now appreciate the influence fathers have on their daughters' development. Girls raised in one-parent families have more difficulty relating to men later on. In one study, girls from divorced families were more flirtatious, sexually precocious, and seductive, while girls raised in widowed families were more withdrawn (Hetherington, 1972). Therefore, paternal absence affects daughters as well as sons.

Family Discord and Behavior Problems

Family turmoil itself, whether it ends in divorce or not, creates problems for children. Research indicates that family turmoil is related to children's behavior problems (Emery, 1982). The more open and intense the hostility, the more serious the children's problems. Marital turmoil is also related to underachievement in school. Fortunately, research indicates that a very good relationship with at least one parent may minimize the problems.

The extent to which a divorce has long-term effects depends on the quality of the family life after the divorce as well as on how well the children can work through their own problems. Children must accept the divorce, work through their feelings, reestablish routines, and reformulate relationships with both parents (Wallerstein, 1983). They must disengage from the conflict and resume their normal activities. If parents make an effort to maintain good relationships with the children, reestablish stable patterns, agree on the child-rearing issues, and understand what the children are going through, the negative effects of divorce can be minimized.

Children do best when both parents are involved, when there is minimum conflict, and when parents agree on child-rearing techniques (Abarbanel, 1979). Based on these findings, new custody arrangements, such as shared custody, are now being tried. When both parents have custody, the child is not a stranger in either house and the father shows greater interest and involvement in the child's life. Most fathers see their role as diminished after divorce, and joint custody may be one way to increase their involvement (Greif, 1979).

Stepparenting: Myths and Facts

When their parents remarry, many children being raised in one-parent families may have to adjust to another change. The problems of stepparenting are now becoming more noticeable as more children find themselves sharing a home in which one parent is not a biological parent.

Most parents who divorce will remarry. Five out of six men and three in four women eventually remarry, with half of all remarriages taking place within three years of the divorce (Cherlin, 1981). About one out of six children under eighteen years of age is a stepchild, and half a million parents annually become stepparents (Visher and Visher, 1979). Yet comparatively little is known about stepparenting.

Stepparenting is not a comfortable role, although it has always been with us. In the past, the percentage of widowed people remarrying exceeded the number of divorced people marrying for the second time. By 1975, however, some 84 percent of all brides and 86 percent of all grooms remarrying had been previously divorced (Cherlin, 1978).

The wicked stepparent conception as shown in fairy tales is inaccurate.

Stepparenting and stepfamilies are surrounded by myths (Visher and Visher, 1979). Often people see stepfamilies as identical to nuclear families, but they are very different. Not only are children living with a new parent, but each individual comes to the new family after having experienced a loss. The child must adjust to a new set of rules, and the parents must learn to share the child with a biological parent who lives in another home. The problems of readjustment can be difficult. In addition, each parent may have his or her own children as well, so two or more children may be living with one biological parent and one stepparent.

In such fairy tales as "Cinderella" and "Sleeping Beauty," the stepmother is wicked and the father is good but weak. This stereotype has come down to us, and many people regard the state of being a stepmother as the epitome of wickedness. Although our estimation of the stepfather's role is not as bad, it is hardly healthy. In reality, stepparents are neither as bad as Cinderella's nor as good as what was portrayed on the "Brady Bunch."

The last myth is that of instant love—that the nuclear family once torn asunder by divorce is now back together and living happily ever after. This conflicts with the wicked stepparent myth, but it is just as false. Stepparents may not instantly fall in love with their stepchildren, and stepchildren may resent or merely tolerate the presence of the stepparents.

Stepparenting presents unique problems, especially in the area of discipline. Imagine marrying into a family with a parent and two children. They have been a one-parent family for some time and have established certain patterns. You, the new parent, must learn how to discipline the children and which patterns can change and which must be left alone. It is a difficult job, and one for which little training is available.

In summary, while the stereotypes are false, the problems are real. Some stepparents will fit in well and develop positive relationships with children, while others will have more difficulty. Stepparenting is a challenging state that requires both skill and patience.

PEERS AND FRIENDS

The family's influence on the school-age child is great, but one of the important features of middle childhood is the growing influence of others, including peers, friends, and teachers.

Relationships Between Children

As children mature, they spend more time with their peers. At age two, about 10 percent of a child's social interactions involve other children, while by age eleven the percentage increases to 50 percent (Barker and Wright, 1955). Peer interactions are very different from adult-child interactions. Child-child interactions involve companionship and amusement, adult-child interactions involve protection, care, and instruction (Damon, 1983). Children understand this difference. They see adults and older children as more helpful, but they look to age-mates for play. Their behavior reflects these perceptions. They show more submission and appeal when interacting with adults, and more social behavior and domination when interacting with peers (Edwards and Lewis, 1979).

Children learn a great deal from their peers. They learn social skills and obtain information by comparing themselves with others, and such interaction fosters a sense of group belonging (Rubin, 1980). Peer interaction allows children to gain a better understanding of social events (Hartup, 1979) and to learn self-control.

But a peer and a friend are not the same. Although **peer** once meant someone of equal status, the word is now used to indicate anyone of similar age (Hartup, 1983). **Friendship** connotes a positive, reciprocal relationship (Shantz, 1983). Children in the same class are peers, yet a particular child may have few, if any, friends. In fact, 5 to 10 percent of all elementary school children are named by no one in their class as a friend (Asher and Renshaw, 1981), and about 12 percent are named by only one person as a friend (Gronlund, 1959). Such a lack of popularity may have many undesirable consequences for the child.

peer
Any person of a similar age.

friendship
A positive, reciprocal interpersonal relationship.

Popularity and Unpopularity

Children who are not popular are more likely to be low achievers and dropouts (Putallaz and Gottman, 1981) and to suffer from emotional difficulties (Newman, 1982; Hartup, 1970). Teachers can identify children who are popular, as well as those who have difficulty relating to other children (Vosk et al., 1982). Popularity and rejection are also fairly stable patterns across time (Bukowski and Newcomb, 1984).

Can you remember your elementary school years? Who were the most popular and least popular children? Why were they popular or unpopular? Physical

Psychologists have found that physical attractiveness, shared interests, friendliness, and interpersonal skills lead to popularity with classmates.

appearance, names, interests, characteristics, and behavior patterns are some of the factors that psychologists have found affect peer acceptance and popularity.

Physical Features.   Children quickly learn society's standards of beauty. Children as young as three years old reflect adult standards when asked to choose which children are prettier or cuter (Dion, 1973). Physical attractiveness is related to acceptance. Children attribute positive social behavior, such as friendliness, to attractive children and more negative behaviors to unattractive peers. In one study, ten- and eleven-year-olds were asked to rank order those peers most liked and least liked. Subjects were shown pictures of "normal" children as well as children with various physical differences. Children's rankings looked like this: normal child, child with crutches and a brace, a child in a wheelchair, a child with a left hand missing, a child with a facial disfigurement, and last, an obese child (Richardson et al., 1961). It is clear that in middle childhood stereotypes of beauty are well established and that children deviating from the norm are likely to be rejected.

What's in a Name?   Draw an Egbert or a Hugo, a Gertrude or a Priscilla. When people mention these unusual names, do pictures or stereotypes flash into your mind? Although it would be a mistake to overemphasize this factor, research indicates that the desirability of a name is related to popularity (Hartup, 1983; Asher et al., 1977). Perhaps children with strange names are more likely to be avoided by their peers. Perhaps parents who give their children unusual names are themselves offbeat and do not teach their children adequate social skills.

RESEARCH HIGHLIGHT *First Aid for the Unpopular Child*

Bobby and Jamie are both unpopular with their class-mates. Bobby's parents notice that he doesn't know how to sustain a conversation, so they work with him on these skills. Jamie's parents involve him in all sorts of team sports, hoping the exposure will show the other children he is worth their attention after all. Both parents are unhappy when neither strategy works.

These parents have some reason for concern. Children who are rejected by their peers suffer greatly. Peers take on an increasingly important role during middle childhood, and rejection is linked to adjustment problems in adolescence. Many unpopular children do not have the social skills necessary to communicate effectively with their peers.

Recent studies show that coaching programs can successfully teach children new social skills, but the success of such programs is mixed, especially for preadolescents. Other researchers take a different approach by engineering group activities in which children must work together as a team to accomplish some goal. This, they reason, will change peer attitudes and behavior. But research on this strategy indicates that acceptance gained this way is temporary and fades quickly.

Perhaps a combination approach would be best. Karen Bierman and Wyndol Furman decided to test this possibility. They identified unaccepted fifth- and sixth-graders with poor interpersonal skills and randomly assigned them to one of four treatment conditions: (1) individual coaching, (2) positive peer involvement in a group experience, (3) combined treatment, and (4) no treatment. The coaching consisted of training in conversation skills, such as asking others about themselves and sharing information. The peer-involvement group was given opportunities to interact with one another while making video films.

The results of this study were that the children who received the coaching did show improvement in conversational skills. Six weeks later, the coached children were talking more, and their newfound social skills stayed with them. However, they showed no gain in peer acceptance. Peer involvement itself did not have a major impact on conversational skills. It did produce significant improvements in classroom status, rates of peer interaction at lunchtime, and other measures of acceptance, but the improvement was temporary. Children in the combination treatment showed improvements both in social skills and in peer acceptance, and these improvements were lasting.

Social-skills training by itself, then, may not be sufficient. Children also need to share cooperative experiences. The researchers hypothesize that the experience in which children cooperate to reach a goal maximizes the probability that unpopular children will get an opportunity to use their social skills. If they do not have these skills, they will continue to be rejected. Children who receive only social-skills training may never get the opportunity to show them off, because their peers will continue to reject them out of habit. In this case, involvement makes it possible for the other children to see that the unpopular children are socially acceptable after all.

So we can conclude that only the combination of social-skills training and shared group experiences is sufficient to alter the unpopular child's social acceptance. Only when children both are involved with one another and have adequate social skills can we expect lasting improvements.

Source: K. L. Bierman and W. Furman, "The Effects of Social Skills Training and Peer Involvement on the Social Adjustment of Preadolescents," *Child Development,* 1984, *55,* 151–162.

Similarity. Children relate to others who share their interests (Byrne, 1961). Those who have the same interests are more likely to start a conversation and play together. In addition, if children share similar attitudes and backgrounds, they meet on common ground and accept one another. Children also choose their friends among peers who are similar in race, sex, and achievement level (Hallinan, 1980).

Personal Attributes. Peer acceptance is also related to friendliness (Hartup, 1970). Children who are outgoing, who know how to give positive reinforcement, and who are enthusiastic and accepting are popular. Deviant and negative reactions to others are related to rejection (Hartup, 1983). Late in middle childhood, such traits as loyalty and empathy become important.

Interpersonal Skills.   Not everyone has the social skills necessary to interact successfully with peers. These skills involve giving positive social responses, attending to what others are saying, giving affection and acceptance, sharing, and being able to communicate (Asher et al., 1977). Popular children are more likely to initiate positive interactions and to receive more positive comments (Benson and Gottman, 1975). These children interact in a nonpunitive manner with many different children (Masters and Furman, 1981). Children who are unpopular are likely to have deficits in social skills (Asher and Renshaw, 1981). They do not interact well with other children, are aggressive, and criticize others. One way to help unpopular children is to teach them the social skills they lack.

The comparative importance of these personal factors for popularity has been researched. Reaves and Roberts (1983) found that physique, personality attributes, and similarity in personal preferences and attitudes contributed to popularity ratings for a sample of 160 second-grade children. Personality attributes, such as telling the truth, not teasing others, and not fighting, were most important to children in the age-range of six and a half to eight years of age. Although popularity in class is beneficial, having a few close friends is probably more important to a child's overall development.

Friendship: A Developmental Perspective

> We're friends now because we know each other's name.
>
> —Tony, age three and a half
>
> Friends don't snatch or act snobby, and they don't argue or disagree. If you're nice to them, they'll be nice to you.
>
> —Julie, age eight
>
> A friend is someone that you can share secrets with at three in the morning with Clearasil on your face.
>
> —Deborah, age thirteen
> (Rubin, 1980, p. 31)

Although children interact with other children in infancy, they first begin to form friendships in early childhood. Like all preschool interpersonal relationships, however, these friendships are fragile (Corsaro, 1981) and fleeting. When four-year-olds were asked why they liked their friend, 47 percent mentioned common activities, 43 percent mentioned play, 28 percent mentioned propinquity (being there), and 25 percent mentioned possessions (Hayes, 1978). When asked why they did not like some children, 46 percent mentioned aggression, 32 percent mentioned deviant behavior, and 28 percent mentioned violation of particular rules. Preschoolers see friends in terms of playmates, and friendship is defined by momentary interactions. The main factors in preschool friendships are physical characteristics and transitory play (Selman, 1981). The qualification for friendship is simply being physically present and willing to play (Rubin, 1980). Friendships form and disintegrate very quickly, and relationships are not based on any real intimacy.

In the early school years, a gradual change takes place. Furman and Bierman (1983) investigated the change in children's perceptions of friendship between four and seven years of age. Common activities, affection, support, and propinquity were all found to be important, but expectations concerning affection and support increased with age, while references to physical characteristics decreased. Older children saw prosocial support, helping, sharing, and affection as more important than common activities. Children in the early grades of elementary school are likely to form friendships on the basis of sharing and helping (Bigelow, 1977). By the second grade, they are aware of the differences between friends and mere acquaintances (Furman and Bierman, 1984). Friendships gradually become more stable. As children mature, they begin to look at psychological compatibility (Rubin, 1980) and see friends as people with whom they can share good times and problems. Friendships are based on deeper values, such as intimacy, trust, loyalty, and faithfulness (Berndt, 1981).

A useful model describing the development of friendship devised by Robert Selman (1981) is summarized in Table 12.1. Selman sees children as developing their conceptions of friendships in stages. In stage 0, friendship is based on proximity. Stage one (called one-way assistance) involves a rather selfish view in which friends are seen as important if they satisfy the child's own needs. Our friend knows what we like and don't like. When children enter stage two—fairweather cooperation—they see friendship as a two-way street. However, these reciprocal relationships are tenuous, and simple arguments often wreck the relationship. In stage three—intimate and mutually shared relationships—some understanding of continuity, affection, mutual support, and the sharing of personal problems exists. On the negative side, possessiveness is apparent in this type of close relationship. Finally, stage four—autonomous interdependent friendships—involves both independence and dependence, accepting each other's needs to have separate friendships outside the relationship.

The major developmental changes are nicely summarized by Shantz (1983). Friendship changes from defining it in terms of concrete behaviors to looking at it in more abstract terms. Adolescents conceive of friends as people who care for one another, share thoughts and feelings, and comfort each other. It changes from the self-centered orientation of perceiving friends as satisfying one's own needs to perceiving friendship as a mutually satisfying relationship, and from momentary or transient positive interactions between individuals to a relationship that endures over time and conflict. In order for these changes to occur, advances in cognitive functioning are necessary. For instance, children cannot develop mutuality unless they can take a friend's point of view into consideration, an ability that develops in middle childhood.

Friendship Patterns and Gender

Same-sex friendships are the rule during middle childhood. Boys and girls do talk with each other, but their relationships lack intimacy and involvement. Active rejection of the opposite sex is rare; avoidance is the usual course of action (Hartup, 1983). Whatever cross-sex friendships do develop are less stable than same-sex relationships (Tuma and Hallinan, 1979). This segregation reaches its peak during the late elementary school or early junior high school years (Schofield, 1981). Of course, individual differences do exist, and some fast-developing seventh-graders may be ready to develop cross-sex friendships.

TABLE 12.1   **How Children Perceive Friendship**
Children's understanding of friendship changes as they mature and affects how they will behave towards their companions.

Stages of Reflective Understanding of Close Dyadic Friendships

Stage 0: Momentary physicalistic playments. Conceptions of friendship relations are based on thinking which focuses upon propinquity and proximity (i.e., physicalistic parameters) to the exclusion of others. A close friend is someone who lives close by and with whom the self happens to be playing with at the moment. Friendship is more accurately playmateship. Issues such as jealousy or the intrusion of a third party into a play situation are constructed by the child at Stage 0 as specific fights over specific toys or space rather than as conflicts which involve personal feelings or interpersonal affection.

Stage 1: One-way assistance. Friendship conceptions are one-way in the sense that a friend is seen as important because he or she performs specific activities that the self wants accomplished. In other words, one person's attitude is unreflectively set up as a standard, and the "friend's" actions must match the standard thus formulated. A close friend is someone with more than Stage 0 demographic credentials; a close friend is someone who is known better than other persons. "Knowing" means accurate knowledge of other's likes and dislikes.

Stage 2: Fair-weather cooperation. The advance of Stage 2 friendships over the previous stages is based on the new awareness of interpersonal perspectives as reciprocal. The two-way nature of friendships is exemplified by concerns for coordinating and approximating, through adjustment by both self and other, the specific likes and dislikes of self and other, rather than matching one person's actions to the other's fixed standard of expectation. The limitation of this Stage is the discontinuity of these reciprocal expectations. Friendship at Stage 2 is fair-weather—specific arguments are seen as severing the relationship although both parties may still have affection for one another inside. The coordination of attitudes at the moment defines the relation. No underlying continuity is seen to exist that can maintain the relation during the period of conflict or adjustment.

Stage 3: Intimate and mutually shared relationships. At Stage 3 there is the awareness of both a continuity of relation and affective bonding between close friends. The importance of friendship does not rest only upon the fact that the self is bored or lonely; at Stage 3, friendships are seen as a basic means of developing mutual intimacy and mutual support; friends share personal problems. The occurrence of conflicts between friends does not mean the suspension of the relationship, because the underlying continuity between partners is seen as a means of transcending foul-weather incidents. The limitations of Stage 3 conceptions derive from the overemphasis of the two-person clique and the possessiveness that arises out of the realization that close relations are difficult to form and to maintain.

Stage 4: Autonomous interdependent friendships. The interdependence that characterizes Stage 4 is the sense that a friendship can continue to grow and be transformed through each partner's ability to synthesize feelings of independence and dependence. Independence means that each person accepts the other's need to establish relations with others and to grow through such experiences. Dependence reflects the awareness that friends must rely on each other for psychological support, to draw strength from each other, and to gain a sense of self-identification through identification with the other as a significant person whose relation to the self is distinct from those with whom one has less meaningful relations.

Source: S. R. Asher and J. M. Gottesman, eds., 1981.

Why do boys stay with boys, and girls associate with girls, during this period? Freud explained it in terms of the resolution of the Oedipal situation, as described earlier in this chapter. Other interpretations for gender segregation have been advanced. These include lack of compatibility in play, encouragement from parents to form friendships with children of the same sex, and the formation of sex-role stereotypes (Hartup, 1983). For example, boys do not expect girls to want to join in their games (Schofield, 1981). They perceive girls as having different interests and participating in different activities. They may also be aware of the relationships between the genders that await them during adolescence, including dating, romance, and sex. Peer pressure may also be a factor. A sixth-grade boy interested in forming a relationship with a girl may find himself under peer pressure not to do so. The young girl may also be the butt of rumors and jokes and find it easier to avoid a boy than to risk her friends' criticism. Whatever the reason, the growth of same-sex friendships during this period helps the child develop the ideals of friendship and intimacy that prove so important when the child begins to form cross-sex relationships in adolescence.

MASCULINITY AND FEMININITY

Sex Stereotypes

By the time children enter school, they have acquired a sense of gender consistency. They now understand that even if a boy wore a dress, changed his hairstyle, or played the part of a girl in a play, he will remain a boy forever. They also know what activities are associated with males and females. Young elementary school children are inflexible in their assignment of sex-appropriate activities (Williams and Stith, 1980) and have now acquired their initial stereotypes (Emmerich and Shepard, 1982). Kindergarteners and second- and fourth-graders were presented with a story and a list of adjectives that adults had previously evaluated as applying more to males or females. Subjects were asked to indicate whether a boy or a girl was involved. Almost all the kindergarten children associated aggression with males. Although second-graders knew more about sex-stereotypes than kindergarten children, the differences between second- and fourth-graders were small. Awareness of masculine stereotyped behaviors, such as aggression, was acquired earlier than awareness of stereotyped female characteristics, reflected by such adjectives as "emotional" or "appreciative" (Williams et al., 1975).

As children mature, they become less rigid in their stereotypes (Huston, 1983). Children after about age seven no longer accept such stereotypes as absolute and are willing to make exceptions (Carter and Patterson, 1982; Garrett et al., 1977). This tendency should not be overemphasized. Children have limits in what they will accept, and the resistance of boys to change is likely to be greater than that of girls.

The Experience of Being a Boy or a Girl

A few years ago, a commercial appeared in which a mother stated her approval of her little girl's attempt to emulate her older brother. A picture showed her daughter in pigtails sliding safely into third base. Since the idea of any commercial is to sell the product, it must mean that being a tomboy—having what we might call male stereotyped interests—is acceptable for elementary school children. I doubt the opposite would ever be shown. Can you imagine a commercial showing a little boy playing with dolls with a little girl and mother saying, "When my little boy wants to keep up with his sister I let him"? Girls are allowed to take on some of the characteristics usually assigned to males during elementary school, but boys are not encouraged to take on the stereotyped competencies of females.

During middle childhood, girls are allowed to engage in stereotyped masculine activities. Is the same freedom given to elementary school boys?

6. *True or False:*
As children progress through middle childhood, their conceptions of sex stereotypes become more rigid.

7. *True or False:*
Girls have stricter ideas about
sex roles than boys do.

Whereas boys show an increased preference for male stereotyped activities, girls do not show the same growing preference for stereotyped female activities (Carter and Patterson, 1982). Boys have much stricter ideas about sex-role preferences than girls do (Nadelman, 1974), and boys greatly value their own stereotyped competencies. In one study, sixth-grade boys and girls were shown tasks that were actually neutral but were presented to them as appropriate for boys, girls, or both sexes. Boys did best on those tasks considered masculine and worst on those tasks considered feminine. Girls performed equally well on the feminine tasks and those considered appropriate for both sexes, but worse on those considered masculine (Stein et al., 1971).

In middle childhood, parents treat sons and daughters differently. Parents allow their sons more freedom. A study performed in England found that four- to seven-year-old girls were more often picked up by their parents at school, played in the house more than on the street, had more restrictive rules about how far from home they could go alone and how much they were to inform their parents about where they were, and were less often allowed to go to parks and libraries alone (Newson and Newson, 1976). Children who are kept so close may miss opportunities to develop a sense of competence and may internalize their parents' fears as they mature (Huston, 1983).

The most obvious behavioral sex differences in middle childhood is in the area of aggression, which will be covered later in the chapter. Males are more aggressive both verbally and physically all through childhood (Parke and Slaby, 1983), but it is unwise to think of a particular behavior as completely dominant in one gender and absent in the other. A great deal of overlap exists. As children become more aware of sex differences in attitudes, interests, or behaviors (whether real or imagined), they consider them almost solely a province of one gender or the other, thus overemphasizing the difference. One study of fifth- and sixth-graders found that girls had high reputations for altruism (doing things for others without expecting a reward) but that their actual behavior differed only slightly from that of boys (Shigetomi et al., 1981). In other words, these children considered girls more helpful by a larger margin than their behavior actually indicated. These stereotypes affect behavior. The desire to fit in with same-sex peers pressures children to act in these "sex-appropriate" ways. Parental treatment and encouragement, as well as sex stereotypes portrayed on various television programs and commericals, add to the tendency of the school-age child to learn and act out sex-stereotyped behavior. Finally, the school itself has an effect both on the child's view of sex-appropriate behavior and upon the child's self-concept.

THE SCHOOL EXPERIENCE

Almost every child in the Western world is exposed to many years of schooling. By the time children have graduated from high school, they have spent 10,000 hours in the classroom (Busch-Rossnagel and Vance, 1982), where they are exposed to many new influences, including a new set of peers and adults. They are encouraged to achieve, and their progress is compared with that of others. They enter a new world of rules and regulations. The school experience affects both children's views of themselves and what they perceive as behavior appropriate for their gender.

Sex Roles in School

Schools contribute to sex-role stereotyping in a number of ways. Teacher-student interactions, unequal access to programs, and sexist treatment of people in school materials all contribute to sex-role stereotyping. Finally, the role models available to children in schools are often limiting (Minuchin and Shapiro, 1983). Before looking at these factors, one caution is in order. Children's conceptions of appropriate behavior is not likely to be based on one statement or one event. Rather, they are accumulations of what they see around them and experience. The school is only one influence in this area.

Recall the behaviors and traits that are valued in elementary school. You are expected to sit still and be neat, very polite, and quiet. Elementary school is perceived as a feminizing experience by most children (Minuchin and Shapiro, 1983). Girls are more likely to have these abilities. They adjust more easily to school, show superior achievement, and express less criticism of the school (Minuchin and Shapiro, 1983).

Teachers react differently to boys and girls. Although elementary school teachers interact more with boys than with girls, much of this interaction is critical. Teachers are more likely to reprimand boys (Serbin et al., 1973). Teachers also have very well defined concepts of sex roles, and both expect and desire the orderly, dependent behavior that is in conflict with the traditional stereotyped sex roles of males (Lee and Groper, 1974). Boys are more likely to be seen as causing trouble, and girls do not receive as much harsh discipline in school as boys (Williams and Stith, 1980). In addition, teachers are more likely to reinforce boys engaged in task-oriented behaviors (Shepherd-Look, 1982). They also tend to concentrate on different areas when evaluating the sexes. One study of second-graders found that teachers were more likely to spend time with boys on math and with girls on reading. By the end of the year, the girls were ahead of boys on reading (Leinhardt et al., 1979). Teachers are also likely to attribute failure to different causes. Boys' failures are often perceived by teachers as being due to lack of motivation, while girls' failures are attributed to lack of ability (Dweck et al., 1978; Dweck and Bush, 1976). This may lead to a condition called **learned helplessness** in females, the state in which a person believes that nothing can be done to change a situation. If a girl believes that she lacks ability, she simply won't try very hard. These differences in teacher-student interactions may contribute to sex-stereotyping.

Many school materials communicate the message that females are less important. Some elementary school texts do not portray women in positive roles and do not show women holding major positions or performing important tasks (Shepherd-Look, 1982). Although texts are now showing less restrictive gender roles, women's contributions in many fields are still undervalued.

Unequal access to various programs is seen mostly on the high school level, where students are differentially encouraged to take various subjects. However, even in the elementary school, girls may be told that physical education is not as important for them or not to worry as much about science and math.

Finally, role models in the schools are quite stereotyped. Some 87 percent of the elementary school teachers are female, while 85 percent of the school principals are men (Busch-Rossnagel and Vance, 1982). Almost all the school secretaries are female, and almost all the custodians are male. This reinforces the male view that school is a female-oriented experience.

8. *True or False:*
Girls receive more attention from elementary school teachers than boys.

learned helplessness
A state in which people believe that there is nothing they can do to improve a distressing situation.

It is clear that boys and girls experience school differently. Teachers admire and reinforce feminine-stereotyped behavior in elementary school. Traditionally, this feminizing experience has been seen as affecting boys far more than girls, because the latter's adjustment and achievement in school is superior (Busch-Rossnagel and Vance, 1983). The various problems males develop in elementary school are sobering. Twice as many boys as girls show articulation errors, three times as many boys are stutterers, the incidence of reading problems is three to five times as common in boys, mental retardation is higher in males, the ratio of boys to girls who are referred for emotional and/or behavior problems is two to one, and boys have a higher rate of schizophrenia, delinquency, academic under-achievement, hyperactivity, enuresis (bed-wetting), and autism (Shepherd-Look, 1982). Two-thirds of all students left back are male (Davis, 1983). These differences are large and disturbing. Males are far more vulnerable than females. Perhaps they have more difficulty adjusting to the school environment, are not as ready physically or mentally, or find school a stifling experience not consistent with their idea of what a male should be doing.

However, authorities have recently reevaluated their analysis of the differential experiences of males and females in school (Busch-Rossnagel and Vance, 1982). Despite these figures, most males seem to recover in secondary school to compete successfully with females. In fact, the long-term negative effect may be greater for girls, since the stereotyped behaviors, which include dependency, submission, obedience, and conformity, are negatively correlated with later academic success. Despite their impressive success in elementary school, girls may suffer later. Perhaps the soundest conclusion is that sex-typing behavior affects boys and girls differently but probably injures both in the long run.

The School and the Self-concept

By the time children enter elementary school, their self-concept is partially formed. However, they get more feedback from a variety of new sources. The feedback may be contradictory, as peers may reinforce one behavior and teachers reinforce another. Sometimes even teachers and parents may be in conflict. Children may have been taught to think for themselves at home, while the teacher wants them to obey orders without question.

How a child performs in school affects his or her self-concept. If children do well in music and not in science, they may see themselves in these terms. Some children must cope with failure for the first time. School failure leads to feelings of shame and distress, embarrassment and incompetence. Negative effects are likely to be greatest when children have studied but still fail, convincing them that they lack ability in this area. This illustrates how important study skills may be. Children may do poorly on a test because they studied the wrong material or did not know how to study effectively. They may then incorrectly conclude that they are not capable in math or reading and develop a negative concept of their academic self in this area. This in turn reduces the amount of time these children devote to learning the material. Self-esteem (the value a person puts on himself or herself) is likely to be greatest when one is convinced that one's success is due to ability and effort.

THE DEVELOPMENT OF MORALITY

The school joins with friends, family, and the mass media in transmitting values to children. During middle childhood, children are challenged by situations that demand that they decide what behaviors are morally correct. Consider the following situations:

■ Charles sits next to his best friend in math. During his last math test, his friend signaled that he didn't know some of the answers. All Charles had to do is uncover his paper and put it on his desk in such a way that his friend could get a good look at it.

■ Shirley found a wallet in the hall with a ten-dollar bill in it. Although she has decided to return the wallet, she could use the ten dollars. She rationalizes that she is entitled to a reward.

■ Seth was told to take a test paper home and have it signed. He knows his parents look only at the grade. He can easily change the six to an eight, making his score 85 rather than 65 and avoiding a host of problems.

■ Everyone has been teasing Henry because he can't catch a ball very well. Jim likes Henry and really doesn't like all this teasing, but he also wants to fit in with the other boys. He doesn't know what to do.

We would all like our children to develop a solid sense of right and wrong, the ability to think for themselves, an orientation toward helping people, and an ability to limit the use of aggression to get what they want. Children are faced with moral decisions every day. Cheating, lying, and stealing are daily temptations in school. Decisions about when to obey and when to disobey, when to fight back and when to turn away, and whether to return some lost article, are fairly common. These areas have recently become the focus of much attention.

Kohlberg's theory stresses the importance of the reasoning behind an act—why this boy sneaked these cookies—rather than the act of "stealing" itself.

Moral Questions

A question involving morality arises anytime a person can do something that helps or injures another individual (Carroll and Rest, 1982). Three distinct approaches to the study of morality are most important. The first studies the child's **moral reasoning**, ideas about justice and right and wrong. This approach is typified by the work of Jean Piaget and Lawrence Kohlberg. The second is the psychoanalytic viewpoint, which stresses the development of a child's conscience. The third is a rather diverse social-learning and behavioral tradition, which emphasizes how such behaviors as honesty and altruism are learned. Each approach looks at moral development in a different way and is perhaps tapping different elements of morality.

moral reasoning
An approach to the study of moral development, stressing the importance of the child's ideas and reasoning about justice and right and wrong.

Piaget on Moral Reasoning

If you have access to five-, eight-, and twelve-year-old children, try this experiment. Present the children with the following problem: "Janet broke one dish trying to sneak into the refrigerator to get some jam. Jennifer broke five dishes trying to help her mother. Who was naughtier?" Piaget (1932) investigated a child's sense of right and wrong through a series of interviews in which he presented children of various ages with such problems as this. The reasoning of young children was in sharp contrast to that of older children. Young children simply stated that the girl who broke five dishes was naughtier than the girl who broke one. They had difficulty taking intent into consideration when evaluating moral questions. Older children had less difficulty understanding intent and answered, as adults would, that Janet's behavior was worse than Jennifer's.

Piaget looked at morality in terms of how a child develops a sense of justice and a respect for the social order (Maccoby, 1980). He did not see it as arising from formal education or simply learning the rules from one's parents. Rather, it is an active process that depends on one's cognitive abilities and experiences with peers.

The Rules of the Game.   Children's understanding of rules follows a general sequence. Preschoolers and children in the early school years consider rules sacred and untouchable and created by an all-powerful authority figure. In this stage of **moral realism**, rules are inflexible, and justice is whatever authority or law commands. The letter, not the spirit, of the law is important (Mussen and Eisenberg-Berg, 1977), and children will become upset if people try to change these rules. Children believe in the absoluteness of values—things are either right or wrong. It is during these years that children evaluate acts on the basis of their consequences not on the basis of an individual's intent or motivation.

At about age seven or eight, the intermediate stage is reached. Children now interact with peers and develop some type of reciprocal give-and-take understanding. What is fair is more important than the position of authority. Punishments may or may not be fair, depending on the crime committed.

The stage called **moral relativism** emerges at about age eleven or twelve. Children can now take extenuating circumstances into account and weigh them in their moral judgments. Children become more flexible, and rules are changeable.

Children gain a better understanding of morality through social interaction and cognitive growth (Piaget, 1932). For instance, as children progress through the concrete stage of cognitive development, they become less egocentric and are able to understand another person's intentions and motivations. They can also take more than one element into consideration at a time when evaluating a complex dilemma. But just because children are able to do so does not necessarily mean they will take intent into account in every situation. Even adults don't. For example, some parents may become very angry at their children for making a mess in the kitchen even though they were just trying to help.

Evaluating Piaget's Ideas.   Age-related differences in children's understanding of consequences and intent are well established. Children younger than seven years old rely primarily on consequences when evaluating another person's actions. Children older than ten or so rely on intentions. Between about seven and ten, children rely on either one of these (Ferguson and Rule, 1982).

But Piaget's ideas have been criticized on a number of grounds. First, making judgments such as who is naughtier is a very special type of moral judgment. Piaget does not deal with questions about what a child should do in a particular situation. He emphasizes degrees of "badness" (Rest, 1983). Second, Piaget's methodology raises many questions. A number of studies have varied such factors as the amount of damage, the degree of intentionality, and the order in which the sto-

---

9. *True or False:*
As children progress through the elementary school years, they are more likely to judge right and wrong on the basis of the consequences of an action rather than intent.

moral realism
The Piagetian stage of moral reasoning during which rules are viewed as sacred and justice is whatever the authority figure says.

moral relativism
The Piagetian stage of moral reasoning in which children weigh the intentions of others before judging their actions right or wrong.

ries are presented (Rest, 1983). These studies generally show that a number of factors affect the evaluation of a story like the one described previously. Under some conditions, even small children understand that deliberate damage is naughtier. When children are asked to evaluate stories one at a time, many studies have found both intent and damage had significant effects across age-groups from four-year-olds to college students. Using this strategy, Leon (1982) found that most children applied an additive rule: they added intent, damage, and rationale in deciding how naughty children were. If only one outcome is presented at a time, and the intent and outcome are explicitly stated, young children can show more advanced moral reasoning than Piaget thought possible (Gottlieb et al., 1977). They are capable of distinguishing between injuring human beings and property damage and judge the former as worse (Elkind and Dabek, 1977). Children as young as four years old can sometimes understand the moral intention of others if the language and cognitive demands are reduced (Keasey, 1978).

Finally, the idea that somehow young preschoolers are amoral is troublesome. Turiel (1978) found that young children resisted any attempts to convince them that it was acceptable to hit someone even if the rules said so. Children have an understanding of some very basic rules of conduct.

From Piaget's work we can conclude that children acquire an appreciation of the rules and a concept of justice in an orderly sequence. However, Piaget's methodology is quite specific, and his theoretical area of interest is narrow here. In short, although his findings are interesting and have some value, his approach does not fully describe the development of moral reasoning. In this area the most complete theory was developed by Lawrence Kohlberg.

Kohlberg's Theory of Moral Reasoning

Heinz's wife has cancer. There is a drug that might cure her, but the only dose is owned by a pharmacist who wants a great deal of money for it. Heinz doesn't have the money. Should he steal it? Lawrence Kohlberg (1976, 1969) presented dilemmas like this one to many subjects and after careful study proposed a model that describes the development of moral reasoning. Kohlberg sees moral reasoning as developing in a three-level, six-stage sequence, which is summarized in Table 12.2. The stages are sequential and universal, that is, they are applicable to every culture, and no stages are ever skipped. Each stage requires more sophisticated skills than the one that preceded it.

How would you have answered the dilemma described above? Most students state immediately that Heinz should steal it. However, Kohlberg is not interested in the answer itself. It is the *reasoning* behind the choice that is of interest and that determines what stage of moral reasoning a person is in.

To illustrate, let's take a more personally relevant example: Barbara wants to be a doctor. She studied very hard for her anatomy and physiology examination but finds that she isn't sure of the answers to some of the questions. She knows that a few points on this exam may make the difference between acceptance or rejection at medical school. She has the opportunity to cheat on the test by copying from the best student in the class, who is sitting next to her. Should Barbara do it?

As Kohlberg's three levels and six stages are reviewed below, keep in mind that it is the moral reasoning, not the answer itself, that determines one's stage of moral development.

TABLE 12.2   **Summary of Kohlberg's Stages of Moral Reasoning**
Lawrence Kohlberg views the development of morality in terms of moral reasoning. The stage of moral reasoning at which people can be placed depends upon the reasoning behind their decisions, not the decisions themselves.

I. Preconventional Level

The child is responsive to cultural rules and labels of good and bad, right or wrong, but interprets these either in terms of the physical or hedonistic consequences of action (punishment, reward, exchange of favors), or in terms of the physical power of those who enunciate the rules. The level is divided into two stages:

Stage 1: Punishment and obedience orientation. The physical consequences of action determine its goodness or badness regardless of the meaning or value of these consequences. Avoidance of punishment and unquestioning deference to power are valued in their own right, not in terms of respect for an underlying moral order (the latter being Stage 4).

Stage 2: Instrumental relativist orientation. Right action is that which instrumentally satisfies one's own needs and occasionally the needs of others. Human relations are viewed in terms of the marketplace. Fairness, reciprocity, and equal sharing are present, but are always interpreted in a physical, pragmatic way. Reciprocity is a matter of "you scratch my back and I'll scratch yours," not of loyalty, gratitude, nor justice.

II. Conventional Level

Maintaining the expectations of the individual's family, group, or nation is perceived as valuable in its own right, regardless of consequences. The attitude is not only one of *conformity* to personal expectations and social order but also of loyalty to it, of actively *maintaining,* supporting, and justifying it, of identifying with the persons or group involved in it. This level has two stages:

Stage 3: Interpersonal concordance or "good boy/nice girl" orientation. Good behavior is that which pleases or helps others and is approved by them. There is much conformity to stereotypical images of what is majority or "natural" behavior. Behavior is frequently judged by intention—"he means well" becomes important for the first time. One earns approval by being "nice."

Stage 4: "Law and order" orientation. Orientation is toward authority, fixed rules, and the maintenance of the social order. Right behavior consists of doing one's duty, showing respect for authority, maintaining the social order for its own sake.

III. Postconventional, Autonomous, or Principled Level

The person makes a clear effort to define moral values and principles that have validity and application apart from the authority of the groups or persons holding these principles, and apart from the individual's own identification with these groups. This level has two stages:

Stage 5: Social-contract, legalistic orientation. Generally with utilitarian overtones. Right action is defined in terms of general individual rights and standards that have been critically examined and agreed upon by society. The person is clearly aware of the relativism of values and opinions and so emphasizes procedural rules for reaching consensus. Aside from what is constitutionally and democratically agreed upon, right is a matter of personal "values" and "opinion"; emphasis is thus on the "legal point of view," but with the possibility of changing law in terms of rational considerations of social utility rather than freezing in terms of Stage 4. Outside the legal realm, free agreement and contract is the binding element. This is the "official" morality of the American government and Constitution.

Stage 6: Universal ethical principle orientation. Right is defined by the decision of conscience in accord with self-chosen *ethical principles* appealing to logical comprehensiveness, universality, and consistency. These principles are abstract and ethical (the Golden Rule, the categorical imperative); they are not concrete moral rules like the Ten Commandments. At heart, these are universal principles of *justice of the reciprocity and equality of human rights,* and of respect for the dignity of human beings as individual persons.

Source: L. C. Jensen, 1985.

Level One: Preconventional Morality.   At the **preconventional level**, people make decisions on the basis of reward and punishment and the satisfaction of their own needs. If Barbara reasons at this level, she might cheat because it satisfies her immediate desires. On the other hand, she might refrain from cheating if she is afraid she might get caught and punished.

Stage one: punishment and obedience orientation.   An individual in stage one avoids breaking rules because it might lead to punishment. This person shows complete deference to rules. The interests of others are not considered.

Stage two: instrumental relativist orientation.   In stage two, the right actions are those that satisfy one's own needs and only sometimes the needs of others. However, the only reason for helping others is that they will then owe you something—a debt to be collected at a later time. There is a sense of fairness in this stage, and a deal is acceptable.

Level Two: Conventional Morality.   At the **conventional level**, conformity is the most important factor. The individual conforms to the expectations of others, including the general social order. Barbara might cheat if she reasons that everyone else is doing it. She might not if she reasons that it is against the rules and she would not be doing the "right" thing.

Stage three: interpersonal concordance or "good-boy/nice-girl" orientation.   Living up to the expectations of others and being good are the important considerations for a person in stage three. There is an emphasis on gaining approval from others by being nice.

Stage four: "law-and-order" orientation.   A person in stage four is oriented toward authority and toward maintaining the social order. The emphasis is on doing one's duty and showing respect for authority. Sometimes people in this stage reason, "If everyone did it, then. . . ."

Level Three: Postconventional Morality.   People in the **postconventional level** have evolved moral values that have been internalized. These values are individualized and not dependent on one's membership in any particular group. If Barbara is reasoning at this level, she may think that achievements are worthwhile only if one is true to one's own values, among which are honesty and integrity. On the other hand, Barbara might reason that if she became a doctor she could help people, and that this overriding principle is more important than whether she checks her answers or not.

Stage five: social contract, legalistic orientation.   In stage five, correct behavior is defined in terms of individual rights and the consensus of society. Right is a matter of personal values and opinions, but an emphasis on the legal point of view is present here.

Stage six: universal ethical principle orientation.   In this highest stage, stage six, the correct behavior is defined as a decision of conscience in accordance with self-chosen ethical principles that are logical, universal, and consistent. These are very abstract guidelines (Kohlberg and Kramer, 1969).

People rarely reason solely in one stage. More often, they may be predominantly in one stage but also partly in the stages before and after. A person may be

preconventional level
Kohlberg's first level of moral reasoning, in which satisfaction of one's own needs and reward and punishment serve as the bases for moral decision-making.

conventional level
Kohlberg's second level of moral reasoning, in which conformity to the expectations of others and society in general serve as the bases for moral decision-making.

postconventional level
Kohlberg's third level of moral reasoning, in which moral decisions are made on the basis of individual values that have been internalized.

40 percent in stage three, 30 percent in stage two, and 30 percent in stage four. Change involves a gradual shift in the percentage of reasoning from one stage to the next, rather than a wholesale switch from one stage to the next higher stage (Carroll and Rest, 1982). Kohlberg's theory has spurred a great deal of research, much of it investigating the following five questions.

Are the Stages Really Universal?   Kohlberg's stage theory has been successfully applied to many cultures (Snarey et al., 1985; Nisan and Kohlberg, 1982; Edwards, 1977). In one of the more recent studies, Nisan and Kohlberg (1982) studied rural and city subjects ages ten through twenty-eight in Turkey and found evidence for the universality of the stage sequence. However, city subjects were well ahead of the villagers in development. The rate of development may vary with one's experiences. Sequential development in non-Western cultures, at least through stage four, has been reported (Carroll and Rest, 1982). Cross-cultural studies have not been clear in finding level three (postconventional) moral reasoning in non-Western cultures.

Are the Stages Really Sequential?   Any stage theory must demonstrate that its stages appear in an invariant order and that no skipping occurs. The fact that people enter and leave stages at varying times in their lives or that not all reach the highest stages does not provide any evidence against the stage concept. In this area, evidence indicates that Kohlberg's sequence holds (Walker et al., 1984; Walker, 1982; Kohlberg et al., 1978).

Are Moral Reasoning and Cognitive Level the Same Thing?   The relationship between cognitive abilities and moral reasoning is obvious. For example, comprehension of the stages is cumulative, with stage one concepts easiest to understand and then stage two concepts, and so on. The ability to understand the basic concepts at each stage forms a barrier to a person who has not attained this ability (Carroll and Rest, 1982). There is a relationship among moral reasoning, cognitive development, and the ability to take someone else's point of view (Krebs and Gillmore, 1982). The ability to empathize and to understand someone else's perspective develops largely during middle childhood. Cognitive development is probably a necessary but not a sufficient condition for attainment of a particular moral stage (Walker and Richards, 1979). So although there is a relationship between cognitive and moral development, they are not the same.

How and Why Do People Move to Higher Stages?   Suppose a child was considering a moral dilemma and was exposed to reasoning different from that child's own reasoning. Would this child be influenced by it? It would depend partly on whether the child understood the reasoning and experienced some type of conflict. If the reasoning was too high, that is, beyond the child's level of understanding, it would not cause any conflict. On the other hand, if it was too low, it would be rejected.

Children move to higher stages of moral reasoning as they experience social interaction that causes cognitive conflict (Carroll and Rest, 1982). As children are able to understand the higher reasoning of another child, they now experience a conflict that impels them to accept the newer, higher-level judgments.

But evidence for this mechanism of change is tenuous. Turiel (1966) found that arguments one level above a child's predominant stage of moral reasoning induced cognitive conflict and change. Subjects rejected the lower-stage reasoning and could not understand or appreciate stages more than one stage beyond. However, research has been contradictory and confusing on this point, with some studies showing that exposing subjects to moral reasoning two stages above was as effective or more effective in inducing cognitive conflict (Walker, 1982). Therefore, Kohlberg's mechanism for explaining change in moral reasoning is questionable at the present time.

What Is the Relationship Between Moral Reasoning and Moral Behavior? Would a person reasoning at a stage five level act differently from a person reasoning at a stage one level? Although nothing in Kohlberg's theory necessitates a link between moral reasoning and moral behavior, it is an important question (Kurtines and Grief, 1974). As Blasi (1980, p. 1) notes, "Few would disagree that morality ultimately lies in action and that the study of moral development should use action as the final criterion." A relationship certainly makes sense. As the individual progresses toward stage six, one would think that moral behavior, such as honesty, resistance to temptation, and not behaving in an aggressive manner, would increase.

Most studies find a relationship between moral reasoning and moral action (Blasi, 1980), but the strength of the relationship varies from area to area. It is very strong for the hypothesis that moral reasoning differs in delinquents and nondelinquents, that is, nondelinquents are more likely to show higher levels of moral reasoning than delinquents. Some support is found for the idea that people at the higher moral stages are more honest, but there is little support for the idea that people in the postconventional level resist social pressure to conform in their actual moral actions. Only relatively weak associations are found between progressing to higher levels of moral reasoning and whether a child will cheat, yield to temptation, or behave altruistically if there is a personal cost attached to it (Maccoby, 1980). Therefore, although a relationship between moral reasoning and moral behavior exists, other factors help determine whether a person will perform an act.

Evaluating Kohlberg's Theory.   Perhaps the case of Heinz bothers you because it seems so unreal. As Bressler (1976, pp. 5–6) notes, "He [Kohlberg] has presented us with a wife in desperate throes, a husband of unimpeachable virtue and a druggist who appears never to have absorbed a single ethical maxim. What we are asked to decide is whether the law may be violated to support the claim to life as against property symbolized by an uncommonly venal and corrupt custodian. The crime itself is highly contained—as far as we know, besides absconding with the drug the felon does not covet so much as a pocket comb." The case appears too simple, too pat. Bressler asks, What if the pharmacist has already promised the vial to another person with an identical illness? One wonders about the relevance of Kohlberg's ethical dilemmas. In real life, most of us face problems that are more complicated and personally relevant.

The discrepancy between reasoning and action is also a problem. For whatever reason, people sometimes do and sometimes do not proceed in ways they think are best (Chandler and Boyes, 1982). In addition, as was demonstrated in the case of Barbara, an individual could reason at any of the levels and still find a reason to cheat or not. More predictability is needed.

Perhaps the greatest problem with Kohlberg's theory is that moral reasoning may be only a part of the overall process by which someone converts environmental information into an action sequence. A more complete picture was advanced by James Rest (Rest, 1983; Carroll and Rest, 1982).

The Larger Picture: Rest's Model

Rest argues that morality involves four major psychological components. First, there is recognition and sensitivity. If an individual is to respond at all, he or she must recognize another person in need and be sensitive to that person's problems. Such variables as the time of exposure and the complexity and clarity of the information are important. People who are confused in an emergency may stand passively by, not because they are not willing to aid the victim but because they are confused. They do not read the situation properly. A person faced with the decision of whether to cheat must be aware that a moral question is involved.

The second component—moral judgment—involves determining what course of action would be best to fulfill a moral ideal. In other words, we decide what ought to be done. This is where Kohlberg's theory fits in well.

The third component involves consideration of the individual's values and environmental influences. This entails devising a plan of action that takes into consideration nonmoral values and goals and situational pressures. The person now decides what he or she actually wants to do. Consider our cheating example. Barbara may realize what the ideal moral answer is, but take other factors into consideration. What if Barbara believes that getting a good grade or showing superiority over the other students are more important than the ideal moral solution? She might then cheat anyway. Her final decision takes into consideration many factors beyond the moral ideal.

Finally, there is the execution and implementation of some action. This involves behaving according to one's goals, despite distractions. Such factors as assertiveness and motivation are involved here.

Using this model, we can better understand the entire process of moral behavior. Failure to behave morally may be the result of a deficiency in any of these components. In the future, fuller descriptions of moral behavior will probably need to use a model that includes, but is not limited to, an analysis of moral reasoning.

Can We Teach Moral Values?

How can we encourage moral values in children? Obviously, we can preach to them and demand that they parrot our speeches. However, since these sentiments will not be internalized, this is ineffective. Another approach, which arises from Kohlberg's theories, holds more promise. Students are challenged by various moral dilemmas and encouraged to discuss them from a variety of viewpoints. In theory, children will be challenged by the reasoning of other children, impelling them towards higher stages of reasoning. The teacher's job is to present the moral dilemmas, facilitate the discussions and role playing, and see that each side is presented.

values clarification courses Educational approaches to improving moral decision-making skills based on presenting students with problems and helping them view the issue from many different viewpoints and consider many different solutions.

Evaluations of these programs, often called **values clarification courses**, are mixed. Some show moderate success (Blatt and Kohlberg, 1975). However, it is difficult to raise the average level of moral judgment of any group, and thus a number of studies show no changes (Rest, 1983). When change does occur it is relatively slight but always in the upward direction. A reasonably long term is required to produce any changes—usually at least three months.

Why have these programs, though somewhat successful, failed to fulfill their full promise? One reason may lie in the nature of the school community. Perhaps a program divorced from student's everyday life is too narrow to make any real difference. The school climate and the child's experiences in society exert a stronger influence than any classroom learning (Etzioni, 1977). It is impossible to dismiss the moral context of the home and school from the development of morality. If the school environment fosters undemocratic values it must affect the child. This, in part, is the thinking behind the "just community" programs which attempt to impart a different attitude in the classroom and school. Teachers are encouraged to be more open and democratic, to discuss moral issues with their students, to hold class meetings, and to encourage an atmosphere conducive to facilitating individual responsibility and moral development. The change in atmosphere is successful, especially in small schools which stress participation in school affairs. However, more research is needed in larger urban schools.

The Psychoanalytic Conception of Morality

Kohlberg and Piaget stress the importance of moral reasoning, while Rest's model is based on an information-processing approach. Freud also saw morality as involving thought processes, but these differ from those we have already discussed.

The Superego: The Ego Ideal and the Conscience. When children are considering an action, do they hear a "small critical voice" exhorting them to improve their behavior? Do they experience guilt if they perform some forbidden act? Psychologists who follow Freud believe so. Morality is viewed as involving the development of the **superego**. Children between the ages of about four to six years resolve their sexual fantasies toward their parents, called the Oedipal situation, by identifying with the parent of the same sex. The superego arises out of this identification. The superego consists of two parts: the **ego ideal** and the **conscience**. The ego ideal consists of the individual's standards of perfect conduct, which are formed when the child identifies and internalizes the ideals and values of the adults around. The second part of the superego is the child's conscience, which causes the child to experience guilt when misbehaving (Eidelberg, 1968; Freud, 1933). Before the superego is formed, all resistance to temptation exists outside the individual (Solnit et al., 1979). The child is afraid that he or she will lose the parents' love or that they will punish the child. After the formation of the superego, the regulation is internalized. Even if the parents are not present, the child acts in ways that would make the parents proud and experiences guilt when acting badly. The attitude that "I shall be as my parents would like me to be if they were here" (Solnit et al., 1979, p. 186) guides behavior.

Evaluating Freud's Views. Research on the psychoanalytic conception of morality is mixed. Children do identify with older people, including their parents (Kline, 1972), but their moral values are hardly carbon copies of their parents' values. Although some similarity exists, the idea that children totally copy their parents is unacceptable (Damon, 1983). In addition, if identification is so important, various aspects of moral behavior, such as honesty and generosity,

superego
The portion of the mind in psychoanalytic theory in which the conscience is found as well as standards of conduct internalized from parental teachings.

ego ideal
Part of the superego which consists of the individual's standards of perfect conduct.

conscience
Part of the superego which causes an individual to experience guilt when transgressing.

should show a strong correlation, because they are formed through the same process of identification. However, only a moderate correlation between these behaviors is found, and the inconsistency in moral actions is difficult to explain using only the process of identification. Thus, identification may be one factor, but it certainly is not by itself sufficient to explain moral development.

The Learning Approach to Morality: Studying Behavior

Up to this point we have been looking at moral reasoning and judgment. Some psychologists approach morality by studying behavior itself, including sharing, helping, and giving, as well as lying, stealing, and being aggressive. They explain moral behavior in terms of the situation, the child's background, the models available to the child, and the reinforcements that are present in the environment.

Learning theorists argue that moral behavior is learned like any other behavior. Operant conditioning explains some of it. Children who are reinforced for giving and sharing are more likely to give and share. Social-learning theorists add imitation to the picture. Much of behavior is influenced by watching how others—both adults and peers—deal with life's challenges. If we observe people we respect helping others or giving to charity, we are more likely to do so ourselves. Of course, this may not always be the case. We do not imitate everything we see. Factors such as the character of the models, the consequences of the behavior, and our own characteristics affect imitation (Bandura, 1977). Cognitive factors are also involved. How we perceive the situation and process the information, as well as how competent we are to deal with the challenge, enter the picture (Mussen and Eisenberg-Berg, 1977). Suppose you see a person collapse. How you react will depend on your ability to size up the situation as well as on your training. If you know how to help such victims, you may administer first aid. If not, you may call the authorities and wait.

PROSOCIAL BEHAVIOR

Children show a wide range of individual differences in their prosocial behavior. Some children are willing to share, keenly feel other children's pain, and are always consoling them. Other children seem oblivious to the plight of peers around them. Are some children simply more caring, more helpful, or more honest than others?

Does Honesty Exist?

It is tempting to simply divide the world into those who are honest and helpful and those who are not, those who give and share and those who are selfish. In our everyday conversations, we are likely to do so—labeling one child as honest, another as selfish. This trait-like approach has not worked. In their landmark studies, Hartshorne and May (1928) tested thousands of children on a number of different tasks. They concluded that children's behavior varied with the situation. A child could be honest in one situation and not in another. One who cheated on an athletics test might or might not cheat on an arithmetic examination (Cairns, 1979).

For quite some time, this situational view of honesty prevailed, but further research using statistical techniques not available to Hartshorne and May discovered a carryover of honesty from one situation to the next, although it was not very strong (Burton, 1963). In summary, although some people are more honest than others, we cannot say that a person will be honest in every situation.

Factors Influencing Prosocial Behavior

Prosocial behavior is complicated by many factors (Yarrow et al., 1983), and simple explanations have failed to explain it. The individual's culture, upbringing, cognitive abilities, emotional state, and the situation itself all affect the child's behavior.

Culture.   We pride ourselves on being a prosocial society. Indeed, Americans donate much money to charity. We value such behavior and preach it to our children. Yet American children are not as willing to share or to give as children in other societies. In one study, children from six different cultures—India, Kenya, Okinawa, Mexico, the Philippine Islands, and the United States—were observed (Whiting and Whiting, 1975). One hundred percent of the Kenyans and 73 percent of the Mexican children showed prosocial behavior in amounts that exceeded the median of all children in the study, while only 8 percent of the American children exceeded this median. Differences were found among the three societies that showed the most prosocial behavior (Kenya, Mexico, and the Philippines) and the other three. Those cultures in which children lived in extended families and had greater responsibilities and in which the structure of the society was simpler encouraged these behaviors.

Parents.   Certain child-rearing practices lead to the internalization of values and prosocial behavior. Parents who use reasoning techniques mixed with affection outside the discipline situation raise children who practice proscocial behavior (Hoffman, 1979). This is especially true if parents take the effort to point out to children the effect of this behavior on the other person (Eisenberg, 1982). Parents also serve as models for their children. If children observe their parents helping and sharing, they are more likely to do the same.

Age.   Are older children more likely to share or give things to others than younger children? One of the most-cited findings in this area is that children become more altruistic with age (Peterson, 1983). Older children have developed cognitive skills that enable them to understand and feel what other children are experiencing. However, such generalizations should be made with care. Although this increase in altruism with age is a general trend, there are many individual differences, and not all studies have shown this to be true (Yarrow et al., 1983).

10. *True or False:*
As children mature, they tend to share with other children more often.

Mood and Emotions.   Generally, children in happy moods show more prosocial behavior than children who are sad (Mussen and Eisenberg-Berg, 1977), but the source of the emotion makes a difference. Barnett and colleagues (1979) manipulated the source of the emotion, namely, whether the children were happy, sad, or neutral about themselves or others. If children were sad about something that had happened to themselves, they were not as generous as

11. *True or False:*
Children who are happy generally give more than those who are sad.

children who were sad about something happening to other children. Children who had experienced happy events, though, were the most generous.

The Situation.   Any look at the factors that influence prosocial behavior must take the child's perception of the situation into account. For example, a child will be more likely to help another if the personal cost is low than if it is high. If children are faced with a situation in which helping another will cause them great pain or trouble, they will be less willing to do so than if it is a minor inconvenience. Asking a five-year-old to share his or her green beans is likely to be greeted with joy, but ask the same child to share a piece of cake and you may witness a different expression. The reinforcement properties of the situation are also important. Children will help and share more if they are rewarded for it (Mussen and Eisenberg-Berg, 1977). In addition, although adults are more responsive to people in distress when they are alone, studies of first- and second-graders show that they are more likely to help if they are with one other person. Fifth- and sixth-graders help about the same whether they are alone or in pairs (Mussen and Eisenberg-Berg, 1977). All in all, the characteristics of the situation affect prosocial behavior.

Encouraging Prosocial Behavior

Prosocial behavior can be encouraged. Using rational methods of discipline and pointing out how a child's prosocial behavior helps others encourages it. Since models are also important, showing children the way, and rewarding their behavior through nodding, affection, and the like, may be helpful. In some areas of prosocial behavior, such as aiding others in distress, developing a feeling of competence is important. Finally, the developmental changes in empathy should be taken into consideration. As children mature, they are better able to read subtle cues and react in ways that take the other person's perspective into consideration. This perspective-taking can be encouraged, as long as one realizes that the younger the child the clearer and less complicated the signals must be.

AGGRESSION

Prosocial behavior is positively regarded by society, and psychologists try to find ways to increase such behavior. The situation is precisely the reverse with aggression, as psychologists strive to reduce antisocial aggressive behavior. The same factors that affected prosocial behavior—namely, culture, socialization, emotionality, age, and situational factors—affect aggression as well.

How Common Is Aggression?

12. *True or False:*
Aggression is one of the most common types of interactions between children.

A casual look at the newspapers may convince you that childhood aggression is one of the more common types of interpersonal interactions. In fact, it is not. A study of highly aggressive boys found that only 2 to 3 aggressive actions occur per 1,000 social interactions (Patterson and Cobb, 1971). Yet the behavior is common enough. Almost all parents have to handle aggression in their young children (Sears et al, 1957). Aggression in the classroom is a serious problem, and the aggressive-disruptive behavior pattern is one of the most common problems presented in mental health facilities (Cullinan and Epstein, 1982). Children are also the recipients of much aggression. Between 84 percent and 97 percent of all parents use physical punishment on a child at some point (Parke and Slaby, 1983).

The social consequences of aggression are great. Aggressive children are generally unpopular (Clarizio and McCoy, 1976) and are more likely to be targets of aggression (Dodge and Frame, 1982). Aggressive children are also likely to be male. Between three and six times as many boys are referred to mental health agencies for aggressive behavior as girls (Cullinan and Epstein, 1982). Boys are also more likely to be the targets of aggression (Cairns, 1979). The sex differences are rather constant across age and culture (Maccoby and Jacklin, 1980; Maccoby and Jacklin, 1974). There is some disagreement on just why this is so. Some argue that hormones predispose males toward aggression (Maccoby and Jacklin, 1980), and the evidence for this hormonal theory in animals is strong. The question is whether it holds for human beings. On this question, authorities disagree. Some argue that the evidence does not indicate such a link (Tieger, 1980), others note that, although inconclusive, research does lean toward the existence of such a relationship (Maccoby and Jacklin, 1980). This argument will continue for many years, but both sides readily acknowledge that social factors are involved in aggression.

Some people believe that the aggressive child will grow out of it, but this is just wishful thinking (Cullinan and Epstein, 1982). Aggression is rather stable over long periods of time for both boys and girls (Olweus, 1982, 1979, 1977), but the nature of the aggression is likely to change.

To understand the developmental nature of aggression, Hartup (1974) divided aggressive behaviors into two categories. **Instrumental aggression** involves struggles over possessions. It is not personal, and its aim is to secure an item. **Hostile aggression**, on the other hand, is person-oriented. This aggression is aimed at injuring the other party. Most young children act aggressively in order to wrench a toy from someone else or to gain space (Hay and Ross, 1982). In a study of preschoolers and first- and second-graders, Hartup (1974) found that aggression generally decreased with age. This pattern is caused by the striking decrease in instrumental aggression. As children mature, verbal alternatives replace physical means (Parke and Slaby, 1983). Only by looking at the factors that produce aggression can we understand these developmental patterns.

instrumental aggression
Aggression that involves struggles over possessions.

hostile aggression
Aggression that is aimed at injuring another person.

13. *True or False:*
As a rule, the frequency of aggressive acts declines throughout the elementary school years.

Factors Affecting Aggressiveness

The Family.   Consider the children who watch their parents argue violently, are hit hard and often, and discover that they get what they want by being aggressive toward others. We could predict that these children would be aggressive, and research confirms our hypothesis.

Certain child-rearing strategies are related to aggression in children, according to a study performed by Sears and his colleagues (1957). These include permissiveness and punitiveness. Parents who were very permissive tended to raise aggressive children. In addition, the more punishing the parents, the more aggressive their children. The combination of permissiveness and punitiveness led to the most aggressive children. If parents allow their children to vent their aggressive impulses, children think it is acceptable. Then they are harshly punished

Children learn how to solve their disputes partly by observing how their parents deal with interpersonal problems.

for it, which causes frustration and anger, which in turn leads to further aggression. This aggressiveness does not remain confined to the home. In a sample of third-graders, parental use of physical punishment was related to the child's aggressiveness at school (Eron et al., 1971).

Violence is often used to solve interpersonal disputes at home, and children learn to use it to get their own way. In families where husbands and wives use verbal or physical aggression to resolve disputes, parents also use such aggression against their children, and children use it against their siblings (Parke and Slaby, 1983). Violence between siblings is the most common type of home violence. However, aggression does not just occur; it is often provoked by someone.

Modeling.   Aggression can also be learned through modeling. A child who witnesses authority figures being aggressive may act aggressively too. In a series of studies, children were exposed to live or filmed models acting aggressively against a Bobo doll. They were then given the opportunity to play with the materials. Usually the children imitated whatever acts they saw. If exposed to aggressive actions, they acted aggressively, if shown constructive actions, they imitated those actions (Bandura, 1977; Bandura et al., 1961). Children who witness aggression in their homes or feel that aggression is condoned are more likely to be aggressive.

Television.   Since children may learn to be aggressive by viewing violent behavior, the question of television violence and children's aggression is an important one. Indeed, children do witness quite a bit of aggression on television (see Table 12.3 and Figure 12.4). By the time a child graduates from high school, he or she has seen 13,000 violent deaths on television (Gerbner and Gross, 1980). Most children watch between three and four hours of television each day

---

TABLE 12.3   **How Violent Are Your Favorite Shows?**
Does the number of violent acts per hour on some of these shows surprise you?

Program	Violent Acts/Hour	Program	Violent Acts/Hour
V: Movie & Series (NBC)	49	Dallas (CBS)	2
The A Team (NBC)	46	Night Court (NBC)	2
Mike Hammer (CBS)	44	Love Boat (ABC)	1
Fall Guy (ABC)	41	St. Elsewhere (NBC)	1
Hunter (NBC)	32	Dynasty (ABC)	0
T. J. Hooker (ABC)	27	60 Minutes (CBS)	0
Miami Vice (NBC)	25	Trapper John, M.D. (CBS)	0
Matt Houston (ABC)	24	The Jeffersons (CBS)	0
Magnum, P.I. (CBS)	21	Alice (CBS)	0
Simon & Simon (CBS)	20	Newhart (CBS)	0
Scarecrow & Mrs. King (CBS)	20	Kate & Allie (CBS)	0
Hardcastle & McCormick (ABC)	19	Three's Company/Crowd (ABC)	0
Knight Rider (NBC)	18	Punky Brewster (NBC)	0
Dukes of Hazzard (CBS)	18	The Cosby Show (NBC)	0
Remington Steele (NBC)	14	Gimme a Break (NBC)	0
Hill Street Blues (NBC)	11	Different Strokes (NBC)	0
Cagney & Lacey (CBS)	6	Silver Spoons (NBC)	0
Fantasy Island (ABC)	6	Family Ties (NBC)	0
Murder, She Wrote (CBS)	3	Cheers (NBC)	0
Falcon Crest (CBS)	3	Webster (ABC)	0
Knot's Landing (CBS)	2	Benson (ABC)	0

Source: National Coalition on Television Violence, 1984.

(Cairns, 1979). Children spend more time watching television than engaging in any other single activity (Parke and Slaby, 1983). Over 70 percent of prime-time television contains violence (Parke and Slaby, 1983), and two-thirds of all television programming aimed at children is violent (Gerbner and Gross, 1980). Despite the concerns expressed by many authorities, televised violence has not been reduced much (Lefkowitz and Huesmann, 1980). Violence is commonly shown not only on dramatic series but also in cartoons and on the nightly news.

If every child exposed to violence on television imitated it, there would be a great public outcry, and parents would exercise considerable care in what their children watch. But this is not the case. The decision to be aggressive is not a simple one, and it is difficult to factor out what caused a violent action (Cairns, 1979). However, the evidence indicates that viewing television increases the probability of violent action (Parke and Slaby, 1983; Singer and Singer, 1983; McCarthy et al., 1975). After reviewing the studies on exposure to violence and aggressive behavior, Andison (1977) found that 77 percent found a positive relationship, 20 percent could not come to a definite conclusion, and less than 5 per-

14. *True or False:*
There is a scientifically recognized relationship between watching violence on television and aggressive behavior.

FIGURE 12.4   Violent Acts per Hour During Network Prime-Time Television
Violence is prevalent on television. The main question is how does it affect the viewer?

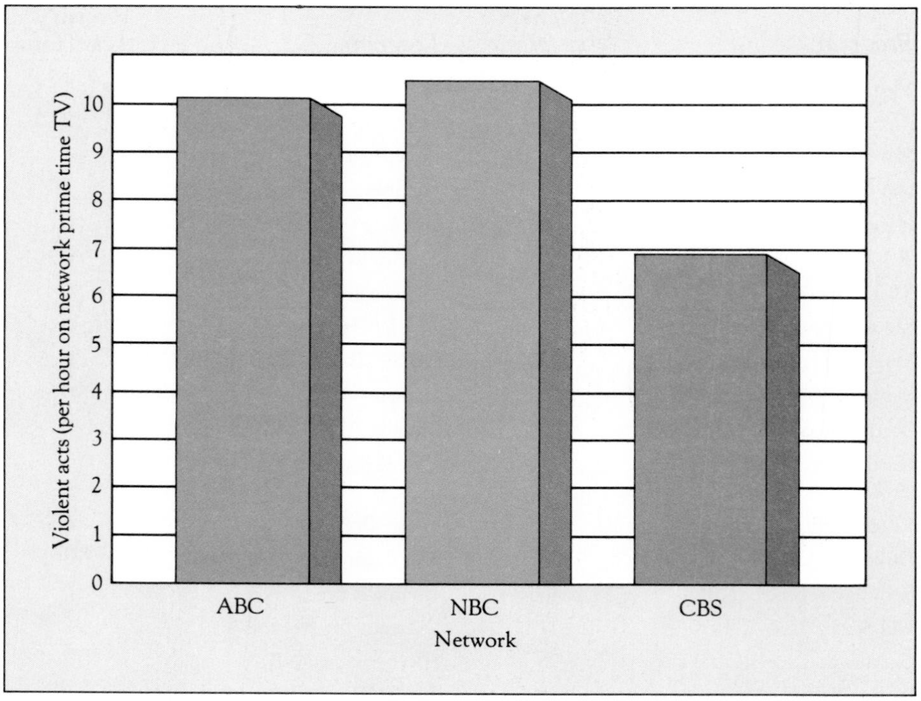

Source: National Coalition on Television Violence, 1984.

cent found the opposite. Most experts now agree that there is a relationship between aggressive behavior and viewing violence on television (Rubinstein, 1980). This should put to rest the argument that viewing violence on television satisfies a child's aggressive impulses. There is little or no evidence supporting this position (Rubinstein, 1980; Comstock, 1980). The opposite conclusion is more tenable.

Another explanation for the relationship between aggressiveness and watching television is more interesting. Perhaps aggressive children simply watch more television. This in and of itself cannot explain the relationships that have been found (Singer and Singer, 1983), but it may contain some truth. In an analysis of two very large long-term studies, Eron (1982) concluded that television violence is indeed one cause of aggressive behavior. However, aggressive children also prefer to watch more and more violent behavior, establishing a circular pattern. Eron reasons that aggressive children are unpopular and spend more time watching television. The violence that they see reassures them that their behavior is appropriate, and teaches them new ways to act aggressively. This makes them even more unpopular and sends them back to the television for another dose of violence. Whatever the reasons, the link between aggression and viewing violence on television is well established.

15. *True or False:*
Aggressive children are likely to choose to watch violent television programs.

One of the most researched questions in history is whether viewing violence on television contributes to children's aggressive behavior.

But television violence has another, more subtle effect on us. We get used to violence on television and come to accept it as a normal part of life (Drabman and Thomas, 1975). We become desensitized to violence and no longer take it seriously (Thomas et al., 1977; Cline et al., 1973). This desensitization may explain the difficulty we have arousing the public to action to stop violent crime, as well as part of the reason people may not be as willing to help a victim of crime.

Variables Affecting the Influence of Television.   What variables affect aggression? Obviously, the nature of the televised aggression and the viewer are important. One expert in this field, George Comstock (1980), suggests that if the violence is socially approved the viewer comes to believe that it is acceptable to be violent. The viewer's ideas about what is and is not socially acceptable may change, especially if the perpetrator of the violence is not criticized for it. This is one reason parents should be actively concerned about their children's television viewing experience; some suggestions for parental involvement can be found in Figure 12.5. The second factor is efficacy or the ability to achieve results. When aggressors get what they want, viewers are likely to believe that aggressiveness is a preferred strategy. If the violence is more realistic or causes the individual to become aroused, it may also encourage viewers to be more violent.

Although some people seem to be more susceptible to violent suggestion than others, children of both sexes and of all ages, social classes, ethnic groups, and personality characteristics may be affected (Huesmann et al., 1984; Lefkowitz and Huesmann, 1980; Dorr and Kovaric, 1980). Both males and females may be equally influenced, with people who are more aggressive within each sex being more affected than others. Although children at every age are susceptible, a particularly sensitive period during late middle childhood, around eight or nine years of age, has been found (Eron et al., 1983). Exposure to violence peaks at about the third grade, but the correlation between aggressiveness and viewing violence increases until ages ten to eleven, suggesting a cumulative effect beyond this sensitive period.

FIGURE 12.5 A Guide to T.V. Viewing

Not every program shown on television is fit for children, nor should children be encouraged to sit for endless hours in front of the television set. Yet, if parents plan their family's viewing activities with an eye to using the time in a constructive fashion, television can have its positive side.

Hints for Viewing Television

Know when children are watching television. Today, many American families have more than one television set, the second one being used almost exclusively by the children and sometimes found in their rooms or the basement. Thus, parents don't always know how much time their children are spending in front of the television set. If this is a question, parents may ask their children to keep a log noting the time they started and stopped watching television. Parents may then keep closer track of how many hours per day their children spend watching television.

Know what children are watching. Not all television programs are suitable for youngsters. In addition, some programs may contain material that requires parental explanation. It is a good idea to check on the type of programs the child is watching.

Choice or chance. When children sit down to watch television, do they have a specific program in mind? Do they enjoy a particular program, or do they watch television merely to pass the time? If children are merely passing time, there may be more profitable activities available for them.

Family viewing. Television viewing is often a passive experience. However, it need not be. As you watch television as a family, encourage children to question the values being portrayed on the screen. Spend time discussing these values, being certain to listen to your children's opinions. Don't be afraid to point out the consequences of an action on television or criticize behaviors that aren't proper. Many television shows raise moral, ethical, and behavioral questions which can lead to profitable family discussions.

No television when . . . Since television often provides an easy escape for children, it is important to set limits on when children can watch programs. For example, watching television during meals is usually not a good idea. Tranquil discussion is better. In addition, when children's friends are around, an afternoon of play is in order, not a full afternoon of television viewing.

Beware of using the television as a babysitter. Parents of very young children frequently leave their children in front of the television set for hours while they do their house work. The television set is no substitute for active interaction.

Be aware of growth opportunities. Sometimes new words or concepts are presented on a television program. Television viewing can offer surprising ways of increasing knowledge.

Look for programs that are entertaining and valuable. Some programs have successfully combined entertainment and education. Some of these programs are especially produced with young people in mind. Others, such as some nature programs, appeal to a broader audience. Be on the lookout for such programs.

Television tied to reading. Some successful television specials and series have been taken from books. Children should be encouraged to read the original. In addition, seeing a program on the old west, for example, may interest a youngster enough to go to the library and read a book on the subject. A television program may excite interest which can be carried over into reading.

Be flexible. In an attempt to limit television time some parents become inflexible. Limiting television watching on school nights is a reasonable policy but, at times, a special program may be shown which children may wish to watch. Rules should not be inflexibly administered.

Television violence, then, is a real factor in increasing the likelihood that people will act aggressively. However, not all people who watch violent television programs become aggressive. So television is only a part of the total picture.

Peer Groups.   Peer groups also influence aggressive behavior (Parke and Slaby, 1983). This may occur in three ways. Children may model themselves after a violent individual, especially if the model gains something of value through violence. Second, the peer group may reinforce the violent deeds. Although aggressive individuals are often rejected by the majority of children, they may find a group in which this behavior is acceptable. This leads us to the third point—the social norms of the peer group. Some groups reject violence more than others.

The Neighborhood.   In some neighborhoods, violence is an everyday occurrence. Children from lower-income groups often live in areas in which violence is a part of life. In addition, a subculture may respect and reinforce the hit-first-talk-later attitude. This is intensified by a physical environment of overcrowding, poverty, and at times a sense of hopelessness.

Cognitive Factors.   Imagine yourself sitting in class when someone steps on your foot. How would you react? Your answer probably would depend on whether you thought the act was intentional. If you reason that it was accidental you respond one way, if you deem it deliberate you respond in a totally different manner. Dodge (1980) presented second-, fourth-, and sixth-graders with a situation in which a frustration was caused by a child with either a hostile, nonhostile, or ambiguous intent. Children in each group reacted with more hostility when the intent was communicated as being hostile. When the intent was ambiguous, however, only the boys rated more aggressive reacted as though the intent was really hostile.

The ability to perceive intent changes with age. Seven-, nine-, and twelve-year-old boys were presented with hypothetical aggressive situations, and the intensity of their reactions was measured. The stories varied as to the intentionality of the action. Nine- and twelve-year-olds responded much less aggressively when they thought it was accidental, while the seven-year-olds reacted similarly to both types. Twelve-year-olds responded less aggressively to intentional verbal provocations than to intentional physical provocations, while nine-year-olds and seven-year-olds did not (Shantz and Voydanoff, 1973).

The child's reputation can also serve as a cue for aggression. Rotenberg (1980) found that second- and fourth-graders felt that a child who had hurt another child intentionally in one situation would do so in the future in another situation. Kindergarten children did not seem to have such long-term, generalized expectations.

Working with the Aggressive Child

There are no magic solutions to reducing aggression in children. Clarizio and McCoy (1976) suggest that at times a behavioral approach that reinforces prosocial behaviors such as sharing and ignores aggressive behavior may be successful. Obviously, the second part of this prescription is often impractical if the aggression will injure another child. Therefore, when ignoring the behavior is impossible, impractical, or undesirable, the child must know what behaviors will not be tolerated and the consequences of misbehavior. Punitiveness and firmness are not the same, and it is best to avoid generating additional frustration and anger through physical punishment. Clarizio and McCoy suggest social isolation for aggressive behavior and explaining the reasons for the punishment. Since children are more likely to accept punishment if the relationship between the authority figure and the child is warm, building a positive relationship may make discipline and punishment more effective.

Since aggression is learned through operant conditioning and imitation, children must be provided with rewards for prosocial behavior and none for antisocial acts. Finally, aggressive children should be exposed to models who are constructive, competent, and rewarded for nonaggressive but assertive actions.

MIDDLE CHILDHOOD IN PERSPECTIVE

The school-age period is often considered one of horizontal growth. Unlike the early years, when cognitive physical and social growth are obvious, changes during middle childhood are more gradual. But significant changes *are* taking place. The child's social world is expanding as friends and teachers become more important. Children are given more freedom and responsibility at home. No longer can supervision be complete, and they must develop their own sense of right and wrong. They also must decide how they will handle their interpersonal relationships.

Up to this point we have been looking at the mythical "normal" child. However, there has recently been more interest in children who differ either mentally or physically from the average child. These include the gifted and mentally retarded, children who are deaf or visually impaired, and children who have learning disabilities or behavior disorders. Years ago, these children were segregated from their peers, but today they are more visible and are being integrated into society. Psychologists and educators have become deeply interested in the plight of children with exceptional needs, and our next chapter will look at their problems and potential.

Chapter Summary

1. According to Erik Erikson, the positive outcome of middle childhood is the development of a sense of industry, while the negative outcome is viewed in terms of inferiority.

2. Freud noted that children resolving the Oedipal situation next enter a latency phase, when sexuality is hidden. Boys' and girls' groups are segregated.

3. During middle childhood, children get feedback from many different people. Their self-concept develops from a combination of this feedback and their own evaluation of their subjective experiences.

4. Children's relationship to their parents changes during middle childhood. Children become more independent and, later in the stage, are greatly influenced by peers. They also become more argumentative and question parental judgment more often.

5. Children's immediate reaction to divorce involves anger, depression, and guilt. Normally children recover from the initial shock after a year or so, but the long-term effects of divorce can be serious if parents continue to argue, if serious financial problems exist, and if social supports are

unavailable. Generally, boys are more adversely affected than girls.

6. Children who are popular tend to be friendly, have good social skills, share interests with their peers, and be physically appealing. Children's conceptions of friendship change over time as they become more cognitively sophisticated.

7. In middle childhood, boys show an increased preference for male stereotyped activities, while girls do not show such a preference for stereotyped female activities. Parents continue to treat sons and daughters differently. Sex typing in schools is also well documented.

8. Piaget and Kohlberg both advanced theories of moral reasoning. Piaget noted that young children do not take intent into consideration when judging actions, and see rules as unchangeable. Older children are more flexible and take intent into consideration.

9. Lawrence Kohlberg explained the development of moral reasoning in terms of three levels, each of which contains two stages. It is the reasoning behind the moral decision, not the decision itself, that determines the level of moral reasoning.

10. Freud viewed morality in terms of the development of the superego. This occurs through identification.

11. Behaviorists are more interested in studying moral behaviors, such as cheating and altruism, than in the reasoning behind the behavior. The environment as well as the situation itself affects moral behavior.

12. Prosocial behavior is encouraged when parents use rational methods of discipline and point out how the child's behavior helps others. The models children observe around them, as well as the reinforcements they experience or witness, are also important.

13. Instrumental aggression involves struggles over possessions, hostile aggression is more person-oriented. Instrumental aggression decreases significantly with age.

14. Children who observe a great deal of aggression at home, are harshly disciplined, or are taught that aggression is an acceptable method of gaining what they want tend to be violent. Aggressive behavior can also be imitated.

15. Most studies indicate that observing violent behavior on television increases the likelihood that the child will act aggressively. It also desensitizes children to violence.

■ *Answers to True or False Questions*

1. *False.* Correct statement: Boys and girls tend to avoid each other during middle childhood.

2. *True.* Not only do parents show less physical affection, but they also spend less time with their children now.

3. *False.* Correct statement: Children raised in permissive environments tend to be impulsive and aggressive.

4. *True.* A common complaint of the custodial parent is that the other parent is now playing the part of candy man/woman and constantly taking the child's side in disputes.

5. *True.* Although the reasons are not really known for this phenomenon, boys do not recover from divorce as easily as girls do.

6. *False.* Correct statement: Although children are aware of the sex-role stereotypes, they tend to become more flexible as they progress through this stage.

7. *False.* Correct statement: Boys have much more rigid conceptions about what is appropriate for each sex than girls do.

8. *False.* Correct statement: Surprisingly, boys get more attention, but much of it is negative.

9. *False.* Correct statement: One of the important developments in the area of moral reasoning is the child's ability to take the intent and motivation of another person into consideration when judging right and wrong.

10. *True.* Generally speaking, children show more prosocial behavior as they mature.

11. *True.* Children who are in a happy mood are more generous than those who are sad.

12. *False.* Correct statement: Aggression is fairly uncommon in child-child interactions.

13. *True.* This decline is due to the decrease in instrumental aggression—merely taking things from others by force.

14. *True.* Most studies find a relationship between watching violence on television and aggressive behavior.

15. *True.* Children who are aggressive tend to gravitate toward the more violent television shows.

CHAPTER THIRTEEN

The Exceptional Child

■ Are the Following Statements True or False?

Try the True-False Quiz below. See if your answers correspond to the information in this chapter. Each question is repeated opposite the paragraph in which the answer can be found. The True-False Answer Box at the end of the chapter lists complete answers.

____ **1.** According to the law, every exceptional child must be mainstreamed, that is, placed in a class with "normal" students.

____ **2.** Subnormal intellectual ability is the sole criterion for being labeled mentally retarded.

____ **3.** Children who are intellectually gifted tend to be socially backward.

____ **4.** The majority of the legally blind can see nothing at all.

____ **5.** Hearing aids improve the quality of the sound as well as amplifying it.

____ **6.** Cerebral palsy is caused by a virus that is transmitted in a way unknown to medical science at this time.

____ **7.** Handicapped children usually describe themselves realistically.

____ **8.** More girls than boys are considered learning disabled.

____ **9.** Hyperactivity can be cured through the correct use of medication.

____ **10.** Children who act aggressively are not very popular with their peers.

THE EXCEPTIONAL CHILD TODAY

Phil was frightened when he entered the classroom for the first time. His new classmates were curious. Phil suffers from cerebral palsy and must spend his days in a wheelchair. He attended a special school for two years and has never been in a regular classroom before. While some of his classmates stare, most ignore him.

Until recently, few people have had personal contact with exceptional children like Phil, but that is changing. In the past, a deliberate attempt was made to separate the educational and social worlds of disabled and nondisabled children, but through the efforts of parent groups, legislative action, and court orders, these children are no longer closeted away. The modern trend is to integrate the exceptional child into society as much as possible.

If this attempt to better the lives of these children is to succeed, we must both understand their similarities to the developmental norm and appreciate their special needs. Knowledge of these conditions has increased dramatically, as has the awareness that these special children can become fully functioning members of society.

Why Interest in the Exceptional Child?

But why an entire chapter devoted to the exceptional child in a text that concentrates on "normal" childhood and adolescent development? Years ago, the exceptional child was defined in terms of his or her disability (Milk, 1980), but today professionals concentrate on the abilities a child does have and the extent to which the child can function in society. In other words, we are moving away from definition by handicap, with its generalities and half-truths, and stressing the potential of the child to lead a meaningful and productive life. This more positive stance means that the similarities between the disabled and the nondisabled become more important, thereby fitting into our perspective.

Second, the trend toward integrating the exceptional child into society means that many readers of this text will become involved in these children's lives, either in the workplace, at school, or at home. In addition, many career opportunities are open in the area of services for the exceptional child, and these deserve some attention too. Third, as our ability to diagnose these conditions both correctly and at an early age increases, we have become aware of the significant number of children who can be labeled exceptional. Estimates of the number of exceptional children are found in Table 13.1.

Defining Terms

Below you will find brief descriptions of five children. Which of these children would you label exceptional, disabled, and/or handicapped?

1. Leonard has an IQ of 140 and seems to enjoy school.
2. Sarah is deaf and requires an interpreter in order to attend regular classes.
3. Tony is hyperactive and requires medication in order to behave properly in class.
4. Cheryl is very mechanically inclined and would like to build her own engine.

TABLE 13.1   **Prevalence of Exceptional Children in the U.S.**
The number of exceptional children in the population is significant, usually more than most people would think.

Exceptionality	Percent of Population	No. of Children Ages 5–18*
Visually impaired (includes blind)	0.1	55,000
Hearing impaired (includes deaf)	0.5 to 0.7	275,000 to 385,000
Speech handicapped	3.0 to 4.0	1,650,000 to 2,200,000
Orthopedic and health impairments	0.5	275,000
Emotionally disturbed	2.0 to 3.0	1,100,000 to 1,650,000
Mentally retarded (both educable and trainable)	2.0 to 3.0	1,100,000 to 1,650,000
Learning disabilities	2.0 to 3.0	1,100,000 to 1,650,000
Multihandicapped	0.5 to 0.7	275,000 to 385,000
Gifted and talented	2.0 to 3.0	1,100,000 to 1,650,000
*Totals	12.6 to 18.0	6,930,000 to 9,900,000

*Number of children based on 1985 population estimates.
Source: B. R. Gearheart and M. W. Weishahn, 1984.

5. Bill has not been able to walk since he was involved in a car accident. He cannot get to and from his job without asking his friends for a lift.

The terms *exceptional*, *disabled*, and *handicapped* are often used interchangeably and incorrectly. An **exceptional child** is a child whose intellectual, emotional, or physical performance falls either above or below that of his or her "normal" peers (Haring, 1982). Everyone deviates from the mythical average, but there is a range of normal performance expected from children at particular stages in their lives, and children who deviate from this norm appreciably are considered "exceptional."

The term **disabled** refers to a total or partial behavioral, mental, physical, or sensorial loss of functioning (Mandell and Fiscus, 1981), whereas the term **handicapped** refers to the difficulty an individual may have in adjusting to the environment (Haring, 1982). The term *handicapped* is often used in connection with an environmental restriction that results from the exceptionality and may well depend on the situation. When he grows up, Bill may be handicapped in climbing stairs, but he may not have any handicap when it comes to performing office work where ramps are available.

Each of the five children described above could be labeled exceptional, and with the exception of Leonard and Cheryl, they are disabled. On the surface at least, only Bill would seem to be handicapped in the situations described. The environmental restriction placed on Bill by his disability has created a handicapping condition. If Bill were able to take a bus to work, or even adapt a car so that he could drive, his disability would remain, but at least in this situation it would not be a handicap.

exceptional child
A child whose intellectual, emotional, or physical performance falls substantially above or below that of "normal" peers.

disability
A total or partial behavioral, mental, physical, or sensory loss of functioning.

handicap
The difficulty an individual has adjusting to the environment.

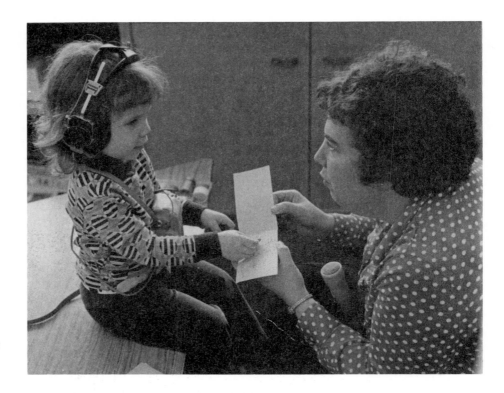

Early identification and assessment of a problem are important steps in designing the best program for disabled children.

The Law and the Exceptional Child

The year is 1960. The place is the school district superintendent's office. The parents of Mickey, a learning-disabled child, are vainly trying to find a way to educate him for life. The superintendent tells them that the district does not have a program for Mickey. Another professional tells them that Mickey cannot learn and that if he were allowed to attend a regular school he would take too much time away from the normal children. A day school would be possible, but the parents would have to pay the entire cost for educating him, even though Mickey's parents pay taxes in the community. Mickey's parents leave the office feeling dejected and helpless.

Across town, the Smiths hear that their daughter Loretta is being placed in a class for the mentally retarded on the basis of results on an intelligence test. The parents know that Loretta becomes very nervous when tested and sometimes gives up. She dislikes the teacher, and the feeling is mutual because Loretta is sometimes disruptive. The principal tells Mr. and Mrs. Smith that placing Loretta in a class for the retarded would be best for everyone. The Smiths are not so certain, but they are told there is nothing they can do about it.

These scenes were not uncommon years ago, when exceptional children were often denied an education, given an inferior education, or simply separated from the mainstream of children as a matter of policy. But this is no longer the case. Beginning in the late 1960s, a number of court decisions resulted in improvements in conditions for exceptional children across the United States. Yet in 1975 Congress received a report that, despite these improvements, over 1.75 million children with handicaps were being excluded from public education, and over half the 8 million disabled children were not receiving the services they needed and were entitled to. Just as disturbing was the finding that children were being misclassified and placed in unsuitable environments (Abeson and Zettel, 1977). These findings, and a great deal of pulic pressure, prompted Congress to pass the most important legislation for the exceptional child. Public Law 94-142, also called the Education for All Handicapped Children Act, legislated a new day for the exceptional child, although it has brought new problems and conflicts.

The law calls for every child to receive a free, appropriate education and provides for procedures to safeguard the rights of disabled children. The major provisions are summarized in Table 13.2. A district can no longer claim that no pro-

---

TABLE 13.2   Major Provisions of PL94-142 (The Education for All Handicapped Children Act)
Public Law 94-142 ensured that all handicapped children would receive a free and appropriate education.

Each State and Locality Must Have a Plan to Ensure:

Child identification	Extensive efforts must be made to screen and identify all handicapped children.
Full service, at no cost	Every handicapped child must be assured an appropriate public education at no cost to the parents or guardians.
Due process	The child's and parents' rights to information and informed consent must be assured before the child is evaluated, labeled, or placed, and they have a right to an impartial due process hearing if they disagree with the school's decisions.
Parent consultation, parent surrogate	Parents or guardian must be consulted about the child's evaluation and placement and the educational plan; if parents or guardian are unknown or unavailable, a surrogate parent to act for the child must be found.
LRE	The child must be educated in the least restrictive environment that is consistent with his educational needs and, insofar as possible, with nonhandicapped children.
IEP	A written individualized education program must be prepared for each handicapped child. The plan must state present levels of functioning, long- and short-term goals, services to be provided, and plans for initiating and evaluating the services.
Nondiscriminatory evaluation	The child must be evaluated in all areas of suspected disability and in a way that is not biased by his language or cultural characteristics or his handicaps. Evaluation must be by a multidisciplinary team, and no single evaluation procedure may be used as the sole criterion for placement or planning.
Confidentiality	Results of evaluation and placement must be kept confidential, and parents or guardian may have access to records regarding their child.
Personnel development, in-service	Training must be provided for teachers and other professional personnel, including in-service training for regular teachers in meeting the needs of the handicapped.

There are detailed rules and regulations of the federal government regarding the implementation of each of these major provisions. The definitions of some of these provisions—LRE and nondiscriminatory evaluation, for example—are still being clarified by federal officials and court decisions.

Source: D. P. Hallahan and J. M. Kauffman, 1982.

grams are available for a disabled child or that a child cannot be educated. It is the district's responsibility to educate the child. In addition, the guarantee that "due process" be used in placing a child in some educational program means not only that a legal procedure must be followed but also that all testing must be non-discriminatory. A Spanish-speaking child can no longer be given an intelligence test written in English, nor can only one test be relied on for any decision. The law also requires educational accountability, because educators must develop what is called an **individualized education program**, or IEP, which states the goals of the schooling and the methods for attaining them. Parents also have the right to participate in all phases of their children's placement and education. Finally, the law mandates that each child be placed in the *least restrictive environment* (Heward and Orlansky, 1984). Figure 13.1 shows various placement alternatives. The most restrictive are found at the top while integration into the normal classroom is the least restrictive possible. When disabled children are put in a regular classroom, they are said to be *mainstreamed*.

individualized education program (IEP)
An individual plan outlining educational goals and methods for attaining them.

FIGURE 13.1   A Continuum of Educational Services
This figure shows the many alternatives available for placing handicapped children. Notice the continuum of services ranging from placing the child in a regular classroom with few or no supportive services (1) to placement in a hospital or institution (10). Children are placed in the least restrictive environment in which they can effectively function.

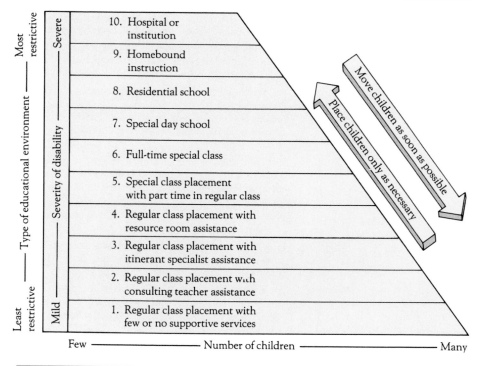

Source: Deno, 1973.

Mainstreaming: Problems and Potential

The most controversial part of the law has to do with the practice of **main-streaming.** Actually, mainstreaming is not really part of the law at all. The law mandates that a child be placed in the least restrictive environment, but it does not require that all children be mainstreamed. Still, for many children P.L. 94–142 has meant integration into regular classrooms.

The thinking behind such integration is obvious. Both the disabled child and the nondisabled child benefit from being exposed to and interacting with each other. The disabled child learns to live in the nondisabled world and gains the social skills necessary for independent living. The nondisabled child becomes less prejudiced and more accepting of the disabled. In short, part of the thinking behind mainstreaming was to improve the social and psychological development of children, which certainly affects what they learn in class (Johnson and Johnson, 1980). (See the Research Highlight "How Do Children Really Perceive the Disabled" on page 496.)

Right from the start, however, problems arose on all levels. From the teacher's standpoint, the program rarely took teachers' concerns into consideration, yet they were blamed for the problems. Teachers walked into class to find that they had disabled children to teach, but they received little or no training in how to meet their special needs. There was little, if any, time included in the day to work with experts in special education. And the exceptional child was not given much preparation for entering the mainstream (Tolkoff, 1981). This inevitably led to problems, and the exceptional child suffered.

For the first time, parents had been given rights and responsibilities but they were faced with bewildering decisions. For example, parents can disagree with the views of the professionals who have tested their child and appeal their decision. However, parents must be quite sophisticated to analyze data from tests and to disagree with professionals. Parents of exceptional children require training to familiarize themselves with all the problems and alternatives open to them. Some districts have found themselves in the position of having a parent demand a course of action which, in all good faith, the school considers ill-advised. The appeal process is expensive, and some districts may just give in rather than fight.

From the exceptional child's point of view, social integration became a problem. Little if any social skills training was available to exceptional children. When this combined with peer ignorance or prejudice, it led to rejection.

There has been some backlash against mainstreaming. Mainstreaming has apparently not led to a reduction in prejudice or increased acceptance on the part of the nonhandicapped (Gresham, 1982). In other words, despite being placed in regular classrooms, exceptional children have not been integrated into the social framework of the classroom.

Does this mean that mainstreaming or the concept of the "least restrictive environment" is a failure? The answer is no. All it means is that we cannot merely throw disabled students into regular classrooms and expect events to take their course. Proximity gives us only an opportunity to help. It does not ensure better acceptance. Strategies aimed at enhancing cooperation between the disabled and the nondisabled are required (Johnson, 1983; Johnson and Johnson, 1980). In addition, exceptional children must be taught appropriate social skills, including conversation and listening skills, so that they can handle social situations

mainstreaming
A term used to describe the process by which exceptional children are integrated into classes with "normal" peers.

1. *True or False:*
According to the law, every exceptional child must be mainstreamed, that is, placed in a class with "normal" students.

RESEARCH HIGHLIGHT   **How Do Children Really Perceive the Disabled?**

The reception that disabled children are greeted with when they are mainstreamed varies considerably. To some degree, acceptance of these children depends on the attitudes and knowledge that nondisabled peers have of the disabled. For example, what if a child believes that a disability is communicable or that most retarded children cannot talk? This would affect relationships with the disabled. In addition, the belief that disabled children want people to give them special attention, or that they act very differently from other people, might also affect how the nondisabled interact with their disabled peers.

Just how do the nondisabled see their disabled peers, and how do their knowledge and attitudes vary according to age, sex, and previous experience with the disabled? The answers to these questions are vital if we are to counter stereotypes and improve chances for successful mainstreaming. Ann Hazzard asked 411 students in grades three through six to answer three questionnaires measuring their experience with disabled people, their knowledge of disabilities, and their attitudes toward disabled people. Attitudes were assessed by a social-distance scale, which measured the extent to which children were willing to interact with a disabled peer.

An analysis of the knowledge scale indicated that knowledge was not related to previous experience or to gender. Perhaps the subjects' experience with the disabled was so limited that it did not help them understand the variety of disabilities covered by the scale. Knowledge scores did increase with age. Attitudes, as measured by the social-distance scale, were related to previous experience with the disabled. Children with more experience showed a greater willingness to interact with disabled peers. However, although this relationship was positive, it was weak, probably because the effects of such experience de-

pend on many factors, such as the nature of the contact. Age was not a factor, but gender was. Girls were generally more willing to interact with the disabled than boys. Perhaps girls prize their nurturance, and this quality comes through. Perhaps the male stereotype is more challenged by the stereotype of the disabled, who may be viewed as weak and helpless. The relationship of knowledge to attitudes was positive but weak.

Looking at the children's answers to the questions on the knowledge scale, Hazzard noted that the major problem was their belief in the "pathetic stereotype of the disabled person" (p. 137). Some subjects viewed the disabled as helpless, different, and deserving pity. On the social-distance scale, children were more accepting of children in school activities, such as eating in the cafeteria with them, than in more personal activities, such as sleeping over at their home.

The implications of this study are clear. Anyone seeking to successfully mainstream disabled children will have to counter the stereotype of the "pathetic" disabled person. In addition, although the relationship between previous experience and attitude was positive, it was weak. This indicates that we need to look at the type of experience with the disabled that increases knowledge and produces positive attitude change. Different experiences with people with various disabilities may be helpful in this regard. Although more specific research is needed, we are beginning to appreciate the complications involved in the process of successful mainstreaming. Improving knowledge and changing attitudes are a proper start.

Source: A. Hazzard "Children's Experience with, Knowledge of, and Attitude Toward Disabled Persons," *Journal of Special Education,* 1983, *17,* 131–139.

(Wanat, 1983; Gresham, 1982). Perhaps all children could use a dose of such skill training, but it is vital to the success of the exceptional child, who is negotiating a new situation at an initial disadvantage. The programs that have been most successful in mainstreaming have (1) developed specific criteria indicating who should and should not be mainstreamed and to what extent, (2) prepared disabled students and their nondisabled peers, (3) promoted communication among educators, and (4) continually evaluated their progress and provided teacher in-service training to enable them to deal better with the challenge of serving students with exceptional needs (Salend, 1984). Perhaps we should have

Preparing a Child for Class

Lynn is a fourth-grader. She has spent the past three years in a special school for children with physical disabilities. Lynn suffers from cerebral palsy and must spend her days in a wheelchair. She can read and write and is now ready for mainstreaming. Her parents are a bit concerned and Lynn is nervous. It was their choice to mainstream the child. She really has not been exposed to a complicated situation like this, and they are not sure whether it was the right decision.

It is unfortunate that Lynn could not attend her new class for the first two weeks of the fall semester. Now a decision must be made. Ms. Rodriguez, her teacher, met her in the morning before school and introduced herself. The principal of the school asked Ms. Rodriguez how she plans to introduce Lynn to the class. She isn't sure. Should she explain Lynn's condition to the class (perhaps some students will think that what she has is catching and avoid her)? Should she do nothing and allow Lynn to make her own way? (Why raise issues that may not be in the class' mind?)

1. If you were Lynn's teacher, what would you do?
2. If you were Lynn's parents, what would you suggest?

expected these problems. Integration of the disabled is a fairly new procedure, and problems might best be considered challenges.

In this chapter we will deal with a number of exceptionalities, including the mentally retarded, the gifted, and children who have visual and auditory problems, as well as those who suffer from learning and behavioral disorders. It is a mistake to center merely on their problems and define the children by their disabilities. Noting that a child has very limited vision is different from calling the child a "blind child." A child is more than a disability. It may affect the child in some areas but not in others, and by centering on a weakness we may overlook someone's strengths. With this in mind, we turn to the first of our exceptionalities, children who are mentally retarded.

THE MENTALLY RETARDED

You are told that a group home for mentally retarded people will be established in your neighborhood. One of your neighbors asks you to sign a petition opposing its opening. The neighbor tells you that these people will bring an "undesirable element" into the community and will depress home values. Would you sign the petition?

Such scenes are repeated in hundreds of communities around the nation. Community opposition appears even after data showing that property values will not suffer and that neighborhoods will not be adversely affected is presented (Landesman-Dwyer, 1981). Even with large-scale educational programs, the home is still not accepted. Why is the prejudice against the mentally retarded so great?

Many retarded individuals can learn to earn their own living and live independently.

mental retardation
A condition marked by subnormal intellectual functioning and adjustment difficulties which occur before a person is eighteen years of age.

2. *True or False:*
Subnormal intellectual ability is the sole criterion for being labeled mentally retarded.

Who Are the Mentally Retarded?

To understand this, we must look at just who is considered **mentally retarded**. In order to be considered mentally retarded, three criteria must be met. First, the individual must show an intelligence score of below 70 on an individualized intelligence test given in the child's primary language. Second, the retardation must occur before the age of eighteen. Third, a substantial failure in adjustment must be present (President's Commission on Mental Retardation, 1977).

Intelligence testing is not an exact science, and a child's intelligence score may change over time. Gains of as much as 15 to 20 points have been noted after periods of intensive instruction (Heward and Orlansky, 1984). Thus, borderline children should be labeled with care. In addition, some authorities argue that even our best intelligence tests are culturally biased against children from minority groups. Thus, defining anyone simply on the basis of intelligence is dangerous.

The second criterion, that the retardation develop before age eighteen, keeps such conditions as brain damage caused by automobile accidents in adulthood from being considered mental retardation. The definition used today is essentially an educational one.

The requirement that some adjustment problem be found is more subjective. Objective tests that measure adjustment problems are of questionable validity (Brown, 1983). Even so, this criterion is important. Adjustment problems relate to the individual's performance in the areas of social responsibility and self-sufficiency (Grossman, 1973). A child who shows a lack of reasoning or an inability to communicate with others certainly has an adjustment problem.

This definition assures that an individual will not be considered mentally retarded merely on the basis of a score on an intelligence test irrespective of how the child functions at home and in school. On the other hand, an individual cannot be considered retarded simply because some behavior problem is apparent.

It is estimated that there are somewhere between 1,100,000 and 1,650,000 mentally retarded children in the United States. Between 2 and 3 percent of all children are mentally retarded (Gearhart and Weishahn, 1984).

Classification Systems

Years ago the mentally retarded were classified into the categories of idiot, imbecile, and moron, which have negative connotations. Then the terms *educable, trainable,* and *custodial* were introduced and are still in use. The problem here is the connotation that children who are trainable cannot be educated. Today many authorities simply use the terms *mild, moderate, severe,* and *profound* to indicate levels of retardation (see Figure 13.2). Even so, you may find the older educable, trainable, custodial categories used, especially in educational circles. About 85 percent of the mentally retarded are in what was called the educable category, with about 12 percent considered trainable and 3 percent custodial.

FIGURE 13.2   Comparison of Classifications Based on I.Q. Score
The classifications of "mild", "moderate", "severe" and "profound" have replaced "educable", "trainable" and "custodial," although you will still see the latter terms used occasionally.

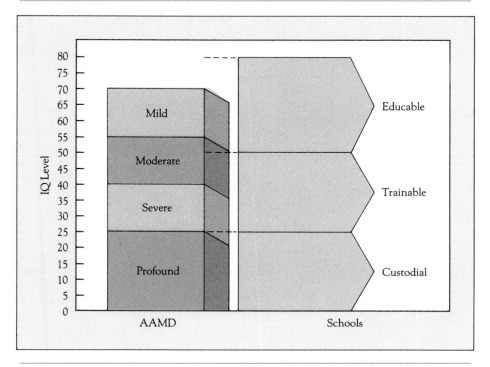

Source: C. J. Mandell and E. Fiscus, 1981.

Thus, the great majority of retardates are found in the upper levels, nearer the normal intelligence levels. The histories and educational possibilities of these children vary with their level of retardation.

Causes of Mental Retardation

Our knowledge of the causes of mental retardation, especially of mild and higher-level moderate mental retardation (educable), is limited. Identifiable causative agents have been discovered in fewer than 20 percent of the cases (Pollaway and Patton, 1981). As the intelligence scores decrease, however, the number of cases that are caused by known organic/genetic factors increase. Some of these known causes include infection, trauma, metabolic and nutritional problems, gross brain disease, prenatal problems, and chromosomal abnormalities (Grossman, 1977).

The Mildly Retarded

Most mildly retarded individuals do not look any different from the general population. The cause of their retardation is generally unknown, but it may be linked to environmental factors. For that reason, the cause is often listed as "cultural-familial." There is no evidence that long-term memory is worse in the mildly retarded, but any learning situation that might require a definite strategy, such as using a mnemonic device, taxes the abilities of the retarded. Although teaching memory strategies to retarded children is effective, the benefits are limited because these children do not generalize the strategies to other situations (Campione and Brown, 1977). Mentally retarded individuals at this level also have difficulty with abstractions and show slower cognitive development.

What is distressing, however, is that many retardates are working at levels below their abilities (Kirk and Gallagher, 1983). Perhaps they have experienced so much failure that they are now used to it and give up easily (Zigler, 1973). Generally, they have a poor self-image and are the victims of rejection. They are often rejected by their peers, regardless of whether they are placed in regular classrooms (mainstreamed) or special classrooms (Gottlieb and Budoff, 1973).

Despite these problems, if they receive the right care the mildly mentally retarded may learn to lead independent, productive lives (see Table 13.3). The mildly retarded were once placed exclusively in self-contained classrooms, but this is slowly disappearing. With the push toward integrating these children with "normal" students, many mildly mentally retarded are found in at least some regular classes, depending on academic performance and behavior.

For many of these students, vocational training is quite important. Vocational training includes behavioral and social training as well as learning occupational skills. Since these children have adjustment problems, some improvement in their general demeanor may be necessary. Behavior modification is often used to improve attention span and reduce misbehavior. In addition, the mentally retarded are frequently deficient in social skills, which may prevent them from obtaining a job.

Think of all the social skills required for most jobs. You must be responsive when people talk to you, maintain eye contact, and get along with people (Foss and Peterson, 1981). In addition, such skills as getting to work on time and han-

TABLE 13.3 **Educational Achievement among the Mentally Retarded**
The mentally retarded are frequently able to surprise people with what they can achieve if given the best educational and familial environments possible.

Degree of Mental Retardation	Potential for Educational Achievement	Potential for Adult Functioning
Mildly retarded: IQ approximately 51–65	"Educable"; capable of 3rd to 6th grade educational achievement; able to read and write and use basic mathematics	Able to be independent personally and socially; able to be self-supporting; frequently lose identification as retarded and blend into "normal" population
Moderately retarded: IQ approximately 36–50	"Trainable"; capable of kindergarten through 3rd grade achievement; typically not able to read and write	Able to be employed in unskilled occupations if supervision available; typically incapable of independent living or marriage
Severely retarded: IQ approximately 21–35	Able to acquire some self-care skills; able to talk and express self; unable to acquire any academic skills	Need permanent care from family or society; some are capable of performing simple chores under total supervision
Profoundly retarded: UQ approximately 20 or lower	Unable to speak; some are capable of self-ambulation but many remain bedridden throughout their lives	Incapable of any self-maintenance; require permanent nursing care

Source: B. G. Suran and J. V. Rizzo, 1983.

dling small problems are necessary. The educable mentally retarded need training in these social skills if they are to lead productive lives.

These children can achieve very steady employment in unskilled or semi-skilled levels, and new research shows that they are effective workers. They are reliable and steady, and their turnover rate is lower. They generally succeed in private industry. A great example of this was the "experiment" performed by McDonald's restaurants. McDonald's trained seventeen mentally retarded people to work in their restaurants. The turnover rate for the mentally retarded was about 40 percent, compared with 175 percent for regular employees (Brickey and Campbell, 1981).

The Moderately Retarded

While our analysis of the mildly retarded stressed the possibilities of developing an independent existence, this is not the case with moderately retarded youngsters. About one-third of the children in this category have known brain dysfunctions, and another one-third suffer from Down's Syndrome. In the past, these children were immediately institutionalized, but today many are raised at home.

As you would expect, the progress of the moderately retarded child is very slow, especially in language development. An educational program for these children usually stresses self-help skills, proper behavior, and limited simple verbal communication (Telford and Sawrey, 1981). It is possible that Down's Syndrome youngsters can be mainstreamed in preschools if they have been stimulated and received excellent care since birth (Harris, 1977). After nursery school, however, special instruction is required. The vast majority of the moderately retarded continue to need care throughout their lives, but here again they can become productive individuals.

Moderately retarded individuals are most often employed in sheltered workshops. Such workshops have demonstrated their value (Rusalem and Malikin, 1976). The workshop environment is noncompetitive and friendly. The child receives very specific instruction and is closely supervised. The jobs may include sorting and packaging. For example, one workshop might require workers to take one item from three or four piles and place them in a bag, which is then brought to another worker who seals it. Such labor gives workers a sense of satisfaction and feeling of productivity, along with a few extra dollars for enjoyment. However, some parents report that their adolescents are bored on such jobs (Hirst, 1983).

The Severely and Profoundly Retarded

Most of the severely and profoundly retarded are found in institutions and traditionally have received only custodial care. Many suffer from multiple disabilities, such as sensory or motor problems. In recent years, advancements in behavioral methods have improved their chances of learning. Gold (1973) showed that the severely retarded could be taught to perform workshop tasks, such as putting together a bicycle brake, by using behavioral techniques. Tasks are first broken down into their simplest components, then the learner is taken physically through each step. Little or no verbal communication is offered, and a technique called **fading** is utilized. In this technique, the individual is first taken through each step, and the instructor's direct participation is slowly reduced until the learner can do the task on his or her own.

Helping the Mentally Retarded

Attempts to help mentally retarded children center on their educational experiences. Today an emphasis is placed on developing the social and personal skills necessary for success in the outside world. Since many mildly retarded individuals can live productive lives if they have the proper education, such an emphasis is well placed. The educational experience does not start in kindergarten. For the mentally retarded child, as with other exceptional children, early identification and treatment is important. Most retarded children benefit from preschool experiences designed for their specific needs.

Many of the retarded children who were once institutionalized are now raised with their own families. In some communities, parents are allowed to place a moderately retarded child in a community residence for as long as three weeks in order to be able to take a vacation from their arduous duties. This allows the parents time for renewal.

There is also a movement toward community-based group homes, where the mentally retarded can live in dignity and with a degree of independence. In this area, the watchword is **normalization**, that is, the current trend is to try to inte-

fading
A teaching technique in which the student is first taken through each step of a process, then the instructor slowly reduces direct participation until the learner can perform the task alone.

normalization
The process by which disabled people are integrated into the mainstream of society as much as possible.

The federal government defines gifted children as those who have high potential in intellectual ability, creative pursuits, the performing or visual arts, and/or specific academic areas, or show leadership qualities.

grate the individual as much as possible into normal society. The degree to which this can be accomplished depends on the severity of the retardation, the education and social training the person receives, and public acceptance of the retarded as individuals with full rights in the community.

THE GIFTED AND TALENTED

Pretend that you're an expectant parent who has learned that a certain treatment will ensure that your child will have an IQ of 160 safely and without any danger. Would you seek out this treatment?

I often ask my students this question, and after assuring them that safety was no problem, the stereotypes begin to unfold. "He would be a misfit," one told me. "She would be socially backward," another noted. The stereotypes of the gifted are probably as great for them as for any other exceptionality. You can examine your beliefs about the gifted by answering the questionnaire in Figure 13.3 on page 504.

Who Are the Gifted?

At first glance, defining **giftedness** would seem to be an easy task. The gifted, most people think, are those who have very high intelligence. Children who score greatly above average on intelligence tests are indeed gifted, but is that all there is to it? What of the child who is athletically or artistically gifted? What of the child who is very creative?

When I taught in a junior high school some years ago, I assigned my students the task of designing their own city. One student who had no better than a 75

giftedness
People who either have demonstrated or have the potential for high ability in the intellectual, creative, academic, or leadership areas or the performing or visual arts.

FIGURE 13.3   **Examine Your Beliefs About the Gifted**

These questions allow you to look at your beliefs regarding gifted and talented children. Before each statement place the number that most closely describes how you react to each one. Be as open as you can.

1—I strongly agree   4—I disagree
2—I agree   5—I strongly disagree
3—I have no opinion

_____ 1. The term *gifted* can mean different things to different people and often causes much confusion and miscommunication.

_____ 2. Intelligence can be developed and must be nurtured if giftedness is to occur.

_____ 3. We seldom find very highly gifted children or children we could call *geniuses*; therefore, we know comparatively little about them.

_____ 4. Thinking of, or speaking of, gifted children as superior people is inaccurate and misleading.

_____ 5. Gifted children, while interested in many things, usually are not gifted in everything.

_____ 6. Difficulty conforming to group tasks is often the result of the unusually varied interests and curiosity of a gifted child.

_____ 7. Because gifted children have the ability to think in diverse ways, teachers often see them as challenging their authority, disrespectful, and disruptive.

_____ 8. Some gifted children have been found to use their high level of verbal skill to avoid difficult thinking tasks.

_____ 9. The demand for products or meeting of deadlines can inhibit the development of a gifted child's ability to integrate new ideas.

_____ 10. Work that is too easy or boring frustrates a gifted child just as work that is too difficult frustrates an average learner.

_____ 11. Most gifted children in our present school system are underachievers.

_____ 12. Commonly used sequences of learning are often inappropriate and can be damaging to gifted learners.

_____ 13. Gifted children, often very critical of themselves, tend to hold lower than average self-concepts.

_____ 14. Gifted children often expect others to live up to standards they have set for themselves, with resulting problems in interpersonal relations.

_____ 15. The ability of gifted learners to generalize, synthesize, solve problems, and engage in abstract thinking most commonly differentiates gifted from average learners. Therefore, programs for gifted children should stress utilization of these abilities.

_____ 16. The persistent goal-directed behavior of gifted children can result in others perceiving them as stubborn, willful, and uncooperative.

_____ 17. If not challenged, gifted children can waste their ability and become mediocre, average learners.

_____ 18. Gifted children often express their idealism and sense of justice at a very early age.

_____ 19. Not all gifted children show creativity, leadership, or physical expertise.

_____ 20. People who work with, study, and try to understand gifted children have more success educating the gifted than those who have limited contact and have not educated themselves as to the unique needs of these children.

_____ 21. I would be pleased to be considered gifted, and I enjoy people who are.

The questionnaire you have just completed should give you some indication of opinions of gifted children that are supportive to their educational growth. The more "1—I strongly agree" answers you were able to give, the more closely your opinions match those who have devoted their energy to understanding gifted children.

Source: B. Clark, 1983.

percent average, not only in social studies but also in math, science, and English, produced an incredible design. After working nonstop for days, he brought his project to school. It contained many new ideas. For example, he placed ambulances in specific areas where they could respond quickly to the needs of the community, and he created an elaborate transportation system with brilliantly considered transfer points. In addition, he incorporated theme parks into the plan, that is, various parks had different themes—not just swings and slides.

After some investigation I found that this child had made $100 the summer before and spent countless hours designing and building a bank in the shape of an elephant—patiently gluing the pennies together. He also had taken all the old carpeting he could find in the trash and, using different colored strips, created a scene of people dueling in the streets, which proudly decorated the wall of his bedroom. With all this, his IQ was certainly not in the category we would call gifted, although his performance would certainly be categorized that way. If giftedness is defined simply in terms of an intelligence score in the top 20 percent (a very liberal criterion), about 75 percent of those children who score very high on tests of creativity would not be identified (Torrance, 1962), and this would include my student.

Older definitions considered giftedness only in terms of IQ, but newer definitions have expanded the concept greatly (Passow, 1981). The federal government defines the gifted as children who either have demonstrated or seem to have the potential for high capabilities in intellectual, creative, specific academic, or leadership areas or in the performing and visual arts (Gifted and Talented Children's Act of 1978). Not only general intellectual ability is considered in this definition, but also aptitudes, creative thinking, leadership ability and talent (Torrance, 1980). Approximately 2 to 3 percent of the school population is considered gifted (Gearheart and Weishahn, 1984).

Characteristics of the Gifted

When I ask my students whether they would like to parent a gifted child, a number of stereotypes show up. These stereotypes prevent society from meeting the needs of the gifted (Treffinger, 1982). For example, many people believe that the gifted are socially backward, with little or no common sense, and that they look down on other people. This is often the stereotype portrayed on television and in some movies (Rickert, 1981).

These stereotypes should be laid to rest. In a longitudinal study of about 1,000 children, Terman and his colleagues (Terman and Oden, 1959; Terman, 1925) found that gifted children who had an IQ of 130 or more were fast learners and interested in school. They also tended to be the oldest child in the family, well adjusted, energetic, and physically healthy. They are also more curious. In another study, the gifted were found to be intuitive, perceptive, a bit rebellious, and original (MacKinnon, 1978).

3. *True or False:*
Children who are intellectually gifted tend to be socially backward.

The gifted child usually has a positive self-concept (Maddux et al., 1982), but what of his interpersonal skills? In this area, controversy exists. After a review of the literature, Austin and Draper (1981) suggest that at some points in their school career the gifted are popular and do well socially, but at other times they experience some difficulty. Gifted preschoolers interact well with their peers, but spend more time with older children and adults. In elementary school, however, a relationship between intelligence and peer acceptance exists, although generalizations are difficult and other factors may also become important. Still, gifted children tend to be popular and do well socially in elementary school. In adolescence, the status of gifted girls decreases greatly, and that of boys somewhat. Gifted boys regain some of their popularity in the later years of high school. Girls do not, and their abilities remain devalued. Austin and Draper note that this sequence may not hold for children whose IQ is above 160, because these children are very precocious and may not fit in. But the vast majority of gifted children whose intelligence scores fall between 120 and 160 have good interpersonal relationships.

Any picture of the gifted must be painted with care. The gifted are not a homogeneous population (Juntune, 1982), and even though most seem well adjusted, some are not. Overgeneralizations can be dangerous. For example, although most gifted children are quick learners, we should not equate being smart with being fast (Sternberg, 1982). Very intelligent people may spend more time planning how they are going to solve a problem instead of merely jumping into a solution.

acceleration
An educational program in which a gifted child skips a grade or a particular unit.

enrichment
An educational program in which a gifted child is given special challenging work that goes beyond the usual.

Helping the Gifted Achieve

Two approaches—acceleration and enrichment—are widely used to help the gifted. **Acceleration** involves skipping a grade or a particular unit and placing the child in a more challenging situation. **Enrichment** involves staying on grade level but assigning work that goes beyond the usual. In addition, children may either be kept in their normal classroom, be placed in a special room for a few hours a day

---

ACTION/ REACTION

Sure I'm Happy But . . .

Barry Duncan has never been a problem in school, if you define problems in terms of overt behavior. On the contrary, he is a pleasant ten-year-old who always has a smile on his face. But Barry is bored in school. He daydreams constantly, and finishes his work quickly but often sloppily. Yet he usually does well on tests and reads at a very high level. His scores on intelligence tests show him to be intellectually gifted.

Barry's report card is good, but he is not doing as well as his teacher, Mr. Carson, thinks he should. Each time Mr. Carson succeeds in motivating Barry, he is surprised by the boy's excellent analytical mind and ability to solve unusual problems. He suggests that Barry be put in a class for very bright and talented children. This class meets three mornings a week, while the rest of the time is spent in the regular class.

Mr. and Mrs. Duncan are not certain this is the right course of action. Although they know Barry is bright, his grades do not show it. They also believe that the same problems of boredom, disinterest, and daydreaming will haunt him in the gifted program. They also admit to some social concerns. Barry is not the most popular student in class, because he is unathletic. He has been taunted as "the brain" in a previous year's class, which bothered him a lot. Barry's parents even caught him making mistakes on his homework on purpose in order not to appear too smart. They are afraid that putting him in this class would accentuate his problems.

1. If you were Barry's parents, what actions would you take?
2. If you were Barry's teacher, suggesting the change, how would you allay their fears?

or week, or even be placed in separate classes. In any case, gifted children require a program that is qualitatively different from the normal school environment (Wolf and Stephens, 1979).

THE VISUALLY IMPAIRED

Blind. Just the term itself is enough to upset most people. Of all the exceptionalities, nothing strikes terror into our hearts more than this one. We are justly concerned about our eyesight, for it is responsible for much of the information we take in from our environment—90 percent, according to some (Kakalik et al., 1974).

Yet blindness and visual impairment are low-prevalence exceptionalities. According to a government survey, about 36,800 children under the age of seventeen are considered severely visually impaired (Kirchner et al., 1979), and it is estimated that the rate of visual impairment is 7 out of 1,000 people under the age of forty-five (DeMott, 1982). The rate for people aged sixty-five and older is 44.5 in 1,000 (Kirchner and Peterson, in DeMott, 1982). In 1975, the U.S. Office of Education reported that approximately 0.1 percent of the children in the United States were visually handicapped (Hallahan and Kauffman, 1982).

Who Are the Visually Impaired?

The definitions of blindness and visual impairment are based both on **visual acuity**, the ability to see an object well at prescribed distances, and or disturbances in an individual's field of vision. Almost everyone is familiar with the Snellen Chart. You stand at a distance of 20 feet and are asked to read the letters on the chart. The letters get smaller and smaller with each line. Average vision is considered 20/20, meaning that you can see at 20 feet what most people can see at that distance. To be considered **legally blind**, you would have to have 20/200 vision in the best eye even with correction. In other words, a legally blind person would see at 20 feet what most of us see at 200 feet. The vision of the **partially sighted** falls between 20/70 and 20/200 in the better eye with correction.

However, an individual may have 20/20 eyesight and still be legally blind. Some people have such poor peripheral vision that it is as if they are seeing out of a keyhole. If a child's entire field of vision is less than 20 degrees, the child is also considered legally blind (Ashcroft et al., 1980). Most blind people have at least some sight and can see something. This **residual vision** is of great importance today, for the trend is to teach the partially sighted and the legally blind to use what they can see to the utmost.

What Causes Visual Problems?

Visual problems can be caused by many things. Disease, hereditary conditions, and accidents are three prominent causes. Years ago, a condition called retrolental fibroplasia was very common among premature babies given too much oxygen (see page 116) and was a major cause of blindness. With better techniques for caring for premature infants, it does not occur as often.

visual acuity
The ability to see an object well at various distances.

legally blind
A person with a visual acuity of 20/200 in the best eye with correction or with peripheral vision that subtends less than 20 degrees of the field.

partially sighted
A person with a visual acuity of 20/70 to 20/200 in the best eye with correction.

residual vision
The remaining sight in people who are legally blind or partially sighted.

4. *True or False:*
The majority of the legally blind can see nothing at all.

One would think that a relationship exists between the degree of visual impairment and the child's educational handicap—the worse the vision, the lower the child's academic achievement. But this is not the case. Remember that the vast majority of visually impaired children have some sight. According to Barraga (1976), some children use their residual sight better than others, and one cannot determine what aid a visually impaired child requires just by considering visual acuity. Barraga (1973, 1964) argues that many visually handicapped children are not taught to use their remaining vision, and studies show that visual training can help these children use their residual vision to its fullest.

Most blind children have their blindness discovered shortly after birth, when they showed obvious signs such as a lack of focusing and retardation in reaching. But the discovery that a child is only partially sighted is another matter. This is of special importance if we realize that development of the remaining vision is so important. The younger the child is when the problem is discovered, the earlier the training can start, and the less affected by the disability the child may be.

Teachers and parents should be able to recognize some of the warning signs of visual problems. If a child frequently complains of eyes hurting, crosses the eyes, squints, holds the head at an awkward angle, or rubs the eyes, the child should have an eye examination. In addition, children who always seem to be copying schoolwork incorrectly may have visual problems.

Portrait of the Population

Although making generalizations about any population is difficult, we can make some general points about the blind. Normally, blind infants develop more slowly than sighted infants (see Figure 13.4) (U.S. Department of Health, Education, and Welfare, 1972). Blind children are limited in their experience, because they are not attracted to objects in their visual field. Blind babies are very late in reaching for noise-making objects, and their independent exploration of the environment is retarded (Bower, 1977; Adelson and Fraiberg, 1974).

The evidence on the cognitive and social development of the visually impaired is difficult to evaluate. While some evidence indicates that the visually impaired are socially immature (Reynell, 1978), other authorities claim that this is because of the way they are treated rather because of the disability itself (DeMott, 1982). Indeed, people are basically uncertain about how to treat a blind person. In addition, some blind children are sheltered by their parents and not permitted to interact with other youngsters. Blind children do have more social problems than sighted children, but again these problems are probably not inevitable (Jan et al., 1977).

No one doubts that not being able to see is a handicap from the very beginning. Blind children cannot make contact with their parents through eye contact as sighted children can, and this inhibits the development of attachment (Fraiberg, 1977). They begin to smile, but smile much less because they cannot obtain visual feedback.

The blind and partially sighted do not fare particularly well in school. Some studies show that they are quite behind their sighted peers in achievement (Kirk and Gallagher, 1983). The visually handicapped process information differently. The information they collect is fragmented, and it is especially difficult for them

FIGURE 13.4   **Comparative Development of Blind and Sighted Babies**
Blind infants fall behind sighted infants in motor development.

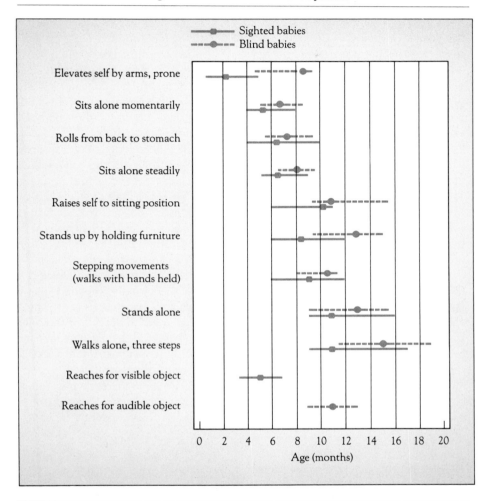

Source: T. G. R. Bower, 1977.

to gain the total picture. But these problems can be addressed. Stephens and Grube (1982) tested seventy-five sighted and congenitally blind children on a number of Piagetian reasoning tasks. The blind were significantly behind the sighted in these tasks, but after two years of specialized education, their performance was equal to that of their sighted peers.

The evidence in the realms of social and cognitive development for the visually impaired is much more distressing. They are underachieving greatly (Suran and Rizzo, 1983) and display significant adjustment problems (Myerson, 1971). Perhaps the partially sighted do not fit in very well with either the blind or the sighted. In addition, when an infant or child is blind, parents must accept it. This is not so for the visually impaired. They may indeed function in an obvious sense, while needing some form of intervention to reach their potential.

Intervention with the Visually Impaired

Three important areas stand out clearly in improving the lot of the visually impaired. First, the visually impaired must be identified early, and their parents must be taught how to meet their needs. Much of the lag in the development of the visually impaired is the result of lack of visual stimulation. Parents can learn new ways to stimulate the child. They can learn to communicate through words and touch, and to deliberately introduce children to their environment instead of waiting for the child to do it. In addition, as Kastein and her colleagues (1980, p. 37) note, "The fact that the baby cannot see may often tempt the parents to do less for and with him, less touching, less talking, less cuddling, when he needs not only what the sighted baby does, but much more."

Second, blind individuals must learn self-help skills (Hatlen, 1976) in order to become independent. They are often socially isolated, and their parents are apt to be restrictive. Dependence, passivity, and a lack of initiative may be the result (Jan et al., 1977). We are often overwhelmed by stories in the media showing how blind people take care of their children and lead "normal" lives, but this is too rosy a picture, for not all blind people get the opportunity to learn the skills needed to become independent. The most important skill—the ability to get around—requires mobility training in using either a cane or a seeing eye dog.

Third, the blind and partially sighted require some special consideration in their learning environments. Most people think the visually impaired all use **Braille**, a form of reading based on touch, but Braille is not the answer for most visually impaired youngsters because it is a very slow method of reading (Henderson, 1973). Large-print books, improving listening skills, and the use of readers are probably better. The Kurzweil Reading Machine, which converts print into speech, is a wonderful breakthrough and can be found on some college campuses.

Visual impairment is a serious disability, but the negative effects do not seem to be inevitable. With early intervention, appropriate self-help skill training, and classroom aids, the visually impaired can live and function independently in society.

Braille
A tactile system of reading designed for the blind.

Most people think that all the visually impaired use Braille, but this isn't true; many use large-print books.

THE HEARING IMPAIRED

The Unappreciated Disability

Put your hands over your ears tightly and ask a friend to talk to you in a moderately low voice. Now try reading your friend's lips. Your friend should not speak any differently from usual. After a couple of minutes, repeat what you think was said.

If you do this exercise properly, you may appreciate what it is like to be hearing impaired. Reading lips is not easy, and although you may improve with practice, even experienced lip-readers can understand only about 50 percent of what they see. Because sounds in English are sometimes very similar to each other in physical production (viewed from the outside), it is estimated that a deaf listener can perceive only 30 to 40 percent of the sounds spoken by a speaker (Gallaudet College, 1975).

In many ways, a hearing impairment is more of a liability than a visual impairment is, for it often leads to speech problems. In order to learn to communicate using speech, children need to listen to, and actively become involved in, conversation. Children who cannot hear human speech do not receive this stimulation. They cannot hear themselves talk. The natural process by which speech is developed does not occur.

Most deaf people use sign language to communicate with the outside world. This is very limiting, since relatively few hearing people understand sign language. Let's say you were deaf and trying to communicate to a hearing individual. How would you do it? The normal answer to this question involves communicating through gestures. Try it! Spend a few minutes trying to communicate with someone in your class using gestures. You will probably find that it is very difficult. The hearing impaired spend a large part of their day interacting with people who do not know such language and who do not have much experience interacting with them. In one study, hearing adults did try to communicate with deaf children by touch, gestures, and simpler speech, but they were successful only a little less than half the time, compared with about 70 percent of the time with young hearing children (Lederberg, 1984).

The deaf also find themselves limited in other ways, since our daily lives are filled with sound. The ringing of the telephone, the whistling of a teakettle, even the warning tone of a smoke alarm, are lost. Today the spotlight is on the use of technology to overcome some of these problems. A teletypewriter (TTY) enables deaf people to send and receive messages over telephone lines. Smoke detectors are designed with lines running to vibrators on the wrist, which may help the deaf cope with this emergency.

The Hearing Impaired Child

We can look at hearing loss in terms of the child's age at onset as well as its type. The onset may be at the prelingual or postlingual stage. The distinction is crucial. Children who lose their hearing at age seven or eight still have had the opportunity to develop reasonably mature speech patterns, but a child who is born deaf (congenitally deaf), or becomes deaf due to an accident or illness before the age of two or three, has not had these language experiences and has a more diffi-

Deaf children in the United States learn to communicate using American Sign Language (ASL). Many deaf children can be mainstreamed if a sign interpreter is available.

conduction hearing loss
Hearing loss caused by mechanical problems in conducting vibrations within the ear.

sensorineural hearing loss
Hearing loss caused by nerve damage.

cult time developing speech. In addition, the type of hearing disorder makes a difference. Problems that are due to mechanical problems in the ear, called **conduction losses,** can be helped by a hearing aid. **Sensorineural losses** involve nerve damage, and hearing aids are usually relatively ineffective in reducing these hearing problems.

Auditory ability is measured not only by an individual's ability to hear faint tones but also by one's ability to hear sounds of different pitches. A person with a hearing loss in the range of human voices has a considerable handicap, while a person who loses the ability to hear either very high or very low pitches may not be greatly handicapped. Table 13.4 shows the effects of hearing impairments on the child's abilities and the educational programming most often used. As with visual impairment, a hearing impaired child must learn to use any residual ability to the utmost.

Estimating the number of deaf and hard-of-hearing children in the population is difficult. The deaf and severely hard of hearing show such great delays in language acquisition that they are readily identified, but many children suffering from less-severe hearing deficits compensate for their problem. They may be labeled very slow or even mentally retarded, and then later be discovered to suffer from a hearing disability (Mollick and Etra, 1981). The lack of attention to what is said, and the processing of partial information, leads one to suspect mental retardation. One child's parents did not realize her auditory problem until her mother noticed that she always switched the telephone from her right ear to her left, even though she was right-handed. These children often receive negative

TABLE 13.4   **The Effects of Hearing Loss**
Hearing loss may affect speech and the ability to communicate.

Average Hearing Loss (500–2000 Hz)	Probable Causes	Ability To Hear Speech Without a Hearing Aid	Extent of Communicative Handicap	Auditory Rehabilitative Considerations
0–20 dB *Normal Range*	May have slight, fluctuating conductive loss Child with central auditory disorder will show normal hearing	No difficulty in any conversational setting Child with central auditory disorder will seem to hear but not understand	None, except for child with central auditory disorder or with speech/language disorders from other causes	Probably needs no rehabilitative treatment Child with central auditory disorder will need intensive therapy
20–40 dB *Mild Loss*	Most likely conductive from otitis media Sensorineural loss may result from mild illness or disease	Hears in most settings, misses soft or whispered speech, will hear vowels but may miss unvoiced consonants, says "huh?" wants TV turned up loud	Mild handicap, may have speech disorder or mild language delay, may omit final and voiceless consonants	If conductive and medically or surgically treatable, needs favorable classroom seating Child with sensorineural problem may need hearing aid, speech reading, and auditory training
40–60 dB *Moderate Loss*	Conductive from otitis media or middle ear problem; maximum conductive loss is 60 dB Sensorineural loss from ear disease or illness	Hearing is a problem in most conversational settings, groups, or when there is background noise; hears louder voiced consonants, may need TV and radio up loud, and have difficulty on the phone	Possible disorder in auditory learning, mild to moderate language delay; articulation problems with final and voiceless consonants; may not pay attention	All of the above may apply May also need special class for the hearing impaired or special tutoring
60–80 dB *Severe Loss*	Probably sensorineural, although mixed is also possible Rubella, meningitis, Rh, heredity are possible causes	Misses all but very loud speech, unable to function in conversation without help, can't use telephone	Probable severe language and speech disorder; learning disorder; may have no intelligible speech	All of the above may apply May need placement in school for the deaf
80 dB or more *Profound Loss*	Sensorineural, or mixed with large sensorineural component Rubella, meningitis, Rh, heredity, ear disease, etc. are causes	Unable to hear speech except loud shout, does not understand spoken language, can't hear TV or radio, can't use the telephone	Severe speech and language deficit, probably no oral speech, learning disorder, "deaf-like" speech and voice	All of the above may apply Will need placement in deaf-oral school or school for the deaf

Source: W. H. Berdine and A. E. Blackhurst, 1985.

feedback for their inattention and delayed development. In some cases, the hearing loss may never be discovered. About one child in 1,000 is deaf, and another 3 or 4 children in 1,000 are severely hard of hearing (Kirk and Gallagher, 1983). Estimates for the slightly hard of hearing are much greater, but the exact number is unknown.

Hearing loss may be caused by many factors. An epidemic of rubella in the 1960s left between 10,000 and 20,000 children with severe hearing impairments

(Green, 1981). Other causes include Rh incompatibility, meningitis, infections of the middle ear, influenza, and hereditary factors.

Portrait of the Population

Because deafness affects communication so greatly, you might expect deaf pupils to have difficulty in school and in social adjustment. This is so. The deaf often suffer from language deficits (Green, 1981). Although they have normal abilities, their communicational deficits cause them much difficulty in school (Green, 1981; Sanders, 1980). Those with mild disorders usually do better than those with more severe disorders, because they suffer a smaller language deficit. Their progress in reading lags as well, but it is not because of any native inability, but rather because of the speech/language/hearing impediment and the lack of an appropriate teaching and learning environment. As the severity of hearing disability increases, so do the child's educational problems (Davis et al., 1981).

The deaf are an isolated minority, and many psychologists argue that this leads to some adjustment problems (Sanders, 1980). Most of these problems are not severe (Hallahan and Kauffman, 1982) and probably relate to the difficulty communicating in a hearing world. Some characteristics, such as impulsivity, hyperactivity, rigidity, and suspiciousness, attributed to the deaf are actually found more in those with multiple disabilities rather than the deaf, whose sole problem is one of hearing. Chess and Fernandez (1980) found that, with the exception of impulsivity, none of these other characteristics could be found in a sample of children they followed from early childhood through adolescence as long as deafness was the only handicap. Even the one significant characteristic, impulsivity, was found in only 20 percent of the sample.

Intervention with the Hearing Impaired

How should the deaf be taught? One school of thought argues that the deaf need a language of their own to communicate with the outside world and that sign language is the most practical method. Others argue that sign language is reasonable when communicating with other deaf children but that the hearing world does not understand sign language. These authorities emphasize the oral method—teaching the deaf to speak. The third school, known as total communication, combines the two. One survey found that about two-thirds of the classes for the hearing impaired use the total communication method (Jordan et al., 1979).

The deaf have been helped by a number of mechanical and human aids. Machines that allow the deaf to use the telephone, such as the TTY (teletypewriter), interpreters who sign for them in class, and hearing aids have all helped the deaf enter the mainstream. As mentioned earlier, hearing aids are not the answer for everyone. They merely amplify the sound, they do not improve the quality. Another form of help is now available to the deaf in the form of hearing ear dogs (Zisman and Harrison, 1981). Almost everyone is aware of seeing eye dogs for the blind. Hearing ear dogs alert their owners to sounds in the environment, including the cry of a baby, the tones of a doorbell, and the sound of the alarm clock.

Just as in the case of visually handicapped children, hearing impaired children have special needs. The children must learn to communicate with their parents and siblings. Lip-reading, although not an efficient technique, is an appro-

5. *True or False:*
Hearing aids improve the quality of the sound as well as amplifying it.

priate skill to have, as is signing. It is more difficult to conquer the problem of social isolation and rejection which arises from the inability to communicate effectively with hearing children who do not know sign language.

Identification of children with mild to moderate hearing losses is vital to their educational success. Many hearing disabilities remain undiscovered, and parents should watch for certain warning signs. These include inattention, seeming not to listen, placing the head so that one ear is closer to the source of the sound, talking loudly or very softly, constant complaining of earaches, or liquid draining from the ear. The sooner a hearing loss is discovered and corrective action is taken, the greater the chance the child can be helped.

THE ORTHOPEDICALLY DISABLED

The Child in a Wheelchair

When asked to describe a handicapped child, many people picture a youngster in a wheelchair. But the orthopedically disabled are a varied group. Approximately 275,000 children suffer from either total or partial paralysis, or suffer from disorders in which they have chronic limitations on their activities. In the past decade, one of the most significant achievements for the orthopedically disabled has been the reduction of architectural barriers that bar the progress of those who must use wheelchairs. Today most public establishments have facilities for the handicapped, but it is truly difficult to appreciate the plight of the orthopedically handicapped unless

Cerebral palsy is a common cause of physical handicap. The mental abilities of children with cerebral palsy vary considerably.

you have experienced something of the kind. You and I rarely think about a curb or a step, yet these may be insurmountable to a child in a wheelchair.

To appreciate this experience, one student used a wheelchair for a day. She wheeled herself from her apartment in the city to some stores a few blocks away. She noticed that people changed expressions when they approached her, and she had to crane her neck to look at the people passing in the street. The doors of some of the stores were too narrow, and the aisles were difficult to wheel through. She also experienced difficulty even with slanted curbs. (One curb was so difficult that she kept sliding down. The car in the nearest lane, filled with teenagers, waited impatiently for her to negotiate it. She got tired of trying, and to their astonishment got up out of the wheelchair and pushed it up on the curb. Their expressions, as you can imagine, were unbelievable.)

The federal government estimates that approximately 5 children out of every 1,000 have a physical handicap that requires some special services or equipment. Half these children suffer from crippling conditions, the other half have chronic health problems (Hallahan and Kauffman, 1982). Here we will concentrate on those with physical impairments.

Portrait of the Population

Because this group is so varied, it is difficult to find any generalizations that fit. For example, a common cause of physical problems is **cerebral palsy**, a disorder that results from brain damage. It may be caused by infection, trauma, or anoxia at birth. The damage shows itself in a number of possible symptoms, including motor problems, paralysis, lack of coordination, and poor speech. It may or may not result in losses in intelligence. The severity of the disorder differs widely. Some victims require braces, speak clearly, and are gifted, others must spend their days in wheelchairs and have severe intellectual and speech problems. The vast majority are somewhere in the middle. So generalizations are dangerous. The disorder does not get worse with time, that is, it is not progressive.

The type of help required by the physically disabled is determined by the severity of the disorder. The emotional problems that may interfere with development must also be mastered. Educational expectations must be in line with the child's abilities. For instance, some victims of cerebral palsy are gifted even though they have difficulty speaking. They may not be labeled as gifted, though, because of their disability.

Another major cause of physical problems is accidents. Many young children are badly injured in traffic accidents because they are not restrained properly. Teenagers are also likely victims of such crashes. In addition, sports accidents, especially those involving diving, may lead to physical disabilities.

Physical Disability and the Self-concept

How well do the physically disabled adjust, and how do they see themselves? The child in a wheelchair or wearing braces suffers from a visible handicap, but the evidence is that these children do not differ qualitatively in adjustment from other children (Lewandowski and Cruickshank, 1980), nor do they show significant emotional maladjustment as a group.

But what of their self-concept? Studies show that handicapped children usually describe themselves realistically. They understand the stereotypes of beauty

---

cerebral palsy
A disability caused by brain damage, usually at birth, marked by motor problems, poor speech, paralysis, and sometimes losses in intelligence.

6. *True or False:*
Cerebral palsy is caused by a virus that is transmitted in a way unknown to medical science at this time.

7. *True or False:*
Handicapped children usually describe themselves realistically.

and physical abilities and are aware of their limitations (Burns, 1979). The chief problem is in the field of interpersonal relations, where the lack of experience and social involvement can lead to problems. The extent of the problem does not always depend solely on the type and severity of the handicap, although these are important. Certainly the loss of both legs is more significant than the loss of one's little finger. But the closeness of the physical deficit to the core of the individual's personality is a vital factor. A person who defines himself in terms of playing the piano will find the loss of a finger catastrophic. A person who leads an athletic life may find the need to use a brace most distressing. In other words, the effect of the disability on the self-concept depends on the severity of the disability and its relationship to the manner in which the individual defines himself or herself. It also depends on the feedback that person receives from others. If the individual is labeled "handicapped" and receives feedback accordingly, personality and abilities may never be fully developed.

Helping the Orthopedically Disabled

The greatest problem faced by the physically handicapped is their lack of mobility. The importance of removing architectural barriers is obvious. In addition, training in independent living is necessary. Remember that children suffering from cerebral palsy differ greatly in their skills. Some may require considerable attention and be unable to live independent lives, while others can become self-sufficient. The training these youngsters receive in skills necessary for independent living is critical. Today, with architectural barriers coming down, they can begin to live fuller, more satisfying lives.

Children who suffer from physical handicaps are afflicted with a visible handicap, but many children suffer from essentially invisible handicaps, including learning disabilities, hyperactivity, and emotional disturbances.

THE LEARNING DISABLED

No matter how hard Carla tries, she can't seem to learn to read. She often mispronounces words, cannot tell the difference between sounds, and lags behind in most subjects. As her attempts meet with failure, Carla feels very discouraged and stops trying. School is a painful experience, and she considers herself a disappointment to her family.

Carla has a learning disability. There have always been children like Carla who, despite their best efforts, simply "could not" achieve in schools. Fifty years ago, such children from poverty backgrounds simply dropped out of school, while those from wealthy families found their way to the psychiatrist's couch for their "unwillingness" to try in school. Today we are beginning to understand the strange malady called learning disabilities.

What Is a Learning Disability?

One of the greatest frustrations is attempting to define a **learning disability**. Many definitions compete with each other, and numerous labels are available. For instance, children who show problems in school achievement, most often as-

learning disabilities
A disorder in which some basic psychological processes involved in understanding or using language manifest themselves in impaired academic performance.

sociated with lack of progress in reading, have been designated perceptually handicapped, minimally brain damaged, or dyslexic, or have been put in at least thirty-eight other categories (Cruickshank and Paul, 1980). Each term has its own problem. For instance, some define such children in terms of perceptual or process handicaps. Indeed, learning-disabled youngsters process information more slowly, show poorer discrimination, and show storage and retrieval memory deficits (Cermak, 1983). These children process information differently (Cruickshank, 1977). For example, they may see a *b* as a *d* or be unable to translate the *d* into the "di" sound. Others disagree with the information-processing approach, arguing that not all learning-disabled children show these differences and that not all children with reading problems process information differently (Stephens and Magliocca, 1978). The problem with minimal brain dysfunction definitions is that not all learning-disabled children show these neurological signs, and many children who do not have a learning disability show them. The term *dyslexia* has also been used. **Dyslexia** is an inability to read with understanding. Such an inability is not related to general intelligence (Weiss and Weiss, 1976). It is clearly too broad and deals only with the symptoms, not with any cause.

dyslexia
An inability to read with understanding.

The federal government defines a learning disability in this manner:

> Specific learning disability means a disorder in one or more of the basic psychological processes involved in understanding or in using language, spoken or written, which may manifest itself in an imperfect ability to listen, think, speak, read, write, spell or to do mathematical calculations. The term includes such conditions as perceptual handicaps, brain injury, minimal brain dysfunction, dyslexia and developmental aphasia. The term does not include children who have learning problems which are primarily the result of visual, hearing or motor handicaps or mental retardation or emotional disturbance or of environmental, cultural or economic disadvantage. (*Federal Register*, December 29, 1977, p. 65083).

This lengthy definition is far from perfect. Today some evidence indicates that economic disadvantage and poor teaching may have an effect on the development of learning disabilities. In addition, a child who suffers from mental retardation or an emotional disturbance can also be learning disabled. Perhaps the best definition was cogently given by Hagin and Silver (1977), when they noted that a "learning disability is a broad term used to encompass a variety of cognitive disorders that produce school achievement inappropriate to the child's age, intelligence, and previous educational opportunities. Its symptoms are heterogeneous, affecting singly or in combination the perception, reception, comprehension, storage, retrieval, and expression of language in all its forms" (p. 9).

While the exact cause of learning disabilities is unknown, most psychologists believe that they are neurological in origin. However, what causes these neurological differences is open to question.

Portrait of the Population

8. *True or False:*
More girls than boys are considered learning disabled.

Because definitions differ so much, estimates of the learning-disabled population vary considerably. Hallahan and Kauffman (1982) note that estimates as low as 1 percent and as high as 30 percent can be found. They favor about a 2 to 3 percent prevalence rate. About four to six times as many boys are affected as girls (Lerner, 1976).

It is difficult to draw a picture of the learning-disabled population for they are a varied group. Perhaps the most important similarity between all children with learning disabilities is that they are not achieving as much as their intelligence and school experience would seem reasonable. In other words, they are underachieving substantially. In a study of 500 children labeled dyslexic, Klasen (1972) found that 26.8 percent were hyperkinetic, 39 percent showed poor concentration, 44.2 percent showed faulty dominance, 49.2 percent showed dyskinesia, 67.2 percent showed visual perceptual problems, and 10.2 percent showed auditory perceptual deficiencies. Dominance relates to sidedness, or one's preference for using a hand, ear, foot, or eye. When children show a preference for the use of the right eye but the left hand, they are said to show mixed cerebral dominance (Weiss and Weiss, 1976). While some suggest that this pattern is found in children with learning problems, the evidence is contradictory, with others claiming that no such relationship exists (Lerner, 1976). Dyskinesia or motor dysfunction involves general awkwardness, poor coordination, and a lack of dexterity (Klasen, 1972). There was no one symptom that every child in Klasen's study shared.

Many learning-disabled children must learn to cope with failure at every level, and they are keenly aware of their deficits (Cohen, 1983). Can you imagine always lagging behind in academic skills, feeling that you are a disappointment to your family, being insulted by other children, and suffering unflattering comparisons to your peers—and all this without any visible deficit? According to Erikson, the psychosocial crisis of the middle years involves industry versus inferiority. A sense of industry develops when a child values his or her own work. This sense of industry is difficult to develop if one compares oneself to classmates and always comes out a poor second. We might expect such a child to suffer from a lack of recognition and satisfaction in achievement. Cruickshank and Paul (1980, p. 525) put it well:

> The concept of self is learned and is directly related to experience. Children who consistently fail and who have negative experiences with themselves in the world, particularly at a time when they are beginning to learn who they are, develop low and defeating self-concepts. As that experience of failure continues, that low self-view is maintained and reinforced even more strongly. This low self-appraisal, then, becomes the foundation for the development of perceptions and behavior to protect a weak and fragile sense of self.

Peer relationships also present problems. Children asked to choose with whom they wanted to be friends rarely chose a child who suffered from a learning disability (Bryan, 1976). The learning-disabled child both gives and receives more negative comments (Bryan and Bryan, 1978).

Intervention Strategies

The learning-disabled child suffers from two disabilities. First, a specific cognitive deficit causes poor achievement. Second, poor interpersonal relationships often follow, with both family and friends. These problems need be attacked in an intervention program.

The first step in helping the child is to discover exactly where the problems are. Just being told that a child has a learning disability tells you nothing about how that child learns. Children must be tested to uncover their specific problems. One child may have difficulty with auditory perception and be unable to hear the difference between a "p" and a "b." For another child the problem may lie in the visual areas, in memory, or in any of a number of different areas.

Once the problem is located, a number of strategies may be used. Telford and Sawrey (1981) identify two main approaches to helping the learning disabled. The first, the basic abilities approach, stresses the importance of such skills as auditory discrimination and memory. After the child's strengths and weaknesses are found, programs are designed to strengthen weak areas and capitalize on stronger ones. If a child is strong in the auditory area but weak in the visual, training exercises would be designed to improve the visual area while instruction takes advantage of the child's auditory strengths (Telford and Sawrey, 1981).

The task-analytic approach looks at learning as a mastery of specific tasks from the simple to the more complex. The attempt here is to break down the task we want to teach the child into the simplest possible steps and then teach the child the skill. Myers and Hammill (1976) use the example of teaching a child to count from one to ten. What skills are necessary for success in this endeavor? The child must be able to say the words, to see or feel objects, and so on. The teacher must recognize what skills are present and absent. If the child does not have these skills, the teacher must return to teaching an earlier task, such as the names of the numbers. (It is possible that in some cases these skills must also be task-analyzed.) Task-analysis shows how the sequence is taught. For example, the child probably should learn the number sequence one through ten in order before proceeding to learning the concept of a one-to-one correspondence between object and number.

Because the learning-disabled child frequently suffers from low self-esteem and interpersonal problems, family counseling, behavior modification, and social-skills training may be required to help the child develop to potential in these areas. The child with a learning disability is often rejected. It is not only academic failures that cause this, but also sometimes the child's own behavior. One of the most common troublesome behaviors is hyperactivity.

THE HYPERACTIVE CHILD

Timothy does not pay attention in class. He walks around the room, touches everything, seems out of control, and is easily distractible. He is impulsive and always in motion.

Spend a few minutes with a hyperactive child and you will begin to appreciate the patience and skill required to deal with these children. Many, but certainly not all, learning-disabled children are hyperactive. Hyperactivity is an invisible handicap because the cause of the problem is not visible. But these children are anything but invisible.

Portrait of the Population

hyperactivity
Children whose behavior is impulsive, overly active, highly distractible, and inattentive.

Hyperactive children are impulsive, highly distractible, inattentive, and show a great deal of inappropriate activity (Ross and Ross, 1976). They have difficulty in school, and their relationship with teachers is often strained. Put yourself in the teacher's shoes for a moment. How would you handle a child who cannot sit still, does not pay attention, and disrupts the clasroom? Such children are criticized and rejected for their behavior. They are also considered aggressive and annoying and are not accepted by their peers. Most hyperactive children are male. It is estimated that the ratio of males to females is between 3 to 1 and 9 to 1 (Gelfand et al., 1982). Prevalence estimates vary greatly, from 5 to 10 percent of the general school population (Sroufe and Stewart, 1973) to a more accepted lower percentage of a bit more than 1 percent.

Causes of Hyperactivity

Before looking into the causes of hyperactivity, a caution is required. Some normally active children are incorrectly labeled hyperactive because their parents and teachers simply cannot cope with them. Some have even been given drugs to calm them down. Misdiagnosis of this disorder is troubling, although the extent to which this is a problem is unknown at the present time.

The causes of hyperactivity are controversial. In one survey, Johnson (1981) found that although excellent laboratory evidence suggests that activity level is partially inherited, there is little direct evidence that hyperactivity is genetically caused. The evidence connecting hyperactivity and minimal brain dysfunction is also weak. While some studies indicate that hyperactive children show abnormal brain-wave patterns, other studies do not. Remember that some children who are physically and mentally healthy show abnormalities in their brain waves. Environmental causes have also been argued. Perhaps the child becomes hyperactive as a result of poor or inconsistent reinforcement. Although this can worsen the situation, Johnson (1981) again finds insufficient evidence to consider this a direct cause of the disorder. Some evidence indicates that lead poisoning and food additives cause hyperactivity, but these explain only a small number of known cases. Hyperactivity may be caused by a complex combination of factors.

Treating the Hyperactive Child

Nowhere is the debate over the proper treatment of an exceptional child more heated than in the area of hyperactivity. Three basic approaches are currently used to treat the hyperactive child—drugs, diet, and environmental manipulation.

Drugs.   Hyperactive children are often treated with stimulants to reduce the symptoms of the disorder. Under such medications, these children become calmer and more attentive (Clampit and Pirkle, 1983). More than half a million children are receiving these drugs (Sprague and Gadow, 1976), and this has become a matter of great concern. Some have criticized the use of these drugs because they treat only the symptoms, not the underlying cause, and may produce unpleasant side effects. Finding the correct dosage is often a problem (Varley and Trupin, 1983). Others question their effectiveness (Gadow, 1983). No one claims that drug therapy will improve intelligence or even schoolwork, but medication can reduce the symptoms so that the child can learn. An analysis of 135 studies of stimulant use with hyperactive youngsters concluded that stimulants are effective (Kavale, 1982). This does not mean that drugs are always the treatment of

9. *True or False:*
Hyperactivity can be cured through the correct use of medication.

choice, however. The very idea of a child taking drugs over the period of years should make us cautious. Some authorities claim that medication should only be used as a last resort and then always in combination with another type of treatment. In any event, since medication only reduces its symptoms, other techniques must be used to compensate for the child's academic and social problems.

Diet.   The search continues for nondrug treatments, and one of the most popular is the **Feingold diet.** In 1973, Dr. Norman Feingold presented a paper to the American Medical Association showing the relationship between hyperactivity and food additives, such as preservatives and artificial flavors. Feingold also noted that some natural chemicals, such as salicylates, might also be implicated and suggested that hyperactive children may be genetically predisposed to react to these additives. He claimed that when hyperactive children are put on a diet free of these compounds, 30 to 50 percent improved (Johnson, 1981; Feingold, 1975).

The Feingold diet consists of two stages. In the first, many natural foods that contain salicylates, such as oranges, are prohibited, along with artificial colorings, flavorings, and additives. Later, these natural foods are slowly returned to the diet while only additives remain forbidden. This diet can be difficult to follow. The next time you are shopping, take a look at the ingredients on the food packages and note just how many foods contain these chemicals. Practitioners of the Feingold diet have grouped together to offer help to others. Their literature includes lists of approved foods, which makes shopping simpler.

Some clinical support for the Feingold diet has been found (Holborow et al., 1981), but controlled studies have been difficult to perform, and each has been criticized on methodological grounds. Johnson (1981) suggests that a scarcely significant relationship exists between diet and behavior, especially among younger hyperactive children, and that success rates with the Feingold diet are lower than claimed. Others either argue that the diet is generally ineffective or note that it is successful in only a small number of cases (Kavale and Forness, 1983; Mattes, 1983). Some authorities argue that this negative assessment is premature and may well be inaccurate (Rimland, 1983). More research is needed in this area. It is reasonable to conclude at this point that the diet may be effective for some children but not for as many as first thought.

Environmental Manipulation.   The third approach (which may be used with either of the first two) involves manipulating the environment and its reinforcements. For example, providing structure and solid routines and using positive reinforcements are helpful (Walden and Thompson, 1981). Some claim that behavioral intervention is superior to medication (Gadow, 1983).

THE BEHAVIORALLY DISORDERED

Hyperactivity and learning disabilities are two of the more common exceptionalities found in our society, but if we consider teachers' estimates, the most common would be the behaviorally disordered child. About 2 to 3 percent of the children in elementary schools have behavioral difficulties that require attention (Kirk and Gallagher, 1983). Again, boys greatly outnumber girls in this category.

Feingold diet
A diet developed by Dr. Norman Feingold for the treatment of hyperactivity, consisting mainly of elimination of preservatives and artificial flavors.

Teachers define the seriousness of a child's difficulty in terms of how the child disrupts the class.

Portrait of the Population

Some behaviorally disturbed children are easy to identify. Certainly a child who shouts out in class or is aggressive needs help, but the child who is acting out is not the only troubled youngster. Children who are overly withdrawn or very anxious are also behaviorally disturbed and may need treatment.

Behavioral problems are usually thought to be caused by the interaction between the child and the environment. In other words, they do not appear to be genetically caused in the overwhelming majority of cases. Children are likely to misbehave if they are reinforced for aggression, see it at home, have found it useful in obtaining their own ends, or gain social status and acceptance from indulging in these behaviors. Withdrawal and anxiety are also environmentally determined.

Some people point an accusing finger at the parents of these children, blaming them for the problem, but such an approach oversimplifies the situation. First, although the early relationship between parents and children is important, predicting later behavioral problems from these relationships is not a simple matter. In one study, Lewis and his colleagues (1984) found that although insecurity of attachment in boys at one year was related to later behavioral problems at six, it only partially predicted later problems. Other factors, such as life stresses including death, divorce, and family moves, are quite important. Making predictions concerning the later behavior of those who have problems in preschool is also hazardous (Fischer et al., 1984). Although some continuity may be found in large samples, it simply is not possible to look at a particular child with problems

Aggressive children can be taught to control their aggressive tendencies.

Children who are withdrawn do not draw attention to themselves. Yet, they often need help in developing self-confidence and learning interpersonal skills.

10. *True or False:*
Children who act aggressively are not very popular with their peers.

time-out procedure
A behavior modification technique in which a person is removed from the environment in which he or she has misbehaved until the offending behavior has ceased.

at age six and state with certainty that that child will have serious problems at age fifteen. Experience is cumulative. In addition, the relationship between parent and child is reciprocal, that is, the child affects the parent and the parent affects the child (Kendall et al., 1984). If we are to understand family relationships, this basic point must be kept in mind. In summary, the cause of a behavioral problem may be very difficult to pin down. In addition, blaming the parent creates defensive attitudes that do not help the child. Most treatment programs require the active participation of the parents, and simply criticizing them is counterproductive.

The Aggressive Child

Children who act aggressively are easy to identify and receive an enormous amount of criticism. They are also often difficult to work with, and their very behavior produces negative feedback. They may be attracted to others who act like them, since they are rejected by many of their peers.

Behavior modification is effective in helping these children. Their aggressive behavior must be modified. **Time-out procedures**, in which children are removed from troublesome situations until they no longer show the offending behavior, are useful. For example, children who throw temper tantrums may be put in their room until they calm down. They may leave the room any time they stop misbehaving. Behavior modification is effective in a number of cases, but other forms of therapy may also be used successfully.

The Withdrawn Child

Children who are withdrawn do not stand out. They may go unnoticed because they do not disturb the class. Their work may be acceptable. They never volunteer and may even refuse to answer questions in class.

These children need to form a close, trusting relationship with adults who can help them develop social skills. A trusting teacher may rehearse an answer with a child and then, when appropriate, call on that child. Such children require a great deal of patience and should be brought along slowly. Many are afraid of rejection and failure and may need to practice how to converse with others. The social environment of the school may be overwhelming for them, and involve competition for attention that is difficult for this kind of child. Making friends in the context of an activity in which a child excels may be best. A child in the band may feel more confident in this environment and find it easier to strike up a conversation and make friends there.

The Anxious Child

Anxious children certainly need help too. Often these children have not lived up to expectations or are afraid of failing. They may show a number of nervous habits and react to pressure in a self-defeating manner. For such children, reducing the pressure they feel and working with the parents can be helpful. In addition, teaching relaxation exercises gives immediate temporary relief. Finally, a number of behavioral approaches are helpful in reducing anxiety related habits. For example, pulling one's own hair is related to anxiety. Azrin and colleagues (1980) successfully treated children who practiced hair-pulling through the use of habit

Psychologists have ways of helping anxious children overcome their problem.

reversal. These children were taught a competing reaction of clasping their hands for three minutes when hair-pulling had occurred, were taught to become aware of the movements involved in hair-pulling, learned which behaviors come before this activity and which situations preceded it, and also learned how to relax.

Most behaviorally disturbed children show these symptoms. By describing the child in terms of the symptoms, we do not label the child for life as "emotionally disturbed." Indeed, some of these children will improve if given a change in environment, and a definite stigma surrounds the label.

CHILDREN WITH MULTIPLE DISORDERS

For the sake of simplicity, each disorder described in this chapter has been treated as if it always existed alone, but this is not the case. For example, as noted previously, some children who suffer from cerebral palsy are not only orthopedically handicapped but also mentally retarded. Some people who are deaf are also blind. Most people who suffer severe disorders demonstrate multiple deficits (Hardman et al., 1984). Many severely or profoundly mentally retarded people suffer from physical and behavioral problems.

The presence of multiple problems complicates the educational and caregiving process. The child who is blind and deaf experiences great difficulties learning to communicate with others. The mentally retarded child with a hearing problem demonstrates not only very slow learning but also significant communication problems. Many of these children are in residential institutions, but with proper training some of them can live in their communities (Kirk and Gallagher, 1983).

Work with children suffering from multiple handicaps must begin early in childhood and continue throughout life. The educational plan centers around fundamental skills, such as those in the areas of self-help and communication. It often requires input from a wide variety of professionals and presents child development specialists with special problems and challenges.

MEETING THE NEEDS OF THE EXCEPTIONAL CHILD

We have made great strides in understanding and helping the exceptional child. Some people do not accept the title "exceptional child," preferring "child with exceptional needs" instead. Indeed, the child with a behavioral problem or a learning disability, or a child who is gifted or mentally retarded, has unique needs that require individual help. This aid should start as soon as possible, and the trend toward early identification and intervention is an important step forward.

At the same time, we also know that these children must fit into the mainstream of society if they are to reach their potential. They must cope with their particular disabilities and make the most of what they have to work with. Thus, while appreciating their deficits and special needs, these children must develop their strengths.

By law, exceptional children must be educated in the least restrictive environment, which in many cases is the regular public school classroom. However, the rush to mainstream without looking both at the child's needs and at the child's abilities is a mistake. While the teacher requires additional support, the exceptional child must also be prepared to take a place in the educational environment. This is the thinking behind the new approach that emphasizes the importance of teaching these children social skills.

While we attempt to improve the lot of children who suffer from various disabilities, we are also trying to prevent the occurrence of disabilities. For instance, we now know the dangers of giving too much oxygen to premature infants, and a vaccine to prevent rubella is routinely administered. Genetic counseling has also been used, as have educational programs that communicate the dangers of such activities as drinking alcoholic beverages during pregnancy to expectant parents.

Despite many problems, the future for these children is brighter than ever before. Advancements in teaching methods, medicine, and psychology all aim at improving the lot of these children, and more and more exceptional children will take their places as well-functioning individuals in our society. As members of our society, these children have the right to expect that they will receive the care and education necessary to allow them to develop their considerable potential to the fullest.

Chapter Summary

1. A disability is a total or partial loss of functioning. A handicap refers to the difficulty a person has in adjusting to the environment. An exceptional child is one whose intellectual, physical, or emotional performance falls either much above or below that of peers.

2. Public Law 94–142 requires districts to provide an appropriate free education for every child. It also mandates nondiscriminatory testing and educational accountability through an Individualized Educational Plan. Finally, it requires that children be placed in the least restrictive educational environment. Mainstreaming is the process by which disabled children are placed in regular classrooms.

3. Most retarded individuals are mildly retarded, and the cause of their retardation is unknown. Many can be educated to lead productive, independent lives. The moderately retarded can be taught self-care, but only rarely can they live independent lives. The severely and profoundly retarded require institutional care.

4. Gifted children are those who have superior intellectual, creative, or academic abilities, or manifest talent in leadership or the performing and visual arts. The gifted are generally well adjusted.

5. A child is legally blind if there is 20/200 vision in the best eye with correction or severely restricted peripheral vision. Blind children develop more slowly than sighted children. With excellent care, the blind can lead independent lives.

6. Many hearing-impaired children have difficulty learning to talk. Many schools for the deaf teach both sign language and oral communication.

7. Cerebral palsy is a disorder resulting from brain damage, usually at birth, causing motor problems, poor speech, and sometimes retardation. If orthopedically disabled people are to lead independent lives, environmental barriers must be removed.

8. Children achieving much below what their intelligence and educational experience indicate they should be achieving are considered learning disabled. These children have difficulty learning to read or doing math. They often suffer from low self-concepts because of their failure. Educational and psychological methods of intervention are now available to aid these children.

9. Hyperactive children are impulsive and distractible. They are treated by medication, changes in diet, and behavior modification.

10. Children who are overly aggressive, withdrawn, or anxious suffer from behavioral disorders. Behavior modification and other forms of psychotherapy and counseling may be helpful.

■ *Answers to True or False Questions*

1. *False.* Correct statement: The law demands that the child be placed in the "least restrictive environment." This may or may not mean the regular classroom setting.

2. *False.* Correct statement: Subnormal intellectual functioning is only one of the criteria for labeling a child mentally retarded.

3. *False.* Correct statement: Most intellectually gifted children are socially well adjusted.

4. *False.* Correct statement: The majority of the legally blind have some vision.

5. *False.* Correct statement: Hearing aids amplify sound, but they do not improve its quality.

6. *False.* Correct statement: Cerebral palsy is caused by brain damage, most often at birth.

7. *True.* Most handicapped people are aware of their limitations.

8. *False.* Correct statement: Four to six times as many boys as girls are learning disabled.

9. *False.* Correct statement: Medication may reduce the symptoms, but it does not cure the disorder.

10. *True.* Aggressive children are usually rejected by the majority of their peers.

PART FIVE

Adolescence

CHAPTER FOURTEEN

Physical Development in Adolescence

■ *Are the Following Statements True or False?*

Try the True-False Quiz below. See if your answers correspond to the information in this chapter. Each question is repeated opposite the paragraph in which the answer can be found. The True-False Answer Box at the end of the chapter lists complete answers.

____ **1.** The sequence of developmental changes in adolescence is still largely a mystery.

____ **2.** Menstruation is one of the earliest signs of puberty in females.

____ **3.** Twelve- or thirteen-year-old girls are generally taller and heavier than the average boys of that age.

____ **4.** If a boy is tall compared with his peers prior to puberty, chances are he will be comparably tall following puberty.

____ **5.** The tendency for each new generation to become taller and heavier than the previous one is accelerating in the United States.

____ **6.** Early-maturing boys have a social advantage during adolescence.

____ **7.** Early-maturing adolescent girls have a clear social advantage during adolescence which lasts well into early and middle adulthood.

____ **8.** Obese teens usually become obese adults.

____ **9.** More than 90 percent of the sufferers of anorexia nervosa, a condition marked by self-starvation, are female.

____ **10.** During the last twenty years, the sexual attitudes of females have changed much more than those of males.

____ **11.** Adolescent sexual attitudes are more liberal than their actual behavior.

____ **12.** The most common reason female students drop out of school is lack of achievement motivation and any goal in life.

____ **13.** Contraceptive use decreases with age.

____ **14.** Exposure to sex education in the schools reduces the probability of sexual experimentation.

Children develop at their own rate. This is more obvious in the late elementary school and early junior high school years, when some of the children are much more physically developed than others.

1. *True or False:*
The sequence of developmental changes in adolescence is still largely a mystery.

Watch a group of seventh- or eighth-graders as they come streaming out of a junior high school. Some of them are already physically well developed, while others have a childish quality. Most adolescents are acutely aware of their physical selves. Early adolescence is a time of tremendous physical change that affects the adolescent's self-concept and behavior. Although the sequence of this physical change is predictable, the timing of the change varies considerably from person to person. For example, the average age for the first menstrual flow among American teens is approximately 12.8 years (Tanner, 1970), but a girl may begin menstruating anytime between ten and sixteen and a half years and still be within the normal range (see Figure 14.1).

In this chapter, we will examine these rapid physiological changes, concentrating on how they affect the adolescent's self-concept and behavior. While reading this material, try to recall how you experienced and coped with these changes.

FIGURE 14.1   **Average Age of Maturational Changes in Males and Females**
The sequence of maturational change is relatively fixed, but the age at which any physical change occurs varies. The chart below shows the ages during which these changes typically occur. The range of ages within which each charted event may begin and end is indicated by the figure placed directly below its start and finish.

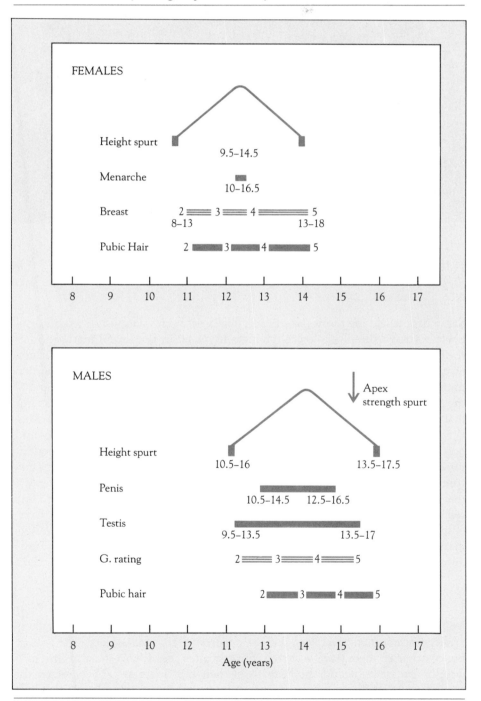

Source: J. M. Tanner, 1974.

Girls experience their growth spurt about a year and a half to two years before boys.

PUBERTY AND ADOLESCENCE

Defining the Terms

puberty
Physiological changes involved in sexual maturation, as well as other body changes that occur during the teen years.

primary sex characteristics
Body changes directly associated with sexual reproduction.

secondary sex characteristics
Physical changes that are not associated with sexual reproduction yet distinguish males from females.

adolescence
The psychological experience of the child from puberty to adulthood.

2. *True or False:*
Menstruation is one of the earliest signs of puberty in females.

Some people use the terms *puberty* and *adolescence* synonymously. Actually, **puberty** refers to the physiological changes involved in the sexual maturation of the individual, as well as other body changes that occur during this period (Sommer, 1978). Body changes directly related to sexual reproduction are called **primary sex characteristics**. These include maturation of the testes in males and of the ovaries in females. Changes that are not directly related to reproduction but that distinguish boys from girls are called **secondary sex characteristics** (Forisha-Kovach, 1984). Secondary sex characteristics include beard growth in males and breast development in females. When the term *puberty* is use to mark an event in someone's life, it refers to the time at which the reproductive system becomes mature and sexual reproduction is possible (Chumlea, 1982). In females puberty is marked by the onset of menstruation. In males it is not as easily determined and relates to the ability to ejaculate mobile sperm. Puberty, then, is a "biological ripening." Adolescence, on the other hand, is a behavioral-cultural ripening (Krogman, 1980). **Adolescence** refers to the stage from puberty to adulthood and covers the entire psychological experience of the child during that period.

The Female Adolescent Develops

Many people believe that menstruation is the first sign of puberty. Actually, menarche, the first menstrual flow, is a late occurrence that takes place after a number of other changes have occurred. Shortly after the growth spurt begins, girls develop breast buds and the breadth of their hips increases. Then, when the growth spurt is at its maximum, changes in the genital organs take place. These include the development of the uterus, vagina, labia, and clitoris as well as the breasts. When growth slows considerably, menarche takes place. At this point, a number of other changes in fat and muscle composition are also occurring. Following menarche, most of the changes are nonsexual, including further changes in body shape and voice (Krogman, 1980). These changes are outlined in Table 14.1.

Even though all normal females progress through these physical changes, each adolescent girl experiences them as novel and challenging. Each pubescent female develops within her own environment, specific culture, and subculture and is exposed to a different set of peers and parents. The importance of her subjective experience should not be lost in any biological discussion of general physical development or norms.

The Growth Spurt.   The growth spurt is one of the earliest and most recognizable body changes. Because this spurt begins about two years earlier in girls than in boys, twelve-year-old girls are generally taller and heavier, and have larger muscles, than twelve-year-old boys (see Table 14.2 and Table 14.3). (Tanner, 1970). Although all structures grow at this time, they do not enlarge at the same rate. The hands and feet reach adult size first, causing many adolescents to complain about having hands or feet that are too big. Parents can alleviate some of this distress by simply telling their children that when they are fully grown their proportions will be correct.

If girls of twelve or thirteen are physically more advanced than boys the same age, why do early-adolescent boys outshine girls in sports? The answer may involve differences in physiology, but different interests and training—both environmental factors—are probably the keys. In our society, males are encouraged to develop their bodies through athletic competition, while females are not. With the growth in popularity of such sports as tennis and jogging, as well as new federal government requirements for colleges, which mandate more emphasis on

3. *True or False:*
Twelve- or thirteen-year-old girls are generally taller and heavier than the average boys of that age.

TABLE 14.1   **Maturation in Girls**

Although, as in the case of boys, there may be normal variations in the sequence of physical and sexual maturation in girls, a typical sequence of events is:

1. Adolescent growth spurt begins.
2. Downy (nonpigmented) pubic hair makes its initial appearance.
3. Elevation of the breast (the so-called bud stage of development) and rounding of the hips begin, accompanied by the beginning of downy axillary (body) hair.
4. The uterus and vagina, as well as labia and clitoris, increase in size.
5. Pubic hair is growing rapidly and becoming slightly pigmented.
6. Breasts develop further; nipple pigmentation begins; areola increases in size. Axillary hair is becoming slightly pigmented.
7. Growth spurt reaches peak rate and then declines.
8. Menarche, or onset of menstruation, occurs (almost always *after* the peak rate of growth in height has occurred).
9. Pubic hair development is completed, followed by mature breast development and completion of axillary hair development.
10. Period of "adolescent sterility" ends, and girl becomes capable of conception (up to a year or so after menarche).

Source: J. J. Conger and A. C. Petersen, 1984.

TABLE 14.2   **Growth During Adolescence**
Stature is given in centimeters. To convert to inches multiply by .39.

Sex and Age	5th	10th	25th	50th	75th	90th	95th
				Percentile			
Male				*Stature in centimeters*			
12.0 years	137.6	140.3	144.4	149.7	154.6	159.4	162.3
12.5 years	140.2	143.0	147.4	153.0	158.2	163.2	166.1
13.0 years	142.9	145.8	150.5	156.5	161.8	167.0	169.8
13.5 years	145.7	148.7	153.6	159.9	165.3	170.5	173.4
14.0 years	148.8	151.8	156.9	163.1	168.5	173.8	176.7
14.5 years	152.0	155.0	160.1	166.2	171.5	176.6	179.5
15.0 years	155.2	158.2	163.3	169.0	174.1	178.9	181.9
15.5 years	158.3	161.2	166.2	171.5	176.3	180.8	183.9
16.0 years	161.1	163.9	168.7	173.5	178.1	182.4	185.4
16.5 years	163.4	166.1	170.6	175.2	179.5	183.6	186.6
17.0 years	164.9	167.7	171.9	176.2	180.5	184.4	187.3
17.5 years	165.6	168.5	172.4	176.7	181.0	185.0	187.6
18.0 years	165.7	168.7	172.3	176.8	181.2	185.3	187.6
Female							
12.0 years	139.8	142.3	147.0	151.5	155.8	160.0	162.7
12.5 years	142.7	145.4	150.1	154.6	158.8	162.9	165.6
13.0 years	145.2	148.0	152.8	157.1	161.3	165.3	168.1
13.5 years	147.2	150.0	154.7	159.0	163.2	167.3	170.0
14.0 years	148.7	151.5	155.9	160.4	164.6	168.7	171.3
14.5 years	149.7	152.5	156.8	161.2	165.6	169.8	172.2
15.0 years	150.5	153.2	157.2	161.8	166.3	170.5	172.8
15.5 years	151.1	153.6	157.5	162.1	166.7	170.9	173.1
16.0 years	151.6	154.1	157.8	162.4	166.9	171.1	173.3
16.5 years	152.2	154.6	158.2	162.7	167.1	171.2	173.4
17.0 years	152.7	155.1	158.7	163.1	167.3	171.2	173.5
17.5 years	153.2	155.6	159.1	163.4	167.5	171.1	173.5
18.0 years	153.6	156.0	159.6	163.7	167.6	171.0	173.6

Source: P. V. V. Hamill, et al., 1977.

female athletics, some changes are taking place. We might also expect that, because of different rates of maturation, female athletes may be capable of developing their potential at an earlier age than men. Indeed, women champions in gymnastics are often much younger than their male counterparts. The earlier growth spurt and maturation, combined with excellent training, allows them to develop their full potential at an earlier age than males.

Menstruation.   "Now you're a woman and can have children," one mother told her daughter after her first menstrual experience. Since the average teen is not fertile for about a year following the first menses, the statement is really untrue. Equating menstruation with womanhood is even more debatable, but this is not an unusual statement for a teenager to hear.

Of all the body changes that occur in adolescence, menstruation is the most dramatic (Logan, 1980). It is also the most ritualized. Various societal laws and customs prescribe what may and may not be done during the time of the men-

TABLE 14.3 **Changes in Weight During Adolescence**
All data is given in kilograms. To convert to pounds multiply by 2.2.

Sex and Age	Percentile						
	5th	10th	25th	50th	75th	90th	95th
Male				*Weight in kilograms*			
12.0 years	29.85	31.46	35.09	39.78	45.77	52.73	58.09
12.5 years	31.64	33.41	37.31	42.27	48.70	55.91	61.52
13.0 years	33.64	35.60	39.74	44.95	51.79	59.12	65.02
13.5 years	35.85	38.03	42.40	47.81	55.02	62.35	68.51
14.0 years	38.22	40.64	45.21	50.77	58.31	65.57	72.13
14.5 years	40.66	43.34	48.08	53.76	61.58	68.76	75.66
15.0 years	43.11	46.06	50.92	56.71	64.72	71.91	79.12
15.5 years	45.50	48.69	53.64	59.51	67.64	74.98	82.45
16.0 years	47.74	51.16	56.16	62.10	70.26	77.97	85.62
16.5 years	49.76	53.39	58.38	64.39	72.46	80.84	88.59
17.0 years	51.50	55.28	60.22	66.31	74.17	83.58	91.31
17.5 years	52.89	56.78	61.61	67.78	75.32	86.14	93.73
18.0 years	53.97	57.89	62.61	68.88	76.04	88.41	95.76
Female							
12.0 years	30.52	32.53	36.52	41.53	48.07	55.99	60.81
12.5 years	32.30	34.42	38.59	43.84	50.56	58.81	64.12
13.0 years	34.14	36.35	40.65	46.10	52.91	61.45	67.30
13.5 years	35.98	38.26	42.65	48.26	55.11	63.87	70.30
14.0 years	37.76	40.11	44.54	50.28	57.09	66.04	73.08
14.5 years	39.45	41.83	46.28	52.10	58.84	67.95	75.59
15.0 years	40.99	43.38	47.82	53.68	60.32	69.54	77.78
15.5 years	42.32	44.72	49.10	54.96	61.48	70.79	79.59
16.0 years	43.41	45.78	50.09	55.89	62.29	71.68	80.99
16.5 years	44.20	46.54	50.75	56.44	62.75	72.18	81.93
17.0 years	44.74	47.04	51.14	56.69	62.91	72.38	82.46
17.5 years	45.08	47.33	51.33	56.71	62.89	72.37	82.62
18.0 years	45.26	47.47	51.39	56.62	62.78	72.25	82.47

Source: P. V. V. Hamill, et al., 1977.

strual flow. For example, one tribe in Borneo confines girls going through menarche in dark cells suspended by poles for long periods of time. When they conclude menarche, they are again introduced to the sun, flowers, earth, and so forth. One South African cattle-rearing tribe believes that the cattle would die instantly if they walked over ground on which even a drop of menstrual blood had fallen. To prevent this, special paths are available for women to use so that they will not have contact with the ground cattle may frequent (Williams, 1977).

It is easy to dismiss these customs as primitive and chalk them up to ignorance, but even in our own society, taboos are plentiful. In some homes, women are considered too unclean to touch food or utensils during their period, and daughters are often taught to be ashamed of menstruation. This contrasts with the experience of male adolescents, who are taught to focus on their body changes as symbols of sexual strength (Breit and Ferrandino, 1979). The reproductive function of the menstrual cycle is underscored, while female sexuality is denied. A number of cultural "don'ts" appear, such as swimming, going barefoot, and participating in sports during the menstrual period, and girls are told that no one should know that they are having their period.

Some teens know little about this important change, and the ignorance is shared by both sexes. As a class experience, I often ask one student to act the part of a teenager while another takes the parental role. The parent is then asked to explain menstruation to her child. Most students find such explanations unusually difficult and admit their lack of knowledge. When a male is asked to play the role of a father explaining menstruation to his daughter, he is likely to admit complete ignorance of the subject, and a spirited discussion often follows.

Some educational progress has been made in this area. Today, most female adolescents have at least been given some biological information about what is happening (or about to happen) to them. They are subjected to fewer restrictions, and discussion today is likely to be more honest. Just how are young people prepared? Friends, mothers, and teachers are the most likely sources of information. At times, older siblings may help. This contrasts with the experience of some girls in other societies. A study of ninety-five young adults from twenty-three countries found a wide variety of preparatory experiences. None of the subjects from Zambia and only half the Asians were given any instruction by their mothers. The Zambians learned from other relatives, the Japanese from teachers. Fathers of girls from Iran and Western Europe were also more likely to be involved than American fathers. Once menstruation begins, both American and foreign girls depend almost exclusively on their mothers (Logan, 1980).

How do teenage girls evaluate the experience? Most American women consider it a negative or, at best, neutral experience. Many feel insufficiently prepared and experience surprise, embarrassment, or fright (Logan, 1980). At the same time, they often feel pride (Whisnant and Zegans, 1975). In one study, 639 girls in fifth and sixth grades (elementary school), seventh and eighth grades (junior high), and eleventh and twelfth grades (high school) were asked for their reactions to their first menstrual period. Their reactions were decidedly mixed, but most reported some physical distress and an immediate desire for secrecy. Girls who were less prepared or began menstruating very early were most likely to evaluate the experience negatively. The researchers conclude that although the experience produces some confusion and ambivalence (especially in those who are very young or not well prepared), it is not as traumatic as once thought (Ruble and Brooks-Gunn, 1982; Brooks-Gunn and Ruble, 1982). The initial reaction to the first menstrual period may be anxiety, but this decreases rapidly as the months pass (Rierdan and Koff, 1980). In summary, if young girls are prepared for menstruation, they will probably experience some ambivalence and anxiety, but these feelings will dissipate with time.

The Menstrual Blues.   The physical discomfort, though, may not dissipate with time. Premenstrual discomfort or pain is a fact of life for millions of women. Surveys have differed widely on how many women suffer negative premenstrual symptoms, with some reporting as many as 95 percent of the women questioned becoming irritable and others reporting between 15 and 20 percent (Paige, 1973). In one survey, 12 percent of the high school girls questioned stated that their menstrual cramps were so severe that they were kept home from school on three or more occasions (Bakwin and Bakwin, 1972).

The premenstrual syndrome is a group of symptoms that women experience, including headache, anxiety, depression, crying, insomnia, and others (Lerner and Spanier, 1980). These range from mild to severe. Although fluctuating hormones cause some of the discomfort, the young woman's attitude toward menstruation is also a factor. Attitude may affect how a woman interprets and copes with premenstrual symptoms.

The Male Adolescent Develops

The first signs of puberty in males are the growth of the testes and scrotum along with the appearance of pubic hair (see Table 14.4). This is followed about a year later by a spurt in height and growth of the penis. The prepubertal growth spurt in males occurs approximately two years after the average female has experienced her growth spurt. Again, the sequence of events is predictable, but the time at which they occur varies from person to person. The trunk and legs elongate. Leg length reaches its adult proportions before body breadth. Growthwise, the last change to occur is a widening of the shoulders (Stolz and Stolz, 1951). This progression demonstrates why a young adolescent boy grows out of his trousers a year before growing out of his jackets (Tanner, 1970). Muscles develop, in part because of the secretion of testosterone, and the heart and lungs increase dramatically, as does the number of red blood cells. Physical development is variable. For instance, penis growth begins at thirteen years in most boys but may start as early as eleven or as late as fourteen and a half. It may end as early as thirteen and a half for some or as late as seventeen for others (Stolz and Stolz, 1951).

The Growth Spurt.   The male growth spurt takes the adolescent boy well beyond the height of the average female. Often a male who has not started his growth spurt will see friends pulling away and yearn to recover his status in the group. Generally, if he was tall compared with his peers before puberty, he will return to this relative position after puberty (Tanner, 1970).

Development of the Sex Organs.   Boys are sometimes self-conscious about the size of their sex organs. A large penis and a hairy chest are sometimes considered signs of great sexual potency in our culture (Verinis and Roll, 1970). For a

4. *True or False:*
If a boy is tall compared with his peers prior to puberty, chances are he will be comparably tall following puberty.

TABLE 14.4   **Maturation in Boys**

Although there may be some individual—and perfectly normal—variations in the sequence of events leading to physical and sexual maturity in boys, the following sequence is typical:

1. Testes and scrotum begin to increase in size.
2. Pubic hair begins to appear.
3. Adolescent growth spurt starts; the penis begins to enlarge.
4. Voice deepens as the larynx grows.
5. Hair begins to appear under the arms and on the upper lip.
6. Sperm production increases, and nocturnal emission (ejaculation of semen during sleep) may occur.
7. Growth spurt reaches peak rate; pubic hair becomes pigmented.
8. Prostate gland enlarges.
9. Sperm production becomes sufficient for fertility; growth rate decreases.
10. Physical strength reaches a peak.

Source: J. J. Conger and A. C. Petersen, 1984.

ACTION/
REACTION

Why Am I So Short?

Lou has always been short. Usually he is the shortest person in his class. But it never seemed to bother him too much until he got to eighth grade. He is now definitely the shortest person in the entire grade, and even most of the seventh-graders are taller than he is. Lou had hoped that the growth spurt his parents had promised would come would at least make his height "respectable," but it doesn't seem to be working out that way.

Lou's parents thought that he was only going through a stage so they ignored his pining about his height. After all, what could be done anyway? Both Lou's parents are small. About four years ago they took him to a growth clinic, at his insistence, but the doctors there told them nothing was wrong.

Lately, Lou has been sullen and angry. He is acting the part of the big man with his friends, often suggesting antisocial acts such as knocking over mailboxes and throwing stones. He is also acting out in class, making little unnecessary remarks about his teachers. His older brother, a high school senior who is also relatively short, has a good relationship with Lou but doesn't seem to know what to do. Lou's parents were called to the school last week, only to be told that Lou cut twice to play video games with his friends at the shopping mall. His parents are concerned.

1. If you were Lou's parents, what would you do?

---

variety of reasons, this is incorrect. First, there are greater differences between nonerect penises than erect ones. Second, the size of one's organs has little if anything to do with the sexual satisfaction of either partner in a relationship (Shope, 1975). It is sometimes reassuring for boys to have such information.

Shaving with a Deeper Voice. The most noticeable changes in boys are the appearance of facial and underarm hair and a deepening of the voice. Shaving is a sign of growth and maturation, and a young adolescent may argue with his parents that he must shave to look neat. Later, he may grow a beard or a mustache as a sign of masculinity. The red badge of courage, the inevitable Band-Aid proving that he must shave, is often found in junior high schools.

Changes in voice are more obvious in males than in females. The all-state tenor walks in after a summer's vacation to find that his voice cracks and breaks. He may be embarrassed by its quality, but he can take solace in the fact that this too shall pass.

Acne

One change that hits both males and females hard during adolescence is acne. Watch any television program beamed at young teenagers and you are almost guaranteed to see commercials about teenage skin problems. The sebaceous glands become enlarged and can easily become infected or blocked, causing irritation of the skin and the acne condition. The condition is encouraged by the presence of various male hormones, making the problem a bit more serious in males than in females. Teenagers with severe cases require medical attention. While there is no guarantee that medical treatment will alleviate the condition, it may keep it from getting worse. These teens may also feel that they are at least doing something about it. The advent of acne at a time when teens often feel that people are constantly observing them and evaluating their appearance and actions can cause many anxious moments.

The Secular Trend: Taller, Earlier, and Heavier

In the last 100 years or so, each new generation has been taller and heavier than the preceding one. In addition, each new generation has entered puberty at a slightly earlier age. These developmental tendencies, known collectively as the **secular trend,** have been the focus of much research. The trend is unmistakable. Since 1900, children have been growing taller at the rate of approximately one centimeter and heavier by half a kilogram (1.1 pounds) each decade (Katchadourian, 1977).

    Menstruation is also occurring at an earlier age as shown in Figure 14.2. In Norway in the 1840s, the average age was 17; in 1950 it was 13 years, 4 months. In Germany in 1860 it was 16 years, 6 months; in 1935 it was 13 years, 5 months. Generally, among European populations the age of menarche has decreased over the past century from a range of 15 to 17 years to 12 to 14 years today (Roche, 1979). There is some evidence that these trends are either leveling off or stopping in the United States (Frisch and Revelle, 1970).

    How can we explain the secular trend, and why is it leveling off in some countries? Most scientists argue that improved health, nutrition, and improvements in the environment encourage earlier maturation and increased growth. Specifically, a decline in growth-retarding illnesses during the first five years of life, improved vitamin intake, and better medical care (Krogman, 1980) promote growth and maturation. The leveling off may indicate that there are limits to how much these factors can affect the onset of puberty and course of the physical changes that occur during puberty.

What Causes Puberty?

Although we do not yet understand exactly what triggers puberty, three structures are thought to be primarily responsible. These are the hypothalamus (a part of the brain), the pituitary gland, and the gonads, or sex organs—the testes in males and the ovaries in females (Sommer, 1978). The hypothalamus produces chemicals known as "releasing factors" into the bloodstream. These factors are carried to the pituitary gland, stimulating it to produce substances called gonadotropins, which stimulate the gonads. The gonads then produce the sex hormones that cause changes in the body (see Figure 14.3) (Sommer, 1978).

    The level of hormones in the body is kept in balance. During childhood, the level of gonadotropins is quite low, but for some reason in later childhood the secretion of these hormones increases. The gonads grow and produce more sex

5. *True or False:*
The tendency for each new generation to become taller and heavier than the previous one is accelerating in the United States.

secular trend
The trend toward earlier maturation today, compared with past generations.

hormones. The hypothalamus is sensitive to sex hormones circulating in the body. As the amount of sex hormones increases, the output of the hypothalamus' releasing factors decreases, thereby reducing the pituitary's output of gonadoptropins and regulating the amount of sex hormones in the body.

FIGURE 14.2 **Average Age of Menstruation in Selected Countries (1840–1980)**
The average age at which an adolescent female begins to menstruate has decreased noticeably over the past hundred years.

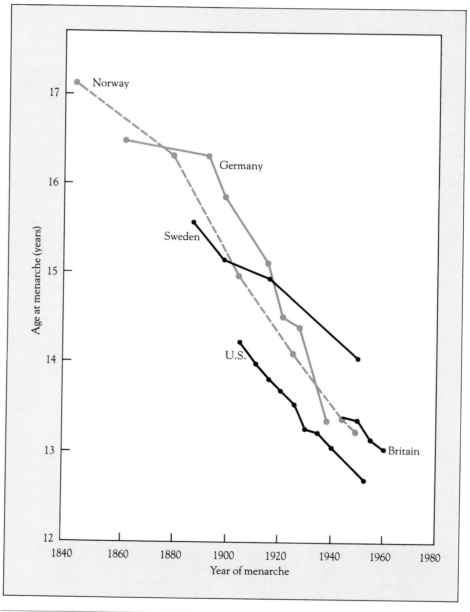

Source: Adapted from J. M. Tanner, 1968.

FIGURE 14.3   **Observable Effects of Sex Hormones**

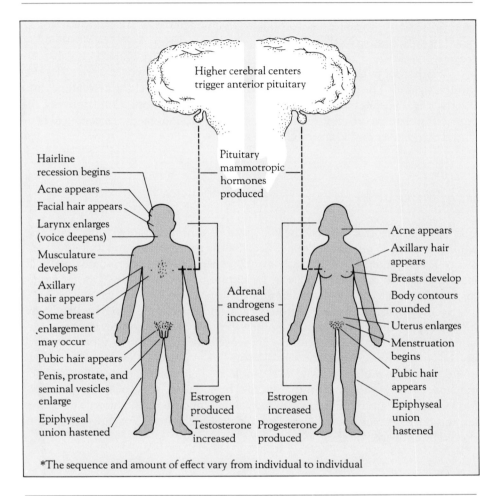

Source: L. C. Jensen, 1985.

Just why these changes are triggered by the hypothalamus remains a question. Scientists now believe that during childhood the hypothalamus is extremely sensitive to the amount of sex hormones secreted. As puberty approaches, however, the central nervous system matures and becomes less sensitive to the hormone levels, causing the hormones to appear in greater concentrations (Chumlea, 1982).

The changes that take place during adolescence, then, are largely determined by hormones. One group of such hormones are the sex hormones. Scientists use the term **androgens** to refer to the group of male hormones including testosterone, and **estrogens** to denote a group of female hormones including es-

androgens
A group of male hormones including testosterone.

estrogens
A group of female hormones including estradiol.

tradiol (Kalat, 1980). Although both males and females produce both sets of hormones, females produce more estrogens and males produce more androgens. During adolescence, the sex hormones are secreted into the bloodstream in great quantity. The androgens cause secondary sex characteristics, such as lower voice, beard growth, and growth of hair on the chest, underarms, and pubic area. Estrogens encourage breast development and broadening of the hips (Kalat, 1980).

Another set of hormones affecting metabolism and growth is secreted by the pituitary gland. The growth hormone is produced in cycles rising and falling during the day. Recent evidence shows that the growth hormone alone does not directly stimulate growth but requires the action of somatomedin, a chemical produced by the liver and kidneys (Chumlea, 1982).

EARLY AND LATE MATURATION

Can you imagine what it would be like to see all your friends physically maturing while you seem to remain childlike? Because the age at which any individual enters or leaves puberty varies greatly from one person to another, some teens will mature early, while others must wait for nature to take its course. Does the timing of puberty affect the personality and self-concept of adolescents?

Studies focusing on the question of early and late maturation have produced interesting results. Before launching into a review of them, however, some caution is required. Most of the studies concerned with the timing of puberty looked at teens who were very early or considerably late in physical development and ignored the entire middle group. Most people are neither very early nor very late, but hover somewhere around the middle. In addition, most of the studies performed used longitudinal data collected at the University of California at Berkeley and have been criticized for methodological problems. Thus, any conclusion should be tempered by these cautions.

Early and Late Maturation in Males

6. *True or False:*
Early-maturing boys have a social advantage during adolescence.

Early-maturing males seem to have a substantial social advantage over late maturers. Jones and Bayley (1950) studied a group of early- and late-maturing boys from Oakland, California. Adults rated the early maturers more positively than the late maturers. Early-maturing boys were considered more masculine, more attractive, and better groomed. Late maturers were considered tense and childish and were seen as always seeking attention. Peers saw them as bossy, restless, less attractive, and having less leadership ability.

A follow-up study found that these later maturers were viewed as more rejecting, rebellious, and dependent, as measured by a projective personality test administered later in their teens (Mussen and Jones, 1957). The fact that they were both more rebellious and dependent demonstrates a basic conflict in their personalities.

In another study, Weatherley (1964) investigated 234 male and 202 female college students' personality traits and their recollections of their physical development. The results for his male sample were similar to those obtained in earlier studies. Late-maturing males of college age had not yet resolved their basic conflicts from childhood, tended to seek both attention and affection, and did not gain positions of dominance or leadership. They were also more rebellious. The late maturer psychologically separates himself from both his parents and his peers. Weatherley also found that early- and average-maturing boys were very similar in personality structure. This might mean that early maturation itself may not be the benefit it has been thought to be. Rather, it may be the lack of late maturation that has been measured in previous studies.

The problems of the late maturer last. Jones (1957) found that differences between early- and late-maturing boys continued into their thirties. The late maturers were less settled, less self-controlled, still more rebellious, and had a lower self-concept. Not all the findings were negative, however, as late maturers were also more assertive and insightful. In addition, when looking at these early and late maturers at about age forty, the differences diminished greatly, and some personality advantages in favor of late maturers were found. The early maturers were more conforming and rigid, whereas the late maturers were more flexible and again insightful (Jones, 1965).

Other studies have also hinted at some advantages for the late maturer. Peskin (1973, 1967) found that early maturers became less active, more submissive, and less curious as they matured. Whereas the early maturing boy may have a social advantage, the later maturer was superior in some intellectual areas. In another study, Ames (1957) again found that early maturers had more personal and social success but were not as happy in their marriages as later maturers. Peskin notes that the problems that seemed to arise in early maturers in middle age—namely, inflexibility and being very conforming—were present even in adolescence.

To summarize, early-maturing boys seem to have a social advantage during adolescence and early adulthood, but their personalities are more rigid and prevent personal growth in the middle years. In addition, the late maturers who had to master the social problems of adolescence may begin to show the advantages of solving early problems.

Early and Late Maturation in Females

The effects of early and late maturation in adolescent girls is less clear. Some studies do find early maturation in females advantageous. Weatherley (1964) found late-maturing girls more likely to suffer from anxiety. Peskin (1973) argues that early-maturing girls were better adjusted in young adulthood as measured at the age of about thirty. However, a number of studies do not find any advantages for early-maturing females (Jones and Mussen, 1958; Jones, 1949). Some evidence even indicates disadvantages for the early maturer. Staffieri (1972) found that early-maturing girls are not considered attractive because they were fatter, whereas later maturers were thinner and judged more conventionally attractive.

In an attempt to make sense out of this material, Faust (1960) suggests that whether the physical changes take place in elementary or junior high school might make a difference. Early-developing girls in elementary school receive fewer positive comments, but the situation is reversed in junior high school, where the early-developing female receives more positive feedback.

7. *True or False:*
Early-maturing adolescent girls have a clear social advantage during adolescence which lasts well into early and middle adulthood.

In summary, the evidence is mixed regarding the effects of early and late maturation in females. The differences that do exist seem to be less important and more transient than those found in males.

THE ADOLESCENT'S BODY IMAGE

A picture many of us hold of the adolescent is a teen standing in front of the bathroom mirror forever trying on new looks and styles. Just about every television situation comedy has a scene in which the entire family is waiting for the teenager to leave the bathroom after just having broken the "total time spent in the bathroom" contest. Yet behind this comedy lies something deeper. Teenagers' bodies are changing so fast that they must make allowances. Although some teens cope very well with these changes, many are not completely at home in their new bodies. Many want to change aspects of their physical selves, mostly their height, weight, and complexion (Burns, 1979). The combination of peer pressure and media advertising encourages them to try to change what can be changed to meet some stereotyped, socially approved image. It may take time for them to become comfortable with their bodies and accept those elements, such as height, that cannot be changed. During these years, parents sometimes forget what it was like to experience these changes and lose patience.

Attaining a positive physical self-image takes time and experimentation. Some parents want to disassociate themselves from the way their teenagers wear their hair or clothing. They may shake their heads at the way teenagers hold themselves or walk or talk. By experimenting with different styles and mannerisms, the teen creates a physical image and style in keeping with that of the peer group. As the adolescent matures, a compromise in physical appearance is often struck, and a positive body image is attained.

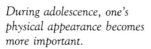

During adolescence, one's physical appearance becomes more important.

When the adolescent has attained a positive physical identity, the self-concept and self-esteem improve (Jourard, 1980). Physical attractiveness in females and muscular physiques in males are related to positive self-concepts (Lerner, et al., 1974). Failure to attain a physical image in keeping with what is valued by the peer group and subculture affects the teen adversely. For instance, Lerner and Korn (1972), in an investigation of body-build stereotypes among males, found that athletic, muscular males normally developed a positive self-concept, while overweight males often suffered from a negative self-concept. Obese teens also have more difficulty developing a coherent identity (Shestowsky, 1983).

People who are ashamed of their bodies lack self-confidence, and then the self-fulfilling prophecy may operate. They may expect people to react negatively to them, which causes them to act in a socially inappropriate manner, which in turn leads to peer rejection. This rejection validates a teen's thoughts about himself or herself. For example, overweight teens may not be able to dress fashionably or attend social functions. This can lead to peer rejection and cause them to rationalize that they were right all the time. Sometimes the fear of rejection itself is sufficient to discourage a teen from attending some social function or trying out for a school team.

NUTRITION AND EATING PROBLEMS

Since teens are so concerned with body image, it stands to reason that eating would be a major concern. The diets of many teens are deficient (Whitney and Hamilton, 1984; Miller, 1980), and severe dieting is a common but often ineffective way to lose weight. Eating disorders are not uncommon. In one study of 2,004 high school students, about 2 percent of the sample were found to suffer from disordered eating, including binging, purging, and feeling that they cannot control their eating (Kagan and Squires, 1984). Although obesity is the most talked about problem, other eating disorders, including anorexia nervosa and bulimia, are also serious concerns.

Obesity

About 15 percent of all Americans under thirty are obese (Hamilton and Whitney, 1979). This figure includes about 10 million teens (Zakus et al., 1979). Those who are 10 percent over chart weight are considered overweight, and those who are 20 percent over are considered obese (Lerner and Spanier, 1980). Obesity is not solely dependent on weight. Body build and age should also be taken into account. It is more than a medical problem, because obese individuals often have negative body images and poor self-concepts. Obesity creates a social problem for the teen. Because our society's view of beauty and attractiveness is equated with being thin, the obese person is out of step with current fashion.

There is no single reason for obesity. As one expert in the area notes, "The onset and degree of overweight are determined by a combination of genetic, metabolic, psychological and environmental events" (Rodin, 1981, p. 370).

Obese children become obese teens, and obese teens become obese adults. Obese teens with a history of overweight have a 28 to 1 chance of becoming and

8. *True or False:*
Obese teens usually become obese adults.

There is a significant concern about the diets of adolescents.

remaining obese adults (Zakus et al., 1979). But people may become obese at any age. Parental supervision of eating habits during the teen years usually wanes as the adolescent gains personal freedom. Social and academic pressure during adolescence may lead to increased caloric intake (Hubble et al., 1969). Many students use food to quiet their anxiety, and the less physically active life many older teens lead runs counter to the active life some led in childhood.

There is no easy cure for obesity. Certainly nutritional information is needed because teens eat an enormous amount of junk food and their diet is often rich in starch but deficient in basic nutrients (Miller, 1980). However, not everyone appreciates or accepts such information. Schafer (1979) found a relationship between self-concept, choice of diet, and acceptance of nutritional information. Women with positive self-concepts both chose better diets and were more influenced by nutritional information than women with poor self-concepts. It is often difficult to get obese people, who generally have poor self-concepts, to accept nutritional information and to change their eating patterns.

Popular diets for teens include crash dieting, semi-starvation, and fad diets. Some diets can cause physical damage, especially kidney damage, and are ineffective in the long run. They may also rob the body of the nutrients necessary for healthy development.

Perhaps a combination of increased physical activity under a doctor's care, nutritional information, reduction in the consumption of junk food, and psychological support provided by the peer group and family members can help the obese teen lose weight and keep it off. It is often easier to prevent obesity than to cure it. But some modest success in weight reduction has been reported for a program, that included nutritional information, the identification of behaviors contributing to obesity, and the alteration of these behaviors as well as an increase in physical activity (Brandt et al., 1980). However, long-term weight loss is difficult, and the battle against fat is a lifelong process.

Anorexia Nervosa

Another eating problem is **anorexia nervosa,** which literally means loss of appetite (Wenar, 1982). However, the name is misleading. It is a disorder marked by self-imposed starvation. It involves an abnormal fear of becoming obese, a disturbance of body image, significant weight loss, and refusal to maintain even a minimal normal body weight (American Psychiatric Association, 1980). Anorexics often have an appetite but are proud of being able to hold out against their hunger. It is one of the few psychological problems that can be fatal. The mortality rate lies between 15 and 21 percent (Halmi, 1978). The overwhelming number of anorexic sufferers are female—about 96 percent (Halmi, 1978)—and the onset of the condition is typically between the ages of twelve and eighteen. These adolescents usually show little overt rebellion toward their parents and suffer deep conflict on the dependent-independent dimension. Anorexics are often raised in educated, success-oriented, middle-class families that are quite weight-conscious. They are also perfectionistic (Whitney and Hamilton, 1984) and are described as model children (Smart et al., 1976).

Once the anorexic has achieved significant weight loss, she does not stop, but continues until she is too slim. Losing weight becomes an obsession. She is afraid she will be out of control if she eats a normal diet, and her weight becomes the controlling passion in her life. Changes in her physiology, thinking, and personality show. Her condition becomes serious as her body begins to waste away. She ceases to menstruate, becomes ill and anemic, cannot sleep, and suffers from low blood pressure, and her metabolism rate decreases (Bruch, 1978).

Anorexics misperceive their own body weight, often claiming that they are fat or about to become so. Development of anorexia nervosa can be divided into three phases (Casper and Davis, 1977). In phase one, the teen shows an increasing concern about her physical appearance, emphasizing her weight. She is afraid of becoming fat and enters phase two, in which the anorexia becomes noticeable. In this phase, anorexics feel a satisfaction at their weight loss and develop a fear of eating. They often use distractions to keep themselves from eating, perhaps by becoming physically active. They exist on a very low calorie diet and water and deny that they have any problem. Parents become alarmed by the continuous weight loss and refusal to eat. Sometimes anorexics concentrate their attention on one or two foods to the exclusion of all others. In phase three, the adolescent begins to admit the problem but remains anxious that she will gain weight if she stops the regimen. She fears losing control and not being able to stop eating. Hospitalization is sometimes necessary to reverse this condition.

Anorexia is not rare. About 1 in 250 female adolescents suffers from the condition (American Psychiatric Association, 1980). The treatment is varied. The first priority is to stabilize and begin the process of increasing body weight to a normal level. This may be accomplished through a behavioral or learning theory approach (Bemis, 1978). Consider the case of a thirty-seven-year-old woman who had been steadily losing weight for more than fifteen years (Bachrach et al., 1965). She was hospitalized and put in a bare room without pictures, chairs, a radio, or any normal comforts. Her social contacts were sharply restricted. All the sources of pleasure for her—magazines, television-viewing, and visits from friends—were used as rewards for eating. For example, only if she ate was she permitted to watch television. At first, just eating was reinforced, but as the treatment progressed she had to show some weight gain before being rewarded. By the time that treatments stopped, she had gained more than 40 pounds.

anorexia nervosa
A condition of self-imposed starvation most often found among adolescent females.

9. *True or False:*
More than 90 percent of the sufferers of anorexia nervosa, a condition marked by self-starvation, are female.

Anorexia nervosa, a disorder in which the individual refuses to eat, is potentially life-threatening.

bulimia
An eating disorder marked by episodic binging and purging.

genital stage
The fourth and last psychosexual stage, occurring in adolescence, during which mature heterosexual behavior develops.

Individual and family therapy are often necessary as well. Some therapists base their approach on the belief that the anorexic teen is experiencing difficulty accepting the challenges of assuming an adult body image and role (Altrocchi, 1980). Other therapists advocate family therapy, which focuses on the relationships among family members and attempts to alter parental expectations. The combination of therapies can be successful.

Bulimia

Another serious eating disorder among teens involves periodic binging and then purging the system (Voget, 1985). **Bulimia** is a disorder that involves episodic binging often followed by induced vomiting. The sufferer is aware that her behavior is abnormal and is afraid of losing control over her eating. Depression and extreme self-criticism is common after the binging period. Often the food is sweet and easy to chew, highly caloric, and eaten very quickly (American Psychiatric Association, 1980). The binging may be preceded by a diet (Whitney and Hamilton, 1984).

Bulimics binge secretly. They stop their eating when they experience stomach pain, require sleep, are interrupted by someone, or induce their own vomiting. Just as in the case of anorexia, these teens have an obsession with their body image. The fluctuations in weight, however, are rarely extreme enough to be as life-threatening as they are in anorexia. Bulimics are concerned about pleasing men and being attractive and perfect.

The treatment for bulimia involves group therapy, in which bulimics gain the support of others to overcome their problems. They often need to be taught how to handle stress and to define femininity in a broader context (Rosenhan and Seligman, 1984).

ADOLESCENT SEXUALITY

Adolescents' reactions to the physical changes that occur depend on their own views of themselves as well as on the feedback they get from peers and parents. Coping with these changes is not easy, yet most adolescents manage fairly well, finally developing a reasonable view of their physical selves and accepting their newfound powers and abilities. These physical changes affect both behavior and interpersonal relationships. They raise new issues that require personal decisions. Nowhere is this clearer than in the area of sexuality.

During adolescence, adult sexuality asserts itself. Freud viewed the **genital stage** as a time in which the libido, hidden during the latency phase, reappears. The physical drives are strong and cannot easily be repressed. Therefore, adolescents turn their attention to heterosexual relationships (Freud, 1920).

The Revolution in Attitudes

Whether one accepts Freud's psychosexual theory or not, the importance of sexuality during adolescence is obvious. Yet only in the past twenty years or so has sexuality taken its place as an important aspect of personality. Sexuality has come into the open, social sanctions have lessened (Calderone, 1976), and our attitudes toward sexuality have changed.

> ## RESEARCH HIGHLIGHT   *The Ideal Male and the Ideal Female*
>
> What do early adolescents see as the ideal male or ideal female? The young teen is just experiencing the physical and social changes that encourage thinking about masculinity and femininity. Yet the beliefs of early adolescents in this area have rarely been investigated. John Curry and Robert Hock sought to rectify this situation.
>
> A measuring instrument designed to identify sexual stereotypes for the ideal male and the ideal female was administered to 65 junior high school students (33 males and 32 females) ages 12 years to 13 years 11 months. The results indicated that altruistic understanding, intelligence, leadership, emotional integration and expression, and independence were most important in their ratings of the "ideal male." Altruistic understanding is composed of such factors as kindness, understanding of others, having a strong personality, and being interested in one's appearance. Emotional integration includes such diverse factors as hiding emotions, being able to devote oneself to others, and gentleness. For females rating the ideal female, the most important factors were competent independence, emotional expression, altruistic understanding, and confidence.
>
> Although both sexes viewed altruistic understanding as descriptive of the "ideal male," girls rated it as more important than boys did. Only one trait, however, completely differentiated males' from females' ratings of the ideal male. Females viewed expression of tender feelings as masculine, males viewed that trait as feminine.
>
> Looking at the ratings for "ideal female," we find that the sexes differed in their ratings in the areas of altruistic understanding and emotional expression. Girls rated these two more important than boys did. However, girls also rated the competence and confidence factor, including such areas as not giving up easily, decision-making, leadership, and self-confidence,
>
> more important than boys did. Again, both sexes rated the "ideal female" as being competent and confident. However, girls saw these as much more descriptive of the "ideal female" than males did.
>
> A comparison of the ratings of both sexes shows that girls did not see differences in competency, including decision-making, leadership, and assertiveness, whereas boys did. The researchers suggest that early adolescent girls are accepting the change in societal norms on the competency dimension, viewing themselves just as competent as males. Adolescent females consider leadership and assertiveness descriptive of the "ideal female" to a greater extent than early adolescent boys do. Only in the narrow, traditional areas of aggressiveness, sensitivity, and empathy do girls admit to sex-role differences. Adolescent boys, on the other hand, see many more differences. They view the ideal male as being more confident, more competent in decision-making and leadership, less emotionally dependent, more assertive, and less affiliative than the ideal female. Adolescent girls are more in step with the changing status of females in our society than early adolescent males.
>
> This study shows that there are differences between how early adolescent boys and girls rate the ideal male and female, but it does not explain why. Are the differences between gender ratings due to maturational differences (females maturing before males), a male tendency to see more sex-role discriminations (fathers are often more concerned with sex differentiations in behavior than mothers), or some other factor? Whatever the reasons, changes in how society views the female role are having a substantial impact on the ideals of girls in early adolescence.
>
> *Source:* J. F. Curry and R. A. Hock, "Sex Differences in Sex Role Ideals in Early Adolescence," *Adolescence*, 1981, *16*, 779–789.

The traditional attitude concerning sexuality reflected the double standard. Boys were permitted sexual freedom, while girls were denied it. Males were encouraged to experiment, yet sanctions against female sexuality were great. The sexual needs of males were recognized, but females' needs were denied, even during marriage. The double standard has, at least to some degree, been reduced (Shope, 1975). Attitudinal differences between males and females have narrowed as illustrated by the results of a questionnaire given over the years to groups of college students and summarized in Figure 14.4.

FIGURE 14.4   The Drift Toward More Liberal Attitudes

Depicted below are the percentages of college students in 1965, 1970, 1975, and 1980 strongly agreeing with certain statements regarding the morality of premarital sexual relationships.

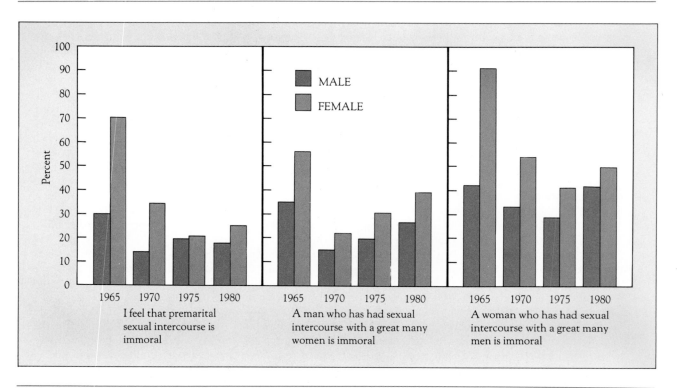

Source: Data from Robinson and Jedlicka, 1982.

The attitude change is in the direction of greater acceptance and a live-and-let-live orientation to sex. In a widely quoted nationwide survey of sexual attitudes, Sorenson (1973) found that adolescents did not believe that premarital sex, in and of itself, was right or wrong. As long as both partners were willing (force was unacceptable) and it occurred within an affectionate relationship, no negative sanctions were attached to it. Sorenson's report contains some 530 tables with data, and many of them are fascinating. When asked whether they agree or disagree with the statement "Anything two people want to do sexually, as long as they both want to do it and it doesn't hurt either one of them, is all right," 71 percent of the males and 66 percent of the females agreed. When faced with the statement "I wouldn't want to marry a girl who isn't a virgin at marriage," 30 percent of the males agreed, 5 percent weren't sure, and 65 percent disagreed.

The attitudes of adolescents are likely to be much more permissive than those of their parents. Whether parents were virgins at the time of their marriage is not the issue, for in many cases parents feel it is necessary to warn against conduct that some parents may have engaged in. As people enter a new role, their perspective changes. Often the recognition that they might have become pregnant or been emotionally hurt is now better understood in retrospect. Sorenson

(1973) noted that 72 percent of the young people in his sample believed their parents thought that sexual intercourse before marriage was immoral, while 12 percent thought their parents would like them to live with their prospective marriage partner before marrying. In addition, only 28 percent of the males and 44 percent of the females believed their attitudes toward sex were similiar to those of their parents. At the same time, adolescents respected their parents' ideas about sex even if they did not agree with them. Some 56 percent of the males and 75 percent of the females indicated they had a great deal of respect for their parents' ideas about sex.

The revolution in attitudes appears to have been greater for females than males, probably because women had more conservative attitudes to start with. Yet the idea that sex itself is taken casually or that the attitudes of males and females are identical is false. Females are still more conservative than males and are more likely to see sex as a part of a loving relationship. To about half the males and about two-thirds of the females in Sorenson's study, sex meant something more than mere physical enjoyment. When faced with the statement "I wouldn't want to have sex with a girl/boy unless she/he loved me," 44 percent of the males and 75 percent of the females agreed. A twist on the same statement, "I wouldn't want to have sex with a girl (boy) unless I loved her/him," found 47 percent of the males and 76 percent of the females agreeing. Females still have a more conservative attitude toward sexuality than males.

Yet casual sex is not viewed positively by the majority of adolescents. When asked whether it would be wrong to have sex with a girl or a guy they had just met and hadn't gotten to know, 51 percent of the males and 79 percent of the females agreed. In a study of adolescent sexual attitudes and behavior patterns in a middle-class sample, Chess and colleagues (1976) found a less fearful and more matter-of-fact attitude than found in the previous generation, and less moral conflict or guilt about sex. But sexual affairs were still not viewed as casual encounters.

Adolescent attitudes are much more liberal than their actual behavior. While their attitudes are tolerant of other people's sexuality, their personal stan-

10. *True or False:*
During the last twenty years, the sexual attitudes of females have changed much more than those of males.

11. *True or False:*
Adolescent sexual attitudes are more liberal than their actual behavior.

We live in a society that surrounds adolescents with sexual messages and innuendos.

dards are stricter. For example, Hass (1979) found that in a study of fifteen- to nineteen-year-old males and females, 95 percent of the males and 83 percent of the females approved of heavy petting such as genital touching, but only 55 percent of the males and 43 percent of the females had participated in such activities. As for sexual intercourse, 83 percent of the males and 64 percent of the females approved of it, while only 56 percent of the males and 44 percent of the females had participated in sexual intercourse.

Four conclusions are indicated by the data. First, adolescent sexual attitudes are quite tolerant. Second, male attitudes are still more liberal than female attitudes (although the gap may be narrowing). Third, sex is not seen as a casual act. And fourth, adolescents seem to be more conservative in their behavior than in their attitudes.

Sexual Behavior

If attitudes have changed quite a bit, what of actual rates of sexual behavior? A summary of the research evidence on the sexual behavior in adolescence is offered in Table 14.5.

TABLE 14.5   Sexual Behavior in Adolescence: A Tentative Summary
This summary is based upon a review of many studies performed by Diepold and Young (1979) which summarized three decades of data by looking at specific sexual behaviors. The following is an abridged summary of their main conclusions.

Behavior	Summary
Dating	There were no data reported in the 1940s or 1950s which dealt directly with adolescent dating practices. However, when the few studies reported during the 1970s are compared to the single study reported during the 1960s, an increase of only a few percentage points is found for both sexes. There is general agreement that almost all adolescents have participated in dating at least once by the time they are 18–19 years of age. By that age the cumulative percentages range from 77% to 100% and there is relatively little difference between males and females. What little data is available indicates that by age 14–15 roughly half of the adolescents have dated.
Kissing	From the studies in the 1970s it can be speculated that there has been a slight increase (approximately 10%) for males engaged in kissing since the 1940s. There is no data on females during the previous three decades but the 1970 data suggest that the onset of experience of females is practically identical to that of males. Heterosexual kissing by middle adolescence is a nearly universal phenomenon and there are few differences between males and females, blacks and whites. There is a suggestion that both black and white male homosexuals report a much lower percentage of heterosexual kissing than any other sample.
Petting	The act of petting has often been divided into "light" petting which is typically restricted to those activities above the waist and "heavy" petting which involves genital contact but not sexual intercourse. From age 16 to 19, no differences have been found in the amount of light petting reported by both sexes over the past 30 years. At age 14,

Behavior	Summary
Petting— continued	however, in more recent studies there is evidence to suggest that both males and females are beginning their involvement at an earlier age. This is especially evident for females who report an increase of approximately 40% over their 1940 counterparts. The overall data for the studies indicates that approximately 60% have engaged in light petting by the age of 15, whereas about half that percentage have been involved in heavy petting. By age 18–19 nearly 90% of the males and 80% of the females reported light petting. For heavy petting there are important but gradual increases over time in the reported experience for both sexes at each age level. At age 14, the 1970s male and female samples reported an increase over the 1940 samples of 68% and 83% respectively.
Masturbation	Overall there appears to be no marked changes in the reported practice of masturbation during the past 30 years for either sex. There is some suggestion, however, that more females are gradually beginning to engage in masturbation by age 18. The data indicate that almost all males have masturbated to orgasm during their teens. Even with the old myths surrounding the feared consequences of masturbation, e.g., acne, mental retardation, insanity, weak heart, etc., there appears to be little behavioral inhibition of this behavior. Nearly 80% of the males sampled have engaged in masturbation by age 14, with an increase throughout the later adolescent years to where 90–98% report the experience by age 18.
Pre-marital coitus	A great deal has been written during the past decade or so about a kind of "sexual revolution." While it may be true that attitudes and an openness to talk about sexual behaviors have occurred, there is little evidence of any sudden massive change in adolescent sexual behavior in terms of pre-marital coitus. The data indicate that while males have remained fairly stable, females have gradually increased their pre-marital involvement and have begun to close the gap between the sexes. . . . The 1970 studies indicate that male involvement has not markedly changed since the 1940 data. For females, however, there has been a gradual and significant increase in reported pre-marital coitus over the past 30 years. By age 19, the 1940 data indicated that more males engaged in premarital coitus at a ratio better than 3:1 over the females. In the 1970s, however, the females are 1:1 with the males from age 16 on up. At age 15, the 1970 data show a 500% increase in engagement compared to their 1940 counterparts, and a 300% increment at age 18. For both sexes, the incidence of pre-marital coitus doubled between the ages of 17 and 18. (Diepold and Young 1979, 49–63)

Source: L. C. Jensen, 1985.

Masturbation.   The most common type of sexual experience for adolescents is masturbation. Society seems to accept masturbation as a sexual activity for males more than it accepts it for females (Wagner, 1980). Most authorities believe that virtually every male has masturbated to orgasm in his teens (Diepold and Young, 1979; Hunt, 1974). Hass (1979) reports that four-fifths of the males he sampled had masturbated to orgasm by the age of fifteen or sixteen. There is no reason to believe that masturbation is physically harmful, but a disturbing sense of guilt still permeates the experience. Sorenson (1973) found that 32 percent of his subjects who reported masturbating felt some guilt and another 17 percent often experienced guilt. Religious condemnations account for some of the guilt, as do some strange beliefs. Rumors that masturbation leads to sterility, lower intelligence scores, hair growing on palms and a number of physical disturbances abound. Some people believe that, the number of ejaculations or orgasms any male can experience is sharply limited and suppress masturbation for this reason.

Evidence indicates that a lower percentage of teenage girls masturbate (Diepold and Young, 1979). Kinsey found that 20 percent of his sample masturbated to organism by age fifteen and 33 percent by nineteen years (Kinsey and Gebhard, 1953), as against 85 percent of males in his sample by age fifteen and 92 percent by age nineteen (Kinsey et al., 1948). Hass (1979) reported that 50 percent of the females in his sample had masturbated by age fifteen or sixteen. In a study of college women, Gagnon and Simon (1969) found that two-thirds had reported masturbating, about double Kinsey's total. If an increase in masturbation among women has occurred, it may be due to the increasing emphasis today on the recognition of female sexuality itself. On the other hand, women may simply be more honest in their approach to sexuality or feel less of a need to hide it from researchers.

Sexual Intercourse.   When people speak of the sexual revolution, they are usually referring to what they see as the tremendous increase in sexual intercourse. Has there been a revolution in sexual behavior?

After reviewing a number of studies on the subject, Dreyer (1982) notes that between 1925 and 1973 the percentage of high school girls reporting premarital sex tripled from 10 percent to 35 percent, and the rate for college females rose from 25 percent to 65 percent. Recent studies show that approximately 44 percent of the high school females and 74 percent of the college women reported engaging in premarital sex. For males the rates have risen, but since the initial rates were higher, the rise is not as dramatic. In 1925, about 25 percent of the high school boys and 55 percent of the college men reported having premarital sex. Today, about 56 percent of the high school men and 74 percent of the college men report experiencing sex. The most recent studies indicate that high school males are more likely to be sexually active than high school females, but that the virginity rates among college men and women are almost the same (Dreyer, 1982). Zelnik and Kantner (1977) conducted studies of adolescent sexuality in both 1971 and 1976 and found an increase even in this five-year period. The percentage of females between the ages of fifteen and nineteen experiencing sex increased from 26.8 percent in the 1971 study to 34.9 percent in the 1976 study. In another study, the average age for the first sexual experience was fifteen years seven months in males and sixteen years two months in females (Zelnik and Shah, 1983).

The increase in premarital sexuality is now accepted by most researchers. However, whether one wants to call this a revolution or an evolution depends on one's personal point of view. Certainly, the change in attitudes has been more radical than the change in behavior (Lerner and Spanier, 1980).

Yet the picture of adolescent sexuality is not one of rampant promiscuity. In Hass' (1979) study, one-fifth of the sexually active boys and almost half the girls age fifteen to nineteen reported having sex with only one partner. In Zelnik and Kantner's (1977) study, only about 10 percent of the subjects reported having sex with more than one partner, and only about half had had intercourse within a month of being interviewed. Less than 30 percent had engaged in sex as often as three times a month, and 15 percent had experienced it only once.

Some explain increasing rates of sexual intercourse in terms of its more open coverage by the media, the reduction of sanctions against premarital sex, the movement toward women's equality, the increase in availability of birth control and abortion, earlier maturation, and the faster pace of our society. Whatever the reasons, sex will probably remain an issue, if not always a very openly discussed issue, between parents and adolescents.

Teenage Pregnancy

One of the paradoxes that abound in our society's treatment of sexuality is that as the sexual information and birth control methods available to teens have proliferated, the number of teenage pregnancies has also increased to a point where teenage pregnancy is now considered a very significant problem.

When sixteen-year-old-Nadine found out she was pregnant, she didn't know what to do. She tried to hide it but couldn't. Her mother cried, and her father yelled at her and only wanted the name of the boy. Although a number of her friends were engaging in sexual relations, Nadine told them, "I just got caught." She had thought of the possibility that she might get pregnant but dismissed it. The subject had never come up in the conversations between Nadine and her boyfriend, Brian. She is now faced with a number of problems, as is seventeen-

Teenage pregnancy is a national problem. More than 1 million teenagers become pregnant each year.

The trend is toward young mothers keeping and raising their babies, perhaps with the help of their parents.

year-old Brian. They can marry or not. She can bear the child, turn it over for adoption, or make some agreement with her parents about raising her child. She can abort. Nadine is confused, and since she is now in her fourth month of pregnancy, she has a time limit. She is overwhelmed.

The Trend.   Nadine and Brian are not alone. The statistics are staggering. One in five fourteen-year-old girls today will become pregnant before reaching the age of eighteen. Most of these pregnancies will occur within six months of becoming sexually active (Ooms, 1981; Jones and Placek, 1981). Over one million teenagers become pregnant each year (Allgeier and Allgeier, 1984). The odds are quite high that a second pregnancy will occur within the subsequent three years. In fact, in one study, one half of the pregnant teens became pregnant again within three years (Furstenberg, 1979). Women who are poor or very young are the most likely to become pregnant again. The number of early pregnancies may be a surprise. However, of the eight million thirteen- and fourteen-year-olds in the United States, one and a half million are believed to have experienced sexual intercourse (Guttmacher Institute, 1976). The figures on pregnancies for females under thirteen years of age are fragmentary, but the evidence indicates that these pregnancies are also becoming more common. It is estimated that of the million fifteen- to nineteen-year-old girls who were pregnant in 1974, 59 percent carried to term, 27 percent had abortions and 14 percent had miscarriages. Teen mothers are also keeping their babies—a fairly recent trend. Ninety-five percent of the teen mothers are keeping their infants (Connoly, 1978). Pregnancy figures in the United States are higher than most other industrial nations and many developing ones. The United States ranks fourth highest with fifty-eight births per thousand females aged fifteen to nineteen versus the low of Japan's five per hundred thousand.

The Consequences   The consequences of adolescent pregnancies are serious for the entire family. If the pregnant teen decides to get married, the odds against a successful marriage are great. The rates of separation and divorce are much greater among couples where the woman was pregnant at the time of the marriage than among couples where she was not pregnant (Kelly, 1982). Teenage marriages are generally less stable, and if the extra stress of pregnancy is added, the potential for discord increases. Whether there is a marriage or not, an adolescent pregnancy affects the future of everyone concerned—baby, mother, father, and grandparents.

The baby.   Infants born to teenage mothers have more health problems than the average infant. They have a 30 percent greater risk of dying before their first birthday, compared with babies of mothers between the age of twenty and twenty-four years (Foster and Miller, 1980). Babies born to teenagers have lower birth weights, are more often premature, and have a greater chance of having a birth defect. These problems are caused by poor nutrition, drugs, and lack of prenatal care. Although there may be some problems due simply to the immaturity of the childbearing system in some very young females, many of these problems are not inevitable. But ignorance, denial and other psychological factors combine to prevent the pregnant adolescent from seeking out the best care for herself and her infant during the crucial prenatal period. As we have seen in other chapters, the rates of child abuse are higher in young families, as is the chance that living circumstances will be inadequate and at the poverty level.

The mother.   Pregnancy is the most common reason that female students drop out of school. Somewhere between 50 percent and 66 percent of female dropouts claim pregnancy as the reason for failure to finish school (Guttmacher Institute, 1976). Some 80 percent of pregnant women who become mothers at seventeen or younger never finish high school. The younger a woman is when she bears her first child, the fewer the years of education she will receive (Moore and Waite, 1977). At ages twenty-three and twenty-nine, mothers who had babies when they were teenagers have lower incomes and hold lower-prestige jobs than their classmates, and also express less satisfaction with their jobs. They often suffer from depression and experience a conflict between independence from and submission to their parents, who helped them through the trying time (Zougher, 1977).

Perhaps the most quoted study in this area was performed at a Baltimore hospital by Furstenberg (1981, 1976). He interviewed 350 pregnant adolescents and followed them for six years, comparing them with a control group who were not pregnant. The results indicated that pregnant teens were much more likely to marry before the age of eighteen and that 60 percent of those marriages ended within six years. The pregnant group averaged two fewer years of schooling, and half these pregnant teens became pregnant again within three years: In the pregnant sample, Furstenberg also found that parent and child had been unable to communicate directly about sexual matters.

Although there were problems attached to early pregnancy, some women adapted well to the challenge. Successful coping was related to the amount of support provided by their families (Furstenberg, 1981). Many of the pregnant subjects expressed regret at their past, and some did succeed in picking up the pieces and achieving.

The father.   Not much has been written about the father of the out-of-wedlock child. As Connolly (1978, p. 40) notes,

> The unmarried father has been a shadow figure cloaked in a fog of prejudice and misinformation. It has been the young pregnant girl who has held center stage, literally taking the rap for pregnancy, since Nathaniel Hawthorne's *Scarlet Letter.* It has been she who has received the uneasy mixture of concern, moral outrage and medical, social and education services. Notice, for example, how the expression "unwed mother" settles easily, while "unwed father" jolts one's expectations and priorities. The burden of parentage has rarely shifted beyond identifying the father and grilling the mother.

Little information concerning the adolescent father is available. We are usually most interested in identifying him and forcing him to accept his legal responsibilities, not in finding out more about him.

The stereotype of the adolescent father as uncaring, uninterested, and immature is often inaccurate. One study of young fathers found that they are more similar to adolescents who had not fathered a child than they are different (Earls and Siegel, 1980). The profiles of the unwed father that do exist show that he is frightened, withdrawn, confused, and often feels guilty about his girlfriend (Barret and Robinson, 1981), but out of fear he may not come forward. In one study, about 95 percent of young fathers expressed a willingness to attend counseling sessions if offered the opportunity (Hendricks, 1980).

There are many variations on the triangle of father, mother, and mother's family. At times, the girl's parents do not permit the father to visit her or the

12. *True or False:*
The most common reason female students drop out of school is lack of achievement motivation and any goal in life.

child. At other times, an attempt is made to increase the ties of the father to his child by giving the child the father's name (Furstenberg and Talvitie, 1980). This is somewhat effective, as research shows that when this occurs mother and child are more likely to have regular contact and to receive financial support from him. It is impossible to generalize about the future relationships between father and child because there are so many variables involved and the information available is so limited.

The consequences of early parenthood can be severe for the father too. Both mothers and fathers are educationally retarded, and it is an uphill climb to succeed in the world of work (Card and Wise, 1978). Often they are found in dead-end jobs. They also may not have the maturity necessary to handle the situation, whether they get married or not.

The extended family.   Most parents are shocked to learn that their unwed daughter is pregnant (Furstenberg, 1976). Teens who seek abortions do not normally consult their parents, but those who carry their pregnancies to term almost always do (Fox, 1981). When the decision is made to bear the child, a definite progression is seen. First, there is anger and disappointment. This is followed by a stage of gradual acceptance and a growing closeness between mother and daughter. The quality of the relationship between the pregnant teen and her parents during the pregnancy determines what will happen after the birth. If the bond is close, marriage is much less likely to occur, and young mothers frequently stay with their parents (Furstenberg, 1981). Most young mothers will stay if their mother signals a desire to help them. In fact, young mothers who are helped by their parents, especially until the child is attending school, are in a better economic position than others who leave to be on their own. Grandmothers provide much of the care in these situations (Forbush, 1981). Many young mothers who return to school are better off years later. Furstenberg cautions that these benefits should not be overstated. Many parents of unwed mothers stated that they would not be so charitable if a second pregnancy occurred (which it often did), and sometimes, as the child matured, a deterioration in family relationships took place. Mother remains in a subordinate position because she is dependent on her family. Even considering these problems, though, it is clear that the young parents need help. Whether they live at home or marry, or whether the new mother tries to make it on her own, the young parent needs counseling and support from the time the pregnancy begins through the prenatal period and delivery and into the early years of parenthood. Since subsequent pregnancies are common, sex education is also required.

Why the Increase?   But why in an atmosphere in which sexual information appears to be plentiful and contraception is readily available has there been an increase in teenage pregnancies? The accepted reasons for teenage pregnancies have changed over the years. In the 1920s it was bad company and immorality; in the 1930s it was poverty and broken homes; in the 1940s the emphasis was on psychological factors. The sick society and delinquent behavior was blamed in the 1950s, and in the 1960s too. In the 1970s and 1980s, however, researchers explain the increase in pregnancies by referring to a combination of factors: the lower age of sexual maturity, the fact that teens begin their sexual experiences earlier, the increase in premarital sex, and the loosening of sanctions against premarital sex (Foster and Miller, 1980). However, these factors do not explain why teenagers do not use contraceptive devices and teenagers' appalling lack of sexual knowledge.

Contraceptive Use

Just as in every other area of sexuality, we see paradoxes in contraceptive use as well. Some 61 percent of the adolescents questioned in Sorenson's (1973) study believed that people are more casual about sex because birth control is easily available. Yet statistics show that contraceptives are not used by a large percentage of the teens engaging in sexual intercourse. Zelnik and Kantner (1977) report that only 30 percent of their sample always used contraception, 45 percent sometimes used some method of preventing pregnancy, and 25 percent reported never having used any method of contraception at all. Younger teens are less likely to use contraception than older teens, and it is also usually left up to the male. In 1978, an estimated 8.4 million women were either unintentionally pregnant or ran a great risk of becoming pregnant, either because they used no contraception or because they used an ineffective method. This included more than 40 percent of the sexually active teens (Dryfoos, 1982). In one startling study, Zabin (1979) found that the majority of teens do not look for any contraceptive assistance until they have been sexually active for about a year. This is distressing, because so many pregnancies occur during the first six months after teens begin engaging in intercourse. Only about 45 percent of sexually active teens use any contraceptive technique during their first intercourse, and most have had intercourse at least once without protection (Dreyer, 1982). Although some increases in contraceptive use during the late 1970s and the early 1980s may have occurred (scientifically valid studies are absent), these increases are not significant. We can conclude that many teens are experimenting with sex and not protecting themselves against pregnancy. Why?

Reasons for Not Using Contraceptives.   Many teens simply do not consider the possibility of becoming pregnant, and if they do it is only a passing thought. A full 40 percent of the females in Sorenson's (1973) study stated that sometimes they do not really care whether they get pregnant or not. Asked "Do you ever worry about the possibility that you might become pregnant?" 16 percent of the nonvirgin girls said "Never," 14 percent said "Hardly ever," 41 percent said "Sometimes," and 29 percent said "Often." When Sorenson asked the nonvirgin males whether they ever worry about the possibility of causing a girl to become pregnant, 18 percent said "Never," 6 percent said "Hardly ever," 48 percent said "Sometimes," and 28 percent said "Often." Some 25 percent of the males also stated that they always trusted to luck that the girl would not become pregnant. It is clear that pregnancy is not a prime concern of either the male adolescent or the female adolescent.

Contraceptive use increases with age (Kantner and Zelnik, 1972), and the use of an oral contraceptive increases in steady relationships and in marriage (Luker, 1975). There are a number of reasons why so many teens do not use birth control methods. Luker (1975) found that many did not believe they could get pregnant and that some were afraid of using an oral contraceptive; a number noted that they were not involved in a continuous love relationship. The fact that contraception must be planned and that planned sex seems to lose its romantic quality and its spontaneity may also be one reason for the sporadic use of contraceptives (Reichelt, 1976). Oskamp and Mindick (1981) argue that viewing

13. *True or False:*
Contraceptive use decreases with age.

oneself as not sexually active, having an external locus of control (believing that luck and chance determine your fate rather than your own actions), not having a future orientation, ignorance, and fear of contraceptives are all involved. In summarizing the results of many studies, Dreyer (1982) argues that the most prominent reason is the denial that one is sexually active. The adolescent may not be mature enough to accept the fact that he or she is engaging in intercourse. The first encounter is rationalized as an accident, a moment of passion, or a chance event.

Sex Education

If you ever want to start a great debate in your community, just bring up the topic of sex education at a school board meeting. You're sure to get a variety of opinions forcefully presented. Some will claim that sex education is a necessary response to the consequences of teenage sexuality. Others will claim that it is the parents' job to explain the facts of life to their children and that the schools should stay out of it. Still others will state with conviction that if you do not dwell on sex, children will forget about it, while a small minority still see sex education as a Communist plot to encourage teenage immorality.

The majority of people have had no formal sex education from either teachers or parents; they learned about sex from their peers (DeLora et al., 1981). Most parents do favor sex education in the schools (Shope, 1975), but the controversial question is what to teach. Most parents want their own values taught (Libby, 1970). Once you get past the biological aspects of sexuality, the questions of contraception and values arise. Some parents do not want contraception taught or birth control devices made available to students, although most do (Rinck et al., 1983). Other parents are afraid that the teacher will encourage sexuality or teach values that are different from those "taught" at home. All in all, sex education is a difficult area.

Most people agree that sex education in the broadest sense ought to take place within the home and a possible sex education program that parents can use with their adolescents is outlined in Table 14.6. Yet parents do not often talk to their children about contraception, morals, or ethics, or help them learn decision-making skills. Rather, the information given is often in the form of an explicit warning: "Don't do it."

What should be taught and how the information should be presented are formidable questions. Of course, students need the biological information. Only 40 percent of Kanter and Zelnick's (1972) sample had any idea when there was the greatest risk of pregnancy. The majority thought it was during their menstrual period, and many thought they could not become pregnant easily. Every so often a columnist publishes examples of teenagers' beliefs about sex and pregnancy—including such ideas as if certain positions are used or the second time a couple has intercourse in a night the girl cannot become pregnant. However, sex education goes beyond biological information. Most adolescents want to discuss values and the meaning of sexuality.

Just what can a sex education program accomplish? Any program that is based on the ideas that it relieves parents and the religious establishment of responsibility for education about values, that it will either lessen promiscuity or stimulate sexual play, that it will automatically reduce venereal disease and preg-

TABLE 14.6   **Sex Education During Adolescence**
This table shows one suggestion for a sex education program that parents can use. However, sex education does not begin in adolescence. It begins early in childhood.

Early Adolescence

Developmental Stages of Children's Understanding	Concepts That Parents Can Teach	Suggested Ways To Teach
Age 11–15		
1. Increased interest in the body and in relating a person's body to such things as popularity, athletic skill, and attraction to opposite sex	1. Teach about the changes that occur in puberty (i.e., menstruation, rapid growth that can be related to poor coordination, widening of shoulders and narrowing of hips for boys, widening of hips for girls, enlargement of breasts for both boys and girls, development of body hair under arms, in pubic area, and on boys' face and arms)	1. Obtain good reading and other information to use with your family (elementary schools will have a good filmstrip)
2. Increased awareness of physical changes and comparing themselves with others. They notice voice change, breast development, height, and hair on the body		2. Reinforce changes in children as positive by paying positive attention to their growth (e.g., "you sure have broad shoulders")
3. Increased self-consciousness about appearance and ability to relate how they look to other things, such as others' respect and social values	2. Teach that good looks do not make a good person and one must develop good values, standards of personal conduct, and modesty	3. Create teaching times during which children are told how puberty affects boys and girls
4. More importance is given to opinions of peers	3. Teach social skills (e.g., how to make friends, how to talk with others, and achievement) so that popularity can be achieved on some basis other than physical attraction	4. Share some of your own experiences with puberty and its changes
5. Children experience strong sexual desire for the first time	4. Teach that individuals go through puberty at different rates—some early, some later, some rapidly, some slowly	5. Initiate numerous conversations to ensure development of positive attitudes about the body, social success, and personal standards
6. Children can mentally see the logic behind reasons; they perceive cause and effect relationships	5. Teach how hormones change in the menstrual cycle and how they increase and decrease sexual desire	6. Frequently ask what ideas your children have about themselves

Late Adolescence

Age 15–18		
1. Children can observe how they relate to others	1. Teach relationship of sex as a commitment to another person in marriage	1. Share personal experiences showing correct choice
2. Reasons and ideas must appear logical to be accepted	2. Reinforce that too much sexual involvement too early cheapens and can ruin the companionship	2. Ask children to tell you their decisions about premarital sex
3. Perceived ability to make their choices is necessary for development of personal values. Attempts to force ideas will evoke resistance	3. Teach that physical attractiveness used to increase popularity will achieve temporary results. Personality and social skills will result in more permanent success	3. Emphasize positive affection, sex, and relationships with others
4. Social success increases in importance, especially attention from the opposite sex. Personal esteem is closely tied to feelings of being socially successful	4. Explain how to hold expressions of intimacy within appropriate limits according to the state of responsible and legal commitment	4. Express confidence, support, and love
5. Children require abundant positive emotional support from parents	5. Convey that well-managed sexual desire is a major part of preparing for success in marriage	5. Avoid critical comments about their looks, choices, or actions. Instead, focus on desirable things you want them to do
6. Although children can understand correct principles, most have difficulty acting according to what they believe		

Source: L. C. Jensen, 1985.

14. *True or False:*
Exposure to sex education in
the schools reduces the
probability of sexual
experimentation.

nancies, or that it will prevent ill-advised marriages is unrealistic (Dale and Chamis, in Scales, 1981). Rather, the purpose should be to "equip young people with the skills, knowledge and attitudes that will enable them to make intelligent choices and decisions" (Scales, 1981, p. 220). The decision itself as to whether to have sex, does not appear to be influenced by sex education. However, there is evidence that sexually active young women who have been exposed to sex education courses are less likely to become pregnant (Zelnik and Kim, 1982). In summary, sex education is likely to continue to be a controversial topic, but the need for it remains great.

Lessons from the Present

In any discussion of sexuality, it is difficult to steer a middle course. On one side there is the seeming freedom and tolerance so noticeable in today's media. The old idea of sex as inherently sinful is not accepted any more, and it is now well established that sex plays a significant part in life, both before and after adolescence. This side views the sexual activities of adolescents as a natural outgrowth of the age, something that implies less hypocrisy and more openness and honesty. The opposing side sees only the problems involved in sexual activity—not only the "immorality" but also the teenage pregnancy, the venereal disease, the lack of adequate information, and the problems of abortion, adoption, or rearing a child and early marriage. These people advocate injunctions against sex, but they have no program to counter these problems except to say "Don't do it"—a strategy that is ineffective. A middle line seems most appropriate. Teenage sexuality is a fact of life, and teens must be helped to make responsible decisions. Today, some teens may be under pressure to experience sexual intercourse in much the same way that years ago the opposite was true. Help in decision-making skills

ACTION/
REACTION

But I Know It All Anyway

Parents often find telling their children about the facts of life difficult. Mr. and Mrs. Adams found it impossible. Every time they tried to talk to their fifteen-year-old son, Ray, about it, he looked bored and said, "I know all that." Yet Ray's parents aren't so sure.

They became very concerned when one of Ray's friends became pregnant. They held their breath, hoping Ray wasn't the father, and thankfully he wasn't. But they are not certain Ray knows as much as he thinks he does. This suspicion was heightened when his older sister told them Ray had made a few comments about the male and female anatomy that were factually incorrect.

One problem Mr. and Mrs. Adams have is finding a way how to tell Ray about the facts of life. They find the subject difficult to talk about. Their parents didn't tell them much. They learned from "the street." They think things are different now and that they should do their best. But how?

1. If you were Ray's parents, how would you proceed?

and in value clarification, as well as a knowledge of basic sexuality and contraception, is necessary. Parents cannot abdicate their responsibility in the values area, for no sex education program can take the place of the parents' input.

The physical changes that take place in adolescence in the areas of body image and sexuality are important. During adolescence, however, cognitive changes are also occurring, and these affect how teens cope with the physical changes they are experiencing and make decisions in a variety of areas, including sexuality. It is to these changes in cognitive development that we now turn.

Chapter Summary

1. *Puberty* refers to the physiological changes leading to sexual maturity, while *adolescence* refers to the individual's psychological experiences during this period of life.

2. The sequence of physical development during adolescence is predictable, although the ages at which they occur vary from individual to individual.

3. Females normally experience their growth spurt before males. After the growth spurt, the genital organs and breasts develop. After these changes, menstruation occurs.

4. In males, pubic, body, and facial hair appear after the growth spurt. At about the same time, the sexual organs mature. Deepening of the voice and enlargement of the shoulders occurs later.

5. The fact that each new generation for the past hundred years or so has been taller and heavier and menstruated earlier than the previous one is known as the secular trend. It is leveling off or even stopping in the United States.

6. Early maturation in males is a social advantage during adolescence and early adulthood. However, in middle adulthood early maturers are less flexible and insightful. The effects of early and late maturation in females is unclear.

7. Nutrition and eating disorders are not uncommon in adolescents. Obesity is a major medical and social problem. Anorexia nervosa, a disorder involving self-imposed starvation, can be fatal. Another eating disorder, bulimia, involves binging and purging.

8. Adolescent attitudes toward sexuality are more liberal than in the past. Females are still more conservative than males, although the gap is narrowing.

9. Adolescents are more conservative in behavior than their attitudes would indicate. However, there has been an increase in premarital sex over the past fifty years.

10. Teen pregnancy is a widespread problem for everyone concerned, including the infant, mother, father, and the extended family. Infants born to teenage mothers have more health problems. Teenage mothers are more likely to drop out of school. Teenage fathers are often found in dead-end jobs.

11. Contraceptive use increases with age. Many teens either do not use any contraceptive device or use an ineffective method because they deny their sexuality, do not believe they can become pregnant, or are ignorant of the biological facts of life.

12. Studies show that exposure to sex education courses does not affect the decision as to whether to engage in premarital sex. However, sexually active girls who have taken a sex education course are less likely to become pregnant. Sex education courses do not relieve the home of its responsibility in this area.

■ *Answers to True or False Questions*

1. *False.* Correct statement: The general sequence is quite predictable, although the age at which any particular change occurs varies with the individual.

2. *False.* Correct statement: Menstruation is actually one of the later changes in puberty.

3. *True.* Girls experience their growth spurt before boys, which makes them taller and heavier at this age.

4. *True.* If he was tall compared with his peers before the growth spurt, he will probably recover his position afterward.

5. *False.* Correct statement: The tendency in the United States for each generation to be taller and heavier is slowing or perhaps even stopping.

6. *True.* Although new research shows early maturation to be a mixed blessing, there is a social advantage during adolescence.

7. *False.* Correct statement: The results of research on early and late maturation in females is mixed.

8. *True.* Obese teens normally become obese adults.

9. *True.* About 96 percent of all anorexics are female.

10. *True.* Female sexual attitudes have changed more than those of males, probably because they were more conservative to begin with.

11. *True.* Most studies find that adolescent behavior is more conservative than their attitudes.

12. *False.* Correct statement: Pregnancy is the number-one reason females drop out of school.

13. *False.* Correct statement: Contraceptive use actually increases with age.

14. *False.* Correct statement: Although it does reduce the probability that sexually active females will become pregnant, it does not prevent early sexual experimentation.

CHAPTER FIFTEEN

Cognitive Development in Adolescence

■ *Are the Following Statements True or False?*

Try the True-False Quiz below. See if your answers correspond to the information in this chapter. Each question is repeated opposite the paragraph in which the answer can be found. The True-False Answer Box at the end of the chapter lists complete answers.

____ **1.** The ability to interpret proverbs or political cartoons develops during adolescence.

____ **2.** Not all adolescents or adults show reasoning at Piaget's highest stage, that of formal operations.

____ **3.** People from non-Western cultures usually do better on tests of formal operations than adolescents from Western cultures.

____ **4.** One hallmark of adolescent cognitive growth is adolescents' ability to differentiate their own thoughts from those of others.

____ **5.** Adolescents believe that what they are experiencing in life is unique and different from everyone else's experiences.

____ **6.** The values of today's adolescents are similar to those held by their parents.

____ **7.** In high school, females generally show a decline in academic achievement, while males show an improvement.

____ **8.** Adolescent women show lower achievement motivation than adolescent men.

____ **9.** The earlier one makes a commitment to a career path, the better.

____ **10.** Vocational interest inventories tell the test-taker what careers should be considered.

____ **11.** The percentage of women doctors in the United States more than doubled in the decade between 1971 and 1981.

____ **12.** As a rule, school counselors are less stereotyped in their views of women and work than the females they counsel.

____ **13.** Middle-class youngsters tend to think that their lives are governed by chance and outside factors, whereas lower-income youngsters believe they are in charge of their own lives.

AT THE DEMONSTRATION

I leaned on the police barricade, watching the demonstrators. I had seen many demonstrations before, and they were all similar. The fervor and conviction of demonstrators always impressed me. Television reporters were busy interviewing one demonstrator. On the evening news they would call him a leader, even though he had not been elected as such. They were a diverse lot, most in their late adolescence.

The man standing next to me shouted, "Why don't you go to work, you bums?" I straightened up. The police looked at him—and at me. Some of the demonstrators looked up, but didn't respond. I had seen confrontations start over much less. I wanted to move away, but the man next to me motioned to the police indicating he would keep quiet. "What's wrong with them?" he asked me. "Nothing. Why?" was my reply. He shook his head. "What happens to them when they hit adolescence? What disease do they catch that makes them so difficult, so pigheaded? They don't listen any more." I just looked at him, waiting. "What do they know?" the stranger continued. "They're idealistic," I replied. The rest of my words were drowned out by the sounds coming from the loudspeaker that were too garbled for me to hear, but they ended with a loud ". . ., and no compromise." "Sure," said the stranger, "they have their ideals, but they don't have the experience to go along with them."

With that he left, and I never saw him again. However, I have heard many adults express similar opinions. People often have difficulty understanding adolescent reasoning and coping with the resulting behaviors. They pine for the good old days, when their children listened to them without challenging their explanations. This chapter will investigate the adolescent's emerging cognitive abilities and look at the development of reasoning, ideals, morals, and values in adolescence. It is hoped that some light will be shed on some of the questions stated or implied in my brief interaction with the stranger at the demonstration.

THE STAGE OF FORMAL OPERATIONS

formal operational stage
The last Piagetian stage of cognitive development, in which a person develops the ability to deal with abstractions and reason in a scientific manner.

Between the ages of about eleven or twelve and fifteen, children enter the **formal operations stage** and develop some important abilities (Piaget, 1972; Inhelder and Piaget, 1958). As with all the other Piagetian abilities, these develop over time, and an adolescent may show one skill but not another at a particular point in development.

Combinational Logic

Give elementary school children a problem in which they must find all the possible alternatives. It may surprise you to find that they do not approach the task in a scientific manner. For example, Inhelder and Piaget (1958) presented subjects of varying ages with five jars of a colorless liquid and told them that some combination of two of these chemicals would yield a yellow liquid. Preschoolers who are in the preoperational stage simply poured one into another, making a mess, while children in the concrete stage of operations combined the liquids but showed no real strategy. Adolescents formed a strategy for combining the liquids and finally solved the problem.

You can easily test this yourself. Write a number on each of four cards, then ask children of varying ages to find all the combinations possible (Busse et al., 1974). Most elementary school children do not systematize their approach, but many adolescents do. This finding can be extended to other situations. Adolescents can give all the possible solutions to a particular problem. If asked why something might happen, they understand that there are many different motives behind behavior. If you ask adolescents to answer the question "Why didn't Justin do his homework?" you'll get a number of answers, some possible and many improbable. This demonstrates another similar skill—being able to divorce oneself from what is real.

Separating the Real from the Possible

"What if human beings were green?" Ask a child this question, and the youngster may insist that human beings are not green. But adolescents can accept a proposition and separate themselves from the real world (Ault, 1977). They can form hypotheses and test them out, which entails separating oneself from the real and considering the possible (McKinney et al., 1982). Adolescents can reflect on a verbal hypothesis, and its elements do not have to exist in real life.

The ability to do this affects behavior. Parents may have difficulty with adolescents who can and do suggest alternatives that may not be feasible or that parents simply do not like. The separation of what *is* from what *can* or *could be* allows the adolescent to begin to think about a better world. Their "why" questions are based on possibilities divorced from reality, and they are capable of suggesting other alternatives. But their lack of experience in the real world limits their ability to think some of these alternatives through.

Adolescents in the formal stage of cognitive development often develop ideals and can cogently argue political questions.

*ACTION/
REACTION*

If You Say Another Word or Ask Another Question—I'll Scream

Fifteen-year-old Patty Jordan had always been bright and verbal. Her parents delighted in her achievements, and Patty's teachers were always pleased with her performance. They still are, but Patty's parents can't take it any more.

If Mr. Jordan says something, you can count on Patty to disagree. If Mrs. Jordan asks Patty to do something, you can guarantee that there will be a long discussion and a number of why questions. Patty has become quite argumentative. Last week, when company came over for dinner, things became embarrassing. During a simple conversation about politics, Patty became enraged when a few of her facts were corrected, and she made a scene. She has also become hypercritical of everything, including her parents' religious convictions, railing against organized religion. At this point, the Jordans are concerned about Patty's ever-increasing argumentativeness and her new passion for privacy.

Patty spends hours on the telephone talking with friends. This the Jordans can understand, even though Patty doesn't seem to believe her parents were ever her age. But when they ask her to limit the telephone calls, she shoots back, "You don't have to, so why do I?" Her parents have gotten to the point that they simply say "Because I say so and it's my house," an answer based on their power as parents. This is not the reasoned approach they like, but they see no other alternative.

1. If you were Patty's parents, how would you handle the situation?

Using Abstractions

The ability adolescents have to separate themselves from the trappings of what is real stems partly from their newfound ability to create and use abstractions. Children in the stage of concrete operations have difficulty understanding political cartoons and adages such as "You can lead a horse to water, but you can't make him drink." They are still reality-bound and have difficulty with abstract thought. They may actually picture a horse being led to water. But adolescents develop an ability to interpret abstractions, allowing them to develop internal systems of overriding principles. They can now talk in terms of ideals and values. Freedom, liberty, justice, and other such concepts take on additional significance when they are separated from their situational meaning. As we shall see in another section, adolescents can now form their own values based on these overriding principles.

The ability to form and use abstractions also shows itself in the ability to succeed in some areas of mathematics. Seventh- and tenth-grade students were tested on both the acquisition and application of problems from various school subjects, including science and social studies. Both groups performed similarly on measures of acquisition, but the tenth-graders were superior on application that involves a higher level of abstract reasoning (Stone and Ausubel, 1969).

1. *True or False:*
The ability to interpret proverbs or political cartoons develops during adolescence.

Hypothetical-Deductive Reasoning

These emerging abilities allow the adolescent to engage in what Piaget called hypothetical-deductive reasoning. Basically, this is the ability to form a hypothesis, which then leads to certain logical deductions. Some of these may be untestable, such as "What if all humans were green?" while others may be capable of scientific investigation. This type of reasoning is necessary for scientific progress. No one has ever seen an atom, but the developments in atomic theory have greatly affected our lives (Pulaski, 1980).

The ability to (1) use combinational logic, (2) separate the real from the possible, (3) interpret abstractions, and (4) engage in hypothetical-deductive logic combine to allow adolescents to reason out problems on a higher level than they could during childhood. Adolescents are capable of accepting assumptions in the absence of physical evidence, developing hypotheses involving if-then thinking, testing out these hypotheses, and reevaluating them (Salkind, 1981). The thinking of adolescents is also more flexible, because they can consider a number of alternatives, weigh them, and then discard those that do not fit the situation. This ability to attack problems logically has great value in math and science, and in life generally.

Thinking About Thinking

Adolescents also develop the ability to think about thinking (Ault, 1977). Teens often think back on their own thought processes and consider one thought the object of another. This ability allows them to consider the development of their own concepts and ideas.

Adolescents progressing through the stage of formal operations, then, develop a number of impressive abilities. They can use abstractions, are not tied to concrete objects, can formulate hypotheses using if-then logic, consider their own thought processes, and generate a number of alternative solutions to a problem. With these newfound abilities, it is natural for adolescents to question, to consider what may be rather than what is, to look at their own system of beliefs, and to be concerned with abstract questions involving overriding principles. (See Research Highlight "Jumping to Conclusions" on page 574.)

FUNCTIONING AT THE FORMAL OPERATIONAL LEVEL

These abilities sound quite impressive, and they are. But not all adolescents, or even all adults, reason on this level (Neimark, 1982, 1975). Not everyone is able to separate the real from the possible, or formulate and test hypotheses in a scientific manner. Although older adolescents tend to be further along in using formal operational thinking, they do not use it on every problem where it would be appropriate. Martorano (1977) tested sixth-, eighth-, tenth-, and twelfth-graders on a battery of ten Piagetian tasks associated with formal operations. Although there was general improvement with age, even the oldest group did not use formal operational reasoning in attacking all ten tasks. Roberge and Flexer (1979) presented eighth-grade students (about fourteen years old) and adults (twenty-two to forty-eight years old) who were college graduates attending graduate school with tests measuring various aspects of formal operational thinking. Some

2. *True or False:*
Not all adolescents or adults show reasoning at Piaget's highest stage, that of formal operations.

RESEARCH HIGHLIGHT   *Jumping to Conclusions*

Suppose one hundred adolescents are told that a certain young boy steals hubcaps, and then a short time later are told that the same boy donates four hours a week to the local hospital reading to elderly patients? Which impression of the boy would remain with them? Most studies find that the primacy effect—the effect of being influenced by the first information received rather than waiting for other information—is strong. Most people, then, would form their opinion based mostly on the information they received first.

But the cognitive skills the listener uses, demonstrated by whether the listener is engaged in concrete or formal operational reasoning, might make a difference. Wendy Palmquist reasoned that, for people using concrete operational reasoning, reality is more important than possibility. Such people would expect later information to merely validate and extend earlier information and would not take all the logical possibilities into consideration. Such reasoners would immediately evaluate the first set of information without waiting for more data.

Formal operational reasoners, however, understand the various possibilities involved. They might be able to suspend judgment and wait until all the information is received. For them, the possibility that there might be conflicting information is dominant over the concrete information received earlier.

To test this hypothesis, Piagetian tests of formal operations were administered to sixty-eight eighth-graders. On the basis of their performance on these tests, subjects were considered either formal operational thinkers or concrete operational thinkers. Each subject was then called into a room and shown pictures of a boy performing a number of activities. Subjects were told to pay attention to the pictures because they would shortly be asked their opinion of the boy. The pictures showed a thirteen-year-old male either performing prosocial behaviors, such as

playing basketball with a younger child or helping a fallen bicycle rider, or antisocial behaviors, such as breaking a car antenna or shoplifting. The order of presentation was varied, so that some subjects saw the antisocial behaviors first while others viewed the prosocial behaviors first.

The findings demonstrated that formal operational thinkers were less taken in by the primacy effect. The concrete reasoners jumped to a conclusion based on the first information, showing the primacy effect. When asked to write a description after receiving the positive block of information followed by the all-negative information, they wrote highly positive evaluations. When presented with the negative information followed by the positive block, they wrote descriptions in very negative terms.

The formal operational reasoners did not follow this pattern. They waited and were unaffected by the order of presentation. The concrete thinkers based their conclusions on the early evidence and were seemingly incapable of waiting and watching, or realizing that conflicting evidence might be presented.

Concrete operational thinkers, then, jump to conclusions more quickly. At this point, we can only hypothesize that people reasoning at the formal or concrete operational levels might differ in their response to sales pitches or their ability to weigh evidence in a trial. Such possibilities require further investigation.

The differences between formal and concrete operational thinkers are not always obvious, but this study demonstrates that the differences can affect a person's judgment and evaluations of others, which in turn affect one's behavior.

Source: W. J. Palmquist, "Formal Operational Reasoning and the Primacy Effect of Impression Formation," *Developmental Psychology,* 1979, *15,* 185–189.

---

57 percent of the eighth-graders and 67 percent of the adults were considered formal operational in their approaches. Notice that neither one of the percentages approaches 100, although the use of formal operational thought increases with age. More adults than teens were considered to be operating on this level. Indeed, other studies show this improvement with age as well. In a study of sixth-grade girls, female college students, and older women, Tomlinson-Keasey (1974) found that 32 percent of the girls' responses, 67 percent of the college students' responses, and 54 percent of the older women's responses showed formal operational reasoning on a test of such skills. As is common in these studies, older

students do better than younger students, but when adults are used, they do better than younger teens but not as well as college students.

Factors Affecting the Use of Formal Operations

Why doesn't everyone show formal operational reasoning? Is it that some people do not have the ability, or does some other factor interfere with such high-level reasoning? Three explanations for this phenomenon have been advanced: (1) the competency-performance argument, (2) cultural differences, and (3) individual differences.

The Competency-Performance Argument

Many psychologists turn to the competency-performance argument for the answer (see pages 215–219). They say that some people have the competency (the necessary ability and skills) to succeed on a task but for one reason or another do not perform successfully (Flavell and Wohlwill, 1969). They fail because of fatigue, the structure of the problem, or a lack of experience with problems requiring such abilities. Danner and Day (1977) presented teenage subjects with tasks requiring formal operational reasoning. Originally, none were able to perform, but when taught how to deal with these problems, 85 percent of the thirteen-year-olds and 95 percent of the seventeen-year-olds showed formal operational reasoning. In another experiment, Kuhn and colleagues (1979) found that initially none of the preadolescents or young adults in their sample demonstrated formal operational reasoning when tackling problems. After being presented with problems requiring such reasoning for three months, however, their preadolescent sample made some modest gains, but the young adults improved tremendously. Perhaps the ability is present in the older group but for some reason does not show itself (Stone and Day, 1978).

Cross-cultural Differences

Evidence showing great cross-cultural differences in the attainment of formal operations has accumulated, but any cross-cultural comparisons must be made with extreme care. Such comparisons are complicated by the general characteristics of the environment, the appropriateness of the task, and the values of the society (Laboratory of Comparative Human Cognition, 1979). Studies of formal operations in non-Western cultures show that people in these cultures generally perform poorly when presented with Piagetian tasks (Dasen and Heron, 1981). It may be that Piaget's stage of formal operations is basically applicable only to adolescents in Western technological societies who are exposed to a great deal of formal education.

We can interpret these failures in two ways. First, the Piagetian tasks presented to these people may be inappropriate. Second, this type of reasoning may not be necessary for functioning in most societies. Piaget viewed it as the ultimate achievement, but it may be an ideal only in Western culture. We have little idea of what may constitute the ideal last stage of cognitive growth in some other societies.

Four points are important here. First, not all Western adults and adolescents function at this level (Ashton, 1975). Second, some adolescents function at this

3. *True or False:*
People from non-Western cultures usually do better on tests of formal operations than adolescents from Western cultures.

stage some of the time, using formal operational reasoning to solve some problems but not others. Third, cross-cultural studies show that this stage is not as universal as Piaget's other stages have been shown to be. This conclusion may be tempered if you believe that if a researcher changed the tests to make them more appropriate for people from these non-Western groups, they might then show this reasoning. Fourth, schooling seems to be an important variable in determining whether people reach the formal operational stage. Schooled non-Western adolescents do better on these tests than unschooled non-Western adolescents (Rogoff, 1980). Such evidence led Piaget (1972) to reevaluate this area of his theory. He recognized that education, vocational interests, and one's society and culture determine performance on tests of formal operations. Perhaps the environments necessary to progress from sensorimotor to preoperational to concrete operational thinking are basic and exist in the overwhelming majority of societies, but formal operational reasoning may require a more technological, structured environment. It requires a specific type of stimulation that perhaps is found most often at the upper levels of schooling. The nature of the environment may be more important in performing at this level than it is at earlier levels.

Individual Differences

Even within the same age-groups in Western societies, some students perform better on tasks requiring formal operations than others. Since people mature at different rates and are exposed to different challenges, individual differences in attaining formal operational skills should be expected. However, the evidence that not all adolescents or adults, even in Western society, use formal operational reasoning begs the question of why some do and others do not. A great deal of controversy exists here. For instance, some studies discovered sex differences in formal operational performance, with males generally being superior to females (Dale, 1970; Elkind, 1962), but other studies failed to find these differences (Overton and Meehan, 1982). Most studies have shown no relationship between intellectual ability (as long as it is within the normal range) and the development of formal operations (Kuhn, 1976). However, mentally retarded people do not develop these skills (Neimark, 1982). The evidence on the gifted is conflicting, with some studies showing them to be advanced in this area (Keating, 1975; Keating and Schaefer, 1975) and others failing to find this (Neimark, 1982). Socioeconomic status does not appear to be related to this ability either (Neimark, 1975). Students of lower socioeconomic status do receive formal schooling, and this probably is sufficient for at least the initial development of such skills. A positive finding concerns the relationship of cognitive style and the development of formal operations. Adolescents who use a more reflective style do better on tasks that measure formal operations than teens who use an impulsive cognitive style (Neimark, 1982).

The explanations as to why some develop these formal operational skills and others do not revolve around these three areas. First, one can claim that some adolescents are capable of these skills but that the tasks are not structured to bring out their performance. Second, cultural factors may affect these abilities. Third, personal characteristics and environmental factors can affect the development of formal operational thought. For example, we know that a certain degree of maturation is necessary and that cognitive style affects formal operational reasoning. We also recognize the importance of formal education and the presence of a stimulating environment that presents adolescents with problems requiring this approach.

FORMAL OPERATIONS AND BEHAVIOR

The development of formal operational thought makes advanced thinking in school possible, especially in social studies, science, and math, but it also explains many other aspects of adolescent thought and behavior.

Adolescent Egocentrism

When teaching at a junior high school some years ago, I received a strange note from a mother. All it said was to please call her that morning concerning her daughter Jennifer's absence from school the day before. Jennifer appeared to be well, but she was acting a bit shy. When I called her mother, I was surprised to learn that Jennifer had played hookey from school for the first time in her life. The reason? Jennifer had gone to the hairdresser and was not pleased with her new look. She refused to be seen, even though her mother said she looked fine. Her mother made certain Jennifer attended school the next day. Jennifer's evaluation of her new look was anything but positive, and she had imagined that every student in the class would be staring at her and evaluating her the same way she evaluated herself.

The concern of adolescents with their appearance is a hallmark of the teenage years, as is their tendency to imagine that everyone is looking at them when they walk into a room, evaluating their actions, and the like. These thought patterns are explained partly by the development of formal operational thought (Elkind and Bowen, 1979; Elkind, 1967). Adolescents can now think about thoughts—both their own and those of others, but they often fail to differentiate between what others are thinking and their own thoughts. Since teenagers are interested in their own appearance, they believe that *everyone* is interested in it and behaves accordingly. It is this reasoning that Elkind (1967) believes constitutes **adolescent egocentrism**. It leads to two other interesting phenomena: the imaginary audience and the personal fable.

The Imaginary Audience.   The phenomenon of the imaginary audience is illustrated by Jennifer's feelings about her appearance, which caused her to miss school. Jennifer anticipated the reactions of her classmates, but those anticipations were biased, because Jennifer was convinced that her classmates would see her the way she saw herself. Elkind argues that adolescents construct an **imaginary audience**, believing that they will be the focus of attention. Other people constitute the audience, but it is imaginary because most of the time the adolescent is not really the focus of attention.

The imaginary audience phenomenon can help us understand adolescents' self-consciousness and mania for privacy. The self-consciousness stems from the conviction that others are seeing and evaluating them in the same way that they see themselves. The mania for privacy may come either from what Elkind calls a "reluctance to reveal oneself" or from a reaction to being constantly scrutinized by others. Privacy is a vacation from evaluation.

Adolescents may seek privacy as a vacation from the feeling that everyone is evaluating them.

4. *True or False:*
One hallmark of adolescent cognitive growth is adolescents' ability to differentiate their own thoughts from those of others.

adolescent egocentrism
A difficulty, usually found in adolescence, involving failure to differentiate between what one is thinking and what others are considering.

imaginary audience
A term used to describe adolescents' belief that they are the focus of attention and being evaluated by everyone.

Adolescents, then, are deeply involved with how others will evaluate them. As they dress, act, and groom, they imagine how others will see them. Elkind notes that when the boy who combed his hair for hours and the girl who carefully applied makeup meet, both are more concerned with being observed than with being the observer.

The imaginary audience slowly disappears during later adolescence to a considerable extent. Teens begin to realize that people may not react to them the way they think. They also come to accept the fact that people are not as interested in them as they thought. However, another phenomenon caused by adolescent egocentrism lasts much longer—that of the personal fable.

The Personal Fable.   As noted, adolescents can reflect on their own thoughts and experiences. They come to believe that what they are thinking and experiencing is absolutely unique in the annals of human history. This belief that what they are experiencing and thinking is original, new, and special is known as the **personal fable**.

I can remember the parents of a ninth-grader in junior high school who were having a particularly difficult time with their son. He had fallen in love with a girl who did not know that he existed. The quality of his work had fallen, and he was confused. When his parents tried to talk to him, he answered, "You can't know how it feels." He was convinced that only he could suffer such feelings of unrequited love, of loneliness, of despair. Elkind notes that evidence of the personal fable is also found in the diaries of adolescents. The personal fable declines somewhat as the adolescent enters young adulthood, but it may never be completely extinguished.

personal fable
The adolescents' belief that their experiences are unique and original.

5. *True or False:*
Adolescents believe that what they are experiencing in life is unique and different from everyone else's experiences.

When two adolescents meet, they are often interested in how they are being evaluated by the other.

"You can't understand how it feels." Teenagers often feel they are the only ones ever to suffer rejection.

Adolescent Morality

The demonstrators described at the beginning of this chapter were idealistic and uncompromising. They were demonstrating against expulsion of a student convicted of a serious breach of university rules. They were certain they were right. They expressed themselves in terms of overriding principles instead of merely demonstrating against what they saw as a misapplication of the rules against one individual.

In Chapter Twelve, we looked at the development of morality, the sense of right and wrong. At that time, two particular strategies were noted. One looked at moral behavior and focused on the situational factors associated with such behaviors as helping others, lying, cheating, and giving to charity. The other tradition emphasized the development of moral reasoning, the way people make their decisions, and is best exemplified by the work of Lawrence Kohlberg (1969).

Cognitive Development and Moral Reasoning. Kohlberg argued that moral reasoning is related to cognitive growth and development. The upper stages of moral reasoning require more sophisticated cognitive abilities. If this is true, adolescents progressing from concrete to formal operations should show an increased ability to reason at higher levels. Indeed, research has demonstrated a correlation between cognitive level and moral reasoning (Carroll and Rest, 1982). Adolescents operating at the formal operations stage have the ability to reason at Kohlberg's higher stages. In one study, the intelligence and level of moral reasoning were found for thirty-three fifth-grade boys. The boys' peers were asked about their moral conduct, and a test of honesty was administered. The results? Not only were cognitive ability and level of moral reasoning related, but higher reasoners also demonstrated more resistance to temptation and were seen by their peers as more caring about the welfare of others (Harris et al., 1976).

A number of studies have demonstrated that moral reasoning correlates well with cognitive development (Langford and George, 1975; Tomlinson-Keasey and Keasey, 1974). The higher stages of moral reasoning require at least the beginnings of formal operations (Weiss, 1982).

Specific cognitive skills, such as the ability to take another's point of view, are also related to moral reasoning (Yussen, 1976). Moir (1974) presented eleven-year-old girls with tests of role-taking and moral reasoning. The ability to take another's role was related to the level of moral reasoning. The ability to put oneself in the position of another person is an important one. Adolescents are attempting to find their place in society, and some authorities argue that this requires an ability to see the world from different perspectives (Lerner and Shea, 1982).

The Higher Stages of Moral Reasoning.   Just what is the nature of these higher stages of moral reasoning? According to Kohlberg (1969), stage four involves reasoning that is oriented toward doing one's duty and maintaining the social order for its own sake. Stage five involves a contractual legalistic orientation that emphasizes not violating the rights of others and a respect for the welfare and majority will of others. Stage six is a more individualistic orientation in which decisions are made involving individual conscience and one's own principles. Adolescents who can deal with abstractions and understand possibilities are better able to reason at the higher levels of moral reasoning. Even if they have this ability, however, many adolescents do not function at this level. In fact, most people do not develop beyond stage four (Shaver and Strong, 1976).

Factors Affecting the Level of Moral Reasoning.   Why do some people use stage six reasoning while others do not? Perhaps the best way to understand this is to invoke the competency-performance argument. Cognitive advancement makes more sophisticated moral reasoning a possibility but does not assure it. Other factors may enter the picture. The content of the problem is one variable (Fischer, 1980), as are the consequences of the moral decision. When people are faced with a dilemma in which the personal consequences are great, they are likely to demonstrate lower-level moral thinking (Sobesky, 1983). Generally, when people are confronted with a problem, their cognitive skills form the upper limit of their abilities to reason, but the situation itself will affect the actual behavior.

The adolescent's moral reasoning cannot be neatly placed in one stage (Kohlberg, 1969). At times adolescents operate on a higher level, at other times they operate on a lower one (Holstein, 1976). Thus, moral reasoning may be inconsistently applied to various problems.

Moral Reasoning and Personal Background.   Are the backgrounds of moral reasoners in higher stages any different than the backgrounds of reasoners in lower stages? According to much research, the answer is yes. For instance, a test of moral reasoning was administered to five hundred University of California students. On the basis of the results from Kohlberg's scale, these students were categorized according to their predominant stage of moral reasoning. The researchers also obtained a number of background and personality measures for

According to the research, the reasons these adolescents are demonstrating may vary from individual to individual.

these students. Norma Haan and her colleagues (1968) found background and personality differences among principled reasoners (stages five and six), conventional reasoners (stages three and four) and preconventional reasoners (stages one and two). The principled reasoners were more likely to be on their own, to be politically active, and to support the protest movement. They belonged to more organizations and were active participants in group action. When asked to describe their own personality, they saw themselves as being idealistic and viewed the ideal man in society as being empathetic and altruistic. Principled women saw themselves as restless, altruistic, guilty, and doubting, and the ideal woman as rebellious and free.

The conventional reasoners were more conservative politically. Although, they approved of the protest movement, they were the least supportive of it. These reasoners were politically inactive and did not join many organizations. Their self-descriptions mirrored their traditional values. Men saw themselves as conventional, ambitious, sociable, practical, and orderly. Women saw themselves as ambitious and foresightful. Both men and women saw the ideal individual as one who had social skills and self-control.

Preconventional reasoners strongly supported the protest movement. While the men joined a moderate number of groups, the women joined a great number yet tended to be inactive. Both sexes viewed themselves as rebellious. The men's descriptions of themselves showed a complete lack of involvement with others. Their ideal person was aloof, stubborn, uncompromising, playful, and free. Women saw themselves as stubborn and aloof and viewed the ideal person as practical and stubborn.

The family backgrounds of these individuals were also different. Preconventional men experienced great conflict with their fathers. Conventional men showed little or no conflict, and those men in higher levels of moral reasoning showed moderate conflict. For women, some conflict with mothers was correlated with higher moral reasoning.

Moderate levels of conflict between child and the same sexed parent were related to higher moral reasoning. However, great levels of conflict were not. In addition, personality differences were present. The preconventional thinker tended to join the protesters to get something for themselves. Perhaps it was a way to show their rebelliousness. The conventional thinkers did not join the protest possibly due to their conservative values and respect for authority. The postconventional reasoners joined demonstrations for different reasons. They were interested in what they saw as an improvement to society.

The development of formal operations gives the adolescent the tools with which to solve a problem at the higher levels of moral reasoning. It does not mean that these tools will be used. All we can say is that formal operations are necessary but not sufficient for the development of higher moral reasoning processes. Many other factors, including personal qualities, family background and the characteristics of the situation, determine whether these abilities will be used.

Moral Reasoning and Prosocial Behavior.   Are high levels of moral reasoning related to more prosocial behavior? This is a very controversial question. Kohlberg answers yes (Kohlberg and Turiel, 1971), while others are skeptical (Wonderly and Kupfersmid, 1980). You may remember Milgram's (1968) famous study, in which he asked students to obey a researcher and deliver what they thought were painful shocks to an innocent subject whose only crime was answering a question incorrectly on a learning-memory test. No shocks were really delivered, but the "teachers" did not know this. The study was really one of obedience. Kohlberg and Turiel (1971) reported that 75 percent of the stage six subjects tested on Milgram's obedience tests did not comply, while only 13 percent of the subjects reasoning at the other moral stages refused to deliver the shocks. This sounds impressive, but notice that 25 percent of the stage six sample delivered the shocks. In addition, some studies have failed to find differences between the behavior of children reasoning in the upper stages and those in the lower stages (Wonderly and Kupfersmid, 1980). All we can say at this point is that there is a positive relationship between level of moral reasoning and behavior, but it has not been found in all studies, and even where it has been found, it is far from perfect.

ADOLESCENT VALUES

So far, we have noted that the development of formal operations is related to new cognitive abilities. The degree to which these abilities are used varies from person to person. Formal operational abilities also allow adolescents to discover their own values and to be guided by these values in their everyday activities. But what values do most adolescents hold, and have these changed over the years?

What Are Values?

Values are constructs that serve as internal guides for behavior (McKinney and Moore, 1982). They are beliefs that certain patterns of conduct or end states are better than others (Rokeach, 1973). To some extent, values are culturally determined. For example, many hunter/gathering societies require teamwork to survive. The values of cooperation and sharing are crucial. Obedience was a value greatly admired by the Pilgrims and the Puritans. Sometimes certain values seem strange to us. In the Soviet Union, the value of the state above the family is taught constantly. For example, during the forced agricultural collectivization of the 1930s, a young adolescent named Pavel Morozov informed on his father, who was storing grain against government policy. Pavel was soon killed by outraged townspeople for the act, but he is honored in Russia as a great hero, and his tomb is always kept neatly decked with flowers by schoolchildren. Pavel's story is told in Soviet schools as an example (Smith, 1976), but Pavel would not be viewed as a hero in the United States. Values, then, are culturally determined and may differ from society to society.

values
Constructs that serve as internal guides for behavior.

What Values Do Adolescents Have?

Bachman and Johnston (1979) conducted a poll of 17,000 high school students to find out what values American adolescents have. Over three-quarters of the students expressed the goal of having a good marriage and family life. Over two-thirds thought that having strong friendships was important. Only 16 percent of the college students and 19 percent of noncollege students thought having a great deal of money was as important, and only 4 percent of noncollege youth and 10 percent of college freshmen thought that being a community leader was important. Bachman and Johnston note that this generation adhered to conventional values of marriage, parenthood, friendships, and meaningful work above money. Their lack of community involvement is somewhat of a disappointment. However, their parents are probably in agreement with these values.

Factors Affecting Values

Values change with the times. Perhaps some of your grandparents were raised during the Great Depression of the 1930s. For such people, security tends to be most important. The 1960s were a time of social upheaval in the United States, involving civil rights and great changes in sexual attitudes. When adolescent values in the 1960s and 1970s are compared, some interesting trends appear (McKinney et al., 1977). In the late 1960s, students were more interested in social interpersonal morality. Values relating to one's relationship with society were most important. By 1975, however, the climate had changed, and students were more interested in personal achievement and less involved with society.

Age also affects values. Beech and Schoeppe (1974) administered a survey of values to students in the fifth, seventh, ninth, and eleventh grades. At all grades, the values of freedom, honesty, love, and a world at peace were ranked high by both males and females. However, the survey also found an increase in some values and a decrease in others. The older students valued a sense of accomplishment, self-respect, wisdom, ambition, and being broadminded and responsible. Certain values, such as cheerfulness, helpfulness, and obedience, decreased, which suggests that students were looking for their own values rather than merely following those of their parents. As students age, some of their values remain, others become more important, and some become less so.

Adolescent values, then, are neither identical with nor completely different from their parents' values. Each generation faces different tasks and experiences a different history, and each must adapt its values accordingly. For example, conservation of energy is a relatively new value in American society, as is concern for a clean environment. Not all value changes are negative (Kaplan and Stein, 1984). And many of the values adolescents hold are similar to those of their parents.

As formal operational abilities develop, early adolescents enter junior high school and continue through high school. Personal achievement values become more important, and future plans are formed. The choices become more important, and mistakes carry greater consequences. To a considerable extent, lives of the adolescents revolve around school experiences, and the experiences of males and females in secondary school differ.

6. *True or False:*
The values of today's adolescents are similar to those held by their parents.

GENDER AND ACHIEVEMENT IN HIGH SCHOOL

Adolescent girls and boys do not achieve identically in secondary schools, even though there are no significant differences in intelligence. In elementary school, girls do at least as well as boys, and perhaps better, but in high school their achievement slips. Even among very bright women, the number who get the training necessary to reach top levels of professional fields are few. In Terman's famous study of gifted children, about half the gifted men became professionals in high-status occupations, while only 11 percent of the women entered these careers, and those that did usually became teachers (Terman and Oden, 1959). These bright women married men who were very high achievers. Even today, the gap between males and females closes rapidly in high school, with males finally surpassing females in achievement, especially in science and math. In elementary school, girls do better and are perceived as better students than males (Bernard et al., 1981). Elementary school teachers value female competencies, and boys receive more punishment, but a drastic change occurs in secondary school: males begin to value school achievement more, and teachers value the sex-role competencies of males more highly (Bernard, 1979). In other words, in elementary school, females may be more comfortable and find that their noncompetitive, highly social, more obedient behavior brings them praise and is greatly valued by teachers, but in secondary school, males become more aware of their future and take school more seriously. Teachers begin to value the aggressiveness and competitiveness of males more, while the opposite is true for females.

7. *True or False:*
In high school, females generally show a decline in academic achievement, while males show an improvement.

Reasons for Differences in Achievement

The fact that males catch up and females decline in academic achievement does not tell us anything about why this is so. There are many theories, but few real facts. Women have an achievement orientation equal to that of men. They are also as persistent, and their general self-esteem is just as high (Richmond-Abbott, 1983). However, men and women sometimes value achievement in different areas. Women tend to see their achievement in terms of interpersonal competen-

8. *True or False:*
Adolescent women show lower achievement motivation than adolescent men.

cies and skills, while men look for achievement in the more objective, academic-oriented areas. Women do not expect to do as well as men in math and science, even though they may have done well previously (Richmond-Abbott, 1983).

Women's achievement motivation is different, not less. This may be a function of socialization practices. Competition and achievement in the world of work is deemphasized for females, while women are encouraged to take marriage and their future family into consideration. In addition, males do not like to compete with females, and women who do try to compete are often less popular (Williams, 1977). It is obvious that expectations are different for men and women in this age-group. Women may be discouraged from taking higher-level courses, such as physics or calculus, while males are expected to do so (Schaffer, 1981).

We are all probably aware of the scene in which someone tells a bright adolescent female that she should not bother taking an advanced math course because it's a waste of time. After all, what is she going to do with it anyway? This type of blatant sexism has been held up to public scrutiny and criticized, as it should be. But such statements are probably less common than the subtle communication of expectations. In many schools and homes today, females are not actively restricted from these areas, they are simply not encouraged to take such courses. Female career choices may be restricted by a number of factors, including the lack of available role models in the sciences, socialization practices that tend to run counter to achievement, and the encouragement of interpersonal competence over academic competence. Females do not have to be actively dissuaded from achieving. Lack of encouragement produces the same result.

In high school, attitudes toward specific subjects also change. Until about eighth grade, the types of math courses taken by males and females are just about the same. By eleventh grade, however, males take more advanced courses. Some

Why are there so few female students in advanced science and math courses? The answer may lie in society's expectations and the lack of encouragement many females receive from friends, family, and school.

claim that this mathematical superiority in adolescence can be attributed to better spatial perception, but this factor, even if important to some degree, could not account for the large differences in achievement in the sciences found in research studies. In one study, Sherman (1980) found that although boys' ability in this area increased slightly more than girls', the difference was not significant. However, male and female attitudes toward math were very different. Females considered math a province of males, and their attitudes were less positive toward it than those of their male peers. These differing expectations and attitudes contribute to the lack of female achievement in the sciences.

This restriction shows itself in the things males and females take into account when making a career choice in the early years of college. In an informal survey, I asked college students what factors were considered in their choice of a career. The standard factors, as you might expect, were interest, money, benefits, and the like. However, many women considered their future family responsibilities and the possibility that they would not have the time to devote to careers that required either great time commitment or commuting long distances. Men did not take such things into account when choosing their careers. Many women seem to have family responsibilities in mind when deciding on a career. Perhaps this understanding that their life plans differ from those of males is present even in high school when considering various vocational possibilities.

One last point is in order. In adolescence, boys do not suddenly become great scholars while females become failures. Rather, males as a group begin to surpass females, especially in the more technical subjects, and the number of underachieving females increases during adolescence (Schaffer, 1981).

Fear of Success

Matina Horner (1968) raised quite a stir when she noted that women feared that success was not in keeping with femininity. If women succeed, they face punishment rather than reward, because they may be rejected by society. Horner asked female college students to write a story about Anne, a top student in her medical school class. Males were asked to write a story about John, also a top medical student. Horner found that 65 percent of the women wrote stories showing that Anne was not happy with her success or had negative experiences. Only 10 percent of the men wrote stories indicating that such academic success led to negative consequences for John.

fear of success
A term used to describe the fear that success in nontraditional spheres of life reflect negatively on one's masculinity or femininity.

Newer research shows that **fear of success** can be found in men as well. In one study, while only 41 percent of the men indicated any fear of success for John in medical school, about 63 percent saw John as having problems if he entered nursing school (Cherry and Deaux, 1975). Some 50 percent of the women wrote fear-of-success stories for Anne in medical school, but only 13 percent wrote them for her in nursing school. Other studies have shown that fear of success is situational and depends on the field one enters (Feather, 1975). It may be that women fear succeeding in male-stereotyped occupations and vice versa (de Charms and Muir, 1978).

In addition, some studies also find fear of success for men entering male-oriented fields. In a repetition of Horner's study, Hoffman (1974) found approximately the same percentage of women fearing success, but over three-quarters of men also expressing such a fear. Perhaps these men had begun to question the value of putting achievement above everything else in life. Not all studies attempting to show fear of success have been able to do so (Zuckerman and Wheeler, 1975). In addition, some studies find that this is changing, especially among women whose mothers work. Gibbons and Kopelman (1977) found that, when asked to write a story about Anne, women whose mothers work had much less fear of success than daughters of nonworking mothers. Because more women are working than ever before, fear of success will probably decrease even further. Fear of success, then, can be found in both sexes when each is entering areas that they do not see as reflecting society's sex-role expectations for them. However, we can expect it to decrease generally among both sexes in the future.

CAREER CHOICE

Students begin thinking about their vocational futures long before high school begins. The process of vocational development starts in childhood as children observe the occupations around them and imagine themselves working in them (Super, 1953), but it is in high school that students begin to realize that a career decision is facing them. This decision is a vital part of forming an identity in adolescence.

The Importance of Career Choice

For many, choosing a vocation is difficult. A vocation determines not only how much money you will make but also your lifestyle (McIlroy, 1979). The average male will spend approximately 80,000 hours, or about 30 percent, of his total life at work (Miller, 1964). Because women are entering the full-time job market at an increasing rate, this figure has meaning for them too. In adolescence, career choice also complements newfound mental abilities, as students can now deal with such hypotheses as what if they do this or that, and plan for their future more constructively.

   The two most important factors in career choice are knowledge of oneself and of the job market. Knowing yourself includes understanding what you want in a job or career, and a realistic appraisal of your abilities and personal resources. Knowing the job market involves understanding the vocational alternatives and the requirements for entry-level positions.

Factors in Making a Career Choice

What causes someone to decide to become a teacher or an auto mechanic? Personal characteristics enter into the decision, and intellectual ability and achievement in high school have an effect on vocational choice too. The student who cannot pass chemistry would probably not go into chemical engineering, nor would someone with two left feet decide to be a dancer. On the other hand, there is a relatively large span of intelligence levels found in most careers. Cronbach (1970) found that although accountants are generally more highly intelligent than miners, some miners are brighter than some accountants. Although general relationships hold, the relationship between intelligence and vocational choice should not be overemphasized.

Hawkeye Pierce, on the popular television show "M*A*S*H*," always wanted to be a doctor and made his career choice very early in life. What would have happened if he had not been accepted by a medical school?

9. *True or False:*
The earlier one makes a commitment to a career path, the better.

Personal experiences are also factors. Suppose your father truly dislikes his job and comes home every night disheartened and consumed by this aversion. It might affect your feelings about your father's occupation. The same would be true if your parents loved their work. Your personal needs, many of which may have been based on experiences during childhood, may cause you to enter one field of study rather than another (Roe, 1964, 1957). In addition, personality and problem-solving orientation may affect career choice. Holland (1973) identified six different characteristics and found them related to different careers. For example, people who are task-oriented or who prefer to work independently tend to enter scientific vocations. Other factors might be practical ones, such as the desire to enter the work force early. Knowing that it takes eight years to earn a doctorate in a particular field might deflate one's enthusiasm if early earning power were a factor. Other practical factors involve being able to pay for training, meet entrance requirements, and the like. Finally, gender and socioeconomic status are factors in career selection, as we will see.

Sometimes career choice is due to chance. A person may merely be at the right spot at the right time. Baumgardner (1975) surveyed college alumni and found that 72 percent had entered their occupations on the basis of circumstantial factors or some combination of circumstances and planning. Only 28 percent felt that career planning had led directly to their job. Baumgardner's work reminds us that chance, once-in-a-lifetime opportunities, and nonplanned factors enter into career choice. Another interesting finding is that adolescents are more certain of what they do not want to be than what they do want to be (Housely, 1973). Career planning, then, may be seen as a process of elimination.

Myths of Career Planning

For many, career planning is fraught with anxiety. A number of misunderstandings and myths surround the vocational choice of adolescents seeking a career that is tailor-made for them. Some of these include:

1. The earlier a person chooses a vocation the better
Some 61 percent of the high school juniors in a national sample believed that the earlier a career choice is made the better (Noeth et al., 1975). Students admire those who make definite career commitments early. But sometimes teens make these decisions too early. Super and Overstreet (1960) found that ninth-graders did not have the maturity to make these decisions. I call this the Hawkeye Pierce myth (after the character of that same name on the popular television show M*A*S*H*). Hawkeye, son of a physician, had wanted to be a doctor since early childhood. He never thought of anything else. What if Hawkeye had not had the ability to become a physician, had discovered he couldn't stand the sight of blood or couldn't get into medical school? What would he have done then? The person who has made a career commitment early in life and stuck to it is envied by many, but these people are rare. Most people change their minds, and the early foreclosure of career possibilities is generally counterproductive.

2. There is only one right choice
Adolescents often believe that there is only one right career for them. Many students coming for help in career planning expect the counselor to suggest one particular occupation that will be *the* answer to all the client's prayers (Thompson,

1976). There are probably a number of correct alternatives, and complete certainty is unrealistic, and perhaps undesirable, because it reduces flexibility.

3. Give me a test and tell me what I should be
Vocational interest inventories often compare the test-taker's answers with the answers of people in various fields who say they are happy in their work. The result is a profile showing how your interests match those of others in particular careers. These tests do not tell you what you should be.

4. What I'm interested in I'll be good at, and what I'm good at I'll be interested in
There is a relationship between interests and abilities, but it is far from perfect (Thompson, 1976). The excellent math student may not be interested in the subject, or in entering a career in which math plays a large part. On the other hand, the fair math student may decide to enter a field like engineering for different reasons. In the late 1960s, many students entered engineering programs because the starting salaries were good and the social status was high, but many flunked out. In choosing a career, abilities should be kept in mind.

5. A mistake in career planning would be catastrophic
Many people see the job they are preparing for as being final, but people often end up in other fields, or at least not in the positions they had been trained for. In the study by Noeth and colleagues (1975), 61 percent of the sample also believed that most people remain in the same job throughout their lives. This is simply untrue (Hazler and Roberts, 1984).

Impatience and Future Orientation

Adolescents are also impatient. Most people have more time to make career choices than they realize. Career decisions occur over a lifetime and involve many smaller decisions. Entrance into a premed program is not a lifelong commitment, it is a one-term choice. Super and Hyde (1978) report that at the age of twenty-five one-fourth of all adults are still not positive about their vocational choices. For most students, prematurely closing the doors on a decision is a poor strategy.

The tendency to look too far ahead is demonstrated by the question a high school junior asked: "How will I pass the bar exam?" Sometimes people look at career step number 24 instead of focusing on steps 1, 2, and 3 (Thompson, 1976). That high school junior should be concerned about finding a college with a good record of helping students get into law school. Worrying about passing the bar exam is premature.

Many adolescents subscribe to one or more of the myths or misunderstandings stated above. This increases their anxiety unnecessarily and narrows their field of vision when just the opposite should be happening.

SEX, SOCIOECONOMIC STATUS, AND CAREER CHOICE

Adolescents today have a variety of choices open to them. While these choices should be dictated by abilities, interests, practical factors, and lifestyle considerations, too often gender and socioeconomic status variables enter the picture.

10. *True or False:*
Vocational interest inventories tell the test-taker what careers should be considered.

The Wrong Choice?

Richard is a sophomore in college. He is a fair student and his strongest subjects are social studies and English, so his parents and friends were surprised when he chose to major in physics. After all, his high school grades in math and science averaged about 80. Richard believes that the best jobs are in the sciences and wants to be part of the technological revolution.

During the first semester, Richard did fairly well. He studied very hard and got a B in math and a C in physics. He was encouraged by his grades, although his parents and older brother (who is majoring in math) are not. In his second semester, Richard began having difficulty, but he came through with a C in math, a D in chemistry, and a C − in physics. He is starting to doubt himself, but he still wants to major in the sciences.

Richard's parents believe that he has made a mistake and is getting deeper into trouble. If his grades don't improve, he'll be put on probation. They have spoken to him about it, but do not want to push the issue because they want Richard to choose a vocation. Yet flunking out of college is a drastic way to learn. They also don't want to be blamed if their son changes his major and isn't happy with it.

1. If you were Richard, what would you do?
2. If you were Richard's parents or brother, would you intervene or stay out of the picture?

Careers for Women

Years ago, one could say with certainty that a girl would grow up, get married, and lead a rather conventional existence. Women who did work often chose nonprofessional jobs. This is not so today. Studies predict that, by the year 1990, nine of every ten women can expect to work outside the home sometime in their lives (Clarey and Sanford, 1982). In addition, although women are still overrepresented in certain fields, such as clerical and service positions, more women are entering what might be called nontraditional fields (see Figure 15.1). A nontraditional field is one in which the overwhelming majority of workers are men, such as engineering.

Nontraditional Careers for Women: Two Views. The trend for women to enter nontraditional fields can be analyzed in two ways. The first is pessimistic. For example, although the increase in female engineers between 1971 (1 percent) and 1981 (4 percent) may seem impressive, it is only because of the relatively few female engineers in the nation in 1971. There are fewer women in engineering than in any other profession (*New York Times*, November 13, 1981). Some also believe that the progress overall has been too slow. Lueptow (1981) studied a group of high school seniors in Wisconsin in 1964 and 1975. In 1964, he found that 80 percent of the women wanted to enter twelve rather traditional fields. In 1975, fewer opted for these professions, but instead looked into new ones, which

FIGURE 15.1 **Employed Women by Occupation, 1973 and 1983 Annual Averages**

More women are working in the managerial and technical areas than ever before. Women are now entering fields which were once largely closed to them. Many of these occupations require post-high school education.

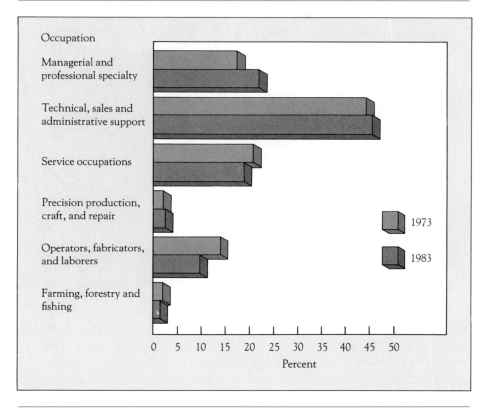

Source: Bureau of Labor Statistics, 1984.

were still predominantly female. There was some change in the number of women wishing to enter nontraditional fields, such as the sciences, but it was a relatively small change overall.

The other evaluation is more optimistic, seeing women as making substantial though uneven progress. For example, in 1971 women accounted for 9 percent of the doctors in the United States but in 1981 they accounted for 22 percent (*New York Times*, November 13, 1981). One-third of all students in law school and one-quarter of students in medicine, veterinary medicine, and business administration were women (Wilson et al., 1982). These figures show that women are beginning to enter these male-dominated fields in large numbers.

The Trend Toward Women Working.   Although women still value marriage and family life, significant changes have occurred. For example, the birth rate has declined. There were 19.4 births per 1,000 population in 1965, compared with 15.8 in 1981 (Bureau of the Census, 1985). Women now find that their

11. *True or False:*
The percentage of women doctors in the United States more than doubled in the decade between 1971 and 1981.

There are now more career opportunities open to women than ever before.

child-bearing and child-raising years are fewer than in past generations. Women are also more likely to become heads of households through divorce or by remaining single than in the past. The inflationary cycle has forced many families to depend on dual incomes. In addition, more women are attending professional programs that require great commitments in time. After devoting so much effort to career preparation, these women are less likely to stop working for long periods of time. Finally, many women are now looking to employment as part of their lifestyle.

For whatever reason, adolescent women need to prepare for careers, and the statistics show that many are doing so. Yet there are certain problems that females, but not males, face in career planning.

Career Decisions for Females

Men are socialized to accept the role of breadwinner, but women have developed a dual role as mother and worker, and this often limits their career choices. Women are sometimes reluctant to enter careers in the sciences because they see problems combining family life and a career in this area (McLure and Piel, 1978). Women are, however, entering some nontraditional careers today. The female doctor or lawyer is becoming common, but the woman entering chemistry, physics, and engineering is still a rarity. Why?

We all know stories about people who have been discouraged by some remark from a professional or even a peer concerning the inappropriateness of achieving in some area. The media demonstrate such sexism too. Television and movies rarely show women in scientific fields, and when they do, the women seem to be incapable of having normal family lives and a career too. The occupational literature can also be biased (Heshusius and Gilsdorf, 1975). Parents sometimes propagate sexist attitudes by discouraging daughters from achieving in certain fields. School counselors are also blamed for discouraging females from developing their potential, but the students often are the ones who already have a sexist view of career choice. In many instances, counselors of both sexes are less stereotyped in their views of work and sex roles than the females they are counseling (Hawley, in Hawley and Even, 1982).

12. *True or False:*
As a rule, school counselors are less stereotyped in their views of women and work than the females they counsel.

Personal experience is one factor that can counter stereotypes, but personal experience involves more than just meeting a woman physicist or medical doctor once. Stereotypes are pervasive and their effects are cumulative.

Women Who Enter Nontraditional Careers. Are there differences between women who choose more traditional careers and those who do not? Auster and Auster (1981) argue that there are. The family plays a role in influencing career decisions. Women who achieve in male-dominated professions have mothers who worked and acted as role models for them. The higher the social status of the position held by the mother, the less traditional the choice made by their daughters (Treiman and Terrell, 1975). The father also influences this decision. Daughters choosing nontraditional careers often have close relationships with their fathers and model themselves after the male parent as well. Both parents also supported their daughter's decision to enter a nontraditional field. Socioeconomic status is important too. There is a positive relationship between higher socioeconomic status and a nontraditional career choice. Women choosing nontraditional careers also tend to be oldest or only children and come from relatively small families. Peers may exert a positive or negative influence on the choice of a nontraditional career.

Other studies have found a correlation between androgyny in females (those whose personalities comprise both masculine and feminine traits) and choice of nontraditional careers (Clarey and Sanford, 1982). Other people besides parents can be important, including mentors and husbands (Wilson et al., 1982). Women choosing nontraditional careers also have beliefs in a more equitable division of labor in marriage and have less-conventional attitudes generally (O'Donnell and Andersen, 1978), including less-traditional sex role attitudes (Keith, 1981).

We can conclude that more females will be working in the future and that many more will be entering male-dominated occupations. Women must be prepared for these new areas. Although a growing number of both men and women state that they do not wish to have children, the overwhelming majority still want families. These women need vocational information concerning the problems and possibilities in this area.

Career Decisions for Males

Because men are expected to make career choices and become the main breadwinner in the family, fewer changes in the career histories of men should be expected. Even so, some are appearing.

Both men and women who enter nontraditional career areas must deal with special difficulties. What additional problems do you think this female mechanic and male nurse will encounter because of their gender?

Many of the stereotypes that surround vocational choice for men can be seen as operating in their favor (Skovholt and Morgan, 1981). For example, personal characteristics such as strength and determination are rated positively. So are men's job choices, such as engineer and electrician. In addition, the rewards that include power, money, and status are positively evaluated by society. For men, occupational success often means high self-esteem. Success in life is often measured by success in vocational pursuits.

We can look at this in two ways. First, these advantages explain why men are less willing than women to explore nontraditional life and career patterns (Hawley and Even, 1982). Because they choose high-status positions, men experience less urgency to question their lifestyles.

However, two negative factors are becoming evident. First, not all men are going to succeed, and vocational failure often leads to self-esteem problems in men. Other problems, including violence in the family, deterioration in health, family trauma, and stress, follow this narrow focus in life. Second, even if males succeed, their lives may become narrow (Kaplan and Stein, 1984). In many cases, they have not developed the relationships with their families that they would have liked. In addition, for many men nontraditional lifestyles and careers would seem appropriate, but they hesitate to enter female-dominated occupations and perhaps therefore do not develop their true potential.

If men are given an advantage by their status, it is a two-edged sword. Consciousness-raising will be necessary if men are to go beyond their narrow base and balance their affiliative and leisure activities with their work. In addition, female-dominated occupations must be opened to men who have the talents to succeed in them. This again entails a change in attitude and values on the part of society.

Socioeconomic Status and Career Choice

Career choice is also affected by socioeconomic status. Adolescents from higher-socioeconomic-status families have higher aspirations than adolescents who come from lower-socioeconomic-status homes (Bachman, 1978).

Teachers and other professionals often have difficulty understanding why children from poor economic backgrounds, even when they are very bright, fail to plan effectively for their futures. While such answers as lack of belief that they can succeed, inability to make the system work for them, and the absence of economic backing from their families are reasonable, one other important characteristic that prevents planning must be noted.

Most middle- and upper-class youngsters believe that they can influence their own futures, that is, they have an **internal locus of control**. But this is not the case with poorer children, who have an **external locus of control** and believe that they are at the mercy of the system, the outside world, or luck. They are more fatalistic in their view (Farmer, 1978). If they do not believe they have the power to change things, why plan?

All in all, the poor face barriers of discrimination and a history of lack of success with the system. This does not mean that they lack motivation to succeed, only that in order to succeed there must be some belief in the effectiveness of one's own efforts. For example, let's say you want to become a chemist but don't believe that even if you study hard you can make it. You might not even know what is necessary. The first problem is one of changing a view toward life, while the second requires adequate vocational information. The disadvantaged also face the problem of poorer reading skills and less opportunity.

The failure in this area is reflected in the tremendous unemployment rate among minority group teenagers. Any programs that aim at promoting reasonable vocational choices must deal with the lack of information concerning vocations and the problems associated with poverty. They must also change basic attitudes, which often run counter to the planning necessary to succeed in obtaining upper-level jobs.

internal locus of control
The belief that one is in control of one's own fate.

external locus of control
The belief that one is at the mercy of other people or of fate.

13. *True or False:*
Middle-class youngsters tend to think that their lives are governed by chance and outside factors, whereas lower-income youngsters believe they are in charge of their own lives.

NEW ABILITIES, NEW FREEDOM

Everyone accepts the fact that adolescence is a time of physical change, yet comparatively few people realize the tremendous cognitive changes that occur at this time. The development of formal operational abilities allows adolescents to come up with their own internal morals and ethics and to decide for themselves what they ought to be and what they want to do with their lives. In many ways, these newfound abilities mean a new freedom to be themselves and to consider what they want to stand for in life. It also contributes to the development of an identity and a new relationship with parents and peers. It is to these areas that we turn next.

Chapter Summary

1. During the stage of formal operations, adolescents develop the ability to find all possible alternatives to a problem, separate the real from the possible, form hypotheses and test them out, understand propositions, interpret abstractions, and think about their own thoughts.

2. Not everyone shows formal operational thinking. This may be explained by the competency-performance argument, cross-cultural differences, or individual differences, such as cognitive style.

3. Adolescents often have difficulty differentiating between their own thoughts and those of others, leading to egocentric thinking. Out of this egocentrism comes the imaginary audience, in which adolescents often think everyone is looking at them, and the personal fable, in which they believe their experiences and thoughts are absolutely unique in the annals of human history.

4. According to Kohlberg, the upper stages of moral reasoning require more sophisticated cognitive abilities. The ability to take someone else's point of view is also related to moral reasoning. Although advanced cognitive abilities may make it possible to function at a higher level of moral reasoning, most people do not develop past Kohlberg's stage four.

5. Values serve as internal guides for behavior. Adolescents appear to value marriage and family life as well as friendships. The values of teenagers today are similar though not identical to those held by their parents.

6. Although there is evidence that females do better in elementary school than males, this changes in high school, where males surpass females, especially in the areas of math and science. The lack of encouragement for females to take courses in these areas, and other situational factors, probably account for the lack of interest females show in these subjects. This reduces their range of occupational choices.

7. Some women fear success in male-dominated occupations because it may not be in keeping with their view of femininity. Males may also fear success in female-dominated occupations. Fear of success is decreasing.

8. The choice of a vocation affects one's entire lifestyle. Although money is an important factor in vocational choice, so is interest and other nonmonetary factors. Such factors as intelligence, interest, personal experiences, practical factors such as the need to enter the work force early, gender, and socioeconomic status also affect career choice.

9. More women are now entering male-dominated occupations. Vocational choice of nontraditional careers requires family support and adequate models.

10. Both males and females from the middle and upper socioeconomic levels have higher vocational aspirations than their peers from poor families. Many poor children do not believe they can succeed, are not able to make the system work for them, or lack the necessary economic backing from their families. Finally, poor children are less likely to believe that they can affect their own fate.

■ Answers to True or False Questions

1. *True.* The ability to interpret proverbs and political cartoons develops during adolescence.

2. *True.* Not everyone develops formal operational thought.

3. *False.* Correct statement: People from non-Western cultures usually do not perform as well on these tasks as Western subjects.

4. *False.* Correct statement: Adolescents frequently cannot differentiate their own thoughts from what others are thinking.

5. *True.* Adolescents often believe that their experiences are truly unique.

6. *True.* By and large, their values are similar but not identical to those of their parents.

7. *True.* During the high school years, females show a decline in academic achievement while males show improvement.

8. *False.* Correct statement: Their motivations are not any lower, but they may differ qualitatively.

9. *False.* Correct statement: Early commitment reduces flexibility, and some may not be vocationally mature enough to make such commitments.

10. *False.* Correct statement: Vocational interest inventories tell test-takers how similar their interests are to those of people currently in the field.

11. *True.* The percentage of women doctors more than doubled during that time and continues to increase.

12. *True.* Females seeking career counseling often have a more stereotyped view of work and sex roles than their counselors.

13. *False.* Correct statement: Middle-class youngsters generally believe they are largely in control of their lives, while lower-income teens believe their lives are governed by chance.

CHAPTER SIXTEEN

Social and Personality Development in Adolescence

CHAPTER OUTLINE

WILL THE REAL ADOLESCENT PLEASE
    STAND UP?
THE SEARCH FOR A PERSONAL IDENTITY

*RESEARCH HIGHLIGHT   Self-Esteem: Wading
    Through the Confusion*

ACTION/REACTION   What Am I To Be?

RELATIONSHIPS WITH PARENTS AND
    PEERS

DRUGS
PRESCRIPTIONS FOR A CHANGING
    RELATIONSHIP

*ACTION/REACTION   Freedom for One, Slavery for
    the Other*

■ *Are the Following Statements True or False?*

*Try the True-False Quiz below. See if your answers correspond to the information in this chapter. Each
question is repeated opposite the paragraph in which the answer can be found. The True-False Answer Box
at the end of the chapter lists complete answers.*

___ **1.** It is more difficult to achieve an identity today
than it was a century ago.

___ **2.** Periods of confusion in adolescence usually
signal the probability of mental illness.

___ **3.** People who have achieved an identity are better able to commit themselves to other people than
people who have not yet achieved one.

___ **4.** Cults use sophisticated psychological techniques to convert people to their way of thinking.

___ **5.** Most adolescents who enter cults are suffering from severe psychological problems.

___ **6.** Conformity to peers increases throughout
adolescence.

___ **7.** Most adolescents rate themselves as very rebellious.

___ **8.** Most adolescents think the generation gap is
wider than it really is.

___ **9.** Alcohol is the most popular drug used by adolescents.

___ **10.** Over the past twenty years, the percentage
of female teens smoking has decreased modestly,
while the percentage of male teens beginning the
habit has increased significantly.

___ **11.** Antismoking campaigns have been more
successful at preventing teens from beginning to
smoke than at motivating people to stop smoking.

WILL THE REAL ADOLESCENT PLEASE STAND UP?

What adjectives would you use to describe a teenager? Do such terms as rebellious, conforming, searching, peer-oriented, sensitive, insensitive, confused, irreverent, independent, stressful, alienated, private, ambivalent, moody, insecure, and tense come to mind? Some of these seem contradictory. The well-known striving for independence is matched by the need for security and dependence. The hopefulness and future orientation accompanies feelings of hopelessness and confusion.

The period of adolescence is usually perceived as a time of confusion, stress, and rebellion. In one of the first major modern works on adolescence, G. Stanley Hall (1904) described the period as one of "storm and stress." This has remained the popular conception of adolescence, especially in Hollywood films, which often portray adolescents as confused, alienated, and isolated, buffeted between the old and useless standards and beliefs of the older generation and the more modern but dangerous examples of their peers. Relationships with parents are viewed as argumentative, and slavish devotion to peers is shown as the norm.

Yet such simplistic notions of adolescents often meet with murmurs of disagreement, especially among adolescents themselves. Many adolescents have good relationships with their parents and are not totally conforming to peers. They make their own decisions and do not seem very confused. Which of these two views of adolescence comes closest to describing what really occurs during the teen years? This chapter will explore adolescent social and personality development, investigate parental and peer relationships, and look at some of the major challenges confronting adolescents in the 1980s.

THE SEARCH FOR A PERSONAL IDENTITY

Which view of the adolescents' relationship with their parents is correct? Is it one of continual conflict, or one of constructive involvement—or is it a little of both?

Adolescents are negotiating a transitional stage between the simpler elementary school years and the commitments of early adulthood. They must somehow integrate the lessons of the past with the realities of the present and the possibilities of the future. They must evaluate and develop their unique abilities and choose a

lifestyle, vocation, and personal definition. In other words, the adolescent must search for and form a personal identity.

Identity vs. Role Confusion

Who am I?
Do I belong?
Where am I going?

These three questions typify the adolescent's search for a personal identity (Ruittenbeck, 1964). Erik Erikson (1959) saw the positive outcome of adolescence as the formation of a solid, personal **identity**, while the negative outcome of adolescence is an aimlessness known as **role confusion** or **role diffusion** (the state of not knowing who one really is). Adolescents are walking a tightrope. Their task is to surrender the older dependent ties and childhood identifications with their parents and develop a separate identity, while continuing a healthy relationship with their elders (Siegel, 1982). If they are to function as adults, they must be able to make their own decisions. They cannot simply be carbon copies of their parents. On the other hand, the attitudes and values gained from parents during childhood serve as anchors, providing security in a sea of change. Total abandonment of these values may lead to bewilderment and utter confusion. In addition, surrendering older ideals assumes them all to be dysfunctional, a conclusion that is difficult to support. Adolescents, then, may have a difficult course to chart. But is it more difficult today than it was years ago?

Finding an Identity in Today's World

The development of an identity involves choosing from various alternatives. A knowledge of the alternatives available, as well as some freedom to choose, are important considerations. Imagine yourself a farmer in the plains of the old American West in the early 1800s. Your life is mapped out for you. You will marry the boy or girl a few farms down the road, buy a farm in the same area, and have as many children as possible so that the land can be worked efficiently. News travels slowly. Your knowledge of the alternatives available is minimal, and your freedom to act is even less.

Now let's look at the situation in that same Western environment today. Television, the print media, and the movies have brought almost instant information to the community from all over the world. Schooling is universal, and farming has become so technological that it requires higher education. Along with this information explosion, different values and many new choices surround teenagers. No longer is the young teenage girl expected to bear as many children as possible. No longer is farming the only vocation available. No longer are you so isolated that other possibilities are unknown. You now have many more choices, and a greater degree of freedom to choose your own course. And with choice comes doubt and anxiety.

These factors—more choices and a greater degree of freedom to choose—combine to make forming an identity more difficult today than it was years ago. One last factor is also important. Many contemporary observers believe that society is changing at a faster rate than ever before (Toffler, 1970). The skills necessary to prosper in the years ahead are likely to change with our society. For in-

One of the most important challenges in adolescence is developing a personal identity.

identity
The sense of knowing who you are.

identity vs. role confusion or diffusion
The psychosocial crisis of adolescence.

role confusion or diffusion
According to psychosocial theory, the negative outcome of adolescence, which involves the failure to develop a personal identity and feelings of aimlessness.

1. *True or False:*
It is more difficult to achieve an identity today than it was a century ago.

Finding an identity one hundred years ago was easier than it is today, simply because there were fewer alternatives available.

crisis
In psychosocial theory, a time in which a person actively faces and questions aspects of his or her own identity.

commitment
In psychosocial theory, making a decision concerning some question involved in identity formation, and following a plan of action reflecting this decision.

identity diffusion
An identity status resulting in confusion, aimlessness, and a sense of emptiness.

identity foreclosure
An identity status marked by a premature identity decision.

identity moratorium
An identity status in which a person is actively searching for an identity.

identity achievement
An identity status in which a person has developed a solid, personal identity.

stance, it was not long ago that a high school education was considered relatively unnecessary, that computers were the toys of science fiction writers, and that manufacturing jobs were considered secure. The lack of stability in society means that teens must predict what vocations and skills will be needed in a changing world if they are to prepare adequately for it.

The Four Identity Statuses

Achieving an identity in a fast-changing world is not an easy task. It depends on two variables: **crisis and commitment** (Marcia, 1967). A **crisis** refers to a time in which one actively faces and questions aspects of one's personal identity. For instance, a student may be faced with a number of choices concerning a college major and be coping with such decisions when approaching the junior year in college. In the personal sphere, the student may be dating someone for a while and may have to decide whether to get more deeply involved. The second aspect, **commitment**, involves making a firm decision concerning some question and following a plan of action that reflects this decision. A person who investigates many vocational choices and decides on a business career follows the appropriate course of study. The decision to end a relationship or to become engaged leads to different behavioral paths.

Adolescents differ in the extent to which they have experienced crises or made commitments. A prominent researcher in this field, James Marcia (1980, 1967), grouped adolescents into four statuses according to their experiences with crises and commitments (see Table 16.1). One group of adolescents, termed **identity diffused**, consisted of adolescents who may or may not have experienced a crisis but have not made any commitments. The **identity foreclosed** group consisted of teens who had not experienced a crisis but had made commitments anyway. The **identity moratorium** group contained adolescents who were presently experiencing a crisis but had not yet made any commitments. The **identity achievers** group consisted of adolescents who had already experienced crises

TABLE 16.1   **The Four Identity Statuses**

Identity Status	Definition
Identity Achievement	An Identity Achiever has experienced doubt (crisis) in personal goals and values, has considered alternatives, and is committed at least tentatively to some expressed value positions and career plans.
Foreclosure	A Forecloser displays a commitment similar to that of the Identity Achiever but has not appraised alternatives to personal goals and values; choices often express parental preferences.
Moratorium	A Moratorium has questioned goals and values and considered alternatives but is still doubtful and uncommitted; predominating is an active effort to become informed and to make suitable choices.
Identity Diffusion	An Identity Diffuser might or might not have experienced doubt over goals and values; he or she does not evidence a serious or realistic inclination to examine concerns about goals and values; he or she expresses no commitments to an ideology or to career plans.

Source: R. Hummel and L. L. Roselli, 1983.

and made their commitments. It is worth taking a more detailed look at each of these statuses.

Identity Diffusion.   In this status, an individual has not made any commitments and is not presently in the process of forming any. The adolescent may or may not have experienced a crisis. Even if there has been a crisis, it has not resulted in any decisions (Waterman, 1982). Identity-diffused people may actively seek noncommitment, actually avoiding demanding situations. They may also appear aimless, aloof, drifting, and empty (Orlofsky et al., 1973). But people in this status are not mentally ill. Their psychological profiles appear normal (Oshman and Manosevitz, 1974), although their self-esteem is not very high.

Some students become alarmed at this description, because they have experienced periods in which the descriptions fit them well. But identity diffusion is negative only when an individual leaves adolescence without making commitments. A period of confusion often precedes the establishment of a firm identity. Adolescents face decisions in many areas of identity formation, including sexual intimacy, occupational choice, and psychosocial self-definition at the same time, and periods of bewilderment are not uncommon (Erikson, 1959). Overprotected adolescents may find themselves challenged in college when they are exposed to many different people espousing different attitudes and moral standards. They have to evaluate these people and their attitudes in the light of past learning and experiences. At the same time, they may be faced with vocational and political considerations, such as which groups to join or which positions of leadership to vie for. We might expect a period of diffusion to occur, and indeed it often does.

2. *True or False:*
Periods of confusion in adolescence usually signal the probability of mental illness.

Identity Foreclosure.   Do you know people who always seem to have it "all together," who knew what they wanted at a very early age and appear very confident and secure? These seemingly lucky people have formed a commitment, but it may not be their own. It may be one handed down to them by their parents. They identify very well, perhaps too well, with their parents. For example, since childhood, a boy may have known that he was destined to enter his father's business. He doesn't consider anything else, and he refuses to develop any talents that lie in another direction. In another situation, a young woman may have chosen her mate very early in life and not explored other possible choices or other alternatives to marriage.

Identity foreclosure is a secure status. These people appear to function well and do not suffer through periods of crisis. They show little anxiety (Marcia and Friedman, 1970). Identity-foreclosed people are often envied by their peers. After all, they have a direction in life and are following a definite path. But this security is purchased at a price. Their path is not one they have chosen themselves, and foreclosed individuals may find themselves mired in an unhappy lifestyle later. As Petitpas (1978, p. 558) notes, "This outward appearance might only be a temporary veneer that could age and crack in time leaving the individuals with a crisis of being locked into an occupation or marriage in which they can no longer function." We can only wonder how many adults are unhappy because they failed to discover what they really wanted in life and instead merely followed a path laid out for them by someone else.

There is another side to identity foreclosure. Some adolescents may be foreclosed because they do not have the opportunity to search or the knowledge of what is available. Many poor and minority group youths simply do not believe they have many choices. Some must enter the labor force as soon as possible to support themselves and their families. Others may not have the basic academic skills necessary for more advanced study that would open up better vocational opportunities. For these teens, foreclosure is forced on them by circumstances, by lack of knowledge about their choices, or by their belief that they do not have any power to control their own destinies.

Identity Moratorium.   Adolescents who are presently experiencing a crisis but whose commitments are vague are considered to be in the moratorium status. This is a period of delay in which a person is not yet ready to make a definite commitment (Erikson, 1968). During this tentative period, many possibilities are explored, some of them radical. However, final commitments tend to be more conservative. Many who were radicals during the 1960s are now living very conservative lives and are members of the political establishment. The moratorium state is not a happy one. The adolescent may be dissatisfied with everything and everyone. The campus reformer may indeed be searching for something. This reformer sees everything that is wrong, but is less successful in suggesting what realistic steps can be taken to alleviate the problems.

People in this status are active and troubled. Quick to debate and frequently in opposition to their parents, they are often hostile toward their peers. They are engaged in what seem like perpetual struggles with authority figures (Donovan, 1975).

Identity moratorium is the least stable of all the statuses (Waterman, 1982), but it may be a necessary status, for when a person makes a commitment it is that individual's own, made after a period of searching for one's own answers. Studies show that about three-quarters of college students who were in this status when they began college could later be said to have achieved an independent identity by graduation (Waterman and Waterman, 1971).

Identity Achievement.   Identity achievers have made it. They have experienced their crises, solved them, and made their commitments. Their goals are realistic, and they can cope with shifts in the environment (Orlofsky et al., 1973). These independent personal identities are not carbon copies of their parents' identities, nor are they totally the opposite of their parents' (Donovan, 1975). Their identity includes some of the parents' values and attitudes, while omitting others. Identity achievers tend to be well adjusted (Bernard, 1981) and achieve the highest grade point averages of any of the other statuses (Cross and Allen, 1970). They also have good relationships with both peers and authority figures (Donovan, 1975).

Identity in Perspective

The concept of identity status extends Erikson's concept in the area of identity formation. Using the variables of crisis and commitment, we can follow adolescents more closely in their quest for a personal identity. Obviously, a person can move from one group to another as he or she experiences a crisis and makes a commitment. This change, though, can occur even with individuals who can be placed in the identity achiever group. Although the identity achiever status is comparatively stable, it can change (Douvan and Adelson, 1966). Some unusual experience might lead one back to a moratorium. For example, one young adult was badly injured in a severe automobile accident and could no longer walk. He had to search for his vocational and even his personal identity again. But the event need not even be that severe. After spending a number of years preparing to become a newspaper reporter, one young woman found that she could not find a job and had to search for an occupational identity all over again. A divorced man or woman may have to search anew for a personal or social identity because the original one is no longer viable.

Identity formation, then, should not be considered something that occurs only in adolescence. The seeds of one's identity are planted in childhood through interactions with parents, peers, and teachers. Experiences during adulthood may test the boundaries of one's identity, causing a reconsideration and further searching. The achievement of a personal identity has many behavioral implications, especially in the area of later interpersonal relations.

Identity and Intimacy

The ego crisis of young adulthood can be expressed as **intimacy vs. isolation** (Erikson, 1968). **Intimacy** normally involves the development of very close personal relationships, often marriage. **Isolation** involves the lack of commitment typified by Simon and Garfunkel's famous song "I Am a Rock, I Am an Island," in which isolation is seen as a safe haven from the gamble of intimacy. However, someone who is having difficulty deciding on his or her own identity may choose to enter into a sort of pseudo-intimacy. For instance, a girl may choose to marry early and establish a traditional home before actually deciding who she is or what she wants. Since intimacy involves a sharing of two identities rather than a

intimacy vs. isolation
The psychosocial crisis of the young adult years.

intimacy
The positive outcome of the psychosocial crisis of young adulthood, involving development of very close interpersonal relations, most often typified by marriage.

isolation
The negative outcome of the psychosocial crisis of young adulthood, resulting in a lack of commitment to others.

RESEARCH HIGHLIGHT   *Self-Esteem: Wading Through the Confusion*

What happens to self-esteem, the value a person puts on himself or herself, during adolescence? Research findings are decidedly mixed on this question. While some studies find an increase with age, others find no increase. Psychology students are often frustrated by such mixed results. Why can't psychologists answer questions definitely? By looking at the research on self-esteem and aging, we can gain some insight into this annoying inability to answer what seem like simple questions directly.

On the surface, it does seem easy to investigate the influence of age on self-esteem. A researcher has two choices. The first is to collect data on self-esteem from a group of adolescents of various ages and compare them. This cross-sectional approach (see pages 19–21) is quick and easy, but it presents difficulties. Because children of various ages are being compared, not the same children over an extended time period, it is difficult to equate our sample of subjects.

The second method is to choose a group of students and periodically test them year after year. This longitudinal method (see pages 21–22) is superior for demonstrating developmental changes in any area, but difficult to execute for a number of reasons. The dropout rate is one concern. Many subjects will take the first test but not later ones. Another problem is the possible practice effects from taking the same test on many different occasions. Subjects may simply get used to the questions, and this may affect how they answer them. Another problem is carelessness. Perhaps some subjects are careless or inattentive and randomly answer the questions on the initial testing. The answers to self-esteem questionnaires tend to be highly positive. A few silly or overly negative answers on the initial testing may create a difficulty. For instance, what if a subject was careless and untruthfully answered some of the questions negatively on the initial administration of a questionnaire? The total score for that person on the self-esteem questionnaire would be low. But what if a year later the same subject takes the questionnaire seriously and scores positively. We might then conclude that the subject's self-esteem actually increased dramatically—which would not be true under the circumstances.

John McCarthy and Dean Hoge examined the relationship between self-esteem and aging with these problems in mind. They noted that the overwhelming majority of studies that showed no relationship between aging and self-esteem were performed using a cross-sectional strategy, testing children of various ages at one time. However, studies performed longitudinally, testing the same children over a period of time, have generally found increasing self-esteem with age. So the research strategy used may determine the results. Longitudinal studies are generally better at determining changes over time than cross-sectional studies. The cross-sectional studies somehow missed the changes.

But are the positive results of longitudinal studies real, or are their results contaminated by the problems of attrition, practice, and carelessness described earlier? The researchers did a longitudinal study of the self-esteem and age. They administered a questionnaire measuring self-esteem to 1,970 junior and senior high school students in thirteen public and parochial schools in two cities. The next year, the same questionnaire was administered to 1,852 of these original subjects. The results demonstrated statistically significant increases in self-esteem over the year.

The researchers now looked at the objections to these findings. They compared the scores for the dropouts with the scores of those who completed both questionnaires and found no differences. Therefore, attrition could not explain their findings. They conducted a second study to test the practice effects of retesting. Some 214 ninth-grade subjects were assigned to an experimental group or a control group. A self-esteem questionnaire was administered to the experimental group twice in a seven-month period. A series of attitude questions not related to self-esteem was administered to the control group at the first testing, and the self-esteem questionnaire was given at the second, seven months later. No significant differences between the two groups at the second testing was found. Therefore, testing or practice effects cannot explain their positive findings.

What of carelessness? The researchers identified careless subjects and estimated the possible error introduced by this factor. First, they repeated a question once near the beginning and then near the end of the test. Second, each test booklet was scanned for silly and thoughtless responses. They then divided the sample into two groups: the careful group and the careless group. The differences in the amount of change between the two testing sessions was minimal. Again, the researchers were able to exclude this factor.

The researchers concluded that age is related to an increase in self-esteem across adolescence, but the real importance of this study goes beyond this finding. The study demonstrates how sensitive variables, such as self-esteem, can be to research strategies. Sometimes variations in research procedures can explain mixed results. It also shows that researchers can deal with criticisms by designing studies that tease out the effects of such possible problems as attrition, practice, and carelessness and reinterpret questions in a new light. In the recent past, the idea that age was unrelated to self-esteem gained considerable support. Now, because of this careful work, we can reevaluate the question.

Source: J. D. McCarthy and D. R. Hoge, "Analysis of Age Effects in Longitudinal Studies of Adolescent Self-Esteem," *Developmental Psychology*, 1982, *18*, 372–379.

complete merging of selves, future problems may arise. Perhaps you know people who chose early marriage as a way out of an identity dilemma. They really haven't solved their identity problem. It is probably still on the back burner, waiting for an opportunity to show itself. Identity problems can be delayed, but not necessarily shelved forever.

3. *True or False:*
People who have achieved an identity are better able to commit themselves to other people than people who have not yet achieved one.

Identity status and the degree of achieving intimacy are related. People in the moratorium and achievement statuses experience deeper levels of intimacy than people in the other two statuses (Fitch and Adams, 1983). In a landmark study, Orlofsky and colleagues (1973) determined the identity status of fifty-three junior and senior male students at a university in New York. The researchers also rated the subjects on the presence or absence of close interpersonal relationships, and the degree of openness, closeness, and commitment that was present in these relationships. Some additional data on personality and social relationships was also collected.

The results indicated that identity achievers scored very high on measures of intimacy, while the identity-diffusion and foreclosure subjects scored poorly. The foreclosure and diffusion subjects were the most isolated. The moratorium subjects were somewhere in the middle. Identity foreclosure subjects had the greatest need for social approval, were least autonomous, and had not modified their family ties. Autonomy and intimacy were related. Identity achievers were found to have successful, mature, intimate relationships, and moratorium subjects were similar to achievement subjects but a bit behind. Most moratorium subjects had intimate relationships with male friends but had not formed enduring heterosexual love relationships. Foreclosure and diffused subjects were involved in some relationships, but these lacked the depth and genuine closeness of the achievement groups. The results of this study confirm that progress toward achieving a mature identity is related to the ability to achieve intimacy.

The Process of Identity Formation

How does a person form an identity? A healthy identity must be fused from past, present, and future considerations. Taking everything from one's past may lead to identity foreclosure, yet taking nothing may lead to identity diffusion. Most people who progress through a moratorium do develop a solid identity (La Voie, 1976), and periods of role diffusion do not necessarily indicate any lasting personality problems. The years between eighteen and twenty-one seem especially crucial for development of an identity. Before this time, the overwhelming num-

What Am I To Be?

Kim had wanted to be a writer as long as her parents could remember. She excelled in writing all through her elementary, junior high, and high school years. Now in college, she finds herself with a problem. She did well in her early writing courses, but she notes that the other students in her more advanced classes are superior to her. After looking into the employment opportunities available in journalism, she decided to seek a new major.

Kim has also lost interest in school. She goes to classes, but is not doing well. She has a good relationship with her parents. She told them that without a goal there seems little reason to go to school. "Everyone needs a purpose." She is confused and unhappy.

This is complicated by the pressures of her boyfriend, Mark. Mark wants to get married as soon as possible. He is in graduate school, and they both will have to work for some time to survive financially. Before this semester, Kim told Mark that she wasn't ready. Now she is wavering.

Kim's parents have nothing against Mark. In fact, they like him. But they are afraid that once she goes to work she'll never go back to school. In addition, they're concerned that this radical change in Kim's marriage plans is associated with her change of major. When they confronted Kim with this, she admitted that could be so. However, she was quick to add that she and Mark would be getting married in a few years anyway.

1. If you were Kim, what would you do?
2. If you were Kim's parents, what would you do?
3. If you were Mark, what would you suggest to Kim?

ber of young people are either foreclosed or diffused (Archer, 1982; Meilman, 1979; Trent and Medsker, 1968), and only very limited changes occur prior to or during the high school years (Waterman, 1982). The experience of schooling, especially college, seems to encourage people to question. If forced to describe the one activity that seems to be most important, it would have to be personal searching. This may take effort and cause much anxiety. It is not unusual for students to envy people who seem to have already made up their minds, but the shortcuts to identity formation can be dangerous. Two such shortcuts include totally accepting the values and aspirations of other people and suspending one's search for a personal identity by blindly adopting a cause or totally accepting an ideology.

Shortcut One: Total Acceptance of Others' Values.   One shortcut has already been mentioned—that of foreclosure, accepting someone else's ideas and aspirations, whether parents or peers. The peer group may be a loose confederation of friends or a closely knit gang. Group belongingness increases one's sense of power and provides acceptance and security. In and of itself, this is not bad, but when blind conformity replaces questioning, there is a delay in exploration and a failure to develop one's own sense of personal identity.

Shortcut Two: Total Acceptance of an Ideology.   In the search for an identity, adolescents often yearn for a cause that requires complete devotion. In the search for meaning in life, nothing seems as satisfying as finding something that one can believe in. Newly developing cognitive abilities (see Chapter Fifteen) allow adolescents to find higher meanings in civil affairs and religion. This can be considered a positive development, and indeed for most it is. However, absolute, unconditional acceptance of a political movement or religious ideology which discourages questioning and doubt can be harmful. The individual is giving up the search. A member of such a religious group once told me that he "no longer needed to question, and doubt was impossible." He had found his identity as a member of a particular religious group. The more the newspapers railed against this group's teachings, the stronger his commitment and his belief that he had found everything became. He had stopped searching, doubting, and questioning and began to look down on all who disagreed with him.

Cults

Both the attempt to find something to believe in and the need for an accepting group may lead an adolescent to become involved in one of the most controversial of all phenomena—cults. Everything written about cults becomes controversial, even the use of the term itself. A **cult** is a group that "calls for a totally new and unique life style under the direction of a charismatic leader" (Eshleman and Cashion, 1983, p. 563). A **sect**, by contrast, is a group that has broken away from a parent church and usually emphasizes rigid doctrines such as "otherworldly" rewards. It is often difficult to differentiate between the two, but cults are usually more radical and based on the leadership of a single individual. The charismatic leader of a cult is usually considered a very special being. He or she represents a kind of prophet or interpreter who has unusual powers and rules

cult
A radical group that advocates a unique lifestyle under the direction of a leader who is believed to have special abilities or insights.

sect
A splinter group that has broken away from the main church and usually emphasizes rigid doctrines.

A number of teens join cults in order to find their identity.

with an iron hand. Religious cults often operate outside the mainstream of the society. The term *cult* is so negative that it is often applied to any religious group that is disliked.

    Why Adolescents Join Cults.   Cults seem to have a special significance for adolescents (Doress and Porter, 1978). Almost all their adherents are older adolescents. No children and few older adults are present during the ceremonies. Why are adolescents so vulnerable to cults?

    The vulnerability may be due to the in-between nature of the stage (Doress and Porter, 1978). Adolescence is a transitional period between absolute acceptance of parental values learned in childhood and emergence of the adolescent's own values. Religious cults fill the gap, or void, between the two periods of life. Adolescents may join cults to achieve an instant family, spiritual rebirth, security, adventure, and structure, or to escape from their problems. Many cults are structured to take advantage of these needs. Adolescents are searching for meaning and purpose in life, for an identity of their own, and cults may provide this (Albrecht et al., 1980). Potential converts are often alienated or isolated from their families and have few friends. Cult members are taught to be interested and highly supportive of potential new members, thus providing the companionship desperately yearned for by some adolescents. The cult becomes a secure place, compared with the changing, often cold and unaccepting world. The message of peace, love, or the purity of the cult as opposed to the ugliness of the outside world is often delivered amid religious trappings and satisfies the spiritual needs of the individual. The cult also provides its members with structure, often through rules laid down by the leader and enforced through peer reinforcement and pressure. Most often the cult is structured to keep outside influences at a minimum, in order to encourage the convert to rely more and more on the cult for support as well as for the basics of life. The cult is almost always stricter than the environment in which the individual was raised. Finally, the cult gives each individual an identity—no more thinking or searching is required. Easy answers are supplied to most of the questions of adolescence, and the anxiety of the search is ended. Cult members are taught to repeat answers over and over until they become a way of thinking, blotting out contrary thoughts (Conway and Siegelman, 1978).

    Cults and Controversy.   Cults offer adolescents a way out of the identity dilemma, but their methods are quite controversial. Some people claim they use brainwashing (Conway and Siegelman, 1978), others deny the charge (Robbins and Anthony, 1978). That their techniques are well founded on the psychological principles of persuasion is accepted by all parties. Cults are very proficient at finding potential converts by identifying individuals who are adrift or isolated. The conversion procedure differs among groups, but frequently the first step is giving affection and understanding. Then the neophyte is moved to isolation from nonmembers, and all sorts of rituals and disciplines, many of which serve to reduce the individual's physical and emotional resistance and increase commitment, are introduced. The foot-in-the-door technique is also used effectively. Small commitments are asked first, then larger and larger commitments, until the final conversion is completed. For example, the individual may be asked to give a dollar to the cult and to stay for an extra hour at a meeting, then asked to

4. *True or False:*
Cults use sophisticated psychological techniques to convert people to their way of thinking.

give more and stay longer. All this is done under the watchful eye of the leader or a surrogate and with the support of the group. Finally, when the individual moves into the cult home, he or she is increasingly isolated both physically and psychologically from family and older values, and the flow of information is controlled by the cult.

Although some people who have joined cults suffer from severe psychological problems at the time of their initiation, most are simply a bit depressed, alienated, and isolated from their families (Singer, 1979). Cult members discover the potential convert's needs and weaknesses and make their pitch when the person is particularly lonely or depressed (Singer, 1979).

5. *True or False:* Most adolescents who enter cults are suffering from severe psychological problems.

Few cult members have been forced to stay through the use of physical force. It usually is not needed. The cult member becomes dependent on the cult for physical as well as psychological support, and group pressure can be a powerful force encouraging the convert to stay. Guilt and fear are the primary reasons people remain in cults even after they show a desire to leave them (Singer, 1979).

Often people who drop out of these cults need help readjusting to the world. The problems these adolescents had before entering the cult life are still present (Singer, 1979). They have become used to regimentation and extreme support, and leaving this controlled environment often leads to aimlessness and loneliness. In addition, some former cult members must relearn how to think for themselves, a skill they did not develop or use in cult life.

Cults, then, have a special meaning and attraction for the searching adolescent who may be lonely and isolated. The danger is that total belief and devotion to cult life may end the individual's personal search for an identity and stunt development in other areas. People who join cults gain security, but at the terrible price of giving up their individuality. It is unfortunate that some adolescents will purchase security, a reduction in anxiety, and an identity by suspending their critical faculties and submitting totally to the will of the group.

Adolescents in a cult repudiate their parents' values and teachings. This represents one end of the spectrum. At the other end of the spectrum are identity-foreclosed individuals, who have adopted an identity derived from their parents without much independent searching. Most teens will neither totally reject nor totally accept their parents' teachings. Rather, they will accept some of their parents' values and modify or reject others. This compromise and movement toward independent thought and action requires a change in the parent-child relationship.

RELATIONSHIPS WITH PARENTS AND PEERS

■ "I wish my parents would get off my back. They're always criticizing everything I do. They must have been saints when they were in their teens. If they would just leave me alone, I'd be okay."

■ "My parents and I get along pretty well. They listen to me and I listen to them—although we don't agree on everything. I have a good set of friends, and my parents like them."

■ "I feel guilty when I do things that I know my parents wouldn't be happy about, so I don't talk about what I do with my friends when I'm with my parents. I live in two worlds—one of friends and the other of family."

■"The one problem I have with my parents is that they don't seem to trust me. They think I'm still eleven years old. They don't want to discuss rules, they just want to lay down the law. They repeat everything four hundred times, especially the warnings."

These are some of the responses I received from fourteen- and fifteen-year-olds when asked about their relationships with their parents. During adolescence, the relationship between parents and children changes. After all, one of the tasks of adolescence is to establish a firm and independent identity, and this necessitates some separation between parent and child and involves attaining some degree of independence and autonomy. Parents are often put in the position of criticizing the same behavior they indulged in when they were adolescents and fully expect from their teens (Petersen and Offer, 1979). The stereotype of the adolescent-parent-peer triangle is often one of tremendous conflict between parent and child and the almost total replacement of parental influence by peers. This stereotype, so popular in the movies and on television, has largely been discarded by psychologists as not in keeping with the facts.

Parental vs. Peer Influences

Peer influence increases during middle childhood and into adolescence. The amount of time spent with parents declines, and the sheer quantity of time spent with friends increases. Yet the picture of slavish devotion to peers does not fit the facts.

Berndt (1979) presented 251 children from third, sixth, ninth, and eleventh or twelfth grades with hypothetical situations in which a child was encouraged by peers to perform antisocial acts such as stealing or cheating, neutral acts such as choosing hobbies, entertainment, and eating places, or prosocial acts such as performing charitable deeds. In a related study, situations involving conformity to parents on prosocial and neutral behaviors were added. Conformity to peers for antisocial behavior peaked at the ninth-grade level and declined afterward. By late adolescence, a decrease in conformity to peer expectations occurred.

In third grade, conformity to parents was greater than conformity to peer expectations. Berndt found evidence of conflict, but third-graders usually decided in the direction of their parents. Peer influences became more pronounced between the third grade and the sixth grade, yet Berndt found no increase in parent-peer conflict. In this period, children can isolate the peer world from the familial environment. Many early adolescents use language with their peers that they do not use at home. When I taught junior high school, I found that many girls who were not allowed by their parents to wear jeans or makeup in school would change into a pair of jeans or apply makeup they had hidden in their lockers. At the end of the school day they would change back and scrub their faces clean. While some had argued with their parents over these issues, many simply decided to live in two worlds. Early adolescents seem to be able to separate their worlds—not discussing with their parents what they do with their peers, and vice versa. By ninth grade, peer conformity is at its peak, and conflict between parents and adolescents is common. Berndt believes that two factors are involved in this increasing conflict. First, antisocial conformity is at its peak here, and parents, who may be able to look the other way concerning hairstyles and taste in music (more neutral stimuli), cannot disguise their concern about antisocial acts.

6. *True or False:*
Conformity to peers increases throughout adolescence.

Second, the push toward independence is particularly strong at this age. Berndt cites studies showing that adolescents at this point often report the greatest number of disagreements with their parents. By the junior and senior years of high school, some conflict remains, but peer influence seems to decline somewhat, and conventional behavior increases. This pattern continues into young adulthood.

The rebelliousness of youth, then, may be overemphasized. Balswick and Macrides (1975) asked 417 college students to rate their own rebelliousness. Some 21 percent of the males and 23 percent of the females claimed to be very rebellious, while 65 percent of the males and 58 percent of the females claimed to be only slightly rebellious. In addition, most adolescents report having fairly good relationships with their parents (Douvan and Adelson, 1966). Other studies have shown that adolescents seek out and consider the advice of their parents even more often than their peers (Kandel and Lesser, 1972).

7. *True or False:*
Most adolescents rate themselves as very rebellious.

Differences in Attitudes and Values

The term **generation gap** became popular a few decades ago. It was used to explain what was seen as the ever-widening gap between the standards, values, and opinions of the generations. Just as in the case of adolescent-parental conflict, the evidence just does not fit the stereotype of generations continually at odds with each other.

generation gap
The difference in attitudes among various generations.

A number of studies have measured the differences in attitudes and values between the generations. Most of these studies find that the generations do differ on a number of issues, but this difference is one of intensity rather than of attitude direction. In other words, the differences in attitudes are not qualitative— one generation believing one thing while the other finds itself at the opposite extreme. The differences are a matter of degree, with one generation agreeing or disagreeing more strongly with a position than the other. The generation gap is more apparent than real (Lerner et al., 1975). Two issues where qualitative differences of opinion do exist are sex and drugs (Chand et al., 1975). Even though the gap between the generations on most issues is not great, adults and teens do not perceive it that way. The generations perceive a more significant gap.

Lerner and his colleagues (1975) asked undergraduate students and their parents to note their feelings on a number of issues, such as racism, war, sex, and drug use. Subjects checked the alternative from number one, meaning "strongly agree," to seven, indicating "strongly disagree." They were asked to rate not only statements that reflected their own attitudes but also those mirroring the beliefs of their parents and peers. Parents were asked to rate their own stands on issues as well as their perception of their children's and other teens' attitudes. The results? Most actual differences were in the direction of intensity. Parents were more conservative than their children. However, the generation gap did exist in the perceptions each group had of the attitudes of the other. Adolescents overestimated the gap between their parents and themselves, while parents consistently underestimated it. Each group tended to see the other as more conservative than it actually was. If we are to talk about a generation gap, we should note whether it is the small actual one or the somewhat larger perceived gap.

8. *True or False:*
Most adolescents think the generation gap is wider than it really is.

Why should the perceived gap be so much greater? Perhaps parents want to see themselves as closer to their children, and adolescents are motivated to separate themselves more from their parents. But this could also be a reflection of poor communication between the generations. This study points toward a need for more direct and honest communication between parents and adolescents, for each group is not reading the other's attitudes accurately.

The evidence, then, shows that adolescents and their parents are not as distant in their attitudes and values as first thought. Many psychologists have now discarded the old theory, which emphasized the continuous rejection of parental attitudes and values in favor of peers (Peterson and Offer, 1979). Yet that does not mean that peers have little influence. In fact, the evidence shows that adolescents are influenced by both generations (Floyd and South, 1972). The question remains: In what areas are peers more important than parents, and vice versa?

Areas of Parental and Peer Influence

If teenagers have questions concerning the newest styles or musical trends, whom would they consult—parents or peers? If they had questions concerning their future occupation, would they ask peers or seek out some older person? Once we rid ourselves of the idea that parents are unimportant and that the peer group means everything, things become much clearer. We can give the peer group its due and reserve for authority figures other areas.

The influence of either generation depends on the situation (Brittain, 1969, 1963). Adolescents perceive peers and parents as competent guides in different areas (Brittain, 1963). The peer group is viewed as more knowledgeable in surface and social areas, such as styles and feelings about school, but in deeper values adolescents report being closer to their parents. This meshes well with common experience. Adolescents are influenced by the opinions of people who they believe have superior knowledge in a particular area. For instance, I have found students eager for vocational information from perceived sources of expertise, often older adults. This does not mean that they do not discuss career options with their friends, just that in this area they seem to realize that some older people know more.

The peer influence in adolescence is great, especially in such areas as music and dress. However, the influence of peers in other areas is sometimes overestimated.

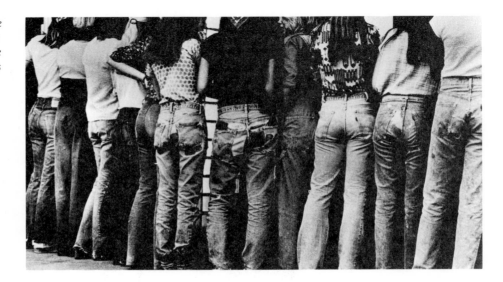

It is a mistake to see adolescents as completely buffeted between parents and peers without minds of their own. Decisions adolescents make are often based on a reasoned sense of independence. They are able to sort alternatives into levels, assigning priority to various questions (Larson, 1972). In other words, in less important areas, such as whether to go to a party, adolescents will accept the opinions of parents or peers, but in more important issues, such as whether to tell the principal who broke the door, they are likely to make an independent decision (Larson, 1972). Even so, the influence of the peer group is impressive.

The Function of the Peer Group

The peer group has a number of functions during adolescence. It often gives support for adolescents striving for independence, since peers are facing the same challenges. As one fifteen-year-old told me, "My friends understand me. I can talk to them. We're interested in the same things." Parent and peer communication patterns differ. Parents are more directive, sharing their wisdom, whereas communication with peers often shows more mutuality and sharing of similar experiences (Hunter, 1984). The peer group also helps adolescents develop social skills and an identity (Coleman, 1981). It serves as a reference group and helps give teens another evaluation of their actions.

The importance of peers is not difficult to observe. All one has to do is look into any high school in the nation and notice the amount of social interaction that goes on. Belonging to a particular group may mean a great deal to adolescents, and the more committed they are to this group, the more they will identify with its standards (Costanzo, 1970). The peer group enforces conformity in attitudes, dress, and conduct, using fear of ostracism as weapons. Simply put, to fit in with the crowd you must speak the same language and be concerned with the same problems. All in all, despite its pull toward conformity, the peer group plays its part in the development of an adolescent's striving toward independence.

Because the peer group is so important, parents are often concerned about the character of their children's friends. During a child's younger years, parents can easily influence who the child's friends are, but during adolescence this is more difficult. Whether parents and adolescents experience conflict on this issue depends on the way parents perceive the values of their children's friends (Newman, 1982). For instance, parents who are concerned about drinking may fight with their adolescents over their choice of friends who drink. However, it is by no means established that parents and peers differ on everything to the extent that they are forces on the opposite sides of the street. Indeed, peers and parents may even complement each other at times. The adolescent's relationships with both peers and parents are not static throughout the teen years. The very nature of these relationships changes as the adolescent faces the many challenges of the period.

Changes in Interpersonal Relationships

Hunter and Youniss (1982) looked at changes in three functions of interpersonal relationships in students from the fourth, seventh, and tenth grades and in college. The control function involved being told what to do and disagreeing. The intimacy function described self-disclosure and empathy, among other aspects of the relationship. The nurture function referred to giving and helping acts.

Peer acceptance is very important to adolescents.

The control function was found to be greater in the parent-adolescent relationship across all age-groups. In other words, parents try to control the behavior of adolescents much more than friends at every age. The attempts at control, though, lessen as the adolescent enters college. The intimacy function showed a change as the adolescent matures. It was greater for parents at fourth grade but was surpassed by peers by tenth grade. By mid-adolescence to late adolescence (seventh to tenth grade), friendship patterns become more intimate, and there is a decrease in this function for parents. Then there is a characteristic increase.

Again we see the pattern in which mid-adolescence seems to be the most trying period for parent-child relationships, with improvement occurring later on. Even though friendships continue to become more intimate in later adolescence, the increase in parental intimacy demonstrates that the growing intimacy with age-mates need not interfere with that portion of the relationship with parents. The nurturance factor remains very high throughout adolescence for the parent-child relationship. Although there is an increase in this helping function for friends, it never surpasses the level of helpfulness in parent-child interactions.

The most interesting change is in intimacy. Sharabany and her colleagues (1981) investigated changes in this area in fifth-, seventh-, ninth-, and eleventh-graders. Intimacy involves frankness and spontaneity, sensitivity and knowing, attachment, exclusiveness, imposing and taking, trust and loyalty. Male relationships generally show a lower degree of intimacy than those formed by females. Females are more expressive and report more giving and sharing than males. Females also develop intimacy with the opposite sex faster than males do. In the fifth grade, boys and girls relate to the opposite sex with little intimacy. By the seventh grade, girls report far more intimacy toward boys than boys toward girls. This discrepancy is maintained through the eleventh grade. Intimacy with same-sex friends remains strong, but with maturity a reduction in attachment and exclusiveness takes place. By the eleventh grade the differences in intimacy between same-sex and opposite-sex friends is reduced. It appears that girls in mid-adolescence are more ready to commit themselves to intimate friendships than boys. Perhaps the socialization of males away from expressiveness partly explains this finding. Since boys may not be as ready to form relationships at this age, it may be wise for a girl to understand that she may be more ready to share than the average male of her age-group.

These studies show that the relationships with parents and with peers are dynamic, changing with maturity and experience. Montemayor (1982) found that parents and peers provide different social worlds for adolescents. Adolescents interact with their parents in such activities as shopping, eating, and doing chores, but spend more time with peers playing games and talking. Most of the free time spent with parents involved watching television, for which many adolescents did not show much enthusiasm. Perhaps parents would do better if they reduced the amount of time they spend watching television with their adolescents and directed their efforts to more active social activities.

Still, there is some good news in this for parents. The restructuring of relationships during early and middle adolescence may be difficult, but it does not put parents out in the cold. In addition, by late adolescence an improvement in the parent-child relationship occurs, and there is less conflict.

The Same Old Problems?

When running some parent-child rap sessions in junior high school a number of years ago, I was surprised at how similar the problems discussed there were to those my friends and I had experienced with our parents. The themes of trust, independence, being treated as an individual, respect for differences, and the like seem to be common to every generation. The day-to-day problems do not seem

During adolescence, teens discuss deeply personal subjects with their friends.

to change much. Even the questions concerning sexual intimacy and decision-
making were common to many previous generations, although attitudes and behavioral standards have changed (see pages 550–557). However, drugs are now
more prevalent, and decisions in this area are much more complicated.

DRUGS

As Tables 16.2 and 16.3 show, adolescent drug use is common. According to a
survey conducted by the National Institute on Drug Abuse, 93 percent of the
high school seniors sampled had used alcohol, 57 percent had used marijuana, 16
percent had used cocaine, 14 percent had used sedatives and 35 percent had used
stimulants. Various studies yield different percentages, but the pattern of significant drug use is apparent.

TABLE 16.2   High School Senior Drug Use, 1975–1983
The following table shows the percentage of high school seniors from the classes of 1975
through 1983 who have used drugs of abuse. These numbers were gathered in annual
nation-wide surveys conducted for the National Institute on Drug Abuse by the
University of Michigan Institute for Social Research. The 1983 survey involved more
than 16,300 high school seniors from public and private schools.

| | | | | | *Ever Used* | | | | |
| | | | | | *Class of* | | | | |
	'75	'76	'77	'78	'79	'80	'81	'82	'83
Marijuana	47%	53%	56%	59%	60%	60%	60%	59%	57%
Hallucinogens	16	15	14	14	14	13	13	13	12
LSD	11	11	10	10	10	9	10	10	9
PCP	NA	NA	NA	NA	13	10	8	6	6
Cocaine	9	10	11	13	15	16	17	16	16
Stimulants	22	23	23	23	24	26	32	36	35
Sedatives	18	18	17	16	15	15	16	15	14
Barbiturates	17	16	16	14	12	11	11	10	10
Tranquilizers	17	17	18	17	16	15	15	14	13
Alcohol	90	92	93	93	93	93	93	93	93
Cigarettes	74	75	76	75	74	71	71	70	71

| | | | | | *Daily Users* | | | | |
| | | | | | *Class of* | | | | |
	'75	'76	'77	'78	'79	'80	'81	'82	'83
Marijuana	6%	8%	9%	10.7%	10.3%	9.1%	7%	6.3%	5.5%
Hallucinogens	0.1	0.1	0.1	0.1	0.1	0.1	0.1	0.1	0.1
LSD	0.0	0.0	0.0	0.0	0.0	0.0	0.1	0.0	0.1
PCP	NA	NA	NA	NA	0.1	0.1	0.1	0.1	0.1
Cocaine	0.1	0.1	0.1	0.1	0.2	0.2	0.3	0.2	0.2
Stimulants	0.5	0.4	0.5	0.5	0.6	0.7	1.2	1.1	1.1
Sedatives	0.3	0.2	0.2	0.2	0.1	0.2	0.2	0.2	0.2
Barbiturates	0.1	0.1	0.2	0.1	0.0	0.1	0.1	0.1	0.1
Tranquilizers	0.1	0.2	0.3	0.1	0.1	0.1	0.1	0.1	0.1
Alcohol	5.7	5.6	6.1	5.7	6.9	6.0	6.0	5.7	5.5
Cigarettes	26.9	28.8	28.8	27.5	25.4	21.3	20.3	21.1	21.2

					Used in Last Year				
					Class of				
	'75	'76	'77	'78	'79	'80	'81	'82	'83
Marijuana	40%	45%	48%	50%	51%	49%	46%	44%	42%
Hallucinogens	11	9	9	10	10	9	9	8	7
LSD	7	6	6	6	7	7	7	6	5
PCP	NA	NA	NA	NA	7	4	3	2	3
Cocaine	6	6	7	9	12	12	12	12	11
Stimulants	16	16	16	17	18	21	26	26	25
Sedatives	12	11	11	10	10	10	11	9	8
Barbiturates	11	10	9	8	8	7	7	6	5
Tranquilizers	11	10	11	10	10	9	8	7	7
Alcohol	85	86	87	88	88	88	87	87	87
Cigarettes	NA	NA	NA	NA	NA	NA	NA	NA	NA

Note: Separate questions about the use of PCP (angel dust) and amyl and butyl nitrites (poppers) were not asked until 1979.

NA indicates data not available

Terms: Ever Used: Used one or more times.

Daily Users: Used 20 or more times in the month before survey.

Used in Last Year: Used in the 12 months prior to survey.

Source: Drugs and American High School Students, 1975–1983. National Institute on Drug Abuse.

Drug Use: A Problem of Adolescence?

Drug abuse is sometimes considered exclusively a problem of adolescence, but this is not true. It should be viewed within a societal context. We are a drug-taking society, and the figures are astounding. Some 12 billion doses of amphetamines are consumed each year (Coon, 1980). Four billion doses of tranquilizers were taken in 1977, including 3.2 billion doses of Valium (Hughes and Brewin, 1979). Between 5 and 10 percent of the work force suffers from alcoholism. Three to 7 percent of the employed population use some form of illicit drug on a daily basis (Quayle, 1983). Two-thirds of all adults drink occasionally (Goode, 1972). In one recent survey, 92 percent of undergraduates at a midwestern university had had a drink in the past month, and 21 percent were classified as heavy drinkers (fifty-six drinks or more during the past month) (Conye, 1984). Alcoholics Anonymous has more than 1 million members. The simple fact is that drug-taking is not restricted to adolescents, or for that matter any specific age-group. Some elementary schools report drug problems. However, the controversy over marijuana, the publicity given to heroin addicts, and the more recent public outcry against drunk driving have encouraged people to think of the drug problem in terms of adolescence, a proposition that is only partially true.

If you were asked which drugs are used most frequently in adolescence, which would you name? If you said alcohol, tobacco, and marijuana, you'd be right.

Alcohol

Alcohol abuse by teenagers mirrors societal use of the drug. Many parents don't even consider it a problem. When I served as a counselor in a junior high school, a teacher reported a young student who constantly reeked of alcohol. His mother was called to school. When I told her that her son had a drinking problem, she sighed with relief. "Gee, I thought he was on drugs" was her reply.

TABLE 16.3   **Annual Prevalence of Use of Eleven Types of Drugs by Subgroups**

	Marijuana	*Hallucinogens*	*LSD*	*PCP*	*Cocaine*
All seniors	44.3	8.1	6.1	2.2	11.5
Sex:					
Male	47.2	9.6	7.4	2.8	13.1
Female	40.8	6.1	4.3	1.6	9.6
Region:					
Northeast	50.9	11.4	8.0	3.6	16.9
North Central	45.6	9.1	7.3	1.5	9.0
South	36.7	4.6	3.9	2.3	6.3
West	45.5	7.8	4.8	1.6	17.9

9. *True or False:*
Alcohol is the most popular drug used by adolescents.

Just like this parent, many other adults think it is quite natural for teens to become drunk once in a while or to have a drink or two. Males look at it as a rite of passage, a sign of maturity. Although females drink less, their rate of alcohol consumption has risen over the past decade (Lowney et al., 1981). The figures on adolescent alcohol use show that it is by far the most popular drug used by youths between the ages of twelve and seventeen (Nathan, 1983). The overwhelming majority of adolescents have used it at some time in their lives, but frequently this is in the presence of their parents—one interesting difference between the use of this drug and others. Many adolescents drink only occasionally. Still, the figures on daily use of alcohol show that it is a significant problem. Between 2 and 6 percent of the adolescent population are classified as problem drinkers (Braucht et al., 1973). About 5.5 percent of all high school seniors use alcohol on a daily basis (Office of Drug Abuse Policy, 1978).

Alcohol is the drug of choice because it is readily available and socially acceptable in many circles. Its use is often modeled by parents. Parental use of alcohol is related to adolescent use (Blum et al., 1970). Parental attitudes are also important. Adolescents who think their parents have permissive views about drug-taking in general are more likely to drink (McDermitt, 1984). However, peer pressure is also a factor. Jessor and Jessor (1975) followed a group of 218 junior high school students, none of whom claimed to drink in 1969. When they reached the senior year of high school, 59 percent were drinking. Significant differences were found between drinkers and nondrinkers. Nondrinkers placed a greater value on academic achievement and less value on independence relative to achievement, showed greater intolerance of deviant behavior, were more religious, were more involved with parents, had friends whose general outlook was similar to that of their parents, and had fewer friends who drank or who approved of drinking. This pattern of abstention diminishes as the adolescent years progress. The unraveling of these more-or-less traditional attitudes explains the onset of drinking behavior. In our society, drinking alcoholic beverages is often seen as an adult activity, as a sign that one has matured into adulthood.

One problem associated with alcohol is drunk driving. In 1982, more than 25,000 people died from traffic accidents and 1.5 million more were injured. Half the fatal accidents were alcohol-related, and many of the dead and injured were

Stimulants* (adjusted)	Sedatives	Barbiturates	Tranquilizers	Alcohol	Cigarettes†
20.3	9.1	5.5	7.0	86.8	14.2
19.6	10.0	5.9	6.9	88.5	13.1
20.3	8.0	5.0	7.1	85.3	14.7
21.5	9.5	5.6	7.8	92.3	15.6
24.1	8.9	5.4	6.2	90.7	17.3
16.4	10.3	6.3	7.4	80.7	13.3
18.7	6.5	3.9	6.4	81.9	7.1

*Adjusted for overreporting of the non-prescription stimulants.
†Based on 30-day prevalence of a half-pack-a-day of cigarettes, or more.
Annual prevalence is not available.
Source: L. D. Johnston, J. G. Bachman, and P. M. O'Malley, *Student Drug Use, Attitudes, and Beliefs: National Trends 1975–1982* (Rockville, Md.: National Institute on Drug Abuse, 1982), 26.

under twenty-five years old (Hardert, 1984). The carnage on our highways has caused an outcry, with people demanding action.

How do we combat the problem of teenage alcoholism and drunk driving? A number of programs have been offered. Some states have raised the legal age for drinking. Educational programs, both those preventive in nature and those aimed at people arrested for various alcohol-related crimes, have become more common both in high school and in college. These programs have not been overly successful (Nathan, 1983). The high cost of drinking in human terms and productivity will continue until we find some way of redrawing the image of the drinker and getting people to take the teenage alcohol problem seriously.

Smoking

One interesting phenomenon of our time is that despite all the evidence linking smoking with cancer, heart disease, and the like, smoking is still a national health problem. Between 1968 and 1974, the percentage of males who smoked stayed relatively constant, rising from 17 percent to 18 percent, but the number of females who smoked doubled, increasing from 10 percent to 20 percent (Silverstein et al., 1982). The number of adolescents who have tried cigarettes at one time or another is much larger, of course, though somewhat less than the number of twelve to seventeen-year-olds who have tried alcohol (Abelson et al., 1977). Most adolescents state that they will quit in a few years, but this is not so. It is paradoxical that while so many adults are trying to kick the habit more and more teens are starting—and they are beginning at earlier ages (U.S. Department of Health, Education, and Welfare, 1978).

The increase in females smoking has been especially great. In a fascinating study, Silverstein and his colleagues (1980) suggested that this increase was due to the availability of low-nicotine cigarettes. Females generally experience great pressure to smoke and they are likely to feel sick when they first smoke. They resolve these contrary pressures by switching to low-nicotine cigarettes. Another

10. *True or False:*
Over the past twenty years, the percentage of female teens smoking has decreased modestly, while the percentage of male teens beginning the habit has increased significantly.

possible reason for the increase involves general rebellion and the movement toward throwing off the shackles of conventionalism. For instance, girls who smoke are more socially outgoing but much more rebellious. They report getting drunk more often, having lower grades, disliking school, having sexual relations, and using marijuana more than their nonsmoking peers (Jarvik et al., 1977). Smokers generally score higher on extroversion but lower on other personality measures such as agreeableness and strength of character (Smith, 1969). The cigarette ads for women are now following the same pattern as those for men. The men's ads show the macho image, the ads directed toward females show the independent, sexy, outgoing, have fun, rebellious attitude that often is attractive to females seeking an identity in a world that now gives them more choices. Smoking follows the same pattern as alcohol consumption. Adolescents who do not smoke tend to have friends that don't and vice versa. When both parents smoke, children are more likely to do so.

Antismoking campaigns have been directed at various segments of the population, including pregnant women, fathers who have young children who may imitate them, teenage girls who are trying to maintain an image, and so on. These campaigns have been more successful in motivating adults to quit smoking than in encouraging teens not to start. One reason may be that adults and adolescents may smoke for different reasons. Studies suggest that smoking is perceived as having social benefits for adolescents (Leventhal and Cleary, 1980). Whether an adolescent smokes may depend on his or her view of the social image of the smoker. If it is close to a teenager's view of the ideal person, that teen is likely to smoke. One study found that sixth- and eighth-graders had mixed views of smokers (Barton et al., 1982). Smokers were rated as less healthy, less wise, less obedient, and less likely to act their age. The sixth-graders also perceived smokers as less likely to achieve in school and less desirable as friends. However, smokers were also rated as tougher, more interested in the opposite sex, and wanting to be with the group more than nonsmokers. These are powerful positive attributes in early and mid-adolescence. Both grades believed that smokers were more likely to drink—a negative quality for sixth-graders but not for eighth-graders. Findings for males and females were similar. According to Barton and his colleagues, smoking in the younger grade is associated with the negative image of the smoker. The more negative the image, the less likely the sixth-graders were to smoke. But in the eighth grade, smoking is related to the positive qualities of the smoker, especially interest in the opposite sex, wanting to be with the group, and the idea of being relaxed. Perhaps antismoking campaigns directed at younger children should stress the negative view of the smoker, while those directed at the mid-adolescent must improve the image of the nonsmoker. Only time will tell whether this strategy will be effective.

Marijuana

Marijuana is used much more frequently by adolescents than by adults (Archer and Lopata, 1979). Perhaps more than any other drug, marijuana symbolizes adolescent rebellion. Whereas marijuana use tends to decline as generations age, alcohol and cigarette use continue.

According to a National Institute on Drug Abuse study (1983), 57 percent of their sample of high school seniors had used marijuana once and 5.5 percent were daily users. According to this survey, about the same percentage of adoles-

11. *True or False:*
Antismoking campaigns have been more successful at preventing teens from beginning to smoke than at motivating people to stop smoking.

Perhaps more than any drug, marijuana symbolizes adolescent rebellion.

cents use marijuana as drink alcohol on a daily basis. Most users do so only occasionally for recreational purposes and do not differ much from nonusers. Nonusers have more affectionate relationships with their fathers (Brook et al., 1981). In addition, adolescent males who identify with nonuser fathers are less likely to use the drug (Brook et al., 1984). However, many differences are found at the extremes (Archer and Lopata, 1979). Regular users are more rebellious and angry, show a lack of responsibility, and score high on a measure of sensation-seeking (Brook et al., 1981). An adolescent's first drink is usually in the family setting, but peer pressure is very important in determining the initial use of marijuana (Sorosiak et al., 1976).

It is easier to cite the health risks involved in alcohol and tobacco use than those in marijuana use, because the studies on marijuana are especially difficult to evaluate. In fact, you can find studies showing just about anything concerning marijuana. There are two strong research findings, however. Marijuana use is related to short-term memory problems, and it causes driving impairments (Archer and Lopata, 1979). One major controversy concerns marijuana and the **amotivational syndrome**. Does marijuana use reduce motivation to achieve? The evidence is mixed here, and you can answer the question either way, depending on which studies you consider most important. Carlin and Post (1974) found that users had lower levels of achievement. Kolansky and colleagues (1978) found that marijuana users were sluggish both mentally and physically, had a lack of goals, showed a loss of interest, had slower reaction times, and suffered short-term memory deficits. A relationship between these symptoms and the frequency of marijuana use exists. When users withdrew from the weed, the symptoms decreased. The time necessary was related to the frequency and duration of the smoking (Kolansky and Moore, 1978). However, other studies have

amotivational syndrome
A condition, controversially linked to heavy marijuana use, involving a lack of ambition and mental sluggishness.

not found such evidence (Archer and Lopata, 1979), and the amotivational syndrome remains a question mark.

Does Marijuana Use Lead to Harder Drugs?   One of the most controversial questions concerning marijuana is its relationship to the use of other drugs. We know, for instance, that people who use marijuana are more likely to experiment with other drugs, but that does not necessarily mean that the next step from marijuana is becoming a heroin addict. The large majority of marijuana users will stop short of that. In a study conducted with New York State high school students, Kandel (1975) found that drug use began not with marijuana but with legal drugs—beer and wine, then cigarettes or hard liquor. Some stopped here, others went on to marijuana and from marijuana to other illicit drugs. We need to know more about why some stop at one level of drug use while others progress to higher levels.

Is drug use associated with a specific personality pattern, peer pressure, or poor relationships with parents? Actually, each of these factors contributes independently to drug use (Brook et al., 1983). The personality pattern of risk-taking, lower achievement orientation, rebelliousness—basically a nonconventional personality pattern—is related to drug-taking. A pattern of parental drug-taking, lack of warmth, and lack of harmony in the home is also related to drug-taking, as is peer use of drugs.

Drug Education

When asked how to combat drug problems, most people cite education. Indeed, education is one important consideration. Yet what kind of education is needed? Some advocate simply presenting the dangers of drug-taking. But this in itself is ineffective, for a variety of reasons. First, these facts often run counter to people's experiences. Most teens know people who drink, smoke, or use marijuana and seem to be achieving and coping reasonably well. The "I know a guy who smokes like a chimney and is eighty-six years old" argument is difficult to counter, since drug research is based on probabilities. There are always exceptions to the rules. Second, teens are very likely to deny or rationalize. Denial is shown in the "It can't happen to me attitude." Rationalization is demonstrated in the common argument "I can get hit by a bolt of lightning tomorrow." Third, information offered by authority figures is not likely to be effective in countering peer pressure, especially with adolescents who see their parents using drugs, have drug-taking friends, or are attracted to drugs as a sign of rebellion.

Accurate information is needed, but so is teaching decision-making skills and educating for individuality. Adolescents need to be taught to think for themselves and to improve their decision-making abilities. This is not necessarily a popular strategy, because their conclusions on various issues are not always going to be identical to those of their elders. Nevertheless, it remains one option for increasing responsibility and countering the drug problem that is so pervasive.

PRESCRIPTIONS FOR A CHANGING RELATIONSHIP

In the last three chapters, the physical, cognitive, and social development of the adolescent have been examined. Even if we do not consider the period of adolescence one of storm and stress, it is one of change. The physical changes are well known, and as we have seen, important changes in the cognitive and social realms are also taking place. Contrary to popular opinion, parents continue to be important factors in their children's development throughout adolescence. Yet parent-child relationships change, and some parents and adolescents negotiate these changes better than others. Knowledge gleaned from research studies on adolescence can be combined with the theoretical perspectives introduced in Chapter Four and applied throughout this text to produce suggestions that can reduce parent-child conflict and improve familial relationships. These suggestions are not cures for all the problems of this period, but they can help each party understand the other better.

Adolescents and Parents

It is popular to dwell on the influence parents have on adolescents, but adolescents also affect their parents' behavior. During counseling sessions, I have often been impressed by adolescents' complaints that their parents do not listen to them, a charge that is frequently true, but I have also found that teens themselves do not listen to what their parents say. In addition, parents often feel unappreciated. I remember the case of one single parent who, despite a number of problems, drove her adolescent daughter here and there without complaint. She told me that she sometimes felt angry because her daughter never once said thank you. Finally, adolescents often know what answers are certain to create problems with their parents. They may say or do things that elicit strong reactions from their parents, perhaps to gain attention or to provoke an argument that masks the real problem. The principle of reciprocal interaction (see page 153) notes that each party in a relationship influences the behavior of the other. Just as parents influence their adolescents, adolescents' verbal and nonverbal behavior influence the behavior of their parents.

Adolescents can use this principle effectively by reinforcing their parents and understanding how their verbal pronouncements will affect their parents. For example, showing appreciation when parents go out of their way to help them can be very reinforcing to parents. In addition, phrasing opinions in ways that are more likely to sway parents can also help. Many disagreements occur because of confused communication. Teenagers often believe they understand what their parents are saying, but this may not actually be the case. If a parent says "You can't go to the dance on Saturday," an adolescent may misunderstand this and interpret it as "You can't go anywhere on Saturday." If adolescents reflect on what their parents are really saying, misunderstandings can be reduced. If the adolescent in the above example had said, "You mean I can't go anywhere?" the parent could have corrected the misunderstanding. There are enough sources for conflict in parent-child relationships without adding misunderstanding to them.

Parents and Adolescents

Research in child development can help parents deal with their adolescents more effectively. Each of the following suggestions is based on the fact that the basic relationship between parents and their children changes during the adolescent years.

Freedom for One, Slavery for the Other

Pamela is on strike. As far as she's concerned, she is a second-class citizen in her home and she is tired of it. She's sixteen now and, according to Pam, her parents treat her like a nine-year-old. She has a strict curfew of eleven o'clock on weekends and must always tell her parents where she is and what she will be doing. When she gets home, what she calls "the inquisition" begins.

What bothers Pamela most is that her seventeen-year-old brother can come and go when he pleases and is not subject to "the inquisition." This is especially frustrating because Pam thinks she is more mature than her brother. Another source of contention are the daily chores. Again, Pam's brother seems to get away with murder, while she has chores that take up a lot of time.

Pam's parents had once seen a counselor, and they agreed to see the counselor again with Pam in hopes of straightening the situation out. They told the counselor that they were strict with Pamela, but not overly so. They give her privacy, but they feel a responsibility to know where she is and what she's doing. If Pam is at a friend's house, she can stay out later, but they don't want Pam "hanging out" anywhere. They live in a tough neighborhood and are afraid something will happen to her.

As for allowing the brother more freedom, they note that he works part-time and he "can't get pregnant or raped." When it was suggested that he could get a girl pregnant, they shook their heads. "He's too smart for that." Pam's parents also claim that both children have chores. He mows the lawn and takes out the garbage. Pam helps her mother cook and clean. Both children are responsible for their own rooms and laundering their own clothes.

1. If you were the counselor, what would you suggest?
2. If you were Pam's parents, what changes, if any, would you agree to?
3. If you were Pam, what would you do?

1. In Chapter Fifteen, the changes in the cognitive abilities of adolescents were discussed, including teens' attempts to formulate their own values. Parents may not listen to their adolescents, especially if their children are taking positions that are different. On the other hand, parents may counter these unwanted views with a long lecture, which is usually an ineffective method of communication. Some evidence indicates that parents tend to concentrate more on explaining their own viewpoints than in trying to understand their child's views (Hunter, 1985). Parents can show their understanding by repeating the feelings or sentiments of their children, thus demonstrating that they are listening. For example, restating a teenager's views by beginning a sentence "So you feel that . . ." both shows parental interest and allows the teen to correct any problem in communication. Before making judgments about a child's ideas and beliefs, it is best for parents to make certain that they first understand them.

2. Despite the teen's striving for independence, the family remains a potent force in a teen's life. Dealing with this independence is challenging. Some parents mistakenly believe that they must take a hands-off approach. Others are reluctant to allow any freedom or responsibility. Adolescents are often ambivalent about freedom and responsibility—wanting it and fearing it at the same time. The same is true for independence. One possible course is to allow the adolescent freedom and responsibility in slow steps. This gradual progression must begin in childhood.

3. The differing perspectives of children of various ages and their parents have been noted throughout this text. As children journey through middle childhood and into adolescence, many parents want to offer their children their wisdom, and this is understandable. One parent once asked me why her daughter had to make the same mistakes she had. It is important to understand that parents are viewing life from one perspective but that adolescents are viewing it from another.

4. Adolescence is often divided roughly into early, middle, and late periods. Most parents have little or no patience with early adolescents, who appear so secretive and immature. When early adolescents consider something vital and parents know better, it becomes difficult to treat the subject with the seriousness these teens think it deserves. Early adolescents are often misunderstood and ridiculed. In middle adolescence, parents often want to talk with their children about important issues and are surprised to find the lines of communication cut. It is important to accept the concerns of early adolescents as genuine for their age and to respect their privacy, while trying to show them the wider view.

5. The adolescent culture often differs from that of their parents in many surface characteristics, such as hairstyles, music preferences, and clothing styles. Conformity to peers in these areas is quite strong, while adolescents' deeper values are often not as much at odds with those their parents hold as is sometimes thought (see pages 613–615). Trying to argue against most of these surface differences is a waste of time. The deeper values are more important.

6. The question of independent identity formation is sometimes one that haunts parents. Some parents want their children to be clones of themselves, but adolescents need to find their own identities. As we have seen, this does not preclude parental influence.

7. Most parents want their children to develop a sense of responsibility and internal controls. This can best be accomplished by using what is called an authoritative approach to child-rearing, as noted in Chapters Ten and Twelve. This involves allowing discussion, using reason whenever possible, being issue-oriented, explaining policies, setting sensible standards, and valuing autonomy (Lunde and Lunde, 1980).

8. Social-learning theory emphasizes the importance of the models children see around them. Adolescents are excellent at noting hypocrisy, and parents are more likely to be imitated if they model what they preach.

9. One responsibility parents have is to be certain that their children have the correct information concerning drugs and sexuality. We have seen that many teens do not have factual, up-to-date information. Simple prescriptions such as "Don't do it" are usually ineffective. At the same time, adolescent decision-making skills need to be strengthened, for in the end adolescents must make their own decisions.

10. During adolescence, the peer group takes on a special importance, and parents must be sensitive to this. Criticizing adolescents in front of their peers is a common mistake. Since the peer group is so important, these adolescents often attempt to save face and will actively challenge their parents and teachers. It is best, whenever possible, to criticize children and adolescents in private.

11. "All my parents ever do is criticize me." This is a common complaint. Some parents aren't even aware that they are constantly nagging their children. In Chapter Four, the importance of positive reinforcement was noted. Noting the positive as well as criticizing the negative is vital. One way of checking this is to keep track of the ratio of positive remarks to negative comments.

As you can see, parents need not abdicate their special relationship with their children to be effective. Supervision and guidance are part of the parents' responsibilities, but so is the preparation of children for independent adulthood. Constant criticism, harsh punishment, and strict warnings are often ineffective, especially if they occur in a cold, hostile environment. Adolescents will be most affected by what they see and experience. As Haim Ginott (1969, p. 243) said, "Character traits cannot be taught directly; no one can teach loyalty by lectures, courage by correspondence, or manhood by mail. Character education requires presence that demonstrates and contact that communicates. A teenager learns what he lives, and becomes what he experiences. To him, our mood is the message, the style is the substance, the process is the product."

Chapter Summary

1. Erik Erikson viewed the formation of a personal identity as the positive outcome of adolescence. Identity diffusion, the failure to answer the fundamental questions of identity, is the negative outcome of the stage.

2. Marcia extended Erikson's conception of identity to include four identity statuses: identity achievement, identity moratorium, identity diffusion, and identity foreclosure. Identity diffusion is a status in which a person has not begun to make any commitments, although he or she may or may not have faced identity crises in life. Identity diffusion is considered negative only when an individual leaves adolescence without forming an identity. Identity foreclosure is a status in which a person has made commitments prematurely. Identity moratorium is a temporary status in which an individual is not ready to make commitments but may be exploring possibilities. Identity achievers have experienced these crises and made their commitments.

3. People who have achieved a personal identity are more ready to form intimate relationships.

4. Forming a personal identity involves searching, and this effort may create anxiety in many people. Some try shortcuts, such as totally accepting others' values, fervently taking on a cause, or joining a group that is very strict and does not allow questioning, such as a cult.

5. The popular picture of adolescence as a period of continuous conflict between parents and children and the replacement of parental influence by peers is not in keeping with findings of studies in this area. Although peer influence is significant, it does not replace that of parents. Most adolescents have good relationships with their parents.

6. The generation gap is not as wide as first thought. Differences in the way the generations see the world are often a matter of degree, but each misperceives the opinions of the other.

7. Peer influence appears to be greater in the areas of social interaction, styles, and attitudes toward schools than in the realm of deeper values. On important issues, adolescents do make independent decisions.

8. Adolescent drug use is common, with alcohol, tobacco, and marijuana leading the list. Alcohol is the most abused drug, and its social acceptability makes combating excessive use difficult. Cigarette smoking has increased greatly among females. Despite the health hazards, the social image of the smoker to many teens is positive. Much of the research on marijuana is contradictory. However, marijuana usage is associated with short-term memory defects and driving impairments. The question of whether its use leads one to become less motivated to achieve is unclear at the present time.

9. Factors such as peer pressure, a personality pattern of risk-taking, rebelliousness, lower achievement motivation, parents who use drugs, and lack of a warm relationship between parents and their children are associated with adolescent drug use.

10. Adolescents may improve relationships with their parents by showing appreciation for their parents' efforts and demonstrating an understanding of their parents' ideas and concerns. Parents may improve their relationships by showing an understanding of the adolescents' concerns, allowing them additional freedom and responsibility as they mature, appreciating the fact that adolescents cannot be clones of their parents, and modeling the behavior they advocate in their adolescents.

■ *Answers to True or False Questions*

1. *True*. There are more alternatives open to adolescents today, making identity formation more difficult.

2. *False*. Correct statement: Periods of confusion are not unusual in adolescence and do not necessarily signal mental illness.

3. *True*. Identity achievers are better able to form intimate relationships.

4. *True*. Cults use very sophisticated persuasive devices.

5. *False*. Correct statement: Cults recruit new members from the ranks of the confused and isolated, but these neophytes are not mentally ill.

6. *False*. Correct statement: Conformity to peers peaks during mid-adolescence and declines thereafter.

7. *False*. Correct statement: Most adolescents do not rate themselves as very rebellious.

8. *True*. Most adolescents believe that there is a wider gulf between them and their parents than there actually is.

9. *True*. Alcohol is the most commonly used drug among adolescents.

10. *False*. Correct statement: Over the past few decades, the percentage of female teens who smoke has dramatically increased, while the percentage of males smoking has stayed about the same.

11. *False*. Correct statement: Antismoking campaigns are more successful in motivating people to stop smoking than in preventing adolescents from starting to smoke.

acceleration An educational program in which a gifted child skips a grade or a particular unit.

accommodation The process by which one's existing structures are altered to fit new information.

adolescence The psychological experience of the child from puberty to adulthood.

adolescent egocentrism The adolescent failure to differentiate between what one is thinking and what others are considering.

amniocentesis A procedure in which fluid is taken from a pregnant woman's uterus and fetal cells are checked for genetic and chromosomal abnormalities.

amotivational syndrome A condition, controversially linked to heavy marijuana use, involving a lack of ambition and mental sluggishness.

anal stage The second psychosexual stage, in which sexuality is centered on the anal cavity.

androgens A group of male hormones including testoterone.

androgyny The state of possessing the best characteristics of masculinity and femininity.

animism The preschooler's belief that inanimate objects possess a consiousness or are alive.

anorexia nervosa A condition of self-imposed starvation most often found among adolescent females.

anoxia A condition in which the infant does not receive a sufficient supply of oxygen.

anxious/ambivalent attachment A type of attachment behavior shown during the "strange situation," in which the child both seeks close contact and yet resists it during the mother's reentrance after a brief separation.

anxious/avoidant attachment A type of attachment behavior show in the "strange situation," in which the child avoids reestablishing contact with mother as she reenters the room after a brief separation.

anxious attachment A general classification of insecure attachment shown in the "strange situation," consisting of either avoidant behavior or ambivalent attachment behavior.

Apgar Scoring System A relatively simple system giving a gross measure of infant survivability.

artificialism The belief that natural phenomena are caused by human beings.

assimilation The process by which information is altered to fit into one's already existent structure.

associative play A type of play seen in preschoolers who are actively involved with one another but cannot sustain these interactions.

attachment An emotional tie binding people together over space and time.

attachment behavior Actions that result in a child's gaining proximity to caregivers.

authoritarian parenting style A style of parenting in which parents rigidly control their children's behavior by establishing rules and value obedience while discouraging questioning.

authoritative parenting style A style of parenting in which parents establish limits but allow open communication and some freedom for children to make their own decisions in certain areas.

autism A severe mental disorder involving a lack of responsiveness to others, communication disabilities, and bizarre behavior.

autonomy vs. shame or doubt The second psychosocial stage, in which the positive outcome is a sense of independence, and the negative outcome is a sense of doubt about being a separate individual.

babbling Verbal production of vowel and consonant sounds strung together and often repeated.

Babinski reflex The reflex in which stroking the soles of the feet results in the toes fanning out.

Bayley Scales of Infant Development A test of intelligence administered to infants between two months and two and a half years of age.

behavior genetics The study of how genetic endowment influences behavior.

behavior modification The use of learning theory to alter behavior.

bilingual A term describing people who can function in more than one language.

Black English A dialect spoken throughout the United States by lower-income blacks but understood by the overwhelming majority of blacks.

blastocyst The stage of development in which the organism consists of layers of cells around a central cavity forming a hollow sphere.

blind experimental designs An experimental design in which researchers do not know whether a subject they are working with belongs to the experimental group or the control group.

Braille A tactile system of reading designed for the blind.

Brazelton Scale A rather involved system for evaluating the infant's reflexes and sensory and behavioral abilities.

bulimia An eating disorder marked by episodic binging and purging.

canalization The self-righting process in which the child shows a catch-up in growth despite a moderate amount of stress or illness.

case study A method of research in which one person's progress is followed for an extended period of time.

castration anxiety A male's fear of castration, usually used to indicate a boy's anxiety during the phallic stage.

centering The tendency to attend to only one dimension at a time.

cephalocaudal principle The growth principle stating that growth proceeds from the head downward to the trunk and feet.

cerebral palsy A disability caused by brain damage, usually at birth, marked by motor problems, poor speech, paralysis, and sometimes losses in intelligence.

Cesarean section The birth procedure by which the fetus is surgically delivered through the abdominal wall and uterus.

child abuse A general term used to denote an injury intentionally perpetrated on a child.

chromosomes Rod-shaped structures that carry genes.

chronological age The person's age according to birthdays.

classical conditioning A learning process in which a neutral stimulus is paired with a stimulus that elicits a response until the originally neutral stimulus elicits that response.

classification The process of placing objects in different groupings.

clinical method A method of studying children which relies on both observation and individual questioning.

cognitive development A general term denoting intellectual development.

cognitive style The stable ways that children process information, whether the source is internal or external.

cohort effort The effect of belonging to a particular generation, of being raised in a historical time.

commitment In psychosocial theory, making a decision concerning some question involved in identity formation, and following a plan of action reflecting this decision.

communication The process of sharing information.

compensatory education The use of educational strategies in an attempt to reduce or eliminate some perceived difference between groups.

comprehension The understanding of language.

computer literacy The knowledge and computer skills an individual needs to function in a technological society.

concordance rate The degree of similarity between twins on any particular trait.

concrete operational stage Piaget's third stage of cognitive development, lasting roughly from seven through eleven years of age, in which children develop the ability to perform logical operations, such as conversation.

conduction hearing loss Hearing loss caused by mechanical problems in conducting vibrations within the ear.

conscience Part of the superego which causes an individual to experience guilt when transgressing.

conscious Freudian term for thoughts or memories of which a person is immediately aware.

conservation The principle that quantities remain the same despite changes in their appearance.

contact comfort The need for physical touching and fondling.

conventional level Kohlberg's second level of moral reasoning, in which conformity to the expectations of others and society in general serve as the bases for moral decision-making.

convergent thinking A type of thinking in which people solve problems by integrating information in a logical manner.

cooing The verbal production of single-syllable sounds, like "oo."

cooperative play A type of play seen in the later part of the preschool period and continuing into middle childhood, marked by group play, playing specific roles, and active cooperation for sustained periods of time.

correlation A term denoting a relationship between two variables.

creativity The ability to approach problems in novel, original ways.

crisis In psychosocial theory, a time in which a person actively faces and questions aspects of his or her own identity.

critical period The period during which a particular event has its greatest impact.

cross-sectional design A research design in which children of different ages are studied to obtain information about changes in some variable.

crossing over The process occurring during meiosis in which genetic material on one chromosome is exchanged with material from the other.

crowning The point in labor at which the baby's head appears.

cult A radical group that advocates a unique lifestyle under the direction of a leader who is believed to have special abilities or insights.

cystic fibrosis A severe genetic disease marked by digestive and respiratory problems.

deciduous teeth The scientific term for "baby teeth."

deductive reasoning Reasoning that begins with a general rule and then is applied to specific cases.

defense mechanism An automatic and unconscious process that reduces or eliminates anxiety or emotional conflict.

deferred imitation The ability to observe an act and imitate it at a later time.

delivery of the placenta The third and last stage of birth in which the placenta is delivered.

dependent variable The factor in a study which will be measured by the researcher.

deprivation dwarfism Growth retardation due to emotional factors such as stress.

despair The second stage in prolonged separation from the primary caregivers, in which the child becomes apathetic.

detachment The last stage in prolonged separation from the primary caregivers, in which the child cannot place trust in anyone else and becomes detached from other people.

developmental psychology The study of how organisms change over time.

diethylstilbestrol (DES) A drug taken during pregnancy to prevent miscarriage and responsible for some cases of cancer in the offspring during late adolescence or early adulthood.

digestive reflexes A group of reflexes such as hiccuping and burping.

dilation The first stage in labor, in which the uterus contracts and the cervix flattens and dilates to allow the fetus to pass.

disability A total or partial behavioral, mental, physical, or sensory loss of functioning.

discipline An attempt to control others in order to hold undesirable impulses in check and encourage self-control.

displacement The process by which an emotion is transferred from one object or person to another more acceptable substitute.

distant-figure-style grandparents Grandparents who are basically uninvolved with their grandchildren and have little contact with them.

divergent thinking A type of thinking in which people see new and different relationships between elements of a problem which are still relevant to the situation.

dizygotic or fraternal twins Twins who develop from two fertilized eggs and are no more genetically similar than any other sibling pair.

dominant traits Traits that require the presence of only one gene.

Down's Syndrome (mongolism) A disorder caused by the presence of an extra chromosome, leading to a distinct physical appearance and mental retardation.

dramatic play A type of play in which children take on the roles of others.

dyslexia An inability to read with understanding.

eclectric Picking and choosing elements from many different theories rather than depending solely on one theory to explain human behavior or development.

ego The part of the mind in Freudian theory which mediates between the real world and the desires of the id.

ego ideal The individual's positive and desirable standards of behavior.

egocentrism A thought process described by Piaget in which young children believe everyone is experiencing the environment in the same way they are. Children who are egocentric have difficulty understanding someone else's point of view.

Electra complex In Freudian theory, the female equivalent to the Oedipal complex, in which the female experiences sexual feelings toward her father and wishes to do away with her mother.

embryonic stage The stage of prenatal development beginning at about two weeks and ending at about eight weeks, when bone cells begin to replace cartilage.

emotional abuse Psychological damage perpetrated on a child over an extended period of time by a parent.

enrichment An educational program in which a gifted child is given special challenging work that goes beyond the usual.

enuresis The scientific term for bedwetting.

epigenetic principle The preset developmental plan in Erikson's theory consisting of two elements: that personality develops according to maturationally determined steps and that each society is structured to encourage challenges that arise during these times.

equilibration In Piagetian theory, the process by which children seek a balance between what they know and what they are experiencing.

eros In Freudian theory, the positive, constructive sex instinct.

estrogens A group of female hormones including estradiol.

evoked potentials A technique of measuring the brain's response to particular stimuli.

exceptional child A child whose intellectual, emotional, or physical performance falls substantially above or below that of "normal" peers.

experimental method A research strategy using controls which allows the researcher to discover cause and effect relationships.

expressive children Children who use words involved in social interactions, such as "stop" and "bye."

expulsion The second stage of birth, involving the actual delivery of the fetus.

external locus of control The belief that one's destiny is determined by others or by fate.

extinction The weakening and disappearance of a learned response.

fading A teaching technique in which the student is first taken through each step of a process, then the instructor slowly reduces direct participation until the learner can perform the task alone.

fear of strangers A common phenomenon beginning in the second half of the first year, consisting of a fear response to new people.

fear of success A term used to describe the fear that success in nontraditional spheres of life reflect negatively on one's masculinity or femininity.

Feingold diet A diet developed by Dr. Normal Feingold for the treatment of hyperactivity, consisting mainly of elimination of preservatives and artificial flavors.

fetal alcohol syndrome A number of characteristics, including retardation, facial abnormalities, growth defects, and poor coordination, caused by maternal alcohol consumption.

fetal monitor A machine that monitors the condition of the mother and the fetus.

fetal stage The stage of prenatal development, beginning at about eight weeks until birth.

field dependent style The use of information absorbed from the environment as the principal guide in processing information.

field independent style The use of internal, independent factors as guides in processing information.

fine-tuning theory A theory noting that parents tune their language to a child's linguistic ability.

fontanels The soft spots on the top of a baby's head.

formal operational stage The last Piagetian stage of cognitive development, in which a person develops the ability to deal with abstractions and reason in a scientific manner.

formal-style grandparents Grandparents who, although interested, are uninvolved in the raising of their grandchildren.

friendship A positive, reciprocal interpersonal relationship.

fun-seeking grandparents Grandparents who play with their grandchildren and enjoy many activities with them.

gametes The scientific term for the sex cells.

gender consistency Children's knowledge that they will remain a boy or a girl regardless of how they act, dress, or groom.

gender identity One's awareness of being a male or a female.

gender stability Children's knowledge that they were of a particular gender when younger and will remain so throughout life.

gene The basic unit of heredity.

generation gap The difference in attitudes among various generations.

generativity vs. stagnation The seventh psychosocial stage, occurring during middle adulthood, in which the positive outcome is a sense of giving to others, while the negative outcome is self-absorption and stagnation.

genital stage The final psychosexual stage, occurring during adolescence, in which adult heterosexual behavior develops.

genotype The genetic configuration of the individual.

germinal stage The earliest stage of prenatal development, lasting from conception to about two weeks.

giftedness People who either have demonstrated or have the potential for high ability in the intellectual, creative, academic, or leadership areas or the performing or visual arts.

grasping reflex A reflex in which a stroke on the palm causes the infant to make a fist.

guilt The negative outcome of the psychosocial crisis of the early childhood period, resulting in a sense that the child's acts and desires are bad.

habituation The process by which organisms spend less and less time attending to familiar stimuli.

handicap The difficulty an individual has adjusting to the environment.

Hawthorne effect The tendency for people to act differently when extra attention is paid them.

hemophilia A sex-linked inherited blood disease.

heritability A term used to describe how much of the variation seen in any particular trait within a population is due to genetic endowment.

holophrase The use of one word to stand for an entire thought.

HOME Scale A scale that provides a measure of the quality and quantity of the emotional and cognitive elements in the home.

hospitalism A condition in children found in substandard institutions, marked by emotional disturbances, failure to gain weight, and retardation.

hostile aggression Aggression that is aimed at injuring another person.

Huntington's Chorea A dominant genetic disorder affecting the central nervous system.

hyperactivity Children whose behavior is impulsive, overly active, highy distractible, and inattentive.

hyperplastic obesity Obesity caused by the formation of an excessive number of fat cells.

hypertrophic obesity Obesity caused by the swelling of fat cells with fat.

hypothesis An educated guess made after examining the literature in the field.

id The portion of the mind in Freudian theory which serves as the depository for wishes and desires.

identification The process by which children take on the characteristics of another person, often a parent.

identity The sense of knowing who you are.

identity achievement An identity status in which a person has developed a solid, personal identity.

identity diffusion An identity status resulting in confusion, aimlessness, and a sense of emptiness.

identity foreclosure An identity status marked by a premature identity decision.

identity moratorium An identity status in which a person is actively searching for an identity.

identity vs. role confusion The fifth psychosocial stage, in which the positive outcome is a sense of knowing who one is, while the negative outcome is a sense of purposelessness.

imaginary audience A term used to describe adolescents' belief that they are the focus of attention and being evaluated by everyone.

imprinting An irreversible, rigid behavior pattern of attachment.

impulsive cognitive style A cognitive style marked by a cursory examination of a problem and answering questions very quickly.

independent variable The factor in a study which will be manipulated by the researcher.

individualized education program (IEP) An individual plan outlining educational goals and methods for attaining them.

inductive reasoning Reasoning that proceeds from specific cases to the formation of a general rule.

industry The positive outcome of the psychosocial crisis in the middle years of childhood, involving a feeling of self-confidence and pride concerning one's achievements.

industry vs. inferiority The fourth psychosocial stage, in which the positive outcome is a sense of confidence concerning one's accomplishments, while the negative outcome is a sense of inadequacy concerning one's achievements.

inferiority The negative outcome of the psychosocial crisis in the middle years of childhood, involving the child's belief that his or her work and achievements are below par.

initiative The positive outcome of the psychosocial crisis of the early childhood period, involving development of a respect for one's own wishes and desires.

initiative vs. guilt The third psychosocial stage, in which the positive outcome is a favorable view of one's own desires and actions, the negative outcome a sense of guilt over one's actions.

instrumental aggression Aggression that involves struggles over possessions.

integrity vs. despair The eighth and last psychosocial stage, occurring during old age, in which the positive outcome is a sense of satisfaction with one's life while the negative outcome is a sense of bitterness concerning lost opportunities.

intelligence A measure of one's rate of development relative to the rate of development of one's peers. The ability to profit from experience. A cluster of abilities, such as reasoning and memory. In the Piagetian view, any behavior that allows the individual to adapt to the environment.

intelligence quotient A method of measuring intelligence by dividing the mental age by the chronological age and multiplying by 100.

internal locus of control The belief that one is in control of one's own destiny.

intimacy The positive outcome of the psychosocial crisis of young adulthood, involving development of very close interpersonal relations, most often typified by marriage.

intimacy vs. isolation The sixth psychosocial stage, occurring during young adulthood, in which the positive outcome is a development of deep interpersonal relationships, while the negative outcome is a flight from close relationships.

isolation The negative outcome of the psychosocial crisis of young adulthood, resulting in a lack of commitment to others.

kwashiokor A nutritional problem often found in toddlers and preschoolers who are newly weaned and then subjected to a protein-deficient environment.

labor A term used to describe the general process of expelling the fetus from the mother's uterus.

Lamaze method A method of prepared childbirth that requires the active participation of both parents.

language The use of symbols to represent meaning.

language-acquisition device An assumed biological device used in the acquisition of language.

language production The ability to verbalize language.

lanugo The fine hair that covers a newborn infant.

latency stage The psychosexual phase, occurring during middle childhood, in which sexuality is hidden.

learned helplessness A state in which people believe that there is nothing they can do to improve a distressing situation.

learning Relatively permanent changes in behavior due to interaction with the environment.

learning disabilities A disorder in which some basic psychological processes involved in understanding or using language manifest themselves in impaired academic performance.

legal blindness A person with a visual acuity of 20/200 in the best eye with correction or with peripheral vision that subtends less than 20 degrees of the field.

Leboyer method A method of childbirth emphasizing the importance of the birth experience for the child and encouraging such practices as dim lights, low voices, delay in cutting the umbilical cord, a bath, and a massage.

libido In Freudian theory, the energy emanating from the sex instinct.

linguistic deficit hypothesis The belief that a dialect, for example, Black English, is a hindrance to learning.

linguistic difference hypothesis The belief that a dialect such as Black English is different from standard English but not a deficit.

longitudinal design A research design in which subjects are followed over an extended period of time to note developmental changes in some variable.

love-oriented discipline A type of discipline relying on the use of reasoning or love.

mainstreaming A term used to describe the process by which exceptional children are integrated into classes with "normal" peers.

marasmus A condition of severe underweight, heart irregularities, and weakened resistance caused by malnutrition.

mass to specific The developmental principle stating that the larger muscles develop before the fine muscles.

maturation A term used to describe changes that are due to the unfolding of an individual's genetic plan. These changes are relatively immune to environmental influence.

maturational age The child's level of maturation relative to his or her peers.

meiosis The process by which sex cells divide to form two cells, each containing 23 chromosomes.

Mendelian traits Traits that follow a rather simple dominant-recessive pattern.

mental age The age at which an individual is functioning.

mental retardation A condition marked by subnormal intellectual functioning and adjustment difficulties which occur before a person is eighteen years of age.

metacognition People's awareness of their own cognitive processes.

metamemory People's knowledge of their own memory processes.

mistrust The negative outcome of Erickson's first psychosocial stage, an attitude of suspiciousness.

monozygotic or identical twins Twins who develop from one fertilized egg and have an identical genetic structure.

moral realism The Piagetian stage of moral reasoning during which rules are viewed as sacred and justice is whatever the authority figure says.

moral reasoning An approach to the study of moral development, stressing the importance of the child's ideas and reasoning about justice and right and wrong.

moral relativism The Piagetian stage of moral reasoning in which children weigh the intentions of others before judging their actions right or wrong.

Moro reflex A reflex elicited by a sudden loud noise or momentary change in position, causing the back to arch, an extension of the arms and legs, and finally their contraction into a hugging position.

motherese The use of simple repetitive sentences with young children.

mothering A general term used to describe the caregiving activities of *all* interested parties, not just the mother.

multifactorial traits Traits that are influenced both by genes and the environment.

nativist explanation An explanation of language development based on biological or innate factors.

naturalistic observation A method of research in which the researcher observes organisms in their natural habitat.

neonate The scientific term for a newborn infant.

normalization The process by which disabled people are integrated into the mainstream of society as much as possible.

object permanence The understanding that an object exists even when it is out of one's visual field.

Oedipal complex The conflict during the phallic stage in which a boy experiences sexual feelings toward his mother and wishes to do away with his father.

onlooker play A classification of play in which the child watches others play and shows some interest, but is unable to join in.

operant conditioning The learning process in which behavior is governed by its consequences.

oral stage The first psychosexual stage, in which sexuality is centered on the oral cavity.

overextension A type of error in which children apply a term in a wider manner than is correct.

overgeneralization A type of error in which children overuse the basic rules of the language. Once they learn to use plural nouns, they may say "mans" instead of "men."

parallel play A type of play common in two-year-olds in which they play in the presence of other children but not with them.

partially sighted A person with a visual acuity of 20/70 to 20/200 in the best eye with correction.

peer Any person of a similar age.

permissive parenting style A style of parenting marked by open communication and a lack of parental demand for good behavior.

personal fable The adolescents' belief that their experiences are unique and original.

phallic stage Freud's third psychosexual stage, occurring during early childhood, in which the sexual energy is located in the genital area and the Oedipal or Electra conflicts take place.

phenotype The observable characteristics of the organism.

phenylketonuria (PKU) A recessive genetic disorder marked by the inability to digest a particular protein. If the disorder is not treated it leads to mental retardation.

phocomelia A condition in which the infant is born without arms or legs or with underdeveloped extremities.

play An activity dominated by the child and performed with a positive feeling.

polygenic or multigenic traits Characteristics that are influenced by more than one pair of genes.

postconventional level Kohlberg's third level of moral reasoning, in which moral decisions are made on the basis of individual values that have been internalized.

power-assertive discipline A type of discipline relying on the use of power, such as physical punishment or forceful commands.

preconscious Freudian term for thoughts or memories that although not immediately conscious can easily become so.

preconventional level Kohlberg's first level of moral reasoning, in which satisfaction of one's own needs and reward and punishment serve as the bases for moral decision-making.

prematurity Any infant weighing less than 5 1/2 pounds or born less than 37 weeks after conception.

preoperational stage Piaget's second stage of cognitive development, marked by the appearance of language and symbolic function and the child's inability to understand logical concepts, such as conservation.

preterm infants Any infant born before 37 weeks of gestation.

primary circular reactions Actions that are repeated over and over again by infants.

primary process The process by which the id seeks to gratify its desires.

primary sex characteristics Body changes directly associated with sexual reproduction.

Project Head Start A massive federal compensatory education project aimed at reducing or eliminating the differences in educational achievement between poor and middle-class youngsters.

protein-calorie deficiency The most common nutritional deficiency in the world, in which neither the number of calories nor the protein consumed is sufficient.

protest The initial reaction to separation in which the infant cries and refuses to be cared for by substitutes.

proto-conversations The infant's responses to verbal and nonverbal cues which resemble turn-taking, as in a conversation.

proximodistal principle The growth principle stating that development occurs from the inside out, that the internal organs develop faster than the extremities.

psycholinguistics The study of the nature of language.

psychosexual stages Stages in Freud's developmental theory.

puberty Physiological changes involved in sexual maturation, as well as other body changes that occur during the teen years.

punishment The process by which some physical or emotional pain is inflicted in order to reduce the probability that misbehavior will reoccur.

qualitative changes Changes in function or process.

quantitative changes Changes that can be considered solely in terms of increases or decreases, such as changes in height or weight.

rapid eye movements (REM) The movements of the eyes during sleep that are related to dreaming.

readiness The point in development at which a child has the necessary skills to master a new challenge.

reading-readiness tests Tests that measure a child's attainment of the skills necessary for success in reading.

recall A way of testing memory in which the subject must produce the correct response given very limited cues.

recessive traits Traits that require the presence of two genes.

reciprocal interactions The process by which an organism constantly affects and is affected by the environment.

recognition A way of testing memory in which the subject is required to choose the correct answer from a group of choices.

referential children Children whose early language is used to name objects, such as "dog" or "bed."

reflective cognitive style A cognitive style marked by a thorough exploration of a problem, a consideration of various alternatives, and, finally giving an answer to the question or performing the task.

reflex A relatively simple automatic reaction to a particular stimulus.

reinforcement An event that increases the likelihood that the behavior that preceded it will reoccur.

replication The scientific necessity that experimental procedures should be capable of being reproduced by others.

representation The ability to create a mental picture of what is transpiring in the environment.

repression A defense mechanism in which memories are barred from consciousness.

reservoir-of-family-wisdom grandparents An older style of grandparenting in which the grandparents, most often the grandfather, serve as titular head of the family.

residual vision The remaining sight in people who are legally blind or partially sighted.

retrolental fibroplasia A disorder involving blindness caused by an oversupply of oxygen most often administered to premature infants.

reversibility Beginning at the end of an operation and working one's way back to the start.

Rh factor An antibody often, but not always, found in human beings.

risk-benefit analysis A detailed analysis of the risks versus the benefits of a particular choice.

role confusion or diffusion According to psychosocial theory, the negative outcome of adolescence, which involves the failure to develop a personal identity and feelings of aimlessness.

rooting reflex The reflex in young infants in which a stroke on a cheek causes them to turn in the direction of the stimulus.

rubella (German measles) A disease responsible for many cases of birth defects.

scheme A method of dealing with the environment which can be generalized to many situations.

schizophrenia A severe mental disorder marked by hallucinations, delusions, and emotional disturbances.

secondary circular reactions Repetitive actions that are intended to create some environmental reaction.

secondary or reality process The process by which the ego satisfies the organism's needs in a socially appropriate manner.

secondary sex characteristics Physical changes that are not associated with sexual reproduction yet distinguish males from females.

sect A splinter group that has broken away from the main church and usually emphasizes rigid doctrines.

secular trend The trend toward earlier maturation today, compared with past generations.

secure attachment A type of attachment behavior in which the infant in the "strange situation" uses the mother as a secure base of operations.

self-concept The picture people have of themselves.

self-esteem The value people put on various aspects of their self.

self-fulfilling prophecy The concept that a person's expectations concerning some event affect the probability of its occurrence.

sensorimotor stage The first stage in Piaget's theory of cognitive development, in which the child discovers the world using the senses and motor activity.

sensorineural hearing loss Hearing loss caused by nerve damage.

separation anxiety Fear of being separated from caregivers, peaking at between twelve and sixteen months.

seriation The process of placing objects in size order.

sex chromosomes The twenty-third pair of chromosomes, which determines the gender of the organism.

sex differences The differences between males and females that have been established through scientific investigation.

sex-linked traits Traits that are inherited through genes found on the sex chromosomes.

sex roles Behaviors expected of people in a given society on the basis of whether they are male or female.

sex-role stereotypes Groups of characteristics that people believe characterize one gender more than the other.

sex typing The process by which people acquire, value, and behave in a manner appropriate to one sex more than the other.

sickle cell anemia An inherited defect in the structure of red blood cells.

small-for-date babies Infants born below the weight expected for their gestational age.

social-learning theory A theory of learning emphasizing the importance of imitation and observation learning.

stimulus deprivation The absence of adequate environmental stimulation.

stimulus discrimination The process by which a person learns to differentiate among stimuli.

stimulus generalization The tendency of an organism which has learned to associate a certain behavior with a particular stimulus to show this behavior when confronted with similar stimuli.

strange situation An experimental procedure used to measure attachment behaviors.

sucking reflex A reflex found in young infants, in which they automatically suck when something is placed in their mouths.

superego The part of the mind in Freudian theory which includes a set of principles, violation of which leads to feelings of guilt.

surrogate-parent grandparents Grandparents who take on the parental role often so the mother can work.

survey A method of study in which data is collected through written questionnaires or oral interviews from a number of people.

symbol Anything that can represent something else, such as words symbolizing an object.

synchrony The coordination between infant and caregiver in which each can respond to the subtle verbal and nonverbal cues of the other.

syntax The way words are put together to form sentences in a particular language.

Tay-Sachs disease A fatal genetic disease.

telegraphic speech The child's use of sentences in which only the basic words necessary to communicate meaning are used and helping words such as "a" or "to" are left out.

temperament A group of characteristics reflecting an individual's way of responding to the environment and thought to be genetic.

teratogens Any agent that causes birth defects.

tertiary circular reactions Repetitive actions with some variations each time.

thalidomide A drug taken to combat nausea during pregnancy and responsible for birth defects.

time-out procedure A behavior modification technique in which a person is removed from the environment in which he or she has misbehaved until the offending behavior has ceased.

transductive reasoning Preoperational reasoning in which young children reason from particular to particular.

transition A period late in labor in which the contractions become more difficult.

transitive inferences Statements of comparison, such as "If X is taller than Y, and Y is taller than Z, then X is taller than Z."

trust The positive outcome of Erikson's first psychosocial stage, a feeling that one lives among friends.

unconscious Freudian term for memories that lie beyond normal awareness.

underextension A type of error in which children apply a term in a narrower manner than is correct.

validity The extent to which a test measures what it is designed to measure.

values clarification courses Educational approaches to improving moral decision-making skills based on presenting students with problems and helping them perceive the issue from many different viewpoints and consider many different solutions.

values Constructs that serve as internal guides for behavior.

vernix caseosa A thick liquid that protects the skin of the fetus.

visual acuity The ability to see clearly at various distances.

visual cliff A device used to measure depth perception in infants.

zygote A fertilized egg.

Chapter One

American Psychological Association (APA). *Careers in Psychology.* Washington, D.C.: American Psychological Association, 1975.

American Psychological Association (APA). *Ethical Principles in the Conduct of Research with Human Beings.* Washington, D.C.: American Psychological Association, 1973.

Appelbaum, M. I., and McCall, R. B. Design and Analysis in Developmental Psychology, in P. H. Mussen (ed.), *Handbook of Child Psychology* (4th ed.), vol. 1. New York: Wiley, 1983, 415–477.

Baumrind, D. Research Using Intentional Deception: Ethical Issues Revisited. *American Psychologist*, 1985, *40*, 165–175.

Berti, A. E., and Bombi, A. S. The Development of the Concept of Money and Its Value: A Longitudinal Study. *Child Development*, 1981, *52*, 1179–1183.

Bettelheim, B. *The Empty Fortress.* New York: The Free Press, 1967.

Birch, L. L. Effects of Peer Models' Food Choices and Eating Behaviors on Preschoolers' Food Preferences. *Child Development*, 1980, *51*, 489–496.

———. Preschool Childrens' Preferences and Consumption Patterns. *Journal of Nutritional Education*, 1979, *11*, 189–192.

Birren, J. E., Kinney, D. K., Schaie, K. W., and Woodruff, D. S. *Developmental Psychology: A Life-Span Approach.* Boston: Houghton Mifflin, 1981.

Blanck, P. D., Rosenthal, R., Snodgrass, S. E., DePaulo, B. M., and Zuckerman, M. Longitudinal and Cross-sectional Age Effects in Nonverbal Decoding Skill and Style. *Developmental Psychology*, 1982, *18*, 491–498.

Borstelmann, L. J. Children Before Psychology: Ideas About Children from Antiquity to the Late 1800s, in P. H. Mussen (ed.), *Handbook of Child Psychology* (4th ed.), vol. 1. New York: Wiley, 1983, 1–41.

Bower, T. G. R. *A Primer of Infant Development.* San Francisco: Freeman, 1977.

Bowlby, J. *Attachment.* New York: Basic Books, 1969.

Bronstein, P. Differences in Mothers' and Fathers' Behaviors Toward Children: A Cross-Cultural Comparison. *Developmental Psychology*, 1984, *20*, 995–1004.

Brophy, J. E. Research on the Self-Fulfilling Prophecy and Teacher Expectations. *Journal of Educational Psychology*, 1983, *75*, 631–661.

Brown, A. L., Bransford, J. D., Ferrara, R. A., and Campione, J. C. Learning, Remembering, and Understanding, in P. H. Mussen (ed.), *Handbook of Child Psychology* (4th ed.), vol. 3. New York: Wiley, 1983, 77–167.

Cairns, R. B. The Emergence of Developmental Psychology, in P. H. Mussen (ed.), *Handbook of Child Development* (4th ed.), vol. 1. New York: Wiley, 41–103.

Chaikin, A. L., Sigler, E., and Derlega, V. G. Non-Verbal Mediators of Teacher Expectancy Effects. *Journal of Personality and Social Psychology*, 1974, *30*, 144–149.

Clarke, A. M., and Clarke, A. D. S. (eds.). *Early Experience: Myth and Evidence.* New York: The Free Press, 1976.

Conger, J. J., and Petersen, A. C. *Adolescence and Youth: Psychological Development in a Changing World.* New York: Harper and Row, 1984.

Cooke, R. A. The Ethics and Regulation of Research Involving Children, in B. B. Wolman (ed.), *Handbook of Developmental Psychology.* Englewood Cliffs, N.J.: Prentice-Hall, 1982, 149–175.

Dennis, W. The Effect of Restricted Practice upon the Reaching, Sitting and Standing of Two Infants. *Journal of Genetic Psychology*, 1935, *47*, 17–32.

Diaz, R. M., and Berndt, T. J. Children's Knowledge of a Best Friend: Fact or Fancy. *Developmental Psychology*, 1982, *18*, 787–794.

Dusek, J. B. Implications of Developmental Theory for Child Mental Health. *American Psychologist*, 1974, *29*, 19–25.

Eisenberg-Berg, N. and Roth, K. The Development of Children's Prosocial Moral Judgment: A Longitudinal Follow-up. *Developmental Psychology*, 1980, *16*, 375–376.

Freidel, F. *America in the Twentieth Century* (4th ed.). New York: Knopf, 1976.

Furth, H. G., and Milgram, N. A. Labeling and Grouping Effects in the Recall of Pictures by Children. *Child Development*, 1973, *44*, 511–518.

Harlow, H. F. *Learning to Love.* San Francisco: Albion Pub. Co., 1971.

Harris, N. S. Whatever Happened to Little Albert. *American Psychologist*, 1979, *34*, 151–160.

Harrison, N. S. *Understanding Behavioral Research.* Belmont, Calif.: Wadsworth, 1979.

Hayes, D. S., Chemelski, B. E., and Palmer, M. Nursery Rhymes and Prose Passages: Preschoolers' Liking and Short-Term Retention of Story Events. *Developmental Psychology*, 1982, *18*, 49–56.

Holmes, D. S. Debriefing After Psychological Experiments, I: Effectiveness of Post-Deception Dehoaxing. *American Psychologist*, 1976a, *31*, 858–868.

———. Debriefing After Psychological Experiments, II: Effectiveness of Post-Experimental Desensitization. *American Psychologist*, 1976b, *31*, 868–876.

Hottinger, W. Early Motor Development: Discussion and Summary, In C. B. Corbin (ed.), *A Textbook of Motor Development* (2nd ed.). Dubuque, Iowa: Wm. C. Brown, 1980, 31–41.

Kail, R., and Hage, J. W. Memory in Childhood, in B. B. Wolman (ed.), *Handbook of Developmental Psychology.* Englewood Cliffs, N.J.: Prentice-Hall, 1982, 350–367.

Keppel, G. *Design and Analysis: A Researcher's Handbook* (2nd ed.). Englewood Cliffs, N.J.: Prentice-Hall, 1982.

Kiesler, S. B. Federal Policies for Research on Children. *American Psychologist*, 1979, *34*, 1009–1017.

Labouvie, E. W. Issues in Life-Span Development, in B. B. Wolman (ed.), *Handbook of Developmental Psychology.* Englewood Cliffs, N.J.: Prentice-Hall, 1982, 54–63.

Lesser, G. S. Applications of Psychology to Television Programming: Formulation of Program Objectives. *American Psychologist*, 1976, *31*, 135–137.

Maier, N. R. F., and Verser, G. C. *Psychology in Industrial Organizations* (5th ed.). Boston: Houghton Mifflin, 1982.

McGraph, J. E. *Social Psychology: A Brief Introduction*. New York: Holt, Rinehart and Winston, 1964.

Milgram, S. Behavioral Study of Obedience. *Journal of Abnormal and Social Psychology*, 1963, *67*, 371–378.

Moely, O. H., Olson, F. A., Halwes, T. G., and Flavell, J. H. Production Deficiency in Young Children's Clustered Recall. *Developmental Psychology*, 1969, *1*, 26–34.

National Commission for the Protection of Human Subjects of Biomedical and Behavioral Research (eds.), *Report and Recommendations: Research Involving Children*. Washington, D.C.: U.S. Government Printing Office, 1977 (DHEW Pub. No. 77–0004).

Nunnally, J. C. The Study of Change: Measurement, Research Strategies and Methods of Analysis, in B. B. Wolman (ed.), *Handbook of Developmental Psychology*. Englewood Cliffs, N.J.: Prentice-Hall, 1982, 133–149.

Palmer, E. L. Application of Psychology to Television Programming: Program Execution. *American Psychologist*, 1976, *31*, 137–139.

Peterson, P. E., Jeffrey, D. B., Bridgwater, C. A., and Dawson, B. How Pronutrition Television Programming Affects Children's Dietary Habits. *Developmental Psychology*, 1984, *20*, 55–64.

Polermo, D. S., and Molfese, D. L. Language Acquisition from Age Five Onward. *Psychological Bulletin*, 1972, *78*, 409–428.

Pulaski, M. A. S. *Understanding Piaget* (rev. and exp. ed.). New York: Harper and Row, 1980.

Rachlin, H. *Introduction to Modern Behaviorism*. San Francisco: Freeman, 1976.

Rosen, R., and Rosen, L. R. *Human Sexuality*. N.Y.: Knopf, 1981.

Rosenthal, R., and Fode, K. L. The Effect of Experimenter Bias on the Performance of the Albino Rat. *Behavioral Science*, 1963, *8*, 183–189.

Rosenthal, R., and Jacobson, L. F. Teacher Expectations for the Disadvantaged. *Scientific American Offprints*, 1968, *218*, 3–7.

Rutter, M. Maternal Deprivation, 1972–1978: New Findings, New Concepts, New Approaches. *Child Development*, 1979, *50*, 283–305.

Sarason, I. G., and Sarason, B. R. *Abnormal Psychology* (3rd ed.). Englewood Cliffs, N.J.: Prentice-Hall, 1980.

Schaie, K. W., and Hertzog, C. Longitudinal Methods, in B. B. Wolman (ed.), *Handbook of Developmental Psychology*. Englewood Cliffs, N.J.: Prentice-Hall, 1982, 91–116.

Seitz, V. Psychology and Social Policy for Children: Introduction. *American Psychologist*, 1979, *10*, 1007–1009.

Selman, R. L. The Child as a Friendship Philosopher, in S. R. Asher and J. M. Gottman (eds.), *The Development of Children's Friendships*. Cambridge: Cambridge University Press, 1981, 242–273.

Shirley, M. N. *The First Two Years* (Institute of Child Welfare Monograph 7). Minneapolis: University of Minnesota Press, 1933.

Society for Research in Child Development (Development Interest Group). *Ethical Standards for Research With Children*. Chicago: Society for Research in Child Development, 1977, 39.

Stevenson, H. How Children Learn: The Quest for a Theory, in P. H. Mussen. *Handbook of Child Development* (4th ed.), vol. 1. New York: Wiley, 1983, 213–237.

Stewart, M. J. Fundamental Locomotor Skills, in C. J. Corbin (ed.), *A Textbook of Motor Development*. Dubuque, Iowa: Wm. C. Brown, 1980, 44–52.

Sue, D., Sue, D. W., and Sue, S. *Understanding Abnormal Behavior*. Boston: Houghton-Mifflin, 1981.

Vasta, R., and Copitch, P. Simulating Conditions of Child Abuse in the Laboratory. *Child Development*, 1981, *52*, 164–170.

Watson, J. B., and Rayner, R. Conditioned Emotional Reactions. *Journal of Experimental Psychology*, 1920, *3*, 1–14.

Wehrabian, A. Measures of Vocabulary and Grammatical Skills for Children up to Age Six. *Developmental Psychology*, 1970, *2*, 439–446.

Wikler, L., Wasow, M., and Hatfield, E. Chronic Sorrow Revisited: Parent vs. Professional Depiction of the Adjustment of Parents of Mentally Retarded Children. *American Journal of Orthopsychiatry*, 1981, *51*, 63–70.

Wood, G. *Fundamentals of Psychological Research*. Boston: Little, Brown, 1974.

Zelazo, R. R., Zelazo, N. A., and Kolb, S. Walking in the Newborn. *Science*, 1972, *176*, 314–315.

Chapter Two

Altrocchi, J. *Abnormal Psychology*. New York: Harcourt Brace Jovanovich, 1980.

Anastasi, A. Heredity, Environment, and the Question of "How?" *Psychological Review*, 1958, *65*, 197–208.

Apgar, V., and Beck, J. *Is My Baby All Right?* New York: Pocket Books, 1974.

Arehart-Treichel, J. Down's Syndrome: The Father's Role. *Science News*, December 1, 1979, 381–382.

Berdine, W. H., and Blackhurst, A. E. *An Introduction to Special Education* (2nd ed.). Boston: Little-Brown, 1985.

Blackhurst, A. E., and Berdine, W. H. (eds.). *An Introduction to Special Education*. Boston: Little, Brown, 1981.

Bouchard, T. J., and McGue, M. Familial Studies of Intelligence: A Review. *Science*, May 29, 1981, 1055–1059.

Bridges, F. A., and Cicchetti, D. Mothers' Ratings of the Temperament Characteristics of Down's Syndrome Infants. *Developmental Psychology*, 1982, *18*, 238–244.

Carter, C. O. *Human Heredity*. Baltimore: Penguin Books, 1970.

Crandall, B. F., and Tarjan, G. Genetics of Mental Retardation, in M. A. Sperber and L. S. Jarvik (eds.), *Psychiatry and Genetics*. New York: Basic Books, 1976, 95–119.

Cratty, B. J. *Perceptual and Motor Development in Infants and Children*. New York: MacMillan, 1970.

Curtis, H. *Biology* (2nd ed.) New York: Worth, 1975.

Daniels, D., and Plomin, R. Origins of Individual Differences in Infant Shyness. *Developmental Psychology*, 1985, *21*, 118–122.

Farber, S. Telltale Behavior of Twins. *Psychology Today*, January, 1981, 58–62, 79–80.

Feldman, M. W., and Lewontin, R. C. The Heritability Hang-up. *Science*, 1975, *190*, 1163–1168.

Fischman, S. E. Psychological Issues in the Genetic Counseling of Cystic Fibrosis in S. Kessler (ed.), *Genetic Counseling: Psychological Dimensions*. New York: Academic Press, 1979, 153–165.

Fogel, A. *Infancy*. St. Paul: West Publishing Co., 1984.

Fuller, J. L., and Thompson, W. R. *Foundation of Behavior Genetics.* St. Louis: C. V. Mosby, 1978.

Gardner, H. *Frames of Mind.* New York: Basic Books, 1983.

Gardner, L. I. Deprivation Dwarfism. *Scientific American*, July 1972, *227*, 76–82.

Goldsmith, H. H. Genetic Influences on Personality from Infancy to Adulthood. *Child Development*, 1983, *54*, 331–355.

Goldsmith, H. H., and Gottesman, I. I. Origins of Variation in Behavioral Style: A Longitudinal Study of Temperament in Young Twins. *Child Development*, 1981, *52*, 91–103.

Gottesman, I. I. Genetics and Personality (1966), in J. J. Hutt and C. Hutt (eds.), *Early Human Development.* London: Oxford University Press, 1973, 17–25.

_____. Schizophrenia and Genetics: Where Are We? Are You Sure? in L. C. Wynne (ed.), *The Nature of Schizophrenia.* New York: Wiley, 1978.

Gottesman, I. I., and Shields, J. *Schizophrenia and Genetics: A Twin Study Vantage Point.* New York: Academic Press, 1972.

Hardy-Brown, K., Plomin, R., and DeFries, J. C. Genetic and Environmental Influences on the Rate of Communicative Development in the First Year of Life. *Developmental Psychology*, 1981, *17*, 704–717.

Health, Education and Welfare (HEW) (U.S. Dept. of). *Facts About Mongolism for Women Over 35.* Washington, D.C.: Department of Health, Education, and Welfare (N.I.H.), no. 74–536, 1973.

_____. *Mongolism (Down's Syndrome): Hope Through Research.* Washington, D.C.: Department of Health, Education, and Welfare (N.I.H.), no. 72–72, 1971.

Heston, L. L. Psychiatric Disorders in Foster-Home-Reared Children of Schizophrenic Mothers. *British Journal of Psychiatry*, 1966, *11*, 819–825.

Hicks, R. E., and M. Kinsbourne. Human Handedness: A Partial Cross-Fostering Study. *Science.* May 28, 1976, *193*, 908–910.

Hirsch, J. G. Helping the Family Whose Child Has a Birth Defect, in J. D. Noshpitz (ed.), *Basic Handbook of Child Psychiatry*, 1979, vol. *4*, 121–128, New York: Basic Books.

Holden, C. Twins Reunited: More Than the Faces Are Familiar. *Science*, November 1980, *197*, 55–59.

Horn, J. M. Bias? Indeed! *Child Development*, 1985, *56*, 779–781.

Jencks, C. *Inequality: A Reassessment of the Effects of Family and Schooling in America.* New York: Basic Books, 1972.

Jensen, A. R. How Much Can We Boost I.Q. and Scholastic Achievement? *Harvard Educational Review*, 1969, *39*, 1–123.

Kalat, J. W. *Biological Psychology.* Belmont, Calif.: Wadsworth, 1980.

Kamin, L. J. *The Science and Politics of I.Q.* Hillsdale, N.J.: Erlbaum, 1974.

Kermis, M. D. *The Psychology of Human Aging.* Boston: Allyn and Bacon, 1984.

Kirk, S. A., and Gallagher, J. G. *Educating Exceptional Children* (2 ed.). Boston: Houghton Mifflin, 1979.

Lappe, M., and Brody, J. A. Genetic Counseling: A Psychotherapeutic Approach to Autonomy in Decision Making, in M. A. Sperber and L. F. Jarvik (eds.). *Psychiatry and Genetics: Psychosocial, Ethical and Legal Considerations.* New York: Basic Books, 1976, 129–146.

Lazar, I., and Darlington, R. Lasting Effects of Early Education: A Report from the Consortium for Longitudinal Studies. *Monographs of the Society for Research in Child Development*, serial number 195, 1982, *47*, nos. 2–3.

Lips, J. C., and Colwill, J. A. *Sex and Sex Roles.* Englewood Cliffs, N.J., 1979.

Liston, E. H., and Jarvik, L. F. Genetics of Schizophrenia, in M. A. Sperber and L. F. Jarvik (eds.), *Psychiatry and Genetics.* New York: Basic Books, 1976, 76–95.

Loehlin, J. C., Lindzey, G., and Spuhler, J. N. *Race Differences in Intelligence.* San Francisco: Freeman, 1975.

Longstreth, L. E. Revisiting Skeel's Final Study: A Critique. *Developmental Psychology*, 1981, *17*, 620–625.

Maccoby, E. E., and Jacklin, C. N. *The Psychology of Sex Differences.* Stanford, Calif.: Stanford University Press, 1974.

Magenis, R. E. Parental Origin of the Extra Chromosome in Down's Syndrome. *Human Genetics*, 1977, *37*, 7–16.

Mange, A. P., and Mange, E. J. *Genetics: Human Aspects.* Philadelphia: Saunders, 1980.

March of Dimes Foundation. *Genetic Counseling.* New York: March of Dimes Birth Defect Foundation, 1980.

Martin, B. *Abnormal Psychology: Clinical and Scientific Perspectives.* New York: Holt, Rinehart and Winston, 1977.

Matheny, A. P. A Longitudinal Twin Study of Stability of Components from Bayley's Infant Behavior Record. *Child Development*, 1983, *54*, 356–360.

Matheny, A. P., Riese, M. L., and Wilson, R. S. Rudiments of Infant Temperament: Newborn to 9 Months. *Developmental Psychology*, 1985, *21*, 486–495.

McBroom, P. *Behavioral Genetics.* National Institute of Mental Health Science Monograph. Washington, D.C.: Department of Health, Education, and Welfare, 1980.

McCall, R. B. Nature-Nurture and the Two Realms of Development: A Proposed Integration with Respect to Mental Development. *Child Development*, 1981, *52*, 1–12.

Mischel, W. *Introduction to Personality* (2nd ed.). New York: Holt, Rinehart and Winston, 1976.

Pai, A. C. *Foundations of Genetics.* New York: McGraw-Hill, 1974.

Plomin, R., and DeFries, J. C. Genetics and Intelligence: Recent Data. *Intelligence*, 1980, *4*, 15–24.

Rainer, J. D. Genetics and Psychiatry, in A. M. Friedman and H. I. Kaplan (eds.), *Human Behavior: Biological, Psychological and Sociological Perspectives.* New York: Atheneum, 1972, 1–29.

Reed, E. Genetic Anomolies in Development, in E. M. Hetherington, S. Scarr-Salapatek, and G. M. Siegel (eds.), *Review of Child Development Research*, vol. 4. Chicago: University of Chicago Press, 1975, 59–100.

Roberts, J. A. F. *An Introduction to Medical Genetics* (5th ed.). London: Oxford University Press, 1970.

Rose, R. J., and Ditto, W. B. A Developmental-Genetic Analysis of Common Fears from Early Adolescence to Early Adulthood. *Child Development*, 1983, *54*, 361–368.

Rosen, R., and Rosen, L. R. *Human Sexuality.* New York: Knopf, 1981.

Scarr, S., and Kidd, K. K. Developmental Behavior Genetics, in P. H. Mussen (ed.), *Handbook of Child Psychology* (4th ed.), vol. 2. New York: Wiley, 1983, 345–433.

Scarr, S., and McCartney, K. How People Make Their Own Environments: A Theory of Genotype-Environment Effects. *Child Development*, 1983, *54*, 424–435.

Scarr, S., and Weinberg, R. A. The Minnesota Adoption Studies: Genetic Differences and Malleability. *Child Development*, 1983, *54*, 260–267.

Scarr-Salapatek, S. Genetics and the Development of Intelligence, in E. M. Hetherington, S. Scarr-Salapatek, and G. M. Siegel (eds.), *Review of Child Development Research*, vol. 4. Chicago: University of Chicago Press, 1975, 1–58.

Scarr-Salapatek, S., and Weinberg, R. A. IQ Test Performance of Black Children Adopted by White Females. *American Psychologist*, 1976, *31*, 726–739.

Schafer, A., and Gray, M. Sex and Mathematics. *Science*, January 16, 1981.

Schaffer, H. R., and Emerson, P. E. The Development of Social Attachments in Infants. *Monographs of the Society for Research in Child Development*, 1964, *29*, no. 3.

Schild, S. Psychological Issues in Genetic Counseling of Phenylketonuria, in S. Kessler (ed.), *Genetic Counseling: Psychological Dimensions*. New York: Academic Press, 1979, 135–151.

Shaw, M. W. Legal Issues in Medical Genetics, in M. A. Sperber and L. F. Jarvik (eds.), *Psychiatry and Genetics*. New York: Basic Books, 1976.

Sibinga, M. S., and Friedman, C. J. Complexities of Parental Understanding of Phenylketonuria. *Pediatrics*, 1971, *48*, 216–224.

Skeels, H. M. Adult Status of Children with Contrasting Early Life Experiences: A Follow-up Study. *Monographs of the Society for Research in Child Development*, 1966, *31*, no. 3.

Smith, R. M., and Neisworth, J. T. *The Exceptional Child: A Functional Approach*. New York: McGraw-Hill, 1975.

Sperber, M. A. Psychiatry and Metacommunication in Genetic Counseling, in M. A. Sperber and L. F. Jarvik (eds.), *Psychiatry and Genetics: Psychosocial, Ethical and Legal Considerations*. New York: Basic Books, 1976, 119–128.

Sutton, H. E. *An Introduction to Human Genetics* (3rd ed.). Philadelphia: Saunders, 1980.

Thomas, A. Chess, S., and Birch, H. G. The Origins of Personality. *Scientific American*, August 1970, *223*, 102–109.

Vandenberg, S. Hereditary Factors in Normal Personality Traits, in J. Wortis (ed.), *Recent Advances in Biological Psychiatry*, 1967, *9*, 65–105.

Wachs, T. D. The Use and Abuse of Environment in Behavior-Genetic Research. *Child Development*, 1983, *54*, 396–407.

Walker, E., and Emory, E. Commentary: Interpretive Bias and Behavioral Genetic Research. *Child Development*, 1985, *56*, 775–779.

Walzer, S., Richmond, J. B., and Gerald P. S. The Implications of Sharing Genetic Information, in M. A. Sperber and L. F. Jarvik (eds.), *Psychiatry and Genetics: Psychosocial, Ethical and Legal Considerations*. New York: Basic Books, 1976, 147–162.

Weisfeld, G. E. The Nature-Nurture Issue and the Integrating Concept of Function, in B. B. Wolman (ed.), *Handbook of Developmental Psychology*. Englewood Cliffs, N.J.: Prentice-Hall, 1982, 208–230.

Whitten, P., and Kagan, J. Jensen's Dangerous Half-Truth. *Psychology Today*. August 1969, *3*, 18.

Willerman, L. *The Psychology of Individual and Group Differences*. San Francisco: Freeman, 1979.

Williams, J. W., and Stith, M. *Middle Childhood: Behavior and Development* (2nd ed.). New York: Macmillan, 1980.

Wilson, R. S. The Louisville Twin Study: Developmental Synchronies in Behavior. *Child Development*, 1983, *54*, 298–316.

Wilson, R. S., and Matheny, A. P. Assessment of Temperament in Infant Twins. *Developmental Psychology*, 1983, *19*, 172–183.

Zigler, E., and Trickett, P. K. IQ, Social Competence, and Evaluation of Early Childhood Intervention Programs. *American Psychologist*, 1978, *33*, 978–999.

Chapter Three

Alexander, G. J., Miles, B. E., Gold, G. M., and Alexander, R. B. LSD: Injection in Early Pregnancy Produces Abnormalities in Off-Spring of Rats. *Science*, 1967, *157*, 459–460.

Annis, L. F. *The Child Before Birth*. Ithaca, N.Y.: Cornell University Press, 1978.

Apgar, V., and Beck, J. *Is My Baby All Right?* New York: Pocket Books, 1974.

Avery, C. S. A DES Daughter Fights Back—and Wins. *Mademoiselle*, October 1981, 78.

Balinsky, B. I. *An Introduction to Embryology* (3rd ed.). Philadelphia: Saunders, 1970.

Berezin, N. *The Gentle Birth Book*. New York: Simon and Schuster, 1980.

Birch, H. G. Functional Effects of Fetal Malnutrition. *Hospital Practice*, March 1971, 134–148.

Birch, H. G. Health and the Education of Socially Disadvantaged Children (1968), in H. Bee (ed.), *Social Issues in Developmental Psychology*. New York: Harper and Row, 1976, 269–291.

Birch, H. G., and Gussow, J. D. *Disadvantaged Children*. New York: Harcourt, Brace and World, 1970.

Blackhurst, A. E., and Berdine, W. H. *An Introduction to Special Education*. Boston: Little, Brown, 1980.

Bottoms, S. F., Rosen, M. G., and Sokol, R. J. The Increase in Caesarean Birth Rate. *New England Journal of Medicine*, March 6, 1980, 559–563.

Brackbill, Y. Lasting Effects of Obstetrical Medication on Children, in J. Belsky (ed.), *In the Beginning*. New York: Columbia University Press, 1982, 50–55.

Brackbill, Y. Obstetrical Medication and Infant Behavior, in J. D. Osofsky (ed.), *Handbook of Infant Development*. New York: Wiley, 1979, 76–125.

Brazelton, T. B. Effects of Prenatal Drugs on the Behavior of the Neonate. *American Journal of Psychiatry*, 1970, *126*, 95–100.

Brazelton, T. B. *On Becoming a Family: The Growth of Attachment*. New York: Delacorte Press, 1981.

Bulmer, M. G. *The Biology of Twinning in Man*. London: Oxford University Press, 1970.

Butler, N., Goldstein, H., Ross, K. Smoking in Pregnancy and Subsequent Child Development. *British Journal of Medicine*, 1972, *4*, 573–575.

Caputo, D. V., and Mandell, W. Consequences of Low Birth Weight. *Developmental Psychology*, 1970, *3*, 363–383.

Cave, V. G. The Role of Immunoglobulins in the Early Diagnosis of Congenital Syphilis, in L. Nicholas (ed.), *Sexually Transmitted Diseases*. Springfield, Ill.: Thomas, 1973.

Clarren, S. K., and Smith, D. W. The Fetal Alcohol Syndrome. *New England Journal of Medicine*, 1978, *298*, 1063–1067.

Cogan, R. Effects of Childbirth Preparation. *Clinical Obstetrics and Gynecology*, 1980, *23*, 1–14.

Coleman, A. D. Psychological State During First Pregnancy. *American Journal of Orthopsychiatry*, 1969, *39*, 788–797.

Copans, S. A. Human Prenatal Effects: Methodological Problems and Some Suggested Solutions. *Merrill-Palmer Quarterly*, 1974, *20*, 43–52.

Counseling and Personnel Services Clearinghouse. *Teenage Pregnancy Factsheet*, Winter 1982, Eric/Caps.

Cox, F. D. *Human Intimacy: Marriage, the Family and its Meaning*, (3rd ed.). St. Paul, Minnesota: West Publishing Co., 1984.

Curtis, H. *Biology* (2nd ed.). New York: Worth, 1975.

Dakshinamurti, K., and Stephens, M. Pyridoxine Deficit in Neonatal Rats. *Journal of Clinical Neurology*, 1969, *16*, 1515–1522.

Dalby, J. T. Environmental Effects on Prenatal Development. *Journal of Pediatric Psychology*, 1978, *3*, 105–109.

Davies, R., Butler, N., and Goldstein, H. *From Birth to Seven*. London: William Clowes, 1972.

Davies, P., and Stewart, A. L. Low Birth-Weight: Neurological Sequelae and Later Intelligence. *British Medical Bulletin*, 1975, *31*, 85–91.

DeHirsch, K., Langford, J., and Jansky, W. S. Comparison Between Premature and Maturely Born Children at Three Age Levels. *American Journal of Orthopsychiatry*, 1966, *36*, 61–78.

Drillien, C. M. *The Growth and Development of the Prematurely Born Infant*. Edinburgh: Livingstone, 1964.

Drugs and Pregnancy. Washington, D.C.: U.S. Department of Health, Education, and Welfare, October 1978, HEW Publication Number (FDA) 79–3083.

Dudgeon, J. A. Breakdown in Maternal Protection: Infection, in L. J. Stone, H. J. Smith, and L. B. Murphy (eds.), *The Competent Infant*. New York: Basic Books, 1973, 159–169.

Eichorn, D. H. Physical Development: Current Foci of Research, in J. Osofsky (ed.), *Handbook of Infant Development*. New York: Wiley, 1979, 253–283.

Fadiman, A. Too Soon and Too Small. *LIFE*, February 1981, 46–52.

Field, T. M. Effects of Early Separation, Interactive Deficits, and Experimental Manipulation on Mother-Infant Interactions. *Child Development*, 1977, *48*, 763–771.

Fitzgerald, H. E., Strommen, E. A., and McKinney, J. P. *Developmental Psychology: The Infant and Young Child* (rev. ed.). Homeword, Ill.: Dorsey Press, 1982.

Fogel, A. *Infancy: Infant, Family and Society*. St. Paul: West Publishing Co., 1984.

Fosburgh, L. The Make-Believe World of Teen-Age Pregnancy. *New York Times Magazine*, August 7, 1977, 14.

Furey, E. M. The Effects of Alcohol on the Fetus. *Exceptional Children*, September 1982, *49*, 30–34.

Gelles, R. J. The Social Construction of Child Abuse. *American Journal of Orthopsychiatry*, 1975, *45*, 365–372.

Gleicher, N. Caesarean Section Rates in the United States. *Journal of the American Medical Association*, Dec. 21, 1984, *252*, 3273–3277.

Golanty, E., and Harris, B. B. *Marriage and Family Life*. Boston: Houghton Mifflin, 1982.

Goldberg, S. Premature Birth: Consequences for the Parent-Infant Relationship (1979), in E. M. Hetherington and R. D. Parke (eds.), *Contemporary Readings in Child Psychology*. New York: McGraw-Hill, 1981, 12–21.

Goldberg, S. Prematurity (1978), in J. Belsky (ed.), *In the Beginning*. New York: Columbia University Press, 1982, 65–74.

Goldstein, M. Parenthood After 30. *Long Island*, November 1980, 20–24, 64.

Gorsuch, R. L., and Key, M. A. Abnormalities of Pregnancy as a Function of Anxiety and Life Stress. *Psychosomatic Medicine*, 1974, *36*, 352–362.

Greenberg, M., Rosenberg, I., and Lind, R. J. First Mothers' Rooming-in with Their Newborns and Its Impact upon the Mother. *American Journal of Orthopsychiatry*, October 1973, *43*, 783–788.

Grossman, M., and Drutz, D. J. Venereal Diseases in Children. *Advances in Pediatrics*, 1974, *21*, 97–137.

Hamilton, E. M. N., and Whitney, E. N. *Nutrition: Concepts and Controversies*. St. Paul: West Publishing Co., 1982.

Hanson, J. W. Unpublished manuscript, cited in *The Child Before Birth* by L. F. Annis. Ithaca, N.Y.: Cornell University Press, 1978.

Hanson, J. W., Jones, K. L., and Smith, D. W. Fetal Alcohol Syndrome: Experience with 41 Patients. *Journal of the American Medical Association*, 1976, *235*, 1458–1466.

Harlap, S., and Shiono, P. Alcohol, and Incidence of Spontaneous Abortions in the First and Second Trimester. *The Lancet*, July 26, 1980, 173–176.

Helms, D. B., and Turner, J. S. *Exploring Child Behavior*. Philadelphia: Saunders, 1976.

Henig, R. M. Saving Babies Before Birth. *New York Times Magazine*, February 28, 1982, 18–22.

Herbst, A. L. Diethylstilbestrol Exposure: 1984. *New England Journal of Medicine*, November 29, 1984, *311*, 1433–1435.

Hooke, J. G., and Marks, P. A. Characteristics of Pregnancy. *Journal of Clinical Psychology*, 1963, *18*, 316–317.

Householder, J., Hatcher, R., Burns, W., and Chanoff, I. Infants Born to Narcotic-Addicted Mothers. *Psychological Bulletin*, 1982, *2*, 453–468.

Hutchins, F. L., Kendall, N., and Rubino, J. Experience with Teenage Pregnancy. *Obstetrics and Gynecology*, July 1979, *54*, 1–6.

Jacobson, J. L., Jacobson, S. W., Fein, G., Schwartz, P. M., and Dowler, J. K. Prenatal Exposure to an Environmental Toxin: A Test of the Multiple Effects Model. *Developmental Psychology*, 1984, *20*, 523–533.

Jones, K. L., Smith, D. W., Streissguth, A. P., and Myrianthopoulus, N. Outcomes in Offspring of Chronic Alcoholic Women. *The Lancet*, 1974, *1*, 1076–1078.

Kennell, J. H., Voos, D. K., and Klaus, M. A. Parent-Infant Bonding, in J. Osofsky (ed.), *Handbook of Infant Development*. New York: Wiley, 1979, 786–799.

Klaus, M., and Kennell, J. H. *Maternal-Infant Bonding*. St. Louis: C. V. Mosby, 1976.

Kline, J., Shrout, P., Stern, Z., Susser, and Warburton, D. Drinking During Pregnancy and Spontaneous Abortion. *The Lancet*, July 26, 1980, 176–180.

Knox, D. *Human Sexuality: The Search for Understanding*. St. Paul: West Publishing Co. 1984.

Kopp, C. B., and Parmelee, A. H. Prenatal and Perinatal Influences on Infant Behavior, in J. D. Osofsky (ed.), *Handbook of Infant Development*. New York: Wiley, 1979, 29–75.

Lamaze, F. *Painless Childbirth*. Chicago: Regnery, 1970.

Landesman-Dwyer, S., and Emanuel, I. (1979). Smoking During Pregnancy, in J. Belsky (ed.), *In the Beginning*. New York: Columbia University Press, 1982, 37–45.

Lawson, K. R. Auditory Responsiveness in Full-Term and Preterm Infants. *Developmental Psychology*, 1984, *20*, 120–127.

Leavitt, F. *Drugs and Behavior*. Philadelphia: Saunders, 1974.

Leboyer, F. *Birth Without Violence*. New York: Knopf, 1975.

Lefkowitz, M. M. Smoking During Pregnancy: Long-Term Effects on Offspring. *Developmental Psychology*, 1981, *17*, 192–195.

Leifer, M. Psychological Changes Accompanying Pregnancy and Motherhood. *Genetic Psychology Monographs*, 1977, *95*, 55–96.

Lenz, W. Malformations Caused by Drugs in Pregnancy. *American Journal of Diseases of Children*, 1966, *112*, 99–106.

Lester, B. M., Heidelise, A., and Brazelton, T. B. Regional Obstetric Anesthesia and Newborn Behavior: A Reanalysis Toward Synergistic Effects. *Child Development*, 1982, *53*, 687–692.

Levy, A. The Thalidomide Generation. *Life*, July 26, 1968, 42.

March of Dimes, Robert Matousek, Statistician. Personal correspondence concerning estimates of number of pregnant women who smoke, 1985.

March of Dimes. *Drug, Alcohol, Tobacco Abuse During Pregnancy*. White Plains, N.Y.: March of Dimes, 1983a.

March of Dimes. *Be Good to Your Baby Before It Is Born*. White Plains, N.Y.: March of Dimes, 1983b.

Martin, J. C. Drugs of Abuse During Pregnancy: Effects upon Offspring Structure and Function. *Journal of Women in Culture and Society* (Signs). Winter 1976, *2*, 357–368.

Mascola, L., Pelosi, R., Blount, J. H., Binkin, N. J., Harris, C. M., Jarman, B., Landon, G. P. and McNeil, B. J. Congenital Syphilis. *Journal of the American Medical Association*, October 5, 1984, *252*, 1719–1723.

McGlothlin, W. H., Sparkes, R. S., and Arnold, D. O. Effects of LSD on Human Pregnancy. *Journal of the American Medical Association*, 1970, *212*, 1483–1487.

McIntosh, I. D. Smoking and Pregnancy: Attributable Risks and Public Health Implications. *Canadian Journal of Public Health*. March/April, 1984, *75*, 141–148.

Miller, R. W. Susceptibility of the Fetus and Child to Chemical Pollutants. *Science*, 1974, *184*, 812–813.

Mills, J. L., Braubard, B. I., Harley, E. E., Rhoads, G. G., and Berendes, H. W. Maternal Alcohol Consumption and Birth Weight: How Much Drinking During Pregnancy Is Safe? *Journal of the American Medical Association*, October 12, 1984, *252*, 1875–1879.

Monif, G. R. G. *Viral Infections of the Human Fetus*. London: Macmillan, 1969.

Montagu, M. F. A. *Prenatal Influences*. Springfield, Ill.: Thomas, 1962.

Moya, F., and Thorndike, V. Passage of Drugs Across the Placenta. *American Journal of Obstetrics and Gynecology*, 1962, *84*, 1778–1798.

Murray, S. F., Dolby, R. M., Nation, R. L., and Thomas, D. B. Effects of Epidural Anesthesia on Newborns and Their Mothers. *Child Development*, 1981, *52*, 71–82.

Nelson, N. M., Murray, W. E., Saroj, S., Bennett, K. J., Milner, R., and Sackett, D. L. A Randomized Clinical Trial of the Leboyer Approach to Childbirth. *New England Journal of Medicine*, March 20, 1980, *302*, 655–660.

New York State Department of Health. *DES: The Wonder Drug Women Should Wonder About*. New York: New York State Department of Health, 1979.

Nichols, P. Minimal Brain Dysfunction: Association with Perinatal Complication, cited in Landesman-Dwyer, S., and Emanuel, I., Smoking During Pregnancy, in J. Belsky (ed.), *In the Beginning*. New York: Columbia University Press, 1982.

Orenberg, C. L. *DES: The Complete Story*. New York: St. Martin's Press, 1981.

Paul, R. H. *Fetal Intensive Care: Intrapartum Monitoring Case Examples*. Los Angeles: University of Southern California, USC Medical Center, 1971.

Peterson, G. H., Mehl, L. E., and Leiderman, P. T. The Role of Some Birth-Related Variables in Father Attachment. *American Journal of Orthopsychiatry*, 1979, *49*, 330–339.

Planned Parenthood. *Daughters of DES Mothers*. New York: Planned Parenthood Federation of America, 1979.

Planned Parenthood. *If You Were Born After 1940 You May Be a DES Daughter and Need Special Health Screening*. San Francisco: Coalition for the Medical Rights of Women and Planned Parenthood, 1977.

Rector, J. M. Prenatal Influences in Rickets. *Journal of Pediatrics*, 1935, 6, 16.

Reich, W. T., and Smith, H. *On the Birth of a Severely Handicapped Infant*. New York: Institute of Society, Ethics, and the Life Sciences, 1973.

Rhodes, A. J. Virus Infections and Congenital Malformations. *Papers Delivered at the First Conference on Congenital Malformations*. Philadelphia: Lippincott, 1961, 106–116.

Ricciuti, H. N. Adverse Environmental and Nutritional Influences on Mental Development: A Perspective. *Paper Delivered at the American Dietetic Association*, Atlanta, 1980.

Rice, R. D. Neurophysiological Development in Premature Infants Following Stimulation. *Developmental Psychology*, 1977, *13*, 69–76.

Rosenberg, L., Mitchell, A. A., Parsells, J., Pashayan, H., Lovik, C., and Shapiro, S. Lack of Relation of Oral Clefts to Diazepan Use During Pregnancy. *New England Journal of Medicine*, Nov. 24, 1983, *309*, 1185–1188.

Ross Laboratories. *Becoming a Parent*. Columbus, Ohio: Ross Laboratories, 1979.

———. *Your Premature Infant*. Columbus, Ohio: Ross Laboratories, 1977.

Rugh, R., and Shettles, L. B. *From Contraception to Birth: The Drama of Life's Beginnings*. New York: Harper and Row, 1971.

Sameroff, A. J., and Chandler, M. J. Reproductive Risk and the Continuum of Caretaker Causality, in F. D. Horowitz (ed.), *Review of Child Development Research*, vol. 4. Chicago: University of Chicago Press, 1975.

Scarr-Salapatek, S., and Williams, M. L. The Effects of Early Stimulation on Low Birth Weight Infants. *Child Development*, 1973, *44*, 94–101.

Simpson, W. J. A Preliminary Report on Cigarette Smoking and the Incidence of Prematurity. *American Journal of Obstetrics and Gynecology*, 1957, *73*, 808–815.

Solkoff, N., Jaffe, S., Weintraub, D., and Blase, B. Effects of Handling on the Subsequent Development of Premature Babies. *Developmental Psychology*, 1969, *1*, 765–768.

Singer, S. and Hilgard, H. R. *The Biology of People*. San Francisco: Freeman, 1978.

Sontag, L. W. War and the Fetal-Maternal Relationship. *Marriage and Family Living*, 1944, 6, 3–4.

———. The Significance of Fetal Environmental Differences. *American Journal of Obstetrics and Gynecology*, 1941, *42*, 996–1003.

Spelt, D. K. The Conditioning of the Human Fetus in Utero. *Journal of Experimental Psychology*, 1948, *38*, 338–346.

Stechler, G. and Halton, A. Prenatal Influences on Human Development, in B. B. Wolman (ed.), *Handbook of Developmental Psychology*. Englewood Cliffs, N.J.: Prentice-Hall, 1982, 175–189.

Stevenson, R. E. *The Fetus and Newly Born Infant: Influences of the Prenatal Environment.* St. Louis: C. V. Mosby, 1973.

Streissguth, A. P. Maternal Alcoholism and the Outcome of Pregnancy (1977), in J. Belsky (ed.), *In the Beginning.* New York: Columbia University Press, 1982, 45–50.

Streissguth, A. P., Martin, D. C., Barr, H. M., Sandman, B. M., Kirchner, G. L., and Darby, B. L. Intrauterine Alcohol and Nicotine Exposure: Attention and Reaction Time in 4-Year-Old Children. *Developmental Psychology,* 1984, *20,* 533–542.

Suffet, F., Bryce-Buchanon, C., and Brotman, R. Pregnant Addicts in a Comprehensive Care Program: Results of a Follow-up Survey. *American Journal of Orthopsychiatry,* 1981, *51,* 297–307.

Thompson, M. Estimate of Opiate-Addicted Births. National Institute on Drug Abuse: Services Research Branch Notes, March 2–3, 1979, cited in Suffet, F., Bryce-Buchanon, C., and Brotman, R., Pregnant Addicts in a Comprehensive Care Program: Results of a Follow-up Survey. *American Journal of Orthopsychiatry,* 1981, *51,* 297–307.

Thompson, W. R., and Grusek, J. A. Studies of Early Experience in P. H. Mussen (ed.), *Carmichael's Manual of Child Development.* New York: Wiley, 1970.

Trotter, R. J. Born Too Soon. *Science News,* October 11, 1980, 118, 234–235.

_____. The New Face of Birth. *Science News,* September 15, 1975, 113, 106–108.

Tucker, T., and Bing, E. *Prepared Childbirth.* New Canaan, CT.: Tobey Publishing Co., 1975.

U.S. Department of Health and Human Services. *Child Health and Human Development: An Evaluation and Assessment of the State of the Science,* Washington, D.C.: National Institute of Health, NIH PUBLICATION NUMBER 82-2304, 1981.

U.S. Department of Health and Human Services. *The Health Consequences of Smoking For Women: A Report to the Surgeon General.* Washington, D.C.: U.S. Department of Health and Human Services, 1981.

U.S. Department of Health, Education, and Welfare (HEW). *Smoking and Health: A Report of the Surgeon General.* Washington, D.C.: DHEW, no. PHS 79-50066, 1979.

University of California, *Berkeley Wellness Letter,* vol. 1. Issue 5, Caffeine.

Vore, D. A. Nutrition and Postnatal Intellectual Development. *Merrill-Palmer Quarterly,* 1973, *19,* 253–260.

Wenar, C. *Psychopathology from Infancy Through Adolescence.* New York: Random House, 1982.

Whitney, E. N., and Hamilton, E. M. N. *Understanding Nutrition* (3rd ed.). St. Paul: West Publishing Co., 1984.

Williams, J. H. *Psychology of Women: Behavior in a Biosocial Context.* New York: W. W. Norton, 1977.

Wilson, J. G. *Environment and Birth Defects.* New York: Academic Press, 1973.

Winick, M. *Malnutrition and Brain Damage.* New York: Oxford University Press, 1976.

Wyne, M. D., and O'Connor, P. D. *Exceptional Children: A Developmental View.* Lexington, Mass.: D.C. Heath, 1979.

Chapter Four

Adler, L. L. Cross-Cultural Research and Theory, in B. B. Wolman (ed.), *Handbook of Developmental Psychology.* Englewood Cliffs, N.J.: Prentice-Hall, 1982, 76–91.

Arndt, W. B., Jr. *Theories of Personality.* New York: Macmillan, 1974.

Baldwin, A. L. *Theories of Child Development.* New York: Wiley, 1967.

Bandura, A. *Social Learning Theory.* Englewood Cliffs, N.J.: Prentice-Hall, 1977.

_____. *Principles of Behavior Modification.* New York: Holt, Rinehart and Winston, 1969.

Bandura, A., Grusec, J. E., and Menove, F. L. Vicarious Extinction of Avoidance Behavior. *Journal of Personality and Social Psychology,* 1967, *5,* 16–23.

Bandura, A., Ross, D., and Ross, S. Transmission of Aggression Through Imitation of Aggressive Models. *Journal of Abnormal and Social Psychology,* 1961, *63,* 575–582.

Bandura, A., and Walters, R. H. *Social Learning and Personality Development.* New York: Holt, Rinehart and Winston, 1963.

Bell, R. Q. Parent, Child, and Reciprocal Influences. *American Psychologist,* 1979, *34,* 821–827.

_____. A Reinterpretation of the Direction of Effects in Socialization. *Psychological Review,* 1968, *75,* 81–95.

Bijou, S. W., and Baer, D. M. *Child Development: The Basic Stage of Early Childhood.* Englewood Cliffs, N.J.: Prentice-Hall, 1976.

Bijou, S. W., and Baer, D. M. *Child Development, vol. 1: A Systematic and Empirical Theory.* New York: Appleton-Century-Crofts, 1961.

Bowlby, J. *Attachment.* New York: Basic Books, 1969.

_____. *Attachment and Loss,* vol. 3: *Sadness and Depression.* New York: Basic Books, 1980.

Brainerd, C. J. *Piaget's Theory of Intelligence.* Englewood Cliffs, N.J.: Prentice-Hall, 1978.

Bransford, J. D., and Franks, J. J. The Abstraction of Linguistic Ideas. *Cognitive Psychology,* 1971, *2,* 331–350.

Brenner, C. *An Elementary Textbook of Psychoanalysis.* Garden City, N.Y.: Doubleday/Anchor, 1955.

Bringuier, J. C. *Conversations with Jean Piaget.* Chicago: University of Chicago Press, 1980.

Cairns, R. B. The Emergence of Developmental Psychology, in P. H. Mussen (ed.), *Handbook of Child Development* (4th ed.), vol. 1. New York: Wiley, 1983, 41–103.

_____. *Social Development: The Origins and Plasticity of Interchanges.* San Francisco: Freeman, 1979.

Chodorow, N. Oedipal Asymmetries and Heterosexual Knots, in S. Cox (ed.), *Female Psychology: The Emerging Self.* New York: St. Martin's Press, 1981, 228–248.

De Leon, G., and Mandell, W. A Comparison of Conditioning and Psychotherapy in the Treatment of Functional Enuresis. *Journal of Clinical Psychology,* 1966, *22,* 326–330.

Deutsch, H. *The Psychology of Women,* vols. 1 and 2. New York: Bantam Books, 1973 (first published 1945).

Dicaprio, N. S. *Personality Theories: A Guide to Human Nature* (2nd ed.). New York: Holt, Rinehart and Winston, 1983.

Dusek-Girdano, D., and Girdano, D. A. *Drugs: A Factual Account* (3rd ed.). Reading, Mass.: Addison-Wesley, 1980.

Eidelberg, L. *Encyclopedia of Psychoanalysis.* New York: The Free Press, 1968.

Erikson, E. *Life History and the Historical Moment.* New York: W. W. Norton, 1975.

_____. *Identity: Youth and Crisis.* New York: W. W. Norton, 1968.

_____. *Gandhi's Truth.* New York: W. W. Norton, 1969.

_____. *Childhood and Society.* New York: W. W. Norton, 1963.

_____. *Young Man Luther: A Study in Psychoanalysis and History*. New York: W. W. Norton, 1958.

Fine, R. *The Development of Freud's Thought*. New York: Jason Aronson, 1974.

Flavell, J. H. On Cognitive Development. *Child Development*, 1982, *53*, 1–10.

_____. *Cognitive Development*. Englewood Cliffs, N.J.: Prentice-Hall, 1977.

_____. *Development of Role-Taking and Communication Skills in Children*. Huntington, N.Y.: Krieger, 1975.

Freud, S. *The Ego and the Id*. New York: W. W. Norton, 1962 (originally published 1923).

_____. *New Introductory Lectures on Psychoanalysis*. New York: W. W. Norton, 1961 (originally published 1933).

_____. *The Interpretation of Dreams*, in J. Strachey (ed.), *The Standard Edition of the Complete Psychological Works of Sigmund Freud*, vol. 4. London: Hogarth Press, 1957 (originally published 1900).

_____. *An Outline of Psychoanalysis*. New York: W. W. Norton, 1949 (originally published 1940).

Furth, H. G., and Wachs, H. *Thinking Goes to School*. New York: Oxford University Press, 1975.

Gesell, A. *Youth: Years from Ten to Sixteen*. New York: Harper and Row, 1956.

_____. The Ontogenesis of Human Behavior, in L. Carmichael (ed.), *Manual of Child Psychology*. New York: Wiley, 1954.

_____. *The First Five Years of Life*. New York: Harper, 1940.

_____. *Infancy and Human Growth*. New York: Macmillan, 1928.

Gesell, A., and Ilg, F. L. *Child Development: An Introduction*. New York: Harper and Row, 1949.

Gesell, A., Thompson, H., and Amatrada, C. S. *The Psychology of Early Growth*. New York: Macmillan, 1938.

Gray, F., with P. S. Graubard and H. Rosenberg. Little Brother Is Changing You. *Psychology Today*, March 1974, 42–46.

Hagen, J. W., Jongeward, R. H., Jr., and R. V. Kail, Jr. Cognitive Perspectives on the Development of Memory, in *Advances in Child Development and Behavior*, vol. 10, H. W. Reese (ed.). New York: Academic Press, 1975, 57–104.

Hall, C. S., and Lindzey, G. *Theories of Personality*. New York: Wiley, 1957.

Harlow, H. F., and Harlow, M. K. Learning to Love. *American Scientist*, 1966, *54*, 244–272.

Hilgard, E. R. *Theories of Learning* (2nd ed.). New York: Appleton-Century-Crofts, 1956.

Hjelle, L. A., and Zeigler, D. J. *Personality*. New York: McGraw-Hill, 1976.

Hunt, J. McVic. Psychological Development: Early Experience. *Annual Review of Psychology*, 1979, *30*, 103–143.

Ilg, F. L., and Ames, L. B. *Child Behavior*. New York: Harper and Row, 1955.

Jenkins, J. J. Remember That Old Theory of Memory? Well, Forget It! *American Psychologist*, November 1974, *29*, 785–795.

Kline, P. *Fact and Fancy in Freudian Theory*. London: Methuen, 1972.

Laughlin, H. P. *The Ego and Its Defenses*. New York: Appleton-Century-Crofts, 1970.

Lips, J. C., and Colwill, J. A. *Sex and Sex Roles*. Englewood Cliffs, N.J.: Prentice-Hall, 1979.

May, R. (ed.). *Existential Psychology*. New York: Random House, 1969.

Mowrer, O. H., and Mowrer, W. M. Enuresis: A Method for Its Study and Treatment. *American Journal of Orthopsychiatry*, 1938, *8*, 436–459.

Mullahy, P. *Oedipus: Myth and Complex*. New York: Grove Press, 1948.

Noam, G. G., Higgins, R. O., and Goethals, G. W. Psychoanalytic Approaches to Developmental Psychology in B. B. Wolman (ed.), *Handbook of Developmental Psychology*. Englewood Cliffs, N.J.: Prentice-Hall, 1982, 23–40.

Nye, R. D. *Three Views of Man*. Monterey, Calif.: Brooks/Cole, 1975.

Phillips, J. L., Jr. *The Origins of Intellect: Piaget's Theory* (2nd ed.). San Francisco: Freeman, 1975.

Piaget, J. Intellectual Evolution from Adolescence to Adulthood. *Human Development*, 1972, *15*, 1–12.

_____. *Genetic Epistemology*. New York: Columbia University Press, 1970.

_____. *The Child's Conception of Movement and Speed*. New York: Basic Books, 1969.

_____. *The Child's Conception of Number*. New York: Humanities Press, 1952.

_____. *The Moral Judgment of the Child*. London: Routledge and Kegan Paul, 1932.

Piaget, J., and Inhelder, B. *The Child's Conception of Space*. London: Routledge and Kegan Paul, 1956.

Pulaski, M. A. S. *Understanding Piaget: An Introduction to Children's Cognitive Development*. New York: Harper and Row, 1980.

Rogers, C. R. *A Way of Being*. Boston: Houghton Mifflin, 1980.

Rychlak, J. F. Eclecticism in Psychological Theorizing: Good and Bad. *Journal of Counseling and Development*, 1985, *63*, 351–354.

Sachs, S., and De Leon, G. Conditioning Two Types of Enuretics. *Behavior Research and Therapy*, 1973, *11*, 653–654.

Salkind, N. J. *Theories of Human Development*. New York: Van Nostrand, 1981.

Sarnoff, I. *Testing Freudian Concepts: An Experimental Social Approach*. New York: Springer, 1971.

Skinner, B. F. *About Behaviorism*. New York: Knopf, 1974.

Thibault, J. P., and McKee, J. S. Practical Parenting with Piaget. *Young Children*, November, 1982, *38*, 18–27.

Thomas, R. M. *Comparing Theories of Child Development*. Belmont, Calif.: Wadsworth, 1979.

Trabasso, T. Representation, Memory, and Reasoning: How Do We Make Transitive Inferences, in A. D. Pick (ed.), *Minnesota Symposia on Child Psychology*, vol. 9. Minneapolis: University of Minnesota Press, 1975, 135–173.

Watson, J. B. *Behaviorism*. Chicago: University of Chicago Press (rev. ed.), 1930.

Yelon, S. L., and Weinstein, G. W. *A Teacher's World: Psychology in the Classroom*. New York: McGraw-Hill, 1977.

Chapter Five

Ainsworth, M. D. S., and Bell, S. M. Infant Crying and Maternal Responsiveness: A Rejoinder to Gewirtz and Boyd. *Child Development*, 1977, *48*, 1208–1216.

Alley, T. R. Headshape and the Perception of Cuteness. *Developmental Psychology*, 1981, *17*, 650–655.

Apgar, V. A Proposal for a New Method of Evaluation of the New-born Infant. *Current Researches in Anesthesia and Analgesia*, 1953, *32*, 260–267.

Apgar, V., Holaday, D. A., James, L. S., Weisbrot, I. M., and Berien, C. Evaluation of the Newborn Infant: Second Report. *Journal of the American Psychological Association*, 1958, *168*, 1985–1988.

Apgar, V., and James, L. S. Further Observations of the Newborn Scoring System. *American Journal of the Diseases of Children*, 1962, *104*, 419–428.

Aslin, R. N., Pisoni, D. B., and Jusczyk, P. W. Auditory Development and Speech Perception in Infancy, in P. H. Mussen (ed.), *Handbook of Child Development* (4th ed.), vol. 2. New York: Wiley, 1983, 573–689.

Azrin, N. H., and Foxx, R. *Toilet Training in Less Than a Day*. New York: Pocket Books, 1976.

Ball, W., and Tronick, E. Infant Responses to Impending Collision: Optical and Real. *Science*, 1971, *171*, 818–820.

Banks, M. S., Aslin, R. N., and Letson, R. D. Sensitive Period for the Development of Human Binocular Vision. *Science*, 1975, *190*, 675–677.

Banks, M. S., and Salapatek, P. Infant Visual Perception, in P. H. Mussen (ed.), *Handbook of Child Development* (4th ed.), vol. 2. New York: Wiley, 1983, 435–573.

Bee, H. *Social Issues in Developmental Psychology* (2nd ed.). New York: Harper and Row, 1978.

Bell, S. M., and Ainsworth, M. D. Infant Crying and Maternal Responsiveness. *Child Development*, 1972, *43*, 1171–1190.

Berg, W. K., Adkinson, C. D., and Strock, B. D. Duration and Frequency of Periods of Alertness in the Newborn. *Developmental Psychology*, 1973, *9*, 434.

Berg, W. K., and Berg, K. M. Psychophysiological Development in Infancy: State, Sensory Functioning and Attention, in J. Osofsky (ed.), *Handbook of Infant Development*. New York: Wiley, 1979, 283–344.

Birns, B. The Emergence and Socialization of Sex Differences in the Earliest Years. *Merrill-Palmer Quarterly*, 1976, *22*, 229–257.

Birren, J. E., Kinney, D. K., Schaie, K. W., and Woodruff, D. S. *Developmental Psychology: A Life-Span Approach*. Boston: Houghton Mifflin, 1981.

Blass, E. M., Ganchrow, J. R., and Steiner, J. E. Classical Conditioning in Newborn Humans 2–48 Hours of Age. *Infant Behavior and Development*, 1984, *7*, 223–235.

Block, J. H. Assessing Sex Differences: Issues, Problems and Pitfalls. *Merrill-Palmer Quarterly*, 1976, *22*, 283–308.

Bond, E. Form Perception in the Infant. *Psychological Bulletin*, 1972, *77*, 225–245.

Bornstein, M. H. Infants Are Trichromats. *Journal of Experimental Child Psychology*, 1976, *21*, 425–445.

———. Qualities of Color Vision in Infancy. *Journal of Experimental Child Psychology*, 1975, *19*, 401–419.

Bower, T. G. R. *Principles of Infant Development*. San Francisco: Freeman, 1977.

Bower, T. G. R., Broughton, J. M., and Moore, M. K. Infant Response to Approaching Objects: An Indication of Response to Distal Variation. *Perception and Psychophysics*, 1970, *9*, 193–196.

Brackbill, Y. Extinction of the Smile: Responses in Infants as a Function of Reinforcement Schedule. *Child Development*, 1958, *29*, 115–124.

Brackbill, Y., Adams, G., Crowell, D. H., and Gray, M. G. Arousal Level in Neonates and Preschool Children Under Contingent Auditory Stimulation. *Journal of Experimental Child Psychology*, 1966, *14*, 174–178.

Brazelton, T. B. *On Becoming a Family: The Growth of Attachment*. New York: Delacorte Press, 1981.

Brierly, J. *The Growing Brain*. Windsor, Eng.: NFER Publishing Co., 1976.

Butterfield, E. C., and Siperstein, G. N. Influence of Contingent Auditory Stimulation upon Non-Nutritional Suckle, in J. F. Bosma (ed.), *Third Symposium on Oral Sensation and Perception: The Mouth of the Infant*. Springfield, Ill.: Thomas, 1972.

Campos, J., Langer, A., and Krowitz, A. Cardiac Responses on the Visual Cliff in Prelocomotor Human Infants. *Science*, 1970, *170*, 196–197.

Cherry, L., and Lewis, M. The Pre-School Teacher-Child Dyad: Sex Differences in Verbal Interaction. *Child Development*, 1976, *46*, 532–535.

Cohen, L. B. Our Developing Knowledge of Infant Perception and Cognition. *American Psychologist*, 1979, *34*, 894–899.

Cohen, L. B., Deloache, J. S., and Strauss, M. S. Infant Visual Perception, in J. Osofsky (ed.), *Handbook of Infant Development*. New York: Wiley, 1979, 393–439.

Condry, J. G., and Condry, S. Sex Differences: A Study of the Eye of the Beholder. *Child Development*, 1976, *47*, 812–819.

Cratty, B. *Perceptual and Motor Development in Infancy and Childhood*. New York: Macmillan, 1970. Second edition 1979.

Curtis, H. *Biology* (2nd ed.). New York: Worth, 1975.

Dayton, G., Jones, M., Aiu, P., Rawson, R., Steele, B., and Rose, M. Developmental Study of Coordinated Eye Movements in the Human Infant, 1: Visual Acuity in the Newborn Human: A Study Based on Induced Optokinetic Nystagmus Recorded by Electro-Oculography. *Archives of Ophthalmology*, 1964, *71*, 865–870.

DeCasper, A. J., and Fifer, W. P. Of Human Bonding: Newborns Prefer Their Mothers' Voices. *Science*, 1980, *208*, 1174–1176.

DeFrain, J., Taylor, J., and Ernst, L. *Coping with Sudden Infant Death*. Lexington, MA: D.C. Heath, 1982.

Dennis, W., and Dennis, M. G. Cradles and Cradling Customs of the Pueblo Indians. *American Anthropologist*, 1940, *42*, 107–115.

Dennis, W., and Najarian, P. How Reversible Are the Effects? in S. J. Hutt and C. Hull (eds.), *Early Human Development*. London: Oxford University Press, 1973, 274–288.

Desor, J. A., Maller, O., and Turner, R. E. Taste in Acceptance of Sugars by Human Infants. *Journal of Comparative and Physiological Psychology*, 1973, *84*, 496–501.

DiFranco, D., Muir, D., and Dodwell, P. Reaching in Very Young Infants. *Perception*, 1978, *7*, 385–392.

Dobbing, J. Human Brain Development and Its Vulnerability (1975), in R. L. Smart and M. S. Smart (eds.), *Readings in Child Development and Relationships* (2nd ed.). New York: Macmillan, 1977, 49–61.

Dobson, V., and Teller, D. Y. Visual Acuity in Human Infants: A Review and Comparison of Behavioral and Electrophysiological Stimulation. *Vision Research*, 1978, *18*, 1469–1484.

Dworetzsky, J. P. *Introduction to Child Development* (2nd ed.). St. Paul, Minnesota: West Publishing Co., 1984.

Eichenwald, H. F., and Fry, P. G. Nutrition and Learning. *Science,* 1969, *163,* 644–648.

Eichorn, D. H. Physical Development: Current Foci of Research, in J. Osofsky (ed.), *Handbook of Infant Development.* New York: Wiley, 1979, 253–283.

Eisenberg, R. B. The Organization of Auditory Behavior. *Journal of Speech and Hearing Research,* 1970, *13,* 461–464.

Elkind, D. *A Sympathetic Understanding of the Child: Birth to Sixteen.* Boston: Allyn and Bacon, 1978.

Engen, T., Lipsitt, L. P., and Peck, M. B. Ability of Newborn Infants to Discriminate Sapid Substances. *Developmental Psychology,* 1974, *10,* 741–744.

Epner, M. (pediatrician and pediatric endocrinologist). Personal communication, 1982.

Etzel, B. C., and Gewirtz, J. L. Experimentation Model of Caretaker-Maintained Heart-Rate Operant Crying in a Six and a Twenty Week Old Infant: Extinction of Crying with Reinforcement of Eye Contact and Smiling. *Journal of Experimental Child Psychology,* 1967, *5,* 303–317.

Eveloff, H. H. Some Cognitive and Affective Aspects of Early Language Development. *Child Development,* 1971, *42,* 1895–1907.

Fagot, B. I. The Influence of Sex of Child on Parental Reactions to Toddler Children. *Child Development,* 1978, *49,* 459–465.

Fantz, R. L. The Origin of Form Perception. *Scientific American,* May 1961, 16–21.

————. Pattern Vision in Newborn Infants. *Science,* 1963, *140,* 296–297.

Fantz, R. L., and Miranda, S. B. Newborn Infant's Attention to Form of Contour. *Child Development,* 1975, *46,* 224–228.

Feldman, J. F., Brody, N., and Miller, S. A. Sex Differences in Non-Elicited Neonatal Behaviors. *Merrill-Palmer Quarterly,* 1980, *26,* 63–73.

Fogel, A. *Infancy: Infant, Family and Society.* St. Paul: West Publishing Co., 1984.

Freedman, D. G., and Freedman, N. C. Behavioural Development Between Chinese-American and European-American Newborns. *Nature,* 1969, *224,* 1227.

Friedman, S., and Carpenter, G. C. Visual Response Decrement as a Function of Age of Human Newborn. *Child Development,* 1971, *42,* 1967–1973.

Gardner, L. I. Deprivation Dwarfism. *Scientific American,* 1962, *227,* 76–82.

Garn, S. M., Clark, D. C., McGuire, K. E. Growth, Body Composition and Development of Obese and Lean Children, in M. Winick (ed.), *Childhood Obesity.* New York: Wiley, 1975, 23–46.

Geber, M., and Dean, R. F. A. The State of Development of Newborn African Children. *The Lancet,* 1957, *272,* 1216–1219.

Gesell, A., Halverson, H. M., Thompson, H., Ilg, F. C., Castner, B. M., Ames, L. B., and Amatruda, C. S. *The First Five Years of Life: A Guide to the Study of the Preschool Child.* New York: Harper and Row, 1940.

Gewirtz, J. The Course of Infant Smiling in Four Child-Rearing Environments in Israel (1965), in B. M. Moss (ed.), *Determinants of Infant Behavior 3.* New York: Wiley, 1975, 205–261.

Gewirtz, J., and Boyd, E. F. Does Maternal Responding Imply Reduced Crying: A Critique of the 1972 Bell and Ainsworth Report. *Child Development,* 1977, *48,* 1200–1207.

Gibson, E. J., and Walk, R. D. The "Visual Cliff." *Scientific American,* April 1960, *202,* 64–71.

Goldberg, S., and Lewis, M. Play Behavior in the Year-Old Infant: Early Sex Differences. *Child Development,* 1969, *40,* 21–31.

Guntheroth, W. G. *Crib Death: Sudden Infant Death Syndrome.* Mount Kisco, N.Y.: Futura Publishing Co., 1982.

Haith, M. M. *Rules Babies Look By: The Organization of Newborn Visual Activity.* Hillsdale, N.J.: Erlbaum, 1980.

————. The Response of the Human Newborn to Visual Movement. *Journal of Experimental Child Psychology,* 1966, *3,* 235–243.

Hamill, P. V. V. NCHS Growth Curves for Children. Vital and Health Statistics: Series 11, Data from the National Health Survey, No. 165. Washington, D.C.: U.S. Government Printing Office (DWEH no. 78-1650), 1977.

Hamilton, E. M. N., Whitney, E. N., and Sizer, F. S. *Nutrition: Concepts and Controversies* (3rd ed.). St. Paul, Minnesota: West Publishing Co., 1985.

Hamilton, E. M. N., and Whitney, E. N. *Nutrition: Concepts and Controversies* (2nd ed.). St. Paul: West Publishing Co., 1982.

Hayes, L. A., and Watson, J. S. Neonatal Imitation: Fact and Artifact. *Developmental Psychology,* 1981, *17,* 655–561.

Haynes, H., White, B. L., and Held, R. Visual Accommodation in Human Infants. *Science,* 1965, *148,* 528–530.

Hirsch, J., and Knittle, J. L. Cellularity of Obese and Nonobese Human Adipose Tissue (1970), cited in Einhorn, D. H., Physical Development: Current Foci of Research, in J. Osofsky (ed.), *Handbook of Infant Development.* New York: Wiley, 1979, 253–282.

Hofsten, C. von. Eye Hand Coordination in the Newborn. *Developmental Psychology,* 1982, *18,* 450–462.

Hutt, S. J., and Hutt, C. R. *Early Human Development.* London: Oxford University Press, 1973.

Illingworth, R. S. *The Development of the Infant and Young Child: Normal and Abnormal.* Edinburgh: Livingstone, 1974.

Intons-Peterson, M. J., and Reddel, M. What Do People Ask About a Neonate? *Developmental Psychology,* 1984, *20,* 358–360.

Jackson, J. F., and Jackson, J. H. *Infant Culture.* New York: Crowell, 1978.

Jacobson, J. L., Fein, G. G., Jacobson, S. W., and Schwartz, P. M. Factors and Clusters for the Brazelton Scale: An Investigation of the Dimensions of Neonatal Behavior. *Developmental Psychology,* 1984, *20,* 339–354.

Jensen, K. Differential Reaction to Taste and Temperature Stimuli in Newborn Infants. *Genetic Psychology Monographs,* 1932, *12,* 363–479.

Kalat, J. W. *Biological Psychology.* Belmont, Calif.: Wadsworth, 1981.

Kaye, H. The Conditioned Babkin Reflex in Human Newborns. *Psychonomic Science,* 1965, *2,* 287–288.

Kearsley, R. B. The Newborn's Response to Auditory Stimuli: A Demonstration of Orientation and Defensive Behavior. *Child Development,* 1973, *44,* 582–590.

Keefer, C. S., Dixon, E., and Tronick, L. B., and Brazelton T. B. Gusii Infants' Neuromotor Behavior: Use of the Neonatal Behavioral Assessment Scale in Cross-Cultural Studies (1978), cited in B. M. Lester and T. B. Brazelton, Cross-Cultural Assessment of Neonatal Behavior, in D. A. Wagner and H. W. Stevenson, *Cultural Perspectives on Child Development.* San Francisco: Freeman, 1982, 20–54.

Kirk, S. A., and Gallagher, J. G. *Educating the Exceptional Child* (3rd ed.). Boston: Houghton Mifflin, 1979.

Kisilevsky, B. S., and Muir, D. W. Neonatal Habituation and Dishabituation to Tactile Stimulation During Sleep. *Developmental Psychology*, 1984, *20*, 367–374.

Korner, A. F. Sex Differences in Newborns with Special Reference to Differences in the Organization of Oral Behavior. *Journal of Child Psychology and Psychiatry*, 1973, *14*, 17–29.

Korner, A., and Thoman, E. The Relative Efficacy of Contact and Vestibular Proprioceptive Stimuli in Soothing Neonates. *Child Development*, 1972, *43*, 443–454.

Kreminitzer, J. P., Vaughn, H. G., Kurtzberg, D., and Dowling, K. Smooth-Pursuit Eye Movements in the Newborn Infant. *Child Development*, 1979, *50*, 442–448.

Lester, B. M., and Brazelton, T. B. Cross-Cultural Assessment of Neonatal Behavior, in D. A. Wagner and H. W. Stevenson (eds.), *Cultural Perspectives on Child Development*. San Francisco: Freeman, 1982.

Lewis, M., Bartels, B., Campbell, H., and Goldberg, S. Individual Differences in Attention: The Relation Between Infants' Condition at Birth and Attention Distribution Within the First Years (1967), in L. J. Stone, H. T. Smith, and L. B. Murphy (eds.), *The Competent Infant: Research and Commentary*. New York: Basic Books, 1973.

Lipsitt, L. Perinatal Indicators and Psychophysiological Precursors of Crib Death (1978), in J. Belsky (ed.), *In the Beginning: Readings on Infancy*. New York: Columbia University Press, 1982, 74–83.

Lipsitt, L. P., Engen, T., and Kaye H. Developmental Changes in the Olfactory Threshold of the Neonate. *Child Development*, 1963, *34*, 37–46.

Lipsitt, L. P., and Kaye, H. Conditioned Sucking in the Newborn. *Psychonomic Science*, 1964, *1*, 29–30.

Lipsitt, L. P., and Levy, N. Electrotactual Threshold in the Neonate. *Child Development*, 1959, *30*, 547–554.

Little, A. H. Eyelid Conditioning in the Human Infant as a Function of Interstimulus Interval, cited in Lipsitt, L. P., and Reese, H. W., *Child Development*. Glenview, Ill.: Scott, Foresman, 1979.

Lowrey, G. *Growth and Development of Children* (7th ed.) Chicago: Year Book Medical Publishers, 1978.

Maccoby, E. E., and Jacklin, C. N. *The Psychology of Sex Differences*. Stanford, Calif.: Stanford University Press, 1974.

MacFarlane, A. Olfaction in the Development of Social Preferences in the Human Neonate (1975), cited in Brazelton, T. B., *On Becoming a Family: The Growth of Attachment*. New York: Delacorte Press, 1981.

Martin, G. B., and Clark, R. D. Distress Crying in Neonates: Species and Peer Specificity. *Developmental Psychology*, 1982, *18*, 3–9.

Maurer, D., and Salapatek, P. Developmental Changes in the Scanning of Faces by Young Infants. *Child Development*, 1976, *47*, 523–527.

McKay, H., Sinisterra, L., McKay, H. G., Gomez, H., and Lloreda, P. Improving Cognitive Ability in Chronically Deprived Children. *Science*, 1978, *200*, 270–278.

Meltzoff, A. N., and Moore, M. K. Newborn Infants Imitate Adult Facial Gestures. *Child Development*, 1983, *54*, 702–709.

———. Imitation of Facial and Manual Gestures by Human Neonates. *Science*, 1977, *198*, 75–78.

Meyer, J., and Sobieszek, B. Effect of a Child's Sex on Adult Interpretations of Its Behavior. *Developmental Psychology*, 1972, *6*, 42–48.

Milewski, A. E. Infants' Discrimination of Internal and External Pattern Elements. *Journal of Experimental Child Psychology*, 1976, *22*, 229–246.

Minard, J., Coleman, D., Williams, G., and Ingledyne, E. Cumulative REM of Three to Five Day Olds: Effect of Normal External Noise and Maturation. *Psychophysiology*, 1968, *5*, 232.

Morris, D. *Manwatching: A Field Guide to Human Behavior*. New York: Abrams, 1977.

Moss, H. Early Sex Differences and Mother-Infant Interaction, in R. C. Friedman, R. M. Richart, and R. L. Van de Weile (eds.), *Sex Differences in Behavior*. New York: Wiley, 1974.

———. Sex, Age and State as Determinants of Mother-Infant Interaction. *Merrill-Palmer Quarterly*, 1967, *13*, 19–37.

Nisbett, R., and Gurwitz, S. Weight, Sex and the Eating Behavior of Human Newborns. *Journal of Comparative and Physiological Psychology*, 1970, *73*, 245–253.

Osofsky, J. D., and Connors, K. Mother-Infant Interaction: An Integrative View of a Complex System, in J. Osofsky (ed.), *Handbook of Infant Development*. New York: Wiley, 1979, 519–549.

Parmelee, A. H., and Sigman, M. D. Perinatal Brain Development and Behavior, in P. H. Mussen (ed.), *Handbook of Child Development* (3rd ed.), vol. 2. New York: Wiley, 1983, 95–157.

Parmelee, A., and Stern, E. Development of States in Infants, in C. B. Clemente, D. P. Purpura, and F. E. Mayer (eds.), *Sleep and the Maturing Nervous System*. New York: Academic Press, 1972.

Parmelee, A. H., Wenne, W. H., and Schulz, H. R. Infant Sleep Patterns from Birth to Sixteen Weeks of Age. *Journal of Pediatrics*, 1964, *65*, 576–582.

Parton, D. A. Learning to Imitate in Infancy. *Developmental Psychology*, 1976, *47*, 14–31.

Patrusky, B. Diagnosing Newborns. *Science*. July 1980, 26–39.

Pedersen, F. A., and Robson, K. S. Father Participation in Infancy. *American Journal of Orthopsychiatry*, 1969, *39*, 466–472.

Pratt, K. C. The Neonate, in L. Carmichael (ed.), *Manual of Child Psychology* (2nd ed.). New York: Wiley, 1954.

Reese, H. W., and Lipsitt, L. P. *Experimental Child Psychology*. New York: Academic Press, 1973.

Rheingold, M. L., and Cook, K. V. The Contents of Boys' and Girls' Rooms as an Index of Parents' Behavior. *Child Development*, 1975, *46*, 49–63.

Ricciuti, H. N. Adverse Environmental and Nutritional Influences on Mental Development: A Perspective. Paper presented at American Dietetic Association Meeting, Atlanta, 1980a.

Ricciuti, H. N. Developmental Consequences of Malnutrition in Early Childhood (1980b), in E. M. Hetherington and R. D. Parke (eds.), *Contemporary Readings in Child Psychology* (2nd ed.). New York: McGraw-Hill, 1981, 21–25.

Richardson, S. A. The Relation of Severe Malnutrition in Infancy of School Children with Differing Life Histories (1976), cited in Ricciuti, S. A., Developmental Consequences of Malnutrition (1980b), in E. M. Hetherington and R. D. Parke (eds.), *Contemporary Readings in Child Psychology* (2nd ed.). New York: McGraw-Hill, 1981.

Ridenour, M. V. Contemporary Issues in Motor Development, in *Motor Development: Issues and Applications*. Princeton: Princeton Book Co., 1978, 39–63.

Roffwarg, H. P., Muzio, J. N., and Dement, W. C. Ontogenic Development of the Human Sleep-Dream Cycle. *Science*, 1966, *152*, 604–619.

Rogan, W., Bagniewska, A., and Damstra, J. Pollutants in Breast Milk. *New England Journal of Medicine*, 1980, *26*, 1450–1453.

Rosenzweig, M. R., Bennett, E. L., and Diamond, M. C. Brain Changes in Response to Experience. *Scientific American*, February 1972, *226*, 22–29.

Rubelsky, F., and Hanks, C. Fathers' Verbal Interactions with Infants in the First Three Months of Life. *Child Development*, 1971, *42*–48.

Ruff, H. A., and Halton, A. Is There Directed Reaching in the Human Neonate. *Developmental Psychology*, 1978, *14*, 425–426.

Rushworth, G. On Postural and Righting Reflexes, in C. B. Kopp (ed.), *Readings in Early Development: For Occupational and Physical Therapy Students*. Springfield, Ill.: Thomas, 1971, 6–21.

Salk, L. The Effects of the Normal Heartbeat Sound on the Behavior of Newborn Infants: Implications for Mental Health. *World Mental Health*, 1960, *12*, 168–175.

Sameroff, A. J. Can Conditioned Responses Be Established in the Newborn 1971? *Developmental Psychology*, 1971, *5*, 1–12.

Sameroff, A. J., and Cavanaugh, P. J. Learning in Infancy: A Developmental Perspective, in J. Osofsky (ed.), *Handbook of Infant Development*, 1979, 344–393.

Schmitt, M. H. Superiority of Breast-Feeding: Fact or Fancy. *American Journal of Nursing*, July 1970, 1488–1493.

Sears, R. R., Maccoby, E. E., and Levin, H. *Patterns of Child Rearing*. New York: Harper and Row, 1957.

Self, P. A., and Horowitz, F. D. The Behavioral Assessment of the Neonate: An Overview in J. Osofsky (ed.), *Handbook of Infant Development*. New York: Wiley, 1979, 126–165.

Semb, G., and Lipsitt, L. P. The Effects of Acoustic Stimulation on Cessation and Initiation of Non-Nutritive Sucking in Neonates. *Journal of Experimental Child Psychology*, 1968, 6, 585–597.

Shirley, M. M. *The First Two Years: A Study of Twenty-Five Babies*, vol. 2, *Intellectual Development*. Minneapolis: University of Minnesota Press, 1933.

———. *The First Two Years: A Study of Twenty-Five Babies*, vol. 1, *Postural and Locomotor Development*. Minneapolis: University of Minnesota Press, 1931.

Simner, M. Newborn's Response to the Cry of Another Infant. *Developmental Psychology*, 1971, *5*, 136–150.

Siqueland, E. R. Response Patterns and Extinction in Human Newborns. *Journal of Experimental Child Psychology*, 1968, 6, 431–442.

Siqueland, E. R., and Lipsitt, L. P. Conditioned Headturning in Human Newborns. *Journal of Experimental Child Psychology*, 1966, *3*, 356–376.

Smith, C., and Lloyd, B. Maternal Behavior and Perceived Sex of Infant: Revisited. *Child Development*, 1978, *49*, 1263–1265.

Super, C. M. Cross-Cultural Research on Infancy, in H. C. Triandis and A. Heron (eds.), *Handbook of Cross-Cultural Psychology*, vol. 4, *Developmental Psychology*. Boston: Allyn and Bacon, 1981, 17–55.

Tanner, J. Physical Growth, in P. H. Mussen (ed.), *Carmichael's Manual of Child Psychology* (3rd ed.). New York: Wiley, 1970.

Thoman, E. B., Leiderman, P. H., and Olson, J. P. Neonate-Mother Interaction During Breast Feeding. *Developmental Psychology*, 1972, 6, 110–118.

Waddington, C. H. *The Strategy of the Genes*. London: Allen and Unwin, 1957.

Wade, N. Bottle-Feeding: Adverse Effects of a Western Technology. *Science*, 1974, *184*, 45–48.

Webster, R. L., Steinhardt, M. H., and Senter, M. G. Changes in Infants' Vocalizations as a Function of Differential Acoustic Stimulation. *Developmental Psychology*, 1972, *7*, 39–43.

Weitz, S. *Sex Roles: Biological, Psychological and Social Foundations*. New York: Oxford University Press, 1977.

Wertheimer, M. Psycho-Motor Coordination of Auditory-Visual Space at Birth. *Science*, 1961, *134*, 1692.

Wesley, F., and Sullivan, E. *Human Growth and Development: A Psychological Approach*. New York: Human Sciences Press, 1980.

Whitehurst, G. J., and Vasta, R. *Child Behavior*. Boston: Houghton Mifflin, 1977.

Whitney, E. N., and Hamilton, E. M. N. *Understanding Nutrition* (3rd ed.). St. Paul: West Publishing Co., 1984.

Wiesel, T. N., and Hubel, D. H. Extent of Recovery from the Effects of Visual Deprivation in Kittens. *Journal of Neurophysiology*, 1965, *28*, 1060–1072.

Williamsen, E. *Understanding Infancy*. San Francisco: Freeman, 1979.

Winick, M., Meyer, K. K., and Harris, R. C. Malnutrition and Environmental Enrichment by Early Adoption: Development of Adopted Korean Children Differing Greatly in Nutritional Status Is Examined. *Science*, 1975, *190*, 1173–1175.

Winick, M., and Russo, P. Head Circumference and Cellular Growth of the Brain in Normal and Marasmic Children. *Journal of Pediatrics*, 1969, *74*, 774–778.

Winick, M., Russo, P., and Waterloo, J. Cellular Growth of Cerebrum, Cerebellum and Brain Stem in Normal and Marasmic Children. *Experimental Neurology*, 1970, *21*, 393–410.

Wolff, P. H. The Development of Attention in Young Infants (1965), in L. J. Stone, H. T. Smith, and L. B. Murphy (eds.), *The Competent Infant: Research and Commentary*. New York: Basic Books, 1973, 307–314.

———. The Natural History of Crying and Other Vocalization in Early Infancy, in B. M. Foss, *Determinants of Infant Behaviour*, 4. London: Methuen, 1969, 81–111.

———. Observations on Newborn Infants (1959), in L. J. Stone, H. T. Smith, and L. B. Murphy (eds.), *The Competent Infant: Research and Commentary*. New York: Basic Books, 1973, 257–269.

Woodruff, C. W. The Science of Infant Nutrition and the Art of Infant Feeding. *Journal of the American Medical Association*, 1978, *240*, 657–661.

Zelazo, P. R., Zelazo, N. A., and Kolb, S. "Walking" in the Newborn. *Science*, 1972, *176*, 314–315.

Chapter Six

Anastasi, A. *Psychological Testing* (4th ed.). New York: Macmillan, 1976.

Ault, R. *Children's Cognitive Development*. New York: Oxford University Press, 1977.

Barrera, M. E., and Maurer, D. Recognition of Mother's Photographed Face by the Three-Month-Old Infant. *Child Development*, 1981, *52*, 714–716.

Bayley, N. *The Bayley Scales of Infant Development*. New York: Psychological Corp., 1969.

———. Development of Mental abilities, in P. H. Mussen (ed.), *Carmichael's Manual of Child Psychology*. New York: Wiley, 1970.

Bayley, N., and Oden, M. H. The Maintenance of Intellectual Ability in Gifted Adults. *Journal of Gerontology*, 1955, *10*, 91–107.

Bee, H. L., Barnard, K. E., Eyres, S. J., Gray, C. A. Hammond, M. A. Spietz, C. S., and Clark, B. Prediction of IQ and Language Skill from Perinatal Status, Child Performance, Family Characteristics, and Mother-Infant Interaction. *Child Development*, 1982, *53*, 1134–1156.

Beller, E. K. Early Intervention Programs, in J. Osofsky (ed.), *Handbook of Infant Development*. New York: Wiley, 1979, 852–897.

Belsky, J., and Most, R. K. Infant Exploration and Play, in J. Belsky (ed.), *In the Beginning: Readings on Infancy*. New York: Columbia University Press, 1982, 109–121.

Bower, T. G. R. *A Primer of Infant Development*. San Francisco: Freeman, 1979.

———. The Object in the World of the Infant. *Scientific American*, 1971, *225*, 30–38, offprint no. 539.

———. The Visual World of Infants. *Scientific American*, 1966, *215*, 80–92.

Bower, T. G. R., and Wishart, J. G. The Effects of Motor Skill on Object Permanence. *Cognition*, 1972, *1*, 165–172.

Bradley, R. H., and Caldwell, B. The HOME Inventory and Family Demographics. *Developmental Psychology*, 1984, *20*, 315–321.

Bradley, R. H., and Caldwell, B. M. The Relation of Home Environment, Cognitive Competence and IQ Among Males and Females. *Child Development*, 1980, *51*, 1140–1148.

Bradley, R. H., Caldwell, B. M., and Elardo, R. Home Environment and Cognitive Development in the First Two Years: A Cross-Lagged Analysis. *Developmental Psychology*, 1979, *15*, 246–250.

Brainerd, C. J. *Piaget's Theory of Intelligence*. Englewood Cliffs, N.J.: Prentice-Hall, 1978.

Brody, L. R. Visual Short-Term Recall Memory in Infancy. *Child Development*, 1981, *52*, 242–250.

Carew, J. V., Chan, I., and Halfar, C. Observed Intellectual Competence and Tested Intelligence: Their Roots in the Young Child's Transactions with His Environment (1975), in S. Cohen and T. J. Comiskey (ed.), *Child Development: Contemporary Perspectives*. Itasca, Ill.: Peacock Publishers, 1977, 29–44.

Cataldo, C. Z. Very Early Childhood Education for Infants and Toddlers. *Childhood Education*, January/February 1982.

Clarke, A. M., and Clarke, A. D. B. *Early Experience: Myth and Evidence*. New York: The Free Press, 1977.

Cohen, L. B., DeLoache, J. S., and Strauss, M. S. Infant Visual Perception, in J. Osofsky (ed.), *Handbook of Infant Development*. New York: Wiley, 1979, 393–439.

Dasen, P., and Heron A. Cross-Cultural Tests of Piaget's Theory, in H. C. Triandis and A. Heron (eds.), *Handbook of Cross-Cultural Psychology*, vol. 4. Boston: Allyn and Bacon, 1981, 295–343.

Diamond, N. Cognitive Theory, in B. B. Wolman (ed.), *Handbook of Developmental Psychology*. Englewood Cliffs, N.J.: Prentice-Hall, 1982, 3–23.

Dunst, C. J., Brooks, P. H., and Doxsey, P. A. Characteristics of Hiding Places and the Transition to Stage 4 Performance in Object Permanence Tests. *Developmental Psychology*, 1982, *18*, 671–681.

Elardo, R., Bradley, R., and Caldwell, B. M. A Longitudinal Study of the Relation of Infants' Home Environments to Language Development at Age Three. *Child Development*, 1977, *48*, 595–603.

———. The Relation of Infants' Home Environments to Mental Test Performance from Six to Thirty-Six Months: A Longitudinal Analysis. *Child Development*, 1975, *46*, 71–76.

Elkind, D. Infant Intelligence (1973), in D. Elkind and D. C. Hetzel (eds.), *Readings in Human Development: Contemporary Perspectives*. New York: Harper and Row, 1977, 39–40.

Endler, N. S., Boulter, L. R., and Osser, H. *Contemporary Issues in Developmental Psychology* (2nd ed.). New York: Holt, Rinehart and Winston, 1976.

Fagen, J. F. Infants' Long Term Memory for Stimulus Color. *Developmental Psychology*, 1984, *20*, 435–441.

———. Infant Recognition Memory: Studies in Forgetting. *Child Development*, 1977, *48*, 68–78.

———. Infants' Delayed Recognition Memory and Forgetting. *Journal of Experimental Child Psychology*, 1973, *16*, 424–450.

Flavell, J. H. *Cognitive Development*. Englewood Cliffs, N.J.: Prentice-Hall, 1977. Second edition 1985.

Goldberg, S., Perlmutter, M., and Myers, N. Recall of Related and Unrelated Lists by 2-Year-Olds. *Journal of Experimental Child Psychology*, 1974, *18*, 1–8.

Golden, M., and Birns, B. Social Class and Cognitive Development in Infancy. *Merrill-Palmer Quarterly*, 1975, *21*, 183–195.

Goldfarb, W. The Effects of Early Institutional Care on Adolescent Personality. *Journal of Experimental Education*, 1943, *12*, 106–129.

Gratch, G. The Development of Thought and Language in Infancy, in J. Osofsky (ed.), *Handbook of Infant Development*. New York: Wiley, 1979, 439–461.

Gratch, G., Appel, K. J., Evans, W. F., LeCompte, G. K., and Wright, N. K. Piaget's Stage 4 Object Concept Error: Evidence of Forgetting or Object Conception? *Child Development*, 1974, *45*, 71–77.

Harris, P. L. Infant Cognition, in P. H. Mussen (ed.), *Handbook of Child Development* (3rd ed.). New York: Wiley, 1983, 689–783.

———. Perseverative Errors in Search by Young Children. *Child Development*, 1973, *44*, 28–33.

Horner, T. M. Test-Retest and Home-Clinic Characteristics of the Bayley Scales of Infant Development in Nine- and Fifteen-Month-Old Infants. *Child Development*, 1980, *51*, 751–758.

Hunt, J. McV. *Intelligence and Experience*. New York: Ronald Press, 1961.

Kagan, J. Overview: Perspectives on Human Infancy, in J. Osofsky (ed.), *Handbook of Infant Development*. New York: Wiley, 1979a, 1–29.

———. The Form of Early Development (1979), in P. H. Mussen, J. J. Conger, and J. Kagan, *Readings in Child and Adolescent Psychology: Contemporary Perspectives*. New York: Harper and Row, 1980b, 18–22.

Kagan, J., and Lapidus, D. R. Infant Antecedents of Cognitive Functioning: A Longitudinal Study. *Child Development*, 1978, *49*, 1005–1023.

Kramer, J., Hill, K., and Cohen, L. Infants' Development of Object Permanence: A Refined Methodology and New Evidence for Piaget's Hypothesized Ordinality. *Child Development*, 1975, *46*, 149–155.

Labarba, R. C. *Foundations of Developmental Psychology*. New York: Academic Press, 1981.

Lewis, M., and McGurk H. Evaluation of Infant Intelligence. *Science*, 1972, *178*, 1174–1177.

Lingle, K. M., and Lingle, J. H. Effects of Selected Object Characteristics on Object-Permanence Test Performance. *Child Development*, 1981, *52*, 367–369.

Lunde, D. T., and Lunde, M. K. *The Next Generation: A Book on Parenting*. New York: Holt, Rinehart and Winston, 1980.

Martin, B. Parent-Child Relations, in F. D. Horowitz (ed.), *Review of Child Development Research*, vol. 4. Chicago: University of Chicago Press, 1975, 320–339.

McCall, R. B. The Development of Intellectual Functioning in Infancy and the Prediction of Later I.Q., in J. Osofsky, *Handbook of Infant Development*. New York: Wiley, 1979, 707–742.

McCall, R. B., Hogarty, P. S., and Hurlburt, N. Transitions in Infant Sensorimotor Development and the Prediction of Childhood I.Q. *American Psychologist*, 1972, *27*, 728–748.

McGowan, R. J., Johnson, D. L., and S. E. Maxwell. Relations Between Infant Behavior Ratings and Concurrent and Subsequent Mental Test Scores. *Developmental Psychology*, 1981, *17*, 542–553.

Miller, D. J., Ryan, E. B., Short, E. J., Ries, P. G., McGuire, M. D., and Culler, M. P. Relationships Between Early Habituation and Later Cognitive Performance in Infancy. *Child Development*, 1977, *48*, 658–661.

Nyiti, R. M. The Validity of "Cultural Differences Explanations" for Cross-Cultural Variation in the Rate of Piagetian Cognitive Development, in D. A. Wagner and H. W. Stevenson (eds.), *Cultural Perspectives on Child Development*. San Francisco: Freeman, 1982, 146–166.

Petersen, G. A. Cognitive Development in Infancy, in B. B. Wolman (ed.), *Handbook of Developmental Psychology*. Englewood Cliffs, N.J.: Prentice-Hall, 1982, 323–333.

Phillips, J. L. *The Origins of Intellect: Piaget's Theory* (2nd ed.). San Francisco: Freeman, 1975.

Piaget, J. *On the Development of Memory and Identity*. Worcester, Mass.: Clark University Press, 1968.

———. *Six Psychological Studies*. New York: Random House, 1967.

———. The Stages of Intellectual Development of the Child. *Bulletin of the Menninger Clinic*, 1962, *26*, 120–128.

———. *The Construction of Reality in the Child*. New York: Basic Books, 1954 (originally published 1937).

———. *The Origins of Intelligence in Children*. New York: International Universities Press, 1952 (originally published 1936).

Rader, N., Spiro, D. J., and Firestone, P. B. Performance on a Stage 4 Object-Permanence Task with Standard and Nonstandard Covers. *Child Development*, 1979, *50*, 905–910.

Ramey, C. T., Farran, D. C., and Campbell, F. A. Predicting I.Q. from Mother-Infant Interaction. *Child Development*, 1979, *50*, 804–814.

Restak, R. M. Newborn Knowledge. *Science*, January/February 1982, 58–65.

Rose, S. A. Developmental Changes in Infants' Retention of Visual Stimuli. *Child Development*, 1981, *52*, 227–233.

Rubin, R. A., and Balow, B. Measures of Infant Development and Socioeconomic Status as Predictors of Later Intelligence and School Achievement. *Developmental Psychology*, 1979, *15*, 225–227.

Ruddy, M. G., and Bornstein, M. H. Cognitive Correlates of Infant Attention and Maternal Stimulation over the First Year of Life. *Child Development*, 1982, *53*, 183–188.

Scarr, S., and Weinberg, R. A. The Influence of "Family Background" on Intellectual Attainment. *American Sociological Review*, 1978, *43*, 674–692.

Siegel, L. S. Infant Tests as Predictors of Cognitive and Language Development at Two Years. *Child Development*, 1981, *52*, 547–557.

Spitz, R. Hospitalism: An Inquiry into the Genesis of Psychiatric Conditions in Early Childhood. *Psychoanalytic Study of the Child*, 1945, *1*, 53–74.

Starkey, D. The Origins of Concept Formation: Object Sorting and Object Preference in Early Infancy. *Child Development*, 1981, *52*, 489–497.

Strauss, M. S., and Curtis, L. E. Infant Perception of Numerosity. *Child Development*, 1981, *52*, 1146–1152.

Super, C. M. Cross-Cultural Research on Infancy, in H. C. Triandis and A. Heron (eds.), *Handbook of Cross-Cultural Psychology*, vol. 4. Boston: Allyn and Bacon, 1981, 17–55.

Thibault, J. P., and McKee, J. S. Practical Parenting with Piaget. *Young Children*, November 1982, *38*, 18–27.

Tulkin, S., and Kagan, J. Mother-Child Interaction in the First Year of Life. *Child Development*, 1972, *43*, 31–41.

Uzgiris, I. C. Patterns of Cognitive Development in Infancy. *Merrill-Palmer Quarterly*, 1973, *19*, 181–204.

Uzgiris, I. C., and Hunt, J. McV. *Assessment in Infancy: Ordinal Scales of Psychological Development*. Urbana: University of Illinois Press, 1975.

Vernon, P. E. Environment and Intelligence, in V. P. Varma and P. Williams (eds.), *Piaget, Psychology and Education*. Itasca, Ill.: Peacock 1976, 31–42.

Wachs, T. D. Utilization of a Piagetian Approach in the Investigation of Early Experience Effects: Research Strategy and Some Illustrative Data. *Merrill-Palmer Quarterly*, 1976, *22*, 11–30.

Wachs, T. D., Uzgiris, I. C., and Hunt, J. M. Cognitive Development in Infants of Different Age Levels and from Different Environmental Backgrounds: An Explanatory Investigation. *Merrill-Palmer Quarterly*, 1971, *17*, 283–317.

Wesley, F., and Sullivan E. *Human Growth and Development: A Psychological Approach*. New York: Human Sciences Press, 1980.

White, B. L. *The First Three Years of Life*. Englewood Cliffs, N.J.: Prentice-Hall, 1975.

———. *Human Infants: Experience and Psychological Development*. Englewood Cliffs, N.J.: Prentice-Hall, 1971.

Willemsen, E. *Understanding Infancy*. San Francisco: Freeman, 1979.

Willerman, L. Effects of Families on Intellectual Development. *American Psychologist*, 1979, *34*, 923–929.

Wingfield, A., and Byrnes, D. L. *The Psychology of Human Memory*. New York: Academic Press, 1981.

Zinsser, C. The Preschool Pressure Cooker. *Working Mother*, October 1981, 61–64.

Chapter Seven

Adams, R. E., and Passman, R. H. The Effects of Preparing Two-Year-Olds for Brief Separations from Their Mothers. *Child Development*, 1981, *51*, 1068–1071.

Ainsworth, M. D. S. Infant-Mother Attachment. *American Psychologist*, 1979, *34*, 932–938.

Ainsworth, M. D. S. The Development of Infant-Mother Attachment, in B. Caldwell and H. Riciutti (eds.), *Review of Child Development*, vol. 3. Chicago: University of Chicago Press, 1974.

———. *Infancy in Uganda: Infant Care and Growth of Attachment*. Baltimore: Johns Hopkins University Press, 1967.

Ainsworth, M. D. S., Bell, S. M., and Slayton, D. J. Individual Differences in the Strange Situation Behavior of One-Year-Olds, in H. R. Schaffer (ed.), *The Origins of Human Social Relations*. London: Academic Press, 1971.

Ainsworth, M. D. S., Blehar, M. C., Waters, E., and Wall, S. *Patterns of Attachment*. Hillsdale, N.J.: Erlbaum, 1978.

Allnut, B. L. The Motherless Child, in J. D. Call, J. D. Noshpitz, R. L. Cohen, and I. N. Berlin (eds.), *Basic Handbook of Child Psychiatry*, 1979, 373–378.

Alvarez, W. F. The Meaning of Maternal Employment for Mothers and Their Perceptions of Their Three-Year Old Children. *Child Development*, 1985, 56, 350–361.

American Council of Life Insurance. *Factsheet on Women*. Washington, D.C.: American Council of Life Insurance, 1982.

American Psychiatric Association. *Diagnostic and Statistical Manual of Mental Disorders* (3rd ed.). Washington, D.C.: American Psychiatric Association, 1980.

Anderson, C. W., Nagle, R. J., Roberts, W. A., and Smith, J. W. Attachment to Substitute Caregivers as a Function of Center Quality and Caregiver Involvement. *Child Development*, 1981, 52, 53–61.

Arend, R. A., Gove, F. L., and Sroufe, L. A. Continuity of Early Adaptation: From Attachment in Infancy to Ego-Resiliency and Curiosity at Age 5. *Child Development*, 1979, 50, 950–959.

Bank, S. P., and Kahn, M. D. *The Sibling Bond*. New York: Basic Books, 1982.

Baskett, L. M. Sibling Status Effects: Adult Expectations. *Developmental Psychology*, 1985, 21, 441–445.

Bell, R. Q. Parent, Child, and Reciprocal Influences. *American Psychologist*, 1979, 34, 821–827.

Belsky, J. *In the Beginning*. New York: Columbia University Press, 1982.

Belsky, J., and Steinberg, L. D. What Does Research Teach Us About Day Care? *Children Today*, July–August 1979, 8, 21–26.

———. The Effects of Daycare: A Critical Review. *Child Development*, 1978, 49, 929–949.

Biller, H. B. Fatherhood: Implications for Child and Adult Development, in B. B. Wolman (ed.), *Handbook of Developmental Psychology*. Englewood Cliffs, N.J.: Prentice-Hall, 1982, 702–720.

Blehar, M. C. Anxious Attachment and Defensive Reactions Associated with Day Care. *Child Development*, 1974, 683–692.

Bowlby, J. Attachment and Loss: Retrospect and Prospect. *American Journal of Orthopsychiatry*, 1982, 52, 664–678.

———. *Attachment and Loss*, Vol. 2, *Separation: Anxiety and Anger*. New York: Basic Books, 1973.

———. *Maternal Care and Mental Health*. New York: Columbia University Press, 1951.

Brazelton, T. B., Koslowski, B., and Main, H. The Origins of Reciprocity: The Early Infant-Mother Interaction, in M. Lewis and L. A. Rosenblum (eds.), *The Effect of the Infant on Its Caretaker*. New York: Wiley, 1974, 49–76.

Bridges, K. M. B. A Study of Social Development in Early Infancy. *Child Development*, 1933, 4, 36–49.

Bronson, G. The Development of Fear. *Child Development*, 1968, 39, 409–432.

Chess, S., and Thomas, A. Infant Bonding: Mystique and Reality. *American Journal of Orthopsychiatry*, 1981, 52, 213–222.

Chibucos, T. R., and Kail, P. R. Longitudinal Examination of Father-Infant Interaction and Infant-Father Attachment. *Merrill-Palmer Quarterly*, Winter 1981, 27, 81–97.

Clarke-Stewart, A. The Day-Care Child. *Parents*, September 1982.

Clarke-Stewart, K. A. And Daddy Makes Three: The Father's Impact on Mother and Young Child. *Child Development*, 1978, 49, 466–478.

Cohen, L., and Campos, J. Father, Mother and Stranger as Elicitors of Attachment Behavior in Infancy. *Developmental Psychology*, 1974, 10, 146–154.

Cohen, S. E. Maternal Employment and Mother-Child Interaction. *Merrill-Palmer Quarterly*, 1978, 24, 189–197.

Donovan, W. L., Leavitt, L. A., and Balling, J. D. Maternal Physiological Response to Infant Signals. *Psychophysiology*, 1978, 15, 68–74.

Dunn, J. *Distress and Comfort*. Cambridge: Cambridge University Press, 1977.

———. Studying Temperament and Parent-Child Interaction: Comparison of Interview and Direct Observation, in S. Chess and A. Thomas (eds.), *Annual Progress in Child Psychiatry and Child Development*. New York: Brunner/Mazel, 1981, 415–430.

Easterbrooks, M. A., and Lamb, M. E. The Relationship Between Quality of Infant-Mother Attachment and Infant Competence in Initial Encounters with Peers. *Child Development*, 1979, 50, 380–387.

Eckerman, C. O., Whatley, J. L., and Kutz, S. L. Growth of Social Play with Peers During the Second Year of Life. *Developmental Psychology*, 1975, 11, 42–49.

Egeland, B., and Sroufe, L. A. Attachment and Early Maltreatment. *Child Development*, 1981, 52, 44–52.

Erikson, E. *Childhood and Society*. New York: W. W. Norton, 1963.

Etaugh, C. Effects of Nonmaternal Care on Children: Research Evidence and Popular Views. *American Psychologist*, 1980, 35, 309–319.

Farber, E. A., and Egeland, B. Developmental Consequences of Out-of-Home Care for Infants in Low-Income Population (1982), cited in Zigler, E., and Muenchow, S., Infant Day Care and Infant-Care Leaves: A Policy Vacuum. *American Psychologist*, 1983, 38, 91–94.

Fischoff, J., Whitten, C. F., and Pettit, M. A Psychiatric Study of Mothers of Infants with Growth Problems Due to Maternal Deprivation. *Journal of Pediatrics*, 1971, 72, 209.

Freud, S. *A General Introduction to Psychoanalysis*. New York: Doubleday, 1953 (originally published 1935).

Friedrich, W. N., and Boreskin, J. A. The Role of the Child in Abuse: A Review of the Literature. *American Journal of Orthopsychiatry*, 1976, 46, 580–591.

Gerson, M. J., Alpert, J. L., and Richardon, M. S. Mothering: The View from Psychological Research. *Signs*, 1984, 9, 434–453.

Grossman, K., Thane, E., and Grossman, K. E. Maternal Tactual Contact of the Newborn After Postpartum Conditions of Mother-Infant Contact. *Developmental Psychology*, 1981, 17, 158–169.

Harlow, H. F. *Learning to Love*. San Francisco: Albion Publishing Co., 1971.

———. Love in Infant Monkeys. *Scientific American*, July 1959, 68–74.

Harlow, H. F., and Harlow, M. K. Social Deprivation in Monkeys. *Scientific American*, 1962, 207, 136–146.

Harlow, H. F. and Suomi, S. J. Social Recovery by Isolation-Reared Monkeys. *Proceedings of the National Academy of Science*, 1971, 68, 1534–1538.

Hay, D. F. Cooperative Interactions and Sharing Between Very Young Children and Their Parents. *Developmental Psychology*, 1979, 15, 647–653.

Hazen, N. L., and Durrett, M. E. Relationship of Security of Attachment to Exploration and Cognitive Mapping Abilities in 2-Year-Olds. *Developmental Psychology*, 1982, *18*, 751–759.

Heinicke, C. M., Diskin, S. D., Ramsey-Klee, D. M., and Given, K. Pre-Birth Parent Characteristics and Family Development in the First Year of Life. *Child Development*, 1983, *54*, 194–208.

Hock, E. Working and Nonworking Mothers and Their Infants: A Comparative Study of Maternal Caregiving Characteristics and Infant Social Behavior. *Merrill-Palmer Quarterly*, 1980, *26*, 79–101.

Hodapp, R. M., and Mueller, E. Early Social Development, in B. B. Wolman (ed.), *Handbook of Developmental Psychology*. Englewood Cliffs, N.J.: Prentice-Hall, 1982, 284–298.

Hoffman, L. W. Maternal Employment. *American Psychologist*, 1979, *34*, 859–865.

————. Effects of Maternal Employment on the Child: A Review of the Research. *Developmental Psychology*, 1974, *10*, 204–228.

Jacobson, A. L. Infant Day Care: Toward a More Human Environment, *Young Children*, July, 1978.

Joffe, L. S., and Vaughn, B. E. Infant-Mother Attachment: Theory, Assessment, and Implications for Development, in B. B. Wolman (ed.), *Handbook of Developmental Psychology*. Englewood Cliffs, N.J.: Prentice-Hall, 1982, 190–204.

Kagan, J. Emergent Themes in Human Development. *American Scientist*, 1976, *64*, 186–196.

Kahana, E., and Kahana, B. Theoretical and Research Perspectives on Grandparenthood. *Aging and Human Development*, 1971, *2*, 261–268.

Kammerman, S. B. *Parenting in an Unresponsive Society: Managing Work and Family Life*. New York: The Free Press, 1980.

Kennel, J. H., Voos, D. K., and Klaus, M. H. Parent-Infant Bonding, in J. Osofsky (ed.), *Handbook of Infant Development*. New York: Wiley, 1979, 786–799.

Klaus, M. H. and Kennel, J. H. *Maternal-Infant Bonding*. St. Louis: C. V. Mosby, 1976.

Klein, R. P. Caregiving Arrangements by Employed Women with Children Under 1 Year of Age. *Developmental Psychology*, 1985, *21*, 403–406.

Kotelchuck, M. The Infant's Relationship to the Father: Experimental Evidence, in M. Lamb (ed.), *The Role of the Father in Child Development*. New York: Wiley, 1976, 329–344.

————. The Nature of the Child's Tie to His Father (1972), cited in Kotelchuck, M., The Infant's Relationship to the Father: Experimental Evidence, in M. Lamb (ed.), *The Role of the Father in Child Development*. New York: Wiley, 1976, 329–344.

Lamb, M. Paternal Influences and the Father's Role: A Personal Perspective. *American Psychologist*, 1979, *34*, 938–944.

————. Interactions Between Eight-Month-Old Children and Their Fathers and Mothers, in M. E. Lamb (ed.), *The Role of the Father in Child Development*. New York: Wiley, 1976, 307–329.

Lamb, M. E., Frodi, M., Hwang, C. P., and Frodi, A. M. Effects of Paternal Involvement on Infant Preferences for Mothers and Fathers. *Child Development*, 1983, *54*, 450–458.

Lamb, M. E., Frodi, A. M., Hwang, C. P., Frodi, M., and Steinberg, J. Mother- and Father-Infant Interaction Involving Play and Holding in Traditional and Non-Traditional Swedish Families. *Developmental Psychology*, 1982, *18*, 215–221.

Lewis, M., and Brooks-Gunn, J. The Reactions of Infants to People (1972), in J. Belsky (ed.), *In the Beginning*. New York: Columbia University Press, 1982, 167–177.

Lewis, M., and Kreitzberg, V. S. Effects of Birth Order and Spacing on Mother-Infant Interactions. *Developmental Psychology*, 1979, *15*, 617–625.

Londerville, S., and Main, M. Security, Compliance and Maternal Training Methods in the Second Year of Life. *Developmental Psychology*, 1981, *17*, 289–299.

Lorenz, K. The Companion in the Bird's World. *AUK*, 1937, *54*, 245–273.

Maccoby, E. E. *Social Development: Psychological Growth and the Parent-Child Relationship*. New York: Harcourt Brace Jovanovich, 1980.

Maccoby, E. E., and Martin, J. A. Socialization in the Context of the Family: Parent-Child Interaction, in P. H. Mussen (ed.), *Handbook of Child Development* (4th ed.), vol. 4. New York: Wiley, 1983, 1–103.

Main, M. Exploration, Play and Cognitive Functioning as Related to Child-Mother Attachment (1973), cited in Sroufe, L. A., Socio-emotional Development, in J. Osofsky (ed.), *Handbook of Infant Development*. New York: Wiley, 1979, 462–519.

Main, M., and D. R. Weston. The Quality of the Toddler's Relationship to Mother and to Father: Related to Conflict Behavior and the Readiness to Establish New Relationships. *Child Development*, 1981, *52*, 932–940.

Matas, L., Arend, R., and Sroufe, L. A. Continuity of Adaptation in the Second Year: The Relationship Between Quality of Attachment and Later Competence. *Child Development*, 1978, *49*, 547–556.

Metcalf, D. R. Organizers of the Psyche and EEG Development: Birth Through Adolescence, in R. L. Noshpitz (ed.), *Basic Handbook of Child Psychiatry*, vol. 1. New York: Basic Books, 1979, 63–72.

Meyerhoff, R. Infant Depression Due to Separation from Siblings Syndrome or Depression, Retardation, Starvation and Neurological Symptoms: A Re-Evaluation of the Concept of Maternal Deprivation. (Psychiatrica Clinica, 1971, *4*, 321–335), cited in S. P. Bank and M. D. Kahn, *The Sibling Bond*. New York: Basic Books, 1982.

Moore, T. Exclusive Early Mothering and Its Alternatives (1975), Scandinavian Journal of Psychology, 1975, *16*, 255–272, cited in Hoffman, L. W., Maternal Employment. *American Psychologist*, 1979, *34*, 859–865.

Morgan, G., and Riccuiti, H. Infants' Responses to Strangers in the First Year, in B. M. Foss (ed.), *Determinants of Infant Behavior* 4. London: Methuen, 1969.

Moss, F. Esq. Personal communication, 1985.

Mueller, E. C., and Vandell, D. Infant-Infant Interaction, in J. Osofsky (ed.), *Handbook of Infant Development*. New York: Wiley, 1979, 591–603.

Neugarten, B. L., and Weinstein, K. K. The Changing American Grandparent. *Journal of Marriage and the Family*. 1964, *26*, 19–206.

New York Times. Day Care Linked to Ills of Children. *New York Times*, June 27, 1984, C7.

Osofsky, J. D., and Connors, K. Mother-Infant Interaction: An Integrative View of a Complex System, in J. Osofsky (ed.), *Handbook of Infant Development*. New York: Wiley, 1979, 519–549.

Parke, R. D. *Fathers*. Cambridge, Mass.: Harvard University Press, 1981.

_____. Perspectives on Father-Infant Interaction, in J. D. Osofsky (ed.), *Handbook of Infant Development*. New York: Wiley, 1979, 549–591.

_____. Father's Role in Infancy: A Reevaluation. *The Family Coordinator*, 1976, *25*, 365–371.

Pederson, F. A., and Robson, K. S. Father Participation in Infancy. *American Journal of Orthopsychiatry*, 1969, *39*, 466–472.

Ragozin, A. S., Basham, R. B., Crnic, K. A., Greenberg, M. T., and Robinson, N. M. Effects of Maternal Age on Parenting Role. *Developmental Psychology*, 1982, *18*, 627–635.

Rheingold, H. L., and Eckerman, C. O. Fear of the Stranger: A Critical Examination, in H. W. Reese (ed.), *Advances in Child Development and Behavior*, vol. 8. New York: Academic Press, 1973.

Rheingold, H. L., Hay, D. F., and West, M. J. Sharing in the Second Year of Life. *Child Development*, 1976, *47*, 1148–1158.

Ricciuti, H. Fear and Development of Social Attachments in the First Year of Life, in M. Lewis and L. A. Rosenblum (eds.), *The Origins of Human Behavior: Fear*. New York: Wiley, 1974.

Robertson, J., and Bowlby, J. Responses of Young Children to Separation from Their Mothers. *Courrier Centre Internationale Enfance*, 1952, *2*, 131–142.

Rode, S. S., Chang, P. N., Fisch, R. O., and Sroufe, L. A. Attachment Patterns of Infants Separated at Birth. *Developmental Psychology*, 1981, *17*, 188–191.

Ross, H. S. Establishment of Social Games Among Toddlers. *Developmental Psychology*, 1982, *18*, 509–518.

Rubin, J. Z., Provenzano, F. J., and Luria, Z. The Eye of the Beholder: Parent's View on Sex of Newborns. *American Journal of Orthopsychiatry*, 1974, *43*, 720–731.

Ruopp, R., Travers, J., Glantz, F., and Coelen, C. Children at the Center (Final Report of the National Day Care Study), cited in Zigler, E., and Muenchow, S., Infant Day Care and Infant-Care Leaves: A Policy Vacuum. *American Psychologist*, 1983, *38*, 91–95.

Rutter, M. Social-Emotional Consequences of Day Care for Preschool Children. *American Journal of Orthopsychiatry*, 1981, *51*, 4–29.

_____. Maternal Deprivation, 1972–1978: New Findings, New Concepts, New Approaches. *Child Development*, 1979, *50*, 283–305.

Saltz, R. Effects of Part-Time "Mothering" on IQ and SQ of Young Institutionalized Children. *Child Development*, 1973, *44*, 166–170.

Schachter, F. F. Toddlers with Employed Mothers. *Child Development*, 1981, *52*, 958–964.

Schaffer, H., and Emerson, P. The Development of Social Attachments in Infancy. *Monographs of the Society for Research in Child Development*, 1964, *29*, (3, serial no. 94).

Schaffer, R. *Mothering*. Cambridge, Mass.: Harvard University Press, 1977.

Skarin, K. Cognitive and Contextual Determinants of Stranger Fear in Six- and Eleven-Month-Old Infants. *Child Development*, 1977, *48*, 537–544.

Smith, A. N., and Spence, C. M. National Day Care Study: Optimizing the Day Care Environment. *American Journal of Orthopsychiatry*, 1980, *50*, 718–721.

Spitz, R. *The First Year of Life: A Psychoanalytic Study of Normal and Deviant Development of Object Relations*. New York: International Universities Press, 1965.

_____. Hospitalism: An Enquiry into the Genesis of Psychiatric Conditions in Early Childhood. *Psychoanalytic Study of the Child*, 1945, *1*, 53.

Spock, B. *Raising Children in a Difficult Time*. New York: W. W. Norton, 1974.

Sroufe, L. A. Socioemotional Development, in J. D. Osofsky (ed.), *Handbook of Infant Development*. New York: Wiley, 1979a, 462–519.

_____. The Coherence of Individual Development: Early Care, Attachment and Subsequent Developmental Issues. *American Psychologist*, 1979b, *34*, 834–842.

Sroufe, A., and Waters, E. Attachment as an Organizational Construct. *Child Development*, 1977, *48*, 1184–1189.

Stines, J. A Daycare Checklist (1983) and Personal Communication, 1985.

Stuckey, M. F., and McGhee, P. E., and Bell, N. J. Parent-Child Interaction: The Influence of Maternal Employment. *Developmental Psychology*, 1982, *18*, 635–644.

Svejda, M. J. Campos, J. J., and Emde, R. N. Mother-Infant "Bonding": Failure to Generalize. *Child Development*, 1980, *51*, 775–779.

Tavris, C. Women: Work Isn't Always the Answer. *Psychology Today*, September 1976, 78.

Thomas, A., Chess, S., and Birch, H. G. The Origins of Personality. *Scientific American*, August 1970, *223*, 102–109.

Thompson, R., Lamb, M., and Estes, D. Harmonizing Discordant Notes: A Reply to Waters. *Child Development*, 1983, *54*, 521–524.

_____. Stability of Infant-Mother Attachment and Its Relationships to Changing Life Circumstances in an Unselected Middle-Class Sample. *Child Development*, 1982, *51*, 144–148.

Tracy, R. L., and Ainsworth, M. D. S. Maternal Affectionate Behavior and Infant-Mother Attachment Patterns. *Child Development*, 1981, *52*, 1341–1343.

Tulkin, S. R., and Kagan, J. Mother-Child Interaction in the First Year of Life. *Child Development*, 1972, *43*, 31–41.

U.S. Department of Labor, Bureau of Labor Statistics. *Handbook of Labor Statistics*. Washington, D.C.: Bureau of Labor Statistics, 1976.

Vaughn, B., Egeland, B., Sroufe, L., and Waters, E. Individual Differences in Infant-Mother Attachment at Twelve and Eighteen Months: Stability and Change in Families Under Stress. *Child Development*, 1979, *50*, 971–975.

Waters, E. The Stability of Individual Differences in Infant Attachment: Comments on the Thompson, Lamb, and Estes Contribution. *Child Development*, 1983, *54*, 516–520.

_____. The Reliability and Stability of Individual Differences in Infant-Mother Attachment. *Child Development*, 1978, *49*, 483–494.

Waters, E., and Deane, K. E. Theories, Models, Recent Data and Some Tasks for Comparative Developmental Analysis, in L. Hoffman, R. Gandelman, and R. Schiffman (eds.), *Parenting: Its Causes and Consequences*. Hillsdale, N.J.: Erlbaum, 1982, 19–54.

Waters, E., Wippman, J., and Sroufe, L. A. Attachment, Positive Affect and Competence in the Peer Group: Two Studies in Construct Validation. *Child Development*, 1979, *50*, 821–829.

Watkins, H. D., and Bradbard, M. R. The Social Development of Young Children in Day Care: What Practitioners Should Know. *Child Care Quarterly*, Fall 1984, *11*, 169–187.

Whitney, E. N. W., and Hamilton, E. M. N. *Understanding Nutrition* (3rd ed.). St. Paul, Minnesota: West Publishing Co., 1984.

Wise, S., and Grossman, F. K. Adolescent Mothers and Their Infants: Psychological Factors in Early Attachment and Interaction. *American Journal of Orthopsychiatry*, 1980, *50*, 454–468.

Wolins, M. Young Children in Institutions. *Developmental Psychology*, 1970, *2*, 99–109.

Yarrow, L. J. Emotional Development. *American Psychologist*, 1979, *34*, 951–957.

Yarrow, M. R., Scott, P., de Leeuw, L. D. and Heinig, C. Child Rearing in Families of Working and Non-Working Mothers (1962), in H. Bee (ed.), *Social Issues in Developmental Psychology* (2nd ed.). New York: Harper and Row, 1978, 112–129.

Zigler, E., and Muenchow, S. Infant Day Care and Infant-Care Leaves: A Policy Vacuum. *American Psychologist*, 1983, *38*, 91–95.

Chapter Eight

Aitchison, J. *The Articulate Mammal: An Introduction to Psycholinguistics.* New York: Universe Books, 1978.

Akiyama, M. M. Are Language-Acquisition Strategies Universal? *Developmental Psychology*, 1984, *20*, 219–229.

Anglin, J. M. *Word, Object, and Conceptual Development.* New York: W. W. Norton, 1977.

Becker, W. C., Engelmann, S., and Thomas, D. R. *Teaching: A Course in Applied Psychology.* Chicago: Science Research Associates, 1971.

Bee, H. *Social Issues in Developmental Psychology* (2nd ed.). New York: Harper and Row, 1978.

Bloom, L. M., Language Development, in F. D. Horowitz (ed.), *Review of Child Development Research*, vol. 4. Chicago: University of Chicago Press, 1975.

———. Talking, Understanding and Thinking, in *Language Perspectives: Acquisition, Retardation, and Intervention*, ed. R. L. Schifeilbusch and L. L. Lloyd. Baltimore: University Park Press, 1974.

Bohannon, J. N., and Marquis, A. L. Children's Control of Adult Speech. *Child Development*, 1977, *48*, 1002–1008.

Bowerman, M. Language Development, in H. C. Triandis and A. Heron (eds.), *Handbook of Cross-Cultural Psychology*, vol. 4. Boston: Allyn and Bacon, 1981, 93–187.

Braine, M. D. S. The Ontogeny of English Phrase Structure: The First Phase. *Language*, 1963, *39*, 1–13.

Brown, R. Development of the First Language in the Human Species. *American Psychologist*, 1973, *28*, 97–106.

Brown, R., Cazden, C., and Bellugi-Klima, U. The Child's Grammar from 1 to 11, in J. P. Hill (ed.), *Minnesota Symposia on Child Psychology*, vol. 2. Minneapolis: University of Minnesota Press, 1969.

Bruner, J. Learning the Mother Tongue. *Human Nature*, September 1978a, P11–19.

———. Learning How to Do Things with Words, in J. S. Bruner and A. Garton (eds.), *Human Growth and Development: Wolfson College Lectures.* Oxford: Clarendon Press, 1978b, p. 62–85.

Caratz, J. C. A Bi-Dialectical Task for Determining Language Proficiency in Economically Disadvantaged Negro Children. *Child Development*, 1969, *40*, 889–901.

Cazden, C. B. Language Development and the Preschool Environment, in C. B. Cazden (ed.), *Language in Early Childhood Educa-*

tion. Washington, D.C.: National Association for the Education of Young Children, 1981.

Chomsky, N. *Language and Mind* (enl. ed.). New York, Harcourt Brace Jovanovich, 1972.

———. *Aspects of the Theory of Syntax.* Cambridge, Mass.: M.I.T. Press, 1965.

———. A Review of B. F. Skinner's *Verbal Behavior. Language*, 1959, *35*, 26–58.

Clark, E. V. Strategies for Communicating. *Child Development*, 1978, *49*, 953–959.

Condon, W. S., and Sander, L. W. Synchrony Demonstrated Between Movements of the Neonate and Adult Speech. *Child Development*, 1974, *65*, 456–462.

Dale, P. S. *Language Development: Structure and Function.* Hinsdale, Ill.: Dryden Press, 1972. Second edition 1976.

deVilliers, J. G., and deVilliers, P. A. *Language Acquisition.* Cambridge, Mass.: Harvard University Press, 1978.

Dodd, B. J. Effects of Social and Vocal Stimulation on Infant Babbling. *Developmental Psychology*, 1972, *7*, 80–83.

Francis, H. *Language in Childhood: Form and Function in Language Development.* New York: St. Martin's Press, 1975.

Frauenglass, M. H., and Diaz, R. M. Self-Regulatory Functions of Children's Private Speech: A Critical Analysis of Recent Challenges to Vygotsky's Theory. *Developmental Psychology*, 1985, *21*, 357–365.

Garnica, O. K. Some Prosodic and Paralinguistic Features of Speech Directed to Young Children, in C. E. Snow and C. A. Ferguson (eds.), *Talking to Children: Language Input and Acquisition.* Cambridge: Cambridge University Press, 1977.

Genosce, F., Tucker, G. R., and Lambert, W. E. Communication Skills of Bilingual Children. *Child Development*, 1976, *47*, 1010–1014.

Goldberg, S., and Lewis, M. Play Behavior in the Year-Old infant: Early Sex Differences. *Child Development*, 1969, *40*, 21–30.

Hess, R., and Shipman, V. Parents as Teachers: How Lower and Middle Class Mothers Teach (1967), in C. S. Lavatelli and F. Stendler (eds.), *Readings in Child Behavior and Development* (3rd ed.). New York: Harcourt Brace Jovanovich, 1972, 436–446.

Holmes, D. L., and F. J. Morrison. *The Child: An Introduction to Developmental Psychology.* Monterey, Calif.: Brooks/Cole, 1979.

Hovell, M. F., Schumaker, J. B., and Sherman, J. A. A Comparison of Parents' Models and Expansions in Promoting Children's Acquisition of Adjectives. *Journal of Experimental Child Psychology*, 1978, *25*, 41–57.

Huttenlocher, J. The Origins of Language Comprehension, in R. L. Solso (ed.), *Theories in Cognitive Psychology.* Potomac, Md.: Erlbaum, 1974.

Labov, W. *The Study of Nonstandard English* (1970), in V. P. Clark, P. A. Eschholz, and A. F. Rosa (ed.), *Language* (2nd ed.). New York: St. Martin's Press, 1977, 439–450.

Lenneberg, E. H. *Biological Foundations of Language.* New York: Wiley, 1967.

Lenneberg, E. H., Rebelsky, F. G., and Nichols, I. A. The Vocalizations of Infants Born to Deaf and Hearing Parents. *Human Development*, 1965, *8*, 23–37.

Luria, A. R. The Directive Function of Speech in Development and Dissolution. *Word*, 1959, *16*, 341–352.

Maccoby, E. E., and Jacklin, C. N. *The Psychology of Sex Differences.* Stanford, Calif.: Stanford University Press, 1974.

Macnamara, J. Cognitive Basis of Language Learning in Infants. *Psychological Review*, 1972, 79, 1–14.

McCarthy, D. A. Language Development in Children, in L. Carmichael (ed.), *Manual of Child Psychology*. New York: Wiley, 1954.

McCartney, K. Effect of Quality of Day Care Environment on Children's Language Development. *Developmental Psychology*, 1984, 20, 244–261.

McLaughlin, B. *Second Language Acquisition in Childhood*. Hillsdale, N.J.: Erlbaum, 1978.

_____. Second-Language Learning in Children. *Psychological Bulletin*, 1977, 84, 438–459.

Mc Neill, D. The Development of Language, in P. H. Mussen (ed.), *Carmichael's Manual of Child Psychology* (3rd ed.)., John Wiley, 1970.

Meichenbaum, D. H., and Goodman, J. Training Impulsive Children to Talk to Themselves: A Means of Developing Self-Control. *Journal of Abnormal Psychology*, 1971, 77, 115–126.

Menyuk, P. *Language and Maturation*. Cambridge, Mass.: M.I.T. Press, 1977.

Miller, S. A., Shelton, J., and Flavell, J. H. A Test of Luria's Hypotheses Concerning the Development of Verbal Self-Regulation. *Child Development*, 1970, 41, 651–665.

Millisen, R. The Incidence of Speech Disorders, in L. E. Traves (ed.), *Handbook of Speech Pathology and Audiology*. New York: Appleton-Century-Croft, 1971.

Molfese, D. L., Molfese, V. J., and P. L. Carroll. Early Language Development, in B. B. Wolman (ed.), *Handbook of Developmental Psychology*. Englewood Cliffs, N.J.: Prentice-Hall, 1982, 301–323.

Moskowitz, B. A. The Acquisition of Language. *Scientific American*, 1978, 239, 92–108.

Nelson, K. Individual Differences in Language Development: Implications for Development and Language. *Developmental Psychology*, 1981, 17, 170–188.

_____. Structure and Strategy in Learning to Talk. *Monograph of the Society for Research in Child Development*, 1973, 38 (1–2, serial no. 149).

_____. Concept, Word, and Sentence. *Psychological Review*, 1974, 81, 267–285.

Nelson, K., Rescorla, L., Gruendel, J., and Benedict, H. Early Lexicons: What Do They Mean? *Child Development*, 1978, 49, 960–968.

Newport, E. L., Gleitman, H., and Gleitman, L. R. Mother, I'd Rather Do It Myself: Some Effects and Non-Effects of Maternal Speech Style, in C. E. Snow and C. A. Ferguson (eds.), *Talking to Children: Language Input and Acquisition*. Cambridge: Cambridge University Press, 1977.

Olim, E. G., Hess, R. D., and Shipman, V. C. Role of Mothers' Language Styles in Mediating Their Preschool Children's Development. *School Review*, 1967, 75, 414–424.

Peckham, C. S. Speech Defects in a National Sample of Children Aged Seven Years. *British Journal of Disorders of Communication*, 1973, 8, 2–8.

Piaget, J. *The Grasp of Consciousness: Action and Concept in the Young Child*. Cambridge, Mass.: Harvard University Press, 1976.

Raloff, J. Reports from the 1982 meeting of the American Speech Language Hearing Association's Meeting in Toronto, Canada. *Science News*, 1982, 122, 360.

Raspberry, W. Should Ghettoese Be Accepted? *Today's Education*, April 1970, 59, 30–31, 34–41.

Rheingold, H. L., and Adams, J. L. The Significance of Speech to Newborns. *Developmental Psychology*, 1980, 16, 397–403.

Roe, K. V., Drivas, A., Karagellis, A., and Roe, S. Sex Differences in Vocal Interactions with Mother and Stranger in Greek Infants: Some Cognitive Implications. *Developmental Psychology*, 1985, 21, 372–378.

Schachter, E. F., Shore, E., Hodapp, R., Chalfin, S., and Bundy, C. Do Girls Talk Earlier? Mean Length of Utterance in Toddlers. *Developmental Psychology*, 1978, 14, 388–392.

Segalowitz, N. S. Issues in the Cross-Cultural Study of Bilingual Development, in H. C. Triandis and A. Heron (eds.), *Handbook of Cross-Cultural Psychology*, vol. 4. Boston: Allyn and Bacon, 1981, 55–93.

Shatz, M. Communication, in P. H. Mussen (ed.), *Handbook of Child Psychology* (4th ed.). New York: Wiley, 1983, 841–891.

Sinclair-de-Zwart, H. Language Acquisition and Cognitive Development, in T. Moore (ed.), *Cognitive Development and the Acquisition of Language*. New York: Academic Press, 1973.

Skinner, B. F. *Verbal Behavior*. New York: Appleton-Century-Croft, 1957.

Slobin, D. I. Children and Language: They Learn the Same Way All Around the World. *Psychology Today*, July 1972, 18 + .

_____. Cognitive Prerequisites for the Development of Grammar, in C. A. Ferguson and D. I. Slovin (eds.), *Studies of Child Language Development*. New York: Holt, Rinehart and Winston, 1973.

Smith, M. E. An Investigation of the Development of the Sentence and the Extent of Vocabulary in Young Children. *University of Iowa Studies in Child Welfare*, 1926, 3 (no. 5).

Snow, C. E. The Development of Conversation Between Mothers and Babies. *Journal of Child Language*, 1977, 4, 1–22.

Stern, D. N., Spieker, S., and MacKain, K. Intonation Contours as Signals in Maternal Speech to Prelinguistic Infants. *Developmental Psychology*, 1982, 18, 727–736.

Thomson, J. R., and Chapman, R. S. Who Is "Daddy"? The Status of Two-Year-Olds Overextended Words in Use and Comprehension (1975), cited in deVilliers, J. G., and deVilliers, P. A., *Language Acquisition*. Cambridge, Mass.: Harvard University Press, 1978.

Time Magazine, If Slang Is Not a Sin. *Time*, November 8, 1982, 91.

Tinsley, V. S., and H. S. Waters. The Development of Verbal Control over Motor Behavior: A Replication and Extension of Luria's Findings *Child Development*, 1982, 53, 746–754.

Trehub, S. Infants' Sensitivity to Vowel and Tonal Contrasts. *Developmental Psychology*, 1973, 9, 81–96.

U.S. Bureau of the Census. *Statistical Abstract of the United States, 1980*. Washington D.C.: U.S. Government Printing Office, 1980.

U.S. Commission on Civil Rights. *A Better Chance to Learn: Bilingual-Bicultural Education*. Clearinghouse Publication no. 51, May 1975.

Vygotsky, L. S. *Thought and Language*. Cambridge, Mass.: M.I.T. Press, 1962.

Weiss, C. D., and Lillywhite, H. S. *Communication Disorders: A Handbook for Prevention and Early Intervention*. St. Louis, Missouri: C. V. Mosby, 1976.

Whitehurst, G. J. Language Development, in B. B. Wolman (ed.), *Handbook of Developmental Psychology*. Englewood Cliffs, N.J.: Prentice-Hall, 1982, 367–384.

Whitehurst, G. J., and Vasta, R. *Child Behavior*. Boston: Houghton Mifflin, 1977.

Wiig, E. H. Communication Disorders, in N. G. Haring (ed.), *Exceptional Children and Youth* (3rd ed.). Columbus, Ohio: Charles E. Merrill, 1982, 81–111.

Wolff, P. H. Observations on the Early Development of Smiling in B. M. Foss (ed.), *Determinants of Infant Behavior*, vol. 2. London: Methuen, 1963.

Chapter Nine

Adler, R. P. Children's Television Advertising: History of the Issue, in *Children and the Faces of Television: Teaching, Violence, Selling*. New York: Academic Press, 1980, 237–251.

Allen, A. W., and Herley, D. *Art Through Your Child's Eyes*. New York: Allen and Herley, 1975.

Anastasi, A. *Psychological Testing* (4th ed.). New York: Macmillan, 1976.

Appel, L. F., Cooper, R. G., McCarrell, N., Sims-Knight, J., Yussen, S. R., and Flavell, J. H. The Development of the Distinction Between Perceiving and Memorizing. *Child Development*, 1972, *43*, 1365–1381.

Atkin, C. K. Effects of Television Advertising on Children, in E. L. Palmer and A. Dorr (eds.), *Children and the Faces of Television: Teaching, Violence, Selling*. New York: Academic Press, 1980, 287–307.

Atkin, C. K., and Gibson, W. Children's Nutrition Learning from Television Advertising, (1978), cited in Atkin, C. K., Effects of Television Advertising on Children, in E. L. Palmer and A. Dorr (eds.), *Children and the Faces of Television: Teaching, Violence, Selling*. New York: Academic Press, 1980, 287–307.

Ault, R. *Children's Cognitive Development*. New York: Oxford University Press, 1977.

Ball, S., and Bogatz, G. *The First Year of "Sesame Street": An Evaluation*. Princeton: Educational Testing Service, 1970.

Barcus, F. E. The Nature of Television Advertising to Children, in E. L. Palmer and A. Dorr (eds.), *Children and the Faces of Television: Teaching, Volence, Selling*. New York: Academic Press, 1980, 273–284.

Bereiter, C., and Engelmann, S. *Teaching the Disadvantaged Child in the Preschool*. Englewood Cliffs, N.J.: Prentice-Hall, 1966.

Bernstein, A. C., and Cowan, P. A. Children's Conception of How People Get Babies. *Child Development*, 1975, *46*, 77–91.

Beyer, N. R., and Morris, P. M. Food Attitudes and Snacking Patterns of Young Children. *Journal of Nutrition Education*, 1974, *6*, 131–134.

Bogatz, G., and Ball, S. *The Second Year of "Sesame Street": A Continuing Evaluation*. Princeton: Educational Testing Service, 1971.

Brainerd, C. J. *Piaget's Theory of Intelligence*. Englewood Cliffs, N.J.: Prentice-Hall, 1978.

Breslow, L. Reevaluation of the Literature on the Development of Transitive Inferences. *Psychological Bulletin*, 1981, *89*, 325–351.

Briggs, C., and Elkind, D. Cognitive Development and Early Reading. *Developmental Psychology*, 1973, *9*, 279–280.

Brown, A. L., Bransford, J. D., Ferrara, R. A., and Campione, J. C. Learning, Remembering, and Understanding, in *Handbook of Child Psychology* (4th ed.), ed. J. H. Flavell and E. M. Markman. New York: Wiley, 1983, 77–167.

Brown, F. G. *Principles of Educational and Psychological Testing*. New York: Holt, Rinehart and Winston, 1983.

Bryant, P. E., and Trabasso, T. Transitive Inferences and Memory in Young Children. *Nature*, 1971, *232*, 456–458.

Bullock, M. Animism in Childhood Thinking: A New Look at an Old Question. *Developmental Psychology*, 1985, *21*, 217–226.

Bureau of the Census. *Statistical Abstract of the United States*, 1985. Washington, D.C.: U.S. Department of Commerce, 1985.

Busch-Rossnagel, N. A., and Vance, A. K. The Impact of the Schools on Social and Emotional Development, in B. B. Wolman (ed.), *Handbook of Developmental Psychology*, 1982, 452–471.

Chazan, M., and Cox, T. Language Programmes for Disadvantaged Children in V. P. Varma and P. Williams (eds.), *Piaget: Psychology and Education*. Itasca, Ill.: Peacock, 1976, 182–299.

Clarke-Stewart, K. A., and Fein, G. G. Early Childhood Programs, in M. M. Haith and J. J. Campos (eds.), *Handbook of Child Psychology*, vol. 2. New York: Wiley, 1983, 917–1001.

Coates, B., Pusser, H., and Goodman, I. The Influence of "Sesame Street" and "Mister Rogers' Neighborhood" on Children's Social Behavior in the Preschool. *Child Development*, 1976, *47*, 138–144.

Cohen, D. J. *Serving Preschool Children*. Washington, D.C.: Department of Health, Education and Welfare, 1975, DHEW no. 76–31057.

Cole, L. Basic Ideas of the Montessori Method (1950), in S. Coopersmith and R. Feldman, *The Formative Years: Principles of Early Childhood Education*. San Francisco: Albion, 1974, 114–122.

Cook, T. D., Appleton, H., Conner, R. F., Shaffer, A., Tomkin, G., and Weber, S. J. *"Sesame Street" Revisited*. New York: Russell Sage Foundation, 1975.

Cooke, R. E. Introduction in E. Zigler, and J. Valentine (eds.), *Project Head Start: A Legacy of the War on Poverty*. N.Y.: The Free Press, 1979.

Corbin, C. B. *A Textbook of Motor Development* (2nd ed.). Dubuque, Iowa: Wm. C. Brown, 1980.

Cratty, B. J. *Perceptual and Motor Development in Infants and Children*. New York: Macmillan, 1970.

Darlington, R. B., and Royce, J. M., Snipper, A. S., Murray, H. W., and Lazar, I. Preschool Programs and the Later School Competence of Children from Low-Income Families. *Science*, 1980, *208*, 202–204.

Davis, G. A. *Educational Psychology: Theory and Practice*. Reading, Mass.: Addison-Wesley, 1983.

Deasey, D. *Education Under Six*. New York: St. Martin's Press, 1978.

Elkind, D. *The Hurried Child, Growing Up Too Fast, Too Soon*. Reading, MA.: Addison-Wesley, 1981.

Flavell, J. H. *Cognitive Development*. Englewood Cliffs, N.J.: Prentice-Hall, 1977.

Flavell, J. H., Flavell, E. R., Green, F. L., and Wilcox, S. A. The Development of Three Spatial Perspective-Taking Rules. *Child Development*, 1981, *52*, 356–358.

Flavell, J. H., and Wellman, H. M. Metamemory, in R. V. Kail and J. W. Hagen (eds.), *Perspectives on the Development of Memory and Cognition*. Hillsdale, N.J.: Erlbaum, 1977.

Ford, M. E. The Construct Validity of Egocentrism. *Psychological Bulletin*, 1979, *86*, 1169–1188.

Friedrich, L., and Stein, A. Aggressive and Prosocial Television Programs and the Natural Behavior of Preschool Children. *Monographs of the Society for Research in Child Development*, 1973 (4, Serial number 151).

Galst, J., and White, M. A. The Unhealthy Persuader: The Reinforcing Value of Television and Children's Purchase-Influencing Attempts at the Supermarket. *Child Development*, 1976, *47*, 1089–1096.

Gelman, R. Conservation Acquisition: A Problem of Learning to Attend to Relevant Attributes. *Journal of Experimental Child Psychology*, 1969, *7*, 167–187.

Gelman, R. Preschool Thought. *American Psychologist*, 1979, *34*, 900–905.

Gelman, R., and Baillargeon, R. A Review of Some Piagetian Concepts, in P. H. Mussen (ed.), *Handbook of Child Psychology* (4th ed.), vol. 3. N.Y.: Wiley, 1983, 167–231.

Gelman, R., Bullock, M., and Meck, E. Preschoolers' Understanding of Simple Object Transformations. *Child Development*, 1980, *51*, 691–699.

Goodenough, F. L. Mental Testing (1949), cited in J. M. Sattler, *Assessment of Children's Intelligence* (rev. repr.). Philadelphia: Saunders, 1974.

Gray, S. W., and Klaus, R. A. The Early Training Project—A Seventh Year Report. *Child Development*, 1970, *51*, 908–924.

Hamill, P. V. V. *NCHS Growth Curves for Children*. Vital and Health Statistics: Series 11, Data from the National Health Survey, No. 165. Washington, D.C.: U.S. Government Printing Office (DHEW no. 78–1650), 1977.

Hamilton, E. M. N., and Whitney, E. N. *Nutrition: Concepts and Controversies* (2nd ed.). St. Paul: West Publishing Co., 1982.

Hawkins, J., Pea, R. D., Glick, J., and Scribner, S. "Merds That Laugh Don't Like Mushrooms": Evidence for Deductive Reasoning by Preschoolers. *Developmental Psychology*, 1984, *20*, 584–595.

Hayes, D. S., Chemelski, B. E., and Birnbaum, D. W. Young Children's Incidental and Intentional Retention of Televised Events. *Developmental Psychology*, 1981, *17*, 230–233.

Heinicke, C. M. Development from Two and One-Half to Four Years, in J. D. Noshpitz (ed.), *Basic Handbook of Child Psychiatry*, vol. 1. New York: Basic Books, 1979, 167–178.

Heinz, J. National Leadership for Children's Television. *American Psychologist*, 1983, *38*, 817–820.

Inhelder, B., and Piaget, J. *The Early Growth of Logic in the Child*. N.Y.: Norton, 1964.

Istomina, Z. M. The Development of Voluntary Memory in Preschool-Age Children (1975), cited in S. G. Paris and B. K. Lindauer, The Development of Cognitive Skills During Childhood, in B. B. Wolman, *Handbook of Developmental Psychology*. Englewood Cliffs, N.J.: Prentice-Hall, 1982, 333–349.

Jensen, A. R. *Bias in Mental Testing*. New York: The Free Press, 1980.

Judd, S. A., and Mervis, C. B. Learning to Solve Class-Inclusion Problems: The Roles of Quantification and Recognition of Contradiction. *Child Development*, 1979, *50*, 163–169.

Kail, R., and Hagen, J. W. Memory in Childhood, in B. B. Wolman (ed.), *Handbook of Developmental Psychology*. Englewood Cliffs, N.J.: Prentice-Hall, 1982, 350–367.

Katz, L. G. Should You Be Your Child's Parents? *Parents*, August 1980, 88–90.

Keeney, T. J., Cannizzo, S. R., and Flavell, J. H. Spontaneous and Induced Verbal Rehearsal in a Recall Task. *Child Development*, 1967, *38*, 953–966.

Kellogg, R. *Analyzing Children's Art*. Palo Alto, Calif.: Mayfield, 1970.

Kingsley, R. C., and Hall, V. Training Conservation Through the Use of Learning Sets. *Child Development*, 1967, *38*, 111–126.

Kister, M. C., and Patterson, C. J. Children's Conceptions of the Causes of Illness: Understanding of Contagion and Use of Immanent Justice. *Child Development*, 1980, *51*, 839–846.

Koocher, G. Childhood, Death and Cognitive Development. *Development Psychology*, 1973, *9*, 369–375.

Koslowski, B. Quantitative and Qualitative Changes in the Development of Seriation. *Merrill-Palmer Quarterly*, 1980, *26*, 391–405.

Lazar, I., Darlington, R., Murray, H., Royce, J., and Snipper, A. Lasting Effects of Early Education: A Report from the Consortium for Longitudinal Studies. *Monographs of the Society for Research in Child Development*, 1982, *47* (2–3, serial no. 195).

Lempers, J. D., Flavell, E. R., and Flavell, J. H. The Development in Very Young Children of Tacit Knowledge Concerning Visual Perceptions. *Genetic Psychology Monographs*, 1977, *95*, 3–53.

LeShan, E. J. *The Conspiracy Against Childhood*. New York: Athenium, 1974.

Lesser, G. S. Applications of Psychology to Television Programming: Formulation of Program Objectives. *American Psychologist*, 1976, *31*, 135–137.

Levin, S. R., Petros, T. V., and Petrella, F. W. Preschoolers' Awareness of Television Advertising. *Child Development*, 1983, *53*, 933–937.

Liebert, R. M., Neale, J. M., and Davison, E. S. *The Early Window: Effects of Television on Children and Youth*. New York: Pergamon Press, 1973.

Lindberg, M. The Role of Knowledge Structures in the Ontogeny of Learning. *Journal of Experimental Child Psychology*, 1980, *30*, 401–410.

Lyle, J., and Hoffman, H. R. Explorations in Patterns of Television Viewing by Preschool-Age Children, in E. A. Rubinstein, G. A. Comstock, and J. P. Murray (eds.), *Television and Social Behavior 4: Television in Day to Day Life: Patterns of Use*. Washington, D.C.: U.S. Government Printing Office, 1972.

Maeroff, G. I. Making 4-Year-Olds Work. *New York Times*, September 20, 1983, Cl, 10.

Mandler, J. M. Representation, in P. H. Mussen (ed.) *Handbook of Child Psychology* (4th ed.), vol. 3. New York: Wiley, 1983, 420–495.

Mann, M. J., Harrell, A., and Hurt, M. A. *A Review of Head Start Research Since 1969 and an Annotated Bibliography*. Washington, D.C.: U.S. Government Printing Office, 1978, No. 017–092–00037–5.

McClinton, B. S., and Meier, B. G. *Beginnings: The Psychology of Early Childhood*. St. Louis: C. V. Mosby, 1978.

McGhee, P. E., Kopp, C. B., and Krakow, J. B. Cognitive Development, in C. B. Kopp and J. B. Krakow (ed.), *The Child Development in a Social Context*. Reading, MA.: Addison-Wesley, 1982, 158–212.

Miller, L. B. Development of Curriculum Models in Head Start, in E. Zigler and J. Valentine (eds.), *Project Head Start: A Legacy on the War on Poverty*. New York: The Free Press, 1979, 195–221.

Miller, L. B., and Bizzell, R. P. Long-Term Effects of Four Preschool Programs: Ninth- and Tenth-Grade Results. *Child Development*, 1984, 1570–1587.

Miller, L. B., and Bizzell, R. P. Long-Term Effects of Four Preschool Programs: Sixth, Seventh, and Eighth Grades. *Child Development*, 1983, *54*, 727–741.

Miller, L. B., and Dyer, J. L. Four Preschool Programs: Their Dimensions and Effects. *Monographs of the Society in Child Development*, 1975, *40*, (5–6, serial number 162).

Minuchin, P. P., and Shapiro, E. K. The School as a Context for Social Development, in E. M. Hetherington (ed.), *Handbook of Child Psychology* (4th ed.). New York: Wiley, 1983, 197–275.

Montessori, M. M. *Education for Human Development: Understanding Montessori*, ed. L. P. Lillard. New York: Schocken Books, 1977.

Moore, R. S., and Moore, D. R. How Early Should They Go to School? *Childhood Education*, October 1973.

New York Times. Death of a Character Is "Sesame Street" Topic. *New York Times*, August 31, 1983.

O'Bryan, K. G. The Teaching Face: A Historical Perspective, in E. L. Palmer and A. Dorr (eds.), *Children and the Faces of Television: Teaching, Violence, Selling*. New York: Academic Press, 1980, 5–16.

Palmer, F. H., and Andersen, L. W. Long-Term Gains from Early Intervention: Findings from Longitudinal Studies, in *Project Head Start: A Legacy of the War on Poverty*, ed. E. Zigler and J. Valentine. New York: The Free Press, 1979, 495–509.

Paris, S. G., and Lindauer, B. K. The Development of Cognitive Skills During Childhood, in B. B. Wolman (ed.), *Handbook of Developmental Psychology*. Englewood Cliffs, N.J.: Prentice-Hall, 1982, 333–350.

Parke, R. D., and Slaby, R. G. The Development of Aggression, in E. M. Hetherington (ed.), *Handbook of Child Psychology* (4th ed.). New York: Wiley, 1983, 547–643.

Perlmutter, M., and Myers, N. A. Recognition Memory Development in Two- to Four-Year-Olds. *Developmental Psychology*, 1979, *15*, 73–83.

Peters, D. L. Early Childhood Education: An Overview and Evaluation, in H. L. Hom and P. A. Robinson (eds.), *Psychological Processes in Early Education*. New York: Academic Press, 1977, 1–23.

Phillips, J. L. *The Origins of Intellect: Piaget's Theory* (2nd ed.). San Francisco: Freeman, 1975.

Piaget, J. Piaget's Theory, in P. H. Mussen (ed.), *Handbook of Child Psychology* (4th ed.), vol. 1, 103–129. New York: Wiley, 1983, (originally published 1970).

———. *Understanding Causality*. New York: W. W. Norton, 1974.

———. *Six Psychological Studies*. New York: Random House, 1967.

———. *The Moral Judgment of the Child*. New York: The Free Press, 1965 (originally published 1932).

———. *The Child's Conception of Physical Causality*. Totawa, N.J.: Littlefield, 1960 (originally published 1927).

Piaget, J., and Inhelder, B. *The Child's Construction of Quantities: Conservation and Atomism*. London: Routledge and Kegan Paul, 1974 (originally published 1942).

———. *The Psychology of the Child*. New York: Basic Books, 1969.

Pulaski, M. A. S. *Understanding Piaget: An Introduction to Children's Cognitive Development* (rev. ed.). New York: Harper and Row, 1980.

Richmond, J. B., Stipek, D. J., and Zigler, E. A Decade of Head Start, in *Project Head Start: A Legacy of the War on Poverty*, ed.

E. Zigler and J. Valentine. New York: The Free Press, 1979, 135–155.

Rossiter, J. R. Children and Television Advertising: Policy Issues, Perspectives, and the Status of Research, in E. L. Palmer and A. Dorr (eds.), *Children and the Faces of Television: Teaching, Violence, Selling*. New York: Academic Press, 1980, 251–271.

Rubin, K. H., Fein, G. G., and Vandenberg, B. Play, in E. Hetherington (ed.), *Handbook of Child Development* (4th ed.). New York: Wiley, 1983, 693–775.

Rubinstein, E. A. Television and Behavior: Research Conclusions of the 1982 NIMH Report and Their Policy Implications. *American Psychologist*, 1983, *38*, 820–826.

———. Television and the Young Viewer. *American Scientist*, November/December 1978.

Sattler, J. M. *Assessment of Children's Intelligence* (rev. repr.). Philadelphia: Saunders, 1974.

Scarr, S. Testing for Children: Assessment and the Many Determinants of Intellectual Competence. *American Psychologist*, 1981, *36*, 1159–1167.

Shane, H. G., and Nelson, W. N. What Will the Schools Become? *Phi Delta Kappan*, 1971, *52*, 59–68.

Shantz, C. U. Social Cognition, in J. H. Flavell and E. M. Markman (eds.), *Handbook of Child Psychology* (4th ed.), vol. 3, 1983, 495–556.

Singer, D. G. A Time to Reexamine the Role of Television in Our Lives. *American Psychologist*, 1983, *38*, 815–817.

Singer, D. G., and Singer, J. L. Family Television Viewing Habits and the Spontaneous Play of Preschool Children. *American Journal of Orthopsychiatry*, 1976, *46*, 496–502.

Singer, J. L., and Singer, D. G. Psychologists Look at Television: Cognitive, Developmental, Personality, and Social Policy Implications. *American Psychologist*, 1983, *38*, 826–835.

Sjolund, A. The Effect of Day Care Institutions on Children's Development: An Analysis of International Research (1971), cited in Clarke-Stewart, K., and Fein, G. G. Early Child Programs, in P. H. Mussen (ed.), *The Handbook of Child Psychology* (3rd ed.), vol. 2. New York: Wiley, 1983, 917–1001.

Smart, M. S., and Smart, R. C. *Preschool Children: Development and Relationships* (2nd ed.). New York: Macmillan, 1978.

Stoneman, Z., and Brody, G. H. Peers as Mediators of Television Food Advertisements Aimed at Children. *Developmental Psychology*, 1981, *17*, 853–858.

Talbot, N. B., and Guthrie, A. Health Care Needs of American Children, in N. B. Talbot (ed.), *Raising Children in Modern America: Problems and Prospective Solutions*. Boston: Little, Brown, 1976.

Tanner, J. M. *Foetus into Man: Physical Growth from Conception to Maturity*. Cambridge, Mass.: Harvard University Press, 1978.

Tower, R. B., Singer, D. G., Singer, J. L., and Biggs, A. Differential Effects of Television Programming on Preschoolers' Cognition, Imagination, and Social Play. *American Journal of Orthopsychiatry*, 1979, *49*, 265–281.

Trabasso, T. Representation, Memory, and Reasoning: How Do We Make Transitive Inferences? in A. D. Pick (ed.), *Minnesota Symposia on Child Psychology*, vol. 9. Minneapolis: University of Minnesota Press, 1975.

Trabasso, T. The Role of Memory as a System in Making Transitive Inferences in R. V. Kail and J. W. Hagen (eds.), *Perspectives on the Development of Memory and Cognition*. Hillsdale, New Jersey: Erlbaum, 1977.

Vernon, P. E. Environment and Intelligence, in V. P. Varma and P. Williams (eds.), *Piaget, Psychology and Education*. Itasca, Ill.: Peacock, 31–43.

Ward, S., and Wackman, D. Television Advertising and Intrafamily Influence: Children's Purchase Influence Attempts and Parental Yielding, in E. A. Rubinstein, G. A. Comstock, and J. P. Murray (eds.), *Television and Social Behavior 4: Television in Day-to-Day Life: Patterns of Use*. Washington, D.C.: U.S. Government Printing Office, 1972, 516–525.

Watkins, B. A., Huston-Stein, A., and Wright, J. C. Effects of Planned Television Programming, in E. L. Palmer and A. Dorr (eds.), *Children and The Faces of Television: Teaching, Violence, Selling*. New York: Academic Press, 1980, 49–71.

Weinberg, R. A. Early Childhood Education and Intervention: Establishing an American Tradition. *American Psychologist*, 1979, *34*, 912–916.

Westinghouse Learning Corporation. *The Impact of Head Start: An Evaluation of Effects of Head Start on Children's Cognitive and Affective Development*. Executive Summary. Ohio University. Report to the Office of Economic Opportunity. Washington, D.C. Clearinghouse for Federal Scientific and Technical Information, June, 1969, (EDO93497).

Whitener, C. B., and Kersey, K. A Purple Hippopotamus? Why Not! *Childhood Education*, November/December, 1980, 18–20.

Wright, J. C., and Huston, A. C. A Matter of Form: Potentials of Television for Young Viewers. *American Psychologist*, 1983, *38*, 835–844.

Wright, J. C., Huston, A. C., Ross, R. P., Calvert, S. L., Rolandelli, D., Weeks, L. A., Raeisse, P., and Potts, R. Pace and Continuity of Television Programs: Effects on Children's Attention and Comprehension. *Developmental Psychology*, 1984, *20*, 653–667.

Zigler, E. Head Start: Not a Program But an Evolving Concept, in *Project Head Start: A Legacy of the War on Poverty*, ed. E. Zigler and J. Valentine. New York: The Free Press, 1979, 367–374.

Zigler, E., and Anderson, K. An Idea Whose Time Had Come: The Intellectual and Political Climate, in *Project Head Start: A Legacy of the War on Poverty*, ed. E. Zigler and J. Valentine. New York: The Free Press, 1979, 3–21.

Zigler, E., and Berman, W. Discerning the Future of Early Childhood Intervention. *American Psychologist*, 1983, *38*, 894–907.

Zigler, E., and Butterfield, E. C. Motivational Aspects of Changes in IQ Test Performance of Culturally Deprived Nursery School Children. *Child Development*, 1968, *39*, 1–14.

Zigler, E., and Trickett, P. K. IQ, Social Competence, and Evaluation of Early Childhood Intervention Programs. *American Psychologist*, 1978, *33*, 789–799.

Zigler, E., and Valentine, J. *Project Head Start—A Legacy of the War on Poverty*. New York: The Free Press, 1979.

Zinsser, C. The Preschool Pressure Cooker. *Working Mother*, October 1981.

Chapter Ten

Acus, L. K. Quarreling Kids? How to Handle Them. *Long Island*, January 24, 1982, Newsday, 16 ff.

Adams-Tucker, C. Proximate Effects of Sexual Abuse in Childhood: A Report on 28 Children. *American Journal of Psychiatry*, 1982, *139*, 1252–1256.

Altrocchi, J. *Abnormal Psychology*. New York: Harcourt Brace Jovanovich, 1980.

Alvy, K. T. Preventing Child Abuse. *American Psychologist*, 1975, *30*, 921–928.

Axline, V. M. *Play Therapy*. New York: Houghton, 1947. Rev. ed., Ballantine Books, 1969.

Bandura, A., Grusek, J. E., and Menlove, F. L. Vicarious Extinction of Avoidance Behavior. *Journal of Personality and Social Psychology*, 1967, *5*, 516–523.

Bandura, A., and Menlove, F. L. Factors Determining Vicarious Extinction of Avoidance Behavior Through Symbolic Modeling. *Journal of Personality and Social Psychology*, 1968, *8*, 99–108.

Bardwick, J. *The Psychology of Women*. New York: Harper and Row, 1971.

Baskett, L. M. Ordinal Position Differences in Children's Family Interactions. *Developmental Psychology*, 1984, *20*, 1026–1032.

Baumrind, D. New Directions in Socialization Research. *American Psychologist*, 1980, *35*, 639–652.

_____. Parental Disciplinary Patterns and Social Competence in Children. *Youth and Society*, March 1978, *9*, 239–276.

_____. Current Patterns of Parental Authority. *Developmental Psychology Monograph*, 1971, *4* (1, Part 2).

_____. Child Care Practices Anteceding 3 Patterns of Preschool Behavior. *Genetic Psychology Monographs*, 1967, *75*, 43–88.

Becker, W. C. Consequences of Different Kinds of Parental Discipline, in M. L. Hoffman and H. W. Hoffman (eds.), *Review of Child Development Research*, vol. 1. New York: Russell Sage Foundation, 1964.

Belsky, J. Child Maltreatment: An Ecological Integration. *American Psychologist*, 1980, *35*, 320–335.

Bem, S. Sex-Role Adaptability: One Consequence of Psychological Androgyny. *Journal of Personality and Social Psychology*, 1975, *31*, 634–643.

_____. The Measurement of Psychological Androgyny. *Journal of Consulting and Clinical Psychology*, 1974, *42*, 155–162.

Berbaum, M. L. Explanation and Prediction: Criteria for Assessing the Confluence Model. *Child Development*, 1985, *56*, 781–784.

Berbaum, M. L., Markus, G. B., and Zajonc. A Closer Look at Galbraith's "Closer Look." *Developmental Psychology*, 1982, *18*, 174–181.

Berbaum, M. L., and Moreland, R. L. Intellectual Development within Transracial Adoptive Families: Retesting the Confluence Model. *Child Development*, 1985, *56*, 207–216.

Berdine, W. H., and Blackhurst, A. E. *An Introduction to Special Education* (2nd ed.). Boston: Little-Brown, 1985.

Best, D., Williams, J. E., Cloud, J. M., Davis, S. W., Robertson, L. S., Edwards, J. E., Giles, H., and Fowles, T. Development of Sex-Trait Stereotypes Among Young Children in the U.S., England and Ireland. *Child Development*, 1977, *48*, 1375–1384.

Blakemore, J. E. O. Age and Sex Differences in Interaction with a Human Infant. *Child Development*, 1981, *52*, 386–388.

Block, J. H. Socialization Influences on Personality Development in Males and Females. *American Psychological Association's Master Lecture Series*. Washington, D.C.: American Psychological Association, 1979.

_____. Issues, Problems, and Pitfalls in Assessing Sex Differences: A Critique of the Psychology of Sex Differences. *Merrill-Palmer Quarterly*, 1976, *22*, 283–308.

Brackbill, Y., and Nichols, P. L. A Test of the Confluence Model of Intellectual Development. *Developmental Psychology*, 1982, *18*, 192–199.

Brody, G. H., Zolinda, S., MacKinnon, C.E., and MacKinnon, R. Role Relationships and Behavior Between Preschool-Aged and School-Aged Siblings. *Developmental Psychology*, 1985, *21*, 124–129.

Broverman, I., Vogel, S., Broverman, D., Clarkson, F., and Rosenkrantz, P. Sex-Role Stereotypes: A Current Appraisal. *Journal of Social Issues*. 1972, *28*, 59–78.

Bruner, J. The Nature and Uses of Immaturity, *American Psychologist*, 1972, *27*, 687–708.

Canavan, J. W. Sexual Child Abuse, in N. S. Ellerstein (ed.). *Child Abuse and Neglect: A Medical Reference*. N.Y.: Wiley, 1981, 233–253.

Carper, L. Sex Roles in the Nursery, *Harper's*, April 1978, 35–42.

Chafetz, J. S. The Bringing-up of Dick and Jane (1974), in S. Cohen and T. J. Comisky (eds.), *Child Development: Contemporary Perspectives*. Itasca, Ill.: Peacock, 1977, 196–201.

DeVine, R. A. Sexual Abuse of Children: An Overview of the Problem in *Sexual Abuse of Children: Selected Readings*. Washington, D.C.: U.S. Department of Health and Human Services, DHHS Pub No 78-30161. November 1980, 3–7.

DiPietro, J. Rough and Tumble Play: A Function of Gender. *Developmental Psychology*, 1981, *17*, 50–58.

Dunn, J., and Kendrick, C. *Siblings: Love, Envy and Understanding*. Cambridge, MA.: Harvard University Press, 1982.

Eagly, A. H. Sex Differences in Influenceability. *Psychological Bulletin*, 1978, *85*, 86–116.

Eaton, W. O., and Von Bargen, D. Asynchronous Development of Gender Understanding in Preschool Children. *Child Development*, 1981, *52*, 1020–1027.

Erikson, E. H. The Problem of Ego Identity (1959) in L. D. Steinberg (ed.), *The Life Cycle: Readings in Human Development*. New York: Columbia University Press, 1981, 189–198.

———. *Youth and Crisis*. New York: W. W. Norton, 1968.

———. *Childhood and Society* (2nd ed.). New York: W. W. Norton, 1963.

Etaugh, C., Collins, G., and Gerson, A. Reinforcement of Sex-Typed Behaviors of Two-Year-Olds in a Nursery School Setting. *Developmental Psychology*, 1975, *11*, 255.

Fagot, B. Sex Differences in Toddler's Behavior and Parental Reactions. *Developmental Psychology*, 1974, *10*, 554–558.

Finkelhor, D. How Widespread is Child Sexual Abuse? *Children Today*, July–August, 1984, 18–20.

Fontana, V. J. When Systems Fail: Protecting the Victim of Child Sexual Abuse. *Children Today*, July–August, 1984, 14–18.

Frasher, R., and Walker, A. Sex Roles in Early Reading Textbooks. *The Reading Teacher*, 1972, *25*, 741–749.

Freud, S. *New Introductory Lectures on Psychoanalysis*. N.Y.: Norton, 1965 (originally published 1933).

Friedrich, W. N., and Boriskin, J. A. The Role of the Child in Abuse: A Review of the Literature. *American Journal of Orthopsychiatry*, 1976, *46*, 580–591.

Frodi, A. M., and Lamb, M. E. Child Abusers' Responses to Infant Smiles and Cries. *Child Development*, 1980, *51*, 238–241.

Frueh, T., and McGhee, P. E. Traditional Sex Role Development and Amount of Time Spent Watching Television. *Developmental Psychology*, 1975, *11*, 109.

Galbraith, R. C. Sibling Spacing and Intellectual Development: A Closer Look at Confluence Models. *Developmental Psychology*, 1982, *18*, 151–174.

———. Just One Look Was All It Took: Reply to Berbaum, Markus and Zajonc. *Developmental Psychology*, 1982b, *18*, 181–192.

Galston, R. Preventing the Abuse of Little Children: The Parents' Center Project for the Study and Prevention of Child Abuse. *American Journal of Orthopsychiatry*, 1975, *45*, 372–382.

Garvey, C. *Play*, Cambridge, MA: Harvard University Press, 1977.

Gelles, R. J. Violence Towards Children in the United States. *American Journal of Orthopsychiatry*, 1978, *48*, 580–593.

General Mills American Family Report. Raising Children in a Changing Society, 1976–1977. Minneapolis, Minnesota: General Mills, Inc.

Green, A. H., Gaines, R. W., and Sandgrund, A. Child Abuse: Pathological Syndrome of Family Reaction. *American Journal of Psychiatry*, 1974, *131*, 882–886.

Harlow, H. F., and Harlow, M. K. Learning to Love. *American Scientist*, 1966, *54*, 244–272.

Harris, I. D. *The Promised Seed: A Comparative Study of Eminent First and Later Sons*. Glencoe, Ill.: The Free Press, 1964.

Hartup, W. W. Peer Interaction and Social Organization, in P. H. Mussen (ed.), *Carmichael's Manual of Child Development* (3rd ed.). New York: Wiley, 1970.

Hetherington, E. M. The Effects of Familial Variables on Sex Typing, on Parent-Child Similarity, and on Imitation in Children (1967), in P. H. Mussen, J. Conger, and J. Kagan (eds.), *Basic and Contemporary Issues in Child Development*. New York: Harper and Row, 1977.

Hoffman, L. Effects of Maternal Employment on the Child: A Review of the Research. *Developmental Psychology*, 1974, *10*, 204–228.

Horney, K. *Feminine Psychology*. New York: W. W. Norton, 1967.

———. *New Ways in Psychoanalysis*. New York: W. W. Norton, 1939.

Hyde, J. S. How Large Are Gender Differences in Aggression: A Developmental Meta-Analysis. *Developmental Psychology*, 1984, *20*, 722–736.

Ilg, F. L., and Ames, L. B. *Child Behavior*. New York: Harper and Row, 1955.

Jennings, S. Effects of Sex Typing in Children's Stories on Preference and Recall. *Child Development*, 1975, *46*, 220–223.

Josselyn, W. D. Androgen-Induced Social Dominance in Infant Rhesus Monkeys. *Journal of Child Psychology and Psychiatry*, 1973, *14*, 137–145.

Kempe, C. H., and Helfer, R. E. (eds.). *Helping the Battered Child and His Family*. Philadelphia: Lippincott, 1972.

Kempe, R. S. and Kempe, C. H. *Child Abuse*. Cambridge, MA.: Harvard University Press, 1978.

Kendrick, C., and Dunn, J. Sibling Quarrels and Maternal Responses. *Developmental Psychology*, 1983, *19*, 62–71.

Kinard, E. M., and Klerman, L. V. Teenage Parenting and Child Abuse: Are They Related? *American Journal of Orthopsychiatry*, 1980, *50*, 481–488.

Kline, P. *Fact and Fantasy in Freudian Theory*. London: Methuen, 1972.

Kohlberg, L. Stages and Sequences: The Cognitive-Developmental Approach to Socialization, in D. Goslin (ed.), *Handbook of Socialization Theory and Research*. Chicago: Rand McNally, 1969.

———. A Cognitive-Development Analysis of Children's Sex-Role Concepts and Attitudes, in E. Maccoby (ed.), *The Development of Sex Differences*. Stanford, Calif.: Stanford University Press, 1966.

Kuhn, D., Nash, S., and Brucken, L. Sex Role Concepts of Two and Three-Year-Olds. *Child Development*, 1978, *49*, 445–451.

Lamb, M. E. Paternal Influences and the Father's Role: A Personal Perspective. *American Psychologist*, 1979, *34*, 938–944.

Lystad, M. H. Violence at Home: A Review of the Literature. *American Journal of Orthopsychiatry*, 1975, *46*, 328–345.

Maccoby, E., and Jacklin, C. *The Psychology of Sex Differences*. Stanford, Calif.: Stanford University Press, 1974.

Maccoby, E. E., and Martin, J. A. Socialization in the Context of the Family: Parent-Child Interaction, in P. H. Mussen (ed.), *Handbook of Child Development* (4th ed.) vol. 4. New York: Wiley, 1983, 1–103.

Martin, B. Parent-Child Relationships, in F. D. Horowitz (ed.). *Review of Child Development Research*, vol. 4. Chicago: University of Chicago Press, 1975, 463–540.

Martin, H. A Child-Oriented Approach to Prevention of Abuse, in A. W. Franklin (ed.), *Child Abuse: Prediction, Prevention and Follow-up*. London: Churchill-Livingston, 1978, 9–20.

McCall, R. B. The Confluence Model and Theory. *Child Development*, 1985, *56*, 217–218.

McGhee, P. E. Television as a Source of Learning Sex-Role Stereotypes (1975), in S. Cohen and T. J. Comiskey (eds.), *Child Development: Contemporary Perspectives*. Itasca, Ill.: Peacock, 1977, 208–214.

McGuinness, D. How Schools Discriminate Against Boys (1977), in S. Hochman and P. Kaplan (eds.), *Readings in Psychology: A Soft Approach* (rev. ed.). Lexington, Mass.: Ginn, 1979, 74–79.

———. Sex Differences in the Organization of Perception and Cognition, in B. Lloyd and J. Archer (eds.), *Exploring Sex Differences*. London: Academic Press, 1976, 123–157.

McLaughlin, B. Child Compliance to Parental Control Techniques. *Developmental Psychology*, 1983, *19*, 667–674.

Mead, M. On Freud's View of Female Psychology, in J. Strouse (ed.). *Women and Analysis*. N.Y.: Grossman, 1974.

Minton, H. L., and Schneider, F. W. *Differential Psychology*. Monterey, Calif.: Brooks/Cole, 1980.

Mischel, W. *Introduction to Personality* (2nd ed.). New York: Holt, Rinehart and Winston, 1976.

———. Sex-Typing and Socialization, in P. H. Mussen (ed.), *Carmichael's Manual of Child Psychology* (3rd ed.). New York: Wiley, 1970.

Money, J., and Ehrhardt, A. *Man and Woman, Boy and Girl*. Baltimore: Johns Hopkins University Press, 1972.

Mullahy, P. *Oedipus: Myth and Complex*. New York: Hermitage Press, 1948.

Munroe, R. H., Shimmin, H. S., and Munroe, R. L. Gender Understanding and Sex-Role Preference in Four Cultures. *Developmental Psychology*, 1984, *20*, 673–683.

New York Times. Abuse of Children Reported Up in '84. Feb. 17, 1985, p. 30.

Parke, R. D., and Collmer, C. W. Child Abuse: An Interdisciplinary Analysis, in E. M. Hetherington (ed.), *Review of Child Development Research*, vol. 5. Chicago: University of Chicago Press, 1975.

Parten, M. B. Social Play Among Preschool Children. *Journal of Abnormal and Social Psychology*, 1932, *27*, 243–269.

Plomin, R., and Foch, T. T. Sex Differences and Individual Differences. *Child Development*, 1981, *52*, 383–385.

Poznansky, E. O. Children with Excessive Fears. *American Journal of Orthopsychiatry*, 1973, *43*, 428–438.

Queens Bench Foundation. Sexual Abuse of Children: A Guide for Parents (1977), in *Sexual Abuse of Children: Selected Readings*.

Washington, D.C.: U.S. Department of Health and Human Services, DHHS Pub No (OHDS) 78-30161. November 1980, 173–181.

Rheingold, H., and Cook, K. The Contents of Boys' and Girls' Rooms as an Index of Parents' Behavior. *Child Development*, 1975, *46*, 459–463.

Richmond-Abbott, M. *Masculine and Feminine: Sex Roles Over the Life Span*. Reading, MA.: Addison-Wesley, 1983.

Rodgers, J. L. Confluence Effects: Not Here, Not Now! *Developmental Psychology*, 1984, *20*, 321–331.

Rogers, L. Male Hormones and Behaviour, in B. B. Lloyd and J. Archer (eds.), *Exploring Sex Differences*. London: Academic Press, 1976, 185–213.

Ross Laboratories. *Your Child's Fears*. Columbus, Ohio: Ross Laboratories, 1979.

Rubin, K. H., Fein, G. G., and Vandenberg, B. Play, in P. H. Mussen (ed.), *Handbook of Child Psychology* (4th ed.), vol. 4. N.Y.: Wiley, 1983, 693–775.

Ruble, D. N. Balaban, T., and Cooper, J. Gender Constancy and the Effect of Sex-Typed Televised Commercials. *Child Development*, 1981, *52*, 667–673.

Russell, G. The Father's Role and Its Relation to Masculinity, Femininity, and Androgyny. *Child Development*, 1978, *49*, 1174–1181.

Sage, W. Violence in the Children's Room. *Human Behavior*, July 1975, 24–29.

Sarafino, E. P. An Estimate of Nationwide Incidence of Sexual Offenses Against Children. *Child Welfare*, February, 1979, 127–135.

Schaffer, K. F. *Sex Roles and Human Behavior*. Cambridge, Mass.: Winthrop Publishers, 1981.

Schultz, L. G., and Jones, P. Sexual Abuse of Children: Issues for Social and Health Professionals. *Child Welfare*, March/April 1983, *62*, 99–109.

Sears, R. R., Rae, L., and Alpert, R. *Identification and Child Rearing*. Stanford, Calif.: Stanford University Press, 1965.

Simmons, B. Teachers Be(a)ware of Sex-Stereotypes (1976), in *Readings in Early Childhood Education*. Guilford, Conn.: Dushkin Publishing Co., 1979, 253–255.

Sjolund, A. The Effect of Day Care Institutions on Children's Development: An Analysis of International Research (1971), cited in Clarke-Stewart, K. A., and Fein, G. G. Early Child Programs, in P. H. Mussen (ed.), *The Handbook of Child Psychology*, N.Y.: Wiley, 1983, 917–1001.

Slaby, R. G., and Frey, K. S. Development of Gender Constancy and Selective Attention to Same Sex Models. *Child Development*, 1975, *46*, 849–856.

Smart, M. S., and Smart, R. C. *Preschool Children: Development and Relationships* (2nd ed.). New York: Macmillan, 1978.

Smith, P. K. A Longitudinal Study of Social Participation in Preschool Children: Solitary and Parallel Play Reexamined. *Developmental Psychology*, 1978, *14*, 517–523.

Smith, P. K., and Green, M. Aggressive Behavior in English Nurseries and Play Groups: Sex Differences and Responses of Adults. *Child Development*, 1975, *46*, 211–214.

Spence, J. H., Helmreich, R., and Stapp, J. Ratings of Self and Peers on Sex-Role Attribution and Their Relationship to Self-Esteem and Concept of Masculinity and Femininity. *Journal of Personality and Social Psychology*, 1975, *32*, 29–39.

Sprigle, J. H., and Schaefer, L. Longitudinal Evaluation of the Effects of Two Compensatory Preschool Programs on Fourth Through Sixth-Grade Students. *Developmental Psychology,* 1985, *21,* 702–709.

Starr, R. Y. Child Abuse. *American Psychologist,* 1979, *34,* 872–878.

Steinberg, L. D., Catalano, R., and Dooley, D. Economic Antecedents of Child Abuse. *Child Development,* 1981, *52,* 975–985.

Stewart, R. B. Sibling Attachment Relationships: Child-Infant Interactions in Infancy. *Developmental Psychology,* 1983, *19,* 192–200.

Sutton-Smith, B., and Roberts, J. M., Play, Games and Sports, in H. C. Triandis and A. Heron (eds.), *Handbook of Cross-Cultural Psychology,* vol. 4. Boston: Allyn and Bacon, 1981.

Sutton-Smith, B., and Rosenberg, B. G. *The Sibling.* New York: Holt, Rinehart and Winston, 1970.

Switzky, H. N., Haywood, H. C., and Isett, R. Exploration, Curiosity, and Play in Young Children: Effects of Stimulus Complexity. *Developmental Psychology,* 1974, *10,* 321–329.

Trabasso, T. The Role of Memory as a System in Making Transitive Inferences, in R. V. Kail and J. W. Hagen (eds.), *Perspectives on the Development of Memory and Cognition.* Hillsdale, N.J.: Erlbaum, 1977.

Turbak, G. Suffer the Children (1979), in *Readings in Child Development.* Guilford, Conn.: Dushkin Publishing Co., 1982, 189–192.

Vandenberg, B. Play and Development from an Ethological Perspective. *American Psychologist,* 1978, *33,* 724–739.

Vandenberg, S. G., and Kuse, A. R. Spacial Ability: A Critical Review of the Sex-Linked Major-Gene Hypothesis, in M. Whittig and A. Petersen (eds.), *Determinants of Sex Related Differences in Cognitive Functioning.* New York: Academic Press, 1979.

Verville, E. *Behavior Problems of Children.* Philadelphia: Saunders, 1967.

Weisler, A., and McCall, R. B. Exploration and Play: Resume and Redirection. *American Psychologist,* 1976, *31,* 492–508.

Westinghouse Learning Corporation. *The Impact of Head Start: An Evaluation of the Effects of Head Start on Children's Cognitive and Affective Development.* Executive Summary. Ohio University. Report to the Office of Economic Opportunity. Washington, D.C. Clearinghouse for Federal Scientific Technical Information, June, 1969. (EDO93497).

Whiting, B. B., and Whiting, W. M. *Children of Sex Cultures: Psychocultural Analysis.* Cambridge, Mass.: Harvard University Press, 1975.

Williams, J. E., Bennett, S. M., and Best, D. L. Awareness and Expression of Sex Stereotypes in Young Children. *Developmental Psychology,* 1975, *11,* 635–642.

Zajonc, R. B. Family Configuration and Intelligence. *Science,* 1976, *192,* 227–236.

Zajonc, R. B., and Bargh, J. Birth Order, Family Size and Decline of SAT Scores. *American Psychologist,* 1980, *35,* 662–669.

Zajonc, R. B., and Markus, G. B. Birth Order and Intellectual Development. *Psychological Review,* 1975, *82,* 74–88.

Zigler, E., and Berman, W. Discerning the Future of Early Childhood Intervention. *American Psychologist,* 1983, *38,* 894–907.

Zigler, E., and Valentine, J. *Project Head Start—A Legacy of the War on Poverty.* N.Y.: The Free Press, 1979.

Chapter Eleven

American Dental Association. *Your Child's Teeth.* Chicago, Illinois: American Dental Association.

Anderson, R. C., and Faust, G. W. *Educational Psychology: The Science of Instruction and Learning.* New York: Dodd, Mead and Co., 1974.

Anderson, R. E., Klassen, D. L., and Johnson, D. C. Why We Need to View Computer Literacy Comprehensively. *The Education Digest,* March 1982, 19–21.

Antonak, R. F., King, S., and Lowy, J. J. Otis-Lennon Mental Ability Test, Stanford Achievement Test, and Three Demographic Variables as Predictors of Achievement in Grades 2 and 4. *Journal of Educational Research,* 1982, *75,* 366–373.

Arlin, P. K. Piagetian Tasks as Predictors of Reading and Math Readiness in Grades K–1. *Journal of Educational Psychology,* 1981, *73,* 712–721.

Athey, I. Language Development Factors Related to Reading Development. *Journal of Educational Research,* 1983, *76,* 197–203.

Ault, R. *Children's Cognitive Development.* New York: Oxford University Press, 1977.

Bailey, D. A. The Growing Child and the Need for Physical Activity (1975), in M. S. Smart and R. C. Smart (eds.), *School-Age Children: Development and Relationships.* New York: Macmillan, 1978, 50–61.

Barron, F., and Harrington, D. M. Creativity, Intelligence and Personality, in M. R. Rosenzweig and L. W. Porter (eds.), *Annual Review of Psychology,* 1981, *32,* 439–477.

Becker, D. J., and Drash, A. L. Endocrinology, in J. D. Noshpitz (ed.), *Basic Handbook of Child Psychiatry,* vol. 1. New York: Basic Books, 1979, 601–621.

Bernstein, H. T. The Information Society: Byting the Hand That Feeds You. *Phi Delta Kappan,* October 1983, 108–109.

Bersoff, D. N. Test Bias: The Judicial Report Card. *New York University Educational Quarterly,* 1981a, *13,* 2–9.

———. Testing and the Law. *American Psychologist,* 1981b, *36,* 1047–1057.

Bettelheim, B, and Zelan, K. Why Children Don't Like to Read. *Education Digest,* March 1982, 2–6.

Biehler, R. F., and Snowman, J. *Psychology Applied to Teaching* (4th ed.). Boston: Houghton Mifflin, 1982.

Blank, M. Intelligence Testing, in C. B. Kopp and J. B. Krakow (eds.), *The Child: Development in a Social Context.* Reading, Mass.: Addison-Wesley, 1982, 708–715.

Blank, M., and Klig, S. The Child and the School Experience, in C. B. Kopp and J. B. Krakow (eds.), *The Child: Development in a Social Context.* Reading, Mass.: Addison-Wesley, 1982, 456–508.

Bloom, B. S. *Human Characteristics and School Learning.* New York: McGraw-Hill, 1976.

Borkowski, J. G., Peck, V. A., Reid, M. K., and Kurtz, B. E. Impulsivity and Strategy Transfer: Metamemory as Mediator. *Child Development,* 1983, *54,* 459–473.

Brainerd, C. J. Young Children's Mental Arithmetic Errors: A Working-Memory Analysis. *Child Development,* 1983, *54,* 812–830.

———. Cognitive Development and Concept Training: An Interpretive Review. *Psychological Bulletin,* 1977, *84,* 919–939.

Bringuier, J. C. *Conversations with Jean Piaget.* Chicago: University of Chicago Press, 1980.

Brody, J. E. Exercise for Children: Noncompetitive and Solo Activities Can Be for Everyone. *New York Times,* November 19, 1980a, C18.

———. Tending to Obesity, Inbred Tribe Aids Diabetes Study. *New York Times,* February 5, 1980b, C1, C5.

Brodzinsky, D. M. Relationship Between Cognitive Style and Cognitive Development: A 2-Year Longitudinal Study. *Developmental Psychology*, 1982, *18*, 617–626.

Brophy, J. Successful Teaching Strategies for the Inner-City Child. *Phi Delta Kappan*, April 1982, 527–530.

Brophy, J. E. Research on the Self-Fulfilling Prophecy and Teacher Expectations. *Journal of Educational Psychology*, 1983, *75*, 631–661.

Brown, A. L., Bransford, J. D., Ferrara, R. A., and Campione, J. C. Learning, Remembering and Understanding, in P. H. Mussen (ed.), *Handbook of Child Psychology* (4th ed.), vol. 3. New York: Wiley, 1983.

Brown, A. L., Campione, J. C., and Barclay, C. R. Training Self-Checking Routines for Estimating Test Readiness: Generalization from List Learning to Prose Recall. *Child Development*, 1979, *50*, 501–512.

Brown, A. L., and Smiley, S. S. Rating the Importance of Structural Units of Prose Passages: A Problem of Metcognitive Development. *Child Development*, 1977, *48*, 1–8.

Brown, F. G. *Principles of Educational and Psychological Testing*. New York: Holt, Rinehart and Winston, 1983.

Bullen, B. A., Read, R. B., and Mayer, J. Physical Activity of Obese and Non-Obese Adolescent Girls Appraised by Motion Picture Sampling, *American Journal of Clinical Nutrition*, 1964, 211–215.

Burstein, B., Bank, L., and Jarvik, L. F. Sex Differences in Cognitive Functioning: Evidence, Determinants, Implications. *Human Development*, 1980, *23*, 289–313.

Busch-Rossnagel, N. A., and Vance, A. K. The Impact of the Schools on Social and Emotional Development, in B. B. Wolman (ed.), *Handbook of Developmental Psychology*. Englewood-Cliffs, N.J.: Prentice-Hall, 1982, 452–471.

Bush, E. S., and Dweck, C. S. Reflections on Conceptual Tempo: Relationship Between Cognitive Style and Performance as a Function of Task Characteristics. *Developmental Psychology*, 1975, *11*, 567–574.

Carter, A., and Stokes, W. T. What Children Know About Reading Before They Can Read. *Journal of Education*. 1981, *65*, 173–184.

Cavanaugh, J. C., and Perlmutter, M. Metamemory: A Critical Examination. *Child Development*, 1982, *53*, 11–28.

Centra, J. A., and Potter, D. A. School and Teacher Effects: An Interrelational Model. *Review of Educational Research*, 1980, *50*, 273–290.

Chaikin, A. L., Sigler, E., and Derlega, V. J. Nonverbal Mediator of Teacher Expectancy Effects. *Journal of Personality and Social Psychology*, 1974, *30*, 144–149.

Chall, J. *Reading 1967–1977: A Decade of Change and Promise*. Bloomington, Ind.: Phi Delta Kappan Educational Foundation, 1977.

Clifford, M. M., and Cleary, T. A. The Relationship Between Children's Academic Performance and Achievement Accountability. *Child Development*, 1972, *43*, 647–655.

Cohen, M. Effective Schools: Accumulating Research Findings. *American Education*, January 1982, 13–16.

Cole, N. S. Bias in Testing. *American Psychologist*, 1981, *36*, 1067–1078.

Coleman, J. S., et al. *Equality of Educational Opportunity Survey*. Washington, D.C.: U.S. Government Printing Office, 1966.

Cooper, H. Pygmalian Grows Up: A Model for Teacher Expectation Communication and Performance Influence. *Review of Educational Research*, 1979, *49*, 389–410.

Cooperman, P. *The Literacy Hoax: The Decline of Reading, Writing, and Learning in the Public Schools and What We Can Do About It*. New York: William Morrow and Co., 1978.

Copeland, R. W. *How Children Learn Mathematics: Teaching Implications of Piaget's Research*. New York: Macmillan, 1971.

Corbin, C. B. Childhood Obesity, in C. B. Corbin (ed.), *A Textbook of Motor Development*. Dubuque, Iowa: W. C. Brown, 1980a, 121–128.

———. The Physical Fitness of Children: A Discussion and Point of View, in C. B. Corbin (ed.), *A Textbook of Motor Development*. Dubuque, Iowa: W. C. Brown, 1980b, 100–107.

Cratty, B. J. *Perceptual and Motor Development in Infants and Children*. New York: Macmillan, 1970.

Curtis, M. E. Development of Components of Reading Skill. *Journal of Educational Psychology*, 1980, *72*, 656–659.

Daigon, A. Toward Righting Writing, *Phi Delta Kappan*, December 1982, 242–246.

Dasen, P., and Heron, A. Cross-Cultural Tests of Piaget's Theory, in H. C. Triandis and A. Heron (eds.) *Handbook of Cross-Cultural Psychology: Developmental Psychology*, vol. 4. Boston: Allyn and Bacon, 1981.

Davis, G. A. *Educational Psychology: Theory and Practice*. Reading, Mass.: Addison-Wesley, 1983.

Davis, J. K., and Frank, B. M. Learning and Memory of Field Independent-Dependent Individuals. *Journal of Research in Personality*, 1979, *13*, 469–479.

Dembo, M. H. *Teaching for Learning: Applying Educational Psychology in the Classroom* (2nd ed.). Santa Monica, Calif.: Goodyear Publishing Co., 1981.

DeOreo, K., and Keough, J. Performance of Fundamental Motor Tasks, in C. B. Corbin (ed.), *A Textbook of Motor Development* (2nd ed.). Dubuque, Iowa: W. C. Brown, 1980, 76–91.

Dempster, F. N., and Rohwer, W. D., Age Differences and Modality Effects in Immediate and Final Free Recall. *Child Development*, 1983, *54*, 30–41.

Diamond, N. Cognitive Theory, in B. B. Wolman (ed.), *Handbook of Developmental Psychology*. Englewood Cliffs, N.J.: Prentice-Hall, 1982, 3–23.

Dirks, J., and Neisser, U. Memory for Objects in Real Scenes: The Development of Recognition and Recall. *Journal of Experimental Child Psychology*, 1977, *23*, 315–328.

Dodd, D. H., and White, R. M. *Cognition: Mental Structures and Processes*. Boston: Allyn and Bacon, 1980.

Donaldson, M. *Children's Minds*. New York: W. W. Norton, 1978.

Durkin, D. Confusion and Misconceptions in the Controversy About Kindergarten Reading (1970), in S. Coopersmith and R. Feldman (eds.), *The Formative Years: Principles of Early Childhood Education*. San Francisco: Albion, 1974, 228–235.

Elam, S. M. The Gallup Education Surveys: Impressions of a Poll Watcher. *Phi Delta Kappan*, September 1983, 26–47.

Elashoff, J. D., and Snow, R. E. *Pygmalian Reconsidered*. Worthington, OH.: Charles E. Jones, 1971.

Entwisle, D. R., and Baker, D. P. Gender and Young Children's Expectations for Performance in Arithmetic. *Developmental Psychology*, 1983, *19*, 100–209.

Etaugh, C., and Hughes, V. Teachers' Evaluations of Sex-Typed Behaviors in Children: The Role of Teacher Sex and School Setting. *Developmental Psychology*, 1975, *11*, 394–395.

Flavell, J. H. *Cognitive Development*. Englewood Cliffs, N.J.: Prentice-Hall, 1977.

Flavell, J. H., Beach, D. H., and Chinsky, J. M. Spontaneous Verbal Rehearsal in Memory Tasks as a Function of Age. *Child Development*, 1966, *37*, 283–299.

Flavell, J. H., Friedrichs, A. G., and Hoyt, J. D. Developmental Changes in Memorization Processes. *Cognitive Psychology*, 1970, *1*, 324–340.

Forman, G. E., and Kuschner, D. S. *The Child's Construction of Knowledge: Piaget for Teaching Children*. Monterey, Calif.: Brooks/Cole, 1977.

Forrest, D. L., and Waller, T. G. Cognitive and Metacognitive Aspects of Reading (1979), cited in Paris, S. G., and Lindauer, B. K., The Development of Cognitive Skills During Childhood, in B. B. Wolman (ed.), *Handbook of Developmental Psychology*. Englewood Cliffs, N.J.: Prentice-Hall, 1982, 333–349.

Fulkerson, K. F., Furr, S., and Brown, D. Expectations and Achievement Among Third-, Sixth-, and Ninth-Grade Black and White Males and Females. *Developmental Psychology*, 1983, *19*, 231–236.

Gallup, G. H. The 15th Annual Gallup Poll of the Public's Attitudes Toward the Public Schools. *Phi Delta Kappan*, September 1983, 333–336.

Gardner, H. *Frames of Mind: The Theory of Multiple Intelligences*. New York: Basic Books, 1983.

Gelfand, D. M., Jenson, W. R., and Drew, C. J. *Understanding Child Behavior Disorders*. New York: Holt, Rinehart and Winston, 1982.

Gelman, R., and Baillargeon, R. A Review of Some Piagetian Concepts, in P. H. Mussen (ed.), *Handbook of Child Psychology* (4th ed.). New York: Wiley, 1983.

Gelman, R., and Gallistel, C. R. *The Child's Understanding of Number*. Cambridge, Mass.: Harvard University Press, 1978.

Goetzels, J. W., and Jackson, P. W. *Creativity and Intelligence*. New York: Wiley, 1962.

Greaney, V. Factors Related to Amount and Type of Leisure Time Reading. *Reading Research Quarterly*, 1980, *15*, 337–357.

Groen, G. J., and Parkman, J. M. A Chronometric Analysis of Simple Addition. *Psychological Review*, 1972, *79*, 329–343.

Guilford, J. P. *The Nature of Human Intelligence*. New York: McGraw-Hill, 1967.

Hamachek, D. E. Characteristics of Good Teachers and Implications for Teacher Education. *Phi Delta Kappan*, 1969, *50*, 341–345.

Hamill, P. V. V. NCHS Growth Curves for Children. Vital Health Statistics: Series 11, Data from the National Health Survey, No. 165 Washington D.C.: U.S. Government Printing Office (DHEW no. 78-1650), 1977.

Hamilton, E. M. N., and Whitney, E. N. *Nutrition: Concepts and Controversies* (2nd ed.). St. Paul: West Publishing Co., 1982.

Harrison, P. L. Mercer's Adaptive Behavior Inventory, The McCarthy Scales, and Dental Development as Predictors of First-Grade Achievement. *Journal of Educational Psychology*, 1981, *73*, 78–82.

Harter, S. Developmental Perspective on the Self-System, in P. H. Mussen (ed.), *Handbook of Child Psychology* (4th ed.), vol. 4. New York: Wiley, 1983, 275–387.

Hattie, J. Should Creativity Tests Be Administered Under Testlike Conditions? An Empirical Study of Three Alternative Conditions. *Journal of Education Psychology*, 1980, *72*, 87–98.

Hechinger, F. M. After a Year of Criticism, Whither the Schools? *New York Times*, December 27, 1983, C6.

Heilman, A. W. *Principles and Practices of Teaching Reading* (2nd ed.). Columbus, Ohio: Charles E. Merrill Publishing Co., 1967.

Hirsch, J., and Knittle, J. L. Cellularity of Obese and Nonobese Adipose Tissue (1970), cited in C. B. Corbin Childhood Obesity, in C. B. Corbin (ed.), *A Textbook of Motor Development* (2nd ed.). Dubuque, Iowa: W. C. Brown, 1980, 121–126.

Holt, J. *How Children Fail*. New York: Pitman, 1964.

Horowitz, A. B., and Horowitz, V. A. The Effects of Task-Specific Instructions on the Encoding Activities of Children in Recall and Recognition Tasks (1975), cited in R. S. Siegler, Information Processing Approaches to Development, in P. H. Mussen (ed.), *Handbook of Child Psychology* (4th ed.), vol. 1. New York: Wiley, 1983, 129–213.

Hyde, J. S. How Large Are Cognitive Gender Differences? *American Psychologist*, 1981, *36*, 892–901.

Ilg, F. L., and Ames, L. B. *School Readiness*. New York: Harper and Row, 1972.

Johnson, R. R., Cooper, H., and Chance, J. The Relation of Children's Television Viewing to School Achievement and I.Q. *Journal of Educational Research*, 1982, *76*, 294–297.

Juraschek, W. Middle School Mathematics and Piaget. *Education Digest*, September 1983, 58–60.

Kagan, J. Reflectivity-Impulsivity and Reading Ability in Primary Grade Children. *Child Development*, 1965, *36*, 609–628.

Kail, R., and Hagen, J. W. Memory in Childhood, in B. B. Wolman (ed.), *Handbook of Developmental Psychology*. Englewood Cliffs, N.J.: Prentice-Hall, 1982, 350–367.

Kaplan, P. S. It's the I.Q. Tests That Flunk. *New York Times*, March 13, 1977, 26.

Kegan, R. *The Evolving Self: Problem and Process in Human Development*. Cambridge, Mass.: Harvard University Press, 1982.

Knittle, J. L., and Hirsch, J. Effect of Early Nutrition on the Development of Fat Epididymal Fat Pads: Cellularity and Metabolism. *Journal of Clinical Investigation*, 1968, *47*, 2091.

Kogan, N. Stylistic Variation in Childhood and Adolescence: Creativity, Metaphor and Cognitive Style, in P. H. Mussen (ed.), *Handbook of Child Psychology* (4th ed.). New York: Wiley, 1983.

Kohen-Raz, R. *Psychophysiological Aspects of Cognitive Growth*. New York: Academic Press, 1977.

Kreutzer, M. A., Leonard, C., and Flavell, J. H. An Interview Study of Children's Knowledge About Memory. *Monographs of the Society for Research in Child Development*, 1975, *40*, 1 (serial number 159).

Krogman, W. M. *Child Growth*. Ann Arbor: University of Michigan Press, 1980.

Laboratory of Comparative Human Cognition. Culture and Cognitive Development, in P. H. Mussen (ed.). *Handbook of Child Development* (4th ed.), vol. 1. New York: Wiley, 1983, 295–357.

Lezotte, L. W. Characteristics of Effective Schools and Programs for Realizing Them. *Education Digest*, November, 1982, 27–29.

Licht, B. G., and Dweck, C. S. Determinants of Academic Achievement: The Interaction of Children's Achievement Orientations with Skill Area. *Developmental Psychology*, 1984, *20*, 628–636.

Maehr, M. L. Culture and Achievement Motivation. *American Psychologist*, 1974, *29*, 887–896.

Mandell, C. J., and Fiscus, E. *Understanding Exceptional People*. St. Paul: West Publishing Co., 1981.

Marjoribanks, K., and Walberg, H. J. Ordinal Position, Family Environment and Mental Abilities. *Journal of Social Psychology*, 1975, *95*, 77–84.

Markman, E. M. Realizing That You Don't Understand: A Preliminary Investigation. *Child Development,* 1977, *46,* 986–992.

———. Facilitation of Part-Whole Comparisons by Use of the Collective Noun "Family." *Child Development,* 1973, *44,* 837–840.

Marsh, M. Computer Assisted Instruction in Reading. *Journal of Reading.* May 1983, *26,* 697–701.

Masters, J. C. Developmental Psychology, in M. R. Rosenzweig and L. W. Porter (eds.), *Annual Review of Psychology,* 1981, *32,* 117–153.

Mayer, R. E. *Thinking and Problem Solving: An Introduction to Human Cognition and Learning.* Glenview, Ill.: Scott, Foresman, 1977.

McGuinness, D. How Schools Discriminate Against Boys, in S. Hochman and P. S. Kaplan (eds.), *Readings in Psychology: A Soft Approach* (rev. ed.). Lexington, Mass.: Ginn, 1979, 74–79.

Meichenbaum, D. H., and Goodman, J. Training Impulsive Children to Talk to Themselves: A Means of Developing Self-Control. *Journal of Abnormal Psychology,* 1971, *77,* 115–126.

Mendelson, B. K., and White, D. R. Development of Self-Body in Overweight Youngsters. *Developmental Psychology,* 1985, *21,* 90–97.

Messer, S. Reflection-Impulsivity: Stability and School Failure. *Journal of Educational Psychology,* 1970, *61,* 487–490.

Micklos, J. Reading Achievement in the United States. *Journal of Reading,* 1982, *25,* 760–762.

Milgram, R. M., Milgram, N. A., Rosenbloom, G., and Rabkin, L. Quantity and Quality of Creative Thinking in Children and Adolescents. *Child Development,* 1978, *49,* 385–388.

Moore, R. S., and Moore, D. R. How Early Should They Go to School? *Childhood Education,* June 1976, 13–18.

Moynahan, E. D. The Development of Knowledge Concerning the Effect of Categorization upon Free Recall. *Child Development,* 1973, *44,* 238–246.

Neuman, S. B. Television Viewing and Leisure Reading: A Qualitative Analysis. *Journal of Educational Research,* 1982, *75,* 299–304.

Nicholls, J. G. Quality and Equality in Intellectual Development: The Role of Motivation in Education. *American Psychology,* 1979, *34,* 1071–1084.

Packer, J., and Bain, J. D. Cognitive Style and Teacher-Student Compatibility. *Journal of Educational Psychology,* 1978, *70,* 864–871.

Paris, S. G., and Lindauer, B. K. The Development of Cognitive Skills During Childhood, in B. B. Wolman (ed.), *Handbook of Developmental Psychology.* Englewood Cliffs, N.J.: Prentice-Hall, 1982, 333–350.

Parsons, J. B. The Seductive Computer: Can It Be Resisted? *Education Digest,* November 1983, 46–49.

Paulsen, K., and Johnson, M. Sex Role Attitudes and Mathematical Ability in 4th-, 8th-, and 11th-Grade Students from a High Socioeconomic Area. *Developmental Psychology,* 1983, *19,* 210–214.

Perkins, H. V. *Human Development.* Belmont, CA.: Wadsworth, 1975.

Phillips, J. L. *The Origins of Piaget's Theory* (2nd ed.). San Francisco: Freeman, 1975.

Piaget, J. *Six Psychological Studies.* New York: Vintage, 1967.

———. *The Child's Conception of the World.* Totowa, N.J.: Littlefield, 1965.

———. *The Child's Conception of Number.* London: Humanities Press, 1952.

———. *Judgment and Reasoning in the Young Child.* New York: Harcourt, Brace and World, 1928.

Piaget, J., and Inhelder, B. *The Psychology of the Child.* New York: Basic Books, 1969.

Piaget, J., and Szeminska, A. *The Child's Conception of Number.* New York: Humanities Press, 1952 (originally published 1941).

Posner, J. K. The Development of Mathematical Knowledge in Two West African Societies. *Child Development,* 1982, *53,* 200–208.

Prawat, R. S., and Jarvis, G. Gender Difference as a Factor in Teachers' Perceptions of Students. *Journal of Educational Psychology,* 1980, *72,* 743–749.

Pulaski, M. A. S. *Understanding Piaget: An Introduction to Children's Cognitive Development* (rev. ed.). New York: Harper and Row, 1980.

Purves, A. C. What Is Being Achieved in Reading and Writing. *New York University Educational Quarterly,* 1977, *9,* 8–14.

Reschly, D. J. Psychological Testing in Educational Classification and Placement. *American Psychologist,* 1981, *36,* 1094–1103.

Resnick, L. B. Instructional Psychology, in M. R. *Rosenzweig and L. W. Porter* (eds.). *Annual Review of Psychology,* 1981, *32,* 659–704.

Richardson, S. A., Goodman, U., Hastoff, A. H., and Dornbusch, S. A., Cultural Uniformity in Reaction to Physical Disabilities. *American Sociological Review,* 1961, *26,* 241–247.

Roberts, F. The First, Great, First-Grade Year. *Parents,* September, 1980.

Rogoff, B., Newcombe, N., and Kagan, J. Planfulness and Recognition Memory. *Child Development,* 1974, *45,* 972–977.

Rosenthal, R., and Jacobson, L. *Pygmalion in the Classroom: Teacher Expectations and Pupils' Intellectual Development.* New York: Holt, Rinehart and Winston, 1968.

Ruhland, D., Gold, M., and Feld, S. Role Problems and the Relationship of Achievement to Performance. *Journal of Educational Psychology,* 1978, *70,* 950–959.

Rutter, M. School Effects on Pupil Progress: Research Findings and Policy Implications. *Child Development,* 1983, *54,* 1–29.

———. School Influences on Children's Behavior and Development: The 1979 Kenneth Blackfan Lecture, Children's Hospital Medical Center, Boston. *Pediatrics,* 1980, *65,* 208–220.

Samuels, S. J. A Cognitive Approach to Factors Influencing Reading Comprehension. *Journal of Educational Research,* 1983, *76,* 261–265.

Scarr, S. Testing for Children: Assessment and the Many Determinants of Intellectual Competence. *American Psychologist,* 1981, *36,* 1159–1167.

Schofield, H. L. Sex, Grade Level, and the Relationship Between Mathematics Attitude and Achievement in Children. *Journal of Educational Research,* 1982, *75,* 280–284.

Siegler, R. S. Information Processing Approaches to Development, in P. H. Mussen (ed.), *Handbook of Child Psychology* (4th ed.), vol. 1. New York: Wiley, 1983, 129–213.

Skinner, B. F. *The Technology of Teaching.* New York: Appleton-Century-Crofts, 1968.

Slater, C. Writing: The Experience of One School District. *Journal of Reading,* October 1982, 24–32.

Smart, M. S., and Smart, R. C. *School-Age Children: Development and Relationships* (2nd ed.). New York: Macmillan, 1978.

Staffieri, R. J. A Study of Social Stereotype of Body Image in Children. *Journal of Personality and Social Psychology,* 1967, *7,* 101–104.

Steele, K. J., Battistia, M. T., and Krockover, G. H. The Effects of Microcomputer-Assisted Instruction on the Computer Literacy of Fifth Grade Students. *Journal of Education Research*, 1983, 76, 298–301.

Sternberg, R. J., and Powell, J. S. The Development of Intelligence, in P. H. Mussen (ed.), *Handbook of Child Psychology* (4th ed.), vol. 3. New York: Wiley, 1983, 341–420.

Stewart, O., and Tei, E. Some Implications of Metacognition for Reading Instruction. *Journal of Reading*, 1983, 26, 36–42.

Stigler, A. E., Shin-Ying, L., Lucker, G. W., and Stevenson, H. W. Curriculum and Achievement in Mathematics: A Study of Elementary School Children in Japan, Taiwan, and the United States. *Journal of Educational Psychology*, 1982, 73, 315–322.

Tanner, J. M. *Foetus into Man: Physical Growth from Conception to Maturity.* Cambridge, Mass.: Harvard University Press, 1978.

Vaidya, S., and Chansky, N. Cognitive Development and Cognitive Style as Factors in Mathematics Achievement. *Journal of Educational Psychology*, 1980, 73, 326–330.

Wadsworth, B. Misinterpretations of Piaget's Theory. *Educational Digest*, September 1981, 56–58.

_____. *Piaget's Theory of Cognitive Development.* New York: David McKay, 1971.

Walker, D. F. Reflections of the Educational Potential and Limitations of Microcomputers. *Phi Delta Kappan*, October 1983, 103–107.

Wall, W. D. *Constructive Education for Children.* London: Harrap and Co., 1975.

West, C., and Anderson, T. The Question of Preponderant Causation in Teacher Expectancy Research. *Review of Educational Research*, 1976, 46, 613–630.

Wheeler, T. C. *The Great American Writing Block: Causes and Cures of the New Illiteracy.* New York: Viking, 1979.

White, K. R. The Relation Between Socioeconomic Status and Academic Achievement. *Psychological Bulletin*, 1982, 91, 461–481.

Williams, J. Reading Instruction Today. *American Psychologist*, 1979, 34, 917–923.

Williams, J. P. Teaching Decoding with an Emphasis on Phoneme Analysis and Phoneme Blending. *Journal of Educational Psychology*, 1980, 72, 1–15.

Williams, J. W., and Stith, M. *Middle Childhood: Behavior and Development* (2nd ed.). New York: Macmillan, 1980.

Wingfield, A., and Byrnes, D. L. *The Psychology of Human Memory.* New York: Academic Press, 1981.

Winick, M. Introduction, in M. Winick (ed.), *Childhood Obesity.* New York: Wiley, 1975, 1–12.

Witkin, H. A. Cognitive Styles in the Educational Setting. *New York Education Quarterly*, 1977, 8, 14–21.

Witkin, H. A., and Moore, C. A. Cognitive Style and the Teaching-Learning Process (1974), cited in M. H. Dembo, *Teaching for Learning: Applying Educational Psychology in the Classroom.* Santa Monica, Calif.: Goodyear, 1981.

Yussen, S. R., and Levy, V. M. Developmental Changes in Predicting One's Own Span of Short-Term Memory. *Journal of Experimental Child Psychology*, 1975, 19, 502–508.

Zigler, E., and Berman, W. Discerning the Future of Early Childhood Intervention. *American Psychologist*, 1983, 38, 894–907.

Chapter Twelve

Abarbanel, A. Shared Parenting After Separation and Divorce: A Study of Joint Custody. *American Journal of Orthopsychiatry*, 1979, 49, 320–329.

Andison, F. S. TV Violence and Viewer Aggression: A Cumulation of Study Results 1956–1976. *Public Opinion Quarterly*, 1977, 41, 314–331.

Asher, S. R., Oden, S. L., and Gottman, J. M. Children's Friendship in School Settings (1977), cited in M. Putallaz and J. M. Gottman, Social Skills and Group Acceptance in School Setting, in Asher, S. R., and Gottman, J. M., *The Development of Children's Friendships.* Cambridge: Cambridge University Press, 1981, 116–149.

Asher, S. R., and Renshaw, P. D. Children Without Friends: Social Knowledge and Social Skill Training, in S. R. Asher and J. M. Gottman (eds.), *The Development of Children's Friendships.* Cambridge: Cambridge University Press, 1981, 273–297.

Bandura, A. *Social Learning Theory.* Englewood Cliffs. N.J.: Prentice-Hall, 1977.

Bandura, A., Ross, D., and Ross, S. A. Transmission of Aggression Through Imitation of Aggressive Models. *Journal of Abnormal and Social Psychology*, 1961, 63, 575–582.

Barker, R. G., and Wright, H. F. *The Midwest and Its Children.* New York: Harper and Row, 1955.

Barnett, M. A., King, L. M., and Howard, J. A. Inducing Affect In Self or Other: Effects on Generosity of Children. *Developmental Psychology*, 1979, 15, 164–167.

Barnett, M. A., Matthews, K. A., and Howard, J. A., Relationship Between Competitiveness and Empathy in 6- and 7-Years-Olds. *Developmental Psychology*, 1979, 15, 221–222.

Barrie, J. M. *Peter Pan: A Fantasy in Five Acts.* London: Samuel French, 1956/1928.

Baumrind, D. Current Patterns of Parental Authority. *Developmental Psychology Monographs*, 1979, 41, 1, Part 2.

_____. Current Patterns of Parental Authority. *Developmental Psychology*, 1971, 4, 1–103.

_____. Child Care Practices Anteceding Three Patterns of Preschool Behavior. *Genetic Psychology Monographs*, 1967, 75, 43–88.

Benson, C. S., and Gottman, J. M. Children's Popularity and Peer Social Interaction, (1975) cited in Putallaz, M., and Gottman, J. M. Social Skills and the Group Acceptance, in Asher, S. R., and Gottman, J. M. (ed.), *The Development of Children's Friendships.* N.Y.: Cambridge University Press, 116–150.

Berndt, T. J. Relations Between Social Cognition, Nonsocial Cognition and Social Behavior: The Case of Friendship, in J. H. Flavell, and L. Ross (eds.), *Social Cognitive Development.* Cambridge: Cambridge University Press, 1981.

Bierman, K. L., and Furman, W. The Effects of Social Skills Training and Peer Involvement on the Social Adjustment of Preadolescents. *Child Development*, 1984, 55, 151–162.

Bigelow, B. J. Children's Friendship Expectations: A Cognitive-Developmental Study. *Child Development*, 1977, 48, 246–253.

Blasi, A. Bridging Moral Cognition and Moral Action: A Critical Review of the Literature. *Psychological Bulletin*, 1980, 88, 1–45.

Blatt, M., and Kohlberg, L. The Effects of Classroom Moral Discussion upon Children's Level of Moral Judgment. *Journal of Moral Education*, 1975, 4, 129–161.

Bower, E. M. School-Age Issues of Prevention, in J. D. Noshpitz (ed.), *Basic Handbook of Child Psychiatry*, vol. 4. New York: Basic Books, 1979, 139–149.

Bressler, M. Kohlberg and the Resolution of Moral Conflict. *New York University Education Quarterly*, Winter 1976, 7, 2–9.

Bukowski, W. M., and Newcomb, A. F. Stability and Determinants of Sociometric Status and Friendship Choice: A Longitudinal Perspective. *Developmental Psychology,* 1984, *20,* 941–953.

Burns, R. B. *The Self-Concept: Theory, Measurement, Development and Behaviour.* London: Longman, 1979.

Burton, R. V. Generality of Honesty Reconsidered. *Psychological Review,* 1963, *70,* 481–499.

Busch-Rossnagel, and Vance, A. K. The Impact of the Schools on Social and Emotional Development, in B. B. Wolman (ed.), *Handbook of Developmental Psychology.* Englewood Cliffs, N.J.: Prentice-Hall, 1982, 452–471.

Byrne, D. Interpersonal Attraction and Attitude Similarity. *Journal of Abnormal and Social Psychology,* 1961, *62,* 713–715.

Cairns, R. B. *Social Development: The Origins and Plasticity of Interchanges.* San Francisco: Freeman, 1979.

Carroll, J. L., and Rest, J. R. Moral Development, in B. B. Wolman (ed.), *Handbook of Developmental Psychology.* Englewood Cliffs, N.J.: Prentice-Hall, 1982, 434–452.

Carter, D. B., and Patterson, C. J. Sex Roles as Social Conventions: The Development of Children's Conceptions of Sex-Role Stereotypes. *Developmental Psychology,* 1982, *18,* 812–825.

Chandler, M., and Boyes, M. Social-Cognitive Development, in B. B. Wolman (ed.). *Handbook of Developmental Psychology.* Englewood Cliffs, N.J.: Prentice-Hall, 1982, 387–400.

Cherlin, A. The Trends: Marriage, Divorce, Remarriage (1981), in Skolnick, A. S., and Skolnick, J. H., Family in Transition (4th ed.). Boston: Little, Brown, 1983, 128–137.

_____. Remarriage as an Incomplete Institution (1978), in Skolnick, A. S., and Skolnick, J. H. *Family in Transition* (4th ed.). Boston: Little, Brown, 1983, 388–402.

Clarizio, H. F., and McCoy, G. F. *Behavior Disorders in Children* (2nd ed.). New York: Crowell, 1976.

Cline, V. B., Croft, R. G., and Courrier, S. Desensitization of Children to Television Violence. *Journal of Personality and Social Psychology,* 1973, *27,* 360–365.

Comstock, G. New Emphases in Research on the Effects of Television and Film Violence, in E. L. Palmer and A. Dorr (eds.), *Children and the Faces of Television: Teaching, Violence, Selling.* New York: Academic Press, 1980, 129–144.

Coopersmith, S. *The Antecedents of Self-Esteem.* San Francisco: Freeman, 1967.

Corsaro, W. A. Friendship in the Nursery School: Social Organization in a Peer Environment, in S. R. Asher and J. M. Gottman (eds.), *The Development of Children's Friendships.* Cambridge, Mass.: Cambridge University Press, 1981, 207–242.

Cullinan, D., and Epstein, M. H. Behavior Disorders, in N. G. Haring (ed.), *Exceptional Children and Youth* (3rd ed.). Columbus, Ohio: Charles E. Merrill, 1982, 207–239.

Damon, W. *Social and Personality Development.* New York: W. W. Norton, 1983.

Damon, W., and Hart, D. The Development of Self-Understanding from Infancy Through Adolescence. *Child Development,* 1982, *53,* 841–864.

Davis. G. A. *Educational Psychology: Theory and Practice.* Reading, Mass.: Addison-Wesley, 1983.

Dion, K. K. Young Children's Stereotyping of Facial Attractiveness. *Developmental Psychology,* 1973, *9,* 183–188.

Dodge, K. A. Social Cognition and Children's Aggressive Behavior. *Child Development,* 1980, *51,* 162–170.

Dodge, K. A., and Frame, C. L. Social Cognitive Biases and Deficits in Aggressive Boys. *Child Development,* 1982, *53,* 620–635.

Drabman, R. S., and Thomas, M. H. Does TV Violence Breed Indifference? *Journal of Communication,* 1975, *25,* 86–89.

Dweck, C. S., and Bush, E. S. Sex Differences in Learned Helplessness, 1: Differential Debilitation with Peer and Adult Evaluators. *Developmental Psychology,* 1976, *12,* 147–156.

Dweck, C. S., Davidson, W., Nelson, S., and Enna, B. Sex Differences in Learned Helplessness, 2: The Contingencies of Evaluative Feedback in the Classroom, and 3: An Experimental Analysis. *Developmental Psychology,* 1978, *14,* 268–276.

Edwards, C. P. The Comparative Study of the Development of Moral Judgment and Reasoning, in R. Monroe, and B. B. Whiting (eds.). *Handbook of Cross-Cultural Human Development.* New York: Garland, 1977.

Edwards, C. P., and Lewis, M. Young Children's Concepts of Social Relations: Social Functions and Social Objects, in M. Lewis and L. A. Rosenblum (eds.), *The Child and Its Family: Genesis of Behavior,* vol. 2. New York: Plenum, 1979.

Eidelberg, L. (ed.), *Encyclopedia of Psychoanalysis.* New York: The Free Press, 1968.

Eisenberg-Berg, N. Development of Children's Prosocial Moral Judgment. *Developmental Psychology,* 1979, *15,* 128–138.

Eisenberg-Berg, N., and Neal, C. Children's Moral Reasoning About Their Own Spontaneous Prosocial Behavior. *Developmental Psychology,* 1979, *15,* 228–230.

Elkind, D. *A Sympathetic Understanding of the Child: Birth to Sixteen* (2nd ed.). Boston: Allyn and Bacon, 1978.

Elkind, D., and Dabek, R. F. Personal Injury and Property Damage in Moral Judgments of Children. *Child Development,* 1977, *48,* 518–522.

Emery, R. E. Interparental Conflict and the Children of Discord and Divorce. *Psychological Bulletin,* 1982, *92,* 310–330.

Erikson, E. H. *Childhood and Society.* New York: W. W. Norton, 1963/1950.

Eron, L. D. Parent-Child Interaction, Television Violence, and Aggression of Children. *American Psychologist,* 1982, *37,* 197–212.

Eron, L. D., Huesmann, L. R., Brice, P., Fischer, P., and Mermelstein, R. Age Trends in the Development of Aggression, Sex Typing, and Related Television Habits. *Developmental Psychology,* 1983, *19,* 71–78.

Eron, L. D., Walder, L. O., and Lefkowitz, M. M. *Learning of Aggression in Children.* Boston: Little, Brown, 1971.

Fine, M. A. Moreland, J. R., and Schwebel, A. I. Long-Term Effects of Divorce on Parent-Child Relationships. *Developmental Psychology,* 1983, *5,* 703–714.

Ferguson, T. J., and Rule, B. G. Influence of Inferential Set, Outcome Intent, and Outcome Severity on Children's Moral Judgments. *Developmental Psychology,* 1982, *18,* 843–851.

Freud, S. *New Introductory Lectures on Psychoanalysis.* New York: W. W. Norton, 1965/1933.

Furman, W., and Bierman, K. L. Children's Conceptions of Friendship: A Multimethod Study of Developmental Changes. *Developmental Psychology,* 1984, *20,* 925–932.

Furman, W., and Bierman, K. L. Developmental Changes in Young Children's Conception of Friendship. *Child Development,* 1983, *54,* 549–556.

Garrett, C. S., Ein, P. L., and Tremaine, L. S. The Development of Gender Stereotyping of Adult Occupations in Elementary School Children, *Child Development,* 1977, *48,* 507–512.

Gerbner, G., and Gross, L. The Violent Face of Television and Its Lessons, in E. L. Palmer and A. Dorr (eds.). *Children and the Faces of Television: Teaching, Violence, Selling.* New York: Academic Press, 1980, 149–162.

Gottlieb, D. E., Taylor, S. E., and Ruderman, A. Cognitive Bases of Children's Moral Judgments. *Developmental Psychology,* 1977, *13,* 547–556.

Greif, J. B. Fathers, Children, and Joint Custody. *American Journal of Orthopsychiatry,* 1979, *49,* 311–320.

Gronlund, N. E. *Sociometry in the Classroom.* New York: Harper, 1959.

Hallinan, M. T. Recent Advances in Sociometry, in Asher, S. R., and Gottman, J. M. (ed.), *The Development of Children's Friendships.* N.Y.: Cambridge University Press, 1981, 91–116.

Harter, S. Developmental Perspectives on the Self-System, in E. M. Hetherington (ed.), *Handbook of Child Psychology.* New York: Wiley, 1983, 103–197.

Hartshorne, H., and May, M. A. *Studies in the Nature of Character,* vol. 1. New York: Macmillan, 1928.

Hartup, W. W. Peer Relations, in P. H. Mussen (ed.), *Handbook of Child Psychology: Socialization, Personality, and Social Development,* vol. 4 (4th ed.). New York: Wiley, 1983, 103–197.

————. The Social Worlds of Childhood. *American Psychologist* 1979, *34,* 944–951.

————. Aggression in Childhood: Developmental Perspectives. *American Psychologist,* 1974, *29,* 336–341.

————. Aggression in Childhood: Developmental Perspectives, in P. Mussen (ed.), *Carmichael's Manual of Child Psychology* (3rd ed.). New York: Wiley, 1970.

Hay, D. F., and Ross, H. S. The Social Nature of Early Conflict. *Child Development,* 1982, *53,* 105–113.

Hayes, D. Cognitive Bases for Liking and Disliking Among Preschool Children. *Child Development,* 1978, *49,* 906–909.

Hess, R. D., and Camara, K. A. Post-Divorce Family Relationships as Mediating Variables in the Consequences of Divorce for Children. *Journal of Social Issues,* 1979, *35,* 4.

Hetherington, E. M. Divorce: A Child's Perspective. *American Psychologist,* 1979, *34,* 851–859.

————. Effects of Father Absence on Personality: Development in Adolescent Daughters. *Developmental Psychology,* 1972, *7,* 313–321.

Hoffman, M. L. Development of Moral Thought, Feeling, and Behavior. *American Psychologist,* 1979, *34,* 958–967.

————. Empathy, Its Development and Prosocial Implications, in C. B. Keasey (ed.), *Nebraska Symposium on Motivation,* vol. 25. Lincoln, Neb.: University of Nebraska Press, 1978.

Huesmann, L. R., Lagerspetz, K., and Eron, L. D. Intervening Variables in TV Violence- Aggression Relation: Evidence from Two Countries. *Developmental Psychology,* 1984, *20,* 746–776.

Huston, A. C. Sex-Typing, in E. M. Hetherington (ed.), *Handbook of Child Psychology* (4th ed.), vol. 4. New York: Wiley, 1983, 387–469.

Jensen, L. C. *Adolescence: Theories, Research, Applications.* St. Paul, Minnesota: West Publishing Co., 1985.

Kalter, N., and Rembar, J. The Significance of a Child's Age at the Time of Parental Divorce. *American Journal of Orthopsychiatry,* 1981, *51,* 85–100.

Kaplan, P. S., and Stein, J. *Psychology of Adjustment.* Belmont, Calif., Wadsworth Pub. Co., 1984.

Keasey, C. B. Children's Developing Awareness and Usage of Intentionality and Motivation, in C. B. Keasey (ed.), *Nebraska Symposium on Motivation,* vol. 25. Lincoln, Neb.: University of Nebraska Press, 1978.

Kelly, J. B., and Wallerstein, J. S. The Effects of Parental Divorce: Experiences of the Child in Early Latency. *American Journal of Orthopsychiatry,* 1976, *46,* 20–33.

Kline, P. *Fact and Fantasy in Freudian Theory.* London: Methuen, 1972.

Kohlberg, L. Moral Stages and Moralization: The Cognitive-Developmental Approach, in T. Lickona (ed.), *Moral Development and Behavior.* New York: Holt, Rinehart and Winston, 1976.

————. Stage and Sequence: The Cognitive-Developmental Approach to Socialization, in D. Goslin (ed.), *Handbook of Socialization Theory and Research.* Skokie, Ill.: Rand-McNally, 1969.

Kohlberg, L., Colby, A., Gibbs, J., Speicher-Dubin, B., and Powers, C. *Assessing Moral Development Stages: A Manual.* Cambridge, Mass.: Center for Moral Education, 1978.

Kohlberg, L., and Kramer, R. Continuities and Discontinuities in Childhood and Adult Moral Development. *Human Development,* 1969, *12,* 83–120.

Krebs, D., and Gillmore, J. The Relationship Among the First Stages of Cognitive Development, Role-Taking Abilities, and Moral Development. *Child Development,* 1982, *53,* 877–886.

Kurdek, L. A. An Integrative Perspective on Children's Divorce Adjustment. *American Psychologist,* 1981, *36,* 856–866.

Kurdek, L. A., Blisk, D., and Siesky, A. E. Correlates of Children's Long-Term Adjustment to Their Parents' Divorce. *Developmental Psychology,* 1981, *17,* 565–580.

Kurtines, W., and Greif, E. B. The Development of Moral Thought: Review and Evaluation of Kohlberg's Approach. *Psychological Bulletin,* 1974, *81,* 453–470.

Lee, P. C., and Gropper, N. B. Sex-Role Culture and Educational Practice. *Harvard Educational Review,* 1974, *42,* (no. 3), 369–410.

Lefkowitz, M. M., and Tesiny, E. P. Dejection and Depression: Prospective and Contemporaneous Analyses. *Developmental Psychology,* 1984, *20,* 776–786.

Leinhardt, G., Seewald, A. M., and Engel, M. Learning What's Taught: Sex Differences in Instruction. *Journal of Educational Psychology,* 1979, *71,* (no. 4), 432–439.

Leon, M. Rules in Children's Moral Judgments: Integration of Intent, Damage and Rationale Information. *Developmental Psychology,* 1982, *18,* 835–842.

Livesley, W. J., and Bromley, D. C. *Person Perception in Childhood and Adolescence.* London: Wiley, 1973.

Loeb, R. C., Horst, L., and Horton, P. J. Family Interaction Patterns Associated with Self-Esteem in Preadolescent Girls and Boys. *Merrill-Palmer Quarterly,* 1980, *26,* 203–217.

Maccoby, E. E. *Social Development: Psychological Growth and the Parent-Child Relationship.* New York: Harcourt Brace Jovanovich, 1980.

Maccoby, E. E., and Jacklin, C. N. Sex Differences in Aggression: A Rejoinder and Reprise. *Child Development,* 1980, *51,* 964–980.

————. *The Psychology of Sex Differences.* Stanford, Calif.: Stanford University Press, 1974.

Maccoby, E. E., and Martin, J. A. Socialization in the Context for Social Development, in E. M. Hetherington (ed.), *Handbook of Child Development,* vol. 4. New York: Wiley, 1983, 1–103.

MacKinnon, C. E., Brody, G. H., and Stoneman, Z. The Effects of Divorce and Maternal Employment on the Home Environments of Preschool Children. *Child Development*, 1982, *53*, 1392–1399.

Masters, J. C., and Furman, W. Popularity, Individual Friendship Selection, and Specific Peer Interaction Among Children. *Developmental Psychology*, 1981, *17*, 344–350.

McCarthy, E. D., Langner, T. S., Gerstein, J. C., Eisenberg, J. G., and Porzeck, L. Violence and Behavior Disorders, *Journal of Communication*, 1975, *25*, 71–85.

Minuchin, P. P., and Shapiro, E. K. The School as a Context for Social Development, in E. M. Hetherington (ed.), *Handbook of Child Psychology: Socialization, Personality and Social Development*, (4th ed.), vol. 4. New York: Wiley, 1983, 197–275.

Mussen, P. H., and Eisenberg-Berg, N. *Roots of Caring, Sharing and Helping*. San Francisco: Freeman, 1977.

Nadelman, L. Sex Identity in American Children: Memory, Knowledge and Preference Tests. *Developmental Psychology*, 1974, *10*, 413–417.

National Coalition on TV Violence Newsletter. March/April, 1984.

Newman, P. R. The Peer Group, in B. B. Wolman (ed.), *Handbook of Developmental Psychology*. Englewood Cliffs, N.J.: 1982, Prentice-Hall, 526–536.

Newson, J., and Newson, E. Seven Years Old in the Home Environment (1976), cited in Huston, A. C., Sex-Typing, in E. M. Hetherington (ed.), *Handbook of Child Psychology* (4th ed.), vol. 4. New York: Wiley, 1983, 387–467.

Nisan, M., and Kohlberg, L. Universality and Variation in Moral Judgment: A Longitudinal and Cross-Sectional Study in Turkey. *Child Development*, 1982, *53*, 865–876.

Olweus, D. Development of Stable Aggressive Reaction Patterns in Males, in R. Blanchard and C. Blanchard, *Advances in the Study of Aggression*, vol. 1. New York: Academic Press, 1982.

———. Stability and Aggressive Reaction Patterns in Males: A Review, *Psychological Bulletin*, 1979, *86*, 852–875.

———. Aggression and Peer Acceptance in Adolescent Boys: Two Short-Term Longitudinal Studies of Ratings. *Child Development*, 1977, *48*, 1301–1313.

Parke, R. D., and Slaby, R. G. The Development of Aggression, in E. M. Hetherington (ed.), *Handbook of Child Psychology: Socialization, Personality and Social Development*, (4th ed.), vol. 4. New York: Wiley, 1983, 547–643.

Patterson, G. R. A Performance Theory for Coercive Family Interaction, in R. Cairns (ed.), *Social Interaction: Methods, Analysis, and Evaluations*. Hillsdale, N.J.: Erlbaum, 1979.

Patterson, G. R., and Cobb, J. A. A Dyadic Analysis of "Aggressive" Behaviors, in J. P. Hill (eds.), *Minnesota Symposium on Child Psychology*, vol. 5. Minneapolis: University of Minnesota Press, 1971.

Peterson, L. Influence of Age, Task Competence, and Responsibility Focus on Children's Altruism. *Developmental Psychology*, 1983, *19*, 141–148.

Piaget, J. *The Moral Judgment of the Child* (M. Gabain, trans.). New York: The Free Press, 1965 (originally published 1932).

Powell, G. J. Psychosocial Development: Eight to Ten Years, in J. D. Noshpitz (ed.), *Basic Handbook of Child Psychiatry*. New York: Basic Books, 1979, 190–199.

Prawat, R. S., and Jarvis, R. Gender Differences as a Factor in Teacher's Perceptions of Students. *Journal of Educational Psychology*, 1980, *72*, 743–749.

Putallaz, M., and Gottman, J. M., Social Skills and Group Acceptance, in S. R. Asher and J. M. Gottman (eds.), *The Development of Children's Friendships*. Cambridge: Cambridge University Press, 1981, 116–149.

Reaves, J. Y., and Roberts, A. The Effect of Type of Information on Children's Attachment to Peers. *Child Development*, 1983, *54*, 1024–1031.

Rest, J. R. Morality, in P. H. Mussen (ed.), *Handbook of Child Psychology: Cognitive Development* (4th ed.), vol. 3 New York: Wiley, 1983, 556–630.

Rheingold, H. L., Hay, D. F., and West, M. J. Sharing in the Second Year of Life. *Child Development*, 1976, *47*, 1148–1158.

Richardson, S. A., Goodman, U., Hastorf, A. H., and Dornbusch, S. A. Cultural Uniformity in Reaction to Physical Disabilities. *American Sociological Review*, 1961, *26*, 241–247.

Rotenberg, K. J. Children's Use of Intentionality in Judgements of Character and Disposition. *Child Development*, 1980, *51*, 282–284.

Rubin, Z. *Children's Friendships*. Cambridge, Mass.: Harvard University Press, 1980.

Rubinstein, E. A. Television and Behavior: Research Conclusions of the 1982 NIMH Report and Their Policy Implications. *American Psychologist*, 1983, *38*, 820–826.

———. Television Violence: A Historical Perspective, in E. L. Palmer and A. Dorr (eds.), *Children and the Faces of Television: Teaching, Violence, Selling*. New York: Academic Press, 1980, 113–125.

Sagi, A., and Hoffman, M. L. Empathic Distress in the Newborn. *Developmental Psychology*, 1976, *12*, 175–176.

Schofield, J. W. Complementary and Conflicting Identities: Images and Interaction in an Interracial School, in S. R. Asher and J. M. Gottman (eds.), *The Development of Children's Friendships*. Cambridge: Cambridge University Press, 1981, 53–91.

Sears, R. R., Maccoby, E. E., and Lewin, H. *Patterns of Child Rearing*. Evanston, Ill.: Row and Peterson, 1957.

Selman, R. L. The Child as a Friendship Philosopher, in S. R. Asher and J. M. Gottman (eds.), *The Development of Children's Friendships*. Cambridge, Mass.: Cambridge University Press, 1981, 242–273.

Serbin, L. A., O'Leary, K. D., Kent, R. N., and Tonick, I. J. A Comparison of Teacher Response to the Preacademic and Problem Behavior of Boys and Girls. *Child Development*, 1973, *44*, 796–804.

Shantz, C. U. Social Cognition, in P. H. Mussen (ed.), *Handbook of Child Psychology: Cognitive Development*, (4th ed.), vol. 4 New York: Wiley, 1983, 495–556.

Shantz, D. W., and Voydanoff, D. A. Situational Effects on Retaliatory Aggression at Three Age Levels. *Child Development*, 1973, *44*, 149–153.

Shepherd-Look, D. L. Sex Differentiation and the Development of Sex Roles, in B. B. Wolman (ed.), in *Handbook of Developmental Psychology*. Englewood Cliffs, N.J.: Prentice-Hall, 1982, 403–434.

Shigetomi, C. C., Hartmann, D. P., and Gelfand, D. M. Sex Differences in Children's Altruistic Behavior and Reputations for Helpfulness. *Developmental Psychology*, 1981, *17*, 434–438.

Shipler, D. K. *Russia: Broken Idols, Solemn Dreams*. New York: Random House, 1983.

Simner, M. L. Newborn's Response to the Cry of Another Infant. *Developmental Psychology*, 1971, *5*, 136–150.

Singer, J. L., and Singer, D. G. Psychologists Look at Television: Cognitive, Developmental, Personality, and Social Policy Implications. *American Psychologist*, 1983, *38*, 826–835.

Skolnick, A. S., and Skolnick, J. H. *Family in Transition* (4th ed.). Boston: Little, Brown, 1983.

Snarey, J. R., Reimer, J., and Kohlberg, L. Development of Social-Moral Reasoning Among Kibbutz Adolescents: A Longitudinal Cross-Cultural Study. *Developmental Psychology*, 1985, *21*, 3–18.

Solnit, A. J., Call, J. D., and Feinstein, C. B. Psychosexual Development: Five to Ten Years, in J. D. Noshpitz (ed.), *Basic Handbook of Child Psychiatry.* New York: Basic Books, 1979, 184–190.

Spurlock, J., and Lawrence, L. E. The Black Child, in J. D. Noshpitz (ed.), *Basic Handbook of Child Psychiatry*, vol. 1. New York: Basic Books, 1979, 248–256.

Stein, A. H., Pohly, S. R., and Mueller, E. The Influence of Masculine, Feminine, and Neutral Tasks on Children's Achievement Behavior, Expectancies of Success and Attainment Values. *Child Development*, 1971, *42*, 196–207.

Surber, C. F. Separable Effects of Motives, Consequences, and Presentation Order on Children's Moral Judgments. *Developmental Psychology*, 1982, *18*, 257–266.

Surgeon General's Scientific Advisory Committee on Television and Social Behavior. *Television and Growing Up: The Impact of Violence.* Washington, D.C.: U.S. Government Printing Office, 1972.

Thomas, M. H., Horton, R. W., Lippincott, E. C., and Drabman, R. S. Desensitization to Portrayals of Real-Life Aggression as a Function of Exposure to Television Violence. *Journal of Personality and Social Psychology*, 1977, *35*, 450–458.

Tieger, T. On the Biological Basis of Sex Differences in Aggression. *Child Development*, 1980, *51*, 943–963.

Tuma, N., and Hallinan, M. T. The Effects of Sex, Race and Achievement in School Children's Friendships. *Social Forces*, 1979, *57*, 1265–1285.

Turiel, E. Distinct Conceptual and Developmental Domains: Social-Convention and Morality in C. B. Keasey (ed.), *Nebraska Symposium on Motivation* vol 25. Lincoln, NE.: University of Nebraska Press, 1978.

Turiel, E. An Experimental Test of the Sequentiality of Developmental Stages in the Child's Moral Judgment. *Journal of Personality and Social Psychology*, 1966, *3*, 611–618.

Visher, J. S., and Visher, E. B. Stepfamilies and Stepchildren, in J. D. Noshpitz (ed.), *Handbook of Child Psychiatry.* New York: Basic Books, 1979, 347–354.

Vosk, B., Forehand, R., Parker, J. B., and Rickard, K. A Multimethod Comparison of Popular and Unpopular Children. *Developmental Psychology*, 1982, *18*, 571–575.

Walker, L. J. Sources of Cognitive Conflict for Stage Transition in Moral Development. *Developmental Psychology*, 1983, *19*, 103–110.

_____. The Sequentiality of Kohlberg's Stages of Moral Development. *Child Development*, 1982, *53*, 1330–1336.

Walker, L. J., De Vries, B., and Bichard, S. L. The Hierarchical Nature of Stages of Moral Development. *Developmental Psychology*, 1984, *20*, 960–967.

Walker, L. J., and Richards, B. S. Stimulating Transitions in Moral Reasoning as a Function of Stage of Cognitive Development. *Developmental Psychology*, 1979, *15*, 95–104.

Wallerstein, J. S. Children of Divorce: The Psychological Tasks of the Child. *American Journal of Orthopsychiatry*, 1983, *53*, 230–243.

Wallerstein, J. S., and Kelly, J. Effects of Divorce on the Visiting Father-Child Relationship. *American Journal of Psychiatry*, 1980, *137*, 1534–1539.

_____. Divorce and Children, in J. D. Noshpitz (ed.), *Basic Handbook of Child Psychiatry*, vol. 4. New York: Basic Books, 1979, 339–347.

White, C. B. Moral Development in Bahamian School Children: A Cross-Cultural Examination of Kohlberg's Stages of Moral Reasoning. *Developmental Psychology*, 1975, *11*, 535–536.

Whiting, B. B., and Whiting, J. W. M. *Children of Six Cultures.* Cambridge, Mass.: Harvard University Press, 1975.

Williams, J. E., Bennett, S. M., and Best, D. L. Awareness and Expression of Sex Stereotypes in Young Children. *Developmental Psychology*, 1975, *11*, 635–642.

Williams, J. W., and Stith, M. *Middle Childhood: Behavior and Development* (2nd ed.). New York: Macmillan, 1980.

Yarrow, M. R., Waxler, C. Z., and Chapman, M. Children's Prosocial Dispositions and Behavior, in P. H. Mussen (ed.), *Handbook of Child Psychology* (4th ed.), vol 4. New York: Wiley, 1983, 469–547.

Chapter Thirteen

Abeson, A., and Zettel, J. The End of the Quiet Revolution: The Education for All Handicapped Children Act of 1975. *Exceptional Children*, 1977, *44*, 114–130.

Adelson, E., and Fraiberg, S. Gross Motor Development in Infants Blind from Birth. *Child Development*, 1974, *45*, 114–126.

Ashcroft, S. C., and Zambone-Ashley, K. Mainstreaming Children with Visual Impairments. *Journal of Research and Development*, 1980, *13*, 22–36.

Austin, A. B., and Draper, D. C. Peer Relationships of the Academically Gifted: A Review. *Gifted Child Quarterly*, 1981, *25*, 129–133.

Azrin, N. H., Nunn, R. G., and Frantz, S. E. Treatment of Hairpulling (Trichotillomania): A Comparative Study of Habit Reversal and Negative Practice Training. *Journal of Behavior Therapy and Experimental Psychiatry*, 1980, *11*, 13–21.

Barraga, N. *Visual Handicaps and Learning: A Developmental Approach.* Belmont, Calif.: Wadsworth, 1976.

_____. Utilization of Sensory-Perceptual Abilities, in B. Lowenfeld (ed.), *The Visually Handicapped Child in School.* New York: John Day, 1973.

_____. *Increased Visual Behavior in Low Vision Children.* New York: American Foundation for the Blind, 1964.

Bloom, B. S. The Role of Gifts and Markers in the Development of Talent. *Exceptional Children*, 1982, *48*, 510–521.

Bower, T. G. R. *A Primer of Infant Development.* San Francisco: Freeman, 1977.

Brickey, M., and Campbell, K. Fast Food Employment for Moderately and Mildly Mentally Retarded Adults. *Mental Retardation*, 1981, *19*, 113–116.

Bryan, T. H. Peer Popularity of Learning Disabled Children: A Replication. *Journal of Learning Disabilities*, 1976, *9*, 307–311.

Bryan, T. H., and Bryan, J. H. Social Interactions of Learning Disabled Children. *Learning Disability Quarterly*, 1978, *1*, 33–38.

Burns, R. B. *The Self-Concept: Theory, Measurement, Development and Behaviour.* London: Longman, 1979.

Busse, T. V., and Mansfield, R. S. The Blooming of Creative Scientists: Early, Late and Otherwise. *Gifted Child Quarterly*, 1981, 25, 63–66.

Campione, J. C., and Brown, A. Memory and Metamemory Development in Educable Retarded Children, in R. V. Kail and J. W. Hagen (eds.), *Perspectives on the Development of Memory and Cognition*. Hillsdale, N.J.: Erlbaum, 1977.

Cermak, L. S. Information Processing Deficits in Children with Learning Disabilities. *Journal of Learning Disabilities*, 1983, 16, 599–605.

Chess, S., and Fernandez, P. Do Deaf Children Have a Typical Personality? *Journal of the American Academy of Child Psychiatry*, 1980, 19, 654–664.

Cohen, R. L. Reading Disabled Children Are Aware of Their Cognitive Deficits. *Journal of Learning Disabilities*, 1983, 16, 286–289.

Cromer, R. F. Receptive Language in the Mentally Retarded: Processes and Diagnostic Distinctions (1974), cited in S. A. Kirk and J. J. Gallagher, *Educating Exceptional Children* (4th ed.). Boston: Houghton Mifflin, 1983.

_____. Conservation by the Congenitally Blind. *British Journal of Psychology*, 1973, 82, 241–250.

Cruickshank, W. M. Myths and Realities in Learning Disabilities. *Journal of Learning Disabilities*, 1977, 137–145.

Cruickshank, W. M., and Paul, J. L. The Psychological Characteristics of Children with Learning Disabilities, in W. M. Cruickshank (ed.), *Psychology of Exceptional Children and Youth*. Englewood Cliffs, N.J.: Prentice-Hall, 1980, 497–542.

Davis, J. M., Shepard, N. T., Stelmachowicz, P. G., and Gorga, M. P. Characteristics of Hearing-Impaired Children in the Public Schools. *Journal of Speech and Hearing Disorders*, 1981, 25, 130–143.

DeMott, R. M. Visual Impairments, in N. G. Haring (ed.), *Exceptional Children and Youth*. Columbus, Ohio: Charles E. Merrill, 1982, 271–299.

Dettmer, P. Improving Teacher Attitudes Toward Characteristics of the Creatively Gifted. *Gifted Child Quarterly*, 1981, 25, 11–16.

Federal Register. Procedures for Evaluating Specific Learning Disabilities. Washington, D.C.: Department of Health, Education and Welfare, December 29, 1977, 65,083.

Feingold, B. F. Hyperkinesis and Learning Disabilities Linked to Artificial Food Flavors and Colors. *American Journal of Nursing*, 1975, 75, 797–803.

Feldhusen, H. Teaching Gifted, Creative, and Talented Students in an Individualized Classroom. *Gifted Child Quarterly*, 1981, 25, 109–111.

Fischer, M., Rolf, J. E., Hasazi, J. E., and Cummings, L. Follow-Up of a Preschool Epidemiological Sample: Cross-Age Continuities and Predictions of Later Adjustment with Internalizing and Externalizing Dimensions of Behavior. *Child Development*, 1984, 55, 137–150.

Foss, G., and Peterson, S. Social Interpersonal Skills Relevant to Job Tenure for Mentally Retarded Adults. *Mental Retardation*, 1981, 19, 103–106.

Fraiberg, S. *Insights from the Blind*. New York: Basic Books, 1977.

Gadow, K. D. Effects of Stimulant Drugs on Academic Hyperactive and Learning Disabled Children. *Journal of Learning Disabilities*, 1983, 16, 290–299.

Gallaudet College. *Deafness Briefs: Information on Deaf Adults*. Washington, D.C.: Gallaudet College, 1975.

Gearheart, B. R., and Weishahn, M. W. *The Exceptional Student In The Regular Classroom* (3rd ed.). St. Louis: Times Mirror/ Mosby, 1984.

Gelfand, D. M., Jenson, W. R., and Drew, C. J. *Understanding Child Behavior Disorders*. New York: Holt, Rinehart and Winston, 1982.

Gifted and Talented Children's Act of 1978, P.L.-95-561, Section 902.

Gold, M. Research on the Vocational Habilitation of the Retarded: The Present and the Future, in N. Ellis (ed.), *International Review of Research in Mental Retardation*. New York: Academic Press, 1973.

Gottlieb, J., and Budoff, M. Social Acceptability of Retarded Children in Nongraded Schools Differing in Architecture. *American Journal of Mental Deficiency*, 1973, 78, 15–19.

Green, W. W. Hearing Disability, in A. E. Blackhurst and W. H. Berdine (eds.), *An Introduction to Special Education*. Boston: Little, Brown, 1981, 150–202.

Gresham, F. M. Misguided Mainstreaming: The Case for Social Skills Training with Handicapped Children. *Exceptional Children*, 1982, 48, 422–430.

Grossman, H. J. (ed.), *Manual on Terminology and Classification in Mental Retardation*. Washington, D.C.: American Association on Mental Deficiency, 1973 and 1977 editions.

Guilford, J. P. *The Nature of Human Intelligence*. New York: McGraw-Hill, 1967.

Hagin, R. A., and Silver, A. A. Learning Disability: Definition, Diagnosis, and Prevention. *New York University Education Quarterly*, Winter 1977, 2, 9–16.

Hallahan, D. P., and Kauffman, J. M. *Exceptional Children: Introduction to Special Education* (2nd ed.). Englewood Cliffs, N.J.: Prentice-Hall, 1982.

Hardman, M. L., Drew, C. J., and Egan, M. W. *Human Exceptionality: Society, School and Family*. Boston: Allyn and Bacon, 1984.

Haring, N. G. (ed.). *Exceptional Children and Youth*. Columbus, Ohio: Charles E. Merrill, 1982.

Harris, M. The Child with Down's Syndrome. *Daycare and Early Education*. May-June, 1977.

Hart, V. Crippling Conditions, in M. S. Lilly (ed.), *Children with Exceptional Needs: A Survey of Special Education*. New York: Holt, Rinehart and Winston, 1979, 195–238.

Hatlen, P. Priorities in Educational Programs for Visually Handicapped Children and Youth. *Division for the Visually Handicapped Newsletter*, Winter 1976, 8–11.

Hechtman, L. and Weiss, G. Long-Term Outcome of Hyperactive Children. *American Journal of Orthopsychiatry*, 1983, 53, 532–541.

Henderson, F. Communication Skills, in B. Lowenfeld (ed.), *The Visually Handicapped Child in School*. New York: John Day, 1973.

Heward, W. L., and Orlansky, M. D. Exceptional Children (2nd ed.). Columbus, OH.: Charles E. Merrill, 1984.

Hirst, M. A. Young People with Disabilities: What Happens After 16? *Child Care, Health and Development*, 1983, 9, 273–284.

Holborow, P., Elkins, J., and Berry, P. The Effect of the Feingold Diet on "Normal" School Children. *Journal of Learning Disabilities*, 1981, 14, 143–147.

Jan, J. E., Freeman, R. D., and Scott, E. P. *Visual Impairment in Children and Adolescents*. New York: Grune and Stratton, 1977.

Johnson, D. W., and Johnson, R. T. Integrating Handicapped Students into the Mainstream. *Exceptional Children*, October 1980, 47, 335–343.

Johnson, J. A. The Etiology of Hyperactivity. *Exceptional Children*, 1981, 47, 348–354.

Johnson, R. T. Integrating Severely Adaptively Handicapped Seventh-Grade Students into Constructive Relationships with Nonhandicapped Peers in Science Class. *American Journal of Mental Deficiency*, 1983, 87, 611–618.

Jordan, I. K., Gustason, G., and Rosen, R. An Update on Communication Trends in Programs for the Deaf. *American Annals of the Deaf*, 1979, 124, 350–357.

Juntune, J. Myth: The Gifted Constitutes a Single Homogeneous Group! *Gifted Child Quarterly*, 1982, 26, 9–10.

Kastein, S., Spaulding, I., and Scharf, B. *Raising the Young Blind Child: A Guide for Parents and Educators.* New York: Human Sciences Press, 1980.

Kavale, K. The Efficacy of Stimulant Drug Treatment for Hyperactivity: A Meta-Analysis. *Journal of Learning Disabilities*, 1982, 15, 280–289.

Kavale, K. A., and Forness, S. R. Hyperactivity and Diet Treatment: A Meta-Analysis of the Feingold Hypothesis. *Journal of Learning Disabilities*, 1983, 16, 324–330.

Kendall, P. C., Lerner, R. M, and Craighead, W. E. Human Development and Intervention in Childhood Psychopathology. *Child Development*, 1984, 55, 71–82.

Kirchner, C., Peterson, R., and Suhr, C. Trends in School Enrollment and Reading Methods Among Legally Blind School Children, 1973–1978. *Journal of Visual Impairment and Blindness*, 1979, 73, 373–379.

Kirk, S. A., and Gallagher, J. J. *Educating Exceptional Children* (4th ed.). Boston: Houghton Mifflin, 1983.

Klasen, E. *The Syndrome of Specific Dyslexia.* Baltimore: University Park Press, 1972.

Landesman-Dwyer, S. Living in the Community. *American Journal of Mental Deficiency*, 1981, 86, 223–234.

Lederberg, A. R. Interaction between Deaf Preschoolers and Unfamiliar Hearing Adults. *Child Development*, 1984, 55, 598–606.

Lerner, J. W. *Children with Learning Disabilities* (2nd ed.). Boston: Houghton Mifflin, 1976.

Lewandowski, L. J., and Cruickshank, W. M. Psychological Development of Crippled Children and Youth, in W. M. Cruickshank (ed.), *Psychology of Exceptional Children and Youth* (4th ed.). Englewood Cliffs, N.J.: Prentice-Hall, 1980, 345–381.

Lewis, M., Feiring, C., McGuffog, C., and Jaskir, J. Predicting Psychopathology in Six-Year Olds from Early Social Relations. *Child Development*, 1984, 55, 123–136.

Maddux, C. D., Scheiber, L. M., and Bass, J. E. Self-Concept and Social Distance in Gifted Children. *Gifted Child Quarterly*, 1982, 26, 77–81.

Mandell, C. J., and Fiscus, E. *Understanding Exceptional People.* St. Paul: West Publishing Co., 1981.

Mattes, J. A. The Feingold Diet: A Current Reappraisal. *Journal of Learning Disabilities*, 1983, 16, 319–323.

Milk, L. Into the Mainstream: Behind the Mask of Pity. *Forum*, November 1980, 37–38.

Mollich, L. B., and Etra, K. S. Poor Learning Ability . . . or Poor Hearing? *Teacher*, 1981, 98, 42–43.

Myers, P. I., and Hammill, D. D. *Methods for Learning Disorders*, (2nd ed.). New York: Wiley, 1976.

Myerson, L. Somatopsychology of Physical Disability, in W. M. Cruickshank (ed.), *Psychology of Exceptional Children and Youth* (3rd ed.). Englewood Cliffs, N.J.: Prentice-Hall, 1971.

Myklebust, H. R., and Boshes, B. *Minimal Brain Damage in Children*, Final Report, Contract 108-65-142, Neurological and Sensory Disease Control Program. Washington, D.C.: Department of Health, Education and Welfare, 1969.

New York State Education Department. *Serving the Learning Disabled Child in New York State.* Albany, N.Y.: Office for Education of Children with Handicapping Conditions, October 1982.

Passow, A. H. The Nature of Giftedness and Talent. *Gifted Child Quarterly*, 1981, 25, 5–10.

Patton, J. M., and Payne, J. S. Mild Mental Retardation, in N. G. Haring (ed.), *Exceptional Children and Youth.* Columbus, Ohio: Charles E. Merrill, 1982, 111–143.

Polloway, E. A., and Patton, J. R. Psychosocial Causes of Mental Retardation, cited in J. M. Patton and J. S. Payne, Mild Mental Retardation, in N. G. Haring (ed.), *Exceptional Children and Youth.* Columbus, Ohio: Charles E. Merrill, 1982, 111–143.

President's Commission on Mental Retardation. *Mental Retardation: Past and Present.* Washington, D.C.: U.S. Government Printing Office, 1977.

Renzulli, J. Myth: The Gifted Constitutes 3–5% of the Population! *Gifted Child Quarterly*, 1982, 26, 11–14.

Reynell, J. Developmental Patterns of Visually Handicapped Children. *Child Care Health and Development*, 1978, 4, 291–303.

Rickert, E. S. Media Mirrors of the Gifted: E. Susanne Richert's Review of the Film "Simon." *Gifted Child Quarterly*, 1981, 25, 3–4.

Rimland, B. The Feingold Diet: An Assessment of the Reviews by Mattes, by Kavale and Forness and others. *Journal of Learning Disabilities*, 1983, 16, 331–333.

Ross, D. M., and Ross, S. A. *Hyperactivity: Research, Theory and Action.* New York: Wiley, 1976.

Rusalem, H., and Malikin, D. *Contemporary Vocational Rehabilitation.* New York: New York University Press, 1976.

Salend, S. J. Factors Contributing to the Development of a Successful Mainstreaming Program. *Exceptional Child*, 1984, 50, 409–416.

Sanders, D. R. Psychological Implications of Hearing Impairment, in W. M. Cruickshank (ed.), *Psychology of Exceptional Children and Youth* (4th ed.). Englewood Cliffs, N.J.: Prentice-Hall, 1980, 218–255.

Sprague, R. L., and Gadow, K. D. The Role of the Teacher in Drug Treatment, in J. J. Bosco and S. S. Robin (eds.), The Hyperactive Child and Stimulant Drugs: Definitions, Diagnosis and Directives. *School Review*, 1976, 85, 109–140.

Sroufe, L. A., and Stewart, M. A. Treating Problem Children with Stimulant Drugs. *New England Journal of Medicine*, 1973, 289, 407–413.

Stephens, B., and Grube, C. Development of Piagetian Reasoning in Congenitally Blind Children. *Journal of Visual Impairment and Blindness*, 1982, 76, 133–143.

Stephens, T. M., and Magliocca, L. A. The Tenth Myth: A Rejoinder to Cruickshank's Myths. *Journal of Learning Disabilities*, 1978, 10, 141–149.

Sternberg, R. J. Lies We Live By: Misapplication of Tests in Identifying the Gifted. *Gifted Child Quarterly*, 1982, 26, 157–161.

Sue, D., Sue, D. W., and Sue, S. *Understanding Abnormal Behavior.* Boston: Houghton Mifflin, 1981.

Suran, B. G., and Rizzo, J. V. *Special Children: An Integrative Approach* (2nd ed.). Glenview, Ill.: Scott, Foresman, 1983.

Telford, C. W., and Sawrey, J. M. *The Exceptional Individual* (4th ed.). Englewood Cliffs, N.J.: Prentice-Hall, 1981.

Terman, L. M. *Mental and Physical Traits of a Thousand Gifted Children.* Stanford, Calif.: Stanford University Press, 1925.

Terman, L. M., and Oden, M. H. *The Gifted Group at Mid-Life: Genetic Studies of Genius,* vol. 4. Stanford, Calif.: Stanford University Press, 1959.

Tolkoff, E. Mainstreaming: A Promise Gone Awry. Albany: New York State United Teachers, 1981.

Torrance, E. P. Psychology of Gifted Children and Youth, in W. M. Cruickshank (ed.), *Psychology of Exceptional Children and Youth* (4th ed.). Englewood Cliffs, N.J.: Prentice-Hall, 1980, 469–497.

———. *Guiding Creative Talent.* Englewood Cliffs, N.J.: Prentice-Hall, 1962.

Treffinger, D. J. Demythologizing Gifted Education: An Editorial Essay. *Gifted Child Quarterly,* 1982, 26, 3–8.

U.S. Department of Health, Education and Welfare. *Serving Children with Special Needs.* Washington, D.C.: U.S. Department of Health, Education and Welfare, 1972.

Varley, C., and Trupin, E. W. Double-Blind Assessment of Stimulant Medication for Attention Deficit Disorder: A Model for Clinical Application. *American Journal of Orthopsychiatry,* 1983, 53, 542–547.

Walden, E. L., and Thompson, S. A. A Review of Some Alternative Approaches to Drug Management of Hyperactivity in Children. *Journal of Learning Disabilities,* 1981, 4, 213–217.

Wanat, P. E. Social Skills: An Awareness Program with Learning Disabled Adolescents. *Journal of Learning Disabilities,* 1983, 16, 35–38.

Weiss, H. G., and Weiss, M. S. *Home Is a Learning Place: A Parents' Guide to Learning Disability.* Boston: Little, Brown, 1976.

Whalen, C. K., Henker, B., Dotemoto, S., and Hinshaw, S. P. Child and Adolescent Perceptions of Normal and Atypical Peers. *Child Development,* 1983, 54, 1588–1598.

Wolf, J. S., and Stephens, T. M. Gifted and Talented, in N. G. Haring, *Exceptional Children and Youth* (3rd ed.). Columbus, Ohio: Charles E. Merrill, 1982, 339–367.

Zigler, E. The Retarded Child as a Whole Person, 1973, cited in J. M. Patton and J. S. Payne, Mild Mental Retardation, in N. G. Haring, *Exceptional Children and Youth* (3rd ed.). Columbus, Ohio: Charles E. Merrill, 1982, 111–139.

Zisman, M., and Harrison, A. Hearing Ear Dogs. *The Deaf American,* January 1981, 33, 14–21.

Chapter Fourteen

Akinboye, J. O. Secondary Sexual Characteristics and Normal Puberty in Nigerian and Zimbabwian Adolescents. *Adolescence,* 1984, 74, 483–492.

Allgeier, E. R., and Allgeier, A. R. *Sexual Interactions.* Lexington, MA.: D.C. Health, 1984.

Altrocchi, J. *Abnormal Psychology.* New York: Harcourt Brace Jovanovich, 1980.

American Psychiatric Association. *Diagnostic and Statistical Manual of the American Psychiatric Association* (DSM3). Washington, D.C.: American Psychiatric Association, 1980.

Ames, R. Physical Maturing Among Boys as Related to Adult Social Behavior: A Longitudinal Study. *California Journal of Educational Research,* 1957, 8, 69–75.

Bachrach, A. J., Erwin, W., and Mohr, J. P. The Control of Eating Behavior in an Anorexic by Operant Conditioning Techniques, in L. P. Ullman and L. Krasner (eds.), *Case Studies in Behavior Modification.* New York: Holt, Rinehart and Winston, 1965.

Bakwin, H., and Bakwin, R. M. *Behavior Disorders in Children.* Philadelphia: Saunders, 1972.

Barret, R. L., and Robinson, B. E. Teenage Fathers: A Profile. *Personnel and Guidance Journal,* 1981, 60, 226–228.

Bemis, K. M. Current Approaches to the Treatment and Etiology of Anorexia Nervosa. *Psychological Bulletin,* 1978, 85, 593–617.

Brandt, G., Maschoff, T., and Chandler, N. S. A Residential Camp Experience as an Approach to Adolescent Weight Management. *Adolescence,* 1980, 60, 807–822.

Breit, E. B., and Ferrandino, M. M. Social Dimensions of the Menstrual Taboo and the Effects on Female Sexuality, in J. H. Williams (ed.), *Psychology of Women: Selected Readings.* New York: W. W. Norton, 1979, 228–241.

Brooks-Gunn, J., and Ruble, D. N. The Development of Menstrual-Related Beliefs and Behavior During Adolescence. *Child Development,* 1982, 53, 1567–1577.

Bruch, H. *The Golden Cage: The Enigma of Anorexia Nervosa.* Cambridge, Mass.: Harvard University Press, 1978.

Burns, R. B. *The Self Concept.* London: Longman, 1979.

Calderone, M. S. Introduction: The Issues at Hand. *Personnel and Guidance Journal,* 1976, 54, 350–354.

Card, J. J., and Wise, L. L. Teenage Mothers and Teenage Fathers: The Impact of Early Childbearing on the Parents' Personal and Professional Lives. *Family Planning Perspectives,* 1978, 10, 199–205.

Casper, R. C., and Davis, J. M. On the Course of Anorexia Nervosa. *American Journal of Psychiatry,* 1977, 134, 974–978.

Chess, S., Thomas, A., and Cameron, M. Sexual Attitudes and Behavior Patterns in a Middle-Class Population. *American Journal of Orthopsychiatry,* 1976, 46, 689–702.

Chumlea, W. C. Physical Growth in Adolescence, in W. W. Wolman (ed.), *Handbook of Developmental Psychology.* Englewood-Cliffs, N.J.: Prentice-Hall, 1982, 471–486.

Connolly, L. Boy Fathers. *Human Behavior,* January 1978, 40–43.

Coopersmith, S. *The Antecedents of Self Esteem.* San Francisco: Freeman, 1967.

Curry, J. F., and Hock, R. A. Sex Differences in Sex Role Ideals in Early Adolescence. *Adolescence,* 1981, 64, 779–789.

Dale, G., and Chamis, G. C. (1971), cited in Scales, P., Sex Education and the Prevention of Teenage Pregnancy: An Overview of Policies and Programs in the United States, in T. Ooms (ed.), *Teenage Pregnancy in a Family Context: Implications for Policy.* Philadelphia: Temple University Press, 1981, 2133–2153.

Darabi, K. F., Jones, J., Varga, P., and House, M. Evaluation of Sex Education Outreach. *Adolescence,* 1982, 65, 57–64.

DeLora, J. S., Warren, C. A. B., and Ellison, C. R. *Understanding Sexual Interaction* (2nd ed.). Boston: Houghton Mifflin, 1981.

Diepold, J., and Young, R. D. Empirical Studies of Adolescent Sexual Behavior: A Critical Review. *Adolescence,* 1979, 53, 44–63.

Dreyer, P. H. Sexuality During Adolescence, in B. B. Wolman (ed.), *Handbook of Developmental Psychology.* Englewood Cliffs, N.J.: Prentice-Hall, 1982, 559–602.

Dryfoos, J. G. Contraceptive Use, Pregnancy Intentions and Pregnancy Outcomes Among U.S. Women. *Family Planning Perspectives*, March-April 1982, *14*, 81–94.

Earls, F., and Siegel, B. Precocious Fathers. *American Journal of Orthopsychiatry*, 1980, *50*, 469–480.

Faust, M. S. Developmental Maturation as a Determinant in Prestige of Adolescent Girls. *Child Development*, 1960, *31*, 173–184.

Forbush, J. B. Adolescent Parent Programs and Family Involvement, in T. Ooms (ed.), *Teenage Pregnancy in a Family Context: Implications for Policy*. Philadelphia: Temple University Press, 1981, 254–277.

Forisha, Kovach, B. *The Experience of Adolescence: Development in Context*. Glenview, Ill.: Scott, Foresman, 1983.

Foster, C. D., and Miller, G. M. Adolescent Pregnancy: A Challenge for Counselors. *Personnel and Guidance Journal*, 1980, *59*, 236–241.

Frisch, R. E., and Revelle, R. Height and Weight at Menarche and a Hypothesis of Critical Body Weights and Adolescent Events. *Science*, 1970, *169*, 397–399.

Furstenberg, F. F. Implicating the Family: Teenage Parenthood and Kinship Involvements, in T. Ooms (ed.), *Teenage Pregnancy in a Family Context: Implications for Policy*. Philadelphia: Temple University Press, 1981, 131–165.

———. Premarital Pregnancy and Marital Instability, in G. Levinger and O. Moles (eds.), *Divorce and Separation: Context, Causes and Consequences*. New York: Basic Books, 1979.

———. The Social Consequences of Teenage Parenthood. *Family Planning Perspectives*, 1978, *10*, 233–235.

Furstenberg, F. Jr. The Social Consequences of Teenage Parenthood. *Family Planning Perspectives*, 1976, *8*, 148–164.

Furstenberg, F. F., and Talvitie, K. G. Children's Names and Paternal Claims: Bonds Between Unmarried Fathers and Their Children. *Journal of Family Issues*, 1980, *1*, 31–57.

Gagnon, J. H., and Simon, W. They're Going to Learn in the Streets Anyway. *Psychology Today*, March 1969, 46–47.

Gelfand, D. M., Jenson, W. R., and Drew, C. J. *Understanding Child Behavior Disorders*. New York: Holt, Rinehart and Winston, 1982.

Guttmacher Institute. *11 Million Teenagers: What Can Be Done About the Epidemic of Adolescent Pregnancies in the United States*. New York: Planned Parenthood Federation, 1976.

Halmi, K. A. Anorexia Nervosa: Recent Investigations. *Annual Review of Medicine*, 1978, *29*, 37–149.

Hamill, P. V. V. NCHS Growth Curves for Children. Vital and Health Statistics: Series 11, Data from the National Health Survey, No. 165. Washington, D.C.: U.S. Government Printing Office (DHEW no. 78-1650), 1977.

Hamilton, E. M., and Whitney, E. *Nutrition: Concepts and Controversies*. St. Paul: West Publishing Co., 1979.

Hass, A. *Teenage Sexuality: A Survey of Teenage Sexual Behavior*. New York: Macmillan, 1979.

Hendricks, L. E. Unwed Adolescent Fathers: Problems They Face and Their Sources of Social Support. *Adolescence*, 1980, *15*, 861–871.

Hubble, J., Wilder, R., and Kennedy, C. E. The Student as Physical Being. *Personnel and Guidance Journal*, 1969, *48*, 229–233.

Hunt, M. *Sexual Behavior in the 1970s*. New York: Dell Books, 1974.

Jensen, L. C. *Adolescence: Theories, Research, Applications*. St. Paul, Minnesota: West Publishing Co., 1985.

Jones, A. E., and Placek, P. J. Teenage Women in the United States: Sex, Contraception, Pregnancy, Fertility, and Maternal and Infant Health, in T. Ooms (ed.), *Teenage Pregnancy in a Family Context: Implications for Policy*. Philadelphia: Temple University Press, 1981, 9–49.

Jones, M. C. Psychological Correlates of Somatic Development. *Child Development*, 1965, *36*, 899–911.

———. The Later Careers of Boys Who Are Early and Late Maturers. *Child Development*, 1957, *28*, 113–128.

———. Adolescence in Our Society: Anniversary Papers of the Community Service Society of New York, in *The Family in a Democratic Society*. New York: Columbia University Press, 1949, 70–82.

Jones, M. C., and Bayley, N. Physical Maturing Among Boys as Related to Behavior. *Journal of Educational Psychology*, 1950, *41*, 129–148.

Jones, M. C., and Mussen, P. H. Self Conceptions, Motivations and Interpersonal Attitudes of Early- and Late-Maturing Girls. *Child Development*, 1958, *29*, 491–501.

Jourard, S. M., and Landsman, T. *Healthy Personality* (4th ed.). New York: Macmillan, 1980.

Kagan, D. M., and Squires, R. L. Eating Disorders Among Adolescents: Patterns and Prevalance. *Adolescence*, 1984, *73*, 15–31.

Kalat, J. W. *Biological Psychology*. Belmont, Calif.: Wadsworth, 1980.

Kantner, J., and Zelnik, M. Sexual Experiences of Young Unmarried Women, in *U.S. Family Planning Perspectives*, 1972, *4*, 9–17.

Katchadourian, H. *The Biology of Adolescence*. San Francisco: Freeman, 1977.

Kelly, J. B. Divorce: The Adult Perspective, in B. B. Wolman (ed.), *Handbook of Developmental Psychology*. Englewood Cliffs, N.J.: Prentice-Hall, 1982, 734–750.

Kinsey, A. C., and Gebhard, P. H. *Sexual Behavior in the Human Female*. Philadelphia: Saunders, 1953.

Kinsey, A. C., Pomeroy, W. B., and Martin, C. E. *Sexual Behavior in the Human Male*. Philadelphia: Saunders, 1948.

Krogman, W. M. *Child Growth*. Ann Arbor: University of Michigan Press, 1980.

Lerner, R. M., and Karabenick, S. A. Physical Attractiveness, Body Attitudes, and Self-Concept in Male and Female College Students. *Journal of Youth and Adolescence*, 1974, *3*, 307–316.

Lerner, R. M., and Korn, S. J. The Development of Body Build Stereotypes in Males. *Child Development*, 1972, *43*, 912–920.

Lerner, R. M., Iwawaki, S., Chihara, T., and Sorell, G. T. Self-Concept, Self-Esteem, and Body Attitudes Among Japanese Male and Female Adolescents. *Child Development*, 1980, *51*, 847–855.

Lerner, R. M., and Spanier, G. B. *Adolescent Development: A Life-Span Perspective*. New York: McGraw-Hill, 1980.

Libby, R. Parental Attitudes Towards High School Sex Education Programs. *The Family Coordinator*, 1970, *19*, 234–247.

Libby, R. W., Gray, L., and White, M. A Test and Reformulation of Reference Group and Role Correlates of Premarital Sexual Permissiveness Theory. *Journal of Marriage and the Family*, 1978, *40*, 79–92.

Logan, D. D. The Menarche Experience in Twenty-Three Foreign Countries. *Adolescence*, 1980, *58*, 247–257.

Luker, K. C. (1975), cited in Dreyer, P. H., Sexuality During Adolescence, in B. B. Wolman (ed.), *Handbook of Developmental Psychology*. Englewood Cliffs, N.J.: Prentice-Hall, 1982, 559–601.

Miller, M. J. Cantaloupes, Carrots and Counseling: Implications of Dietary Interventions for Counselors. *Personnel and Guidance Journal*, 1980, *58*, 421–425.

Minuchin, S., Rosman, B., and Baker, L. *Psychosomatic Families: Anorexia Nervosa in Context*. Cambridge, Mass.: Harvard University Press, 1978.

Moore, K. A., and Waite, L. F. Early Childbearing and Educational Attainment. *Family Planning Perspectives*, 1977, *9*, 220–225.

Mussen, P. H., and Jones, M. C. Some Conceptions, Motivations and Interpersonal Attitudes of Late- and Early-Maturing Boys. *Child Development*, 1957, *28*, 242–256.

Ooms, T. Introduction, in *Teenage Pregnancy in a Family Context*, ed. T. Ooms. Philadelphia: Temple University Press, 1981, 9–49.

Oskamp, S., and Mindick, B. Personality and Attitudinal Barriers to Contraception, in D. Byrne and W. A. Fisher (eds.), *Adolescents, Sex and Contraception*. New York: McGraw-Hill, 1981.

Paige, K. E. Women Learn the Menstrual Blues. *Psychology Today*, September 1973, 41–48.

Peskin, H. Influences of the Development Schedule on Learning and Ego Functioning. *Journal of Youth and Adolescence*, 1973, *2*, 273–290.

_____. Pubertal Onset and Ego Functioning. *Journal of Abnormal Psychology*, 1967, *72*, 1–15.

Reichelt, P. (1976), cited in Dreyer, P. H., Sexuality During Adolescence, in B. B. Wolman (ed.), *Handbook of Developmental Psychology*. Englewood Cliffs, N.J.: Prentice-Hall, 1982, 559–601.

Rierdan, J., and Koff, E. The Psychological Impact of Menarche: Integrative Versus Disruptive Changes. *Journal of Youth and Adolescence*, 1980, *9*, 49–58.

Rinck, C., Rudolph, J. A., and Simkins, L. A Survey of Attitudes Concerning Contraception and the Resolution of Teenage Pregnancy. *Adolescence*, 1983, *72*, 923–929.

Robinson, I. E., and Jedlicka, D. Change in Sexual Attitudes and Behavior of College Students from 1965 to 1980: A Research Note. *Journal of Marriage and the Family*, 1982, *44*, 237–240.

Roche, A. F. Secular Trends in Stature, Weight and Maturation, in A. F. Roche (ed.), Secular Trends in Growth, Maturation and Development of Children. *Monographs of the Society for Research in Child Development*, 1979, *44*, 3–27.

Rodin, J. Current Status of the Internal-External Hypothesis for Obesity: What Went Wrong? *American Psychologist*, 1981, *36*, 361–373.

Rosenhan, D. L., and Seligman, M. E. P. *Abnormal Psychology*. New York: W. W. Norton, 1984.

Ruble, D. N., and Brooks-Gunn, J. The Experience of Menarche. *Child Development*, 1982, *53*, 1557–1566.

Scales, P. Sex Education and the Prevention of Teenage Pregnancy: An Overview of Policies and Programs in the United States, in T. Ooms (ed.), *Teenage Pregnancy in Family Context: Implications for Policy*. Philadelphia: Temple University Press, 1981, 213–254.

Schafer, R. The Self-Concept as a Factor in Diet Selection and Quality. *Journal of Nutrition Education*, 1979, *11*, 37–39.

Shestowsky, B. Ego Identity Development and Obesity in Adolescent Girls. *Adolescence*, 1983, *71*, 550–559.

Shope, D. F. *Interpersonal Sexuality*. Philadelphia: Saunders, 1975.

Smart, D. E., Beumont, P. J., and George, G. C. Some Personality Characteristics of Patients with Anorexia Nervosa. *British Journal of Psychiatry*, 1976, *128*, 57–60.

Sommer, B. B. *Puberty and Adolescence*. New York: Oxford University Press, 1978.

Sorenson, R. C. *The Sorenson Report: Adolescent Sexuality in Contemporary America*. New York: World Publishing Co., 1973.

Staffieri, J. R. Body Build and Behavioral Expectancies in Young Females. *Developmental Psychology*, 1972, *6*, 125–127.

Stolz, H. R., and Stolz, L. M. *Somatic Development of Adolescent Boys*. New York: Macmillan, 1951.

Tanner, J. M. Physical Growth, in P. H. Mussen (ed.), *Carmichael's Manual of Child Development* (3rd ed.). New York: Wiley, 1970, 77–155.

_____. Early Maturation in Man. *Scientific American*, 1968, *218*, 21–27.

_____. *Growth at Adolescence*. Oxford: Blackwell, 1962.

Teitze, C. Teenage Pregnancies: Looking Ahead to 1984. *Family Planning Perspectives*, 1978, *10*, 24–28.

Verinis, J. S., and Roll, S. Primary and Secondary Male Characteristics: The Hairiness and Large Penis Stereotype. *Psychological Reports*, 1970, *26*, 123–126.

Voget, F. X. Bulimia. *Adolescence*, 1985, *20*, 46–50.

Wagner, C. A. Sexuality of American Adolescents. *Adolescence*, 1980, *59*, 567–580.

Weatherley, D. Self-Perceived Rate of Physical Maturation and Personality in Late Adolescence. *Child Development*, 1964, *35*, 1197–1210.

Wenar, C. *Psychopathology from Infancy Through Adolescence*. New York: Random House, 1982.

Whisnant, L., and Zegans, L. A Study of Attitudes Towards Menarche in White Middle-Class American Adolescent Girls. *American Journal of Psychiatry*, 1975, *132*, 809–814.

Whitney, E. N., and Hamilton, E. M. N. *Understanding Nutrition* (3rd ed.). St. Paul: West Publishing Co., 1984.

Williams, J. H. *Psychology of Women: Behavior in a Biosocial Context*. New York: W. W. Norton, 1977.

Zabin, L. S., Kantner, J. L., and Zelnik, M. The Risk of Adolescent Pregnancy in the First Months of Intercourse. *Family Planning Perspectives*, 1979, *4*, 215–222.

Zakus, G., Chin, M. L., Keown, M., Herbert, F., and Held, M. A Group Behavior Modification Approach to Adolescent Obesity. *Adolescence*, 1979, *55*, 481–491.

Zelnik, M., and Kantner, J. F. First Pregnancies to Women Aged 15–19: 1976 and 1971. *Family Planning Perspectives*, 1978, *10*, 11–20.

_____. Sexual and Contraceptive Experience of Young Unmarried Women in the United States, 1976 and 1971. *Family Planning Perspectives*, 1977, *9*, 115–134.

Zelnik, M., and Kim, Y. J. Sex Education and Its Association with Teenage Sexual Activity, Pregnancy and Contraceptive Use. *Family Planning Perspectives*, May-June 1982, *14*, 117–126.

Zelnik, M., and Shah, F. K. First Intercourse Among Young Americans. *Family Planning Perspectives*, March-April 1983, *15*, 64–70.

Zougher, C. E. The Self-Concept of Adolescent Girls. *Adolescence*, 1977, *12*, 477–488.

Chapter Fifteen

Ashton, P. T. Cross-Cultural Piagetian Research: An Experimental Perspective. *Harvard Educational Review*, 1975, *45*, 475–506.

Ault, R. *Children's Cognitive Development*. New York: Oxford University Press, 1977.

Auster, C. J., and Auster, D. Factors Influencing Women's Choice of Nontraditional Careers: The Role of Family, Peers, and Counselors. *Vocational Guidance Quarterly,* 1981, *29,* 253–265.

Bachman, J. G. *Youth in Transition, Vol. 2: The Impact of Family Background and Intelligence on Tenth Grade Boys.* Ann Arbor, Mich.: Institute for Social Research, 1970.

Bachman, J. G., Green, S., and Wittanen, I. D. *Youth in Transition, Vol. 3: Dropping Out—Problem or Symptom?* Ann Arbor, Mich.: Institute for Social Research, 1971.

Bachman, J. G., and Johnston, L. D. The Freshmen. *Psychology Today,* September 1979, 78–87.

Bachman, J. G., O'Malley, P. M., and Johnston, J. *Adolescence to Adulthood: Change and Stability in the Lives of Young Men.* Ann Arbor, Mich.: Institute for Social Research, 1978.

Baumgardner, S. R. Rational Career Planning and Nonrational Career Realities (1975), cited in Baumgardner, S. R., Vocational Planning: The Great Swindle. *American Personnel and Guidance Journal,* 1977, *56,* 17–23.

Beech, R. P., and Schoeppe, A. Development of Value Systems in Adolescence. *Developmental Psychology,* 1974, *10,* 644–656.

Bernard. M. E., Keefauver, L. W., Elsworth, G., and Naylor, F. D. Sex-Role Behavior and Gender in Teacher-Student Evaluations. *Journal of Educational Psychology,* 1981, *73,* 681–696.

Busse, T. V., Mansfield, R. S., and Messinger, L. J. *Activities in Child and Adolescent Development.* New York: Harper and Row, 1974.

Carroll, J. L., and Rest, J. R. Moral Development, in B. Wolman (ed.), *Handbook of Human Development.* Englewood Cliffs, N.J.: Prentice-Hall, 1982, 434–452.

Cherry, F., and Deaux, K., (1975) Fears of Success Versus Fear of Gender-Inconsistent Behavior: A Sex Similarity, cited in K. F. Schaffer, *Sex Roles and Human Behavior.* Cambridge, Mass.: Winthrop, 1981.

Clarey, J. H., and Sanford, A. Female Career Preference and Androgyny. *Vocational Guidance Quarterly,* 1982, *20,* 258–265.

Cronbach, L. J. *Essentials of Psychological Testing* (3rd ed.). New York: Harper and Row, 1970.

Dale, L. G. The Growth of Systematic Thinking: Replication and Analysis of Piaget's First Chemical Experiment. *Australian Journal of Psychology,* 1970, *22,* 277–286.

Danner, F. W., and Day, M. C. Eliciting Formal Operations. *Child Development,* 1977, *48,* 1600–1606.

Dasen, P., and Heron, A. Cross-Cultural Tests of Piaget's Theory, in H. C. Triandis, and Heron, A. (ed.), *Handbook of Cross-Cultural Psychology: Developmental Psychology* vol 4. Boston: Allyn and Bacon, 1981, 295–343.

DeCharms, R., and Muir, M. S. Motivation: Social Approaches. *Annual Review of Psychology,* 1978, *29,* 91–113.

Elkind, D. Egocentrism in Adolescence. *Child Development,* 1967, *38,* 1025–1034.

Elkind, D. Quantity Conceptions in College Students. *Journal of Social Psychology,* 1962, *57,* 459–462.

Elkind, D., and Bowen, R. Imaginary Audience Behavior in Children and Adolescence. *Developmental Psychology,* 1979, *15,* 38–44.

Farmer, H. S. Career Counseling Implications for the Lower Social Class and Women. *Personnel and Guidance Journal,* 1978, *56,* 467–472.

Feather, N. T. *Values in Education and Society.* New York: The Free Press, 1975.

Fischer, K. W. A Theory of Cognitive Development: The Control and Construction of Hierarchies of Skills. *Psychological Review,* 1980, *87,* 477–531.

Flavell, J. H. *Cognitive Development.* Englewood Cliffs, N.J.: Prentice-Hall, 1977. Second edition 1985.

Flavell, J. H., and Wohlwill, J. F. Formal and Functional Aspects of Cognitive Development, in D. Elkind and J. H. Flavell (eds.). *Studies in Cognitive Development.* New York: Oxford University Press, 1969, 67–120.

Forisha-Kovach, B. *The Experience of Adolescence: Development in Context,* Glenview, Ill: Scott, Foresman, 1983.

Gallup, G. H. The Gallup Poll of Teachers' Attitudes Toward the Public Schools. *Phi Delta Kappan,* October 1984, 97–107.

Gallup, G. H. The 16th Annual Gallup Poll of the Public's Attitudes Towards the Public Schools. *Phi Delta Kappan,* September 1984, 23–39.

Haan, N., Smith, B., and Block, J. Moral Reasoning of Young Adults: Political-Social Behavior, Family Background, and Personality Correlates. *Journal of Personality and Social Psychology,* 1968, *10,* 183–201.

Harris, S., Mussen, P., and Rutherford, E. Some Cognitive, Behavioral, and Personality Correlates of Maturity of Moral Judgement. *Journal of Genetic Psychology,* 1976, *128,* 123–135.

Havighurst, R. J. The World of Work, in B. B. Wolman (ed.), *Handbook of Human Development.* Englewood Cliffs, N.J.: Prentice-Hall, 1982, 771–791.

Hawley, P. The State of the Art of Counseling High School Girls, Ford Foundation Faculty Fellowship for Research on Women's Role in Society, Project No. 0675P, June 1975, cited in Hawley, P., and Even, B., Work and Sex-Role Attitudes in Relation to Education and Other Characteristics. *Vocational Guidance Quarterly,* 1982, *31,* 101–109.

Hawley, P., and Even, B. Work and Sex-Role Attitudes in Relation to Education and Other Characteristics. *Vocational Guidance Quarterly,* 1982, *31,* 101–109.

Hazler, R. J., and Roberts G. Decision Making in Vocational Theory: Evolution and Implications. *Personnel and Guidance Journal,* 1984, *62,* 408–410.

Heshusius-Gilsdorf, L. T., and Gilsdorf, D. L. Girls Are Females, Boys Are Males: A Content Analysis of Career Materials. *American Personnel and Guidance Journal,* 1975, *54,* 206–212.

Hoffman, L. W. Fear of Success in Males and Females, 1965 and 1971. *Journal of Consulting and Clinical Psychology,* 1974, *42,* 353–358.

Holland, J. *Making Vocational Choices.* Englewood Cliffs, N.J.: Prentice-Hall, 1973.

Holstein, C. B. Irreversible, Stepwise Sequence in the Development of Moral Judgement: A Longitudinal Study of Males and Females. *Child Development,* 1976, *47,* 51–61.

Horner, M. Towards an Understanding of Achievement-Related Conflicts in Women. *Journal of Social Issues,* 1972, *28,* 157–176.

————. Sex Differences in Achievement Motivation and Performance in Competitive and Non-Competitive Situations. Unpublished Doctoral Dissertation. University of Michigan, 1968.

Housely, W. F. Vocational Decision Making: A Function of Rejecting Attitudes. *Vocational Guidance Quarterly,* 1973, *21,* 288–293.

Inhelder, B., and Piaget, J. *The Growth of Logical Thinking.* New York: Basic Books, 1958.

Kaplan, P. S., and Stein, J. *Psychology of Adjustment*. Belmont, Calif.: Wadsworth, 1984.

Keating, D. P. Precocious Cognitive Development at the Level of Formal Operations. *Child Development*, 1975, *46*, 276–280.

Keating, D. P., and Schaefer, R. A. Ability and Sex Differences in the Acquisition of Formal Operations. *Developmental Psychology*, 1975, *11*, 531–532.

Keith, P. M. Sex-Role Attitudes, Family Plans, and Career Orientations: Implications for Counseling. *Vocational Guidance Quarterly*, 1981, *29*, 244–253.

Kohlberg, L. Stage and Sequence: The Cognitive-Developmental Approach to Socialization, in D. A. Goslin (ed.), *Handbook of Socialization Theory and Research*. Chicago: Rand-McNally, 1969.

Kohlberg, L., and Kramer, R. Continuities and Discontinuities in Childhood and Adult Moral Development. *Human Development*, 1969, *12*, 93–120.

Kohlberg, L., and Turiel, E. Moral Development and Moral Education, in G. Lesser (ed.), *Moral Development and Moral Education*. Chicago: Scott, Foresman, 1971.

Kuhn, D. Short-Term Longitudinal Evidence for the Sequentiality of Kohlberg's Early Stages of Moral Development. *Developmental Psychology*, 1976, *12*, 162–166.

Kuhn, D., Ho, V., and Adams, C. Formal Reasoning Among Pre- and Late Adolescents. *Child Development*, 1979, *50*, 1149–1152.

Laboratory of Comparative Human Cognition. Cross-Cultural Psychology's Challenges to Our Ideas of Children and Development. *American Psychologist*, 1979, *34*, 827–834.

Langford, P. E., and George, S. Intellectual and Moral Development in Adolescence. *British Journal of Educational Psychology*, 1975, *45*, 330–332.

Lerner, R. M., and Shea, J. A. Social Behavior in Adolescence, in B. B. Wolman (ed.), *Handbook of Human Development*. Englewood Cliffs, N.J.: Prentice-Hall, 1982, 503–526.

Lueptow, L. B. Sex-Typing and Change in the Occupational Choices of High School Seniors, 1964–1975. *Sociology of Education*, 1981, *54*, 16–24.

Martorano, C. S. A Developmental Analysis of Performance on Piaget's Formal Operations Tasks. *Developmental Psychology*, 1977, *13*, 666–672.

McClure, G. T., and Piel, E. College Bound Girls and Science Careers: Perception of Barriers and Facilitating Factors. *Journal of Vocational Behavior*, 1978, *12*, 172–183.

McIlroy, J. H. Career as Life-Style: An Existential View. *American Personnel and Guidance Journal*, 1979, *57*, 351–356.

McKinney, J. P., Fitzgerald, H. E., and Strommen, E. A. *Developmental Psychology: The Adolescent and Young Adult* (rev. ed.). Homewood, Ill.: Dorsey Press, 1982.

McKinney, J. P., Hotch, D. F., and Truhon, S. A. The Organization of Behavioral Values During Late Adolescence: Change and Stability Across Two Eras. *Developmental Psychology*, 1977, *13*, 83–84.

McKinney, J. P., and Moore, D. Attitudes and Values During Adolescence, in B. B. Wolman (ed.), *Handbook of Human Development*. Englewood Cliffs, N.J.: Prentice-Hall, 1982, 549–559.

Milgram, S. Some Conditions of Obedience to Authority (1968), in R. Flacks (ed.), *Conformity Resistance and Self-Determination: The Individual and Authority*. Boston: Little, Brown, 1973, 225–239.

Miller, D. C. Industry and the Worker, in H. Borow (ed.), *Man in a World at Work*. Boston: Houghton Mifflin, 1964.

Moir, D. J. Egocentrism and the Emergence of Conventional Morality in Preadolescent Girls. *Child Development*, 1974, *45*, 299–304.

Moshman, D. Development of Formal Hypothesis-Testing Ability. *Developmental Psychology*, 1979, *15*, 104–112.

———. Consolidation and Stage Formation in the Emergence of Formal Operations. *Developmental Psychology*, 1977, *13*, 95–100.

Murphy, C. Today's Children and Education. *Wilson Quarterly*, Autumn 1982, 61–82.

Neimark, E. D. Adolescent Thought: Transition to Formal Operations, in B. B. Wolman (ed.), *Handbook of Human Development*. Englewood Cliffs, N.J.: Prentice-Hall, 1982, 486–503.

———. Intellectual Development During Adolescence, in F. D. Horowitz (ed.), *Review of Child Development Research*, vol. 4. Chicago: University of Chicago Press, 1975.

Noeth, R. J., Roth, J. D., and Prediger, D. J. Student Career Development: Where Do We Stand? *Vocational Guidance Quarterly*, 1975, *23*, 210–220.

O'Donnell, J. A., and Andersen, D. G. Factors Influencing Choice of Major and Career of Capable Women. *Vocational Guidance Journal*, 1978, *26*, 214–222.

Overton, W. F., and Meehan, A. M. Individual Differences in Formal Operational Thought: Sex Role and Learned Helplessness. *Child Development*, 1982, *53*, 1536–1543.

Palmquist, W. J. Formal Operational Reasoning and the Primacy Effect of Impression Formation. *Developmental Psychology*, 1979, *15*, 185–189.

Piaget, J. Intellectual Evolution from Adolescence to Adulthood. *Human Development*, 1972, *15*, 1–12.

Pulaski, M. A. S. *Understanding Piaget*. New York: Harper and Row, 1980.

Ravitch, D. The Debate About Standards: Where Do We Go from Here? *American Educator*, Fall 1981, 14–19.

Richmond-Abbott, M. *Masculine and Feminine: Sex Roles over the Life Cycle*. Reading, Mass.: Addison-Wesley, 1983.

Roberge, J. R., and Flexer, B. K. Further Examination of Formal Operational Reasoning Abilities. *Child Development*, 1979, *50*, 478–484.

Roe, A. Personality Structure and Occupational Behavior, in H. Borow (ed.), *Man in a World at Work*. Boston: Houghton Mifflin, 1964, 196–215.

———. *The Psychology of Occupations*. New York: Wiley, 1957.

Rogoff, B. Schooling and the Development of Cognitive Skills, in H. C. Triandis and A. Heron, *Handbook of Cross-Cultural Psychology*, vol. 4: *Developmental Psychology*. Boston: Allyn and Bacon, 1981, 233–295.

Rokeach, M. *The Nature of Human Values*. New York: The Free Press, 1973.

Salkind, N. J. *Theories of Human Development*. New York: Van Nostrand, 1981.

Schaffer, K. F. *Sex Roles and Human Behavior*. Cambridge, Mass.: Winthrop, 1981.

Shaver, J. P., and Strong, W. *Facing Value Decisions: Rationale-Building for Teachers*. Belmont, Calif.: Wadsworth, 1976.

Sherman, J. Mathematics, Spacial Visualization, and Related Factors: Changes in Girls and Boys, Grades 8–11. *Journal of Educational Psychology*, 1980, *72*, 476–482.

Skovholt, T. M., and Morgan, J. I. Career Development: An Outline of Issues for Men. *Personnel and Guidance Journal*, 1981, *60*, 231–237.

Smith, H. *The Russians*. New York: Ballantine, 1976.

Sobesky, W. E. The Effects of Situational Factors on Moral Judgments. *Child Development*, 1983, *54*, 575–584.

Stone, C. A., and Day, M. C. Levels of Availability of a Formal Operational Strategy. *Child Development*, 1978, *49*, 1054–1065.

Stone, M. A., and Ausubel, D. P. The Intersituational Generality of Formal Thought. *Journal of Genetic Psychology*, 1969, *115*, 169–180.

Super, D. E., and Hyde, D. T. Career Development: Exploration and Planning. *Annual Review of Psychology*, 1978, *29*, 333–372.

Super, D. E., and Overstreet, P. L. *The Vocational Maturity of Ninth Grade Boys*. New York: Teachers College Press, 1960.

Terman, L. M., and Oden, M. H. *Genetic Studies of Genius, 1: Mental and Physical Traits of a Thousand Gifted Children*. Stanford, Calif.: Stanford University Press, 1959.

Thompson, A. P. Client Misconceptions in Vocational Counseling. *American Personnel and Guidance Journal*, 1976, *55*, 30–34.

Tomlinson-Keasey, C., and Keasey, C. B. The Mediating Role of Cognitive Development in Moral Judgment. *Child Development*, 1974, *45*, 291–298.

Treiman, D., and Terrell, K. Sex and the Process of Status Attainment: A Comparison of Working Women and Men. *American Sociological Review*, 1975, *40*, 174–200.

Vondracek, F. W., and Lerner, R. M. Vocational Role Development in Adolescence, in B. B. Wolman (ed.), *Handbook of Human Development*. Englewood Cliffs, N.J.: Prentice-Hall, 1982, 602–617.

Weiss, R. J. Understanding Moral Thought: Effects on Moral Reasoning and Decision Making. *Developmental Psychology*, 1982, *18*, 852–861.

Weitz, S. *Sex Roles: Biological, Psychological and Social Foundations*. New York: Oxford University Press, 1977.

Williams, J. H. *Psychology of Women: Behavior in a Biosocial Context*. New York: W. W. Norton, 1977.

Wilson, J., Weikel, W. J., and Rose, H. A Comparison of Nontraditional and Traditional Career Women. *Vocational Guidance Quarterly*, 1982, *31*, 109–117.

Wonderly, D. M., and Kupfersmid, J. H. Promoting Postconventional Morality: The Adequacy of Kohlberg's Aim. *Adolescence*, 1980, *15*, 609–631.

Yussen, S. R. Moral Reasoning from the Perspective of Others. *Child Development*, 1976, *47*, 551–555.

Zuckerman, M., and Wheeler, L. To Dispel Fantasies About the Fantasy-Based Measure of Fear of Success. *Psychological Bulletin*, 1975, *82*, 932–946.

Chapter Sixteen

Abelson, H. I., Fishburne, P. M., and Cisin, I. *National Survey on Drug Abuse*. Rockville, Md.: National Institute on Drug Abuse, 1977.

Adams, G. R., and Jones, R. M. Female Adolescents' Identity Development: Age Comparisons and Perceived Child-Rearing Experience. *Developmental Psychology*, 1983, *19*, 249–257.

Albrecht, S. L., Thomas, D. L., and Chadwick, B. A. *Social Psychology*. Englewood Cliffs, N.J.: Prentice-Hall, 1980.

Altrocchi, J. *Abnormal Psychology*. New York: Harcourt Brace Jovanovich, 1980.

American Psychiatric Association. *Diagnostic and Statistical Manual of Mental Disorders* (3rd ed.). Washington, D.C.: American Psychiatric Association.

Archer, J., and Lopata, A. Marijuana Revisited. *American Personnel and Guidance Journal*, 1979, *57*, 244–252.

Archer, S. L. The Lower Boundaries of Identity Development. *Child Development*, 1982, *53*, 1555–1556.

Balswick, J. O., and Macrides, C. Parental Stimulus for Adolescent Rebellion. *Adolescence*, 1975, *10*, 253–266.

Barton, J., Chassin, L., Presson, C. C., and Sherman, T. J. Social Image Factors as Motivators of Smoking Initiation in Early and Middle Adolescence. *Child Development*, 1982, *53*, 1499–1511.

Bernard, H. S. Identity Formation During Late Adolescence: A Review of Some Empirical Findings. *Adolescence*, 1981, *16*, 349–356.

Berndt, T. Developmental Changes in Conformity to Peers and Parents. *Developmental Psychology*, 1979, *15*, 608–617.

Blum, R. H., et al. *Society and Drugs*, vol. 1. San Francisco: Jossey-Bass, 1970.

Bond, T. T. Identity Development of the Traditional Female Client. *American Personnel and Guidance Journal*, 1982, *60*, 532–535.

Braucht, G. N., Brakarsh, D., Follingstad, D., and Berry, K. L. Deviant Drug Use in Adolescence: A Review of Psychosocial Correlates. *Psychological Bulletin*, 1973, *79*, 92–106.

Brittain, C. V. A Comparison of Rural and Urban Adolescents with Respect to Peer vs. Parent Compliance. *Adolescence*, 1969, *13*, 59–68.

———. Adolescent Choices and Parent-Peer Cross-Pressures. *American Sociological Review*, 1963, *28*, 385–391.

Brook, J. S., Whiteman, M., Gordon, A. S., and Brook, D. W. Identification with Parental Attributes and Its Relationship to the Son's Personality and Drug Use. *Developmental Psychology*, 1984, *20*, 1111–1119.

Brook, J. S., Whiteman, M., and Gordon, A. S. Stages of Drug Use in Adolescence: Personality, Peer and Family Correlates. *Developmental Psychology*, 1983, *19*, 269–277.

Brook, J. S., Whiteman, M., Brook, D. W., and Gordon, A. S. Paternal Determinants of Male Adolescent Marijuana Use. *Developmental Psychology*, 1981, *17*, 841–848.

Carlin, A. S., and Post, R. D. Drug Use and Achievement. *International Journal of the Addictions*, 1974, *9*, 401–410.

Chand, I. P., Crider, D. M., and Willets, F. K. Parent-Youth Disagreement as Perceived by Youth: A Longitudinal Study. *Youth and Society*, 1975, *6*, 365–375.

Coleman, E. Counseling Adolescent Males. *American Personnel and Guidance Journal*, 1981, *60*, 215–219.

Conway, F., and Siegelman, J. *Snapping: America's Epidemic of Sudden Personality Change*. Philadelphia: Lippincott, 1978.

Conye, R. K. Primary Prevention Through a Campus Alcohol Education Project. *Personnel and Guidance Journal*, May 1984, *62*, 524–529.

Coon, D. *Introduction to Psychology: Exploration and Application*. St. Paul: West Publishing Co., 1980.

Cross, H. J., and Allen, J. G. Ego Identity Status, Adjustment, and Academic Achievement. *Journal of Consulting and Clinical Psychology*, 1970, *34*, 288.

Donovan, J. M. Identity Status and Interpersonal Style. *Journal of Youth and Adolescence*, 1975, *4*, 37–55.

Doress, I., and Porter, J. N. Kids in Cults. *Society*, 1978, *15*, 69–71.

Douvan, E., and Adelson, J. *The Adolescent Experience*. New York: Wiley, 1966.

Erikson, E. H. *Identity, Youth and Crisis*. New York: W. W. Norton, 1968.

_____. The Problem of Ego Identity, in *Identity and the Life Cycle* (1959). New York: W. W. Norton, 1980.

Eshleman, J. R., and Cashion, B. G. *Sociology: An Introduction*. Boston: Little, Brown, 1983.

Federal Bureau of Investigation. *Uniform Crime Reports: Crime in the United States*. Washington, D.C.: U.S. Government Printing Office, 1976.

Fitch, S. A., and Adams, G. R. Ego Identity and Intimacy: Replication and Extension. *Developmental Psychology*, 1983, *19*, 839–845.

Floyd, H. H., Jr., and South, D. R. Dilemma of Youth: The Choice of Parents or Peers as a Frame of Reference for Behavior. *Journal of Marriage and the Family*, 1972, *34*, 627–634.

Freud, S. *A General Introduction to Psychoanalysis*. New York: Permabooks, 1953, (originally published in 1935).

Ginott, H. G. *Between Parent and Teenager*. New York: Macmillan, 1969.

Goode, E. *Drugs in American Society*. New York: Knopf, 1972.

Hall, G. S. *Adolescence: Its Psychology and Its Relations to Physiology, Anthropology, Sociology, Sex, Crime, Religion and Education*. New York: Appleton, 1904.

Hardert, R. A., Gordon, L., Laner, M. R., and Reader, M. *Confronting Social Problems*. St. Paul: West Publishing Co., 1984.

Huesmann, L. R., Eron, L. D., and Lefkowitz, M. M. Stability of Aggression Over Time and Generations. *Developmental Psychology*, 1984, *20*, 1120–1134.

Hughes, R., and Brewin, R. *The Tranquilizing of America*. New York: Harcourt Brace Jovanovich, 1979.

Hummel, R., and Roselli, L. L. Identity Status and Academic Achievement in Female Adolescents. *Adolescence*, 1983, *18*, 18–26.

Hunter, F. T. Adolescents' Perception of Discussions with Parents and Friends. *Developmental Psychology*, 1985, *21*, 443–440.

Hunter, F. T. Socializing Procedures in Parent-Child and Friendship Relations During Adolescence. *Developmental Psychology*, 1984, *20*, 1092–1100.

Hunter, F. T., and Youniss, J. Changes in Functions of Three Relations During Adolescence. *Developmental Psychology*, 1982, *18*, 806–812.

Jalali, B., Jalali, M., Crocetti, G., and Turner, F. Adolescents and Drug Use: Toward a More Comprehensive Approach. *American Journal of Orthopsychiatry*, 1981, *51*, 120–131.

Jarvik, M. E., Cullen, J. W., Gritz, E. R., Vogt, T. M., and West, L. J. (eds.). *Research on Smoking Behavior*, U.S. Department of Health, Education and Welfare, NIDA Research Monograph 17. Washington, D.C.: U.S. Government Printing Office 1977.

Jessor, R., and Jessor, S. L. Adolescent Development and the Onset of Drinking (1975), in R. E. Muuss (ed.), *Adolescent Behavior and Society: A Book of Readings* (3rd ed.). New York: Random House, 1980, 455–474.

Johnston, L. D., Bachman, J. G., and O'Malley, P. M. *Drug Use Among American High School Students, 1975–1977*. Rockville, Md.: National Institute on Drug Abuse, DHEW Pub. No. 78619, 1977.

Kandel, D. Stages in Adolescent Involvement in Drug Use. *Science*, November 28, 1975, *190*, 912–914.

Kandel, D. B., and Lesser, G. S. *Youth in Two Worlds*. San Francisco: Jossey-Bass, 1972.

Kolansky, H., and Moore, W. T. Sufficient for Alarm, in J. P. Brody and H. K. Brody (eds.), *Controversy in Psychiatry*. Philadelphia: Saunders, 1978, 881–904.

_____. Toxic Effects of Chronic Marijuana Use. *Journal of the American Medical Association*, 1972, *222*, 35–41.

Larson, L. E. The Influence of Parents and Peers During Adolescence: The Situation Hypothesis Revisited. *Journal of Marriage and the Family*, 1972, *34*, 67–74.

La Voie, J. C. Ego Identity Formation in Middle Adolescence. *Journal of Youth and Adolescence*, 1976, *4*, 371–385.

Leadbeater, D. J., and Dionne, J. P. Adolescent's Use of Formal Operational Thinking in Solving Problems Related to Identity Resolution. *Adolescence*, 1981, *61*, 113–121.

Lerner, R. M., Karson, M., Meisels, M., and Knapp, J. R. Actual and Perceived Attitudes of Late Adolescents and Their Parents: The Phenomenon of the Generation Gaps. *The Journal of Genetic Psychology*, 1975, *126*, 195–207.

Lerner, R. M. and Spanier, G. B. *Adolescent Development: A Life-Span Perspective*. New York: McGraw-Hill, 1980.

Levanthal, H., and Cleary, P. The Smoking Problem: A Review of the Research and Theory in Behavioral Risk Modification. *Psychological Bulletin*, 1980, *88*, 370–405.

Lowney, J., Winslow, R. W., and Winslow, V. *Deviant Reality: Alternative World Views* (2nd ed.). Boston: Allyn and Bacon, 1981.

Lunde, D. T., and Lunde, M. K. *The Next Generation: A Book on Parenting*. New York: Holt, Rinehart and Winston, 1980.

Marcia, J. Identity in Adolescence, in J. Adelson (ed.), *Handbook of Adolescent Psychology*. New York: Wiley, 1980.

_____. Ego Identity Status: Relationship to Change in Self-Esteem, "General Maladjustment," and Authoritarianism. *Journal of Personality*, 1967, *35*, 118–133.

_____. Development and Validation of Ego-Identity Status. *Journal of Personality and Social Psychology*, 1966, *3*, 551–558.

Marcia, J. E., and Friedman, M. L. Ego Identity Status in College Women. *Journal of Personality*, 1970, *38*, 249–263.

Margolis, R., and Popkin, N. Marijuana: A Review of Medical Research with Implications for Adolescents. *Personnel and Guidance Journal*, 1980, *59*, 7–15.

McCarthy, J. D., and Hoge, D. R. Analysis of Age Effects in Longitudinal Studies of Adolescent Self-Esteem. *Developmental Psychology*, 1982, *18*, 372–379.

McDermitt, D. The Relationship of Parental Drug Use and Parents' Attitude Concerning Adolescent Drug Use to Adolescent Drug Use. *Adolescence*, 1984, *73*, 89–97.

Meilman, P. W. Cross-Sectional Age Changes in Ego Identity Status During Adolescence. *Developmental Psychology*, 1979, *15*, 230–231.

Montemayor, R. The Relationship Between Parent-Adolescent Conflict and the Amount of Time Adolescents Spend Alone and with Parents and Peers. *Child Development*, 1982, *53*, 1512–1519.

Nathan, P. E. Failures in Prevention: Why We Can't Prevent the Devastating Effects of Alcoholism and Drug Abuse? *American Psychologist*, 1983, *38*, 459–468.

Newcomb, M. D., Huba, G. J., and Bentler, P. M. Mothers' Influence on the Drug Use of Their Children: Confirmatory Tests of Direct Modeling and Mediational Theories. *Developmental Psychology*, 1983, *19*, 714–727.

Newman, P. The Peer Group, in B. B. Wolman, *Handbook of Developmental Psychology.* Englewood Cliffs, N.J.: Prentice-Hall, 1982, 526–537.

Office of Drug Abuse Policy. Report Prepared by the White House Committee on Drug Abuse for the President, 1978.

Orlofsky, J. L., Marcia, J. E., and Lesser, I. M. Ego Identity Status and the Intimacy Versus Isolation Crisis of Young Adulthood. *Journal of Personality and Social Psychology,* 1973, *27,* 211–219.

Oshman, H., and Manosevitz, M. The Impact of the Identity Crisis on the Adjustment of Late Adolescent Males. *Journal of Youth and Adolescence,* 1974, *3,* 207–216.

Peterson, A. C., and Offer, D. Adolescent Development: Sixteen to Nineteen Years, in J. D. Noshpitz (ed.), *Basic Handbook of Child Psychiatry,* vol. 1. New York: Basic Books, 1979, 213–233.

Petitpas, A. Identity Foreclosure: A Unique Challenge. *American Personnel and Guidance Journal,* 1978, *56,* 558–562.

Quayle, D. American Productivity: The Devastating Effect of Alcoholism and Drug Abuse. *American Psychologist,* 1983, *38,* 454–458.

Robbins, T., and Anthony, D. New Religions, Families and Brainwashing. *Society,* 15, May-June 1978.

Robinson, I. E., and Jedlicka, D. Change in Sexual Attitudes and Behavior of College Students from 1965 to 1980: A Research Note. *Journal of Marriage and the Family,* 1982, *44,* 237–240.

Ruittenbeck, H. M. *The Individual and the Crowd: A Study of Identity in America.* New York: New American Library, 1964.

Sharabany, R., Gershoni, R., and Hofman, J. E. Girlfriend, Boyfriend: Age and Sex Differences in Intimate Friendship. *Developmental Psychology,* 1981, *17,* 800–809.

Siegel, O. Personality Development in Adolescence, in B. B. Wolman (ed.), *Handbook of Developmental Psychology.* Englewood Cliffs, N.J.: Prentice-Hall, 1982, 537–549.

Silverstein, B., Feld, S., and Kozlowski, L. T. The Availability of Low-Nicotine Cigarettes as a Cause of Cigarette Smoking Among Teenage Females. *Journal of Health and Social Behavior,* 1980, *21,* 383–388.

Silverstein, B., Kelley, E., Swan, J., and Kozlowski, L. T. Physiological Predisposition Toward Becoming a Cigarette Smoker: Experimental Evidence for a Sex Difference. *Addictive Behaviors,* 1982, *7,* 83–86.

Singer, M. T. Coming Out of the Cults. *Psychology Today,* January 1979, 72–82.

Smith, G. M. Relations Between Personality and Smoking Behavior in Preadult Subjects. *Journal of Consulting and Clinical Psychology,* 1969, *33,* 710–715.

Smith, H. *The Russians.* New York: Ballantine, 1976.

Sorosiak, F. M., Thomas, L. E., and Balet, F. N. Adolescent Drug Use: An Analysis. *Psychological Reports,* 1976, *38,* 211–221.

Toffler, A. *Future Shock.* New York: Random House, 1970.

Trent, J. W., and Medsker, L. L. *Beyond High School: A Psychological Study of 10,000 High School Graduates.* San Francisco: Jossey-Bass, 1968.

U.S. Department of Health, Education, and Welfare. *Smoking and Health: A Report of the Surgeon General.* Washington, D.C.: U.S. Government Printing Office, 1978.

Walker, B. A., and Mehr, M. Adolescent Suicide—A Family Crisis: A Model for Effective Intervention by Family Therapists. *Adolescence,* 1983, *18,* 285–292.

Waterman, A. S. Identity Development from Adolescence to Adulthood: An Extension of Theory and a Review of the Literature. *Developmental Psychology,* 1982, *18,* 341–359.

Waterman, A. S., and Waterman, C. K. A Longitudinal Study of Changes in Ego Identity Status During the Freshman Year at College. *Developmental Psychology,* 1971, *5,* 167–173.

Acknowledgments

Page 28, Figure 1.3, From *Guidelines for Research Involving Human Subjects* from the State University of New York at Stony Brook.

Page 36, Opening story paraphrased from *Is My Baby All Right?*, by Virginia Apgar and Joan Beck. Copyright © 1972 by Simon and Schuster Inc. Used by permission.

Page 62, Table 2.2, From "The Origin of Personality," by A. Thomas, S. Chess and H. G. Birch. Copyright © 1970 by Scientific American, Inc. All rights reserved.

Page 64, Table 2.3, From "The Origin of Personality," by A. Thomas, S. Chess and H. G. Birch. Copyright © 1970 by Scientific American, Inc. All rights reserved.

Page 89, Table 3.2, Reprinted by permission from *Infancy*, by Alan Fogel. Copyright © 1984 by West Publishing Company. All rights reserved.

Page 133, Table 4.2, Adapted from *Childhood and Society*, 2nd Edition, by Erik H. Erikson, by permission of W. W. Norton and Company, Inc. Copyright © 1950, © 1963 by W. W. Norton and Company, Inc.

Page 140, Table 4.3, From "Practical Parenting with Piaget," by J. Thibault and J. McKee, In *Young Children*, November 1982, by permission of the author.

Page 144, Dialog from *Conversations with Jean Piaget*, by Jean-Claude Bringuier. Copyright © 1980 by the University of Chicago. All rights reserved.

Page 146, From "Remember That Old Theory of Memory? Well, Forget It," by J. J. Jenkins in the *American Psychologist*, November 1974, 791. Copyright © The American Psychological Association. Used by permission of the author and the American Psychological Association.

Page 152, Table 4.4, From *Special Children*, by B. G. Suran and J. V. Rizzo. Copyright © 1983 by Scott, Foresman and Company. Reprinted by permission.

Page 155, Photos courtesy of Albert Bandura

Page 166, Figure 5.1, From "The Origin of Form Perception," by R. L. Fantz. Copyright © 1961 by Scientific American. All rights reserved.

Page 168, Photo courtesy of William Vandivert and Scientific American.

Page 173, Photos courtesy of Andrew Meltzoff and the American Association for the Advancement of Science. From A. N. Meltzoff and M. K. Moore, *Science*, 1977, Vol. 198.

Page 175, Table 5.1, From *Introduction to Child Development*, 2nd Edition, by J. P. Dworetzky. Copyright © 1984 by West Publishing Company. All rights reserved.

Page 180, Table 5.3, From *Cultural Perspectives on Child Development*, D. A. Wager and H. W. Stevenson, eds. W. H. Freeman and Company. Copyright © 1982.

Page 184, Figure 5.3, Reprinted by permission from *Nutrition: Concepts and Controversies*, 3rd Edition, by E. M. N. Hamilton, E. N. Whitney, and F. S. Sizer. Copyright © 1985 by West Publishing Company. All rights reserved.

Page 192, Figure 5.4, From *The First Two Years: A Study of Twenty-Five Babies*, by M. M. Shirley. Copyright © 1933, University of Minnesota. Original Edition published by University of Minnesota Press, Minneapolis, Minnesota.

Page 216, Table 6.1, From *The Origins of Intellect*, by J. L. Phillips. W. H. Freeman and Company. Copyright © 1975.

Page 241, Table 7.2, From "Socioemotional Development," by L. A. Sroufe. In *Handbook of Infant Development*, J. D. Osofsky, ed. Copyright © John Wiley and Sons, Inc., 1979. All rights reserved.

Page 247, Photo courtesy of the Harlow Primate Laboratory, University of Wisconsin.

Page 252, Table 7.3, *From Infant Day Care: Toward a More Human Environment*, by A. L. Jacobson. Copyright © 1978 National Association for the Education of Young Children. All rights reserved.

Page 285, Table 8.1, Adapted and abridged from *Communicative Disorders: A Handbook for Prevention and Early Intervention*, by C. D. Weiss and H. S. Lillywhite. St. Louis, 1976. Used by permission of the C. V. Mosby Company and the author.

Page 292, Figure 8.1, From *The Acquisition of Language*, by B. A. Moskowitz. Copyright © 1978 by Scientific American, Inc. All rights reserved.

Page 294, Quotation from "Language Development," by G. J. Whitehurst in *Handbook of Developmental Psychology*, B. B. Wolman ed. Copyright © 1982. Reprinted by permission of Prentice-Hall, Inc. Englewood Cliffs, New Jersey.

Page 314, Photo Copyright © 1985 Children's Television Workshop. Used by permission of Children's Television Workshop.

Page 318, Table 9.3, From *A Textbook of Motor Development*, 2nd Edition, by Charles B. Corbin. Copyright © 1980 Wm. C. Brown Publishers, Dubuque, Iowa. All rights reserved. Reprinted by permission.

Page 320, Table 9.4, From *Perceptual and Motor Development in Infants and Children*, by J. Bryant. Copyright © 1979. Reprinted by permission of Prentice-Hall, Inc., Englewood Cliffs, New Jersey.

Photo Credits

searchers, Inc.; **263** Jeffrey Blankfort, Jeroboam, Inc.; **271** Hella Hammid, Photo Researchers, Inc.; **273** Michael Rothstein, Jeroboam, Inc.;

279 Ellen Warner, Black Star; **280** Elizabeth Crews; **283** Elizabeth Crews; **289** Rick Smolan, Stock, Boston; **293** (*left*) Steve Maines, Stock, Boston; (*right*) Hazel Hankin, Stock, Boston; **296** Elizabeth Crews; **297** Robert V. Eckert, Jr., EKM-Nepenthe; **306** Elizabeth Crews;

312 Peter Menzel, Stock, Boston; **314** Courtesy of Children's Television Workshop; **321** Paul Conklin, Monkmeyer; **323** Suzanne Szasz, Photo Researchers, Inc.; **325** Elizabeth Crews; **331** Mimi Forsyth, Monkmeyer; **342** Jean-Claude Lejeune, Stock, Boston; **344** Randy Matusow, Archive Pictures, Inc.; **346** Courtesy of Family Communications, Inc.; **348** Bill Grimes, Black Star;

358 George B. Gibbons, III, FPG; **361** Karen R. Preuss, Jeroboam, Inc.; **367** Robert Pacheco, EKM-Nepenthe; **369** (*left*) Karen Rosenthal, Stock, Boston; (*right*) Michael Weisbrot, Stock, Boston; **371** Erika Stone, Photo Researchers, Inc.; **374** James R. Holland, Stock, Boston; **379** B. Kliewe, Jeroboam, Inc.; **385** Shirley Zeiberg, Taurus, Photos; **386** Peter Menzel, Stock, Boston;

395 Michael Hayman, Black Star; **396** Ann McQueen, Stock, Boston; **400** Martin M. Rotker, Taurus Photos; **404** Elizabeth Crews; **413** Burk Uzzle, Woodfin Camp & Associates; **416** Will McIntryre, Photo Researchers, Inc.; **417** Elizabeth Crews; **418** Michal Heron, Woodfin Camp & Associates; **422** Michal Heron, Woodfin Camp & Associates; **436** Robert V. Eckert, Jr., EKM-Nepenthe;

440 Jim Anderson, Woodfin Camp & Associates; **442** Mary Evans Picture Library, Photo Researchers, Inc.; **444** (*left*) Owen Franken, Stock, Boston; (*right*) Shirley Zeiberg, Taurus Photos; **450** Deborah Kahn, Stock, Boston; **456** Mary Evans Picture Library, Photo Researchers, Inc.; **458** Elizabeth Crews; **463** Victor Biller, Photo Trends; **467** Mimi Forsyth, Monkmeyer; **480** Randy Matusow, Monkmeyer; **483** Cary Wolinsky, Stock, Boston;

488 Mitchell Payne, Jeroboam, Inc.; **492** Elizabeth Crews; **498** Anestis Diakopoulos, Stock, Boston; **503** (*left*) Michal Heron, Woodfin Camp & Associates; (*right*) Cary Wolinsky, Stock, Boston; **510** (*left*) Jean-Claude Lejeune, Stock, Boston; (*right*) Abraham Menashe, Photo Researchers, Inc.; **512** Kathy Sloane, Black Star; **515** Abraham Menashe, Photo Researchers, Inc.; **523** Peter Vandermark, Stock, Boston; **524** Terry McKoy, Taurus Photos; **526** Phyllis Graber Jensen, Stock, Boston;

529 Jeffry W. Myers, FPG; **530** Peter Vandermark, Stock, Boston; **532** Elizabeth Crews; **534** Donald Dietz, Stock, Boston; **546** James H. Karales, Peter Arnold, Inc.; **548** Gale Zucker, Stock, Boston; **550** Susan Rosenberg, Photo Researchers, Inc.; **553** Lynne Jaeger Weinstein, Woodfin Camp & Associates; **557** Arthur Tress, Woodfin Camp & Associates; **558** Ginger Chih, Peter Arnold, Inc.;

568 Frank Siteman, Stock, Boston; **571** Sybil Shelton, Monkmeyer; **577** Timothy Eagan, Woodfin Camp & Associates; **578** Shirley Zeiberg, Taurus Photos; **579** Sybil Shelton, Peter Arnold, Inc.; **581** Erika Stone, Peter Arnold, Inc.; **585** Sybil Shelton, Monkmeyer; **588** Photo Trends; **592** Bruce Roberts, Photo Researchers, Inc.; **594** (*left*) Marilyn Sanders, Peter Arnold, Inc.; (*right*) Kit Hedman, Jeroboam, Inc.;

598 Eric Kroll, Taurus Photos; **600** (*left*) Stock, Boston; (*right*) Sylvia Johnson, Woodfin Camp & Associates; **601** Frank Siteman, Jeroboam; **602** Mary Evans Picture Library, Photo Researchers, Inc.; **609** Christopher Brown, Stock, Boston; **614** Nancy J. Pierce, Photo Researchers, Inc.; **616** Paul Conklin, Monkmeyer; **617** Elizabeth Crews; **623** Jim Anderson, Woodfin Camp & Associates.